St John's College Cambridge

A HISTORY

The head of Lady Margaret Beaufort, the foundress of the College.
From the tomb effigy by Pietro Torrigiano in the Lady Chapel, Westminster Abbey

St John's College Cambridge

A HISTORY

Edited by Peter Linehan

COLLEGIUM SANCTI JOHANNIS
EVANGELISTÆ IN ACADEMIA
CANTABRIGIENSI.

THE BOYDELL PRESS

First published 2011
The Boydell Press, Woodbridge

ISBN 978 1 84383 608 7

The Boydell Press is an imprint of Boydell & Brewer Ltd
PO Box 9, Woodbridge, Suffolk IP12 3DF, UK
and of Boydell & Brewer Inc.
668 Mount Hope Ave, Rochester, NY 14620, USA
website: www.boydellandbrewer.com

A CIP catalogue record for this book is available from the British Library

The publisher has no responsibility for the continued existence
or accuracy of URLs for external or third-party internet websites
referred to in this book, and does not guarantee that any content
on such websites is, or will remain, accurate or appropriate.

Papers used by Boydell & Brewer are natural, recyclable products
made from wood grown in sustainable forests

Designed and typeset in Adobe Caslon Pro by
David Roberts, Pershore, Worcestershire

Printed in Great Britain by
MPG Books Ltd, Cornwall

CONTENTS

vii

ILLUSTRATIONS

Frontispiece The head of Lady Margaret Beaufort: From the tomb effigy by Pietro Torrigiano in the Lady Chapel, Westminster Abbey. Photograph by the Warburg Institute, University of London. Reproduced by permission.

COLOUR PLATES

The plates appear between pp. 396 and 397.

BLACK-AND-WHITE FIGURES

CONTRIBUTORS

DEREK BEALES
Fellow of Sidney Sussex College and of the British Academy,
Professor Emeritus of Modern History in the University

PETER HENNESSY
Fellow of the British Academy,
Attlee Professor of Contemporary British History
at Queen Mary, University of London

BOYD HILTON
Fellow and Steward of Trinity College, Fellow of the British Academy,
Professor of Modern British History in the University

PETER LINEHAN
Fellow of St John's College and of the British Academy, sometime Dean

MARK NICHOLLS
Fellow and President of St John's College

RICHARD REX
Fellow of Queens' College,
Reader in Reformation History in the University

FOREWORD

ST JOHN'S COLLEGE in Cambridge came into being on 9 April 1511 as the result of a benefaction in the will of Lady Margaret Beaufort, Countess of Richmond and Derby. Lady Margaret, the mother of King Henry VII, had decided to re-found as a college the ancient Hospital of St John the Evangelist, which had fallen into disrepair, but had died in 1509 before her plans could be realized. Thereafter her wishes were fulfilled by her loyal and devoted adviser, John Fisher, bishop of Rochester and chancellor of the University. Over the next five years, the College's first buildings were constructed around a single court, now First Court although much altered since that time. They incorporated the heavily refurbished thirteenth-century chapel of the old Hospital, along with a newly built Hall and Library, and residential accommodation for Fellows and students, the whole entered by a splendid gatehouse that stands today almost unchanged.

The original foundation of the College allowed for a Master and fifty Fellows and Scholars, and St John's remained about that size throughout its early years. Over the course of five centuries, however, the College has received many further generous gifts and benefactions, allowing it to expand in size and numbers. The present College buildings cluster around ten courts, spanning the River Cam and now extending to the far side of St John's Street, and represent a magnificent range of architectural styles and fashions. They are set in incomparably beautiful grounds that have been progressively extended to become the largest of any college in Cambridge or Oxford. The College now numbers some 140 Fellows and over 850 undergraduate and graduate students who, along with more than 200 staff, make it one of the two or three largest in either of the ancient universities, with members drawn from nearly sixty countries, illustrating its international standing and reputation and reflecting in large part the remarkable achievements of the men and women who have passed through its courts.

For St John's is the college of statesmen such as William Cecil, Lord Burghley, the all-powerful adviser to Queen Elizabeth I throughout much of her long reign, Lord Palmerston, one of the most influential of nineteenth-century England's prime ministers, and Dr Manmohan Singh, current Prime Minister of India and leader of the largest democracy the world has ever known and of nearly one-fifth of its population. It is also the College of some of the world's best-known writers and poets, including William Wordsworth, Samuel Butler, Douglas Adams and Louis Cha, and of many of its greatest scientists, including John Dee, William Heberden, Paul Dirac and Frederick Sanger. It has produced some of the greatest humanitarians of all time, notably Thomas Clarkson and William Wilberforce, whose efforts led to the abolition of the slave trade in 1807, and countless more men and women who have achieved distinction in all walks of life. Indeed, within sight of the effigy of Lady Margaret on her tomb in Westminster Abbey are memorials to many of the great figures that her illustrious foundation has educated, and a remarkable one person in fifty of those whose lives are described in the *Dictionary of National Biography* is a Johnian.

It comes as a surprise, therefore, to discover that despite its influence and the achievements of its alumni, no comprehensive history of the College exists. That deficiency is now rectified in this our Quincentenary Year, with the present volume edited by Peter Linehan, a Fellow of the College for forty-five years, with contributions from him and four other distinguished historians. As Dr Linehan says of this history in his introduction, 'The chronicling of those Great Johnians whose statues adorn the exterior of the Chapel's nave ... is not its purpose.' Instead, as you will discover, this volume provides a fascinating glimpse of the people who have lived, taught and studied within its walls, and the ways in which they reacted to, and influenced, the times in which they lived: times which were often turbulent, with the College having to cope with the challenges caused by religious strife, popular unrest, financial depressions, civil wars, global conflicts and social upheavals. Yet cope it did and more, emerging ever stronger and more self-confident, and with a renewed determination to remain at the forefront of education, scholarship and research both nationally and internationally.

Indeed, as this history indicates in so many different ways, St John's has often been in the vanguard of reform within the academic world, and has contributed in no small way to the outstanding reputation that the University of Cambridge now enjoys. And, although the modern College is very different from the institution that was established at the beginning of the sixteenth century, its powerful ethos and strong sense of tradition can be traced back to those early years. Great emphasis is placed on promoting independence of thought and action on the part of all who work and study here, and on encouraging excellence in whatever form it emerges in any given individual. There remains a profound appreciation of the enormous value of collegiate activities in preparing young people for success in an increasingly competitive world, including living and dining together and participating as a community in sport, music and drama.

The College of today has been shaped by the characters and values of its previous inhabitants, and it transmits much of their qualities and beliefs to each new generation of Johnians. An intense feeling of shared experience and of joining a large family of like-minded men and women is undoubtedly one of the origins of the unique ties that exist between Johnians of all ages, and of the deep affection in which the College itself is held by so many of its members. Few would disagree with the words of one nineteenth-century undergraduate quoted in this history: 'We are in the best college in the best university ... in the world', or as one more elderly Johnian said to me recently, 'I've never in my life come across anyone who went to St John's and wished that they had been anywhere else' – surely the greatest accolade that any institution could receive. As we look forward with confidence to the future I hope that you will enjoy this splendid account of the first half millennium of St John's.

Christopher Dobson, 44th Master
1 January 2011

PREFACE

'I HAVE BEEN writing for some years on College history', R. F. Scott informed the Librarian of Windsor Castle at the end of 1910. The College's thirty-fifth Master, Scott was seeking permission to include the Royal Library's Holbein drawing of Bishop Fisher in the College's quatercentenary memorial volume.

The object of that volume, it was stated on its publication in the following year, was not 'to tell again the history of the College' – since that, it was alleged, 'has been written by others'.[1] But this was hardly so. Nor did Scott's own historical contribution – his 'Notes from the College Records' printed in the *Eagle* over many years – invaluable though they are, provide what was looked for. Neither did his slim volume on the subject (sufficiently attractive though it was for someone to purloin the University Library's copy during that quatercentennial year) so much as scratch the surface of the subject.[2]

Indeed, as Edward Miller stated in his Preface to the perceptive and elegant account of the College published on the 450th anniversary, the history of St John's was 'still to be written on the scale and in the detail the subject warrants'.[3] Thomas Baker's snappily entitled *Succinct and Impartial Account of St John's House and St John's College, with some occasional and incidental account of the affairs of the University, and of such private colleges as held communication or intercourse with the old House or College*, completed in 1707, had taken the story up to the time of Peter Gunning, twenty-second Master (1661–70). Writing at a time when, more so even than now, it was not politic to continue one's narrative up to the present, the non-juring 'ejected Fellow' knew all too well when history had to end and where embarrassment (or legal action) might begin.[4]

Together with its continuation by the learned antiquarian, William Cole, who died in 1782 during the mastership of John Chevallier, Baker's *Account* remained in manuscript until J. E. B. Mayor's 1869 edition of both authors' works, with massive additional jottings of his own covering the time down to Ralph Tatham, thirty-second Master, the whole running to 1,235 pages in two volumes.[5] Thereafter, the indefatigable Mayor and, after him, Scott published the admissions records for the years 1629–1802.[6]

---

[1] Letter dated 28 Dec. 1910 (M.2.1); *Collegium Divi Johannis Evangelistae 1511–1911*, p. v.

[2] R. F. Scott, *St John's College, Cambridge* (London, 1907). And no one surrendered to the temptation to steal J. B. Mullinger's *St John's College* (London, 1901), which although more substantial, found it 'hard to find room for more than a summary catalogue of persons and events' and ends raggedly in 1885–6. Cf. J. Twigg, 'Evolution, obstacles and aims: the writing of Oxford and Cambridge college histories', *History of Universities* viii (1989), 184.

[3] *Portrait of a College: A History of the College of Saint John the Evangelist Cambridge* (Cambridge, 1961), p. xi.

[4] Linehan, 'Commemoration of Benefactors, 4 May 1997', 12–14.

[5] *History of the College of St. John the Evangelist, Cambridge*, ed. J. E. B. Mayor (Cambridge, 1869).

[6] *Admissions to the College of St John the Evangelist in the University of Cambridge*, 3 vols. (Cambridge, 1882–1931).

So in 1910 there was no shortage of material. All that was needed was what Mullinger and Scott, and Cole before them, had all lacked. Cole was willing to leave the creation of a narrative to future writers 'who have not had the drudgery to collect, but have all ready to their hands'.[7] And in the century since then the amount of raw material has both multiplied and been made manageable thanks to the labours of Malcolm Underwood and Jonathan Harrison in the College's Archive and Library.

Times change and with them so too do readers' expectations. For example, and regrettably perhaps, in a College History published in 2011, Baker's inclusion of a catalogue of Johnian bishops as supplementary information might not be thought the strongest selling-point. After all, Johnians are notoriously good at finding fault. So what *is* appropriate? Consider the opinion of Edgar Woodhead in 1912, for example. It is not clear whether it was to Mullinger's History or Scott's that Woodhead was referring but, whichever it was, he didn't think much of it. Reading it after running with the eight during the Mays (which he *did* enjoy), he wrote to J. R. Tanner that he was

> fain to confess that it does not give me what I should like in such a history. In details of the buildings and struggles for election as master, I fail to find a picture of the actual life of the collegians, their studies and recreations, their social aims and the impression they made on national life as a whole. (...) The history brought home to me very forcibly the difference between the two schools of historians – the analysts and staticians (*sic*) and those who aim at vivid portraiture.
>
> I read Lord Acton's French Revolution pari passu with Carlyle and felt that the latter gives you the rush and swing of the period, you cannot help being carried away with the crowd, whereas Acton with his cold omniscience not only fails to arouse sympathy but repels and saddens by leaving a general impression of human folly and madness.

After his towpath apotheosis, Woodhead opted for the Carlylean alternative, and thought that, best of all, maybe Tanner would fill the historian's role. But Tanner had other plans for his middle and later years, notably satisfying a very Johnian urge to improve his golf handicap,[8] so the History of St John's remained unwritten.

Even so, Edgar Whitehead's exigent prescription remains, and parts of it remain relevant. For, as Whitehead showed, with Acton not thought good enough and more 'rush and swing of the period' called for, Johnians are also fussy. It had therefore better be plainly stated sooner rather than later what this book is (or tries to be) and what it does not. What it is not (and this is not unusual)[9] is a Carlylean collective biography of 500 years of Great Men who, if they really are distinguished, will be found where they belong, in the new

---

[7] Cooper (1808–66), *Athenae Cantabrigienses.*, i.vi.

[8] TU 12.14.146; below, p. 454.

[9] Likewise, Clare Hopkins, *Trinity: 450 Years of an Oxford College Community* (Oxford, 2005), ix.

Dictionary of National Biography.[10] It will therefore fail to satisfy the shade of Edgar Whitehead. The chronicling of those Great Johnians whose statues adorn the exterior of the Chapel's nave (with one or two situations vacant awaiting even Greater Johnians yet to come) and the luminaries adorning its ceiling (from St Ignatius of Antioch to Dr James Wood) is not its purpose. Its agenda therefore will include only five of the ten memorialized in brass by the southeast door of that building, two of whom, celebrated for their rowing feats, the carnage of the Great War deprived even of entries in the *ODNB*. For all its distinction, the trio of William Gilbert, C. A. Parsons and J. A. Fleming will not be recorded in the pages that follow, the purpose of which might better be described as providing a narrative for those whose tastes lie somewhere between Baker-Mayor and what Colin Bertram once referred to as 'history written for the non-specialist, the Arthur Bryant level of sufficient scholarship'[11] – though, of course, for all too many Johnian readers down the centuries even that level of aspiration might have proved rather a tall order.

Fifty years ago the Editors of the *Eagle* described the defining character of those readers as 'quiet, unassuming competence' and wrote of Johnians *en vacances* blossoming in the French Alps.[12] But it wasn't always so. Time was when it would not have been safe to allow Fellows of the College to wander even so far as Trinity. 'Oh, you have a list of the deformities of the College', Lord Chief Justice Mansfield enquired 'with a smile' of the College's counsel in 1757 in the matter of Thomas Todington's appeal against his exclusion from the Fellowship on account of his withered hand,[13] in the course of legal proceedings that revealed the existence of an entire conventicle of the afflicted, referring to particulars 'of cases of deformed and mutilated persons, who had been f(ellows) or sch(olars)', and whose association even with a wooden leg might be regarded as a detail capable of oblivion.[14] Later in the century the very sanity of certain senior Fellows was at issue.[15]

As Derek Beales makes clear in his account of the matter, we would be sorely mistaken were we to allow that, or any particular, impression of the eighteenth-century history of This Great College to dominate our view of the age.

---

[10] Where accounts of 1,063 Johnians will be found, which since R. F. Scott, E. A. Benians and J. S. Boys Smith are all omitted, ought to be 1,066 at least.

[11] 'Antarctica sixty years ago. We the obligate Pinnipedophagi', *Polar Record*, 32, no. 181, p. 151.

[12] 'Animae naturaliter Johnianae', *Eagle* lviii (1958), 1–3.

[13] SJCA, D89.199, fo. 7; below, p. 186. (The reason why this condition might have disqualified him from the Fellowship derived from the requirement of medieval canon law that ordained clergy have all their parts in working order.)

[14] 'The F(ellows) mentioned were Mr Kenyon, Mr Shaw, & Dr Waller, the Scholar Christopherson with a hump back, Shuttleworth, Twells & Benson all remarkably lame, and Barton with a wooden leg. Ferne also now sch(olar) remarkably deformed. To the 3 cases of F(ellows) I answered (...) that Shaw had only one eye, but that whether he lost it before or after his election was not remembered, that Dr W. was lame, but not mutil(ated) or deformed. Conc(erning) the Sch(olars) I answered that Sh., T. and B. were all lame, that Chr. was deformed (...) that Barton, if I remember'd right, had not a wooden leg ...': SJCA, D89.197.

[15] 25 May 1768: below, p. 202.

As well as Samuel Ogden's the eighteenth century was William Heberden's. Every century provides such contrasts. At one time or another, St John's has harboured the unlikeliest of soul-mates. The College of Matthew Prior and Paul Dirac is also that of Jimmy Edwards and Titus Oates. Difference and contrast, then, is another thing that the rest of this volume will seek to describe.

Like all works of history, this one is only a temporary palliative. Allowing hard-headedness to be counted as a Johnian characteristic (which I think is what our Trinity contributor to this volume means to imply by his reference to 'the true Johnian passion for empirical overkill'),[16] there will surely be better to come. For, to paraphrase Thomas Baker, the College's finest historian of all: 'If everyone will add somewhat to what we have done, it may be a complete work in time.'[17]

P.A.L.

27 December 2010,
The Feast of St John the Evangelist

ACKNOWLEDGEMENTS

Warm thanks are due to all those who provided information as well as to the larger number who promised to do so and to the one or other essential contributor whom at the end of an enterprise of this kind there is a real risk of failing to remember. This category includes the generous Benefactor who has enabled copies of it to be provided to as many Old Johnians as are curious about where they came from, Rosemary Barratt (for discussion of the diary of her father, Hilary Macklin), Katie Birkwood and Kathryn McKee for organizing the illustrations, Dr Dawn Dodds, Mrs Barbara Dring (widow of Sid Dring, Kitchen Manager), the Master and Fellows of Emmanuel College Cambridge for permission to quote from the unpublished papers of H. M. Gwatkin, Paul Everest for photography, Hugo Hinsley for material concerning his father Sir Harry Hinsley, Prof. Keith Jeffery, Dr Hilary Larkin, the Master and Fellows of Magdalene College, Cambridge and Dr Richard Luckett (Pepys Librarian) for permission to quote from the unpublished Diaries of A. C. Benson, Senator Martin Mansergh, Sue Mansfield (for setting my margins as well as for many other kindnesses), Richard Nolan (for legal advice), Roy Papworth (former Chief Clerk of the College), Julian Reid (Archivist, Merton College, Oxford), Dr Lucy Rhymer, Stephanie Rucker-Andrews for all her statistical work, and Alex Stannard (the unmasker of Algy on p. 441).

For the gift or loan of material I am immeasurably indebted to the kindness of Mrs Elisabeth Benians and the late the Rev. Martin Benians, and to Mr Ken Blythe and Mr Stephen Boys-Smith.

---

[16] Below, p. 334.
[17] Baker-Mayor, 10.

Lines from Sir John Betjeman's poem, 'I. M. Walter Ramsden ob. March 26, 1947' [Collected Poems, by John Betjeman © The Estate of John Betjeman 1955, 1958, 1962, 1964, 1968, 1970, 1979, 1981, 1982, 2001], cited at p. 654, are reproduced by permission of John Murray (Publishers). The letter of 16 May 1943 from J. W. Davidson to E. M. Davidson cited at p. 557 is reproduced by permission of the National Library of Australia.

Without Malcolm Underwood's assistance in the College Archive this book could quite simply not have been written. The same goes for the staff of the College Library (Fiona Colbert, biographical librarian, and Jonathan Harrison in particular, *sine quibus non*) whose cheerful and untiring assistance have regularly relieved the tedium ordinarily associated with such exercises. Siân Smith proved no less of a blessing at the indexing stage. The genial group of alumni and undergraduates who gathered in May Week 2009 to discuss the College's last forty-odd years – Emma Beauclerk, Nick Charlwood, Sarah Dickson, Graham Harding, Peter Hennessy, Ben Hoyle, Ben Macintyre, Elliot Ross, Derica Shields, David Smellie, Malcolm Schofield and Suzanne Szczetnikowicz – helped probably more than they knew to inform the content of the Epilogue.

The Editor is above all indebted, and so is the College, to the other six contributors to the volume for so stoically putting up with his pestering and chivvying. Particular thanks are due to Peter Hennessy who came to the volume's rescue when the twentieth-century author had to withdraw, and to Derek Beales, who, at very short notice, came to the rescue and saved the College's eighteenth century from undeserved oblivion.

P.A.L.

ABBREVIATIONS

BC	Buildings Committee
Benson Diary	Diaries of A. C. Benson
BL	British Library
CB	SJCA, Conclusion Book
CUA	Cambridge University Archives
CUL	Cambridge University Library
BSLB	Boys Smith Letter Book(s)
BSP	Boys Smith papers
CBD	Cecil Beaton Diaries
CM(M)	Council minute(s)
CR	*Cambridge Review*
CUR	*Cambridge University Reporter*
EABP	Benians papers
EC	Entertainments Committee
GAC	General Athletic Club
GB	Governing Body
GC	Glover Correspondence
	(letters to T. R. Glover in process of classification, SJCL)
GD	Diaries of T. R. Glover
GEDD	Glyn Daniel, 'Commonplace Book mit Journal'
JCR(C)	Junior Combination Room (Committee)
KCC	Kitchen Consultative Committee
LMHD	Hilary Macklin Diaries
ODNB	*Oxford Dictionary of National Biography*
PBA	*Proceedings of the British Academy*
SBF	Senior Bursar Files
SBFG	Senior Bursar's Files, General
SBFP	Senior Bursar Files, Personnel
SBR	Samuel Butler Room
SJCA	SJC Archives
SJCL	SJC Library
SJMC	Senior and Junior Members Committee
SLB	Scott Letter Books, 2 vols. (SJCA, M2.1–2)
TNA	The National Archives

St John's College Cambridge

A HISTORY

BY WAY OF PROLOGUE

I<small>T</small> might so easily have been otherwise. By 1511 the site by the river on which the College now stands might already have been occupied by others – by other academics, that is, with a prior claim on the place, the members of a college which would have been Cambridge's oldest and able to date its foundation to the year 1280. For it was in that year that the bishop of Ely, Hugh of Balsham, secured a charter from King Edward I allowing him to establish a group of scholars in the Hospital of St John, the foundation of Augustinian canons[1] opposite the church of All Saints in the Jewry, the quarter from which in 1275 the Jews had been expelled and sent packing to Norwich.[2] But 'for various causes', we are told, after just three years the scheme failed and the bishop's scholars were relocated to the balmy south of the city in the place that was to become Peterhouse.[3] We are not told what the causes were for their failure to put down roots amongst the hospital's custodians and the sleep-starved sick whom they tended, though anyone in residence throughout a modern May Week may well imagine. The proposition that the hospital itself 'was part of the credit system in Cambridge from the very first years of its existence', 'founded immediately and literally across the street from the Cambridge Jewry in order to check the economic influence of the latter, to offer a Christian alternative to both its religious and its financial attractions' is perhaps no more than a tantalizing possibility.[4] The evidence may be said to be unstable. And even if it be sounder than that, over the next two centuries both aspects of the hospital's functions withered while the pleasures of the flesh took precedence over the application of remedies for the failings thereof, and its ghosts steadily accumulated upon what in 1511 became the College's exclusive territory. That reflection provides a starting-point which is salutary. But it is not novel. For, as Thomas

---

[1] Not of the Military Order of the Hospital, as urged by K. Scott, 'The foundation of the Hospital of St John the Evangelist', *Eagle* lxvii, no. 283 (1975), 3–4: a startling misconception recently restated by Professor G. R. Evans, *The University of Cambridge: A New History* (London, 2009), 130. For the rule of the Hospital of St John see M. Rubin, *Charity and Community in Medieval Cambridge* (Cambridge, 1987), 300–1.

[2] R. B. Dobson, 'The Jews of medieval Cambridge', *Transactions of the Jewish Historical Society of England* xxxii (1990–92), 16.

[3] Rubin, 271–3; *Cartulary of the Hospital of St John the Evangelist, Cambridge*, ed. M. Underwood (Cambridge, 2008), xiv–xvii; R. Lovatt, 'Hugh of Balsham, bishop of Ely 1256/7–1286', in *Pragmatic Utopias. Ideals and communities, 1200–1630*, ed. R. Horrox & S. Rees Jones (Cambridge, 2001), 75–6. As to the possible specifically missionary objectives of the bishop's strategy, the remarks of C. N. L. Brooke ('The churches of medieval Cambridge', in *History, Society and the Churches: Essays in Honour of Owen Chadwick*, ed. D. Beales and G. Best [Cambridge, 1985], 59–60) are germane.

[4] Rubin, 217–26; cf. Dobson, 15.

Baker acknowledged long ago: 'Whatever virtues we may have are founded upon the transgressions of others.'[5]

P.A.L.

---

[5] Baker-Mayor, 50.

I

THE SIXTEENTH CENTURY

Richard Rex

Fisher's College

1. THE KING'S MOTHER

THE foundation of St John's College was the eventual outcome of a meeting in 1495 that only just made it into the historical record. In one of the earliest surviving account books in the archives of the University of Cambridge are found some stray entries for the expenses of the Senior Proctor on a trip to London, where he had been lobbying on the University's behalf in one of those intractable 'town and gown' disputes that make up so much of Cambridge history. The first of these entries records a boat trip one Tuesday to Greenwich, where the Senior Proctor lunched with 'my lady the King's Mother' and later dined with the Lord Chancellor.[1] The 'King's Mother' was Lady Margaret Beaufort, Countess of Richmond and Derby, the most powerful woman in the land. The Senior Proctor was John Fisher, a rising young academic administrator.

The attraction, it seems, was instantaneous and reciprocal. Fisher was a striking man, a full six foot in height, loose-limbed and muscular without an ounce of fat on him, sallow skinned with dark hair, grey eyes, and a square jaw. With his measured manner and evident personal austerity he could even be a somewhat disconcerting figure. Years later, renewing her personal vow of chastity in his presence, Lady Margaret recalled that she had recognized in him her future 'cheffe trustye counselloure' since 'the first tyme I see you'.[2] She in turn was diminutive but forceful, with a brilliant and expensive taste in fashion. In the years that followed her son's accession to the throne she was one of the most dazzling figures at his court, outshining even his queen. No doubt Fisher was star-struck at the time, and as their friendship grew she became one of the most important people in his life. He was, he later said, 'as beholden to her as to my own mother'.[3]

Fisher's meeting with Lady Margaret was the start of a process which saw her patronal, or maternal, instincts drawn towards both England's universities.

[1] *Grace Book B*, ed. M. Bateson, 2 vols. (Cambridge, 1903–5), I. 68. The immediately preceding pages of the manuscript, which might have enabled us to date the journey precisely, no longer survive.

[2] SJCA, C7.11, Thin Red Book, fo. 47r. For Fisher's physique and physiognomy, see *Vie du bienheureux martyr Jean Fisher*, ed. F. van Ortroy (Brussels, 1893), 355–6.

[3] *Early Statutes of the College of St. John the Evangelist in the University of Cambridge*, ed. J. E. B. Mayor (Cambridge, 1859), 242.

By 1498 Fisher was her closest adviser, in effect her spiritual director, and she was supporting a theology lecturer in each university. In 1502 these positions were formally established and endowed as the Lady Margaret's readerships (now professorships), with John Fisher himself the first Cambridge incumbent. As he rose in the University's hierarchy and the Lady Margaret's household, her patronage inclined more and more heavily towards Cambridge. Cambridge alone was chosen for the Lady Margaret's preachership in 1504, by which time Henry VII himself had taken notice of the University's rising star. For Henry was undergoing a crisis of conscience. Having lost his eldest son, his youngest son, and his wife in quick succession, he fell seriously ill himself, and in a spasm of guilt over his harsh and exploitative ruling style, promised God that, if he was spared, he would reform. In particular, he would henceforth nominate only exemplary candidates to serve as bishops. Fisher was the chief beneficiary of this worthy but short-lived vow, and was plucked from Cambridge to become bishop of Rochester. The University, its nose tingling with the scent of royal favour, promptly elected him Chancellor, a position he would occupy for the next thirty years.

The King's Mother had already shown some interest in the foundation of a Cambridge college, having lent financial and personal support in the 1490s to the project of transforming the old nunnery of St Radegund's into Jesus College. By 1503 she was far more deeply involved in a project to rescue an existing college, God's House, that had fallen into financial difficulties. She already had her son's permission to make substantial endowments at Westminster Abbey. In 1504, with Fisher advising her, as he later put it, as to 'what seemed most conducive to the welfare of her soul', she secured further permission to divert some of that endowment to Cambridge, so as to refound God's House on a more stable footing as Christ's College.[4] The dilapidated site was largely rebuilt and, towards the end of 1506, what was in effect a new college was granted new statutes by Lady Margaret, who came in person to preside over its opening ceremonies that autumn.[5]

The third foundation with which she was involved at Cambridge was that of St John the Evangelist. Like Christ's College, St John's was to be a refoundation. In this case the original institution was the Hospital of St John the Evangelist, which dated from the twelfth century. Towards the end of Henry VII's reign the hospital had fallen on hard times. Heavily in debt, its actual disposable income was barely half its theoretical £70 a year. Lady Margaret's Cambridge advisers had their eye on the place even as the new buildings of Christ's College were going up. In February 1507 the bishop of Ely, James Stanley, put the hospital into administration, relieving its prior, William Thomlyn, of his responsibilities, which he entrusted to a committee consisting of two of Lady Margaret's advisers and two of his own diocesan officials. The stated reason for this was

---

[4] Fisher to the University, 26 Feb. [1529], in J. Lewis, *The Life of Dr. John Fisher*, ed. T. H. Turner, 2 vols. (London, 1855), II. 305.

[5] B. Dobson, 'The Foundation', in D. Reynolds (ed.), *Christ's: A Cambridge College over Five Centuries* (London, 2004), 3–34. See also M. K. Jones and M. G. Underwood, *The King's Mother: Lady Margaret Beaufort, countess of Richmond and Derby* (Cambridge, 1992), 215–29.

Thomlyn's negligence and mismanagement, the same grounds that would justify the eventual suppression of the hospital.[6] Lady Margaret's men doubtless already had some hopes of redeploying its buildings and estates for the maintenance of poor scholars. The initiative for the bishop's intervention was almost certainly theirs, not his: James Stanley had only been bishop since the previous November, and was not quite such an exemplary prelate as John Fisher.[7] That he acted in this case so promptly and decisively is explained entirely by his relationship to Lady Margaret. He was her stepson, he owed his promotion to her, and while she lived he did what he was told, otherwise content to live happily on the episcopal manor at Somersham, where his housekeeper bore him three children.

2. ORIGINS AND OBSTACLES

Cambridge hopes, however, were not destined for immediate fulfilment. Lady Margaret's attention was for the moment centred upon Christ's College, where construction and repair work, together with the costs of equipping the place, were mopping up most of her available resources. A graver problem was that she also had Oxford advisers, most notably Dr Edmund Wilsford, Provost of Oriel College, who was her usual confessor in her last years. Inspired by what had been achieved at Cambridge, they were seeking to interest her in transforming one of Oxford's religious houses, St Frideswide's, into a college. They were to be disappointed, although in the 1520s none other than Cardinal Wolsey would take up the project, refounding the priory as Cardinal's College (in turn to be acquired by Henry VIII and refounded as Christ Church). If we can believe an encomium of John Fisher penned at St John's in the 1520s, his was the crucial influence which frustrated the plans of the Oxford men in Lady Margaret's entourage.[8]

It is only in 1509 that we find clear evidence that Lady Margaret had committed herself to the new venture, and this as her health began to decline. Plans were well under way by March, when the 'comptroller' (or chief accountant) of her household, Hugh Ashton, made three trips to London 'aboute the alteracion of Sainctt Johns house in Cambrige into a colleige of secular studentes', while his assistant, Thomas Bellingham, went to Cambridge itself on the same business.[9] These trips resulted in an agreement with the bishop of Ely, by which he surrendered his rights as patron of the hospital to Lady Margaret in return for the right to nominate candidates for a Fellowship in the new college. Shortly after the death of her son, Lady Margaret petitioned the new king, Henry VIII, for permission to proceed. The petition makes her general intentions plain, but no specific plans were set down in her lifetime, nor even outlined in her last will and testament (although her agreement with James Stanley was summarized in

[6] SJCA, D3.75 (3 Feb. 1507).

[7] There is no surviving official register for the eight years of Stanley's light-touch episcopate; *ODNB* (D. G. Newcombe).

[8] Lewis, *Dr. John Fisher*, II. 293.

[9] SJCA, D102.1, fo. 8r.

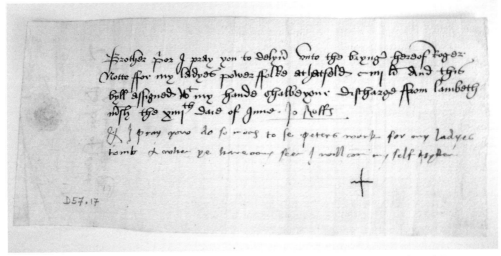

1 Request of Fisher to the prior of St Bartholomew's Smithfield (William Bolton) to deliver money for Lady Margaret's almsfolk and inspect the work on her tomb at Westminster Abbey: 'Brother prior I pray you to delyv[er] unto the bring[er] hereof Roger Notte for my ladyes power folke at Hatfeld iiij l[ibr]i And this byll assigned w^t my hande shalbe your discharge from lambeth m[er]sh the xiiij daie of June. Jo Roffs & I pray yow do so moch to se Peters work for my ladyes tomb & when ye have oons seen I will com[e] my self thyder.' (?1512): SJCA, D57.17

a codicil).[10] This was most uncharacteristic of such a determined and organized woman, perhaps reflecting the uncertainties and anxieties that surrounded the passing of the old king and the accession of a new. Partly in consequence of the inadequacy of the documentation, the foundation of St John's was to be plagued with legal problems and challenges.

Her original vision for the College has to be reconstructed from scattered hints. The papal bull which authorized the transformation of the hospital into a college specified that it was to consist of a Master and fifty Scholars (a term which in that context includes both Fellows and Scholars, the terms used in Lady Margaret's petition to Henry VIII of 1509).[11] Interestingly, this means that she envisaged St John's on a more modest scale than Christ's, which consisted of a Master and sixty Scholars (twelve Fellows and forty-eight Scholars). The funding for the project is first mentioned in a letter written by Henry Hornby in February 1510. He states that it was her will that 'the issues and profits of 600 marks [i.e. £400] of land of her inheritance beinge in feoffment' should be used to establish the College. And he is already worried that, if the College is not founded, Henry VIII will resume Lady Margaret's inheritance.[12] This fear led the executors to lobby Lords and Commons in Parliament, in the hope of

---

[10] *Collegium Divi Johannis Evangelistae, 1511–1911* (Cambridge, 1911), 103–26, for her will, dated 6 Jun. 1508. The codicil was dated 10 Mar. 1509.

[11] *Calendar of Entries in the Papal Registers Relating to Great Britain and Ireland: Papal Letters* (London, 1893–), XVIII. nos. 55, 63 (24 Jun. 1510). For the full Latin text, see pp. xxxiii–xxxvii.

[12] Hornby to the brethren of the Hospital of St John: SJCA, D105.94.

securing an exemption should the new king pass an Act of Resumption, a stat-ute clawing former royal lands back to the crown.[13] A posthumous codicil added to Lady Margaret's will in 1512, under the authority of the archbishop of Can-terbury's probate jurisdiction, set out what the funding was meant to achieve: clearing the hospital's debts; repairing its properties and estates; erecting new collegiate buildings; securing a sufficient landed endowment; and adequately equipping the library, kitchens, and other essential offices. But with the excep-tion of clearing the debts, these objectives were ill defined. It was left unclear when, or under what conditions, her executors would cease to enjoy the use of the revenues from her enfeoffed lands, releasing them back to the crown.[14]

The path was beset with obstacles. Fisher later wrote a plaintive memoran-dum enumerating the problems the executors had faced. He was particularly irked by the disloyalty shown towards his patroness's memory and intentions by her relatives and former servants. Unexpected obstruction came almost at once from her stepson, James Stanley. He had been co-operative enough while she lived, but he dug in his heels after her death, protesting that as yet 'he hadde not sealide' any promises in binding form. He refused to sign anything else until the bishop of Winchester brokered a deal that gave him financial compensation ('to our great charge', Fisher recalled) for signing away his patronal rights.[15] Stanley drove a hard bargain. His original agreement with Lady Margaret allowed him to nominate three candidates to the College, from whom one would be elected to a Fellowship. Now he was to be allowed simply to nominate three Fellows.[16]

At the same time, the brethren of the hospital fought fiercely to safeguard their interests. They found technical flaws in the first copy of the papal bull for the closure of their house, which cost the executors more time and expense.[17] They also lobbied Stanley for support. However, in a letter of 15 December 1510 he urged them to reconcile themselves to the inevitable, claiming credit for securing them good pensions.[18] He did his best by them. In the agreement he signed with Lady Margaret's executors on 12 December, a last-minute alteration raises the pension allocated to each of the three former brethren from £5 6s 8d

---

[13] SJCA, D6.12.

[14] *Collegium Divi Johannis Evangelistae*, 124–5.

[15] Lewis, *Dr. John Fisher*, II. 277–82, at pp. 277–8.

[16] The evolution of the agreement is seen in two copies in the College archives. One (SJCA, D6.4), signed 'Margaret', is plainly what was first agreed. The other (SJCA, D6.5) was originally identical except for an additional clause recording the date (14 March 1509), and was signed by Stanley ('Ja. Elien.') in the same place as Marga-ret's, bottom left. But on this second copy, the provision for the Ely Fellowship is subsequently altered by deletions and insertions. It carries Stanley's signature a second time (bottom right). The presence of the signatures of Fox, Fisher, Hornby, and Ashton (four of Lady Margaret's executors) suggests that they were attesting the alterations made to the original text. When the College was first constituted in April 1511, there were three Fellows – Stanley's nominees. Thomas Baker, *History of the College of St John the Evangelist, Cambridge*, ed. J. E. B. Mayor, 2 vols. (Cambridge, 1869) [henceforth Baker-Mayor], I. 281.

[17] This may be why there are two copies in the papal registers. See above, n. 11.

[18] Stanley to the brethren of the hospital: SJCA, D105.96.

to £6 13s 4d (a 25 per cent increase).[19] At last, early in 1511, the brethren were escorted from the premises and transferred to another hospital in Ely.[20] They may not have been very happy there, as later that year each of them received a papal licence (doubtless at the expense of the executors) to live in the outside world and hold an ecclesiastical benefice without loss of their pension.[21]

Technical difficulties also beset the foundress's last will and testament. It was, Fisher opaquely remarks, 'thought expedient by the juges' that Lady Margaret's will should be proved not only in the Prerogative Court of Canterbury but also, unusually, in Chancery. A Chancery process of Dickensian dilatoriness ensued, involving 'myche tyme and labore taken, more then I can tell in a few words', with 'so many writts, so many Dedimus potestatem … so many suyts to the Kyngs sollicitour, the Kyngs attorney, the King's sergeants' that it took a year and a half to sort out, leaving Fisher himself, like most Chancery petitioners in history, 'right sory that ever I toke that besones upon me'.[22]

Meanwhile, as turmoil engulfed the project, many of Lady Margaret's household servants, disappointed of their expectations by her late decision to found a new college, complained to the king, insinuating that Fisher had exerted undue influence upon her in her final months and pointing out that Henry, too, was a loser from the plan for a new college. In Fisher's words, this made the king 'verray hevy lorde agaynst me', suspecting that the bishop was trying to defraud him.[23] As a result, the executors were harried by royal auditors to give an account of their handling of Lady Margaret's goods and to prove their right to spend the revenues from her lands. They managed to persuade the chief auditor of the Exchequer, Sir Robert Southwell, that everything was in order, but he died in 1514 before he could certify this to the king, and his less sympathetic successor, Sir Edward Belknap, reopened the case.[24] In the end, Lady Margaret's executors had to surrender the revenues of her enfeoffed lands into the king's hands on 11 July 1515.[25]

Later tradition viewed this as in effect a confiscation of endowment, an impression derived from Fisher's aggrieved reference in the statutes of 1530 to the 'subtraction of revenues worth £400 a year' from the College.[26] But while Fisher was convinced that a wrong had been done, there is no reason to believe that either Lady Margaret or he had envisaged her lands as constituting the College's endowment. The codicil to her will gives her executors disposal of the

---

[19] The sum of 106s 8d has been struck through, and £6 13s 4d has been inserted above it: SJCA, D3.85.

[20] Richard Henrison to Fisher, 13 Mar. 1511: SJCA, D6.6.

[21] *Calendar of Papal Letters*, XVIII, nos. 145–7 (18 July 1511).

[22] Lewis, *Dr. John Fisher*, II. 278–9.

[23] Ibid., 279.

[24] Ibid., 280–81. Belknap was a real favourite of Henry VIII in those early years. He was appointed successor, with Sir John Daunce, to Sir Robert Southwell as 'general surveyor' by a grant of 17 Nov. 1514: *Letters and Papers, Foreign and Domestic, of the Reign of Henry VIII*, ed. J. S. Brewer *et al.*, 21 vols. (London, 1862–1910), I. 3499, g. 49.

[25] Jones and Underwood, *The King's Mother*, p. 246, n. 46, citing *Calendar of Ancient Deeds* IV. 23 (A6312).

[26] *Early Statutes*, 240.

revenues of those lands until the new college was on a firm footing. The same codicil refers to the manor of Malton (Cambridgeshire) as granted to Christ's College, an entirely and transparently different transaction.[27] Had she wished to endow St John's from her own estates, she would have said so. The misfortune of her executors was that Sir Edward Belknap, under pressure to restore order to royal finances after the spending spree of Henry VIII's early years, adopted a narrow interpretation of the objectives specified in the codicil. Fisher, reasonably enough, felt that the removal of this revenue stream even before the College had opened for business, and long before the landed endowment was adequate to its support, was in contravention of the foundress's will.

3. CONSTRUCTION AND CONSOLIDATION

Despite the obstacles impeding the executors, distinct progress was made in these years, and the College of St John the Evangelist came into legal existence on 9 April 1511, with Robert Shorton its first Master.[28] Shorton was Fisher's choice for the post, and he justified his appointment by assiduous efforts during the building programme that followed. At the suggestion of Henry Hornby, Oliver Scales was appointed Master of the Works, though Shorton had reservations, feeling that while Scales would be excellent as long as he was in Cambridge, he might have too much business on hand to allow him to be present at all times. Shorton wanted someone on site all the time to make sure the works went forward expeditiously. He need not have worried. Serious building operations presumably commenced later in 1511, when Richard Reculver of Greenwich started delivering some of the 800,000 bricks ordered in February that year.[29] With regular supplies of cash from Fisher, acting for Lady Margaret's executors, Shorton seems to have been able to keep Scales's mind on the task. Work proceeded apace through 1512 and 1513.[30]

The building conformed to the usual pattern for a medieval college: a single court or quadrangle, bounded on one side by a chapel, on another by a hall and kitchens, and on the others by residential chambers, a library, and a gatehouse. In this case, the chapel of the old hospital was retained (though extended and substantially modified), as was the shell of the old infirmary that stood beyond the chapel to the north-east. Everything else was newly built, at a cost of about £5,000.[31] First Court has undergone considerable changes since that time, with the partial classicization of facades in the eighteenth century, and in the nineteenth the demolition of the medieval chapel and its replacement in gigantesque neo-Gothic. But through the sixteenth and seventeenth centuries First Court presented a largely homogenous aspect in Tudor red brick, a grander version of

[27] *Collegium Divi Johannis Evangelistae*, 125.

[28] SJCA, D4.17: charter of foundation issued by Lady Margaret's executors.

[29] Bond with Richard Reculver, 1 Feb. 1511: SJCA, D57.173.

[30] SJCA, C17.23 presents the accounts of Oliver Scales for 1512 and 1513, spending just over £2,450.

[31] A. C. Crook, *From the Foundation to Gilbert Scott: A History of the Buildings of St John's College, Cambridge 1511 to 1885* (Cambridge, 1980), 8–14.

the Old Court at Queens' College. John Fisher had been President of Queens' for a few years (1505–8), and this may have been the decisive influence on the early design of St John's.[32]

The loss of the profits from Lady Margaret's lands in 1515 was a grievous blow. By clearing debts and carrying out repairs the executors had raised the income from the old hospital's estates to about £80 a year, and they had added some further lands, notably the manor of Bassingbourne in Fordham that Lady Margaret had acquired for this purpose, but by 1515 the total income was only about £100 a year, nothing like adequate for the college they envisaged.[33] The executors petitioned the king for support, perhaps with the assistance of Catherine of Aragon. Henry allocated them some of the profits of a wardship (a grant of the administration and profits of the estates of a feudal tenant of the Crown who was below the legal age of majority). He obliged the countess of Devonshire, who held the wardship of the young Viscountess Lisle, to make over the sum of £2,800 to the College in regular instalments, but this income ended abruptly when the viscountess died. Probably only half the projected sum had been received by then, and the countess argued that it was not fair to expect her to make up the remainder of the sum when she no longer enjoyed the profits of the lands. The tone of Fisher's comment on this does not indicate that he agreed with her, but he was probably wise not to take on such a powerful noblewoman in the courts.[34]

Better still, in March 1516 Henry gave permission for the College to acquire the property of a failing religious house. It was doubtless Fisher's local knowledge that had led the executors to the Maison Dieu at Ospringe (just outside Faversham, down the road from Rochester). In theory, this brought an additional £70 a year, but no land transaction in Tudor times was ever as simple as that, and in this case the business was bungled. The Maison Dieu surrendered direct to the College, rather than via the king (the ultimate feudal overlord), and a few years later the College found it necessary to secure their title to the estates by surrendering them to the king, who regranted them on 1 August 1519.[35] Revenue from the Ospringe estate was uncertain and variable for years, and had to meet the heavy transaction costs. Some College accounts for 1519 include an entry for moneys paid 'to the cardinal and sundry others for various matters relating to Ospringe': an extraordinary £93 in fees and douceurs for officials from Cardinal Wolsey downwards.[36]

It was on 29 July 1516 that St John's College finally made the transition from construction project to educational institution. Fisher himself came to Cambridge for the opening ceremonies, and had probably hoped to add lustre to

---

[32] V. H. Morgan, *A History of the University of Cambridge*, II. *1546–1750* (Cambridge, 2004), 23.

[33] SJCA, M3.1, Master's account 1514–15. Gross income, including £80 arrears now collected, stood at just over £200, but allowing for those arrears and necessary charges, the net disposable income for collegiate purposes was around £100.

[34] Lewis, *Dr. John Fisher*, II. 281. SJCA, D56.147 (24 Jun. 1519), acknowledging 2,000 marks (£1,333 6s 8d) received thus far.

[35] SJCA, D4.8.

[36] SJCA, Roll M3.2, visus 1518–23, membrane 2.

2 Henry VIII in majesty. Initial of licence for College to acquire
site and possessions of Ospringe Hospital, 1519: SJCA D4.8

the occasion by bringing with him the greatest scholar of the age, Desiderius
Erasmus of Rotterdam, who was visiting England that summer (but Erasmus
did not come). He consecrated the chapel and then, with Henry Hornby, set
about constituting the Fellowship. Thirty-one Fellows were admitted that day,
starting with James Spooner and John West, the two survivors of the three Fellows nominated by James Stanley in 1511. They were followed by another nine
MAs and twenty BAs. But financial difficulties afflicted the College in its early
years. Until the early 1520s the Fellows received no stipends, only their allowances for 'commons' (meals in Hall) and 'livery' (academic dress). Part of the
reason for this lay in one Christopher Wright, the sturdy survivor of the hospital brethren, who continued to draw his £6 13s 4d pension (equivalent to the
stipend of ten Fellows) until 1531. So the Fellowship shrank. By 1519 there were
twenty-six Fellows, along with twenty-three Scholars, and the College stayed
that size for the next few years.[37]

St John's College was more and more becoming one man's dream. With the
aid of other Cambridge men in Lady Margaret's household, John Fisher had
concentrated her patronage on Cambridge. With the aid of her other executors,

[37] SJCA, C17.24 (1518) and D107.8; Jones and Underwood, *The King's Mother*, 243, n. 38,
for the cessation of Wright's pension.

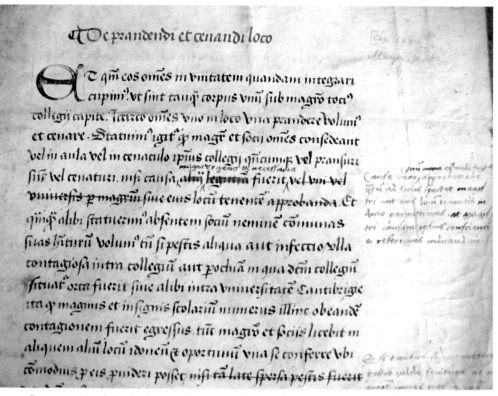

3 Commensality. Marginal corrections to the College Statutes in the hand of John Fisher, 1516. The section requires the Master and Fellows to dine together in Hall 'that they all be as one body beneath the Master': SJCA, C1.40.2

he had brought her plan for St John's to fruition. From 1516 onwards, when the other executors devolved onto Fisher the task of drafting its statutes, the College was the project closest to his heart. Its most pressing need was for further endowment, and he dedicated his efforts to amassing it.

Two centuries later, Thomas Baker was to remark, with a touching naivety about the dynamics of fundraising, that in the College's early years 'private founders were crowding in'.[38] It would be fairer to say that they were rounded up, and the man mostly responsible for this was Fisher, who, like all great fundraisers, was ruthless in turning personal connection to corporate profit. It is especially noteworthy that the crowd of private founders melted away abruptly after his death. Fisher's role is most evident in the case of the Constable Fellowship. Since his youth at Cambridge, Fisher had been a friend of John Constable, scion of the Yorkshire magnate family, the Constables of Flamborough.[39] When John's brother, Sir Marmaduke, the head of the family, decided to establish a chantry foundation to pray for his soul, it can only have been this connection with Fisher that led it to be placed down south in St John's College. Sir

[38] Baker-Mayor, I. 95.
[39] R. Rex, *The Theology of John Fisher* (Cambridge, 1991), 23–6.

Marmaduke's lifetime gifts in cash were supplemented after his death with the manor of Millington in Yorkshire, made over to the College by his executors, who were led by his brother John.[40]

The East Riding of Yorkshire furnished a clutch of early benefactions which were most probably garnered through Fisher's personal connections. Dame Joan Rokeby, who endowed a Fellowship in 1525, and who for reasons of status retained her name from her first marriage (to Sir Richard Rokeby), had by that time outlived her second husband, Thomas Creyk, one of the wealthiest burghers of Beverley, Fisher's home town, where she ended her days. Robert Halitreholme, an ageing canon lawyer who endowed a Fellowship the same year, was also from Beverley. John Dowman, whose benefaction supported nine 'sizars', was from Pocklington, halfway between Beverley and York, where he founded the grammar school. John Ripplingham, a former Fellow of Queens' College who founded two scholarships at St John's in 1516, was from Hull, and Robert Duckett, who founded two scholarships in the few years before he died in 1522, was from Keyingham in Holderness. As he was not only a Cambridge graduate, quite possibly from Fisher's own college of Michaelhouse, but also parish priest of Chevening, which lay in the Rochester diocese, we can conclude that Fisher was able to work on almost all his loyalties in securing that benefaction.[41]

All of the male donors just named had graduated from Cambridge in the later fifteenth century, and Cambridge connections were probably just as important in their decisions. Dr Thomas Thompson, Master of Christ's College, had a long association with Fisher which presumably accounts for his donation of rents in Cambridge to support a chantry in St John's and thus supplement the income of two Fellows. Hugh Ashton's foundation, supporting four Fellows and four Scholars, of course reflected his own personal connection with the foundress and his role as one of her executors. The endowment of a Fellowship by Dr William Fell, formerly Lady Margaret's almoner, doubtless reflected personal loyalty to the foundress, but probably also the connection with Fisher through service in her household.[42] Edward Gregson, whose gift of nearly £400 was intended ultimately to support two Fellows and two Scholars, had been a founding Fellow of Jesus College, which should have had the greater claim on him. Robert Simpson and Thomas Thimbleby, who each founded a Fellowship, were also Cambridge men, though without demonstrable links to Fisher. The generosity of other early benefactors is less easy to account for. The Staffordshire benefactors James Beresford and John Bayly had no known

---

[40] *Early Statutes*, 404–6, for Constable's original foundation; SJCA, D58.4 for the agreement with the executors to expand it.

[41] Foundation deeds at SJCA, D58.13, 2 (Duckett, 26 Feb. 1521); D59.40 (Halitreholme, 18 Jun. 1525); D59.45 (Rokeby, 11 Jul. 1525); D59.57 (Dowman, 28 Apr. 1526); D59.91 (Ripplingham, 10 Sept. 1516). Career details of the Cambridge graduates in this paragraph and the next from J. and J. A. Venn (comp.), *Alumni Cantabrigienses: A Biographical List of all Known Students, Graduates, and Holders of Office at the University of Cambridge … to 1900*, Part I in 4 vols., Part II in 6 vols. (Cambridge, 1922–54).

[42] Foundation deeds at SJCA, D58.15 (Thompson, 20 Mar. 1523); D94.266 (Ashton, 21 Sept. 1520 and 27 May 1521); D58.57 (Fell, 1 May 1533).

connections with Lady Margaret or Fisher, nor yet did Dr John Keyton (canon of Salisbury).[43]

Two of the largest gifts confirm the general sense of Fisher's role behind the scenes in building up the College's endowment. The medical lectureship founded by the great humanist scholar and physician Thomas Linacre must have been based in St John's because of Fisher's influence, as they shared a wide circle of friends including Thomas More, John Colet, and Cuthbert Tunstall. The most generous of all the early benefactors was Roger Lupton, provost of Eton, who had amassed immense wealth through a lifetime of royal service and ecclesiastical pluralism. In total, his gifts to St John's supported two Fellowships and eight Scholarships. His acquaintance with Fisher would have dated back to the early years of the century, when he was prominent in Henry VII's service, and the personal nature of the connection between them is indicated by the story that he had to resign his position at Eton after having publicly lamented Fisher's execution in 1535.[44]

It is always easier to persuade others to give if you lead by example, and Fisher's greatest contribution to building up the endowment of St John's was his own massive personal investment. Around 1520 he spent over £1,000 acquiring three manors (Holbeach, Ramerick, and Ridgewell) to support his personal chantry foundation in the College, to consist of four Fellows and two Scholars, which was initially established on 6 March 1521.[45] He thought it more worthwhile to devote the money to saving his soul through educating theologians, than to fritter it away, as he later put it, 'on my relatives or other vanities'. Fisher was a famous preacher, and no doubt his rhetorical talents helped him to communicate his profound sense of the religious value of education to the benefactors he reeled in for the College. Perhaps his most remarkable success was in winning the support of Henry VIII himself. Notwithstanding the inauspicious start to their relationship in the disputes over Lady Margaret's will, Fisher rose sharply in Henry's estimation during the 1520s thanks to the king's decision to take on Martin Luther in print. It was Fisher who preached the keynote sermon in May 1521 announcing that Henry had written an *Assertion of the Seven Sacraments* against Luther. When Luther penned a furious rejoinder, Fisher hastened to the king's defence, publishing three books against Luther over the next few years. So when Henry passed through Rochester in 1522, Fisher was treated to the full force of the royal charm: the king 'callyd of my loord as soyn as he wer cum to hys logyng and he talkyd luffyngly [lovingly] wyth my loord all the way betweyn the pales [the bishop's palace] and hys chamber in the abbay'.[46] In return Fisher took full advantage of royal favour in seeking permission to

[43] Foundation deeds at SJCA, D58.1 (Gregson, 27 Apr. 1527); D59.92 (Simpson, 26 Jul. 1529); D58.38 (Beresford, 12 Feb. 1520); D58.33 (Bayly, 13 Sept. 1526); D59.94 (Keyton, 27 Oct. 1530); D59.41 (Thimbleby, 5 Jun. 1534).

[44] For Linacre and Lupton, see *ODNB* (V. Nutton; S. Wright). The Linacre foundation agreement is SJCA, D59.75 (19 Aug. 1524). Lupton gave the College £600 in May 1527 (D59.72). The Lupton agreements are D59.56 (9 Mar. 1528) and D59.39 (23 Feb. 1537).

[45] SJCA, D58.58 (6 Mar. 1521), Fisher's agreement with SJC for the foundation. See D14.170 for his grant to the College of the manors of Ridgewell and Thorrington.

[46] SJCA, D105.53.

suppress two more failing religious houses for the College's benefit, the nunneries of Broomhall in Berkshire and of Higham, just outside Rochester.[47] He had probably had his eye on the latter for some time: there were only three nuns, and two of them had fallen pregnant by the local vicar, Edward Stirrup.[48] Systematic lobbying was necessary: for example, a brief was drawn up in May 1521 for Henry Courtenay, earl of Devon, then one of the king's boon companions, so that he could argue their case in the privy chamber.[49] As with Ospringe, the process of acquisition was lengthy and expensive, and Wolsey exacted his customary tribute. The mortmain licence (royal permission for an institution to hold property) for the nunneries cost £200. The nuns were pensioned off and posted to convents of their choice, and by the middle of the decade St John's was receiving about £50 a year each from the estates of Broomhall and Higham, and about £66 from Ospringe.[50]

The success of Fisher's fundraising efforts is easily summed up. In 1515, St John's was worth about £100 a year, around the average for a Cambridge college. By the time he was executed in 1535, it was valued at just over £500 a year, second only to King's College.

4. LECTURES AND LANGUAGES

After the College was formally opened in the summer of 1516, academic life was soon under way despite the financial worries. In the broadest terms, the course of study at Cambridge was defined by the statutes of the University, which set out a programme of study in the 'liberal arts' that led after four years to the degree of BA and after a further three years to the MA. In theory, teaching was provided centrally by the 'regent masters', recently graduated MAs, but in practice, by Tudor times, teaching was increasingly provided within colleges, partly by college lecturers chosen from the Fellows, and partly through the tutorial system, by which groups of students were assigned to a Fellow of MA status who would combine pastoral responsibility with an oversight of their academic studies. It is difficult to find out much about what was taught, and how, because college lecturing was defined only in the most general terms, if at all, in college statutes, while the tutorial system was largely informal and has therefore left even fewer traces in the historical record. Nevertheless, some impressions

---

[47] Letters patent granting both convents to the College were issued in November 1522: SJCA, D6.16.

[48] Lewis, *Dr. John Fisher*, II. 310, 312–14.

[49] SJCA, D13.94.6, 'Artycles of consyderation for my lorde of Devonshyer'. The date is from D106.13, 13, noting 2s paid 'for making a boke to my shewe to my lorde of devonshire', 23 May 1521. The same page notes 'a supplicacion to my lorde Cardinall for bromehall' on 28 May. For the earl of Devon, see D. Starkey, *The Reign of Henry VIII: Personalities and Politics* (London, 1991), 95; and *ODNB* (J. P. D. Cooper).

[50] SJCA, D106.13, 22 (8 Feb. 1522, for the licence); SJCA, M3.4, Master's accounts, 1525–6; SJCA, SB3.1, Bursars' accounts, 1526–7. Dame Jane Rawlyns, prioress of Broomhall, drew her pension of £5 a year until 1548. D106.18, fo. 85v, is the last payment. There was no payment to her in 1549: fo. 140r.

of academic life can be put together from a range of scattered and fragmentary sources, which are richer for St John's than for most other Cambridge colleges.

The most helpful sources are the successive recensions of the College statutes that were drawn up by Fisher in 1516, 1524, and 1530.[51] The first version was particularly indebted to the 1506 statutes for Christ's College, which he had presumably also played a significant part in drafting. One innovation adopted almost word for word was the institution of an official College lecturer, defined, as at Christ's, as playing the part in the corporate body of the College of 'that organ by which new offspring are procreated', a metaphor which then as now must have lent itself to ribaldry. The lecturer was to provide four two-hour lectures a week (straight after morning mass), one in 'sophistry', one in logic, and two in natural philosophy, on texts to be set by the Master and Seniors.[52] He had to devote another two hours a day to 'repetitions' and 'examinations', in which he took the students through lecture material in more detail and made sure that they had understood it. In addition to this he had to preside at various scholarly exercises in the afternoons and evenings, probably occupying another twelve hours a week. The Fellow selected for this onerous task was, wisely, forbidden to refuse it, on pain of losing his Fellowship. Despite the annual salary of 53s 4d, this was a post with a high turnover in the sixteenth century, though occasionally the same man might fill it for several years. The first lecturer on record was one of the founding Fellows, Thomas Wearsdale, but we know nothing of the content or style of his teaching.[53]

The work of the College lecturer (later known as the 'domestic' or 'principal' lecturer) was envisaged in terms of the traditional training in the liberal arts, which focused heavily on Aristotelian logic and philosophy. But the University had already set out on a long road that would lead ultimately to two Cambridge specialities: mathematics and astronomy. By 1500 the University was already providing lectures in mathematics, and Fisher stipulated that the College was to appoint four Fellows to teach mathematics through the Long Vacation, between 'commencement' (degree day for MAs) and the start of the Michaelmas Term. These four Fellows, who were also to offer lectures on the ecclesiastical festivals that fell in other terms, were to lecture respectively on arithmetic, geometry, perspective, and the sphere (or cosmography).[54] This last subject may have been interpreted rather broadly. In 1519–20 a 'tabula de cosmographia' was purchased for the Hall, along with a standard textbook, Pomponius Mela's treatise *De cosmographia*. But as this book was actually a description of the world (geography rather than cosmography, in modern terms), the 'tabula', for which

---

[51] A few pages survive of an earlier version of the statutes, but it is not clear whether these represent an earlier code that actually governed the College, or merely an earlier draft of the code promulgated in 1516: M. G. Underwood, 'Behind the early statutes', *Eagle* lxix, no. 291 (1983), 4.

[52] The wording of the 1516 statute, as at Christ's, could give the impression that the lecturer is to offer four two-hour lectures a day! See Dobson, 'Foundation', 21. But this is beyond the bounds of possibility, and the more precise wording of the 1524 statute shows that one lecture each working day is intended: *Early Statutes*, 328 (1524) and 383 (1516).

[53] SJCA, D107.8, 24 (1518–19).

[54] *Early Statutes*, 385.

a very high price was paid (6s 8d – most books could be bought for a few pennies or a couple of shillings), was most likely a map of the world, perhaps the *Universalis cosmographia* published on twelve sheets in 1507.[55]

The statutes underwent substantial and relatively rapid revision in the early years. The second recension was issued on 24 July 1524,[56] but College accounts and correspondence show that it had been in preparation for several years. John Watson was paid 2 marks on Fisher's instructions in October 1522 'for busynes that he had concernyng our statutes'.[57] The following year, Fisher's chaplain was reporting to the Master that John Bottell had been commissioned to write out 'your statutes'.[58] The forum for drafting and correcting the statutes was evidently the bishop's household rather than the College itself, and Fisher's personal involvement in the task is evident from the heavy marginal annotations in his own hand.[59] A copy of the statutes of one of Oxford's most humanist colleges, Corpus Christi, is bound after a copy of the 1524 statutes in a volume in the archives, and verbal resemblances show that Fisher was influenced by them in his 1530 recension.[60]

The later recensions of the statutes specified in increasing detail the academic provision of the College, and introduced a number of features that helped to establish St John's as one of England's foremost centres for what historians now call 'Renaissance humanism', but what was generally referred to at the time as *bonae literae* (literally, 'good letters'), an intellectual movement focused on the study of the languages and literature of classical antiquity. Fisher's own commitment to humanism had long been evident. In 1511 he had brought Desiderius Erasmus to Cambridge to lecture in Greek, a subject not previously available at either University. Even in his 1516 statutes he voiced the hope that some Fellows would set about the study of Greek and Hebrew.[61] This was not allowed to remain a dead letter. With his characteristic indefatigability as a fundraiser and academic entrepreneur, Fisher secured the services for both his College and his University of two rising young English scholars, Richard Croke and Robert Wakefield, at royal expense. Richard Croke had left England to study Greek abroad and by 1518 was lecturing at the University of Leipzig. But the promise of a position in Cambridge lured him back in 1519, and while he lectured in the University he resided in St John's, probably as a Fellow-Commoner. Robert

[55] SJCA, D107.8, 61.

[56] *Early Statutes*, 341–2.

[57] SJCA, D106.13, 32.

[58] SJCA, D105.44; also D105.41. John Bottell was the rector of Cuxton, near Rochester, who acted as a scribe for Fisher: *Vie du bienheureux martyr Jean Fisher*, 71–2, 362.

[59] SJCA, C1.40.7, fo. 1r–v, is the 1516 statute concerning the lecturer. The long marginal alteration in Fisher's hand in the margin (fo. 1v) is integrated into the 1524 version (*Early Statutes*, 327). C1.40.2 shows Fisher's amendments on an early draft of the 1516 statutes. See fig. 3.

[60] SJCA, C1.2. The chapter on allocation of rooms in the Corpus Christi statutes is found at fo. 105v, and differs entirely from the chapter on the same subject in the 1524 statutes for St John's (fo. 10r). However, the relevant chapter in the 1530 statutes opens with the same words as the Corpus Christi statute (*Early Statutes*, 164).

[61] Ibid., 375.

Wakefield was taken on to meet the need for Hebrew. Elected to a Fellowship in 1519, which was doubtless connected with the purchase of 'two books of Hebrew' that year,[62] he was then granted two years of paid leave by Fisher so that he could 'goo by yonde the sea to thentent thatt he may be the more expolite and perfite in the tonge of hebrew', and thus, when he returned, 'be more able to perfite [perfect] other in the sayme learnyng and to doo honour both to your Colleg and to the hoolle reame'.[63] He studied at Louvain and Tübingen before returning in 1524 to serve in the University as 'the king's reader in Hebrew', on much the same basis as Croke in Greek. Both men's stipends were paid direct from the royal coffers, a further indication of the extent to which Fisher was able to exploit royal favour to support his academic projects in the early 1520s.

Meanwhile, in a reorganization of his personal foundation in St John's formalized in an indenture of April 1525, Fisher established college lectureships in Greek and Hebrew.[64] The intention was, no doubt, that Croke and Wakefield would fill these posts for some years, but this was frustrated by events. Wakefield and Croke were ambitious and prickly individuals, and in the mid-1520s both men were to turn against Fisher as they graduated from his patronage to that of the king. Croke made enemies in College, as he did almost everywhere he went, and we can see the final breakdown of his relationship with Fisher in a furious letter from the bishop, the only surviving part of an evidently ill-tempered exchange. Croke had written twice to Fisher, accusing him variously of unduly favouring northerners in the statutes, of embezzling funds entrusted to him by Lady Margaret's executors, of taking the credit for her foundation, and of filling the College with his relatives. In reply, Fisher protested that the northern bias was exactly what the foundress had wanted, and that nobody could have done more than he had himself to ensure that the College reflected glory on her name. Going onto the offensive, he reprimanded Croke for his habit of absenting himself from Hall in favour of private dinner parties with his cronies in his rooms, though even this might have been borne had Croke shown a proper dedication to lecturing. Had he himself wished to use the College to provide comfortable berths for his needy relatives, Fisher added, with biting sarcasm, he had enough of those to fill every nook and cranny of the place, which might have been preferable to wasting space on ingrates.[65] None of this did Croke much harm, as thanks to the connections Fisher had made for him at court, he was plucked from the College in 1526 to become tutor to Henry VIII's illegitimate son, Henry Fitzroy.

Robert Wakefield's break with Fisher came a little later, when, in 1527, he was recruited to the team of scholars working on Henry VIII's divorce from Catherine of Aragon. His expertise in Hebrew was of especial value in an argument that focused on the interpretation of key texts from the Old Testament. The fact

---

[62] SJCA, M3.2, visus 1518–23, membrane 2, 'Et in denariis solutis in duobus libris de Ebrue'.

[63] SJCA, C7.11, Thin Red Book, fo. 219r (Baker-Mayor, I. 358).

[64] *Early Statutes*, 250–52 (1530), embodying the substance of the 1525 agreement, for which see SJCA, D58.59.

[65] SJCA, C7.11, Thin Red Book, fos. 49r–50v, Fisher to Croke (no date). For Croke's career, see *ODNB* (J. Woolfson).

4 Initial of royal licence for the College to acquire land, 1526,
showing the figure of St John holding the poisoned chalice and
expelling the poison in the form of a winged serpent: SJCA D5.4

that Fisher was already the leading scholar arguing for the validity of Catherine's marriage to Henry must have made Wakefield's *démarche* look to him like a personal betrayal. The fact that Wakefield continued to draw his stipend as a Fellow on Fisher's foundation in St John's until 1532 added injury to insult. His position at court presumably made him impossible to dismiss even though he can no longer have been carrying out his duties. Only when Henry rewarded him with a Fellowship at his new, and shortlived, King Henry VIII's College, in Oxford, did Wakefield finally have to vacate his Fellowship at St John's.[66] By that time Richard Croke was also working full time on Henry VIII's divorce, and was also a Fellow of King Henry VIII's College. Fisher would not have savoured the irony of having gone to all the trouble of founding lectureships in the sacred languages only to see their first incumbents switch horses so adroitly and, from his point of view, prostitute their talents to their prince.

Notwithstanding the defection of Croke and Wakefield, the study of Hebrew survived and that of Greek even flourished in St John's, although this can only

---

[66] King Henry VIII's College was the continuation under new management of Cardinal's College (Wolsey's foundation in Oxford), and would in turn be refounded as Christ Church in 1546.

be inferred from a few scraps of evidence. The torch was carried for Hebrew by Ralph Baynes, a Fellow on Fisher's foundation who went on to become professor of Hebrew at the prestigious Collège du Roi in Paris. But it would take a generation for the language of the Old Testament to take firm root in the curriculum at St John's. Greek developed far more swiftly. Croke's successor was George Day, and it is a sufficient tribute to him that he was the Tutor of John Cheke, the greatest Greek scholar of the College's second generation. In the 1530s, Day was succeeded as the College lecturer in Greek first by John Redman and then by Cheke, the two men whom Ascham credited with inaugurating the academic golden age of St John's.[67] Another of the leading early Grecians was Robert Pember, a Fellow from 1524, who became a close friend of Roger Ascham, and, eventually, a founding Fellow of Trinity College in 1546. A tincture of Greek learning can be discerned in the sermons of one of the founding Fellows, Henry Gold.[68] And during one of his own absences from College, Richard Croke wrote to Gold (who was looking after his pupils) telling him to make them translate half of page of Lucian a day from Greek into Latin.[69] Enthusiasm for Greek can also be seen in the books students owned. One of the Fellows, Richard Brandsby, was buying Greek books from the University bookseller, Garrett Godfrey, in the 1520s.[70] Leonard Barton, a Fellow who died in 1531, owned a copy of Theodore of Gaza's Greek grammar (probably in an edition by Erasmus).[71] The most revealing evidence comes from the accounts kept for Matthew White, a nephew of John Fisher who was granted a scholarship on his uncle's foundation. In his second year of study (1531–2), White was equipped with a Greek grammar and dictionary, which suggests that the subject was becoming a standard requirement in College.[72]

John Fisher also used his personal foundation to support the work of the College lecturer by funding four 'examiners' in the main areas of study: rhetoric, dialectic, mathematics, and philosophy. The task of the examiners was to hold classes every day on which lectures were given, in which they would test the students on what they had learned. Master and Seniors were to fix the timetable. With stipends of 40 shillings a year these were sought-after appointments, and they were to be filled annually on 10 September by the Master and Seniors, with preference, *ceteris paribus*, to Fellows on Fisher's foundation.[73] The establishment of the examiner in rhetoric was of particular importance, as this was not a subject that was covered by the College lecturer. By 1529 the rhetoric lecture was being given by John Seton, who was not yet an MA, but who showed his

---

[67] R. Ascham, *Scolemaster*, in *The Whole Works of Roger Ascham*, ed. J. A. Giles (London, 1856), IV. 142.

[68] L. E. Whatmore, 'A sermon of Henry Gold, vicar of Ospringe, 1525–27, preached before Archbishop Warham', *Archaeologia Cantiana* lvii (1944), 34–43, esp. pp. 35, 36, 41.

[69] Croke to Gold, no date: TNA SP1/34, fo.±32r.

[70] *Garrett Godfrey's Accounts, c. 1527–1533*, ed. E. Leedham-Green, D. E. Rhodes, F. H. Stubbings (Cambridge, 1992), 22–3, 36–7.

[71] CUA, VCCt Wills I, fo. 54r.

[72] SJCA, D106.6, fos. 52r, 55r.

[73] *Early Statutes*, 244–50.

humanist attainments by signing a receipt for his stipend in a fine italic hand.[74] The books found in the hands of students and teachers at the College show the impact the position made. Christopher Jackson, a Fellow who died in 1528, and whose memorial can still be seen in the chapel, owned all four volumes of Erasmus's *Adagia* as well as a work of Lorenzo Valla's – this latter almost certainly Valla's *Elegantiae latinae linguae*, the endlessly reprinted definitive style-guide to humanist latinity.[75]

It was the pursuit of elegant Latin that stood at the heart of the Renaissance curriculum, and St John's was in the vanguard of this in Cambridge, though it must be emphasized that this movement was at work throughout the University. The University's most self-conscious gesture towards *bonae litterae* was to establish the post of University Orator in the academic year 1521–2. The Orator's duties included writing formal letters on behalf of the University to powerful patrons and making stylish addresses to welcome visiting dignitaries or mark special occasions. The first Orator, Richard Croke (1521–7), was from St John's, as indeed were four of the first five Orators.[76] His first successor, George Day (1527–37), had proved his credentials by turning out some tolerably classicizing Latin verses to decorate the early pages of John Fisher's most important book, his *Assertionis Lutheranae Confutatio* (Antwerp, 1523), and he was very probably the author of an elegant Latin encomium of Fisher as University and College benefactor that survives among the archives.[77]

For all his commitment to Renaissance humanism, Fisher came to have misgivings about the extent to which, in some circles, it was driving out more traditional scholastic studies and exercises. So his examiners supported tuition in logic and philosophy as well as in rhetoric. In one draft statute he stipulated that a second lecturer should be appointed to teach from the 'questions of Antonius', the medieval commentaries of Antonius Andreae on the logic of Aristotle and Porphyry.[78] In another he voiced anxiety over the decline of scholastic disputation, and set out instructions for all members of the College to practise this art regularly, with candidates for the BA working from Antonius Andreae; candidates for the MA from Buridan, Pierre Tartaret or Joannes de Magistris; junior Fellows on Scotus; and senior Fellows on Aristotle or Plato. One similar change that he introduced in 1530 was to give the College discretion to change his Hebrew lectureship for a while into a lectureship on the works of Duns Scotus (the scholastic theologian who was the bugbear of thoroughgoing humanists), 'if they can be turned into better Latin'.[79] In fact, Scotus's days were numbered,

[74] SJCA, D106.6, fo. 45v.

[75] CUA, VCCt Wills I, fo. 46v.

[76] *Grace Book B*, II. 101 (Croke, 1521–2), 141–2 (Day, 1527–8), 212 (Thomas Smith, Queens', 1537–8), and 238 (Cheke, 1541–2). For the fifth Orator, Ascham, in 1547–8, see *Grace Book Δ*, ed. J. Venn (Cambridge, 1910), 53.

[77] J. Fisher, *Assertionis Lutheranae Confutatio* (Antwerp, 1523), sig. A2r–v; Lewis, *Dr. John Fisher*, II. 290–97.

[78] Baker-Mayor, I. 343. A book of 'Antony questions' was bought for Matthew White (SJCA, D106.6, fo. 62r): SJCA, C7.11, Thin Red Book, fos. 8v (logic) and 9r–v (second lecturer). Marginal annotations in the 1524 statutes (*Early Statutes*, 326–7) indicate that the second lecturer was appointed.

[79] *Early Statutes*, 252.

and Fisher need not have lost sleep over the decline of disputation. Not only did the *viva voce* disputation remain a staple of teaching and examining long into the seventeenth century, but, for all the stirring of new intellectual currents, Aristotelianism continued to dominate natural philosophy in Cambridge, as in most of Europe, until the new empirical and mathematical approaches of Bacon, Galileo, Descartes, and eventually Newton left it looking merely ridiculous.

5. TUTORS, PREACHERS AND PLAYS

One of the most obscure aspects of collegiate life in the Tudor University is the tutorial system. All scholars and students below the status of MA were assigned to a tutor, yet tutorial arrangements were largely personal and informal, and therefore almost invisible in the statutes and archives. Tutors really were *in loco parentis*, and as such responsible for the education, welfare, and financial arrangements of their pupils. Thus kitchen bills were settled by tutors, who had to recoup the costs from their students themselves. We catch occasional glimpses of the tutorial relationship, as in the accounts kept for Edward and Matthew White, the nephews of John Fisher who were Scholars on his foundation around 1530. John Seton, Matthew's Tutor, clearly provided for most of his needs, buying his books and clothing and allowing him spending money, and he sought reimbursement from the Master, who managed the funds.[80] But our knowledge of the tutorial system is scanty, based on a few surviving letters and passing references in other sources. Thus John Cheke's father, Peter, appointed his son's Tutor, George Day, as the supervisor of his own last will and testament when he was dying in 1530.[81] As with everything in Tudor England, personal relationships and patronage were vital. Fathers or friends would write to college heads and others seeking appropriate tutors and scholarships for their sons or clients. For example, Henry Ediall wrote to the Master seeking a place on the foundation of Cardinal Morton for a relative of the cardinal's, William Morton. He was clearly successful, as William Morton is listed as a Scholar of the College in the year 1522–3.[82] Hugh Ashton sent a young boy to the College as a Scholar on his foundation in 1520, and the President, John Smith, allotted him John Rudd as his Tutor.[83]

Education was not, for Fisher, an end in itself, nor had he persuaded the foundress and so many other benefactors to invest in St John's College simply to foster the cultivation of the mind. The higher purpose was the training of priests to serve God and the Church. In an age when the reform of the priesthood was seen as the key to the reform of Christian society, there could be no more meritorious work in the eyes of God. This was the basis on which Fisher

---

[80] SJCA, D106.6, fos. 52r, 65v.

[81] CUA, VCCt Wills I, fo. 50v.

[82] SJCA, D105.254, 31 Oct. no year given. A very badly damaged valuation of the entire University for tax purposes, listing all fellows and students by their colleges, survives at TNA SP1/233, fos. 187–223. See fo. 195r for St John's.

[83] SJCA, D56.25, John Smith to Nicholas Metcalfe, 19 Apr. 1520.

could urge people not merely to endow prayers and masses for their souls in the traditional way, but to do so through the specific vehicle of an academic college. The foundress's wish, he stated, was that the College should bring forth 'theologians who would communicate the fruit of their learning to the people' through preaching. This was reflected in the most innovative provision in his statutes, which required that a quarter of the Fellows were to be charged with the task of preaching the Word of God to the people.[84] Establishing and endowing preacherships was by no means unprecedented. Lady Margaret had established a preachership at Cambridge in 1504, and around the same time the University had obtained papal authority to license twelve of its theologians each year to preach anywhere in the kingdom. Other benefactors had endowed preaching positions in colleges, as Dame Alice Wyche had done at Queens', but all they usually required was a single sermon a year at a particular place.[85] This was the first time that extensive popular preaching was defined as part of a college's mission. It would be some time before the target of a quarter of the Fellowship would be met, but the first preachers are recorded in 1520: Thomas Hall, Nicholas Darington, and Thomas Arthur. Over the next few years they were joined by Henry Gold, who was later a preacher on the staff of the archbishop of Canterbury, and by the first two Presidents of the College, John Smith and William Longford. Fellows of St John's also appeared increasingly among the University's licensed preachers. All those just named received this privilege, and they were joined by many colleagues, including Richard Croke and Ralph Baynes, most of whom probably held a College preachership at some point (the records are very patchy for the 1520s and early 1530s).[86] Preacherships brought an additional stipend of 13s 4d a year, a welcome perquisite, and were mostly monopolized by the Seniors. It is clear, however, that not everyone took the preachership as seriously as the bishop. In his second recension of the statutes, he not only had to insist that preachers carry out their duties in person, but also to warn that all theology students should attend and refrain from 'mocking the preacher by words or gestures, or by making faces'.[87]

The preachership was to give Fisher perhaps the gravest shock he was to face in the development of St John's, in an episode which looked ahead to a future he would never have contemplated. For in 1527 one of the preachers, Thomas Arthur, was arrested in the company of a licensed preacher of the University, Thomas Bilney, on suspicion of heresy. They had made a preaching tour together from Cambridge to London that summer, delivering sermons that challenged aspects of traditional devotion such as the veneration of images and the intercession of the saints. They were in due course charged before a tribunal headed by Cardinal Wolsey, and abjured their controversial propositions in

---

[84] *Early Statutes*, 377.

[85] For Dame Alice Wyche's foundation, see S. Wabuda, *Preaching during the English Reformation* (Cambridge, 2002), 55–6.

[86] SJCA, D107.8, 60 (1520), 94 (1521), and 120 (1523). For University preachers see *Grace Book B*, II. 105, where at least four of the twelve named for 1522–3 were from St John's (Brandsby, Bradshaw, Longford, and Gold); and 137, where three of the four named for 1526–7 were from St John's (Brewer, Baynes, and Fletcher).

[87] *Early Statutes*, 316.

December.[88] Among the range of purposes with which Fisher originally credited Lady Margaret in founding the College was 'the increase of the faith'. In 1524, already perhaps reacting against Lutheranism, he amended this to 'the corroboration of the faith'.[89] Preaching heresy did not correspond to either of these, and the anxiety it occasioned him is most evident in an amendment he made to the statutes in the third revision of 1530, giving the Master and Seniors power to expel any member of College 'on the slightest suspicion' of heresy.[90]

The most unexpected aspect of Fisher's own involvement with St John's is the fact that he stood at the origin of the College's vigorous tradition of sixteenth-century drama. The President, John Smith, wrote to the Master in December 1521 'And [i.e. 'if'] owr company myght have the play that my lorde made thei wold provyde to play yt', from which it would appear that he had written something for the Christmas season.[91] Sadly there is no hint as to what the subject of this drama might have been, though it would have been written in Latin, and was probably no comedy. The earliest reference to a play in the accounts is for Christmas 1524, when we find 7s 8d spent on costumes, including a 'playing gown' each for a man and a woman.[92] Around that time Richard Brandisby bought a copy of the neo-Latin comedy *Acolastus*. Another Fellow of the 1520s, Thomas Arthur, actually wrote two tragedies, *Microcosmus*, and *Mundus Plumbeus* ('The Leaden World').[93] He is named in passing in a receipt for expenses on a play, which suggests that his plays were probably performed in College.[94] The Fellows were certainly committed to the educational value of drama. John Redman, John Cheke, John Hatcher and Richard Wade were all involved in putting on plays in 1535, by which time the expenses of such events included setting up and taking down a stage.[95] By the 1540s, plays were to be almost annual events, and were recognized as such in the statutes of 1545, which laid down that each Fellow was to take a turn, year by year, as the 'Lord of Christmas', with responsibility for organizing the entertainments.[96]

---

[88] S. Brigden, *London and the Reformation* (Oxford, 1989), 111–13; J. Foxe, *The Acts and Monuments*, ed. J. Pratt (London, [1877]), IV. 619–25. Arthur's last appearance as a College preacher is in 1525–6 (SJCA, SB3.1). It is likely that his arrest in 1527 abruptly terminated his appointment, after several years of continuous service, so that his name was not included when the 1527 accounts were made up at the end of the year.

[89] *Early Statutes*, 373 (1516) and 309 (1524).

[90] Ibid., 212: 'levissima quavis suspicione'. This amendment was removed in 1545: p. 213.

[91] SJCA, D105.47 (9 Dec. 1521). See also D105.49 (13 Dec.), 'the company wolde gladly have my lordes play'.

[92] SJCA, D106.11, fo. 39r (early 1525). These entries are struck through, but identical entries are scattered in D106.12, fos. 146v, 149v, 150v, and 153v, an account covering the same period, and probably relating to a play for Christmas 1524.

[93] J. Bale, *Scriptorum illustrium Majoris Brytanniae catalogus* (Basel, 1557–9), I. 709–10. Neither play survives. Bale had been at Cambridge in the 1520s, so may perhaps have seen them performed.

[94] SJCA, D57.136. See A. H. Nelson (ed.), *Records of Early English Drama, Cambridge*, 2 vols. (Toronto, 1989), II. 842, 931.

[95] Nelson, *Records of Cambridge Drama*, I. 109.

[96] *Early Statutes*, 139.

6. NICHOLAS METCALFE
AND THE PROBLEMS OF GOVERNANCE

The continuing evolution of the statutes in the early years reflected not only theological anxieties and academic developments but also administrative realities. On the opening day of the College in 1516, a new Master was appointed to replace Robert Shorton, who had supervised the construction works. The new man was Alan Percy. Lacking in academic distinction and administrative experience, he was a surprising choice, explicable only as a failed fundraising gambit. For Alan Percy was a younger brother of the earl of Northumberland, whose broad estates in the East Riding of Yorkshire put him at the pinnacle of the social hierarchy in Fisher's native region. But the gesture did not draw in the patronage of that great family, and a couple of years later Percy was bought out on a generous pension of £10 a year, to be replaced by Dr Nicholas Metcalfe, who, as archdeacon of Rochester, had been Fisher's right-hand man since 1512.

Metcalfe brought to the Mastership an energy that Percy devoted only to the accumulation of ecclesiastical benefices. The correspondence that survives in the College archives is probably only a tithe of what was written, but it is enough to indicate the wide range of problems he had to deal with. There was scandal. In one letter to the Master, John Smith reported that one of the founding Fellows, Nicholas Darington, was

> diffamed with a woman in the countre the which is now with childe and itt is seid that itt schulde be his nott onlie here with vs thorowght all Cambridge butt also in the countre with diuerse probacions of that same the which is to the grett diffamacion of owr colliege and allso to vs all.[97]

As Darington remained a College preacher until 1522, when he went abroad to study at Louvain, it seems that neither his nor the College's reputation was unduly damaged by this rumour.[98] But it will have been something Metcalfe was anxious to hush up while he worked on sealing deals with donors and vendors. Those deals were endless. There were lands and woods to survey, manorial courts to hold, rents to collect, and accounts to audit. Not that there was not also plenty to do at home. The later 1520s and the 1530s saw not only the fitting out of Fisher's lavish chantry chapel, which Metcalfe supervised, but still more importantly the construction of a second court, Metcalfe Court, to house the growing student numbers. By 1523 the College was already much larger than has previously been thought. To the fifty or so Fellows and Scholars supported by the foundation there had already been added about the same number of pensioners and Fellow-Commoners, giving a total membership just under a hundred that year. By the end of Henry's

[97] SJCA, D105.247 (18 Jul. 1519).

[98] Darington to Henry Gold, from Louvain, 16 Jul. 1522: TNA SP1/25, fo. 51r. Darington relies on Gold's goodwill in sorting out a disagreement between him and Metcalfe over money, admitting that 'I was perhaps a little more vehement than he would have liked in demanding what was mine'. Metcalfe's accounts have an entry for 21 Nov. 1522 paying Darington's agent £3 6s 8d in arrears for the year ending the previous August: SJCA, D106.13, 35.

reign, total membership was around 170, with about forty Fellows and sixty Scholars.[99]

The most significant constitutional change in the 1524 statutes was evidently the fruit of Metcalfe's hectic experience in office. For the establishment of a permanent President to deputize for the Master (the 1516 statutes provide merely for a temporary deputy) recognizes the prodigious time that Metcalfe spent away on business in these early years.[100] Detailed accounts of his personal expenses for 1521 and 1522 make it hard to believe at first glance that he spent any time at all in Cambridge. His life was an endless round of the king's courts, with almost continual business in Common Pleas, King's Bench, Chancery, and the Exchequer. For variety, there was occasional business in the Court of Arches, the archbishop of Canterbury's appeal court. There were innumerable attorneys and officials to be briefed or consulted; writs, warrants, deeds, letters, and indentures to be drafted and copied and checked; fees to be paid and palms to be greased. In 1521 he was away on four lengthy tours totalling nearly eight months, as he sorted out the affairs of Ospringe and the nunneries. He was back at St John's for the Fellowship elections on the fourth Monday of Lent (11 March 1521), but was off again before Easter, returning for June and for the second half of August and most of September. Then he was away again until a couple of weeks before Christmas, during which odyssey he had to follow Cardinal Wolsey to Calais in the hope of expediting some paperwork. In the long hours waiting on the cardinal's attention he managed to lose at chess to Thomas Goodrich.[101] The following year Metcalfe claimed expenses for a total of 339 days away, though again he seems to have been at St John's for the Fellowship elections, which that year took place on 31 March.[102]

In 1527, events such as Henry's petition for a divorce and Thomas Arthur's abjuration for heresy were straws blown about in the wind of change, but few people could yet see where those changes would lead. Henry VIII's opposition to Lutheranism was still unhesitating, and the religious structures of late medieval England seemed unshakeable. St John's College, one of the latest of those structures, had emerged from the uncertainties of its early years and now stood as the finest monument to John Fisher's decades of service to the University. In 1528 the University wrote to inform their former chancellor that, on account of his many services, most notably in securing them the munificent patronage of Lady Margaret, they had voted on 30 January to accord him the honour of an

---

[99] SJCA, M3.2, Master's accounts for the foundation members in 1523–4; TNA SP1/233, fo. 195r for the 1523 total of ninety-eight; Ascham, *Whole Works*, I. 143, for the total in 1547; and SJCA, D106.18, fos. 16r–23v, for the foundation that year. For Metcalfe Court see Crook, *Foundation to Gilbert Scott*, 24.

[100] *Early Statutes*, 281–2 (1524); compare pp. 358–9 (1516).

[101] SJCA, D106.13, 25: 7 shillings 'For our passage from Calis when I was with my lorde Cardinall for the nonnes'. D106.8, fos. 4r–6v contains full accounts of the trip to Calais, 15–26 Oct., including at fo. 6r, 'ffor a quarte of wyne that ye lost to Mr goodreke at the chesse' (22 Oct.). A good deal of wine was quaffed in the long hours of waiting.

[102] Figures based on Metcalfe's accounts of his business expenses for those years: SJCA, D106.13, 11–36.

annual votive mass for his soul in perpetuity.[103] In his reply, Fisher went out of his way to emphasize that it was Lady Margaret rather than he who merited their gratitude: 'In these matters I was merely a servant, doing nothing more than I was bound to by all human and divine laws.'[104] The obsequies, he insisted, should be hers, not his, though he gratefully accepted a share in their prayers. Yet setting aside his commendable self-deprecation, we can see that of all Lady Margaret's legacy to Cambridge, it was St John's College which owed the most to Fisher. But for that meeting back in the 1490s, her attention might never have been drawn so decisively towards England's younger university. To found one college was remarkable: to found a second was unprecedented. And for all the hectic activity in the months before her death, her intentions for that second college were far from legally settled when she died. Although many of her executors played their part in what followed – most notably Richard Foxe, Hugh Ashton, and Henry Hornby – they recognized, as much as did their contemporaries, Fisher's pre-eminent role in the establishment of the College, most evidently in delegating to him the patronal privileges of the foundress for his lifetime. In reality, and for all his humility, he deserved at least as much credit for its foundation as she did. For the first phase of its history, until his execution in June 1535, St John's was Fisher's College.

---

[103] Lewis, *Dr. John Fisher*, II. 301–3, 303–5.
[104] Ibid., II. 305–7, esp. p. 305.

St John's College and the Crisis of the Reformation

1. THE IMPACT OF THE 'BREAK WITH ROME'

The history of the College, like the history of England, was changed utterly by the 'King's Great Matter', Henry VIII's midlife crisis over Anne Boleyn. Her refusal to settle for the dubious honour of being the royal mistress led Henry to start looking for a way out of his first marriage. Under other circumstances, his decision to trade in his first wife for a newer model might have had few implications beyond making work for lawyers. But the king's hypertrophied conscience fastened onto the pleasing notion that his marriage to Catherine of Aragon was directly contrary to the express Word of God. Catherine had been married to his elder brother Arthur, Prince of Wales (d. 1502), and the book of Leviticus forbade marriage to a brother's wife. Henry's insistence that marriage to the widow of his brother was 'incest' offers a nice contrast to his insouciance about marriage to the sister of his mistress (he had previously had a lengthy affair with Mary Boleyn). But his conscience turned a matter of law into a question of theology. John Fisher was sounded out for his opinion, and soon concluded that, notwithstanding the royal scruples, Henry's marriage to Catherine of Aragon was valid.[1]

Although the pull of royal patronage led to some defections, Fisher's influence over the College remained paramount. Over the winter of 1529–30 several Fellows engaged in a pulpit controversy with the University chaplain, Hugh Latimer, then emerging as a leading Evangelical preacher. Although the argument was about doctrine, it was said that their animus against Latimer was fuelled by his support for Henry's divorce, and that their attacks were fomented by friends of Fisher's such as John Watson, a former Fellow who was by this time Master of Christ's College.[2] Throughout the early 1530s St John's proved durably loyal to its godfather, though it must have received a shock when one of its founding Fellows became one of the first victims of Henry's Reformation. Henry Gold (Fellow 1516–25) had become chaplain to William Warham, Archbishop of Canterbury, and in this role he had witnessed the dramatic rise of the so-called 'Holy Maid of Kent', Elizabeth Barton, a serving-girl whose miraculous cure from epilepsy at a Kentish shrine in the 1520s had led to a new life as a nun and visionary at the convent of St Sepulchre's in Canterbury. Archbishop Warham investigated her cure and declared it authentic. Her fame spread as her revelations extended to matters of religion and high politics. Her message that the king should remain faithful to his wife and to his church won her the credence of Fisher and many others. Henry Gold was one of her inner circle

---

[1] Rex, *Theology of John Fisher*, 165.

[2] Edward Fox to the Vice-Chancellor, 24 Jan. 1530, in J. Lamb (ed.), *A Collection of Letters, Statutes, and Other Documents ... Illustrative of the History of the University of Cambridge* (London, 1838), 14–15. On 29 January 1530, the Vice-Chancellor censured four men for their attacks on Latimer: ibid., 15–18. Three of them, Ralph Baynes, John Briganden and Thomas Greenwood, were Fellows of St John's and College preachers for that academic year: SJCA, SB3.4.

rounded up in autumn 1533. With them, in spring 1534, he was declared guilty of treason by Act of Attainder and executed on Monday 20 April at Tyburn.

Shortly before Gold's execution, Fisher had been invited to swear the new oath to the succession, and thus to recognize Henry's marriage to Anne Boleyn and implicitly repudiate the papacy. Upon his refusal, he was consigned to the Tower of London with other dissidents. Despite this, the College continued to communicate with him, sending a deputation to console him with letters and gifts, and seeking his approval for further alterations to the statutes. One letter included this outspoken declaration of support:

> We judge it wicked indeed and disgraceful, in this state of affairs, not to manifest our affection to you and demonstrate our proper concern for you. Since all who, in these times, either rejoice in the noble name of a Christian or care for their fatherland and commonwealth, grieve at your troubles and afflictions, we would be the most ungrateful of all, devoid of any shadow of reputation for honesty, if whatever adversity you face did not also torment us and inflict upon our hearts the utmost pain (…) When we call to mind and consider how great a sign of divine favour it is in this world to undergo tribulation for the sake of righteousness, our minds are seized at once with heartfelt joy, for then we grasp what we never really doubted, that you please God rather than men.

This is the sort of thing that Marian exiles and martyrs wrote to each other a generation later, and the College's letter closes with an invocation of the supreme sacrifice:

> But if indeed anything should happen which would seem harsh and bitter by the judgement of this world, we hope that God will make it easy, gentle, joyous, and honourable for you, just as he transmuted the shame and ignominy of the Cross into the ultimate honour and glory.[3]

The letter is undated, but the accounts for Fisher's foundation in the College have an entry from spring 1534 recording 5s for Matthew White, Fisher's nephew, a Scholar on the foundation, 'when he went to my lord of Rochester', presumably with his tutor John Seton and Richard Brandisby, on their mission concerning the statutes.[4]

For all their moral support, however, none of the Fellows, with one known exception, emulated their patron in refusing the oath to the succession. That exception was Ralph Baynes, a Fellow on Fisher's personal foundation and a vocal opponent of Hugh Latimer. He received his stipend for the last time in the first quarter of 1534, and is next heard of in Paris as a refugee.[5] There he spent twenty years, ending up as professor of Hebrew at the Collège du Roi, not

[3] Lewis, *Dr John Fisher*, II. 356–8.

[4] SJCA, D106.6, fo. 65v; *Vie du bienheureux martyr Jean Fisher*, 281.

[5] Ibid. for the last payment to Baynes on Fisher's foundation, for the first quarter of 1534. Simon Heynes to Thomas Cromwell, from Paris, 2 Oct. 1535, reported the presence there of 'Mr Bayne, whiche departed owt of Englond sumwhat before the deth of my lorde of Rochester, his good lord', and noted that although Baynes used to be a 'gret adversari', he is not 'busy of his tonge' and 'medlith of no maters': TNA SP1/97, fo. 84r. See *ODNB* (J. Wright) for a summary of his career.

to return to England until the reign of Mary, when he became bishop of Coventry and Lichfield. Having fled the realm rather than take the oath, he was the first of many members of St John's to choose exile for the sake of conscience in the Tudor century.

John Fisher's resistance, of course, led him to the scaffold on 22 June 1535. Even after that the College showed a degree of loyalty to his memory. Prayers were offered for his soul on that day each year thereafter, in accordance with the indentures he had agreed with the College, even though his goods and chattels, legally their property but on loan to him until his death, were in fact confiscated to the exchequer. John Cheke made a note against the date in the calendar of his prayer-book, reminding himself to turn up for the dole of 3s 4d awarded to each Fellow who attended Fisher's annual exequies.[6] The loss which most upset the Fellows was of Fisher's peerless library, of which now not a single book can be definitely identified. It was rumoured at the time that the collection was parcelled out among cronies of Thomas Cromwell.[7] For years afterwards the College's letters to power-brokers at court lamented this loss and appealed in vain for the delivery of the books or appropriate compensation.[8]

2. THE FALL OF METCALFE

Such loyalty was gradually eroded by direct political interference in both University and College. This began with the royal visitation of the University in October 1535, the main purpose of which was to elicit the personal subscription to the royal supremacy of every last member. No one in Cambridge dared refuse. The royal agents were also aware, however, of the role of academic studies in the political and ideological games that were being played. The abolition of papal jurisdiction required more than the stroke of a pen. Papal authority was literally inscribed in the corpus of canon law by which the Church was regulated; and it was endorsed in the system of scholastic theology that represented the highest form of knowledge in Fisher's world. The teaching of canon law was simply abolished by the injunctions which the Visitors imposed, and the teaching of theology was abruptly reformed. Henceforth, lectures were no longer to focus on the *Sentences* of Peter Lombard, or on the multifarious scholastic commentaries on that core medieval text. Instead, theology lectures were all to be on the Bible itself, a provision inspired by the official rhetoric that identified Henry's new-found royal supremacy quite literally with the 'Word of God'.[9]

---

[6] BL Additional MS 6059, fo. 6v. This calendar, which later belonged to William Cecil, is all that survives of the prayer-book, and I am grateful to Stephen Alford for his advice on interpreting it. For Fisher's dole see *Early Statutes*, 256.

[7] *Vie du bienheureux martyr Jean Fisher*, 46; Rex, *Theology of John Fisher*, 192.

[8] SJC to the Lord Protector (21 Nov. 1547): Ascham, *Whole Works*, I. 137–44, esp. p. 140. See also SJC to Queen Mary (no date), congratulating her on her accession: Baker-Mayor, I. 377–8.

[9] F. D. Logan, 'The first royal visitation of the English universities, 1535', *English Historical Review* cvi (1991), 861–88; R. Rex, 'The crisis of obedience: God's word and Henry's reformation', *Historical Journal* xxxix (1996), 863–94, at p. 889.

The visitation had a delayed impact upon St John's. Dr Metcalfe had dutifully conformed to everything required of him but he, with a few others, was singled out by the Visitors as one of the old guard of college heads who showed 'greate pertinacite ... to their olde blindenes', and whom it would be better to replace with men 'of a good upryght judgement'.[10] He remained in office another year, but the gravest political crisis of Henry's reign, the 'Pilgrimage of Grace', made his position untenable. The 'Pilgrimage' was the greatest rebellion ever faced by a Tudor monarch, a rising of tens of thousands of armed men across almost all of northern England. Judicious parleying and offers of concessions had defused the military threat by Christmas 1536, and in 1537, after one or two feeble aftershocks of sedition, Henry was able to move decisively against the erstwhile leaders of the movement.[11] But its deep northern roots left St John's suspect in the aftermath. Too many of the Fellows, Scholars, and pensioners came from families that had taken a prominent part in the rising. Metcalfe himself was summoned to London for a personal interview with Cromwell. What passed between them is unknown, but on his return Metcalfe convened the Fellows in the chapel and announced, 'with weepyng teares' (as an eye-witness later recalled) that he had been 'commaunded' to resign the Mastership.[12] In a touching display of his affections, his memorial brass in the chapel records not the date of his death, but the day he stepped down: 4 July 1537.[13] John Caius, a Cambridge student of that generation, was in no doubt that this amounted to expulsion, and gleefully noted that all those responsible were themselves subsequently visited by divine vengeance.[14] Even some of those who did not share Metcalfe's religious views were sorry to see him go. As Roger Ascham observed many years later:

> He was a Papist indeed; but would to God, among all us Protestants, I might once see but one that would win like praise, in doing like good, for the advancement of learning and virtue.[15]

Metcalfe's resignation precipitated a crisis. Letters were sent from court indicating that the king's preferred choice for the mastership was George Day, one of the Fellows who had traded in Fisher's patronage for Henry's.[16] This did not go down well. On 15 July two Fellows were in London with Hugh Latimer, by then bishop of Worcester, showing him what they claimed was a statute

[10] TNA SP1/98, fo. 48r.

[11] R. W. Hoyle, *The Pilgrimage of Grace and the Politics of the 1530s* (Oxford, 2001).

[12] Statement by Thomas Watson (15 Oct. 1565): SJCA, D48.307, answer to question 5.

[13] The inscription reads as follows (italics indicate words scored through): Nicolaus Metcalfus huius Collegii magister viginti annos quarto die Iulii magistratu excessit *et vestras* ad deum *preces vehementer expetit* Anno domini mᵒ ccccᵒ xxxviiᵒ. Metcalfe died in 1539.

[14] J. Caius, *Historiae Cantabrigiensis Academiae* (London, 1574), 75–6. See also the contemporary reference in the Thin Red Book, SJCA, C7.11, end cover, referring to 'Doctor Metcalffe qui fuit dimissus'.

[15] Ascham, *Whole Works*, IV. 234.

[16] Wilson to Thomas Wriothesley, 3 Aug. 1537: TNA SP7/1, fo. 87r, refers to 'what my lord [Cromwell] had wrytyn to them both of the kynges hyghnes mynde and his own and also for one of there own college'.

5 Chapel plaque to Nicholas Metcalfe with religiously objectionable words hammered out:
'Nicholas Metcalfe for twenty years Master of this college abandoned the rule of it
on 4 July 1537 ~~and fervently begs your prayers~~ to God ~~for him~~.'

that empowered the king simply to appoint a Master. Their statute was spuri-
ous, but their anxious presence in London shows that Day's cause was faring
badly.[17] Next day the Fellows and Scholars gathered in the chapel for a votive
mass invoking the guidance of the Holy Spirit upon the election. Then, having
cleared the chapel of all but the Fellows, the President took their personal oaths
to give their votes in the best interests of the College, before proceeding to the
ballot. Each Fellow submitted a slip of paper bearing the name of his preferred
candidate. If there was a unanimous choice or an absolute majority, then the
candidate was to be declared duly elected.[18] In this case, we know that the vote
was divided, and that a clear majority chose a certain Dr Nicholas Wilson. This
was an astonishingly provocative gesture. Wilson was a Yorkshireman, from
near Beverley (Fisher's home town), a former Master of Michaelhouse (Fisher's
original college) who in 1521 had written an enthusiastic preface for one of Fisher's books.[19] By the late 1520s he was a chaplain and confessor to Henry VIII,
but despite this he had been a busy and popular preacher in the early 1530s, tour-
ing England to rally support for Catherine of Aragon and the pope. In 1534 he
was one of the few men to follow Fisher and More to the Tower for refusing the
oath to the succession. However, early in 1537 he had finally capitulated, earning
himself a royal pardon on 29 May 1537. As he explained in an anguished letter to
Cromwell's secretary, the election was to his 'noo small grefe and hevynes', and

[17] Latimer to Cromwell, 5 Jul. 1537: H. Latimer, *Sermons and Remains of Hugh Latimer*,
ed. G. E. Corrie (Cambridge, 1845), 377–9.

[18] For the electoral process, see *Early Statutes*, 6–10.

[19] J. Fisher, *Concio quam anglice habuit* (Cambridge, 1521 [*recte* 1522]), sigs. A1v–B3r.
This was a Latin translation of a sermon Fisher preached in London against Martin
Luther's doctrines on 12 May 1521.

something that he had no more expected than 'to haue be made the bushope of rome'. Of course he refused to accept the position, and second time round, on 27 July 1537, the Fellows took the hint and George Day was duly elected.[20]

Notwithstanding this imprudent demonstration, the College was by no means a haven of unalloyed conservatism in religion. Roger Ascham was elected a Fellow in 1534 despite a rebuke from the Seniors over his open support for the royal supremacy.[21] Certain Fellows were already beginning to cultivate connections with the Evangelical faction at the king's court. In 1535 John Cheke sought Anne Boleyn's help when William Bill, presumably a pupil of his, was precluded by his debts from taking up the Fellowship to which he had been elected that Lent. She probably helped, as Bill was admitted to the Fellowship in November, and she also funded the studies of William Barker, who was elected to a Fellowship in 1539.[22] An equally powerful connection is evident in the fact that one of Thomas Cromwell's nephews, a lad named William Wellyfed, came to study at the College, probably from October 1536. Although his letters to his uncle show him to have been a less than entirely satisfactory student, sprinkled as they are with apologies and regrets over wasted time and opportunities, his presence will have given his Tutor (whom, regrettably, Wellyfed does not identify) a direct line to the heart of England's Evangelical establishment.[23] Robert Neville, who was lobbying Hugh Latimer in 1537 on behalf of a small group of Fellows worried about the defiance of their colleagues in the first election that year, was soon benefiting from Latimer's patronage. Latimer himself hinted darkly that, even in the wake of George Day's election, St John's was not free from 'factions and affections'.[24] The existence in College of a group more sympathetic to the new order would explain Latimer's comment.

Day might in some ways have seemed as compromised as Wilson. He had been a Fellow on Fisher's foundation in the 1520s, and had contributed encomiastic Latin verses to adorn one of his patron's refutations of Luther. It was probably Fisher's support that secured him appointment as the first Linacre lecturer in 1525.[25] But like Robert Wakefield, Day switched horses during the divorce controversy and became a royal chaplain. Moreover, he was no northerner (he came from Shropshire), and by 1537 was high in royal favour. Nothing in his brief Mastership was as momentous as his election. He was busy at court, and barely a year later was promoted Provost of King's. Although King's was a

---

[20] Wilson to Wriothesley, 3 Aug. 1537: TNA SP7/1, fo. 87r–v; SJCA, C7.11, Thin Red Book, fo. 172r, copy of notification to Cromwell, as Chancellor of the University, of Day's election (27 Jul. 1537).

[21] Ascham, *Whole Works*, IV. 234–5.

[22] Cheke to Matthew Parker (the queen's chaplain), 28 Sept. 1535, in Ascham, *Whole Works*, I. 1–2. See also Baker-Mayor, I. 283.

[23] William Wellyfed to Cromwell, from SJC (5 Oct. 1536): TNA SP1/106, fo. 261r. Another letter (undated) mentions but does not name his Tutor (fo. 262r). Further undated letters at fos. 264r and 266r.

[24] Latimer to Cromwell, 6 Sept. 1527, in his *Sermons and Remains*, 381–2. For Neville, see p. 378.

[25] SJCA, M3.3, computus roll for 1524–5, records £5 for Mr Day 'Lectori de physyk' for that year. £5 was half the annual stipend for the post, which therefore clearly began that year.

smaller college, the Provost's stipend of £66 13s 4d eclipsed the £6 13s 4d of the Master of St John's.[26] Day paid an inward price for his abandonment of his first patron. Having reconciled himself enthusiastically to 'mother Church' under Queen Mary, he was twitted by the Protestant martyr John Bradford for his readiness to conform under Henry to what he now condemned as heresy. Day's response is deeply revealing: 'You were but a child when this matter began. I was a young man, and then coming from the university, I went with the world: but, I tell you, it was always against my conscience.'[27] The chief significance of his election is as one of the first signs of how the new-found royal supremacy would, for generations, shape collegiate life through intervention in elections. For a century or more elections of the heads of Oxford and Cambridge colleges were prone to be short-circuited by something akin to the *congé d'élire* long customary for the election of bishops.[28]

3. JOHN TAYLOR AND THE EVANGELICAL TURN

A grovelling letter to the king shows that royal intervention secured the succession of Dr John Taylor as Master on 4 July 1538, after Day's transfer to King's.[29] Taylor came from a Fellowship at Queens' College, and his arrival added impetus to the Evangelical tendency in College.[30] Through the previous dozen years Queens' had been much more affected than St John's by Evangelical religious doctrines. The President of Queens' in the mid-1520s, Dr Thomas Farman, had been at the centre of a ring that ran forbidden books to Oxford and Cambridge, and died in captivity in 1528 while under investigation for heresy. Other early Evangelicals there included Simon Heynes, Richard Wilkes, and Sir Thomas Smith. Taylor's affiliation with this grouping can perhaps be discerned in the fact that he owed his first ecclesiastical promotion – the plum benefice of St Peter's Cornhill in London – to the patronage of Henry VIII's physician, Dr William Butts, a close friend of Hugh Latimer and a key figure in the Evangelical politicking at court in the 1530s and 1540s. That said, it will hardly do to call Taylor, as Mullinger did a hundred years ago, a 'staunch Lutheran'.[31] He was far from staunch: like Cranmer, he signed up to Henry VIII's decidedly anti-Lutheran summary of Christian doctrine, the 'King's Book', in 1543. Nor is 'Lutheran' a helpful term. The English Evangelical movement under Henry VIII was eclectic and hesitant, not a thing of clear-cut party lines.[32]

---

[26] *Early Statutes*, 168; Lamb, *Documents*, 61. The Provost's total remuneration was £74 10s, the Master's £10 3s 4d.

[27] Foxe, *Acts and Monuments*, VII. 176.

[28] Morgan, *History of the University of Cambridge*, 388–436.

[29] TNA SP1/134, fo. 100r–v, avowing their obedience to Henry's letters. See also the copy at SJCA, D105.342, with the signatures of the Fellows, perhaps for the record.

[30] Taylor was not, as has been thought, a complete outsider. Though a Fellow of Queens' since 1523, he had previously been a Scholar at St John's: TNA SP1/233, fo. 195r, 'Ioannes Taylour', listed among the Scholars.

[31] J. B. Mullinger, *St John's College* (London, 1901), 32.

[32] D. MacCulloch, *Thomas Cranmer: A Life* (New Haven & London, 1996), 2.

Under Taylor firm steps were taken in the new direction. The Chapel had been furnished at Fisher's personal expense, so that his rebus, the fish and ear of corn ('fish ear': Fisher), was carved and plastered all over it.[33] The accounts for the first quarter of 1540 record 3d 'for takyn downe of Doctor Fyscher armes apon ye tumme', 4d 'for takyng downe of the fysshes', and 3s to a joiner for 'transformyng of the fysches'.[34] This latter entry referred to the fish that were carved into the ends of all the choir stalls, which were changed into 'monstrous and ugly antiks' on the personal orders of Thomas Cromwell.[35] Fisher's corpse had a traitor's burial, and so never came to Cambridge, and in due course his tomb was dismantled when his chantry chapel was converted for use as accommodation. The pieces were left in a dark corner of the chapel until the eighteenth century, when they were moved outside, soon to be reduced to rubble by rain and frost.[36] The deletion of Fisher did not stop there. His statutes were taken in once more for revision in the 1540s, and every reference to him was excised. His Fellowships were rolled up into Lady Margaret's foundation, and the provisions for his soul were downgraded sometimes to 'Dr Fisher' even before the abolition of the mass and of prayers for the dead in the reign of Edward VI.[37] When Queen Elizabeth visited the College in 1564 Fisher's name was conspicuous by its absence from the list of benefactors that was presented to her.[38] Although, to their credit, some Fellows sustained Fisher's memory over the ensuing centuries, it was not until the nineteenth century that the College could once again officially recognize his role in its history. Even after that, hostility from Nonconformist Fellows resulted in the new buildings of the 1930s being named North Court rather than Fisher Court.[39]

Taylor set about using his power in Fellowship elections to reshape the College, making it gradually less hospitable to those of more traditionally Catholic leanings. The first Fellow admitted under the new regime rejoiced in the name of William Taylor, and there is more than a suspicion that he was a relative of the Master. Thereafter followed a series of names which, though obscure today, were to be prominent in the annals of the English Reformation – the Pilkington brothers, Andrew Perne, Roger Hutchinson, Thomas Lever, and Roger Kelke.[40] It may be risky to read back into the 1540s the later committed Protestantism of these men, as to some extent the rising proportion of Protestants in this generation of Fellows was simply a matter of chronology: Evangelical Protestantism in general was making a distinct if slow advance in England. But the eruption of at least two disputed Fellowship elections during Taylor's regime suggests that there is more to the story than the mere passage of time.

[33] Construction of 'my lordes chapell' finished by 1529: SJCA, D106.9, fo. 39r. The parts of his tomb were made in spring 1533: D106.6, fo. 63r.

[34] SJCA, D106.17, fos. 56r, 66v.

[35] *Vie du bienheureux martyr Jean Fisher*, 45.

[36] R. Willi and J. W. Clark, *The Architectural History of the University of Cambridge* (Cambridge, 1886) 285–6, reproducing an eighteenth-century sketch of the tomb.

[37] *Early Statutes*, 238–56.

[38] CUL, MS Mm.2.23, 110.

[39] Below, p. 543.

[40] Their careers are all summarised in *ODNB*.

Lent 1540 saw Roger Ascham, with the able assistance of John Cheke and some of the younger Fellows, lobbying for the election of his pupil, John Thomson, to a vacant Fellowship on Fisher's foundation, apparently with success, despite the fact that he was running Thomson against the candidates of more senior colleagues. The influential figure of Dr John Redman, Lady Margaret Professor and probably a Senior, was backing one Richard Burton (an exact contemporary of Thomson), while Thomas Crosley was backing a man named Fisher (probably Henry Fisher, MA 1539), who may well have been a relative of John Fisher.[41] While Ascham was a known favourer of the 'new learning', Redman and Crosley were both conservatives in matters of religion. The likelihood is that there was some element of religious difference in this contest. But the Fellows were constitutionally quarrelsome. During a fraught campaign over the Vice-Chancellorship late in 1539, it was two Fellows of St John's, Richard Cumberford and Richard Swayne, who led a conspiracy of regent masters in taking control of the Senate House in an attempt to prevent an adjournment of the election. When Cumberford gave the signal, 'nowe play the men and I will begyne', Swayne barred the doors and there was a rush to assault Dr Geoffrey Glyn, who was presiding over the assembly. Andrew Perne (a Scholar of St John's) yanked his hood back, and other confederates included Robert Horne and Edwin Sandys, who later boasted 'we had shearpyd our dagers', and that his 'wold have beyn yn D[r]. Harvie'.[42] It was not long afterwards that another Scholar, Leonard Metcalfe, presumably a relative of the former Master, was tried at the Cambridge Assizes for the murder of William Lambkyn, a burgess of the town who was in some capacity his servant. As Lambkyn owed him money, it is not hard to see how their quarrel might have arisen. For once, the privileges of the University were unequal to the task of protecting their own, and Metcalfe was convicted and hanged.[43]

A more serious dispute broke out at the Fellowship election of 1542, an episode shot through with religious tension. Almost all we know of the matter comes from the brief court record of the outcome of an appeal against the Master heard before the bishop of Ely, as Visitor of the College, and thus in effect its appeal judge. The row had arisen over the award of a Fellowship on Hugh Ashton's foundation to Thomas Lever at the election in March 1542. This had provoked fierce opposition, led by three of the Fellows, Henry Sanderson (or Saunders), Richard Becke, and Richard Fawcett, whom the Master had as a result dismissed from the Fellowship. Twenty Fellows (out of thirty-nine) signed an appeal to the Visitor. His adjudication, though embodying wise elements of compromise, upheld their appeal. He reinstated the dismissed Fellows with full seniority and annulled Lever's election, but made all the Fellows promise to elect him the following year. Instead, he awarded the Ashton Fellowship to John Christopherson, who had presumably polled more votes in the original election.

---

[41] See Ascham's letters of March 1539 to Taylor, Cordingley, and Cumberford in Ascham, *Whole Works*, I. 6–15.

[42] Lamb, *Documents*, 47–8.

[43] C. H. Cooper, *Annals of Cambridge*, 5 vols. (Cambridge, 1842–1908), I. 398–9. SJCA, D57.190–207 are various bills for expenses in riding out to College estates, in which Leonard Metcalfe was often accompanied by Lambkyn.

Although the spark for this conflagration was a disputed election, the fact that a majority of the Fellowship subscribed to the appeal hints at underlying tensions. Thomas Baker saw a 'north–south' divide at work, an inference based on revisions to the College statutes a few years later, which much reduced the privileges of northerners.[44] But as both Lever and Christopherson came from Lancashire (Ashton's foundation gave first preference to Lancastrians), while northerners and southerners were found on both sides, there is not much to support this analysis. Emerging religious differences offer a better explanation. Thomas Lever rapidly emerged as a fiery Protestant preacher under Edward VI, and fled the country for the sake of religion when Mary Tudor took the throne. John Christopherson left the country in Edward's reign and only returned under Mary, to become bishop of Chichester, in which capacity he sentenced numerous Protestants to death by burning. The future religious affiliations of the Fellows of 1542 correlate remarkably closely with the factional division of the Fellowship that year. Of the twenty 'appellants', none can be shown to have had distinctly Protestant inclinations, while eleven displayed strong Catholic convictions in the generation following Henry's death. Of the nineteen Fellows who did not subscribe to the appeal, none subsequently showed strong Catholic sympathies, while eleven displayed strongly Protestant convictions during the next dozen years.[45]

The bishop of Ely's settlement called upon all the Fellows to 'submit themselves humbly to the Master and show him due obedience', but this pious aspiration was in vain. Before long, Sanderson was after Taylor again, this time petitioning the Visitor about the 'pretended election' of Richard Alvey as one of the seven Seniors. All we know of this dispute is one side of the argument, a lengthy justification written by Sanderson in reply to Dr Taylor's defence against his original charges. Sanderson made this dispute the peg on which to hang a general indictment of Taylor's regime. In his view, Taylor played fast and loose with the statutes to achieve his ends, and it was impossible to do business with him as 'no bonds will hold him'. He was, in short 'the principal author of all contention in our college'. The real issue is painfully obvious: Alvey had been made a Senior, an honour Sanderson wanted for himself. As he had been elected five years before Alvey, and had served as a Bursar for three years, he felt slighted. The Master's reasons for preferring Alvey were probably partly religious and partly personal. Alvey, like many others, would choose exile under Mary Tudor rather than face the choice between denying his faith or dying for it, and he would achieve fame under Elizabeth as 'Father Alvey', Master of the Temple, a patriarch of English Protestantism.[46] Taylor's counter-charges against Sanderson, that he was was 'given to riot' and to 'unlawful games' smacks partly of Evangelical moralism and partly of continuing resentment over Sanderson's role in the events of 1542: Taylor also alluded to 'words used against him in the last visitation'. The remaining Seniors were evenly split over this election, and

---

[44] Baker-Mayor, I. 118.

[45] For Lever and Christopherson, see *ODNB* (B. Lowe; J. Wright). The analysis of the religious sympathies of the Fellowship is based on evidence too disparate and voluminous to summarize here.

[46] For Alvey's career see *ODNB* (C. S. Knighton).

Taylor had evidently given a casting vote in favour of Alvey. The statutes did not offer guidance for resolving disputed elections of this kind, but Taylor's solution was entirely equitable, and the Visitor would have had no particular reason to uphold Sanderson's appeal against it.[47]

Although Roger Ascham told John Cheke rather ruefully of his father's advice to get away from the place and its endemic in-fighting, St John's was not yet riven from top to bottom by religious strife.[48] Ascham's own ample correspondence testifies to a far more complex reality, in which emerging disagreements over theology were simply one axis among many on which the interrelationships of the Fellows were plotted. College politics, personal ties, and academic commitments interacted to kaleidoscopic effect. Ascham enjoyed a pension from one of England's most conservative clergymen, Edward Lee (archbishop of York). And after Lee's death, he angled for the patronage of the equally conservative Stephen Gardiner. In 1549, when the Protestant Reformation was in full swing, he wrote to the College from Cheshunt and sent greetings not only to Protestants such as Lever, Hutchinson, and the Pilkingtons, but to conservatives such as Alban Langdale, George Bullock, and Richard Fawcett.[49] Nor did close personal relationships necessarily translate into religious discipleship. John Bland, the future Protestant martyr, was Tutor in the 1530s to both Edwin Sandys and Richard Fawcett. But while Sandys became a prominent Evangelical, Fawcett served as an official at Bland's trial for heresy. Fawcett urged him to recant, appealing to the fact that they were 'brought up both in one house [i.e. St John's] and born both in one parish', and the presiding judge offered him time to confer with 'your friend Dr Faucet'. And Bland no doubt raised a laugh with his observation, 'though I was never able to do him good, yet once I was his tutor'.[50] Clearly Bland's tutorial influence had not been enough to turn Fawcett from the old ways; but equally clearly, the religious dividing lines were by no means as firmly drawn in the 1530s as they were by the 1550s.

The tidal flow quickened through the 1540s. Fellowship elections ran increasingly in favour of Evangelical candidates, and the appellants of 1542 drifted gradually away to friendlier havens. By the time he died, late in 1545, Henry Sanderson had bailed out to King's Hall, where the new Warden was a former colleague at St John's, John Redman. Fellowships at King's Hall were rather more lucrative than at St John's, and easier to hold along with plum benefices outside, though Sanderson did not live long enough to enjoy these benefits. Two of the leading appellants, John Seton and Thomas Watson, attached themselves to Stephen Gardiner, bishop of Winchester, eventually resigning their Fellowships in 1548. Only seven of the appellants were left by 1549, an increasingly beleaguered minority.[51]

---

[47] *Early Statutes*, 32; *Eagle* xxxi (1909–10), 291–9.

[48] Ascham, *Whole Works*, I. 48.

[49] Ibid., I. 168. For Langdale and Bullock, see *ODNB* (J. Wright; R. Rex).

[50] Foxe, *Acts and Monuments*, VII. 287 (Sandys) and 300–1 (Fawcett). For Sandys, see also *ODNB* (P. Collinson).

[51] CUA, VCCt Wills I, fo. 71r, for Sanderson's death in 1545; Foxe, *Acts and Monuments*,

4. THE TRIUMPH OF RENAISSANCE HUMANISM

While the religious life of the College became increasingly contentious, its academic life flourished. Henry VIII's break with Rome accelerated the substitution of Renaissance humanist scholarship for medieval scholasticism in the University curriculum. The injunctions of 1535 swept away the medieval textbooks which had long underpinned the teaching of logic. The principal lecturer of St John's, John Seton, filled the gap by compiling his own introduction to the subject, which spread through the University in manuscript and note form until, at the urging of friends such as Cheke and Watson (friendships were still holding across the religious divide), he published it in 1545. His work drew on recent humanist scholars such as Erasmus, Rudolph Agricola, and even the Lutheran Philip Melanchthon. Melanchthon's textbook on logic was particularly popular in Cambridge, but Seton regarded it as more useful for teachers than for students, and he may also have looked askance on its theological tendentiousness. The examples which Melanchthon set out often inculcated Protestant doctrine as well as illustrating the point in question. Seton gives a wide berth to theology, though he often sets out moral lessons in his examples: all prudent people are temperate; no hedonists are temperate; therefore no hedonists are prudent.[52] Given a new lease of life in a revised edition by another Fellow of St John's, Peter Carter, in the 1560s, Seton's work remained a standard textbook throughout the century.[53]

John Cheke, John Redman, Roger Ascham and their contemporaries represented a golden generation of classical pedagogy in the College. The decade between the royal injunctions of 1535 and the foundation of Trinity College in 1546 saw St John's at the forefront of humanist learning, and Ascham looked back on them in a roseate glow of nostalgia and sheer Johnian patriotism in his most famous work, the posthumously published *Scholemaster* (1570). Under the leadership of Cheke and Redman, he boasted, the College nurtured more genuinely learned men than the entire University of Louvain. Closer to home, he also tried to put the College's upstart neighbour in its place:

> Yea, St. John's did then so flourish, as Trinity College, that princely house now, at the first erection was but *colonia deducta* out of St. John's, not only for their master, fellows, and scholars, but also (which is more) for their whole both order of learning and discipline of manners.[54]

When Ascham returned to St John's in 1543 after two years' absence through illness, he must have been disappointed to find that he had missed the excitement occasioned by his friend, Cheke, in pioneering a new pronunciation of Greek with the eager support of the students but in the teeth of opposition from the Chancellor, Stephen Gardiner. Some scholars have seen the controversy over

---

VI. 151–3 and 199–200 for Watson and Seton. Their stipends as Fellows ceased in 1548: SJCA, D106.18, fos. 80v–81r.

[52] J. Seton, *Dialectica* (London, 1545), sigs. A2v for the critique of Melanchthon; A4v for Greek verses contributed by Cheke; H8v for the syllogism.

[53] W. S. Howell, *Logic and Rhetoric in England, 1500–1700* (Princeton, 1956), 50–56.

[54] Ascham, *Whole Works*, IV. 142, 235.

Greek pronunciation as a sort of surrogate religious conflict, because Cheke and Smith were Evangelicals while Gardiner was a determined Catholic.[55] But Ascham's account of St John's at this time shows that enthusiasm for humane studies and the new pronunciation ran across incipient confessional divisions. Among his Johnian friends of that era he picks out for special praise not only Cheke but also Thomas Watson, who wrote a classical tragedy in Latin which, Ascham tells us, he refrained from publishing because of a handful of 'false quantities' (technical errors in the versification).[56] Where Cheke became a notorious Protestant in the reign of Edward, Watson was a leading figure in Mary I's Catholic restoration, and ended his days in 1584 as a prisoner of conscience under Elizabeth.

This golden generation was responsible for a remarkable level of literary production, but it is important to understand why this was. Academic publication was orientated towards escape, to promotion outside and beyond the University. Scholarly performance was a sort of rain-dance to bring patronage from above. John Seton dedicated his *Dialectica* to Stephen Gardiner, and was soon a personal chaplain to the bishop, who bestowed a couple of lucrative benefices upon him.[57] John Cheke specialized in elegant renderings of Greek texts into Latin, which he wrote out in his peerless italic for presentation to the king, at first in gratitude for the Regius professorship of Greek, and then as New Year's presents. His fine edition of a couple of John Chrysostom's sermons in Greek, followed by his own Latin translations, was also put into print, together with its fulsome dedication to Henry.[58] Such eye-catching gifts and gestures doubtless helped secure him appointment in 1544 as tutor to the young prince of Wales, Edward, a connection which in turn tightened links between the College and the court for the next decade. William Grindall and Roger Ascham followed Cheke into royal service as tutors to Edward's sister, Elizabeth. Roger Ascham and John Christopherson sent their respective showpieces, *Toxophilus* (a handbook on archery) and *Jephtha* (a Greek tragedy on a biblical theme) to a range of potential patrons.[59] Although one or two of these efforts made it into print, it is important to remember that they were usually presented in manuscript form. Christopherson's dedication to Cuthbert Tunstall is in trademark Johnian italic. When Ascham was trying to mend fences with Redman in 1543, he told him how happy he would have been to copy out for him the treatise on justification which he had presented to Henry VIII the previous

---

[55] W. S. Hudson, *The Cambridge Connection and the Elizabethan Settlement of 1559* (Durham NC, 1980), 43–60, implies a convergence of humanist scholarship and evangelical religion, largely by ignoring Catholic humanists such as Thomas Watson and John Christopherson.

[56] Ascham, *Whole Works*, IV. 240–41. For Watson's play, see *A Humanist's Trew Imitation: Thomas Watson's Absalom*, ed. J. H. Smith (Urbana, IL, 1964), esp. p. 12 for the identification of the surviving text as his work.

[57] Seton, *Dialectica*, sig. A2r.

[58] *D. Ioannis Chrysostomi homiliae duae*, trans. J. Cheke (London, 1543).

[59] Ascham, *Whole Works*, I. 77–83, for presentation copies to a clutch of courtiers and bishops; J. Christopherson, *Jephthah*, ed. F. H. Fobes (Newark, DE, 1928), 19 (William Parr) and 24 (Cuthbert Tunstall). See SJCL, MS 284 for the copy Christopherson sent to Tunstall.

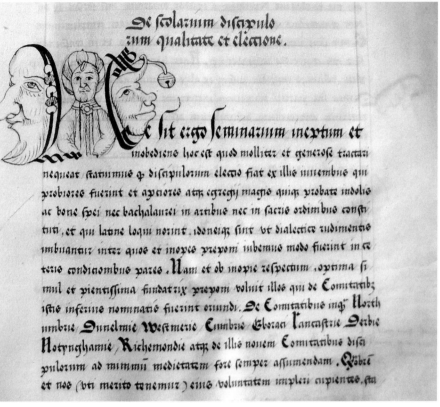

6 Grotesques illustrating the statute giving preference to those from the nine
Northern counties for election as scholars on Lady Margaret's foundation:
'other things being equal, the poorest are to be preferred.' SJCA, C1.40.7

year.[60] Like Cheke and Christopherson, Ascham wrote a very fair italic hand,
which could add prestige value to a presentation manuscript. His beautiful cal-
ligraphy is seen to best effect in the elegant signature he cut into the stone fireplace in the Old Treasury above the great gate.[61]

Henry VIII's final intervention in the life of the College was to authorize the
fourth recension of the statutes, which were promulgated in 1545. The impetus
for this doubtless came from inside the College, and some of the changes may
even reflect ideas mooted during the work on Fisher's unfinished fourth recension of his statutes in the early 1530s. But the two major changes in this revision
can probably be attributed to the king personally. The excision of all references
to the late bishop of Rochester, which completed the process of 'non-personing'
that had begun with the erasure of his heraldic emblems in the chapel, testifies to the continuing resentment of a king to whom the memory of Fisher
and More must always have occasioned a pang of conscience. The foundress's

[60] Ascham, *Whole Works*, I. 46.

[61] M. G. Underwood, 'The Old Treasury and its graffiti', *Eagle* lxviii, no. 288 (1980),
23–6. The reasons why Ascham and others carved their names in that fireplace
remain obscure.

preference for the north was deleted from the statutes on the qualifications of Fellows and Scholars, while the provisions that at least half the Seniors and Fellows should be northerners were amended to make that proportion a maximum. This reining in of the privileges of the nine northern counties is likely to reflect furious royal memories of the Pilgrimage of Grace.[62]

5. ST JOHN'S UNDER THE 'YOUNG JOSIAH'

The death of Henry VIII in January 1547 introduced an era of revolutionary change for College and realm alike. Archbishop Cranmer's address at the coronation of the young King Edward VI cast him as an infant Josiah, who would take up where his father had left off and set about uprooting all remnants of idolatry and popery from the land.[63] The levers of power were soon in the hands of Edward's uncle, the duke of Somerset, under the title of Lord Protector of the Realm. The new regime had an immediate impact on St John's. John Taylor had for some time been hoping to find a better benefice than the Mastership to hold alongside his position as dean of Lincoln, and once he was required to become properly resident at Lincoln in August 1546, he was obliged to resign from St John's.[64] His successor, William Bill, was elected on 10 March 1547 at the specific request of the duke of Somerset. This may have owed something to the presence at court of William Bill's older brother, Thomas, whose role as a royal physician gave him access to the prince and the duke. The elevation to the Mastership of a leading figure among the Evangelical Fellows raised the religious temperature in College at exactly the moment that the government sharply changed England's religious direction. Cranmer's Reformation programme was soon under way, and his Evangelical *Homilies* of 1547 were supplemented by the royal ecclesiastical injunctions of September 1547, which required the wholesale removal of religious imagery from England's churches. St John's College rushed headlong on the course Cranmer had set. A list survives that names eighty men who were licensed by the government in the summer of 1547 to preach anywhere in the kingdom. It includes not only the new Master, Dr Bill, but the President (Dr John Madew), with four current and three former Fellows.[65] St John's alone provided a remarkable 10 per cent of that particular taskforce. But it is also worth noting that Madew was the only one of them who was also a College preacher that year. Almost all the other College preachers had been among the

---

[62] *Early Statutes*, 30–33 (Seniors), 48–51 (Fellows), and 68–9 (Scholars). For the fate of Fisher's foundation, see pp. III, 238–56.

[63] T. Cranmer, *Miscellaneous Writings and Letters*, ed. J. E. Cox (Cambridge, 1846), 126–7. For the Reformation under Edward, see D. MacCulloch, *Tudor Church Militant: Edward VI and the Protestant Reformation* (London, 1999); and S. Alford, *Kingship and Politics in the Reign of Edward VI* (Cambridge, 2002).

[64] For Taylor's residency at Lincoln, see *ODNB* (M. Bowker). Taylor to William Butts (one the king's physicians), 31 Oct. 1545: SJCA, D105.305, outlines the problem he will face when he takes up residency at Lincoln, and begs his help in getting a better benefice in place of the mastership.

[65] *Calendar of State Papers Domestic Series of the Reign of Edward VI*, ed. C. S. Knighton (London, 1992), no. 74.

'appellants' in 1542.[66] From the time that we can identify the Seniors reliably, the start of 1547, only two of the seventeen Seniors elected in Edward VI's reign were conservatives.[67] The College rapidly aligned itself with the expectations of the regime, not least because the education of the young king was in the hands of their charismatic former colleague, John Cheke. By the end of the year an official letter to the Lord Protector in the name of the entire College defined its mission as firstly 'to spread the Gospel of the Lord to the People of God', and secondly to expel 'all human doctrine, that is, popery, with all its hypocrisy, superstition, and idolatry'.[68]

The emergence of a regime dominated by the duke of Somerset and given theological direction by Thomas Cranmer led to an ebullition of Protestant zeal in many parts of southern England, especially London. Whether this was because Henry's death took the lid off the pot or because Cranmer was stoking the flames beneath it offers a choice of metaphor between which it is needless to judge. But Henry's machinery of censorship and repression was dismantled, and the excitement went to many heads, including that of Thomas Dobbe, who had been elected a Fellow of St John's at the divisive election in Lent 1542.[69] Early in the new reign Dobbe appears in St Paul's Cathedral, interrupting the celebration of mass at the elevation of the consecrated wafer, inveighing against the sin of idolatry that the members of the congregation were committing, in his view, by venerating it as the body of Christ. He was arrested by the Mayor of London, brought before Cranmer, and consigned to the Counter prison, where he fell ill and died soon after. What adds interest and complexity to his story is that he had only just been ejected from the College, and that his sad history is related, with a misleading twist, in the epic narrative of the early English Reformation that forms a large part of John Foxe's *Book of Martyrs*. As Foxe tells it, Dobbe had 'resorted to a certain maiden' in Cambridge, and, despite 'intending with himself and addicting his mind to the christian state of matrimony', had been hounded out of College over the affair by three other Fellows, Hutchinson, Pynder, and Taylor. Foxe presented Dobbe's death in gaol as tantamount to martyrdom, and blamed it upon the 'malicious handling' of those who had driven him from the College, implying that they were papists.[70] There is no reason to doubt that Dobbe expelled, for his stipend was paid right up to Christmas 1546, after which his name disappears from the accounts.[71] What is intriguing is the circumstance that, of Dobbe's three foes, 'Hutchinson' was certainly Roger Hutchinson, a convinced Protestant, while 'Taylor' can only have been the Master himself (expulsion was the Master's prerogative).[72] It was therefore not the College's religious conservatives but its Evangelicals

---

[66] SJCA, D106.18, fo. 29v.

[67] SJCA, C3.1, Register, 11–12.

[68] SJC to the Lord Protector, 21 Nov. 1547: Ascham, *Whole Works*, I. 137–44, at p. 138.

[69] Baker-Mayor, I. 284; SJCA, D106.17, fo. 119v.

[70] Foxe, *Acts and Monuments*, V. 704–5; Brigden, *London and the Reformation*, 426–7.

[71] SJCA, D106.17, fos. 247–8 and 288–9; D106.18, fos. 24–5.

[72] The third, John Pynder, was a friend of Ascham who conformed under Mary, but was himself expelled from the College in 1557 after a prolonged row with the Master, George Bullock. See below, p. 55, nn. 112–14.

who drove Dobbe out, which in turn suggests that moral rather than doctrinal considerations caused his expulsion. While Foxe assures us that Dobbe's intentions were strictly honourable, we are entitled to doubt that. The truth is most probably that the Evangelicals wanted to get him out of the College because his affair was embarrassing their cause.

The rising tide of Protestant antagonism to the mass provoked some free-lance iconoclasm in the College chapel later that year.[73] On Thursday 22 September, the rope which suspended the pyx above the altar was cut in a calculated insult to the consecrated eucharistic wafer that it contained. This was the work of a young French Protestant refugee named Joseph, then a servant to Mr Robert Stafford, one of the College's noble Fellow-Commoners. The scandal was seized upon by some of the conservative Seniors as an opportunity to make a stand. The episode was brought to the attention of the government in London, by 'certain persons' who, Roger Ascham reckoned, 'cannot stomach the decline and fall of superstition and strive any way they can to cloud over the new dawn of the gospel in our time, and therefore hope to exploit this event to diminish the credit of this college'. Ascham gave his opinion in a letter he wrote to Archbishop Cranmer two days later, in which he promised that Thomas Lever would soon tell him the whole story.[74] Lever was entrusted with the task of taking Joseph to London to appear before the Privy Council, while payments to George Bullock and William Barker for trips to London suggest that perhaps other interest groups in the College sought to have their say.[75] The College's anxious efforts to smooth over this scandal were helped not only by their existing link to the king through the person of Cheke, but also by the emergence of a former pensioner, William Cecil, as a rising star of the Lord Protector's regime. The Master's servant delivered ingratiating letters to both of them in December 1547, along with several sets of gloves as presents.[76]

What had begun as mere youthful high spirits soon turned into a theological showdown. In December, Thomas Lever and Roger Hutchinson, zealous Protestants who lectured respectively in rhetoric and logic, took as the focus of one of their regular disputations in College the question of whether or not the mass was the Lord's Supper.[77] Presumably they colluded in arguing that the 'mass' – the Catholic celebration of the eucharist, understood by Catholic theologians as a sacrifice – was nothing to do with the 'Lord's Supper', the appellation which Protestant theologians preferred for what they took to be a memorial meal. As Hutchinson had been one of the Seniors since 28 March 1547, the disputation seemed to carry College backing, and it sparked off controversy across the University. A rematch was planned in the Old Schools, probably organized by Catholics hoping to set the record straight. But the Vice-Chancellor, John

---

[73] For this hostility, see J. N. King, *English Reformation Literature* (Princeton, 1982).

[74] Ascham to Cranmer, 24 Sept. 1547: Ascham, *Whole Works*, I. 118–19.

[75] SJCA, D106.18, fo. 43r.

[76] Letters to Cecil and Cheke, 28 Dec. 1547: SJCA, C7.12, Thick Black Book, 191–2. For the delivery of the 'glooffes' and their purchase – twelve pairs each: SJCA, D106.18, fos. 43r, 49r.

[77] SJCA, D106.18, fos. 26r–27v; Ascham, *Whole Works*, I. 154. Mullinger erroneously states that the disputation provoked Joseph's iconoclasm: *St John's College*, 39–40.

Madew, who was also the President of St John's and himself inclined towards the Reformation, refused to allow that second disputation to take place. The furore spurred Roger Ascham to pen a lengthy treatise on the subject, in which he sets out firm Protestant convictions for the first time. It was yet another bid for patronage on his part, as he wrote to William Cecil for advice on whether to dedicate the book to Somerset or to Cheke, but it was also the clearest of indications of how the wind was blowing both nationally and through the College.[78]

Nevertheless, the first steps towards Protestantism are clearly recorded. Early in 1548 the College bought copies of the royal injunctions of 1547, together with Cranmer's Protestant homilies. They also acquired English psalters for chapel services, along with copies of the new English translation of the canon of the mass, Cranmer's halfway house on the road to an English liturgy. Then 1549 saw the purchase of the first copies of the new Book of Common Prayer itself, along with over a dozen more psalters.[79]

Our last clear view of the College under Edward comes in summer 1549, with the royal visitation of the University. The chief objective of this visitation was to make sure that the Book of Common Prayer was accepted throughout the University, and its wider aims were as far as possible to weaken the Catholic party and to consolidate the Protestant party. The Visitors themselves were led by the bishops of Ely and Rochester (Thomas Goodrich of Jesus College and Nicholas Ridley of Pembroke College), assisted by the dean of St Paul's (William Mey, Trinity Hall and Queens') and four laymen – Sir William Paget (Trinity Hall), Sir Thomas Smith (Queens'), John Cheke (St John's and King's) and Thomas Wendy (Gonville Hall). They bullied and hectored those of Catholic inclinations, dislodged selected heads of house and other malcontents, and promoted Protestants. At St John's, the leading Catholic Fellows, 'Mr Crosley, Mr Langdale, Mr Browne with others of their faction' were called in for a dressing-down.[80] The Fellowship elections that Lent had been suspended in anticipation of the arrival of the royal commissioners, who filled the vacant Fellowships by appointment that summer. Heading their list was one 'Perosen' or 'Perusinus', an Italian Protestant refugee from Perugia, whose given name was Pietro Bizzarri.[81] This was an unmistakable declaration of intent, and there were certainly no committed Catholics among that year's new Fellows, only one of whom, Christopher Tatham, retained his place in Mary's reign. Bizzarri has left few other traces in Cambridge, but one was his contribution to one of the more remarkable publications of Edward's reign: a volume of classicizing verses specially printed in memory of another Protestant exile, Martin Bucer, who died at Cambridge in 1551. A similar collection was printed not long afterwards for two of the contributors to that volume, the young duke of Suffolk, Henry

---

[78] Ascham, *Apologia pro coena dominica contra missam* (London, 1577); Ascham to Cecil, 5 Jan. 1548: Ascham, *Whole Works*, I. 157.

[79] SJCA, D106.18, fos. 87v–88r, 142r.

[80] William Rogers to Sir Thomas Smith, 14 May 1559: TNA SP10/7, fo. 39v. They were not expelled from their Fellowships, just taught 'a lesson'.

[81] SJCA, C3.1, Register, 133 (4 Jul. 1549) and D106.18, fo. 134r ('d. Perosen'). For his eponymous career, see M. Firpo, *Pietro Bizzarri: esule italiano del cinquecento* (Turin, 1971), esp. pp. 24–34 for his years in England under Edward VI.

Brandon, and his brother Charles. They had come to study at St John's in 1549, but died within half an hour of each other in summer 1551, victims of another outbreak of the 'English Sweat', a form of influenza that devastated the population on several occasions in the sixteenth century.[82] Both collections included numerous contributors from the College, and both were intended to persuade contemporaries that the causes of 'good letters' (Renaissance humanism) and the 'new learning' (Reformation Protestantism) were inextricably bound together.

Sadly, the full course of the Edwardine Reformation in St John's cannot be plotted, as no bursarial accounts survive for the years 1550–55. This gap in the records is itself eloquent testimony to the disruption of institutional life in a period which saw two monarchs, four Masters, and almost continuous religious alteration. One imagines either that the last Edwardine Bursars took the recent papers with them as they fled in autumn 1553, or that those who gleefully took possession of their rooms threw them out with the rubbish as they moved in. However, the extent of reconstruction and re-equipping that had to be undertaken in restoring Roman Catholic worship under Mary shows that the 'stripping of the altars' seen throughout England was carried out in College – and probably with rather more expedition and enthusiasm than in many other places.[83] By this stage, William Bill had been promoted to the Mastership of Trinity (whose first three Masters were all former Fellows of St John's), and he had been succeeded on 10 December 1551 by the fiery Thomas Lever. Both were devout Protestants, but while William Bill simply weathered the storm of Mary's reign, keeping his head down in retirement on family property in Ashwell, Lever was to lead a minor exodus from Cambridge to Strasbourg and eventually Geneva. He had already made a name for himself as an uncompromising preacher. It was probably his preaching at the court of the young king in 1550 that earned him his promotion.[84]

Lever no doubt relished the demolition of the Chapel's altars as well as the great bonfires of Catholic liturgical books that took place in 1550 and 1551. Vestments and other now redundant ornaments were sold off, and some of this stuff found its way into the hands of the University Registrary, John Mere. In 1552 some of the revenue from those sales was presumably used to purchase copies of the second, still more decisively Protestant, Book of Common Prayer. Finally, as disaster overwhelmed royal finances in the closing years of the reign, Edward VI's government confiscated practically all the gold and silver plate that had been accumulated over centuries for the adornment of Catholic worship. The sacred vessels given by Lady Margaret, Fisher, and others will have been carted off with the rest.

The headlong Reformation of Edward VI's reign came to an abrupt end in the summer of 1553. Under the guidance of the Lord President of his Council

---

[82] *De obitu doctissimi Martini Buceri* (London, 1551), L1r; *Vita et obitus duorum fratrum Suffolciensium* (London, 1551); Alford, *Kingship and Politics*, 124–31.

[83] E. Duffy, *The Stripping of the Altars* (New Haven & London, 1992), 448–77, for the assault on traditional religious practices under Edward. For Bill and Lever see *ODNB* (C. S. Knighton; B. Lowe).

[84] T. Lever, *A Sermon Preached the Thyrd Sondaye in Lente before the Kynges Maiestie* (London, 1550).

(John Dudley, duke of Northumberland), the ailing king sought to overrule the Act of Succession of 1544, by which the throne was to pass to his sisters, Mary and then Elizabeth. Instead, he diverted the succession to the next in line, the descendants of Henry VIII's younger sister, Mary. The lucky girl was Jane Grey, whose hand in marriage the Lord President had been shrewd enough to secure for his eldest son, Guildford Dudley. The point of this desperate manœuvre was to prevent the overthrow of Protestantism which everyone knew would follow upon the succession of Mary Tudor, who, almost alone in England, had refused to accept the newfangled English worship of the Books of Common Prayer. The coup looked unstoppable, but Mary had other ideas. Issuing a bold call to arms when news of Edward's death leaked from the court, she saw supporters hasten from all sides to a rendezvous at Framlingham in Suffolk. Cambridge, though, with its levers of power in Protestant hands, was loyal to Lady Jane. So when the duke of Northumberland led his troops northwards to give battle to Mary, he made his headquarters at Cambridge, and was feted by the Vice-Chancellor and the heads of houses, prominent among them William Bill, John Cheke, and Thomas Lever. On Sunday 16 July the Vice-Chancellor preached in support of the duke, and on Monday morning Lever was waiting at St Catharine's College to ride with the manuscript to a printing shop in London so that it could be printed when news came that the duke's army was retreating in disarray. Within days the Vice-Chancellor was sampling the hospitality of the Tower of London, and many others in the University were giving anxious consideration to their future. After his prominent role in the events of the summer, Lever made himself scarce. By February 1554 he was in Strasbourg, at the head of a group of students from both universities.[85]

6.   THE RESTORATION OF ROMAN CATHOLICISM

One of Mary's first acts as queen was to strike down all injunctions and new statutes given to the universities in the name of Edward VI, instructing them to restore the *status quo* pertaining at Henry VIII's death. In Cambridge, Stephen Gardiner was immediately restored to the Chancellorship of the University, in place of the duke of Northumberland. Preoccupied with matters of State, Gardiner sent his chaplain, Thomas Watson, former Fellow of St John's, to let the University know his wishes.[86] These seem to have included Watson's own appointment as Master of St John's, an office to which he was elected on 28 September 1553. Watson brought with him a copy of John Fisher's 1530 statutes, and it is these, rather than Henry VIII's statutes of 1545, which appear to have governed the College under Mary.[87] The fact that Fisher's statutes gave the Master and Seniors power to expel Fellows on mere suspicion of heresy may have helped precipitate the most rapid turnover in the Fellowship in the College's history.

---

[85] H. C. Porter, *Reformation and Reaction in Tudor Cambridge* (Cambridge, 1958), 75–6.

[86] Gardiner to the University, 25 Aug. 1553: *The Letters of Stephen Gardiner*, ed. J. A. Muller (Cambridge, 1933), 456.

[87] *Early Statutes*, xxiv.

The total Fellowship at that time varied between forty and forty-five. Whether voluntarily by flight or compulsorily by expulsion, it was roughly halved over the winter of 1553–4. In 1556, the first year of Mary's reign for which we have a full list, only fifteen of the forty-five men who were Fellows that year had been elected before Mary came to the throne. Perhaps as many as nine of those who were Fellows in 1553 opted for exile. We can be sure that Leonard Pilkington (and probably James too, though this is uncertain), Thomas Fowle, Roger Kelk, Ralph Lever, Nicholas Shepherd, Percival Wiburne and Thomas Wilson were expelled, because they were restored by the next royal visitation (conducted by Protestants) in 1559. The full extent of the disruption, though, can be seen in the fact that 21 new Fellows were admitted in 1554.[88]

Thomas Watson stayed at St John's only long enough to preside over this purge. He had been appointed dean of Durham in November 1553, and had left for his new home by 12 May 1554, when George Bullock was chosen to replace him, to the bitter amusement of his former colleagues, who vented their frustrations from the uncomfortable safety of their European havens by penning scurrilous Latin verses against him.[89] St John's produced an impressive proportion of the Marian Protestant exiles, especially those from Cambridge. Of seventy-six exiles with a background at Cambridge University, a quarter were connected with St John's, fourteen of these having certainly been Fellows (though some had left the College years before).[90] The most illustrious of them was Sir John Cheke, who had been allowed to leave the country in 1554, but then incurred royal displeasure through his involvement in the production of propaganda against Mary's restoration of Catholicism. As a result, he was kidnapped in the Netherlands in May 1556, bound hand and foot, and forcibly repatriated to England, where, after a sojourn in the Tower, he was compelled to recant his beliefs at the queen's court.[91] The exiles are significant not so much for what they achieved abroad, which was mainly impotent fulmination against Mary's regime and the Catholic faith, but for what they tell us about the level of Protestant commitment that had been attained in the College by the end of Edward's reign, and for what they would achieve after their return, when many of them went on to play influential roles in the restored Church of England.

The often repeated suggestion that the academic standing of the College fell dramatically thanks to the Marian expulsions does not stand up to analysis. Despite the expulsions, numbers certainly held up. With forty-one Fellows, fifty-one Scholars and eight sizars in 1556, the establishment of the College was much the same size as in 1545. A complete list of the membership compiled for

[88] SJCA, Register, C3.1, 137.

[89] Bale, *Catalogus*, I. 728.

[90] These figures are ultimately derived from C. H. Garrett, *The Marian Exiles: A Study in the Origins of Elizabethan Puritanism* (Cambridge, 1938), and are summarized by Porter, *Reformation and Reaction*, 76–9. Garrett counted twenty-one Johnian exiles, but one of them, Thomas Becon, had no connection with the College, while two others (William Jackson and Richard Luddington) can only be dubiously identified with its known members. Porter adds a Johnian whom Garrett missed, William Birch: *Reformation and Reaction*, 77.

[91] For Cheke's story see *ODNB* (A. Bryson).

the royal visitation in 1559, and including the pensioners (or paying students), numbers 150. Given the heavy mortality from an influenza epidemic in the late 1550s, this compares well to the total of 170 boasted in 1547.[92]

Standards, as well as numbers, were maintained. The golden generation of Ascham, Cheke, and Watson had broken up long since under the impetus of ambition and promotion, but the College did not therefore lapse into a leaden dullness. The Marian Fellowship included veterans of the Ascham era such as Christopher Browne, who held the Hebrew lectureship, and Ascham's pupil and friend Edward Raven, ensconced as the Linacre lecturer until his death in 1558. The Master, George Bullock, was a genuinely learned man, who compiled a massive concordance to the Bible, which he eventually published in Antwerp. The still more learned Bartholomew Dodington, Regius Professor of Greek from 1562 until 1585, had entered St John's as a Scholar in 1547, becoming a Fellow in 1552 and remaining throughout Mary's reign before migrating to Trinity in Elizabeth's.[93] The students of the College were able to produce a handsome sheaf of classical verses to mark the burning of Martin Bucer's bones in the market place on 6 February 1557.[94] But the scholarly interests of the College at this time can be appreciated from evidence that survives thanks to the influenza epidemic that afflicted England in the closing years of Mary's reign. Infection carried off half a dozen Johnians, and the inventories of their movable property compiled for probate include detailed lists of their books, through which we get a glimpse of the breadth and depth of their learning. One of the victims, ironically, was the Linacre lecturer in Physick, Edward Raven. His library of over 200 books was a prodigious collection, half of it Latin and Greek literature, the other half medical books (and no theology barring a few copies of the Bible). The rather younger Thomas Hartley (d. 1557) owned a good measure of Latin and a little Greek, with a handful of books by Erasmus. William Gockman (d. 1558) had 150 books, mostly theological, and with a large block of recent Catholic polemics, but also evincing a good grounding in Greek. Christopher Browne added a clutch of Hebrew texts to a respectable classical and theological library. And Miles Buckley, who died in the summer of 1559, likewise boasted Greek and Hebrew volumes, leaving his Greek copy of Plato's works to the library.

[92] SJCA, D106.17, fo. 246r names fifty-one Scholars and eight sizars in summer 1545, and fo. 248r names forty-two Fellows; SB4.1, fo. 9r–v, for 1556. These lists did not include pensioners. CUA, College I.7 (for 1559). SJC to the Lord Protector, 21 Nov. 1547; Ascham, *Whole Works*, I. 137–44, at p. 143: 'We are 170 or more'. The 1559 list was made in July, probably the lowest point in the annual cycle.

[93] For Dodington's career see *ODNB* (E. Leedham-Green and N. G. Wilson).

[94] Lamb, *Documents*, 215, for mention of 'a great nombre of verses against Bucer's brennyng' brought to the Visitors by Bullock. H. C. Porter understandably misinterpreted this as referring to verses 'in favour of Bucer' (*Reformation and Reaction*, 56). But in Tudor English 'against' can mean 'towards' or 'in advance of' (e.g. 'against his coming'), as well as 'contrary to'. See for example references in the accounts for 1564 for expenditure 'against Mr Secretaryes Cummynge to the colledge' and 'against the quenes cumminge' (SJCA, SB4.1, fo. 266r–v). In this case, where the verses were handed over two days before the burning, they were evidently intended to join other verses in condemnation of Bucer that had already been posted up on church doors. Had the Master found verses in favour of Bucer written by his Scholars, there would have been serious repercussions.

The best evidence for study in Marian St John's comes from the inventory of William Johnson, who matriculated in 1555 and died shortly after graduating BA in spring 1559. He had an impressive eighty books, with the inevitable logic and Aristotle supplemented by Plautus, Cicero, Livy, Sallust, Caesar, Virgil, Horace, Juvenal, Martial, and Ovid among the Latins; Homer, Demosthenes, Lucian, and Aristophanes in Greek, with a dictionary and a grammar; and a clutch of humanist texts including Erasmus's *Adages*, More's *Utopia*, Ramus's dialectic, and John Cheke's tract on the pronunciation of Greek. St John's under Mary was evidently still producing the sort of scholars of whom Ascham would have been proud.[95]

As in the 1520s, so in the 1550s much of the focus of collegiate activity was on equipping and beautifying the Chapel. The top priority was restoring Catholic worship to its pre-Reformation glory. The earliest stages of this process are concealed from us by the gap in the College accounts, but we know that George Bullock went to law to reclaim from the University Registrary, John Mere (a closet Protestant and a close friend of Matthew Parker, future archbishop of Canterbury) various 'ornamentes' of which the College had been 'shamfully spoyled'. This seemed to have backfired when Mere lodged a counterclaim with the Vice-Chancellor on the grounds that Bullock's recourse to the queen's courts infringed University privileges. This resulted in the Master's excommunication. The issue eventually came before Stephen Gardiner, Chancellor of both the University and the realm, and he took Bullock's side, mainly because 'he hathe byn ever noted Catholike'. He may also have recalled that Bullock appeared as a witness on his behalf in the lengthy proceedings which resulted in his removal from the bishopric of Winchester in Edward's reign. Gardiner ordered the Vice-Chancellor (Dr John Young, himself a former Fellow of St John's) to absolve him and then to negotiate some compromise settlement which would return the chapel goods but compensate Mere.[96]

By the time the accounts resume in 1556, the Catholic restoration was in full swing. The celebration of the traditional Catholic liturgy required books, vestments, and utensils. In some cases, the debris of the Edwardine Reformation was still on the market. Old vestments could still be purchased, having been bought up in the turmoil of the previous reign, sometimes no doubt by those with pious hopes of an eventual Catholic Restoration, but perhaps more often by those with an eye for a bargain. Successive sacristans purchased old copes and paid for them to be mended and restored. Special attention was given to restoring service at the high altar. In autumn 1555 a joiner was paid 'for setting up the Roode', that is, the crucifix on the screen which separated the chapel from the antechapel (in effect the choir from the nave). A complete 'sute of vestimentes with a cope' was purchased for £4 6s 8d in spring 1556.[97]

[95] E. Leedham-Green, *Books in Cambridge Inventories* (Cambridge, 1986), I. 166–8 (Hartley), 209–15 (Raven), 218–22 (Gockman), 224–8 (Browne), 228–30 (Johnson), and 245–9 (Buckley).

[96] Gardiner to Young, 17 Jun. 1554: *Letters of Stephen Gardiner*, 469; Foxe, *Acts and Monuments*, VI. 225–6.

[97] SJCA, SB4.1, fo. 17v.

Every reign now seemed to bring a major visitation of the University, and on Wednesday 20 January 1557 a visitation under the authority of Cardinal Reginald Pole (though without his presence) reached St John's early in the morning, commencing with a mass of the Holy Spirit, before getting down to serious investigative work the next day.[98] George Bullock was on good terms with the Visitors, and St John's produced little if any evidence of real dissent. On Thursday 4 February he had to present to them the inventories of the personal libraries of all the Fellows and Scholars, and the collection of one Fellow, John Lakyn, was brought round for closer inspection, perhaps because his brother Thomas was a Protestant refugee abroad.[99] But Lakyn seems to have been conforming happily enough, as he was involved next year in purchasing for the chapel two old copes and some silk to make new altar hangings.[100] Another Fellow, Robert Dakyns, had to do penance for eating flesh on a fast day.[101] But the conscientious objectors had fled years before. The visitation in general found the College in good health. A statement of the College's income and outgoings produced for the occasion presented a balance sheet of just over £635.[102]

The visitation spurred the colleges to renewed zeal, and in spring 1557 Bullock went down to London to purchase more than £5 worth of vestments, including a fine cope emblazoned with an image of the Assumption of the Blessed Virgin Mary. It might be thought that such emphasis on liturgical display was misplaced at a time when the priority might perhaps have been given to preaching and teaching, in order to entrench Catholic doctrine in the face of the challenge of Protestantism. But liturgical display was very much a part of Catholicism, and the devotion of the fairest fruits of human artifice to divine service was an essential part of the religious identity that Catholics wished to establish in defiance of the new creed. Nor should one underestimate the impact of such display in an era in which cultural life still contained relatively little of image and colour. The Counter-Reformation's vigorous reassertion of the value of beauty in divine service enjoyed success in much of Europe, and even earned the backhanded compliment of a kind of imitation in the pursuit of the 'beauty of holiness' in the Church of England in the time of Charles I and William Laud.

The accounts for Mary's closing years saw a torrent of such expenditure. A fine pyx was cast and gilded to hold the blessed sacrament at the high altar.[103] A 'faire Antiphoner bownd in whyte lether' was purchased in summer 1558 from Goodman Watson, the stationer, at the prodigious cost of £3 13s 4d, an enormous sum for a book. This may perhaps be identified with the beautiful manuscript antiphoner, originally from Spain, that still survives in the library. Not satisfied with that, next term saw the purchase of another antiphoner for £4 5s,

---

[98] Lamb, *Documents*, 206–7.
[99] Ibid., 216 (Lakyn). For Bullock and the Visitors, see pp. 209, 215, 222, 227.
[100] SJCA, SB4.1, fo. 76r.
[101] Lamb, *Documents*, 222.
[102] SJCA, C17.2, account roll dated 31 Jan. 1557.
[103] SJCA, SB4.1, fo. 44r (1557).

and a further £8 spent on other liturgical books.[104] The antiphoner was the basic text required for singing the daily services of matins and evensong (and the other 'hours' of prayer), and the renewed place of music in the chapel is indicated by the purchase of a lectern for the organ. Elaborate church music, which had been rapidly going out of fashion under Edward (as it would again, though not totally, under Elizabeth), was definitely back in fashion under Mary. The high altar was finished with the installation of an altarpiece depicting Christ's Passion. Attention then switched to the 'low altars', the subordinate altars in the chantry chapels endowed by Ashton, Fisher, and Thompson before the Reformation set in. Here they had to cut corners. Plain canvas was bought and stained to provide relatively cheap hangings and altar cloths, with four 'papers of crucifixes' (presumably woodcut prints) as a substitute for carvings. Four sets of liturgical vessels ('cruets') and 'sacring bells' were purchased for a relatively cheap 5s 8d – one set for each of the chantry altars.[105] In John Fisher's chapel a 'table' (in this context, usually a board with writing painted on it) was set up there, probably to record his benefactions to the College but perhaps also his martyr's fate.[106]

Restoration of the old ways was not, however, all about spending long hours in a dark and dank chapel. The accounts for 1558 record the regular purchase of gallons of wine that enabled holy days, or holidays, to be marked in Hall as well. Besides Christmas, Candlemas, Ascension, Whitsun, and All Saints, there was special attention for the two feasts of St John the Evangelist, on 27 December and 6 May ('St John at the Latin Gate'). In summer the Fellows and students cheered themselves around bonfires to mark the feasts of Midsummer, St Peter's, St Thomas's Eve, and the Assumption.[107] At Christmas in both 1557 and 1558 they reported 2s 6d given to the town waits 'according to the old custome', a pointed observation from which we may infer that, at least in St John's, this custom had been abrogated under Edward.[108] Christmastide also saw the appointment each year of the 'Lord in Christinmas', whose substantial fee of 20 shillings was doubtless intended to cover the expenses of the entertainments he laid on.[109] The evidence for drama in the College during Mary's reign is thinner than in earlier reigns, but the 'Lord in Christmas' was clearly responsible for organizing performances, as is evident from the inventory of 'Plaiers Apparell' that was entrusted in 1547 to Thomas Lever, the 'Lord' for that year, to hand on to his successor the year after.[110] In Mary's reign the Master seems to have

[104] SJCA, SB4.1, fo. 76r. The surviving antiphoner is SJCL MS 263; the identification is speculative.

[105] SJCA, SB4.1, fo. 76r (1558); and fo. 80v for the lectern.

[106] SJCA, SB4.1, fo. 80r.

[107] SJCA, SB4.1, fo. 80v.

[108] SJCA, SB4.1, fos. 45r, 81r.

[109] SJCA, SB4.1, fos. 45r (Bartholomew Dodington) and 76v (William Baronsdale).

[110] Nelson, *Records of Cambridge Drama*, I. 159–62. See SJCA, D106.18, fo. 49r, for Lever's role as 'lord yn chrystmas' in 1547 (not 1548–9, as erroneously suggested in *Records*, I. 159). The *Records* reference to a Christmas lord at St John's for '1549–50' (I. 165) in fact belongs to 1548, and the payment to 'the weightes vppon saynt Iohns day' given for '1550–51' (I. 168) in fact belongs to 1549. Interestingly, there is no

looked after the stage wardrobe, and Mr Lakyn put on a play at Christmas in 1556.[111]

Like so many Tudor Masters after Metcalfe, Bullock had problems with his Fellowship. In the wake of his lawsuit against John Mere he got into a row with some of the senior Fellows, led by John Pynder, who were trying to undermine him on grounds of his refusal to seek absolution from the excommunication that Dr Young had pronounced against him, but who may well also have been resentful of the fact that the presidency of the College was awarded to one of the new Fellows of 1554, George Hunter. Bullock attempted to expel Pynder and his supporters from the College, but on appeal to the Chancellor, Stephen Gardiner, they were reinstated. Bullock then opened a new front over Pynder's role in some shady dealings relating to the lease of the manor of Hilton in Huntingdonshire. Hilton, twelve miles north-west of Cambridge, was the customary refuge of the Fellows and Scholars 'in all tyme of sykenes'. The implication is that Pynder had collaborated with the then Master, Lever, in underhand and somehow advantageous dealings which included lending the lessee £18 for his entry fine and reducing or omitting the College's rights of use in times of plague. Pynder's counterplea that the lease was in its customary form does not seem entirely consistent with his claim that there was 'no interlynynge or rasinge of the seid lease but by the hole consent of the seid Mr fellowes and Skollers'!![112] As with Mere, Bullock sued Pynder in the royal rather than the University courts, and, like Mere, Pynder fought back by claiming privilege of the University. The battle was still raging when Cardinal Pole's visitation arrived in January 1557, and on Wednesday 3 February Pynder exhibited to the Visitors a subpoena that Bullock had procured against him, seeking permission to leave Cambridge to answer it. Upon his return, a series of hearings before the Visitors went Bullock's way, and Pynder was sentenced to expulsion on 16 February. Having kicked Pynder out, Bullock proceeded to kick him while he was down, once more hauling him before the Visitors in a suit for eviction and debt which resulted in an award of £6 4s 1d against Pynder on 2 March.[113] The Master also won the lawsuit over the lease of Hilton: the register copy in the College archives is annotated 'frustrate by law'.[114] Pynder did not suffer unduly, though. He promptly found a new berth at Magdalene.

The disruption to the life of the College that arose in the mid-Tudor years from political and religious changes and from the consequent chopping and changing of the statutes was exacerbated both by the deteriorating economic

payment to a Christmas lord for 1549. The practice was probably abandoned in the wake of the visitation of spring 1549.

[111] Nelson, *Records of Cambridge Drama*, I. 195 for Lakyn's play (SJCA, SB4.1, fo. 45r). *Records*, I. 196–8 prints the inventory of 'players Garmentes' in Bullock's custody.

[112] SJCA, D57.90: Pynder's answer to Bullock's complaints. The register copy of the lease may lend substance to Bullock's suspicions. The text falls naturally into two parts: the lease itself, specifying term and rent; and the covenants, including that reserving use of the manor house to the College in times of plague. The covenants are written in a markedly different hand, so may have been added later. SJCA, C7.12, Thick Black Book, 306–8.

[113] Lamb, *Documents*, 215, 219, 223, 229.

[114] SJCA, C7.12, Thick Black Book, fo. 306.

situation of the country and by a period of poor stewardship. Nicholas Metcalfe had been tireless in his devotion to the College's financial interests, travelling extensively to get a grip on the rapidly growing landed endowment. His immediate successors, as Henry Howard showed in his history of the College finances, were not always so scrupulous.[115] A demoralization of society's attitude towards ecclesiastical endowments was perhaps inevitably occasioned by Henry VIII's pillage of the monasteries. The age-old taint of sacrilege attached to despoiling the Church was wiped away, and, led by a king who compelled bishops and cathedrals to engage in unfavourable land exchanges with him, acquisitive landowners viewed church property, including that of colleges, as fair game. Churchmen, equally demoralized, became far more willing to enter into deals on leases which gave advantageous terms to friends, relatives, and patrons in return for personal payments under the table. The statutory restraints on granting leases were routinely disregarded by John Taylor, Richard Longworth, and Nicholas Shepherd, who all seem to have regarded the Mastership as little more than an opportunity for profit. It was only towards the end of the century, with the return of political stability and perhaps also with the rise of Puritanism, that improvement began to be seen in the management of College leases.

Much of Bullock's time, however, was also consumed in one of the College's longest-running lawsuits, against the aptly named Snagge, a Bedfordshire gentleman determined by fair means or foul to take possession of 16 acres of woodland belonging to the College that stood squarely within the lands of a manor which he had acquired a few years before. The woodland was by this time an appurtenance of the neighbouring manor of Ramerick, acquired by St John's in 1521. Thomas Snagge was understandably incredulous to find that the woodland was not his, sat as it was in the midst of his property, though it is easy to imagine a previous lord of the manor alienating woodland, a long-term asset, in order to mitigate short-term cash flow difficulties. So he set out to give the College's tenant, Robert Godlington, a hard time, plundering timber and seeking to draw him into an unequal fight. The College swung into action on its tenant's behalf, with Mr Bill of Ashwell (the brother of the former Master, Dr Bill) as their attorney as the case ground its way through King's Bench, Chancery, and Star Chamber.[116] In 1556 Bullock spent nearly four months at London on this business, and about three months in 1557. The case long outlasted the reign, dragging on for years, but once William Cecil was at the heart of government, Snagge's defeat was only a matter of time.[117]

By the end of Mary's reign the College was returning to what Fisher and Metcalfe would have regarded as normality. The Chapel was not the brilliantly decorated place of worship they had left, but Catholic worship was restored, prayers and obits for benefactors were once more being celebrated, and the

---

[115] H. F. Howard, *An Account of the Finances of the College of St John the Evangelist in the University of Cambridge, 1511–1926* (Cambridge, 1935), 28–32.

[116] SCJA SB4.1, fos. 47r, 79r.

[117] For a statement of the case see TNA SP12/20, fo. 32r–v. For Bullock's travels and expenses on the case, SJCA, SB4.1, fos. 21r, 78r. For further expenses in the next reign, e.g. fos. 111r and 293r (costs in Star Chamber, 1559 and 1565). Snagge's case is summarized at TNA SP12/20, fo. 32r–v, in a paper for William Cecil.

combination of Catholic theology and Renaissance scholarship that they had sought to introduce was once more evident in the personnel of the College and their books. Yet the Catholic Restoration at Cambridge was not as deeply rooted as at Oxford. The Marian regime had concentrated its fire, in every sense, on Oxford. It was at Oxford that Cranmer, Ridley and Latimer – Cambridge men, all three – were first humiliated in disputation and then condemned to a horrific death at the stake. It was in Oxford that theology teaching was entrusted to foreign experts. Juan de Villagarcía and Pedro de Soto made an impact there comparable to that of the Protestant Martin Bucer in Edwardine Cambridge. One might question the tactical wisdom of not taking more trouble over Cambridge, which had certainly sent forth more of the movers and shakers of the English Reformation than Oxford over the previous twenty-five years. The effects were to become plain under Elizabeth. Oxford saw more Catholics expelled from their colleges and more crypto-Catholics hanging on to fight another day. The impressive publishing campaign mounted by Catholic refugees from the University of Louvain in the 1560s was staffed almost entirely by Oxford men. St John's College, Oxford, which had only been founded in Mary's reign, was especially prominent in the Catholic resistance.[118] St John's College, Cambridge, in contrast, like Cambridge in general, displayed less opposition to the next turn of fortune's wheel.

---

[118] E. Duffy, *Fires of Faith* (New Haven & London, 2009), 200.

William Cecil's College

THE accession to the throne of Elizabeth I in November 1558 not only gave another spin to the wheel of religious change but also brought to power, as her closest adviser and chief minister, one of the most eminent statesmen ever sent forth by St John's. Almost at once, William Cecil, a pensioner of the College from 1535 until 1540, was offered the Chancellorship of the University, an office that was to prove far more onerous than he could ever have imagined.[1] The University and its colleges were in continual contact with him for nearly forty years on matters great and small. No college cost him more time and trouble than St John's. His 'honorable good affection to benefitt it all kynde of wayes' was notorious, and his filial loyalty sustained endless provocation.[2] For the history of the College in Elizabeth's reign was a volatile mixture of religious zeal and personal ambition which exploded on numerous occasions. Cecil was cast as the umpire or the peacemaker in the recurrent games and battles played out by domineering Masters and troublesome Fellows.

I. THE ELIZABETHAN SETTLEMENT

Elizabeth's first Parliament saw the prompt restoration to the statute book of the royal supremacy and the Book of Common Prayer. Only then could the government turn to the implementation of the new religious arrangements in the Church of England. The universities were a special priority for the royal commission of visitation entrusted with this task in the summer of 1559. Cecil himself, in theory, headed the commissioners, who also included the new archbishop of Canterbury, Matthew Parker, but they were too busy elsewhere to take an active part in proceedings at Cambridge. All but one of the commissioners were Cambridge graduates, three of them former Fellows of St John's: James Pilkington, Robert Horne, and William Bill.[3] Five of them had been forced out of headships or Fellowships at Cambridge, so when they arrived in July they set about their task with a vengeance.

The Marian Master, George Bullock, refused to take the required oath to the royal supremacy, and was deprived of both his Mastership and the Lady Margaret professorship of divinity, which he had held for less than a year. Sadly, the records of the visitation of the province of Canterbury do not survive, but those for the province of York do, and in them we hear Bullock's voice. He retreated from Cambridge to Durham, where he held a prebend in the cathedral. When the Visitors caught up with him again, on 25 September, he was

---

[1] S. Alford, *Burghley: William Cecil at the Court of Elizabeth I* (New Haven & London, 2008), 12–23; Porter, *Reformation and Reaction*, 102.

[2] Andrew Perne to Cecil, 18 Oct. 1585: BL Lansdowne MS 45, fo. 130r. The Lansdowne manuscripts preserve the bulk of Cecil's voluminous correspondence with Cambridge and St John's. It is this archive that permits the College's history in Elizabeth's reign to be reconstructed in remarkable detail.

[3] Porter, *Reformation and Reaction*, 104.

blunt and outspoken, as he had presumably been before. Invited to acknowledge the queen as Supreme Governor of the Church of England, he responded that 'the bisshope of Rome hath and ought to have the iurisdiction ecclesiasticall within this realme'. Thus 'by playne and flate wordis', the Visitors reported, 'he affirmed that the sea of that bisshope was the sea Apostolicke'.[4] Ejected from his last resort in England, he took refuge abroad, though his misfortunes continued. Pirates boarded the ship on which he was crossing the Channel, took everything he owned, and stranded him on the northern coast of France. Retiring to the abbey of Ninove in the Netherlands, he spent his days compiling a massive concordance to the Bible, which he published shortly before his death in 1572.[5]

It was one of the Visitors, James Pilkington, who was appointed Master in Bullock's place on 20 July. A thorough purge of the College ensued, although the process was not quite so drastic as appears at first sight. The fortunate survival of a full list of the membership of the College compiled for the visitation enables us to reconstruct the process more accurately than can be done for 1553.[6] Of thirty-seven Fellows that summer, only eighteen were still in place a year later. However, of the nineteen departures, one came about by death and another five were career moves.[7] Seven Fellows seem to have been expelled that summer, of whom one, Philip Sherwood, later fled the country to become one of the 'seminary priests' who so troubled the Elizabethan authorities. Valentine Taylor likewise fled to the sanctuary of the Catholic university at Louvain, accompanied by one Cuthbert Ellison, a priest who had entered St John's as a Fellow-Commoner late in 1558.[8] The President, Thomas Willan, was almost certainly expelled with them. Five other Fellows held on until the end of the year, but then disappear from the records both of the University and of the Church of England, and therefore may well have left for reasons of conscience. Below the level of the Fellowship the process is obscure, as no regular records of the College's Scholars and pensioners survive from that time. One of the recently matriculated Scholars, William Clibburn, was reported to Cecil for calling Elizabeth a 'rascal'. The informants were two College pensioners, George Bond (soon to become a Fellow) and George Withers, who had just been elected to a Fellowship at Queens'.[9] Clibburn is never seen again in the University records,

---

[4] *The Royal Visitation of 1559: Act Book for the Northern Province*, ed. C. J. Kitching (Gateshead, 1975), 25.

[5] G. Bullock, *Oeconomia Methodica Concordantiarum Scripturae Sacrae* (Antwerp, 1572): sigs.+3r–+4v provide details of his flight from England.

[6] CUA, College I.7.

[7] Henry Warren, Nicholas Cobb, and Henry Cockcroft turn up in University records in the 1560s, while Christopher Tatham served in the Elizabethan Church. The last, John Berryman, was re-elected to the Fellowship in 1562. Miles Buckley died that summer and was buried in the Chapel at the steps of the altar, for which see his will at CUA, VCCt Wills II, fos. 19v–20v (probate 8 Aug. 1559).

[8] *Matricule de l'Université de Louvain*, ed. E. H. J. Reusens *et al.* (1903–80), IV. 610 (10 Oct. 1560). Ellison's forename is given there as 'Luthbert'. See SJCA, SB4.1, fo. 65v, for Ellison's entry fee into Fellows' commons.

[9] *Calendar of State Papers Domestic Series of the Reigns of Edward VI, Mary, Elizabeth* (London, 1856), 127. See CUA, Matr. 1, 172, for Clibburn's matriculation, 27 May 1559.

and was probably sent packing. Another of the Scholars, John Rames, turns up among the Catholic refugees at Louvain in 1566.[10]

There were, no doubt, other departures for reasons of conscience, but probably not very many. One of the leavers would in due course be canonized by the Roman Catholic Church. Richard Gwyn left the University and returned to the Welsh Marches, where he served as schoolmaster at 'Orton Madoc' (Overton, by the Dee, a few miles south of Wrexham), composing widely circulated Welsh carols in defence of the old faith against the new.[11] Arrested in 1580 amidst growing hysteria occasioned by the activities of two Catholic missionary priests, Edmund Campion and Robert Parsons, Gwyn was charged in 1582 under new legislation making it high treason to seek to convert people to Roman Catholicism. After being tortured under the aegis of the Council of the Marches, he was hanged, drawn, and quartered at Wrexham in 1584 by a particularly inexpert executioner.[12] Recently discovered evidence corroborates the story told in the contemporary account of his martyrdom that he had studied at St John's thanks to the charity of Dr Bullock and that while there he went under the Anglicized version of his name, Richard White. For in the roster of the College compiled in 1559 there is a 'Richard Whyte' among the 'sizars', the poorest students.[13]

Some of the resulting vacancies were filled instantly, as Thomas Fowle, Roger Kelke, Ralph Lever, Nicholas Shepherd, Percival Wiburn, and Thomas Wilson were restored by the Visitors to the Fellowships from which they had been ejected at the start of Mary's reign, with Wilson replacing the Marian President Thomas Willan.[14] It has been imagined that the changing of the guard was not entirely without humanity. The accounts record a dinner held 'for owre Mr and other that hade bene fellowes', and this has been taken as a gracious farewell to Bullock and his followers.[15] However, as these accounts were always written up at the end of the year, 'owre Mr' would by then have meant James Pilkington, while those that 'had bene fellowes' probably meant those who, like him, had been expelled under Mary, making it not a generous gesture towards the departing losers but a celebration for the returning victors.

It was a particular priority of the Elizabethan regime to embed the new religion in England's institutions, most of all in the universities on account of their

---

[10] CUA, College I.7. *Matricule de l'Université de Louvain* IV. 710, as 'Joannes Reyms, Anglus, in theologia' (18 Jun. 1566).

[11] 'The carols of Richard White' in *Unpublished Documents Relating to the English Martyrs*, I. *1584–1603*, ed. J. H. Pollen (London, 1908), 90–99.

[12] 'A True Report of the Life and Martyrdom of Mr. Richard White, Schoolmaster', in *The Rambler*, III, part VII (May 1860), 233–48, 366–88.

[13] CUA, College I.7. Venn (*Alumni Cantabrigienses*, I.iv. 388) identifies the martyr with a Richard White who matriculated as a pensioner at Christ's in 1571 and graduated BA in 1575 and MA in 1578, but this cannot be the man who had spent at least sixteen years in and around Overton by the time his troubles began ('True Report', 234).

[14] SJCA, SB4.1, fo. 130r has Mr Wilson as President for 1560, replacing Willan, who had held that office in 1559 (fo. 101v; see also CUA, College I.7).

[15] SJCA, SB4.1, fo. 109r; Baker-Mayor, 1.144. The former Master is referred to as 'd. bullocke' (Dr Bullock) on fo. 109v.

role in training the clergy.[16] Pilkington was certainly the man for the job. As Master he published a commentary on the prophet Haggai, which doubtless reflects the sort of teaching he delivered in Cambridge as Regius Professor of Divinity and which gives us a sense of how he aspired to guide the College. His commentary is suffused with a deep gratitude for the passing of the Marian persecution, which he interprets as a divine chastisement for the lukewarm reception the English people had accorded the 'gospel' when it was first offered to them under Henry VIII and Edward VI. Pilkington aims to stir his readers 'to an earneste furtheryng of Gods true relyigyon' so that the failings of the 'colde gospellers' will not once more bring down the wrath of God on their heads.[17]

The leitmotif of his commentary is 'buylding God's house' (Haggai 1:2), and the accounts testify to Pilkington's efforts to build it in St John's.[18] As so often, building God's house necessitated some preliminary demolition work. Shortly after the change of regime, one John Waller and his man were paid for pulling down the high altar and Hugh Ashton's altar. Later in the year, an 'alter on the southe side of the lower chappell' was also ripped out.[19] Notwithstanding the statutes and the official provision of a Latin edition of the Book of Common Prayer for use in college chapels, English was the language of worship. English psalters were bought, and the chapel's English Bible had to be rebound in 1562 and replaced in 1566.[20] A board with the Ten Commandments painted on it in English was put up in the Chapel in summer 1564, for the instruction of the younger students.[21] Pilkington had only contempt for organ music in church, scorning the provision of 'swete Organes for the eare' as popish idolatry.[22] The musical tradition of chapel worship changed dramatically. A lectern had been purchased for the organ in Bullock's last year, but after 1558 there is no reference to any organ in chapel until a new one was ordered in 1635.[23] The old organ was probably scrapped with the altars, as within a few years the organ-chamber had been converted into an extra room for the use of the Master.[24] There was still some music in chapel. In summer 1563, ten Geneva Psalters were bought for use there, and another batch of ten was purchased towards Christmas, clear signs of the growing attachment in Elizabethan Cambridge to the model of theology and worship established by John Calvin in Geneva.[25] But the singing now was simple, accessible and unaccompanied hymnody rather than the elaborate polyphony beloved not only of Queen Mary but also of her Protestant sister Queen Elizabeth.

[16] N. Jones, *The English Reformation* (Oxford, 2002), 115–24.

[17] J. Pilkington, *Aggeus the Prophete declared* (London, 1560), sigs. A2v and A4v.

[18] Pilkington, *Aggeus*, sig. C8r.

[19] SJCA, SB4.1, fo. 104r.

[20] SJCA, SB4.1, fos. 194v, 320r. The Chapel bible was mended again in 1569, and a large copy of the 'Bishops' Bible' was bought in 1572: fos. 427v, 466r.

[21] SJCA, SB4.1, fo. 258v.

[22] Pilkington, *Aggeus*, sig. L1r.

[23] SJCA, SB4.1, fo. 80v. N. Thistlethwaite, 'St John's College Organs 1528–1994', *Eagle* (1995), 54. The organ had been mended in 1547: SJCA, D106.18, fo. 32r.

[24] Willis and Clark, *Architectural History*, 283.

[25] SJCA, SB4.1, fo. 258v.

Although James Pilkington was soon to be made bishop of Durham, his religious sympathies, like those of many of the first generation of Elizabethan bishops, inclined towards what would later be known as Puritanism. The naming of his four children – Joshua, Isaac, Deborah, and Ruth – evinces a systematic preference for Old Testament names over the saints' names favoured in Catholic cultures, a Puritan habit of Calvinist origin. He even voiced distaste for the pagan names of the days of the week, although he saw little hope of remedying them.[26] And when we hear the Master of St John's denouncing bishops and other patrons who appoint incompetent clergymen to parishes as murderers of the souls lost through their heedlessness, it is easy to see where the two giants of early Cambridge Puritanism, William Fulke and Thomas Cartwright, both of them then members of St John's, contracted some of their habits of thought.[27] Equally, though, Pilkington did accept appointment as a bishop, which warns us against exaggerating the extent of his 'Puritanism'. But at its heart Puritanism was merely a commitment to further reform within the Church of England, and that commitment was one to which he wholeheartedly subscribed.

Pilkington's Puritanical tendencies did not stamp out all good fun and Fellowship in the College, though they certainly changed the tone. The bonfires which had been lit to celebrate the major feasts of the year in Mary's reign disappear abruptly from the accounts after 1559.[28] But the custom of marking the festival of St John at the Latin Gate (6 May) with a feast in Hall, which may have been introduced in the reign of Mary, was maintained. The feast is first seen in the College record for 1558, with the purchase of two gallons of 'clared [claret] and whyte wyne upon Sanct John Port Latynes daye'.[29] But plenty of wine was drunk in spring 1562, celebrating Easter, the Port Latin, and Whitsun in quick succession, while malmsey as well as claret was bought for the following Christmas.[30] The 'Port Latin' became a regular and grander celebration, with generous expenditure on food and wine: £2 11s 5d in 1587. In 1595 they even paid musicians to perform.[31] The waits continued their visits throughout the reign, and the College began a custom of spending heavily on dinners in honour of visiting guests, especially (though not exclusively) former Fellows. A prodigious £3 13s 9d was spent on supper for the marquess of Northampton in 1562.[32] Pilkington himself was entertained at the cost of a gallon of 'Hipocrace' (hippocras, a drink akin to mulled wine) when he revisited the College as bishop of Durham in 1571.[33] Later that year, Elizabeth and her court came to Audley End, and some of her council made the trip to Cambridge during

---

[26] Pilkington, *Aggeus*, sig. B7r–v. For the names of his children see *ODNB* (D. Marcombe).

[27] Pilkington, *Aggeus*, sig. E3v.

[28] SJCA, SB4.1, fo. 109r for the last 'bone fyer of St peters even' (31 July); Midsummer bonfire, fo. 108v.

[29] SJCA, SB4.1, fo. 80r.

[30] SJCA, SB4.1, fos. 198v–200v.

[31] See e.g. SJCA, SB4.1, fos. 425v (1570) and 448r (1571); and SB4.2, fos. 247v (1587), 353r (1592), and 423v (1595).

[32] SJCA, SB4.1, fo. 198v.

[33] SJCA, SB4.1, fo. 448r.

her stay. The College took the opportunity to ingratiate themselves further with William Cecil, presenting him, too, with 'a gallon of hipocrace', and his son, Thomas, with 'a boxe of marmolet' [marmalade].[34] The 1570s also saw the addition to the calendar of another celebration, the anniversary of Elizabeth's accession (17 November), which is first specifically mentioned in 1574, with 2s 2d 'bestowed on the quenes daye in wine and suger and apples'.[35] By the time of William Whitaker's mastership these celebrations included an oration in Hall and bonfires in both courts.[36]

2. THE FIRST STIRRINGS OF FACTION

After James Pilkington had been consecrated bishop of Durham on 2 March 1561, he held onto the Mastership of St John's long enough to bequeath it, in effect, to his younger brother Leonard, who needed to take his BD degree that summer in order to become eligible for the post. The bishop's evident favour at court secured the backing of William Cecil for his brother's succession, which was also supported by the Vice-Chancellor, Robert Beaumont, who assured Cecil that under Leonard's rule, 'licentious youthe' would be 'kepte in awe, learning floorishe, and pure religion take better roote'.[37] With this kind of backing, Leonard Pilkington was duly elected. His brief Mastership was uneventful until it began to draw to a close. With the promise from his brother of one of the ripest ecclesiastical plums in his gift, the rectory of Whitburn (just north of Sunderland), he decided to retire from Cambridge.[38] The farcical chaos that ensued made a mockery of Beaumont's complacent prediction.

The first anyone in College learned of the Master's proposed departure was on 23 July 1563, when the President, Richard Longworth, convened the Fellows in the chapel, announced Pilkington's resignation, and read out a letter from Queen Elizabeth. This authorized them to proceed to an immediate election, notwithstanding their statutes, and warmly recommended none other than Longworth himself. What was evidently a carefully prepared coup at once came unstuck. Only sixteen out of forty-six Fellows were in residence, but they refused to be bounced, not least because Longworth was a cousin of the Pilkingtons, and the mastership seemed to be turning into a hereditary fief. Two other candidates were proposed, and one of them, Roger Kelke, swept the board with eleven votes. Robert Horne, the bishop of Winchester, took one vote, while there were four abstentions. Longworth himself polled not a single vote (though the five who did not support Kelke were probably his party). The Fellows promptly wrote to Queen Elizabeth and William Cecil justifying their

---

[34] SJCA, SB4.2, fo. 448v. See Cooper, *Annals of Cambridge*, II. 278 for the visit.

[35] SJCA, SB4.1, fo. 538r.

[36] Whitaker to Cecil, 14 May 1590: BL Lansdowne MS 63, fo. 211r.

[37] Beaumont to Cecil, 24 Sept. 1561: TNA SP12/19, fo. 104r.

[38] See *ODNB* (R. L. Graves) for Leonard Pilkington's career, and this promotion in particular. Whitburn was valued at just under £40 a year. See *Valor Ecclesiasticus* (London 1810–34), V. 313. In the 1545 statutes, the Master's stipend had been raised to £12, and his total remuneration to £18 4s: *Early Statutes*, 153, 169, 173.

actions. To Elizabeth they explained that Longworth's proceedings were in breach of their statutes, and that, bound as they were by oath to choose the best candidate, they preferred Kelke as a man older, wiser and more upright than her candidate. Remarkably, they did not even apologize for disregarding her wishes, merely assuring her of their confidence that her well-known goodwill towards scholarship would lead her to endorse their decision.[39]

They favoured Cecil with a rather fuller account, hoping that he would help square things with the queen. They enumerated the ways in which Longworth's proceedings had contravened their statutes, in particular the revelation, after the event, that the Master's resignation was conditional upon Longworth's own election. It would be a 'pytyfull presydent', they pleaded, if Masters were allowed to force successors upon the College by such means. This was evidently the nub of the matter, as they complained that Pilkington had only clung to office 'to place therin his countreyman and kinsman'. But for good measure they launched into a personal attack, claiming that he had *de facto* vacated his office through non-residence and that his prolonged absences were damaging the College by encouraging predators like Snagge to set upon their estates.[40]

Cecil's reaction suggests that he had not been privy to the original coup, as he did what he could to promote Kelke's cause. He may have remembered Kelke from his own time at St John's, whereas Longworth had not come to the College until 1549, years after Cecil had left. A letter from Kelke to Cecil a few days later reported a meeting in which he had called on Longworth, in Cecil's name, to back down. But Longworth would have none of it, and raised all sorts of objections to the electoral process which had not occurred to him when he thought he would end up as Master. Kelke explained what Elizabeth and Cecil now wanted, but Longworth refused to believe him unless he received a 'mandatory' letter (which Kelke urged Cecil to procure). Something, he concluded, had to be done, as strife was intensifying and studies were suffering.[41]

At this point Longworth played a master-stroke, urging that Cecil make an example of the recalcitrant Fellows for 'so little regarding the Queen's Majesty's so favourable letters'.[42] Cecil could not be seen to countenance open disobedience to his sovereign, so he changed tack and called in the bishop of Ely, Richard Cox, to adjudicate in his capacity as Visitor. In August 1563, Cox brusquely ruled Kelke's election invalid and soundly rebuked the Fellows for proceeding 'so rashly and disorderly' with an election contrary to their statutes.[43] A month or so later he reported that Pilkington was still keen to resign, but advised against allowing the Fellows 'ffree election according to their Statutes' on the

---

[39] SJC to Elizabeth (23 Jul. 1563): BL Lansdowne MS 7, fo. 4r. The details on voting come from the letter to Cecil (see next note).

[40] SJC to Cecil, 23 Jul. 1563: BL Lansdowne MS 7, fo. 6r, enclosing a list of eight specific complaints (fo. 8r), from which the citations are drawn. The case against Snagge ground on at vast expense: SJCA, SB4.1, fos. 111v (1559) and 293v (1565).

[41] Kelke to Cecil, 27 Jul. 1563: BL Lansdowne MS 7, fo. 10r.

[42] Longworth to Cecil, 28 July 1563: BL Lansdowne MS 7, fo. 12r. Longworth's letter enclosed a statement impugning the validity of Dr Kelke's election (fo. 13r), signed by himself and five other Fellows (doubtless the five who had not voted for Kelke).

[43] Cox to Cecil, 15 Aug. 1563: BL Lansdowne MS 6, fo. 164r.

grounds that 'in this contentiouse tyme' the outcome was unpredictable. Instead he urged that a Master be appointed by royal prerogative, concluding by recommending Longworth.[44]

Which is exactly what happened. The Fellows wrote to Cecil on 5 January 1564 to announce that, having considered his merits fairly, they had now unanimously elected the man whom they had originally opposed.[45] In expressing their fulsome gratitude to Cecil for having brought peace to the College, however, they were premature. It was on Longworth's watch that St John's entered one of the most turbulent periods in its early history, as a tide of youthful enthusiasm for further Reformation beat itself fruitlessly against the rock of Elizabeth's idiosyncratic religious preferences.

Nevertheless, the peace lasted long enough to make a success of the ceremonial highlight of the College's Tudor history, a royal visit. In August 1564 the court came to Cambridge, and Elizabeth was received and entertained in one college after another. As the *alma mater* of her chief minister, St John's played a prominent part in proceedings. Richard Curteys, the President of St John's, was also the Senior Proctor that year, and welcomed Cecil to the College, where he stayed for the duration of the visit. On Wednesday 9 August Elizabeth herself came to St John's, and rode into the Hall to be greeted with a Latin oration by one of the older Fellows, Humphrey Bohun, which yet again recited, to no avail, the College myth about the loss of Lady Margaret's lands. A former Fellow, Edward Lewkenor, who now held a minor position in the royal household, delivered an encomium in verse, and classicizing verses in the queen's honour written by more than forty Fellows and students were posted around the walls.[46] Only Trinity College produced more verses in Greek for the queen, and not even Trinity matched St John's in offering a few verses in Hebrew and even Syriac.[47]

The 1560s were a period of rapid growth for the College. After the inflation and influenza of the previous reigns, England's economy and population had stabilized and returned to growth. This was reflected in student numbers, which rose sharply. This is approximately visible in the matriculation statistics, which averaged about thirty-six a year in the 1550s, but rose to nearly seventy a year in the 1560s, with a distinct increase in the annual totals visible from 1565. When the queen visited in August 1564 there were 183 Fellows and students, but by December 1565 this had risen to 283, with an unparalleled 114 matriculations in the intervening year.[48] More accommodation must have been provided to make this expansion possible, and the accounts for 1564–5 indicate that various of the

[44] Cox to Cecil, 17 Sept. 1563: BL Lansdowne MS 6, fo. 177r.

[45] SJC to Cecil, 5 Jan. 1564: BL Lansdowne MS 7, fo. 159r, signed by Richard Curteys and thirteen others.

[46] Baker-Mayor, I. 157–61; Cooper, *Annals of Cambridge*, II. 184–208, at p. 198.

[47] *Verses Presented to Queen Elizabeth I (CUL MS Add. 8915)*, ed. E. Leedham-Green (Cambridge, 1993), 1–8 (Trinity) and 9–15 (St John's).

[48] Matriculation statistics are derived from the University's matriculation book, CUA, Matr. 1, 116–255. The totals for 1564 and 1565 come respectively from Cooper, *Annals of Cambridge*, II. 207 and TNA SP12/38, fos. 104r–105. The latter list also includes the Master and three servants, bringing its grand total to 287.

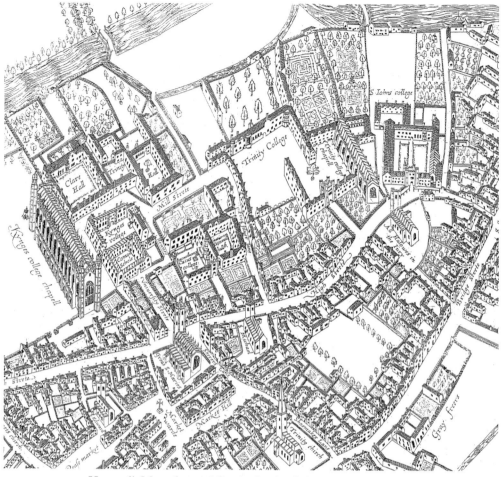

7 Hamond's Map of central Cambridge (1592) showing Metcalfe Court
(soon to be destroyed to make way for Second Court) and Rath Hall by the river

hospital's surviving outbuildings were being converted to provide residential chambers. A great deal of work went into 'the chambers over the wheate lofte' and into the 'chambers by the water sydes'.[49] The latter can be identified with the largest of three buildings on the College's riverside visible on Hamond's map of Cambridge drawn in 1592, and records of room allocations from the seventeenth century indicate that the building, which came to be known as Rath Hall, contained six sets of rooms. The chambers over the wheat-loft are not so easy to locate, although they are almost certainly the same as the 'studyes and chambers over the Backhouse' [that is, the bakehouse], which seems to

[49] SJCA, SB4.1, fos. 295v–299r, under both 'Expensa necessaria' and 'Reparaciones domi'. 20,000 bricks were ordered in 1565: fo. 295v. See also fo. 266v for the start of these works towards the end of 1564. The references seem to be to different projects, rather than two different ways of describing the same project. Cf. Crook, *Foundation to Gilbert Scott*, 25.

have been part of the property facing the front of the College across St John's Street.[50]

The absolute expansion in numbers can be seen in the complete lists of the membership of the College which were compiled on a number of occasions in Elizabeth's reign. The figure of 150 at the visitation in 1559 was perhaps unusually low, with political uncertainty exacerbating the seasonal slump in numbers seen every summer. In December 1565 the roster stood at 287 members (48 Fellows, 235 students). In 1575 it was a more modest 242 (55 Fellows, 187 students), but evidently it could vary dramatically, as in 1581 it stood at a prodigious 335 (51 Fellows, 284 students).[51] Not all of those named on these lists can be found in the University's matriculation registers, which warns us that estimates of student numbers based on the registers in fact provide only a minimum figure. The list for 1565 is especially interesting, because it groups students under their Tutors. Tutorial groups ranged between one and nineteen, with the average around five students per Fellow. Eight Fellows had ten or more students, and the largest group was that of Oliver Carter (Fellow, 1562–71). Most Fellows had one or more pupils. Even the Master had one. This may have been at least in part for reasons of accommodation. Chambers were normally shared. Fellows without pupils could be required to share two to a chamber. Only Fellows of doctoral rank or College preachers might have a room to themselves, with the special permission of the Master. The students were squeezed in, sometimes two to a bed, or else in 'truckle beds' that were tucked under the larger beds in the day, or perhaps in a bed in the 'cockloft' under the eaves, reached by a ladder. The chambers were fitted with small individual studies in which to work, but the atmosphere would have been friendly at best, oppressive at worst. From 1545 the norm was fixed at four students per chamber.[52]

The surge in student numbers had other consequences for the College infrastructure. By 1569 there was an urgent need for improved sanitation, and masons and labourers spent the year constructing a capacious privy by the river, a project which cost £50 and involved a dam to hold back the waters while works were completed. The privy stood just downstream of the Water Side chambers, the north end of which was described in the seventeenth century as 'by the

---

[50] SJCA, SB4.1, fo. 297r. This reference to chambers over the bakehouse is, as such, unique, but it would make sense for the wheatloft and the bakehouse to be in the same place. A new bakehouse was built on that site in the early seventeenth century (Baker-Mayor, I. 453).

[51] BL Lansdowne MS 20, fo. 212r–v (1575); BL Harleian MS 7039, fo. 245r (1581). Caius, *Historiae Cantabrigiensis Academiae*, 77, gave the total membership as 271 (Master, 51 Fellows, 78 Scholars, 89 pensioners, 46 sizars, 6 servants). Some totals include the servants (always 6), some do not.

[52] *Early Statutes*, 164–7. In 1545 preachers and Seniors were given the right not to share with another Fellow, but at the price of accommodating two students: p. 167. In 1580, the privilege of doctors was reduced to that of the preachers and Seniors. The 1580 statutes are printed in *Fifth Report from the Select Committee on Education* (London, 1818), 404–62; for this point, see p. 445. The seventeenth-century 'prizing books' give a sense of the layout and capacity of the rooms, e.g. SJCA, Prizing Book 1, C12.1, 19, for the 'Chamber nexte the librarie' when it was transferred from Mr Boys to Mr Allenson (29 Apr. 1597). It contained seven studies.

water side next the Boggards' ('boggards' being then a synonym for 'privy').[53] It is presumably the smallest of three buildings clearly visible on the 1592 map on ground now occupied by the river frontage of Third Court. The Master and the President, however, did not have to venture so far, but enjoyed private and doubtless better-appointed provision. The Master's privy was given windows in 1571, while the President's facilities had been upgraded in 1565.[54]

As has often been remarked before, in order to understand the nature of collegiate life in Tudor England it is vital to understand how young they all were.[55] When William Cecil lectured the heads of house on the importance of keeping control of 'inordinate youth' he was not just thinking of the students, he was thinking of the Fellows as well. When Cecil had come to St John's aged fourteen in 1535, his Tutor, John Cheke, was just seven years his senior.[56] The senior Fellow in 1565, Richard Curteys, was barely thirty, having matriculated in 1550 at the typical age of about fifteen and become a Fellow at the age of eighteen. Over forty of his forty-eight colleagues had only joined the Fellowship in the reign of Elizabeth. Their average age was not much above twenty. The Master, Richard Longworth, was only thirty-three. No wonder the College employed an informer to report on Fellows and students visiting Barnwell in search of loose women.[57]

Tutors were responsible for their young charges, but must often have found them hard to manage. The more successful Tutors provided entertainment as well as instruction. William Fulke kept a small menagerie in his rooms, with dogs, rats, and rabbits as well as the birds that he and his students snared.[58] Everard Digby, another of the College's characters, was accused by his Puritan enemies of taking his students out fishing when they should all have been in Chapel. As he was the author of England's first textbook on swimming, he probably took them into the river as well as along it, notwithstanding the University's ban on swimming in 1571. Indeed, his book is dedicated to one of his former students, Richard Wortley.[59] Archery was another favoured pastime. Matthew White had a bow bought for him as a Scholar in the early 1530s, and bows and arrows are found mentioned in several of the inventories made at the deaths of Fellows in the sixteenth century.[60] As early as 1530 it was necessary to forbid shooting arrows, as well as throwing balls, within the court or the

---

[53] SJCA, Prizing Book 2, C12.2, 270.

[54] SJCA, SB4.1, fo. 298v, records 13d for a mason 'makinge a place to avoide urine by Mr Presidentes Chamber'; see fo. 448v, 12d for 'glassing our Masters pryvye'.

[55] Porter, *Reformation and Reaction*, 108, 112.

[56] BL Add. MS 6059, fos. 6v (Cheke, 1514) and 9v (Cecil, 1521) for their birthdays.

[57] Below, p. 74, n. 79.

[58] Articles against William Fulke: TNA SP12/38, fo. 67r.

[59] P. Lake, *Moderate Puritans and the Elizabethan Church* (Cambridge, 1982), 172; E. Digby, *De arte natandi* (London, 1587); Cooper, *Annals of Cambridge*, II. 277; Venn, *Alumni Cantabrigienses*, I.iv. 466, for Richard 'Wortle', matriculated 1578 as a pensioner.

[60] SJCA, D106.6, fo. 47r for White's bow; Leedham-Green, *Books in Cambridge Inventories*, I. 33 (Henry Sanderson, 1545), 58 (William Porter, 1546), 210 (Edward Raven, 1558), 313 (Robert Smith, 1571), 344 (Edmund Roberts, 1580), 537 (Stephen Thompson, 1599).

8 Doggy paddle, sixteenth-century style. From Everard Digby's *De arte natandi*,
England's first textbook for swimmers (1587): SJCL, Aa.6.19

garden.[61] Roger Ascham's book on archery, *Toxophilus*, is framed as a dialogue
between two students which arises when one of them, Philologus, is surprised
while out for a walk to find the other, Toxophilus, reading a book rather than
going out with some others 'to shoot at the pricks'.[62] Presumably butts were
set up in the meadows across the river. Indoor games were also in vogue. Playing cards was in general frowned upon, as an occasion for gambling, though it
was generally permitted at Christmas. More cerebral games were encouraged.

[61] *Early Statutes*, 138 (repeated in 1545, p. 141).
[62] R. Ascham, *Toxophilus*, in *Whole Works*, III. 1–163 (second pagination series), esp.
p. 11.

Both William Gockman and Edward Raven, victims of influenza in 1558, had chess sets, as did Stephen Thompson (d. 1599),[63] while another Fellow, Ralph Lever, wrote a handbook for the arcane 'philosophers' game' (a chess-like strategy game in which the pieces and moves were based on arithmetical and geometrical principles) which, as his title emphasized, had been 'invented for the honest recreation of students, and other sober persons'.[64] When the Edwardine Visitors forbade cards altogether in 1549, they specifically recommended chess and the 'philosophers' game' instead.[65]

But discipline could be hard to maintain. Students under fourteen could be beaten for their misdemeanours. Older students were liable to be fined by the Deans, and this produced a steady income throughout the century. Drinking and dicing were endemic among the gentry sons who were swarming to Cambridge as pensioners, and the increasingly puritanical seriousness of the University was seen by some as a discouragement to genuine scholarship as well as an unrealistic expectation of maturity from youth. As the Elizabethan student Thomas Nashe put it:

> If at the first peeping out of the shell a young Student sets not a grave face on it, or seemes not mortifiedly religious, (have he bever so good a witte, be hee never so fine a Scholler), he is cast of [off] and discouraged.[66]

Nashe, who studied at St John's from 1582 until 1588, lived in the Cambridge of the University wits, such as Robert Greene and Christopher Marlowe, with its dash and style, its hints of wantonness, homosexuality, popery, and espionage, and its obsession with words and rhetoric, verse, drama, and romance fiction.[67] There were two Cambridges under Elizabeth, and the tension between them was evident in St John's throughout her reign.

3. WILLIAM FULKE AND THE VESTMENTS CONTROVERSY

By the middle of the 1560s agitation for further reform within the Church of England had come to focus on what seems at first sight a marginal issue, the proper clothing for clergymen in church. Queen Elizabeth, whose tastes favoured a certain formality, had issued injunctions in 1559 stipulating that the clergy were to 'wear such seemly habits, garments, and such square caps, as were most commonly and orderly received in the latter year of the reign of King

---

[63] Leedham-Green, *Books in Cambridge Inventories*, I. 210, 218, 537.

[64] R. Lever, *The Most Ancient and Learned Playe, Called the Philosophers Game* (London, 1563). Andrew Perne had a set: Leedham-Green, *Books in Cambridge Inventories*, I. 422.

[65] Cards were permitted at Christmas under the statutes of 1530 and 1545: *Early Statutes*, 138–9. This permission was withdrawn by the Visitors in 1549, who nevertheless added 'scaccis aut ludo philosophorum nativitatis tempore in aula ludant': SJCA, C1.4, fo. 62. But the statutes of 1580 returned to the more relaxed earlier situation: *Fifth Report*, 438.

[66] Cited by C. Nicholl, *A Cup of News: The Life of Thomas Nashe* (London, 1984), 25.

[67] Ibid., 29–32.

Edward VI'.[68] The problems that zealous Protestants had with this requirement were summed up in a letter from James Pilkington to William Cecil, lamenting that such trouble was being taken over such trifles 'in this libertie of godds truth'. But like most opponents of the prescribed vestments, while he objected to the injunction as an infringement of Christian liberty, his real issue was that the vestments themselves were redolent of the old religion. He reminded Cecil that 'all cuntries which have refourmed religion have cast away that popishe apparell with the pope', and maintained that it was 'necessarie in apparell to have a shewe how a protestant is to be knowen from a papist'.[69] Ironically, the queen's visit to Cambridge in 1564 may have made this issue more sensitive, as Cecil, in his capacity as Chancellor of the University, had given special instructions for the maintenance of 'uniformity … in apparel and religion' for the duration of the visit.[70]

The fact that St John's College emerged in 1565 as the epicentre of Cambridge dissent over vestments was part of the Pilkingtonian legacy. It was the achievement of one man, William Fulke, one of the last Fellows admitted by Leonard Pilkington, who immediately made him a College preacher, disappointing the expectations of more senior colleagues. After Pilkington's departure, Fulke rapidly established a moral ascendancy over his successor, Richard Longworth. That summer he called for the removal of the steps at the east end of the Chapel – doubtless because their very existence was a reminder of the altar that had once stood upon them – and the Master was prompt to comply. This gave even more offence to the older Fellows because the demolition work turned up the bones of their friend, Miles Buckley, who had been laid to rest there five years previously.[71]

Next year Longworth secured Fulke's appointment as principal lecturer, and Fulke used his growing influence to advance the cause of further reform in a series of sermons attacking the celebration of communion with unleavened bread, the practice of kneeling to receive the sacrament, the wearing of the cope for its celebration, and, finally, the wearing of surplices by clerics in church services, which he dismissed as 'popish trumpery'. He led the way in abandoning the surplice. At his instigation the College's fine copes, so lovingly retrieved or replaced in Mary's reign, were now sold for a song, once more to the offence of the senior Fellows, who recalled that James Pilkington, when Master, had turned down an offer of £40 for them as too little. At every turn Fulke carried Longworth with him. Ordinary bread was introduced for communion, kneeling was abandoned, and after Fulke preached at the start of the Michaelmas Term, Longworth came into chapel and took communion without a surplice, thus legitimizing a protest which rapidly caught on.

With Longworth's connivance, Fulke instigated direct action. On the first Saturday of term, his tutorial pupils formed the core of a large group of students

[68] *Visitation Articles and Injunctions of the Reformation Period*, ed. W. H. Frere (London, 1910), III. 20.

[69] Pilkington to Cecil, 25 Oct. 1564: BL Lansdowne MS 7, fo. 212r.

[70] Baker-Mayor, I. 158.

[71] Waller spent ten days 'taking downe the grades [steps] in the chapell and lyinge the stones againe' (SJCA, SB4.1, fo. 299v). For the bones, see TNA SP12/38, fo. 67r.

who intimidated the rest by hissing anyone who came into chapel wearing a surplice. When Longworth openly declared that they had right on their side, the tone was set for the entire term. Longworth forbade George Bond to hold a disputation on whether it was permissible to wear vestments at the command of the prince. (Bond took the hint, and by 1566 had migrated to the more congenial and liturgically conservative environment of Gonville and Caius College.) Thus, by the end of 1565, Fulke was hand in glove with the Master, hugely popular with the students and younger Fellows, and pretty generally loathed by the Seniors, who resented the way that Pilkington and Longworth had promoted him over their heads.

Beaumont and the heads of house (including Longworth) felt unable to control the situation, and wrote to Cecil petitioning for a relaxation in Cambridge of the requirements relating to vestments. But when Cecil heard rumours of events in his own college, he wrote demanding an explanation. Longworth's decision to send Fulke to explain was perhaps unwise – a man of his brazen self-confidence was not the best choice of ambassador – and he was sent back with a brusque summons to London for the Master himself. It was at this point, when they surmised that the abandonment of the surplice was not going to be condoned by Elizabeth and Cecil, that a faction of the senior Fellows saw and seized the opportunity for a counter-attack not only against the upstart Fulke, but also against a Master whose election they had originally opposed. Longworth was detained in London while Cecil, after a personal audience with Elizabeth on 9 December, wrote to the College the next day summoning Fulke back to London and charging Richard Curteys, the President, with the task of restoring order. The Seniors handed over Fulke with glee, and rapidly drew up detailed indictments against him and Longworth, in the hope of having them both removed.[72]

These indictments were the inevitable ragbag of gossip and grievance. Every aspect of Longworth's governance was challenged. His enemies cast doubt on his election, his admission, and his integrity, claiming that he took bribes, notably a grey gelding allegedly offered as an inducement to grant the lease of a College manor, and insinuating that he and one of his supporters had misappropriated a cope worth 50 shillings. The charges became more damaging when it was alleged that he and his adherents attended Chapel without surplices, and that he had arbitrarily altered the statutes from the condition in which they had been conveyed to the College by royal commissioners. They also complained about his habit of taking credit for all preferments in the College while blaming all disappointed hopes on the Seniors. There is real bitterness in the complaint that 'he preferreth to lectures and chambers in the house unlearned bachylors, before learned Masters of Arte'. They accused him of currying favour with the 'youthe of the howse' by allowing extra fires and feasts in Hall, and by suspending punishments handed out by the Deans.

---

[72] Curteys to Cecil, 12 Dec. 1565: TNA SP12/38, fo. 61r, enclosing articles against Longworth, fos. 63r–66r; and Fulke, fo. 67. See also fos. 2–3 and 11–12 for earlier articles against them, that had been sent to Cecil by Humphrey Bohun. These four sources, transcribed in *Eagle* xxviii (1906–7), 141–7, 149–57, furnish the details for the narrative of this episode unless otherwise indicated.

He had defended the bakehouse Bursar, John Linsay, against charges of purveying short measure. Finally, with enormous disdain, they concluded that 'he dothe never studie, and prechethe soe negligentlie' that he was an offence to his hearers and a disgrace to his office. They particularly resented his promotion of Fulke, on whom they launched a parallel attack, detailing his part in the events of that term, and emphasizing a pulpit invective he had delivered on All Saints' Day against a sermon preached earlier the same day in which the Vice-Chancellor, Robert Beaumont, had urged obedience to the queen's instructions.

William Cecil responded to this deluge of information and insinuation with a clutch of furious letters, announcing his determination to 'quench this wilde furye, broken loose in that Colledge of St John's, which I do and ought to esteeme as my nurse' and offering Curteys his full support in restoring order. Cecil gave free rein to his rhetoric and decried the 'ryotous insolencye' of 'these rash young heades', worrying that men who were so nearly 'rype to clyme into pulpittes' would 'contente themselves with no limittes either in the Church or in the pollicy [i.e. state]'. A veiled threat against those who so little 'esteme my poore favor and good will' did the trick.[73] Within a few days Curteys wrote back with a fascinating document, a complete list of the membership of the College, with the students listed under their Tutors, marked up to indicate compliance, absence, or non-compliance. This is the only such complete list we have for the Tudor college, and comes to the remarkably high total of 287 names. Slightly more than half had attended chapel at the weekend wearing surplices, and another thirty-three were away from College. That Curteys reported it as a major success that the number of non-conformists was down to 107 shows just how widespread the rebellion must have been before.[74]

The December coup was only partially successful. Fulke was expelled from his Fellowship, but Longworth survived as Master. Fulke was evidently the scapegoat, though he may well have taken on this role willingly. For he was still around College and in Longworth's inner circle during 1566, and in Lent 1567 was triumphantly re-elected to the Fellowship, once more to enjoy the Master's favour. The price of Longworth's survival was to read out in Hall a public retraction, personally drafted for him by Cecil.[75] But, as Curteys complained, he interwove his own commentary with the retraction, minimizing the extent of his own humiliation and making it all too clear that he held a grudge.[76] The Master's miseries, however, were not at an end. Later that year he was complaining to Cecil of the insubordinate attitude of two of the Seniors, Humphrey Bohun and William Baronsdale, and another of Cecil's

---

[73] TNA SP12/38, fos. 71r–73v, copies of letters from Cecil to the Vice-Chancellor and to Curteys, and of a letter to forward to the bishop of Ely, all of 13 Dec. 1565. See also *Eagle* xxviii (1906–7), 157–60.

[74] Curteys to Cecil, 17 Dec. 1565: TNA SP12/38, fos. 102r–103r (letter) and 104r–105r (list).

[75] BL Lansdowne MS 8, fo. 157r.

[76] Curteys to Cecil, 24 Dec. 1565, enclosing further articles against Longworth, TNA SP12/38, fos. 136r–137v.

correspondents reported that the College that summer was riven with personal vendettas.[77]

The lengths to which Longworth and his allies would go in their counter-offensive emerges from a defamation case brought in the Vice-Chancellor's court by Curteys at the end of October 1566. Curteys opened the case with a long complaint to the effect that the Master's cousin, Thomas Longworth, was wandering around Cambridge telling anyone who would listen that Curteys was the man who, about two years before, had been surprised *in flagrante delicto* with a woman in a house in Barnwell. Thomas Longworth, he alleged, had repeated this slur in the presence of Mr Grundy and Mr Fulke. Various further details transpired, notably that Thomas was then called before the Master in the presence of Mr Carter, Mr Smith, and Mr Fulke. Fulke's presence is an intriguing detail that shows he still enjoyed Longworth's confidence and suggests that he remained a resident member of College, even though no longer a Fellow (as Thomas Baker would almost two centuries after him):[78] otherwise the Master and Fellows would have been in breach of the statutes by discussing confidential College business with an outsider. Thomas was then commissioned to make further enquiries in Barnwell. It is obvious that the Master's party hoped to gather enough evidence to expel Curteys from the Fellowship for gross immorality. However, their efforts proved fruitless. Although they traced the story back to its source, John Rust of Barnwell and his son, Nicholas, Curteys called their bluff by bringing his case before the Vice-Chancellor. John Rust had previously been generous with his information. 'Is not this good gere?', he had asked the local constable, 'Was it not Mr Curtesse that was taken at Ionson house?' Faced with Curteys's estimation of the damage to his good name at 500 marks (£333 6s 8d), Rust experienced sudden amnesia, while his son flatly denied having ever spoken about the matter. The witnesses from St John's closed ranks, refusing to answer questions about internal College affairs on the grounds that this was contrary to their statutes, to which they were bound by oath. They admitted only that Thomas Longworth had a roving brief to gather gossip from Barnwell,[79] which had long been a resort of choice for members of the University (the proctors' accounts regularly featured expenses for items such as 'searching out whores in Barnwell [...] and expelling them'[80]). Unsupported by either the good folk of Barnwell or the Fellows, but with everyone agreeing that he had told the story, Thomas Longworth was found guilty, though the damages awarded were not the 500 marks demanded, but a more modest £10 and a grovelling retraction.

March 1567 seemed to mark the turning of the tide for Longworth, as it saw both the departure of Richard Curteys to become dean of Chichester and the triumphant re-election of William Fulke to the Fellowship. Fulke's ascent to the degree of BD next year raised him to fourth in the seniority list, and with

---

[77] Longworth to Cecil, 29 May 1566: TNA SP12/39, fo. 204r; and John Wells to Cecil, 11 Jun. 1566: TNA SP12/40, fo. 20r.

[78] Below, p. 157.

[79] This narrative is derived from the case papers in CUA, VCCt IV.22, Oct. and Nov. 1566.

[80] *Grace Book B*, II. 198, for 1536.

his election as President for 1569, the College should have settled down under a united regime. Yet by June that year Longworth was complaining to Cecil that false rumours of his intention to resign were being put about by Fulke, whose 'busy head' was doing nothing but 'rippe up my doings' and 'deface me with untruths'.[81] The Master's explanation was that it all arose out of a quarrel between them over the leasing of a College property, and that because of this Fulke had his sights on the top job. Fulke orchestrated a petition of twenty-one Fellows against the Master's regime, while Longworth dragooned another twenty-three Fellows into petitioning for its continuance. As in 1563, Cecil called in the Visitor. The weary bishop of Ely could find no better solution than to call down a plague on both houses, persuading Fulke and Longworth that only the resignation of both could bring peace to the College. Fulke took his departure with good grace, but the Master fought on so doggedly that Cox had to resort to expulsion.[82] Even then Longworth refused to lie down, but rode to London in December for a personal interview with Cecil in a last-minute bid for a reprieve, armed with a letter of support signed by twenty-three Fellows (though fifteen of them had been elected within the past two years). But Cecil was less pliant in 1569 than he had been in 1565, and on 17 December a new Master was elected.

The election in December 1569 gave the Fellows another opportunity to show their contrariness. William Cecil wrote recommending the man he had quietly and unsuccessfully supported back in 1563, Dr Roger Kelke, Master of Magdalene, who was also favoured by the Visitor, the Vice-Chancellor, and other heads of house.[83] So on 16 December the Fellows convened in chapel under the chairmanship of the senior Fellow, John Beacon, and elected Nicholas Shepherd, a former Fellow of St John's who had moved to Trinity in 1561.[84] Almost the first problem he had to deal with was the election of William Fulke to the Fellowship for a third time, a record that has probably never been equalled. The vote in the chapel was overwhelming, but Shepherd was understandably nervous about declaring Fulke elected until he had sought Cecil's advice. This was apparently favourable, as Fulke was once more in receipt of his stipend from spring 1570 until summer 1571, when he finally renounced his Fellowship in order to get married.[85]

[81] Longworth to Cecil, 18 Jun. 1569: BL Lansdowne MS 11, fo. 163r.

[82] Cox to Cecil, 3 Dec. 1569: BL Lansdowne MS 11, fo. 154r.

[83] Vice-Chancellor *et al.* to Cecil, 18 Nov. 1569: BL Lansdowne MS 11, fo. 183r; Cox to Cecil, 3 Dec. 1569: ibid., fo. 154r. Cecil's preference is acknowledged by a letter from various Fellows to Cecil, no date: ibid., fo. 193r.

[84] CUA, CUR 93, item 2, notice to Vice-Chancellor of election (16 Dec. 1569).

[85] Shepherd to Cecil, 14 Mar. 1570, BL Lansdowne MS 12, fo. 94r. See also fo. 96r for a supporting letter from the Fellows, 15 Mar. 1570: SJCA, SB4.1, fo. 440v, for the cessation of Fulke's stipend.

4. THE RISE OF THE 'PENSIONERS'

The rising numbers in College were continuing to put pressure on space, and from some point further students, no doubt mainly paying students or 'pensioners', seem to have been given accommodation on the site across the road, in a building known from around 1580 as the Pensionary, where the Old Divinity School (once known as the New Divinity School) now stands. This derelict site had been repaired and leased to the College cook, Roger Harrison, as the 'new house afore the College gates' in 1561, and it seems that he began to rent out rooms. His lease was not renewed when it expired in the 1580s, and instead the College rented out the rooms there directly. From that time income from this property is recorded as received from 'diverse tenants' and the property itself is described as a 'new hospice', a term also used for the old building on the north side of the chapel which was converted to residential uses in the 1580s. The name 'pensionary' first appears in the accounts in 1581, when repairs were done to its gate.[86] Despite the name it was not solely for pensioners. One of the Fellows, Richard Webster, had chambers there in 1583.[87] What shows that the building was already in residential use for the College, however, is that another Fellow, Edmund Roberts, had a room there when a *post mortem* inventory of his goods was made in February 1580.[88] This was before Harrison's lease had expired. It looks very much as though the cook was making money out of the College's need for accommodation, and that when his lease expired the College decided to take the property under its own management for the same purpose.

Other changes were also undertaken with an eye to the pensioners, many of whom came from the leisured classes. Most remarkable was the introduction of the College's first dedicated sports facility – the tennis court. Standing on ground now occupied by the north range of Second Court, this walled and paved construction, for the game now known as real tennis, was set up in 1574. The almost annual need to repair the paving offers backhanded testimony to its success, and when the contracts for the construction of Second Court were made, the works included the provision of a new tennis court beyond the river (visible in one of Loggan's famous views of Cambridge). Players paid a fee to use it, and despite the cost of repairs it provided a regular income that was used to supplement the wages of the porter and the laundress. Later on the tennis court was joined by a bowling alley, which seems to have been laid out in 1589.[89]

The most prestigious entertainments in College were undoubtedly the plays that were regularly staged, which might be performances of classic comedies and tragedies, such as Plautus's *Persa* in 1583, but which were sometimes specially written.[90] The most famous play staged at St John's in the sixteenth century was undoubtedly the Latin tragedy *Richard III*, written on the model of Seneca's tragedies by the Master of Gonville and Caius College, Dr Thomas

[86] SJCA, SB4.2, fos. 123v, 124r.

[87] SJCA, SB4.2, fo. 165v.

[88] Leedham-Green, *Books in Cambridge Inventories*, I. 344.

[89] SJCA, SB4.2, fo. 290r, the work of three men over four days.

[90] Nelson, *Records of Cambridge Drama*, I. 311.

Legge, and performed in the Hall of St John's in three instalments on successive nights in March 1579. The play survives in numerous manuscripts, and the inaugural performance was a triumph remembered for years, that gave Legge's name an honoured place in the literary firmament of Shakespearean England.[91] His account of Richard III anticipated Shakespeare's in drawing its material from Holinshed. Remarkably, the cast list survives, naming forty-seven members of College, the clear majority of them Fellows, and several of the rest future Fellows. It brought together almost all the College's most interesting characters, and it is striking how few of those who appeared in the play were ever numbered among the Puritans in the internecine disputes that ran through the reign. The title role fell to one John Palmer, who ended his life as dean of Peterborough in a debtor's prison. According to the Stuart antiquarian Thomas Fuller, Palmer's spendthrift ways derived from the 'Princelike humor' that filled his head from the time he played that part. The curious entry in the accounts for that year, 'for suger Candye and other thinges to preserve Sir Shepardes voyce', suggests that the young pensioner Leonard Shepherd, chosen to play Edward IV's queen, Elizabeth, may have been something of a *prima donna*.[92] The extrovert Everard Digby was there, as was the promising young Scholar Abraham Fraunce, who would earn a doubtful reputation endeavouring to establish the hexameter as the standard measure for English verse. Most brilliant of them all was the Fellow-Commoner Mr Henry Constable, who was to matriculate only a month later, and graduated first among the BAs in 1580. A few years later he wrote one of the first sonnet sequences in the English language, and not long after that he reverted to the Catholicism of so many of his relatives, to spend the rest of his life composing religious poetry and polemics in exile in France.[93]

5. TYRANTS AND REBELS

The histrionics of the Fellows were not restricted to the stage. By 1573 the new Master, Nicholas Shepherd, found himself under heavy attack as a lengthy indictment was presented against him by a substantial faction of the Fellowship. He was charged with 'unsatiable' financial exploitation and abuse of office, tireless sowing of contention and maintenance of faction, 'tyrannye' in conducting elections, and 'untollerable negligence in governing the colledge'. Much of this was typical of the mutterings and grumblings that abounded in an age when the Fellowship was incapable of transacting business without engendering schism. But some charges reveal either monumental misconduct on Shepherd's part or the grossest defamation on the part of his enemies. There is a ring of truth about the opening claim, that two of the Seniors went to Berkshire to survey a wood with a view to purchase, struck a good deal at £80, and were then outmanoeuvred by Shepherd, who negotiated a purchase for his own benefit at

---

[91] Ibid., I. 283–4; II. 918–19.

[92] Ibid., II. 944–6 for the cast lists; and I. 286 for Palmer. SJCA, SB4.2, fo. 80v for Shepherd's voice. This entry seems to refer to a play for Christmas 1579 rather than to *Richard III*, but presumably Shepherd was still cast for a female part.

[93] For Fraunce and Constable see *ODNB* (W. Barker; C. Sullivan).

£100. The rest of the financial allegations focus on attempts to favour friends and relatives with College leases, which will have done little damage at a time when such favour was almost a moral duty. The fact that such behaviour appears in the indictment is a symptom rather than a cause of the situation, summed up in the observation that the Master was 'generallye misliked of all the fellowes'.[94]

This time the Fellows excelled themselves. Declaring that Shepherd had vacated the Mastership *ipso facto* through spending more time absent from College than was permitted by the statutes, they proceeded to an election, against the explicit instructions of the bishop of Ely. Still more remarkably, their choice now fell upon Richard Longworth, who was supported not simply by his former allies but even by some of those who had sought to remove him in 1569, who now had 'the warmest recollection of his goodness'. Of fifty-eight Fellows on the books that summer, thirty-one signed petitions to Cecil in favour of Longworth's reinstatement, albeit to no avail.[95] Cecil once again called in the Visitor, who, inevitably, annulled the election and investigated the charges against Shepherd for himself. Most of them he dismissed as mere matters of opinion, such as the accusation that he had forced through the election to the Fellowship of his half-brother, Samuel Todd. Only the question of Shepherd's alleged excessive absence merited serious attention, but even this came down to a technicality on which the Master was given the benefit of the doubt. The statutes allowed three months' absence a year without specific permission from the Seniors, and Shepherd's enemies interpreted this narrowly as meaning twelve weeks, which Cox deemed unreasonable.[96]

However, one further line of attack seems to have been pressed home successfully in the aftermath of the visitation. The charges against Shepherd included the claim that 'he hath a longe time mainteyned a faction of those that oppugne the state and present governmente of the churche established by lawfull authorytye of parliamente'.[97] This lay outside the purview of the Visitor, but its potency lay in tarring Shepherd with the brush of presbyterianism, a Calvinist model of ecclesiastical government which aimed to replace the episcopal and hierarchical structure of the Church of England with a more elective and federal system. English agitation for presbyterianism had originated in Cambridge just a few years before, in the lecturing of Thomas Cartwright, the former Fellow of St John's who was by that time a Fellow of Trinity and Lady Margaret Professor of Divinity. The ensuing controversy had cost Cartwright his Fellowship and his chair, and had led him to flee the country. This attack on Shepherd was opportunistic in the extreme. His enemies included men of stronger Puritan sympathies than his, such as Thomas Leache, who had signed a petition in support of Cartwright in 1570, and Maurice Faulkner, whose Puritanism led him to clash

[94] BL Lansdowne MS 17, fos. 145–6. The document is endorsed '1573'.

[95] Ibid., fos. 155r, 157r (quoted), for two letters to Cecil, both 18 July 1573, with the same twenty signatories; and fo. 159r for another of late July, with twenty-two signatories, half of them different from before.

[96] Cox's handling of the situation is reported in a letter from Thomas Byng to Cecil, 26 Sept. 1573: ibid., fo. 169r.

[97] Ibid., fo. 146v.

with Shepherd's successor.[98] Nevertheless, some of the mud stuck, as is evident from the fact that Shepherd underwent close questioning about his views on ecclesiastical government and had to sign a paper affirming wholehearted conformity with the Book of Common Prayer and the Thirty-Nine Articles, and distancing himself at a number of points from Cartwright's agenda.[99] It seems that he was so badly discredited that he had no choice but to resign.

The choice of his successor tends to confirm that Shepherd departed under the suspicion of presbyterian leanings. Unlike the previous ten Masters, John Still (elected on 21 July 1574) had no prior connection with St John's. But he had been appointed Lady Margaret Professor in succession to the presbyterian Cartwright, and was always noted for his confirmity to the Church of England's established order. Still's election heralded a rare outbreak of peace, but a short one. He decided to take on some of the College's vested interests, and by the end of 1575 was embroiled in a controversy over the Linacre lectureship, having picked a fight with the most senior figure in the College. Thomas Randall, a Fellow since 1561, had held the Linacre lectureship since Michaelmas 1568, and looked upon it as his personal property. Dr Still thought it time for him to exchange academic life for private practice, making way for a younger student of medicine, William Lakyn. On several occasions he negotiated for Randall to vacate the post, notably when he was elected Senior Proctor for the academic year 1575–6, during which Still himself was serving as Vice-Chancellor. According to Still, Randall more than once agreed conditions under which he would step down, but never actually did so. In consequence, Still vetoed his re-election but, unsurprisingly, Randall had a considerable following in the College, especially among the Seniors.[100] When one of Randall's leading supporters, Maurice Faulkner, spoke in chapel to reprove both the Master and the Seniors for their stubbornness, it is not clear whether he was trying to pour oil on the waters or on the flames.[101] But the Master, in particular, was stung, and nursed his grudge. When Faulkner preached along similar lines in Great St Mary's in December, Still persuaded the University authorities to imprison him for contempt.[102]

Still won both his battles, for his preferred candidate, William Lakyn, held the Linacre lectureship from 1577.[103] But the episode was significant not so much for its outcome as for one of its underlying causes. Even before this contretemps, Bishop Cox of Ely, reflecting on a decade or more of constant intervention in

[98] TNA SP12/73, fo. 31r: petition in support of Cartwright. For Faulkner, see below, nn. 101–2.

[99] Scott, 'Notes', *Eagle* xxix (1907–8), 30–33, transcribed from a manuscript in the library of the Inner Temple.

[100] Still's reasons for not accepting Randall's election are set out in BL Lansdowne MS 23, fos. 103r–104r, and in a letter of his to Cecil of 17 Apr. 1576 (fo. 36r). Randall's supporters wrote two letters on his behalf (fos. 32r and 34r), signed by 29 Fellows in total.

[101] Lansdowne MS 23, fos. 91r–92r, notes of a sermon preached by Faulkner in the Chapel in July 1576.

[102] Faulkner to Cecil, 25 Jan. 1577: BL Lansdowne MS 24, fo. 40r, a covering letter for the text if his sermon, found at Lansdowne MS 23, fos. 93r–97v.

[103] SJCA, SB4.2, fo. 32r, shows Lakyn in receipt of the stipend.

the affairs of St John's, thought he had got to the bottom of the problem. Writing to Cecil in June 1575, he had argued that the troubles had arisen partly from 'the foly and stoutnesse of unbridled youth', and partly from the physical condition of the statutes, which had been so heavily amended by erasure, insertion, and annotation during the royal visitations of the previous thirty years that it was no longer possible to be sure what they were meant to say. His timely suggestion of a royal commission to 'bringe the sayde Statutes into good order' was, unfortunately, ignored, and by the end of the year he was getting desperate as he sensed a fresh storm brewing.[104] Although under the new Master ('a worthie, learned, and a zelous man') the 'uncleane spirit' of contention had been driven out, 'alas he begynnethe to enter agayne with seven spirites wursse then himself.' Cox foresaw a 'new broyle' unless urgent steps were taken.[105]

The Visitor busily sought to build up a head of steam behind his proposal. It was doubtless at his instigation that the archbishop of Canterbury, Edmund Grindal, wrote to Burghley that there was 'no original authentic book of statutes in the treasury' at St John's, but that the only copies were 'rased, blotted, interlined, and corrupted with marginal additions, so as indeed no man can certainly affirm what is statute, what not'.[106] The observation was a fair one. These copies of the statutes are still to be seen, and the various manuscripts constitute almost a palimpsest of the difficult history of the English Reformation. What with Fisher's almost endless tinkerings; the Henrician revisions designed to expunge Fisher, reduce the 'northern' predominance in the College, and mitigate 'popery'; the more determined purge of 'popery' under Edward followed by the attempt to return to Fisher's statutes under Mary – and the quires into which the statutes were broken for editorial purposes can still be seen – and the final return to the Edwardian situation under Elizabeth, it is a wonder that more disputes were not generated. In 1559 two of the Fellows, the recently restored Ralph Lever and the newly elected John Coldwell, had travelled to visit Sir Henry Grey 'to enquire for King Edward's statutes', that is, for a copy of the statutes as amended by the royal Visitors of 1549.[107] It seems as though their journey was in vain.

The eruption of the latest 'broyle' at St John's led Cecil to follow Cox's advice. On 13 July 1576 a royal commission was established, headed in theory by Cecil himself, and manned by Cox, and six Cambridge heads of house – Thomas Byng (Clare), Henry Harvey (Trinity Hall), Edward Hawford (Christ's), Thomas Ithell (Jesus), Andrew Perne (Peterhouse), and John Whitgift (Trinity).[108] The commission's remit was broadly conceived, and its powers were extensive. It was not merely to revise the statutes, but to restore good order in the College. To this end, it could overrule the normal mechanisms of government, nominating and removing officers and Fellows at will. The commission took several years

[104] Cox to Cecil, 29 Jun. 1575: BL Lansdowne MS 20, fo. 158r.

[105] Cox to Cecil, 4 Dec. 1575: BL Lansdowne MS 20, fo. 168r. See also a similar letter of 19 Feb. 1576: TNA SP12/107, fo. 80r.

[106] Grindal to Cecil, 23 Apr. 1576: *The Remains of Edmund Grindal*, ed. W. Nicholson (Cambridge, 1843), 358.

[107] SJCA, SB4.1, fo. 110v.

[108] CUA, CUR 93, item 4.

to accomplish its principal task, but its impact was more immediate in other ways. No new Fellows were elected in 1576 or 1577.[109] In the latter case, the commissioners simply suspended the elections. What happened in Lent 1576 is less clear. It is possible that the commission retrospectively annulled that year's elections, but it is more likely that the process was a casualty of the stand-off between the Master and the Seniors and helped precipitate the appointment of the commission.

John Still must have been a much relieved man when, in May 1577, he was nominated Master of Trinity in place of Whitgift, and was able to set down the poisoned chalice of St John's. All sorts of names were mooted for the succession, including current and former Fellows. Thomas Ithell sent Cecil a summary of the field. It was led by Andrew Perne, the Master of Peterhouse, who had been a Scholar of the College back in 1540 and was by now one of the venerable ancients of Cambridge, a survivor of every religious change.[110] Another favourite was Richard Howland, Dr Kelke's successor as Master of Magdalene. The two current Fellows were brusquely dismissed by Ithell. Robert Rhodes was an unworldly academic, 'an honest man and learned, but not so fitt for governement, as is to be wished'. As for Thomas Smith, Ithell laconically reminded Cecil that 'he hath bene some partye in the late trobles in St Johns and before your L[ordship] in them'. The final candidate was John Knewstub, a Puritan who had ruled himself out by resigning his Fellowship rather than conform to the full requirements of the Book of Common Prayer.[111]

The man chosen was Howland. John Whitgift had hoped to see Howland succeed him at Trinity, and it was probably his backing, as one of the commissioners for the College, that secured St John's as a consolation prize. Whitgift's choice proved wise, and Howland presided over the most peaceful interlude in the history of St John's since the days of Metcalfe. This was partly thanks to the new statutes, which were ready by summer 1579 and were formally promulgated by royal authority in 1580.[112] But, as we shall see from the troubles under his successor, this was not the whole story. It is also a tribute to the new Master's practical wisdom. The Fellows wrote to Cecil in praise of Howland's handling of the Fellowship elections when these resumed in spring 1578.[113] There was a whisper of College faction in 1580, but the remarkable thing is that no more was heard of it, which suggests that the problem, which cannot now be identified, was swiftly and consensually settled.

The new statutes purposefully strengthened the Master's hand and diminished the hitherto immense influence of the Seniors, whose numbers were

---

[109] SJCA, Register of Admissions, C3.1, 151–2. The dates in the register are confusing because they are given 'old style', dating the new year from 25 March. SJCA, SB4.1, 530r confirms that three new Fellows were admitted in 1575, while SB4.2, fos. 12r, 31v show that none were admitted in 1576 or 1577.

[110] See P. Collinson, D. McKitterick, and E. Leedham-Green, *Andrew Perne: Quatercentenary Studies* (Cambridge, 1991).

[111] Ithell to Cecil, 3 Jun. 1577: TNA SP12/114, fo. 5r.

[112] SJCA, SB4.2, fo. 102v, 20s paid for the 'wrytinge of the new statutes'. Another copy was made early in 1581, for the bishop of Ely: SJCA, SB4.2, fo. 123r.

[113] SJC to Cecil, 29 Mar. 1578: BL Lansdowne MS 25, fo. 165r.

sensibly reduced from an unwieldy twelve to a manageable eight. Earlier ambiguities and obscurities were resolved, often in laborious detail, but usually with good sense. Thus the statute regarding the election of the President, which had given rise to the quarrel over the Linacre lectureship in 1576, now set out a series of sufficient conditions for election, in descending order of preference. The agreement of the Master with all or most of the Seniors was best. But failing this, the Master could elect with the agreement of half the Seniors, or indeed just three of them. If the Master could not put together even this degree of consensus, then the Seniors could appoint without his consent if all or all but one of them agreed. However, if they could not agree among themselves, then in the last resort the Master could simply appoint by prerogative.[114]

The changes to the College's statutes offer some parallels to the changes in the University's statutes around 1570, which reduced the power of the Regent House and concentrated authority in the hands of the Vice-Chancellor together with the heads of house.[115] But while the changes in the University narrowed the focus of power from democracy to oligarchy, the alterations in the College narrowed the focus from oligarchy to monarchy, and simultaneously reduced the accountability of that monarch to external authorities. As long as this power was in the hands of a moderate and clubbable man such as Howland, to be exercised only to keep the peace, all was well. But in the hands of the zealous Whitaker it was to become the engine with which he would strive to remould the College in his own image, turning it into a Puritan seminary.

The task of bringing harmony to College was made easier by an Act of Parliament which brought more financial benefit to the colleges of Oxford and Cambridge than any individual founder: the Corn Rents Act of 1576. This Act empowered colleges to demand that a third of the rent payable to them under any lease be paid in kind, or else be paid in cash at a rate determined in terms of a quantity of corn valued at the price then current in the Cambridge (or Oxford) market.[116] In an era when inflation was constant and at times rampant, but was ill understood, while rents customarily remained fixed, this statute in effect 'index-linked' a large proportion of collegiate rental income. The purpose of the Act was to relieve the evident necessity that was afflicting most colleges by the middle of Elizabeth's reign, as inflation gnawed at the real value of their mostly fixed rents. The severe impact of inflation can be seen in the fate of one of the Elizabethan endowments in the College. In 1574 John Gwynne, a former Fellow, left a charge of £40 a year payable to the College out of the profits of lands he bequeathed to a relative, in order to fund three Fellowships and six Scholarships for students from Wales. This charge, not being a rent, was not protected by the Act, and its real value plummeted. In 1584 Gwynne's executors agreed to reduce the foundation to two Fellowships and three Scholarships, and in the 1650s it was further cut, to simply three Scholarships.[117]

[114] *Early Statutes*, 29–31. For 1580 see *Fifth Report from the Select Committee on Education*, 421–2.

[115] Morgan, *History of the University of Cambridge*, 77–9.

[116] Ibid., 271.

[117] SJC D64.3 and 64.33, agreements with executors.

The legislation for corn rents brought immediate and enduring benefits. St John's was starting to amend its leases before the end of the year, and by the time Thomas Baker was writing his history of the College, a century or more later, the corn rent was worth far more than the cash rent.[118] Colleges profited still more in times of dearth, when prices rocketed. Before long, these increased revenues were not only facilitating building projects, such as the conversion of the infirmary and the construction of Second Court, but also permitting the distribution of an annual dividend to the Fellows, which soon became the most important element in their remuneration.[119] The credit for this boost to collegiate fortunes belongs primarily to Sir Thomas Smith, the former Fellow of Queens' and friend of John Cheke who by this time was Elizabeth's principal Secretary of State. It was him that the University thanked for introducing and promoting the bill in Parliament.[120] But as a 'public' rather than a 'private' bill, this legislation proceeded with the sanction of the government, which means that Cecil also must have supported it.

Cecil's personal interest in the well-being of the students was shown in 1581 when he granted the College £30 a year, which was to be spent chiefly in augmenting the commons of the foundation Scholars, bringing their allowance to a full shilling a week where they had previously received only 7 pence. Of that grant, however, 16 shillings were to go on improving the annual feast for the Master, Fellows, and Scholars on the Sunday after the feast of St John the Evangelist in the Christmas season.[121] He would have remembered the hard times evoked with perhaps some exaggeration by Thomas Lever in a famous sermon in the presence of the young Edward VI, the times when, in order to get warm enough to sleep, students had to walk or run up and down for half an hour at night before going to bed. In 1578 his second wife, Mildred, had already done something about this problem, giving £20 to provide the fuel for fires every Sunday and feast day between All Saints and the Annunciation (from 1 November until 25 March).[122] Even so, cold feet remained a problem. The late Elizabethan Fellow, John Bois, used to recall three rules that William Whitaker prescribed to young academics: the third was, 'Never to go to bed with cold feet'.[123] Both Cecil and his wife demanded similar service in return for their largesse. Mildred required four sermons a year to be given in the parish church of Cheshunt, near their residence of Theobalds, while Cecil himself called for two sermons, one at Cheshunt and the other at Stamford, near Burghley House. But in addition to the 'Burghley Sermons', the Scholars were to demonstrate their gratitude by offering, every year, classical Latin verses on suitably sombre or admonitory scriptural themes, such as 2 Timothy 2:22–6, 'Flee also youthful lusts ...', and Ecclesiasticus 7:40, 'In all thy works remember thy last end, and

[118] Baker-Mayor, I. 170–71: 'such an improvement as usually makes the third part more than the whole'.

[119] Morgan, *History of the University of Cambridge*, 272.

[120] G. R. Elton, *The Parliament of England, 1559–1581* (Cambridge, 1986), 226.

[121] Baker-Mayor, I. 415–16.

[122] Baker-Mayor, I. 404.

[123] A. Walker, 'The Life of Mr. John Bois', in F. Peck (ed.), *Desiderata Curiosa* (London, 1779), II. 325–42, at p. 339.

thou shalt never sin'.[124] Thomas Nashe composed some of the verses presented to Cecil in 1585.[125] The Burghley Verses endured as long as the classical tradition coloured English education, and ceased only in 1988.

6. WILLIAM WHITAKER AND THE PURITAN COLLEGE

The Mastership of Richard Howland began to draw towards its close early in 1585, when on Whitgift's recommendation the queen appointed him bishop of Peterborough. His consecration at Whitgift's hands on 7 February 1585 heralded a period of lengthy and complex manœuvring over the succession at St John's. Lobbying was soon under way and rumours were rife. Cecil was immediately suspicious, and wrote to Cambridge's leading theological conservative, Andrew Perne, reproaching him with seeking royal intervention in the election – a charge Perne indignantly rebutted. Cecil's suspicions may not have been entirely unfounded, however, as Perne admitted having been in contact, albeit on other matters, with Lord Lumley, whose chaplain, Anthony Watson (a former Fellow of Christ's, later bishop of Chichester), was one of those whose name was being mentioned in connection with the Mastership.[126] Nor was Cecil's intervention entirely innocent, as he had his own candidate, William Whitaker, an ambitious Cambridge academic whose influential uncle, Alexander Nowell, dean of St Paul's, had secured him Cecil's patronage some years before. This had helped him to the Regius professorship of Divinity in 1580, and Whitaker had repaid his patron by dedicating to him two of his polemical treatises against Roman Catholicism. However, there were concerns in some quarters about Whitaker's Puritan leanings, and Perne made damaging insinuations to this effect, hinting that Whitaker's recent reluctance to take his doctorate in divinity was a sign of dangerous and deepening Puritan sympathies.[127] By the summer of 1586 Howland was reporting that Lumley's chaplain was only a stalking-horse for an internal candidate, Laurence Stanton, whose faction was strong enough to make Whitaker's election difficult and would subsequently, he feared, 'greatlie hinder his governement and alter the quiett state of the Colledge'.[128] Not until February 1587, two years after Howland's promotion was the election held. Whitaker was chosen, but by his own account, only 'with the utmost difficulty and contention'. The election was, he added, being challenged on procedural grounds, but he relied on Cecil's support, with good reason.[129]

For almost four centuries following his death in 1595, William Whitaker was known to history as a fainéant Master under whose aegis the College was really run by Henry Alvey. While Whitaker had his nose forever in his books and filled his time penning voluminous polemics against the Papists, it was thought,

---

[124] Baker-Mayor, I. 415–16.

[125] Nicholl, *Cup of News*, pp. vii and 36; and document 5, a copy of TNA SP15/29, fo. 130r.

[126] Perne to Cecil, 18 Oct. 1585: BL Lansdowne MS 45, fo. 130r.

[127] Perne to Cecil, 1 Sept. 1585: BL Lansdowne MS 45, fo. 125r.

[128] Howland to Cecil, 27 Jun. 1586: BL Lansdowne MS 50, fo. 82r.

[129] Whitaker to Cecil, 26 Feb. 1587: BL Lansdowne MS 51, fo. 132r.

Alvey manipulated elections to put together a Puritan power-base from which he would in due course launch his own bid for the Mastership. This view was first suggested by anti-Puritan Fellows during the electoral struggle that followed Whitaker's death, and rapidly gained currency. But it has been entirely overturned by Peter Lake's definitive analysis of his Mastership. Although Alvey was always a loyal supporter of Whitaker, having lobbied for his election, and from 1591 was his right-hand man, he was no *eminence grise*. It was Whitaker himself who exploited the powers of the Master under the new statutes to construct a dominant Puritan caucus among the Fellows. Only eleven out of about fifty Fellows had petitioned for Whitaker in the manœuvres preceding the 1587 election, but thirty-four were to petition for Alvey's election in 1596.[130]

Whitaker was undoubtedly the protagonist in the first crisis of his regime, the attempted dismissal of one of the Seniors, Everard Digby. Everard Digby was everything that Whitaker was not. Where Whitaker was a Calvinist and a Puritan, consumed with fear of 'popery' and dedicated to the preaching of the 'word', Digby was more Renaissance man than Reformation theologian, hostile to both Calvinism and Puritanism, a master of the fine italic handwriting that was still a hallmark of Johnian humanism.[131] A Senior since 1585, and thoroughly at home under the relaxed regime of Howland, he had been part of the opposition to Whitaker's election. Indeed, from the bitterness with which Whitaker subsequently pursued him, he probably led it. Notwithstanding his promise to Cecil that he would be a fount of 'peace, concord and consensus' and would cut off 'occasions of faction', Whitaker seized upon a technical infringement of the statutes as a pretext for expelling a man for whom he evidently had a deep personal and ideological antipathy. The technical infringement was a quarrel over payment of a kitchen bill. The real issue, as Whitaker later put it, was 'Papistrie'. Digby's contempt for Calvinism, which he was not afraid to voice in sermons, was part of an eclectic and idiosyncratic intellectual synthesis that embraced medieval scholastic theologians and philosophers as well as early Christian fathers, the 'hermetic' writings of Greek Neoplatonism, and much Renaissance scholarship. This heady mixture left him open to suspicions of 'popery' that were only exacerbated by the fact that he was a cousin of the Digbys of Rutlandshire, notorious Catholic recusants.[132] That said, Everard Digby was no papist. But Calvinist Cambridge was swift to equate 'the anti-Puritan (...) with the pro-Catholic'.[133] Digby's emphatic acceptance of the three articles that Whitgift employed to prise hardline Puritans out of the Church of England was offensive enough to many of his colleagues, and his taste for religious ceremonial more so. He liked to attend divine service in King's College

---

[130] Lake, *Moderate Puritans*, esp. p. 191. Lake has ten Fellows petitioning in favour of Whitaker, but see BL Lansdowne MS 50, fo. 142r, a letter to Cecil, undated, but endorsed 1586, signed by eleven Fellows.

[131] See his unsuccessful petition to Cecil for the rectory of Tinwell, near Stamford (26 Jan. 1581; perhaps 1582): BL Lansdowne MS 34, fo. 27r.

[132] The head of his family, also named Everard Digby, was a Catholic recusant whose son, another Everard Digby, would be executed in 1606 for his part in the Gunpowder Plot.

[133] Nicholls, *Cup of News*, 28.

Chapel, doubtless savouring the polyphony and organ music performed there even at the high tide of Cambridge Puritanism, and certainly not available in St John's. Along with his approval for the use of ornate copes in cathedral worship, this marks him as an adherent of the curiously dressy and theologically understated style of Protestantism favoured by Queen Elizabeth herself. Finally, he was immune from Puritan neuroses about popery and the mass. Thus he ostentatiously refrained from preaching against the 'Romish Antichrist' – a subject almost *de rigueur* for aspiring Elizabethan preachers – and a contemptuous aside about 'their Christide' showed what he thought of those who hated the Catholic mass so intensely that they even wished to excise the mere echo of the word, in 'Christmas', from their calendar.[134]

The precise legal course of the Digby affair is not recorded, but the broad outlines can be reconstructed from references in the ample correspondence it later generated. Early in 1588, a personal spat over the settlement of a kitchen bill escalated thanks to Digby's pigheadedness. Digby refused not to pay the bill, but to call upon the Steward to do so, insisting that, as he was a Senior, by the custom of the College the Steward should call upon him in order to collect his money. It was all somewhat childish, and the Steward, showing remarkable restraint, went so far as to agree, one evening in Hall, to call upon Digby. But Digby, evidently a man of confrontational temperament, attempted to push home his advantage still further. Rising from the table at once, he invited the Steward to come and get his money that minute, declaring before the students, 'By god I will make you waite on mee.' At this the Steward changed his mind, refusing to lose face. From there the process was mechanical, with informal and formal warnings before Digby's name was crossed off from the lists in the buttery and, as he remained recalcitrant, the Master in due course expelled him.[135]

Predictably, Digby did not go quietly, but appealed. A commission was established to review the case, and a pained letter from Whitaker to Cecil reveals his fears that it had been rigged to secure Digby's vindication. In particular he regretted the appointment to it of Dr Thomas Legge, Master of Gonville and Caius. The appointment was in truth reasonable enough, because Legge was a civil and canon lawyer who served as the University's 'commissary' (a law officer). But Legge had himself undergone lengthy investigation on a range of charges back in 1582, at which time Whitaker, as he recalled in his letter, gave evidence against him 'for Papistrie', leading him now to fear, probably rightly, that Legge would not be 'altogeather soe indifferent … as were requisite'. It was now also that he played the 'no popery' card, earnestly (if somewhat implausibly) assuring Cecil that 'Papistrie doth secretely encrease' in the College, and ascribing this to 'among others Mr Digbeie a man notoriously suspected'. Pending the appeal, Digby actually returned to College and resumed eating at the Fellows' table, boasting that he had been reinstated (which was not yet the case) and even presuming to sit as presiding Fellow. Whitaker thought that if his decision were to be overturned, he might as well himself retreat from both the College

---

[134] Lake, *Moderate Puritans*, 172–6.

[135] 'The answers of William Whitaker to the objections offered by Everard Digby': BL Lansdowne MS 57, fos. 175r–76r, esp. fo. 175v. Further details are found in a supplementary paper, fos. 177r–78r.

and the University.[136] In his zeal to discredit his foe, he heaped up allegations and accusations of every kind, from Digby's scornful attitude towards Calvinists and unpatriotic dislike of Sir Francis Drake to his habit of taking students fishing on Sundays and his mischievous tendency 'to blow an horn often in the Colledge on the day time and hollow [halloo] after it'.[137]

Whitaker did not act on his veiled threat of resignation as the commission, which included Whitgift and Cecil, headed towards a decision in Digby's favour that April. Instead, he frantically set about lobbying Puritan sympathizers at court, such as the earls of Leicester, Warwick, and Essex, protesting that Digby was a 'lewd fellow', 'verie unsound and factious', a Papist and a 'seducer of the youth in the College', whose removal was essential 'for religion's sake'.[138] But, as Whitgift observed, the Master had acted not only in breach of the statutes but also 'contrary to the rule of Charitee'. And if Digby's real offences were religious, then he should have been charged with them formally.[139] Digby was doubtless just as busy contacting anti-Puritans such as Sir Christopher Hatton, his 'most honorable and singuler good Patron', to whom he had dedicated a book in 1579, and would dedicate another in 1589.[140] Although almost every account of this case published so far has concluded that Digby's expulsion was upheld, this was not so.[141] He was evidently restored to his Fellowship, receiving his stipend for the second and third quarters of 1588.[142] Whitaker was still blustering in a letter to Cecil that summer, pleading with him to uphold his decision against Whitgift's, insisting that he was right all along, and offering 'to procure the opinions of as good lawiers as any are in England' to prove it.[143] But Digby himself had realized that Whitaker's college was no place for an outed anti-Puritan. Having enjoyed his brief triumph, he left at Michaelmas 1588 to end his days as a comfortable pluralist with a chip on his shoulder.

[136] Whitaker to Cecil, 18 Feb. 1588: BL Lansdowne MS 55, fo. 135r.

[137] Whitaker to Cecil, 4 Apr. 1588, BL Lansdowne MS 57, fo. 174r, covering his reply to Digby's objections, fos. 175r–76r; and further details, fos. 177r–78r; Porter, *Reformation and Reaction*, 186.

[138] Leicester to Cecil, 6 May 1588: BL Lansdowne MS 57, fo. 202r for some comments about Digby evidently fed to him by Whitaker; and Whitgift to Cecil, 30 Apr. 1588: ibid., fo. 160r, for further denigration and the bid to involve the earls.

[139] See Whitgift's letters to Cecil and to Leicester, 30 Apr. 1588: BL Lansdowne MS 57, fos. 160r, 161r.

[140] *Theoria Analytica* (London, 1579) and *Dissuasive from Taking away the Lyvings and Goods of the Church* (London, 1589). In each case, a fine woodcut of Hatton's heraldic bearings is found on the title page verso, opposite the dedication. Digby's dedication of the latter work is a superb philippic against the Puritans ('smoth dissemblers') and their pretensions to 'reforme the supperstitious braunches of the sweete auncient welblowne Rose of England'.

[141] Porter, *Reformation and Reaction*, 186. See also the entry on Digby in *ODNB* (N. Orme).

[142] SJCA, SB4.2, fo. 263v (1588). It has been suggested that his reappearance on the payroll reflects the adoption of a compromise suggested by the earl of Leicester, namely that he be allowed a brief respite and then be removed: Lake, *Moderate Puritans*, 180. But this does not take adequate account of the fact that Digby's appeal was upheld (p. 178); and that there is no hint of any second process or sentence against him.

[143] Whitaker to Cecil, 1 Jun. 1588: BL Lansdowne MS 57, fo. 202r.

Whitaker found a willing lieutenant in Henry Alvey. Alvey had been present at several of Whitaker's interviews with Digby, and was rewarded with rapid promotion, becoming Junior Bursar in December 1588, a Senior in January 1589, Senior Dean in December 1589, Senior Bursar in December 1590, and principal lecturer in July 1590.[144] His election to the disciplinary office of Dean actually came in the very month that he led a demonstration through the streets of Cambridge to Peterhouse to protest to the Senior Proctor (one Richard Betts) against the expulsion from the University of a leading Puritan figure, Francis Johnson of Christ's College. Johnson, with his colleague Cuthbert Bainbridge, had been brought before the Vice-Chancellor's court for preaching in Great St Mary's against the established structure of the Church of England. Johnson was the more intractable of the pair, and in December a petition in support of his reinstatement attracted sixty-eight signatures. A dozen were Fellows of St John's, and the first signatures were those of Daniel Munsey and Henry Alvey.[145] This was the largest contingent from a single college. They probably had Whitaker's tacit support, as he himself wrote to Cecil regretting that Johnson had been denied leave to appeal.[146]

Alvey was at the heart of the most contentious episode in Whitaker's Mastership, the convening in St John's College, probably in the Master's chambers, of nothing less than a 'national synod' of England's most committed presbyterian theologians.[147] The timing could not have been worse. Staged in the wake of the 'Marprelate Tracts', a series of scurrilous pamphlets that had convulsed the nation in 1588 and 1589 with their scabrous satire of the bishops, this gathering met as Queen Elizabeth's inquisitor-general, Archbishop Whitgift, was unleashed upon the Puritans with redoubled vigour. Whitaker's anti-Puritan opponents in the College saw a golden opportunity. If he and his disciples could be convicted of organizing a 'presbytery' in the College itself, they would be finished. The clandestine meeting, tendentiously described as a 'presbytery', was made the highlight of a litany of grievances despatched to Cecil by discontented elements within the Fellowship. Even though Whitaker had been away from St John's when the meeting took place, this was a career-threatening charge, and he acted decisively to deflect it, sending Cecil a detailed refutation of the charges against him, mobilizing support from those heads of house with moderate Puritan sympathies (they wrote to Cecil on 20 October 1590), and inducing about two-thirds of the Fellowship to write to Cecil the same day denying all knowledge of any 'presbytery' in College. As Lake points out, although this petition included a number of non-puritan signatories, the names of Whitaker's leading opponents – such as John Palmer, Eleazar Knox (ironically enough, the son of the Scottish Reformation hero John Knox), and Robert Booth – were not among them, which enables us to guess who it was that drew up the charges against him. That charge-sheet, fascinatingly, is no longer extant. It is tempt-

---

[144] SJCA, Register C3.1, 14 (Senior), 27 (Dean), 53 (Bursars), 107 (lecturer). For his role as President 1592–5, see SJCA, SB4.2, fos. 346v, 367v, 388v, 414v. Lake has Alvey elected President in Dec. 1590: *Moderate Puritans*, 189. This actually occurred in Dec. 1591.

[145] Porter, *Reformation and Reaction*, 188, referring to BL Lansdowne MS 61, fo. 57r.

[146] Ibid., 163, referring to BL Lansdowne MS 62, fo. 90r.

[147] Ibid., 189–94; Lake, *Moderate Puritans*, 192–7.

ing to speculate that Cecil, who was a faithful patron to Whitaker, regarded it as too dangerous to his client to permit it to survive. Whitaker asked Cecil to let him see it so that he could reply to it, saying he would return it: maybe he kept it. The tone of Whitaker's letter to Cecil (24 October 1590) is defiant and slightly arrogant, the tone of a man accustomed to treat the entire world like an unruly classroom.[148] Cecil may not have been entirely deceived by the precise equivocation with which Whitaker specifically denied and indeed disproved the claim that a 'presbytery' had been established in St John's. But it was very much in his interests to accept what he was told, not only because of the loss of face on his part in the event of the disgrace of a man whom he had promoted so far, but also because of his loyalty to his old College, whose reputation would have been severely damaged.

Thanks to Whitaker, Alvey survived this crisis, and was soon raised to the office of President, which he held for four consecutive years (1592–5). In the wake of Whitaker's death, his dramatic rise and tightening grip struck his rivals as deeply sinister: 'Mr Alvey for the space of 7 or 8 years last past, hathe in all elections and bringinge younge students to the howse, ambitiouslye contryved a plotte for the Mastershippe.'[149] However, their retrospective conspiracy theory is hardly to be credited. No doubt Alvey was purposefully advancing Puritans, but he could neither have foreseen Whitaker's premature death nor have expected him to achieve timely promotion: Whitaker's abrasive Puritanism and inflexible management style were considerable handicaps in the race for preferment when Whitgift was entrenched at Canterbury with the still more rabidly anti-Puritan Richard Bancroft (soon to be Bishop of London) as his right-hand man. Despite reservations over his practical prudence, Whitaker remained a respected theologian, and when Cambridge became embroiled in controversy over the Calvinist doctrine of predestination in 1595, he was inevitably one of those summoned to Lambeth by Whitgift for a conference intended to determine the Church of England's position on the subject. The Lambeth Articles of autumn 1595, which took up an essentially Calvinist position on all the main points in dispute, were largely Whitaker's work, and as he rode back to Cambridge in November he must have reckoned them a triumph.[150] But he contracted a fever on his way home, and died on 4 December, not yet fifty years old. As the Church of England's foremost theologian he was accorded a public funeral in Great St Mary's by the University, with the Vice-Chancellor preaching the sermon.[151]

This outpouring of public grief for Whitaker turned Alvey, his favourite, into his heir presumptive. His bid for the Mastership was more opportunism than conspiracy, but he had more support than any previous internal candidate, and in a free election would certainly have prevailed, as even his

---

[148] BL Lansdowne MS 63, fo. 225r.

[149] BL Lansdowne MS 79, fo. 154v.

[150] Porter, *Reformation and Reaction*, 364–75; Lake, *Moderate Puritans*, 201–29. Whitaker's triumph was illusory, but he did not live to learn that Queen Elizabeth had taken against the Lambeth Articles and refused to endorse them.

[151] Porter, *Reformation and Reaction*, 201–3.

enemies frankly acknowledged.[152] In their desperation to prevent his almost inevitable election, they heaped up accusations of Puritanical non-conformity against him and his allies, who in turn bombarded Cecil with excuses, indignantly if somewhat unconvincingly repudiating the slur of Puritanism.[153] Cecil decided to intervene. Royal letters were procured, giving the Fellows a choice between two former colleagues, Laurence Stanton (Fellow 1572–87) and Richard Clayton (Fellow 1578–93). The Vice-Chancellor, Roger Goad, summoned the Seniors and other key Fellows to a pre-election meeting on 21 December, no doubt laying down the law from London. Next day, Clayton was their unanimous choice.[154] The detailed information about the Puritan activities of Alvey and his followers that had been supplied to Cecil probably gave him the leverage he needed to conjure up this unanimity. The significance of this moment is richly symbolized in the way that Cecil chose to reward their submission, by bestowing upon them a set of fine silver plate for the celebration of communion. The relevance of the Christian sacrament of memory and unity spoke for itself. As the new Master and the Seniors wrote in their letter of thanks, whenever they looked upon those silver vessels they would call to mind his generosity towards them and his achievement in having reconciled their long warring factions in peace and charity.[155] Yet there was a still wider significance to his gift, invisible to them but visible in the perspective of hindsight. For it was in the 1590s that a new movement stirred within the Church of England, setting out once more to invest religious worship with dignity and even beauty after three decades in which the theologically driven liturgical minimalism of the Puritans had set the agenda. Though Cecil had begun the reign in the religious company of men such as James Pilkington, old age saw even him inclining towards the more mellow style of religion which his queen had always favoured.[156]

The Puritan tide had ebbed and flowed in St John's during the reign of Elizabeth. The first surge came under the leadership of William Fulke over the wearing of the surplice in 1565. A few Fellows stood up for Thomas Cartwright, formerly of St John's, when his advocacy of presbyterian church government got him into trouble in 1570. Throughout the reign the College turned out a stream of Puritan preachers to evangelize within the Church of England, and was a major element in the strength of the Puritan cause. Out of eighty-one Puritan preachers identified by Patrick Collinson as active in Suffolk in the 1580s, thirty

[152] Lake, *Moderate Puritans*, 197.

[153] BL Lansdowne MS 79, fos. 154–6, 160.

[154] Goad to Cecil, 22 Dec. 1595: BL Lansdowne MS 79, fo. 162r. A stray note relating to this election is misfiled with Cecil's papers from the 1560s at BL Lansdowne MS 8, fo. 158r. It lists five candidates (Clayton, Bowreman, Webster, Webbs, and Stanton). Intriguingly, it notes which were married and which not: only Clayton was unmarried. This suggests that Elizabeth had an interest in the election, because she had a marked preference for unmarried clergy. For more on the election see Porter, *Reformation and Reaction*, 201–5.

[155] Letter to Cecil, 21 Jan. 1596: BL Lansdowne MS 80, fo. 145r. SJCA, SB4.2, fo. 444r details the costs of bringing Cecil's gift from London.

[156] K. Fincham and P. Tyacke, *Altars Restored: The Changing Face of English Religious Worship, 1547–c. 1700* (Oxford, 2007), 82–97.

had been members of St John's College, mostly in the years around 1570.[157] The 'doyen of the Suffolk preachers', John Knewstub (Fellow 1567–74), a friend of Cartwright's, had left the College because of conscientious scruples over the Book of Common Prayer, and there were those who hoped to see him return as Master. Edward Lewkenor, a Suffolk gentleman who was one of the most active Puritan MPs in Parliament from the 1570s onwards, was himself a former Fellow (1561–6); and the leader of Suffolk's Puritan gentry, Sir Robert Jermyn, encouraged benefactions to St John's, even though it was not his college.[158] Howland's years saw the tide ebb, but he took many of the leading anti-Puritans away with him to Peterborough when he became bishop, and under Whitaker it surged again, to its high watermark.

19. RICHARD CLAYTON AND SECOND COURT

The passing of William Whitaker was a turning-point. Though a prig and a bully, he was mourned. His voluminous works of theological controversy had made him famous throughout Protestant Europe, and his name had brought lustre to the College. After his death, his disciples in St John's rushed his remaining writings into print, supplementing them with a sheaf of funeral verses as well as a brief biography penned by Abdias Ashton.[159] Whitaker summed up the ambiguities of Elizabethan Protestantism and Puritanism. As the nephew of Alexander Nowell, dean of St Paul's, and a client of William Cecil, he stood in some ways at the heart of the establishment. For a while he even enjoyed the patronage of John Whitgift, the scourge of the Puritans. Yet he seemed to grow more radical with the years, and his Mastership represented the high tide of Puritanism in St John's. His successor, Richard Clayton, brought in from Magdalene, was wished upon the Fellows, not wanted by them. Yet he worked some strange magic on the College. By now, the Church of England was developing a tradition and an identity of its own. In 1595 few could remember the reign of Mary Tudor, and almost none the splendours of the pre-Reformation Church. The words of the Book of Common Prayer were becoming part of the background-noise of life and there was nothing strange, as there had been a hundred years before, about an English Bible. Clayton was a man for these more normal times.

Clayton's great achievement was the construction of Second Court, which has traditionally been regarded as a decisive response on his part to the problem of growing student numbers.[160] However, by the end of the century there was no such problem, nor was Second Court the answer to it. Matriculation numbers had come down from their peak and had steadied, while accommodation needs

---

[157] P. Collinson, *The Elizabethan Puritan Movement* (Oxford, 1967), 128.

[158] For Jermyn and Lewkenor, see *ODNB* (J. Craig; J. W. Brigden). Jermyn's sister Frances endowed a scholarship in 1581, to which he nominated during his lifetime (Baker-Mayor I. 417–18).

[159] W. Whitaker, *Praelectiones*, ed. J. Allenson (Cambridge, 1599). Abdias Ashton's biography is in an appendix, on pages numbered 27–51.

[160] Thus Mullinger, *St John's College*, 90; Crook, *Foundation to Gilbert Scott*, 30.

had been met through the conversion of the Waterside chambers, the Pensionary, and the Labyrinth.[161] Second Court was not the fruit of a far-sighted policy decision, but a prestige project undertaken out of pure opportunism. It was Robert Booth, an enemy of Whitaker's who had left the Fellowship in 1592 for service as steward in the household of the earl of Shrewsbury, who brought the College the opportunity in the person of Mary Talbot, née Cavendish, daughter of the famous Bess of Hardwick, and now herself countess of Shrewsbury. Even though the money delivered, at £2,760, fell short of the £3,400 she had pledged, it was still a magnificent donation, and enabled the College to replace the slightly ramshackle Metcalfe Court with an altogether grander edifice, albeit one that was itself under-specified. By 1603 the new chambers were in occupancy, and matriculation numbers, which had dipped for the duration of the project, returned to their normal level.[162]

Second Court marked the end of the Tudor era for St John's, with Fellows and students moving in almost as Queen Elizabeth breathed her last. Religious tensions were defused as differences were sunk in the common project. Whitaker's right-hand man, Henry Alvey, adapted to the new regime, and was soon back in office as President, and personally paid for a new bridge 'towardes the feildes' in the grounds at the back of the College.[163] The College's first century was thus book-ended by two powerful female benefactors. Lady Margaret had provided First Court. The countess of Shrewsbury provided Second Court, with a new back gate every bit as splendid as that at the front. Finally, as a sense of tradition developed a deeper hold on minds after a century of revolutionary change, the College's greatest icon was acquired. The fine panel painting of Lady Margaret that still presides in Hall was hung there for the first time in 1598.[164]

---

[161] For matriculations, see the chart in Crook, *Foundation to Gilbert Scott*, 145, though his interpretation of the chart (p. 144) is called into doubt by some of the returns for total College numbers cited above.

[162] The story of the construction is well told in Crook, *Foundation to Gilbert Scott*, 30–40. It seems as though Second Court enabled the College to abandon the Pensionary across the road, which was leased out anew shortly afterwards (Baker-Mayor, I. 453).

[163] SJCA, SB4.2, fos. 476r, 503r (bridge, 1597 and 1598); fos. 496v, 522r, 548r (Alvey was President from some time in 1598 and through the next two years).

[164] SJCA, SB4.2, fo. 505v.

9 Mary Talbot, countess of Shrewsbury, the donor of Second Court
Artist unknown

II

THE SEVENTEENTH CENTURY

Mark Nicholls

IT is a paradox that the revolutionary seventeenth century – shaped by political instability, religious ferment, and profound social dislocation – ultimately brings consolidation to both the University and its colleges. Cambridge's role in the English Establishment and its place within wider English society seem to alter only slowly; the turmoil occasioned by Civil Wars, Republics, Restoration and Glorious Revolution has, on the face of things, little lasting effect. Within the small world of the University, the later seventeenth century can be regarded as a golden age in the history of St John's. In size, in facilities and in prestige it outstrips every rival. Yet what is good for a college is not always good for a university. Such change as there is leaves an impression of drift rather than progress. Cambridge begins to appear more inward looking. Still the nursery of clergymen and the landed gentry, it is rather less noticeably the nursery of bureaucrats and statesmen. The university dominated numerically by St John's in 1700 is no longer the vigorous, enquiring, dynamic force so important to the politics, religion and cultural life of Jacobean England.

I. ESTATES

Early in the reign of James I the College estates were scattered across sixteen English and Welsh counties. Predictably, the highest concentration is found in Cambridgeshire. Tenants in a sweep of villages around the city – including Coton, Dry Drayton, Barkway, Cottenham, Horningsea, Thriplow, Histon and Steeple Morden – paid rents according to the usual quarterly, half-yearly or annual cycles. Or else, having their own lives to lead and fortunes to make, they failed to pay them, for all sorts of different reasons. In nearby Suffolk, St John's owned property in Great Bradley and Glemham, while in Essex, the College drew rents from land in Clavering, Thorrington and Rawreth. In Hertfordshire there was property in prosperous Ashwell, as well as an income from the Cecil manor of Theobalds. Huntingdon brought modest returns from Stukeley, Paxton and Hilton. Bromehall in Berkshire yielded a notional £27 a year. And so the list goes on, covering Bedfordshire, Norfolk (always rather thinly represented in the list of estates, despite its proximity to Cambridge), North Stoke in Oxfordshire, Northampton, Warwickshire, and even distant Caernarvon. Particularly profitable concentrations of College land lay in Kent, Lincolnshire, Yorkshire and Nottinghamshire: the ancient holdings amid the fruit-fields and hedgerows at Ospringe, the rich returns from Marfleet on the Humber, the steady profits from Markham, and from Ireton.[1] Then there were urban tenements, no more than a foothold bringing in £15 or so a year, in rapidly expanding London: in Knight Rider Street, in Wood Street, and in Mark Lane.

In 1602–3, all these properties and other rents generated an income of around £675 through the year.[2] By 1671 the figure for a very similar list of properties had risen to £945, and by 1683 the total stood at £970.[3] That increase reflected the acquisition of significant new estates, at Leighfield, Rutland, in 1640, in accordance with a bequest from Edward Mountstephen and John Highlord, and particularly at March and Wootton Rivers in Wiltshire, received in the 1680s and 1690s from the duchess of Somerset.[4] The duchess's property proved particularly important to College finances, one reason why her portrait still hangs in the twenty-first century College Hall.

Land was, and remains, vital to the College, but then as now the cash income from land was structured and guaranteed through sub-leases and diversification. The most straightforward course, often followed, was to lease land to a local landowner with some coercive power in a county, who might sublet and make a profit in turn.[5] However, the key to the College's steady generation of wealth lay in management of returns from a corn-rent system, prudently adopted in the previous century. An Act passed in Queen Elizabeth's day had insisted that one-third of all college rents should be paid in kind, or from commutation payments on the same produce.[6] In their season, the College thus benefited from vast quantities of wheat and malt. During 1634, for example, St John's received wheat to the value of £854, and malt worth £140. Some of this was processed and consumed in College, but over £828 by value was put on sale.[7] Whatever might happen to fixed monetary rents, in an era of unheralded inflation, consumables would always attract the market rate, and the market rate, over time, steadily improved. Thomas Baker went so far as to term the Elizabethan Act a second endowment to every college.[8] Measured over centuries, it proved crucial in ensuring their prosperity.

That collegiate prosperity helped in various ways to maintain and feed resident members. Throughout the seventeenth century, Fellows and Scholars both profited from the 'gain' or profits made in the previous year by the brewhouse and bakehouse, the relevant figure, or corn-money, being carefully recorded in

---

[1] In 1617 the College's tenant Edward Master recommended swift action in replacing a recently deceased rector, for otherwise the tithes might be sequestered to other purposes, and there would shortly be 'sum pretty sum of money due for the tithe cherryes and other fruit': SJCA, D105.123.

[2] SJCA, SB4.3, fo. 61v.

[3] SJCA, SB4.8, fos. 112r, 394r.

[4] Howard, *Finances*, 81.

[5] See the hint of this pragmatic practice identified by R. F. Scott, 'Notes', *Eagle* xxxvi (1914–15), 22–6.

[6] 18 Elizabeth c. 6. V. H. Morgan, *A History of the University of Cambridge*, II. *1546–1750* (Cambridge, 2004), 220.

[7] SJCA, SB4.4, fo. 341v.

[8] See Howard, *Finances*, 34.

the Bakehouse and Brewhouse Bursar's accounts.[9] This practice endured deep into the nineteenth century, and provided the model for the annual dividends paid out of fines. College payments and accounting processes being what they were, it is never quite straightforward to assess the extent of such bounty. Certainly, the long series of accounts tell a great deal about the College's receipts and payments. But of course these documents never set out to meet modern statistical needs. There was little or no attempt, for example, to total or balance the sequence of rentals, which sweep through the century and run on, indeed, to the reforms of 1770, classifying financial outlay and income.[10] Balances of the various officers are to be found in the Balance Books, but these are given in general, bald totals, most probably compiled from loose papers and private books, long since discarded.

The rentals tell so much, but no more. They make no mention of the dividend payments crucial to Fellows. These are found in the Dividend Books; by 1645 the practice of paying dividends out of total fine money, first noted in 1629, had to all intents and purposes been established.[11] Still more insidious, the figures for money rents on the College estates become increasingly obsolete. Fines – in this period amounting to around one year's full rental value, and frequently calculated with help from members of the College who possessed some local knowledge – were far more important. Just the same, the sources are immensely rich. As with any detailed set of institutional accounts they open a window on the past. Their unchanging format, presenting comparable information at a high level of detail, year after year, sheds light on practice, custom and change in a long-vanished world.

Ambitious, growing colleges all harboured designs to build on, enclose and otherwise develop land in Cambridge. At times these ambitions conflicted with the interests of their neighbours, and on such occasions the parties involved either went to court, in the best Jacobean tradition, or deployed their influential supporters in a courteous but telling exchange of letters. When Trinity decided to enclose land west of the river, on Garret Hostel Green, land on which tenant farmers of St John's claimed rights of common, the dispute took years to resolve. Along the way, Trinity enlisted support from a former Master, John Whitgift, by that time archbishop of Canterbury, who wrote pointedly about his hopes for his old college and his belief that St John's would 'have a speciall regard of this my Motion unto you in the behalf thereof'. In a later letter, trying a slightly different approach, he advised the College 'as a frend … not to stand any longer with [the tenant farmers] in this present case', while later still he declared that the queen was also displeased at their 'unkynde and un-neighbourly dealing with Trinitie College in so small a matter'.[12] In those days archbishops could be as persuasive as Mafia dons, especially when they invoked the queen's name, but Richard Clayton, then Master of St John's, was no pushover. The College just as courteously declined to give way, and the matter remained unresolved long after

---

[9] SJCA, BB2 and 3.

[10] With only a short experimental hiatus in the early 1690s.

[11] Howard, *Finances*, 84–5.

[12] Scott, 'Notes', *Eagle* xvi (1889–91), 467, 474, 517.

10 David Loggan's print of a three-court College with provision
for tennis court across the bridge: *Cantabrigia Illustrata* (1690)

Whitgift's death in 1604. Collaboration was, however, far more common than dissent. Despite the high-profile disputes, relations with Trinity in respect of these borderlands seem for the most part to have been marked by a quiet, necessary, co-operation. Neither side wished to squander money in the courts. When boundary ditches needed scouring, one college or the other might take up the task, the costs being split evenly.[13]

Beyond the Cam, and to the north of Garret Hostel Green, lay the real tennis court, the fishponds tucked between St John's Ditch and the Bin Brook, clearly marked in David Loggan's print, and the sweep of the Paddock with its walks out into what we now call the Wilderness.[14] The tennis court depicted by Loggan was built in 1602–3, to replace a sixteenth-century predecessor lost in the construction of Second Court.[15] As for the Wilderness, it came to St John's piecemeal. When the College acquired the 'bowling green' from the Corporation of Cambridge in 1610, it dropped its longstanding objections to Trinity's enclosure of Garret Hostel Green.[16] The rest of the western grounds, all bar a

---

[13] For example, see SJCA, 4.8, fo. 237v.

[14] St John's Ditch used to run under the site of New Court, roughly on the line from the current I Staircase to A Staircase. The fishponds, carefully hedged off from those belonging to Merton College, were leased out to Cambridge merchants in our period, and appear still to have been commercially viable. See E. Miller, 'Fish Ponds Close and its pondyards', *Eagle* lix (1962), 353–62.

[15] R. Willis and J. W. Clark, *The Architectural History of the University of Cambridge* (Cambridge, 1886), II. 321.

[16] A few of the issues in this long-running dispute are rehearsed in the documents reprinted by Scott, 'Notes', *Eagle* xxxi (1909–10), 306–13.

small plot in the north-west and the causeway alongside Trinity, were acquired nearly fifty years later in a pragmatic deal cut with Corpus Christi College, yet another act of intercollegiate rationalization. In 1658 St John's leased to Corpus 2.5 acres in Trumpington in exchange for 'the upper walkes', paying generous compensation to the dispossessed tenant, one Henry Brown.[17] This lease was renewed, the rents went unpaid and, in the eighteenth century, the *de facto* swap was recognized by both colleges.[18]

2. BUILDINGS AND BENEFACTORS:
THE FABRIC OF THE COLLEGE

With status at stake and with benefactors and wealthy parents to attract, the College took pains to present a smart and imposing face to the world. From the earliest times, St John's ensured that the frontage of the College, together with that other high-profile frontier the Back Lane alongside Trinity College, were maintained in good order.[19] Early in the seventeenth century, 'Goodwife Neede' was paid to keep 'the streetes cleane' outside the College,[20] and she and her successors feature in accounts throughout the period. By 1632, in a sensible combination of work, 'Megg' was sweeping both the street and the new Library, for a total of just under ten shillings a quarter.[21] The courts, too, were gravelled, or 'pebbled' or 'paved' in the parlance of the time. Smartness naturally extended to the fabric of buildings. In 1615 the plumber was paid for 'leading the eagles before the gates' and a joiner was remunerated for 'cutting a Crowne in wood to set upon the posts of the gate'.[22] The Great Gate was lit, both for security and for the sake of appearance. Charges 'for a Lanterne and Lanterne lyne for the gates' feature in the rentals, contending against the darker months of the year.[23]

The original College buildings very soon proved too modest for a growing, and more affluent, population. First Court, Metcalfe's Court, Rath Hall, the Infirmary and the Pensionary failed to cope with the stream of new undergraduates, and new Fellows. Indeed, John Hamond's map of 1592 – the first really reliable cartographical representation of Cambridge – shows the limitations on available built space particularly well. Hamond, in the best Tudor tradition, presents an angled, bird's-eye view of the city. First Court stands alone, apart from the gabled appendage of Metcalfe's Court, attached asymmetrically to its south-western corner. The gravelled court is divided into two by a path leading east–west from the Great Gate to the screens passage.

[17] SJCA, SB4.6, fo. 253v.

[18] Howard, *Finances*, 83. See also SJCA, D17.170; Willis and Clark, *Architectural History*, II. 238.

[19] Note the payment to 'Goodman Danyell for fowre hundred and seaventy yards paveinge in the Lane towards Trinity Colledge' among many other such payments on the accounts: SJCA, SB4.3, fo. 73r.

[20] SJCA, SB4.3, fo. 121r, among other references.

[21] SJCA, SB4.4, fo. 313r.

[22] SJCA, SB4.3, fos. 354r, 355r.

[23] SJCA, SB4.4, fo. 100r.

The Infirmary clings close to its ancient twin, the old Chapel, while the Master's Lodge stretches westwards by a few yards from the back of the court, protruding into a walled garden. On the site of the northern end of Second Court, and of the seventeenth-century Old Library, an orchard with dovecote extends down to the river. Across what looks like an open meadow, west of Metcalfe's Court, Rath Hall and two smaller buildings – privies perhaps – stand on the river, near a single-railed bridge. But the most obvious feature of the map is the space so obviously available for new building. Hamond's view of Cambridge represented a challenge to the authorities in St John's, and the challenge was taken up. Late in the 1590s, the College resolved on a striking, costly response, the erection of an entirely new court.

Thomas Baker, writing in the first half of the eighteenth century, endorsed a contemporary view that 'as the College beg[a]n to rise in buildings, so it declined in learning'. The College, he insists, was for a time 'so overbusied with architecture, that their other studies were intermitted and the noise of axes and hammers disturbed them in their proper business'. Baker here expressed the antiquarian's nostalgia for a remote past: nothing is ever quite as good as it used to be, and the decline in learning is open to debate, but there can be no question about the building work. The Mastership of the Lancastrian bachelor Richard Clayton is now remembered for the construction of Second Court. Masters like to leave their mark, and the Court was, as Baker concedes, Clayton's project, though he adds, correctly, that the Master was assisted by 'the unwearied agency of Mr R[obert] Booth our best solicitor'.[24] Booth, former Fellow and Bursar, was at this point Chaplain to the countess of Shrewsbury, and he was indeed both indefatigable and persuasive. Surviving coloured plans and elevations for the new Court, drawn up and signed by Ralph Symons the architect (whose other works include parts of Emmanuel and Sidney Sussex Colleges, and the plans for Trinity's Great Court) with the builder Gilbert Wigge, show a familiar outline. Superficially the court today looks much as it did 400 years ago. But of course there are differences; the kitchen range and the Shrewsbury Tower, for example, have been considerably rebuilt in the past century, as any close inspection of the brickwork will show, while the two buttresses on the western range, now inside Third Court, were added out of necessity in 1691.[25]

Articles of agreement for the build were concluded in 1598, and work pressed ahead over the next four years, sweeping away Metcalfe's Court in the process. The north range was finished first, and within a year. Financing the project, however, proved less straightforward. What follows is a tale repeated with variations on several occasions through the next 300 years. Booth's new connections were exploited, albeit with due caution. In February 1599 he wrote to the Master, suggesting that no mention be made of the new building to the earl of Shrewsbury at that point, as his lordship had not yet been primed to make

---

[24] Baker-Mayor, I. 190–1.

[25] A. F. Torry, *Founders and Benefactors of St John's College, Cambridge* (Cambridge, 1888), 16; SJCA, SB4.9, fo. 171v. Willis and Clark, *Architectural History*, II. 321. Clayton's and Boys Smith's arms on the spandrels of the Shrewsbury Tower commemorate the two phases of twentieth-century restoration.

a contribution!²⁶ But of course Shrewsbury's wife was fully behind the project, and Shrewsbury himself, as a member of the ever shrinking high nobility in Elizabethan England – Elizabeth was sparing with promotions to the peerage – and as a member of the Privy Council, was just the sort of wealthy patron the College hoped to attract. The closet Catholicism of the earl, his countess, and members of their household, hardly mattered, and it has to be noted that, even in a time of war with Catholic Spain, it made no particular difference to Elizabeth either.²⁷ In 1600 the Seniors had broken cover, writing to Shrewsbury and asking if he would underwrite the remaining work.

In the end, the foundation of Second Court, as it came to be known during the seventeenth century, was credited to the countess of Shrewsbury. Booth monitored the work closely, complaining in the summer of 1600 when word spread that the 'new gatehowse', contrary to the agreed design, would not in fact be 'so large and fayre as the ould one towards the streat'.²⁸ That, he said, would not be countenanced; the countess, he implied, expected equal prominence and would not be outshone by Lady Margaret. With some justification, Booth came to look on the project as his own, and he hoped to leave his own stamp on the final design. That stamp took a precise form: Booth bequeathed £300 to the College in order to build a 'conduytt within the new Court … and to bring water thereunto from some fitting spring'. Clean water was always precious in towns, and particularly so in a stagnant urban environment on the edge of the Fens. It is said that Trinity would not grant permission for a pipe from their conduit. The College, however, may also have felt that water conduits in courts, along the lines of the near-contemporary fountain in Trinity Great Court, were a little over-flamboyant for St John's, or perhaps just a waste of an inadequate sum of money.²⁹ They put Booth's bequest, when it was eventually received in 1627, to other uses, including a contribution towards the new Chapel organ and a subsidy towards the deficit on the building account.³⁰ The College still awaits its fountain.

In all, Second Court cost the College a little over £3,600, of which the 'foundress' and her understanding husband, whose fortunes took a nosedive early in the seventeenth century, paid some 75 per cent.³¹ Their reward was the estimation in which such gestures are held. Daughter of the redoubtable Bess of

---

²⁶ SJCA, D94.8.

²⁷ On the earl's turbulent career see G. R. Batho, 'Gilbert Talbot, seventh earl of Shrewsbury (1553–1616): the "great and glorious earl"?', *Derbyshire Archaeological Journal* xciii (1973), 23–32. On the late Elizabethan court see N. Mears, 'Regnum Cecilianum? A Cecilian perspective of the court', in J. Guy (ed.), *The Reign of Elizabeth I: Court and Culture in the Last Decade* (Cambridge, 1995), 46–64. In 1616 the countess lobbied Owen Gwyn, as Vice-Chancellor, for help to incorporate the Catholic physician John Hawkins, on the basis of his Doctorate of Medicine from Padua: Scott, 'Notes', *Eagle* xxxvi (1914–15), 17.

²⁸ Scott, 'Notes', *Eagle* xxiii (1901–2), 14–15.

²⁹ Willis and Clark, *Architectural History*, II. 262. On Trinity's reluctance see SJCA, D105.266 and 269.

³⁰ Scott, 'Notes', *Eagle* xvi (1889–91), 465–6, 467–8; xxv (1903–4), 271–9.

³¹ SJCL, Bb.7.6, a collection of architects' drawings, accounts and letters relating to the building operations.

Hardwick, perhaps the most formidable woman in Tudor history, the countess was a pretty formidable character herself. She lived at the heart of court, understood its politics, and was not afraid to take great risks as the occasion demanded. When her niece Arbella Stewart – a descendent of Henry VIII's older sister Margaret whose royal blood made her a potential rival to King James I for the throne of England – contracted a clandestine marriage with the earl of Hertford's grandson, who also enjoyed a claim to the throne through King Henry's younger sister Mary, the political implications could not be overlooked by the Jacobean regime. The countess connived in Arbella's deception and was imprisoned in the Tower of London as a result. There she lobbied successfully for the release of her famous fellow prisoner Sir Walter Ralegh.[32] Baker and other commentators and historians equally well placed to know suggest that, in the seventeenth century, the concept of a joint foundation, along the lines of Queens', was taken seriously.[33]

Building work on this scale – the Court measures 137 feet north to south by 165 east to west – is a precarious business. Baker, who always enjoys a cautionary tale, dwells on the problems created by the construction of Second Court. Wigge and Symons made no profit from the build, indeed they were left in debt to the College, and the College pursued them determinedly through the University Vice-Chancellor's Court.[34] The principle of the matter apart, St John's could not afford to lose money in the venture; even without the builders' arrears, the College was left with nearly £1,000 to find, over and above the benefaction. It was left, too, with a 'slight and crazy building ... which can never live up to the age of the first court'. Thus Baker, but he was, of course, writing about a First Court as yet unscarred by James Essex's stone cladding, and not yet dismembered by the destruction of the medieval Chapel.[35] Though built on the cheap, just as Baker implies, Second Court has stood up well against time. While some walls have crumbled and while others have been propped up, several later buildings in the College have required more expensive maintenance. And while hardly revolutionary in scope or design, the Court offered something new. To be sure, a large portion – the first floor along the whole northern range – went to the Master, and more to the Fellows, who lived in the tried and tested way with their pupils lodging in rooms within their sets. But in Second Court the staircases ran right up into the attics, allowing students their own uninterrupted access to the Court. Moreover, the Court was sufficiently spacious to permit some undergraduates to keep chambers of their own, a great attraction to the sons of noblemen and the wealthier gentry, and their status-conscious fathers. As in any college, certain rooms soon acquired a particular cachet, especially when combined into handsome apartments. Henry, Lord Maltravers, a Fellow-Commoner from 1624, enjoyed five rooms at the request of his father the earl of Arundel, and the next year young Maltravers himself

---

[32] N. E. McClure (ed.), *The Letters of John Chamberlain*, 2 vols. (Philadelphia, 1939), I. 618.

[33] Even in the early nineteenth century she is described by Charles Yate as 'Foundress of Second Court': SJCL, MS H.31.

[34] Willis and Clark, *Architectural History*, II. 258–9.

[35] Baker-Mayor, I. 191–2.

wrote to the Master, suggesting that his old set might now prove suitable for the earl of Southampton.

Metcalfe's Court may have been brushed aside by Second Court, but in the provision of undergraduate accommodation other sixteenth-century arrangements enjoyed a longer life. Rath Hall survived until the completion of Third Court in the 1670s, while chambers were occupied in both Infirmary and Pensionary far into the nineteenth century. For generations of undergraduates the Infirmary was 'the Labyrinth', a reference both to the twisting, covered pathway round the Chapel which, from 1636–7, offered the most convenient access to the old building, and also to the convoluted, medieval structure itself.[36]

The long gallery of the Master's Lodge was the new Court's most remarkable feature. It was in this long gallery – perhaps in a partitioned central section, if Symons' plans were followed in detail – that the papers of betrothal between Prince Charles and Henrietta Maria of France were duly ratified by the king, the duke of Buckingham, and the Secretary of State Sir Edward Conway. The event is commemorated there in a stained-glass roundel.[37] Parts of this splendid chamber seem to have been used early on as an art gallery, emphasizing an impression that, while within the Lodge, this was a collegiate space measured for the grand occasion. Curtains of 'changeable taffaty' were made for the pictures hanging there in 1614, and new pictures were added, and indeed curtained, while that fashion lasted.[38] Fabric and fittings nearly always received prompt attention in rooms where guests were received. Sixteen fine 'Russia chaires' were provided for the refurbishment of the Audit Chamber in 1657–8.[39]

For a century the College Library had occupied the first floor of the south range, by the Great Gate, but in 1616 the books were moved out, the old Library chamber and the precious but hitherto inaccessible attic above were converted into accommodation, and temporary storage was arranged over the kitchens, on the western side of First Court. As these moves suggest, the College was thinking not simply of replacing lecterns with bookcases, but of building a completely new library, even though it lacked, for the moment, the necessary resources. Ambitions were driven by the offer of a substantial collection of books, a collection that easily eclipsed the 700 or so titles already owned by St John's. This was the fine library assembled by William Crashaw, the Puritan scholar and preacher, father of the less-than-Puritan Pembroke poet Richard Crashaw. William, a former undergraduate and Fellow of the College, had served as preacher at the Temple Church in London, and had amassed a working collection of titles to inform his labours.[40] Now enjoying a quieter Yorkshire

[36] 'Payd Mr Broxolme the income of his Chamber by the east end of the Chappell where the new passage was made to the lodgeings behind the Chappell ix li.' SJCA, SB4.5, fo. 81v.

[37] TNA SP14/176, fo. 91; G. Watson, 'Charles and Henrietta', *Eagle* (1998), 40–8.

[38] SJCA, SB4.3, fo. 332r. After it became the Fellows' Combination Room in the nineteenth century, and well into the 1900s, the long gallery retained its role as a showcase for pictures. See the 1919 painting by Hugh Buss, in the College collection.

[39] SJCA, SB4.6, fo. 254r.

[40] P. J. Wallis, *William Crashawe: The Sheffield Puritan* (Sheffield, 1963); Wallis, 'The library of William Crashawe', *Transactions of the Cambridge Bibliographical Society* ii (1954–8), 213–28.

benefice, and unable or unwilling to move his library north, he concluded a deal whereby he would sell certain desirable volumes to another Johnian, Henry, third earl of Southampton, so that the earl might present the books to their old college. In 1615, 200 manuscripts and 2,000 printed books (out of at least 3,000 in Crashaw's library) were duly transferred to Southampton House in the Strand.[41] Like Crashaw, the earl was keen to see a home fit for these treasures. Shakespeare's one-time patron knew a good thing when he saw it. Little more than a decade after the construction of Second Court, with all its attendant frustrations, the College was now obliged to identify someone willing to meet the cost of major new building work.[42]

That requirement was satisfied by the generosity of a former sizar and Fellow of the College, John Williams, a pugnacious, erudite Welshman. One of the last ecclesiastics to hold high political office in England, Williams combined the bishopric of Lincoln with the keepership of the Great Seal – he was in effect Lord Chancellor without the title.[43] He was also one of the foremost literary patrons of his day, supporting and encouraging poets, playwrights and writers, including the extremely popular Latin epigrammatist John Owen. Though we cannot be quite certain, it seems as though Williams took the initiative over the Library. The first approaches were extremely cautious. To begin with Williams acted anonymously, his interests represented by a friend and fellow Johnian bishop, Valentine Carey. In the course of time, however, he threw off his anonymity and revelled in his role as founder of the Library, studying plans and bringing expertise gained while carrying out improvements at Lincoln and while founding a town library at Leicester to bear on the new task. The costs rose, and then rose again; Williams's generosity was thoroughly tested. Appreciating his interest, and the way in which interest encourages money, the College took pains to submit their proposals for Williams's approval, whenever possible through well-wishers such as Carey. In June 1624 Carey raised the possibility of a further subvention. 'After hard words', the intermediary reported, Williams 'gave these good, that for the perfecting of it he would strayne himself for £100 more.'[44] In all, Williams poured over £2,000 into the building of the Library, some two-thirds of the total expenditure.[45]

The design matured slowly. Initially, the benefactor envisaged a central staircase, but by October 1623 he and Carey were agreed that 'the ascent to the Library must needs be at one of the ends of the building, by a stayrecase cast out, for it is [to be] considered that if it were in the midst of the building, the landing, and ingress, would cause the loss ether of a light, or of a stall for bookes'.[46]

[41] Scott, 'Notes', *Eagle* xxiii (1901–2), 22–5.

[42] In this and what follows I am indebted to the researches of Elizabeth Quarmby-Lawrence, formerly Special Collections Librarian at St John's.

[43] For Williams's career see K. Fincham, *Prelate as Pastor: The Episcopate of James I* (Oxford, 1990); N. Tyacke, *Anti-Calvinists: The Rise of English Arminianism, c. 1590–1640* (Oxford, 1987).

[44] Carey to Gwyn, 25 June 1624: Scott, 'Notes', *Eagle* xvii (1891–3), 348.

[45] The summary account is found in SJCA, C13.1, fo. 283v. Just under £200 from the gift of Sir Ralph Hare was also committed.

[46] SJCA, D105.231; Scott, 'Notes', *Eagle* xvii (1891–3), 145.

So 24 feet were trimmed off the Master's long gallery and a splendid staircase – now the first two flights of E Second Court – was added to the plan. No one seems to have objected. The Master, Owen Gwyn, was an accommodating man, who never forgot the bigger picture. At a late stage, the two bishops discussed a model of the building, rejecting as 'over conceited' a peristyle, poring over the design of the ground-floor chambers, the high windows to north and south, and the oriel window overlooking the Cam – which Williams accepted for the sake of appearance, though sensibly concerned about 'the inconveniency of the air from the river'. They agreed, again sensibly, that lead was best on the roof, 'albeit the charg thereof were something more'.[47]

Every penny was well spent, for even Baker could not call the new Library 'slight' or 'crazy'. This was a building on the grand scale. 120 feet long, and some 30 feet wide, it demanded, and received, a fine oak front door. The lovely Jacobean ceiling of the then long gallery continues through E Staircase to the chamber used until recently as the Librarian's Office, and it may even be that for a time the Library's door opened directly out of the gallery.[48] Much about the Upper Library remains unchanged to this day. There have been one or two small modifications. The door on the first-floor landing of E Second Court is now accompanied by a somewhat incongruous (and no longer functioning) doorbell. The central bookcases, and modestly effective heaters, are nineteenth-century additions, as is the sprawl of heraldry in the fine oriel window, a Victorian 'development-office' initiative. With the exception of a pair at the eastern end of the Library, the curiously high intermediate cases were raised by one shelf in the 1740s to accommodate the many books bequeathed by Thomas Baker. But using imagination the visitor can easily see the splendid Gothic chamber as it was when first opened in 1628: the layout of cases, the stone-facing, the oak ceiling, the grilled, lockable doors to protect valuable classes, the 'windowed' shelf-lists on the principal cases, and the classification system were all established either at the time of building, or very soon after.[49]

The intention was that Williams's books should adorn Williams's library – in 1638 more than £40 was spent by the College in cataloguing and transferring them from the bishop's house at Buckden to another property.[50] In the end, however, inertia, over-complex arrangements, and a change in political fortunes frustrated the College's hopes.[51] The bishop's later career was as turbulent as his character: never favoured by Charles I, and borne down by the steady enmity of Charles's archbishop of Canterbury, William Laud, Williams lost the Great

---

[47] Carey to Gwyn, 29 May and 19 Nov. 1623: Scott, 'Notes', *Eagle* xvii (1891–3), 11 and 343–4. The oriel window was, of course, of clear glass, as in the fine nineteenth-century print by Ackermann. The present-day clutter of armorial stained glass – a selective catalogue of benefactors – was added in the 1880s as a memorial to the Revd H. H. Hughes (Torry, *Founders and Benefactors*, 32). The arms of Thomas Baker and James Wood, who surely merited places at the 'top table', were moved to the smaller oriel window in the Lower Library.

[48] Torry, *Founders and Benefactors*, 16.

[49] Perhaps the Mr Mathewes who made the wainscoting at Audley End was responsible for the splendid bookcases: SJCA, D105.146. It is impossible now to be certain.

[50] SJCA, SB4.5, fo. 104r.

[51] Scott, 'Notes', *Eagle* xxxiv (1912–13), 161–9.

Seal early in the reign, and was eventually imprisoned in the Tower from 1637 to 1640. With Laud's fall he enjoyed an all-too-brief triumph, in his translation to the archdiocese of York on the eve of the Civil Wars. But then the entire bench of bishops was abolished in the First Civil War by a House of Commons desperate for an alliance with the Presbyterian Scots.[52] Williams retired to Wales, and there he died, in 1650. His library was depleted by Richard Kilvert, an industrious official who acted for the Crown against Williams in Star Chamber litigation. After Williams's death the College secured what was left, only to find that the collection essentially duplicated volumes already held in the Library. Happily, however, some of these books, still readily identified by his coat of arms stamped on the binding, did indeed find a home in St John's. Though lacking the armorial binding, a fine copy of the Great Bible of 1538, believed to have once been in the possession of Thomas Cromwell, may also have come from Williams's collection.

The Library did not exhaust Williams's generosity. He also funded a foundation of two Fellowships and four Scholarships, though the rent of land at Raveley, Huntingdonshire, and certain advowsons set aside for this purpose very soon proved inadequate. While Williams Scholars continued to be elected to 1859, the last Fellow on Bishop Williams' foundation vacated his Fellowship in 1645 at the height of the Civil War. The College, as it later insisted, may have been led to underwrite an inadequate foundation in the expectation of further donations, frustrated by the eclipse in Williams' fortunes.[53] Alas, these things happen.

When Southampton's gift was at last incorporated into the collection, the College Library instantly tripled in size, and, luxuriating in its spacious new quarters, it continued to expand rapidly.[54] The rentals detail a procession of significant gifts. Just occasionally, they also record attempts to manage stock. In 1628, the Library sent 'the bookes which wee had double to My Lord of Litchfeilde', packing them up and paying for a hamper.[55] Even with such rationalization, the Upper Library collection had grown to 4,000 books by 1640, following major donations from Thomas Morton, bishop of Lichfield (and later of Durham), Lord William Howard, John Carey Viscount Rochford, and – the foundation of the College's medical collections – from John Collins, the Regius Professor of Physic. In 1631 the College also possessed at least two globes, located in the Library.[56] Though ornamental, and elegant in their depiction of exciting recent geographical discoveries documented by the likes of the Johnian Samuel Purchas, the globes were never very robust, or perhaps readers spun them too fast. They are already under repair in 1633.[57]

---

[52] E. Vallance, '"An holy and sacramentall faction": federal thought and the Solemn League and Covenant in England', *English Historical Review* cxvi (2001), 50–75.

[53] Scott, 'Notes', *Eagle* xvii (1891–3), 352; xxxiii (1911–12), 101–36.

[54] The expansion still started from a very low base. It cost just two shillings to move the existing library across from First Court.

[55] SJCA, SB4.4, fo. 245v.

[56] SJCA, SB4.4, fo. 291r.

[57] SJCA, SB4.4, fo. 338v. A few years later, reference is made in the accounts to mending 'one of the old and one of the new globes' (SB4.5, fo. 271), while later still one of them

The Library proved a great asset to St John's in more ways than one. Allowing space for significant gifts and bequests of books, it encouraged generosity, developed the scholarship of Fellows and students, and also attracted important visitors, ready to be impressed by this demonstration of the University's scholarly credentials. On the eve of the Civil Wars Charles I viewed both Chapel and Library, dined al fresco in Second Court and on his departure from the Great Gate took leave of the Vice-Chancellor. Among friends, he glanced into the future: 'Whatsoever becomes of me', the king said, 'I will charge my Sonn, upon my blessing, to respect the University.'[58] When thirteen years later, in the exhausted, noncommittal peace of Protectorate England, John Evelyn came to Cambridge in the course of a summer tour, he 'went first to see St John's Colledge and Librarie, which I think is the fairest of that Universitie'. Alongside 'some faire Manuscripts' Evelyn noted the 'vast', early sixteenth-century Antiphoner, still on display in the Upper Library.[59] Evelyn's friend and fellow diarist, Samuel Pepys, visited the Library in 1662, while Charles II was shown round in 1681.[60] John Gibson, whose letters offer a particularly vivid insight into Cambridge undergraduate life in the 1660s, records in May 1669 a visit from the 'Prince of Tuscany', later Cosimo III. The visitor was treated to speeches of welcome and a philosophy Act in the Old Schools. 'An anthem appointed with pleasant musick' was sung in King's Chapel, while Trinity laid on a Latin comedy in the Master's Lodge. Before this evening's entertainment, however, the prince 'took a walk into our Library and the Doctors along with him'.[61] From the 1690s, Trinity's new Wren Library, and later the University Library embellished by copyright legislation and the collection presented by George I, became the sights to see, but the College's collections have never stopped growing, and diversifying, away from the public eye.

With gifts come responsibilities. From that day to this, a member of the College has been paid to look after the books. Mindful of the obligation to honour benefactors, St John's paid £10 for a massive portrait of Williams, by Gilbert Jackson, which originally went on display in the Library. Williams' portrait now hangs at the lower end of the Hall, together with the equally substantial images of his contemporaries Thomas Morton and another Library benefactor, the capable diplomat Sir Ralph Hare. There, until very recently, they kept company with the much smaller portrait of another Jacobean benefactor, William, Lord Maynard of Wicklow, who founded a logic lecture in 1620, trading on his generosity to secure numerous favours for connections. For a time, chambers over the long gallery were reserved for Maynard's posterity, should they come up to the College.[62]

No one in seventeenth-century St John's was particularly disconcerted by these demands. Colleges have always invested time and trouble in cultivating

---

was equipped with a brass pulley (e.g. SB4.5, fo. 8or). A globe 'invented by the Earle of Castlemane' is purchased for the Library in 1681 (SB4.8, fo. 353v).

[58] Cooper, *Annals of Cambridge*, III. 321–2.

[59] J. Bowle (ed.), *The Diary of John Evelyn* (Oxford, 1985), 163.

[60] C. Sayle, 'Bibliotheca loquitur', *Eagle* xvii (1891–3), 376–7.

[61] G. C. M. Smith (ed.), 'John Gibson's manuscript', *Eagle* xvii (1891–3), 265–6.

[62] Scott, 'Notes', *Eagle* xxxvi (1914–15), 132–40.

benefactors, and have usually appreciated that the process demands both flex-ibility and a close attention to detail. In 1628 a trifling sum was spent on 'gilt paper to writ letters for the College'.[63] One 'Favell', presumably a townsman with calligraphic skills, was employed in 1638 to write elegant letters, designed to impress.[64] In 1622–3 John Scott was paid 10 shillings 'for writing and col-ouring' and a frame for a table of benefactors in the Chapel, while a 'staple' to hang it on cost the College a penny in 1638.[65] Large sums were laid out in decorating the Library's book of benefactors, both with rather fine portraits of the most generous, and also with the arms of many other significant donors, expertly drawn.[66] Ralph Hare's gift in 1623 – the juxtaposition of his portrait with that of Williams is doubly significant since his generosity helped make up the shortfall on the Library – is confirmed by the comings and goings of the donor and his servants (duly rewarded, at over the odds), and by reciprocal visits from the President and other Fellows. The all-important legal documents, which preserved record and title to so many benefactions, were placed in a new, specially made box, and kept under lock and key.[67] Benefactors to colleges enjoy a measure of immortality. In St John's their generosity is still commemorated at the beginning of May each year, when a long if necessarily selective list of names is read out by the deans during a service in the Chapel.

Despite the traditional cast of the administrative documents, there was noth-ing static about the appearance and fabric of a seventeenth-century college. The impression, much as today, is of engagement with the challenge posed by the maintenance of an already extensive Cambridge estate. Details of this engage-ment are often mundane, but those same details contain enlightening clues to both the layout and the operational routine of St John's before and after the Civil War. How, for example, did the College that rejected Booth's fountain provide water to its residents? Looking at both the Rentals and the Loggan prints – often a revealing combination – the strategic locations of hand-pumps becomes obvious. Specific reference is made to '3 poumps in the Colledg' in 1608–9.[68] There was a pump in the Bakehouse yard, which occupied the site now occupied by the old Divinity School.[69] Another stood in the kitchen. A third was located in the 'boggards' (that is, the privies) by 1651, and most prob-ably long before.[70] There is a pump in the Back Lane behind the Kitchen, and one 'by the waterside' by 1630.[71] Others are found in the 'M[aste]r his yard' in 1647, in Upper Court, and also, of necessity, in the Brewhouse.[72] Reliant on

[63] SJCA, SB4.4, fo. 245v.

[64] SJCA, SB4.5, fo. 105v.

[65] SJCA, SB4.4, fo. 99v; SB4.5, fo. 102r.

[66] The 'Liber Memorialis' is held in the Library to this day, at SJCL, MS K.18.

[67] SJCA, SB4.4, fo. 99v. Hare is also commemorated in a window in Chapel, and in the older oriel window in Hall. The large portrait hanging above the screens in Hall was purchased by the College in 1632.

[68] SJCA, SB4.3, fo. 220.

[69] SJCA, SB4.4, fo. 75v; SB4.8, fo. 190r.

[70] SJCA, SB4.3, fo. 118v; SB4.6, fos. 22v, 23r.

[71] SJCA, SB4.4, fo. 221v.

[72] SJCA, SB4.5, fo. 341r; SB4.6, fo. 217r; SB4.9, fo. 147v; SB4.3, fos. 51v, 52r, 122r.

impermanent leather flaps, the seventeenth-century pump was frequently in need of repair; this was cheap, low-grade technology, absolutely essential to the supply of water throughout the College.

The detail also tells us that there was, early in the century, a 'rownde table' in Hall, while the 4 shillings 'paid for pasting and bynding a bible' in 1621 supports the theory that diners were still at this point treated to regular mealtime readings.[73] Kitchen routine is preserved in a long series of entries in the Rentals. Chimneys are swept, and vessels scoured. New plates are bought, if infrequently. The brawn cauldron sees good service, and is regularly 'seethed' using firewood – precious stuff in Cambridgeshire – bought at Stourbridge Fair and elsewhere.[74] Kitchen records were once kept still more systematically in the Buttery Book, but no such volume survives for this period in the College Archives.[75]

What of those other staples in Cambridge life, now so curiously absent from St John's: clocks and bells? A large clock, which apparently did not work particularly well, was repaired more or less every year. New wheels as well as springs, and ropes are all fitted, and then refitted. The clock is first recorded very early in the history of the College, certainly from 1530, and it is obvious that it was positioned at a significant height from the ground, driven as it was by heavy weights. It could strike the hour, for there are references to a hammer. Timepieces in this period had their limitations, and the College clock was necessarily regulated by older technology: in 1609 the College bought 'a dial to sett the clocke by', while another 'sunn diall for the clock loft' was purchased in 1639.[76] The precise location of this College clock is now unknown, though it seems to have been placed in its own, lockable clock-tower.[77] In 1633 the will of a former Fellow, John Nevinson, included a legacy to provide payments to the clock-keeper, along with the chapel clerk and the bellringer, perhaps another clue to a location in or near the Chapel. The Loggan prints of 1690 show no clock, but early in the eighteenth century a consumptive sizar, Ambrose Bonwicke, had to find a boy to take on some of his duties as clock-keeper, since the effort involved in winding the mechanism caused the poor young man to cough and spit blood.[78]

The Hall bell, or 'Great Bell', is also mended frequently. So far as we can tell it hung in the Chapel tower.[79] The bell seems to have been recast in 1610, and probably again in 1624, though by this point we may be considering more than one.[80] There was still another recasting in 1635.[81]

---

[73] SJCA, SB4.3, fo. 307r; SB4.4, fo. 49r.
[74] E.g. SJCA, SB4.3, fos. 261v, 176r, 196v.
[75] Several references, e.g. SJCA, SB4.6, fo. 180v.
[76] SJCA, SB4.3, fo. 220r; SB4.5, fo. 130v.
[77] SJCA, SB4.6, fo. 25r.
[78] Crook, *Foundation to Gilbert Scott*, 156.
[79] SJCA, SB 4.5, fo. 283r.
[80] Crook, *Foundation to Gilbert Scott*, 155.
[81] SJCA, SB4.5, fo. 24r.

3. MASTERS, FELLOWS AND CAREERS

The seventeenth-century college was a youthful society. It is often claimed that, in very early times, undergraduates were mere boys, and indeed the occasional thirteen-year-old is found on the books at St John's well into the seventeenth century. However, the claim is based on contemporary perceptions of youth and maturity. Most undergraduates were in fact sixteen or seventeen on arrival in Cambridge, still far from the age of majority, but only a little younger than the eighteen years common today. The real youngsters were the Fellows. As Miller points out, when looking at the College in the 1630s, most men had achieved their Fellowships in St John's by the age of twenty-two, and Fellows tended to move on, to marriage, to clerical promotion, or to both, within ten to fifteen years.[82] While in Cambridge the more fortunate among them would augment their incomes by taking up curacies within riding distance of the University – this pattern is noticeable in many colleges. In so transient a society the more durable Fellow might expect to become a Senior within eight to ten years of election. Even in the later seventeenth century, when it became possible to hold livings (provided they were not college livings) and Fellowships together, the demands of having to be in two places at once meant that Seniors not infrequently delegated their college duties to younger deputies.[83]

College society, as with collegiate life across Cambridge, was rooted in regional distinctions, advantages, and limitations. The deliberate favouring of northern candidates for Fellowships under the original College statutes, which had been modified if not quite abandoned under Henry VIII, gave place to a hotch-potch system in which each particular Fellowship imposed a particular geographical limitation upon candidates.[84] The rule could be circumvented in practice, but it was honoured for centuries in principle. This obedience to the regionalism of founders and benefactors reached down through the ranks of undergraduates, with scholarships and other awards closely tied to a particular town or county. There were seldom sufficient places to accommodate all the worthy young candidates, and the question was frequently decided by pressure from the locality or sometimes by unseemly in-fighting within the College. Migration, from college to college, offered one way round these problems, but only at the cost of weakening an individual's allegiance to a particular house. County origins, of course, could be obscure, or deliberately obscured. The 1570 University statutes pointedly included a definition, but that same definition – 'that county to which it shall appear that their father belonged' – created through its studied vagueness as many problems as it solved.[85] The parsimony of some benefactions also resulted in a situation where certain Scholarships and Fellowships were more poorly remunerated than others, especially after the effects of ongoing inflation are taken into account.

---

[82] Miller, *Portrait of a College: A History of the College of Saint John the Evangelist Cambridge* (Cambridge, 1961), 30.

[83] P. Cunich *et al.*, *A History of Magdalene College Cambridge, 1428–1988* (Cambridge, 1994), 146.

[84] Morgan, *History of the University of Cambridge*, II. 197–8.

[85] Ibid., 215–17.

The seventeenth century saw little change in the size of the Fellowship. In 1602–3 there were fifty-seven Fellows.[86] By 1625 there were sixty-three.[87] In the mid-1670s, however, the number had fallen to just fifty-three.[88] Fellows were formally admitted once a year, in March or April, the change of the year on 25 March regularly confusing the contemporary scribes charged with writing titles for each annual list in the Register. New Fellows – five a year on average through the first decade of the century – duly record their county in accordance with the Statutes, and also the benefactor responsible for their Fellowship.[89] Scholars, admitted usually but not quite invariably in November each year, followed suit.

Stipends of all sorts seem to have been paid promptly, usually on a quarterly basis. A Fellow's annual income amounted to the total of several such sums, together with money received direct from his pupils and augmented by the all-important dividend. The full remuneration escapes us, though one undated calculation from the seventeenth century argues, credibly, that £40 p.a. was a 'favourable value for a fellowship'.[90] Adding the known figures together, an impression of financial comfort consistently emerges. These sums can be done in many ways, for many of the smaller perks of Fellowship had their value. Brawn at Christmas, for example, was deemed to be worth 10 shillings a head. In 1633 Mr Spell, a Senior Fellow, received 13s 4d stipend, 40s as Bursar, £2 13s 4d as a Senior, £5 'Pro Ambrosio Cave', 33s 4d as a dukes of Suffolk Chaplain, 8s 'stipend concionatorum', and 13s 4d in a notional 'clothing allowance' to the Fellowship. Also, perhaps, 6s in 'Comendaco fundatricis'.[91] There is no way of ascertaining the dividend from fines that needs to be added, as the sums paid to individual Fellows are lost before the 1690s. But on the assumption that each Junior Fellow received £1 for every £50 or £60 of fine income, Spell might easily have added £12 or even £15 to his income. In the same year Mr Peyton, a young man low on the list of Fellows, received 13s 4d stipend, the 13s 4d 'liberatura', and the 'comendaco fundatricis' payment, but had not as yet worked his way up into the other remunerative appointments, his dividend excluded. Comfort does not imply certainty of income. While fines were to some extent foreseeable, the income stream was nevertheless irregular, and as the payments in the early eighteenth century show particularly well, the dividend to Fellows fluctuated significantly, year on year.[92] The Seniors, as Spell's case suggests, did best of all. In 1672–3 Mr Morton, long-standing Library-keeper, was receiving over

[86] SJCA, SB4.3, fo. 66r.

[87] SJCA, SB4.4, fo. 163r.

[88] SJCA, SB4.8, fo. 231v.

[89] SJCA, C3.1, pp. 160–4. Emphasizing once again the enduring nature of College procedures, the pattern was almost identical in the final decade of the century (C3.2).

[90] SJCA, D57.100.

[91] SJCA, SB4.4, fos. 331r–333r, 335v. Chaplaincies paid out of a number of foundations were frequently deployed to augment a Fellow's income; for example, two for Dr Thompson, two for Dr Fell, four (at 33s 4d each per annum) in memory of the two young dukes of Suffolk, who had died of influenza on the same day in 1551. Catastrophe for the Brandon family brought some good to the Fellowship of St John's.

[92] Howard, *Finances*, 303–5.

£16 a year in direct payments, including more than £10 for his possibly notional responsibilities in the Library.[93]

Profits from the bakehouse and brewhouse arising out of the 1576 Corn Act were paid at a higher rate to Fellows than to Scholars (the ratio was two to one, initially, though the distinction diminishes as time goes on), at a better rate to Senior Fellows, and at a still more advantageous rate to the Master.[94] In practice, so far as one can tell, the profits were drawn substantially on the working bakehouse. The superficially attractive and long-lived office of Brewhouse and Bakehouse Bursar (its duties were subsumed into those of the Steward in the 1860 Statutes) seems by the seventeenth century to have been something of a misnomer, in that there is no clear evidence for in-house brewing at any stage before the later nineteenth century. Perhaps it is significant that the title is from time to time shortened in the records to 'Bakehouse Bursar', or something very similar.[95] In the 1600s the College was already leasing out a brewhouse, while taking great care to scrutinize the profitability of its bakehouse.[96] The operation of the brewhouse is an obscure business, but some system similar to that known in agriculture as métayage seems to have obtained: the College provided the coals, malt, hops and a sum of ready money, in return for an agreement to provide beer in rented premises, at the Swan in St Clement's parish, for example. In 1609 there seem to be two agreements with different partners: George Bubwith was to hold the brewhouse and look after the fabric of the building, but Anne Cropley accepted responsibility for providing the beer.[97]

Not that everyone found it straightforward to live on these resources. George Bunnington, admitted a Fellow in 1612, ran into debt very soon afterwards and wrote in desperation to the Master, Owen Gwyn, seeking a 'praeter', in this context a 'whip-round' in the College among Fellows and Fellow-Commoners. On the thin evidence available, it seems that the College obliged. Bunnington's debt was around £40, by no means a trivial figure, but his father had friends in very high places, including that rising Jacobean favourite and future Chancellor of the University, George Villiers. So far as one can tell, there seems to have been a personal call on Gwyn for his patronage, a call that carried weight.[98]

One office of great significance in later centuries was steadily acquiring prestige and power within college gates. Tutors enjoyed, to modern eyes, a

[93] SJCA, SB4.8, fo. 167v.

[94] Morgan, *History of the University of Cambridge*, II. 272.

[95] Howard, *Finances*, 39–40. The official is often termed the Bakehouse Bursar or Bread Bursar.

[96] As shown in the detailed, weekly record-keeping that makes up SJCA, BB2. A lease of the brewhouse, 3 Oct. 14 James I, is preserved in SJCA, C8.1, pp. 858–60. The disaffected Fellow Robert Waideson noted that the brewer paid the College 100 marks a year for its custom in his attack on the Master, Dr Arrowsmith, in the 1640s: Scott, 'Notes', *Eagle* xxxiv (1912–13), 23.

[97] Apparently, the Steward himself was not the lessee. None of the providers in the book of receipts from the 1650s to 1760 figures as lessee of the brewhouse, and it would seem that the system petered out during the Commonwealth or even earlier, before the revival of a brewhouse in 1850 (in Globe Passage, Holy Sepulchre's). I owe this information to the researches of the College Archivist, Malcolm Underwood.

[98] SJCA, D105.143 and 144.

remarkable degree of authority over their young charges, balanced only by a remarkable weight of responsibility. They read to their students personally, oversaw academic studies, often on a regular if not daily basis, kept an eye on moral conduct and on religious zeal, watched over health, took financial responsibility for the children – legally all undergraduates *were* then children – *in loco parentis*, reassured worried mothers and fathers, visited family homes, organized instructional visits in the vacations, and played an increasing part in securing for those who wished to work at their books the means so to do. Parents, as a rule, demanded no less. As one correspondent wrote to Owen Gwyn, the tutor chosen for his somewhat wayward son should 'keepe him in more awe, [and] hould him closer to his booke, by restraininge his liberty wherof he hath alredy to much tasted'.[99] The best tutors did just that, though such teaching counted as private, and might be charged for accordingly. A system focused on the individual did in fact allow young men at college – men from all backgrounds – to pursue interests suited to their own abilities and inclinations.

Towards the middle of the century, the tutorial system at St John's changes in a way that we still do not quite understand. Until the Civil War, tutorial burdens and rewards are spread quite widely across the Fellowship, but by the mid-1660s some five tutors and the Master are together responsible for over 80 per cent of undergraduates. The tutorship was becoming a way of life for some Fellows, and its rewards figure increasingly in individual finances. This may be principled rationalization, or it may simply be that the College was playing to particular strengths at a particular time. Here, as in many other aspects of seventeenth-century college life, more research is required.[100]

The early seventeenth-century College was full of 'characters'. There was the remarkable Andrew Downes, Regius Professor of Greek, prickly yet erudite, one of the translators of the Authorized Version. Simonds D'Ewes as an undergraduate called upon Downes 'at his house, near the public Schools', and found the great man reading, with his hat on and his feet up on a table. On D'Ewes's arrival Downes 'stirred neither his hat nor his body, only taking me by the hand'. This the earnest young scholar – D'Ewes never really saw the funny side of anything – characterized charitably as 'homely' behaviour.[101] Richard Senhouse, President in the 1620s, and from 1624 bishop of Carlisle, was a north-countryman, from Cumberland, one of those outwardly unambitious men who nevertheless prosper in the world. As Thomas Baker observed, while Senhouse did not seek advancement, he did not refuse it when it was offered. He had, in John Gauden's words, 'an eloquent tongue and an honest heart', which count for something in life, and he was also very fond of fishing.[102] Other

---

[99] Letter from Thomas Edwardes: SJCA, D94.463.

[100] Howard, *Finances*, 87. I am grateful to Malcolm Underwood for sharing with me the findings of his preliminary work on the subject.

[101] [J. H. Marsden], *College Life in the Time of James the First, as Illustrated by an Unpublished Diary of Sir Symonds D'Ewes* (London, 1851), 31. Fuller once wrote of D'Ewes that he preferred 'rust before brightness'. Simonds was the ancestor of John Dewes, the Middlesex and England cricketer, an undergraduate during the twentieth century. John's sons Tim and Jim also studied at St John's in their turn.

[102] *ODNB* (P. E. McCullough); Marsden, *College Life*, 28.

near-contemporary Johnians published the first English treatises on swimming and bee-keeping.[103]

Amid all these youngsters the Master, the only married man in the College, might stand out – or might not. Even in a small society he would preserve a certain remoteness, dining apart from the Fellows on ordinary nights.[104] On the other hand, the Mastership of a Cambridge college in those days came fairly low on the ladders of preferment and ambition. Many Masters were elected young – before the Civil War Owen Gwyn and William Beale, in their forties, were quite mature selections by the standards of the day – and while some lived many years in the Lodge, others were content to move onwards and upwards, without outstaying their welcome. Much depended on the individual. The offer by the bishop of Coventry and Lichfield of the archdeaconry of Shrewsbury to Owen Gwyn, and Gwyn's refusal, give us a glimpse of perceived career structures in the Church at that time. Generally speaking, Heads of Houses were yet to reach the heights of their careers; in social terms they rubbed shoulders with deans and archdeacons rather than with bishops.[105]

Within his own world, however, a college Master exercised great authority. Throughout the seventeenth century, and far beyond, the government of St John's was defined by the Elizabethan statutes, both of St John's, dating from 1580, and of the University, confirmed in 1570. Together, these statutes established the colleges as important, even dominant forces in Cambridge politics. To some extent they merely reflected reality, of course, for colleges were prospering, and, trading on patronage, were the natural focus of influence and power. In part, however, the changes were calculated, deliberately augmenting the authority of the Heads of Houses, men central to the Elizabethan reforms.[106]

The leap of faith involved in choosing an individual to preside over a house had thus become crucial. Masters could make or mar the fortunes of a college, and consequently its standing in the eyes of patrons and parents. Collectively, they could also shape the reputation of their university. With more turning on the outcome, elections were made with care, and were influenced by pressure from all sides. At St John's, the election of a new Master in 1595, following the death of William Whitaker, was far from straightforward. Left to themselves, the Fellows would probably have opted for Henry Alvey, like Whitaker a strong Calvinist and, unlike Whitaker on his election, a Fellow of long standing. Lord Burghley and the queen had, however, no wish to see the University remain under the influence of extreme Protestantism, and indeed many Fellows probably wished to turn away from the tensions exacerbated by Whitaker's scrupulous Calvinism.[107] In the dangerous political and economic climate of the 1590s, moderation and the *via media* were the order of the day. This was the age of Hooker, and Whitgift's Lambeth Articles; Calvinism may have dominated the theology of the Church, but it dominated a Church firmly controlled

---

[103] Everard Digby and Samuel Purchas the younger.

[104] Morgan, *History of the University of Cambridge*, II. 304.

[105] SJCA, D94.497.

[106] Morgan, *History of the University of Cambridge*, II. 78–9; D. Hoyle, *Reformation and Religious Identity in Cambridge, 1590–1644* (Woodbridge, 2007), 18–19.

[107] Ibid., 44–6, 49–50.

by episcopal hierarchies.[108] There were lines to draw. Elizabeth and Burghley insisted that no election should be made before the College was aware of the queen's preference. In a matter of days, St John's was given a broad hint that the Master of Magdalene, Richard Clayton, was the man she considered best fitted for the office. Hints of this type could never be ignored. Alvey was passed over and Clayton, a man of middle-of-the-road Anglican beliefs, was duly elected.[109] Baker testifies with his usual elegance to the manner in which Clayton 'rooted out' the pervasive Puritanism that had so characterized Whitaker's tenure.[110] The times were changing, even though they were not changing very fast.

On Clayton's death, the Fellows made another extremely significant if rather more straightforward election. Owen Gwyn, Master of St John's from 1612, has never quite received his due. Certainly he was no great scholar. Baker – who disliked Gwyn, perhaps on account of his close association with a fellow Welshman, Baker's *bête noire*, John Williams – writes that his name 'adds no lustre to our annals'. Gwyn is reported to have been idle and negligent, conniving in the annexation of fines and leases to favoured Seniors. Yet these accusations at times resemble the routine contemporary denunciation of venality in office.[111] It is significant that Baker, opinionated but ever conscientious, lists alongside Gwyn's faults of 'intrigue and greater ambition' a tendency to be 'much more concerned for the revenues than the government of the college'.[112] Gwyn had served as Senior Bursar and knew how to keep an account, as Baker also, rather sniffily, admits. Centuries later another Bursar, Henry Fraser Howard, pointed out that many of the record sequences housed among the College archives either begin or take on a new energy under Gwyn's control. There are worse legacies. The 'Dividend Book' initially details fines received for the granting and – just as important – the renewal of leases. As the years pass, it details much else besides, becoming in effect a record of the resources channelled into payment of dividends.[113] The Balance Book runs from 1614; the Prizing Book, valuing College accommodation over time, survives from 1627. New regulations were set in place to govern the allocation of leases, the handling of fine money, and the investigation of debts owing to the College. Moreover, Gwyn never neglected assets. In 1617 he and the Seniors established the post of Library Keeper, decreed that it should be held by a scholar, set an appropriate remuneration, and defined, carefully, the duties involved. Initially this was a temporary arrangement while the books remained in the rooms over the Kitchen, but it soon became obvious that

---

[108] P. Lake, *Anglicans and Puritans? Presbyterianism and English Conformist Thought from Whitgift to Hooker* (London, 1988); 'Calvinism and the English Church 1570–1635', in M. Todd (ed.), *Reformation to Revolution: Politics and Religion in Early Modern England* (London, 1995), 179–207.

[109] The election is touched upon in M. H. Curtis, *Oxford and Cambridge in Transition, 1558–1642* (Oxford, 1959), 218–19.

[110] Baker-Mayor, I. 196.

[111] Morgan, *History of the University of Cambridge*, II. 164–6.

[112] Baker-Mayor, I. 198, 199.

[113] The contents of the Dividend Book, as maintained under successive Bursars, are analysed by Howard, *Finances*, 53–6, Appendix VII.

a need had been identified; St John's was never without a Library Keeper of some kind thereafter.[114]

Building on what may have been a still-born initiative at the very end of the sixteenth century, the College admissions register is effectively launched in 1630, when the Order Book records the adoption of a volume in which the name, the parents, the county, the school and the tutor of every new entrant are to be recorded by a person specifically appointed to the task. This 'clerk' was paid for his work by the new members themselves, receiving 'of each of them for his pains, as the head lecturer and deans do, for their admission'.[115] The splendid biographical sequence is maintained to this day. Indeed, the record in the Admissions Register now defines membership of the College. Gwyn's attention to record-keeping went still further. In a gesture towards transparency, it was decreed in April 1627 that 'a Copy written out of all ... decrees [of the Master and Seniors] ... may be kept in the library with the Statutes, that all fellows may know them, and so enable themselves to observe them'.[116] Gestures go only so far, however. Despite the Master's best endeavours, College orders for the seventeenth century remain scattered, with some found in the Admonition Book and others, for the Commonwealth period, lurking incongruously in the Plate Book. True consolidation did not follow until well into the eighteenth century.

To a more charitable eye, Baker's charges of over-familiarity with the Seniors might be regarded as necessary co-existence. Masters were not infrequently men from relatively straitened backgrounds, with fortunes to make and – since they could now marry – with families to provide for, and of course they worked in accordance with the standards of financial propriety prevailing at the time. Howard sets Baker's statements in perspective, pointing out that 'tactical' grants of leases to Master and Fellows, and to others outside College, had been common practice for years.[117] Gwyn certainly benefited from the potentially very dangerous agreement between the Master and Seniors of 1599 which gave the Master a choice of any lease belonging to the College, that lease subsequently forming a part of the Master's maintenance. Accepting an existing custom is, however, rather different from establishing a preferential new arrangement, and Gwyn's successor William Beale in his turn succumbed to temptation and augmented the Master's income.[118] The hundreds of letters surviving from his correspondence provide an impression of industry, and duty, and there can be no doubt that Gwyn had mastered the black arts of networking and congeniality, essential to a Master in any age. He retained the affection of friends and pupils,

---

[114] Orders dated 30 Sept. 1617, in SJCA, C8.1, p. 863.

[115] SJCA, C5.1, fo. 6r, order dated 21 Jan. 1630. There were, though, earlier books in which were recorded 'the admission of fellows and schollers' (C3.1 and 2).

[116] Howard, *Finances*, 56.

[117] Ibid., 57–9. Senior Bursars stick together: Howard is diligent in defending Gwyn against charges of laxity, incompetence and corruption laid by Baker and Mullinger.

[118] Morgan, *History of the University of Cambridge*, II. 293. The Seniors seem to have shared between them the bribes offered by tenants hopeful for renewals. Expedients, as Miller admits, soon became irregularities in the prevailing circumstances (Miller, *Portrait of a College*, 28).

among them Valentine Carey and his own cousin and former tutorial pupil John Williams.

These letters to Gwyn in the College Archives offer a rare insight into the working life of a Jacobean Master.[119] Their significance was long ago highlighted in the *Eagle*, and needs only the briefest rehearsal here. Gwyn, after so many years in Cambridge, had become the embodiment of St John's to many well-connected outsiders. At the same time he was of course beholden to patrons, and increasingly burdened by administrative tasks in Cambridge. The days in which an absentee Master was tolerated, by Fellows and would-be benefactors, were long past. Gwyn received letters from importunate fathers and courtiers, which mixed flattery with open requests for favours. Those favours included the election of sons and protégés to Fellowships, and advantageous renewals of leases to avaricious courtiers or well-connected friends.[120] The flaws and the utility of this system were acknowledged by Robert Booth in 1614, when requesting a Fellowship for one William Marshall: 'I confess it to be true', he wrote to Gwyn, 'that it doth discourage your studentes, to see strawngers preferred before them, and yet I know that upon speciall occasiones and sutes it hath benne often donne, and very commendablye.'[121] 'God', wrote Laurence Stanton, a former Fellow and dean of Lincoln in a 1612 letter to Gwyn, 'hath placed you where you may doe muche good to manie', and he proceeded without scruple to presume upon their 'ancient acquaintance'.[122] John Williams, then contemplating support for the College's new library, sought a favour for his chaplain, giving assurances that whatever might be done for the man, he, Williams, would 'acknowledge [it] as reflecting upon my intercession'.[123] How could Gwyn say no to that?

Nevertheless, he did say no on occasion. Many if not most of these requests were in vain, even when made by powerful court notables such as the duke of Lennox or by the archbishop of Canterbury, George Abbot.[124] Some were decidedly optimistic in their assessment of the Master's powers. In Richard Clayton's time the influential bishop of Lichfield and Coventry Richard Neile, yet another Johnian prelate, lobbied for a Fellowship on behalf of a protégé from Westminster School, Samuel Harding. But Harding never received the prize.[125] Nor did Michael Wandesforde, the subject of a brisk letter from his kinsman the earl of Northumberland in 1620.[126] The vicissitudes of a career at court were not permitted to stand in the way of such requests: Northumberland wrote from his cell in the Tower of London, while the countess of Shrewsbury also penned

---

[119] In classes D94 and D105.

[120] SJCA, D94.15, 205, 206, 285; D105.3, to cite a few early examples among many.

[121] SJCA, D105.131; Scott, 'Notes', *Eagle* xxvii (1905–6), 336.

[122] SLCA, D105.292; Scott, 'Notes', *Eagle* xix (1895–7), 539–40.

[123] Morgan, *History of the University of Cambridge*, II. 105.

[124] See, for example, SJCA, D94.486. The duke was, however, successful in orchestrating the preferment of George Seton, a Scots connection of Lennox, in 1620: SJCA, D94.490; D105.171.

[125] Scott, 'Notes', *Eagle* xxxvi (1914–15), 13–15. As bishop of Lincoln, Neile enjoyed more success when seeking a scholarship for John Rand in October 1616.

[126] Scott, 'Notes', *Eagle* xxxvi (1914–15), 124–5.

a note while a prisoner in the Tower to endorse another candidate for a Fellowship.[127] Pragmatism overrode sentiment in an age of high and unpredictable mortality: Ralph Bunnington wrote in 1618, recording with formal, fatherly regret the death of the spendthrift George before asking whether the lad's Fellowship might pass to one of his younger brothers.[128]

Those who sought things more easily granted were less frequently disappointed. Gwyn's old friend Robert Hill, now rector of a lucrative parish in the City of London, wrote in 1613 asking if the Master of St John's might find a place in College for the son of an old Cambridge acquaintance, Richard Rutter, 'a grave preacher in the high country'. No doubt the reference is to Derbyshire. Richard Rutter junior matriculated in 1614, and took his BA in 1618.[129] Even at this level, though, success was never guaranteed: Ralph Hare, so generous a benefactor to the new Library, asked Gwyn in 1623 for a chorister's place for 'a pore boy named Daynes', but nothing now suggests that the request was successful.[130] Other writers contented themselves with presents, in line with the courtesy of the age, or perhaps in an attempt to store up good will for the future. Henry Tresham's gift of a buck in the summer of 1613 might be seen in this way; bucks were sent to the College as tokens of 'friendship' throughout the seventeenth century.[131]

While there is of course some truth in the charge laid by Miller among many others, that the weight of patronage reduced Fellowships to just another element in 'the proprietory system, a fee simple for the devolution of which a present incumbent might even make his own arrangements', it remains striking that many elected by these apparently unworthy means turned out to be fine scholars.[132] Patronage did not always favour the rich and untalented. Colleges themselves connived in attempts to place deserving young men in Fellowships elsewhere, when their own resources or statutes would not permit an election closer to home. This process was both resented and essential: St John's complained about an attempt to place a man from another college in one of its Fellowships, pointing out the 'great discouragement to our paynefull students, if forreyners and straungers be admytted to their hopes', but the College also willingly provided letters of recommendation for candidates of their own, Samuel Periam for example.[133] As in Periam's case, such efforts were by no means always successful.

Requests, even from the greatest courtiers, might be politely disregarded, but, in theory, direct orders or mandates from the monarch had to be obeyed. Denounced, then as now, as a mechanism that rewarded well-connected nonentities, and certainly increasingly prevalent in early-Stuart England, mandates were by no means so poisonous. They were granted sparingly, even though the

[127] SJCA, D105.75; Scott, 'Notes', *Eagle* xxxvi (1914–15), 143–4.

[128] SJCA, D105.143; Scott, 'Notes', *Eagle* xxvii (1905–6), 319–22.

[129] Scott, 'Notes', *Eagle* xxxvi (1914–15), 20–2.

[130] SJCA, D105.126.

[131] SJCA, D94.116.

[132] Miller, *Portrait of a College*, 34.

[133] Morgan, *History of the University of Cambridge*, II. 368–9.

six or seven nominations a year could seem a lot in the small world of collegiate Cambridge. The currency, moreover, was not devalued; colleges complained at the loss of autonomy, and at the frustration of well-qualified young men in their own ranks whose career paths were blocked, but the Fellows intruded were by and large sound people from other colleges. If the procedures seemed somewhat breathless and frantic in the first decades of the seventeenth century, this reflected the processes of patronage in a royal court besieged by requests for favour, rather than any insidious authoritarian tendency. Nor was the process inevitable. Even when the king seemed set on intruding a man into the Fellowship, he could at times be persuaded to change his mind, or to decide against pressing the matter. In 1606 Ambrose Copinger, a Trinity graduate frustrated in his efforts to secure a Fellowship in his own House, obtained James's mandate for one at St John's. Having only months earlier acceded to another royal demand along the same lines, the College now fought back, seeking Robert Cecil's help, and again arguing that the king's request was unfair on 'young students of good hope brought up in our house'. Copinger ended up with a Fellowship at St Catharine's instead.[134] When Gwyn was elected Master in 1612, Richard Neile seems to have persuaded the monarch against interfering in the process.[135]

Honorary degrees were less contentious, though James I distributed them in typically liberal fashion when he visited the University in 1624. His liberality aroused some resentment, and not simply within the University, but on this occasion the discontent drew on ancient xenophobic prejudice, being directed principally against the foreign envoys and courtiers so honoured. Charles I nominated sixty mandatory degrees during his own visit to Cambridge eight years later, but for all the University's instinctive hostility – particularly manifested towards new Doctors of Divinity, as D'Ewes records – the passing crowd of visiting courtiers, carrying away their doctorates and MAs, hardly burdened the University.[136] Rather, such largesse strengthened all-important connections with courts, at home and overseas. The squalls over the use of mandates at the royal visits of 1624 and 1632 were significant in their rarity. It may be remembered, too, that mandates were sometimes a convenient means of terminating lengthy and expensive internal debates, particularly over the choice of a new Master. Increasingly, royal intervention in Mastership elections was anticipated, and not altogether despised. By avoiding any undue tampering with the University's powers of self-regulation, Charles I retained a broad loyalty within Cambridge, while carrying through a religious revolution that angered and annoyed many senior members. This was also achieved by the cautious, *ad hoc* placement of suitable men, with suitable political and religious views, as the moment allowed.

The Mastership election in 1633 is a case in point. At Gwyn's death, King Charles was in Scotland, and so the President and Seniors duly sent Dr Ambrose 'to give notice to his Maiestie'. This was a financial blow. Ambrose was not inclined to stint in his journey, and his round trip cost the College the

---

[134] Ibid., 408–9.
[135] Ibid., 417–18.
[136] Ibid., 424.

astonishing sum of £40. It was ill luck that matched the death of a Master to a rare venture north of the border by the Stuart monarchy; Charles had not visited Scotland since his accession.[137] He had postponed his coronation in Edinburgh for eight years, in part because of his own reluctance to leave London, in part because of the self-declared poverty of his northern kingdom.[138] The urgency of Ambrose's mission testifies to a pressing problem, and to a split within College. In a struggle between Seniors and Juniors on the Fellowship, the view of the latter prevailed, and Richard Holdsworth, a Puritan prepared (just about) to tolerate Laud's ceremonial reforms, defeated the President, Robert Lane, even though Lane had secured, through Ambrose's prompt action, a letter of recommendation from Charles I. The Vice-Chancellor declined to admit Holdsworth, but could not accept that Lane had won the election. With both sides throwing as much mud as possible, and exhausting their energies and their credit in the process, the Crown was eventually moved to select a compromise candidate. The choice fell on the Master of Jesus, William Beale, a man broadly sympathetic to the Laudian religious reforms then sweeping across England.[139] Beale was formally admitted in February 1634, and the College provided wine and 'sugar cakes' for the reconciliation party held to celebrate his official arrival.[140] Three years later, the admirable Holdsworth, a charismatic man attractive to students of all religious persuasions, became Master of Emmanuel, but it was the University Library that eventually benefited from his excellent collection of over 10,000 books.[141]

By the mid-1630s, these Laudian reforms were having an impact. Significant sums were being spent to repair and decorate the Chapel, and an organ built by Robert Dallam of Westminster was introduced in 1635. The organ must have been an impressive instrument, for it cost £185, about the same as the one Dallam had built for Jesus a year earlier.[142] By 1637 the College had a surpliced choir. Stained glass was reintroduced – in 1635 the Master himself set Robert Tayler to work placing 'some old painted glasse in the great window'.[143] The roof was painted 'in a skie colour and set full of gilt starrs', and the Chapel adorned with sixteen elaborate hangings. Scaffolding, borrowed from Clare Hall and transported down river at College expense, facilitated this task.[144] Brass candlesticks

---

[137] SJCA, SB4.4, fo. 336r.

[138] M. Kishlansky, 'Charles I: a case of mistaken identity', *Past and Present* 189 (2005), 41–80 at p. 70.

[139] J. Twigg, *The University of Cambridge and the English Revolution, 1625–1688* (Woodbridge, 1990), 27; Hoyle, *Reformation and Religious Identity*, 187–8; A. Foster, 'Church policies of the 1630s', in R. P. Cust and A. Hughes (eds.), *Conflict in Early Stuart England: Studies in Religion and Politics, 1603–1642* (Harlow, 1989), 193–223.

[140] SJCA, SB4.4, fo. 362r.

[141] Morgan, *History of the University of Cambridge*, II. 479.

[142] Scott, 'Notes', *Eagle* xxiv (1902–3), 153–5. R. F. Scott detects the hand of Beale in both transactions. Several 'old and uselesse' pieces of plate were sold to contribute towards the cost, though in the end the organ was paid for 'with Mr Bouthes money': SJCA, SB4.5, fo. 58r. In all, the refurbishment of the Chapel cost in excess of £435: Hoyle, *Reformation and Religious Identity*, 186, 213–14.

[143] SJCA, SB4.5, fo. 24r.

[144] SJCA, SB4.5, fo. 49v.

chosen by the Master adorned the Master's and President's stalls,[145] while a 'velvett cushion on the Altar' cost more than £3.[146] In 1638 a bequest from a former Scholar of St John's, Francis Dee, bishop of Peterborough, added to the growing collection of chapel silver, and presented the College with a selection of religious pictures, as well as an altar cloth.[147] Altar rails, statuary, further candlesticks, a new pulpit and a 'dove of glory' costing 25 shillings enhanced the beauty of holiness.[148] Dr Ashton's Chapel, formerly a chamber, 'but now used and adorned as a Chappell', widened the scope for worship.[149] These extravagant expressions of 'near popery yet no popery' encouraged the crypto-Catholic College President, John Price, to embellish services with a touch of individualistic devotion. At the phrase 'therefore with angels', 'he turned to gaze at images of angels', a gesture which did not escape, and which was probably not meant to escape, some of his more reformed colleagues, left fuming at his apparent idolatry. Just as pointedly, Beale did little to curb his enthusiasm.[150]

4.   TEACHING AND COURSES

The teaching available at Cambridge in those days depended to some extent on whether a student sought the qualifications essential to an academic or clerical career, or whether he was set on putting the finishing touches to a well-rounded, gentlemanly education. That distinction was often far from clear: gentlemen were caught up in academic debates and disputes, while would-be clerics acquired a taste for other professions. Rich young men – and not every future academic survived in Cambridge as an indigent sizar – took advantage of the extracurricular skills imparted by dancing- and fencing-masters. Tutors, moreover, prudently catered for both camps, often at one and the same time, mixing in their tutorial groups the generally less wealthy sizars and sub-sizars with the sons of landed families.[151] By long custom, sizars served both the Fellows and the Fellow-Commoners, lighting fires, performing secretarial tasks, or simply running errands, as Thomas Manning did for Simonds D'Ewes. However, waiting at table was a duty that fell on pensioners and scholars as well as sizars, long into the eighteenth century.[152] A Fellow-Commoner traditionally brought his sizar to Cambridge as companion rather than servant, for the well-to-do man brought servants with him as well; D'Ewes did so, at the start of the seventeenth century. Sizars were full members of the community. In the eighteenth

---

[145] SJCA, SB4.5, fo. 49v.

[146] SJCA, SB4.5, fo. 24r.

[147] SJCA, SB4.5, fo. 107r.

[148] T. Cooper, *The Journal of William Dowsing: Iconoclasm in East Anglia during the English Civil War* (Woodbridge, 2001), 176–7.

[149] SJCA, SB4.5, fo. 54v.

[150] Hoyle, *Reformation and Religious Identity*, 214.

[151] The distinction is drawn between nine 'proper' sizars supported originally by an endowment from John Dowman in 1525, who waited on the Master and Seniors, and sub-sizars maintained by other Fellows and by Fellow-Commoners.

[152] R. F. Scott, 'Some aspects of College life in past times', *Eagle* xliii (1923–4), 160–75.

century they had their own gyps and bedmakers, as the diary of Charles Sutton confirms.[153] These pragmatic arrangements were deployed to tide over a promising student of limited means until a scholarship might be obtained, and menial duties recognized rather than defined the status of such men. Sizars were in any case the most numerous rank of undergraduate: Scott calculates that around the turn of the seventeenth century an average of twenty-five sizars were admitted each year, alongside twenty pensioners, and three Fellow-Commoners.[154] The almost equal balance between the rough and ready meritocracy of the sizarship, and the 'purchase' system of places for sons of the wealthy, is striking.

What these undergraduates actually read, studied, and learnt, however, remains all too often obscure. Surviving tutors' manuals and student journals highlight only the individuality of education at Cambridge in the seventeenth century. The formal academic syllabus still rested heavily on rhetoric and logic, on theology, philosophy, and the classics.[155] But it is actually very hard to write of a 'syllabus': the 1570 statutes hardly mention anything so mundane, while teaching played fast and loose with those skimpy guidelines. Strident calls for reform – notably from Bacon in his *Advancement of Learning*, Hobbes in his attack on the dominance of Aristotle, and Milton in his criticism of the emphasis on dialectic – actually sought a codification of new ways that already prevailed in Cambridge.[156] Much was left to the tutors, and tutors have always had their own ideas about what should be imparted to diligent and to not so diligent youth. Joseph Mede of Christ's, for example, deliberately tailored courses to the capacities of individual students: 'when they were able to go alone, he chose rather to set every one his daily Task'.[157] There was an element of cosy conservatism to all this.[158] Study of the classics, philosophy, and logic underpinned the acquisition of sound religious knowledge, and erudition, while an increased attention to rhetoric sharpened a young man's eloquence. John Ray taught botany in Cambridge during the Interregnum, albeit privately, while the Veronese Giovanni Vigani came to lecture in chemistry during the 1680s. His *materia medica* cabinet survives at Queens' College. Newton's finest mathematical works emerged from his life and experience in Cambridge.[159] Bacon's ideas, and the works of Descartes, were mulled over throughout the second half of the century. Mathematics, and the natural sciences, were a coming force. The Cambridge Platonism of Ralph Cudworth, Benjamin Whichcote and Henry

---

[153] Ibid., 163–4.

[154] Ibid., 166.

[155] James Duport's regulations at Magdalene are specific, and strong in their endorsement of Aristotelian principles, see Cunich, *History of Magdalene College*, 148–50.

[156] E. Leedham-Green, *A Concise History of the University of Cambridge* (Cambridge, 1996), 91.

[157] Morgan, *History of the University of Cambridge*, II. 467–8, 511–22; J. Worthington (ed.), *The Works of the Pious and Profoundly Learned Joseph Mede* (London, 1677), p. iv. John Milton was among Mede's pupils. On elite education at the time, see L. Stone (ed.), *The University in Society* (Princeton, 1975), R. O'Day, *Education and Society, 1500–1800: The Social Foundations of Education in Early Modern Britain* (London, 1982), A. Fox, *Oral and Literate Culture in England, 1500–1700* (Oxford, 2001).

[158] Hoyle, *Reformation and Religious Identity*, 14.

[159] Leedham-Green, *Concise History*, 95.

More easily survived the Restoration, and indeed flourished in the later Stuart Church.[160] Despite the rather anarchic foundations, it all made for a stimulating academic environment. Simonds D'Ewes, son of a Suffolk gentleman, sums up the academic life of a well-to-do student, at no point obliged to pursue a rigorous course of study, but nevertheless enthused by the possibilities inherent in a seventeenth-century education:

> Nor was my increase in knowledge small, which I attained by the ear as well as the eye, by being present at public commencements, at Mr Downes his public Greek lectures, and Mr Harbert's public rhetoric lectures in the University; at problems, sophisms, declamations, and other scholastical exercises in our private college; and my often conversation with learned men of other colleges, and the prime young students of our own.[161]

But the bright young gentleman need never face the ordeal of a Cambridge examination. Some, like D'Ewes, laboured hard, while others, like the idle and unscholarly William Cecil, future second earl of Salisbury, frittered away their time in hunting, pining for the excitements of the court. Ultimately, their futures did not turn on the diligence of their studies.[162] For the aspiring cleric, doctor or lawyer, things were different. The degree they sought was still, in essence, a licence to preach, practice or teach. To that end, they had to pass exams. Examinations in Cambridge were, however, notoriously problematic. One deeply ingrained difficulty was the ancient but enduring system of disputations, in which false arguments were advanced, often vigorously, so that they could be proved incorrect. The age was wedded to classical forms of disputation, and to a world-view which emphasised the deployment of thesis and antithesis, the threat posed by subversive inversion.[163] As Steele noted in *The Spectator*, early in the eighteenth century, 'those who have been present at publick Disputes in the University, know that it is usual to maintain Heresies for Argument's sake. I have heard a Man a most impudent socinian for half an hour, who has been an Orthodox Divine all his Life after.'[164] In these circumstances it was all too tempting to argue a little too vigorously, particularly if the 'false' position in fact had a measure of influential support within the Church. And unorthodox views, expressed with panache, might set the educated listener thinking. It is altogether extraordinary that the authors of the Elizabethan statutes, otherwise so obsessed with the establishment and maintenance of order based on hierarchy, should have neglected the disputation, leaving it to their successors to struggle in vain against the turmoil generated by a vigorously contested argument.

---

[160] Ibid., 92.

[161] Quoted in Morgan, *History of the University of Cambridge*, II. 136.

[162] Around 1605, William Cecil wrote plaintively to his father: 'May it please your Lordship to understande that I never was out of love with my booke, knowinge learninge to be a necessary and an excellent qualyty in any gentleman. For my staying heere it must be as longe as youre Lordship thinkes good, but if your Lordship do leave it to mine owne choice I coulde be very well content to goe from hense as soone as might be': *Eagle* xxx (1908–9), 272.

[163] S. Clark, 'Inversion, misrule and the meaning of witchcraft', *Past and Present* 87 (1980), 98–127.

[164] Quoted in Morgan, *History of the University of Cambridge*, II. 128.

Victor Morgan suggests, plausibly, that they left well alone simply because the whole process was so ingrained in the educated mentality.[165]

Written examinations lie in the future, both for the colleges and the University. They may appear first in Trinity, around the turn of the seventeenth century. In St John's, the survival of one or two 'epistles' suggest that candidates for admission were obliged to make their case in writing, and of course in Latin, to a tutor or other senior member of the College, but this is as far as any modern, written scrutiny intrudes.[166]

5.   STAFF

In every period of the College's history, indispensible staff stayed long in post. Richard Green the Cook, for example, ruled his kitchen for more than twenty years at the start of this century. The terms and conditions under which those staff were employed, however, changed a great deal. Through most of the seventeenth century, staff retained on stipends cost the College a tiny amount, about £23 a year, including around £8 for the baker.[167] Just ten or eleven College servants, including the baker, cook and one (unidentified) porter, were given livery coats at College expense in 1623, and the number hardly changes before 1650.[168] Several other regular members of staff, including the miller and his deputies, waiting staff, laundresses and cleaners, were paid wages entered into the accounts as necessary expenses every quarter, and a great deal of work was completed by outside contractors, with gardeners, ditchers, hedgers, plumbers and tilers all brought in as occasion demanded.[169] Along with a vintner, an apothecary was frequently reimbursed after dinners; he provided the spirits, select refreshments beyond the pockets of ordinary men and women before the days of gin.

Building repairs and improvements were almost invariably carried out by contractors. 'Sinks' or soakaways in the Back Lane and in the Cellars were unblocked, wells were scoured, windows reglazed, walls painted, pumps mended, chimneys repointed, and 'spouts' and gutters cleared, lengthened or repositioned by outside labour. Sometimes the materials to be used – lime, bricks, hair, timber, glass, sand, lead and slates – were purchased directly by the College, sometimes indirectly through those same workmen. Projects to maintain the fabric of a large college, set in extensive grounds, had already become a constant burden, the favoured contractors enjoying almost permanent employment while the weather allowed. College waste was cleared by a scavenger who was receiving 10 shillings a quarter in 1612, with one-off, large-scale

---

[165] Ibid., 129.

[166] SJCA, D30.48, fos. 39v, 81v, 82v.

[167] SJCA, SB4.3, fo. 328v; SB4.6, fo. 341v, and BB2 among many other accounts. Moreover, these figures included around £6 for the Master's servants.

[168] SJCA, SB4.4, fo. 99v; BB2.

[169] For the miller, a skilled and vital employee, who received 10s a week in the early seventeenth century, together with a bushel of wheat a month, see SJCA, BB2.

operations charged piecemeal.[170] The regular nature of the more routine tasks is emphasized by the frequency with which work remains unspecified in the accounts. Other seasonal projects follow a similar pattern. Gardeners are constantly cutting back trees, weeding and trimming quickset hedges and organizing the slaughter of innumerable moles. Molecatching was something of an art: professional molecatchers charged 3d a mole in 1612, and the cost rose later, as costs do. The going rate was 4d by 1640, 8d in 1668, and by the 1660s the necessary molecatcher was paid an annual retainer of 8s or 10s.[171] However, the College was again paying only 4d a mole in 1690 – perhaps they were becoming easier to catch, or was there more competition within the profession?[172]

College employees were themselves expected to benefit from the policy of contracting out. Richard Green organized and was reimbursed for expenditure in respect of major feasts, particularly the Port Latin. He received over £8 for food on this occasion in 1614.[173] Feasts were always expensive affairs, for substantial additional sums were spent on wine, the musicians and other charges. Menus, insofar as we can now tell, followed pragmatically on the season and on seasonal migration: fishponds on the site of present-day New Court provided freshwater fish as a winter supplement, while geese were on the menu for large dinners by the 1640s.[174] As any tourist will soon note, the College has a long and (in the colourful detail of the legend) substantially apocryphal association with swans. But there is a factual basis to all these 'Porterhousian' tales: payment was made for two breeding swans and nine young ones 'to stocke the Colledge swan marke' in 1637. Swans for breeding were purchased in 1691 and payments to the Swanyard and for swan maintenance continue for years afterwards.[175]

Detached outside scrutiny of expenditure added to the list of salaries and payments. The Auditor, in the 1620s a Mr Ridding, received a £2 fee, a figure which, rather surprisingly, did not change through the century.[176] Auditors were of course always made comfortable at College expense, with wine, food and tobacco provided, and the Audit Dinner in January was a grand affair. But in most years they only put the seal upon a thorough internal accounting process. Every now and then the records offer a clue to the diligence, or otherwise, of a particular Bursar. Early in the century, individual names were normally entered against the tennis court rentals received each quarter. When in 1626 these were omitted from the final account, the entry has been neatly and pithily annotated 'remember their names'.[177] The heading 'punishments' is never broken down in this way; a decent veil is drawn over a negligible source of income.

---

[170] SJCA, SB4.3, fo. 287v. 'For Carriage of 10 loads of muck at 3d the load and 3 loads of Rubbish at 2d the load' – 3s 6d (fo. 332v).

[171] SJCA, SB4.3, fo. 287v; SB4.5, fo. 155r; SB4.6, fos. 374v, 435v; SB4.8, fo. 48r. Occasionally, the molecatcher took on other pests, such as the polecats caught during the 1680s: SB4.9, fos. 22v, 49r, 99r.

[172] SJCA, SB4.9, fo. 173v.

[173] SJCA, SB4.3, fo. 332r.

[174] SJCA, SB4.5, fo. 207v.

[175] SJCA, SB4.5, fo. 81v.

[176] SJCA, SB4.4, fo. 142v; SB4.9, fo. 289v.

[177] SB4.9, fo. 159r.

Fines for these essentially petty transgressions usually amounted to little more than a few shillings a quarter.

In an age dependent on horse transport there were stables in the Pensionary, and attached to the Master's Lodge. Stables required servicing too; 'horsemeat' had to be provided, stalls had to be cleaned, mounts had to be groomed and shod. Settlement of the smith's bill is recorded in the rentals for many years: John Graves 'the College Smith' is paid for his quarterly work *and* on a job-by-job basis in 1638. Another essential servant, Katherine Frison, the College 'Laundresse' or washerwoman, was paid a far from ungenerous £2 3s 4d per half-year in the 1650s. The washerwoman worked with, and reimbursed, at least one dependent maid, and the figure had increased to a still more healthy £2 18s 4d a quarter by 1673.[178]

Bedmakers worked in the College in D'Ewes's time, and probably long before. Ever the subject of university rumour and gossip, the employment of these women seems to have provoked no open scandal in St John's to rival the goings on reported by Samuel Ward, a Trinity undergraduate in the 1590s.[179] Bedmakers were the respectable manifestation of one fundamental tension in an all-male society, and that tension was predictably exploited by ambitious young Cambridge ladies. Authority just about accepted that undergraduates might be permitted their pleasures, but it was a shocking thing indeed to see the sons of wealthy gentlemen succumb so far as to propose marriage to women of the town. Alliances of that sort were of course made, from time to time, even if the urgent tone of Royal Injunctions from March 1630, on this subject as on so many others, probably reflects the fear of potential developments rather than current reality.[180]

The staff at St John's enjoyed various perquisites, almost all of them reflecting the traditional relations between master and servant. Many were badges of office. The College Porter's gown was clearly a grand affair. Mr Simpson was paid £3 4s 6d for one in the mid-1660s.[181] At the lavish funeral of Richard Clayton in 1612 every servant received a cloak, while six poor men of the town and six poor women were presented with gowns.[182] Perhaps because of long service, and a small regular payroll, pensions were paid to very few people, commonly one or two. However, payments to sick members of staff are occasionally noticed.[183]

---

[178] SJCA, SB4.6, fo. 219v; SB4.8, fo. 169r; SB4.9, fo. 221v.

[179] Morgan, *History of the University of Cambridge*, II. 318.

[180] Ibid., 319.

[181] SJCA, SB4.6, fo. 463v.

[182] Baker-Mayor, I. 197.

[183] For example, to one Henshaw, a gardening contractor and labourer, in the 1680s: SJCA, SB4.9, fo. 124r. Eventually, a payment was made to his son to bury him (fo. 148r).

6. COLLEGE LIFE

Early in the seventeenth century, at the peak of the Jacobean enthusiasm for a university education, the University society was around 3,000 strong, divided two to one between undergraduates and senior members.[184] This was a very large proportion of the town's population, which has been estimated – perhaps slightly *over*estimated – at 11,000 in the middle of the century.[185] Mirroring a familiar pattern noted in nearly every early modern town, the University's population was constantly refreshed by migration. Matriculations across Cambridge totalled 509 in 1619; setting aside abnormal peaks in 1631 and 1667 following years when University entries had been limited by outbreaks of plague, this figure was not surpassed until the mid-1860s.[186]

In contrast to the earliest days of the College, students admitted during the seventeenth century came from every social class. Over the hundred years, Cambridge witnessed an influx of wealthier students to balance the numbers of boys from less affluent backgrounds.[187] That trend is particularly clear in richer colleges such as St John's. Undergraduate society developed into a mix of the able 'career' scholars and the young men of means, completing their education. The Admissions Registers, where the sons of druggists, goldsmiths, yeomen, shoemakers, curates, butchers, husbandmen, stonemasons, maltsters, ostlers and tailors rub shoulders with the heirs to great estates, only hint at the sheer variety of human circumstance now encountered within the College.[188] Occasionally, as we have seen, the two spheres mixed, especially when clever tutors dovetailed needs and ambitions, but ambitions and prospects were usually quite different. Building on its excellent court connections, fostered by the Cecils and Thomas Howard, St John's remained attractive to the nobility and higher gentry. Men like the future tenth earl of Northumberland, Algernon Percy, the future Lord Deputy in Ireland, Thomas Wentworth, the future Viscount Falkland, Lucius Carey, and the future Parliamentarian general Thomas Lord Fairfax all came and went, bringing their servants and companions, and taking up the most prestigious rooms as Fellow-Commoners.[189]

Even for these privileged young men, undergraduate life was no idyll. The typical seventeenth-century winter, characterizing the 'little ice-age' that gripped northern Europe for 200 years, was bitterly cold, and rooms in the

---

[184] Morgan, *History of the University of Cambridge*, II. 221–2. This compares with a rather lower figure of 2,100 for contemporary Oxford (Tyacke), but the parameters may not be exactly the same.

[185] Ibid., II. 247–8, gives Cambridge's non-University population as 7,750 in the 1620s, and 8,000 at the time of the Hearth Tax census in 1674. It had risen sharply in the late Elizabethan and Jacobean period, from a figure of just over 2,000 at the Ecclesiastical Census of 1563.

[186] Leedham-Green, *Concise History*, 69.

[187] The extensive literature on the social composition of early modern Cambridge is summarized in Hoyle, *Reformation and Religious Identity*, 13–14.

[188] J. E. B. Mayor, *Admissions to the College of St John the Evangelist in the University of Cambridge*, ed. R. F. Scott, 4 parts in 3 vols. (Cambridge, 1882–1931).

[189] For evidence of residence before the days of reliable registers see Scott, 'Notes', *Eagle* xxxvi (1914–15), 117–52.

Labyrinth, even in the main Courts, were seldom easy to heat. Coal fires warmed the College – just as they did until the 1940s – and the accounts repeatedly refer to 'seacoal', brought from Newcastle down the east coast of England and up the Ouse river network. Oxford, further from easily navigable water, was unable to benefit from coal to the same degree.[190] However, an analysis of charges shows that 'coal' in this period still sometimes refers to another, more ancient fuel. The cost of maintaining fires in the College during 1613 amounted to just under £120. Of this, £53 was spent on charcoal, just over £50 on seacoal, £13 on sedge and the balance on 'turves'.[191] The money was recouped directly from those who benefited, the Fellows, Scholars and students, and, as with the wholesale purchase and resale of fish to supplement winter diets, the intention seems to have been to break even.[192] Benefactors from time to time took pity on the freezing scholar, and paid for fires in winter. From the 1580s Lady Burghley's fires warmed the College Hall from November to February.

In those cold winters, snow and slush had to be cleared, sometimes laboriously and quite expensively, from the gutters.[193] Other environmental perils were less predictable, if rather more threatening. St John's was never immune to flooding; the Cam was too close for comfort. Flood-water seriously damaged the contents of the College cellars in 1615 and 1617.[194] The river again took its toll during the wretched winter of 1674 – more than 423 cartloads of earth were brought in to raise the banks that year – and yet again in 1686.[195] Gales also tested the buildings and planted gardens. 'Great winds' in the 1640s swept away many slates in Second Court, damaged the leads and the new oriel window in the Library, toppled chimneystacks, and necessitated extensive repairs.[196]

In summer, plague or the threat of plague, combined with the desirability of country visits in the drier months when roads were in better repair, confirmed the development of a Long Vacation, an 'intermission and a time of breathing', between Commencement in July and the autumnal reassembly marked by Stourbridge Fair.[197] Plague was a real threat, as the savage outbreak of 1630 illustrates, but so too were a host of other contagious and infectious diseases that made towns unhealthy places in early modern England. Smallpox, influenza, as in the dreadful epidemic of 1556–8, the sweating sickness and typhoid fever all visited, time and again.

Other ever-present threats seem to pass the College by. In a city of smouldering hearths and smoky chimneys St John's somehow avoided serious fire damage. The few documented conflagrations were predictably confined to the

---

[190] See J. Hatcher, *History of the British Coal Industry,* I. *Before 1700* (Oxford, 1993).

[191] SJCA, SB4.3, fo. 311v. There are references to turf cupboards and stores in the College Prizing Books (e.g. SJCA, C12.2, p. 158).

[192] E.g. SJCA, SB4.4, fo. 342v, 343r; SB4.5, fos. 158v, 159r.

[193] SJCA, SB4.8, fo. 191r.

[194] See SJCA, SB4.3, fos. 355r, 398v. A 'sellar' is also mentioned in the 1620s (SB4.4, fo. 193v). Reference is made to the 'Master's sellar' during the 1630s (e.g., SB4.5, fo. 79r).

[195] SJCA, SB4.8, fo. 191r; SB4.9, fo. 99r.

[196] SJCA, SB4.5, fos. 341r, 369r, 370r, 429v.

[197] Morgan, *History of the University of Cambridge,* II. 223–4.

kitchens and bakehouse, or at worst to adjacent buildings. They did not cause any widespread damage.[198]

The Prizing Books, maintained from 1606, reveal much about the layout of the Courts.[199] One can walk in the mind's eye from room to room, up stairs and along corridors, peering into coal stores, folding back chamber doors, brushing aside hangings – draft excluders – of every colour and quality. Prizing Books record rooms at moments of transition, when they passed from one resident Fellow to another, and so they do not detail personal items and adornments. Rather, they record basic fabric and fixtures: casements, glass windows, framed and unframed desks and shelves, right down to locks and hinges. Even shelving had its value, a value that 'abates' over time at standardized rates.[200] The books reveal an occasional curiosity, for example the 'deathes head' in the window of the 'lower outward chamber' of the President's lodgings in Second Court, 'nexte to the tower on the northe side'. Though the Prizing Books still illustrate traditional layouts, they also point to a gradual drift away from the particularly crowded and intimate arrangements of the sixteenth-century First Court, in which tutors lived and slept alongside their students, deploying truckle beds, making use of attic rooms called 'excelses', partitioning off study spaces, and controlling access to the second floor chambers through internal staircases. Here is an intimacy outlined by Thomas Nashe in his much-quoted *To the Gentlemen Students* (1589), where he describes how St John's had 'more candles light in it, everie Winter Morning before fowre of the clocke than the fowre of clocke bell gave stroakes'.[201] The new century brought with it some new ways. Second Court preserved the principle that those Fellows who were allocated the first-floor chambers still enjoyed the second-floor chamber above, but now the stairs were public, even though at least one Fellow, attached to the old ways, sought and secured permission to erect a private staircase to his upper rooms.[202]

At the same time, the growing numbers of young gentlemen and aristocrats beating a path to the College's door led to greater expectations, and higher payments to achieve such expectations. The earl of Arundel requested five chambers to accommodate his two sons and their respective entourages, adding, lest the wrong impression were given, that further servants would lodge in the town. Arundel got his rooms, at a price. A Fellow-Commoner around the year 1600 required over £60 a year for his maintenance, excluding the costs of clothes,

---

[198] For instance, see SJCA, SB4.4, fo. 118r; SB4.5, fo. 342v; SB4.9, fos. 99v, 123r. One in the 1650s occurred over the President's rooms: SB 4.6, fo. 251v.

[199] There are earlier records, one or two from the sixteenth century, but the earliest surviving prizing book records that 'another appoyntment was made by the Maister and Seniors for the prisinge of all chambers by the 2 Bursers and the 2 Deanes or there Deputies Decemb. 8. 1606 both in the upper and lower courte': SJCA, C12.1, p. 5.

[200] SJCA, C12.1, p. 9. The system was open to abuse and generated occasional bitterness, as some Fellows claimed that they had carried out unrecognised repairs and improvements, while others insisted that colleagues had shirked their obligations (e.g. C12.2, p. 78).

[201] Quoted in many places, e.g. Torry, *Founders and Benefactors*, 37.

[202] Ibid., 48–9.

furniture and bedding.[203] Algernon Percy came with his servants in 1615, before his thirteenth birthday – his father languished in the Tower of London after crossing King James at the time of Gunpowder Plot, but that setback merely sharpened the earl of Northumberland's ambitions for his son. He particularly asked Gwyn to 'bestow … a carefull eye' on the young man.[204]

The names of the great and good inevitably find their way into the record, yet until the introduction of a comprehensive Admissions Register in 1631, there is no certain means of identifying every Johnian. Tradition, or a casual reference long after the event, can often be the only clue to membership of the College. Given his father's status, it is astonishing that evidence for Robert Cecil's stay at St John's in the 1580s is so meagre, though he expressed later in life a personal affection for the College that surely goes beyond Lord Burghley's long patronage. Thomas Hobbes, an Oxford man, accompanied his patron William Cavendish to St John's, and was incorporated into the BA degree in 1608. And what of Ben Jonson? Thomas Fuller in his *Worthies* asserts unambiguously that Jonson was 'statutably admitted' to the College, presumably in the late 1580s, though the archival evidence is now inconclusive.[205] In 1629 John Williams urged the treasurer of Westminster Abbey to give Jonson £5, when the playwright was old and sick.[206] Perhaps the extended College family was looking after its own.[207]

The usual eye was kept by Authority in all its forms, from the king – James I took a spasmodic if careful interest in the well-being, discipline and order of members of the University – to the coercive agents of the University and colleges. On the account for 1602–3 a small sum is recorded for 'a paper booke to write in the goeinge out and comeing home of fellowes and scholers', surely an exeat book familiar to generations of undergraduates.[208] 'Coming home' is a telling phrase here, for the College specifically set out to be a 'home' for its young people. Homes, though, are governed by rules, some formal, some informal, but together attempting to guide adolescents along sober, sensible paths. In an age when fathers' advices to their sons commanded wide circulation – King James, Burghley, Northumberland, and Sir Walter Ralegh all set pen to paper with this end in view – College authorities strove to do likewise. Richard Holdsworth, for example, set out forthright 'Directions' for the instruction of youth, guidelines which took root in Emmanuel after he became Master there in 1637. Holdsworth's advice focused on moderation: make good use of your evenings, he wrote, and do not get up too early, sound counsel in a Cambridge winter. He allocates subjects to be studied in the morning – logic and philosophy, the shadow of Aristotle still dominant – and in the afternoon – poetry, history, and classical oratory.[209] Holdsworth is modelling the temperate all-rounder, a figure

---

[203] Miller, *Portrait of a College*, 35.

[204] SJCA, D105.55.

[205] J. B. Mullinger, 'Was Ben Jonson ever a member of our College?', *Eagle* xxv (1903–4), 302–5; E. Glasgow, 'Ben Jonson and St John's', *Eagle* lxxi, no. 295 (1987), 66–70.

[206] H. C. Beeching, 'Was Ben Jonson a Johnian?', *Eagle* xxvi (1904–5), 357–8.

[207] Robert Lane's letter to Gwyn *c.* 1615 implies a collegiate intimacy: SJCA, D105.28; *Eagle* xvi (1889–91), 237.

[208] SJCA, SB4.3, fo. 72v.

[209] Morgan, *History of the University of Cambridge*, II. 515.

recognizable, at least as an ideal, throughout the Johnian centuries. Of course, the ideal that he laid down is not necessarily reflected in the reality of manuscript notes and reading lists kept by students, both conscientious and cavalier. But at least it offered a counsel of perfection.

The 'real' University was of course full of human frailty. No society dominated by young men can ever be wholly cool and unemotional. There were numerous spats, inside the College and also between the undergraduates from different Houses, boisterous expressions of the subversive manliness analysed by Dr Alexandra Shepard and others.[210] The winter of 1601–2, for example, was warmed by a festering feud between St John's and Trinity. Causes of this ill feeling may have grown out of the boundary dispute over Garret Hostel Green, but the two sides do not seem to have required much provocation. Records of the Vice-Chancellor's Court detail the usual sordid consequences, of how Gonell of Trinity, 'seeinge a ston lyeinge at or against Trinitye colledge gates; did bringe yt to St Johns Colledge gate, and gave yt to one to be throwen, but cannot tell to whome he gave yt'. Windows were broken, challenges made at sword-point through the College gates, and a mob of twenty Trinity men 'did beate Mr Binlesse into St Johns'. This 'hurlye burley', and other cases of stone-throwing and glass-breaking, came to court because repairing an Elizabethan window was far from cheap.[211] Following the attentions of Trinity 'scholars' in 1602, it cost St John's more than 26 shillings to replace glass in the Library, a prominent and vulnerable range looking out over the public street.[212]

Just as one can exaggerate the degree of hostility that existed between 'town' and 'gown' in the seventeenth century, squabbles with Trinity have an air of the timeless. They grow more interesting on the rare occasions when Fellows, and even Masters, became involved, though the Masters at least limited themselves to more dignified exchanges of letters. In the spring of 1616, for example, John Richardson, Master of Trinity, issued a gentlemanly rebuke to Gwyn for his failure to control rowdy undergraduates intent on carrying war to the enemy's courts and grounds. He would not, he declared, compromise their own friendship, no, not 'for a thousande boyes quarrels, and yet I know that boyes may begin a quarrel which at length will end amongst men of greater place'.[213]

Despite assurances given to anxious parents that the boys were tucked up safe in bed, no college was ever a fortress. 'Night gaddinge' was a perennial problem. Too many colleges were adjudged negligent in failing to close their gates of an evening, or else in closing them far too late.[214] In any case, it is clear that many students, either through choice or economic necessity, lived outside

---

[210] Ibid., 252; A. Shepard, *Meanings of Manhood in Early Modern England* (Oxford, 2003); 'Contesting communities? "Town" and "Gown" in Cambridge, *c.* 1560–1640', in Shepard and P. Withington (eds.), *Communities in Early Modern England: Networks, place, rhetoric* (Manchester, 2000), 216–34.

[211] A. H. Nelson (ed.), *Records of Early English Drama, Cambridge* (Toronto, 1989), I. 385–90. See also pp. 425 *et seq.*, another contretemps between the two Colleges in 1611.

[212] SJCA, SB4.3, fo. 53r.

[213] SJCA, D105.276; Scott, 'Notes', *Eagle* xvi. 525.

[214] Morgan, *History of the University of Cambridge*, II. 111.

college, adding no doubt to tensions with the citizens of Cambridge, but also breaking down barriers, and helping to foster an underlying unity of purpose which, as Shepard shows, can easily be overlooked.

Alarmed by rising numbers, new sins, and the boundless scope of their collective imagination, the University authorities could and did legislate against such licence. William, son of Robert Goffe was barred by the Proctors from proceeding to his degree on account of his bad behaviour, although Robert loyally suspected that the young man's crimes had been blown up out of proportion, that they were 'but juvenilia delicta', that it was not difficult 'to finde a staffe to beate a dogg, especially of such as will seeke a knott in a rush'. Here, clearly, was a father who knew his son.[215]

More ingenious students came up with more sophisticated entertainment. Reacting against the legislation of the Restoration period designed to enforce conformity in the Anglican Church, Lewis Maidwell, admitted as a sizar in 1668, committed treason, counterfeiting the signatures of both King Charles II and his Secretary of State, Lord Arlington, in an elaborate scheme to humiliate an unpopular informer against Nonconformists. Happily, the Master, Francis Turner, managed to mitigate the offence, insisting that Maidwell had no 'malicious designe', that it was 'pure roguery'. The lad, he said, came from a good school, and had 'thought this but a Westminster trick, not consideringe the consequence'.[216]

Music and drama had their place in College life. When we read about it, a good deal of the music was public and celebratory. In the 1590s musicians were rewarded on 'St John's Day', in the depths of December, and at successive celebrations to mark, early in May, the feast of St John *ante portam Latinam*.[217] When the College gathered round an early spring bonfire to mark the peaceful succession of James I, the musicians played then too.[218] Trumpeters were also employed and rewarded. At the visit of the Count Palatine and Prince Charles in March 1613, alongside the usual 'wyne cakes and sugar' laid on for distinguished guests, college trumpeters stood 'uppon the top of their towre' and 'began to sownde' as soon as the visitors came in sight.[219] The next day, during their formal visit to the College, the princes were dogged by trumpeters, who popped up over the Great Gate and again on top of the Shrewsbury Tower.[220]

Plays in colleges across Cambridge were by no means uncommon, and by no means inexpensive. In 1605 St John's paid £30, 'layde out for a Comedie'.[221] Authority could never quite make up its mind about drama. Theatre had its place as an educational tool, so long as the older tongues still prevailed. Plays were laid on during the magnificent 'official visits' as a means of displaying wit and literacy as well as entertaining guests. *Aemilia*, a 'latine Comedy' written

---

[215] SJCA, D105.140.
[216] Scott, 'Notes', *Eagle* xxix (1907–8), 276.
[217] SJCA, SB4.2, fo. 449; Nelson, *Records of Cambridge Drama*, I. 358.
[218] Nelson, *Records of Cambridge Drama*, I. 391.
[219] SJCA, SB4.3, fo. 264v; Nelson, *Records of Cambridge Drama*, I. 505.
[220] Nelson, *Records of Cambridge Drama*, I. 509.
[221] Ibid., I. 401.

by the Johnian Thomas Cecil and performed by Johnian actors, was staged before 2,000 people in the Hall of Trinity College during the king's visit in March 1615, and Latin plays performed in Hall at St John's seem to have been something of a Christmas fixture as late as the 1610s.[222] Roger Ascham recalled the Hall decorated for plays at Christmas. Robert Snowden, bishop of Carlisle, an undergraduate at Christ's during the 1580s, recommended his eldest son to Owen Gwyn, not only for his 'ingenious and studious aptnes to any part of book-learning' but also for his 'skill in vocall and instrumentall musicke, and towardlines to act a part in Comedies or Tragedies, in which kinde of scholarly exercises, your most famous Colledge excelled all others in my time'.[223] Poor Snowden had been unsuccessful in placing his son at Trinity, and he does not stint the flattery, but the Johnian welcome for an all-rounder is taken as read.

The University did not, however, look so kindly on performances in vulgar modern tongues, and they positively frowned on the vernacular. There was often good reason for alarm; dramatic wit could carry a sharp edge. The notorious performance of *Club Law* at Clare Hall, towards the end of the sixteenth century, took for its target senior members of the town corporation, while proposals to stage Jonson's *Ignoramus* before the king in 1615 led to protests from outraged London lawyers.[224] In 1623 the ambassadors from Catholic Spain and from Spanish Flanders, while being entertained and lodged at Trinity College, were warned off attending an Ash Wednesday play in the College, because it consisted principally of debates between a Jesuit and a Puritan.[225] No direct evidence, however, suggests that the theatrical offerings of St John's attracted notoriety on this scale.

Driven on by periodical and generally ineffective programmes of moral reform instigated by the Privy Council, the University was always worried by the scurrility in plays and entertainments, and by their potential to 'withdraw schollers from their learninge'.[226] Sometimes the trouble started even before the performance, as when Trinity turned away 'divers northern tuffe laddes' from St John's, insisting that its hall was already full. Needless to say, these 'tuffe laddes' did not leave quietly.[227] The 'grosse and rude disorder of haukinge, and humminge at Comodyes and disputacions' was denounced by the Heads of Houses in the 1620s, without perceptible effect.[228] At plays if not at disputations, a response from the audience was, of course, expected, and it was possible to control that response only so far. On occasion, particularly when an outbreak

[222] CUL, Add. MS 2677, art. 1, fo. 3; Nelson, *Records of Cambridge Drama*, II. 928. The Jacobean letter-writer John Chamberlain thought little of *Aemilia*, finding it 'drie', though 'larded with pretty shewes at the beginning and end' (*Letters of Chamberlain*, I. 587).

[223] SJCA, D105.18, letter dated 2 May 1620.

[224] Nelson, *Records of Cambridge Drama*, I. 377–8, 382. *Club Law* was, however, printed from a manuscript in St John's College Library (S.62) by G. C. Moore Smith as *Club Law: A Comedy* (Cambridge, 1907).

[225] Nelson, *Records of Cambridge Drama*, I. 587–8. All this fuss did not stop the king seeing, and enjoying, the play a few days later.

[226] PRO, SP 38/8, docquet, 4 Mar. 1605.

[227] Morgan, *History of the University of Cambridge*, II. 39.

[228] Nelson, *Records of Cambridge Drama*, I. 586.

of plague gave them ready cause, the Privy Council tried to take the problem in hand. From the list of what is banned one gains some insight into the leisure pursuits, games and pastimes of four centuries past: 'Bull-bayting, Beare-bayting, common Plaies, Publique shewes, Enterludes, Comodies & tragedies in the English Tongue games at loggetes, & nyneholes & all other sportes and games.'[229] Football was likewise forbidden as a 'hurtfull and unscholarlike exercise' in the 1590s, and the adjectives were accurate enough. Shrove Tuesday football, a traditional, disorganized, sometimes lethal mass-participation event, long endured in the country calendar. There is no sign of organized cricket yet, but the sudden appearance of records referring to matches in Cambridge at the start of the eighteenth century, together with evidence from other parts of England, suggest that some forerunners of the game were common much earlier.[230] The tennis court, on the west bank of the river north of the kitchen bridge, cost the College a little over £28 in 1602–3, as part of ongoing building work.[231] In the account for 1606–7 there is a charge for fifty-five 'heads of willow to make the hedge by the Tennys Court', a hedge well established by the time of David Loggan's prints. The willows were carried up from Trumpington, where they still grow on the flat meadows.[232] Those who used the court (and it does seem to have been a perk for the wealthier student) paid a quarterly fee of around 5s.[233] As Loggan shows clearly at the end of the century, there was also a bowling green on what is now the Fellows' Garden, catering for a less expensive, less socially prestigious, but certainly a far more popular seventeenth-century pastime. When you look for it, bowling is everywhere in the contemporary record.

The injunctions and bans stretched further, following every malignant shift of fashion, whether imagined or real. One decree issued by the Vice-Chancellor and other Heads of Houses in February 1607 fulminates against both drinking and that new, but increasingly popular custom, smoking. 'Excessive drinkinges fowle drunkenness, & taking Tobacco, in Taverns, & shoppes too commonly & immodestly frequented' are all, rather quaintly, gathered together as vices noted only recently among the youth of Cambridge, and, of course, 'not heard of in former better times'.[234] So far as one can tell from these periodic crackdowns, the brothels on the south-eastern edge of Cambridge never lacked custom, while enterprising showmen also saw potential in a ready audience of gullible young men. John Adamson, who attempted to stage an 'Olympic Games' on the Gog Magog Hills in 1619, tempted his clientele with 'horseraces, bull bayting, beare bayting, Loggattes, ninehoales, ryflinge, dicinge', but was warned off by the City authorities determined on propriety – early modern governments were unnerved by large crowds, where high spirits and disorder might lead to serious disturbances. Adamson was not the first to suffer such frustration. An earlier attempt to stage games on the evidently lawless Gogs, back

---

[229] CUA, Lett. 11a.A.8.a; Nelson, *Records of Cambridge Drama*, I. 395.

[230] W. Sugg, *A Tradition Unshared: A History of Cambridge Town and County Cricket, 1700–1890* (Cambridge, 2002–10).

[231] SJCA, SB4.3, fo. 72r.

[232] SJCA, SB4.3, fos. 175r–v.

[233] SJCA, SB4.3, fo. 300r. The fee seems to have varied.

[234] CUA, CUR 44.1 (Art. 145).

in 1580, had likewise been banned by the Vice-Chancellor and the local grandee Roger, Lord North, and other prohibitions had followed in the intervening years.[235] However, the authorities were well aware that less ambitious projects and one-off events were almost impossible to control.[236] As a rule, the louder the protest and the sharper the legislation, the more remote the prospect of enforcement.

Specifically Johnian crimes tended to be rather prosaic, even timeless. Men were occasionally sent down, permanently or temporarily, for repeatedly flouting authority, while first offenders admitted their fault publicly in a book kept for the purpose. There are few surprises on the list of offences: too much drink, scaling the College walls to frequent the town and 'aedium infamium' (houses of ill repute) late at night, fornication, keeping unsuitable company, cheeking the Dean, missing Chapel once or twice too often, the occasional act of violence and, when precision fails, 'furta notabilia' (significant theft) or 'a certaine disorderly sordid act unworthy of a scholler'. Records of expulsions were noted by Master and deans, and by the Seniors too on earlier occasions. The College being ready to forgive, and reluctant to forego fees, temporary rustications were often accompanied by the possibility of a return should evidence be submitted to show that the young man had mended his ways.[237]

All was not excess and riot. There were many 'seemly' customs observed across the University, among them the more or less compulsory 'cattechizing in Colledges betwixt the hours of three and fowre on Sundaies and holy daies', enthusiastically endorsed by James I.[238] Most members of the College knew how to enjoy themselves without descending to unsuitable behaviour. A special dinner was held on Fellows' Election Day and at the Scholars' Election. Wine in the Hall on Christmas Day seems a modest enough indulgence in 1627, especially when the bill was lower than that for wine two nights later, on the Feast of St John.[239] There was indeed a tradition of hospitality, of 'wine in Hall for strangers'.[240] Occasionally the boat was well and truly pushed out. When the Prince Palatine and Prince Charles visited the College, the costs of the banquet laid on in their honour amounted to over £131. £35 levied on bachelors at commencement was credited to this charge, with the balance paid from 'fyne monye'.[241] The Warden and Fellows of Merton College, owners of an adjacent estate on the Backs eventually purchased by St John's over 300 years later, were entertained on an altogether more modest scale in 1622, treated to 'wine and cakes' in the Gallery.[242] When Prince Charles returned safely – and providentially without success, so far as the Protestant majority in England were concerned – from his impulsive attempt to win the hand of the Infanta of Spain in

---

[235] Morgan, *History of the University of Cambridge*, II. 116.

[236] CUA, VCCt.I.9, fos. 211v–212; see also Nelson, *Records of Cambridge Drama*, I. 570–1.

[237] A flavour of seventeenth-century crimes and misdemeanours can be found in the punishments and confessions recorded in SJCA, C5.1, quote at fo. 194v.

[238] Scott, 'Notes', *Eagle* xxxii (1910–11), 31.

[239] SJCA, SB4.4, fo. 198r.

[240] SJCA, SB4.4, fo. 291r.

[241] SJCA, SB4.3, fo. 312v.

[242] SJCA, SB4.4, fo. 77r.

1623, the Fellows celebrated with a special exceeding night,[243] and, as the tit-for-tat games of dynastic politics were played out on a European stage, there were decorous entertainments during the visit of James I and the French Ambassador to conclude the betrothal of Charles to Henrietta Maria in 1624, an event commemorated by a window roundel in what is now the Combination Room. That eminent Johnian Thomas Wentworth, then Lord Deputy in Ireland and Lord President of the North, and later earl of Strafford, was entertained with due style in 1636.[244]

The ceremonial of College, University and nation was also marked with appropriate decorum. Bonfires on 5 November seem to have been relatively straightforward commemorations of a still recent terror, a formal contemplation of the What Might Have Been.[245] St John's celebrated the deliverance of the state from Gunpowder Treason with special dinners throughout the century.[246] The nineteenth-century summary of Simonds D'Ewes's lost diary, which has fallen under some suspicion as a historical source, includes a splendid account of Port Latin festivities during the late 1610s, utterly convincing in its detail:

> Before our good cheer we had an excellent clerum at St Mary's, preached by my good friend Mr Micklethwaite, of Sidney College. And after the feast in Hall was ended, all the fellow-commoners and bachelors of the house, according to their annuary custom, went down the river to a pretty green near Chesterton, accompanied by a band of loud music; and having busied ourselves awhile with honest recreations, we returned to supper.[247]

Any picture of seventeenth-century college life is, of course, based on a myriad individual experiences: one man's St John's has always been different to another's. On the one hand the College turned out public servants like Strafford, and the tenth earl of Northumberland, King Charles's Lord Admiral, but a prominent, uncomfortable supporter of Parliament in the First Civil War. Here were men who lived, and in Wentworth's case died, in the public eye. So too did the poet and diplomat Matthew Prior, one of the driving forces behind the Treaty of Utrecht in 1713. Prior was the only surviving child of a London joiner, and after the father's early death his family fell upon difficult times. Not yet in his teens, Prior went to work in his uncle's Westminster pub, the Rhenish tavern on Channel Row, and it was there that his future patron the earl of

---

[243] SJCA, SB4.4, fo. 100r.

[244] SJCA, SB4.5, fo. 54v.

[245] St John's accounts show 4d spent on 'the booke of thankesgeving after the deliverance from the treason against the Parliament house' (SJCA, SB4.3, fo. 117v), and wine was still being served in Hall to mark 'Powder Treason Day' on the account for 1648 (SB4.5, fo. 371r). On Gunpowder commemoration see J. Sharpe, *Remember Remember the Fifth of November: Guy Fawkes and the Gunpowder Plot* (London, 2005).

[246] See, for example, SJCA, SB4.8, fo. 238r.

[247] [Marsden], *College Life*, 62. In a letter of 1885, pasted into the College copy of his book (Aa.2.16) Marsden claimed to have discovered the diary 'many years ago in an old library in Colchester Castle', but admitted that it was 'now missing'. The internal evidence, however, does not suggest a forgery. Music on Port Latin Day was still a fixture in the calendar after the Restoration, when we also find in the accounts a charge for 'Herbs in the Hall': SJCA, SB4.8, fo. 72r.

Dorset first met him, reading Horace behind the bar. Duly impressed, Dorset sponsored his schooling, and Prior eventually came to St John's in 1683 as the holder of one of the generous scholarships provided by the duchess of Somerset. Then there were some (literally) sober scholars, the almost teetotal John Smith, who devoted a great part of his life to the study of the Venerable Bede, and the even more abstemious Joseph Sparke, 'mad a quarter of a year together in every year', who in the early eighteenth century traced out the history of the see of Peterborough.[248] At the same time the College took in the unambitious sons of clever men – Thomas Daffy was given his education in the 1660s thanks to his father's invention and his brother's marketing of an extraordinarily popular 'elixir salutis' – and nurtured the gentle recluse Henry Welby, who spent the last forty years of his life in beneficent solitude, immured voluntarily within the walls of his Grub Street home.[249]

7.   WORLDS TURNED UPSIDE DOWN

When a balance of forces matched the incompetence of a king against the truculence of a faction in Parliament and led England to war in the late summer of 1642, the Cambridge colleges, full of ambitious men who owed their positions and their future prospects to connections in a royal court, found themselves isolated within hostile territory. The eastern counties, spiritually Puritan, particularly influenced by religious reform on the Continent, and dominated by magnates inclining towards parliament, gradually fell under the control of the London administration, while King Charles set up his court in Oxford. Charles, nevertheless, counted on his friends, and in June 1642 demanded money from loyal Cambridge colleges in order to finance his impending war effort. According to Thomas Baker, St John's contributed over £150. The College received a receipt for the money,[250] and the College Balance Book records that this sum was removed on 2 July from 'the bagg of my Lord of Lincolnes mony' in the Treasury'.[251]

While Oxford offered perhaps £6,000, the returns from Cambridge were meagre, and based on individual college initiatives rather than any concerted response by the University. Nevertheless the king, recognizing for once the geopolitical realities facing Cambridge and also keen to extract further gifts, declared himself pleased with the response of both universities, while reminding colleges again in July that it might be wise to 'deposit their plate into our

---

[248] D. C. Douglas, *English Scholars, 1660–1730* (London, 1951), 62–3, 175–6. Smith, a Westmorland man, was originally destined for the University of Glasgow. However, on the day he was to set out for the north, it rained so heavily that his father declined to let him leave, and started to have second thoughts. Young John came south instead, to the scarcely less inclement Cambridge.

[249] See *ODNB* (D. Souden). Welby is one of very few individuals who owes his place in the *DNB* solely to his prominence as a recluse. Daffy's original 'elixir' was a cold remedy containing the laxative tincture of senna. Other versions cured distemper and (plausibly) cleared internal obstructions.

[250] SJCA, C13.6.1, extract copy of College Balance Book, signed by John Poley.

[251] SJCA, C17.7, fo. 363v.

hands', in order to protect it from parliamentary depredations.[252] The hint was clear enough, and St John's responded early in August, handing over a significant quantity of silver. The surviving memorandum in the College Archives puts the figure at 2,064 ounces, valued at £516.[253] Baker's transcript copy of the receipt, and the order of Seniors with the very detailed description of the plate, are preserved in his College History.[254] 'Pots with two Ears', 'Standing Pieces and other Boules', 'Beakers', 'Salts', and 'A Bason in Ewre having the Col. Arms and twelve Names upon it' were dispatched in 'two Fir Boxes'. Much to the fury of a local cavalry commander, Oliver Cromwell, who is said to have tried to intercept the convoy, the plate reached Charles, but this was the last substantial service that Cambridge colleges were able to perform for the sovereign. A Parliamentary garrison occupied the city and Cromwell, according to Baker, vented his anger on Beale, the Master of Queens' and the Master of Jesus, who were all hauled off to London in disgrace.[255]

Although the Parliamentary garrison at Cambridge was probably no more unruly than any other body of soldiers in the period, the records of most colleges show evidence of vandalism and damage caused by billeted troops. In St John's the recent wear and tear is evident when work to restore the fabric of the College picks up at the end of the decade, but the sums involved were even then relatively small.[256] Physical damage seems to have run second to the psychological blight imposed by a hostile, occupying force. The College was 'insulted, guns were frequently discharged in at the windows, the gates at last broke open by the soldiers together with the bursar's chamber and study door, and a good round sum carried off by violence'.[257] Baker chronicles the actions of an enterprising Captain Mason, who plundered more than £11 from 'the Bursers studye' in April 1643, besides £14 very recently paid in by a tenant.[258] He also reminds us that the College walls 'for some months were turned into a prison'; First Court was used as a gaol before the autumn of 1644.[259] But Baker may also intend a less literal interpretation, referring to the siege mentality that dominated Royalist Cambridge during those difficult months.[260]

Predictably, the Chapel changed most, in part through the more or less

---

[252] Twigg, *Cambridge and the English Revolution*, 72.

[253] SJCA, D57.186, a memorandum of the various sums advanced to the king in 1642, and sent to the Vice-Chancellor to collate the responses of the colleges.

[254] Baker-Mayor, II. 632–3. Baker puts the total weight of the plate a fraction higher.

[255] Hoyle, *Reformation and Religious Identity*, 223.

[256] See Twigg, *Cambridge and the English Revolution*, 144–6.

[257] Baker-Mayor, I. 219.

[258] SJCA, SB4.5, fo. 230v; Twigg, *Cambridge and the English Revolution*, 145. There were dark suspicions in College that the latter theft had resulted from collusion between Mason and the College tenant.

[259] With all the attendant dilapidations: 'Memorandum that the particulars in the Upper Chamber were spoyled or taken away when the [First] Court was made a prison', entry dated 17 Apr. 1647 in SJCA, C12.2, p. 230. See also p. 186, when the dating is a little more precise. There are, however, moments when in reading the Prizing Books one begins to suspect that the forces of Parliament are being blamed for other, subsequent wear and tear.

[260] Baker-Mayor, I. 219–20.

enthusiastic response of Fellows to the changing times – Beale's 'Laudian' reforms had by no means proved universally popular – and in part through the attentions of the Parliamentary agent charged with the task of sweeping away 'all monuments of superstition or idolatry' in the University. This famous and energetic iconoclast, William Dowsing, kept a journal of his work, and although the original has not survived its text is preserved in eighteenth-century transcripts, one of them made by Thomas Baker. Here was a man with his work cut out. While no one may doubt Dowsing's zeal for his cause, his responsibilities covered the whole of East Anglia. Cambridge was chock-full of 'idols', but so too were many country and urban churches, great and small, lost among the hundreds of parishes in the east of England.

Dowsing duly swept through the city in just under a fortnight, during Christmas and New Year 1643–4. He turned his attentions to St John's on 29 December, in the company of the President and two other Fellows. Dowsing's diary rather enigmatically records the removal of '44 with *cujus animae propitietur deus*, and one with *Orata pro anima*; 20 former, ten last'. Trevor Cooper assumes that the entry refers to inscriptions, perhaps some pre-Reformation survivals.[261] It also seems likely that Dowsing ordered the removal of stained glass, since an entry in the College Rentals for January 1644 notes a payment to Daniel Maldon in respect of '220 quarries of glasse and for 149 foot of old glasse which was taken downe banded and soadared'.[262] St John's, like several other colleges, had prudently removed some items beforehand. In 1643 the College authorities had taken down the pictures and the organ, and had whitewashed the walls.[263] Perhaps there had also been some attempt at concealment, just as old glass had been hidden away during the destruction of 1558–61, only to be restored to the East Window in the 1630s. Perhaps! But, if so, the concealed items were not seen again in Chapel for nearly seventeen years, if at all. Even the cross on the Bell Tower was removed.[264]

War brought its own, dramatic changes, across the University. Measured in simple figures, scholarship suffered, just as it suffers in every major conflict that draws upon the youth of a nation. The 1640s were disastrous years for schools all over England – endowment dried up, new foundations withered – and this crisis in education had its impact on the universities, reducing the pool of qualified students.[265] Fathers grew reluctant to commit their sons to a distant university, and saw their own goods and resources snatched away by one side or the other. Henry Newcome recalled that, on beginning his studies at St John's in 1644, he was one of only nine new students that year, and even Newcome promptly intermitted until May 1645, 'by reason of the troubles'.[266] Another

---

[261] Cooper, *Journal of William Dowsing*, 175–8.

[262] SJCA, SB4.5, fo. 252v.

[263] SJCA, SB4.5, fo. 226v. The 'little organ' was removed separately that autumn, at a cost of 4s (fo. 230r). In a final gesture of tidiness, the organ case was removed during the year following (fo. 252v).

[264] SJCA, SB4.5, fo. 256r.

[265] See D. Cressy, 'Levels of illiteracy in England, 1530–1730', *Historical Journal* xx (1977), 1–23.

[266] R. Parkinson (ed.), *The Autobiography of Henry Newcome* (Manchester, 1852), 7.

Johnian undergraduate, the Yorkshireman Matthew Robinson, was obliged to travel to Cambridge by a roundabout route through the Fens in the spring of 1645, staying off the picketed roads and dodging military patrols.[267] These perils, and their effects, were seen across the University. In 1643, as John Twigg points out, only forty-five new matriculations were recorded from all the colleges. War seems to have particularly deterred the wealthier men, so important for the money and prestige that they brought to the University, and perhaps predictably it had its most marked impact on the smaller colleges, some of which seem to have all but ground to a halt. The usually prosperous Emmanuel recorded just one matriculation in 1643–4.[268]

Masters and Fellows who remained loyal to their king were cast aside. In the spring of 1644 Parliament built on its control over the eastern counties, ordering Edward Montagu, earl of Manchester, a local magnate ('Manchester' is in fact an abbreviation for 'Godmanchester') and one of the leading figures in the initial revolt against the king, to take in hand the task of transforming Cambridge into a loyal adjunct of the new regime. Dependent at that time on Scottish military support, Parliament had agreed to impose a form of Presbyterianism on the English Church, but to achieve their aim within any reasonable timescale they needed the backing of compliant universities. Acting under authority of an Ordinance for regulating the University and for removing 'scandalous ministers', Manchester set to work. At St John's William Beale was ejected from his Mastership on 13 March 1644, 'for opposing the proceedings of Parliament, and other scandalous Acts in the University'.[269] There was nothing remotely scandalous about Beale, but in the prevailing climate he could not hope to survive. For a time, Baker tells us, Beale attended Charles in Oxford, before joining the entourage of Lord Cottington, ambassador in Madrid. There he died, anxious at the end lest his body should fall into the hands of the Inquisition. Beale's friends, it is said, buried him under the floorboards of the chamber in which he passed away.[270]

Manchester had removed William Beale, and he also had the task of identifying a replacement. Little is known about the horse-trading that preceded this appointment: it was relatively brief, and it took place against the backdrop of similar upheavals in several other colleges. On 11 April, as part of a process that saw him install four new Masters in the space of two days, the earl came to St John's in person and 'declared and published' as Master John Arrowsmith, once an undergraduate member of the College, more recently a Fellow of St Catharine's and, most significantly in the present context, a Calvinist Puritan divine and loyal member of the Westminster Assembly. Manchester had a taste for direct action; he conducted the ceremony, putting Arrowsmith into the Master's stall, and delivering to him 'the statutes of the said Colledge in testimonie of his actuall investiture and possession of the said charge'.[271]

[267] See SJCL, MS S.26.2.
[268] Twigg, *Cambridge and the English Revolution*, 83.
[269] SJCA, D57.97.
[270] Baker-Mayor, I. 220–1.
[271] SJCA, C3.2, pp. 11–13.

It was a logical choice. Baker – for whom Beale was something of a hero – grudges Arrowsmith any compliment, but even Baker admits that his theological writings were well thought of by discerning readers, and that, 'allowing for the iniquity of the times … he was a good man'.[272] Arrowsmith was in fact a scholar and administrator of stature. He was seldom swayed by party in his appreciation of learning and ability, a point amply made by his support for the Royalist Matthew Robinson, who became a Fellow in 1650. Arrowsmith's eventual translation to the Mastership of Trinity in 1653 testifies to the respect in which he was held, even in the smaller pool of talent that characterized both the 'purged Cambridge' of the English Republic and, indeed, the English Republic itself.

The Fellowship in their turn were obliged to swear an oath upholding Presbyterian doctrines enshrined in the Solemn League and Covenant, and to pursue the 'perfect reformation both of the College and University'. New Fellows named by Manchester subscribed to 'a forme of a solemne promise' prescribed by the earl.[273] Those who could not in conscience take their oath shared Beale's fate. The purge was profound. According to Twigg's carefully compiled figures, thirty-one senior members of the College were ejected in 1644–5, compared with forty-eight at Trinity and twenty-one at Pembroke. Across the University over 200 men were punished in this way.[274] The list of the Fellows given in the Rentals for 1645 looks thin, the names of those ejected splattered with crosses, robustly drawn.[275] Many retired to a private life and survived as best they could, awaiting better times; some indeed recovered their Fellowships, or took up other, higher, preferment when fortune turned in 1660. One or two put up a fight. John Barwick, for example, showed his true colours, composing Royalist propaganda and, with other Cambridge Fellows, publishing a broadside against the Covenant in London, later in 1644, denouncing it as both hypocritical and opportunist.[276]

This purge of 1644–5 set something of a precedent, in that over the next fifteen years the circle of consent from which Parliamentary and University authority was drawn dwindled with each successive political crisis. Sometimes the shrinkage was imperceptible, countered by various *ad hoc* measures in Parliament to ensure that Fellowship quotas might be filled and the various College statutes duly observed. In 1647, for example, St John's witnessed the election of fourteen new Fellows, to supplement the thirty-two 'conformable' men who had survived.[277] However, the execution of the king in January 1649 polarized opinion between those who could accept the new republic, and those who could not. This was a step too far even for Manchester. Having been appointed Chancellor of the University in 1649 he was duly removed from office in 1651.[278]

---

[272] Baker-Mayor, I. 228.

[273] SJCA, C3.2, p. 411.

[274] Twigg, *Cambridge and the English Revolution*, 98, 295.

[275] SJCA, SB4.5, fos. 278v–279r.

[276] Twigg, *Cambridge and the English Revolution*, 97. The pamphlet *Certain disquisitions and considerations representing to the conscience the unlawfulnesse of the oath, entituled, A Solemn League and Covenant* appeared under a bogus Oxford imprint.

[277] SJCA, SB 4.5, fos. 335r, 337r.

[278] He was replaced by Oliver St John, Lord Chief Justice of Common Pleas.

His fate was shared by others lower down the University hierarchy, though it is fair to note that compared with events in 1644–5, these upheavals were limited, and may sometimes even have been nurtured by students hoping to take up vacancies.[279] At St John's three further Fellows, Robert Clerke, Allen Henman and Thomas Wombwell, were ejected in December 1650 for refusing the Engagement – only to regain their Fellowships at the Restoration.

All this to-ing and fro-ing led to tensions in the Fellowship. Matthew Robinson, in his memoirs, recalls bitter factions in 1650, tensions exacerbated by a scholarly form of 'underground resistance'.[280] This had been going on for some time. In 1646 Arrowsmith presented charges in Parliament against Zachary Cawdrey, a son of the vicar of Melton Mowbray, and a Fellow of St John's since 1641. Cawdrey and another Fellow of the College, George Hutton, were tried by the House of Lords, accused of open Royalism, and specifically of publicly endorsing and using the Book of Common Prayer. Both were found guilty in December that year and stripped of their University offices, though it is interesting that both were able to retain their Fellowships, which cannot have made for a contented, cohesive College community. There are signs of robust residual royalism within the University, well into the 1650s. It was certainly evident when England again fell into civil war during the summer of 1648: in June that year the House of Commons noted 'tumults and insurrections' in Cambridge. Throughout the interregnum there were some in the city who, like Cawdrey and Hutton, surreptitiously rejected the Directory of Public Worship in favour of the old prayer book.

But everything is not quite as it seems, for the friction covers some timeless stresses and strains of collegiate life. As Twigg points out, the Cawdrey affair was simply the clearest manifestation of a bitter quarrel within St John's between the older Fellows and the more radical, intruded younger element, with poor Arrowsmith trapped in between.[281] Radicals sought to interpret specific statutes to their advantage, the more conservative faction countering that no parliamentary ordinance had envisaged setting aside the customary readings. A few of these tensions mirrored uncertainties all over England. Victorious in the Civil War, Parliament was uncertain how to exploit the peace. The Army remained unpaid, and threatening – in 1647 a large force camped for the summer on Royston Heath, almost literally looking down on Cambridge. The 'distracted state of the kingdom', and the unpredictability of the times, helped produce a distracted college. From all the evidence, much of it aired – even flaunted – in public, St John's was a deeply unhappy place at this point.

Bitterness is expressed with particular vehemence in an extraordinary pamphlet written and published in 1649 by one of the Fellows, Robert Waideson. In September 1648 Waideson was ejected from his Fellowship and removed from College under the Twenty-fifth and Forty-sixth Statutes then prevailing. His offence had been to arrest another Fellow, William Winterburn, 'within the College precincts by a writt from the Kings-Bench without the leave and

[279] Morgan, *History of the University of Cambridge*, II. 477.
[280] SJCL, MS S.26.2.
[281] Scott, 'Notes', *Eagle* xxxiii (1911–12), 257–300.

contrary to the expresse declaration of the Master and Seniors'. In imposing their punishment the Master and seven Seniors also took into consideration, and perhaps exaggerated for their own purposes, Waideson's 'turbulent disposition and carriage, whereby the Society hath been much and long disquieted'.[282] There was, inevitably, another side to the story, duly told at length and in print. The College had been ordered to pay Waideson £20 in 1649 'by order of the Committee of the Universities for his Charges in Exhibiting and following a peticion against some senior malignant fellowes'.[283] Waideson's *An Accusation of Dr Arrowsmith* is a magnificently vitriolic assault on his Master, who, Waideson believed, had been less than even handed over College appointments, and capricious in his interpretation of the Statutes.[284]

Waideson destroys his own case, and reinforces that of his opponents, through hyperbole and bile. The impetus of disappointed expectations was always too obvious; he lost out in a contest for preferment with John Cleveland, the poet, and quarrelled endlessly with John Bird, formerly of Merton College. But alongside the predictable accusations of alcoholism, ignorance, and bias, there are passages that ring true, corroborated as they are in other sources. Particularly convincing was the accusation that Royalists, and supporters of an Episcopalian church, still held Fellowships with the compliance of Arrowsmith, whose duties in the Westminster Assembly left him dependent on the 'old guard' in College. None of the intruded Fellows, Waideson claimed, was up to very much; they were place-seekers to a man. The eventual settlement of this dispute satisfied neither side. Waideson secured the monetary value of his Fellowship from the College, but was never restored to the Fellowship itself.[285]

The 1580 statutes insisted that no new undergraduate 'aut famulus scholaris' should be admitted without first being assigned to a tutor, 'vel ipsum magistrum, vel ex sociis ejusdem Collegii unum, qui ad solutionem commeatus et sizationis, omnium et singulorum pupillorum suorum, et aliorum onerum intra Collegium debitorum teneri se sciat'. Today, the relevant Statute simply requires that 'no bachelor, not being a Fellow, and no undergraduate member of the College, shall be without a Tutor'.[286] The similarities mask considerable differences, however; working within the broad sweep of statute, the tutorial system has developed over time. Howard suggests that these upheavals in the Fellowship during and after the Civil War might have helped to accelerate that development. The loss of old certainties, and the impermanent nature of many Fellowships, fashioned institutions from expedients. By the second half of the seventeenth century, as we have seen, a smaller number of Fellows were taking responsibility for the welfare of junior members. Mullinger names Watson,

---

[282] SJCA, C5.1, fo. 193v. Waideson had also been censured by the President and Seniors in 1642 for striking another member of the College (ibid.), and there is another incident involving a 'Weightson' referred to on fo. 193r.

[283] SJCA, SB4.5, fos. 400r, 400v.

[284] The tract is reprinted by Scott, who adds several other circumstances and facts relating to the case: Scott, 'Notes', *Eagle* xxxiv (1912–13), 1–48, 149–61.

[285] Twigg, *Cambridge and the English Revolution*, 125–6; Scott, 'Notes', *Eagle* xxxiv (1912–13), 154.

[286] Statute XIV, c. 3.

Roper, and Orchard, who looked after 277, 139 and 363 pupils respectively; these reliable individuals were exercising control over the education of their charges, and, increasingly, over their financial and moral welfare. Just the same, the tutorial system remained an expedient; it was not until 1860 that Tutors were recognized in the statutes as officers of the College, and the administration of tuition fees was for centuries substantially ignored by the College accounting system.[287]

War, and an appalling run of harvests in the later 1640s, left in its wake an impoverished university. The evidence from every college is overwhelming. Rooms fell out of occupation, and into disrepair. Building work stopped across the city. After its income dwindled by 50 per cent during the first five years of the 1640s, Trinity resorted to renting out rooms vacated by ejected Fellows to students. Twigg observes a clear trend towards leaving Fellowships vacant. Gifts dwindled. At St John's, the years after 1642 are characterized by an almost complete absence of benefactions.[288] In this respect, this decade of war was probably the least remunerative in the College's history.

The demands of a military economy also damaged College profits. Fought ostensibly in the name of ancient liberties, the Civil War imposed novel and unprecedentedly heavy taxation, particularly in areas under the control of Parliament. Despite traditional exemptions, College and University property was subjected to war taxation, and while rents and revenues were guaranteed by Parliament in 1644, dividends payable to 'delinquents' – to those, in other words, judged to have shown support for the king – were paid over to local sequestrators.[289] Rents and revenues were in any case hard to come by. The ravages of war prevented some tenants from paying their dues, while also offering a convenient excuse to the unwilling. Fines, as entered in the Dividend Book, dipped sharply, though it must be remembered that there was little or no concerted attempt in the seventeenth century to extract a rising real income from this essentially capricious source.[290] The Rental account for 1644 records a total income from money rents of £601, compared with £879 on more or less the same properties, eight years earlier.[291] The lists of those in arrears lengthened swiftly.[292] Long after hostilities had ceased, St John's was still struggling to recover debts, to offset the depredations of hostile armies in a divided country. The tenant at Leighfield was forced to take refuge in a garrison during the War, and the College lost eight years of rent as a result. In Royalist Derbyshire, 'ejected fellows of the King's party' were accused in 1646 of having appropriated rents due to the

---

[287] Howard, *Finances*, 87–8; Mullinger, *St John's College*, 173–4.

[288] The sole significant benefactor was Robert Mason, former Fellow, Chancellor of the diocese of Winchester, Judge of the Vice-Admiralty Court for the Isle of Wight and South-Hants, who gave the College a valuable and large collection of law books in 1648. He brought the books to College in person, was entertained with some ceremony, and a scribe was paid to enter his donation in the Benefactors' Book (Torry, *Founders and Benefactors*, 28; SJCA, C11.4, p. 18; SB4.5, fo. 400v).

[289] Twigg, *Cambridge and the English Revolution*, 138–9.

[290] See Howard, *Finances*, 69–70, 303–4.

[291] SJCA, SB4.5, fos. 40v, 244v.

[292] SJCA, SB4.5, fos. 288v–293r.

College, while property at Marfleet was reckoned one year later to have been 'drowned at the siege of Hull'.[293]

After the end of the first Civil War, in 1646, the situation began to improve. Cambridge, purged and compliant, won back its exemptions from taxation and began recovering old debts. The Bursar of St John's, for example, was sent by Master and Seniors into Yorkshire, to inspect the soggy fields at Marfleet and to collect arrears.[294] But every college found it necessary to consider the sufferings of tenants; compromises over rents were the order of the day, the cases all the more compelling after so great an upheaval. In 1650 numerous reductions were made in order to allow tenants to pay their own taxes, St John's accepting that the tax burden had been extraordinary.[295] Not that domestic peace took away the more efficient demands for cash – a standing army, on which the authority of first the Commonwealth and then the Cromwellian protectorates rested, had to be paid for, and the fighting did not of course end altogether. With the military demands of the 1650s – campaigns against the Scots and the Irish were followed by wars against the Dutch and the Spanish – large sums of money were once again demanded, with few exemptions on offer. Some concessions were made in the legislation governing taxation for the Spanish War in 1657, but Twigg has calculated that St John's still contributed an average of £80 a year in taxes through the 1650s.[296] During the last quarter of 1651, £56 was paid to meet every form of taxation – parliamentary and local militia.[297] In the first six months of 1653 Parliamentary taxes alone came to £37.[298] The total tax bill in 1656 was £81.[299]

With income reduced, most colleges had little choice but to cut back the size of their Fellowships, usually by leaving vacancies unfilled. Royalist critics sneered that the remaining Fellows were simply enriching themselves, taking a larger share of surplus income, but all the evidence suggests that smaller Fellowships resulted from necessity rather than avarice. The only solutions lay in a swift return to 'normality', and the years following the end of the First Civil War witnessed a determined attempt by the purged Fellowship to, quite literally, put their house in order. In the accounts for 1649 the Bursar, Samuel Heron, and his agents are constantly on the move, pursuing debtors, viewing woods, holding courts, visiting London lawyers and officials, and serving writs.[300] Large sums were spent on repairing dilapidated buildings, in getting the place shipshape. The extensive if inexpensive slating projects across the College in 1654 can also be seen as a statement of intent.[301] The Chapel was cleaned, painted, and smartened up; a new ceiling was erected, complete with a frieze, architrave

---

[293] SJCA, D59.2; Twigg, *Cambridge and the English Revolution*, 140–1; Howard, *Finances*, 65.

[294] SJCA, SB4.5, fo. 340r.

[295] SJCA, SB4.5, fo. 406v. More than £220 was allowed out of a total arrears of £3,200.

[296] Twigg, *Cambridge and the English Revolution*, 203.

[297] SJCA, SB4.6, fo. 26r.

[298] SJCA, SB4.6, fo. 91r.

[299] SJCA, SB4.6, fos. 186r–187v.

[300] SJCA, SB4.5, fo. 397r.

[301] SJCA, SB4.6, fos. 120r–v.

and linings.[302] A great deal of money was spent restoring and renovating the bowling green.[303] Careful thought was clearly given to the layout and maintenance of the College Walks: willows were cut, and a major planting of sweetbriars and honeysuckle enhanced the appearance of the grounds in 1651 and 1652.[304] Refurbishment went hand in hand with instruction. In the Master's Lodge, the purchase of two large maps 'for the Gallery' is recorded in the account for 1648: 'one of England the other of the land of Canaan'. Four maps in the Gallery were 'glossed' by a painter in the following year.[305] With the return of more settled days in the later 1640s, it was perhaps a healthy sign that the College could once again be touched for a good cause: by order of Master and Seniors, £3 was given 'towards the reliefe of a poore Irish Divine ... at the entreaty of Dr Love'.[306]

Amid their many weighty problems, the Master and Fellows were occasionally diverted by lesser concerns. One of Arrowsmith's last acts, before moving on to Trinity, was to challenge the provenance of the portraits of Charles I and Henrietta Maria which still hang in the Lodge. The family of William Beale insisted that the two paintings had been Beale's private property, and submitted a certificate from the ejected Fellow John Barwick, maintaining that Beale had frequently laid claim to them as 'his own goodes bought with his owne money'.[307] This was a plausible argument, but the paintings stayed where they were. Through every vicissitude, moreover, the Fellows retained an easy ability to enjoy themselves. Six quarts of claret wine were drunk in Hall 'upon the day of Thancksgiving for the rowting of the Lord Gorings Forces at Langport, July 22 1645' – Cambridge was close to the 'front line' throughout the First Civil War, Royalist forces seized Huntingdon as late as the autumn of 1645, and so every development that bought the end closer was warmly welcomed.[308] Tenants were still entertained when they brought in their rents; it was the least the College could do. Just as important to the seventeenth-century mind, Fellows who died in College were still given a seemly send off. In 1645, more than £4 was laid out on Mr Broxolme's funeral expenses, and in tending him on his deathbed.[309] The Audit and the election of officers were marked with at least a semblance of the old extravagance, particularly as the decade of war gave way to the more settled and far more prosperous 1650s.

Arrowsmith's successor, elected by a majority of the Fellows in June 1653, was Anthony Tuckney, the son of a Lincolnshire vicar, Scholar, Fellow and then Master of Emmanuel and a learned, highly respected theologian of strong predestinarian Calvinist principles. Highly respected and erudite, even in his youth, Tuckney was an obvious choice, given the temper of the times, for the vacant Regius professorship in Divinity in 1656. While his Emmanuel colleague

[302] SJCA, SB4.5, fo. 366v.

[303] E.g. SJCA, SB4.5, fo. 398v.

[304] SJCA, SB4.6, fos. 24r, 55v.

[305] SJCA, SB4.5, fos. 371r, 399v.

[306] SJCA, SB4.5, fo. 370v.

[307] SJCA, D105.113 and 114; Scott, 'Notes', *Eagle* xxvi (1904–5), 316–17.

[308] SJCA, SB4.5, fo. 283v.

[309] SJCA, SB4.5, fo. 284r.

the Royalist William Sancroft did not think much of Tuckney, many others acknowledged, even applauded, his talents as a scholar and an administrator. He had need of those skills in all the political upheavals that lay ahead: Tuckney was elected shortly after Cromwell's famous ejection of the Rump Parliament, and in the same month that the Nominated Assembly – the so-called Barebone's Parliament, Cromwell's first and most radical attempt at creating a wholly new form of government for England – first met at Westminster. In his eight years as Master, Tuckney was to witness the failure of that particular experiment, Cromwell's two very different models of government by Lord Protector, the experiment in local administration by Major-Generals, the downfall of the Protectorate under Cromwell's eldest surviving son Richard, the very English anarchy of 1659, and the military coup engineered by General George Monck, Commander of the most effective military force in the British Isles, the Army of Occupation in Scotland, which saw the restoration of both Rump Parliament and King Charles II in May 1660.

Through all these vicissitudes, and perhaps in reaction to them, the College strove for Godliness. In January 1655, deans and tutors were ordered to visit the scholars' chambers regularly in order to maintain discipline. Those undertaking such scrutiny were urged to praise students who had settled to diligent study, but, equally, to criticize and punish those engaged in 'eating and drinking, and vaine idle talking and keeping of company'. In December 1658 the Master and Seniors decreed that all bachelors of arts and undergraduates should attend their tutors' prayers at 8 p.m.[310]

Allowing for the gap between documented exhortation and unrecorded practice, these injunctions seem to have addressed a risk rather than a problem. Like many other Cambridge Houses, the College appears to have been well managed during the Commonwealth. The systematic audit of plate in the 1650s – there is no sign of this practice in earlier records – is just one example of good housekeeping. In another, Library rules were overhauled, and orders were laid down 'for the better preserving the Bookes'.[311] St John's certainly remained attractive to parents of prospective undergraduates; here is the first suggestion of a trend that grows ever more noticeable in the years ahead. Remembering the upheavals of the Civil Wars, mindful of social dislocation so openly displayed, fathers and mothers sought to send their sons to the larger, more financially stable colleges. Even in the grim 1640s, admissions at St John's actually rose towards the end of the decade, while in the 1650s they equalled, and even surpassed, the levels prevailing twenty years earlier. For the first time in the century St John's became the largest Cambridge college in terms of admissions, a position that it retained, ever more emphatically, to 1700 and beyond.[312] Constant attempts by the University authorities to offer stability were aided by the more pressing distractions confronting would-be reformers, and the intermittent support of Cromwell and his successive administrations. The powers that be in Westminster, tacitly

---

[310] SJCA, C13.1, fos. 277r, 276r. Commonwealth Orders are preserved in their fullest version at the back of the Plate Book.

[311] Scott, 'Notes', *Eagle* xxiv (1902–3), 165–6.

[312] See J. A. Venn, *A Statistical Chart to Illustrate the Entries at the Various Colleges in the University of Cambridge, 1544–1907* (Cambridge, 1908).

accepting the ever narrower consensual base on which their authority rested, showed no particular interest in establishing new, rival universities, and even less interest in further reform of the colleges. Only the occasional expression of more radical religious sentiment, within and outside Parliament, caused ripples of alarm, to disturb the consensus towards conformity with security. Those who doubted the necessity of an educated clergy were hardly likely to look with any favour on the institutions that taught and prepared clerics for a life in the Established Church.

For their part the colleges, mindful of the ruination seen during the 1640s, were content to play on tradition and to preserve familiar customs. The old ways of St John's, including the employment of trumpeters on St John's Day, were pointedly observed.[313] College records, after the hiatus of the mid-1640s, fall back by design rather than indifference into long-established patterns.[314] The best students worked diligently, encouraged by diligent tutors. Spurred on by 'that darling of men', Zachary Cawdrey, Matthew Robinson resolved 'to study seven hours per day at least: four of these hours he spent in philosophy, his morning study; the afternoon hours he devoted *litteris amoenioribus*, viz. to Greek and Latin poets, until he had left none of moment unread, to history, geography, etc.'

Robinson's work-ethic did not weaken: 'If in any day he had failed of his task by company or term exercises in the schools and college, he would recover it on the night or ere the end of the week, and the university had not a more constant student.' 'The strength of his studies lay in the metaphysics and in those subtile authors for many years ... as to ethics (excepting some solid questions belonging thereunto) and physics (abstracted from anatomy, astronomy, meteorology, and the natural history at large) he thought these jejune studies not exceeding one month's enquiry: and for the new philosophy he was *inter primos*.' Here, of course, is autobiography in the third person, composed many rose-tinted years later. Conceding his real ability, there is something of the quintessential student about Robinson, making his earnest resolutions, and catching up on work through the long hours of the night. In this self-fashioning he was no priggish recluse, just a methodical young man. 'One week in three months he would set apart to town visits, and then he spared no money, appearing always abroad in excellent clothes; but at other times was close shut up in his studies, not to be seen but in the chapel and at his commons ... Yet in his severest studies he could bestow one hour daily upon poetry and poetical exercises.'[315]

Hand in hand with Godliness went caution. The colleges conformed, out of conviction, out of necessity, and out of prudence. Trinity and Corpus marked a 'thanksgiving day' on 30 January 1651, the second anniversary of the king's execution, and later that year more than one college built a bonfire to join the celebrations sanctioned by Parliament for Cromwell's 'crowning mercy', the

---

[313] SJCA, SB4.6, fo. 284r.

[314] See, for example, the Rentals and the formalities of admissions to the Foundation: SJCA, C3.2.

[315] J. E. B. Mayor (ed.), *Autobiography of Matthew Robinson* (Cambridge, 1856), 19–21. The original autobiography is in SJCL, MS S.26. Robinson's *Strena poetica*, his New Year's Gift to Cawdrey, is in the Library at O.65.

comprehensive defeat of Charles II and his Scottish army at Worcester.[316] Flattery kept pace with the changing times. Comparing two books of Latin and Greek verse published to commemorate the accession of Richard Cromwell as Protector in September 1658, and the Restoration of Charles II in May 1660, the authors, drawn from across the University, are substantially the same. When it came, Cambridge greeted the Restoration with somewhat embarrassed junketing and jollity. Restoration in England was a calculated, pragmatic choice, made by lie-low Royalists, disenchanted members of the Long Parliament, and the leading military power in the land. It was this, or anarchy. An undergraduate named Wright caught the mixed emotions in verse, his loyal lines preserved accidentally: the flyleaf was used to draft some eighteenth-century bursarial accounts.

> None, sure, can grudge the Honor of this Day:
> Alass! 'twas purchas'd very dear:
> For, Be the Sun now ne're so clear
> Many a black storm did usher in this May.[317]

The royal achievement was restored to the halls of many colleges – in St John's a Mr Knuckles was paid the not inconsiderable sum of £6 15s for gilding the king's arms[318] – while in Great St Mary's there was music and feasting. St John's, perhaps compensating for their extravagance in regilding, committed the rather modest sum of 30 shillings to wine in Hall.[319] Loyal addresses were rushed off to London, carried by senior figures in the University. Oliver Cromwell came in for a great deal of vilification in sermons and in the University records, and in time-honoured British tradition a minority, on this occasion the Quakers, was picked on by an intoxicated, angry mob. Across Cambridge, the Restoration saw some fifty of the Fellows ejected in 1644 and 1650 restored to their colleges: at St John's Thomas Wombwell, Robert Clerke and William Lacy returned by order of the earl of Manchester, the peer responsible for their ejection, himself now restored as Chancellor.[320] Allen Henman, Amias Reding, Thomas Tyrwhytt, and John Ambrose were likewise reinstated by the Court of King's Bench, the College pointedly noting in the records, over and over again, that their ejection had not been effected by the Master and Fellows, but rather had followed on decisions taken by the Committee for Reformation of the Universities.[321]

The ramifications were not always obvious. In the College register there is a grumpy note written by Nicholas Bullingham, the Fellow usurped by Wombwell in the line of succession to the seniority. Bullingham stood aside, while reserving his next 'right and capacity to be chosen … according to Statute', but it is clear that he did not think much of the way in which Wombwell had

[316] Twigg, *Cambridge and the English Revolution*, 163.
[317] SJCA, D105.135.
[318] SJCA, SB4.6, fo. 315r. The payment was recorded in the second quarter of 1660.
[319] SJCA, SB4.6, fo. 315v, for wine 'upon the thanksgiving day'.
[320] SJCA, C3.2, pp. 323–4.
[321] SJCA, C3.2, pp. 314, 317, 325, 327, 328.

been received into his place, 'uppon noe other account than his returne to his Fellowship by Order upon the change of the times'.[322]

While many Fellows returned, a much smaller number departed; there were fewer academic casualties in 1660. Manchester ordered that no one should lose a Fellowship unless it was clear that the Fellowship in question had been held by an ejected man, and the succession to Fellowships was seldom very clear, especially after the passage of years. So far as one can tell, only Edward Kenyon resigned, his departure concealed under the diplomatic cloak of sickness. But no great political upheaval can ever be bloodless, and in Restoration Cambridge Masters were the scapegoats. Ten Heads of Houses were removed in 1660, and it soon became obvious that Tuckney's days were numbered. Baker, sympathetic in spite of their religious differences, attributes the Master's downfall to the ingratitude of younger Fellows, anxious to secure the goodwill of the new regime, and perhaps to Tuckney's fears that his own resignation was somehow expected. In fact, it seems to have been the practicalities of a collegiate life that finished him off. First, Tuckney refused to accept a royal mandate appointing Ralph Wetherly to the next Foundress or Bye Fellowship to fall vacant, rejecting Wetherly on the grounds of idleness and immorality, 'for drinking and staying all night in a Tavern, with a wench of that house', but also opposing the principle of profligate mandates in that they discouraged 'those that have been stayed up here in hopes of preferment upon there desert'.[323]

This has about it the air of a doomed man's display of principle. Royal patronage could be resisted only with help from friends in very high places, and no one was in the mood to deny a popular new king. Wetherly entered his Fellowship, wench or no wench. Protests were restricted to the private, pointed gesture of entering mandates in the records of the College, to illustrate the necessity of the act.[324] Through his misjudgement, and obvious lack of influence, the Master was shown to be vulnerable. He might indeed be considered a liability to his College. In February 1661, twenty-four Fellows complained to the Crown that the Master had given up his attendance in Chapel since the reintroduction of the Book of Common Prayer.[325] As the fault was manifest, it could hardly be overlooked. That June Tuckney resigned both his Mastership and the Regius professorship, pleading age and infirmity. He retired to London, where he lived relatively quietly, if not without continuing harassment from the Church authorities, until his death in 1670.

No one closely associated with the Cromwellian regime could wholly escape the acts of petty vindictiveness which, rather than any wholesale search for legal vengeance, so characterised the early 1660s. At some point in the Restoration era, Tuckney's name was cut out of the list of Masters in the Register, and though Arrowsmith is spared that indignity, both are omitted from a Royalist numbering of subsequent Masters, added by way of an alternative to the official

---

[322] SJCA, C3.2, p. 34, note dated 13 Nov. 1660. Bullingham had to wait in turn behind other restored Fellows, but he was eventually admitted into the Seniority in April 1662.

[323] Twigg, *Cambridge and the English Revolution*, 267–8.

[324] SJCA, C3.2, p. 151.

[325] Scott, 'Notes', *Eagle* xxix (1907–8), 277–9.

count.[326] That was about as cruel as a college could get, and no one was particularly keen to dwell forever on old grievances. Tuckney's replacement, Peter Gunning, came from the Master's Lodge at Corpus with Crown approval, and in a rare if necessary display of solidarity among the Fellowship was elected unanimously.[327]

8. THE GOLDEN AGE OF ST JOHN'S

Wherever possible, the Restoration settlement sought to turn back the clock, imposing a measure of principled retribution along the way. In February 1661, Charles II issued instructions to the Vice-Chancellor that all orders issued by his father and grandfather relating to the University should be executed, and observed. In addition, however, the orders required a review of licences for University preachers 'granted in these disorderly times since the beginning of the year 1643'. Those licences were to be called in, 'and the persons so licensed be put again to be approved by the vote of the present University in Congregation'.[328] The consequences were easily foreseen: Charles was bombarded with requests for advancement, Fellowships, and degrees by mandate, put forward by petitioners who professed loyalty, and who insisted that they, their fathers and their patrons had suffered for the Royalist cause. The principle might have been worthy enough, but there was scope to satisfy only some of these men, and no particularly robust method of establishing whether their claims were true.[329]

The return of monarchical rule had little immediate effect on the size of the University, which through the Interregnum and Restoration remained close to the peak figures recorded in the 1620s. Among individual colleges, St John's was particularly successful in riding the tide of Cavalier enthusiasm: the 372 Fellows and students within its gates in 1672 actually exceeded, if only just, the total in 1621. Thereafter, numbers declined, in response both to the changing fashions in education for boys from gentry families and the gradual marginalization – or perhaps pigeonholing is a better word – of the University within English political, religious and social life. Nor can one entirely set aside the visceral belief, encountered all over the country during the later seventeenth century, that too much education in the schools and the universities had contributed directly to the 'late unhappy troubles'.[330] By the end of the century, then, Cambridge matriculations stood at about half the level noted at the death of James I. These trends, however, are relative, and they shaped the popularity and size of different colleges at different rates, over different time-scales. Moreover, they do not necessarily indicate any loss of status in the wider world; indeed, Cambridge's European reputation, shaped by the likes of Isaac Newton and Richard

[326] SJCA, C3.2, p. 9.
[327] His arrival in College was celebrated with 'wine and bisket': SJCA, SB4.6, fo. 346v.
[328] Cooper, *Annals of Cambridge*, III. 492; Scott, 'Notes', *Eagle* xxxii (1910–11), 258.
[329] Scott, 'Notes', *Eagle* xxxii (1910–11), 258–74.
[330] See Cressy, 'Illiteracy in England', 22.

Bentley, grew at the very moment that numbers began to fall. Even entering the pudding-time of the early eighteenth century, the popularity of St John's was only marginally diminished. Conservatism and tradition do after all tend to favour larger, richer institutions, most closely identified with the political and religious Establishments. Certainly they favoured St John's. In 1727, for example, and this was not an exceptional year, the total number of resident members, 351, was greater than the next two largest colleges – Trinity and Caius – added together.[331]

Life does not seem to change very fast, at least if change is measured through surviving College records. The same deductions are entered in the Prizing Books, the same payments are made to Fellows, and the same fees are paid to servants. Political disorder in mid-century seems to have fostered a climate in which colleges chose to echo the emphasis placed by successive Restoration administrations on stability and order. This was as noticeable in the 1690s as it had been in the 1660s. The king and queen visited in September 1681, and were entertained by the Master in the Long Gallery, just as Charles's father and grandfather had been welcomed before the Wars.[332] While other sectors of the Establishment looked to the 1630s, rigorously – even viciously – upholding the Church of England against Popery and all forms of Unorthodoxy, and reverting to irregular parliamentary sessions, summoned at the king's need, the University also fell back on known ways and customs.[333] Oxford and Cambridge continued to supply the court and the church with educated men, while the ties developed with the county gentry elites over the past 150 years helped strengthen their position still further as annual parliaments, called in response to the financial stresses of continuous warfare from the 1690s, complemented the old order of a dominant London court. But the whole process had become less dynamic. The universities were important because they formed part of a familiar English world, not because of what they taught. If continuity, rather than stagnation, was the watchword, it was continuity in a conservative vein. Outside Cambridge, things were changing. As Morgan writes, 'the world of the coffee house and the newspaper now reached into the university in the way that the academic exercise had once reached into the provincial pulpit'.[334] Eloquence came to be caricatured as pedantry. The universities no longer set the tone for elite culture in England.

Over both the long and the short terms, economic cycles added to the prevailing defensive mindset. There are signs throughout the later seventeenth century that the lot of a landlord was becoming ever more difficult. In agriculture, there were rather too many awkward years, of abundance rather than scarcity, years in which good harvests held down the price of grain on commercial markets, and in which those low prices created problems for the College's agricultural tenants. Like so many other landowners, the College responded in the

---

[331] Twigg, *Cambridge and the English Revolution*, 289. On the changes in academic fashion see Morgan, *History of the University of Cambridge*, II. 465–6.

[332] Scott, 'Notes', *Eagle* xxxv (1913–14), 172–4.

[333] On the Restoration 'settlement' see P. Seaward, *The Cavalier Parliament and the Reconstruction of the Old Regime, 1661–1667* (Cambridge, 1989).

[334] Morgan, *History of the University of Cambridge*, II. 135.

traditional ways, by increasing or decreasing the fines paid by its tenants when entering new leases, rather than by seeking to adjust annual or quarterly rents. Entry fines were set at Marham, Norfolk, during 1667 'in regard of taxes, cheapness of grain, etc', and at Horningsea in 1672 'in regard of the cheapness of grain and fall of rents'. By the 1690s William III's seemingly endless Continental war – the price England and Scotland paid for their 'Glorious Revolution' – was also having its effect, fines again being fixed at Thorrington in Essex 'in regard of fall of rents and extraordinary taxes and the fines of the Courts reserved to the College'.[335] The conflict with Louis XIV only highlighted a trend noticeable ever since the Civil War: a tenant might now expect allowances to be made by a landlord when bearing the unlooked-for burden of new impositions. Initially the College made contributions at second hand to those obliged to pay these assessments, but with taxation increasingly accepted as one of life's constants, the duties of payment became a standard bargaining counter for tenants when negotiating new leases.

Just the same, too much can sometimes be made of these problems. As has been seen, college income had long been structured so as to balance out fluctuations in the price of corn, and there can be no doubt that St John's did well enough financially after the Interregnum, investing in new land, and profiting from some particularly generous benefactions, notably the March and Wootton Rivers estates acquired from the duchess of Somerset after her death in 1692.[336] The Kentish Town estate bequeathed by William Platt in 1632 finally came to the College out of a proto-Dickensian Chancery quagmire in 1684, and this lucrative property financed the first Fellowships to break the county restrictions that governed – and shackled – all the rest.[337] The College expanded physically as well. The bold stride of the Library in the 1620s, from the north-western corner of Second Court down to the river, prompted the completion of a third court, or 'Library Court', built out across the garden that had until then afforded a rather gentle, rural approach to the Shrewsbury Tower. Construction of the two ranges required began in 1669, and was completed in 1673.[338] This brisk process involved the demolition, in April 1670, of a link with the early College, the three-story Rath – or more popularly 'Rats' – Hall, a hostel

---

[335] Howard, *Finances*, 67.

[336] Sarah, duchess of Somerset (*c.* 1642–92), was the daughter of Sir Edward Alston (admitted to St John's in 1612 and President of the Royal College of Physicians 1655–67). She was married three times, taking her title from her second husband, John Seymour, duke of Somerset. The duchess endowed her father's College with land at March, Cambridgeshire, and with the manor of Wootton Rivers, Wiltshire, to support five scholars to be chosen from the schools of Marlborough, Hereford and Manchester. St John's was not the only educational foundation to profit from her charity. Among her other benefactions were scholarships at Brasenose College Oxford, endowments for the grammar school at Tottenham, Middlesex, and funds for training apprentices from boys native to Wiltshire and from those attending the Green Coat School, Westminster.

[337] The Platt Fellows were nevertheless very much second-class citizens, effectively shut out from participation in College administration until the reforms of the nineteenth century swept away the geographical (though not the school) restrictions.

[338] The date 1671, marking the completion of the first, southern range, may still be noted on the western wall (Torry, *Founders and Benefactors*, 50).

standing at the southern corner of the site.[339] Despite the name, Rats Hall was far from derelict. It was slated and lathed regularly, and 'Chambers over the water' were replastered in 1647.[340] Nevertheless, the Hall's deficiencies, practical and aesthetic, had by now become all too apparent. It was simply not modern enough for Caroline taste.

New buildings almost always change the way in which members of a college think about their Cambridge home. By 1671 Second Court was already being referred to as 'the Middle Court' in the rentals – a sure sign of a shift in the geographical centre of collegiate life. A final, graceful gesture to the 'Foundress' of that central Court was added during the same year in the form of a statue to the countess of Shrewsbury. Like the near contemporary statues of St John and Lady Margaret over the other college gates, the countess stands to this day in her niche, half-way up her splendid tower.[341] Perhaps this gesture has, in addition, an element of apology about it, for while Lady Margaret's gatehouse remained the ceremonial point of entry, the countess's equally fine tower now lost forever its role as the grand 'back gate' to the College.

Architecturally, this new Third Court made a virtue out of diversity; no two sides are alike. While the western range follows, with its rather amateurish cloister, suggestion of a gateway completed by a circular pediment, and other seventeenth-century embellishment, the traditional design of full-width stair-cases and a mixture of full-width and smaller chambers, the southern range takes a very different approach. It was designed on a new model, built around a chimney, two chambers deep, perhaps in an attempt to match the breadth of the Library across the new court, and certainly picking up the contemporary Wren designs for terraced housing.[342] The most noticeable difference to earlier Johnian architecture is that the staircases do not slice right across the building. Doors open into a room facing the Court, while two rear rooms face outwards, running round behind the stairs. There was now some flexibility to house stu-dents apart from Fellows. Here was one model for James Essex's radical recon-struction of the south range in First Court, almost exactly a century later.

More chambers were thus available, but still no perceptible attempt was made to codify all these rooms. Staircase lettering and numbering had to await the rational enlightenment of the eighteenth century. Instead, the Restoration College developed a rationality all its own. Taking forward, so it seems, the original practice in a single-court college, rooms were described geographically, strictly according to their location. Labels of this sort were precise, but often cumbersome and hard to remember. What we now know as D5 Third Court, for example, was then referred to as 'the uppermost chamber or cockloft over the

---

[339] Ibid., 48.

[340] SJCA, SB4.5, fo. 341r; Willis and Clark, *Architectural History*, II. 321. See also SB4.6, fo. 55v.

[341] SJCA, SB4.8, fo. 121r. She actually pre-dates the statue of Lady Margaret in First Court, which was purchased and installed in 1674, replacing a sundial: SB4.8, fo. 191r; Willis and Clark, *Architectural History*, II. 318–19; Crook, *Foundation to Gilbert Scott*, 60.

[342] In 1715 chambers in what are now C to F Staircases in Third Court were prized to the 'College'.

cloyster, being the next save one to the bridge'.[343] A surviving document from the Commonwealth period gives us a glimpse of individual room rents, which from the small sample available seem to vary according to both size and location. 'The Middle Chamber behinde the Chappell over Mr Ducketts chamber' carried an attached income of £8 3s., while the more attractive, more central, warmer 'middle chamber over the kitchin looking in to the backe lane' commanded an income of £15 2s. Actual rents received by the College in no way match these figures, but the list is clearly incomplete, and rents in any case may have been negotiated with tutors.[344]

The cost of these two new ranges demonstrates the impact of higher standards and seventeenth-century inflation: £5,256 was required, compared with £3,600 for Second Court seventy years earlier. There is some evidence that the impetus for building, not for the first or the last time, came from the promise rather than the reality of a benefaction. This sum was eventually raised without much ado, rather less than half coming through an appeal to old members, and the balance, so far as is now known, being drawn from normal College income.[345] There is a timeless quality in the response to College appeals: the earl of Rutland sent £10 in January 1671, noting in his covering letter that 'the widdowes Mite was received as well as the greater offerings'.[346] Received it was, though the College had no doubt hoped for more from a nobleman of Rutland's wealth and status. Donations were solicited, and donors thanked, with period panache: 'perhaps wee may be thought worthy rather to be laughed at than pittyed, who begin to build and know not how to finish … some in their life build their monument and wee hope a stone laid in a College may give as faire and lasting a memory to your name as one placed in the Church.'[347]

Completion of Third Court was no isolated phenomenon. The optimism of the 1660s and early 1670s saw considerable fine-tuning to the fabric and appearance of the College. Large sums were spent, each year, on the never-ending tasks of replastering, retiling, and reglazing. The expense of a new Great Gate is accounted for in 1666: 103 feet of oak boarding cost a trifle more than £1 – a bargain – while a 'Mr Woodroft' (very probably George Woodcroft) received 14s for carving two 'Antilopps heads'.[348] Further work on the Great Gate, the College's face to the world, followed in the later 1670s.[349] The river, in those days very much a working highway, traversed daily by transport barges rather

---

[343] N. F. M. Henry and A. C. Crook (eds.), *Use and Occupancy of Rooms in St John's College* (Cambridge, 1985), I. 27. The indexes to Prizing Books offer detailed lists of College rooms, described in classic seventeenth-century fashion. See particularly SJCA, C12.3, pp. 561–4.

[344] SJCA, SB4.7, fo. 39r. There is a similar but slightly less detailed list from the 1680s in SB4.9, fo. 1v. While the principle of descriptive identification had not altered by that stage, there appears to have been a standardization of rents, with the attic sets priced at exactly half the figure set for rooms on lower floors.

[345] Crook, *Foundation to Gilbert Scott*, 59; Willis and Clark, *Architectural History*, II. 271. In the nineteenth century New Court cost more than fifteen times this figure.

[346] Baker-Mayor, I. 544.

[347] Scott, 'Notes', *Eagle* xxxii (1910–11), 10.

[348] SJCA, SB4.6, fo. 487r (presumably yales).

[349] SJCA, SB4.8, fos. 282r, 283v, 284r.

than punts, was 'cleansed' in 1699.[350] Money was spent furnishing the Master's Lodge in line with the latest fashions: marble fireplaces and a 'Japan skreen' are recorded towards the end of the 1690s.[351] The altar tapestry was covered with a silk curtain by 1690.[352] A more literal fine-tuning was also apparent, as skills lost during the Interregnum were relearnt. Endowment was provided for the Choir. In the accounts for the 1660s and 1670s, Loosmore, the Organist, was paid regularly for 'learneing the Choristers', and even for 'teaching the Organist', while the organ was tuned just as regularly. Once in a while, its case was repainted.[353] The Organist himself seems to have commanded a healthy stipend of £20 by the mid-1670s.[354] Books of Common Prayer, as refashioned in 1662, were purchased and put 'into the old plush covers'.[355] 'Rosemary and Bayes' appear at Christmas on occasion.[356]

On its westwards march across the centuries, the College now overlooked the river, and the old kitchen bridge paid for by Robert Booth a century earlier, the sole crossing point in St John's, was considered inadequate, despite (or perhaps in contrast to) the fine new gateway erected in the mid-1680s.[357] A bequest of £500 from Henry Paman (d. 1695), former Fellow and Bursar of the College, and a prominent physician, made possible something better, but the improvements were a while in coming. Searching for a more imposing solution, the College weighed, and rejected, ambitious plans proposed by Christopher Wren and his pupil Nicholas Hawksmoor for a structure more or less on the line of the nineteenth-century Bridge of Sighs, settling instead for a broad, elegant carriage-road at the site of the old bridge, built by the Cambridge mason Robert Grumbold between 1696 and 1712, which draws on Wren's initial design but adopts Wren's name today out of snobbery alone. The slightly elusive panels in the balustrade, representing Neptune and Father Cam, were carved very skilfully by Francis Woodward.[358] As David Loggan's prints and map of 1688–90 show, the site had compelling logic, serving as it did the old Back Lane, a thoroughfare now severed by the growth of the Kitchens, Buttery and other Catering and Conference operations.[359] Loggan's map, incidentally, gives the College a pleasing symmetry through the three courts, if one disregards the

---

[350] SJCA, SB4.10, fo. 93v.

[351] SJCA, SB4.10, fo. 95v.

[352] SJCA, SB4.9, fo. 169v.

[353] SJCA, SB4.6, fos. 370r, 374v, 401r; SB4.8, fo. 94v; SB4.8. fo. 234v. This would appear to be the George Loosemore who was Organist at Trinity and Jesus in the 1660s. He was replaced briefly by one Hawkins in 1682, which accords with the supposed date of his death (see *ODNB* [I. Payne]; SB4.8, fo. 376v). Hawkins was, presumably, the very young James Hawkins, chorister of St John's, and Organist at Ely from 1682 (see *ODNB* [L. M. Middleton and K. D. Reynolds]). Loosemore's longer-term replacement was Thomas Williams.

[354] SJCA, SB4.8, fos. 238r, 284r.

[355] SJCA, SB4.6, fo. 432r.

[356] SJCA, SB4.8, fo. 94v.

[357] SJCA, SB4.9, fo. 98r.

[358] Willis and Clark, *Architectural History*, II. 274, 276–7.

[359] Loggan was paid £10 15s by the College 'for his Booke of the Cutts of the Colleges in Cambridge, and of the Town of Cambridge': SJCA, SB4.9, fo. 173r.

Labyrinth, and the excrescences still clinging to the back of the Master's Lodge. By this point the two main courts are quartered into gravelled 'panels', while the smaller Third Court is, as today, cut into two.

Unlike the more spectacular upheavals provoked by the Civil War, the religious and political turmoil of the 1680s and 1690s made little immediate impact on the College but left instead a lasting legacy. The College under Gunning's Mastership had followed the prevailing fashions of the post-Restoration years. Samuel Pepys, when visiting Magdalene next door, picked up an accurate sense of Gunning's determined loyalism.[360] There was a strong 'high Church' ethos, a conviction in College both that religious toleration was the back door to a restoration of State Catholicism, and that monarchs might be set aside only by God. As fashions changed, however, many churchmen educated at St John's lacked the Vicar of Bray's willingness to move with the times. The first significant test came with the accession of a Catholic king, James II, in 1685, and with that king's tactical attempt to introduce greater liberty of conscience in the bastions of the Establishment, including the universities. Of the 'Seven Bishops' who so publicly resisted James's Declaration of Indulgence in 1688, three – the former Master Francis Turner, White, and Lake – were Johnians. Together with the Archbishop of Canterbury, William Sancroft, and their three colleagues, the Johnian bishops refused to publish the Declaration, insisting in a widely publicised petition to the king that their refusal was motivated by neither lack of respect nor sympathy for dissenting protestants, but because the king's actions here exceeded his royal authority. They saw – correctly – that the move to grant greater liberty of conscience was a means of ameliorating the penal laws against Catholics. The Catholic James, not surprisingly, regarded their actions as rebellious and disrespectful. The bishops were imprisoned in the Tower of London and prosecuted for seditious libel.[361]

Here James miscalculated. Ten Nonconformist ministers made a point of visiting the prisoners; the judges disagreed on whether the bishops' petition might be construed as a libel; and Sancroft and his colleagues were eventually acquitted at their trial in June 1688, a massive loss of face for the king, and conclusive proof that his strategy had failed. Their acquittal prompted the London mob to wild celebrations. Yet when these bishops insisted, time and again, that they remained loyal subjects of their Stuart king, they and some of their followers meant what they said. It was one thing to resist the spread of 'popery' in England, quite another to reject God's anointed monarch. Of the 400 or so 'nonjurors' who were eventually deprived of their posts for declining to swear an oath of allegiance to William and Mary in 1689, more than twenty were Fellows of the College. The matter was accepted as one of principle, and for this and other more pragmatic reasons any ejections were for the most part handled very gently. In 1693 the Master, Humphrey Gower, actually defied orders to expel the Johnian rebels, arguing *inter alia* that a Fellowship amounted to freehold

[360] See Cunich, *History of Magdalene College*, 137.

[361] See R. Thomas, 'The Seven Bishops and their petition, 18 May 1688', *Journal of Ecclesiastical History* xii (1961), 56–70; G. V. Bennett, 'The Seven Bishops: a reconsideration', in D. Baker (ed.), *Religious Motivation: Biographical and Sociological Problems for the Church Historian* (Oxford, 1978), 267–87.

property, and that 'Magna Carta and many other statutes forbade a man to be put out of his freehold save by due process of law.'[362]

People often invoked the talismanic Charter in a losing cause, but here Gower got away with it – the case fell on a technicality, and King William had other, more pressing things to think about. Gower had himself taken the oath, in part at least. Perhaps he did so out of self-interest; certainly he acted to shield his Fellowship. While it won St John's few friends in William's court, and effectively ended Gower's career, his qualified compliance also bought the College time, for he lingered in his office for well over thirty years and remains the longest-serving Master in the College's history. The surviving Johnian non-jurors were forced from their Fellowships only in 1717, in the tense days that followed the Hanoverian succession when another foreign king demanded loyalty, and at a time when Cambridge witnessed some frightening demonstrations of Jacobite sympathies.[363] Even then, the principle of gentle handling was again observed. As is well known, the antiquary and historian of the College, Thomas Baker, was allowed to keep his rooms in Third Court until his death in 1740, proudly describing himself as 'socius ejectus', ejected Fellow, when scribbling in the hundreds of books that survive from his fine and varied library.[364]

In its late seventeenth-century heyday, the College was governed by a consistently experienced and able group of Seniors, headed by three particularly distinguished Masters. Peter Gunning, son of the Vicar of Hoo in Kent, and educated at Clare College, was a constant Royalist who had not compromised his principles during the vicissitudes of Civil War. Briefly Master of Corpus, he succeeded Tuckney in 1661 as both Master of St John's and also as Regius Professor. Gunning was always destined for preferment, and he left the Mastership in 1670 to become bishop of Chichester, moving on to the richer see of Ely in 1675. A powerful controversialist, he believed, as his *ODNB* biographer K. W. Stevenson points out, in tradition. John Evelyn, who heard him preach, observed that Gunning could 'do nothing but what is well'. This was not an easy time to be Master of a Cambridge college, yet from all the surviving evidence it appears that the great traditionalist, the great upholder of royal authority, did not set out to preside over a divided house. In the restorations to fabric, in the assertions of continuity that so dominate this decade in the College's history, one detects the strong hand of its Master.[365]

Gunning's successor, Francis Turner, came from a generation too young to have been caught up directly in the worst of the Civil Wars. However, as the son of a marriage between Charles I's chaplain and the daughter of his Secretary of State, Francis Windebank, he enjoyed the best Royalist credentials. A graduate of New College, Oxford, Turner prospered at the Restoration, becoming chaplain to the duchess of York, Rector of Therfield, a rich living just down the road from Cambridge, and a Fellow-Commoner at St John's

---

[362] Quoted in Miller, *Portrait of a College*, 45.

[363] Twigg, *Cambridge and the English Revolution*, 286.

[364] F. Korsten, *A Catalogue of the Library of Thomas Baker* (Cambridge, 1990).

[365] H. A. L. Jukes, 'Peter Gunning, 1613–1684: churchman, scholar, controversialist', *Proceedings of the Cambridge Antiquarian Society* lv (1962), 36–52.

in 1666. Gunning's patronage seems to have been a stepping stone to further advancement, and, though never in Gunning's scholarly league, Turner carried his predecessor's restoration of the College fabric to its logical conclusion with the completion of Third Court. Furthering his career in the service of James, duke of York, Charles II's younger brother, he eventually succeeded Gunning yet again, this time as bishop of Ely in 1684. The relationship with his royal patron soured when James, on succeeding to the throne as James II, embarked upon his attempt to introduce some form of religious toleration for Catholics. As has been seen, Turner resisted James, and to the king's chagrin took a stand with his fellow bishops, but like Archbishop Sancroft he was unable to support the Glorious Revolution. Engaging in plots against William and Mary, he was deprived of his see and remained a principal nonjuror for the rest of his life. Some attribute the strongly Jacobite character of St John's in these years to the selections of Scholars and Fellows made during his Mastership.[366]

Unlike his two predecessors, Humphrey Gower never secured preferment to a bishopric, and so remained Master of his College to his death in 1711. A Herefordshire man, he was almost exactly the same age as Turner, though a very different character. A loyalist, cautious, affable, a sound scholar and a great benefactor of St John's, he lived out his assertion made as early as 1682 that he considered himself 'wedded to St John's College'.[367] If, like W. S. Gilbert's peers, he did nothing in particular, he did it very well.

Masters were, of course, men of standing and virtue, destined so often for high promotion in the Church. But college alumni do not all mirror this high ideal. No college is without its black sheep, and for St John's the list is particularly rich and varied in the eighteenth century. However, the greatest Johnian rogue of them all, Titus Oates, was a late seventeenth-century phenomenon. A migrant from Emmanuel, his extraordinary career as a charlatan, turncoat, swindler, liar and impostor, as the man almost single-handedly responsible for the anti-Catholic Popish Plot hysteria which gripped London in 1679–80, is thoroughly familiar, and it is hard to find a good word for him or for any of his actions. Thomas Baker, however, does at least try, suggesting that his fellow Johnian was personally incapable of fabricating the Popish Plot. 'I knew Oates', Baker writes, 'he was dull enough and as impudent as dull … a passionate, rash, half witted Fellow, his want of judgment might run him a little too far.'[368]

By the end of the century there was still a gulf between those undergraduates who came to Cambridge with a view to work, and those – undoubtedly a majority – for whom the experience, the measured brush with learning, and the sheer collegiality of the place sufficed. It is difficult to assess the standards set, but by now there is no such problem identifying those areas in which proficiency was expected.[369] John Gibson describes the College examination to determine scholarships and exhibitions.

[366] See the particularly interesting *ODNB* article by Paul Hopkins.

[367] Quoted by Malcolm Underwood in *ODNB*.

[368] MS note on the flyleaf of SJCL, U.20.68.

[369] Consider the string of orders concerning the observation of residence requirements and academic exercises in late seventeenth-century and early eighteenth-century Orders: SJCA, C5.1.

At the giving in of our Epistles which was on Thursday the last day of October we were examin'd very strictly by Mr Morton one of the senior Fellow's in Aristotle, and in the first book of Homer, after that by the Master, in Burgersdicius, in Aristotle, and in the Greek-testament. On Munday next the 4ᵗʰ of November we did all meet in the Chapple and had A theame given us to make Extemporary, the word's of our subject were these. Aeternitas in bonis, infinitum bonum: in malis infinitum malum. We have read over Burgersdicius and are now going to read Golius Ethicks.[370]

Abraham de la Pryme, later renowned for his history of Hull, tells a not so very dissimilar tale a quarter of a century later. His early impressions of Cambridge in 1694 are as fresh and as vivid as any, and while the College examination in this case seems to have been a measure to put new undergraduates through their paces, the personal involvement of the Master and Senior Fellows is again striking.

We arrived in Cambridge ... on the first of May and I was admitted member of St John's College the day following. First I was examined by my tutor, then by the senior dean, then by the junior dean, and then by the master who all made me but construe a verse or two apiece in the Greek Testament, except the master who ask'd me both in that and in Plautus and Horace too. Then I went to the registerer to be registered member of the College and so the whole work was done. We go to lecturs every other day in logics and what we hear one day we give an account of the next; besides we go to his chamber every night and hear the sophs and junior sophs dispute and then some is called out to conster a chapt. in the New Testament, which after it is ended, then we go to prayers and then to our respective chambers.[371]

The crispness of surviving evidence here can lead to misconceptions. As Daniel Waterland's published advice to his tutorial students at Magdalene College makes clear, the undergraduate curriculum early in the eighteenth century was much broader than the knowledge measured in university examinations. Even though Aristotle had given way to Euclid and, in a resonant underlining of the modern, to Newton, the ghost of the wide-ranging old medieval arts course still lingered, insistently emphasizing grammar and logic. This remained true long afterwards, even as mathematics took its grip on the tripos examinations throughout the remainder of the 1700s and far beyond.[372]

This century ends as it begins. Long after the Restoration, the timeless

[370] G. C. M. S[mith] (ed.), 'John Gibson's manuscript', *Eagle* xvii (1891–3), 246–68 at pp. 256–7. Burgersdicius's Logic was printed at least eight times in Cambridge between 1637 and 1680. Theophilus Golius's *Epitome doctrinae moralis ex libris ethicorum Aristotelis* was edited by Winterton and published in Cambridge in 1634.

[371] C. Jackson (ed.), *The Diary of Abraham de la Pryme, the Yorkshire Antiquary* (Durham, 1870), 19.

[372] Morgan, *History of the University of Cambridge*, II. 338–42; C. Stray, 'From oral to written examinations: Cambridge, Oxford and Dublin 1700–1914', *History of Universities* xx (2005), 76–130.

TESTIS OVAT

TITUS OATES,
From a rare Print.

11 Titus Oates, migrant
from Caius College in 1669,
peregrine presence at SJC,
author of the Popish Plot:
SJCL, Port. VI.7

flavour of College life is still captured through the great series of Rentals. Repairs to the fabric, to the clock, and to the pumps were still noted in every annual account. So too were the never-ending efforts to present a respectable face to the world, renting carts to carry away rubbish, tidying the College walks 'against the comencement',[373] and weeding the courts 'at Sturb[ridge] faire'.[374] Rails were freshly painted in First and Third Courts, while ornate new posts and rails were set up before the College gates in 1686 – they are to be seen in the Loggan prints.[375] A summerhouse in the Master's Garden, useful for entertainments on long, hot afternoons, was recorded by 1695, possibly this is one result of all the significant work on the Lodge in that year.[376] There is still a rural feel to the western fields across the Cam: haymaking is recorded in the Walks,

[373] SJCA, SB4.6, fo. 344v.
[374] SJCA, SB4.6, fo. 345r.
[375] SJCA, SB4.9, fos. 48r, 75v.
[376] SJCA, SB4.9, fos. 267r, 268v. This work coincided with a particular effort to collect arrears in rents, SB4.9, fo. 224v.

with the hay sometimes used in the Master's stable.[377] The City 'character' is never absent. One contractor and jack of all trades, Mr Nottingham, a particularly important Cambridge figure in his day, was paid to bale water out of the cellars.[378] The clock continued to give trouble, and by the 1650s John Wardell, 'clocksmyth' was listed alongside the auditor, the rent collector, the College counsel, and the Seneschal in Essex as a recipient of college fees and retainers. He was paid 10 shillings a year to address a perennial problem.[379] Just once in a while the documentation hints at change, and broader horizons. In the mid-1660s, for example, Mr Dent is paid 9 shillings for 'news books and Bills'.[380] Small adjustments to the routine reflect changes in the habits of English urban society: coffee, for example, begins to feature on the accounts from the 1680s.[381] In 1690, in a radical departure for college record-keeping, the local pubs that supplied wine and other refreshments are identified by name: the Three Tuns served St John's in this way, as did the Mitre, the Dolphin, and the Rose.[382] And late in the century there is a camomile bed that needs constant weeding.[383]

In these dog-days, the high summer of the College's fortunes, our glimpse into the life of seventeenth-century St John's closes with dogs. The accounts reveal that dogs were regularly and 'officially' brought into the College during and after the 1670s, and dogs, like the buildings, required maintenance.[384] On one occasion a rather substandard creature promptly had to be cured of mange, the cure involving a generous allowance of liver.[385] On others, payment was made for 'physicking and blooding' dogs in 1685 and 1693.[386] But what purpose did these sickly beasts and their more robust brothers and sisters serve? Were they hired for security, for pest control, or for sport and companionship? We can say that the demand for dogs seems to have been seasonal: a couple of shillings were spent on a 'young mastive' in 1687, which was kept for twelve weeks.[387] However, the reasons for this to-ing and fro-ing, like so much else about the seventeenth-century College, are nowhere set down on paper. Humans and dogs alike are slaves of the record.

---

[377] SJCA, SB4.9, fos. 49v, 74v.

[378] SJCA, SB4.6, fo. 373r. The ever-present Nottingham also attended successive audits.

[379] SJCA, SB4.6, fo. 213v.

[380] SJCA, SB4.6, fo. 463v.

[381] On the reception and early popularity of the drink see B. W. Cowan, *The Social Life of Coffee: The Emergence of the British Coffeehouse* (London, 2005).

[382] SJCA, SB4.9, fos. 173r, 197v, 220r.

[383] SJCA, SB4.9, fo. 173r.

[384] SJCA, SB4.8, fo. 355r.

[385] SJCA, SB4.8, fo. 216r.

[386] SJCA, SB4.9, fos. 49r, 220r.

[387] SJCA, SB4.9, fo. 99v.

III

THE EIGHTEENTH CENTURY

Derek Beales

I. INTRODUCTION

CENTURIES rarely correspond with distinctive periods of history. Neither the year 1700 nor the year 1800 marked a turning point for England, Cambridge or St John's. But 'the long eighteenth century', from 1689 until perhaps 1830, does correspond with a unique period in the history of the English universities. This was the time when Oxford and Cambridge were most completely identified with the Church of England, its hierarchy, the career opportunities it offered, its teaching, its internal divisions, its development and its limitations.[1] Of all the colleges, none was more involved with these issues than St John's.[2]

England's educational system, like that of almost every Christian country until the twentieth century, was very largely in the hands of clergy, and its principal aim, as usually understood, was to inculcate in students the tenets of Christianity and the precepts of Christian morality. Until the Civil War of the seventeenth century the presumption was that the country had only one Christian Church: before the Reformation, the Roman Catholic Church; after the Reformation, the Protestant Church of England. With the Restoration of the monarchy in 1660 came the restoration of the Church of England. But it was a changed church, having lost the vibrant Puritan element it had included before the War. There now existed in England separate Nonconformist or Dissenting churches, which after 1689 had the right, under certain conditions, to

I have received unstinting help from the Archivist and the Library staff of St John's, from the Editor and Dr Mark Nicholls, and from my wife Sally. Professor Stephen Taylor and Dr Sarah Brewer have been particularly generous with loans of books and of notes taken in archives. Others who have helped me include Mr R. P. Blows, Dr T. J. Hochstrasser, Mr Richard Humphreys, Professor J. P. W. Rogers, Mr Nicholas Rogers and the Rev. Dr Peter Waddell.

[1] Victor Morgan's and Peter Searby's are the relevant volumes in the *History of Cambridge University*. J. Gascoigne, *Cambridge in the Age of the Enlightenment* (Cambridge, 1989) is immensely valuable, as is J. C. D. Clark, *English Society, 1688–1832* (Cambridge, 1985), and, for the influence of party politics and the duke of Newcastle as high steward and chancellor, D. A. Winstanley, *The University of Cambridge in the Eighteenth Century* (Cambridge, 1922). Strangely, there is no study specifically devoted to the relationship between the Church of England and the universities in the eighteenth century.

[2] All the previous histories of St John's have proved most useful: Baker-Mayor; Mullinger, *St John's College*; *Collegium Divi Johannis Evangelistae*; Miller, *Portrait of a College*. Also invaluable, especially for the eighteenth century, is Scott-Mayor.

possess their own chapels and worship in them, and to set up their own schools. No such rights, however, were extended to Roman Catholics until, very tentatively, in the late eighteenth century. The old universities became in principle, and very largely in practice, confined to members of the Church of England: students were required to attend its services daily in their college chapels and, in order to graduate BA, down to 1772, a man had to declare his acceptance of its Thirty Nine Articles and, after that date, that he was '*bona fide* a member of the Church of England as by law established'.[3] Hence, during these years the universities and their colleges were debarred by law from educating not only all women but, effectively, substantial numbers of men too: Roman Catholics, Nonconformists, non-Christians, avowed atheists and some dissident Anglicans. Moreover, nearly all the teachers in the two universities were ordained clergy of the Church of England, and a high proportion of matriculated students were in due course ordained – overall, rather more than a half but, in the case of St John's, nearly three-quarters.[4] The College's special relationship with the Church was emphasized by the fact that, whereas it admitted roughly a quarter of the University's students, its members included more than a third of those who had taken the degrees of Bachelor and Doctor of Divinity.[5]

This was also the period when the total number of students attending the University fell to its lowest level in modern history.[6] At no point in the eighteenth century did the undergraduate population reach as much as half of the total that had been achieved in the 1620s and again around 1670. That second peak was followed by steady and rapid decline to a trough lasting from the 1730s until the end of the century. During that trough Cambridge matriculations amounted to fewer than 200 a year, taking all the sixteen colleges into account, and the average annual intake to St John's was in the thirties or forties, whereas in the seventeenth century it had usually reached the sixties and occasionally the eighties. The College's average entry rose somewhat in the 1770s and 1780s but fell back in the 1790s. It was only from about 1805 that the University's

---

[3] On the oath, Cooper, *Annals of Cambridge*, IV. 366. See below, p. 199.

[4] P. Virgin, *The Church in an Age of Negligence (1700–1840)* (Cambridge, 1989), 135, calculates that just over 50 per cent of Cambridge students were ordained. Other historians have arrived at figures around or above 60 per cent (brought together in Gascoigne, *Cambridge in the Age of the Enlightenment*, 21). Miller, *Portrait of a College*, 60, estimates that four-fifths of eighteenth-century undergraduates of St John's were ordained. My sampling suggests that this proportion is a little high, but that the true figure was well over 60 per cent.

[5] Winstanley, *University of Cambridge in the Eighteenth Century*, 246n., giving a list of the numbers eligible, as holders of these degrees, to vote in the election of the Lady Margaret Professor of Divinity in 1764. While St John's had thirty-six out of 102 electors, King's had only two, though Trinity mustered twenty-five. One College, Trinity Hall, was distinctive in having a *maximum* of two Fellows in Orders, since it had been founded to teach Law.

[6] A very large graph of the movement of all colleges' numbers, based on his *Alumni Cantabrigienses*, was compiled by J. A. Venn. This shows the fall in total student numbers before and during the eighteenth century and also the superiority in numbers of St John's over Trinity, and of both over all other Colleges. There is a copy in the Muniment Room of Sidney Sussex College, which was originally given to me by Professor Peter Mathias, who had inherited a stock of the graphs when he took over Venn's room in Queens'.

numbers at last began to grow significantly. No new Cambridge college opened its doors between Sidney Sussex in 1596 and Downing in 1817. Oxford's numbers too fell in the first half of the eighteenth century, if not quite so markedly, and, though they began to recover earlier than Cambridge's, still remained low by comparison with previous centuries.[7] So in the eighteenth century the universities were manifestly less representative and significant in the life of the country than they had been and would become again.

St John's, however, was easily the largest college in the half-empty University of Cambridge, consistently outstripping Trinity in undergraduate numbers from the 1640s down to the early nineteenth century. But Trinity's Fellowship was slightly larger than St John's – approaching sixty, whereas St John's was just over fifty. Trinity's income, too, was substantially higher for most of the century; and, to judge by the number of noblemen and Fellow-Commoners among its students, its social prestige was generally greater.[8]

It is far from easy to explain such a drastic fall in numbers and the long trough that followed, particularly since the population of England increased by a third or more between 1750 and 1800. The exclusion of Nonconformists must have been a factor, especially since the academies that they were now permitted to found were open to Anglicans and some offered an alternative, cheaper education with a broader syllabus than the universities'. Those who needed legal training could get it at the Inns of Court, and those wishing to be medical doctors commonly went either to Leyden or Edinburgh for at least part of their education. But an important element in the explanation must be that, though very few laymen were actually anti-religious, there was clearly a growing sense among them that Anglican clergy ought not to dominate university teaching as they did. At the beginning of the century two fathers discussing their sons' education came to similar conclusions. Sir William Chaytor declared in 1701: 'We must not think of the University unless they will study divinity.' And in 1704 Frederick Leigh wrote:

> for my part I doe not think of sending my eldest son to either [university], nor any of my Youngest but such whom I design for the Church in which case 'tis absolutely necessary to qualify them for orders, by taking Degrees there.[9]

---

[7] For the comparison with Oxford see Venn's article, 'Matriculations at Oxford and Cambridge, 1544–1906', *Oxford and Cambridge Review* (1908), 48–66.

[8] R. R. Neild, *Riches and Responsibility: The Financial History of Trinity College, Cambridge* (Cambridge, 2008) has been most useful to me, especially since the author makes many comparisons with St John's. I am most grateful for Mr N. Allen for lending me his copy. Howard, *Finances*, is exhaustive. Rather striking evidence of the difference in social standing between the two colleges is to be found in the lists in the published poll books of members of the Senate who voted – and especially of those who did *not* vote, most of them presumably non-resident – in the three contested parliamentary elections for the University in 1780, 1784 and 1790. In 1780, although more Johnians (just) than Trinity men voted, John's produced forty-three non-voters, including five peers, while Trinity had sixty-six, of whom eleven were peers. In 1784 Trinity provided marginally more voters and in 1790 substantially more, but the lists of non-voters convey much the same impression of social difference.

[9] Both quotes from Gascoigne, *Cambridge in the Age of the Enlightenment*, 17.

Throughout the century the possession of an Oxford or Cambridge BA was the basic, and often treated as a sufficient, qualification for ordination in the Church of England. Undergraduates not wishing to become clergymen often left the University without taking the BA.

Probably no choice of a master of a college has ever been more significant than that of Richard Bentley, a Johnian, to be Master of Trinity in 1699. The selection was made by the committee established by William III to advise him on church appointments. Its chairman, Tenison, the archbishop of Canterbury, had tried very hard to get Isaac Newton to agree to stand. Newton, a Fellow of Trinity, had of course won international fame after the publication in 1687 of his *Principia mathematica*, which put forward his theory of gravitation, offering a new explanation of the workings of the solar system. His professorship was one of the very few University posts that a man could hold and remain a layman. Tenison urged him to take Orders so that he could become Master. 'Why will you not?' asked Tenison. 'You know more divinity than all of us together.' Newton replied: 'Why then, I shall do you more service than if I was in orders.'[10]

The two fathers somewhat exaggerated the clerical character of Cambridge education. A significant number of sons of nobles and gentry still came to Oxford and Cambridge in the eighteenth century, mostly as Fellow-Commoners, and very few of them were intended for the Church. Perhaps the grandest examples among Johnians before 1750 were the first marquess of Rockingham (matriculated 1712), two future earls of Exeter (1718, 1744) and the future duke of Chandos (1724). In the second half of the century came two future dukes of Northumberland (1760, 1797) and a future duke of Ancaster (1772), a clutch of future marquesses (Cornwallis (1755), Exeter (1770), Townshend (1770), Huntly (1780), Bath (1785) and Londonderry, better known as Viscount Castlereagh (1788)) together with at least eight earls or earls-to-be. Nearly all the major politicians of the period had attended one or other University: in the last years of the century several who were to be prominent after 1800 came to St John's, including Castlereagh and two future prime ministers, Viscount Goderich (1799, prime minister 1827–8), and the earl of Aberdeen (1800, prime minister 1852–5). Only three years later came Viscount Palmerston, the greatest of them all, prime minister in 1855–8 and 1859–65. Prominent lawyers and medical doctors had often spent some time at Oxford or Cambridge. Moreover, as we shall see, the Church of England itself changed during the century, so that many of its clergy became closer to laymen in their outlook and behaviour.[11]

Despite all these considerations, however, the near-monopoly of University and College posts by mostly bachelor clergymen, many of them working also as parish priests and/or hoping for preferment in the Church, strongly biased the curriculum against preparation for other professions and meant that teaching, scholarship and research were for the majority of dons secondary pursuits. Only a small proportion of Fellows of St John's, as in other colleges, held office as Tutors, with responsibility for teaching students; and less than one Fellow in

---

[10] Ibid., 85–6.
[11] See below, pp. 209.

four published so much as a single sermon.[12] Presumably Newton had hoped that this clerical near-monopoly would be challenged sooner than it was. But the governing classes were convinced that the Revolution of 1688 had created the best form of government in the world, because it prevented the king and the executive from encroaching on their liberties and preserved the established Church from both Catholicism and religious enthusiasm. Hence, during the entire eighteenth century it was never possible to muster a majority for the radical reform of any major institution, whether Parliament, the Church, the law, poor relief or the universities.

The story of Cambridge in the early eighteenth century, and especially the story of St John's, has to be seen against the background of the politico-religious crises of the seventeenth century. As was shown in the previous chapter, the Civil War of the 1640s, the years of republican rule from 1649 to 1660, the Restoration of 1660, the campaign of 1678–9 to exclude the Catholic James from the succession, his attempt after he became king in 1685 to promote Roman Catholicism, and, most recently, the Revolution of 1688 had all led to upheavals in the universities and their colleges. The fact that only the restoration of the monarchy had made possible the restoration of the Church of England, after years of persecution, had bound the Church to royalism. But each of the subsequent constitutional crises had appeared to require from the clergy a different justification of monarchy and a new version of its relation with the Church and religion. The dispute over the exclusion of James from the throne had given birth to the national Whig and Tory parties, the former contending for his exclusion, the latter against it. Anglican clergy as well as laymen had been divided on the issue. Especially after 1689, now that parliament met every year and from 1695 general elections occurred at least every three years (changed to seven years in 1716), political party divisions were of crucial importance within the universities and the Church as well as in Parliament and the country.

Successive governments, whether Whig or Tory, were in no doubt that they needed the support and co-operation of the universities, which educated a good proportion of the governing elite and the great majority of Anglican clergy, who were seen as the guardians and promoters of morality and political deference as well as of religion itself. The latest dilemma posed to their consciences had been the Revolution of 1688 and its aftermath: James's flight from England, chased out by the invading army of William of Orange, followed by the coronation early in 1689 of William as King William III and of his wife Mary, daughter of James, as Queen Mary II. The new parliament passed a law requiring 'any Archbishop or Bishop, or any other person now having any Ecclesiastical Dignity, Benefice, or Promotion' to take new oaths, including a new oath of allegiance to William and Mary, failing which they would automatically be deprived of their posts. Almost all the offices, degrees and college Fellowships in Oxford and Cambridge counted in this category. A significant group of Anglican clergy, known as nonjurors, decided that they could not in conscience swear allegiance to William and Mary. They were often identified with Tories, but most Tories

---

[12] I can confidently give this figure for the proportion of fellows who published anything thanks to the CD compiled by Dr Hilary Larkin.

proved ready to take the oath. Some nonjurors were also Jacobites, working for the return of James to the throne, but others accepted, even if they would not bless, the *status quo*.[13]

The original group of nonjurors included eminent, notably learned and spiritually impressive men, but they numbered in total only 394, that is, perhaps 3.5 per cent of the whole body of clergy.[14] That the proportion was so low is explained largely by the blatancy of James's attempt to intrude Catholics into public positions, including college posts, and by the fact that the oath of allegiance required in 1689 was remarkably unspecific and undemanding. It was only necessary to swear to 'be faithful, and bear true Allegiance to their Majesties, King William and Queen Mary'. Swearers were not required to declare that James II had no claim to the throne or that he had abdicated or been lawfully deposed, or even that William and Mary were the rightful sovereigns. Parish clergy would of course have to lead congregations in more enthusiastically worded prayers for the new sovereigns. But the actual oath could easily be squared with a belief that James had in theory or in principle a better claim to the throne than the *de facto* monarchs, William and Mary.

Within this group of 394 nonjurors were 200 who had been educated at Cambridge, of whom sixty-four were Johnians. As Dr Findon points out in his excellent study of the subject, 'no other College, in either University, produced more than a third of that number'.[15] Among the Fellows of St John's, more than twenty, that is, over a third, failed to take the oath – again, easily the largest number and proportion in any Oxbridge college. The reputation of St John's as a Tory, High Church and perhaps Jacobite college was thus confirmed. Largely because of the stance of St John's, Cambridge University as a whole was understood in 1700 to be more conservative and Royalist than Oxford.

This conservatism was much wider in its scope than the mere issue of allegiance to particular monarchs. Divisions on this matter, and between Tory and Whig, were closely related, in the universities and in the country, to differing views on many broader questions: how far the king should have to defer to the 'sovereignty' of Parliament; whether or not the Church of England had authority deriving from Christ and the Apostles to declare and impose doctrines, namely, the Thirty Nine Articles; how far, if at all, toleration of non-Anglicans should extend; and, ultimately perhaps most important for the universities, whether the new philosophy associated with John Locke and the new scientific discoveries and theories especially associated with Newton were reconcilable with Christianity and, more particularly, with the doctrines of the Church of England. In general it was Tory writers who upheld the authority of the monarch, who asserted the right of the Church to require of its members belief in doctrines it had laid down, who opposed toleration of non-Anglicans and who questioned the new philosophy and science. Whigs, on the other hand, usually stressed the supremacy of parliament, downplayed the doctrinal authority of the

---

[13] On the nonjurors, see J. C. Findon, 'The Nonjurors and the Church of England, 1689–1716' (DPhil diss., Oxford University, 1978). Professor Stephen Taylor generously lent me a copy of this invaluable work.

[14] Ibid., especially chaps. II, V and Table 1.

[15] Ibid., 118 and n.

Church, favoured toleration of Nonconformists, were inclined to accept Locke's justification of Christianity as grounded in reason rather than revelation, and saw Newton as 'vindicating the ways of God to man'.

On all these issues Cambridge, and especially St John's, appeared in the early years of the eighteenth century to support the Tories. But by the 1730s the University, partly because of strong pressure from the government, had changed its stance, and even St John's had become receptive to the Whig approach. By the second half of the eighteenth century it was axiomatic that Oxford was Tory and Cambridge Whig, Oxford High Church and Cambridge 'Latitudinarian' (i.e. relatively undogmatic). This change was associated with a remarkable differentiation between the curricula of the two universities. Oxford became the university that privileged classical studies and logic, Cambridge the home of mathematics and natural philosophy. I shall try to trace and explain this change in outlook as exemplified in St John's.

2. THE ARCH-TORY COLLEGE, TO 1727

It was intended in 1689 that the oath of allegiance to William and Mary would be required of the Masters and Fellows of all colleges, and of all those taking degrees. But, while it was plain from the legislation that the new oath would have to be sworn by those who *in future* took degrees or were elected to Fellowships and other College and University appointments, the position of existing Fellows and those who already had degrees and were holders of College and University offices was not so clear. St John's proved uniquely skilful in exploiting this lack of clarity.

The Master, elected in 1679, was Humphrey Gower. He was known as a strong proponent of the divine right of kings, following in the footsteps of his predecessor, Francis Turner, who had become bishop of Ely and had so remained until he refused to take the oath of allegiance to William and Mary. Gower, however, decided that he could in conscience take it and so retained after 1689, as well as the Mastership, his canonry of Ely Cathedral and the Lady Margaret Professorship of Divinity, to which he had just been elected. He had to cope with the problem presented by the refusal of many Fellows of St John's to swear the oath. The government tried various means of compelling him and the College to act against them, but he proved exceptionally skilful at manipulating legal processes to the advantage of the dissident Fellows. He made famous use of Magna Carta,[16] but it was more significant legally that he could claim not to have official knowledge of the position of individual Fellows in regard to the oath. After two legal cases brought against Gower by the government collapsed, it threw in the towel, and the nonjurors remained Fellows. It was only a matter of time before under the College statutes most of the younger among them would be required to take the degree of Bachelor of Divinity, when they would have to swear the oath or lose their Fellowships. But those who had already taken the degree were apparently secure. This story is a particularly striking

---

[16] See above, pp. 156–7.

instance of the impact of the constitutional changes brought by the Revolution of 1688. The king had been effectively deprived of the power, much used by earlier monarchs, to order the appointment and removal of individual Masters and Fellows. The universities and colleges were now acknowledged to be in principle independent and self-governing, though subject to political pressure, to their statutes, and to a small number of laws made by Parliament and interpreted by the courts.

The nonjuring issue remained of great significance well into the eighteenth century, especially for St John's. According to Dr Findon, indeed, it was well after the Revolution that the nonjurors of St John's exerted their chief influence, abetted by their sympathetic Master.[17] The government tried again to secure from the country's clergy a stronger statement of loyalty to the regime after the death of James II in 1701. An Abjuration Act was passed, which required an oath from clergy that declared William the rightful king and denied any right to the Pretender, James's son. Like the Act of 1689, however, it failed to make provision for identifying recalcitrant Fellows of colleges, and so St John's retained its nonjuring Fellows. The reign of Queen Anne from 1702 to 1714 quietened the issue for the time being because, unlike William III, she was a Stuart and an Anglican; and in her last years her Tory government pleased the High Church by restricting through the Occasional Conformity Act of 1711 and the Schism Act of 1714 the toleration lately granted to Nonconformists.

The rare survival of letters from an undergraduate of St John's to his father – preserved because the young man died before he completed his course – makes it possible to give an unusually intimate picture of the College's life in the reign of Anne, illustrating the significance of nonjuring and the nature of the curriculum.[18] Ambrose Bonwicke was the son of the former head of Merchant Taylors' School in London, who was a graduate of St John's, Oxford, and a nonjuror. The boy was exceptionally bookish and pious – or so he seems by the standards of the twenty-first century – like a Puritan or an Evangelical born out of time. On Saturdays he prepared himself dutifully for Holy Communion on Sundays. As a scholar of Merchant Taylors', he had been required to lead school prayers, but 'he stuck at' the first collect for the king, 'it being indeed one of the most improper prayers in the whole liturgy to be used for a governor whom he thought was not so *de jure*, as well as *de facto*'. He seemed to be sure of a place at St John's, Oxford, but the interviewers there had cold feet when they learned of his nonjuring opinions. So he and his father visited St John's, Cambridge, where he was offered a place as a sizar in 1710. When he got there, he found to his delight that Communion was celebrated in the chapel more often than in any other college in either University except Christ Church, Oxford. He avoided the company of those he called 'the lewder sort' of undergraduates, refusing to be allured to the delights of Stourbridge Fair. A favourite of successive Masters and Tutors, he was soon elected a Scholar, and at daily morning chapel was so punctual that he was asked to stand in for the Chapel Clerk. He was also

[17] Findon, 'Nonjurors and the Church of England', 51–2.
[18] J. E. B. Mayor (ed.), *Cambridge under Queen Anne* (Cambridge, 1911), 1–112.

deputed to deal with the recalcitrant clock.[19] He was grateful for his Tutors' advice and admired their lectures.

He recorded the following list of reading accomplished during his second year:

> Whitbey's *Ethics*, Thirlby against Whiston, Burgerdicius's Ethics, Curcellaeus's *Ethics*, Puffendorf *De Officio Hominis & Civis*, Sanderson *De Obligatione Jur. & Consc.*, the last four books of the *AEneis* [he had read the first nine in the previous year], Eustachius's *Ethics*, and a second time as far as the Passions, the greatest part of Collier's *Essays*, the eight last *Pythian Odes* of Pindar, and the six first *Nemean*, half Vossius's *Partitiones Oratoriae*, Grotius's *De jure Belli & Pacis*, Ray's *Wisdom of God in the Works of Creation*, Allingham's *Use of Maps*, Euripides's *Medea*, and 357 verses of his *Phoenissae*, Milton's *Paradise Lost*, 122 *Epigrams* of Martial, a chapter out of the Greek Testament every day for eighteen weeks, 39 Hebrew *Psalms*, all Sallust, Thomas à Kempis, Brome *Of Fasting*, *Whole Duty of Man*, and Nelson [*Festivals and Fasts*], all a second time on Sundays and other holy-days; Suetonius, Caligula and Claudius; five books of Pliny's *Epistles* a second time, and three more added to them; more than five books of the *Adventures of Telemachus* in French ...; about a third of Heracles's comment on Pythagoras's *Golden Verses*, the prologue and first satire of Persius, the two first *Catilinarian Orations*, that for Milo and the two first *Philippics*; the first volume of Echard's *Roman History*, Howell's *Epistles*, Tyrrell *Of the Law of Nature*, and against Hobb[e]s, part of Clerk's *Physics* and Cheyne's *Philosophical Principles of Religion*, with other books.

In addition, he describes writing many Greek and Latin themes, disputations and verses, translating Latin into Greek and *vice versa*, and French into English and *vice versa*. He was less happy when in his third year he was faced with studying mathematics.[20]

His reading list is exceptionally long, though it includes many works that we know were prescribed and widely read in the University at the time. The list illustrates that the undergraduate course, even for a student destined for the Church, was not so much a course in theology as in classics and philosophy. His letters provide excellent evidence not only of the appeal and significance of nonjuring, but also of the good relationships between dons and students in St John's, of the usefulness of some Tutors' teaching and of the seriousness with which at least some students pursued their studies.

The picture of undisturbed piety and scholarship presented in Bonwicke's account contrasts with the situation after the death of Queen Anne in 1714. The Act of Settlement of 1701 had provided for the succession to the throne of the Protestant House of Hanover if, as turned out to be the case, Anne left no heir. Attempts were made to persuade the Pretender that London was worth giving up the Mass for, but he refused. So George I became king, by Act of Parliament, in 1714. His accession was unchallenged, but the Jacobite rebellion of 1715 in

---

[19] See above, p. 108.

[20] Mayor, *Cambridge under Queen Anne*, esp. 53–6. The works mentioned are identified further in the endnotes of Mayor's book.

Scotland revived government fears of disaffection, especially in the universities. These fears seemed justified in the case of Cambridge by the fact that an address from the University congratulating the king on the suppression of the rebellion, though it was eventually approved, had evoked strong opposition.[21]

So concerned were the new Whig ministers by the strength of Toryism in Oxford and Cambridge that they contemplated a far-reaching reform, under which the Crown would control the appointment of Masters and Fellows of colleges. One promoter of this plan wrote that it was notorious that there could be no peace in England 'if the Youth of the Nobility & Gentry, & especially such as are designed for Holy Orders, are infected with false Principles utterly inconsistent with our happy Establishment in Church and State'. Instead of this grand and impractical scheme, however, the government prudently contented itself with passing a law in 1715 which prescribed yet another new oath of allegiance and stopped up all the legal loopholes that had so far saved nonjuring Fellows from deprivation.[22]

Professor Gower had died in 1711 after the longest tenure of the Mastership in the College's history. He was considered learned and his teaching for the BD was applauded, but he published in total only three sermons. His will included substantial benefactions to the College, including his manor-house at Thriplow for the use of future masters. No doubt his skill and firmness in protecting the nonjurors kept the Fellowship together, but they also ensured that the College would be out of favour with the Hanoverian regime. During his time the College authorities had to cope with the extensive damage caused by the great gale of 1703, 'when Fifteen Stacks of Chimnies fell down into St. John's-Colledge, without hurting any Body'. But the only still visible sign of his long tenure is the elegant stone bridge across the Cam, finally begun in 1709 and finished in 1712.[23]

His successor was Dr Robert Jenkin, who had been a nonjuror in 1690 but had changed his stance shortly before his election as Master, in order to take his DD. He published more than any other eighteenth-century master of the College, including a work called *The Reasonableness and Certainty of the Christian Religion*, 2 vols. (1697–1700), which went through many editions. It was a relatively moderate response to those, like Locke, who argued that Man's reason and nature must be the basis on which Christianity is justified. Jenkin argued rather that the essential tenets of Christianity, though derived from revelation and formulated by the Church, could nonetheless be shown to pass the test of reason.[24] He was sympathetic to the nonjuring Fellows but under the new legislation he could do nothing to save them. On the last permitted day, 22 January 1717, the veteran nonjuring Fellows and the four new ones who had been elected since 1689 were declared to have forfeited their Fellowships because they had not sworn the oath. New elections were made to replace them. Numerous Fellows and a posse of Scholars, having taken Communion according to the rites of the Church of England, now appeared before local magistrates – as many

[21] Cooper, *Annals of Cambridge*, IV. 143–5.

[22] Findon, 'Nonjurors and the Church of England', 120–3.

[23] Cooper, *Annals of Cambridge*, IV. 66; Crook, *Foundation to Gilbert Scott*, 61–5.

[24] Cf. Gascoigne, *Cambridge in the Age of the Enlightenment*, 173.

Tho: Baker Coll: Jo: Socius ejectus

12 Thomas Baker, 'ejected Fellow' (d. 1740). Bibliophile, major benefactor of the College Library, nonjuror and the College's first historian. Although deprived of his fellowship in 1717, he retained his Third Court rooms and spent the last twenty-three years of his life there, recording the fact of his ejection on the fly-leaves of his books.

generations of their successors had to do – to swear the oath of allegiance to the Hanoverian king and to deny the claim to the throne of the Stuart Pretender. But, even then, at least one deprived Fellow was allowed to retain his College rooms: Thomas Baker, the College's unofficial librarian, lived on until 1740 in his spacious set, described by a Continental scholar as a 'museum', writing a major history of the College. On the title page he described himself, with some exaggeration, as Socius Ejectus ('ejected Fellow').[25]

In the meantime, however, the nonjurors had been demonized in a controversy that was to have a lasting impact on the Church. It was believed, or asserted, during the period immediately after the accession of George I that the nonjurors were becoming bolder and more critical of the main body of Anglicans, and some of them certainly sought to establish themselves as a separate church. In 1716 Benjamin Hoadly, a notorious Whig polemicist, newly appointed bishop of Bangor, issued a virulent pamphlet attacking them, entitled *A Preservative against the Principles and Practices of the NONJURORS both in Church and State. Or, an APPEAL to the Consciences and Common Sense of the Christian Laity.* In this diatribe he denounced the nonjurors as enemies of liberty and asserted the right of the government to curb any kind of dangerous opposition, even from clergymen, and hence to deprive nonjurors of their benefices. He went on to argue that the Church of England (like all other churches, he said) had no authority whatever from God, Christ or the Apostles to proclaim and impose new doctrines and new interpretations. There should be no question of a Church presuming to lay down the true faith, as the wicked papacy did; the very existence of a Church was justified only by the sincere devotion of its adherents, founded in their own reading of the Scriptures. 'A bishop,' he wrote elsewhere, 'is only a layman with a crook in his hands.'[26]

This pamphlet shows how dangerous the nonjuring schism seemed to some of the government party. But Hoadly's arguments went far beyond what even liberal Anglicans normally asserted, and were hard to distinguish from the justifications given by Nonconformists for establishing churches distinct from the Church of England. His denial of doctrinal and apostolic authority to the Church so appalled its leaders that, at the annual meeting of its representative

---

[25] Ibid., 121–2, and earlier histories of the College, e.g. Miller, *Portrait of a College*, 44–5; Mullinger, *St John's College*, 214–18; also Mayor, *Cambridge under Queen Anne*, 140–4.

[26] See Gascoigne, *Cambridge in the Age of the Enlightenment*, esp. p. 124.

body, Convocation, in 1717, his views on this point were condemned with no dissentient voice. The government's response was to prorogue Convocation. This was an arbitrary act, and would have seemed more so if anyone had known that Convocation would not be allowed to meet again until the mid-nineteenth century. The collective voice of the clergy had been silenced. Further, the restrictions on toleration of Nonconformists in the legislation of Anne's reign were soon repealed.

The 'Bangorian controversy' that Hoadly had ignited reverberated for decades. Encouraged by Whig governments and the bishops they appointed, more and more Anglican clergy admitted to having no strong notion of the authority of the Church, and were inclined to identify 'Reason' and 'Nature' rather than Revelation as the basis of the Christian religion. As we shall see, some of those who were later to bring St John's over to the Whigs openly avowed their debt to Hoadly.[27]

All the College's Fellows, except two designated as medical and two as legal, were required after seven years to take the BD and be ordained in the Church of England. So, whichever side a Fellow took in this doctrinal controversy, the number of church benefices or 'livings' to which the College had the right of presentation was crucial to his career prospects. Its early benefactors had endowed it with a few livings, chiefly with a view to providing long-term employment for Fellows, especially those who wished to marry, and so reducing the number of Life Fellows. It was of course assumed without argument that it was beneficial to parishes that their rectors or vicars should be of Fellowship calibre, though the clergy concerned often delegated their functions to curates. A Fellow who accepted a College living automatically ceased to be a Fellow, while the considerable number who were presented to livings by patrons other than the College were allowed to keep their Fellowships if they did not marry. Henry Gunning noted in his *Reminiscences* that 'most of the churches within ten miles of Cambridge were served by Fellows of colleges.' St John's, he recorded, unlike Trinity but like many other colleges, did not serve supper, and so the officiating clergy, who were bound to miss their dinners, formed 'Sunday-evening Clubs', that of St John's being called 'The Curate's Club'.[28] The provision of College livings has been described as a sort of pension fund for Fellows, but it often benefited a man much younger than the present-day pensionable age. The average tenure of a Fellowship has been estimated at fifteen years[29] – in other words, many Fellows would have obtained a living by the time they were forty.

How important this provision was in the life of the College is shown by the custom that, when a College living fell vacant, the fact would be announced to the assembled company in Hall by the butler. The benefice would then be offered to the Fellows in order of seniority. Before 1700 the College possessed the considerable number of twenty-one livings, but of these nine had been bought or given to it in the previous decade. Sixteen more were acquired

[27] A less sympathetic account than Gascoigne's of Hoadly's views and activities pervades Clark's *English Society*. See below, pp. 188–9.

[28] H. Gunning, *Reminiscences of the University, Town and County of Cambridge from the Year 1780*, 2 vols. (London, 1854), I. 180–1.

[29] Miller, *Portrait of a College*, 51–3.

between 1700 and 1736. The process had been greatly assisted by benefactions, most importantly the Brackenbury Fund, given in 1692 specifically to enable the College to purchase more livings. It seems that all colleges were trying to pursue the same policy, but St John's was particularly successful. Between 1690 and 1736 it had trebled the number of its livings, thus greatly increasing the attractiveness of its Fellowships.[30] No wonder that people thought the universities were becoming too powerful in the Church, and that opposition in Parliament to colleges' purchase of livings led to its severe restriction by the Mortmain Act of 1736 – although by then the universities in fact controlled no more than 10 per cent of all benefices.[31]

Another peculiar feature of the religious situation in St John's was that the exceptional number of its BDs and DDs gave it the voting power to ensure that the Lady Margaret Professorship of Divinity was held continuously by Johnians from 1688 to 1875. Gower was elected to this chair after some years as Master, and Jenkin succeeded him as both Master and professor in 1711. After him, in 1727, came the brief tenure as Master of Robert Lambert, who did not hold the chair, but he was succeeded in 1735 – for thirty years – by John Newcome, who did. In choosing as masters during this period three men who were or became Lady Margaret professors, the Fellows of St John's ensured that in the seventy-six years between 1689 and 1765 there were only eight years during which the Master of the largest college in the University could become Vice-Chancellor. This was because the prudent founder of the Lady Margaret Chair had specifically laid down that within a few days of the professor taking up the office of Vice-Chancellor he would cease to be the professor and the process of electing his successor must begin.[32] Only a Master could be Vice-Chancellor, and in that capacity he asserted the standing of his College and could exercise some influence on its behalf in the University. So large a college as St John's was no doubt inclined to consider itself more or less self-sufficient; and the concern of most Fellows was for promotion in the Church rather than in the University, which by comparison offered very few career opportunities. But the arrangement must have reduced the potential influence of the College within the University.[33]

Although it was nonjuring and Toryism that were seen to characterize St John's, there were Fellows of the College of a different persuasion. The College was never monolithic. Peter Needham, Fellow from 1698 to 1716, had been a precocious scholar, coming into residence at the age of twelve, who after

---

[30] The College livings are beautifully tabulated in Howard, *Finances*, 296–8. G. F. A. Best, *Temporal Pillars* (Cambridge, 1964), 102, n. 2, compares Howard's figures with those for some other colleges.

[31] The Mortmain Act has been studied chiefly in relation to Queen Anne's Bounty, a state scheme to increase the value of livings. See Best, *Temporal Pillars*, and Virgin, *Church in an Age of Negligence*, chap. 3.

[32] See below, pp. 193–4.

[33] I have tried to discover the names of the annually elected members of the Caput, the body that advised the Vice-Chancellor, in hopes of finding out whether the College exerted influence there. But the records do not appear to contain this information. I owe thanks to Dr Patrick Zutshi, the University Archivist, for his help on this and other matters.

graduating published some respected editions of classical texts and worked intensively on Aeschylus, leaving notes that were exploited by later commentators. In 1716 he preached and published a fine sermon before the University rejecting the view that Christ's words, 'Compel them to come in', justified forcible conversion. He and his patrons were Whigs, and in 1719 he assured Lord Macclesfield, the Lord Chancellor, that 'Disaffection to His majesty's Person and Government … seems to wear off daily, [and] I much hope it will disappear in time.'[34] But it was to be some years before his hope was realized in his own college.

The almost contemporary comments of two Johnians who had made European reputations provide excellent evidence about the College's relationship with its members and with the world outside Cambridge. Matthew Prior, a Fellow of the College from 1688 until his death in 1721, was by 1714 famous both as a poet and a diplomat. He had come from a humble background, though his precocity had attracted aristocratic patronage which enabled him to attend Westminster School. The Fellowship to which he had been elected was one of the two designated for medicine, a subject he was hard put to teach when it was later required of him. He was at first a Whig and a protégé of William III himself. Having played a significant role in the negotiations leading to the Treaty of Ryswick in 1697, he was rewarded with a civil government post. He had written to his superior in 1695: 'I … protest to you I cannot think of returning to my College, and being useless to my country, to make declamations and theses to doting divines there, having drawn up memorials to the States-General in the name of the greatest king in Europe.'[35] Later he supported the Tories and became such an important go-between in the negotiations with France at the end of the War of the Spanish Succession that the Treaty of Utrecht of 1713 was dubbed 'Matt's peace'. Meanwhile he had become successful as a poet and, after a period of imprisonment in 1716–17 for alleged sympathy with the Pretender, received the astonishing figure of £4,000 in subscriptions for the publication of his collected verse in 1718. He famously recorded his annoyance that, when he visited his college in 1713, fresh from conversing amicably with Louis XIV in his palaces, the Master, Jenkin, stayed obstinately seated while talking to him, leaving him to remain standing. The incident certainly provides evidence of a master's status at this time.

Prior was unusual among Fellows in having published a great deal, and one of his rare poetic allusions to scientific life is striking in its acuteness and modernity:

> Man does with dangerous Curiosity
> These infathom'd Wonders try:
> With fancy'd Rule and Arbitrary Laws
> Matter and Motion he restrains,
> And study'd Lines and fictious Circles draws;
> Then with imagin'd Sovereignty

---

[34] Cited in Gascoigne, *Cambridge in the Age of the Enlightenment*, 93.
[35] L. G. Wickham Legg, *Matthew Prior: A Study of his Public Career and Correspondence* (Cambridge, 1921), 31.

> Lord of his new *Hypothesis* he reigns.
> He reigns: How long? 'till some usurper rise,
> And he too, mighty Thoughtful, mighty Wise,
> Studies new Lines, and other Circles feigns.

The reflection applies as well to Hoyle in the twentieth century as it applied to Descartes in the seventeenth.

Richard Bentley is acknowledged as one of the greatest classical scholars who has ever lived. He had come up to St John's as a poor sub-sizar from a Yorkshire school in 1677 and had amply shown during his undergraduate years the intellectual quality required for a Fellowship. But the stipulations in the statutes of St John's (as in those of most colleges) that restricted many Fellowships to persons born in particular counties had meant that no Fellowship had been available to this brilliant young man when he graduated – in the jargon of the day, 'his county was full'. Instead, the College had found him a position as master of Spalding school in 1682. After a year he had gone off to the more promising pastures of London (and Oxford) to make his clerical career in the service of churchmen and noblemen, especially Stillingfleet, the dean of St Paul's, a Johnian clergyman of liberal or 'latitudinarian' tendency, who after 1689 took over the bishopric of Worcester from a nonjuror and made Bentley his chaplain. The best career path to clerical preferment was no longer through the University hierarchy but rather through contacts with powerful laymen and clergy outside. But Bentley was unique among such aspirants in having shown real genius as a classical scholar, demonstrating in 1695 the spuriousness of one notable text, the *Letters of Phalaris*; and he would later provide credible editions of many others, including Manilius, previously almost unreadable. The breadth and depth of his intellectual interests beggar belief. In the 1690s he gave the first Boyle Lectures on the folly of atheism, was called in to resuscitate the ailing Cambridge University Press, which he achieved, and wrote a justification of Isaac Newton's revolutionary scientific work as compatible with religion. He became a Fellow of the Royal Society.

In 1699 the ecclesiastical commission established by the king appointed Bentley Master of Trinity, after Newton's refusal. It was not often that a graduate of another college – and especially of rival St John's – was given this post, which incidentally paid its holder roughly three times as much as the Mastership of St John's. Bentley 'created mayhem' at Trinity by his 'despotic' behaviour during forty-three years as Master, but he had a programme which looked to the future. He had vaingloriously written this defence of his policies as early as 1710:

> It has often been told me by Persons of Sense and Candour, that when I left them I might say of the College [Trinity], what Augustus said of Rome, 'I found it of brick, I left it marble.' The College-Chapel, from a decay'd antiquated Model, made one of the noblest in England; the College Hall, from a dirty, sooty, Place, restor'd to its original Beauty ... The Master's Apartment ... from a Spacious Jail ... made worthy of that Royal foundation ... with an elegant Chymical Laboratory, where Courses are annually taught by a Professor, made out of a ruinous Lumber-Hole; ...

the College Gatehouse rais'd up and improved to a stately Astronomical Observatory ...[36]

These words of Bentley's ring like a retrospective condemnation of St John's, where he had lived as a poor sub-sizar in the cramped and primitive conditions of the Labyrinth, where the new buildings were of brick, where there was virtually no study of natural sciences, no observatory and no intention of remodelling the old hall and chapel. Little seems to have been recorded of Johnians' attitude to Bentley as Master of Trinity, but his conspicuous empire-building and his disputes and litigation with its Fellows must have been a constant source of wonder, gossip and criticism during his forty-three years in office. Early on, his conduct must have strengthened the determination of St John's to have nothing to do with Wren's plan for their new bridge across the river to form part of a grandiose landscaping scheme involving the land of both colleges. Eventually, after numerous attempts to control Bentley had failed, he was in 1733 formally deprived of the Mastership, but the Vice-Master, who alone could carry out the sentence, refused to do so, allowing Bentley nine more years in the Lodge.

It was to be half-a-century before St John's provided itself with an observatory, and more than 150 years before it decided that a new Chapel and Master's Lodge were required. Fortunately, as we shall see, it made only small progress towards converting its brick courts to marble in the 1770s.

In other respects Bentley's vast programme triumphed more quickly. His affiliation of Newtonian philosophy to Christianity was soon widely accepted in Cambridge. So was his commitment to the Whigs. In these senses he was a warning and a threat to his old College, and a harbinger of what the University would become after the middle of the century.

3. TRANSITION, 1727–65

After Jenkin's death in 1727 Robert Lambert became Master. The election had been hotly contested: no candidate received a majority of the Fellows' votes and so the choice devolved on the eight Senior Fellows who (with the Master) ordinarily governed the College. Lambert had been a Tutor in mathematics, Greek and Hebrew, had given regular courses of lectures on the Thirty Nine Articles and had served for the last seven years as Bursar.

This was a critical moment in the story of the University's political relationship with the Hanoverian dynasty and its Whig supporters. Under Walpole, prime minister since 1721, the government was making determined efforts to win over the University, so much so that the royal prerogative was used to grant the scarcely believable numbers of 110 honorary degrees in 1726 and 286 in 1727.[37] Partly as a result of this lavish patronage, at the general election of 1727

[36] This and the Prior poem are quoted in L. and H. Fowler, *Cambridge Commemorated* (Cambridge, 1984), 127, 130. On Bentley see the biographies by J. H. Monk, 2 vols. (London, 1830–3) and R. J. White (London, 1965).

[37] R. Sedgwick (ed.), *The History of Parliament: The House of Commons, 1715–1754* (London, 1970), I. 201–2. The University's Grace Book I in the University Library contains a long list of honorary graduates for 1727 but unfortunately gives the colleges

– consequent on the death of George I – the University replaced its two long-serving Tory MPs by two Whigs, a Finch and a Townshend, who remained its Members until 1768. Lambert had become Master just before this parliamentary election and, though a Tory, was elected a few months later to be the first Johnian Vice-Chancellor for nearly fifty years. He soon found himself heading a deputation to the new king, George II, who was at the Newmarket races, in order to ask him to visit the University. This must have caused heart-searching in the College, especially as the king, when he came, visited King's and Trinity but not St John's. After an interval of a year Lambert was again elected Vice-Chancellor, this time by only one vote: 32 of his 84 votes had come from his own College. Toryism was visibly in decay in the University, as it became apparent that the Hanoverian dynasty was secure, that it was emphatically Whig, and that it was determined wherever possible to promote Whigs in the Church and the University. Lambert, though a Tory, had the sense to display loyalty to the dynasty, thus easing the College's transition to Whiggery.

His Mastership lasted only eight years. He died suddenly in 1735, still under the age of sixty. So there was no period at the end of his tenure when he was physically or mentally impaired – as happened with every other eighteenth-century master of the College because there was as yet no idea of a retirement age or a pension scheme. Lambert's appearance was described as 'not advantageous, being small and not at all bettered by a squint in one of his eyes'.[38] But he was evidently a good man of business, as shown by the facts that he was elected Vice-Chancellor a second time and that in St John's he had started the series of Junior Bursar's accounts in 1720, left copious notes on the College's estates and catalogued its benefactors.

The College Library possesses the commonplace book of William Selwin, who was a student in the days of Lambert's Mastership. He came up in 1730 and was evidently destined from the start for the law rather than the ministry. The book gives a very different impression of undergraduate studies from the account in Bonwicke's letters. Selwin records some of his exercises in Hall, or preparation for them, mostly on classical subjects and often in Latin, but with a dash of mathematics. He also made some study of French, using as texts Fénelon's *Télémaque* (like Bonwicke in this respect) and the *Considerations on the Causes of the Greatness of the Romans and their Decline* by Montesquieu, which Selwin must have read almost as soon as it was anonymously published in 1734 – a remarkably up-to-date and adventurous choice, especially since the book had initially received only a lukewarm reception.[39] Although the percentage of law students was low, the fact that their courses of study were significantly different from those of potential clergy must have helped to broaden the outlook of the College as a whole.

The same applied to the even smaller number of students specializing in

of very few of the candidates, though it identifies some as Johnians. I have not found evidence for the promotion of 1726.

[38] Baker-Mayor, 1018. As with most of the Masters, the extracts from Cole printed in this volume together with Mayor's additions, pp. 1015–21, give by far the fullest account of Lambert.

[39] SJCL, MS O.60.

medicine. As well as the two Fellowships assigned to law, the College had two for medicine. But the numbers studying this subject at Cambridge were declining precipitately. In the 1720s sixty-seven students in the University took their MBs, in the 1730s forty-six, in the 1740s thirty-five, and in the 1750s only fifteen.[40] From 1731 to 1752, however, St John's had a medical Fellow of real distinction in William Heberden, who regularly lectured on *materia medica* and acquired a great reputation both as teacher and physician, which he extended when he married and left Cambridge to practise in London in 1752. Among his patients there were the poet Cowper and Doctor Johnson. In a period when medical science made little progress, Heberden 'advanced knowledge of angina pectoris, arthritis and night-blindness'.[41] He evidently maintained his connexion with St John's, presumably showing a readiness to treat its members, since in 1764 the Master and Seniors agreed that he should be sent every Christmas 'a Collar of Brawn' – a unique provision.[42]

Among the small number of Johnian students of medicine in this period was Erasmus Darwin, two of whose brothers also came to the College. He matriculated in 1750. He took his MB in 1755, having also studied medicine at Edinburgh. He must have made a reputation for himself very early in his time at St John's. It was the custom for the University to send a formal address to the monarch congratulating him or her on accession, marriages, births of children, victories, signature of peace treaties and so on. These addresses were often accompanied by a printed collection of appropriate poems written by members of the University distinguished either by birth or by their offices, usually at least one from each college. The death of Frederick, prince of Wales, in 1751 called forth such an address and a volume of verse. St John's was represented in this collection by several poems in Greek, Latin and English, one of them by Erasmus Darwin, then only a second-year undergraduate.[43] It is not known that he had any connexion with the College after he went down, but he had an important role in the intellectual and scientific history of Britain as a member of the Lunar Society of Birmingham, associating with many of the most creative men of his time such as James Watt, Matthew Boulton, Josiah Wedgwood and Joseph Priestley, men who had no links with the old universities. Darwin's energy and curiosity led him into many areas of enquiry, most notably the classification of plants and the development of different species. His grandson, the great Charles Darwin, wrote a life of him and acknowledged the influence of his proto-evolutionary theories.[44]

It was not only students of law and medicine who broke out of the traditional curriculum. A student contemporary of Selwin, Samuel Squire, who, when he

---

[40] Gascoigne, *Cambridge in the Age of the Enlightenment*, 182.

[41] R. Porter, *The Greatest Benefit to Mankind* (London, 1997), 256.

[42] CB, 27 Dec. 1764.

[43] Cooper, *Annals of Cambridge*, IV. 284. The title of the collection is: *Academiae Cantabrigiensis Luctus in obitum Frederici celsissimi Walliae Principis.* Cf. the list of contributors to the address on the marriage of the Princess Royal in 1734, ibid., 213–14. But Cooper's lists are incomplete.

[44] See on the Lunar Society, J. Uglow, *The Lunar Men* (London, 2002); C. Darwin, *The Life of Erasmus Darwin*, 2nd edn (London, 1887).

came up, was not sure he wanted to be ordained, was able to pursue what he later called 'a miscellaneous course of reading'. But he was highly intelligent and well organized, and took the opportunity to learn not only Hebrew, which was regularly taught, but also Icelandic, Anglo-Saxon and Gothic, qualifying him to become a pioneer writer on Anglo-Saxon history. He was proud of the fact that, taking into account the various Scholarships and Fellowships he earned, and his private tutoring, his Cambridge education cost his father only £314. He was later to amass church preferments and became a force in University politics.[45]

Lambert was succeeded as Master, after a good deal of horse-trading, by John Newcome, who had been an unsuccessful candidate at the previous election. He had, however, then been elected to Jenkin's other post, the Lady Margaret Chair, and retained it when he became Master. He had lectured to Bonwicke on mathematics and was later charged with teaching Greek. He had not at first been known as a Whig, but now he came forward as the Whig candidate. His election was seen to mark a crucial shift in the College's politics.[46] He remained Master for almost thirty years (1735–65), the second longest tenure in the history of the College. He was condemned by an enemy as 'a slow, dull, plodding mortal ... His parts were chiefly confined to low cunning artifice and a desire to overreach ...'[47] It was during his reign that the numbers of undergraduates reached rock-bottom: in 1761 the uniquely low number of twenty-five was admitted.[48] He liked residing at Thriplow and from 1744 he was also dean of Rochester, where he spent much time and money. But he was said to have fulfilled the duties of his chair admirably, at least in the early years of his tenure, when he also presided over modest improvements in college administration.

In his first year of office begins the series of Conclusion Books, the record of the decisions of the Master and Seniors who in practice, under the statutes, governed the College. These books are of great use to historians, as they must have been in the running of the College. The majority of the entries concern the management of the College's considerable estates, with particular reference to renewals of leases. Permissions might also be given, for example, to plough or, especially later in the century, to enclose land. Few of the estates were more valuable or caused as much trouble as Wootton Rivers in Wiltshire, which had been given to the College by the duchess of Somerset in the last years of the seventeenth century. For example, a barn there had to be rebuilt after it had been blown down – not a unique occurrence; 'the estate ... [was] repaired' at a cost of £100; and a gamekeeper had to be appointed. During the next Mastership it was agreed that the lands should be valued; 10 guineas was sent to the

---

[45] *ODNB* (R. Browning). His son presented to the British Museum a four-volume collection of most of his works (now in the British Library), introduced by a handwritten account of his father's life, from which I have drawn much, including the cost of his Cambridge career.

[46] E.g. Gascoigne, *Cambridge in the Age of the Enlightenment*, 100–1.

[47] Baker-Mayor, 1023. Mayor's section on Newcome (pp. 1022–41) is invaluable and includes many quotations from the Conclusion Book.

[48] Scott-Mayor, III. 158–60.

poor of the village; and in 1769 it was decided that the Master must visit the place.[49]

Apart from the estates, the most regular entries concerned presentations to college livings and the appointments of masters at certain schools, most often and most contentiously at Shrewsbury,[50] but also at Sedbergh, Pocklington, Spalding and Aldenham. The small single donations are often especially interesting. A few pounds would be sent to towns or villages connected with the College where people had suffered from a fire.[51] Ranging more widely, money was sent to assist the Protestant University of Debrecen in Hungary and new colleges in Philadelphia and New York.[52] It has been thought highly significant of a change in the College's political stance that it subscribed money towards enlisting troops to fight the Jacobite invasion of 1745. But, while it is true that such a grant would hardly have been made by the St John's of 1715, in 1745 the College was joining the University and many other colleges in contributing.[53]

So far as the running of the College itself was concerned, the Master showed a special interest in the library, which no doubt explains its being reordered, replenished and recatalogued (twice, it seems, the second time alphabetically). He was to leave it a collection of valuable books in his will.[54] The College's stock of church music was also expanded.[55] The most striking administrative change, made in 1755, concerned the Bursar's handling of the College's funds. Previously Bursars had rendered an account of the financial position once only, when they left office. Like government ministers of the day, they had kept the substantial balances of college funds in their own accounts and taken the interest. The Master and Seniors, once they learned how much money was involved, decided that this practice must end and agreed in November 1755 that the Bursar must repay interest on £3,000 at 3½ per cent by 31 January 1756. At the same time it had been ordered that no further investments should be made without the approval of the Master and Seniors. It took more than a year to get these changes fully accepted by the new Bursar, though he had been the original whistle-blower in this affair. But similar difficulties arose again in 1763, it seems with the 'receiver' of college funds in London: an order was given to an agent

> to use proper measures to prevent Mr Hammond from receiving any more of the College money; and that he shall endeavour to get what is in his hands, immediately, except seven hundred and thirty one pounds,

[49] CB, 29 Apr. and 12 Oct. 1751; 5 Dec. 1759; 5 July 1765; 16 (?) Mar. 1767; 7 Nov. 1769.

[50] The College archives contain substantial papers on a lengthy dispute between the College and the town about the revenues and government of the school. See materials assembled in 'Notes from the College records': *Eagle* xxii (1900–1), 297–321; xxiii (1901–2), 141–70.

[51] E.g. 11 June 1736 (Hinxton), 4 June 1737 (Fenny Stanton), 11 Oct. 1737 (Cherry Hinton); 20 Jan. 1738 (Bishop's Stortford).

[52] These entries were reprinted in Baker-Mayor, 1038, 1040.

[53] Miller, *Portrait of a College*, 45; Cooper, *Annals of Cambridge*, IV, 250–4; R. Humphreys, *Sidney Sussex: A History* (Cambridge, 2009), 171.

[54] Baker-Mayor, 1034–6, 1041.

[55] CB, 8 March 1742, 30 Apr. 1760 (Baker-Mayor, 1036, 1039).

fourteen shillings and eight pence, for which sum the Bursar has given us his Security.[56]

Other innovations in the Bursar's domain were to buy a fire engine for £50 and to insure the College buildings for £5,000.[57] As for the buildings, little was done other than maintenance, though new glazing was to be put into the chapel and elsewhere, a wall was to be built 'to hide the necessary house', the street 'in front of the College' was to be paved, a new pump was to be bought for the stable yard and 'a New Leaden pump to be put down in the Back Lane'.[58] Entries concerning the grounds are often difficult to identify, but this one sounds significant: 'Agreed yt a Reed Hedge 8 feet high be plac'd from ye top of ye Garden to ye Cross Walk, yt Shrubs & Evergeens be planted to fill ye Space between ye Trees & ye old Hedge, & yt ye Old Hedge be Splash'd [*sic*] to ye Cross Walk.' The last item was rescinded at the next meeting: 'Instead Plashing [*sic*], Yew Trees in place of it.'[59]

With regard to Fellows' conduct, it was necessary for the Master and Seniors formally to grant the 'year of grace', that is, the extra (eighth) year now often allowed before a Fellow had to proceed to the BD.[60] Their permission was also required for Fellows 'to go abroad'. But many Fellows were absent for long periods in England without such permission, in some cases in order to fulfil their duties as parish clergy. In general, their lives seem to have become steadily more comfortable. Like most landed proprietors', the College's income grew substantially in the eighteenth century. Out of the fines paid for leases, 'dividends' were paid to the Master and Fellows. In 1690 the Master received as his share £30, the Seniors £15 and the Junior Fellows £10 each. Under Newcome £20 became the normal dividend for Junior Fellows, but in 1756 it shot up to £40, which remained the normal figure until 1770. These increases expressed as percentages were far greater than any rise in general prices. The Scholars and sizars also received more than in the past, both in money and in kind – more coal, for example.[61] It is unclear what lies behind the order of 1756 allowing the Fellows a penny a day for green vegetables in their commons, or the purchase in 1762 of 'One groce [*sic*] of knives and one Groce of forks for the use of the president's table.'[62]

During this period the Admonitions Book reports undergraduate misconduct of mostly familiar forms, some of which was punished fairly leniently.

---

[56] On these financial changes see Howard, *Finances*, esp. pp. 78–80; Baker-Mayor, 1037–8; CB, 23 Dec. 1763.

[57] Baker-Mayor, 1036–7.

[58] Baker-Mayor, 1035, 1038; CB, 12 Oct. 1761 [though '1762' in the MS], 29 Jan. and 26 Oct. 1762.

[59] Ibid., 7 Apr. (not, I think, correctly reproduced in Baker-Mayor, 1039) and 12 Apr. 1762.

[60] The College's Statutes allow such an extension. Mullinger, *St John's College*, 224, describes these extensions as an 'institution' by which Newcome 'propitiated the Fellows', but there seems to be no firm evidence that the practice began under him.

[61] Howard, *Finances*, 84–6, 304–5; Baker-Mayor, 1037. Cf. R. F. Scott, 'Some aspects of College life in past times', *Eagle* xliii (1923–4), 160–75.

[62] CB, 22 Nov. 1756, 28 Apr. 1763.

Students missed chapel, swore, got drunk, slept out of college, fornicated, went to London without permission, occasionally rioted. In 1740 the Conclusion Book records the Master and Seniors attempting to take a firmer stand against 'any Scholar in Statu Pupillari' who, after the gates have been closed, 'break open any Door, or by scaling of Walls, leaping of Ditches or any other way get out'. Such Scholars 'shall be *ipso facto* expelled'. Further, it was 'Ordered … that no Scholars ever presume to loiter, or walk backwards & forwards in any of the Courts or Cloysters.'[63] It seems curious that these restrictions apparently applied only to Scholars. To judge from the Admonitions Book, receiving a girl in one's room, whether or not 'disguised as a man', ensured expulsion, as did the single instance of 'melting down a College silver spoon and selling part of it'.[64] It is impossible to tell from the records how much the Master, the Deans or other Fellows disciplined students for lesser offences, or gave warnings that made the solemn procedure of Admonition unnecessary.

The gravest crime attributed to a Johnian in this period was the alleged murder of a sizar called James Ashton, for which another sizar, called John Brinkley, was tried at Cambridge Assizes. The circumstances were peculiar. Ashton and Brinkley had evidently been close friends. On 9 March 1746 at about midnight Brinkley called on an undergraduate described as Mr C, who had the room next to Ashton in the First Court, saying that the porter should be summoned because Ashton was bleeding to death. Brinkley claimed that he and Ashton had been 'lying together' at Ashton's desire, and that Ashton had got out of bed and somehow injured himself on the chamber pot, which was found to be broken into pieces, some of them jagged. It was said by some that Ashton had been trying to shake off the attentions of Brinkley. The state of forensic science at that time left the doctors unable to determine whether the chamber-pot could have done the damage, and the evidence against Brinkley was insufficent to convict him. But he was generally considered guilty, was evidently sent down, and disappeared.[65]

Both inside and outside the University its discipline of its students was considered slack. One of the duke of Newcastle's early initiatives after he became Chancellor in 1748 was to put forward a new set of University regulations about student behaviour. He seems to have acted in order to head off a proposed general enquiry into the state of the universities.[66] There was some opposition, partly on the ground that this was the colleges' and not the University's business; and one of the proposed regulations, which would have required that an annual report should be made on each student to the Chancellor, had to be dropped. But a code of eighteen regulations was eventually accepted by the Senate in June

[63] Admonitions Book, 25 Mar. 1740.

[64] Ibid: the cases of Drake and Talbot in 1750, and Edwards 25 Nov. 1757 (the silver spoon).

[65] Scott-Mayor, III. 546–50, heavily dependent on *Gentleman's Magazine*, vol. xvi, 466–7, 469–71; 'Our Chronicle', *Eagle* xxi (1899–1900), 370–2; Linehan, 'Unfinished business', *Eagle* 2001, 32–9. The Admonitions Book contains no reference to this affair.

[66] Professor Stephen Taylor generously gave me a copy of his article on 'University reform and the Cambridge regulations of 1750', which explains the political context.

1750. Many of them prescribed in detail the proper dress for Fellow-Commoners, BAs, noblemen and Scholars. Others, however, dealt with common forms of misconduct, thus throwing light on the customs of the time. A student, for example, must not keep a servant or a horse, except with the written permission of his parents and the Master of his College.

> Every person *in statu pupillari* who shall be found at any coffee house, tennis court, cricket-ground, or other place of public diversion and entertainment, betwixt the hours of nine and twelve in the morning, shall forfeit … ten shillings …
>
> No person *in statu pupillari* shall be suffered to go out of town on horseback or in any wheel carriage whatsoever without the express consent of his tutor or the Master of his College, under the penalty of forfeiting thirteen shillings and fourpence for the first offence, … and be expelled for the fourth.
>
> Every person *in statu pupillari* appearing with a gun or keeping or procuring other persons to keep sporting dogs for his use during his residence … shall forfeit the sum of ten shillings for every offence.

Taverns and coffee houses figure prominently. Their owners must not give credit beyond 20 shillings and must not serve students alcohol after 11 p.m., on pain of a penalty of £5 for the first offence, and loss of licence for the third.[67] In the end one is left with the impression that students could still get away with most infringements, so long as they had the money to spare for the substantial fines incurred.

Coffee houses deserve special attention. Throughout the eighteenth century they were the centre of many University members' social life outside their colleges. It was assumed that undergraduates would visit them frequently, and so did many dons. Baker, the *socius ejectus*, for example, used to go 'to a coffee-house in an evening after chapel, where he commonly spent an hour with great chearfulness in conversing with a select number of his friends and acquaintance, chiefly upon literary subjects'.[68] James Wood, Fellow of St John's, had a less happy experience at the Union Coffee House in 1788: he was assaulted by a Fellow-Commoner of Corpus, Tom Adkin, a friend of the Whig circle at King's and Trinity. The matter was taken to Court and Adkin was fined £100.[69] Coffee houses provided food and drink and, most notably, newspapers, and gave an opportunity for political as well as more general discussion. Four or five seem to have competed with each other at most periods of the century, but few lasted longer than thirty years. 'The Johnian' operated in All Saints Yard, opposite the front of the College, from the forties, and was apparently superseded there by 'Clapham's' about twenty years later.[70]

---

[67] The regulations are printed in Cooper, *Annals of Cambridge*, IV. 278–81.

[68] Mayor, *Cambridge under Queen Anne*, 420.

[69] Cooper, *Annals of Cambridge*, IV. 432–3. Cooper says this James Wood was the future Master, but there was another James Wood who was a Fellow at the same time, who was about to become Bursar.

[70] See R. Newman, *St John's Triangle, Cambridge: An Archaeological Excavation and Watching Brief*, 2 vols. (Cambridge, 2008), I. 123–8.

Newcome's Mastership was not notable either for internal reform or for good discipline, though, as we shall see, during his rule the College changed in important ways as a result of largely external developments. But in one respect his tenure was unique and prophetic. Soon after he had been elected to his chair in 1727 he had gone to live in the house in the town assigned to the Lady Margaret Professor, and by the end of the year had married Susanna(h) Squire, thus vacating his Fellowship. He was the only Master of St John's in the eighteenth century who was already married when elected. His wife was the aunt of the eclectic student Samuel Squire and the daughter of a rector of Durnford in Wiltshire whose three sons were matriculated members of St John's.[71] It was surprising enough to see a wife in the Master's Lodge at all. What was amazing in that age was that she was not only an attractive and charming hostess but also a learned, literary wife, who published more than her husband on the subject he professed: Divinity. He mustered only a couple of sermons in print. She wrote, anonymously but acknowledging her authorship when presenting copies, *Enquiry into the evidence of the Christian religion* (1729), which went into three editions, and *Plain account of the nature and end of the Sacrament* in two parts (1738). 'Her modesty and humility,' it was said, 'always strove to conceal the great powers and extraordinary improvements of her mind.' The politically reactionary Baker carefully transcribed into his copy of the *Enquiry* this tribute from the German *Acta eruditorum* of 1734:

> She certainly deserves better than the lowest place among female philosophers, since she has treated an important theme, which has exercised the minds of serious scholars, with arguments both sound and clearly expressed, with praiseworthy judgment and in a felicitous style.[72]

Her writing was lively, she was determined to define terms properly, and she proved ready to modify the text of the *Enquiry* in a second edition to take account of further study. According to bishop Squire's son, 'whatever advantage the young student might have derived from the superintending care and protection of the Professor [Newcome], he found a more anxious and perhaps more useful friend in his aunt.' She died in March 1763 after reaching the age of eighty, and the epitaph on her memorial in St Benet's Church, Cambridge, extolled her as 'a woman of an excellent Understanding & an Upright Heart who constantly employed her great Talents to the Honour of God & the good of mankind through the course of a long life'.[73]

It was during Newcome's time as Master that the College fought a battle in the courts which perfectly illustrates the complexity of its legal position, caught between the law of the land, canon law, its outdated statutes and the terms of the ancient benefactions it had received. Two Fellowships and two Scholarships at St John's had been endowed by Dr John Ke(y)ton in 1531, to be filled, if possible, by suitable persons who had been 'Queristers of the Chapiter of Southwell'.

---

[71] See for what follows the MS account of Squire's life described above in n. 45, as well as the works cited below in n. 80.

[72] Baker-Mayor, 1026.

[73] I am grateful to Fabienne Bonnet for uncovering the upper part of this slab and reading it for me.

One of these Fellowships fell vacant in 1755 on the resignation of Theophilus Lindsey, who had had no connexion with Southwell. Thomas Todington, who had come up in 1751 from Southwell, had actually sung in the minster choir and was about to be ordained, offered himself as a candidate. The College, however, elected William Craven, who had been classed as Fourth Wrangler in the Senate House Examination of 1753 but had no connexion with Southwell. When this election was challenged, the College produced a range of arguments to justify their rejection of Todington. The most significant was that he had 'a withered hand'. Canon law ruled out the ordination of persons deformed or mutilated, and Canon Keyton had made the same stipulation about his Scholars, though not explicitly about his Fellows. Todington appealed to the bishop of Ely as Visitor of the College, but the College tried to get round that by saying that the statutes made the bishop Visitor only for certain stated purposes, which did not include Fellowship election disputes.

Powell, the future Master, was deputed to put the College's case to the bishop, who referred it to the Court of King's Bench, which decreed that the bishop was Visitor for all purposes. The bishop then declared Todington eligible because his deformity was only slight, Craven lost his Fellowship and Todington was elected to it. Powell, characteristically, had kept full and careful notes of the proceedings, which survive in the College archives.[74]

The first of the two major changes during the period of Newcome's Mastership which were mainly due to external influences was that the College became reconciled to the Whig hegemony. Great lords with nearby estates had always patronized and influenced the University. In the 1690s the earl of Exeter at Burghley near Stamford had sheltered Jenkin, the future Master, and employed him as domestic chaplain though he was a nonjuror.[75] Several generations of this family were educated at St John's. Anne's Tory prime minister, Robert Harley, earl of Oxford, had lived at Wimpole House, near Royston, where he had gathered his superb library and assisted the Tory cause in the University. His son continued in the same course – for example, he worked with the opposition to Bentley in Trinity.[76] We have seen that the Whig governments of George I and George II did their best to counter these Tory influences, but until the late 1730s they lacked both a local aristocratic dynasty and a formal connexion with the University except for the new Whig MPs. In 1737 they obtained such a connexion when the duke of Newcastle, one of Walpole's secretaries of state since 1724, was elected to the junior of the two University posts open to great outsiders, the high stewardship. This was in these years a more important post than usual because the senior post, the Chancellorship, was held by the duke of Somerset, who was both senile and absentee. Then in 1740 the government had a stroke of good fortune. The second earl of Oxford, bankrupted by drink, building and book-buying, had to sell Wimpole. It was bought in 1740 by lord Hardwicke, Lord Chancellor since 1737, a friend of Newcastle and a stalwart of

[74] SJCA, D89, 194–200 and D108, 119–21; Peter Linehan, 'Commemoration of Benefactors', *Eagle* (1997), 11–12.

[75] Baker-Mayor, 1006.

[76] The correspondence between the younger Harley and Conyers Middleton is revealing here: e.g. BL Add. MSS 32457, Oxford to Middleton, 14 Nov. 1726 and 2 Feb. 1727.

the Whig party, whose office gave him control of considerable patronage in the Church.[77]

Since 1727 the Townshends of Raynham in Norfolk, neighbours and supporters of Walpole, had provided one of the Whig MPs for the University. The MP's nephew, Charles, who as Chancellor of the Exchequer in 1766 was to assert Britain's right to tax the American colonies, had been tutored at home by Powell, the future Master of St John's, in 1741–3.[78] In 1748 Newcastle was elected to succeed Somerset as Chancellor, and in the following year Hardwicke was elected high steward in Newcastle's place. With the backing of the king, these two grandees came as near as possible to controlling the elections and appointments to major posts in the University. When Hardwicke died in 1764, his heir managed to win the tightest of elections to succeed his father as high steward.[79] His younger son Charles Yorke, a prodigiously effective and wealthy lawyer, was already the University's legal counsel and in 1768 joined Townshend as one of its MPs.

It was Newcastle who was the dominant figure. He was one of the great wire-pullers of history, incessantly scheming, making contacts, writing letters, and exploiting government and church patronage to turn the University into a Whig stronghold. To be fair to him, he fervently believed that only the Hanoverian dynasty and the Whig party could maintain the free constitution of Britain; and he genuinely wanted to reform the University curriculum. He endowed medals to be competed for in classical studies; and he wanted the new Regius professorship of Modern History, founded in 1724, to live up to its name, teaching history and the modern languages necessary to study it. But the party-political aim was paramount. He and his colleagues needed support from clergy of Whig opinions in the country and, most particularly, the votes of Whig bishops in the House of Lords. Whenever a mastership or chair fell vacant, or seemed likely to do so, Newcastle mobilized his contacts, probably including the nearby bishops of Ely and Lincoln and perhaps the archbishop of Canterbury, relevant peers and professors, and Fellows of the colleges concerned whom he had already obliged or who hoped for preferment from him. At least so long as George II lived, as more and more dons came to realize, if you sought a good career in the Church, there was no point in being anything but a Whig.

Exactly how these developments related to Newcome's Whig Mastership is an intriguing question. He had been elected before Newcastle obtained the high stewardship, well before the dominance of the Whig government in the University had been fully established. Already in 1743, however, Newcome was asked to preach before the House of Commons and in the next year he was made dean of Rochester. When Newcastle won the Chancellorship in 1748 by a unanimous vote, Newcome gave offence within the University by raising his cap and cheering in the Senate House. His wife and her connexions have an unsung role in the story. Her nephew Samuel Squire, having been ordained and won

[77] See D. Souden, *Wimpole Hall* (London, 1991), chaps. 2 and 3.

[78] Baker-Mayor, 1043.

[79] Winstanley's *University of Cambridge in the Eighteenth Century* is almost entirely concerned with the story of Newcastle's relationship with Cambridge. Pp. 55–138 provide a loving account of the election for the High Stewardship in 1764.

a Fellowship at St John's, became – as well as an Anglo-Saxon scholar and a political pamphleteer – secretary and chaplain to Newcastle. At the great man's installation as Chancellor in 1749 Squire was the preacher. Sycophantically, if not blasphemously, he took as his text: 'Whence has this Man this wisdom?' Squire seems to have retained his position as Newcastle's political secretary while moving at great speed up the ecclesiastical hierarchy: William Cole, the indefatigable and usually accurate commentator on the Cambridge of his day, was so confused by the number of Squire's preferments that he ascribed some of them to a second, non-existent Squire. It was in fact one and the same Samuel Squire who was a prebendary of Wells Cathedral and archdeacon of Bath from 1743 to 1761, rector of St Anne's, Soho from 1750 to 1766, vicar of Greenwich from 1751 to 1766, made dean of Bristol in 1760, and then bishop of St David's in 1761. He was also chaplain to George III when prince of Wales and wrote for him *The Principles of Religion made easy to young persons*, published in 1763. He owed his last preferments as much to the king's favourite, the earl of Bute, as to Newcastle.[80]

Cole said of Newcome as Master:

> He was often made uneasy by the difference of his politics with those of his fellows; especially during the former part of his government: towards the latter end matters cooled; and he had time to model the college, in a long prefecture of 30 years, according to his own system.

Cole's account of Newcome's early difficulties is partly borne out by the report that, in the days before the Chancellorship election of 1748, the Master of St John's 'had occasioned great merriment by closetting his Fellows and being just as wise as he was about their sentiments after it.'[81] The major shift in the Fellows' attitude must have occurred in the 1750s and must have owed as much to outside pressures as to the activities of Newcome and his extended family.

Contemporaries believed that it was Newcome's dearest wish to become a bishop, but despite his services to Whiggery this did not happen. The alumni of St John's, the College with the largest concentration of BDs in the country, naturally hoped for their share of Newcastle's patronage. But such rewards were long in coming. Although by 1750 it was understood that Oxford was the Tory, even Jacobite, University, while, in Newcastle's words, Cambridge's 'Behaviour [was] as meritorious, as the other is justly to be censured',[82] at that date the loyalty of St John's must still have been considered uncertain. Dr John Green, however, who had been one of the Bursars in 1748–50, and was then elected Master of Corpus, was in 1761 made bishop of Lincoln – holding both posts for two years before admitting that he could not fulfil the duties of the bishopric properly if he remained Master. The only other major English see to go to a Johnian in these years also went to one who had become head of another College, Edmund Law, Master of Peterhouse, who in 1768 was appointed bishop

[80] See Scott-Mayor, III. 427–9; Baker-Mayor, 709–10. I owe thanks to Prof. Stephen Taylor for information about Squire's patrons.

[81] Winstanley, *University of Cambridge in the Eighteenth Century*, 39.

[82] Quoted in Taylor's article cited above, n. 66.

of Carlisle but continued as master, living in Cambridge except during the summer. Theologically, both men were near the Hoadlyan end of the spectrum: Law was the only bishop who voted to abolish subscription to the Thirty Nine Articles. Johnians otherwise had to make do, until 1778, with three Irish bishoprics, Welsh St David's and Sodor & Man.[83] But the nomination of Squire to a bishopric at the age of forty-eight in 1761, even though it was only to St David's, would surely have led to his translation to a grander see if he had not died in 1766.

The second major development arising outside St John's which had a huge impact on the College during the Newcome years and beyond – more, perhaps, than on any other college – was the emergence in the University of competitive examinations in mathematics which over some decades were to become written as opposed to oral, and conducted in English as opposed to Latin. Their development was very slow and fitful, but this becomes easier to understand if it is remembered that no such examinations had previously existed in any European University and that their appearance in Cambridge was the product of an organic development from within the University, not a blueprint imposed from above.[84]

In 1700 the University's examinations appear to have been entirely a matter of oral disputations on moral, philosophical or religious propositions or classical literature, conducted in Latin. It seems that just one College, Trinity, had a written element in its examinations for Fellowships, newly strengthened by Bentley. The University published each year an Order of Seniority, largely on the basis of performance in its disputations. In 1710–11 Richard Laughton, a Fellow of Clare and an ardent disciple of Newton, was proctor and so was able to take charge of the examination, and two important changes were made in it. He introduced some Newtonian theses for discussion; and the list of successful candidates was for the first time divided into two classes. In 1730 the examination moved to the newly completed Senate House and became known as the 'Senate House Examination'.

It was seen to be becoming steadily more mathematical, though it would be more accurate to describe it as focusing on mathematics and natural philosophy, with some emphasis on geometry and optics. A growing number of students, especially the brightest, took the examination, though the old disputations continued in parallel with it into the nineteenth century. The process of examination was slowly refined in various ways: students were examined in college groups; then in 1747 the final class-lists were first printed and published; and in 1753 the classes into which the students were divided became three, with the peculiar names of 'Wrangler', 'Senior Optime' and 'Junior Optime'. The examination became more and more prestigious; it was soon taken by nearly half of undergraduates; and to be classed as a Wrangler, especially as Senior Wrangler,

---

[83] Cf. Baker-Mayor, 706–26.

[84] For this and the next two paragraphs see Gascoigne, *Cambridge in the Age of the Enlightenment*, esp. pp. 270–3; Gascoigne's 'Mathematics and meritocracy: the emergence of the Cambridge mathematical tripos', *Social Studies of Science* xiv (1984), 547–84; and C. Stray, 'From oral to written examinations: Cambridge, Oxford and Dublin 1700–1914', *History of Universities* xx (2005), 76–130.

brought a candidate local, if not wider, fame and usually led straight to a Fellowship. In the 1760s two-thirds of Wranglers became Fellows, in the 1770s and 1780s more than 70 per cent.

It is impossible to be sure about all the details of the development of this examination: surviving descriptions commonly take for granted what we would like to have spelled out – for example, it is uncertain when the use of English became normal and when the examination ceased to be entirely or largely oral. But by the 1760s, which was before these changes occurred, the operation of the examination had added greatly to the competitiveness of undergraduate life and had made mathematics and natural philosophy the focus of the studies of almost all those who wished to attain academic distinction. Cambridge was already, to a surprising degree, a scientific University.

It seems strange in an age when religion and science are often declared to be mutually exclusive that in the eighteenth century a University almost entirely staffed by Anglican clergy should have become so dedicated to the study of mathematical and scientific subjects. A part of the explanation was the extraordinary renown in Cambridge of Newton and his work. For some, including Newton himself, his discoveries and theories, though they changed Man's perception of God's role in creating the universe, did not diminish it but rather enhanced it. Addison, a powerful influence on Selwin and on other undergraduates such as the sons of Lord Hardwicke,[85] had published this famous ode or hymn in the *Spectator* of 1712:

> The Spacious Firmament on high,
> With all the blue Etherial Sky,
> And spangled Heav'ns, a shining Frame,
> Their great Original proclaim:
> Th' unwearied Sun, from Day to Day,
> Does his Creator's Power display,
> And publishes to every Land
> The Work of an Almighty Hand.

This simplistic identification of God's work with Newton's theories, innocent of Matthew Prior's scepticism about scientific hypotheses, commanded wide acceptance. More generally, natural philosophy was obviously akin to natural theology, which treated Christianity as natural to men and rationally based. This was the view not only of Hoadly but also of less radical proponents of the tolerant, cool, undemanding Anglicanism which the Whigs saw as the only kind of religion unlikely to cause political upheavals. Mathematics itself had the great advantage in the circumstances that it was theologically neutral. But it was remarkable too how widely 'Divinity' could be understood. Not only subjects that now seem obviously scientific, but also literary and historical subjects, could be accepted as exercises for Doctorates of Divinity: Powell, the future Master of St John's, had earned his DD with a Latin dissertation making a

---

[85] The young Yorkes when students had got together and produced a tiny edition of what they called *Athenian Letters: Residing at Athens during the Peloponnesian War*, 4 vols. (London, 1741–3), which became quite well known and admired, and which relied heavily on Addison. I owe this reference to Dr L. Klein.

comparison between the governments of England and Scotland in the early Middle Ages.[86]

Perhaps even more surprising than the emphasis on mathematics and natural philosophy – and much criticized – was the fact that the study of classics was not equally cherished in Cambridge, although it was still the core of the curriculum in schools. By contrast, Oxford, which largely ignored mathematics, concentrated on logic and classics in its examinations when, later than at Cambridge, they were introduced.

Under Newcome more and more students of St John's distinguished themselves in the Senate House Examination. In 1747, when its list was first published, out of the twenty-four Wranglers and senior Optimes, eight were Johnians. In 1754 the College had four of the twelve Wranglers.[87] There was almost no University-organized teaching: many of the small number of professors employed by the University gave no lectures at all. So the teaching of students and their preparation for examinations were essentially a matter for the colleges. It had become normal for only a few among their Fellows to specialize as lecturers and tutors, and the role of private tutors was growing in importance. Under Newcome two Fellows of St John's became especially notable, in the College and also more widely, as teachers of mathematics and Newtonianism. The senior was Thomas Rutherford, or Rutherforth, who came up as a sizar at the age of fourteen in 1726, became a Fellow in 1733 and Regius Professor of Divinity in 1756, having published in 1748 *A system of natural philosophy* in two volumes. The other was Powell, whom we have already met in several capacities. Powell had come up in 1734 and become a Fellow in 1740. He had pre-empted Rutherforth by publishing in 1746 *Heads of lectures in experimental philosophy*. Unusually, Powell had offered his lectures to the whole University and they had proved remarkably popular.[88] These two Tutors clearly contributed much to the success of members of their College in the Examination.

The dominance of the small number of College Tutors, however, was beginning to be criticized, as for example by John Brown, a Johnian canon of Carlisle, in his *Estimate of the Manners and Principles of his Time* of 1757.

> Professorships [Brown wrote] ... have degenerated into gainful Sinecures ... the *private* lectures of *College-tutors* have usurped and occupied their Place. Thus the great Lines of Knowledge are broken, and the Fragments retailed at all Adventures, by every *Member* of a College who chuseth to erect himself into a *Professor of every Science*. What an Accession of Lustre, Fame, and Knowledge, would our Universities receive were these *Few*, now confined to the narrow Sphere of *particular* Colleges, *ordained* and *appointed* to *illuminate* the Whole?

Brown's book became famous across Europe for its wider arguments. Voltaire

---

[86] This was published by Balguy in his edition of Powell's *Discourses on Various Subjects* (London, 1776).

[87] Mullinger, *St John's College*, 256.

[88] Richard Hurd to Sir Edward Littleton, 24 Nov. 1745, published in *The Early Letters of Bishop Richard Hurd, 1739–1762*, ed. S. Brewer (London, 1995), 146. I am very grateful for the editor's loan of this book.

pretended in 1760 that its critical depiction of Britain's failings in the early days of the Seven Years War had goaded the nation into achieving the triumphs that followed. Now, he said, it was the French who needed the stimulus of such a book.[89] Catherine II invited Brown to Russia to promote educational reform. But his theories were never tested there, since he committed suicide when he was on the point of leaving England in 1766. His ideas did not triumph in Cambridge either. His book, however, is one of many indications that from the 1750s, with the Whig hegemony established and Jacobitism defeated, reform of Britain's institutions, including the universities, became again a matter of serious debate. In 1766, for example, a move was made to mount a petition urging that dons should be allowed to marry, but it was not generally supported, or even taken very seriously.[90]

St John's success in the Senate House Examination aroused envy, with some justice. Richard Watson of Trinity, later bishop of Llandaff and a notable scientist, wrote:

> I was the second wrangler of my year [1759], the leading moderator having made a person of his own college [St John's], and one of his private pupils, the first, in direct opposition to the general sense of the examiners in the Senate House, who declared in my favour. The injustice which was done me then was remembered as long as I lived in the University; and the talk about it did me more service than if I had been made senior wrangler. Our old Master sent for me, and told me not to be discouraged, for that when the Johnians had the disposal of the honours, the 2nd wrangler was always looked upon as the 1st.

In 1763 Watson had the chance, as moderator himself, to make the system fairer. Instead of examining classes made up from members of one college, in future the examiners made up the classes 'according to the abilities shown by individuals in the schools', so that the ablest were matched against each other.[91]

The rivalry between Trinity and St John's extended to every aspect of University and College life. In 1751 the Master of Trinity was surprised to receive a recommendation from the duke of Newcastle for a mere butler's post. The Master replied that he would of course like to gratify the duke.

> But Your Grace may remember perhaps that St John's college always looked upon themselves as the rivals of Trinity, the next great college in the University. And the humour, I find, is still so prevalent among us that … I am not sure whether some of the higher spirits among [the Fellows] would not sooner quarrel with their bread and butter than receive it from the hands of a Johnian butler.[92]

[89] John Brown, *An Estimate of the Manners and Principles of the Times*, 2 vols. (London, 1757); Voltaire to Louise Florence Pétronille de Tardieu d'Esclavelles d'Epinay, 26 Dec. (1760), in T. Besterman, *Correspondance de Voltaire*, vol. 106 (Geneva, 1972), 416. I owe this reference to Mr George Watson.

[90] Cooper, *Annals of Cambridge*, IV. 340–1.

[91] See Stray, 'From oral to written examinations'.

[92] Winstanley, *University of Cambridge in the Eighteenth Century*, 240 and n.

4. THE MASTERSHIP OF WILLIAM POWELL, 1765–75

Newcome was only slightly younger than his wife and became enfeebled in his last years. The election of a new master had therefore been much anticipated and discussed. The duke of Newcastle had taken an interest in the question at least since 1758, when Newcome's life was thought to be endangered by a prolonged bout of hiccups.[93] But, by the time he died in January 1765– according to the poet Gray, 'really raving'[94] – the political situation had greatly changed. The broad Whig government of Pitt and Newcastle had been faced in 1760 with the accession of a new young king, George III, who was determined not to be, as he thought his grandfather George II had been, a puppet of the Whigs. The new king's interventions helped to cause a split in the Whig party: the duke left the government in 1762 and so could no longer control church appointments as he had done for decades. When Hardwicke died in 1764, the election of his less impressive son as high steward of the University was achieved only with the greatest difficulty: the earl of Sandwich, a much-disliked member of the new government whose country seat was at Hinchingbrooke near Huntingdon, stood against him. At the election in the Senate House the votes were tied. In order to resolve the matter, it was necessary to go to the Court of King's Bench, which declared the vote of one of Sandwich's supporters invalid. In beating off this challenge, Newcastle and Hardwicke, though weakened, had shown that they were still formidable.[95] Now that under Newcome Whiggery had triumphed in St John's, they intended and expected to influence the election of his successor.

Newcome had wanted to retire from the chair in his old age because he could no longer fulfil its duties, but Newcastle had helped to prevent this, judging it politically advantageous to have the Mastership and the chair vacant at the same time. The duke had long regarded as the only serious candidates Powell, Rutherforth and another Fellow, Dr Zachary Brooke, all of whom could be considered qualified for both the Mastership and the Lady Margaret Chair. Newcastle had once regarded Powell as an enemy, whereas he had usually been able to rely on Rutherforth. But Brooke had become a client of the earl of Sandwich, and so Newcastle's first priority became to keep him out of the Mastership.

In the event seven candidates came forward for the Mastership, of whom the most plausible were at first, as predicted, Powell, Rutherforth and Brooke. As a result of a deal between the Newcastle and Sandwich factions, Brooke decided to stand only for the chair while inducing a sympathetic Fellow, Frampton, to join the Mastership fray in order to look after his interests. The archbishop of Canterbury and the bishop of Norwich were drawn into the discussions. When Powell saw which way the wind was blowing, he agreed to support Brooke for

---

[93] Ibid., 241.

[94] Gray to Palgrave, Jan. 1765 (*Gray's Letters*, ed. D. C. Tovey, 3 vols. [London, 1900–12]), III. 61. The letter (pp. 61–3) gives a racy account of the election.

[95] The election is the subject of one of Winstanley's set-pieces, *University of Cambridge in the Eighteenth Century*, pp. 240–66. Miller, *Portrait of a College*, 63–5, gives a useful short account, but he is surely wrong to call Powell a Tory.

the chair, and Frampton withdrew his candidature for the Mastership. By this time Newcastle had come out unequivocally for Powell as Master:

> The most likely to carry it on our side [he wrote to the archbishop] is Dr Powell, a very zealous friend and in every respect a most deserving unexceptionable man, was long and lately the first tutor in the College, and has now a very good temporal estate of his own.[96]

The last phrase may well be the key to Newcastle's attitude: the 'temporal estate' in question had been inherited by Powell from a cousin whose mother had been a Pelham, a close relation of Newcastle. In trying to back candidates who were both acceptable to him and likely to be elected, while not offending others, Newcastle got himself into serious difficulties. When he eventually decided to back Powell for the Mastership, he told him so, but his emollient letters to other candidates caused Powell to take umbrage at what he saw as the duke's double-dealing. But he was placated. Rutherforth, however, was permanently alienated. Brooke was duly elected to the chair and Powell to the Mastership. An unsuccessful candidate, Samuel Ogden, wrote to the duke: 'The Lady Margaret, My Lord, as I apprehend, has made the Master.'

Ogden was a Fellow of strong personality, notable for the style and brevity of his sermons in the Round Church, of which he was Vicar: 'his voice,' it was said, 'was growling and morose, and his sentences desultory, tart, and snappish'. He was famous too for his 'uncivilized appearance', his greedy eating (to him was attributed the aphorism 'The goose, Sir, is a silly bird. Too much for one; not enough for two.') and his insatiable pluralism. He thought himself eligible for many chairs in the University and preferments in the Church, and virtually purchased the chair of Geology: he gave £200 to the last surviving executor of its donor, John Woodward, and was duly appointed. Newcastle's opinion of Ogden was that he was 'not producible'.[97]

How far Newcastle's influence was decisive in the election of Powell is hard to judge. We have seen that Powell had the support of another powerful whig connexion in the Townshends, that he had been a notable College Tutor and had even published a well-known textbook. He was the first Johnian Master of the century to be an FRS. He had played an important part in running the College under Newcome, as shown by his having been sent to represent the College before the bishop of Ely in the Todington case. The financial changes made under Newcome bear the stamp of Powell's influence. But he had left Cambridge when he inherited his 'very good temporal estate' in 1761 and resigned his Fellowship two years later. He had published controversial views, which is not usually a recommendation for a Master: he had preached in 1758 against early reforming proposals to abolish the requirement of subscription to the Thirty Nine Articles for those taking degrees, while contriving to offend the orthodox by asserting that it did not matter if young men subscribed to the Articles

---

[96] Newcastle to archbishop of Canterbury, 18 Jan. 1765: Winstanley, *University of Cambridge in the Eighteenth Century*, 262.

[97] On Ogden, Scott-Mayor, III. 478–81; Gunning, *Reminiscences*, I. 236–40; Miller, *Portrait of a College*, 57–9. Gray to Mason (*Gray's Letters*, III. 62n.) also has Newcastle's remark.

Dr Ogden 1776.

13 Samuel Ogden,
Fellow and President,
he purchased the
Woodwardian chair
of Geology in 1764
and, after uttering one
memorable sentence,
died in 1778. Portrait by
Christopher Sharp

without fully grasping their significance. He must have been known within St John's as a rich man, an energetic man, a disciplinarian and a man with plans for the future of the College. He had made enemies, one of whom called him 'a most supercilious, headstrong, positive, passionate and conceited animal'. Cole wrote of him:

> He was a man of rugged and severe discipline, but virtuous, learned, and by no means beloved … he was by nature positive and obstinate, and never to be beat out of what he had once got into his head … Upon all public occasions, and where the honour and reputation of his college or the university was concerned, no one did the honours of both to greater advantage … He was rather a little, thin man, florid and red, with staring eyes, as if almost choked, or as if the collar of his shirt was too tight about his neck.[98]

Perhaps, after the long years of Newcome, the Fellows for once felt the need of a vigorous reforming head. They may also have looked forward to his becoming the first Johnian Vice-Chancellor of the University for more than thirty years, which duly happened a few months after his election as Master. They were never again to elect a master who held the Lady Margaret Chair, and all later masters

[98] Baker-Mayor, 1050 and 1047.

served as Vice-Chancellor until, in the late twentieth century, that office ceased to rotate among Heads of Houses.

Powell's election was followed by a public demonstration of Newcastle's approval of St John's under its new Master. On 28 June 1766 the duke arrived in Cambridge, stayed three days in St John's and held two levees there. He had returned to government office briefly in 1765 as lord privy seal in the ministry of the marquess of Rockingham.[99] The College was now manifestly accepted as part of the Whig ascendancy, in sharp contrast to its position when Lambert had been St John's last Vice-Chancellor.

The new Master did not take long to assert himself in the College. Although the Conclusion Book continues to record routine decisions, it also reports a much higher proportion of new initiatives than under Newcome. At the very first meeting of Powell's tenure he and the Seniors set in train a scheme to build an observatory on the west tower of Second Court, one of several measures he promoted that look like emulation of Bentley's Trinity. In 1769 were duly published *Astronomical Observations made in St John's College, Cambridge in 1767 and 1768*.[100] It was also at this first meeting that Powell made clear that he intended to accept the rectory of Freshwater on the Isle of Wight. It had been given to the College 150 years earlier, with three other livings, 'the Master being allowed "to assume and retain unto himself" one of these "at every avoidance"'. This decision was not popular with the Fellows, since Freshwater was a rich living in an agreeable place and Powell was already wealthy. But he defended himself on the ground that the living had been intended by the donor to be available to the Master and, if he declined it, the next vacancy would be unlikely to coincide with a change of Master.[101] In 1766 he was made archdeacon of Colchester, the town where he had been born. Although so active in College, he spent some summers in the Isle of Wight and attended to his duties as archdeacon, preaching some powerful sermons to the clergy in his charge.[102]

Powell's two major initiatives in College were, first, to introduce a new examination for all students and, secondly, to reform the accounts. Important though the financial changes were, they were not publicized. But his new examination, for which he has always been assigned the full credit, made a considerable stir. He introduced it in his first year of office. Until this time no college had such an examination at all, and the University actually excused noblemen and Fellow-Commoners from its own tests, while all Kingsmen were so excused. Powell did more than merely establish these examinations, overcoming considerable resistance from students. He devised the tests and assessed them himself, keeping a full and clear record of the results.[103]

[99] Cooper, *Annals of Cambridge*, IV. 342.

[100] Mullinger, *St John's College*, 243–4. An instructive exhibition on the observatory was mounted during 2009 by the College Library.

[101] See Cole's remarks in Baker-Mayor, 1056.

[102] Some at least of the sermons were published in T. Balguy (ed.), *Discourses on Various Subjects, by William Samuel Powell, DD* (1776).

[103] Mullinger, *St John's College*, 238–42, is good on the examination. Cf. the articles cited above in n. 84.

14 The Shrewsbury Tower with the College observatory aloft: testimony to the more active Mastership of William Powell (1765–75). Dismantled 1859.

The College's examination, though in part a taster for the University's, was genuinely different: it was broader in its subject-matter as well as including all students. The set topics were announced some months before the examination. The first list available comes from December 1766. It runs:

Year 3 ('for those who will be then Sophs'):
    Hydrostatics and Optics
    Grotius, *De Jure Belli et Pacis*, bk 2
    Xenophon, *Upon the Lacedaemonian and Athenian Commonwealths*
    St Mark's Gospel
Year 2 (Junior Sophs):
    Euclid, [*Elements*,] bks 1–6
    Locke, *Essays*, vol. I
    Livy, bks 1,2
    St Mark's Gospel
Year 1:
    Horace, *Epistles*
    Homer, *Iliad*, bk 9
    St Mark's Gospel.

It seems that one of the Gospels or the *Acts of the Apostles* was always set, and taken very seriously. The examiners reported in 1767 that the Greek Testament

> must always be considered as an important part of the examination. It is expected that such as make but a moderate progress in other parts of

learning, be at least attentive to this. And if those, to whom it is easy, wholly neglect it, little notice will be taken of their other merits.

Prizes were awarded to the best performers, and also to the man who produced the largest 'number of good Themes' during the year.

The actual examination was not the only new procedure laid down to further discipline and scholarship. A prize was established for regular attendance at chapel, and the Scholars were to produce exercises, on a rota determined by the butler, on the first lesson for Evensong of the day, 'in any language, verse or prose', 'as long as can be conveniently written on a half-sheet'.

The innovation of the College examination came to be regarded as a huge success, helping to account for the strength of St John's candidates in University examinations and presenting the College to the world outside Cambridge as a serious, hard-working, scholarly and Anglican establishment. But no other college followed the example of St John's until Trinity did so in 1790. It is easy to see that the examination had serious weaknesses. The syllabus was not especially demanding, and examiners commented that some students did not trouble to deal with all the required texts or to stay for the whole time allocated to the examination. And it encountered opposition from the now conspicuous radical elements in the University. John Jebb, an active Fellow of Peterhouse, was by contemporary standards radical both in religion – questioning some of the Thirty Nine Articles of the Church of England in which he had been ordained – and in politics – supporting some measure of parliamentary reform.[104] In his *Remarks upon the present mode of education in the University of Cambridge* of 1772 he urged that the University should be reformed in numerous ways: by making itself more widely accessible through ceasing to insist on subscription to the Thirty Nine Articles; by diversifying its curriculum; and, to ensure that students worked harder, by subjecting all of them to annual University examinations. While he acknowledged Powell's college examination to be a beneficent reform so far as it went, he argued that it was wrong to leave so much of the teaching and examining to the colleges. He contended that the University and its professors should provide more lectures, which students should be required to attend, and that the University should examine them all, of whatever social and academic standing. Despite considerable support, including that of Newcastle's successor as Chancellor, the duke of Grafton, Jebb's proposal was narrowly rejected.

Powell wrote a pamphlet in answer to Jebb's. He first denied, unconvincingly, that professors' lectures were ill attended. But he argued that in any case the really useful lectures were those of 'the Tutors in the separate Colleges', and that the 'private instruction' that students received in college was also invaluable. It was a great advantage, he claimed, that 'the Governors and Instructors live with their Pupils, whom they teach and examine daily.' It would be very

---

[104] On Jebb and these controversies see the valuable work of A. Page, *John Jebb and the Enlightenment Origins of British Radicalism* (London, 2003), esp. chs 2, 5 and 6. I am most grateful to Dr T. J. Hochstrasser for drawing this book to my attention.

foolish, he concluded, to give over the assessment of students to ill-paid external examiners.[105]

This was one of the earliest bouts in a controversy that continues to this day about the proper relation between the University and the colleges. Although Powell's defence of the existing system was less than wholly convincing, it is hard to see how at this time the University could have been placed in full charge of teaching and examining all students. The colleges supported nearly 400 Fellows and accepted the responsibility of making some of them Tutors charged with teaching undergraduates. The University had a mere handful of professors, some of them unpaid, most of whom were not required to give a single lecture. Powell's arguments were certainly more difficult to sustain for small colleges with ten or a dozen Fellows and a tiny intake. But, until a major reform was contemplated, broadening the University curriculum and providing the staff to teach it, and removing the exemptions of Kingsmen and Fellow-Commoners, Jebb's scheme could not work, while Powell's offered a practical way forward in the circumstances of the time.

Lurking behind these debates was the question of the relationship between the Church of England and the universities. Both Jebb and Powell had religious considerations in mind. Jebb found some of the Thirty Nine Articles unacceptable, and was soon to give up his Orders and attend the Essex Street Unitarian Chapel recently founded by Theophilus Lindsey (matriculated 1741), a Johnian defector from the Church of England. There were a number of such cases among members of the College: for example, James Allen (1751) became a Methodist, Julius Bate (1727) a Hutchinsonian divine, and Edward Perronett (1741) worked with the Wesleys and joined the Countess of Huntingdon's Connexion, an upper-class affiliate of Methodism.[106]

Powell's own religious position is significant. When giving a sermon on the anniversary of the execution of Charles I, he managed to avoid showing the slightest sympathy for the king and instead deplored the violence of seventeenth-century political and religious disputes generally. It is intriguing that his greatest friend, to whom he left £1,000, was Thomas Balguy, a Fellow of St John's and a natural theologian of some note who acknowledged the merits and influence of Hoadly while not conceding his most extreme claims. Both Balguy and Powell saw the maintenance of the national Church of England as essential to politics, religion and society. Both were ready to broaden access to it to a limited extent, by not insisting that those who subscribed to the Thirty Nine Articles had to endorse every word of them. They accepted the change, agreed by the University in 1772, under which a man taking the BA had only to 'declare that I am *bona fide* a member of the Church of England as by law established.' But they would not go so far as to embrace Nonconformists. They evidently agreed with Dr Johnson, who remarked when discussing this debate:

---

[105] [W. S. Powell,] *An Observation on the Design of Establishing Annual Examinations at Cambridge* (Cambridge, 1774). Cf. Gascoigne, *Cambridge in the Age of the Enlightenment*, 175, 204.

[106] See the biographical sketches of these men in Scott-Mayor, III.

'our Universities were founded to bring up members of the Church of England, and we must not supply our enemies with arms from our arsenal.'[107]

The Master had a revealing dispute with a very early Evangelical, a clever and athletic Fellow-Commoner called Rowland Hill, who came up in 1764. Hill was acquainted with the countess of Huntingdon and greatly admired her. He had contacts with a group of Oxford undergraduates who were sent down in 1768 for behaving like Methodists. Hill believed that the University of Cambridge was 'in total darkness' and formed a society of devout students who met for prayer and who taught and preached in the open air in Cambridge and in the country-side nearby. Powell threatened to send him down, but Hill's father, who was a baronet and whose family had given the College some livings, evidently exerted pressure, and the Master climbed down. In surviving letters the young man described with glee to his like-minded sister how Powell sent a Tutor to him to say that he could remain if he 'wd not disturb the town by public conventicles … and [promised] not to teach in the University any doctrine contrary to the 39 Articles'. Hill said he would not have promised never to talk religion to towns-people, and that nothing was said by the Tutor about 'not dispersing Method-istical books, and frequenting houses suspected of Methodism'. He was one of the first Fellow-Commoners to take the Senate House Examination. After he graduated, six bishops declined to ordain him, though he managed to become a deacon. All the same, he contrived to spend a very long life ministering in chapels built for him, describing himself as 'Curate of all the fields, commons etc. throughout England & Wales', starting up Sunday schools and other reli-gious organizations, and both promoting and performing vaccination on a large scale.[108]

Though first and foremost a cleric and divine, Powell was also a historian, a bit of a lawyer, a scientist and an administrator. He showed a rare ability to mas-ter the complications and technicalities of the College's finances and accounts. Shocked by what he learned, he was determined to reform them, thereby mak-ing his second great contribution to the College's development. The historian of its finances regards 1770, when Powell carried through a reorganization of the accounts, as the principal landmark in their whole history.[109] The College's major source of revenue was rents and fines from its landed property. But the Rental did not provide an intelligible account of the financial position. Not only were the headings and some of the details in barbarous Latin, but, as Powell himself wrote in his 'Reasons for altering the form of the accounts' in 1769,

> The accounts are much longer than use requires … Notwithstanding their length, they trust much to the memory, and are immethodical, intricate

---

[107] On Balguy, H. D. Jones, *John Balguy: An English Moralist of the 18th Century* (*Abhand-lungen zur Philosophie und ihrer Geschichte*), Heft 2 [Leipzig, 1907]). Dr Johnson's remark is quoted, e.g. in Peter Searby, *A History of the University of Cambridge*, III. *1750–1870* (Cambridge, 1997), 409. Gascoigne, *Cambridge in the Age of the Enlight-enment*, 132–3.

[108] SJCL, Misc. Letters/Hill: Letters from Rowland Hill to his sister; Scott-Mayor, II. 701–4.

[109] Howard, *Finances*, chap. V, gives an excellent account which is the basis of what follows.

and obscure … they are very defective … They are incorrect; constantly incorrect in small matters, and liable to be so in greater. Such parts as are correct, yet carry in them the appearance of error or fraud. Several parts of the accounts being kept only in the Bursar's private books or on loose papers are liable to be lost … The greatest defect in our accounts is that they bring us to no conclusion. In the great rental no balance ever appears.

This is the authentic 'positive' voice of Powell the Enlightened autocrat, reformer and modernizer.

The rental of 1770, which he masterminded, was in English, was divided into Revenue and Expenditure, and made it easy to produce a certificate showing how far the former exceeded the latter. The document was still complicated, and certain items were still kept out of it, like the accounts of the Platt Fellowships Foundation. But the improvement in clarity and efficiency was enormous.

Powell can also be seen carrying further the policy begun under Newcome, of phasing out the old system of rewarding college employees (partly or wholly) in kind and with perquisites. It was replaced, as opportunity offered, by a new system: the payment of cash salaries or wages. For example, it was decreed in 1769 that the Junior Bursar should no longer make a 'charge for Charcoal beyond what he pays, or for boiling Brawn.' There shall in future be no present from the Charcoal merchant. Old iron and copper shall no longer be a perquisite but they must be sold for the benefit of the College. Instead of these perquisites, the Junior Bursar shall receive £22 p.a. in addition to his meagre stipend of £2, plus his 'fees at the two Commencements', and nothing more. This is just one example of several such reforms made under Powell.[110]

Another of his changes was to modify the position of the sizars, affecting their social as much as their financial status. Previously they had paid to the College less than other students did, in return for performing duties, chiefly waiting at table in Hall. In March 1765 it was agreed that nine of them should wait at table and 'for their trouble' receive the fruits of nine vacant Scholarships. Before long sizars were being admitted without being assigned to a Fellow, as had earlier been required. It was not possible to award a Scholarship to a student until he was in residence, but it seems that promising sizars were being told beforehand that they would be made Scholars or Exhibitioners after coming up. Within a few years they were spared all menial duties.[111]

Powell evidently hoped to get those College statutes changed which restricted Fellowships to students from particular counties – provisions which made it impossible to make elections to Fellowships on merit alone. It was agreed in 1766 that a petition on this matter 'shall be presented to His Majesty if the Master shall find it probable, that such a Petition will succeed'. Since no more was heard of the matter, it must have emerged that the king did not wish to make such a change.[112] I have, however, come across no objection being

---

[110] CB, e.g. 13 Nov. 1766; 16 Feb. 1769; 20 Feb. 1770; 20 and 25 Feb. 1772.

[111] Scott, 'Some aspects of College life in past times'.

[112] CB, 25 Mar. 1768. This item is not, as most of the others are, in the extracts printed in Baker-Mayor, 1070–8. No doubt this explains why Scott's preface to part IV of his *Admissions*, p. viii, says that the attempt to make this change began only later.

made to the statute that required all Fellows to be Englishmen born, a provision that applied in every college except Trinity and King's.

It is curious that under Powell no fewer than three Fellows of the College were declared insane. On 25 May 1768

> The Master and six Seniors being met to elect two Seniors in the Room of Mr Cardale and Mr Ludlam unanimously agreed that the Insanity of the two Fellows next to the Seniority, namely Mr Allen and Mr Stubbs, is a weighty Cause why they should not be elected into the number of Seniors.[113]

Two years later a Fellow called Stephen Fovargue BD horsewhipped and kicked his gyp Thomas Goode, who soon afterwards died, declaring on his deathbed that the injuries inflicted by Fovargue were the cause of his illness. The coroner's inquest returned a verdict of manslaughter. Despite the fact that two surgeons who had examined the body concluded that the cause of death was 'a fever brought on by excessive drinking', Fovargue fled the country, 'being apprehensive of a Cambridge Jury from his known ill character'. He was outlawed and his Fellowship was declared vacant. When he returned to Cambridge in desperation, he found that he could not be tried because he was an outlaw, and so he went to London as a vagrant, and soon died. He was said to be 'a dissipated character and partially insane'.[114]

A Master of Powell's ambitious temperament was bound to cherish plans for improving the College site and buildings. In 1771 or 1772 he proposed a scheme to 'lay out [the College's] gardens, under the direction of the celebrated Mr. [Capability] Brown, and to face with stone the south side of their first court'. He further proposed that old members should be asked to subscribe for this purpose, saying that he himself would give the considerable sum of £500. The scheme was agreed to, and the active local architect, James Essex, began the remodelling of the first court at the beginning of 1773. With the new stone came new sash windows and a new arrangement of the rooms internally, to make available larger, more self-contained sets. The cost was apparently £2,700. Work was beginning on the other sides of the court when Powell died. The Fellows immediately rebelled against it. The result, of course, was to unbalance the Court, and most people now regret that Powell was ever allowed to start emulating another of Bentley's schemes and begin classicizing the College's buildings. But the rooms were larger and more attractive than the old ones and were assigned to rich students who could pay the higher rents. The smaller works mentioned during Powell's reign include other replacements of windows, usually by larger panes, and the addition of new gates, preferably of iron, 'for the end of the walks'.[115]

How much Brown did in the grounds is uncertain. It is surmised that he created the Wilderness, suppressing the bowling green, but the documentary

---

[113] Baker-Mayor, 1073.

[114] Cooper, *Annals of Cambridge*, IV. 372 and n.

[115] On the refacing of part of the First Court and other lesser works see Crook, *Foundation to Gilbert Scott*, 66–72. On the iron gates, CB, 13 Nov. 1766 (Baker-Mayor, 1072). See also on the new internal design of the block Mark Nicholls, above, pp. 153–4.

evidence is absent. In 1772 it was explicitly 'ordered that the bank be repaired under the direction of Mr. Brown', whatever that meant. No payments from the Master or the College are to be found in Brown's accounts, now held by the Royal Horticultural Society, but Powell could perhaps have paid him privately. In 1778, however, the College presented Brown with a piece of plate worth £50.[116]

It may be significant that Brown was a friend of John Mainwaring, who was Bursar from 1768 to 1786 and who must have played more of a role in Powell's Mastership than appears from the record. Although we know that a deputy was brought in to sort out the accounts, Powell could hardly have carried through the reform if Mainwaring had been opposed to it. He had come up in 1742 and had been presented in 1749 to the Rectory of Church Stretton in Shropshire by Lord Weymouth. He could therefore retain his Fellowship. He was a friend of bishop Hurd and the poets Gray and Mason, travelled abroad with Dr Fisher, a Fellow of St John's, and is said to have dined at the table of Cardinal Bernis in Rome. In 1760 he published anonymously the first ever book-length study of a composer – Handel, of course. After his long stint as Bursar he became Lady Margaret Professor and married a charming singer. He had asthma or some other breathing problem that made his sermons difficult to hear; and, because he knew this, he always had them printed. He was often ill but lived to be over eighty.[117]

Powell's 'manner and speech' had been affected by a stroke some years before in January 1775 he had another seizure, which proved fatal, while attending a meeting of the governing body of the new Addenbrooke's Hospital. Masters are rarely as able and effective as he was and, as we shall see, the impact of his reforms was felt for decades to come.

Before, during and after Powell's Mastership, one of his exact contemporaries, Sir Fletcher Norton, was a major figure in the House of Commons, the Johnian most highly placed in national politics between Prior and Castlereagh. He must have maintained some sort of connexion with the College because he sent his son to it in 1760, Powell being designated his Tutor.[118] Sir Fletcher had a justified reputation for greed, self-aggrandizement, ill-temper and bullying. Horace Walpole said of him, 'Nothing can exceed the badness of his character even in this bad age.' But he was acknowledged to be a very good lawyer, and

---

[116] CB, 10 July 1772; J. Clifford, *Capability Brown* (Princes Risborough, 2001), 36; Crook, *Foundation to Gilbert Scott*, 66, 72; two articles by J. S. Boys Smith, 'The alterations made in the Fellows' Garden and the College grounds in 1822–3', *Eagle* liii (1950), 147–61, and 'The College grounds and playing fields', *Eagle* liv (1951), 300–5. Crook says that advice was sought from 'a Mr Miller', but he is spelled 'Millar' in the Conclusion Book (as correctly shown in Baker-Mayor, p. 1071). Perhaps it would be worth investigating whether this was the celebrated landscape gardener, Sanderson Millar or Miller.

[117] Scott-Mayor, III. 526–8. R. Luckett, *Handel's Messiah: A Celebration* (London, 1992), 11, 58, 181–2, also pointing out the book's errors. Mainwaring does not get a mention in Gray's published correspondence, but he figures often in Brewer's edition of Hurd's (see above, n. 88).

[118] On Norton: Scott-Mayor, III. 76–8, appendix, pp. 453–5; P. D. G. Thomas, *The House of Commons in the Eighteenth Century* (Oxford, 1971), 312–25; N. W. Wraxall, *Historical Memoirs of My Own Time*, ed. R. Askham (London, 1904), 434–7; *ODNB* (P. Laundy).

governments found him a dangerous enemy. In the Whig split of 1762 he took the king's side, accepting the office of solicitor-general under Bute in that year and the office of attorney-general under Grenville from 1763 to 1765. He opposed John Wilkes in the dispute over general warrants and, when the Commons passed a motion condemning them in February 1764, he famously declared: 'If I was a Judge I should pay no more regard to this resolution than to that of a drunken porter.' He was then out of office until 1770 but was won over to support the duke of Grafton's government in 1769 by appointment to a sinecure worth £3,000 a year. When Lord North became prime minister and the Speakership of the Commons fell vacant in 1770, Norton was elected to it, although many MPs disapproved of him strongly enough to vote for an alternative candidate (a Townshend) who had made it clear that he would not serve. Horace Walpole thought he could 'do less hurt in the Speaker's Chair than anywhere else'. He did not prove entirely impartial, but much more so than had been expected, and his personality kept the House in order. Towards the end of the seventies, after the beginning of the War of American Independence, he ceased to support the government of Lord North and made another notorious gaffe when the House agreed to pay off the Civil List debt, saying from the Chair that the Commons had 'granted to Your Majesty ... a very great additional revenue; great, beyond example; great beyond Your Majesty's highest expense'. The king and the ministers assailed the Speaker, but the Commons backed him, and he now became so popular with the opposition that he was made a Freeman of the City of London. He was not re-elected Speaker in 1780 and received none of the great offices he had hoped for. But in 1782, in a scene worthy of Gilbert, he was made a peer by the king at a few hours' notice during the Queen's Drawing Room – an unprecedented breach of protocol – because the new prime minister, Rockingham, demanded visible proof that the king would bestow honours on those he recommended, and Norton, as a former Speaker, had the least disputable claim. He became Lord Grantley.

If the career of Norton illustrates the opportunities that politics under George III could offer to an able and rumbustious Johnian lawyer of conservative views, an almost completely contrasting example was given by John Horne, who later added Tooke to his surname.[119] He had come up in 1754 as a sizar, the son of a poulterer who had made enough money to send his son to Eton. The boy never managed to concentrate on a career in one profession. He tried the law without success, was ordained at his father's behest but spent some years tutoring and travelling. Having became curate of St Lawrence, Brentford, he continued to travel. A lively man with interesting views on philosophy and literature, he met many of the greatest men of his age during his travels: Voltaire, D'Alembert, Adam Smith, Hume and so on. But the most important friendship for his later career was that of Wilkes, whose stance on general warrants he supported. When Wilkes stood as MP for Middlesex in 1768, Horne gave him unstinting help in person and in print, becoming known as an effective radical pamphleteer and winning renown when in 1771 he succeeded in overturning a libel

---

[119] A large literature contains references to Horne Tooke. The following are particularly helpful in this context: Scott-Mayor, III. 621–4; C. and D. Bewley, *Gentleman Radical: A Life of John Horne Tooke* (London, 1998).

15 In contrast to Ogden: the radical John Horne Tooke: SJCL, Port. III.6

judgment of the great Lord Chief Justice Mansfield (who had decided against St John's in the Todington case). When Horne came to Cambridge in order to take his MA in 1771, the award was opposed in the Senate House on the ground that he had traduced the clergy. But he was backed by the highly respectable churchman Richard Beadon, his Johnian contemporary and friend, and was allowed the degree. He then took up the cause of the American colonists in the War of Independence and was imprisoned for a year for fomenting sedition. In the early 1780s he became active in the Society for Constitutional Information, in the cause of parliamentary reform. Meanwhile he was writing lively books on grammar and philology, most notably *The Diversions of Purley* (1786). We shall meet him again among the English sympathizers with the French Revolution.

5. NEW ISSUES AND NEW PROSPERITY, 1775–1800

The election of a Master to follow Powell was held under quite different conditions from that of 1765. The duke of Grafton, Newcastle's successor as Chancellor of the University, was never going to bother himself with micro-management of its affairs. In any case he ceased to be prime minister in 1770 and held government office only fitfully thereafter. His great interest in life was horse-racing at Newmarket, which was close to his house at Euston. Furthermore, he turned out to be something of a maverick. He had been an undergraduate at Peterhouse when the Johnian Law had just become its Master and was converting it into a centre of what, by the standards of the University, amounted to religious radicalism. Grafton himself had become a Unitarian and declined to accept the LL.D. usually bestowed on Chancellors because during the ceremony he would have had to affirm belief in the Thirty Nine Articles of the Church of England.[120] In the election of a Master to follow Powell, much of the outside interference recorded came not from politicians but from bishops.[121]

The candidates were three Fellows. One was Samuel Ogden, as usual; another Richard Beadon, who was the University's public orator and a cousin of the late bishop Samuel Squire; and John Chevallier, who had held various minor posts in the College and seems to have specialized in philosophy. Balguy did not stand, though he was regarded by many as a most worthy candidate: he was not well known to the Fellows, since he was archdeacon of Winchester and resided in that diocese. The archbishop of Canterbury and the bishops of Ely, London and Winchester all lobbied for Beadon, as did Lord North, Lord Hyde and the earl of Sandwich. This seems to have been one of those elections in which the younger Fellows rebelled against the Seniors and outsiders and insisted on electing an agreeable man not likely to domineer over them. Chevallier triumphed by one vote, a Fellow having 'come post out of Wales, the night before the election', to support him. Cole paid the new Master this back-handed compliment: he said he was

> the best hearted creature, humane, generous and obliging, I have ever conversed with: a man of integrity and open-heartedness, learned and ingenious, and is deficient in no part of an excellent master but want of health and vigour to manage a large and turbulent society.

As was pointed out when he died, he was unusual in having not received 'any preferment either from the College or from private patronage'. On this account the College paid for his funeral.[122]

It is intriguing that Powell's visits to Freshwater played a part in the story of Chevallier's election. While in the Isle of Wight the Master had got to know the family of a Peterhouse man called Fisher and persuaded him to move to St John's as Fellow and Tutor in 1773, where he became friendly with Mainwaring and made a great impression by 'his various talents, ... the suavity of his manners, and the peculiarly felicitous manner with which he conveyed instruction'. It was he who had organized the party that voted for Chevallier. He had been private tutor in England to a prince Poniatowski, probably the nephew of the king of Poland, only the first of many royal princes and princesses whom he was to take in hand, including Queen Victoria's father and George IV's daughter. He was clearly the smoothest of operators. Both he and Beadon ended up as bishops.[123]

---

[120] See Clark, *English Society*, esp. pp. 311–13 and notes.

[121] For the election of Chevallier see Baker-Mayor, 729, 1078–82; Mullinger, *St John's College*, 252–3.

[122] CB, 17 Mar. 1789.

[123] Baker-Mayor, 731–2, 1081–2. Dr R. Butterwick kindly advised me about Polish princes visiting Cambridge and England at this time.

Chevallier died comparatively young, having gone blind, in 1789. He was succeeded by William Craven, another very mild and modest man. He had been one of the early stars of the new University examinations: Fourth Wrangler in 1753 and winner of one of the medals that Newcastle had just endowed. Deprived of his Keyton Fellowship by the bishop of Ely in the Todington case,[124] he was soon elected to another. He had been Mathematical Tutor and was Senior Bursar and also Professor of Arabic. Whereas Chevallier appears to have published nothing, Craven at least brought out three sermons.[125]

Chevallier's and Craven's reigns were notable for the continuing influence of Powell's reforms and for the impact of political and other external changes rather than for internally generated new developments or masters' initiatives. To take first the effect of Powell's reforms, the last two years of his Mastership had seen the College's intake creep over forty for the first time for decades and, although this figure was not reached in every subsequent year, there were several intakes of over fifty. No doubt this marked increase in admissions, as compared with other colleges, was partly due to the reputation for serious study associated with the new college examination as well as to impressive results in the Senate House Examination. In addition, the incongruous new stone-faced rooms in First Court provided better-class accommodation than other parts of the College and most other colleges, so that they proved very popular with wealthy students.

At the other end of the social spectrum, the existence of sizarships had always been important in giving an opportunity to poor children of talent to rise to the top. It is surprising how many fathers of entrants to St John's were in humble occupations, most often 'husbandmen', who could barely afford the fees of a sizar, let alone a commoner's. Three of the eighteenth-century Masters, Newcome, Chevallier and Craven, had begun as sizars, as had bishops Green and Law. But a considerable number of those admitted as sizars did not stay the course, and their overall numbers – and their proportion of the students – fell markedly during the eighteenth century. Around 1700 about thirty sizars were admitted annually, roughly half the whole intake. Of the much smaller intake of the 1760s about a third, around ten, were sizars. Their average numbers continued to decline, and in 1788–9, for the first time, the number of noblemen and Fellow-Commoners among the intake actually exceeded the number of sizars – a pattern that recurred in several later years. This change, reflected also in the greater number of peers and future peers of high degree who came to St John's in the last decades of the century,[126] marks a distinct shift in the social balance of the College's student body. It seems unlikely that this was Powell's aim when he altered the conditions of sizars, since he was known for assisting poor students out of his own pocket.[127] In any case, the encouragement of social mobility was built into the College statutes: in electing Fellows, the College was required to

---

[124] See above, pp. 185–6.

[125] On Craven and his election, Baker-Mayor, 1088–93; Mullinger, *St John's College*, 261–4.

[126] See above, p. 165; and on the social mix Miller, *Portrait of a College*, 71–2.

[127] Baker-Mayor, 1056.

give preference to 'the more needy candidates'.[128] But, socially, Powell was the best-connected Master of the century so far, and he knew very well the value to the College and its members, especially those looking for Church preferment, of acquaintances among the aristocracy.

Powell had made sure to set a good example to the students, by always attending chapel and by always overseeing the examination he had invented. The testimony of William Wilberforce, who came up as a Fellow-Commoner in 1776, only a year after Powell's death, strongly suggests that a reaction had already set in against his discipline. In this year there was the unusually large number of eleven Fellow-Commoners, plus one nobleman, as against twelve sizars. Wilberforce will have dined with the former:

> I was introduced [he wrote] on the very first night of my arrival to as licentious a set of men as can well be conceived. They drank hard. And their conversation was even worse than their lives ... often indeed I was horror-struck by their conduct.

As if this was not enough discouragement, his Tutors asked him why, since he was rich, he bothered to work hard. 'My tutor,' he wrote, 'never urged me to attend lectures and I never did.' He was told that he was too clever to need mathematics. All in all, he said, 'as much pains were taken to make me idle as were ever taken to make anyone else studious.'[129] It is hard to imagine these attitudes being tolerated while Powell was alive.

So far as the records show, the College examination was set and conducted under Chevallier and Craven in much the same way as under Powell, though it was evidently becoming more of a written examination, with Latin questions giving way to English. Its success was manifest when Trinity copied it in 1790. The first surviving printed examination paper dates from 1794. It is a mathematics paper which begins with a few algebraic equations to solve and continues with half-a-dozen English-language puzzles. This example of the latter, which seems one of the more difficult, shows their rather elementary nature:

> A countryman, being employed by a poulterer to drive a flock of geese and turkeys to London, in order to distinguish his own from any he might meet on the road, pulled 3 feathers out of the tails of the turkeys and 1 out of those of the geese, and upon counting them found that the number of turkey feathers exceeded twice those of the geese by 15. Having bought 10 geese and sold 15 turkeys by the way, he was surprised to find as he drove them into the poulterer's yard, that the number of geese exceeded the number of turkeys in the proportion of 7:3. Required the number of each.[130]

St John's results in the Senate House Examination continued to be excellent. The best years were 1779 – during Wilberforce's time, but he did not take the examination – when ten out of the seventeen Wranglers were Johnians; 1782, when the tally was seven out of eighteen; and 1788 and 1792, when it was six

[128] 1580 Statutes, cap. 12.

[129] W. Hague, *William Wilberforce* (London, 2008), 21–4.

[130] The paper is printed in C. Wordsworth, *Scholae academicae* (Cambridge, 1877), 256.

out of eighteen. A rare Fellow-Commoner to submit himself to this test was Thomas Gisborne, Wilberforce's contemporary and lifelong friend, who was classed as Sixth Wrangler in 1780.[131]

The Conclusion Book for Chevallier's time reports many decisions to repair and maintain aspects of the property: renewing the pavements of the Courts, reslating some of the roofs, painting and reglazing the Hall and so forth. But no major work was undertaken. This modesty kept down the College's expenditure, while returns from property continued to rise. The College's income began to grow more rapidly than Trinity's and come nearer to it. In 1781 the Fellows' dividend was increased to £56 and in 1788 to £60.[132]

Under Craven a little more was done, and much more contemplated. In February 1792 it was agreed, according to the Conclusion Book, 'to make a new staircase leading to the Wilderness – and to make a passage through the turret of the Treasury.' It seems inconceivable that 'the Wilderness' was what was meant. One suspects that the following entry for November 1793 superseded the earlier one: 'Agreed that the Labyrinth be put in habitable repair, and one new stair case be made, under the direction of the Senior Bursar.' It does not say much for previous Bursars that the Labyrinth was not 'in habitable repair' before this time. In 1796 it was agreed to modify some chimneys, at the Bursar's discretion, according to Count Rumford's new plan. By 1800 the dividend had been raised to £90. These successive increases, although they were partially offset by higher living costs, especially during the war against revolutionary France, clearly improved the lot of Fellows.[133] Dons, like beneficed clergy of the Church of England, were becoming richer, living and behaving more like gentlemen. It was during this period that, throughout the country, the number of clergymen JPs was rising fast.

The College was beginning to contemplate new building. A plan for one new block was commissioned in 1789; and the future Sir John Soane, who was in charge of some small improvements in 1792, was asked to produce a scheme for what might be done more generally. Two years later a new building fund was set up, which it was intended would grow as Fellow-Commoners put into it money in lieu of their prescribed gifts of plate. But war and a fall in student numbers diminished the sense of urgency in the later 1790s.[134]

Miscellaneous expenditure included 'altering the pitch of the organ' – presumably raising it – and giving 'a guinea to a poor Turk'. During the war quite frequent doles were given to the poor, 10 guineas 'to the Soup Establishment', the same 'towards the relief of the Widows and Orphans of the Seamen and Marines who fell in the engagement of August 1 1798 [the battle of the Nile] under Admiral Nelson'.[135] The large sum of £500 was contributed 'for the Service of Government' in 1798.[136]

---

[131] Mullinger, *St John's College*, 255–8.

[132] Many of the decisions are quoted in Baker-Mayor, 1082–8, but after 1786, when a new Conclusion Book was begun, one has to go to the original MS volume.

[133] Howard, *Finances*, 313–17; Neild, *Riches and Responsibility*, 75–6.

[134] Crook, *Foundation to Gilbert Scott*, 71–2.

[135] CB, 9 June 1777, 6 Apr. 1778, 10 Feb. and 13 Oct. 1798, 25 Jan. 1800.

[136] CB, 10 Feb. 1798.

Under these two agreeable but uninspiring Masters St John's, in common with all colleges, was being faced with a succession of new challenges. One issue, it is true, had at last gone away: with the death of James, the 'Old Pretender', in 1766, even the pope declined to recognize his son as king of England: instead, he welcomed George III's brothers and sons, one after the other, to Rome. There was now no doubt about the security of the Hanoverian dynasty. But, as we saw, from at least 1762 Britain's foreign and internal policy both became subjects of serious and divisive controversy. Heightened public involvement was seen in the Wilkes affair of the 1760s and then in the disputes over the treatment of the American colonies, culminating in the War of Independence and a disastrous defeat for Britain. In 1780 there were large public meetings in Cambridge as elsewhere, demanding 'Economical Reform' of the administrative system in a spirit reminiscent of Powell's reforms in St John's; and in 1782 there was agitation for a measure of parliamentary reform. Both the petitions produced in these contexts in Cambridge had been drafted by the Regius Professor of Divinity, Richard Watson, the Trinity man who had earlier reformed the Senate House Examination to curb the successes of St John's.

At the general election of 1780 three out of the five candidates for the two University seats were Johnians: the Hon. John Townshend, Lord Hyde and Richard Crofts. Townshend got in. William Pitt, aged twenty-one, son of the great earl of Chatham and a reformer, who had been a student at Pembroke and had become a close friend of Wilberforce, came bottom of the poll. At the same election Wilberforce won a seat for his home town of Hull. After North was forced to resign as prime minister in 1782, George III had to acknowledge the colonies' victory. Three new governments were formed in quick succession, none of which had the full confidence of the king. At the end of 1783, with the peace signed, he dismissed the third, the 'coalition' of Fox and North, and appointed Pitt, now aged twenty-four, prime minister. In the general election following this royal *coup d'état*, Pitt stood again for the University and this time came top of the poll. The second seat was won by the earl of Euston, a Trinity man, son and heir of the Chancellor, the duke of Grafton. In the Commons Euston was inclined to follow Fox and the opposition to Pitt. The majority of voters from St John's backed Pitt, and the majority in Trinity Euston. This was the ideal parliamentary representation for the University, the more so after Pitt was elected High Steward of the University in 1790. He and Euston remained the University's MPs until Pitt died in 1806. In 1784 Wilberforce stood as a supporter of Pitt in the huge county constituency of Yorkshire, defying its great landlords, and won, ensuring himself national fame. Out of the political upheaval of the early eighties had come a new hegemony that lasted nearly as long as Newcastle's had. From 1783 to 1801 Pitt remained prime minister, advising the king whom to appoint to bishoprics and other posts in the Church. In 1789 he made Beadon (by this time Master of Jesus) bishop of Gloucester; and in 1794 William Stuart, son of the earl of Bute, who had come up to St John's in 1772, was made bishop of St David's, being promoted in 1800 to be archbishop of Armagh.

By the 1780s the rise of Evangelicalism was seen as a serious problem by the current leaders of the Church of England. The whole tenor of Anglican history in the eighteenth century – especially in Cambridge – had been to foster a remarkably undogmatic, undemanding piety, avoiding both rigorism and 'enthusiasm'. The upper classes had been mainly scornful of the efforts of John Wesley and his Methodists to take the Gospel as they understood it to places and people which the official Church of England did not reach, of their stress on revelation rather than reason and nature as the basis of Christianity, and of their claim that Christ expected of its adherents conversion to a completely new way of life. Many Anglicans loathed this tendency, though it had not yet clearly separated itself from the Church of England. Powell's hostility was the normal attitude of the University's clergy to Evangelicalism, which was regarded with good reason as an attempt to bring some Methodist attitudes and methods into the Church of England. Another Johnian expression of the same view is to be found in the 400-page will of John Hulse, dated 1777, establishing a fund to pay preachers who will

> demonstrate … the truth and excellence of Christianity, … chiefly against notorious Infidels, whether Atheists or Deists, not descending to any particular sects or controversies (so much to be lamented) among Christians themselves, except some new or dangerous error either of superstition or enthusiasm, as of Popery or Methodism.[137]

The Johnian Bishop Ross of Exeter, appointed in 1778, had been ready to invite John Wesley to dinner, but many Anglican clergy deplored this action.[138] Wilberforce's parents had been horrified when his uncle's and aunt's Methodism had attracted him as a boy, and they had broken off the contact.[139] But, some years after his self-indulgent time at St John's, in 1785, he underwent a conversion of a Methodist character, though emphatically within the growing Evangelical community of the Church of England. The change in his behaviour was less drastic than in some such cases. He prescribed these rules for himself about dining: 'No dessert, no tastings, one thing in first, one in second course. Simplicity. In quantity moderate … Never more than six glasses of wine; my common allowance two or three.'[140] But his theological programme was drastic enough. In his seminal book of 1797 entitled *A practical view of the prevailing religious system of professed Christians in the higher and middle classes in this country contrasted with real Christianity*, he sought to eradicate 'the deadly leaven of Hoadly's latitudinarian views which had spread to an alarming extent among the clergy'.[141]

Within Cambridge the Evangelical movement was at first especially associated with Magdalene and King's Colleges, then with Queens', and not with St John's. Wilberforce himself was deeply influenced by Isaac Milner, with whom he travelled on the Continent in 1785, a Fellow of Queens' who was later to become President of the College. It was in 1785 also that the Vice-Chancellor and Master of Magdalene, Peter Peckard, set as a subject for the University's

---

[137] Cooper, *Annals of Cambridge*, IV. 440.

[138] Baker-Mayor, 726–7.

[139] Hague, *Wilberforce*, 7–16.

[140] Ibid., 101.

[141] Ibid., 268–76.; quotation from Gascoigne, *Cambridge in the Age of the Enlightenment*, 230.

Latin Essay Prize 'Is it right to make slaves against their will?' Thomas Clarkson, a student of St John's as yet unknown to Wilberforce, won the prize and was so stirred by what he learned that he decided to dedicate his life to working to end slavery. He was one of those whose influence helped to persuade Wilberforce to take up the cause in 1787. By the late 1780s the sermons of Charles Simeon of King's, the Evangelical vicar of Holy Trinity, were filling his church with undergraduates; and in London Wilberforce had begun to create the network of Evangelical and benevolent societies, the most prominent of which was the anti-slavery society, aiming to abolish the slave trade and, if possible, slavery itself.[142]

St John's College subscribed 10 guineas to the Abolition Society in 1788. They would not have done so if this had been seen as a purely Evangelical issue. Abolition had much wider support: it was one of the very few reforms which the Senate of the University, encouraged by Pitt, was bold and united enough to support by a petition to the House of Commons in 1788, and again in 1792.[143]

Wilberforce revisited St John's in 1788, insisting that they avoid giving him 'a damp bed and rather let me have one that has been slept in, sheets and all, for a month.' His opinion of the Fellows he met was low:

> They were not what I had expected; they had neither the solidity of judgment possessed by ordinary men of business, nor the refined feelings and elevated principles which become a studious and sequestered life.[144]

Craven did not like Evangelicalism any more than Powell had. In the 1790s the Master required all undergraduates to attend a special course of sermons in College, cunningly arranged at the very time when Simeon would be preaching at Holy Trinity.[145] Henry Ryder, who came up to St John's in 1795, was destined to become the first Evangelical bishop, but he did not convert to this brand of Anglicanism until well after 1800. Much more typical of St John's opinion – though unique in his scholarly achievement as a theologian – was Herbert Marsh, a Fellow who spent many years in the eighties and nineties on leave, working first in the Middle East on the historical origins of the Gospels, and then in Germany to study its recent theological scholarship. In 1799 he ventured into politics, publishing a German-language defence of Pitt's foreign policy towards the Revolution. He remained an opponent of Evangelicalism and, when bishop of Llandaff and later of Peterborough, condemned Bible societies and hymn-singing.[146]

William Wordsworth, sometimes regarded as the greatest Johnian of them all,[147] came up in 1787. It is remarkable how few accounts of undergraduate

---

[142] On Cambridge Evangelicalism in general, Gascoigne, *Cambridge in the Age of the Enlightenment*, 252–62; on Simeon, Gunning, *Reminiscences*, II. 144–50; on Evangelical societies, Hague, *Wilberforce*, e.g. 103–13.

[143] Cooper, *Annals of Cambridge*, IV. 426, 443.

[144] Hague, *Wilberforce*, 162–3; Gunning, *Reminiscences*, I. 326.

[145] Mullinger, *St John's College*, 263–4.

[146] Baker-Mayor, 733–898.

[147] See the celebration volume *Wordsworth at Cambridge* (Cambridge, 1950), 1. K. R. Johnston, *The Hidden Wordsworth* (Bloomington, IN, 1998), chap. 5, is a useful account

life survive from the eighteenth century: the experience does not seem to have evoked the nostalgia so characteristic of modern reminiscences. Apart from Bonwicke's, which is of an utterly different character, no eighteenth-century account of undergraduate life at St John's is so full as Wordsworth's, though the fact that, apart from a few letters, it is all in verse and was repeatedly modified by the author makes it particularly difficult to use.

He had an uncle who was a Fellow of St John's and so, despite having been brought up a poor orphan in the Lake District, knew something about the University. Before he came up he announced: 'I will be either Senior Wrangler or nothing.'[148]

Once in the College

> Questions, directions, counsel and advice
> Flowed in upon me from all sides. Fresh day
> Of pride and pleasure: to myself I seemed
> A man of business and expense, and went
> From shop to shop about my own affairs,
> To tutors or to tailors as befel, ...
> I was the dreamer, they the dream: I roamed
> Delighted through the motley spectacle:
> Gowns grave or gaudy, doctors, students, streets,
> Lamps, gateways, flocks of churches, courts and towers –
> Strange transformation for a mountain youth.

These lines could almost have come from a twenty-first-century freshman.

Wordsworth was a sizar, however, and the room he was assigned, though close to the modern Wordsworth Room, was much smaller and much less attractive:

> The Evangelist St John my patron was;
> Three gloomy courts are his, and in the first
> Was my abiding-place, a nook obscure.
> Right underneath, the college kitchens made
> A humming sound, less tuneable than bees
> But hardly less industrious ...
> Near me was Trinity's loquacious clock
> Who never let the quarters, night or day,
> Slip by him unproclaimed ...
> Her pealing organ was my neighbour too.

As for examinations,

> Such glory was but little sought by me,
> And little won.

Eventually he found himself repelled by two crucial elements of Cambridge life.

---

of the poet's time in Cambridge, mostly in prose, but not adding much. I am grateful to Professor John Kerrigan for this reference.

[148] *The Letters of William and Dorothy Wordsworth*, vol. I, 2nd edn, ed. E. de Selincourt and C. L. Shaver (Oxford, 1967), 11n.

16 H. W. Pickersgill's preliminary study of Wordsworth for the portrait now in Hall; commissioned by the College in or around 1831

First was the overwhelming emphasis on mathematics – despite his reverence for Newton and

> the pleasure gathered from the elements
> Of geometric science …
>   Simple, pure
> Proportions and relations, with the frame
> And laws of Nature.

He became instead absorbed in literature in several languages, but especially in the poetry of great English writers whom he already meant to emulate. He refused to work at mathematics, could not therefore take the Senate House Examination and so abandoned hope of a Fellowship.

Secondly, he bridled at the remorseless round of Anglican services:

> Let Folly and False-seeming (we might say) …
> Let them parade among the schools at will,
> But spare the house of God. Was ever known
> The witless shepherd who would drive his flock
> With serious repetition to a pool
> Of which 'tis plain they never taste?
>   … Be wise,
> Ye Presidents and Deans, and to your bells

Give seasonable rest, for 'tis a sound
Hollow as ever vexed the tranquil air,
And your officious doings bring disgrace
On the plain steeples of our English Church.[149]

The prosperous and mildly reforming early years of Pitt's ministry were inter-rupted by the French Revolution, which broke out just after Craven's election as Master. From the start it was seen as a momentous event, which at first thrilled many Englishmen. For Wordsworth it was a blissful dawn, encouraging him to visit the Continent; and he was one of many who hoped that it would encourage more or less radical reform in England. Cambridge and the Church, however, were more particularly concerned with the fate of the Catholic clergy driven out of France. Large subscriptions were raised to support them: St John's gave £50 in October 1792.[150] Partly because of this changed climate towards Catholics, a Catholic Relief Act of 1791 claimed to allow Catholics to attend Oxford and Cambridge – though not to hold major offices in the universities. Magdalene admitted a few, but there is no sign of any yet at St John's.

By the end of 1792, however, the Revolution had become extreme – demo-cratic, anti-religious and aggressive. Its more enthusiastic English supporters, like Tom Paine, author of *The Rights of Man* (1791–2), came to be seen by many as a threat to property, order and religion. The University and the town both sent addresses to the government applauding its firm measures to limit popular agitation. On 31 December 1792 Paine was burnt in effigy on Market Hill, and the execution of Louis XVI in January 1793 was mourned with 'a dumb peal' of bells at Great St Mary's. Almost immediately after that, France declared war on Britain, which caused opinion to turn still more strongly against France. The irrepressible Horne Tooke, however, was on the scene again in London, sup-ported at first by Theophilus Lindsey. Tooke enjoyed acting the gadfly, applaud-ing the Revolution and applying what he saw as its lessons to Britain, declar-ing that there ought to be no lords and that, while monarchy was desirable, a king should be executed every fifty or a hundred years.[151] Once Britain was at war with France, his involvement with radical societies led the government to prosecute him and other radicals for treason. Arrested in May 1794, they were sent to the Tower. But after a long trial, in which Horne Tooke cross-examined many major public figures, including Pitt, with great skill and humour, the jury acquitted him after only eight minutes' discussion. He had not quite finished mocking the parliamentary system of the time. In 1801 he agreed to stand for the legendary rotten borough, Old Sarum, and was duly elected, but after a short spell in the House was declared incapable of being an MP because he was in Holy Orders of the Church of England.[152]

In Cambridge a small band of sympathizers with the Revolution found

---

[149] These lines come from the version of 1805, as published in J. Wordsworth, M. H. Abrams and S. Gill, *The Prelude, 1799, 1805, 1850* (London, 1979), 92, 94, 192, 112. Wordsworth softened the passage on religion before publication in 1850.

[150] CB, 26 Oct. 1792.

[151] See Bewley, *Gentleman Radical*, chaps. 7–10, esp. p. 100.

[152] Ibid., 211–17.

themselves in danger. One of them, William Frend, was deprived of his Fellow-ship at Jesus for publishing a pamphlet said to have profaned and reviled all the clergy. A succession of hearings and appeals, involving Craven as Master of St John's, confirmed the sentence.[153]

The political situation was now the opposite of that in Newcome's day. It was the self-styled Whigs, those opponents of Pitt who accepted the leadership of Fox, who were now a tiny minority in Parliament; and, in Gunning's words, in reference to the Frend affair, to those who studied the signs of the times it was very evident that

> Whigism would be an unprofitable profession, and that a good oppor-tunity now presented itself for abandoning their principles; thus their apostasy assumed the garb of patriotism, and a regard for the established religion.[154]

St John's had one prominent representative among Fox's colleagues, Samuel Whitbread. But otherwise it was reckoned an anti-whig College. Some already used the name 'Tory' of it and of the Pittites nationally, although it would be a long time before the term was embraced by them. Accidents of personality were crucial of course, but it seems there was an ethos dominant in the College of Powell and his successors which made it fitting that it should contribute so many alumni to what came to be called the Tory party, especially to its 'lib-eral' wing: most prominently Castlereagh, Goderich, Aberdeen and Palmerston. They were churchmen, but moderate; ready to support modest reforms but, until the crisis of 1828–32, no fundamental changes. Meanwhile, Trinity became a nest of Whigs, whose day did not arrive until that crisis came.

Although Craven had come up as a sub-sizar, he succeeded in convincing the world that he was a member of the family of the earls of Craven, a claim which is thought to have encouraged more noblemen to come to St John's. By the end of his tenure there were altogether nearly thirty Fellow-Commoners among the rising overall numbers of the College's undergraduates.[155] In other words, his Mastership continued the process, begun by Powell, of raising the social stand-ing of the College.

By contrast, one of the Senior Fellows throughout Craven's Mastership was Isaac Pennington. Son of a ship's captain, he came up as a sizar in 1762. In 1766 it was agreed to pay him '£15 a year for the care of the Observatory'. He was a Wrangler in the tripos of 1767 and became a Fellow in 1768. In 1775, two years after being made physician to the new Addenbrooke's and elected Professor of Chemistry in a contest between himself and a Trinity man, he was designated a medical Fellow, which spared him the obligation to be ordained. In College he was successively Steward, Junior Bursar and then President and Bakehouse Bur-sar. He was a Senior Fellow for thirty-four years from 1783. In 1793 he became Regius Professor of Physic [i.e. Medicine]. When in 1795 an address was pre-sented by the University to the king, congratulating him on his escape from an

---

[153] E.g. Cooper, *Annals of Cambridge*, IV. 447–50.

[154] Gunning, *Reminiscences*, I. 302.

[155] Mullinger, *St John's College*, 271–2.

attempt on his life, Pennington was knighted. He became active in the Volunteer Movement during the invasion threat of 1803–5. He died in 1817, leaving his house near the College to the Master, helping to consolidate the property of St John's in the 'triangle' opposite the front gate. He made sundry other benefactions, including one to give the Master £200 a year provided that he was Rector of Freshwater. This 'direct encouragement to holding in plurality' was later declared unlawful. He must have been a forceful personality, a pillar of the College and presumably a good physician by the standards of the time. He was a beneficiary of the social engineering of the sizarship system. But he does not appear to have published a line, he would not lecture, and he was clearly no reformer.[156]

Craven remained Master until he died at the age of eighty-five in 1815 – in January, the same month that had proved fatal to Lambert, Newcome and Powell. He left £3,000 to the College, which in time was put towards the cost of New Court.[157]

6. CONCLUSION

In 1792 a new direct coach service from London to Cambridge, presumably daily, was announced. The journey was scheduled to take seven hours and a quarter. There had been services before, but not so regular and taking longer.[158] In 1788 a meeting of 'the nobility, gentry, and freeholders of Hertfordshire, Essex, Cambridgeshire, Huntingdonshire, and the Isle of Ely' had 'by a great majority' urged that 'a canal [be built] from the Stort at Bishop's Stortford by way of Saffron Walden to the Cam at Cambridge.' Another such meeting was held in the following year and made the same demand.[159] But there was too much opposition and it was never built. So the town's communications were poor.

It was small. In 1728 its population was estimated at 6,422. At the first census of 1801 the total was just over 10,000. It may be that these figures are not directly comparable, but there was certainly a significant increase during the century. Physically, though, Cambridge had hardly spread at all during the eighteenth century. Its expansion was inhibited by the huge remaining areas of unenclosed land on almost every side, to the west more than 1,200 acres.[160] It is hard now to imagine a Cambridge in which the Backs, east of what is now Queen's Road, were the limit of College and University occupation and building. Farmland or open land came right up to the road on the west. There were almost no buildings between the Backs and the village of Coton. There were as yet not even any college gardens across Queen's Road: those of Trinity, King's and Caius date from the early nineteenth century, when as part of the enclosure of the Western

---

[156] Scott-Mayor, III. 683–6.
[157] Mullinger, *St John's College*, 264.
[158] Cooper, *Annals of Cambridge*, IV. 442.
[159] Ibid., 432, 436–7.
[160] F. W. Maitland, *Township and Borough* (London, 1898); *Royal Commission on Historical Monuments, England: City of Cambridge*, I (HMSO, 1959), lvii.

Field the colleges obtained some land. Wordsworth in Cambridge missed the hills, but he could

> gallop through the country in blind zeal
> Of senseless horsemanship.[161]

Gunning, an undergraduate in the 1760s, spoke of the pleasure to be had from walking out with a gun: 'In going over the land now occupied by Downing Terrace, you generally got five or six shots at snipe.' Further out, of course, there were 'great varieties of wildfowl'. In 1777 a hunted stag, followed by the hunt, invaded St John's just after dinner, reaching the first court, where a plaque records the event. The College was careful enough about erecting gates to make such events very rare, but the fact that they could ever occur shows how rural west Cambridge was. St John's and other colleges had been promoting enclosure, but it was only in the next century that it happened on a large scale, making possible the expansion first of the town and then of the University.

Inside the town the long-standing refusal of colleges, including St John's, to co-operate had prevented satisfactory paving and lighting being installed until in 1788 a new Act replaced the Paving Act of Henry VIII.[162] This state of affairs makes it easy to understand why such large changes as were required if the University was to be reformed had as yet no hope of success. They required Parliament to act, because the privileges and oddities of the Church of England, as well as of the universities and the colleges, were all enshrined in law. It took decades to found Downing College, not only because the will was contested but also because the founder and executors wanted to set up a new-style college.[163]

There had been little likelihood of such major reforms occurring even in the years before the war with France. But the impact of the French Revolution made change even more difficult. It became the view of many, if not most, people concerned with politics that the events in France had shown the danger of tinkering with a country's constitution, that it was simply too much of a risk to religion and society to embark on reform. Not until after Parliament had reformed itself and sundry other institutions did it face up to the challenge of reforming the universities.

Given this situation, it is surprising that the University innovated as much as it did in the eighteenth century. But the conversion of Cambridge into a University where mathematics was the dominant subject required no change of the law. The new curriculum made Cambridge unsatisfactory to students of literature, history, classics, theology and so forth, but also made it unique – and, as was surely important, different from Oxford. Almost by accident, it led to Cambridge becoming a scientific University. The second major change, the establishment of what came to be the tripos, and of college examinations, also required no change in the law, but it became crucial to later University development at least in the English-speaking world. In both changes St John's had a

---

[161] *Prelude*, line 194.

[162] Cooper, *Annals of Cambridge*, IV. 428–9.

[163] T. J. Hochstrasser, "A College in the Air": myth and reality in the foundation story of Downing College, Cambridge', *History of Universities* xvii (2001–2), 81–120. Dr Hochstrasser generously sent me a copy of this article.

significant role. But they were more important for their future impact than for their effect in the eighteenth century itself. The main contribution of St John's during those years was to supply a larger cohort than any other college of clergy of the Church of England.

IV

THE NINETEENTH CENTURY

Boyd Hilton

I.   INTRODUCTION

PHYSICALLY St John's was transformed during the nineteenth century. In 1800 it comprised little more than one small and two medium-sized courts ranged along a single axis perpendicular to the east bank of the Cam. Except for the south range of First Court, with its classical ashlar coating of a quarter century earlier, its red brick buildings had all been built in the domestic style of the Tudor and Stuart periods. But then a quarter of a century later construction began on New Court, an accommodation block across the river, making St John's the first college to intrude on the 'Backs', and the only one to do so until Queens' followed suit in 1936. New Court, which was bigger than anything built in Cambridge before, maintained the College's axial plan, and was accessed from Third Court by means of a covered alleyway of stone construction that soon became known as the Bridge of Sighs. With its graceful arch and open Gothic fenestration, barred to prevent students from climbing in, it bore no resemblance in either form or function to its Venetian namesake, but the steep and sombre buildings that rise on either side of the narrow stream at that point give off a not dissimilar atmosphere of romantic menace, allowing punters for a few nautical metres to imagine themselves *gondolieri*. A few years before work on New Court began, the Broad Walk had been constructed in a straight line from the Wren Bridge to the Queen's Road, where it terminates in a pair of wrought iron gates, a distance of about 1,000 feet. The view of Third Court from these new gates 'forms a lovely vista', as Alec Crook has pointed out, and was probably meant to emphasize the existing east–west dominance, but in fact, as Crook has also pointed out, this was soon lost, partly because of the unavoidable death of ancient elms, but mainly because of the parallel mass of New Court alongside, a building whose prominent facade creates an unmistakably 'southern orientation'.[1]

The second great architectural intervention of the nineteenth century came in the late 1860s, when the old Chapel was demolished and replaced a few metres to the north by a much taller and more flamboyant building, whose huge square

I am very grateful to the Editor for advice and comment; to Dawn Dodds and Lucy Rhymer for assistance with research; to Jonathan Harrison and other members of the Special Collections staff for much practical assistance willingly rendered; and super-eminently to the College Archivist Malcolm Underwood for his unparalleled expertise, patience, and enthusiasm, not to mention his many stimulating interpretative suggestions.

[1] Crook, *Foundation to Gilbert Scott*, 86–9; J. S. Boys Smith, 'The alterations made in the Fellows' Garden and the College grounds in 1822–3', *Eagle* liii (1948–9), 147–61.

tower at once replaced the Great Gate as the College's defining architectural feature. The new Chapel undoubtedly has flair, but it compromises the visual integrity of First Court, especially in the north-east corner where an awkward gap has been left between it and the extended St John's Street range. Thanks to New Court and the new Chapel, St John's in 1900 had more swagger than in 1800, but spatially it was less harmonious.

These changes in the physical appearance of St John's were striking, but less significant than the functional revolution that affected Cambridge as a whole in the course of the nineteenth century. In 1800 the colleges operated both as sites of passage for gilded youth, and as ladders by means of which poor boys might ascend to respectable jobs, notably in the established Church. By 1900 most of the old religious, not to say monastic, ethos had disappeared, and their most obvious function was to receive the sons of the upper middle classes, and kit them out (quite literally, since team sports now played a central role in daily life) for service in the empire, domestic government, or the professions. The impact of this shift may have been felt with more than usual force in St John's, where the clerical element had been particularly strong, but it was at least evolutionary. More alarming, especially to such a conservative college, was the spirit of nineteenth-century 'reform', which blew with gale force through the rafters and belfries of almost all ancient institutions, not just the universities but also schools, cathedral chapters, almshouses, and hospitals. There were a thousand or more charitable corporations, bound rigidly by law but free from legislative interference, free to govern themselves so long as they kept within the terms of their numerous trust deeds and statutory provisions. In the 1850s, however, and then again in the 1870s, Oxford and Cambridge were subjected to inspection by parliamentary commissioners and forced to put their houses in order. For most colleges, but especially for St John's, this was an acutely painful process. The positions taken on these issues were never morally black or white, of course. Looking back on struggles that, however puny in retrospect, seemed like life-and-death to those involved, one's sympathies are often mixed, as they are on reading *The Warden* and *Barchester Towers*. Trollope set his saga in a cathedral close, but, except for the paucity of female characters, his satires on corruption, nepotism, and the warfare between different types of churchmanship, would have worked just as effectively in a Cambridge college. What is certain is that for Fellows, as for churchmen, reform was an indispensable topic of conversation from the 1830s onwards, a dominant narrative to which all the other pressures and vicissitudes of institutional life seemed but sub-plots.

A central part of the reform agenda was financial. Before the nineteenth century, colleges were statutorily forbidden to exploit the value of their properties to the full. This limited what they could do, but gave them stability. Increasingly as the century progressed, however, they were told to maximize their utility in the public interest by processes that today would be called 'rent-seeking'. It is hardly surprising then that the two most esteemed Fellows of St John's in the Victorian age were not scholars but Senior Bursars, both of whom were rewarded for their skill by afterwards becoming Masters. The new state of affairs also meant that colleges became exposed as never before to the vicissitudes of capitalism, and, because their assets were predominantly in land, this meant that they throve during most of the first and third quarters of the century, and withered during most of the second and fourth. This can be illustrated in St John's case by the way in which the junior Fellows' dividend moved up and down in a series of secular trends, each lasting between twenty and thirty years.[2] There was a long upward movement between 1799 and 1821, during which the dividend rose from £70 to £160, which is where it remained until 1830 when it plunged to £100. It then averaged £125 over the following sixteen years before beginning a long ascent in 1847 – to £160 in 1852, £180 in 1857, and £240 in 1860. It dipped very slightly during the early 1860s, rose again towards the end of the decade, hovered between £290 and £300 throughout the 1870s, and would probably have risen higher had it not been for admonitory warnings against excessive bonuses by the parliamentary commissioners. The fourth and final phase began in 1880 with a steady and rapid decline, till by 1890–2 the dividend stood at only £170. In 1893 it slumped to £130, and then to £110 in 1894–5 before staging a very mild recovery. In 1900 it stood at £150, just half its peak of twenty years before, and exactly where it had been in 1820.[3] These are, of course, nominal rather than real values, and adjusting for movements in cereal and other prices modifies the trends, especially with respect to the first two phases, but it does not modify them by very much. The size of the individual dividend is worth recording because it was a matter of daily concern to those who depended on it, and its rapid decline – which, for reasons that will emerge, was much greater than in other colleges – was an obvious cause of the rancour that poisoned relationships among senior members in the 1890s. However, as a measure of the College's overall financial performance the total amount paid out in dividends is even more significant, and here the decline was even steeper, reflecting the large number of Fellowships that the College could not afford to fill towards the end of the century. That harsh reality helps to explain why the premier college of 1800 – for that is what many considered St John's to be – ended the century in something like crisis.

2. PROSPERITY AND EXPANSION, 1800–30

Getting and spending, we lay waste our powers.
William Wordsworth, *The World Is Too Much with Us* (1807)

The first of the nineteenth century's two periods of expansion was fuelled by steadily increased income from the College's estates as the Continental blockade[4] combined with bad seasons and monetary depreciation to create ever higher food prices and farm rentals. Although the end of the French wars in 1815 led to widespread agricultural depression and markedly increased arrears of rent, some of which had to be written off by the College, it took some time for leases

---

[2] The Junior Fellows' dividend continued to be calculated in the traditional way and amounted to two-thirds of what a Senior Fellow could claim.

[3] See below, p. 379.

[4] The Continental blockade refers to Napoleon's attempt to starve Britain into submission by cutting off her food supplies and other articles of commerce.

to fall in, and so revenue from fines and rents remained buoyant throughout the 1820s. Back in 1770 income had stood at just over half that of Trinity, a college of comparable size, but since then it had risen considerably faster. Like-for-like comparisons are impossible, but it seems that in some of the wartime years St John's income even topped that of its neighbour, though it continued to pay its Fellows (and especially its Masters) much smaller dividends and stipends.

Part of the reason for this relative success may be that Trinity was then enjoying what its financial historian describes as a period of 'passive prosperity',[5] whereas St John's did far more than simply sit back and benefit from rising prices. The country's constantly improving system of road transport made it feasible to inspect estates more frequently, while the process of enclosing open land, commenced under Powell's Mastership, now began in earnest. Over £8,000 (or more than one year's income) was spent on enclosure between 1770 and 1813, the bulk of it from 1798 onwards and mainly affecting the counties of Cambridge and Huntingdon, though some took place in Essex, Yorkshire, Nottingham, and elsewhere. Since enclosures almost always entailed the provision of new farmhouses and other buildings, the total sums expended on improvements were considerable, and mainly financed by the sale of consols or other securities.[6] Whatever amounts were spent on the enclosures themselves could be regarded as 'monies properly converted into landed property', and therefore legitimately disbursed. Monies spent on buildings, on the other hand, were thought to hold 'less permanent advantage', so in such cases it was important to replenish the funds from which they came by the purchase of annual instalments of new stock.[7] The distinction is significant because it reflects the fact that colleges were still bound by the Statute of Mortmain, which protected landed but not commercial or funded property. The rule was that they must never alienate permanent assets, meaning those in real property or land, and that annuities and securities could only be held for temporary or designated purposes, such as a building fund. In St John's case the interest on such financial assets averaged well over £1,000 p.a. between 1817 and 1826, as compared with barely £200 during the previous ten-year period and little more than £70 during the 1830s. Not until the 1860s would income from securities make a serious contribution to college wealth, and not for another century would it make a dominant one. Nevertheless, interest payments made up a significant addition to the revenue account during the decade after 1816, and, together with a broadly corresponding decrease in expenditure thanks to the cessation of the wartime Property Tax, it helped to prolong the sense of economic well-being beyond the peace and into the 1820s.

Meanwhile the political situation was equally propitious thanks to the wave of reaction that set in following the French Revolution. In 1793 the National Convention in Paris had dissolved all French universities on the grounds that they embodied privilege and the 'spirit of corporation', and English radicals

[5] Robert Neild, *Riches and Responsibility: The Financial History of Trinity College, Cambridge* (Cambridge, 2008), 61, 74–5.

[6] Howard, *Finances*, 154–6.

[7] CB, 2 Mar. 1804.

were calling for similar measures on this side of the Channel. Joseph Priestley described Oxford and Cambridge as 'stagnant pools', and from 1809 onwards the *Edinburgh Review* maintained a torrent of abuse from its Whig redoubt in Edinburgh. All this would eventually take its toll, but the immediate impact was rather to strengthen the forces of conservatism and loyalism in Britain. And so, whereas university dons had commanded relatively little public esteem in the so-called 'age of enlightenment', now – like clergymen in general – they found themselves called on by government ministers to use whatever influence they might possess to help rally the people behind throne and altar. They became, in other words, an accepted part of what Coleridge would call 'the clerisy of the nation', by which he meant not just the clergy, or even all the clergy, but 'the learned of all denominations; the sages and the professors of ... all the so-called liberal arts and sciences, the possession and application of which constitute the civilization of a country'.[8]

As staunch conservatives most Fellows of St John's were comfortable with the counter-revolutionary atmosphere of these decades, and only too happy to see their own role in Coleridgean terms. During these decades the criterion for ecclesiastical appointments was gradually shifting from connection to merit, primarily as measured by proficiency in Greek but also by aptitude for mathematics,[9] and this development provided the College with a clear mission to populate the parishes, not just numerically but in terms of quality, something it could claim to do at least as well as any other thanks to its continuing distinguished showing in the tripos. Moreover, no one took the duty to mobilize religion in the cause of social harmony more seriously than James Wood, who succeeded Craven as Master in 1815. He did all he could to focus collegiate life upon the chapel, by instituting reading prizes, by encouraging the foundation of a joint choir school with Trinity, and by securing the erection of a new organ in 1839. He also left £20,000 towards the building of a larger chapel in the future.[10] As Master he delivered many hundreds of sermons, several of which are preserved in manuscript. Beautifully written and logically developed, these minor masterpieces of persuasion dwelt mainly on the need for rich young men to practise charity, not least by helping to educate the poor in 'veracity, humility, and attention'. He presented this as an urgent imperative, partly in order to heal the wounds of the wider community, and partly to ensure that his undergraduate listeners would go on to lead esteemed lives, but mainly because it was 'the will of our Creator, from the wonderful contrivance and design with which our faculties are suited to answer particular purposes'. In their relentless homiletic, Wood's sermons bore some resemblance to Hannah More's *Thoughts on the Importance of the Manners of the Great to General Society* (1788), and also to *A Practical View* (1797), a highly influential text by his Johnian close contemporary, William Wilberforce, but spiritually the tone – sober, unthreatening, this-worldly – was very different.

[8] S. T. Coleridge, *On the Constitution of the Church and State according to the Idea of Each* (1830), ed. John Colmer for *The Collected Works of Samuel Taylor Coleridge*, ed. Kathleen Coburn and Bart Winer (1969–), X. 46.

[9] Christopher Stray, 'Curriculum and style in the collegiate university: classics in nineteenth-century Oxbridge', *History of Universities* xvi (2) (2000), 186.

[10] Miller, *Portrait of a College*, 73–4.

Whereas those two Evangelical moralists would have agonized over the state of the undergraduates' souls, Wood was more concerned about their reputations. Whereas More and Wilberforce emphasized God's providential government above all else, Wood nodded to the doctrine but preferred to stress what human beings should do of their own accord and for themselves. And unlike them, though he lived and breathed religion, 'he never introduced the subject ... into common conversation'. The often-repeated suggestion that Wood was an Evangelical therefore seems very wide of the mark,[11] but were there any doubt on the matter it would be dispelled by the story of Hastings Robinson, a Fellow and Assistant Tutor. Cast down by the death of his father, which gave 'a gloomy turn to his mind', Robinson forsook the society of his College friends 'for that of the soi-disant Evangelicals', meaning the devotees of Charles Simeon of King's and Holy Trinity Church. 'This naturally occasioned displeasure in the Master's mind who could not endure a person of those views in the situation he held in College.' The upshot was that Wood appointed someone else in poor Robinson's College place, while at the same time the bishop of Bath and Wells retracted the offer of a living in Derbyshire.[12]

'Jemmy' Wood was unquestionably a significant figure in the history of St John's, as well as being an important benefactor. As a Lancastrian he exemplified the College's close relations with the north of England. As the son of a handloom weaver and former sizar, he exemplified its traditional pride in promoting social mobility.[13] As a former Senior Wrangler he typified the College's excellence in mathematics, and as an arch-conservative he represented the views of the younger and more assertive members of the society. Like the majority of Johnian Masters to this day, he had worked his way up the College's insides, having been appointed a Tutor in 1789 and President in 1802, so the Fellows who elected him knew what they were getting. As one of them remarked, Wood's 'sound and cautious understanding, seconded by unremitting diligence, by remarkable punctuality and rigid adherence to *order* in all his arrangements, particularly qualified him for the able discharge of the practical duties of life.'[14] Although he was self-effacing and dull of speech, leading one of his more intimate and intelligent friends to comment that 'his merit was of a kind which could not be duly estimated except after intimate acquaintance with him, and by intelligent people',[15] his energy, integrity, cordiality, and reputation for humility more than made up for these inadequacies. Besides, contacts mattered much more in the *ancien régime* than eloquence or wit, and Wood was at the centre of an elaborate network of patronage, especially but not only in the Church. As

[11] Juliet Barker, *The Brontës* (London, 1994), 9; James Wood, 'On Charity' (1786): SJCL, MS S.66, pp. 17, 20–1; Baker-Mayor, II. 1094–1100.

[12] T. W. Hornbuckle to J. W. Whittaker: SJCL, J. W. Whittaker Correspondence, 10.11.

[13] Miller, *Portrait of a College*, 73: 'As an undergraduate he kept in a garret called the Tub at the top of O staircase, second court, and read by a candle on the stairs with his feet in straw, being too poor to afford a light or fire.' He is said still to haunt the staircase in that guise.

[14] Ibid., 74.

[15] Baker-Mayor, II. 1096; Searby, *History of the University of Cambridge*. III. 93–4.

a potential beneficiary put it, 'his influence … is of the most amazing extent. The archbishop of Canterbury, the bishops of Peterborough, Ely, Worcester and Chester, the duke of Northumberland, Lord Clarendon and Lord Palmerston would be inclined to do any thing of this kind that he might request.'[16] For all these reasons Wood was a popular, indeed venerated Master.

'All here as usual, placid and dull, comfortable and sleepy,' wrote a young don in 1821.[17] Yet although the Old House (as Johnians were wont to refer to it) seemed predominantly at ease with itself, there had been a few disconcerting developments. It had suffered a first public setback in 1811 – rather unfairly, it must be said, since the protagonist in the affair was a single individual rather than the Fellowship as a whole – but the distinction was frequently mislaid in the brouhaha that ensued. Like Wood, Herbert Marsh, the Lady Margaret Professor of Divinity (1807–39), was anxious to uphold the Established Church; unlike Wood he preferred to do so the noisy way. Although he was courteous and placable in private, he was a fiercely combative controversialist in public. His own beliefs were too eclectic for him to be neatly labelled, but he was fired by a loathing of Evangelicals within the Church, seeing them (quite wrongly) as a Trojan horse whereby religious Dissenters might infiltrate the Establishment. He particularly disliked the predominantly Evangelical British and Foreign Bible Society, mainly because it distributed copies of the scriptures at home and overseas without an accompanying prayer book to ensure they were interpreted according to Anglican doctrine. So when he heard in 1811 that some 200 undergraduates were organizing to form a local auxiliary of the Society, he went into full bellow. The affair became known as the 'Cambridge controversy', thereby demonstrating that it had attracted national attention. It also resulted in a decisive victory for the Society, as its proposed auxiliary was enthusiastically endorsed, and then set up under the presidency of William Mansel, Master of Trinity.[18] Marsh conceded defeat with reasonably good grace, but the atmosphere of Pentecostal rejoicing and Simeonite smugness that characterized the crucial meeting was widely seen as a blow to St John's prestige.

Another loss of face took place in March 1817 when James Wood, in his role as Vice-Chancellor, and accompanied by Proctors, stormed in on a meeting of the fledgling Union Society at the Red Lion, a fashionable coaching house. According to legend, after he had ordered its members 'to disperse, and on no account to resume their discussions', the Society's president William Whewell, insolently imitating Speaker Lenthall's dismissal of Charles I in 1642, demanded that 'strangers will please to withdraw'. (This encounter, assuming it took place as described, was full of ironies. Whewell, the son of a carpenter, was what Wood the weaver's son had once been – a humble sizar from Lancashire – and he too would one day be Vice-Chancellor in his capacity as Master of Trinity.) The Society appealed, whereupon Wood appears to have acted maladroitly. First

[16] J. W. Whittaker to his mother, 1 Jun. 1820: SJCL, J. W. Whittaker Correspondence, 2.6.

[17] Richard Jones to J. W. Whittaker, 19 Dec. 1821, British Library of Political and Economic Science MSS.

[18] D. M. Thompson, *Cambridge Theology in the Nineteenth Century: Enquiry, Controversy and Truth* (Aldershot, 2008), 43–7.

he accused the Union members of inattention to their studies, when in fact most of them had excelled in tripos and won a number of academic prizes. He then ordered them to discontinue their debates on 'political, literary, or any other subjects', a ban which the Society partly circumvented by reconstituting itself as a reading club until a later Vice-Chancellor, Trinity's Christopher Words-worth, allowed their debates to resume in 1821. To be fair, Wood was in a very difficult position. The end of the French wars two years earlier had released a great deal of pent-up hatred throughout the country against existing institu-tions, a widespread disaffection that had been muted so long as the nation was fighting an external enemy, and government ministers were looking to college heads to nip any signs of student disloyalty in the bud. Even the designation 'Union' was alarming, for although it probably signified nothing more sinis-ter than the fact that it had been formed by amalgamating three pre-existing University clubs, it reminded nervous conservatives of the 150 or more Union Societies that were thought to be fomenting radical disaffection all over the country. National attention focused on London's Spa Fields riots in December 1816, and on the hunger march of the Manchester Blanketeers three months later, while in Cambridgeshire itself no one could forget that, less than twelve months earlier, Ely and Littleport had been briefly but violently taken over by insurgent labourers. Wood's *démarche* against the Cambridge Union came just a few weeks after Parliament had passed a Seditious Meetings Act and suspended *habeas corpus*.[19] In such a context, his limp-fist-in-a-barbed-wire-glove strategy of talking tough for the benefit of outside ears, while turning a blind eye to the Union's continued existence, was probably very sensible, but it made him look weak and caused many non-Johnians to question his judgement. The episode also pointed up the rivalry between Cambridge's two most dominant colleges, and strengthened the impression that St John's was a hotbed of bigoted reac-tion. According to contemporary doggerel, Wood was one whom 'not a Whig will now acknowledge, return his bow, or shake his hand', an alienation which mattered little at the time but which was to have repercussions after the Whigs returned to power in 1830.

As well as becoming embroiled in Cambridge affairs, the College had to address a significant internal problem. Its Fellows might have been conservative, but they were not blindly so. The attack on monarchy, Church, and aristoc-racy in France had been so vicious and effective that it was no longer enough to defend the British version of those institutions on grounds of ancient pre-scription or providential dispensation. Instead they had to be shown to be use-ful, deserving, and fully in accord with newly developing standards of public probity and accountability. This expectation explains the fall-out from the case of Bursar Wood, a complicated story but one worth disentangling for what it shows about changing attitudes to corporate governance. In 1795 another James

---

[19] Ged Martin, *The Cambridge Union and Ireland, 1815–1914* (Edinburgh, 2000), 107–16, on which this paragraph relies heavily. Martin points out also that the Seditious Meetings Act could be construed as giving local magistrates power to disperse the Union Society. Since the University was jealous of its sole jurisdiction in matters of student discipline, here was another reason for Wood to pre-empt any such interven-tion by taking the initiative.

Wood[20] had resigned the Bursarship in protest against an order requiring all college moneys to be deposited with one of its two bankers. These were Gosling & Co., later Goslings and Sharpe, London bankers who had acted in respect of the Platt estate in Kentish Town since 1765, and a newly appointed Cambridge banker, W. Fisher. A conscientious officer, Wood argued that it was improper for such moneys to be held by anyone other than Bursars; that the 3 per cent interest specified by Fisher to be paid to the 'College' would deprive him of a source of revenue that he and his predecessors had traditionally enjoyed; and further that this would come at a time when his own duties in respect of rent collection were about to increase owing to the discontinuance of the post of College Receiver, a post which had until then been held by his brother, Richard. Despite James Wood's misgivings, his other brother William, who was also a Fellow, agreed to succeed him and, in defiance of the order, proceeded to lodge money with his nephew Bell and with Richard Wood. All might have been well had not the latters' speculations failed in the banking crisis of 1797, the consequence being a deficiency in William Wood's bursarial accounts of some £4,000–5,000. The College was forced to sell £3,000 in stock, while more than a quarter of the nominal dividend had to be suspended for three years. Wood was thoroughly disgraced, forbidden to draw any profits from his Fellowship, and sent to live out of College. In 1801, after he had paid back about £5,000, he appealed to the Visitor, who restored his Fellowship, and five years later he was elected to the rectory of Lawford, but his subsequent claims for monetary compensation, and for the sinecure rectory of Aberdavon, were rebuffed.

It is evident from Wood's appeal papers that he felt he had done nothing wrong,[21] and it could indeed be said on his behalf that allowing college money to be used for speculative purposes had traditionally been regarded as a perquisite to compensate for heavy bursarial duties and inadequate stipends. Though they were Fellows, Bursars had also been regarded as in some sense agents, and so long as they did well by the College few questions had been asked about their own finances. Wood had been unluckily caught out by the bank crash of 1797, a crisis so severe that the Bank of England was forced to suspend cash payments, but he subsequently made good almost all the defalcation. Yet he was not forgiven. He fell victim in part to rapidly changing expectations of financial probity that were affecting all departments of public and corporate life. It was a mood-change that Powell had initiated locally when he reconfigured the College's accounts in 1770, and which had been reinforced nationally by the reports of the parliamentary commissioners for investigating the public accounts (1780–86), with their calls for regularity, accountability, and thrift. These changing standards, which owed much to the Evangelical revival of the times, would have taken effect sooner or later, but Wood's disgrace ensured that in St John's they came sooner. An order of 1802 repeated the stipulation that all moneys be deposited on receipt with either the London or the Cambridge banker,[22] and

---

[20] No relation of the eponymous Tutor and future Master.

[21] 'Pamphlets relating to Revd Dr Wood's case': SJCA, D101.4.

[22] The Cambridge banker from 1802 to 1815 was Edward Gilliam, then from 1815 to 1897 Mortlock & Sons. In 1897 both Mortlocks and the London bankers Goslings & Sharpe were absorbed by Barclays.

added four significant provisos: that the balance in the Cambridge account should never be more than double what was held in London; that the interest on what was held in Cambridge should be used to augment the salaries of the four most important working officers, with 50 per cent going to the Senior Bursar and the rest shared equally among the Junior Bursar, Bread Bursar, and Steward; that the principal sums, whether held in London or Cambridge, should be drawn upon 'only as the wants of the College may require'; and that accounts should be presented by each officer once a quarter.[23] The Bursar and his colleagues were now much better provided for, but at the same time their freedom of action was severely circumscribed.

The question of officers' emoluments continued to be troublesome. In 1814 it was decided to augment the Senior Bursar's stipend by the amount of a Junior Fellow's dividend. This was to compensate him for the loss of traditional perquisites such as bacon, hens, sheep, brawn, and capons, now that most farms were being relet on money-terms only and not in kind. Then in 1819 it was decided that cash in the bank could be converted into government securities. The College would make any profit or loss on such transactions, but the officers would divide the interest accruing among themselves in the same proportions as before. Maybe the collapse of share prices following another bank crash in 1825 made this arrangement seem a bad bargain for the College. At any rate, in 1827 it was agreed to pay the officers a fixed sum in lieu of interest: £105 for the Senior Bursar and £35 for the others. The dramatic fall of the dividend in 1830 led to the Senior Bursar being awarded £290 in compensation for his anticipated losses over the next six years, and soon afterwards it was decided to stabilize his income under that head at its 1829 figure of £160.[24] Thus gradually did the College move towards a system of 'pay and not perks', a policy that would later be applied to lesser members of the establishment, such as domestic staff.[25]

The most significant reform of these early years related to the composition of the Fellowship. In 1819 the College petitioned to be allowed to remove from its statutes the stipulation that, of the thirty-two Foundress or Lady Margaret Fellows, there were to be no more than two at any one time who had been born in the same county,[26] and no more than one in the case of certain Welsh dioceses. Wood was almost certainly the moving spirit in this, though there is no evidence of any internal dissension, and it seems likely that rivalry with Trinity played a part in the decision. Decades earlier the Johnian mathematician Thomas Jones, calculating that the only Fellowship open to someone from his native St Asaph was likely to remain blocked for the foreseeable future, had migrated to Trinity, where as Senior Tutor (1787–1807) he is said to have 'raised the reputation' of that College', thereby increasing its numbers to more than those of St John's, and arguably giving it 'the lead in the Cambridge world'.[27] The petition was successful, and as a result, while restrictions on the twenty-one Fellowships

---

[23] CB, 4 Feb. 1802; Howard, *Finances*, 152–4.

[24] CB, 5 Apr. 1827, 30 Mar. 1831, 13 Apr. 1836.

[25] See below, pp. 267–71.

[26] This stipulation had ensured that half, and no more than half, of the Foundress Fellows came from the nine northern counties: above, pp. 43–4.

[27] G. M. Trevelyan, *Trinity College: An Historical Sketch* (Cambridge, 1946), 78.

that had been founded by private benefactors were continued,[28] Foundress Fellows were allowed to transfer without loss of seniority to any such foundation for which they were qualified, thereby creating a vacancy that could be filled by anyone from anywhere of sufficient merit. This would ensure that talent was not lost through accident of birthplace, and also that applicants for privately endowed Fellowships would be stronger than those for the Keton Fellowship in 1775, when notoriously the only two candidates had been a 'Wooden Spoon' and someone who had not even obtained honours.[29] Because this seems now to have been such a sensible change to have made, it is easy to underestimate its significance at the time, but in those days corporations very rarely sought to alter their statutes. Even the College's lawyers were dubious, and everything depended on James Wood being able to win over highly placed politicians such as the Home Secretary, Lord Sidmouth.[30] His success in doing so added to the sense that St John's was snugly ensconced at the heart of the political establishment.[31]

It was then in an atmosphere of economic and political optimism that the Seniors were prompted to undertake the first of the century's two financially disastrous building operations, the creation of New Court. Expansion of the College had been mooted as early as 1774, since when undergraduate admissions had 'increased in a most extraordinary degree',[32] from about forty in 1800 to about ninety in 1820, but for a long time nothing substantial could be done to increase accommodation because colleges were not allowed to borrow on the security of their estates. The situation was transformed in 1824 when an Act of Parliament allowed the universities access to the funds of the loan commissioners, a body that had been set up seven years earlier with the power to advance exchequer bills to individuals, corporations, vestries, and other statutory bodies for the purpose of completing public works schemes authorized by the legislature. With strong prompting from the Master, the Seniors immediately decided on a building big enough for between 100 and 120 Fellows and scholars.

No site being readily available on the east side of the river, it was agreed to plunge westwards, and three architects were directed to draw up plans in 'as nearly as may be the style of the present second court'. The most prominent of the three was William Wilkins who, having recently completed Trinity's New Court, was currently engaged on the south and east ranges of King's. Perhaps for that reason he refused to compete, and so lost the chance to build for all of Cambridge's three largest colleges. St John's turned instead to Messrs. Rickman & Hutchinson of Liverpool, specialists in commissioner churches, though the lead partner Thomas Rickman was mainly famous for his academic treatises on

[28] These twenty-one were sometimes called Foundation Fellowships, having been appropriated to the foundation, but they remained distinct from the thirty-two Foundress Fellowships, as did the eight so-called Bye-Fellowships (seven Platt and one Webster).

[29] Miller, *Portrait of a College*, 75–6.

[30] SJCA, D105.150–9, 255–63; Scott, 'Notes', *Eagle* xxi (1899–1900), 1–23.

[31] In this context it is worth mentioning that the most high-flying Johnian at this time was the Viscount Castlereagh, later the marquess of Londonderry, who was Foreign Secretary from 1812 to 1822 and among the most prominent of European statesmen.

[32] James Wood to Lord Palmerston, 14 May 1826, in J. S. Boys Smith, 'The College seeks help from Lord Palmerston', *Eagle* lvi (1954–5), 185–93.

styles of Gothic architecture. The building that resulted is in the hybrid style typical of the early nineteenth century, more 'Gothic survival' than 'revival', or in other words 'classical with Gothic knobs on' like many of the commissioner churches. The planning is classical, the elevation symmetrical, the roof appears flat behind its castellated balustrade, and the regular fenestration enforces the horizontal emphasis. It would resemble a barracks were it not for a few crockets, a row of fourteen pointed Gothic windows along the cloistered screen that fences the building off from the 'Backs', and for its exotic central cupola, described by Pevsner as 'a glazed lantern with thin flying buttresses and pinnacles'.[33] The last feature dominates the composition and accounts for the building's affectionate designation as the 'Wedding Cake'. The whole development was evidently meant to make an impression, and established beyond doubt that St John's was the pre-eminent college in Cambridge, financially as well as academically. The New Court of Trinity is puny by comparison, not least in its floor heights.

However, anything less like 'the style of the present second court' could hardly be imagined, and this would still have been the case if the College had stuck by the architects' original intention, which was to build in a uniform red brick with stone only for the staircases, dressings, and mouldings. But it was decided at a late stage (June 1827) to use Ketton stone instead on all but the north-facing rear elevation. This naturally swelled the cost, which came eventually to just short of £78,000, as against an original estimate of £42,500 and an extant building fund of only £9,000. The question of how to pay for New Court thus became paramount. In 1826 the College mortgaged 101 sets of its own rooms, as well as a number of estates, in order to borrow £45,000 in exchequer bills from the loan commissioners, but no sooner had they done so than Parliament raised the interest on such advances from 4 to 5 per cent. The reason was clear. The loan commission had been set up in 1817 in an attempt to revive the economy and prevent a post-war slump, yet by 1824, when the decision was taken to allow Oxford and Cambridge to take advantage of the scheme, the economy was over-heating. In December 1825 there occurred the first and worst stock market crash of the century. Blaming these events on over-speculation, the government reacted pro-cyclically rather than counter-cyclically (i.e. in a way that would now be labelled 'quantitative hardening') by raising interest rates. The fact that Trinity, Christ's, and one or two other colleges further up the queue had sneaked under the net, and so avoided the higher rates, no doubt added a sense of injustice to injury. Frantic efforts were made to lobby the local MP and highly placed Johnian, Viscount Palmerston, Secretary at War. He in turn lobbied an even more highly placed Johnian, the Chancellor of the Exchequer, Frederick Robinson, by urging that 'the discipline of the College must suffer from having so many of the Young Men out of the walls.'[34] There was a particular concern that undergraduates would take lodgings in Barnwell, a district notorious for its prostitutes. But Palmerston and Robinson were

---

[33] Nikolaus Pevsner, *The Buildings of England: Cambridgeshire*, 2nd edn (Harmondsworth, 1970), 152.

[34] Palmerston to Robinson, 25 May 1826, in Boys Smith, 'The College seeks help', 187.

powerless against a prime minister determined to cut down on speculative lending. As well as being an Oxford alumnus, Lord Liverpool was worried about a
different type of 'moral hazard' than that which faced the undergraduates in
Barnwell.

Back in Cambridge it was clear by Christmas 1827 that the cost of the works
had been underestimated to a truly alarming extent. Robinson was now prime
minister (as Lord Goderich), but his government was obviously going to fall
at any moment. There was clearly no time to be lost, which might explain why
the Seniors, who very rarely met between Christmas and New Year, took the
unprecedented step of meeting on Boxing Day in order to seal an appeal to the
Treasury for a reduction in the rate of interest. Having been turned down, they
appealed again in 1828 for 'an enlargement of the time for repayment of our
present loan'. This too was refused, though the College was authorized to procure a further £20,000 loan from the commissioners. The following year they
appealed yet again, this time for the interest on this second loan to be lowered
from 5 to 4 per cent *and* for 'an enlargement of the time for the repayment of
the same', and yet again they were rebuffed. Fortunately, they were able to benefit soon afterwards from a Public General Act of Parliament, which reduced
the interest rate to 4 per cent, and the commissioners themselves under powers
available to them agreed to extend the period of the loan.[35] While these two
last moves came as a relief, St John's had traditionally set more store by exploiting private influence. For that reason alone the repeated ministerial rebuffs must
have been humiliating and perhaps even shocking. They registered the extent
to which the political tide was turning against what William Cobbett, a radical agitator, was calling 'The Thing' – old corruption, secret influence, and the
establishment in general.

3. UNDER SIEGE: POLITICAL AND ECONOMIC PRESSURES, 1830–47

Conservative as I am, I seldom speak upon politics, because I know that
the Conservatism of those about me is a rabid mania with which I cannot
sympathise.

Charles Merivale to his father, 1835

By the time that New Court was completed in 1831, far more stock had had
to be sold than was anticipated,[36] hence the drastic diminution in interest on
securities, which had been such a useful source of income in the 1820s. Not until
1832 was any distribution made from general revenues towards the loan charges;
about £5,000 was paid that year, and just over £100,000 in all. Some relief was
provided by James Wood, who chipped in with a loan of £6,000 at 4 per cent 'to
clear off all demands of the Architects and Contractors'.[37] Unfortunately, even

---

[35] CB, 13 Apr., 1 May and 14 Oct. 1826, 26 Dec. 1827, 8 May 1828, 9 Apr. 1829.
[36] CB, 26 Jul. 1828, 29 Mar. 1830.
[37] CB, 14 Jul. 1831.

this gesture led to further trouble, since the Bursar, Charles Blick,[38] neglected to begin repaying instalments of the loan until seven years after Wood's death in 1839. As a result the debts arising from the building of New Court were not finally cleared until 1857, an unnecessary delay that led to grotesquely large interest charges. According to Howard's calculations, 'before the accounts were finally closed the College had to find from its revenues a sum of over £41,000 in interest alone, or more than one-half of the actual cost of the buildings'.[39]

All this would have mattered much less if the national economy had been buoyant, but continuing agricultural depression made for almost permanent crisis. The balance at the audit of 1829 reached rock bottom at £98, and sparked off a number of belt-tightening initiatives, notably a doubling of all room rents in the following year, and a 50 per cent cut in the number of feasts. Arrears of rent averaged more than £3,000 throughout the 1830s, and Blick was forced to take the drastic step of taking farms 'in hand', meaning that for want of willing tenants they were farmed by the College itself, for example at Raveley, Rawreth, Great Stukeley, Longstowe, and Hilton. It is not clear how these farms were financed or administered during their tenantless intervals, though a little more is known about some of the Headcorn farms in Kent. Howard believes that Blick farmed these properties on his own account from 1841 to 1845, 'paying rent to the College, obtaining or granting to himself reductions in that rent and taking any profit or bearing any loss'.[40] It seems certain that there would have been much more loss than profit, except for a suspicion that Blick might have kept the tithes to himself.

By this time it was clear that the College's finances were in a complete mess and, in what seems to have been a moment of high drama, the Seniors chose not to re-elect Blick at the 1846 audit. The coup was almost certainly encouraged by the Junior Fellow who took his place, William Bateson, and Blick seems not to have seen it coming. Ralph Tatham, who had succeeded Wood as Master in 1839, is supposed to have pronounced, after the vote was taken, 'Gentleman, you have done a cruel thing!'[41] Blick was given the Yorkshire rectory of Brandesburton in which to live out his final years, since when he has received almost nothing but obloquy. In College lore it has even been held against him that he enjoyed fishing in the moat of the farmhouse he had taken in hand at Headcorn, the implication being that Bursar Blick fiddled with his rod while the College was drowning. 'The College finances were seriously mismanaged', writes Howard sniffily. 'It is difficult to condone the application to College finance of methods following the lines of the hire purchase system.'[42] Searby refers simply to Blick's 'incompetence' and 'mismanagement'.[43] And undoubtedly Blick

---

[38] The first significant Senior Bursar of the nineteenth century was Robert Boon (1802–9), after whom came five others in rapid succession and then Charles Blick (1816–46), the longest-serving such officer in the history of St John's.

[39] Howard, *Finances*, 169. For a detailed account of the building and financing of New Court, see Crook, *Foundation to Gilbert Scott*, 74–86.

[40] Howard, *Finances*, 159–63.

[41] As recorded by G. D. Liveing, *Eagle* xxxv (1913–14), 85.

[42] Howard, *Finances*, 159, 172.

[43] Searby, *History of the University of Cambridge*, III. 136–7, 140–1.

was less hard-nosed than the straitened times demanded, probably less hard-working, and in his later years possibly negligent. On the other hand, he 'was thought by some of the Fellows to be an extraordinarily good Bursar', and no one seems to have thought him personally dishonest, which is why he was not chased and disgraced like William Wood. On the contrary, he was continually re-elected to office. Apart from Richard Berry and John Mainwaring, who served for twenty-one and eighteen years respectively,[44] none of Blick's ninety-four predecessors had been Bursar for longer than nine years, and most of them had served for very much less, yet Blick was allowed to continue for thirty. If he really was negligent, how much more so were they who re-elected him year after year.

Four other arguments may be urged in mitigation. The first is that, simply by being Bursar for so long, Blick turned it into a full-time job with enhanced expectations, and the latter were almost certainly used against him in retrospect. The second point is an obverse of the first. Although subsequent Bursars wielded enormous influence, including the power to say 'No', Blick was a subordinate for much of his tenure. Bursars had no formal or informal authority independent of the Master and eight Seniors, and most were appointed while they were still juniors. Only three of the first eight Bursars of the nineteenth century were Seniors at the time of their appointments. Three others attained seniority within a few years of taking office, but Blick had to wait until his fourteenth year. Admittedly this was fortuitous – the speed with which any individual Fellow was promoted depended on the departures or deaths of those above him – but it reinforces the point that he was a somewhat subordinate figure, especially given the activism of the Master, who paid 'considerable personal attention' to estate affairs.[45] It is also the case that Blick's reputation has suffered unduly from the hostility of two later Bursars. William Bateson, who was his immediate successor as well as his assassin, had obvious motives for traducing him, including possibly a guilty conscience, while in the case of Henry Howard, his successor but five, the real animus seems to be that of the frustrated financial historian. Unlike the worthy James Wood, when Blick visited College farms he did not make detailed notes of his findings, or if he did they have not survived, and in consequence 'much obscurity attaches to many of the transactions'.[46] Perhaps Blick's real crime, so far as Howard was concerned, was in not anticipating the accounting practices of a later age. Finally, it is luck more than anything that mainly distinguishes a good Bursar from a bad one. Blick took office at the onset of an agricultural depression in 1816, and left it at the onset of recovery in 1846. The only years in which he could have been expected to do anything remarkable with the estates were 1816–17 and 1846, and as it happens these were all bumper years for spending on estate

---

[44] During 1693/4–1714/15 and 1768–86.

[45] Howard, *Finances*, 156–8, 262–3. Wood must also bear the main responsibility for the fact that no loan repayments were made to himself between 1832 and 1839, that is assuming the omission was really down to negligence and not deliberate.

[46] Howard, *Finances*, 159.

improvement.[47] Blick must take at least some of the credit for that. For all the rest of his time he was helpless, and making detailed notes on the estates would not have made a jot of difference.

If the second quarter of the century was problematic financially, it was no less so politically. As already indicated, St John's was a high Tory college with an attachment to the establishment in Church and State that went beyond the conventional conservatism of most other colleges.[48] Given that the prime minister, Lord Liverpool, was also staunchly traditionalist, the Fellows had felt sufficiently at ease to relax their customary procedure of presenting a united front to the world. This was demonstrated during the parliamentary by-election of 1822, when the Master and nine Fellows voted on the losing side, while nine other Fellows 'very reluctantly' sided with the victorious 'anti-Catholic' party.[49] 'Lady Margaret has been torn and shattered', wrote a Junior Fellow, 'perfectly impotent, she lies exposed to the contempt or pity of the world, (…) the dame who for centuries past has been the terror of the wicked.'[50] Yet, as his waggish tone suggests, there was little ill-will on this occasion, since nothing very much was thought to be at stake. Four years later, when Palmerston triumphed in a much more highly charged general election, thirty-eight out of forty-six Fellows voted for Palmerston. It seemed that Lady Margaret was still intact when it mattered.

Immediately afterwards, however, the mood soured, and when in 1829 Wellington's government bowed to the inevitable and carried Catholic emancipation, tensions rose between the conservative majority and a few mainly younger liberals. 'I regret to say', wrote a visiting former Fellow, 'that College is very much changed for the worse, there seems but little harmony amongst the Residents (…) Some *staunch* old Johnians finding the course politics are taking in the Old House *threaten* to send their sons to Oxford, lest their principles should be contaminated.'[51] Worse still for the conservatives, in the following year the College's two most prominent friends at court, Palmerston and Robinson, defected to the Whigs when Lord Grey offered them important ministerial positions in his new government. Consequently, in the highly charged election of 1831, only ninety-nine Johnians supported Palmerston as against more than 200 for each of two Tory and anti-reform candidates.[52] Clearly the College's allegiance was to party rather than to Palmerston himself, and this in itself was a significant pointer to a new political polarization that continued through to the 1847 election. On that occasion, which was especially lively thanks to the opening of a

[47] £7,756 and £8,250 in 1817–18 as compared with an average of £1,063 during 1806–15; £6,956 in 1846 as compared with an average of £1,334 during 1836–45. Blick should also be given some credit for a revival in expenditure on enclosures during 1841–5.

[48] The term 'Tory' came back into common use in the later 1820s.

[49] 'Anti-Catholic' here signifies opposition to Catholic emancipation, an issue that was just starting to bubble.

[50] Edward Bushby to J. W. Whittaker, 28 Nov. 1822: SJCL, J. W. Whittaker Correspondence, 8.3.

[51] L. P. Baker to J. W. Whittaker, 3 Aug. 1829: SJCL, J. W. Whittaker Correspondence, 6.9.

[52] Searby, *History of the University of Cambridge*, III. 477–8.

railway line linking Cambridge to London, non-resident Johnian MAs voted in droves for the only Johnian candidate, the anti-Catholic, anti-reforming conservative Charles Evan Law.[53]

Table 1 Votes of Trinity, St John's, and all MAs in the
Cambridge University general election of 1847

Candidates	St John's	Trinity	All
Law (Conservative)	402	334	1,486
Goulburn (Liberal Conservative)	179	483	1,189
Fielding (Conservative)	292	243	1,147
Shaw-Lefevre (Liberal)	103	397	860

The juxtaposition of St John's and Trinity preferences in this table is appropriate because in these years the rivalry between these two largest colleges turned into real enmity, a reflection in part of the new political polarization in public life generally. Both Whig prime ministers of the 1830s, Lords Grey and Melbourne, were Trinity men, and both led governments that were dependent on supporters who detested the established Church. Another Trinity man was Thomas Spring Rice, Chancellor of the Exchequer during the later 1830s and MP for the town of Cambridge, and it was he who effectively launched the reform campaign by presenting the petition for abolishing University tests – i.e. for allowing Dissenters to graduate – in 1834. Way back in 1787 ten Junior Fellows of Trinity had challenged the authority of their Master and Seniors on a major issue (and won),[54] something that did not happen in St John's until the 1870s. As a result the predominantly Whiggish and relatively secular Trinity Fellowship had cultivated a reformist self-image, and within it a number of active liberals such as Peacock, Hare, Sedgwick, and Thirlwall were seeking to widen access to the University. For alarmist Johnians the political enemy was literally at the gates.

A flavour of senior common room politics at this time can be gained from the following account by a recently elected Fellow, the self-effacing Charles Merivale,[55] in 1835. It had become clear that a by-election was about to occur in one of the University seats, whereupon

> Yesterday at dinner time the Master sent round to us to meet him at the Lodge, immediately after Hall, where when we repaired, he made us a speech upon the state of affairs and probability of an election, in which case he said that it was highly desirable that the College should act in a body as usual, and ended with proposing to us to choose out of three persons who had occurred to him, Sir George Rose, Sir Alexander Grant, and Mr Law, the Recorder of London. All were Johnians, all Tories, and the heaven-directed suffrage fell upon Law – I not saying a word ... The College tactics have long been to fight in phalanx, by which means they frequently are enabled to take the Trinity forces in detail and so cut them to pieces; whereas I, who am not much perverted by college prejudices,

[53] Ibid., 492.

[54] Neild, *Riches and Responsibility*, 82.

[55] Fellow and Tutor, 1833–48.

sometimes am found acting the part of a Trinity man *in partibus*, and annoy them uncommonly in the rear.[56]

These comments seem to confirm something that the rest of Cambridge had long believed, that Johnians 'had a private Commandment: Thou shalt not vote against a Johnian.'[57] At any rate the phalanx was once again victorious, and Charles Law was elected. He was called into action as early as 1837, when the radical Earl Radnor pressed for a parliamentary commission to investigate the colleges and halls at the ancient universities. His intention was to discover how far each of them fulfilled the aims of its founders and benefactors, including help for the poor, the promotion of religion and virtue, and the encouragement of learning and the liberal arts. Resentment turned to panic shortly afterwards when the House of Lords menacingly inquired of each society whether it had the power to alter its statutes, or whether legislation would be required for that to happen. The Seniors replied that they did have such power, and would exercise it whenever 'necessary or expedient', but despite this outwardly haughty response they were desperate to prevent a commission, 'a measure in the present temper of the times to be greatly deprecated'.[58] In a blatant attempt to shut the stable door in case the horse had bolted, Law had inquired whether

> upon examination of the cases in which a departure from the Letter or Spirit of the Statutes without due authority, may be objected [i.e. demonstrated], anything can yet be done under the authority already possessed by the Colleges, their Visitors, or the University at large to effect a strict conformity between the Laws by which they profess to be governed and the actual practice under these laws, not only would the pretended necessity of a Commission be obviated, but in the apprehended event of such a Commission being actually issued, the University at large and the Colleges respectively would occupy a defensive position impregnable to the attacks of the Dissenters and of a Government unhappily leagued with the Dissenters.

In response, Wood agreed on the need 'to look over our Statutes carefully by ourselves and then submit our opinion to the Visitor, and request him to make, in conjunction with us such alterations as may quiet the public mind, which is at present a little excited against us'.[59]

In the event the 'violent attack' anticipated by Wood never took place, and the threat of a commission faded, but the atmosphere remained jittery, and young Merivale began to feel more out of place than ever.

> I have no private quarrel with any of our members, but live on courteous and friendly terms with all of them ... But there is a coarse, illiberal vulgarity in all this which, as a student and a clergyman, I deeply abhor. But I am a quiet and a timid man, and seldom venture even to remark upon it;

[56] Charles Merivale to his father, 22 Feb. 1835: *Autobiography of Dean Merivale, with Selections from his Correspondence*, ed. Judith Anne Merivale (1899), 135–6.

[57] Leslie Stephen, *Life of Henry Fawcett*, 3rd edn (London, 1886), pp. 116–22.

[58] Charles E. Law to Ralph Tatham, 5 May 1837: Scott, 'Notes', *Eagle* xxi (1899–1900), 6.

[59] Wood to Tatham: ibid. 9.

if I do I am easily to be put down by a laugh or a sneer. Conservative as I am, I seldom speak upon politics, because I know that the Conservatism of those about me is a rabid mania with which I cannot sympathise.[60]

Rabid is a very strong word and may not be entirely fair. It needs to be remembered that all senior common rooms consisted of a relatively small number of permanent elderly Fellows and a much larger and fluctuating contingent of men in their twenties and early thirties, but very few in middle age. (In the case of St John's, eight of the thirty-five Foundress Fellows elected in the 1830s left within five years, and fifteen more within eleven.)[61] In the circumstances a young man like Merivale might well have exaggerated the rabidity of his more elderly colleagues. Nevertheless, political feeling clearly ran high, which might explain the fate of George Kennedy, Fellow from 1835 to 1843, an outstandingly successful classic, winner of the Porson Prize and sundry scholarships, by all accounts a brilliant and successful private coach, yet never appointed to a Tutorship or to a share in one, apparently because of his support for Melbourne's government. His brother Benjamin wrote to protest.

> My brother is … a constitutional Whig; opposed to Ballot, to admission of Dissenters into the Universities, to the new Education Scheme, and to all shades of Church spoliation. I ascribe it to the tenacity of party spirit that he continues to place any confidence in those who now miscall themselves Whigs – but when the flimsy ties which now hold them together are dissolved (as they soon must be) and Radical and Conservative principles stand face to face, I know well that my brother's sympathies will be on the right side. Meanwhile I dare pledge myself for him that he would exercise no interference as Tutor one way or the other.[62]

This letter was written not to Wood but to the former President who had succeeded him as Master in 1839, the sixty-one year old Ralph Tatham, about whom surprisingly little is known, other than that he was notably handsome. Contemporaries also spoke of his 'singular dignity of person and courtesy'. '*He brought forth butter*, said the wags, *in a lordly dish*.' This was in marked contrast to his predecessor, who had been revered for his perceived goodness and earnestness rather than for any suavity of manner. Probably Tatham's most important attribute was that in 1809 he had defeated a Trinity man in the contest for the office of Public Orator, a high-profile position to be cherished at a time of party strife. At any rate his election as Master was uncontested and, so far as can be gleaned from the records, it was greeted with acclamation. The archives contain more than seventy letters of congratulation, many of them with a political tinge. 'You will succeed as a matter of course.' 'Your standing and character in the College and University [gives you] a prescriptive right to succeed to the Mastership.' 'Your incomparable claims.' 'Efficient and zealous chief.' 'Rejoice.' 'I shall

---

[60] Merivale to his father, *c*. 1837: *Autobiography of Dean Merivale*, 135–6.

[61] Searby, *History of the University of Cambridge*, III. 106–7.

[62] Rev. George Kennedy to Ralph Tatham, 20 Jul. 1839, and Dr Benjamin Kennedy to Ralph Tatham, 18 Sept. 1839: SJCA, D90.413–15. For Benjamin Kennedy, see below, pp. 249, 327.

have the pleasure in my own mind of contemplating the important College of St John's in the safe keeping of all its ancient privileges as long as it shall please Divine Providence to prolong the days of the present Master.'[63]

Tatham's first duty was to persuade MAs to come up to Cambridge to 'support the College', meaning they should vote for J. J. Blunt in the contest for the Lady Margaret chair of Divinity. This had come to be regarded as little less than a College fiefdom, so for Blunt not to have got it would have been a disaster.[64] His success made everyone a little happier, and most were happier still in 1841 when the Whig government fell and the Conservatives returned to power under Sir Robert Peel. Two years later the young queen and her Prince Consort made a memorable visit, the St John's courts being decked in crimson carpet for the occasion. But in 1846 the Conservative party disintegrated over Peel's decision to repeal the corn laws, itself an alarming move (or so it appeared at the time) for all those institutions that depended for their wealth on agricultural rentals. These events would lead to four decades of unwelcome Liberal political hegemony, and it may well have been desperation that moved the Fellows in 1847 to take the highly unusual step of contesting a nomination for the post of Chancellor of the University. It is unsurprising that they should have opposed Trinity's candidate, Prince Albert, as being too liberal, a bit more surprising that they should have picked on an out-and-out reactionary to oppose him, but Lord Powis, a former nobleman of the College, was particularly popular in Church and University circles just then, by virtue of his successful campaign to prevent the formation of a new diocese of Manchester by combining the sees of St Asaph and Bangor. In the three-day poll that followed, the voting was close – 953 for the Prince and 837 for Powis – sufficiently so, it might be thought, for Johnians to have claimed a moral victory, but in fact not so. In the first place the issue seems to have divided the St John's Fellows; at least it was rumoured that several of them including the Master were anxious to abort before the final day of polling. And perhaps because Powis was notoriously High Church and anti-reformist, political passions ran so high and led to so much resentment (not to mention obstreperous behaviour) that defeat was made to seem all the more devastating. Enemies said that Powis was 'patronised by 3 P's, Punch, Puseyites & Pigs', signifying respectively xenophobic opponents of the Queen's German husband, High Churchmen, and Johnians.[65] 'Piggery' was of course a term of abuse long used to describe St John's. Like 'hog', it had been slipping gradually into desuetude, a sign perhaps of the College's declining fortunes, but in 1847 it was back in force. In Cambridge lore, the Chancellorship debacle marked the moment when that decline became obvious to all.

---

[63] Letters to Tatham in April–May 1839 from George Wray, Samuel Laing, the duke of Northumberland, and Revd Richard Burgess: SJCA, D90.313, 316, 358, 392.

[64] It was held by a Johnian continuously from 1688 to 1875.

[65] *Romilly's Cambridge Diary, 1832–64: Selected Passages from the Diary of the Rev. Joseph Romilly*, ed. J. P. T. Bury, M. E. Bury, and J. D. Pickles (Cambridge, 1967–2000), I. 86, 227; II. 196, 199.

4. 'THE LOWEST, MOST CHILDISH, PIGGISH, PUNNING PLACE'[66]

The College keeps up its reputation as a refuge for the poor, and I do not doubt that in a few years with our new Tutors our character for gentlemanly bearing will improve. At present we have too many representatives, backed by some among the Fellows, of the noisy and dissipated school.

John Mayor to his mother, *c.* 1848,
Trinity College, Cambridge, Library: Mayor Papers, B8/245.

Cambridge's two most influential and glamorous undergraduate institutions of the nineteenth and twentieth centuries were the Union Society and the Apostles. St John's and Trinity could jointly claim to have founded the first of those in 1815, but Trinity quickly seized the initiative, helped no doubt by the fact that it was a Master of St John's who had sought to suppress it. Only four Johnians served as President during the remainder of Wood's lifetime, and it was not until the 1890s that their descendants finally achieved a dominant influence within the Union. Meanwhile eight of the twelve undergraduates who formed the Cambridge Conversazione Society in 1820 were Johnians. Because there were twelve and because they were Evangelicals, they soon became known as the Apostles, but during the course of the 1820s the Evangelicalism was ditched as the society virtually became a preserve of Trinity. That College went on to supply more than 80 per cent of members between 1830 and 1850, and more than 90 per cent in the twenty years thereafter.[67] In both cases Johnians had shown great enterprise but then surrendered to their rival, suggesting a loss of leadership within the University, and perhaps also a loss of social cachet. Could it also be that the dons' despair over the 1832 Reform Act, and over the implications of Whig rule generally, filtered down to the student body? How else might one explain the sudden wave of emigration that occurred? There were, it is true, many practical reasons for changing colleges besides dissatisfaction with one's first choice, but even so it seems telling that, of 302 persons admitted during 1834–6, as many as forty-one should have emigrated, while only three or four joined St John's from other colleges.

So what was the undergraduate body of St John's like? In his survey of St John's at the beginning of the nineteenth century, Edward Miller commented on four significant developments. Academically the College had become 'generous to mediocrity and small endeavour', meaning that under Craven (1789–1815) the high standards set in Powell's day had not been sustained. Very possibly this declension was connected with the fact that 'the range of recruitment, viewed from the social angle, was narrower than in the past'. Only half as many sizars were being admitted in the 1790s as in the 1750s and only a quarter as many as in the 1690s.[68] Persons from artisanal and farming families had virtually

---

[66] 'I thank Fortune daily I was not a Johnian. It is the lowest, most childish, piggish punning place.' *The Letters and Private Papers of William Makepeace Thackeray*, I. *1817–1840*, ed. G. N. Ray (1945), 107.

[67] W. C. Lubenow, *The Cambridge Apostles, 1820–1914: Liberalism, Imagination, and Friendship in British Intellectual and Professional Life* (Cambridge, 1998), 109–10.

[68] See above, p. 207.

disappeared, while there were more sons of peers and gentry than ever before.[69] These were all recent shifts, but Miller was also able to identify a secular trend – literally a secular trend – over the course of the eighteenth century as a whole: whereas in 1700 four-fifths of undergraduates made their careers in the Church, one hundred years later the proportion had fallen to just over one-half. Interestingly all the developments noted by Miller went into reverse during the first half of the nineteenth century. Academic standards recovered, the number of sizars rose, artisans' sons trickled back, aristocrats retreated fast, and a clerical career became once more the preferred destination of most students.

With regard to academic standards, it is true that only about a quarter of undergraduates had sufficient expertise in mathematics to allow them to take honours degrees, about half were poll men who could work as much or as little as they liked, and the rest took no degree at all. However, this was broadly true of other colleges as well, while in terms of honours in the tripos, which was the main source of esteem, St John's hauled itself back and eventually overtook its great rival in the 1840s.

Graph 1 says little about the College's academic performance as a whole, since it takes no account of total numbers, nor of candidates placed in the second and third classes. Given that numbers fluctuated considerably from year to year, and that many undergraduates took no degree at all, it would make no sense to try to construct the equivalent of today's so-called 'Tompkins table', which calculates tripos performance by college. The graph *is* an index of prestige, however, since national as well as local attention focused on the list of Wranglers. It was a source of pride that, having run more or less neck-and-neck with Trinity for forty years, St John's secured many more Wranglers in the 1840s, and over twice as many in the top four. In fact the tide had turned in 1839, an *annus mirabilis* when the College notched all four of the top mathematics places. Johnians also claimed the coveted position of Senior Wrangler on no fewer than twenty-two occasions during the first half of the century, and in seven years out of eight between 1843 and 1850.

Success in mathematics was not matched in the new Classical tripos, in which only seventy-four Johnians obtained first-class honours as against 160 Trinity men during the first twenty-eight years of its existence (1824–51). An ability to attract the best classics has sometimes been put forward as one reason why Oxford as a whole attracted more elite members of society than Cambridge, and a similar differentiation may have taken place as between St John's and Trinity. The former certainly seems to have become less socially exclusive, though all such statements have to be made with caution owing to the incomplete and frequently vague information provided by the admissions register. It is known that of the 320 students who were admitted in the years 1801–6,[70] all but twenty-one were aged between seventeen and twenty, the youngest being sixteen and the oldest thirty; this means that, as in Cambridge generally, the student body was on average somewhat older than in the middle of the eighteenth

[69] Miller, *Portrait of a College*, 71–2.

[70] Though even this figure must be used cautiously, since not all students who were admitted (and therefore entered in the admissions register) actually came into residence.

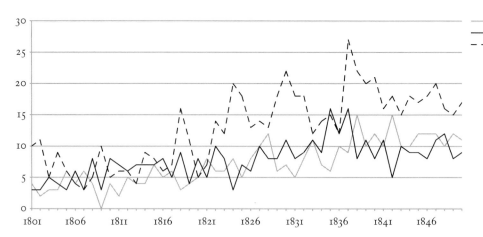

Graph 1 Numbers of Senior Wranglers in St John's, Trinity, and other colleges, 1801–50

century. Of those who recorded a home address, seventy-nine came from the northern half of England, 144 from the south,[71] and only a trickle from elsewhere, mainly the other parts of the United Kingdom and the colonies. In these respects the only change over the succeeding thirty years was a slight hardening of the southern bias. Thus of the 579 students admitted during 1831–6, all but forty fell in the 17–20 age range, 158 were from the north, and 328 from the south.

In terms of schools attended there was a somewhat bigger shift. Of the 193 cases where a school was cited in the earlier period (1801–6), twenty-nine of the entrants were Etonians and twenty-five Harrovians. Of all the other schools, only Rugby with ten and Shrewsbury with seven made any sort of showing. The later cohort (1831–6) also contained a considerable number of Etonians, but proportionately they were much less prominent, just twenty-four out of the 278 who recorded an *alma mater*. The dominant school was now Shrewsbury with forty successful candidates, while Charterhouse scored seventeen, Sedbergh thirteen, Rugby and Uppingham nine apiece. A complication is that, whereas before 1830 the column labelled 'school' in the admissions register is left blank for some candidates, in the 1830s and for some time afterwards it was common to refer to a certificate of fitness to study, many of them signed by a Fellow of St John's or one of the other colleges.[72] A blank entry or reference to a certificate might indicate that the person in question had not been to school, having been privately educated at home instead, but this cannot be relied upon,[73] and so one must be tentative in drawing conclusions. Even so, the declining prominence of

---

[71] Whereas the Elizabethan statutes refer to the nine most northern counties, for this analysis 'the north' signifies the twelve most northern counties and includes Shropshire, Staffordshire, Leicestershire, and Lincolnshire.

[72] During 1831–3 and 1836, for example, 178 entrants cited a school and 122 presented a certificate, but only one certificate is recorded during 1834–5. These sudden shifts presumably reflected a change in bureaucratic practice within St John's, though whether they carry any significance is not known.

[73] A very few instances have been found of Venn citing a school where this was missing from the admissions register.

Eton and the virtual disappearance of Harrow, in favour of much less smart but umbilically connected establishments like Shrewsbury and Sedbergh, is quite striking. And the trend continued. Taking 1841, 1846, and 1851 as sample years, the most successful schools were Sedbergh with eight candidates admitted, Shrewsbury and Manchester Grammar with seven each, Rugby with six, and Uppingham with five. If it meant that St John's lost some of its appeal to *le bon ton*, as the most fashionable and badly behaved echelons of high society were referred to in the Regency period, that would hardly be surprising given that the *beau monde* was now almost entirely a Whig preserve. As a result, blades and rattles – men like the Etonian Edmund Grose, who matriculated in 1801 and was described by Lord Byron (Trinity) as 'a very amiable and clever man (…) in great request for his wit, gaiety, and *chansons à boire*' – became much thinner on the ground.

At the same time there was a falling off in the numbers of noblemen and Fellow-Commoners. There were only two of the former category in the whole of Cambridge in 1795, and both were at St John's; there were again just two in 1850, but both were at Trinity. In 1795 St John's was home to twenty Fellow-Commoners as against forty-two in Trinity and sixteen at Emmanuel; in 1850 there were only four in St John's, while five other colleges had more than that number, including Trinity with twenty-one. The family backgrounds of undergraduates also deteriorated in social terms, though here again, since the only information comes from the admissions register it is necessary to interpret the statistics cautiously. Only 177 out of the 320 students admitted during the first six years of the century wrote down any sort of descriptor in the 'Father's Name and Addition' column, and thirty years later only 291 did so out of 579 admitted.

Table 2 Father's declared status/occupation, 1801–6 and 1833–6

	1801–6	*1831–6*
aristocrats	28	10
esquires, gents, sirs, barts	56	79
clergy	47	110
military	4	21
civil servants, clerks	11	11
law	9	14
medicine	5	14
teachers	5	7
merchants	5	6
manufacturers	0	6
retailers	2	1
other	5	12

The most striking change is that the percentage of aristocratic fathers fell from 15.8 to 3.4 per cent. The correspondingly significant increase in the number of fathers who were ordained reflects the strong religious revival that had set in since the late eighteenth century, and had galvanized both wings of the Established Church, High and Evangelical. The rise in the military component is equally unsurprising given the country's almost continuous involvement in war with France between 1793 and 1815. The most problematic category concerns those fathers who were registered as esquires, gents, sirs, and baronets. It is tempting to think of such designees as members of the landed gentry, leisured rent-receivers in other words, in which case it could be said that their reduced number (in percentage terms) was balanced by the appearance of six manufacturers. Such a conclusion would fit a traditional Marxist social history of the period. Unfortunately, many of the earlier self-styled gents and esquires may well have been horny-handed industrialists, in which case the appearance of manufacturers in the list may signal no more than that such people were willing for the first time to acknowledge themselves as such, manufacturing industry having been valorized to a great extent during the debates on parliamentary reform during 1831–2.[74] Table 3 shows snapshots of parental status or occupation for 1841, 1846, and 1851. Aristocratic fathers have disappeared entirely, clergymen are well represented (though seven of the thirty-six listed were non-Anglicans, a new development), while the mercantile and professional classes figure more prominently than before. Professed manufacturers remain extremely uncommon, but farmers appear in bulk for the first time in 1851, and there are now considerable numbers of artisans. Perhaps the biggest change is the precision with which artisans and retailers were described (e.g. ironmonger, butcher, grocer, wireworker, jeweller, cabinet maker, commercial traveler). It shows that coyness in such matters had gone out of fashion, also that St John's was now heavily patronized by the myriad of occupational types that peopled urban Britain.

Table 3 Father's declared status/occupation, 1841, 1846, and 1851

	1841	*1846*	*1851*
esquires, gents, sirs, barts	9	24	13
clergy	15	21	20
military	9	0	3
civil servants, clerks	3	0	1
law	4	3	7
medicine	3	0	3
teachers	0	0	3
merchants	4	14	7
manufacturers	0	1	1
banker	0	0	1
retailers	4	4	4
artisans	4	3	7
farmers	0	0	11
brewers	0	0	1
surveyors, engineers	0	3	0
undertaker	0	0	1
other	9	0	3

At the bottom of the social tree was the sizar, a category traditionally associated with St John's. There had been a falling off in number during the eighteenth

[74] This suggestion gains some credence from the fact that all six of the students whose fathers were registered as manufacturers during 1831–6 were admitted from 1833 onwards. In the parliamentary debates of 1831–2, reformers successfully helped to establish in the public mind the novel idea that the middle class in general – and the manufacturing middle class in particular – was the backbone of the nation, the source of its moral and economic strength.

century, but a considerable revival after 1800. Taking eleven sample years at five-year intervals between 1801 and 1851, 263 out of 722 persons admitted were sizars, some 36 per cent. Since, in the University as a whole, sizars accounted for no more than 10 per cent of undergraduate numbers, the College's contribution would seem to justify the boast of a young Fellow at mid-century that St John's maintained 'its reputation as a refuge for the poor'. And all the more so in so far as there is evidence from the 1820s that sizars were very heavily subsidized.[75]

Sizars were no longer required to perform menial household tasks, but that they were still the objects of disdain seems evident from Samuel Butler's auto-biographical (but also satirical) novel, *The Way of All Flesh* (1903).

> Behind the chapel (…) there was a 'labyrinth' (this was the name it bore) of dingy, tumble-down rooms, tenanted exclusively by the poorest under-graduates, who were dependent upon sizarships and scholarships for the means of taking their degrees (…) I have seen some of these men attain high position in the world of politics or science, and yet still retain a look of labyrinth and Johnian sizarship. Unprepossessing (…) in feature, gait and manners, unkempt and ill-dressed beyond what can be easily described, these poor fellows formed a class apart, whose thoughts and ways were not as the thoughts and ways of Ernest and his friends, and it was among them that Simeonism chiefly flourished (…) To most of them the fact of becoming clergymen would be the *entrée* into a social posi-tion from which they were at present kept out by barriers they well knew to be impassable; ordination, therefore, opened fields for ambition which made it the central point in their thoughts, rather than as with Ernest, something which he supposed would have to be done some day, but about which, as about dying, he hoped there was no need to trouble himself as yet.[76]

A problem with this passage, which is the most famous depiction of life at St John's in nineteenth-century literature, is that the writer – Salopian, pensioner, classic, author of *Erewhon* and a number of non-Darwinian evolutionary tracts – went up in 1854, eighteen years after Simeon had died, and almost as many after Simeon's type of Anglican Evangelicalism had ceased to be the identifiable religious brand of old. Furthermore, Butler was clearly satirizing the attitudes of mutton-heads like his protagonist (Ernest) rather than offering an objective analysis of sizardom. Nevertheless, his autobiographical novel, together per-haps with the Wilberforce connection,[77] has led some historians to suppose that St John's was then an Evangelical redoubt, much as Magdalene, Queens', and Caius were at different times.

Certainly there were Evangelicals at St John's in Simeon's day, including some notable clergymen such as J. W. Cunningham (who matriculated in 1801), Francis Close (1816), and Henry Melvill (1817). It is impossible to give precise

[75] SJCA, M1.10.1–31.
[76] Samuel Butler, *The Way of All Flesh* (Harmondsworth, 1953), 190–2. Samuel Butler (1835–1902), writer and artist, attended St John's during 1854–8.
[77] Though William Wilberforce was not converted until after he had gone down from St John's.

numbers since definitions of Evangelicalism are notoriously flaky, but it is possible to say that between 1800 and 1840 St John's admitted ninety persons who either were, or would become, Evangelicals beyond a shadow of a doubt, and of these forty-two were sizars.[78] In addition to them, another 106 men were admitted for whom there is *some* (albeit inconclusive) evidence of Evangelicalism, and thirty-nine of them were also sizars. These figures give strong support to Butler's suggested correlation, at least for an earlier period, but it does not mean that Evangelicals influenced the religious tone of the College. The hostility shown by Marsh and Wood has already been noted, and the latter's predecessor Craven had been equally hostile.[79] Moreoever, the very fact that Evangelicalism was linked to sizardom suggests that Evangelicals had a marginal status, given that sizars continued to be treated disdainfully. As Butler went on to point out, they were addicted to tea and prayer among themselves, they attached themselves to a handful of sympathetic Tutors, and taught in local Sunday schools rather than seeking to proselytize among the student body. In fact Evangelicalism no more influenced the religious tone of the College than did the High Church revival, led in Cambridge by Trinity's Hugh Rose. St John's was deeply, seriously religious, but the faith that prevailed was of a sober, middling sort, untinged by enthusiasm or excessive dogma.

An indication of the College's commitment to religion, or at least to a clerical career, is evident from the figures on undergraduates' subsequent occupations (though once again it needs to be said that the information is far from complete).

Table 4 Undergraduates' subsequent careers, 1801–6 and 1833–6

	1801–6	*1831–6*
Clergy	139	345
Military	10	9
Law	33	40
Medicine	3	3
Teachers	10	47
Academics[†]	19	48

† This is a very imprecise category, since it includes not only those who went on to become career academics, in Cambridge and elsewhere, but those who served for just a few years as College Fellows.

The first and wholly unsurprising conclusion to draw from Table 4 is that St John's offered a ladder of upward social mobility. Of those undergraduates with artisanal or mercantile backgrounds or who came out of retailing (the much-despised 'shopocracy'), none went back there. Instead they became professionals of one sort or another. But the most striking statistic is the proportion of

[78] Apart from noblemen and Fellow-Commoners, all undergraduates were admitted as either sizars or pensioners, but many of them (and especially the latter) went on to win scholarships. The peak year for evangelical admissions was 1832, followed by 1818. I am indebted to the unparalleled expertise of Dr Gareth Atkins in the matter of identifying evangelicals.

[79] Miller claims that Craven instituted Sunday lectures on the Gospels and the Acts, partly to keep Johnians away from Simeon's sermons: *Portrait of a College*, 68.

students who went on to take Holy Orders: 65.8 per cent during 1801–6, 77.7 per cent during 1831–6, 80.0, 67.4, and 78.5 per cent in 1841, 1846, and 1851 respectively.[80] It would seem that, after a relatively secular phase during the eighteenth century, the College was once again operating as an Anglican seminary above all else. A related development was the rise of the teaching – and, to a lesser extent, the academic – professions.[81]

Since statistics do not convey what a place was like to live in, the remainder of this section will touch on the undergraduate experiences of five individuals for whom archival evidence is available. The first only ever wanted to be a poll man, but was bullied by his patron (Professor Selwyn) into going in for honours, and it nearly killed him. The other four were 'reading men' who went on to become Fellows, one indeed to be Master.

Quite a lot is known about some studious future Fellows because their papers have ended up in the College Library, whereas the vast majority of undergraduates who were little more than passers by – *qui cum per unum ostium ingrediens, mox per aliud exierit* – are much harder to get to know, but fortunately the diary of Francis Hutton (1846–9) gives a vivid account of how one somewhat harum-scarum young man coped. He never much liked the location – 'Cambridge is at all times, a horrid place, but on a rainy day, it is almost intolerable' – and he found most lectures 'excessively stupid and uninteresting', especially those in classics and mathematics (he longed for more theology). But tea, egg flip, and wine were compensations, as were velocipeding and jumping in the countryside, while 'a pipe generally puts one in good humour'. He hosted parties into the early hours, after one of which a friend 'stayed behind – to puke: which feat he performed to his complete satisfaction, in my "Wife", which is the College sou-briquet for a "*pot de chambre*".' However, 'the great draw-back of parties in Cam-bridge is the want of female society, and a lot of young spirits together need one or two petticoats to keep them within bounds'. (Tell that to the Dean!) He only ever mentions work to record that it has been 'put off' once again. Having been bullied by Selwyn into putting in for honours, he informs his Tutor Edward Brumell of his intentions, but the latter's 'stare of amazement' and 'incredulous laugh' leads him to suppose that he stands no chance of getting them. Accordingly he fritters away the remaining weeks, only to find himself in a 'terrible funk' when the examination looms. 'What a big fool I am. And what a donkey I have been.' One day, exhausted after a morning examination, he relaxed throughout the afternoon and early evening, then returned to his room to revise for the following morning's paper, but could not find his algebra textbook. At this point let him take up the tale.

---

[80] These numbers were significantly higher than in Oxford where, in 1818/19 and 1848/9 alike, only about one-half of undergraduates went on to take Holy Orders: M. C. Curthoys, 'The careers of Oxford men', in M. G. Brock and M. C. Curthoys (eds.), *Nineteenth-Century Oxford*, Part I [vol. VI of *The History of Oxford*] (Oxford, 1997), 503.

[81] Well over one-third of those who took teaching posts were in Holy Orders. Such persons have been counted twice in the above statistics.

It was now 10½ o'C and I had not looked at an Algebra for two years. I rushed down stairs to the man beneath me, and asked him to lend me one – he had no such thing – I got the key of the street door, and off I went over the way to Jones's lodgings, and found him out. However I found an old Algebra – and returned in very good spirits to my rooms, tho' sadly fearful for the morrow. There was no time to lose, so set to work, and read away to the Binomial Theorem by three o'Clock in the morning, when I closed the book, took a pipe, in order to digest what I had read, and also to warm me for I had been so attentive that the fire had gone out, and I felt very cold. When I got into bed, I could not sleep, but rolled from side to side, and counted Morpheus in ones – nay! I took morphine – but all was of no avail. I lay awake – and thought what a great ass I had been not to read when I had time (...) Well, I got out of bed, dreadfully sleepy, at 8 o'C on the Friday, took coffee and started for the Senate House, the rain falling, and the morning consequently dark. I felt in a dreadful state of nervousness when I took my seat in the Senate, and it increased to an awful degree when I got the paper, for sure I was a dead plank – my head fell on my hand and I gave way to despair and fell into a sound sleep. Presently I felt someone tapping me; so I looked up, and saw the Director standing over me "You have been thinking a long time" he said, "so pray set to work, or I fear the consequences for you". I thanked him for his kindness and told him I did not feel very well, which was the fact. However, the sleep had refreshed me, and I began to work (...) I came out as pale as a sheet, and thoroughly knocked up.

In the event Hutton scraped into the second class, an enormous relief, 'for I was reckoned a safe pluck, by most men, and their opinion coincided with my own. Thank God, my University troubles are over, and I am about to commence life in earnest.'[82] In all this Francis Hutton comes across as a universal type of likeable scallywag, but one characteristic nails him to the earlier nineteenth century – his instinctive piety. Although he had no time at all for the Evangelical set, he attended compulsory chapel in an earnest frame of mind. Indeed, one of his grouses against Cambridge was that 'it is so *full* of temptations (...) The only way to guard against them is to be constantly in prayer to our God for help against them.'

More significant for the future of the College was the emergence of a type of undergraduate best described anachronistically as the 'scholarship boy'. It is a term mainly used to describe ferociously hard-working mid-twentieth-century students who were obsessed by examination results and by their own and others' places in the pecking order, but it is equally apposite with respect to the second quarter of the nineteenth century. Conscientious workers had existed before, of course, especially among the sizars; what was new was the pecking order. One historian goes so far as to describe the competitive system as it emerged in Cambridge (but not Oxford) after 1800 as 'a ranking order of unparalleled intensity

[82] Francis Hutton's Journal: SJCL, MS W.33.

and precision'.[83] Those undergraduates who responded eagerly to the challenge were sometimes called 'prizemen', and certainly they collected many prizes, but that is slightly misleading since they were moving beyond the assumptions of an earlier period when a Fellowship had been seen as the ultimate prize, won on the basis of examination honours and carrying entitlement for life, should the honorand so wish, without any obligation to pursue further scholarly or scientific work. By the 1830s the prospect of what might now be called a professional academic career was taking hold among many genteel middle-class families, with the consequence that precocious undergraduates aspired to Fellowships from a very early age. That is the second sense in which the term 'scholarship boy' seems appropriate.

In St John's there were two important prototypes in Samuel Butler (grandfather of the novelist) and Benjamin Hall Kennedy. Butler went up in 1791, won three of the Browne's medals, the Craven Scholarship, and the Members' Prize, as well as being senior classic. He was elected a Fellow in 1797, and one year later became headmaster of Shrewsbury School, a position which was in the College's gift and which he held for almost forty years. His phenomenal success in turning a moribund establishment into one of the leading public schools was widely recognized and envied, and owed much to his innovative introduction of regular examinations. One of his two most stellar pupils was Benjamin Kennedy of *Latin Primer* fame, who, while still at Shrewsbury, entered for the Cambridge Porson Prize. (His entry was so good that the regulations were changed so as to exclude schoolboy contestants in future.) Later, at St John's, he won the Pitt University Scholarship, the Members' Prize, and a host of other prizes including the Porson for a second and third time, before graduating as senior classic and first Chancellor's medallist in 1827. He became a Fellow in the following year but then went off to teach, eventually succeeding Butler at Shrewsbury, where he was headmaster from 1836–66, before returning to Cambridge as Regius Professor of Greek. In his thirty years at Shrewsbury he established himself as 'the greatest classical teacher of the nineteenth century'. The steady stream of high-flying candidates whom he sent up to Oxford and Cambridge benefited his own *alma mater* in particular, and paved the way for what has been called 'the golden age of Johnian classics'.[84] Butler and Kennedy did much to define the academic trajectory of their former college, yet significantly neither of them finished higher than Senior Optime in mathematics. Conflict between mathematics and classics was to be a running sore in St John's for the rest of the century. Although the subject had been included in the College's examinations since 1765, the Classical tripos had operated only since 1824, and until as late as 1857 it was necessary to secure honours in mathematics before being allowed to sit for Classical honours, the effect being to divert many potential classics to Oxford.

One of Butler's brightest pupils was William Henry Bateson, Blick's nemesis,

---

[83] Christopher Stray, 'The shift from oral to written examination: Cambridge and Oxford 1700–1900', *Assessment in Education* 8 (2001), 39. This new obsession with ranking (and shaming) as distinct from merely banding students in the Senate House examinations was symbolized by the adoption of the 'Wooden Spoon' *c.* 1800.

[84] *ODNB* (T. E. Page; J. H. C. Leach).

and a man who had more influence than any other on the direction that St John's would take in the nineteenth century. The fifth son of a Liverpool merchant, he was exceptionally shrewd, ambitious, and calculating from an early age. As a pupil at Shrewsbury he took a sharp account of the values added by different masters, and was disposed to switch subjects if he thought it would improve his prospects. At the age of seventeen he agonized over 'whether it would be more advantageous to incur the expense of another year's tuition with Dr Butler and have the prospect of greater success at Cambridge or to avoid that expense and not have so good a chance of succeeding',[85] and most of his letters home from that time on were about winners and losers in the scholarship stakes. After being unexpectedly rejected by Corpus Christi College, Oxford, he attributed his 'defeat' to the 'chicanery', 'duplicity' and 'roguery of the Corpus gentlemen'. 'There is certainly room for reform here.'[86] Then, when his friend Thomas Brancker unexpectedly beat Robert Scott[87] for Oxford's Dean Ireland Scholarship, Bateson found himself in a dilemma.

> It has (...) put the Dr. [Butler] into this predicament: his plans being laid in this manner that Scott should get it this year, Brancker next & that then some other Shrewsbury man should come in: but he has been disappointed in Scott: & therefore is uncertain with regard to the succession of Shrewsbury men as all the upper boys who are leaving this half year (...) are going to Cambridge. But as we have had such extraordinary success at Oxford he wishes to keep it up: he therefore applies to me to go up to Oxford: certainly no very dishonourable thing to me: and he begins by working on my fears: & says that Harris and I will *clash*: but to that I have had my eyes open all along: he then says there is a Trinity [Oxford] Scholarship or two vacant for which I have a very good *chance* but as you are aware I had a very good *chance* for the Corpus Scholarship in the Dr's opinion: and I understood from him when I was rejected at Corpus that the Trinity gentlemen were just as bad as my friends at Corpus – in addition to these objections, I have a great antipathy to Oxford, a rooted antipathy which I have *always* had. Moreover I do not see that my prospects will be any better at Oxford than at Cambridge (...) It is plain to see that the Dr. only wishes me to go to Oxford to strengthen *his* interest at that University.[88]

In the event Bateson, who was no one's pawn, entered St John's in 1831, and was elected to a scholarship in November. However, it was not many months before his forward-looking mind was calculating whether he ought not to migrate to Pembroke, where Fellowships were worth £220, as against £150, and yet also

---

[85] W. H. Bateson to his father, 1 Nov. 1829: SJCL, Miscellaneous Letters: W. H. Bateson, 2.2.

[86] Bateson to his father, 8 Mar. 1831, SJCL, Miscellaneous Letters: W. H. Bateson, 2.9.

[87] Brancker was the other of Butler's two most stellar pupils. Scott later became Master of Balliol College, Oxford (1854–70) and combined with Liddell to produce the famous *Greek–English Lexicon*.

[88] Bateson to his father, 19 Mar. 1831: SJCL, Miscellaneous Letters: W. H. Bateson, 2.10.

easier to come by, the majority of them being open to laymen, whereas all but four of St John's fifty-three Foundation Fellows were required to vacate six years after taking their MA, unless by then they had also taken Orders. Yet 'no man ought to go into orders with merely the idea of getting a living'. In seeking to persuade his father of the advantages of Pembroke, he reasoned that he would never succeed at St John's, being only the fourth best classic of his year and unlikely to become more than a Senior Optime at mathematics, and as for the two lay law Fellowships, both were occupied and 'not likely to be given up'.[89] 'At a small College', on the other hand, 'on account of the great scarcity of good men they are very glad to get a tolerable man to be Tutor: which you must be aware is a very lucrative office (…) I have been led to take this subject into consideration not from any private pique with any one connected with this College (…) but purely from a desire to forward my own interest.'[90] His father was unconvinced, and so a week later Bateson played the 'private pique' card instead, writing indignantly that he had been gated ('a punishment usually reserved for moral offences') by an Assistant Tutor for refusing to attend some optional trigonometry lectures: 'I immediately went to him and explained but he would not listen to anything: I then said, Mr Evans, if you persist in this punishment which is at the same time needless and intolerable I shall be forced to migrate from the College: he said he could not help that.'[91] Still his father (who held the purse strings) remained intransigent, and Bateson was forced to concede that he must stay put:

> To succeed at this College will require very laborious & diligent exertion, perhaps more than I am master of: at all events I will try the fortune of war: and if I do not eventually succeed, as far as I am concerned, I will endeavour to clear myself of all imputations of bad-generalship: let the town be well garrisoned and prepared for an attack, and there will be little danger of a surprise from the enemy.[92]

Without the benefit of hindsight such sentiments would seem risibly portentous. They certainly reveal the young man's truculent self-esteem and combative view of the world. As it turned out, his biggest enemy would be a seriously life-threatening bout of typhoid fever, which forced him to degrade for a year,[93] and yet despite this setback, and despite dissatisfaction with some of the pedagogy on offer, Bateson did slightly better in examinations that he had predicted, graduating in 1836 as third classic as well as Senior Optime.

He now had to land a Fellowship, a challenge he approached with his usual

---

[89] Bateson to his father, 31 Mar. and 6 Apr. 1832: SJCL, Miscellaneous Letters: W. H. Bateson, 2.12–13.

[90] Bateson to his father, 31 Mar. 1832: SJCL, Miscellaneous Letters: W. H. Bateson, 2.12.

[91] Bateson to his father, 6 Apr. 1832, SJCL, Miscellaneous Letters: W. H. Bateson, 2.13.

[92] Bateson to his father, 25 Apr. 1832, SJCL, Miscellaneous Letters: W. H. Bateson, 2.15.

[93] According to a junior colleague, Bateson's 'severe illness had left its traces on him in a certain loss of elasticity and a slight weakening of memory which, little as they may have been suspected by others, made him conscious in after life that he was never quite the same man after it as before'. J. E. Sandys, 'In Memoriam William Henry Bateson', *Eagle* xi (1879–81), pp. 4–5.

brand of calculating pessimism. None of those who held the three Fellowships assigned to Lancastrians was 'likely to vacate in my time', he warned his father.

> We have just heard that Bailey (…) is married: but there is no great gain in this, as he would have had to vacate in course, next year at farthest, as he is at the bar. There are now three fellowships vacant for next year, but of these one is strictly appropriated to Beverley [School].'[94]

Three months later the prospect looked brighter.

> We are likely to have a considerable number of vacancies in the Fellowship next year. There are already four Foundations and one Platt. Two of the former are appropriated, namely one (Taylor's) to the County of York, and one (Stephenson's) to Beverley men from Beverley School. It is also expected that Whitley will be married before Xmas, whose Fellowship is open to all comers. And Solomon Smith, it is believed, will adopt a similar method of vacating his Platt in a few days.[95]

This is a reminder that, while middle-class sons all over Britain were panting to step into dead men's shoes, in order to become a Fellow one usually had to step into those of a bridegroom. And it seems clear from the correspondence of aspirant scholars that a good deal of interested match-making occurred. At all events, Bateson became a Fellow in February 1837. He read for the Bar but then decided to take Holy Orders and return to Cambridge, though whether this was done for religious reasons or 'with merely the idea of getting a living' is not apparent. He did some school teaching and won a high reputation as a private tutor in classics, but was not offered a College Tutorship, apparently because he was thought to be too 'liberal' in a political sense. Yet his practical acumen must have been evident to everyone, and he was appointed Steward in 1845. This gave him access to information about the running of the College which he used to harry Blick, before usurping the office of Senior Bursar in 1846.

The younger Bateson was evidently high principled. For example, he 'stoutly opposed' the exclusion of sizars from the College boat and cricket clubs.[96] Even so, he comes across in his correspondence at this time as self-absorbed, self-interested, and unlikeable. Yet as Bursar and later as Master he was to strike colleagues as a model of consideration and solicitude for others. According to one obituarist, 'an outward dignity of demeanour was combined with a real simplicity of character, and beneath a certain coldness of manner lay a heart remarkably kind.'[97] Maybe success softened him, maybe marriage did,[98] or it may simply be that Bateson's youthful astringency arose from his having been forced onto a treadmill by self-interested pedagogue-schemers such as Butler, and goaded by parents who, like so many members of the upper middle class

---

[94] Bateson to his father, 20 May 1836: SJCL, Miscellaneous Letters: W. H. Bateson, 2.16.

[95] Bateson to William Drake, 1 Sept. 1836, SJCL, Miscellaneous Letters: W. H. Bateson, 1.1.

[96] Mullinger, *St John's College*, 287.

[97] [T. G. Bonney], 'The Master of St John's: obituary', *CR* ii (1880–1), 258–9.

[98] See below, p. 258.

during the second quarter of the nineteenth century, were increasingly anxious about whether their sons would ever find suitable jobs. Bateson was far from being the last person to worry whether the expensive investment in his own education would turn out to be 'worthwhile'.

Anxieties about their future prospects also troubled Robert, John, and Joseph Mayor, sons of an Evangelical vicar in Cheshire, who unlike Bateson were beset by immediate money worries as well. In 1838 Robert thought of sitting the sizarship examination while a pupil at Manchester Grammar School, but instead enrolled as a pensioner in the expectation that he would win a scholarship, and so be better off. He *did* win a scholarship, an achievement he had 'little reason to be proud of', however, 'as even at the beginning of the examination it was next to impossible that any one would take it from me. In fact if a Manchester man becomes candidate for one of these scholarships, however deficient he may be, and however superior his competitors may be, they cannot pass by his claims.'[99] His father gave him £36 to spend during his first term, and he managed to finish with £1 16s 8d in his pocket, having spent nearly £4 on groceries, £9 on laundry, over £10 on upholstery, £4 on razors, £1 11s 6d on stationery. His College bill included charges for commons (dinner) and 'fines for not keeping Chapels'. ('These two first charges are as moderate as they will ever be, as I have never once at table sized for puddings &c.') There was a standing charge to the cook, £16 for room rent, £2 10 for tuition, and a few further small charges for glasses, candles, and coal. In addition he had to supply whatever furniture had not been left behind by the previous occupant.[100] He just managed to keep on the happier side of Wilkins Micawber's dividing line until his third year, when he was obliged to borrow from friends and beg another £5 from home. Such financial constraints naturally kept him alert to any other scholarships and exhibitions for which he might be eligible. 'How proud shall I be when the time comes that instead of being a burden to my parents, I shall be able to relieve them in the education of some of my brothers.'[101] This was pertinent since at about the same time the second son John, then at Shrewsbury School, was already beginning to calculate his own chances in the scholarship stakes.[102] In 1845 Robert's pleasure in winning a Fellowship at the second attempt was tempered by John's failure to win a Bell [Scholarship]: 'great disappointment, but good may [come], we should have been too much elated if we had each been successful in our aims, it will teach us not to value or reckon too much on such distinctions'.[103] Two years later, when it was Joseph's turn on the treadmill, John received some alarming intelligence from the Welsh Marches. 'The head boy of Shrewsbury a most laborious reader is coming to John's this year – I had supposed that he would defer it for a 12 month – which will very much abridge Joe's chance of ye Port Latin.'[104] The threat led Joe to consider the wisdom of migrating to a smaller

[99] Robert Mayor to his father, 9 Oct. and 5 Nov. 1838: Trinity College, Cambridge, Library, Mayor Papers, B7/34–5.

[100] Robert Mayor to his father, 19 Jan. 1839: Mayor Papers, B7/36.

[101] Ibid.

[102] John Mayor to his father, n.d.: Mayor Papers, B7/42.

[103] Robert Mayor to his mother, 1845: Mayor papers, B8/207.

[104] John Mayor to his mother, 22 Sept. 1847: Mayor Papers, B8/232.

17 'The Latiner' (1872): not a Sicilian brigand, but J. E. B. Mayor: almost certainly the work of Reginald Fawkes (1868; Trinity) SJCL, Port. XVI.12

college, but on becoming second classic in 1848 he was encouraged to stay on and try his luck in St John's.[105] In the event all three brothers became Fellows, though Robert did not reside, moving off first to a post teaching mathematics at Rugby School before become rector of Frating with Thorington, where he remained a devoted 'old boy' of St John's. His brothers both took private pupils and helped to nurture the Moral Sciences tripos, established in 1851. Joseph left Cambridge in 1842, and went on to become Professor of Classical Literature and later Moral Philosophy at King's College London. John Edward Bickersteth Mayor, by far the most eccentric, remained a Fellow for sixty-one years and indeed became a College institution.[106]

Given their pressing need for academic success, it is unsurprising that the Mayors' correspondence should have been dominated by accounts of preparations for, and performance in, examinations. Of course letters home are to be read with a certain scepticism – Robert in particular probably emphasized how hard he worked as an excuse for not writing longer letters – but it is notable that he frequently stayed up during the vacations rather than rejoin what was evidently a loving and fun-loving family. A typical day would have him attending an 8 o'clock lecture following chapel at 7, and then from 10 until 1 there would be further lectures, for many of which he had simply not had time to prepare. Like so many of those undergraduates whose leanings were mainly humanistic, the real bugbears were algebra and calculus, subjects that 'admit of an immense quantity of cram',[107] and indeed he crammed to some effect, ending up Third Wrangler. He also expected, correctly, that his parents would be interested in other students, and reported home on the detailed marks gained by different candidates as though they were cricket scores: 'Simpson's place is due entirely

---

[105] John Mayor to his mother, 1848: Mayor Papers, B8/241.
[106] See below, pp. 319–20, 327.
[107] Robert Mayor to his mother, 1839, Mayor Papers B8/188–9.

to one paper in which he was far from well, and was 200 marks below Cayley. In every other he was either equal or above him' (*ad infinitum*).[108] And if there should be any doubt as to whether these scholarship boys really cared, the following account by Joe Mayor of his friend F. S. Powell's fate should dispel it.

> He had the fullest assurance of a first from both Tutors and lecturers – one indeed who saw some of the papers he sent in told him that judging by those he ought to be from 4th to 6th and there were even reports that he was to have the medal – yet he is only head of the second class. I had been walking with him that morning and just after dinner we rushed to the bookseller's where the list is hung up. There were a great crowd round it and with some difficulty I forced my way through while he stood outside in dreadful suspense as you may imagine. I was horror struck when I saw his place, particularly as the list was large and I had to look a long way. I only made a sort of sign to him that I could not congratulate him. He broke through and caught sight of his own name, then snatching my arm and begged me to come away, so I took him up to my room and there he threw himself into an arm-chair before the fire. In vain I tried to console him by reminding him that those who had far longer experience of him than the examiners had come to a very different opinion, that his object had been to educate himself, not to get a place &c &c. At first he could say nothing, then he fancied that there must have been a mistake, that we had seen it wrong or the examiners had lost papers. I went and brought a list to satisfy him, and two most wretched hours we spent in studying it. Some times he would declare that he could never read or work again, that he had failed in the subject which had occupied the six last years of his life and should never be able to set to any thing else with spirit, that he could have no faith in industry, that he had toiled so many years for nothing, that it was a disgrace never to be forgotten, there was no road to honour left open, and so on.[109]

At one point Charlotte Mayor, clearly alarmed by the relentless regimen of work and fixation on success, mused about 'scholastic life leading to a want of common sense'. Her youngest son hastened to reassure her that, far from making 'a world of one's books', he boated, chatted, and met with people from different walks of life. Moreover, 'we are each of us picking up all we can about the professions we or our friends are to go into, and every now and then hearing news of those who have already started in the race'.[110] This latter comment got to the nub of the matter, which was that younger members of the relatively impoverished genteel classes had their way to make in a world where patronage was increasingly being frowned on, and where Masters and Tutors could no longer prefer favoured pupils into positions as James Wood had once done. Academic performance mattered, which made it all the more galling when the system was perceived to be unfair. In 1841, for example, there was great

[108] Robert Mayor to his parents, 1842, Mayor Papers, B7/41.
[109] Joseph Mayor to his mother, 1850: Mayor Papers, B8/328. Powell had the consolation of being elected to a Platt Fellowship the following year.
[110] Joseph Mayor to his mother, 1847: Mayor Papers, B8/288.

indignation at 'a change *they* made in the system of examination', with disastrous results.

> Every one seems to be disappointed, and Mr Hymers[111] says that he never new [*sic*] a list which surprised him more. Some who were expected to be Wranglers, have been plucked, others are low in the third class. Six of the best Classics are amongst the plucked. The three Colleges which generally stand highest have not done so badly for years. St John's in particular.[112]

There had been similar carnage in the previous year's Classical tripos, when the bottom-placed Johnian on the list had had to be comforted with a friend's reflection that his was only 'a somewhat sad instance of the preponderance of ill luck and examinational destiny over steady scholarship and quiet study'.[113] Of course, people who do badly and those who seek to console them always say that examinations are unfair, but here they probably had a point, since, as Charles Merivale would aver before a Royal Commission a decade later, the 'variable and capricious' practices of the mainly inexperienced examiners in classics had caused grave injustices.[114] Cambridge was increasingly being conceived as a meritocracy, yet its instruments for assessing merit were inadequate. Elections to Fellowships often roused similar indignation, as when Robert Mayor blamed donnish politics for his failure to win one in 1844. In his mother's words,

> Dear Robert was not elected a Fellow; it was a grievous concern occasioned as it appears by a contest between the two Masters[115] of the College – Hymers had boasted of having all the seven Fellows of this year from his side of the College, and this induced the other Master [Thomas Crick][116] to make most strenuous efforts to get Wilson who belonged to his side elected in the stead of Robert (…) So disappointing dear Joe are all earthly expectations (…) However it is the will of our heavenly Father and must be right and good and best.[117]

During the second quarter of the century St John's would appear to have been, for the last time perhaps, an extremely heterogeneous society, so much so that it is impossible to describe a prevailing ethos. It is to be wondered whether there were stand-offs among the respective bodies of bottle-heads, sizars, and Scholarship boys, whether there were friendships across the divides, or whether the different tribes simply failed to notice each other? It is known that reading men like the Mayors despised the 'noisy and dissipated' types, while if Samuel Butler *grand-fils* wrote truly, sizars were a despised minority.

They were rarely seen except in hall or chapel or at lecture, where their

---

[111] Fellow, 1827–53; Tutor, 1832–53.

[112] Robert Mayor to his mother, 27 Jan. 1841: Mayor Papers, B8/202.

[113] Charles Ellicott to George Shaw, 26 Mar. 1840, copy in George Shaw Letter Book: SJCL, MS O.78.24, at pp. 56–7.

[114] *Report of Her Majesty's Commissioners on the State, Discipline, Studies, and Revenues of the University and Colleges of Cambridge*, Parliamentary Papers 1852–3, xliv, 397–8.

[115] Here and below, Charlotte Mayor intends not 'Master' but 'Tutor'.

[116] Fellow, 1825–48; Tutor, 1831–46.

[117] Charlotte Mayor to Joseph Mayor, 1844: Mayor Papers, B16/1.

manners of feeding, praying and studying, were considered alike objectionable; no one knew whence they came, whither they went, nor what they did, for they never showed at cricket or at the boats; they were a gloomy, seedy-looking *confrerie*, who had as little to glory in in clothes and manners as in the flesh itself.[118]

But for all the confusion it was becoming more and more obvious by the 1840s that the future direction of the College would be shaped in a meritocratic direction by men like Bateson and the Mayors. As in public life generally, aristocratic privilege and condescension were no longer to be tolerated. Young Bateson's *Schadenfreude* in reporting home on the failure of one young sprig from Trinity to pass an examination set the tone.

> I have some satisfaction in telling you that a Nobleman Lord Haddo ... underwent the operation of plucking: such things as these occurring at intervals read a very salutary lesson to men of rank, and tend in some measure to support the character of the University. Noblemen at best are not desirable in an University; they promote idleness, expense, and dissipation: and when they are numerous, they are invariably attended by a crowd of persons cognominated toadies, sycophants or tuft-hunters. I believe such a thing as the plucking of a nobleman is never heard of at Oxford, where, you know, they are far more numerous, but, we must conclude, much more intelligent.[119]

5. 'HALCYON DAYS': ESTATE AND HOUSEHOLD REFORM IN THE AGE OF BATESON, 1846–81

> I was astonished ... to learn that there is a system of heavy perquisiting in connexion with the communion Wine. The Chapel clerk asked whether three bottles would be required, or two. I thought he meant for the *term*, but the senior dean tells me that he meant for the day! ... If the wine is paid for out of the offertories it is certainly very unfair to the men whose sixpences and coppers are reverently placed there ... And as for the [Chapel clerk] himself, it is a part of the wretched old plan which made all these men drunkards in the past. Perquisites in drink belong to an order of things that can no longer stand the daylight.
> R. Caldecott to Scott, 3 Nov. 1890: SJCA, D92.1.120.6.

There can be no disputing that the third quarter of the century was the age of Bateson. From the moment he became Senior Bursar he completely overshadowed his former Tutor and current Master, Tatham, who was to some extent discredited by association with the financial irregularities and slackness of Blick's later years. It was therefore no surprise when, in February 1857, Bateson succeeded to the Mastership himself, and with as great a degree of support

---

[118] Butler, *Way of All Flesh*, 190–2.

[119] Bateson to his father, 20 May 1830: SJCL, Miscellaneous Letters: W. H. Bateson, 2.16.

as Tatham had enjoyed in 1839, though for very different reasons. Twenty-five years earlier, while still a freshman, he had conceived of his career in St John's as a military campaign, and had vowed not to let himself down by 'bad-generalship',[120] and true to form the first thing he did after gaining the citadel was to plan a campaign of a very different sort. Just three weeks after his election he wrote to his sister:

> So soon as I had it clear before me that I should be made Master of the College, I inquired of Honora whether Annie Aikin, her great friend, upon whom I had long secretly set my heart, was free, and at all likely to accept any advances from me. I had never made it known to anyone before, much less to the lady herself that such was the state of my affections. Honora could make out nothing except that she was free – so as faint heart &c down I came last Tuesday week and by incessant dedication of myself to the object of my mission I am delighted to tell you that I am now an accepted suitor. I have thought the matter over with all the prudence & coolness that I could command and I can say deliberately that such another wife could not be found. There is literally nothing wanting to complete the group of female virtues and fascinations and I am as happy as possible.[121]

Bateson was what in modern parlance would be called a good committee man, and his influence in part reflected the increasingly bureaucratic nature of institutional life. 'He was especially characterized by a clear logical intellect, by a singularly acute judgment, and by a remarkable faculty for seeing the weak points in any scheme or argument. He was an excellent man of business, of great industry and patience, a first-rate chairman of a meeting, discerning its feeling with marvellous intuition', discerning too the optimal time to put a question.[122] That tribute was written by an admirer but is representative of opinion more generally. Equally important in the eyes of a Fellowship anxious to reassert its importance within the University was Bateson's growing profile outside the College. He was Public Orator from 1848 to 1857, was frequently elected to the Senate, acted for a time as Secretary to its Council, and served on most of the important University syndicates. Even more significant was his appointment to a committee to revise the University's statutes in 1849, while in the following year he became Secretary to the Graham Commission (1850–2). This was the first of three public inquiries in the mid-Victorian period to inquire into 'the state, discipline, studies, and revenues' of both the University and its colleges, and Bateson established a considerable reputation for the meticulous way in which he assembled the 674 pages of evidence and report. In 1872 he

---

[120] See above, p. 251.

[121] Bateson to his sister, 26 Feb. 1857: SJCL, Miscellaneous Letters, 2.17. Anna Aikin is described in the *ODNB* account of her son William (by R. Olby) as 'beautiful and spirited, (...) fond of the arts and a strong advocate for the rights of women'.

[122] [T. G. Bonney], 'Obituary of W. H. Bateson'. One of his tricks was to lull opponents into rhetorical traps by playing dumb, causing one of them to comment, 'I do doubt whether any man is morally justified in looking as stupid as he can on occasion'; T. G. Bonney, *Memories of a Long Life* (Cambridge, 1921), 42.

became one of seven members of the Royal Commission for inquiring into the property and incomes of the ancient universities and their colleges, and five years later he served on the statutory commission to put its recommendations into effect. In short, he was for two decades the most practically influential don in Cambridge.

The circumstances and consequences of Bateson's election as Master are discussed in the next section. As a committed reformer he naturally had the support of most of the younger Fellows, but it is surprising that he was not more vigorously opposed by the old guard. The explanation must be that even they were grateful to him for having restored the College's finances. And since the expansionist policies of the Bateson years were underpinned by rising prosperity, it makes sense to begin this discussion of the reform decades with his work as Bursar.

Very shortly before Bateson was appointed Senior Bursar, the Seniors agreed to the following motions:

> 10 February 1846: *Agreed* that before the renewal of any of our leases the Bursar do furnish the Seniors with all particulars respecting the property intended to be leased, at least a month before any offer is made to the tenant.

> 28 March 1846: *Agreed* that all accounts of every kind, trust funds as well as the general accounts, be examined and prepared at least a week before the final audit, for the inspection and approval of the Seniors, and not be finally passed unless signed by the Master and at least one of the two Deans.

It is impossible to be sure, but these determinations were almost certainly prompted by Bateson, though he was not himself a Senior, and they were almost certainly made with the express intention of ousting Blick, whom he very soon afterwards replaced. In so far as they limited the Bursar's freedom to act independently of the Seniors, it might be said that Bateson tied his own hands. But then he was shrewd enough to appreciate that, in the more bureaucratic world that was emerging, the surest way for a Senior Bursar to exercise power was to do everything by the book, knowing that his superior knowledge and expertise would enable him to carry committee members with him.

The new Bursar made his presence felt at once by insisting that the dividend for 1846 should be lowered to £110, even though it had stood at £130 since 1841 and the College had had a successful year financially. He justified the reduction by pointing out the £3,000 debt to Wood's estate that Blick had failed to provide for, and – like many a Bursar before and since – he prophesied a 'falling off in the income next year', the previous year's success having been due to windfall factors that would not be repeated.[123] Yet he felt able to increase the dividend to £140 in 1847, after which it rose inexorably, hitting £150 in 1848, £160 in 1852, £180 in 1857, £210 in 1858, £240 in 1860, £260 in 1867, and £300 (its recommended

---

[123] Bateson, 'Reasons why the dividend should be diminished': SJCA, D90.471.2. His main justification was that income from renewal/entry fines had totalled £5,349 in 1846, nearly three times as much as the average of the three previous years.

limit) in 1872.[124] In view of this it seems likely that the one-off reduction in 1846 was primarily a move in the game Bateson was playing, which was to discredit Blick as thoroughly as possible and to establish just how bleak financially his own inheritance had been. His very first letter as Bursar was to the land agent James Lake, requiring him to evaluate the properties at Headcorn, including those which Blick had farmed himself. Shortly afterwards he presented a paper demonstrating that, thanks to Blick's inefficiency in failing to call in tithes, certain rentals, and other debts, St John's had 'sacrificed' (taking interest into account) some £14,000.[125] Meanwhile if Blick hoped that he could fish out his remaining time in rectorial peace, he was soon disillusioned. For several years Bateson pestered him with letters demanding to know why he had or had not done this or that, to which Blick invariably replied that he 'could not recollect'. On one occasion Bateson upbraided him for having allowed an unauthorized courier to carry money to London, with apparently unfortunate results. It all helped to establish Bateson's credentials in the Fellows' eyes as the College's redeeming genius.

According to one tenant, Blick had 'assured him' that his property 'was as good as a freehold so long as he kept paying his fines'.[126] Bateson's first task was to signal to the College's lessees and agents alike that those days were over. 'I would wish you to understand that the half-yearly rents should be paid before the expiration of the quarters subsequent to Lady Day and Michaelmas. It is the practice which the College means to adhere to for the future and I expect that it will not be inconvenient to the tenants.'[127] 'I request you [an agent] to inform him [a tenant] that unless the fine be paid within a week from the date of your letter, the College will charge him interest at the rate of 4 per cent per annum from Michaelmas last.'[128] His letters to defaulting tenants were even more peremptory.

> I enclose a stamped receipt for the balance of rent due at Michaelmas last. If you please, you can continue tenant at Leigh Field on the old terms. But the College cannot consent to any abatement of rent. I should recommend you to consider your answer well, as I do not doubt that by improved cultivation the land might be made much more productive than it has been. You can, if you please, quit at Michaelmas next. Let me know your determination within a week.[129]

> The College will remit you the arrear of rent due at Michaelmas last and I hope to hear no more about the failure of your crops. You will not fail to pay the rent due last Lady Day on the 11th of October.[130]

The brusqueness of these communications was no doubt partly calculated. The new Senior Bursar was less than three weeks into the job, and determined to

[124] For the recommended limit, see below, pp. 285, 373.
[125] Bateson, 'Notes on Headcorn rents' [c. 1847]: SJCA, D90.471.1.
[126] Houghton to Bateson, 16 Jan. 1851: SJCA, SB21/Sun/2.14–16.
[127] Bateson to C. Giblin, 24 May 1846: SJCA, SB2.1.
[128] Bateson to J. B. Merriman, 24 May 1846: SJCA, SB2.1.
[129] Bateson to A. Reynolds, 6 Jul. 1846: SJCA, SB2.1.
[130] Bateson to J. Allen, 18 Jul. 1846: SJCA, SB2.2.

make sure that tenants did not expect him to continue in the slapdash ways of his predecessor.

Bateson's task of restoring St John's to prosperity was made immeasurably easier by the so-called 'golden age of English agriculture'. Despite the alarms of all those who had supposed that Corn Law repeal would destroy arable farming, most landowners and their tenants prospered mightily from the late 1840s to the early 1870s, and Cambridge colleges were no exceptions. But even allowing for that, Bateson was undoubtedly an energetic and accomplished Bursar. During his first ten years the amounts laid out on repairing, enclosing, draining, and otherwise improving estates averaged almost £3,500 as compared with just over £1,300 during the last ten years of his predecessor's reign. In addition he greatly accelerated the process whereby beneficial leases were converted into 'rack rents' (i.e. annually renewable tenancies). This was something that the ecclesiastical commissioners and more enterprising colleges such as Pembroke and Queens' had been doing for about fifteen years, and even in St John's, during Blick's later years, it had been agreed that if any lessee failed to renew in full at the proper time, then 'no second offer was made to him, and the lease was suffered to run out'.[131] The results were so impressive in terms of boosting regular income that it was resolved in 1851 to phase beneficial leases out almost entirely, an exception being allowed in a single case where the lessee had himself spent heavily on improvements. Most of the remaining long leases ran out between 1863 and 1868, the last year in which the College derived any income from renewal fines.[132] The process enabled St John's to take advantage of the sustained price rise during the third quarter of the century by increasing rents, but it meant that the estates had to be inspected continuously, a process facilitated by the development of railways and the rising number of professional land agents. It also meant that Bursars had to do business with each individual farmer or sub-lessee, instead of as heretofore simply dealing with the main lessee, who had often been a middle-man rather than a farmer. The new 'hands-on' approach transformed the position of Bursar from that of go-between to one of businessman in his own right, and boosted his status within the Fellowship.

When Bateson became Master, his position as Bursar was taken by the

---

[131] *Report … on the State … of the University and Colleges of Cambridge*, Parliamentary Papers 1852–3, xliv, 629.

[132] CB, 28 Jan. 1851; Howard, *Finances*, 179. Commenting in 1912, the then President G. D. Liveing ('Presentation of the master's portrait', *Eagle* xxxv (1913–14), 85, stated as a reason for the change of policy that the system of periodic fines for renewal was unfair. 'Those fines were divided among those Fellows who were fortunate enough to be on the list when the fines fell in.' In fact, although in some colleges (such as Trinity and Peterhouse) fellows did indeed share the fines among themselves as they came in, and in consequence the dividend often fluctuated violently from year to year, this was not so in St John's, where the dividends tended to be held at a constant level for several years at a time, and then moved upwards (or, very occasionally, downward) by tiny increments. The only occasion of an unusually sharp rise (from £96 in 1807 to £140 in 1808) cannot have been related to fines, which increased only slightly between those years, but was caused by other accidental factors, i.e. vastly increased profits from sales of timber, and a further windfall of £710 for land sold to the Kennet & Avon Canal Company.

enigmatic George Reyner.[133] To Cambridge folk at large the latter was merely
an eccentric figure who rode inexpertly through country lanes every day, lashing
his steed (the equally irascible Plato) with vigorous forward flicks of his whip,
but it was the forward flicks of his tongue that made his colleagues smart. A
stickler for obeying rules to the letter and for wearing formal dress, he was passionately conservative, personally domineering, and quick to raise the temperature of debate, whether privately or in public. He was cordially disliked by the
junior members, who called him 'Betsy' because of a religious tract that landed
in College one day entitled *The Conversion of Betsy Raynor*. They could not know
about the good he did by stealth, for example in secretly funding the studies of
poor scholars. To them he was (in the words of one of his successors) simply 'a
riddle and a thorn'. He could wither with a look, and his way of reproaching a
peccant undergraduate was often 'sharp enough to take his head off'.[134] As Junior Dean he made himself extremely unpopular, and in a notorious incident was
once loudly hissed by a posse of possibly drunken undergraduates as he processed out of chapel.[135] He could be equally intolerant when admonishing colleagues on high table and in the Combination Room, writing to the Master on
one occasion: 'At 20 minutes before midnight, my bedroom window being open,
I heard the sound of feet and voices in the college walks (…) There had been a
feast in the combination room at seven o'clock, and (…) several of the Fellows
had obtained the keys from the porters and adjourned into the grounds. This
appears to me a violation of the good orders and regulations of the College.'[136]
On another occasion he 'nearly brought about a rebellion among the juniors'
when he approached a newly elected Fellow who was smoking a pipe in the
wilderness and barked, 'Take that filthy instrument out of your mouth, sir!' And
yet, when the mood took him he could be high spirited and mirthful, especially
when winding down over dinner at the 4.30 p.m. Hall.

George Bonney, a sworn enemy, acknowledged that Reyner was 'really able',

> but he had risen from the ranks, and seemed as if a consciousness of
> the fact always prevented him from feeling at his ease. The result was
> a self-assertive rudeness, which often made him socially almost intoler-
> able … For a considerable time we spoke only on matters of business. Yet,
> notwithstanding his overbearing habits, there was much in Dr [Reyner]
> worthy of respect.[137]

The reference to Reyner's having risen from the ranks presumably alludes to
the fact that he had been a sizar, yet snobbishness was not a characteristic of St
John's at that time, and one may doubt its significance in this case. More sympathetically, the future Bursar Robert Scott believed that Reyner simply gloried
in his own independence of thought and judgement, and 'feared not the face of
man' in doing so.

[133] Educated at Manchester Grammar School; 4th Wrangler, 1839; Fellow, 1840; Sadlerian Lecturer in Mathematics, 1847–57; Junior Dean, 1849–51; Senior Bursar, 1857–76.
[134] R. F. Scott, 'The Rev George Fearns Reyner DD', *Eagle* xvii (1892–3), 403–8.
[135] Joseph Mayor to his mother [post 1848]: Mayor Papers, B8/308.
[136] Reyner to Bateson, 11 Aug. 1868: SJCA, D90.626.
[137] Bonney, *Memories*, 41.

18 George Fearns Reyner,
Senior Bursar 1857–76.
Sketch by E. H. Palmer

Naturally impulsive and warm-hearted, he occasionally credited his friends with merits far beyond their desert, until there came the inevitable discovery that even they had some of the little foibles of ordinary human nature, when they would be pronounced to have 'deteriorated' (...) Where another might have said, 'There I do not agree with you,' Dr Reyner on one occasion remarked to one of his closest friends, 'Mr H., I perceive you are a man of low moral tone'. Such criticisms are a little difficult to bear, but all knew the critic's worth, and, with generous recognition of it, allowed for plainness of speech and equally significant silence.[138]

Dons learn how to deal with such eccentricities, and even to delight in them. Whatever his faults, Reyner was a card, which explains why letters to him from former and non-resident Fellows were often written in an affectionate and playful tone, as well as from a safe distance, but a College Bursar has to mix with down-to-earth farmers. Bateson had been hard, but at least he was straight, whereas Reyner frequently adopted toying and teasing tactics. Sometimes when would-be purchasers wrote in with offers, they would receive non-committal answers or even none at all. Tenants in particular were infuriated by the new Bursar's idiosyncrasies. Robert Scott first put into print the story, often since alluded to, that one day, after tramping through some unkempt fields, Reyner asked a tenant sarcastically, 'Do you find growing thistles a lucrative occupation, Mr X?' It was presented as a specimen of drollery, but in his private journal Scott gave a less flattering account.

Old William Stutter Frost our tenant at Thorington disliked him so much that when he saw Reyner coming he would deliberately absent himself leaving a bailiff or foreman to shew Reyner round and only just turning up for a minute or two to say good bye and offer a glass of wine. Reyner

---

[138] Scott, 'George Fearns Reyner', 404.

offended him by his remarks. 'Do you call this good farming?' he asked with reference to a field of corn full of thistles. No doubt owing to this dislike the buildings at Thorington were not properly attended to and got into the state in which they were when Pieters[139] came and he and I have had to pay heavily for previous neglect.[140]

Farmer Merriman, agent at Wootton Rivers, told Scott that his men loathed Reyner because he was always 'suspicious of people with whom he came in contact. Merriman's father and uncle hated Reyner for this suspicion.'[141] And to reinforce the impression, Robert Mayor told Scott that 'in the later period of his college and bursarial life Reyner's mind seemed affected. He was so extremely suspicious and abrupt.'[142]

Repetition of the word 'suspicious' might to later generations suggest a degree of paranoia. Even so, the differences of style between Bateson and Reyner should not be made too much of. Despite profound and damaging disagreements in other areas,[143] on financial matters the two men worked in tandem, often going on estate visitations together, and despite a formal pretence that Reyner was in charge ('You must [...] consider yourself as armed with full discretionary powers')[144] it is clear that Bateson was the dominant partner when it came to really important decisions, and that he even continued to undertake some of the donkey work.[145] There is, however, one intriguing piece of evidence that goes the other way. It comes in the form of a postscript to a letter from Reyner to one of the College's land agents, and concerns the appointment of a new tenant for some land at Sunningdale: 'P.S. One (confidential) point I have not mentioned I think: it is this: it is my practice to make it almost a *sine qua non* that any new farm tenant should be a Churchman. The majority of our old tenants are dissenters.'[146] As a champion of Nonconformists' rights and a stickler for maximum economic efficiency, Bateson would surely have been outraged by such a clerically skewed policy. It makes one wonder just whom Reyner's 'confidential' was intended to exclude.

Yet probably the biggest change in policy owed less to personality than to the Universities and College Estate Act 1858, which provided that colleges, which had hitherto held real estate in mortmain, might now sell land for the first time, though with a proviso lasting until the end of the century that the proceeds had to be vested with the Board of Agriculture pending reinvestment in land.[147]

---

[139] Reyner's immediate successor as Senior Bursar.

[140] R. F. Scott, 'MS Diary, 1891–3', 6 Oct. 1892: SJCA, SB1.21.311–16.

[141] Scott Diary, 4 Jan. 1893: SJCA, SB1.21.325–6.

[142] Scott Diary, 6 Oct. 1892: SJCA, SB1.21.311–16.

[143] See below, pp. 339–41, 351–65.

[144] Bateson to Reyner, 8 Jul. 1864: SJCA, Bateson Letter Books, M1.7.

[145] For example, Bateson continued to break the news to long-standing tenants that rack rents had replaced the old system of 'periodical fines and nominal rents'. Bateson to H. J. Adams, 29 May 1861: SJCA, Bateson Letter Books, M1.7.

[146] Reyner to John Clutton, 5 Jun. 1863: SJCA, SB21/Sun/36.2.

[147] The proviso could be circumvented, as could the previous ban on sales, but only by means of expensive special measures: J. P. D. Dunbabin, 'Oxford and Cambridge College Finances, 1871–1913', *Economic History Review*, 2nd ser. xxviii (1975), 631–47.

This change in the law naturally introduced a new calculation into estate policy, one that Reyner exploited in ways that to outside parties made him seem dilatory. At a time of moderate but sustained price rises, there was often a case for sitting tight in the hope of a better deal in a year or two. So when Samson and Albert Ricardo sought to buy the Titness Farm estate in Berkshire, after having been told that their lease would not be renewed on expiry, Bateson advised: 'I do not think it would be well for us to sell. (...) I think I should say that (...) it would be useless to offer any terms which did not considerably exceed an ordinary market value.'[148] 'Only a very advantageous offer would persuade the College to part with the estate', was how Reyner put it to the would-be purchasers, slightly less bluntly,[149] but to another supplicant he was perfectly explicit: 'The position of the College with reference to this [Knowle Hill] property will after a few years be materially improved: and colleges can always afford to wait.'[150]

The legislation of 1858 also allowed colleges to build houses on long ninety-nine-year leases – instead of only forty years as hitherto – prompting Bateson and Reyner to react with extraordinary alacrity.[151] Bateson had made many political contacts through his work on the Graham Commission, and may well have anticipated the move, which would explain why the College spent a lot of money in 1857 on enfranchising its Kentish Town copyholds. The next step was to merge the Platt estates into the general estates of the College, and set about residential development of a 70-acre site east of Kentish Town Road. These grass fields and gardens fetched about £50 per acre, and the houses that went up were mainly of superior quality. From 1862 onwards, and reaching a climax between 1877 and 1885, by which time the development was practically completed, more than 700 house leases were granted on the estate, and almost eighty more for shops, a school, roads, and All Saints Church. It was a prodigious amount of activity, but being managed through London agents it did not impact on the daily work of the College officers. Thanks to the development of Kentish Town, the Platt estates may be regarded as the most remunerative bequest ever made since the foundation – its ground rents were worth £2,887 by 1882, £3,300 by 1893 – and it certainly helped to sustain the College through the ensuing agricultural depression.[152] It has been estimated that the gross income from agricultural land of all Cambridge colleges declined from £135,200 in 1871

Sales of land in the first half of the century were very few, but even before the Act of 1858 good money was made by selling to the Midland and Metropolitan Railway Companies. An important subsequent sale was of land in Cow Cross Street and Red Lion Alley to the City of London for the development of Smithfield Market.

[148] Bateson to Reyner, 20 Jul. 1863: SJCA, D33.3.2.5.

[149] Reyner to Albert Ricardo, 7 Jan. 1863: SJCA, SB21/Sun/10/4.

[150] Reyner to Lt-Col Carleton, 15 Aug. 1861: SJCA, SB21/SY/Eg/1/12.

[151] This is worth stressing in view of Miller's erroneous statement to the effect that Bateson's policy was one of 'relying exclusively upon the fortunes of agriculture': *Portrait of a College*, 96–7.

[152] Howard, *Finances*, 201, 235. Anticipating leasehold reform, a decision was made in 1953 to sell the Kentish Town freeholds house by house, most of them being by then in multiple occupancy. J. S. Boys Smith, *Memories of St John's College Cambridge, 1919–1969* (Oxford, 1983), 169–78.

to £119,800 in 1913, while that from houses rose from £22,600 to £62,500.[153] This is broadly in line with what happened at St John's, where revenue from houses rose by 185 per cent from £4,715 in 1882 (the first date at which different types of property are differentiated in the Rentals) to £13,421 in 1915, while that from land fell by 40 per cent, from £31,595 to £18,945.

Reyner was criticized by his successors for having allowed the College to engage in reckless expenditure, on the assumption that 'the time of prosperity would never end'.[154] Scott was generally appreciative in print, but could be caustic in private about his financial management during the 'halcyon days' of the 1860s and 70s.[155] He even accused Reyner on one occasion of having sold off the family timber.

> Fowler tells me that Reyner had a great sale of timber in the Brookfield Wood and realised a good deal. I see from the accounts that in 1875 he realised £139 net, having previously got about £20 for underwood. That was the worst of Reyner, he inflated the college revenues by doing things his successors cannot repeat. There is no timber now ripe for cutting in the wood except a tree or two and a few rubbishing trees in the hedgerows.[156]

There was even a suspicion of sharp practice. On ceasing to be Senior Bursar in 1876, Reyner married and went off to be rector of Staplehurst where, as Scott later recorded, he erected a dairy and other out buildings for his own use on what was properly College land. 'It is a very singular state of affairs.' Apparently 'no one interfered with him "because he had been Bursar so long".' Worse still, Reyner's predecessor in the living had offered 'to buy the field in front of the rectory house and add it to the glebe', but 'the College would not hear of the proposal, I suppose on the advice of Bateson and Reyner. It is a great pity for the barn is not wanted now there being no glebe and the field is.' The eventual beneficiary of the College's intransigence was Reyner's widow, who bought it for £200.[157] Yet Scott could also appreciate his predecessor's strange charm and sly chutzpah. As an example of the latter trait, he recorded an occasion when Reyner and Pieters, who had succeeded as Bursar, were trudging together over the Staplehurst fields just alluded to, and Pieters was wringing his hands despairingly about the latest bankruptcies and the collapse in College rents. '"It is horrible! it is horrible!" said Dr Reyner. "Yes," was [Pieters'] reply, 'there is a great falling off in the rents." "I perceive a greater falling off in the Bursar," was the unexpected retort, delivered with a kindly twinkle of the eye.'[158]

The third quarter of the century was marked not only by a revolution in College finance but by a thorough overhaul of its internal structures, and in particular of those functions that it shared with a grand hotel, and which were the

---

[153] Dunbabin, 'Oxford and Cambridge College Finances', 658.

[154] Liveing in 'Presentation of the master's portrait', *Eagle* xxxv (1913–14), 86. For these expenditures, see below pp. 345–6.

[155] See below, p. 388.

[156] Scott, 'MS Diary, 1891–3', 22 Aug. 1893: SJCA, SB1.21.467.

[157] Scott Diary, 21 Mar. 1893: SJCA, SB1.21.340–4.

[158] Scott, 'George Fearns Reyner', 407.

immediate responsibility of the Junior Bursar.[159] Until this time it was usual for the latter office to change hands very rapidly – there were twenty-two incumbents between 1800 and 1850 – so it may be significant that Basil Williams (1850–4), Simeon Hiley (1854–60), and Churchill Babington (1860–7) were all relative fixtures in the post. There was also external pressure from the Graham commissioners, one of whose main concerns was the extent to which the high incidental costs of college life were restricting the access of middle-class boys to a university education. For example,

> We think it desirable that college servants should be paid by fixed stipends, and not by perquisites, and in particular that the system of profits on the sale of commodities, wherever it prevails, should, as far as practicable, be discontinued. Care should also be taken, that the prices of all articles supplied for the use of Students, should be frequently revised and made known in the college, and provision made for the frequent information of the Student, as to the amount, and the several particulars, of the liabilities he has incurred.[160]

The commissioners referred here to the practice whereby undergraduates supplemented the servants' meagre salaries by a panoply of *ad hoc* payments: to their bedmakers, to the chapel clerk, to the waiters in Hall when they first dined or changed their status or their table. Worse still were the often extortionate charges levied by the cook for private meals supplied to rooms.[161] In St John's there had already been some modifications to the system, under Powell in the 1760s and 1770s and again in the 1830s, though the latter had had more to do with saving the College's money than that of the students. Thus in 1832 it was ruled that undergraduates should no longer pay fees directly to individual servants but rather to the butler via the Steward for distribution at a fixed rate,[162] and in 1848 the Bakehouse Bursarship was recognized as a statutory office with stipend. Yet despite these changes, the substance of the Graham commissioners' criticisms could not be denied, and so in the early 1850s the Seniors established an internal committee on service, the duty of which was to carry the process of bureaucratic rationalization much further. This was very much in tune with current public opinion, which was just then up in arms against the alleged aristocratic amateurism and incompetence that it blamed for the poor performance of the Army and the War Department in the Crimean War. It also matched the thinking of the radical politicians of the Administrative Reform Association

---

[159] The remainder of this section relies very heavily on Malcolm Underwood, 'Restructuring a household: service and its nineteenth century critics in St John's', *Eagle* lxxii (1985–90), 9–19. See also Searby, *History of the University of Cambridge*, III. 143–6; Rachel Wroth, 'Servants at St John's College, Cambridge, 1850–1900' (dissertation for the Advanced Diploma in English Local History, University of Cambridge Board of Continuing Education, 1998).

[160] *Report ... on the State ... of the University and Colleges of Cambridge*, Parliamentary Papers 1852–3, xliv, 149.

[161] According to popular rumour, the St John's cook was so rich that he offered to lend the Master of Trinity £60,000 for the building of Whewell's Court.

[162] Junior Bursar's Order Book: SJCA, JB2.1.

(1855–7), whose goal was, in the words of a sarcastic historian, to bring 'the public service up to the fabled standards of private enterprise'.[163]

The focus fell at once on the service in Hall, and especially on the two butlers, one of whom tended to the Fellows while the other (sometimes known as the Junior Butler) waited on the Scholars. The committee referred to them as sinecurists on the grounds that they did very little manual labour themselves, and yet neither had 'any practical acquaintance with the usages of a gentleman's table'. Their *modus operandi* was to rake in fees from various sources and subcontract the work to servants. The latter included a number of female bedmakers, many of whom had in recent decades chosen to double up as waitresses, thereby taking the place of the sizars who were no longer required to perform such menial tasks. In the course of a twelve-month period, which the committee chose for investigation, about £1,500 from the profits on sales of beer and butter and on various other trade items, as well as from a medley of fees and allowances, passed through the hands of the Fellows' Butler, Mr Thomas Peach. Against this amount he paid £947 out on sundry purchases and in wages to his staff,[164] leaving him with an income of £299, i.e. about £70 more than that of a Senior Fellow. Despite being salaried, the Junior Butler received fees from each member on taking a degree and from each Fellow on election, and these perks enabled him to pay the wages of Hall and Buttery attendants as well as a clerk (who had until recently been his own son). His net income was estimated at £179 p.a. There was duplication in the kitchens, partly because the Fellows' Cook and the Scholars' Cooks each had his separate staff of underlings, and partly because of demarcation disputes, with specialized plate washers, dish washers, and knife cleaners. Outside of catering the greatest indignation fell on the shoe blacks who, it was claimed, lived high on their tips from the young gentlemen, while employing deputies at journeymen's wages to do the actual work.[165]

Following the committee's investigation and recommendations, the Seniors decided that the Junior Butler's various sources of income should be replaced by a fixed stipend, that in addition to the existing butlers 'a professional should be hired who will dress and keep the tables, linen and plates in order', and (apparently on grounds of propriety) that males rather than females should be employed as waiters. In 1860 the Steward took over the duties of the Bread and Beer Bursars, while the hiring and firing of servants was vested in responsible officers such as the President (put in charge of bedmakers, Hall waiters, and laundresses), the Senior Bursar (coal porter), and the Junior Bursar (Chapel clerk, Chapel washers, shoe blacks, gardeners, and plate cleaners). More important servants such as the butlers, cooks, principal porters, sub-librarian, and baker were placed under the jurisdiction of the Seniority as a whole.[166] The post

---

[163] Olive Anderson, 'The Administrative Reform Association, 1855–1857', in Patricia Hollis (ed.), *Pressure from Without in Early Victorian England* (1974), 262–88.

[164] Who included the equally aptly named Miss Mutton.

[165] 'Reports of committees and other papers about reform of management in St John's, 1854–1916': SJCA, CC4, CC4.1. The members of the Service Committee were Francis France, W. H. Bateson, James Atlay, George Bainbridge and Simeon Hiley.

[166] CB, 17 Mar. 1860.

of Scholars' Cook was abolished on the death of the incumbent in 1861, and in 1868 the Fellow's Butler was placed on a fixed stipend of £300 and forbidden to accept perquisites.[167] More controversially, male gyps were put in charge of groups of rooms, and required to pay the bedmakers where these were their wives. The last move in particular caused tears and tantrums.

> We have had quite a scene with our bedmaker [Mrs Green], who in accordance with new college regulations has been pensioned off. She says the family has been connected with the college for a century, & she has been bedmaker to the Mayors for 18 years. How old it makes us! I paid her an extra quarter's salary and have got her a bible stoutly bound in calf ... According to the new scheme gyps and bedmakers together are to receive only as much as either singly now receive 2£ a quarter; but I cannot turn off Green, who is a great gossip of mine, and so must go on with the extra payment.[168]

Mrs Green had a point. Between 1800 and 1870 the number of servants fell from about 140 (of whom 100 were bedmakers or laundresses) to 110, even while the number of undergraduates in residence rose from 125 to 361, and the number of Fellows remained static at about fifty-five.[169] Whether or not the domestic operation of the St John's 'household' had been made more efficient, it had certainly been rendered leaner.

The culmination of the bureaucratic process came in 1888 when it was ordered that bedmakers, instead of continuing to receive via the Tutor a sum (£8) for each set of student rooms, were instead awarded an equivalent amount in fixed quarterly wages from the service fund. (According to Scott, writing ten years later, 'part of the scheme [was] that their wages may be raised if they give satisfaction'.)[170] Furthermore, in the case of married couples it was resolved to deduct £2 from their joint pay packets, the money to be earmarked as deferred payment against old age and infirmity. Those bedmakers who were receiving only £5 a room would receive pensions, to commence as a rule at age sixty, five years earlier than hitherto. Finally, it was decided that only women should be employed as bedmakers in future, thereby taking the movement towards separate spheres a step further.[171]

Meanwhile the Service Committee had also attempted to address dissatisfaction with the system of 'private supply'. This system was to be summed up pertinently by a member of the 1867 student intake who went on to become the most important memoirist of late Victorian St John's, the classic William Heitland. The kitchens in those days, he recollected, had been 'leased to speculators, who made their profit out of undergraduate luxury. Thus they compensated

[167] SJCA: D104.133.

[168] John Mayor to his mother [*c.* 1859]: Mayor Papers, B8/261.

[169] First Junior Bursar's Account, 1807–29: SJCA, JB3.1; Payments to bedmakers and laundresses, 1839–53: SJCA, TUI.3.2, C5.4; CB, 17 Mar. 1860; Lists of College suppers for servants, 1864–9: SJCA, D33.10.21.

[170] Scott, 'Vacant rooms in College', 25 May 1898: SJCA, C12.10.6.

[171] 'Report of the Service Committee', 29 Feb. 1888: SJCA, D100.155; CM, 212/13 (4 May 1888); 'Notice to bedmakers', 15 Jun. 1888: SJCA, D104.59–61.

themselves for having to provide dinner in hall at a low contract price.'[172] In an attempt to check this exploitation, and in response to a memorial from the undergraduates, the Seniors had already required the Cook (Owen Jones) to 'furnish every member of the College with a book to be filled up by [himself] with the several items of charge incurred in the Kitchen as often as a request may be made to that effect', such book to be 'delivered by the Cook with all the items entered therein as soon as possible after the end of every Term'.[173] Jones had presumably complied, and the new system will have pleased the Tutors, who were anxious to keep tabs on their pupils' levels of spending, but it did not meet the junior members' main complaint, which was the over-charging. When discontent welled up again in 1868, it was magnified by the impression among students that no one in authority ever listened to their complaints, though some of it may have been fomented by the querulous George Bonney as a means to attack the Steward Henry Russell, whom he considered an old fool. The main grievances as stated were:

> The absence of any fixed standard of charges. Not only is no tariff given to the Men to enable them to calculate the cost of any entertainment, but every inquiry into the cost of any commodity or the requisite amount of it is evaded by the Cook (...)
>
> As regards Breakfasts, no sort of economy is practised by the Cook. The quantity sent is always excessive: the quality sometimes bad: the charges too great: while all attempts on the part of individuals to check these abuses bring upon them discredit and almost incivility, because the majority acquiesce in what they consider incurable annoyance (...)
>
> When you want a breakfast for your friends, more fish is served up than you want ... To prevent this extravagance in executing orders, men have tried ... to order fish (for example) for 4 and plates for 8 but this is defeated by the cook, &c &c.[174]

The Seniority's immediate response was to abolish all sizings (Buttery purchases) other than those in beer.[175] Then, five years later, when Jones the Cook ceased work ('died poor' according to Heitland, presumably meaning that he had been deprived of the bonuses enjoyed by his predecessors),[176] his replacement was contracted to supply provisions for private rooms upon a system of 'portions', 'commons', or 'sizings' at prices regulated by a printed tariff, and to provide breakfasts, lunches, and dinners at fixed prices per head. He was forbidden to receive any other payments, perquisites, or allowances. At the same time all kitchen affairs were placed under the control of the Steward, while he and the President, Junior Bursar, Tutors, and Secretary of the Undergraduates'

---

[172] W. E. Heitland, *After Many Years: A Tale of Experiences and Impressions Gathered in the Course of an Obscure Life* (Cambridge, 1926), 103–4.

[173] H. Russell, 'Diary of events connected with St John's College, 1856, 1864–84', 14 Dec. 1865: SJCL, U22.

[174] Russell, 'Diary of events', 27 Oct. 1868.

[175] Ibid., 2 Dec. 1868.

[176] Heitland, review of Bonney's *Memories*, *Eagle* xlii (1921–2), 285; Heitland, *After Many Years*, 104.

Dinner Committee were established as a standing body to regulate charges in Hall and for private supply.[177]

The story so far has been one of increasing regularity, transparency, accountability, and central control, yet something else was evidently going on alongside this 'Whiggish' narrative. The new Cook was to receive no stipend, and was to maintain the kitchen and its equipment at his own expense, and to pay his staff their wages. He was to provide meals in Hall for Fellows and students at fixed prices per head. The main meal could cost a little more than before, but would constitute a complete dinner and not just, as hitherto, a joint to which consumers could add extras ('size up') if they desired. These determinations were the work of a committee headed by the President J. S. Wood, Bonney, and Alfred Marshall, the distinguished economist who was Steward for a few months in 1877. They were almost certainly seeking to raise culinary standards (described by Bonney as 'very plain'),[178] in line with the earlier decision to appoint a third and more 'professional' butler. Great things were expected from this new Cook, Desiré Bruvet, a Frenchman, and shortly after his arrival it was agreed that, for an additional charge, Fellows and students should be able to dine at the more sophisticated hour of 7.15 as well as in the middle of the afternoon. In the same spirit, at the *Ante Portam Latinam* feast in 1873 claret was served for the first time in living memory, alongside sherry and Hattenheim. Yet by 1877 this experiment in private enterprise was deemed to have failed, possibly because the agricultural depression was squeezing many of the undergraduates' pockets, or possibly because (in Heitland's summing up) Bruvet 'made the Kitchens pay, took to money-lending, and had to leave'. His successor (designated 'Head Cook', a linguistic demotion) was to be regarded as a College servant rather than an independent trader, while management of the kitchens was placed in the hands of the new Steward, William Garnett.[179] From now on it became the latter's duty, and not the Cook's, to hire and fire the staff and pay the wages.

Described in the *Oxford Dictionary of National Biography* as 'affable and charming, alert and vigorous', Garnett was an extreme believer in centralization, and tried to run the catering operation as a military campaign. Under his influence, and for a brief period only, the Steward became known informally as the Canteen Manager and his assistant as the Mess Manager, while the Fellows' Butler and other staff became Commissariat Officers in imitation of the Royal Naval and Military Club. A professional kitchen clerk was appointed for the purpose of keeping accounts with the same attention to detail as 'a canteen officer in a military canteen'. Any waste for disposal was ordered to be officially recorded rather than being consumed by staff on or off the premises, perquisites were banned (yet again), while all breakages were to be reported and appropriate sums stopped from wages if negligence was proved. The kitchen staff's response was to resign *en masse*, whereupon Garnett coolly hired replacements from

[177] CB, 6 Jun. 1876.

[178] Bonney, *Memories*, 33.

[179] Garnett became Steward in 1877, but during 1880–2 he was designated Junior Steward with a stipend of £300, while a titular Steward received a mere £50. CB, 17 Mar. 1880. This unusual arrangement probably signalled the College's awareness that Garnett's procedures were experimental and might have to be aborted. See *DNB* (D. Knight).

London. He alone had power to order food, and having rapidly lost patience with the local cartels he decided to source supplies from London at wholesale prices. This was unpopular in the town but delighted the undergraduates, at least to start with, and dinner in Hall became known as 'Garnett's sixpenny blow out'. It was less popular with the Deans, who quickly became concerned at the effect of such luxury on the tone of the College, as Russell (now Junior Bursar) noted in his diary.

> Last day of boat races. 24+ supped in Lecture room IV 3rd Court: Torry Jun Dean, Pres^t of Lady Marg. Boat Club presiding. They had particularly asked Mr Garnett, Steward, to provide an economical supper; he sent them good supper at lowest poss price, and then they took in a bottle of champagne per head beside cups, beer, and punch, and other liquids, had a boy guest whom they made drunk (he threw plates about), spoilt by forcible usage a College silver spoon and fork, and instead of going to their rooms when they broke up made a noise in Court for ½ hour, shouted 'Garnett' in 3rd Court for about a ¼ hour+ (...) Torry said he lost all control over them, took John Edward Marr B.A. 1879 (he had privately taken in 6 bottles of champagne besides the n° ordered by committee) to bed drunk, blanked his face and left him.[180]

However, what finally caused Garnett's experiment to unravel was not its encouragement to licentiousness but its eventual tendency to raise the cost of food. The great benefit of local sourcing was of course its flexibility, whereas bringing supplies in by train on spec. to a kitchen without the means of refrigeration meant that whenever there were dips in demand – quite frequently, since many students were beginning to be financially pinched – the undergraduates had to be charged extra simply in order to enable the kitchen to pay its trade debts. In 1882 Garnett's brave (some said foolhardy) experiment was deemed to have failed. Unfortunately his wares now began to be much missed by those who had been able to afford them, and so the focus of resentment moved from price to quality. Matters came to a head at a two-hour meeting in 1884 when the undergraduates demanded a meeting after Hall. According to one of them,

> A meeting was convened by the Steward of the College at which anyone might attend to discuss the complaints made against 'Hall', it was awful fun, fellows got up and complained about all sorts of little things (gravy, pastry, beer, vegetables &c &c) and sat on the Steward, who is a don; Heitland was there and got very angry with one man which was most amusing, it appears nasty remarks have come out in the *Cambridge Review* and *Truth* which Heitland & Co don't like, I didn't go home till 10.30.[181]

Heitland might not have liked to admit as much in front of the children, but he wrote much later that the department was in a 'very sad plight when W. F. Smith took over; he had a hard task to keep it going in his earlier years'. Smith has

---

[180] Russell, Diary of events', 20 May 1879: SJCL, U22. Marr, the future author of *The Geology of the Lake District* (1916) and FRS, was a pupil of Bonney at the time.

[181] Stephen Abbott Notcutt to his mother, 7 Feb. 1884: SJCL, GBR/0275/Notcutt/A7.

been described as 'a happy schoolboy, (…) a big plump and bearded schoolboy', an expert on Rabelais and with humour to match, for ever 'twinkling, and babbling, and bubbling'.[182] As Steward (1881–92) he gradually turned things round on the catering side by reverting quietly to older methods, and by rebuilding bridges with local suppliers.[183] Unfortunately, he could not master the accounts, the deficits continued, and there were concerns about peculation, which eventually led to a revolt on the Council led by Donald MacAlister and William Bateson junior (the son of the Master). A number of Council resolutions in 1891 stipulated that duplicate counterfoils of all orders to tradesmen were to be preserved by the Steward for inspection by the Audit Committee, which was also to monitor the Kitchen accounts once a month. The Cook was instructed to purchase provisions 'in large quantities from wholesale houses', while his £1 allowance for journeys to London was withdrawn. At the same time all 'outside trade' in wines and spirits was discontinued, as well as the sale of spirits to College members.[184] The immediate effect of these resolutions was the resignation of the Head Cook Mr Cash, to be replaced by Mr Parsley. Shortly afterwards Smith himself was ousted to be replaced by Bateson, who soon found that the kitchen accounts were beyond his comprehension as well.[185]

The equally extreme but wildly contrasting experiments under Bruvet and Garnett should warn against any tendency to suppose that domestic management changed only in one direction during the age of Bateson. On the other hand, nothing exercises a college more than the quality of its 'wittals'. Changes in the management of bedders, porters, and waiters can often be related to national trends and current fashions, but in the case of food quality it is more a matter of veering from one system to another in the hope of finding something that works. One thing that can be said is that the Fellows of St John's showed a new concern for both their stomachs and their palates during the third quarter of the century. The Steward and Junior Bursar had traditionally been paid at the same rate, but the decision to double the former's stipend in 1877 suggests a shift in the relative priority given to board over lodging. But even in other less sensitive departments it is important not to exaggerate the onward momentum of reform. There will have been passive obedience, and many blind eyes will have been turned, while there will also have been protected pockets that escaped the process entirely. The motto at the head of this section describes the shock felt by a newly appointed Dean when he discovered the extent of perquisiting in communion wine. That was in 1890!

External revenue and domestic management are important considerations but supplementary to the core functions of education, religion, and learning. The struggles over academic reform were to prove bitterly disruptive, not so much because of differences of opinion on the issues themselves, though some

---

[182] T. R. Glover, *Cambridge Retrospect* (Cambridge, 1943), 53–6.

[183] Council memoranda: SJCA, SB1.24SJ.

[184] In the Council Minute that records the 1891 resolutions, CM, 322/7 (6 Nov. 1891), the Cook is referred to as the 'Manager', but that seems to have been wishful bureaucratic thinking, since the term Manager was not adopted until 1919.

[185] See below, p. 484.

existed, but because they became entangled with the most basic question of all: the question 'Who governs?'

6. ACADEMIC REFORM
AND THE BATTLE FOR THE STATUTES

We have no wish to deny that such a harmony and connection between the subjects of college study and of university examinations should exist (...) But we cannot but look with the greatest alarm at the prospect of having attempts made to establish such a connection (...) by the action of any power extraneous to the University and the Colleges. We conceive that any attempt to compel the College to appoint teachers or to reward proficients by external agency would be an interference with their internal freedom of a kind utterly unheard of except in the worst times, and altogether destructive of their just and ancient corporate rights.

> Annotated draft petition to Vice-Chancellor against
> the intended Royal Commission on Oxford and
> Cambridge Universities, 1849: SJCA, D90.493.

If St John's opposition to Prince Albert as Vice-Chancellor in 1847 confirmed its reputation for blinkered conservatism, the same might be said of its first set of new statutes, devised in the following year and promulgated in 1849, since all they did was to ratify a small number of changes in working practice that had taken root over previous centuries. Even the fact that they were written in Latin suggested a conscious determination to cling as far as possible to tradition. However, the next set of new statutes in 1860[186] undoubtedly 'represented a substantial breach in the old order',[187] even though they did not go as far as many would have wished. The effect was to force conservatives on to the defensive in the face of younger Fellows impatient for change. Evidently the 1850s was a pivotal decade.

Bateson turned thirty-eight at the mid-century but was a young Fellow at heart, as exemplified for example by his early solicitude for sizars. His reforming impulses were undoubtedly deep and sincere, and throughout the next two decades he was to be a major driving force for change. As Secretary of the Graham Commission he made sure that the College complied with the spirit as well as letter of the inquiry, in contrast to Tatham whose tone was much more snooty, and he emerged from the episode with the status of a University as well as College politician. He then played an even more central role in persuading the politicians to address the academics' chief concerns before legislating on the Commission's recommendations. In his view the resulting Act of Parliament created 'a liberal constitution for our University' that was also workable, while

---

[186] This term has always been used to cover not only the main body of statutes made by the commissioners in 1860, but four others approved by the Crown in 1857 (abolition of preferences in regard to Fellowships and Scholarships), 1858 (incorporation of the Platt estates and Fellowships into the whole), 1859 (Masters' emoluments), and 1861.

[187] Miller, *Portrait of a College*, 86.

the commissioners appointed to monitor its implementation were accorded the highest accolade: 'unexceptionable'.[188] From then on Bateson saw himself as the leader of the 'forward party' in Cambridge, and to the very end he showed himself ready to risk 'civil war' in matters of reform, as for example in his unsuccessful attempts to reduce the influence of heads of houses within the University, and to restrict certain voting rights within the Senate to resident members. He led the move to abolish religious tests, braving much acrimony in the process; he was the first chairman of the board set up in 1869 to promote the establishment of a non-collegiate institution, a pet project of reformers keen to widen access to students too poor to meet the cost of college fees; he pushed for the admission of women; he supported the introduction of Life Fellowships; and most controversially he declared, without any of the usual attempts at obfuscation, that Parliament had the right to revise the terms of college endowments.[189] At the time of his unexpected death in 1881, aged sixty-eight, he had almost completed the major task of reformulating the College statutes yet again in response to commissioners' recommendations.[190]

Since Bateson's liberal politics were almost certainly the reason why he had not been offered a Tutorship or Lectureship, it has often been deemed surprising that he should have won the Mastership so easily. The obvious explanation is that Tutors and Lecturers were chosen by the Seniors whereas the Master was elected by the Fellows at large, including the substantial party of impatient younger men alluded to above. Reminiscing on the 1850s, an elderly John Mayor observed that almost daily during term he had used to sit in Hall 'at the Bursar's table ... among others of the reforming "Caucus", the two Babingtons, Overton, Adams, Todhunter, Bashforth, Liveing; many have gone, but all saw plans, there first broached, take shape and ripen into act'.[191] Still, that does not explain the almost complete unanimity in favour of Bateson. In what was reported to be a friendly election, the only other internal candidate was Archdeacon France,[192] and he stood down once it became clear that his support was limited to a handful of the older Fellows. As suggested above, gratitude for Bateson's bursarial achievements must have constituted a major reason for his success, but another factor may have been the realization by conservatives that the Graham Commission had let them off rather lightly, notably by dropping a proposal for college contributions towards the revenues of the University. That being so, they may have reflected that Bateson's influential role as Secretary to the Commission probably helped to prevent much more damaging recommendations, and if they reflected harder still it might even have crossed their minds that the reform-minded prime minister, Lord John Russell, would never have sanctioned Bateson's appointment as Secretary had the latter not been known to

---

[188] Bateson to ?Edward Strutt, MP, 7 March 1856: SJCA, D90.576.

[189] D. A. Winstanley, *Later Victorian Cambridge* (Cambridge 1947), 263–332.

[190] See below, pp. 365–7.

[191] J. E. B. Mayor, 'In memoriam Charles Cardale Babington', *Memorial Journal and Botanical Correspondence of Charles Cardale Babington* (Cambridge, 1897), li–lvii. Junior fellows sat in the body of the Hall at the Bursar's or President's Table until 1892, when the dais was widened to make space for two high tables.

[192] Fellow, 1840–64; Tutor, 1848–60; President, 1854–64; Archdeacon of Ely, 1859–64.

hold liberal views. Perhaps, given the dangerously radical political mood of the mid-to-later 1850s, there was something to be said for having a member of the liberal establishment as Master.[193]

But what of those Fellows who grumbled and fantasized by turns at the Bursar's table? It would be anachronistic to call them 'Young Turks', yet that was the contemporary light in which two surviving members of the group saw themselves in 1909, when they were invited to reminisce about 'St John's in the 1850s' for the *Eagle* magazine. However, whereas Joe Mayor attributed their ardour to the excitements caused by the 1848 revolutions in Europe, Henry Roby more prosaically ascribed it to the promptings of the Graham Commission.[194] Both men were right according to their lights. Roby was a Fellow for less than seven years, being forced to leave on account of his marriage in 1861. Since religious doubts made ordination out of the question, he would have had to leave anyway, but in his brief time in Cambridge he was very active, not least as the first Secretary of the Local Examinations Syndicate, and within St John's he did more than anyone, in his genial, bluff, and brutally direct way, to shake the Fellowship up. Not the least important of his contributions was to run Bateson's campaign for the Mastership, taking older Fellows by surprise with his vigour and persistence. Nor would many other Junior Fellows have had the self-confidence to circulate 450 copies of a combative pamphlet on University and College reform to interested parties throughout Cambridge.[195] As a future public servant and politician, he was no doubt programmed to emphasize the top-down nature of the reforms of the 1850s, yet he was not wrong in doing so. The Graham Commission's recommendations were subsequently embodied in the Cambridge University Act of 1856, which allowed colleges just two years in which to revise their statutes accordingly, failing which commissioners would be appointed to do the colleges' work for them. Roby was right to see this pistol to the head as a determining factor, without which nothing might have changed.[196]

Seven others might be designated leaders of the reform movement in the 1850s, and thanks to the practice (which seems to have begun about then) of individual dons arranging for multiple copies of their petitions and position papers to be printed,[197] their aims and attitudes are relatively easy to reconstruct.

---

[193] One of the five commissioners was also a Johnian, the liberally inclined Sir John Herschel.

[194] J. B. Mayor, 'College reform in the fifties', and H. J. Roby, 'College reform under the Cambridge University Act of 1856', *Eagle* xxxi (1909–10), 189–209.

[195] Henry John Roby, *Remarks on College Reform* (Cambridge, 1858). It was written in response to an earlier and deeply conservative pamphlet by his friend and antagonist, Henry Latham of Trinity Hall.

[196] It is always a matter of interest to know whether junior members know what is going on among the Fellowship. An undergraduate of the mid-1850s, writing much later, recollected, '[Roby] was one of a brilliant group of young fellows, which included Courtney and J. B. Mayor (...) and J. E. B. Mayor (...) They were reformers, and were our heroes. Of University reform we knew nothing. But we thoroughly understood Roby's fight with the College Cook. (...) College cooks were reported to make enormous profits (...) So a College cook was a worthy foe on whom Roby was to flesh his steel ...': J. M. Wilson, 'H. J. Roby', *Eagle* xxxvi (1914–15), 202–6 at p. 203.

[197] The introduction of this facility seems to have encouraged prolixity in the way that photocopiers did over a century later.

Francis Bashforth, the future expert in ballistics, had come second to John Couch Adams as a Wrangler, had been elected a Fellow in 1843, and left for a College living fourteen years later, a cure which he was able to combine with the post of Professor of Applied Mathematics at Woolwich Artillery College. George Liveing was the first beneficiary of one of St John's most important educational initiatives, being appointed director of the Chemistry Laboratory that opened in 1853, and subsequently Lecturer in Chemistry. Because he had red hair, and because he could swing in a trice from equability to hot temper, he was known as the 'Red Precipitate'. He had strong opinions, and particularly abhorred the practice of bored Fellows clinging on to their College posts in the hope of a rich living (which incidentally was how he pronounced his name). Though Roby subsequently claimed to have been the ringleader of the reformers, Liveing's diagnosis of the situation was more penetrating and his prescriptions more far reaching. Churchill Babington was another who backed Bateson very strongly for Master. He surrendered his Fellowship in 1866, after twenty years, in order to become rector of Cockfield, and having been elected to the Disney Chair of Archaeology in the previous year. Leonard Courtney was a future Liberal MP and junior minister, a staunch believer in proportional representation, the peace movement, women's suffrage, and the wickedness of imperialism. Finally, Robert Hayward, Isaac Todhunter, and Joe Mayor were indefatigable in drumming up support, especially among the non-residents.

Some of the reformers would have liked to abolish all religious tests, and to shift the balance of resources from the colleges to the University, but since the Graham Commission did not pursue these issues it seemed best to start with more immediate matters, which can be considered here under four separate headings. The removal of restrictions on eligibility for Fellowships and Scholarships was the least controversial, though in the case of the latter it involved much painstaking negotiation and legal argument. Attempts to rearrange the system of undergraduate tuition were fraught, and moves to alter the terms of tenure for future Fellows even more so,[198] but the issue that really had the ermine flying was that which Liveing called 'the permanent government of the College'.

The College had chafed for a long time under the restrictions on Fellowships. Whereas, for example, most of Trinity's money was traditionally consolidated into one pot, St John's emoluments were held on different foundations and accounted separately, with little if any prospect of virement between accounts. This meant that the ability to elect to a particular Fellowship, and the stipend attaching to it, depended on the state of each particular fund, a situation that naturally created inequalities. For example, it had been agreed in 1815 that, although the overall financial position was healthy, 'the low state of the Platt Funds' made it inexpedient to fill more than one of the vacant Fellowships on that particular foundation. At mid-century there were eight Platt Fellows receiving lower emoluments and enjoying fewer privileges than Foundation Fellows. In 1856 Bateson's proposal that they should be merged with the main body and enjoy equal rights was carried by 27 votes to 2 in a meeting of

---

[198] There was a general understanding that fellows' existing rights would be respected.

all Fellows, and subsequently carried into effect in the new statutes.[199] As with the simultaneous merging of the Platt estates, this was certainly a measure of rationalization, though it probably worked against the cause of reform by making some elderly and deeply reactionary Fellows (such as Henry Russell) eligible for membership of the Seniority for the first time.[200]

Like Fellowships, Scholarships could only be filled when there was money in the relevant fund. All this made for complexity and endless *ad hoc* adjustments. For example, when James Wood donated funds for nine new exhibitions, their emolument was deemed to be one-fifth of the annual value of the Clavering estate. In the 1850s there were 124 scholarships on offer, only thirty-two of which were open. The remainder were restricted in various ways and worth only £20, much less than at Trinity and many other colleges. A more tangential concern was that parents were deliberately choosing to move to St John's parishes in order to exploit what might be called a nineteenth-century postcode lottery.[201] In these circumstances it naturally occurred to the Graham commissioners that the various scholarships might be consolidated, and all existing preferences and restrictions modified, so as to make them both more open and more lucrative. In his evidence to the Commission Tatham stoutly resisted this proposal. 'It would not be expedient to remove any of the limitations affecting fellowships, Scholarships, or Exhibitions', especially since any vacancies are always swiftly filled up quickly with worthy applicants.[202] Yet two years later, in their official response to the commissioners, the 'Master and Fellows' took a diametrically opposite line.

> We do not hesitate to say that open fellowships and Scholarships are ... more advantageous than restricted ones. We may further observe that the Scholarships in our College, though numerous, are inconsiderable in value; and if, by diminishing their number, their value were increased, they would excite greater emulation, and be regarded by our Students as a higher distinction than at present, but we have no powers which enable us to accomplish this object.[203]

These second thoughts may well have reflected Bateson's growing influence at the expense of Tatham, whose health was gradually failing. Anyway, they were warmly endorsed by the Commission, and proposals to put them into effect were then carried at a meeting of thirty-two Fellows by 24 votes to 8. The new statutes reduced the number of Foundation Scholars to sixty and guaranteed them an income of at least £50. They were to be chosen by examination, either from among existing students of the College or from such other persons as the Master and Seniors might think fit. In addition four minor scholarships were to be awarded each Michaelmas term, again by examination, to youths under

---

[199] See below, p. 290.

[200] Bonney, *Memories*, 39–41.

[201] Mayor, 'College reform in the fifties', 189.

[202] *Report ... on the State ... of the University and Colleges of Cambridge*, Parliamentary Papers 1852–3, xliv, 625–6.

[203] *Correspondence Respecting the Proposed Measures of Improvement in the Universities and Colleges of Oxford and Cambridge*, 12 Jan. 1854, Parliamentary Papers 1854, l, 361.

twenty who had not yet commenced residence at University or were in their first term.

The creation of open scholarships altered the College's relations to what might be called the outside world, though how far this was intended or appreciated is uncertain. Relations with certain schools, particularly in the northern half of England, were central to its historic mission, but several proved problematic in the first half of the nineteenth century, when only Shrewsbury and possibly Sedbergh (with preferences given to two and ten scholars respectively) could be designated 'feeder schools'. Inevitably perhaps, the College tended to be held responsible when things went wrong, yet received no plaudits for institutions that were successful. The two most embarrassing incidents both related to Pocklington Grammar School in Yorkshire, an institution which, despite its connection, sent up no more than forty-six men in the whole of the century. First, it was held up to opprobrium in Henry Brougham's report of 1818 on account of one of its classrooms having been turned into a sawpit. Then in 1839–40 there were protracted complications arising from the unauthorized sale of school land to the Great Northern Railway Company by the master, James Shield. Whether or not such difficulties had anything to do with the matter, St John's gave offence in certain traditionalist circles by not fighting harder to retain its closed scholarships. Bateson's somewhat brusque correspondence with affected schools certainly suggests a willingness to be done with all such *ancien régime* hangovers.[204] James Pycroft, the Antiquary Royal and a self-appointed defender of 'founders' trusts' against parliamentary invasion, wrote to Reyner much later to complain about the 'total disregard paid by [Bateson] to the College's immunities and rights' at this time.[205] In 1867 it was agreed to petition against the Public Schools Bill, but the protest was ineffectual, and in 1871 the College finally lost the right to present head masters to Shrewsbury School.

It must not be supposed from this that all sense of responsibility for schooling was abandoned. Many St John's Fellows shared the widespread belief that, in educational terms, the British working class was falling disastrously behind its counterparts in competitor countries, and reversing that trend seemed much more important to men like Bateson than honouring ancestral dues. During the early decades of the century the Conclusion Books record only three grants of money to schools (in 1818, 1821, and 1824) whereas enormous amounts went towards the building and repairing of churches, but starting in 1839, which was the year in which Lord John Russell established the Privy Council Committee for Education, St John's began to make a large number of annual grants (usually anything between £5 and £30) towards establishing or expanding elementary schools, including many run by the National Society. Naturally, these donations were confined to Cambridge and to districts where the College owned land, but it nevertheless amounted to a substantial commitment, and one that grew from 1850 onwards as the revenues prospered and the sense of relative decline in the nation's educational standards increased. In 1864, for example, upwards of £70

---

[204] W. H. Bateson to Revd. J. H. Evans, 21 Nov. 1856, draft: SJCA, Bateson letter books, M1.6. Or maybe Bateson was just getting his own back on Evans. See above, p. 251.

[205] J. W. Pycroft to Reyner, 4 Feb. and 12 Apr. 1867: SJCA, D88.24, 30.

was distributed to nine schools, in 1870 twenty-four schools shared £360, in 1874 ten more received a total of £119. Admittedly these are not huge amounts in themselves, but the expenditure of bursarial time and effort was considerable, and helped to lock the College more tightly into the life of its scattered communities.[206] A new consideration came into play with the 1870 Education Act, which required local councils to maintain a sufficient number of school places per head of population (though it stopped short of making attendance compulsory). An immediate consequence was that local churchmen often attempted to blackmail colleges into making voluntary contributions by raising the spectre of increased rates and Godless education. Just such considerations were central to a thirty-year wrangle within Cambridge itself. In 1876 Charles Drake, a Johnian curate of All Saints, wrote to Reyner on behalf of the governing body[207] of the Cambridge Elementary Church Schools:

> I meant to ask the College what I am asking my parishioners, viz to pay the rate in addition to the voluntary subscription. I do not suppose that I shall succeed in every case in getting what I want (...) As far as the College is concerned I should be quite satisfied if they were to (...) only acknowledge the principle of a voluntary rate for Church Education, I would gladly lose part of the annual subscription. The fact is that unless the appeal which the Governors are now making is satisfactorily responded to, we shall have a School Board very shortly (...) The Colleges will have to pay a School Board rate, and the question they have to decide is whether they will willingly pay for the support of Education on Church principles what they will be compelled to pay for Education on no religious principles.[208]

All in all it can be said that St John's took its duties to national schooling seriously, but of course its main function was to instruct undergraduates, and here the reformers of the 1850s were in despair. To start with, they felt very strongly the need for Cambridge and Oxford to 'increase their influence over the country, (...) and especially a larger portion of the laity of the country',[209] in order to meet the complaint that colleges were still little better than finishing schools and seminaries. But even in respect of their traditional clientele there were serious reservations both about the quantity and the quality of the teaching on offer. In addition to the twice-yearly college examinations introduced by Powell, undergraduates in mid-stream took the 'previous' or 'little-go' examination (introduced in 1822), and then went on to sit the tripos. Most of them were

[206] SJCA, SB21/Cb/C/73–5 contains eighty-seven items of complex correspondence on such matters relating to parishes in Cambridge and Newnham alone, 1864–1900; SB21/Cb/N/G/5 contains another twenty-six relating to schools in Granchester and Newnham.

[207] Confusingly this governing body was referred to as the 'Old Schools'.

[208] C. B. Drake to Reyner, 28 Mar. 1876: SJCA, SB21/Cb/C/75/29. Was it significant that, despite this appeal, St John's refused Charles Drake's request. Would it have been different if Reyner had not resigned his Bursarship in 1876? Was a Bateson-led Seniority growing indifferent to blackmail on behalf of Anglican schools?

[209] 'Cambridge University Act: 23 Fellows to the Master and Seniors of St John's College', n.d.: SJCA, D44.2.12.

poll men, meaning that they read for the ordinary degree, and while the numbers reading for honours gradually increased, it was not until 1885 that a majority did so. Heitland considered that the former were 'no credit to the University', not least because they were 'shamefully neglected'.[210] College lectures were provided for both sets of students, but their quality was impaired by a reliance on mixed-ability teaching, with the smart and dim boys on each of the tutorial sides being taught together in large school rooms. According to surviving accounts, the mathematics lecturers merely dictated questions and then perambulated the room, offering individual advice and criticism as appropriate.[211] It was widely accepted that ambitious students would have to resort to coaches, yet the cost of private tuition was considerable (about £75 p.a. for a 'whole tutor' and £37 for a 'half tutor'), and was condemned by the Graham commissioners. 'The greatest part of a man's education here consists of what he does by himself and with his *private* tutor', raged Bateson. 'The College Tutors I can assure you are of very little assistance, especially to a classical man.'[212] George Shaw, smarting from his disappointing examination result, denounced the need for private tuition as 'one of the greatest evils'.[213] For their own part the private tutors were no more satisfied. Most were hanging on in the hope of a Fellowship eventually and a sufficient number of pupils to keep them alive in the meantime. They needed the pupils as badly as the pupils needed them, yet many found 'private pupilizing' to be very hard work and 'no real education, only coaching for limited purpose'.[214] 'The effort of straining one's attention for five hours without intermission, so as not to let a single mistake pass, with or without a headache, is what I never tried before till this Long [Vacation] and am not anxious to try again if I can help it.'[215]

The system would have been sufficiently strained even if the syllabus had remained as it was in the 1820s – mainly devoted to mathematics and classics and to the logical analysis of arguments, notably those of Newton, Euclid, Paley, and Locke – but it broke down under the weight of the new knowledge-based courses that were introduced after 1830,[216] partly in response to public demands for more 'useful' instruction. To adopt Malcolm Underwood's apt metaphor, there was a 'slow broadening of the stream of knowledge … into more and more clearly distinguished rivulets'. In 1837 hydrostatics, mechanics, and (presumably as a counterweight) divinity were added to the ordinary degree, which not only necessitated yet more private tuition but also left less time for students to

---

[210] Heitland, *After Many Years*, 126.

[211] T. G. Bonney, 'A septuagenarian's recollections of St John's', *Eagle* xxx (1908–9), 300–1.

[212] Bateson to his father: SJCL, Miscellaneous Letters: W. H. Bateson, 2.13.

[213] George Shaw's note on verso of Richard Wilson to Shaw, 22 Mar. 1840, copy: SJCL, MS O.78. 21(b) at p. 53.

[214] H. J. Roby, *Reminiscences of My Life and Work: For My Own Family Only* (privately printed, Cambridge, 1913), 38.

[215] Joseph Mayor to his mother, ?1851: Mayor Papers, B8/342.

[216] By which time oral disputations had been all but abandoned in favour of written examinations, partly as a result of a shift of emphasis (led by Whewell) from Newtonian geometry and logic to Continental algebraic analysis in the 1820s: Stray, 'The shift from oral to written examination', 33–50.

attend professorial lectures.[217] In 1843 William Whewell, the recently elected Master of Trinity and also Vice-Chancellor, had attempted to shift the balance of instruction from private tuition to professorial lectures, and when his scheme was thwarted he blamed opposition from St John's. (Many others in Cambridge felt that Johnians were unwilling to change a system in which they were so spectacularly successful, taking the four top Wranglerships in 1839, for example. Johnians riposted that their superiority was owing to Powell's reforms, and that they would not take instruction from colleges that had yet to catch up.) Then in 1848 Whewell did persuade the University, with Prince Albert's help, to establish two new triposes (in the Moral and Natural Sciences) which students who had passed the previous could take to obtain honours without having to do any more mathematics or classics. These new courses required knowledge of history, law, and political economy in the first case, and in the second botany, geology, mechanics, and engineering, all subjects that had so far been covered only in professorial lectures, and which college lecturers were rarely equipped to teach. Accordingly in 1852 twenty-two junior Fellows of St John's, led by Bashforth and Todhunter, issued the Master and Seniors with a memorial in which they called for more tutorial provision. Four months later they begged not to 'appear guilty of undue haste or impatience' in asking why nothing had been done in 'a matter so important'.[218]

The Seniors refused to make any changes to basic structures, which meant that educational provision remained in the hands of two tutorial sides, each working independently of the other as though in separate colleges. Each side consisted of a Tutor and two Assistant Tutors (alternatively designated College Lecturers), with each Tutor continuing to receive all fees and to appoint and pay his Assistants. This was a disappointment to Liveing, whose wish was for the two sides to be merged,[219] and for the College to receive and distribute all fees, somewhat along the lines of the household reforms of the same decade. But in 1853 the Seniors did at least move in the direction of 'providing more complete instruction in the various branches of study now recognised by the University'. They added a fourth Lecturer to both sides, while in addition Joe Mayor and Charles Liveing were appointed as Lecturers to teach Moral and Natural Sciences respectively, making ten Lecturers and two Tutors in all.[220]

---

[217] Malcolm Underwood, 'The revolution in college teaching: St John's College, 1850–1926', in Jonathan Smith and Christopher Stray (eds.), *Teaching and Learning in Nineteenth-Century Cambridge* (Woodbridge, 2001), 107–21, on which this account leans heavily.

[218] 'Twenty-two Fellows to the Seniors': SJCA, D103.52; Bashforth, T. E. Cooper, I. Todhunter to R. Tatham, 2 Jun. 1852: SJCA, D90.495. Bashforth also called for higher tuition fees and more specialist lecturing as well. See also D44.2.12 for an identical memorial with an additional signature.

[219] In 1854 the Seniors did at least agree to merge the two sides' separate sizarship examinations.

[220] To help the tuition fund, the fees hitherto paid to specially designated officers for determining certain prizes (e.g. to the 'Father of the College' for superintending the declamations in Chapel), and for conducting the scholarship examination, were abolished. The Tutors were required to carry out these duties (without additional remuneration) and the money saved was transferred to the tuition fund to help cover the additional stipends.

19 The Chemistry Laboratory, opened 1853 behind New Court:
the regular haunt of George Downing Liveing (1827–1924)

Students were to be streamed by ability in the case of arithmetic and algebra, arrangements for examinations and prizes were made more rigorous (or at any rate more bureaucratic), and each Tutor and Lecturer was to 'consider himself bound to employ two hours at least daily in public instruction'.[221] At the same time a small Chemical Laboratory was created behind New Court for student use at a charge of 1½ guineas per quarter to Johnians and 2 guineas to students from other colleges.[222] Given that the building debt had still not been paid off, all this amounted to a substantial effort on the Seniors' part, a point they made forcibly in their written response to the Graham Commission.

Even so, it only scratched the surface as far as the reforming Fellows were concerned. They now pressed the idea that Tutors and their assistants should be replaced altogether by Lecturers, or by what would now be called a teaching staff. Lecturers should be appointed for three years renewable on good perform-ance, and should be paid commensurately with the clerical and legal professions, or at the very least enough to obviate the need for private pupils. After nine years they should be given Fellowships for life, allowed to marry, and allowed

---

[221] CB, 8 Jul. 1853; 'Report on the Education Fund', 1909: SJCA, SBF77.

[222] Liveing was made superintendent of the Laboratory in 1860 on his appointment as Professor of Chemistry.

to escape ordination. It was also deemed essential for the College to give up the practice (arising from habit and prejudice rather than from any statutory necessity) of electing only present and previous members.[223] Six other colleges had elected Johnians, and St John's should have the benefit of the best Lecturers wherever they emerged from. 'It must be really advantageous to the College to elect the best men, as is plainly shewn by the example of the foremost colleges at Oxford.' Of course, if the Tutors were to be abolished, then the pastoral role that they performed *in loco parentis* (such as preventing students from getting into debt) would have to be performed by someone else. Liveing thought that this role might be taken on by the two Deans, though in that case the Master would have to take responsibility for dealing with serious breaches of discipline involving the Proctors or the police, since the Deans in their expanded capacity would be inclined to act like the current Tutors, i.e. to 'become the advisers in such cases, (…) more anxious to screen their pupils than to keep up a high tone and strict discipline'.[224]

In 1860, as in 1853, some limited concessions were made to the reformers' views. Instead of Tutors being abolished, a third Tutor was appointed and a permanent fund established for the payment of Lecturers, using two-thirds of the undergraduate fee for the purpose.[225] The 1860 Statutes gave official recognition for the first time to the ten College Lecturers, and ruled that their classes might be attended by all students and not just by those on a particular side. The Seniors were made responsible for appointing all Tutors and Lecturers, a step which was not necessarily for the better in terms of personal fitness for decision making, but at least it had the merit of putting an end to what had hitherto been a self-selecting oligarchy. At the same time, all those Fellows who were actively engaged in teaching were constituted as an educational board to advise the Seniors on matters to do with tuition.

This was some progress. Yet as fast as St John's ran, the world seemed to be running even faster. In 1865 the University brought forward the previous and general examinations in order to make room for special examinations at the end of the third year in 'law, mechanism, and practical science'. The change necessitated yet further adjustments at college level, as well as the employment of new Lecturers, to be paid for out of corporate revenue. By 1871 St John's was employing eleven Lecturers supported by tuition fees to teach the traditional subjects (mathematics, classics, scripture, and moral philosophy), and another six paid for out of corporate revenue to teach the new triposes and special subjects. Yet the sense of inadequacy that had afflicted the early 1850s seemed still to obtain.

For example, a bitter row was sparked off by a non-resident Fellow, J. M. Wilson, science master at Rugby School, who published an aggressive pamphlet in which he denounced the fact that the Natural Sciences tripos had a much lesser status than the Mathematical. 'The colleges have a mighty power over schools', yet those Johnians who went forth into the classroom were often

---

[223] Only four out of 353 Fellows elected between 1801 and 1870 had not been undergraduates of the College.

[224] G. D. Liveing, 'Memorandum to St John's College Governing Body', 6 Jan. 1857: D44.2.27.

[225] CB, 25 Apr. 1860.

loath to teach science, with the result that France and Germany were steaming ahead of Britain in subjects requisite to the workings of a modern industrial and imperial power. Even Oxford, the supposed home of lost causes, had begun to offer scholarships and exhibitions in the natural sciences and to appoint Lecturers, thereby showing 'finer susceptibilities than Cambridge for the intellectual impulses and convictions of the country. I feel hurt and ashamed that this should come exclusively at present from Oxford. It is at Cambridge that science ought to flourish. There it would find its most congenial home.'[226] Bonney backed Wilson up in print, and complained that the Seniors had sat on their laurels since founding the Chemical Laboratory and lectureship.[227]

In principle Wilson had a strong case. He knew that the College was doing well financially and could have responded to his demands, but there was a problem. Although the 1860 Statutes did not place a strict limit on the size of the dividend, they did stipulate that, if there were to be a surplus beyond the amount necessary 'to afford to each Fellow an average income of £300 a year (exclusive of rooms and commons)', then that surplus might be used, not to increase the dividend, but to promote the core objectives, most obviously by increasing the number of Fellowships. 'Might' here very obviously implied 'ought', which at once set up a conflict between self-interest and altruism. In 1870, the year in which the dividend rose to £290, close to the implied maximum, a fierce debate took place at the annual College meeting of Fellows over an abortive attempt by the University's Physical and Experimental Science Syndicate to establish a new Public Lectureship in Science. Throughout Cambridge, apparently, the opposition of the St John's Seniors to the proposal 'was thought to be a deadlock to it', and while it was agreed that this criticism was unfair, since the College more than pulled its scientific weight, it nevertheless prompted Bonney, Hill, Haslam, and Hudson to argue vigorously for a change of policy. It was, they asserted, a damnable situation that aspirant natural scientists should be forced to go to Oxford, Glasgow, or Edinburgh. Why could St John's not emulate Christ Church, which had recently established readerships in physics, chemistry, and physiology? The difficulty was that, since no existing Fellow was qualified to teach the subjects, either new Fellowships must be created, with consequent loss of dividend to existing Fellows, or else other Fellowships must be suppressed. Bonney wanted to suppress two Fellowships in order to pay for a professor, and Marshall would have done the same but to pay for two scientific Lecturers, yet unfortunately the statutes did not allow for Fellowships to be suppressed at all. The discussion went nowhere angrily, and it was left to the duke of Devonshire to come to the rescue of Cambridge science by donating more than £6,000 towards the building of the new Cavendish Laboratory.

Even in regard to the traditional subjects there was little sense of much progress having been made. When Heitland went up as a pensioner in 1867 he found that 'college lectures and examinations were mostly futile'. It was still

[226] J. M. Wilson, *A Letter to the Master and Seniors of St John's College on the Subject of the Natural and Physical Sciences in Relation to School and College* (1867), 4, 6–11, 14–15. Similar sentiments were expressed from 1869 onwards by the influential Endowed Schools Commission, whose secretary was Henry Roby.

[227] T. G. Bonney, *A Letter to the Master and Seniors of St John's College* (1867).

the case that private coaches with a reputation for 'getting men through' at a charge of £9 per term 'throve on the constant demand for their services', especially for composition, unseen translation, and advanced mathematics.[228] And in classics at least there was still the same old mixed ability teaching in large classrooms, meaning that scholars from advanced sixth forms had to adapt to lower standards alongside oafs who could hardly decipher the Greek alphabet. But the worst thing about the system was that it was too mechanical, too rote-bound, ultimately too fixated on results.

> In the case of Degrees with Honours a competition of the crudest character prevailed. The so-called Order of Merit existed in all Triposes. Merit meant the relative number of marks gained by the several candidates on a particular set of papers at a given date. Marks were added together, and places in the lists determined by the totals (...) Vast pains were taken by the examiners, and Cambridge men regarded their rigid system with pardonable self-satisfaction as the best thing of the kind in the world. To be senior Wrangler was the very crown of Academic distinctions. Now, so long as you understood by 'merit' no more than I have stated above, there was no harm done. The fact of a man's place was indisputable. Error began when the fact of a given moment was regarded as fixing a man's intellectual place in the world for life. This absurdity was a manifestation of the 'sporting instinct' of which English people are grotesquely proud.[229]

It was also of course a self-perpetuating system, since Fellowships were awarded by one's order in the tripos, unlike the situation in Trinity, where Fellowship candidates took special scholarly tests. This meant that at St John's those who flourished under the system went on to teach it, and also that as teachers they sought to do for others what had been done for them, i.e. secure to each pupil the highest number of marks he was capable of acquiring, and no more. Again Heitland made a partial exception of Trinity, where there was more attention to the task of training both for manhood and scholarship, whereas the system seemed to be at its worst – 'a wasteful failure' – at his own college. This sense that there might be something wrong with St John's specifically, as distinct from Cambridge generally, was intensified by Whewell's introduction of intercollegiate lectures. When he first mooted this idea in the 1850s, Joe Mayor could only speculate about the sophisticated intellectual instruction to be had 'on the other side of the wall', meaning from classics such as William Thompson, W. G. Clark, and Edward Cope.[230] In the early 1870s, however, the undergraduate Heitland was actually allowed to visit next door and sit at the feet of Henry Jackson, Richard Jebb, and Henry Sidgwick, and the experience led him to ruminate. 'I came away convinced that there were in a lecture-room possibilities of which much might be made, and that the able and learned Johnian staff were somehow hampered by their system or by the spirit in which it was worked.'[231]

---

[228] Heitland, review of Bonney's *Memories*, *Eagle* xlii (1921–2), 284.
[229] Heitland, *After Many Years*, 126–7, 139–40.
[230] Mayor, 'College reform in the 1850s', 190.
[231] Heitland, *After Many Years*, 140.

The third area of concern for the reformers of the 1850s – the terms and conditions under which Fellowships might be retained – was potentially even more contentious. The Graham commissioners ignored the complex arrangements to be found in different colleges, and simply asked whether continued residence as a Fellow ought to be made depend on 'the discharge of active duty in discipline or tuition, or with the earnest prosecution of private study'. Since 'active duty' in discipline and tuition was sufficient to ensure continued tenure as a Fellow of St John's, the force of the query fell on the phrase, 'earnest prosecution of private study'. The College's official response to this apparently-innocent-but-poisonous suggestion was negative: 'We should have great difficulty in determining from time to time whether a Fellow were or were not earnestly prosecuting his private studies.' Since no one in Queen Victoria's glorious days would have thought of determining such an issue by the length of a Fellow's publications, decisions on whether or not to terminate would inevitably come down to partiality, and that in turn would cast suspicion on any appointments made to Fellowships so vacated. It was also the case that colleges would be less inclined to throw out those officers who proved themselves inadequate to the task of 'discipline or tuition' (or, as it might be, bursaring) if the consequence were to deprive them of their Fellowships as well. Furthermore, the requirement to prosecute private study earnestly would also make Fellowships less worth having, whereupon students would not work so hard to secure them.[232]

These were all wise arguments as well as honest ones, and significantly the Graham commissioners did not press the point, and yet a large number of the Junior Fellows took up their suggestion. The basic problem was that there was 'no sufficient inducement' for the best men to remain and give themselves up to teaching, since 'a college lectureship affords no provision for life, nor even fair remuneration for the work done'. In particular it could not compete with the pecuniary rewards now obtainable in the Church or the Law. Most of those Fellows who stayed on in Cambridge did so either because they enjoyed idle luxury, or because they were on the lookout for a rich living and the opportunity to marry. In order to accrue some savings while they waited their turn, many took on private pupils or – still worse – a college Tutorship or Lectureship. Either way, they were square pegs in round holes, and their very presence had 'a deadening effect'. Moreover, because they were judged as potential clergymen rather than as academics, the best scholars were frequently not chosen for Fellowships. Conversely, those who were chosen gained no practical experience for the clerical profession either. 'It is admitted on all hands that fellows of colleges do not now usually make the most efficient pastors. A lengthened bachelor life in college, in a limited society, it is said, is a bad preparation for a cure of souls, where ministrations to both sexes are needed, and to all ranks.'[233] As for the Seniors who had charge of College governance, they were mostly 'men that had been left stranded in Cambridge', and were generally lacking in wisdom and energy.

Liveing and his co-reformers therefore supported the commissioners'

---

[232] *Correspondence Respecting ... Oxford and Cambridge*, Parliamentary Papers 1854, 1, 362.

[233] Liveing, 'Memorandum to SJC Governing Body', 6 January 1857.

suggestion that, except in the case of Tutors, Lecturers, and Bursars, Fellowships should be terminable 'after a fixed period' unless their holders were 'not merely occupied in *study*, but fairly giving themselves to advance *learning*' (i.e. engaged in original research). They hoped that the danger of partiality might be prevented by handing the decision to 'an independent tribunal (suppose the Master, Visitor, and Vice-Chancellor)'. A corollary of such a change would be to remove any requirement for a Fellow to take Holy Orders. Also, if Fellowships were to be renewable only on condition of good behaviour (i.e. academic achievement) then there would no longer be any need to privilege celibacy (which was presumably a clumsy device for inducing good behaviour).[234] Another way of preventing Fellows from hanging on till a juicy living came up might be to restrict them to only two choices of living (except in the case of the six most impoverished ones).

Ultimately the question of Holy Orders was a distraction from the obvious point that, if better men were to be induced to become academics, they would need to be better paid. But how could this happen at a time when public opinion would clearly not sanction higher charges to students? Liveing simply stated as a matter of fact that, if all newly appointed Seniors were to give up their additional dividends, there would eventually be an annual income of £640 p.a. which, together with what was already paid to Deans and Tutors 'might suffice for an adequate staff of Lecturers'. Roby went slightly further in his pamphlet. 'I looked up the original Statutes of Bishop Fisher (…) and pointed out the great contrast in the distribution of income intended by the founder compared to what it was in our time, the provision of adequately paid Lecturers being now put aside, and the fund being divided among the Fellows with few or no duties (…) My brochure was commended by Todhunter as very smart.'[235] However, it must have been obvious to all that this attack on the distribution was an attack on the principle of seniority itself, a point on which Liveing was the most outspoken. In the following passage, written under the heading 'The permanent government of the college', he made what was surely an oblique allusion to the Blick years.

> The College is fortunate in having at present a more efficient acting Seniority than there has sometimes been. They have in former times too often been indifferent, obstructive, and dilatory, and may be so again. Without any reflection on the present Seniority, there are examples enough in other colleges, in which weakness of mind, indolence, or merely a longing for the biggest living, have brought men to the top of the list; there is one college which has the eminent distinction of a madman on the Seniority; and there has been no lack of instances of men imbecile from old age. Nor are these exceptional cases, but will recur again and again as long as human nature is unchanged.

[234] Ibid. 'Nineteen Fellows to the Cambridge University Comissioners': SJCA, D44.2.24.
[235] Roby, *Reminiscences*, 40.

The reformers' solution was for an elected Council comprising (say) the Master, the Senior Bursar, the two Tutors responsible for undergraduates, and five other (unpaid) Fellows, with all weighty matters, and any other matters by request, referred for decision by the 'whole body [of Fellows], as used to be the case'.[236] But, as in the case of teaching arrangements, the 1860 Statutes fell far short of what they wanted. Tutors, Lecturers, Praelectors, Senior Bursars, and some holders of University posts, including professors, were excused the need to take Holy Orders, but otherwise conditions of tenure remained virtually unchanged, and nothing was done about the requirements of celibacy. On the matter of governance the Seniority was statutorily designated a 'board', but that did nothing to reduce its virtually absolute powers. The most significant innovation was the new Statute LV, which stipulated that there was to be an annual general meeting of all Fellows having MA status, with a view to raising suggestions for the 'more efficient government of the college, or the promotion of its interests'. If after one year the Seniors had failed to implement any such suggestion, it was to be voted on at the following annual general meeting and, if passed by two-thirds of those present, and not contrary to statute, 'it shall become binding on the college'.

Statute LV was almost certainly intended as a sop to the reformers, but in fact it turned out to be a time bomb, the detonator being the simple phrase, 'all Fellows having M.A. status'. This was the phrase used by the Graham commissioners, and by the politicians who drafted the Cambridge University Act of 1856, when they came to define what a 'governing body' was for the purpose of implementing any necessary statutory changes within two years. As a definition it posed no problem for most colleges, where it more or less reflected the reality, but it created confusion in the case of a few, like St John's and Trinity, where according to statute the governing body was vested in the Master and eight most senior resident Fellows. (This peculiarity in their constitution reflected their large size rather than any innate tendency to oligarchy.) Possibly Bateson, the commissioners, and after them the legislators deliberately enfranchised the younger Fellows, possibly they simply sought uniformity across the colleges without thinking about the consequences, but either way it created a situation where, for a brief period, there were two governing bodies in St John's, a permanent executive for day-to-day decision making and a constituent assembly for the purpose of statute revision. In 1856, according to Roby's account, an attempt was made by the ordinary governing body to limit the work of statute revision to the nine Seniors, 'but this attempt was frustrated by petitions from the rest of the Fellows'.[237]

Which meant that the stage was set for a series of what John Mayor described as 'stormy' sessions in which the temporary governing body sought to thrash out the business of statute revision. There were at least twenty such meetings stretching from the autumn of 1856 to the autumn of 1857, and they gave rise to a great deal of grandstanding. Liveing was elected secretary and has left for posterity a much fuller account of proceedings than are available in the Conclusion

[236] Liveing, 'Memorandum to SJC Governing Body'; Roby, 'College reform', 197.
[237] Roby, *Reminiscences*, 40.

Book.[238] His minutes provide a fitting place to close this section, providing as they do a snapshot of opinion at that pivotal time. Thus Bateson's opening proposal to place all the Foundation Fellowships on a uniform footing was carried by 28 to 2. The identities of the dissentients are not revealed, but one was very likely Reyner. Bateson's follow-up proposal to do the same for all scholarships and exhibitions, and to increase their value, was carried more narrowly, by 24 to 8. (At this point he was elected Master, the disposition of votes for and against him being very similar to those on the scholarships statutes.) His subsequent motion to merge the Platt Fellowships into the rest was agreed to without a vote. At one meeting a draft statute was circulated assigning equal dividends to all Fellows without any addition for seniority.[239] Signed by Hayward, John and Joe Mayor, Bashforth, Todhunter, Roby, Liveing, and seventeen other fellows, it claimed to represent 'the major part of the Governing Body of St John's named in the 19 and 20 Vict. c. 88', but when it came to the meeting it was voted down easily. Indeed, it may simply have been a way of letting off steam and making their resentments known, rather than a serious attempt to deprive the Seniors of their bonuses. Hayward's and Liveing's move to end celibacy was lost by 20 to 8, and nine other reform motions, including proposals to abolish compulsory ordination, to extend the initial period of a Fellow's tenure from six to ten years, to abolish the Tutorship system, and to establish an elected council, all went the same way. Liveing's motion that no Fellow should be allowed to turn down more than four College livings (apart from a few impoverished ones) was more narrowly defeated, by 19 to 12; a demand that they acquire some parochial experience before taking a living went down by 22 to 12. Early in the proceedings Reyner, who at times was quite clearly out of control, had to be restricted to one amendment per motion. His frustration will have stemmed, not simply from innate conservatism, but from consciousness of his new duties as Senior Bursar, and from a fear that his more reform-minded colleagues would gladly take advantage of improving finances to let expenditure rip. He wrote in his diary exasperatedly after one particularly imaginative discussion,

> In the governing body committee it seemed to be thought that (i) the Somerset Scholars ought to be paid more by £400 a year, and (ii) the other Scholars more by £1500 a year; (iii) also that £3000 a year should be set aside for a building fund; (iv) and that the dividend should go up to 200£; (v) and that these three things should proceed *pari passu*; (vi) that there should be 60 scholarships at 50£ per annum; (vii) and exhibitions corresponding to Dr Wood's and Sir Ralph Hare's.[240]

Pari passu is of course a Bursar's nightmare, but nevertheless Reyner was beginning to enjoy his new status. He made it clear that he had no fears about

---

[238] 'Minutes of the Proceedings of the Governing Body of St John's College under 19 & 20 Victoria c. 88': SJCA, D104.122; 'Papers concerning the Revision of College Statutes 1856–7': SJCA, D44.3.1–2.

[239] SJCA, D90.613(13).

[240] 'Reyner's diary notes as Senior Bursar, 18 Mar. 1857': SJCA, SB1.6. By 'governing body committee' it is unclear whether Reyner meant the temporary governing body of all MA fellows, or a specially appointed subset of that body.

appearing in a minority of one, though his motion to the effect that Fellows must declare themselves full members of the United Churches of England and Ireland was carried by 26 votes to nil. Very likely his aim on that occasion was to flush out the three Fellows who abstained. Unfortunately Liveing did not record their names. Could one of them have been Bateson?

These meetings of a temporary governing body for the purposes of statute revision gave the Junior Fellows a taste of power, and it remained to be seen whether they would go willingly back into their box. It must surely have been obvious to everyone that there would be trouble ahead, but while all the controversial discussions were taking place, during the late fifties, the effect was rather refreshing. The reformers may have been rebuffed on major issues, and they certainly thought the 1860 Statutes far too cautious, but there was a welcome sense of movement, and at least they felt involved. Statute revision can therefore be seen as part of a much bigger process whereby a new sense of corporate identity was being forged.

7.   THE CREATION OF A COLLEGIATE ETHOS, 1850–1900

> To apply the Word to the solemnity of this day; the 7th Jubilee of our ancient College (…) We must have better divines than Redmayn (…), better preachers than Pilkington (…) We must have better and braver bishops than those four of the noble seven (…), more earnest and eloquent pleaders for the liberty of their fellow men (…) than Wilberforce …, better Heralds of the Gospel than Henry Martyn (…) and Thomas Whytehead. We must have better missionary bishops than Cotterill and Colenso (…) We must have a nobler band of men than this, or at least we must have men like these, and more in number (…) And why should we not have? (…) Is not our College more securely established? our Kingdom more united and firm than it was of old? We have passed through those seasons of trial and trouble, in which other nations are now struggling, and there is good hope that the promise to Joshua shall be fulfilled to us, *In this place will I give peace* (…) The storms of winter and conflicts of early spring have passed away, and the Maytime of our College-life is come.
>
> William Selwyn, *The New Chapel of St John's College Cambridge:*
> *A Word Spoken at the Annual Commemoration of Benefactors, 1861*
> (Cambridge, 1869), 12, 16–20, 22.

Selwyn's confidence that the winter's storms had given way to Maytime was characteristic of the mood of the later 1850s and 1860s. A similar serenity was implicit in the way in which Charles Kingsley revised his Christian socialist novel *Alton Locke*. First published in 1850, it was written in the fashionable genre of social realism and contained some highly derogatory comments about Cambridge, apparently based on his experiences there. (He had been an undergraduate at Magdalene College from 1838 until 1842 when he had, incidentally, employed William Bateson as a private tutor in mathematics.)

The book was reissued in 1862, virtually unaltered except that the Cambridge sections were omitted. Gone were the venal and port-swilling dons, the idle, dissolute, and rowdy students, the Barnwell whores, the antiquated and obscurantist customs. Cynics naturally attributed the omission to the fact that in 1860 Kingsley had been appointed Regius Professor of Modern History in Cambridge. They implied that he could hardly go on berating an institution of which he was now a distinguished ornament. Yet his defenders argued, with some justification, that Cambridge had greatly changed in the meantime. The Barnwell whores really had for the most part been cleared away, religion had begun to be taken more seriously, academic practices were being modernized, while the behaviour of dons and students alike had much improved.

Social transformations rarely occur suddenly, at least without a revolution, but in mid-nineteenth-century Britain it was precisely the absence of a revolution – or (to be more precise) the disappearance of the *fear* of an imminent revolution – that led very rapidly to changes in social attitudes and relationships. 1848 was the 'Year of Revolutions' all over the Continent, but in England the insurrectionary Chartist movement was widely perceived to have collapsed almost overnight after a failed demonstration on 10 June. The reality was more complex, but the impression that this was so led to a marked relaxation of social tension. The dangerous classes – workers, political agitators, criminals, paupers, even raucous undergraduates – seemed to be not so dangerous after all. In such an atmosphere James Wood would not have dreamed of trying to disband the Union Society, and Ralph Tatham would not have fretted over the election of a Whig government. It is also relevant that in 1836 Cambridge, along with 177 other towns, had acquired a municipal corporation elected by rate-payers. As elsewhere this had been followed by the development of a local police force and any number of civic improvements, including a campaign for moral purity. Notably in the 1850s the City authorities, aided by the Evangelical vicar Charles Perry, swept away the Barnwell brothels and replaced them with new churches.

From the 1850s onwards photographs exist to show how mid- and late Victorian undergraduates looked. Most of the early images are of individuals, but by the 1870s it was common for societies and sports teams to seek to immortalize their transient moments of sodality. There they remain, posed and frozen young men against the background of New Court's ivied Gothic 'cloister', two small chaps on the floor in the front with their knees poking upwards, a seated middle row looking intensely into the camera, and the back row standing, sometimes with boaters or tassles, often in profile, and looking at anything but the camera. The captain at centre of the seated row might have a round or oval ball on his lap, or the more languid types in the rear might sport bats and rackets. Judging from this visual evidence, the most striking development during the third quarter of the nineteenth century was the increasing prevalence of facial hair. Of the forty faces preserved from the years 1856–9, thirty-two (or 80 per cent) were clean-shaven, four had neat sideburns, one had sideburns and a moustache, one just a moustache, and two had full beards. Out of eighty-three for the period 1860–3, fifty (or 60 per cent) were hairless, twenty-two had big bushy mutton

chops, six had moustaches only, and five had beards. By the early 1870s the proportion of clean-shaven undergraduates had dropped to about half, and by the
1880s to about one-third. Most of the remainder had clipped moustaches, and
a few had bushy chops, but beards were still very rare. By and large the dons
were hairier. Almost all of them are likely have been clean-shaven before the
1850s, but about three-quarters covered at least part of their faces from the 1860s
onwards. The heaviest and bushiest beards belonged to Whytehead, Todhunter,
Hiern, Hudson, Smith, Wace, Freeman, Heitland, and John Mayor. Also notable were those of Bonney (long), Liveing (long and red), Torry (divided), Taylor
and Sandys (neatly trimmed), and MacAlister (pointed). Foxwell and Tottenham, the latter a notable fop, had the trendiest moustachios. Based on this evidence there is some suggestion of a correlation between large amounts of hair
and extrovert behaviour.[241]

None of the above will seem surprising, since historians have long been
aware of a sudden penchant for facial hair from the 1850s onwards. A traditional
explanation has been the desire of British men at home to emulate hirsute soldiers returning from the Crimea. However, the truth is rather more complex, as
Christopher Moore has shown. In general society moustaches and bushy sideburns had already begun to spread in the decade before 1850, but full beards
were discountenanced because of their association with Chartism and other
forms of radicalism. The sudden decline of the revolutionary threat at mid-
century then led to an equally sudden predilection for full beards. Moore sees
this as a 'movement' rather than a mere fashion because of the constant patter
of philosophizing commentary that accompanied it. Carlyle, for example, and
the Christian Socialist propagandists Kingsley and Hughes, are said to have
'envisioned bearded men as icons of a primal manhood undiminished by modern
industrialism'. Beards may also have represented an attempt to address a crisis
of masculinity caused by awareness that many middle-class women were beginning to assert their intellectual and sexual independence.[242] They spoke of such
masculine qualities as 'independence and hardiness and decisiveness'. Beards
were manly appendages, both 'natural' and Protestant (Jesuit priests were invariably depicted as shaven and shorn, as well as effeminate).[243] But whatever the
underlying causes, it is clearly the case that by the 1870s at least one-half of
British men had full beards, while most of the remainder were heavily whiskered. This fact provokes a reconsideration of the St John's photographs. That
younger dons in the third quarter of the century should have felt impelled to
assert the manliness of their chosen profession by growing facial hair is entirely
understandable. What is more striking is the extent to which undergraduates
resisted the movement, how far their clean-shaven or lightly whiskered faces
differentiated them from the prevailing masculine fashion. And that too seems
right since, although the undergraduates of the 1860s look much more adult

---

[241] For an exemplar, see below, p. 301, n. 264.

[242] Similar anxieties may have led men to substitute 'sleeping suits' for 'night costume' in
the later 1850s and 1860s.

[243] Christopher Oldstone Moore, 'The beard movement in Victorian Britain', *Victorian
Studies* 48 (2005), 7–34.

than those of the 1830s when judged by twenty-first-century visual criteria, in terms of outlook and behaviour they were very-much more juvenile.

This was all part of a powerful change in atmosphere during the 1850s, one effect of which was that college came to be more like school. There was a new emphasis on corporate spirit, team games replaced fishing, and the undergraduate condition began to be seen no longer as the beginning of manhood but as the last stage of boyhood. Thomas Hughes's two novels, *Tom Brown's Schooldays* and *Tom Brown in Oxford*, depict the way in which school life was seen to segue into the undergraduate condition without requiring any great shift in sensibility. An underlying cause of the new mentality, which cannot be developed here, was the mid-century idealization of childhood itself as a condition worth prolonging. The change in atmosphere would have made college life much more cohesive, so that hopefully fewer undergraduates would have felt like Thomas Whytehead, who two decades earlier had got himself 'a little bird in a cage to make some sort of companion for me, as I often feel as if I would give anything for something alive like myself to keep me company'.[244] But it also made college life less special than it had seemed, for example, to the Trinity Apostles of the 1820s and 1830s. Frederick Maurice, John Sterling, Arthur Hallam, and Alfred Tennyson had invested undergraduate relationships with great spiritual significance, and had envisioned themselves as messianic individuals capable of redeeming a morally bankrupt nation, but now in the 1850s the emphasis was rather on corporate endeavour and institutional tradition.

Certain practical changes also worked to make college life seem less esoteric. One of these was the introduction of the penny post in 1839, as Robert Mayor (hypocritically perhaps) complained,

> Formerly one did not write, when there was nothing wherewith to fill the sheet. Letters when written were the spontaneous predilections of a heart full of home, for they were penned when one's thoughts were turned more particularly homewards, and at moments when one felt that it would be no easy thing to refrain from unbending oneself to those one loves. But now alas, for the boasted liberty of the present age, in which it seems to be a merit to trample down the venerable customs of past ages, letters *must* be written for the sake of sending them to the post once a week, however disinclined one may happen to be on that particular day.[245]

If the obligatory weekly letter had the effect of reducing the distance between home and university, then the development of the railways, at its fastest in the 1850s, had a much greater one. Back in the days of the stage coach boys from northern climes had often found it impracticable to get home in the vacations; many stayed away for years and more at a time, perhaps boarding with relatives in the south-east of England. Going up to Cambridge in those days could seem an awfully big adventure, and as a result college life felt as though it was a genuine rite of passage. As Whytehead wrote in 1834, 'college may be animating, but it is not *home*.' Thanks to the railway, however, parents could now visit their sons

---

[244] Whytehead to his sister, Feb. 1834, quoted in *ODNB* (R. Scott).
[245] Robert Mayor to his mother, 17 Mar. 1840: Mayor Papers, B8/194.

in term time, and college was coming to seem more like home from home in consequence. Such changes in habits and outlook naturally affected Cambridge as a whole, but there are grounds for thinking that they affected St John's particularly, and that even more than other colleges St John's came to seem more like school.

The phrase 'like school' does not refer to one particular type of institution, since undergraduates had had very diverse experiences, ranging from the aristocratic and unreformed public schools to the grammar schools and private academies (including some like Dotheboys Hall), while several had not been schooled at all. What is being referred to is rather the reconceptualization of 'school' in books such as Arthur Stanley's *Life of Thomas Arnold* and Hughes's *Tom Brown's Schooldays*. Published in 1857, the latter's account of Rugby School under Arnold became at once, not only a best seller, but an iconic and largely mythical exposition of muscular Christianity and liberal manliness. Arnold and Hughes were Oxford men, and yet their type of broad Christianity was much closer to the default religion of Cambridge University, where Evangelicalism and High Churchmanship had always been strictly for minorities. It is also clear from the *Eagle*, founded in 1858, that their influence was felt consciously by contemporary Johnians. Launched amid much enthusiasm, the magazine attracted subscriptions and contributions but also scepticism and disdain from 'a conservative section', who said it was 'wholly uncalled for; a mere whim; certain to fall through in a term or two'. The first issue, which appeared in 1859, opened with a rousing editorial that sought to rally the troops in the face of the dark and dangerous political forces out to damage the universities.

> Only let us pull together in this concern, with a strong pull and a steady swing, that the Eagle may be a rallying point and a watchword among us; something to fasten College spirit upon when here; something by which we can carry it down with us when we go away; the spirit of old Brookes; the spirit which cracks up its own as the best College in the best University in the best country in the world.[246]

At one level this was simply an expression of the xenophobia or 'Podsnappery' that was typical of the Palmerston years, but the reference to Old Brooke was more precise. He was the heroic captain of School House during Tom Brown's early days at Rugby, the man-boy who gives 'a toast which should bind us all together, and to those who've gone before and who'll come after us here. It is the dear old School-house – the best house of the best school in England.' The *Eagle's* editorial may well have been written by the senior member (and Fellow) on its board of management, Joe Mayor. He had been a boy at Rugby under Arnold, while his brother Robert was currently a master there and would later become a governor. Despite the sneers of the sceptics, the magazine has survived to this day, and is probably the oldest extant college magazine in the world. It is also one of the bulkiest, and from an early stage it generated a collective (and enduring) fascination with the College's history and antiquities. It also played an important part in creating an *esprit de corps* which was (and remains)

---

[246] Editorial, *Eagle* i (1858–9), 1, 4.

quite remarkable for a large college, and which has been wholly absent from the even larger one next door.[247]

In 1865 James Wilson, a non-resident Fellow and current master at Rugby, wrote to recommend one of his pupils for admission.

> I send you one more Rugbeian, a very good gentlemanly fellow who has failed for his scholarship at Oriel, (he was 2nd) and now comes to you. You must find room for him (…) I rejoice in the tide of Rugbeians which is flowing to St John's; they are a right good lot, and do you good, and you do them good; and I expect something handsome from the college as an acknowledgement of my services down here.[248]

Flowing tide was an exaggeration, but the 'Rugby liberals' (as they were known) certainly sent a good number of boys to St John's in these years, besides contributing hugely to its ethos.

Many undergraduates will have been indifferent to the military-religious enthusiasms of the 1850s, but for those who were swept up in them it seemed that something big was stirring. The power of their mood music lay in its combination of optimism and energy, qualities that had not sat together in previous decades. It was optimistic because it was based on the conviction that Britain was the world's greatest nation with a divine mission to perform. It was energetic and urgent because it had its roots in the apocalyptic pessimism of the 'hungry forties'. Back then it really had looked to many God-fearing persons as though society was in turmoil and as though God was preparing vengeance. To the young Fellow William Colenso, writing from St John's in 1843, the 'fearful state of the universities' epitomized the corruption of society in general. The dons were indolent, self-indulgent, and neglectful of their statutory obligations in so far as they had 'generally no connexion with the youths around them but that of mere accident and self-interest'. 'O that some plan could be devised for stirring up under God such a yearning for the souls of men among us.' Fired by reading the works of Maurice and Coleridge, Colenso longed for the awakening of a missionary spirit, and lamented that so few graduates were willing to work overseas among 'the multitudes that perish'. If he had ended his sentence with 'perish', he would have sounded like a thousand Evangelical tub-thumpers preaching that the end of the world was nigh, but instead he continued: '... the multitudes that perish, I say not *eternally*, – which is in the hands of Infinite Truth and Love, – but temporally, in the loss of that light and joy and glorious hope, which quicken by the Grace of God our own hearts'.[249] Broad Churchmen like Colenso rejected the Evangelicals' emphasis on eternal and everlasting

---

[247] The disparity in college spirit between St John's and Trinity remains. For example, there were thirteen fellows present on the touch line at a rugby match between the two colleges in Michaelmas 2009. Twelve of them were Fellows of St John's. The other, a Fellow of Trinity, had formerly been a Fellow of St John's and was shouting for his former college.

[248] J. M. Wilson to S. Parkinson, 15 Jun. 1865: SJCA, TU6(1) [*re* G. L. Bennett, 1865]. The final sentence sounds facetious, but shortly afterwards Wilson did make a large (albeit impersonal) demand on the College. See above, pp. 284–5.

[249] J. W. Colenso to Revd J. P. Ferguson, 14 Sept. and 23 Oct. 1843, George W. Cox, *The Life of John William Colenso* (1888), I. 21–3.

punishment, but many shared their sense of millennial urgency, and their insistence on missionary commitment. Then, a few years later, there had come the relaxation of social tensions alluded to above, and the consequent fusion of urgency and optimism had spawned a new sense of national greatness and a new interest in imperial expansion, sentiments which for churchmen translated into an enthusiasm for colonial mission. There was a feeling that the work had been left too much to individuals, or else to societies run by laymen, or worse still to Nonconformists and Catholics. Such churchmen naturally looked to the ancient universities for a supply of men willing to go out and convert the heathen.

Within this broad scenario the Crimean War had a galvanizing effect. Although not a holy war in geopolitical terms, it was mainly interpreted in that light, and it gave rise to the concept of the Christian soldier marching behind the cross of Jesus, as immortalized in Sabine Baring-Gould's hymn a decade later.[250] In other words, it yoked together the impulses to colonial mission and to muscular Christianity, and Joe Mayor was suitably thrilled, not least by the change it wrought in undergraduates who enlisted.

> What a splendid thing it is for the Army that this war has broken out. One could never have believed that such frivolous fops as one came to fancy them could be changed into such heroes as they have shown themselves. I begin to think the Army is the best school for most men after all. A cannon shot is decidedly a finer stimulant than an imposition and will draw out their faculties if anything will.[251]

The man who expressed these sentiments most memorably was the 'energetic and warlike' George Augustus Selwyn.[252] Elected to a Fellowship in 1833, he had gone off eight years later to become the first bishop of New Zealand, where he founded St John's Theological College in Auckland. He had little time for theological speculation but a tremendous capacity for spiritual fervour, leading Gladstone to call him 'one of the band of great bishops'. Since the establishment of a colonial bishoprics fund in 1841, the number of colonial prelates had increased from six to twenty-eight, five of whom were Johnians,[253] and that statistic, along with the Crimean crisis, provided his theme for a series of barnstorming sermons in Cambridge in 1854. Focusing especially on Australasia's need for missionary clergy, he argued that the recent gold finds in Victoria had been providential. 'When all thinking men were fearing the outbreak of the volcano which lay hid beneath the fair show of English society, He discovered veins of gold at the world's end, so as at once to relieve the old world, and to enrich the new; so increasing abundantly the means of spreading the knowledge of His Name.' Alluding to the 12,000 men who had volunteered for military service since the battle of the Alma, Selwyn exhorted 12,000 more to offer their names to the archbishop of Canterbury, as men who were willing 'to go

---

[250] Olive Anderson, 'The growth of Christian militarism in mid-Victorian Britain', *English Historical Review* lxxxvi (1971), 46–72.

[251] John Mayor and Joe Mayor to their mother: Mayor Papers, 1854, B8/375, 251.

[252] Norman Vance, *The Sinews of the Spirit: The Ideal of Christian Manliness in Victorian Literature and Religious Thought* (Cambridge, 1985), 86.

[253] Including Colenso, who became bishop of Natal in 1853.

anywhere and do anything' as soldiers for Christ. As for the real soldiers at Sebastopol, 'who were now perhaps mounting the bloody breach', he asked, 'was it as a forlorn hope or with a hope full of immortality?' This was almost tantamount to saying that men who died in battle had consecrated deaths, a theme that would largely disappear from view during the last quarter of the century but surfaced again during the First World War. Many will have thought the notion theologically dubious but others, like Joe Mayor, were deeply moved.

> You can't conceive how beautifully [Selwyn] brings out these things. Every one holds his breath and there is a twitching in every face. Old dons one would have thought as dry as a bone use their handkerchiefs plentifully. In fact the enthusiasm is extraordinary in a place like Cambridge where we analyse every thing into common-place. There is no chance here for any got up eloquence but it is impossible to stand a great heart opened so generously to one. St Paul must have been very like him.[254]

Joe Mayor's brother John was no less thrilled by Selwyn's sermons. 'What a pity it is we have no such man in Cambridge. Carus was far too soft and ladylike to have much weight with men of robust minds.'[255] There was further excitement in 1856 when David Livingstone visited St John's, and an ecstatic climax in 1859 with a meeting of the Oxford and Cambridge Great African Mission in the Senate House. Bateson was currently Vice-Chancellor and took the chair, and Gladstone headed a glittering cast of speakers, but for Joe Mayor it was Bishop Selwyn once more who caught the moment best.

> It was a delight and wonder to listen to [Gladstone], and yet I think Bishop Selwyn is still the finest speaker I ever heard. There was a divine enthusiasm about him which I never saw or expect to see in any other man. [Whereas Gladstone and Bishop Wilberforce merely urged] the importance of the mission (…) as a means of doing away with slavery, and opening up a wide field for commerce.[256]

There could be no doubt that in this context the missionary Henry Martyn was deemed to be the noblest Johnian of them all, estimated far ahead of the stay-at-home abolitionist William Wilberforce, and slightly ahead of a more recent tragic missionary, Thomas Whytehead, a full-length painting of whom was shortly to adorn the roof of the new Chapel choir.[257]

It fell to George Selwyn's older brother William, a former Fellow and now the Lady Margaret Professor of Divinity, to preach on the 350th anniversary or seventh Jubilee of the foundation. His sermon (an extract of which appears

---

[254] Joe Mayor to his mother, 1854: Mayor Papers, B8/375.

[255] John Mayor to his mother, 1854: Mayor Papers, B8/251. After Simeon's death in 1836, and until 1851 when he left Cambridge, the Revd William Carus of Trinity was the main upholder of evangelical religion in the University.

[256] Joe Mayor to his mother, 1 Nov. 1859: Mayor Papers, B8/376.

[257] Martyn (1781–1812) and Whytehead (1815–43) were evangelical missionaries who 'burned themselves out for God', dying young and lonely in faraway lands. Martyn's great achievement was to translate the Bible into Arabic, Persian, and Urdu, while Whytehead was sent by the Church Missionary Society to work among the Maoris as Bishop Selwyn's chaplain.

at the head of this section) has gone down in College lore as having provided the stimulus for building a new chapel. That is misleading,[258] but it certainly played its part in sustaining the mood of post-millennial enthusiasm, one effect of which was to induce a collective sense that the existing chapel was architecturally too mean for the spiritual task ahead. Selwyn likened the dark days of the 1830s and 1840s to those of the seventeenth century, and rejoiced that both dangers had been surmounted. 'The storms of winter and conflicts of early spring have passed away, and the Maytime of our College-life is come.'[259]

The missionary movement eventually blew itself out, a fact that the faithful had constant cause to lament in the 1870s. As early as 1857 the so-called Indian Mutiny had challenged many of its underlying assumptions, while immediately afterwards fears of invasion by French ironclad ships led St John's and other colleges to establish volunteer and rifle companies.[260] In these circumstances 'defence of the realm' became more a matter of *Realpolitik* than of Godly mission, while imperialism too became increasingly ensnared in European power politics. So the muscular Christian missionary moment was relatively short-lived, and yet it achieved something important for the College: a sense of autonomy. There is no escaping the fact that, during the second quarter of the nineteenth century, Johnians at all levels had been obsessed by their precarious place in the pecking order, especially with regard to Trinity. In the 1840s the undergraduate George Shaw was only one of many to express exasperation at Cambridge's 'tomfooleries', among which he included the tribal rivalry between two neighbouring colleges. 'I like Trinity quite as well, and if I had been a member of it should have *looked down* upon St John's; they are both capital places however, and it is mere folly to depreciate one in order to aggrandize the other.'[261] The Broad Church and muscular Christian movements of the 1850s and 1860s, for all that many will have been irritated or unmoved by them, at least had the merit of concentrating Johnians on themselves. They helped to create a genuine sense of identity, which, whether one liked it or not, was better than relentlessly measuring oneself against 'the other'.

One reason for the new sense of corporate identity after 1850 is the fact that, for the first time in the nineteenth century, a significant proportion of students came from a select group of public schools. In the twenty years from 1852 to 1871, Rugby sent up sixty men, Shrewsbury fifty-nine, Marlborough College fifty-four, Sedbergh fifty-one. Cheltenham and Uppingham followed with twenty-seven and twenty-two respectively, both scoring very strongly in the 1860s. Eton continued to 'decline' with just twenty-five boys admitted, but Harrow bounced back with twenty-two, and Manchester Grammar School kept its end up with twenty-three. No other institution scored more than sixteen (Charterhouse). It needs to be said at once that the undergraduate body remained fairly diluted,

---

[258] See below, p. 342.

[259] W. Selwyn, *The New Chapel of St John's College Cambridge: A Word Spoken at the Annual Commemoration of Benefactors, 1861* (Cambridge, 1869), 22.

[260] For the Johnian corps, see Heitland, *After Many Years*, 119–24. Heitland observes that most students cheered on the Prussians in the War of 1870, and evidently felt that the French had it coming to them.

[261] G. Shaw to Sidney Smith, 20 Mar. 1840, copy: SJCL, MS O.78.20 at p. 51.

given that in all more than 1,500 young men were admitted during these years, but even so the fact that 273 of them came from just six schools must have had an impact, especially as those schools conformed, with the probable exception of Sedbergh, to a certain type. Rugby, Marlborough, Uppingham, and Tonbridge can all be described as 'reformed' or, in the language of the day, 'Arnoldised'. Marlborough had been founded in 1843 as a Christian boarding school for the children of clergy. After a rocky beginning, which included a notorious rebellion,[262] it was put to rights from 1852 onwards by George Cotton, a Trinity man and the model for the 'Young Master' in *Tom Brown's Schooldays*. Cotton worshipped Arnold and his methods, having been first a pupil and then a housemaster under him at Rugby, and in 1858 he responded to Selwyn's call for episcopal missionaries by accepting the post of bishop of Calcutta. Meanwhile Uppingham was in the process of becoming one of the leading public schools under its Master, Edward Thring, the most explicit post-Arnoldian exponent of manliness and what he always called 'true life'. Shrewsbury was less obviously in the Arnoldian mould, and its college connection was of course historic rather than cultural, but under B. H. Kennedy it was turning into one of the eight leading public schools as recognized by the Clarendon Commission of 1861–4.

In *Tom Brown's Schooldays* Old Brooke, Thomas Hughes's fictional house captain and heroic exemplar, announces to 'frantic cheers' that he would 'sooner win two School-house matches running than get the Balliol scholarship any day'. Although these were undoubtedly Hughes' own sentiments, they were far from being those of his own hero, the non-fictional Arnold, who had had little interest in sport and was by no means a philistine. And yet, because he expressed himself so fervently on moral and religious matters, Arnold could often sound like one, especially if quoted out of context. A notorious remark of his on the question of university entrance demonstrates the point. 'Mere intellectual acuteness, divested as it is, in too many cases, of all that is comprehensive and great and good, is to me more revolting than the most helpless imbecility, seeming to be almost like the spirit of Mephistopheles … What we ought to do is to send up [to university] boys who will not be plucked.'[263] William Selwyn was not an anti-intellectual either. In his Jubilee sermon he gave out a roll call of great Johnians whom he commanded the present generation to surpass. In the extract quoted at the beginning of this section the names cited are nearly all those of divines, and that is certainly where Selwyn's emphasis lay, but he also called for better poets – than Wordsworth for example – better scholars in ancient tongues, better Hebraicists, physicians, naturalists, botanists, and astronomers. He called for a revival of the learning – described variously as 'liberal', 'Baconian', and 'inductive' – that had helped to see the College through the storms of the sixteenth and seventeenth centuries. In this he was undoubtedly sincere, but as with Arnold the ethical aspects of his message proved more resonant than the educational. At any rate, the surviving tutorial archives suggest that in these decades the possession of character allied to Christian manliness counted for

---

[262] John Mayor taught there from 1849 to 1853, which might explain the rebellion (see below, p. 320 on his pedagogic skills), but the ostensible reason for the week of anarchy and tumult was 'chronic hunger'.

[263] Quoted in A. P. Stanley, *The Life and Correspondence of Thomas Arnold* (1845), I. 134–5.

20 1854: Samuel Butler 'requested not to have again a noisy midnight party to annoy neighbours'. Extract from the Junior Dean's books: registering Butler's absences from Chapel. These increased until March 1857, incurring a 'week taken away' for 'continued ~~obstinate~~ irregularity at Chapel by the Dean': SJCA, DS 3.4 (1851–61)

more than cleverness. The fictional Tom Brown is plucky, sturdy, dependable, and honourable without being remotely acute or cultured, and all the indications are that, in the later part of the century, this was the type of boy that St John's cherished, at least in its pensioners.[264]

It was the Tutors' function to admit the pensioners, and their correspondence provides a wealth of insight into contemporary attitudes, containing as it does letters of reference written by schoolmasters, anxious inquiries from parents, and testimonials from patrons. Unfortunately, detailed files only exist for the second half of the century. Before then, either systematic records were not made, the Tutor keeping information in his head or on scraps of paper, or else the records were not conserved in the central archives. Whatever the reason, the survival of admission records is further evidence of the bureaucratic direction in which the College was moving at mid-century. They must be read with caution, since this was a closed world in which teachers would have tailored their remarks according to the tastes of individual Tutors, but with that proviso the referees were often exceedingly frank, especially with respect to academic ability (and its opposite).[265] '[W. Monk, 1851] is favourably progressing in Latin, and has read a little Greek (...) It is however, on moral grounds that I submit his name to your notice.' '[H. H. Bagnall, 1863] may give a little trouble about chapel and lectures, but otherwise you will find him amenable.' 'I wish to enter a pupil of mine [G. F. Dashwood, 1862] under [Joe Mayor] at St John's (...), a very nice high-principled hardworking lad – unfortunately he is rather stupid but for all that he is not at all likely to get plucked.' Of R. G. Hurle, 1862, it was written, 'his talents are moderate ... but the great point in the case is that he is of a most excellent disposition, industrious and high principled'. A housemaster informed Parkinson that '[H. J. Atkins, 1870] is a rough diamond but his father is *very* well to do and a highly respectable man. When you know the lad himself you

---

[264] Whereas one might hazard that Tom's caddish and bounderish tormentor Flashman (since immortalized by the novelist George MacDonald Fraser) was more the Trinity type. An exemplar might be Robert Tennent, who went up from Rugby to Trinity, but then migrated to St John's in 1857 rather than obey an order to remove his moustache. The following appears against his name in the St John's Deans' books: 'Bullies and frightens other lodgers into surrendering rooms. Should testimonials for Orders be given to such a man?' In the event he became a barrister rather than a clergyman.

[265] This frankness distinguishes the references from their grimly inoffensive, not to say formulaic, equivalents in the twentieth-first century.

will I think confess that I have made as much of him as could be made of such material.'[266] Such candour about candidates who were admitted prompts curiosity as to what can have been written about boys who did not get in. Clearly the testimonialists agreed with Arnold that, so long as a man was clever enough not to be 'plucked', then character was a sufficient qualification for a university education. Even parents got the message: 'My son [W. Allen, 1877] is thoroughly principled, will be fully amenable to discipline, and will read steadily. But I don't think he will accomplish more than a pass.'[267] The father of T. E. Nevin [1870] admitted that his son had 'neither the abilities nor energy of some boys, but, with a tutorial, might pass credibly. As an old Johnian, I should wish him to be a member of that College.' A sibling was even more insouciant: 'Hoping that my brother will prove a more successful pupil under you, than I have done under Mr Sandys'.[268] Of course, it is easy to mock such attitudes from the standpoint of a much later culture. The important question is, were such attitudes unusual in a long nineteenth-century context? The probable answer is that the concern for high-principled candidates was especially strong in St John's, whereas the tolerance of academic ordinariness was common throughout Cambridge.

It is obvious from these letters that money was often a complicating factor in the application process. Many better-off parents were desperate that their offspring should 'avoid getting into a fast set of men, who easily would lead him into all sorts of extravagance',[269] and demanded that Tutors should do what they could to prevent it. One indignant uncle almost went so far as to blame Joseph Ward, a wise, sweet, and conscientious Tutor, for the repeated failures of H. Bentley [1893] in chemistry. 'I fear that he finds the social temptations of college life stronger than his good intentions of working … I was rather sorry to find … that his rooms were in the ground floor, and so an easy resort for idle men. Could you move him to others less easily accessible? I fear too that he is forming acquaintances undesirable in other ways besides idleness. He has certainly deteriorated since he came into residence.'[270] Allocation of rooms was a major preoccupation with this type of boy. The private tutor of R. H. Potts [1864] was anxious that his pupil, 'a gentleman of some means', should be placed with 'a nice set of men', having been used to 'good society' at Harrow. 'Please keep [F. W. W. Tunstall, 1879, orphan] as *nice* rooms as possible, as he has been accustomed to every comfort'.[271] Meanwhile, many parents pleaded poverty, especially clerical poverty, and fretted about room and tuition costs. Some hinted that other less distinguished colleges held out a 'superior monetary attraction'.[272] There were anxious inquiries about the prospect of obtaining sizarships, and much anguish when these were not forthcoming.

'I was glad to hear that the moral discipline of St John's is now a great

[266] SJCA, TU4, TU5c, TU6(1).
[267] SJCA, TU6(1).
[268] SJCA, TU6(1), TU6(8).
[269] 22 Mar. 1871: SJCA, TU6(1).
[270] 29 Dec. 1894: SJCA, TU10(2).
[271] SJCA, TU6(8), TU6(11).
[272] 18 Jun. 1868: SJCA, TU6(1).

improvement upon the past', wrote a parent in 1868. 'The Dean of my day was I think too much of a Gallio.'[273] Perusal of the Deans' books, which survive from 1834 as a record of undergraduate peccadilloes, confirms one's impression that over time, as the authorities became more prurient, the students grew more juvenile. Certainly, heterosexual misdemeanours seem mainly to have occurred – or, at least, were recorded as having mainly occurred – in an earlier period. For example, J. P. Royle [1832] was rusticated for being 'in the habit of continually visiting the house of a prostitute at Barnwell'. He later became the vicar of Wellow. J. W. Maltby [1848], the future rector of Morton, was found walking with a prostitute, and A. Drury [1851], who would never make it beyond curate, 'spent a night in a house of ill fame'. He was not rusticated but merely gated on account of 'some mitigating' but unspecified 'circumstances'. J. D. Stone [1848] actually took up residence in a Barnwell bordello, but it is not clear what was done to him. The last three offences all occurred in 1850–1, which may suggest that the year of Britain's glorious Great Exhibition was one of peculiar licence, or merely that the Deans of the day were unusually vigilant. Fewer sexual offences were recorded after 1851, though R. C. Stevens [1857] made a habit of 'sleeping with other men in same bed', and R. W. Wickham [1869] was 'found by a pro-proctor after 11 o'clock holding filthy conversation with two prostitutes at the door of a brothel'. Instead exhibition*ism* seems to have been rife in the 1850s. The records reveal that in 1853 a rowing blue, Herbert Snow, 'frequently (...) exposes himself at his window in unseemly undress with pipe.' He and some friends flashed again on Port Latin day 'as guests were passing to the combination room'. It cannot have been held against him, since he later became a classics Fellow. In the following year J. F. Jenkin is decanally described as 'fond of beer & tobacco & displaying at window of lodgings in the Town, in a low way', while three years later still E. L. Mallory was 'admonished by the Master for some unseemly exposure at his window' (whether the Master's window or Mallory's is unclear). Like windows, doors were frequently manhandled, most commonly by being 'screwed up' or 'nailed up', though there is only a single recorded instance of a Dean's own door being indisposed in that way: in 1854 by J. E. Gorst in revenge for the Dean having intervened the night before to stop him and his friends 'imitating the voices of strange animals from his windows'. (Subsequently Third Wrangler and briefly a Fellow, in 1860 Gorst was sufficiently fired by College spirit to join Bishop Selwyn among the Maori, but he quickly despaired of bringing them up to European standards of civilization, and returned to try his luck with the Conservative Party instead.)[274] In fact the Deans were frequently being insulted, farmyard noises were surprisingly prevalent, and the mood in 1854 appears to have been particularly light-headed. It might have had something to do with the febrile atmosphere of wartime – this

[273] Meaning careless or insouciant in matters of law, after the Roman proconsul of Achaia under the Emperor Claudius. SJCA, TU6(8).

[274] As Central Agent in the 1870s Gorst was largely responsible for mobilizing Conservative Party support in urban areas. Afterwards, in the House of Commons, as one of Lord Randolph Churchill's so-called 'Fourth Party', out to harry the old guard of aristocratic Tory leaders, Gorst misbehaved as raucously as he had when an undergraduate. He was also closely involved in social, and especially educational, reform.

Gorst (α) admonished for a noisy party in his rooms, after Hall; some of w.^h were y.^e
the great annoyance & disgust of the neighbourhood; so much so, as
The actual offenders were such of his friends as H. Snow, rathe
thereof immediately sent off to, and inserted in, one of the Cambridge Newspapers, & t

21 In Oct. 1854: the Senior Dean's door is 'screwed up' on the night after he had
intervened to stop a party in the rooms of J. E. Gorst (with friends 'imitating the voices
of strange animals from the windows'), though 'the actual offenders were such of his
friends as H. Snow rather than Gorst himself', it is recorded, indicating the sort of
skill on Gorst's part which, despite 'a vulgar account' of these incidents being conveyed
to the Cambridge and London papers, succeeded in securing for himself election
as M.P. for the University, Honorary Fellowship of College, and membership of ➚

was a year in which the charge of the Light Brigade put all other acts of lunacy
into the shade – or it might simply have been that the cohort harboured more
than the usual number of bottle-heads. At any rate, that was the year when
E. C. Bramall had to be 'admonished' for making 'noises in imitation of cock-
crowing etc. from W. E. Cresswell's window', and when the son of the archdeacon of Chester was rusticated for throwing stones at the Senior Dean's window. 1854 was also the year of a 'noisy midnight party' hosted by Samuel Butler,
whom the authorities clearly considered a pain, but mainly for his persistent
absence from chapel. Three years later, 'maddened by intoxication', the future
astronomer of distinction, R. A. Proctor, 'burnt Dean's door with a candle' and
'insulted the Dean by violent outcries from 2 to 4'. Alcohol-fuelled behaviour
was a constant worry for the Deans, of course. A future judge, W. Beresford,
was rusticated in 1838 for 'habitual intoxication', but one Williams (unidentified)
got away with an imposition eight years later; he was made to write out Paley's
chapter on drunkenness.[275] Students were frequently caught by the proctors and
bulldogs for breaking gates (i.e. going absent without leave). There was 'smoking
and shrieking in the court' (both forbidden), there were japes involving lighted
squibs and illicit fireworks, but surprisingly little fisticuffs (Tom Brown's Rugby
being evidently not a model in this respect). As for the way in which misdemeanours were reported, it is often the incidental details that catch the eye. In
1860–1, for example: 'G. P. Lane accosted a light girl in College grounds; outing
to Cottenham in dog cart. The propriety of this visit much to be questioned.
Had a bugle with them.'[276]

Some of the reasons for students being hauled up seem trifling now: 'Cracking nuts in chapel' (a future Fellow in 1839), 'Fastens anthem slips on surplices
of men in front of him' (a joker in 1871). On the other hand, the authorities

[275] William Paley (1743–1805), theologian and sometime archdeacon of Carlisle, whose
influence in Cambridge was strong and enduring. His *Principles of Moral and Political
Philosophy* (1785) and *Evidences of Christianity* (1794) remained examinable works in
the tripos until the late Victorian period and inter-war years respectively.
[276] Junior Dean's books, SJCA, DS3.2–6; Senior Dean's books, DS4.2–5.

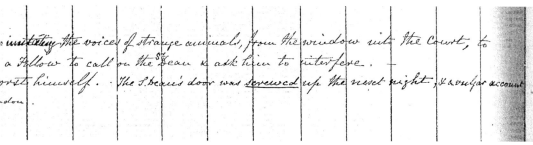

imitating the voices of strange animals, from the window into the Court, to a Fellow to call on the S. Dean & ask him to interfere. — ... himself. The S. Dean's door was screwed up the next night, & a vulgar account ... done.

the Privy Council: SJCA, DS 3.4 (1851–61). In the previous year the miscreant Snow had distinguished himself by frequently firing guns in his rooms; exposing himself 'at his window in unseemly undress with pipe etc.', wearing slippers in the court, again exposing himself with his friends on Port Latin day 'as guests were passing to the Combination Room', and, of course, absenting himself from Chapel. As well as winning a rowing blue, he was elected a Fellow and finished up as Professor of Greek at Durham: ibid.; Venn, II. v. 585

were surprisingly tolerant of firearm misuse. Luxmoore was merely 'reproved for firing a pistol in the grounds', and Tracey was 'advised not to fire pistols in his rooms', both incidents taking place in 1853. Perhaps the previous year's alarms about a possible French invasion made for leniency. Yet Bonney reports that undergraduates were 'constantly, though surreptitiously, shooting' with saloon pistols in the mid-1860s: one miscreant even fired two bullets into Professor Adam Sedgwick's dressing room in Trinity, and got off with an abject apology.[277] But considering the total number of undergraduates in nineteenth-century St John's, the Deans' books record no great catalogue of crime. There is more high-spirited inconsiderateness than wickedness, and the authorities seem to have been suitably indulgent. Indeed, to judge from the reports, only one student *really* got under a Dean's skin.

> J. N. Langley 1875: An unpleasant and rude person; wants to argue in a coolly impudent manner. When spoken to about lolling in an improper manner in chapel on Sunday evening, he demanded, 'Can you show me any written law *against* lolling in chapel?' An exceedingly unpleasant manner.[278]

When someone was to be sent down, the College officers usually did their best to be tactful. In May 1888 an intoxicated freshman, D. Stephens, was 'noisy in Hall and conspicuous in the street'. Knowing that the Junior Dean would rusticate him for the term, his Tutor (Ward) advised him to go down early 'instead of waiting for any formal citation before the Governing Body'. 'I believe the authorities will be satisfied and this will allow the matter to drop.' Stephens was to be allowed to return for a few days to take his examinations, and in a final act of kindness Ward sent the obligatory 'letter home' to his father's

---

[277] Bonney, *Memories*, 101–2.

[278] Later Fellow of Trinity, Professor of Physiology, FRS, and hypnotist, Langley also became 'one of the best skaters in England in the old style'. Devotees of the veteran juvenile William Brown will recognize the self-exculpatory formula: 'It's news to me there's a lor against lolling in Chapel.'

business address (at the son's request).[279] A more serious case arose in 1894 when one evening, shortly before midnight, J. B. Dale appealed to the Junior Dean for protection against J. R. Hole, who had allegedly broken his windows and assaulted his person in the Porter's Lodge. Hole protested his innocence but was condemned on the evidence of a porter, who said he had been 'very excited and evidently the worse for liquor'. The plaintiff, Dale, then begged the Dean to be lenient. 'It would ever be a source of deep regret to me, that the prospects in life of Mr Hole should in any way suffer through me (…) Mr Hole's friends have assured me that he has this term been making a serious effort to reform.'[280] There is no record of Hole being sent down, yet he evidently disappeared without a degree. Presumably he was told to fall on his sword, rather than incur a formal penalty that would blight his 'prospects in life'.

Sometimes it seems as though students were mere pawns in a donnish game. For example, Heitland complained on a famous occasion about noisy behaviour in the Courts, not because he had been discommoded but simply as a way of suggesting that the Deans were failing in their duty to keep the peace. In response the Junior Dean, on gleefully discovering that Heitland's pupils had been among the noisiest, fined them with draconian severity. This had Heitland protesting against decanal dictatorship: 'We have in fact English institutions and Turkish practice.'[281] But while Tutors often sought to protect their pupils against the Deans, whenever possible Tutors and Deans united to protect their charges against prosecution by the police or local council. Such claims to independence in matters of discipline contributed greatly to the resentment habitually felt by town against gown. One such occasion followed the opening concert of the New Corn Exchange in 1875. Several men including Johnians were locked out by the mayor, bailed by their Tutors, then took revenge by smashing the mayor's windows the following night, all of which was much tut-tutted over in the national press.[282] However, the century ended with a signal defeat in this respect. In 1893 the Vice-Chancellor despatched a seventeen-year-old prostitute Daisy Hopkins to the Spinning House for a fortnight. She was shortly released on a technicality and sued unsuccessfully for wrongful imprisonment. Despite the legal victory, the University suffered much adverse publicity, and in the following year it was agreed to surrender the Vice-Chancellor's power to send women to gaol, and also his right to license theatrical entertainments.[283]

The sense of corporate cohesion that had built up over the 1850s and 1860s was retained for the rest of the century, but after about 1870 it had an institutional basis rather than being founded on any one dominant ethos like muscular Christianity, or indeed on a select group of feeder schools. Indeed, a striking

---

[279] SJCA, TU10(5).

[280] J. B. Dale to Caldecott, 9 Jun. 1894, and Caldecott to Charles Taylor, 11 Jun. 1894: SJCA, D92.24.34–5.

[281] Three letters from Heitland to the Master, 16 June 1892: D92.33.4–6.

[282] As still happens, London journalists frequently used Oxford terminology (e.g. 'quad') in their account of Cambridge events.

[283] In 1901 the hated Spinning House was pulled down and a new police station built on the site. See Rowland Parker, *Town and Gown: The 700 Years' War in Cambridge* (Cambridge, 1983), 156.

22 W. E. Heitland in characteristically genial form: SJCL, Port. XIX.8

feature of St John's in the final quarter of the nineteenth century is its increasing heterogeneity, starting with a very wide range of backgrounds. The close-knit circle of schools that had done so much to populate the place in previous decades entirely vanished. It almost seems as though the Tutors adopted a policy of not taking more than one or at most two candidates from a single school. In 1885, for example, the eighty-eight entrants who identified a school in the admissions register came from as many as seventy-one different establishments, in the following year 105 new members came from eighty-eight schools, and these statistics were typical. The smart public schools were now almost invisible. In the cohort of 1881–6, out of 739 freshmen whose school is known, only two were Etonians and only eight came from Rugby.[284] The remainder came from schools all over the country, many of them extremely obscure, though the London schools did relatively well, and also some of the cathedral schools, such as Hereford. This variety of background may help to explain the absence of clique on which contemporaries commented, but another explanation may be that as many as 42 per cent of Johnians admitted during 1881–6 hailed from the northern counties, a much higher percentage than previously.[285] The following

[284] Relations with Rugby had been soured as a result of a 'civil war' (1871–4) in which Bateson, a governor, had played a controversial role in ousting Henry Hayman as headmaster, ostensibly because he was incompetent but really – so many believed – because he was a strong Tory and stout believer in Church defence.

[285] See above, p. 242.

decade brought a marked increase in candidates from overseas – twenty-one out of seventy-nine in 1891 – a welcome resource given the decline in domestic applications.[286]

Table 5 Father's declared status/occupation, 1876, 1881–6, 1891, and 1896

	1876	*1881*	*1886*	*1891*	*1896*
esquires, gents, sirs, barts	11	10	1	4	5
farmers	0	3	2	3	4
clergy	19	15	19	14	10
military	2	2	1	0	0
civil servants, clerks	3	10	9	3	8
law/medicine	14	10	10	10	14
teachers/academics	0	8	11	4	7
merchants/financiers	14	6	12	10	8
manufacturers	6	8	8	0	8
retailers	5	8	5	0	7
skilled artisans		2	3	0	0

Table 5 provides five-yearly snapshots to show the main parental occupations in the later nineteenth century. There is a sprinkling still of manufacturers, artisans,[287] and retailers, but the dominant groups are now civil servants, teachers and academics, lawyers and medics, merchants and financiers. Persons describing themselves simply as esquires or gentlemen fall away sharply after 1881, possibly as a consequence of the agricultural depression, while clergymen, though still well represented, tail off somewhat in the nineties. As for the destinations of those who went down from St John's, the most surprising statistic, and one that surely marks the College out, is the continuing attraction of the Church. Out of 522 persons who were admitted during 1881–6 and whose future occupations are known, 44.4 per cent went on to pursue a religious career, and all but a handful of those became Church of England clergymen.[288] The next most popular categories were school teaching (22.2 per cent), the law (13.8), academia (12.45), and medicine (9.2). These statistics speak for themselves, the main conclusion being that while these students might have had diverse backgrounds, their focus on the future was narrowly concentrated, at least in terms of function. Geographically it was otherwise, since at least 10 per cent went on to have experience of living in India and other parts of the empire, whether as civil servants, teachers, doctors, lawyers, academics, or chaplains.[289] Very few sought careers in manufacturing industry, though the cohort did include A. M. Mond, later Lord Melchett. Graced with family wealth, he did not need a degree and did not take one. Of those who did take degrees, well over a half were content to be 'poll men'. This would change at about the turn of the century, thanks in part to the introduction of attractive new triposes, and by the time of the First

---

[286] See below, p. 382.

[287] One freshman described his father's occupation as 'Engineer (engine-driver)'.

[288] That ratio was maintained in 1891 but fell to 24.3 per cent in 1896. As before, schoolteachers in Holy Orders have been counted twice.

[289] Special encouragement was given to candidates for the Indian Civil Service: Miller, *Portrait of a College*, 93.

23 The Eagles Club in their second year, 1883; the taller man in the
window is C. Aubrey Smith: SJCL, Album 16/9

World War almost everyone would go on to graduate, two-thirds of them with
honours.

In terms of what the future held in store for him, the most colourful member
of the cohort must surely have been Charles Aubrey Smith. He was a famous
cricketer for the University and then for Sussex, an awkward left-arm seamer
who was nick-named 'Round-the-Corner Smith' because of an exaggeratedly
sloping run, which led W. G. Grace to complain that he could not see him
coming. Although pronounced dead by doctors on one occasion while prospect-
ing for gold in South Africa, he recovered well enough to captain an England
eleven (and play in one test match) there and in Australia. He worked during the late Victorian and Edwardian years as an actor and actor manager in
the West End, and was commercially successful if less so critically. (For one
performance he was accused of a 'trivializing lack of inner seriousness' by the
critic Max Beerbohm, hardly a very solemn person himself.) Acting led Aubrey
Smith to Broadway on many occasions, then to Hollywood and the movies,
first silent, then sound. He appeared in scores of films as a character actor, his
'character' being the stereotypical English officer and gentleman, making him
the forerunner of David Niven, whose early talent he fostered. Whatever might
have been the case with Niven, it is clear that Aubrey Smith required no talents
as an actor to succeed in such roles. He soon became the accepted leader of the
'Hollywood Raj', a sour reference to the way in which British actors were seen to
be colonizing Hollywood in the 1930s. His greatest passion in these later years
was to keep alive in America the flame of cricket by more or less insisting that

every visiting Englishman turn out for his side. There is a story that on dropping a sitter of a catch in the slips he called to his butler for his glasses, which were duly brought to him on a silver platter. Then, dropping an even easier catch off the very next ball, he expostulated, 'Damned fool brought my reading glasses!' It is surely pertinent to wonder what Bishop Selwyn would have made of this tall and handsome Johnian doing his best to propagate the values of an English gentleman, not in Bangalore but in Beverly Hills.[290]

An Order of 1880 prescribing new rules of admission confirms the impression gained from correspondence that, from 1870 onwards, Tutors began to show more of a concern for scholarly ability. In addition to being certified as of 'good moral character', all candidates were now to have evidence of 'attainments' from a public examining body or headmaster, failing which it would be necessary to pass a College entrance examination in classics and mathematics.[291] This increased emphasis on the likely tripos performance of pensioners exacerbated concerns that had already begun to be felt with regard to the role of sizars. In the past many of them had gone on to be Scholars, Fellows, even occasionally Masters, but the situation had changed since 1860 when nearly all colleges made open scholarships and minor exhibitions available to persons not already in residence. The cleverest and most assiduous of the poorer students naturally forsook sizarships for these new awards, which were usually more valuable and carried status rather than stigma. The consequence was a remarkable shift in the percentage of Fellows who started out as sizars. Of the 194 Fellows elected between 1801 and 1840, 126 had been admitted as pensioners and sixty-eight as sizars. There had then followed the heyday of the academic sizar, the decades 1841–60, during which fifty-one of their number became Fellows as against forty-nine pensioners. To put that another way, and taking the 1850s alone, 11.6 per cent of those admitted as sizars went on to be Fellows, but only 3.5 per cent of pensioners, a remarkable difference when it is remembered that the latter category included most of those who won scholarships.[292] But then in the 1860s the picture changed, only nineteen sizars making it into the Fellowship as against forty pensioners, and their success rate continued to decline in the following decades. By the later 1870s the fiercely anticlerical Heitland was thundering against 'laxity in election of sizars', and he used his memoirs to denounce those clerical Fellows who were exploiting the system to foist a Cambridge degree (and passport to preferment) on humble boys simply because they were willing to enter the Church of England.[293]

One of the Fellows whom Heitland had in mind must have been Torry, who

---

[290] David Rayvern Allen, *Sir Aubrey: Biography of Charles Aubrey Smith, England Cricketer, West End Actor, Hollywood Film Star* (London, 1982).

[291] As all scholars and other award-holders had had to do since 1860: CB, 7 May 1880.

[292] The sizars' academic achievements clearly did not prevent Samuel Butler (matriculated 1854) from disparaging them in *The Way of All Flesh* (see above, pp. 245, 256–7), but one indication that their status might have improved, at least temporarily, is that in 1856 the blackballing of a sizar from the Lady Margaret Boat Club on snobbish grounds led to widespread protest among the undergraduates, and to the setting up of a rival society, the Lady Somerset (1856–61).

[293] Heitland, *After Many Years*, 107–8.

strongly defended the system on the grounds that it made the College 'one of the chief nurseries of the Church's ministers'.[294] He admitted that the examination performance of sizars had fallen, for the simple reason that many of those who in previous years had obtained firsts as sizars were now minor scholars instead. It was therefore a legitimate question to ask

> Are we doing any good in using these Sizarships as an inducement or encouragement to men to come up, if they are only to obtain a 3rd Class in Honours? I have no hesitation in saying that the Sizarships are *well-used* with this purpose. For 1) There are few men for whom there is a greater demand than these inferior honour men. Not so much as Curates – though there is a scarcity of them – as for under masters in Schools. And 2) Many of them are the sons of ill paid professional men, who, as a Class, know better how to value, and can least afford, the advantages of the Universities. But 3) if many of them are raised from a lower position to be brought up here, so much the better. These are the men, having some ability above others in their station, who would become Masters or Tutors, and perhaps struggle through the examinations of London or of Dublin University, and who will make all the better Masters or Tutors for having been at the University.[295]

In the event sizarships were not abandoned but their holders came under increasing surveillance. An Order of 1877, for example, announced stringent conditions for continuing on the list. In order to retain his entitlement to reduced fees, a sizar was required at the end of his second year to be in one of the first two classes of the College examination in his special subject, or else in the first class of the general examination for the ordinary degree. He also had to be certified by the Master and Tutors as 'economic in his habits', and 'regular in his attendance at lectures'. Another Order in the following year stipulated the need for 'such a standard of attainment and ability as may be consistent with a fair probability of an University Honour being reached at the end of the Course'.[296] Then in 1899 the number of sizarships was reduced to nine, and payments by allowances abandoned.[297] Emphasis was placed instead on entrance exhibitions, though before the twentieth century these were almost all restricted to classics and mathematicians.

As strictly academic matters came to be regarded as the province of the lecturing staff, so the Tutors' pastoral role came to seem more important socially. It has often been said that the Tutorship of John Hymers (1832–53) marked 'an era', and certainly that accomplished mathematician and dedicated teacher had won much affection, but he had remained personally aloof, as had Brumell, Crick, and most others in the earlier period. Later Tutors, by contrast, were expected to play a much bigger public role in the life of the College and to be – at least in appropriate circumstances – familiar with their pupils. There being no College

---

[294] A. F. Torry, *College Economy and University Extension: A Letter to the Master of St John's College, Cambridge* (Cambridge & London, 1868), 14.

[295] A. F. Torry, 'Sizarships and sizarship examinations', 10 Oct. ?1879: SJCA, D104.68.

[296] College Orders on sizarships, 29 Nov. 1877 and 12 Nov. 1878: SJCA, D104.68.

[297] Howard, *Finances*, 223.

nurse or sanitorium, Tutors were also obliged to tend the sick *in loco parentis*, and many such as Heitland did this conscientiously. At the other extreme was Donald MacAlister, whose clinical duties and heavy teaching load in the natural sciences forced him to skimp on the pastoral side of his work, but whose charismatic persona won respect and affection nevertheless.

Hall was the social centre at which the 300 young men hailing from almost as many schools were made to gel, encouraged by alcohol and 'the proverbial "cold gooseberry" of everyday experience'.[298] It was not a very decorous affair, as J. M. Wilson recollected many decades later:

> The dinners in Hall, at 4 p.m., were very expensive and unless one 'sized', *i.e.*, ran up a heavy bill for vegetables and pudding and cheese, they were meagre and ill-served, as well as abominably dear. The joints were placed at intervals on the long tables and the men carved for themselves, for the most part execrably. I have seen a leg a mutton so mangled by the first comer – whom I could name – that no one who came after him could get a well-cut slice from it.[299]

In 1880 it was felt necessary to remind students that they could not take in their own drink (or food), but twice a year, on St John's Day and 6 May, as well as at the Guest Table at other times, they were allowed to order either a pint of claret or a half pint of sherry from the Buttery, as well as similar quantities for their guests. Occasionally things got out of hand, as whenever the Boat Club had to be told off for cheering following a successful row. When Russell was Steward (1865–9) there was a proliferation of petty regulations to be '*strictly observed*', a reminder that those were the days when College was most like school: 'No sizings to be allowed except beer. Joints be not pushed about the table, no one leave Hall till all at the same table are finished, no changing of Hall except by swapping with someone from the other Hall, that you be punctual arriving.'[300] In May 1866 it was promulgated that junior members might not be absent from Hall, nor (despite its recent extension) might they introduce friends from other colleges, a ruling that would have reinforced the inward-looking atmosphere of College life at this time. Russell was a notoriously fussy man, and it is unclear how strictly or for how long attendance at dinner remained compulsory, but it might explain the popularity of private breakfasts.

> A favourite meal was breakfast, a most elaborate affair, at which sometimes as many as ten or a dozen undergraduates would sit down to a copious spread. Beginning at 9, they would not break up till 11 or later. Cups of various kinds and strengths, from cider and claret to ale and 'copas', passed round after the duty of eating was solemnly discharged, and tobacco and lively talk conducted the party to an end.[301]

[298] 'Diary of Joseph Timmis Ward', 6 May 1875: SJCL, W2. In 1884 the Council unanimously agreed to Heitland's motion that sizars should no longer be required to dine at a separate table and at a separate hour: CM, 80/20 (3 Oct. 1884).

[299] J. M. Wilson, 'H. J. Roby', *Eagle* xxxvi (1914–15), 203.

[300] Russell, 'Diary of events', 2 Dec. 1868: SJCL, U22.

[301] Heitland, *After Many Years*, 115–16.

It was also in the 1860s, according to Heitland, that students took to taking wines after Hall 'in imitation of the dons'. Much older and perhaps wiser, he affirmed that liquor had played a larger part in daily life in 1870, when there was far more drunkenness than in 1920.[302]

There is always a danger in relying on old men's memories. Unfortunately, very few undergraduate letters home survive in the archives for this period, but some that do are instructive. Written without artifice by bored young men straining for something to say, they contain details of day-to-day existence that would otherwise be unrecoverable. Particularly helpful, because written by a man whom the Victorians would have regarded as perfectly commonplace, is a batch of thirty letters from Abbott Notcutt of Ipswich.[303] While it is impossible to know just how representative he was, his accounts of goings-on suggest that Johnians were now a fairly outward-looking tribe, especially as compared with the earlier and more intense generation of Bateson, the Mayors, Hutton, and Shaw. Many of Notcutt's missives are simple calls for advice, such as 'How often ought I to change cloth and dinner napkin? Once a week or fortnight?', and 'Is there any danger of catching *consumption* from a man who has had it or is recovering from it or has it?' There is a great deal about his eating habits. Having ordered two plates of meat first thing from the huge range of items available from the kitchens, 'I eat as much breakfast as I can without getting sick' (this by way of reassurance to a mother whose worry was that he would become undernourished). Half a fourpenny loaf spread with treacle and a pint of milk usually kept him going during the day, with the occasional treat such as arrowroot biscuits from home (the main source of his popularity apparently). Then Hall in the evening (he liked the gooseberries, except when they were buried in boiled rice), some beer, phosphorus whenever he has a cold, then bed at 11.15 p.m. He contracts fewer colds in his third year, his Tutor (Heitland) having awarded him capital rooms at the top of the north-eastern corner of Second Court: 'rather low' but 'very large' and with views of both sunrise and sunset. They cost him £17 for the year with another £8 for his gyp, and they have to be furnished, a realization which reminds him with some force that he is a burden on his grandpapa, who is financing his studies. However, he is not a man who can keep remorse up for very long. 'I am afraid it is very doubtful whether I shall do well enough to get [a scholarship] at Xmas but I shall of course do my best; so many of the men here that get scholarships seem to do nothing but work and are rather wretched sort of beings. I shall try and do seven hours a day[304] and keep in good health' (this last a cunning touch, given his mother's apparent anxieties on the subject). In March 1884 he decides to begin shaving 'as I don't like to appear untidy'.

Although by no means an assiduous scholar, Notcutt seems to have entered on the Natural Sciences tripos dutifully enough, while also 'cramming up Paley'. He enjoyed physiology, whether dissecting worms and dogfish or listening

---

[302] Heitland, review of Bonney's *Memories*, 286.

[303] Stephen Abbott Notcutt to his mother, Oct. 1883–Nov. 1885: SJCL, GBR/0275/Notcutt/A1–30. His most inventive excuse for not having written home sooner was the additional legwork caused by the introduction of inter-collegiate lectures.

[304] Assuming that he stuck to it, this compared favourably with the future Fellow T. R. Glover's six to seven hours in the Lent term of 1892: below, p. 650.

to Michael Foster lecture, and he kept his end up in physics, chemistry, and mathematics, but knowing that he intended to become a solicitor, he was keen to switch to law after one year. Unfortunately his grandfather, the paymaster, wanted him to do two years of natural sciences in the hope that he would gain a higher class and win a scholarship. The subsequent letter home had therefore to be very circumspectly argued. He reasoned that if he could only read law in his second year, he would be able to hear Kenny lecture on personal property, and since Kenny was 'far and away the best and clearest lecturer', attendance at his lectures would prevent the need for an expensive coach. However, 'it is not likely, considering the number of other subjects there are for the Law, that he will lecture on personal property again till after the tripos of 1886, so *if* I go in for the Law tripos in 1886, I must go to Kenny now *or* have a coach later on.' Furthermore, although this course of action would lessen his chance of winning a scholarship, it would give him the option of fancy degrees ('I should be able to get a B.A. or Ll.B. or both degrees and might afterwards take M.A. or Ll.M. or both and afterwards perhaps Ll.D.'), which in turn might allow him to skip two expensive years of articles. It is a brilliant letter of a lawyerly kind. Detailed and exact on non-essentials, vague but optimistic on the crucial points, it put the pressure on grandpapa by requesting an immediate answer (because Kenny's lectures started next Thursday), and it implied without actually saying that his Tutor was in agreement.[305] Which very possibly he would have been, since Heitland wrote to Mrs Notcutt at one point, 'Pray do not hurry yourself about the Bill. Your son is one of those who may be safely left mainly to their own judgment ... He is a right good fellow.'[306]

Outside the classroom Abbott attended Union Society debates in the evening, heard Joe Chamberlain, joined in the side-splitting laughter at a fiery Irish speaker, heard a brilliant speech from H. J. Hyndman (ex-Trinity) proposing socialism (and opposed by a Johnian). He went to a performance of *Elektra* at Girton, attended Unitarian meetings, conversed with 'one of the coloured men, such a nice fellow', sang Gilbert and Sullivan songs, read the newspapers avidly, kept abreast of public affairs and local politics in Ipswich. But his great obsession was sport. He played football every day for weeks on end, despite the filthy state of the College pitch, and cricket every day for a week, scoring his first century (110 not out) against Caius. (Whether he ever played with or against 'Round-the-Corner Smith' is not recorded.) He felt stiff after running with the Hare & Hounds ('never again'), and was thrilled to be elected to the Hawks Club (despite which mother still believed him to be sickly). All this serves as a reminder that, while comparisons are hard to establish, St John's was a fairly sporty college. In 1855 it is said to have inaugurated athletic sports with its 'Johnians (only) Derby' held on Fenner's Ground. The events included flat and hurdle races, high and long jumps, throwing the cricket ball, 'sixteen hops', and putting a 14 lb stone.[307] Three years later St John's decided to take advan-

---

[305] Notcutt to his mother, 29 Jan. 1884: SJCL, GBR/0275/Notcutt/A5.

[306] Heitland to Mrs Notcutt, 20 Jan. 1885: SJCL, GBR/0275/Notcutt/A34.

[307] J. R. Jackson, 'The first Athletic Sports in Cambridge', *Eagle* xvi (1890–1), 358–61; Searby, *History of the University of Cambridge*, III. 646.

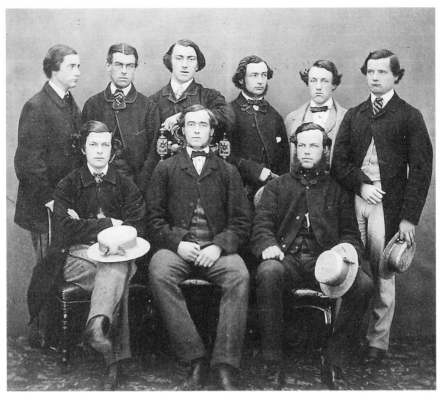

24 An LMBC crew (?1858) including Samuel Butler, standing second left, and Henry Hoare (son of Chapel Tower Hoare), second right: SJCL, Album 14/24 (with the ascription 'Second Lent Boat 1859', which does not correspond with the LMBC crew lists for that term)

tage of its large land holdings west of the river, and became the first college to lay out a playing field. Although cricket and rowing continued to dominate until about 1880, and the May Bumps remained a seasonal highlight of fun and frolic ('crews falling in the river etc.'), there were now at least a dozen different sports that could be said to be 'organized'. Nor was the College even then averse to low cunning. According to an early number of the *Eagle*, on one occasion 'the Corpus men had rather the worst of a closely contested match'. Even so, 'had it not been for the ingenious manœuvre of Mr. Phillips [St John's], who persuaded one of the Corpus men to kick the ball through his own goal, the match might have ended in a tie'.[308]

Possibilities of a different kind of sport opened up with the founding of Newnham and Girton Colleges. It meant the arrival of eligible girls in Cambridge, and must have given new urgency to the tracts that had long been sent to freshmen every October, exhorting them to chastity.[309] Joseph Timmis Ward BA met some girls – his account suggests that it was for the first time – at one

[308] Anon, 'Our Chronicle', *Eagle* vi (1867–9), 254–6.
[309] Heitland, *After Many Years*, 191.

of Dr Bateson's 'perpendiculars'. The latter term was used by students to indicate a stand-up party, generally thought to be very stiff affairs, though this one was meant to be enlivened by two square dances. Ward took part coyly, but recorded that most of the young men present just stared.[310] Notcutt seems to have had more fun on a trip to London a decade later. '2 of the Major girls were there and we all drove to Albion St; the dance was managed splendidly, good music and plenty of introductions. I danced almost every dance; the dances consisted *entirely* of valses with the exception of one solitary lancers (...) I managed to accommodate my step to the prevailing one.'[311] It seems, however, that Cambridge gradually loosened up, sufficiently at least for the introduction of an annual May Ball in the 1890s, after which London girls began to come to Cambridge instead of Cambridge boys going down to London.

Two small events in 1883 may be regarded as pointers to the future. The first was the decision to establish a forum for missionary work in London. After a series of very full and enthusiastic meetings in the Hall, it was agreed that the College should pay for a curate to be attached to a parish in one of the more populous parts of London.[312] This modest response to the 'rediscovery of poverty' in Britain's industrial cities suggests that the Johnian ideal of mission was not dead, but it was now concentrated on home rather than overseas, and on social needs ahead of purely spiritual ones. Then, six months later, a very full meeting of the College Debating Society considered the motion 'that in the opinion of this House the Church of England should be disestablished and disendowed'. It comes as no surprise that the motion was lost, but what might surprise is the narrowness of the margin: 48 votes to 30 with 17 abstentions. If the College had not yet become a secular institution, it was clearly no longer an unthinking adjunct of the Church establishment.

8.   FROM CLERGYMEN TO DONS?

When I became a Fellow, some 24 years ago, I passed into a society very different from the present one ... There were doubtless among the Fellows many men of high merit. But of intimate friendship between them, there was, I venture to say, very little. There was much agreement in what we call 'views', but hardly any sympathy. I do not imagine that the elder men had a notion how dreadful this seemed to a new Fellow, fresh from Undergraduate life.

W. E. Heitland, 'Josiah Brown Pearson', *Eagle*, xix (1895–7), 87–91

The title of this section is something of a cliché but is justified in St John's case, not least by the shift that took place in the nature of Fellows' subsequent careers. As Peter Searby has demonstrated, not one of those elected between 1800 and 1870 later become a landed gentleman in the sense of relying on rentals for a

---

[310] 'Diary of Joseph Timmis Ward', 28 Feb. 1876: SJCL, W2.
[311] Notcutt to his mother, 21 Jan. 1885: SJCL, GBR/0275/Notcutt/A/18.
[312] Russell, 'Diary of events', 23 Apr., 7 and 8 May 1883: SJCL, U22.

living, and very few entered public life, the military, or business of any kind.[313]
Forty-five became doctors or lawyers, but the only striking development was
a switch, at about the middle of the nineteenth century, from becoming an
Anglican clergyman or reverend schoolmaster to becoming a career academic or
a lay school teacher.

Table 6 Final career choices of St John's Fellows, 1800–70

	1801–10	*1811–20*	*1821–30*	*1831–40*	*1841–50*	*1851–60*	*1861–70*
clergy	35	30	31	38	26	10	11
academic	3	4	6	6	24	21	33

Whenever they were not engaged in seeking to advance or resist the cause of
reform, many Fellows had lives to lead as scholars and reverend gentlemen, but
what that entailed in practice changed considerably as the ideal of an academic
profession began gradually to emerge. Searby has also analysed the meagre publication record of the St John's Fellows as exemplifying the fact that dons then
did not, and were not expected to, further the cause of learning by writing books
and papers,[314] but subsequently, as expectations rose, so did output. Indeed, in
the final third of the century the Fellows of St John's could be described as
prolific. And whereas in 1854 there was only one FRS among fifty-four Fellows,
in 1910–11 sixteen out of forty-six were either FRS or FBA. At the other end of
the scale, Bonney contemptuously dismissed about one-fifth of the mid-century
Fellows as 'men of no account', yet that particular species was almost (though
not quite) extinct by 1900.[315]

And yet, considering its size St John's cannot be said to have brimmed
with intellectual distinction in the nineteenth century. Probably only Herschel, Adams, Bateson junior, and Marshall were indisputably of the first rank,
though a strong case might be made for Weldon.[316] This is not a big tally considering the abundance of great minds elsewhere in Cambridge: Maine, Maitland, Frazer, Hort, Westcott, Lightfoot, Whewell, Sidgwick, Smyth, Stephen,
Kingsley, Seeley, Munro, Porson, Jebb, Housman, Milner, Sedgwick, Clerk
Maxwell, Stokes, Kelvin, Thomson, Foster, Balfour, and Clifford, to name but
a few and not to mention such briefer presences as Darwin and Babbage. Cru-
cially, St John's never spawned a constellation of talent such as formed in Trinity

---

[313] Searby, *History of the University of Cambridge*, III. 741 (App. VIII a). One of Todhunter's axioms was that the men who narrowly failed to be elected to a Fellowship were
often those who went on to achieve most in life.

[314] Ibid., III. 111–17, 744 (App. IX a, b). Searby's aim is to describe rather than point an
anachronistic finger. Even so it seems harsh to designate Bateson as 'non-publishing'
('research inactive' in today's terminology), just as it does to credit Reyner with only
two short works and the following reproof: '[It] leaves us wondering how he did
spend his time after discharging his duties as a college lecturer in mathematics.'

[315] Bonney, *Memories*, 39.

[316] This discussion excludes persons whose work mainly came to fruition in the twentieth century, such as the algebraic geometer H. F. Baker. Nevertheless, it is worth
noting that his presence during the closing decades of the century, like that of the
physicist Joseph Larmor, who worked in parallel with J. J. Thompson and in some
respects prefigured Einstein, was evidence of a new intellectual edge in the College.

in the 1830s around Whewell, Hare, Sedgwick, and Peacock. Such clusters can develop accidentally, the result perhaps of one person's ability to germinate imagination in others, and so there is no point in seeking explanations, especially as one of the more plausible reasons hitherto adduced does not on close inspection seem convincing. This is the suggestion that the gift of £12,000 by John Piggott in 1810–11 'enabled [Trinity] to improve the value of its livings at the same time as it was made more unusual for them to be held with Fellowships, and [so] helped to promote the circulation of Fellowships, and to ensure that *only those stayed on who wanted to do so for academic reasons*'.[317] Now, it is not a straightforward matter to compute the relative value of the livings attached to different colleges, but inspection of the published *Clergy Lists* and tithe accounts does not suggest that Trinity's crop offered more tempting financial rewards than those of St John's. On the contrary, the higher dividends available in that college might have led to *greater* retention of Fellowships. Nor would it seem that Fellowships turned over more slowly in St John's, where, between 1824 and 1854 the average duration was less than eight years (though that blurs the difference between those few Fellows who stayed for life and the vast majority who came and went within a year or two). A more meaningful statistic is that the average annual number of vacancies was 4.66. Just three persons elected during the 1820s retained their Fellowship for more than twenty-two years, while of the forty-seven-strong 1830s cohort, three exceeded twenty years, forty served from sixteen to eighteen years, and eight left within three years. It amounted to quite a rapid turnover, and suggests that one cannot blame what Heitland called 'the drowsy simplicity' (and Marx might have called the 'idiocy') of College life for any intellectual shortcomings there might have been.

A real change occurred after 1840. Whereas of eighty Foundation Fellows elected during the years 1811–40, only seventeen remained for more than twenty-five years, thirty out of the 100 elected during 1841–70 did so. This clearly signals the emergence of the 'professional' academic career (to adopt Heitland's approving term), a development that was given further impetus by the provision made for limited six-year Fellowships in the 1860 Statutes. That initiative is not referred to in the earlier section on academic reform, simply because it did not challenge vested rights and therefore did not make a stir. On the contrary it was insinuated into place without much remark. Yet its longer-term implications were profound, as the ever-perceptive Heitland noted.

> For many a long day it had not unnaturally been usual to regard College endowments as a permanent provision for those who won a share in them. Either a man (unmarried of course) remained a Fellow for life, or he went off to a College Living or some other preferment. Tenure for a limited term of years (...) was a new notion.[318]

And it meant, of course, that if he wished to remain a Fellow he had just six years in which to establish the scholarly credentials that could win him a

---

[317] Robert Robson, 'Trinity College in the age of Peel', in Robert Robson (ed.), *Ideas and Institutions of Victorian Britain: Essays in Honour of George Kitson Clark*, (1967), 320 [italics added].

[318] Heitland, *After Many Years*, 146.

lectureship or similar preferment. Another important step towards academic professionalization was taken in 1883 when it was decreed that candidates for Fellowships should submit dissertations or other writings as evidence of independent work, indicating in a cover note wherein lay its originality. Candidates who did not submit written work were informed that they could expect to be examined, either in writing or *viva voce*.

The ways in which certain Fellows contributed intellectually will be considered in what follows, but first it will be well to remember that being a don rather than a clergyman did not just have scholarly implications. It also meant acting a part and behaving in a particular kind of way. Judged by these criteria the Fellowship does not seem to have been a very donnish place at the mid-century. New arrivals were frequently disappointed, and quickly missed the wit and intellectual brilliance of the scholars' table.

> The conversation [at High Table] is certainly no improvement to that at the bachelor's table which was always free and unconstrained for we who knew each other sat always in the same place so that there were 5 or 6 talking together always. At the Fellows' table we sit according as we go in and so often get next stupid or disagreeable men.[319]

By contrast, during the last three decades of the century St John's must have had one of the liveliest common rooms in Cambridge, though admittedly that assessment is based in large part on Terrot Reaveley Glover's nostalgic (albeit barbed) account in *Cambridge Retrospect*. There was certainly no shortage of eccentrics. First prize must go to the man with the 'gleaming, bright, kind eyes', John Mayor,[320] about whom there is only space here to include two of the most famous anecdotes. Finding one day that his copy of Lewis and Short's *Latin Dictionary* was nowhere to be found, he jumped at once to the conclusion that it had been stolen by rival scholars, probably Germans, anxious to set their eyes on many years' worth of Mayor's own marginal emendations, annotations, and corrections. All the likely booksellers in Europe were put onto the alert, when in fact all that had happened was that his bedmaker had used the volume to prop up an ailing chest of drawers. The second story relates to Mayor's diet. He famously subsisted throughout each day on twopenn'orth of food (prunes, a biscuit, and a glass of lemonade), and as a passionate vegetarian he ate very sparingly in Hall. However, one of the cooks was said to comment to G. G. Coulton, 'Prof. Mayor, Sir, 'e thinks 'e eats nothing but vegetables: but we allus puts something in to keep 'im up.' He was also exceptionally unworldly, tutting incredulously on one occasion after being informed that 'many of the football men (…) had libraries of less than 2,000 books'. In telling the story Glover commented, 'This last was true.' Glover's summing up was dismissive: 'Mayor as a professor was virtually useless to students or to the College; except as a lovable, discursive, irrelevant survival of the past (…) People liked him as "a dear old thing", but he was not really a factor in anyone's affairs.'[321]

---

[319] Joe Mayor to his mother, 1852: Mayor Papers, B8/354.

[320] Fellow, 1849–1910; University Librarian, 1864–7; Kennedy Professor of Latin, 1872–1910.

[321] Glover, *Cambridge Retrospect*, 85–8.

Glover was particularly contemptuous of Mayor as a lecturer, producing unstoppable streams of deep but irrelevant learning, wholly unfocused, unargued, and useless for tripos purposes. And certainly he could be boring on pet subjects, such as the lives of Spanish Protestants for whom he harboured a passion that went beyond his habitual antiquarianism. But Glover was much too young to have known Mayor as an ardent romantic. As a young man he had been thrilled by Carlyle's books ('there is so much truth in them, and hatred'), and it was from them that he imbibed the message that 'the greatest good which can fall to a man is labour'. In this he resembled so many early-to-mid-Victorians. Indeed, it was one source of their prodigious activity and vitality. 'If you have men to fight against who you know have a clear aim which they never lose sight of, yourself the while not steadfast, "waiting to see what may turn up", you cannot expect to get the better.'[322] Heitland referred fondly to Mayor's 'sympathetic innocence' and 'humankindness', while his brother Joe remarked half exasperatedly that he was 'overflowing with schemes which he urges upon every one'.[323] His many public campaigns for 'bettering the world' included temperance, vegetarianism, anti-vivisection, animal rights, hygiene, spelling reform (he wished to strike out Latin derivatives), and Pestalozzian object lessons (in place of the utilitarian 3 R's). He even hoped to persuade aristocrats and gentry to act in a 'Christ-like' way by converting their country mansions into retreats for weary and downtrodden city folk.[324] This might have been Utopian, but at least it saved him from the muscular Christian priggishness of his brothers. He was certainly not a man to succumb to any sort of collegiate ethos.

More sinisterly eccentric was the historian J. B. Mullinger,[325] who had served a term in prison in 1871 after having attacked his sister-in-law with a carving knife. 'Always eccentric in his conduct', according to Venn, 'many stories were current about his intolerance of the slightest noise when lecturing and of his threats to those with whom he came unexpectedly in contact.' There was also the fastidious Peter Mason.[326] While serving as President during twenty years of great controversy, he hardly ever voted. Heitland told Glover that 'the old man's elaborate and gesturing old-world politeness had no relation with any old-world manners, but was his own absurd invention', and Glover agreed that 'it was certainly odd (…) But he was not as simple as he looked. Heitland maintained that the simplicity concealed a foxy cunning.'[327]

---

[322] John Mayor to his mother, 1845–6: Mayor Papers, B8/218, 224; Heitland, *After Many Years*, 177. There is an early portrait of him looking more like Garibaldi or an Italian brigand than the Old Testament prophet of later years.

[323] Joseph Mayor to his mother, *c.* 1853: Mayor Papers, B8/372.

[324] J. E. B. Mayor, *Social Changes in Sixty Years* (Manchester, 1897).

[325] University Lecturer in History 1894–1909; below, pp. 450, 481.

[326] Fellow, 1854–1912; Hebrew Lecturer, 1854–1901; Dean, 1864–82; President, 1882–1902; below, pp. 411–12.

[327] Glover, *Cambridge Retrospect*, 81–2.

Which brings in William Heitland himself, the common-room irritant[328] who has been encountered in many guises already – as perceptive commentator, academic reformer, Tutor, Junior Bursar – but whose most important role, according to Glover, was that of 'a character', 'an oddity', 'at once a terror and a delight'. 'The extraordinary freakish humour, the genial fun, the savage fun, the quip, the verse, the incalculable angle, made him always interesting; you were always watching.' One of the first lay Fellows – the abolition of tests came just in time, for he was firmly opposed to his family's wish that he should take Orders – Heitland was above all a self-dramatist, 'apt to be stormy and invariably tragic'. But, on getting to know him, one found

> friendship, humour, irritation, industry, geniality, and once more the tragic touch; things, especially in College, were apt to be *pessimi exempli*. He was periodically immensely vext at things and people in College, and, when he was vext, people knew it; but a kindliness co-existed with his irritability [as when he sat up three nights with his very sick tutorial pupil Dicky Benthall (...) If a tutorial pupil shifted his chair in his daily consultation sessions by so much as an inch there would be a cry of pain, (...) [but] he stood by his pupils, when he was clear that they were right and straight, whether clever or not.[329]

He could certainly be boorish. 'If there was to be breakfast in the Combination Room, it might (...) be planned to go on from 8 a.m. to 6 p.m., and then Heitland would turn up at 5.55 p.m., and if he did not find a sufficient supply of forks, things, we can believe, would be *pessimi exempli* and so forth.' He could fly off the handle if someone inadvertently blocked out his light, yet when a notoriously clumsy colleague flung coffee over his trousers, Heitland genially said that that was why he wore trousers.[330] He averred on every possible occasion that he would rather have been a Fellow of Trinity, but only in a 'because he knows it teases' sort of way. In turn the teased learned how to exploit his contrarian tendencies by urging him to do the opposite of what they really wished him to. Towards the end of the century and beyond he would refer gnomically to the 'great hurt' that had been done unto him, but no one could figure out what he referred to. Possibly his having been asked, or not asked, or asked in the wrong way, to help out with classics teaching in the 1890s when times were difficult, or possibly he was referring to the strange affair of the pillar box.[331] When he was seriously ill in 1893, 'to all appearance dying of typhoid fever', the undergraduate occupants of his New Court staircase all had to hush until he got better – which they willingly did, for he was larger than life and a genuine character.[332]

---

[328] Fellow, 1871–1935; Lecturer in Classics, 1871–85; Tutor, 1883–93; Junior Bursar, 1886–1901. His only rival for the role of irritant was George Bonney, who was certainly mouthy, being described by one of his colleagues as a 'great trencherman' and overawing most of them with his volubility, but he was less capricious than Heitland and also less caustic.

[329] Glover, *Cambridge Retrospect*, 38–9, 42.

[330] Ibid., 43, 56.

[331] See below, p. 390.

[332] Heitland, *After Many Years*, 119.

25 E. H. Palmer, Fellow,
Professor of Arabic, secret
agent, murdered 1882.
SJCL, Album 1/34

Every successful common room should contain a mystic. The most colourful and, in Heitland's opinion, most extraordinary of nineteenth-century Fellows was Edward Palmer. As a local boy, and having no mother to caution him
otherwise, he had played with the gypsies in the wood a good deal, and had
picked up any number of exotic accomplishments, including fluent Romani.
Later as clerk to a London wine merchant he swiftly acquired through conversation various French and Italian dialects. He mingled in prominent theatrical circles, including those of Henry Irving, and became one of the most
powerful mesmerists of the *demi-monde*. Then, back in Cambridge owing to a
consumptive illness, he befriended the local teacher of Hindustani, following
which his progress in any number of near eastern languages was 'phenomenally
rapid'. The prodigy came to the notice of Newbery and Todhunter, Fellows of St
John's, who secured his admission as a sizar in 1863. 'His was a case in which the
College system shewed what it could do best', wrote Heitland long afterwards.
Noticing him for the first time in chapel, Bonney was struck by his 'broad and
ample forehead, delicate features, and rather prominent eyes'.[333] While an
undergraduate, Palmer's extraordinary ability in difficult languages became so
obvious that, despite getting only a third class in classics, he was rewarded with

[333] Bonney, *Memories*, 106–12.

a Fellowship in 1867. Almost immediately he went off to Sinai for the Palestine Exploration Fund, got to know and empathize with Arabs, and learned their languages. He subsequently walked the 600 miles from Sinai to Jerusalem, then to Lebanon and Damascus, and wrote detailed accounts of his experiences under the title *The Desert of the Exodus: journeys on foot in the wilderness of the Forty Years' Wanderings* (1871). (He published much else besides – scientific findings, gazetteers, inscriptions, histories, dictionaries, grammars, transliterations, and translations, most famously of the Koran – all of them interesting but also unconventional and prone to 'unscholarliness'.) He returned into residence and put in a stint as Lord Almoner's Professor of Arabic (1871–82). Described as 'bubbling over with natural mirth', he must have brought great joy and good cheer to the Combination Room, not least because he was the most remarkable conjuror. 'In a crowded room with men touching his elbows he would perform trick after trick, completely baffling the curiosity of the company, doing things that noted professionals would only attempt behind a special table and at some little distance.'[334] He could also draw. But though himself an entertainer, Palmer unsurprisingly found both the lifestyle and his duties dull. He held aloof from the bitter struggles of the day,[335] and according to Heitland he 'loathed' all College meetings.

> What concerns me here is my recollection of him as a singularly unacademic character in an Academic setting (…) There was one emotion – Surprise – which nothing ever seemed able to arouse in him: the commonplace limits of the possible and probable were ignored with unruffled calm. He could give quite different versions of a thing to different men, not from indifference to truth, but rather from an Eastern sense of propriety; thus Messrs A B C etc each got what suited his particular case, in short what he deserved. Each would receive the same gentle smile, backed by the raising of the eyebrows that Palmer's friends knew so well (…) That the greatest linguist in the University, and the man with the deftest fingers, was looking on at all our doings with a calm smile of indifference, is a fact that I cannot forget.[336]

In reflecting on Palmer's personality Heitland was, like many of his generation, responding subconsciously to the lure of the mysterious East. For his part Abdallah Efendi (just one of Palmer's many Bedouin names) may well have been moved by his contempt for warring clerics and academics to place too implicit a trust in Arab tribesmen, not realizing perhaps that the stakes were higher. He left Cambridge, worked as a journalist, was called to the Bar, and then in 1882 was sent by Gladstone's government on a secret service mission to Egypt. His object was to protect the Suez Canal from attack by Arabs owing allegiance to the Egyptian nationalist, Arabi Pasha. His immediate instructions were to detach various tribes from the nationalist cause by bribing them with English gold. But his fate was to be ambushed, along with two English

---

[334] Heitland, *After Many Years*, 153–6.
[335] See below, pp. 339–67.
[336] Heitland, *After Many Years*, 153–6.

companions, and shot in the desert. Like Lawrence of Arabia, Palmer was a supreme individualist, and for that reason it makes little sense to try to fit his career into any sort of pattern, but at a stretch he might be compared to the previous generation's many missionaries, except that Christian endeavour had been replaced by academic fervour. The orientalist Stanley Lane-Poole described him, not only as a linguist without equal, but as 'the quietest and most unassuming of men of genius'.[337]

Finally, every successful common room needed its golden boy, and preferably just one. That part could only have been played by the Highlander Donald MacAlister,[338] whose glittering career alone might have been enough to dispel any doubts about the academic merits of sizars. Known very early on as a 'brilliant boy', it was not simply that he came out Senior Wrangler, but that everyone had always known he would. As a young Fellow he was a perfect match for Reyner. At least, he must surely be the man of 'ready wit and imperturbable temper' whom Bonney credited with the guts to put the old curmudgeon down. On one occasion, after Reyner had countered some remark of his by saying, 'You have not yet cut your wise teeth', MacAlister (presuming that it was indeed he) replied at once: 'The wise teeth, Dr Reyner, are the last to come and the first to go. I have cut mine and have not lost them.'[339] Glover considered him to be 'one of the ablest men in Cambridge'. However, 'the Saxon was perplexed by MacAlister, and was made uneasy by his uncanny cleverness, by the ease with which he did things and by the range of his knowledge and his capacity.' He was equally accomplished in classics, mathematics, and medicine, and also a brilliant (mostly paediatric) clinician. When Benjamin Jowett, Master of Balliol, fell ill, a Fellow's wife begged him to call for MacAlister. 'The cures he has made here are really wonderful, & everyone who has tried him believes in him, as we both do. I always have a feeling now that whoever he takes in hand *must* get well.'[340] According to an obituarist, 'his infinite variety, ability, and power of application would have taken him to the top of any profession he had chosen'.[341] Heitland commented on his 'exceptional cleverness', Bishop Welldon on his 'wonderful equanimity', Glover on his debonair cheerfulness. The latter's summing-up falls little short of hero-worship, and has a heightened intensity not apparent in his mainly playful but invariably mordant remarks on other people.

> He handled University and College business with a quickness that shocked people (...) What other men laboured at, he seemed to do with a

[337] Lane-Poole, quoted in W. S. Sherrington, 'Edward Palmer', *Eagle* xii (1881–3), 238–40.

[338] Sizar; Senior Wrangler, 1877; Fellow, 1877–1934; Lecturer in Natural Sciences (Medical); Tutor; FRCP, 1886; clinician to the Addenbrooke's Hospital; University Lecturer in Medicine; President of the General Medical Council, 1904–31; Principal and Vice-Chancellor of Glasgow University, 1907–29; Chancellor, 1929–34; KCB, 1908; Baronet, 1924; and the recipient of a huge number of other honours and honorary degrees at home and abroad.

[339] Bonney, *Memories*, 41.

[340] Mary Paley Marshall to Jowett, 29 Oct. 1891: *The Correspondence of Alfred Marshall, Economist*, ed. John K. Whitaker (Cambridge, 1996), II. 57.

[341] Humphry Rolleston, 'Sir Donald MacAlister', *British Medical Journal* (1936), 1154.

light touch; it was a burden to them to be accurate; he came naturally by it, and just did the thing, and went on unstaggered to the next. He had a ready pen, and could draft a resolution as readily as he seized the issue. He looked further afield than many of the men he had to work with; he had seen more, and he had realized more; and the local tradition meant less to him than the newer and larger idea (…) Forty years and more of friendship always show the same picture – the friendly, smiling figure, never over-strained, never at a loss, always ready to do the kind thing that materially helped, and always quick to divine what it should be – the sort of friend that surmounts difficulties for you and makes life easier and more delightful.[342]

Many other Fellows of St John's besides the aforementioned had strong personalities, but as scholars and scientists they tended mostly to be extremely laborious and learned, producing works that in different ways would be useful to others rather than breaking new ground or shifting paradigms. Archetypal in this respect were the Babington first cousins once removed, Churchill an archaeologist and Charles Cardale a botanist. The former was famous among other things for his edition of fragments of papyri, and for puncturing some of the more Whiggish claims made by Macaulay against the clergy of the seventeenth century. His *Birds of Suffolk* has been described as a 'storehouse of facts', and in addition he authored many hundreds of articles for the *Dictionary of Christian Antiquities* on such items as medals, glass, gems, inscriptions, seals, rings, and tombs. There was hardly a specialized archaeological journal to which he did not contribute, and he amassed a huge collection of shells. There was a relish to his antiquarian enthusiasm that was infectious, partly because he was thoroughly unpretentious, but the case of Charles Babington, usually known as 'Beetles' owing to his collecting obsession, was sadder. As a young man, having matriculated in 1826, he and Charles Darwin were bitter rivals for the approbation of the Professor of Botany, John Henslow, himself a prodigiously knowledgeable Johnian.[343] It is said that they almost fell over each other in their attempts to prepare and then tidy the great man's laboratory before and after his lectures, and their mutual antagonism was only heightened by their long-standing competition for amassing entomological specimens.[344] However, it was Darwin who sailed to the Galapagos Islands in 1831–6 and proceeded eventually to revolutionize men's understanding, while Babington stayed at home to serve as Henslow's assistant, deputy, and finally successor. He had a passion for collecting and taxonomizing, starting with beetles and moving on to plants and flowers, and he exercised considerable influence on the many amateur practitioners whose ambition was to produce county floras. His most important scientific contribution was his *Manual of British Botany*, a concise but scholarly handbook which brought its subject into line with more modish German, French, and Scandinavian methods, and which in doing so could be 'credibly held to have revolutionized the situation in Britain'. Showered with distinctions,

---

[342] Glover, *Cambridge Retrospect*, 95–8.
[343] Professor of Mineralogy 1822–7, Professor of Botany 1825–61.
[344] Janet Browne, *Charles Darwin*, I: *Voyaging*, (New York, 1995), 124.

he continued to publish prolifically, and to taxonomize ever more minutely into species, sub-species, and sub-subs, but he must have known that Darwin and his closest confidant, John Hooker, disparaged him. 'Poor Babby', they called him, and privately proclaimed his *Flora* far inferior to George Bentham's *Handbook of the British Flora* (1858). 'Look how Babington is eternally changing his mind – or rather his opinion (for mind he has none) as to genera & species', wrote Hooker to Darwin in 1858, and when Babington succeeded Henslow Darwin contented himself with the comment, 'What a contrast!'[345] The problem was that Babington's empirical bent led him to neglect the emerging field of experimental botany, and so left him 'isolated in his interests'.[346] Worse still was the fact that he continued to resist theories of evolution. He was dismayed when, in his presidential address to the British Association for the Advancement of Science at Norwich in 1869, Hooker came out openly in favour of natural selection, and he was still unreconciled to Darwinism at the time of his death in 1895.[347] For that reason alone, his long tenure of the Chair of Botany (1861–95) was from the University's point of view unfortunate.

Babington's willingness to devote himself to the service of a great man seems to have been another Johnian characteristic. William Garnett, for example, sometime Steward, was only too happy to serve as right-hand man to his idol, Clerk Maxwell, before moving off into scientific politics and administration,[348] and in much the same way Herbert Foxwell was devoted to W. S. Jevons. Foxwell was a charming man, amusing company, a good administrator, and a hard worker. He attained nationwide respect for his knowledge of the practical aspects of economics, especially banking, and he exerted much institutional influence, but he resisted theoretical developments and published only one book, in 1919. His most important contribution was to compile a definitive bibliography of economic literature, and to create two great and still intact book collections on the subject.[349] He might be compared to the geometer H. F. Baker or to Edwin Clark, elected in 1883 to a professorial Fellowship in law. The latter was a commanding figure and brilliant administrator, and is credited with making his faculty pre-eminent in legal studies, but although erudite and productive he 'wrote primarily for his students'. His major four-volume treatise on Roman

---

[345] Hooker to Darwin, 13 July 1858 and Darwin to Hooker, 18 May 1861: *The Correspondence of Charles Darwin*, ed. Frederick Burkhardt, James A. Secord, *et al.* (Cambridge, 1985–), VII. 132, IX. 133. Note that Hooker was scornful, not because Babington changed his mind ('we all do') but because he lacked a mind.

[346] D. E. Allen in *ODNB*. On experimental botany, see below, pp. 331–4. A bachelor with private means, Babington was allowed to keep his rooms in college after graduating in 1830, but he did not become a Fellow until 1874, thirteen years after succeeding Henslow as Professor of Botany.

[347] It is important to establish this point because Edward Miller (*Portrait of a College*, 78) cites an unidentified source to the effect that Babington, dubiously described as 'a friend of Darwin', 'displayed "glee over Samuel Wilberforce's discomfiture by young Huxley" at the Oxford meetings of the British Association at Oxford in 1860'. It is conceivable that Babington was gleeful on the grounds of disliking Wilberforce or clerical interferers generally, but the implication that he agreed with Darwin's *On the Origin of Species* is quite wrong.

[348] David Knight in *ODNB*.

[349] A. L. Bowley and Richard D. Freeman in *ODNB*.

private law 'had little impact on subsequent studies', while his other books 'had little influence and are seldom cited'.[350]

Again, few people could have been more learned than the Hebraist Peter Mason, but his 'Grammar' was described by younger men as 'Biblical' on the grounds that it had 'nothing to say to modern theories as to the language'.[351] Edward Palmer produced many imaginative works and translations, but none brought him anything like the esteem due to him for his catalogues of the Persian and Arabic manuscripts at King's and Trinity Colleges and the University Library. J. R. Tanner was a highly respected historian, but his lasting contribution was an edition of documents on Tudor and Stuart constitutional history. It was left to Maitland and others to breathe life into the dry bones.

The writings of the classics exemplify many of the familiar traits. None could have been more famous in his way than Benjamin Kennedy, Regius Professor of Greek, but his main contributions took the form of primers and grammars, immensely influential aids to others, in other words. Criticisms by a rival grammarian, H. J. Roby, of Kennedy's *Public School Latin Primer* (1866), led to a furious spat which was eventually settled in a typically Johnian way – over a bottle of Château Margaux supplied by Kennedy. Incidentally Roby typifies a type of scholar who had no wish to be a clergyman, and yet who was born just too soon to be a don. A genuine scholar of Latin grammar and Roman law, he married out of the Fellowship in 1861, became a schoolmaster at Dulwich, a parliamentary commissioner, an MP, and a Manchester businessman. At several points along the journey he was put up for chairs, only to be pipped by younger candidates with more conventional CVs.[352]

Glover has left a fascinating account of the next generation of classics, the men who taught him towards the end of the century. In his view, Mayor could never concentrate long enough to produce a really great book, 'but making notes towards a project was another thing, an enjoyable task that gave the sensation of valuable work'. Mayor's attempt to trace which other authors had used the same words as Tertullian was dismissed by Glover as lexicographical obsessiveness, telling one nothing about 'the mind or character or theology' of the author. Even so Mayor's massive book on Juvenal, published in 1872, was in keeping with the most current German scholarship, and has been described as being, 'for all its moments of madness, one of the grand edifices of Victorian scholarship'.[353] Glover was much more impressed by Heitland's *Agricola* – 'a fresh inquiry made by a really alert mind' – and also considered his *History of the Roman Republic* to be 'a very big bit of work', but even so it was much less brilliant than Mommsen's because, in Glover's opinion, 'he seems to stop before all is said – a Cambridge habit of mind, perhaps'.[354] With hindsight it cannot be said that either book made much of an impact on the development of the subject. John Sandys, according to Glover, was 'extraordinary (...) even among

---

[350] Wilfrid E. Rumble in *ODNB*.

[351] Glover, *Cambridge Retrospect*, 81.

[352] Christopher Stray in *ODNB*.

[353] John Henderson, *Juvenal's Mayor: The Professor who Lived on 2d. a Day* (Cambridge, 1998); Glover, *Cambridge Retrospect*, 86–7.

[354] Glover, *Cambridge Retrospect*, 40.

scholars of that day, at once for the width and accuracy of his scholarship; he knew so much and knew it so well'. All this made him 'incapable of the untidiness of impressionism'. He edited an enormous number of books and texts, and his work on Euripides and Pindar was outstanding, but once again it was work designed to put others in his debt rather than make a loud splash itself. C. E. Graves was a fine scholar and a successful lecturer whose editions of Thucydides and Aristophanes were valuable for pupils at school and university, 'but he never wrote a big book'. Glover had kind words for all his teachers, including Graves and Haskins, but the man who clearly fascinated him was the only beardless one, Harry Rede Tottenham, formerly of Trinity and one of the very few Fellows to be brought in from the outside, in 1880. 'Everybody liked him, but nobody would have called the picturesque, untidy humourist an energetic character. With his pupils he was shy, and in his own room face to face perhaps shyer still (…) but always with a curious little smile of his own coming and going, and winning him goodwill.' Tottenham was contemptuous of the almost universal solemnity of dons and the idiocy of examiners, holding 'nothing of that sort sacred'. Nor was he supremely interested in grammar and philology, which according to Glover were then regarded dogmatically as a science, superior knowledge of which would help to procure one a College living (so some things had not changed). He wrote brilliant papers, not books or scholarly editions. He was nothing like Jebb or Sandys, but 'full of curious Classical learning, taken as it were sideways'. And he added greatly to 'the gaiety of College life', not least by his limericks and general gift for nonsense.[355] Obviously Tottenham fascinated Glover because he was so out of place in St John's.

Another way in which an academic writer can be useful is in the production of textbooks, definitely a Johnian speciality. James Wood's *Elements of Algebra* remained a standard work for thirty or forty years, while Hymers's various geometrical treatises went through multiple editions. Their works presented no original research but introduced students to French and German mathematical methods. In the following generation, only one of Isaac Todhunter's many books displayed analytical ambition, but his *Euclid* (1862) and his expositions of algebra (1858), trigonometry (1859), mechanics (1867), and mensuration (1869) sold hugely world-wide, and remained standard textbooks until the early twentieth century. He also contributed to the history of mathematics, as Foxwell did to that of economics. In the same way, Stephen Parkinson's *Elementary Treatise on Mechanics* and *Treatise on Optics* became standard undergraduate works, and helped to console those students who could not hire him as a coach.

But though the general run of achievement was worthy more than inspired, and though there was nothing like a constellation of talent at any one time, there were a few indisputably towering intellects about whom something needs to be said. John (later Sir John) Herschel was charming, modest, and deservedly popular. He has been described by his biographer (Michael Crowe) as Britain's 'first modern physical scientist', and a model for the future in that he combined expertise in astronomy, mathematics, chemistry, mechanics, optics, acoustics, and electricity. Thanks to inherited wealth on his mother's side, he

---

[355] Ibid., 58–62.

could afford to be indifferent to academic preferment.[356] He hated 'pupillizing', deplored 'religion established by law' (as distinct from the 'religion of nature'), and took a dim view of the Johnian fascination with 'proselytizing in foreign lands'. If his correspondence is any guide, his bachelor days were largely taken up dreaming of 'charming girls' and 'beautiful women', and all in all he seemed somewhat detached from College life.[357] His most important pedagogic contribution was to combine with younger colleagues such as Babbage and Peacock to form the Analytical Society, the aim of which was to reduce the dependence of mathematics teaching in Cambridge on Newtonian fluxions, and to introduce in its place the Leibnizian analysis fashionable on the Continent. After quitting his Fellowship and moving to London in 1829, Herschel quickly grew in public eminence. Though not by nature a controversialist, he was a notably reforming President of the Mathematical Section of the British Association, and later an equally reforming Master of the Mint (1850–5). Intellectually his work was distinguished by its breadth rather than by any single breakthrough in a particular field, but he was immensely prolific and made important contributions to photography and meteorology. He was equally absorbed by the theory and culture of science, and his *Preliminary Discourse on the Study of Natural Philosophy* (1830) influenced Darwin, Faraday, Whewell, and Mill among others.

However, he is remembered best for his efforts to continue the observations of his father, William, into the nature of clouds. This work involved him and his family in a dramatic five-year stint (1833–8) at the Cape of Good Hope, where he studied celestial objects through his giant reflecting telescope at the British Royal Observatory. It was his equivalent of the voyage to the Galapagos. His initial conclusions led him to endorse his father's hypothesis that stellar systems were subject to Newton's laws of gravitational attraction in the same way as the earth's solar system. He was subsequently moved by Lord Rosse's findings to suppose that all nebulae are composed of stars, but lived long enough to think that maybe his father had been right after all in so far as some nebulae are merely gases. (This willingness to shift with the evidence brought him much respect in an era when scientists were anxious to establish their authority as empirical observers and experimentalists.) Herschel was widely recognized as an international star in his own right, and was buried in Westminster Abbey alongside an earlier Master of the Mint, Isaac Newton.[358]

For all his analytical brilliance, Herschel clearly shared the Johnian bug for collecting and analysing. In a catalogue of 1865 he itemized 5,079 known nebulae, all but 450 of which had been discovered by his father or himself, and at the time of his death he was about publish another list of 10,320 double and multiple stars. Methodologically he therefore stands at the far end of the spectrum from John Couch Adams, a lowly born Cornishman, sizar, and later Senior Wrangler and Fellow (1843). Adams' main, though by no means only, claim to fame was to have discovered the planet Neptune – entirely by mathematical calculation,

---

[356] At different times he refused an invitation to put in for the Savilian Chair at Oxford, and rejected the offer of the presidency of the Royal Society.

[357] J. F. W. Herschel to J. W. Whittaker, 22 May, 26 June, and 2 July 1813: *Calendar of the Correspondence of Sir John Herschel*, ed. Michael J. Crowe (Cambridge, 1998).

[358] Michael J. Crowe in *ODNB*, on which this paragraph relies heavily.

or what he called 'celestial mechanics'. Far from using anything so vulgar as a telescope, he limited himself to pencil and paper. Starting from the well-known observation that Uranus was not following the orbit to be expected according to Newton's calculations, and not for one moment supposing that Newton might be wrong, Adams decided that there must be a large planet beyond Uranus that was causing its perturbations. Using wholly *a priori* methods, he worked out the new planet's orbit, its mass, and its likely position at a future date. It was then necessary for the astronomers (Herschel included) to find a telescope capable of verifying his predictions. Eventually one was found in Berlin, observations were taken, and it transpired that Adams' calculations were accurate to a mere 2° 27′. According to the *Edinburgh Review*, the discovery of Neptune on 23 September 1846 at the spot predicted by Adams 'provided a spectacular confirmation of the power of mathematical theory (…) to tease out the secrets of the creation'. The discovery of Neptune, wrote Herschel, 'by the mere consideration of the recorded perturbations of the remotest planet previously known, by the theory of gravitation, as delivered by Newton, and matured by the French geometers, will ever be regarded as the most glorious intellectual triumph of the present age.'[359] And all this by a young man who had barely taken his final examinations, who was tutoring frantically in order to raise money for his siblings, and who was even finding time to teach his bedmaker, Mrs Ireland, to read. His prediction has been hailed as 'one of the grandest intellectual problems ever tackled'. The aftermath was blurred by the fact that, owing to his own characteristic unassertiveness and to the dilatory disdainfulness of James Challis and George Airy, directors respectively of the Cambridge and Royal Greenwich Observatories, Adams was denied the forthcoming Copley Medal, which went instead to Le Verrier, a Frenchman who had independently arrived by mathematical methods, albeit different ones, at a similar conclusion. No matter, Adams' priority was quickly recognized, he was awarded the Copley two years later, and he and Verrier did not fall out. Adams's reputation, within Cambridge especially, was huge from that time on, and he succeeded to the Lowndean Chair of Astronomy and Geometry in 1859.[360] By then he was no longer a Fellow of St John's unfortunately, having migrated to Pembroke in 1853. He would not take Holy Orders, and the College Seniors could not persuade a lawyer to vacate one of the few Fellowships that would have permitted him to remain.[361]

If Adams continued to be lionized in Cambridge, William Bateson junior was very much an outsider, who had to be fully supported by the College in a variety of offices before the University at last appointed him a Reader in 1907. (It was a sign of the times that experimental scientists were expected now to hold a University as well as a College appointment.) The main reason for his exclusion was that he refused to accept certain key aspects of the Darwinian theory of evolution. During the 1890s and 1900s, especially but not only in Cambridge, the Darwinian paradigm was hardening into a quasi-religious scientific belief in

---

[359] [J. F. W. Herschel], review of Humboldt's *Kosmos*, *Edinburgh Review* lxxxvii (1848), 170–229 at p. 191.

[360] Roger Hutchins in *ODNB*, on which this paragraph relies heavily.

[361] CB, 7 June 1852.

response to what was seen as a rising tide of scientific scepticism. Alfred Russel Wallace, who had been St John the Baptist to Darwin in 1858, now took on the role of St Paul by proclaiming that the theory of natural selection could 'only be compared to Newton's *Principia*' in its demonstration of 'a hitherto unrecognized law of nature'. In standing against this official consensus, therefore, and 'seeking to honour Darwin' by disagreeing with him, Bateson was asking for trouble, and the longer he remained without a University appointment, the more strident and vitriolic he became in defending his ideas. But though he was never fully accepted by the home establishment, he built up a devoted band of younger researchers, and became one of the most eminent and internationally celebrated scientists of his day.

Like many of his generation, he was keen to tackle the problem of variation in the process of species development, and attached himself at first to the school of animal morphology headed by the brilliant Frank Balfour, a Fellow of Trinity, and widely regarded as Darwin's natural successor until his death on Mont Blanc aged thirty in 1882.[362] Bateson's personal tutor – and at this time friend and mentor – was Balfour's close ally Walter Weldon, a Fellow of St John's since 1884. Balfour was charismatic, but it was said of Weldon that he 'lectured as one inspired' and 'had the divine gift of compelling interest'. Both men were committed Darwinians, who started from the assumption that the embryo, in the course of its development, recapitulates the evolutionary history of the species, a theory of descent known as phylogeny. Bateson's own earliest work on worms, which he claimed demonstrated the possibility of transmutation from the invertebrate to the vertebrate, fell squarely within this tradition.

However, shortly after this Bateson fell under the influence of W. K. Brooks, a professor at John Hopkins University and the author of *The Law of Heredity: A Study of the Cause of Variation, and the Origin of Living Organisms* (1883). Brooks rejected the view that natural selection could operate in the way that Darwin had suggested, that is by a myriad of very tiny and piecemeal variations operating over many millennia. Instead he argued that variation was likely to be a phenomenon of the whole organism. This suggestion chimed with Bateson's own growing dislike of Darwin's theory of continuity, or gradual incremental change. He disliked its *a priori* foundations, which offended his sense that science should proceed along the lines of verifiable experimentation. In other words, he wanted biology to be more like physics and chemistry. He was also concerned that Darwinian theory might be used by unscrupulous politicians to support a programme of positive eugenics, as propounded by the geneticist Francis Galton. But most of all he objected to the essentially utilitarian assumption behind the theory that variations only occur because they convey an advantage in the struggle for life, or, as Darwin himself put it, that species never act altruistically.

Bateson's alternative vision of genetic research was centred on the physiology of heredity. This alignment, in Olby's words, 'invited the search for discontinuities in biology analogous to those in chemistry that mark the chemical

---

[362] Helen Blackman, 'A spiritual leader? Cambridge zoology, mountaineering and the death of F. M. Balfour', *Studies in the History and Philosophy of Science Part C: Studies in History and Philosophy of Biological and Biomedical Sciences* 35 (2004), 93–117.

elements'.[363] Fired by this agenda, Bateson revealed how much he had imbibed the Johnian passion for collecting facts. In the search for examples of what seemed to be 'discontinuous variations', he travelled through different parts of Europe, Asia, and North Africa, 'ransacked museums, libraries, and private collections', and 'attended every kind of "show", mixing freely with gardeners, shepherds, and drovers, learning all they had to teach him'. 'Beetles' Babington could not have been more assiduous, but, unlike 'Beetles', Bateson was desperate to understand and explain. The outcome of these investigations was *Materials for the Study of Variation* (1894) in which he attacked head on the recapitulation theory of embryological development.

He now embarked on a major programme of experimental plant hybridization, following the method of Darwin's work on *The Variation of Animals and Plants under Domestication* (1868), but concentrating instead on freaks of nature or monstrosities, which he claimed were variations emanating from within the organism. It was a few years after this project had begun, in 1900, that he was directed to a publication of 1866 by the Moravian monk, Gregor Mendel. It gave Bateson an understanding of how variations could occur independently of both hybridity and the environment, and 'offered an algorithm with which to predict the outcome of experiments in crossing'.[364] The stage was set for one of the most vicious and long-standing disputes in the history of science. It was fought in the first instance between the Mendelians (led by Bateson) and the biometricians (led by Weldon and Karl Pearson), but it was also fought between Bateson and Weldon personally, with each man seeking by institutional means to deprive the other of research funding. This was not quite a case of fratricidal strife since Weldon had left St John's, first for University College London in 1889, and then ten years later for Oxford where he was elected the Linacre Professor of Geology. There was also crossfire from the germ theorists (led by August Weismann), who challenged both the Mendelians and the biometricians, and clung to the ancestral theory of inheritance proposed by Francis Galton.

In his long-standing opposition to Darwinism, Galton had argued in favour of four concepts: discontinuous development, punctuated equilibrium, organic stability, and the phenomenon whereby species revert to the mean. Conceptually therefore he was on the same side as Bateson, but he differed from Bateson methodologically insofar as he espoused statistical methods. In this respect he was closer to the biometrician Weldon, who argued vigorously that 'the questions raised by the Darwinian hypothesis are purely statistical, and the statistical method is the only one at present obvious by which that hypothesis can be experimentally checked'.[365] To Bateson, this strategy amounted to little more than rendering the tired old descriptive methods more sophisticated by applying mathematical models of probability, and he insisted instead on the need to get to understand the processes of heredity by experimental means. His

---

[363] Robert Olby in *ODNB*, on which this and the following paragraphs rely heavily; also Nicholas W. Gillham, 'Evolution by jumps: Francis Galton and William Bateson and the mechanism of evolutionary change', *Genetics*, 159 (2001), 1383–92.

[364] Ibid.

[365] F. W. R. Weldon, 'Some remarks on variations in animals and plants', *Proceedings of the Royal Society of London* lvii (1894–5), 379–82.

discoveries, which had considerable public resonance, helped to persuade the government to establish research centres in plant and animal breeding, and gave him a claim to be regarded as one of the most significant founders of modern genetics.[366] Moreover, in so far as any side can be said to have 'won' the argument, albeit some time after the main protagonists were all dead, it was the Mendelians.

Bateson's most distinguished colleague at St John's was the economist Alfred Marshall, who wrote to him in 1908:

> I cannot – to be frank – see that your facts are inconsistent with the belief that the *quality* of the life of the parents affects every juice and every fibre & every cell inside the genital organs as well as outside. Every rowing man knows that character is as important as physique: the Johnian freshman of my year who, judged by physique, was easily first, turned out to be absolutely useless. After a little while the captain of the sixth boat would not look at him; & mere 'weeds' full of pluck made their way into the first boat.[367]

Much earlier, Marshall had asked Bateson to explain Weismann's opposition to Lamarck's theory regarding the inheritance of acquired characteristics, after which the two men agreed to have 'a thorough good talk on Weismannism in relation to Sociology'.[368] These are the only positive indicators of cross-fertilization between the two men in the whole of Marshall's published correspondence, though it seems more than likely that the economist will have quizzed the geneticist more frequently, and no doubt confessed to feeling puzzled.

In considering Marshall's achievements, it will be helpful to distinguish the positive contribution on which his public career was built, from what might be called his normative philosophy. He had graduated as Second Wrangler in 1865 and been elected to a Fellowship. Three years later he was appointed to lecture on the Moral Sciences tripos. He lost his Fellowship as a result of his marriage in 1877, spent some years at Bristol University College where, as well as being physically ill he was also very unhappy, and then returned to Cambridge in 1884 (and to St John's a year later) when he succeeded Fawcett as Professor of Political Economy. He had few formal qualifications for the post apart from a straightforward textbook, *The Economics of Industry* (1879), which he had written with his wife, but, as Tullberg has pointed out, 'his status as the man who could rescue the "dismal science" from its reputation as a set of natural laws by which the country and a small group of its inhabitants could remain wealthy only at the expense of the majority who must remain poor, ignorant, and hopeless, was widespread among his students and others who had been inspired by his public

---

[366] Despite his adherence to the theory of discontinuity, Bateson was appalled that his middle son should want to be a poet and playwright rather than a scientist, and his evident disapproval was probably one of the (lesser) factors that helped drive the young man to suicide in 1922.

[367] Marshall to Bateson, 26 Oct. 1908: *Correspondence of Alfred Marshall*, III. 202–3.

[368] Marshall to Benjamin Kidd, 6 June 1894: ibid., II. 114–15.

lectures'.[369] He made his name with respect to the wider public in 1890 with a mammoth volume on *The Principles of Economics*. His essential achievements were first to incorporate the insights of Jevons and other marginal utility theorists, so as to transform so-called 'classical economics' into the new paradigm of so-called 'neo-classical economics',[370] and secondly to establish the science on sounder foundations by including algebraic formulae and diagrams in its exposition. While holding firmly to the tenets of individualism, free trade, and free market competition, he sought to humanize those policies by insisting that people were motivated by much else besides a desire for profit-maximization – by desire for status, for example, by a care for those dear to them, or by public approbation. Furthermore, he insisted, even when economic agents *were* motivated by material greed, they were often extremely irrational in the ways they sought to satisfy the urge. In his attempt to provide a comprehensive account of how an economic system worked, an account moreover that balanced theory with empirical evidence, Marshall's only rivals in the Anglophone world have been Adam Smith and J. S. Mill, and as a working hypothesis, commanding general assent, his version lasted roughly as long as theirs.

Meanwhile, Marshall was being drawn more and more into a public role, serving on various Royal Commissions and inquiries including those on labour (1891–4), the aged poor (1893), the Indian currency (1899), and local taxation (1899).[371] All these investigations involved the compilation of statistics. Tullberg emphasizes his own claim to have been 'hungry for facts', and certainly there are passages in his works that display the true Johnian passion for empirical overkill. Yet for all the public fame and academic acclaim, Marshall drew little satisfaction from his achievements.

> I have been some months wading through the detestable mud of international trading statistics. They have little interest for me: because I know that everything in them that is of much importance can be got by 'massive' observation & conjecture, & that the apparent definiteness of those aggregates of hundreds of thousands of guesses at value, which are spoken of as 'facts' by the newspapers offers little real guidance. But that which offers the best guidance to me, is too subjective for external use. So I have to waste time on analysing statistics for other people's benefit. If such work has done me no other good, it has taught me not to try to interpret statistics, unless in a matter as to which I know what the statistics will be like before I read them.[372]

---

[369] Rita McWilliams Tullberg in *ODNB*. In seeking to find an opening for Marshall in St John's as early as 1881, Foxwell had written: 'Perhaps I ought to mention, what may not be so generally known, that he is now recognized in Cambridge and elsewhere as the founder of a distinct economic school, and that a large proportion of his pupils are now holding important educational posts or have in other ways become men of mark', Foxwell to Charles Taylor, 6 Oct. 1881: SJCA, D104.109.

[370] Called so mainly by historians of economic thought. See Donald Winch, *Wealth and Life: Essays on the Intellectual History of Political Economy in Britain, 1848–1914* (Cambridge, 2009), 149–76 and *passim*.

[371] P. D. Groenewegen, *A Soaring Eagle: Alfred Marshall, 1842–1924* (Aldershot, 1995).

[372] Marshall to Bateson, 26 Oct. 1908: *Correspondence of Alfred Marshall*, III. 202–3.

Whether Marshall's disparagement of statistics was made with the Bateson-Weldon quarrel in mind is unclear, but what is certain is that he wanted to be something more than the latest economic synthesizer.

The root problem was a tension between what Marshall wanted to argue and the methods by which he sought to argue. Those methods were essentially mathematical, and were therefore well suited to analysing states of mechanical equilibrium. Yet what he really wanted to do was to explain the economy – and society more generally – in non-static or evolutionary terms. As he put it in an address towards the end of his life,

> At last the speculations of biology made a great stride forwards: its discontinuities fascinated the attention of all men as those of physics had done in earlier years. The moral and historical sciences of this day have in consequence changed their tone, and economics has shared in the general movement.[373]

Whereas Bateson consciously strove to undermine Darwinism, Marshall genuinely believed in the need to incorporate it into political economy. His problem was that, like so many others in Britain, he misinterpreted the theory. The biggest paradox in nineteenth-century intellectual history is that Darwin's work gave an enormous boost to the re-emergence of Lamarckian ideas, simply because in Britain so many non-scientists (especially) interpreted Darwin's work in a Lamarckian light. They assumed, in other words, that the evolutionary processes of natural selection would, without any need for positive eugenics, weed out less desirable specimens and so produce over time 'finer, fitter, and more beautiful beings'. Herbert Spencer had coined the axiom 'survival of the fittest', Darwin had adopted it, and in the general culture it had become a convenient shorthand to describe the principle of evolution, but in the general culture the term 'fittest' was nearly always interpreted in the way that Spencer intended – to mean morally and physically superior – rather than in Darwin's sense of being accidentally most suited to a particular environment. In that respect, Marshall was part of, and contributed to, the general culture.[374]

As to why there should have been such a gross lack of awareness in Britain of the vicious cruelties, randomness, and wastefulness entailed in Darwin's theory of natural selection, the answer must have something to do with the social optimism so prevalent in the third quarter of the century. In such a context evolution seemed to equate naturally with improvement. When the mature Marshall spoke with some regret about his early 'tendency to socialism', he was referring not to Marx but to F. D. Maurice, whose ideas and personality he had found attractive. As an undergraduate in the early 1860s he would have been thoroughly exposed to the Christian socialist blitheness of those years. What Marshall

---

[373] Alfred Marshall, 'The present position of economics', in *Memorials of Alfred Marshall*, ed. A. C. Ryan and J. M. Keynes (1925), 154.

[374] Bonney fell into the same trap, writing: 'We discover the germ of a natural theology in the gradual evolution, through the operation of the environment, of that which is more perfect from that which is less perfect, which leads by means of selection, called natural, to the survival of the fittest': T. George Bonney, *The Influence of Science on Theology* (Cambridge, 1885), 56.

wanted to proclaim was that capitalism and economic individualism could foster altruism. As Winch points out, for all the apparent austerity and scientific professionalism of Marshall's theoretical economics, when reading his accounts of the economic organon, it is 'hard not to feel that [we are] being recruited into an ethical crusade'.[375] He preached, for example, the very un-Darwinian notion that with increased wealth and civilization the wealthy will learn to act altruistically, that economic 'chivalry' will temper the harshness of advanced capitalism, and that for their part the working class will, in Winch's paraphrase, undergo a process of 'character formation as a result of quasi-Darwinian processes of adaptation to changes in the work environment'. It was a noble vision, and very redolent of the Johnian ethos of the early 1860s when Marshall had been an undergraduate, but one must doubt whether it was really any less utopian than John Mayor's belief that vegetarianism could save the world, or that capitalists red in tooth and claw might be persuaded to lie down with their workers.

This survey of intellectual distinction must finally include the name of Joseph Larmor, an applied mathematician and theoretical physicist who was at his creative peak during the 1890s and who, along with J. J. Thomson of Trinity and the Dutchman H. A. Lorentz, played a leading part in the development of electron theory. By recognizing electrons as the electromagnetic basis of matter, he helped to break away from the earlier assumption that there must be a continuous and essentially material ether underlying all physical phenomena. However, because he continued to believe that 'the equations of electromagnetism were not fundamental but were a manifestation of the underlying properties of a universal ether', albeit not a material one, he was resistant to Einsteinian relativity. Nor did he move into quantum theory. Nonetheless, he played a crucial role in establishing the full coherence of what has been called classical physics, as well as in developing insights (e.g. into space-time transformations) that would enable others to challenge it.[376]

With three such luminaries as Bateson, Marshall, and Larmor, the Fellowship in the 1890s was considerably more distinguished than at any time in the century. Unfortunately, there is little evidence of that interdisciplinary fermentation which proponents of the college system rightly trumpet. Marshall was genuinely interested in analogies between the human and the social body, and the fact that he seems to have corresponded so rarely with Bateson means nothing given their proximity, and yet such letters as do exist do not suggest an intimate intellectual acquaintance. Meanwhile Bateson and Larmor took some time to get over a blazing row following the ejection of the physicist G. G. Stokes from the Council of the Cambridge Philosophical Society in 1889. Larmor was the CPS Secretary and put it about that Stokes had been done down 'by a caucus of the biologists', a charge that was vigorously rebutted by the latter.[377] Underlying the personal antagonism was the wider conflict between physicists

[375] Winch, *Wealth and Life*, 270–94 at p. 294.

[376] Isobel Falconer in *ODNB*; A. E. Woodruff in *Dictionary of Scientific Biography*, ed. C. C. Gillispie, 16 vols. (New York, 1970–80), VIII. 39–41.

[377] Bateson to Larmor, 29 and 30 Nov. 1889 and Larmor to Bateson, 30 Nov. 1889, S. F. Harmer to Larmor, 30 Nov. 1889: SJCL, Miscellaneous letters, W1.Ba–Bea.Bateson, 1–6.

and biologists. It was partly a struggle for supremacy, but also resolved into a genuine disagreement about the methods of scientific inquiry, and one moreover that touched directly on Bateson's work. As stated above, the latter was engaged in a great battle on behalf of experiment and induction against Weldon and his band of biometricians. In a letter of 1899, in which he paraphrased Bateson, Weldon pronounced: 'The contention "that numbers mean nothing and do not exist in Nature" is a very serious thing, which will have to be fought. Most other people have got beyond it, but most biologists have not.'[378] It was therefore something of a climbdown on Bateson's part when he felt the need to ask Larmor for a mathematical analysis that might help him to explain an observed phenomenon. Even in asking for help, he could not suppress a sneer. "I don't want a transcendental lead from the physicists. We will do the transcending; all I ask is for your mechanics to give us an idea of how one bit of jelly can by its intrinsic properties divide into two'.[379]

There were also perhaps institutional reasons why intellectual cross-fertilization was slow to develop. Looking back from Scotland on his time in St John's in the nineteenth century, MacAlister used to say how proud he was to have persuaded his colleagues to turn a disused lecture room into an additional small combination room for postprandial smokers.

> After a few years practically the whole body drifted to the smoking-room, [leaving only one or two over port, so port was abolished. When the wine merchant inquired as to what had happened to the usual order for port], there was nothing to answer but that tobacco had killed port drinking. The old order had yielded to the new; smoking was become universal; men enjoyed a cigarette and a chat after dinner, and got back to their rooms – and their work – soon after eight, instead of circulating port in the big room until half past nine or so.[380]

This made a good yarn, and it suited MacAlister to think that this is what had happened. A strong Presbyterian, he regarded smoking as swift and manly whereas drink was effeminate and time-wasting, but the fact is that even before his little revolution the Fellows of St John's, unlike those at Trinity and some other colleges, had rarely combined after dinner on ordinary nights. It was much more the custom for one of them to invite three or four others to take port, sherry, claret, and dessert in his room. It is tempting to think that this was the mark of a factionalized Fellowship. It is time to return to the issues – academic, religious, political, personal – that so divided the society in the final third of the century.

---

[378] Weldon to Karl Pearson, 16 November 1899, quoted in D. R. Cox, 'Biometrika; the first 100 years', *Biometrika* 88 (2001), 3–11.

[379] Bateson to Larmor, 22 Feb. 1913: SJCL, Miscellaneous letters, W1.Ba–Bea.Bateson, 11.

[380] MacAlister, as reported in Edith MacAlister, *Sir Donald MacAlister of Tarbert, by his Wife* (London, 1935), 310–11.

9. 'A BATTLE-FIELD FOR CONFLICTING OPINIONS': CHAPEL WARS, COLLEGE WOES

> The Governing Body (...) in my early College days was controlled by a narrow-minded and bigoted clique. They passed on to it by seniority and were unremovable: and the mischief they did lived after they had ceased to rule.[381]
>
> W. E. Heitland, *After Many Years*, 142

In April 1865 a non-resident Fellow, the Rev. Simeon Hiley, paid two brief visits to College. He wrote to Reyner soon afterwards to express regret that the Bursar's 'beloved countenance' had not been visible on either occasion, and went on to chat merrily about various Fellows and their achievements. His letter ended more portentously than he can have realized.

> At the present the sun seems to be shining beautifully on St John's. May such a state of things long continue! ... Have you heard anything of a serious accident having happened to your friend Henry Hoare? One of our local papers mentioned this as a fact, and it was alluded to in the *Times*, but, I thought, with some uncertainty.[382]

The significance of the last two sentences will become apparent presently. Meanwhile the optimism expressed in the first two was widely shared and is readily understandable. As previous sections of this chapter have shown, revenues were flourishing, internal management was being overhauled, some mildly significant academic reforms had been pushed through without bloodshed, even the least enthusiastic Fellows being more or less acquiescent, while the College as a whole, having got over its obsession with Trinity, had acquired a strong corporate identity. The noisiest members of the awkward squad – Roby, Courtney, Hayward, Bashforth, Joe Mayor, Churchill Babington – all departed between 1857 and 1866, while Liveing, the other strong reformer, was increasingly preoccupied with scientific work. It seemed therefore as though the more conservative Fellows could look forward to a quiet period in the sunshine.

But even without their leaders, it was questionable how long the junior Fellows would remain content with the sop they had been given in 1860. Statute LV allowed them to raise issues at an annual College meeting scheduled for the last Tuesday of October, but this was little more than a talking shop. Signs that the juniors were getting restless became evident in 1864, when the annual meeting passed a motion to the effect that copies of the minutes of the Master and Seniors be sent to all Fellows, at least on those items of business that affected them all.[383] The Seniors would have none of it, but in the following year it *was* agreed that Fellows might inspect the Conclusion Book, or at least a copy of it that was to be kept in the Bursar's office. That was the year in which the dangerously liberal Gladstone made a public speech about allowing all citizens not incapacitated by 'considerations of personal unfitness' to come within the 'pale of the constitution' (he meant, be entitled to vote). The point was no doubt taken

---

[381] Heitland, *After Many Years*, 142.

[382] S. Hiley to Reyner, 8 Apr. 1865: SJCA, D92.1.52.

[383] Russell, 'Diary of events', 25 Oct. 1864: SJCL, U22.

to heart on high table. As any rate, in the following year political and religious tensions within the senior common room blew up to such an extent that for at least fifteen years even the routine running of the College was to be placed in jeopardy.

At a national level the death of Palmerston in 1865 brought to an end a decade and a half in which party strife had been relatively muted. Suddenly battle was resumed between Liberals and Conservatives, as personified by Gladstone and Disraeli. From 1832 and for the remainder of the century the two University seats were held almost continuously by Conservatives,[384] a situation that would once have delighted St John's, but the Fellowship was now politically divided. At the time of the 1868 election one bewildered former member lamented 'the days of old when the Johnians voted in a "pack" [and] one was drawn at once into "committee" &c., but now we are like hounds that have lost the scent.'[385] Had he but known it, the hounds had started to turn on each other, starting with an extraordinary spat at the Cambridge City election in 1865, a spat for which Bateson must surely take most of the blame. It was a very close and tense election, at which the two Conservatives candidates (W. Forsyth and F. S. Powell) secured 762 and 760 votes, narrowly beating the Liberal Colonel Torrens and the Radical W. D. Christie with 726 and 725 votes respectively. Shortly before the poll Christie wrote to Bateson to complain that, of the twenty or so staff members employed by St John's who were entitled to vote, only one was prepared to support either himself or Torrens, and 'that four at least are avowed Liberals and have said that they are afraid to vote for us'. He then requested that Bateson, whom he absolved of any personal malfeasance, should publicly disavow any interference by Fellows with the freedom of College dependents, 'otherwise I see no hope of obtaining the conscientious votes of terrified servants of your College'.[386] Bateson complied, after which Christie exhibited the following placard throughout Cambridge:

Dr Bateson to Mr Christie on Free Voting
College Servants and Tenants

> I can have no hesitation in authorising you to make it known that it is my wish, that any one who is in any way dependent on St John's College may be left free to exercise his right of franchise according to his judgment and discretion, and that I will do all that may be in my power to protect any one who may so exercise it.[387]

Bateson's desire for free elections was undoubtedly sincere, but he might have added (if only *pro forma*) that he saw no grounds for suspecting that any Fellow of St John's had ever thought otherwise. Instead, his use of the terms 'my wish' and 'my power' gave the impression that he thought the imputations to be justified. It elicited the following icy inquiry from six Fellows led by Reyner: 'We

---

[384] One of the seats was held by Liberals during 1856–7 and 1882–5.

[385] L. Stephenson to Reyner, 12 Feb. 1868: SJCA, D92.1.86.

[386] Christie to Bateson, 28 Jun. 1865, copy: SJCL, U22.

[387] The placard contained a similar declaration by Dr James Cartmell, Master of Christ's.

beg to ask on what grounds the charge therein insinuated against the College has received the public sanction of the Master's name.' Bateson replied,

> So far was I from the intention to insinuate any charge against the College that my object and intention was to repudiate, as far as I could, the notion that any undue influence would be exercised by the College in the approaching election of members for the Town. That notion I believed to be a groundless one, and the inquiry which you have addressed to me strengthens the opinion which I had previously formed.

If Bateson thought that this reply would satisfy Reyner and his co-signatories, his usual astuteness must have deserted him. The phrase 'repudiate, *as far as I could*' seemed to admit some truth to the charge that certain Fellows had sought to coerce College servants; while, if he *really* believed the charge to be groundless, how could the protest of Reyner and his colleagues have strengthened that belief? If the latters' earlier missive had been icy, their response to his reply was distinctly sub-zero.

> We beg to thank you for your reply to our letter of the 8th. We exceedingly regret that you authorized publication of a statement calculated to produce an impression inconsistent with the purpose of your letter to us. We presume that we are at liberty to publish this correspondence. We are, Dear Master, Yours faithfully.[388]

This angry exchange (which Reyner and his colleagues did indeed publish, in the *Cambridge Chronicle*) had to be conducted by letter because, while they seethed with anger on high table, and wondered whether they harboured a liberal viper in their bosom, Bateson himself was on holiday in his house at Fylingdales in North Yorkshire. Historians feed on correspondence, but correspondence only occurs when protagonists are physically apart from each other, something that rarely happens in a close-knit community. It is therefore impossible to say whether this passage of arms was a bolt from the blue, or whether relations between the Master and certain Fellows were at permanent breaking point before then. When Joe Mayor revisited St John's in 1869, what he mainly heard were 'grumblings about the rate at which changes were being introduced', the biggest bugbear being the likely admission of Dissenters, but he was reassured by Bateson during a private drink after dinner that the conservatives would never be able to 'agree among themselves on what to make their stand'.[389]

In fact, when Bateson said this, the conservatives had already taken their stand, though he can be forgiven for not yet appreciating just how venomous and protracted the outcome would be. The ostensible *casus belli* was not primarily the admission of Dissenters but the content of sermons in Chapel, which might seem surprising given that St John's Fellows had been operating at a fairly low temperature in theological matters. It was partly the fact that missionary-cum-muscular Christianity had papered over the doctrinal cracks for a decade

---

[388] G. F. Reyner, J. S. Wood, J. E. B. Mayor, A. C. Haviland, W. P. Hiern, and H. Russell to Bateson, 8 and 12 Jul. 1865 and Bateson to Reyner *et al.*, 9 Jul. 1865: SJCL, U22.

[389] Joe Mayor to Robert Mayor, 4 Dec. 1869: Mayor Papers, B11/30.

or so, and that these were now beginning to show again as it lost impetus, but it is also the case that religious disputation was largely a pretext for battles that were becoming increasingly personal, political, and indeed almost tribal.

Before examining the 'battle of the sermons', it is pertinent to point out that the Chapel was anyway a focus of attention because of the momentous decision some years earlier to build a new one. On 27 January 1862 the Seniors decided to set up a building fund, largely on the basis of £20,000 of 3 per cent consols held in the name of James Wood, and to approach the architect George Gilbert Scott. They were responding to seventeen Junior Fellows who had met on 28 May 1861 to petition in favour of a new Chapel, and to sixteen non-resident Fellows who had done the same shortly afterwards.[390] These thirty-three Fellows seem in turn to have been responding to William Selwyn's aforementioned *Ante Portam Latinam* sermon (6 May 1861) in which he hinted at the need for a more uplifting and capacious place of worship. According to College tradition, Selwyn's address provided the 'final impulse' that turned pipedream into reality.[391] The notion gains support from the fact that his 'sermon in stones' first appeared in print in 1869, when it was published under the title, *The New Chapel of St John's College Cambridge*, in a lithographed edition commissioned by the College to coincide with the consecration of the building. Two sentences from Selwyn's address are often highlighted: 'Is there not one improvement more to be desired than all? Long-talked of, long-delayed, for which perhaps *the time is now come* (…) The silver and gold are thine, O Lord; we will not rest until we have raised a chapel more worthy of our College.' On the other hand, only one of the sermon's twenty-five pages is about the Chapel. The phrase 'one improvement to be desired' refers vaguely to changes in the 'material fabric', suggesting enlargement rather than a whole new building, while Selwyn's reference to 'a chapel more worthy of our College' is followed by a warning: 'But we remember (…) the glory of Athens lyeth not in her walls, *but in the worth of her citizens. Buildings may give lustre to a College, but learning giveth life.'*[392] The main point of the sermon was to encourage Godly learning and Christian mission, not investment in bricks and mortar.

In fact the new Chapel did not come about because of any sudden rush of enthusiasm. The idea had been bandied about for years before this. 'Beetles' Babington stated authoritatively that architects had already been consulted, though he did not say who, or how earnestly. Russell recorded later that the idea of a new Chapel was being 'loudly and generally discussed' before Selwyn's intervention.[393] In fact the question of timing may be more prosaically explained by the fact that in 1860 new legislation allowed colleges to borrow money in compensation for having given up the old system of fines. As to who within the Fellowship was mainly responsible for the decision, Heitland (writing much later, but having pumped Liveing for information) laid the blame for what he thought was an architectural 'abomination' on the 'dominant party among the

---

[390] SJCA, D101.5a, 5f–g.

[391] J. S. Wood, 'William Selwyn', *Eagle* ix. (1874–5), 298–322, at p. 315.

[392] Selwyn, *The New Chapel*, 15–17.

[393] [H. Russell], *The New Chapel of St. John's College, Cambridge* (Cambridge, 1869), 1.

Fellows', meaning Reyner, John Spicer Wood,[394] and the President Francis France, though he also condemned Selwyn for egging them on.[395] Conversely Bateson stressed the unanimous nature of the decision, recording in a memorandum that 'there was no division nor disagreement as to the resolutions'.[396] As on the Orient Express, everyone was guilty.

And yet Bateson's own role must not be forgotten. He became Master on 2 February 1857, and Reyner took over as Senior Bursar on the 6th. The very first entry in the diary that Reyner kept as Bursar, dated 7 February, stated simply: 'Master thinks that a Chapel, Hall, and Lodge might be erected at a cost of £40,000. He would have the Hall &c at the *north* of all our present buildings. Thinks the Hall should be built first.'[397] It is hard to know what to make of this cryptic comment, but evidently Bateson was well to the fore among the instigators. That he has not generally been seen as such may be because he was not regarded as pious or devotional. Although of necessity an ordained clergyman, and briefly vicar of Madingley (1843–7), he had never shown much religious commitment, but after becoming Master he took 'to going to chapel regularly morning and evening', partly no doubt from a sense of duty, but also perhaps in the hope of winning over 'the two or three [Fellows] who on Church grounds voted against him'.[398] Maybe he was moved by the corporate spirit of worship that was then so high, and by the muscular Christian appeals of preachers like the Selwyns for colleges to justify their privileges by fitting men for public duty, empire, and God's cause. Whatever the motivation it is abundantly clear from his correspondence that Bateson became extremely enthusiastic about the new Chapel, and that he devoted a considerable amount (£1,000) from his personal funds towards its completion, as did Reyner (£500). The irony here is that, having righted the College's finances following the disastrous debts left over from an earlier building programme, Bateson's own architectural ambitions should have played a big part in bequeathing to his successors an even greater burden. As for opposition to the scheme, there seems to have been very little at first, though Peter Mason and Frederic Wace[399] expressed doubts. Such was the religious enthusiasm, a sense too perhaps that the new statutes marked an epoch, that most people seemed carried along. Former Fellows frequently wrote to Master or Bursar to comment on the College's fortunes, but the only extant letter of protest is from the Rev. Francis Llewellyn Lloyd,[400] who railed against the destruction of venerable buildings. 'If there is a new Chapel on a new site (...) I shall be fain to think it is a new college.'[401]

Having determined to proceed, the College turned (without any thought of a competition) to George Gilbert Scott, who was the leading Gothic church

[394] Fellow, 1847–83; Assistant Tutor and Classical Lecturer, 1853–60; Tutor, 1860–70; President, 1871–82.

[395] Heitland, 'George Downing Liveing', *Eagle* xliv (1924–6), 98.

[396] SJCA, Bateson's Letter Books, M1.7.

[397] Reyner's Estate Diary 1857: SJCA, SB1.6.

[398] John Mayor to his mother, Feb. 1858–9: Mayor Papers, B8/236.

[399] Fellow, 1860–75.

[400] Fellow, 1840–58.

[401] Lloyd to Reyner, 26 Dec. 1862: SJCA, D92.1.35.

architect and restorer of the day, and whose similar commission for Exeter College, Oxford had been completed in 1860. Since the latter is a striking Sainte Chapelle look-alike, which utterly destroys the proportions of the Exeter quadrangle, the Fellows of St John's should have had some idea of what might be in store for them. Scott prepared two plans – one for a new building, the other for a restoration of the existing Chapel and its extension northwards onto the site of the Labyrinth. He recommended the latter, but the Fellows insisted on rebuilding, at which point Scott argued, in a famous memorandum, that the late thirteenth-century English pointed style was the one to go for, partly because it was in his opinion the loveliest and most authentic, but also because it was the style of Gothic predominating at the time when the Hospital of St John had been built, whereas the Gothic prevailing at the time of the College's foundation had been poor and debased.[402]

It would have been possible, and might have been better, to have left the north side of First Court with its old Chapel intact, and to have let the new Chapel rise up majestically behind it. Instead the Fellows determined on a clean sweep, partly because they wished to extend the Hall northwards into the space occupied at ground level by the Combination Room and above it by the Master's dining room. In order to give the Hall extension an oriel window onto First Court, it was necessary to clear the western end of the north range containing other parts of the Master's Lodge, and logically that meant pulling down the old Chapel as well.[403] The full scheme therefore comprised not just the new Chapel but a new Lodge, to be built next to the river and set back a little from Bridge Street, and the restoration, though not to the original length, of the Long Gallery, now the Combination Room. There was to be a mammoth appeal to old members and a limit of £40,000 was placed on the amount that could be taken for the purpose from the corporate funds of the College.

The story of the building of the new Chapel has been told with such skill and in such detail by Alec Crook that it would be pointless to write at length on the topic here.[404] Scott's design was for a huge building – 193 by 52 feet – with a polygonal apse, and with a transeptal ante-chapel at the west end, a feature not found in Cambridge, but having several precedents in Oxford. With one important exception, discussed in the next paragraph, the process of construction went more or less according to plan. Ancaster stone was chosen for the elevations, and the duke of Devonshire supplied red marble for the interior; a stone vaulted ceiling was designed for the ante-chapel but, as a concession to cost, an arched timber ceiling for the Chapel itself. Reyner, who had little faith in the clerk of works ('not a good man') proved the hero of the hour. He took very close control of operations, and in his irritable and inimitable way kept architect, masons, carvers, glaziers, and sub-contractors up to scratch. A committee of Senior Fellows gave earnest consideration to the stained glass windows, responsibility for which was given to the prolific firm of Clayton & Bell, and which

---

[402] He meant the early sixteenth century but would have included the much earlier King's College Chapel (*c.* 1446–1515) in his anathema.

[403] Though this last aspect of the works was not finally decided on until March 1868.

[404] Crook, *Foundation to Gilbert Scott*, 90–114.

were paid for by a subscription, including £2,265 from the earl of Powis, son of the candidate for the Chancellorship in 1847, and £1,510 from junior members. And when it was all done St John's acquired a chapel that was nothing if not imposing, an excellent suburban vicarage for a Master's Lodge, and a 93-foot long Combination Room that remains one of the glories of Cambridge.

The important exception alluded to above concerns the tower. Scott's original design had nothing more up top than a tall and pretty-looking flèche, much like the one at Exeter College. Fatefully, however, the man chosen to lay the foundation stone on 6 May 1864 was Henry Hoare, a friend of Bateson and Reyner and a last-minute substitute for Lord Powis, who was ill. He urged the view that so noble a structure ought to have a tower. The Seniors considered this and decided that it was unaffordable. Bateson conveyed the bad news on 7 June, whereupon Hoare offered to pay the estimated cost himself, £1,000 in five annual instalments, 'subject to the condition of his living so long'.[405] Scott was ecstatic, and so too was Bateson. He might not have kow-towed to aristocrats, but plutocrats had him fawning, and in his brief thank-you letter he managed to squeeze in multiple references to Hoare's 'noble offer', 'princely gift', and 'munificent proposal'.[406] Some Fellows clearly had doubts, but Bateson was desperately eager. He cut short his retreat at Fylingdales, and did everything he could to expedite the deal. On 9 August the Seniors agreed. One of them, Bonney, who was emerging as the main opponent of the whole venture, claimed later that he urged his colleagues to take out insurance on Hoare's life 'on the ground that we were virtually trustees for the College (…) but I obtained very little support, some even saying it would not be like gentlemen to do it. I may add that I was the more urgent about this precaution, because, when standing near Mr Hoare while he was laying the foundation stone, I thought he "was not a good life".'[407] As it happened, Hoare did die, in April 1866, but not through ill health, rather as the delayed consequence of a railway accident thirteen months earlier – the *Times* report referred to above (n. 2) was accurate in that respect. He had paid just one instalment and another would be honoured by his estate, but this still left a deficiency of £3,000 on what he had promised, and of £4,100 on what the tower eventually cost.

Would Hoare's son and heir (also a Henry) step into the breach? A strange correspondence ensued, complicated by the younger Hoare's insistence on negotiating via Gilbert Scott. His basic point was clear: 'I am not so rich a man as my Father, and I am not ashamed to say that I have not the inclination, and do not feel bound in any way to continue the amount of the subscriptions.' However, he added that he was very anxious to purchase from the College the advowson of the living of Staplehurst, which lay adjacent to his own property and to which he hoped to present his brother. He was prepared to offer £4,200 more than the living was worth, that money to be spent on whatever the College pleased, including the tower. Bateson seemed willing to accept the bribe, but Reyner and the other Seniors insisted that such an act of simony would

[405] CB, 9 Aug. 1864.
[406] Bateson to Hoare, 20 Jul. 1864: SJCA, Bateson Letter Books, M1.7.
[407] Bonney, *Memories*, 56.

26 T. G. Bonney ('old cantank'): SJCL, Album 10/26a

be dishonourable to the College, and so Bateson was forced to write to Hoare 'by their request'[408] as follows:

> I regret to say that the embarrassments which would be occasioned by the condition that is proposed are too serious to allow us to accept it (...) However little you might intend it we feel that 'the two ideas of the Living and the Tower' would be unavoidably associated both in our own minds and in the opinions of the outer world (...) We shrink from the idea that the college should sell its advowson in order to obtain aid in building a part of the Chapel.[409]

This refusal meant that Reyner, when he came to retire in 1876, could take the favoured living of Stapleford for himself, though whether that prospect played any part in his decision over the advowson it is impossible to say.

The bare facts are that the final cost of the new Chapel and associated works[410] was £78,319, to which must be added a further £20,000 of interest on a debt that was not paid off until 1896. During that period the Chapel cost the

---

[408] H. Russell, 'Diary of events', 18 Oct. 1866: SJCL, U22.

[409] Scott to Bateson 18 Oct 1866, Bateson to Scott, 24 Oct. 1866, Hoare to Scott, 3 Dec. 1866, Bateson to Reyner, 7 Dec. 1866, Bateson to Hoare, 8 Dec. 1866: SJCA, D33.3.3.28/29; D33.3.3.32/34–7.

[410] Including nearly £9,000 for the Master's Lodge and more than £5,000 for the alterations to Hall.

College £1,735 p.a., which was equal to £30 on the dividend.[411] The parallels with New Court are striking. Both projects were mooted for decades before finally being urged on by dominant Masters. Both cost much more to build than had been anticipated, both left crippling debts, and both were followed by agricultural depressions which made those debts far harder to pay off. But at least New Court was fit for purpose, whereas the new Chapel had the feel of a mausoleum from the start, being already redundant by the time it was completed, thanks to the ending of University Tests and consequent decline in chapel attendance. On top of these financial and functional shortcomings there has been continuous debate ever since about its architectural quality.[412] The Chapel has been criticized for being too tall, too short, and also too wide. The tower – which rises 163 feet and is based, like many of Scott's towers, on that at Pershore – is generally acknowledged to be a noble edifice, but the parapet and pinnacles lack delicacy, and there are doubts about way it relates (or fails to relate) to the main structure. According to Bonney, the ensemble of tower and chapel resembled 'a burly man mounted on a Shetland pony'.[413]

More relevant here than any aesthetic judgments is the lowering effect that the new Chapel had on morale, even while it was being built. Bonney was a fierce opponent of the whole scheme ('From first to last the Chapel is a failure'), and therefore hardly representative of the Fellowship, but even so he was probably correct to discern a growing sense of dismay. 'When it came to pulling down the old Chapel of St. John's, I am sure that many of the Society felt some remorse as the process of demolition gradually revealed the fine early English work that had been hidden for centuries under a mean Perpendicular shell.' And even enthusiasts like Liveing were 'very conscious of the disastrous effect on the once beautiful proportions of the First Court'.[414] More telling were the comments of an enthusiast, J. S. Wood, writing as early as 1875 about another enthusiast, William Selwyn.

> [I] can now only look back with regret on the part which [I] took in the building of a new Chapel for the College. But those were days in which, though clouds were already gathering, men might still hope that a new Chapel would always be, what the old Chapel had never ceased to be, a meet expression, though in nobler and more stately form, of the faith of the Society to which it should belong. And so, not without serious misgivings on the part of some, misgivings which, *sooner even than those who felt them could have anticipated*, were proved to have been only too well-founded, and not without some natural regret on the part of all for the

---

[411] Howard, *Finances*, 209–12, 238–40.

[412] For one particularly jaundiced opinion, see Edward Beckett Denison to Reyner, 22 Aug. 1869: SJCA, D33.3.1.i.78: 'If Scott had somebody over him with a flail to thrash his invariably bad proportions and bits of mongrel Gothic out of him, leaving him to work out details (except window tracery, which he always makes asses of when left to himself) you might have had the finest thing of the kind in England.' However, since Denison (as Lord Grimthorpe) was responsible for the remodelling of the west front of St Alban's Abbey, his taste in such matters might be thought questionable.

[413] Bonney, *Memories*, 56.

[414] Heitland, 'Liveing', *Eagle* xliv (1924–6), 98.

27 The Old Chapel alongside the New, the tower of which (T. G. Bonney's 'burly man mounted on a Shetland pony') was to prove unexpectedly expensive for the College (1869)

loss of the homelier building which had been hallowed by centuries (...) the new Chapel was begun.[415]

Colleges with long histories pass through many troublous times, but most of the difficulties are external ones, which they cope with more or less ably. In this case the Fellowship had to contemplate a self-inflicted blow, and one that had left a gaping wound in the north-east corner of First Court. It all added to the sense of crisis.

The new Chapel had a problematic first decade. As well as dominating the College by its physical bulk, disputes relating to what went on inside it divided

[415] J. S. Wood, 'William Selwyn', *Eagle* ix (1874–5), 315–16 (italics added).

the Fellowship bitterly, and in Bonney's words almost impaired the College's 'usefulness'. The most immediate worry was poor attendance. Fines for non-attendance at chapel ceased – it is not certain why – in 1866. Undergraduates were still required on pain of gating to attend five times a week including once on Sunday,[416] but without the old financial sanctions it is perhaps not surprising that laxity should have set in. Anyway, a building designed to seat 245 rarely accommodated more than thirty, except on special occasions. In August 1873, for the first time anyone could remember, no one turned up to a Holy Communion except the two celebrants (and they barely on speaking terms). Worse still, the few undergraduates who did attend often behaved badly by lounging and talking. In 1871 eight junior Fellows led by Hill and Sandys sought to address the problem by calling for hymns to be introduced into services in place of the Sanctus or an anthem.[417]

> The Sunday morning services [are] wearisome to (…) a majority of the congregation partly because [it] has to leave the performance of a great part of the choral service to the choir and organist alone. The habit of abstaining from joining in the canticles, which is the necessary result of their present elaborate character, is now extending to the non-choral services and the undergraduates are now less hearty than they used to be in taking up the responses. I cannot help thinking that this listlessness might be partly obviated by a discouragement of the present excessive use of 'services' and other non-congregational music and that the introduction of hymns, considered as it has been on former occasions, would, if definitely sanctioned by the governing body, be welcomed by undergraduates and graduates alike, as one step, at any rate, in the right direction.[418]

The problem with this suggestion so far as the Seniors were concerned was that hymns were redolent of 'chapel' culture in its Welsh Baptist or northern mill town sense, not very desirable connotations for those who were anxious about the loss of the Anglican monopoly in the very same year. In 1873 Sandys and his colleagues again requested that hymns be introduced and canticles chanted as a way of rendering worship more 'hearty' and 'devotional', and the Seniors relented so far at least as to allow the singing of a number from the SPCK hymnal on Saturday and Sunday evenings.[419] Two years and very little improvement later, the same dons again raised the question of the canticles, and also demanded that hymns be introduced into the weekday services. To strengthen their case they began by holding meetings with what in the following century would be called the 'God Squad', a group of undergraduates led by a future Fellow, Henry Simpkinson.[420] There was general agreement that introducing music on weekdays would lead to 'increased heartiness', and a majority also wished to make the Sabbath services more 'congregational'. With regard to the latter proposal, there was a stumbling block in the form of the organist

---

[416] The Seniors issued a reminder to this effect in 1876: D51.1, 28 Nov. 1876.

[417] Russell, 'Diary of events', 30 Sept. 1871: SJCL, U22.

[418] Sandys to Bateson, 5 Sept. 1871: SJCA, D103.198.

[419] CB, 12 Jun. 1873; Russell, 'Diary of events', 31 May 1873: SJCL, U22.

[420] Fellow, 1877–87.

Dr Garrett, who was known to oppose any 'simplification' of the music, while, with regard to the former, the introduction of a hymn would lengthen the service and so might deter rather than attract potential worshippers.[421] 'General dread of any lengthening of service by a hymn though hymn desired', noted one of the Fellows present. This meant that when the matter was considered at the annual general College meeting of all the Fellows in 1875, discussion mainly turned on whether the daily services of Morning and Evening Prayer could be shortened so as to accommodate a hymn. Proponents such as Sandys and A. F. Torry argued that almost all other colleges had shortened their services (leading Bateson to comment, 'We cannot stand aloof'), and that undergraduates had become used to short services at school. Predictably, opposition to the proposals came from the two most conservative Fellows. Reyner insisted that any shortening of services would amount to a 'deterioration', and blamed 'bad behaviour' on the prevalence of 'scepticism in books &c which unsettles men's minds'. This was how conservatives always sought to explain the subversive character of the lower orders, but it was self-defeating of Reyner to imply that undergraduates should never have been taught to read. As Junior Dean and the officer responsible for chapel, Henry Russell[422] clearly felt defensive about the allegations of misbehaviour. He protested that it was no worse than it had always been, just that undergraduates could be seen in the new Chapel whereas before they had been hidden behind recesses. He likewise blamed the building for the lack of heartiness in saying the responses: 'Men are more sparse in larger chapels and afraid of their unsupported voices.' Anyway, it would be 'dangerous to teach men that the remedy for bad behaviour (…) is to cut services short.'[423] All such arguments were little more than shadow boxing, however. The conservatives' unanswerable case was procedural, i.e. that the general College meeting's propositions had no standing under Statute LV, that they could not be voted on, and that any discussion of them could only be informal. This is worth noting because, as will be seen, the same argument was used again and again to stifle any meaningful discussion outside the Seniority. Meanwhile, attendance at chapel continued to languish. Twenty-three services were held in January 1879 with an average turn-out of fewer than six, and even in February – i.e. term time – numbers fluctuated between ten and twenty-five, while not a single undergraduate turned up on 6 May 1870. Perhaps these low numbers were just as well, since the new Chapel proved to be an acoustic nightmare for speakers, though musically excellent.[424]

Two decades on, and nothing had changed on this particular front. In 1904 the Dean was forced to concede that 'the Daily Service no longer holds the place in College life which it once held'. Given that the average weekday attendance

[421] 'Diary of Joseph Timmis Ward', 29 Apr. 1875: SJCL, W2; SJCA, D103.189.

[422] Fellow, 1849; Junior Dean, 1868–77; Junior Bursar, 1877–84.

[423] Torry, Sandys, Griffith, Watson, Whitworth to Bateson, 24 Sept. 1875: SJCA, D103.190; Russell, 'Diary of events', 26 Oct. 1875: SJCL, U22.

[424] 'The effort to hear at a distance from the preacher will be considerable wherever the Preacher stands; and that upon the whole a Fellow would probably be best heard from the Lectern, where his being also in sight would probably be a great help to most persons' attention': Russell to Bateson, 2 Feb. 1877: SJCA, D103.170.

was down to three or four, this could be regarded as an understatement. At least one-third of the undergraduates were claiming full exemption, and because sport dominated so many students' early afternoons, medics and natural scientists often had practicals or private tuition between 5 o'clock and 7. Nor were they set any sort of example from on high since, apart from the Master, Deans, and Chaplains, who attended *ex officio*, hardly any senior members ever turned up. The Dean's solution, which was vetoed by the Visitor, was to cut services to 10 minutes, as being 'more in accordance with modern conditions'.[425]

Meanwhile, back in the 1870s, an unholy row broke out between the Master and the Junior Dean. Bateson and Russell were poles apart politically and temperamentally, but the row itself was deliberately provoked by a third party. Alfred Torry was an ambitious and self-important reformer. Naturally he despised Russell, and probably took delight in sneaking to Bateson that Russell had refused dissenting undergraduates admission to the Voluntary Choir. Nothing was more calculated to infuriate Bateson, who took the view that the University Tests Act prohibited any such discrimination. Bateson to Russell:

> I do not know whether I am correctly informed that you disallow the attendance of undergraduates as Volunteer Members of the Choir, who being Nonconformists are yet in the habit of attending the Chapel Services and desire no exemption under the power given by the Tests Repeal Act. If this is the case, I wish to say that I know of no authority under which you can exclude such persons and for my own part I think they ought to be allowed to attend.[426]

In his reply Russell drew a distinction between Nonconformists sitting *among* the choir and 'assisting in the musical part of the Service' (which was acceptable to him, and which he had allowed on one occasion) and being members of it, which all Anglicans and most Dissenters would regard as an anomaly. He then got to the nub:

> The Universities Tests Act has not made the Chapel Service in any the slightest degree a Service for all members of the College regarded as such. It would have been simply impossible to make it so without enacting that it should be varied from time to time to suit the different forms of religion, Christian or not Christian (...) By keeping the Service of the Church of England as the Chapel Service it has kept the Chapel Service as a Service for Churchmen, and not a Service for all members of the College regarded as such. But admission of Non-Churchmen as formal members of the Chapel Choir would be distinctly asserting a principle contrary to this reservation in the Act itself.[427]

The issue in itself was trivial, but like the investiture contest in the eleventh and twelfth centuries it epitomized a fundamental conflict between secular and sacred authority. Bateson's response ignored the theocratic point and went straight to what was, for him, the nub.

[425] F. Dyson to Taylor, 26 Jan. 1904: SJCA, D103.100–1.
[426] Bateson to Russell, 30 Jan. 1877: SJCA, D103.169.
[427] Russell to Bateson, 2 Feb. 1877: SJCA, D103.170.

You have objected to Undergraduates not Churchmen joining the Voluntary Choir (...) You have not deemed it necessary to seek for any distinct
authorisation for adopting such a line of action (...) You appear to me to
have exceeded the discretionary powers which belong to your office, and
I say so without any reference to the repeal of the University Tests and as
though the circumstances were the same as before the Act of the Legislature on that subject. I have no wish to bring questions of this kind before
the Seniority (...) [but] if you cannot give me an assurance that you will
interpose no discouragement on the class of persons adverted to, so far
as relates to their being members of the Voluntary Choir, I shall have no
other course left open to me.[428]

To which Russell's reply was elaborately polite to the point of insolence, and
typically obscurantist, but made quite clear that, in his opinion, a Dean of St
John's had powers to operate within his own sphere without seeking the permission of the Master and Seniors.[429] His problem, as Bateson pointed out, had
nothing to do with the University Tests Act but went back to the fact that there
could only be one governing body, and that was the Seniority. As a Senior himself, Russell was only too happy to use that argument against the pretensions
of the juniors, as will be seen, but he was riled to have it used against himself
qua Dean. Later in 1877 Russell ceased to be Junior Dean, whether of his own
volition or Bateson's is not known, and took up the post of Junior Bursar instead,
while Torry took his place as Junior Dean.

In addition to these particular skirmishes, the College naturally became
embroiled in issues that were dividing Anglican congregations everywhere.
These were of two types, ecclesiological and doctrinal. With regard to the
former, there was great controversy at this time as a result of the Anglo-Catho-
lic or Ritualist movement within the Church of England, but it does not seem
to have been a big issue in St John's. There was a whiff of gunpowder in 1864
when the Seniors divided equally on a proposal by Peter Mason, the Senior
Dean, for weekly Holy Communion, and Bateson, very hostile, gave a casting
vote against. And Russell got mildly worked up once when Mason celebrated
Holy Communion standing in the 'eastward position' in front of the altar and
with his back to the congregation. However, he desisted from doing so in 1871
after the Privy Council (in Herbert *v.* Purchas) condemned it as ritualistic,[430]
and all in all such practices do not seem to have caused much of a problem. But
the case was very different with regard to doctrinal differences. Indeed, it is
not too much to say that theological disputation brought effective governance
almost to a standstill. It cannot, however, be blamed on the new Chapel, being
very much a legacy from the old one.

Two introductory points need to be made here, the first concerning form, the

---

[428] Bateson to Russell, 5 Feb. 1877: SJCA, D103.171.

[429] Russell to Bateson, 7 Feb. 1877: SJCA, D103.172. Russell added that, if he had sought
the permission of the Seniority, 'undoubtedly, I believe, I should have obtained it, at
least at any time before October of last year'. That was when Russell had lost Reyner,
his great ally on the Seniority.

[430] Russell, 'Diary of events', 26. Feb. 1871: SJCL, U22.

second content. Although congregations were not permitted to cheer or boo, attendance or (especially) non-attendance at sermons was a recognized way of making a statement. For example, in 1875 the legendary educationist and former Fellow Edwin Abbott[431] was scheduled to deliver three University sermons on Darwin's *On the Origin of Species* and *Descent of Man*. Many undergraduates were fascinated by the first two and correspondingly disappointed when they turned up to the third lecture to find that Abbott was indisposed, and that his place had been taken by a more conventional preacher dilating on Christ's agony in the garden. The point of this story is that one undergraduate realized immediately on entering St Mary's that 'something had happened', because 'all the old dons' including Reyner had 'returned in full force'.[432] Whether or not to lend one's ears to another was often a highly tactical decision, so it is unsurprising that the civil war in St John's should have taken the form of a 'battle of the sermons'. Admittedly, there was also a fortuitous element in that it was only in 1860, after the University Senate had decided to abolish Sunday morning preaching in Great St Mary's, that the Seniors agreed to introduce sermons after the Sunday evening service in St John's. They were to take place during the six lecturing weeks of each term, and would be preached by either the Master or a Fellow. It is not clear how soon the 'battle of the sermons' started to become bloody, but by 1865 at the latest it was generating so much polemical tension that any attempt to create a numinous atmosphere was impossible. As Heitland commented wittily, 'in order to get any spiritual nourishment out of the Chapel services, you had to take it in with you, and in some highly developed form'.[433]

With regard to content, the same battle was being fought, though rarely so viciously, in chapters, dioceses, parishes, and colleges everywhere. In 1853 the theologian F. D. Maurice had been dismissed from his chair at King's College London, ostensibly for having denied the doctrine of eternal punishment. Two years later Benjamin Jowett's commentary on St Paul caused terrible offence to the orthodox by denying that Christ had in any literal sense died for the sins of mankind. Likewise in 1861 the Anglican contributors to *Essays and Reviews* sought to reinterpret and so rescue Christian faith by distancing it from its more superstitious elements. At that point it was still just possible to dismiss these authors as clerical *enfants terribles* who would grow out of their neological malady once they had matured. But during the course of the 1860s it became obvious that the old Evangelical and High Church orthodoxies were causing people to abandon the faith together, even to the extent of giving up their Fellowships, like Leslie Stephen of Trinity Hall. In consequence, what might be called 'middle opinion' was turning away from orthodoxy and towards broad churchmanship, one central tenet of which was to engage positively with the fashionable scientific ideas including evolutionary biology. In Cambridge this

---

[431]　Senior Classic, 1861; Fellow, 1862. Abbott resigned in 1863 on getting married. In 1875 he was head of the City of London School.

[432]　Ward, 'Diary', 14, 21, and 28 Feb. 1875: SJCL, W2. St John's Library first acquired copies of *On the Origin of Species* (1859) and *The Descent of Man* (1871) in 1876, the year of Reyner's departure. It is impossible to say whether he had prevented their earlier purchase, or whether he decided to leave because they had been purchased.

[433]　Heitland, *After Many Years*, 176.

development was being led by two of the leading theologians of the day, Fenton Hort and Brook Foss Westcott, both of Trinity. It threw traditionalists on the defensive and forced them to become more strident. Hence the fury with which they attacked science, proclaimed the divinely inspired nature (i.e. literal truth) of Holy Scripture, and preached the orthodox Gospel scheme of redemption, based on the doctrines of providence, original sin, justification by faith, atonement, judgment, heaven, and hell.

In St John's this traditional Christianity was represented most forcibly by Reyner, Wood, and Russell. Of the former little more needs to be said except that even his detractor Bonney acknowledged him to be 'a well-read theologian of the old school'. The President John Spicer Wood was instinctively a much less combative man, but he felt passionately on religious matters. Scott, who knew him only by hearsay, dismissed him as 'difficult, (...) one of those men who are never in sympathy with youth and who never realise that a man may be full of mischief but no wickedness. He was thoroughly unpopular.'[434] Yet John Mayor, who knew him personally, described him as delicate, kindly, and conscientious, 'a man of saintly strain, of the type of George Herbert'. It was said that as Proctor he had restored 'several penitent daughters to their homes',[435] while everyone acknowledged that he preached beautifully on the money changers in the temple (John 11:12–16). His later years as a Fellow were made miserable by a conflict for which he was in large part responsible, his rigid adherence to principle having a greater impact than the sweetness of his nature. The last of the trio, Henry Russell, the man who feared that his choir might be defiled, kept personal diaries that provide an unrivalled account of many aspects of college life between 1864 and 1884. They record in the most minute detail such things as attendance at chapel services (with names in the case of Fellows), where different Fellows chose to stand in relation to the altar at different ceremonies, who attended various feasts and dinners, what was eaten, and so on and so forth. One of the pits into which historians can fall is in supposing that, because someone took the trouble to write something down, that person at least must have thought it interesting or significant. In fact it seems clear that Russell wrote things down because he had nothing better to do with his life. At formal meetings his endless appeals to 'points of order', must have made him a tiresome colleague, especially to those on the side of reform. In the words of his obituarist, 'minuteness, or perhaps one should rather say precision, seemed the characteristic of his mind (...) In [committee] his criticisms and amendments were not always welcomed by ardent men eager to press forward their far-reaching plans and wide proposals'.[436] Bonney dismissed him more bluntly: 'He combined an excellent memory for unimportant details with a complete incapacity for grasping principles.'[437] Nevertheless, pedants often make fine witnesses, and without Russell we should know far less about the Chapel wars than we do.

Fighting on the other side in those wars were Bateson, John Mayor, and

[434] R. F. Scott, MS Diary, 1899–1908: SJCA, SB1.23.502.

[435] J. E. B. Mayor, 'The Rev. John Spicer Wood DD', *Eagle* xvii (1891–3), 654–5.

[436] Edwin Hill, 'Obituary of Revd Henry Russell', *Eagle* xxv (1903–4), 198–200.

[437] Bonney, *Memories*, 40.

George Bonney. Bateson's sermons were so broad and so bland theologically that to Reyner and Wood they must have seemed little better than agnostic. There was much about doing duty to God by doing duty in the world, but hardly anything about the need for redemption. There were rebukes for those unchar-itable Christians who denounced each other over words – 'forms of worship, church services, postures, standing, and kneeling'. Even more provocative was his post-Darwinian perspective on the need to adapt Christian belief to human reason.

> It must, I think, be admitted by thoughtful and candid men that the progress of scientific enquiry and the results of philosophical investiga-tion have rudely shaken many things which not many years ago were regarded as important and indisputable, such things, I mean as relate to the origin of our race, the mutations of species, and whatsoever depends on the results of enquiry into pre-historic times.[438]

Likewise the broad-minded Mayor would outrage orthodox believers by telling undergraduates from the pulpit that he hoped to meet Socrates and other virtu-ous pagans in heaven. But the pugnacious Bonney it was who determined on a fight. Already embarked at the age of twenty-six on a career as a geologist, he read Darwin's *Origin of Species* when it first came out, and

> saw at once that though, as the author frankly admitted, he might have to modify, and even correct some of his conclusions, he had made as great an advance in Natural History as Kopernick had done in Astronomy. Since those days (...) we may confidently affirm that evolution expresses a proc-ess which operates not only in all things, whether living or non-living, but also in ethics, theology, civilization, and everything that concerns the progress of mankind.[439]

It followed that 'ministers of religion must expect their teaching to be sub-jected to scientific criticism.'[440] Holding such views, Bonney inevitably gagged on those of his clerical colleagues who clung to the *Genesis* account of the creation. Thanks to Russell's diary we know that seventy-three turned up to hear Bonney in December 1866, including fifty-six undergraduates. This was about three times the usual figure, but whether the congregation was swelled by anticipation of the preacher's message, or by the expectation that he would say something outrageous, or by some contingent factor, is impossible to say.

Matters came to a crisis in 1868. On 10 May Reyner expressed himself even more forcefully than usual against clergymen with latitudinarian views. According to later report he spoke of sermons 'not tending to corroborate the faith but rather to overthrow it'.[441] It may have been this address that elicited 'a slight ironical applause from the benches'.[442] Everyone knew he meant Bonney,

---

[438] W. H. Bateson, *Six Sermons* (Cambridge, 1881), 7, 47.
[439] Bonney, *Memories*, 37.
[440] Bonney, *Influence of Science of Theology*, vi.
[441] Mayor *et al.* to the Visitor: SJCA, D103.73. See below, p. 364.
[442] Heitland, *After Many Years*, 178.

who rose to answer the challenge a fortnight later. In Heitland's words: 'I shall never forget hearing him preach one evening, evidently in a white heat, and pause in the middle of his discourse, only to start again with bated breath: "*You have been told by those who ought to have known better ...*" and so on. Such scenes were not edifying.'[443] Which is why on 12 June, after two feverish discussions, the Seniors voted on a proposal to suspend all preaching in Chapel until further notice. 'For: Parkinson, Reyner, Wood, Mason, Bushby. Against: Mayor, Bonney. Neutral: Russell.'[444] No one would have believed it at the time, but sermons were to remain suspended until 1877.

It must have struck many as symbolic that, just four days before the fateful decision to suspend, work had begun on dismantling the old Chapel, starting with the removal of its ancient woodwork.

In Heitland's account of the matter, the differences between Reyner and Bonney 'were too embittered for even the Master's tact to compose them'.[445] Heitland was hugely impressed with Bateson, his future father-in-law, whom he saw as a mediator, but he was still only an undergraduate in 1869 and failed to appreciate the extent to which Bateson must be regarded as a protagonist. It is true that with regard to the purely doctrinal disputes Bateson was above the fray, but these cannot be separated from the political war that was raging. It was already evident by 1869 that, thanks to him as much as anyone, Dissenters would shortly be admitted on equal terms. When it actually happened Wood was vitriolic, saying that it had turned colleges into 'chance-medleys of churchmen, dissenters and unbelievers'.[446] Such a dilution would have mattered less under the old statutes, but in 1860 the 'College', in the persons of its governing body, had for the first time been placed in charge of every aspect of divine service.

> No City of God, no Church of Christ, is here (...) Faithful men there are but they are not an organised body. An organised body it is, but it not a body of faithful men, still less of men organised in accordance with the ordinance of Christ. Yet such a body it is that now claims to stand in the place of the Body of Christ, a veritable antichrist, to all members of the Church of England in a College.[447]

If Heitland is correct, it was Wood even more than Reyner who insisted on banning sermons, yet despite his success in this respect he seems never to have darkened the chapel doors between 1869 and 1881. 'He stood more and more alone in what he regarded as a fallen society.'[448] Bonney was understandably baffled at Wood's continuing to offer himself every year as President, notwithstanding the terrible example he set to undergraduates by never attending chapel. Bonney

---

[443] W. E. Heitland, 'Thomas George Bonney', *Eagle* xliii (1923–4), 263.

[444] Russell, 'Diary of events', 12 Jun. 1868: SJCL, U22.

[445] Heitland, *After Many Years*, 178.

[446] J. S. Wood, *The Position of Members of the Church of England in a College of the University of Cambridge* (Cambridge & London, 1882), 2.

[447] Ibid., 4–6, 30–1.

[448] Mayor, 'John Spicer Wood', 661.

was even more baffled by the fact that the Seniors year after year 'had not the moral courage' to discontinue him from office.[449]

By comparison with the admission of Dissenters, the move by Bateson, Bonney, Liveing, and Fellows of other colleges to set up a non-collegiate institution in order to enable less well-off men to obtain Cambridge degrees might seem innocuous. Yet emotions were so raw that even this led to bitterness, and, what was worse, it was an almost entirely internecine conflict played out at a public meeting, and reported for an even wider public that read the *Cambridge Chronicle*. Bateson was chairman of the board behind the proposal, and after he had made some amiable remarks, three Johnians stood up to pour cold water on it. On one side was A. F. Torry, who was particularly anxious about the iniquities of lodging-house life and was keen to see the extension of college hostel facilities. He said the scheme did not go far enough. On the other side, Russell protested that 'a collegiate and a non-collegiate system were scarcely compatible with each other in the same University'. And Reyner, as he was sometimes wont to do, went over the top.

> Nothing more was to be required of these men than attendance at examinations (…) As to the principle of the scheme it was infidel. It was a scheme to admit members to this University, who would in no way be brought into contact with religion; they would be simply students seeking a degree here. The apparent motive of the scheme was one of base expediency, a motive which actuated Pontius Pilate *populo satisfacere*; he would not say *populus*, but *plebs* – the *plebs* of newspapers and magazines, which advocated infidelity to make themselves sell – the *plebs* of philosophers, falsely so called. Lastly, it was the scheme urged by Political Dissenters whom he classed with the *plebs* of the whole population of England. It was a scheme for informing the mind and the mind only; a scheme for furnishing the mind with unsanctified knowledge (…) If we are to have godless and infidel education, let it be forced upon us from without, but let not the University itself take the initiatory step.

Bonney immediately got up to remark that 'if anything could show that our scheme of education was imperfect, it was [Reyner's] speech'. Then Bateson, trying to calm things down, said he 'was sorry to hear Mr Reyner use language which in his cooler moments he would possibly regret'. This caused a loud 'No' to erupt from his antagonist.[450] Non-Johnians present shook their heads.

These disputations are relevant to the story of John William Colenso and the consecration of the new Chapel in May 1869. That story is related in almost every history and memoir of the College, and yet, without understanding the context provided by the chapel wars, it cannot be fully appreciated. Colenso was a much revered former Fellow (1837–46) and, as a vigorous and resourceful African missionary, appointed bishop of Natal in 1853, he could be described as the *beau ideal* of a holy Johnian. Unfortunately he was also notorious on account of

---

[449] Bonney, *Memories*, 41–2.

[450] *Cambridge Chronicle*, 28 Mar. 1868; W. W. Grave, *Fitzwilliam College Cambridge 1869–1969: Its History as the Non-Collegiate Institution of the University and its Beginnings as an Independent College* (Cambridge, 1983), 25–31.

his *Pentateuch and the Book of Joshua Critically Examined* (1862) in which, following German biblical analysis, he argued that the first six books of the Bible were
not the word of God, and that their accounts of tribal savagery in fact contra-
dicted the message of God's love. This led his apparent superior, the Evangelical
bishop of Cape Town, to depose and then excommunicate him, but to no effect
since the Judicial Committee of the Privy Council ruled that these actions were
ultra vires. For several years Colenso remained a divisive figure, anathematized
by conservatives and praised by liberals such as Dean Stanley, who pointedly
invited him to preach in Westminster Abbey. In these circumstances it is unsurprising that the Seniority should have instructed Bateson to warn Colenso off
attending the grand ceremony planned for the consecration of the new Chapel,
despite the fact that he had loyally subscribed towards its creation.[451] Unfortunately, the dignitary appointed to preach on that occasion was that 'mighty
militant' George Selwyn, the former bishop of New Zealand, recently installed
as bishop of Lichfield, and brother of William. In the course of offering broth-
erly love to all Johnians absent and present, and unable to restrain himself, he
specifically excluded the 'recreant' bishop from his benison. 'He went out from
us but he is not of us. One thing still remains: we can pray for him.' Later that
evening the Master spoke in a crowded Hall and drew loud cheers with his
words, 'Others there are, who, though unable to be present in body, are present
with us in spirit – not the least the illustrious prelate whom the preacher specially commended to our prayers.' Heitland, recollecting that 'memorable scene',
typically saw it as an example of Bateson's tact, a successful attempt to repair
the damage done by Selwyn. Its real significance lay in showing that a combative Bateson was willing to allude to dirty linen, not merely in public, but on
the most open day in the College's recent history, a day when special trains had
been laid on from King's Cross. It also marks Bateson's genuine admiration of
Colenso, whom (he later predicted) would come to be regarded as a '*grande decus*
[great ornament] of the College'.[452]

   So how significant were these quarrels? For the individuals concerned, once
they had got over their immediate obsessions, perhaps not all that much. Heitland claimed that much later 'the two pulpit adversaries' met on friendly terms
in London, and that Reyner invited Bonney to preach in his church at Staplehurst. This reminds us that many Fellows led discretely consecutive lives.
Whether or not Reyner's bizarre horsemanship had been a sign of sexual frustration, after leaving Cambridge marriage, the clerical vocation, and automatic
deference seem to have removed the edges from his personality. With the help
of considerable private resources, he and his wife contributed munificently to
the needs of his parish, including those of the poor, and they seem to have
been considerably loved in the community. Moreover, although his impact on
St John's had been immense for twenty years, there were only two College representatives among the hundreds at his funeral, and in the summations of his

---

[451] Colenso is reported to have told his son, then in residence at St John's, that 'if Mr
   Reyner helped to administer [Holy Communion], probably he would have openly
   refused it to me'. Mullinger, *St John's College*, 285. Reyner had certainly pressed for his
   exclusion.

[452] Russell, 'Diary of events', 11 Jun. 1880: SJCL, U22.

life that were delivered at that ceremony, the College rated no more than the barest mention, unlike the 2nd V.B. East Kent Regiment, whose acting chaplain he had been, and whose members fired the salute. Wood too found happiness and respect in wife and parish, though more briefly – he died unexpectedly after a few years. Russell and Bonney never married,[453] but the former seems to have been delighted to have swapped the Junior Bursarship for a parish, while the latter forged a wholly new academic life in London before returning to St John's, as opinionated as ever, in 1905. But even if individuals escaped, it is hard to believe that the College did not suffer as a result of such poison among the Fellowship over a period of ten to fifteen years. Indeed, it may be telling that the two most outspoken Fellows of the late nineteenth century could not quite bring themselves to talk about it. Reviewing Bonney's *Memoirs*, Heitland commented on the 'mighty self restraint' shown by the author, and expressed his disappointment that Bonney should have named no names in his account of the chapel wars; yet his own memoirs published four years later were equally reticent, Bonney and Reyner being referred to coyly as 'two of the elders'.[454] Elsewhere, Bonney said that it would be better 'not to go into the reasons' for the damaging disputes, and Heitland wrote that it was too painful to talk about.

Most of all, the battle of the sermons was important because it fed directly into an ongoing and underlying war, between Junior and Senior Fellows, which ushered in the so-called 'revolution' of 1882. Following the Seniority's decision to suspend preaching, a cooling off period ensued, but in September 1869 Pearson and others demanded a College meeting to discuss a decision that was 'not only opposed to the best interests of the College, but also in contravention of the obvious intention of Statute 14'. When that discussion took place in October it seemed as though both parties were anxious to restore a measure of harmony, especially as the dispute was being openly discussed in other colleges, and had even been alluded to in the *Spectator*. Bateson set the tone by saying that all he wanted to do was sound out the views of the twenty Fellows present. The saintly Pearson pleaded with his colleagues to eschew sermons of 'an atheistical and Socinian tendency'; Reyner insisted that sermons should teach the Christian faith and the historical facts of the Old Testament; Whitworth deplored controversial sermons, and claimed that what was needed from the pulpit was not instruction but exhortation; Wace was only prepared to resume sermons if there could be safeguards against a repetition of recent events. Only Mayor spoke strongly on the other side, arguing that 'men could not consent to preach in a groove', but according to Russell 'no one objected to having *some* regulation of sermons'.[455]

---

[453] It is impossible to know whether obituaries in the *Eagle* were sexually coded, but for the record Heitland commented that Bonney's 'fondness for the society of young men was very marked', and Hill thought it sufficiently important to mention Russell's 'influence on the choir boys. He made it his business to go (daily, I believe) into their school and give them personal instruction.'

[454] Heitland, review of Bonney's *Memories*, *Eagle* xlii (1921–2), 284; Heitland, *After Many Years*, 178.

[455] Russell, 'Diary of events', 26 Oct. 1869: SJCL, U22.

When discussion resumed in October 1870, the Seniors having done nothing to break the deadlock in the meantime, those Fellows designated by Bonney as the most 'bigoted' all remained opposed to sermons being restored, Reyner because of Fellows' compulsion to preach politics and not the Gospel, Mason because 'people preached about the Bible who knew o about it', and Wood because of complaints from undergraduates that 'Fellows preached against each other'. On the other side, Mayor referred to Bishop Fisher's concern that young men should be trained to preach to the poor, and Bateson commented gently on the importance of 'liberty of thought'. Unity did not require uniformity, and everything depended on 'forbearance and good feeling'. At the end of the discussion the vote in favour of resuming sermons was carried by 21 to 9, but ominously, of the eleven most Senior Fellows present, only Mayor and Bonney joined the Master in favour of resuming sermons, while of the twenty most junior only one did not vote in favour. The Fellowship was sharply divided between young and old.[456] And when, several weeks later, one of the Seniors – presumably Mayor or Bonney – proposed that Fellows should be asked to preach as in the Old Chapel, Russell moved successfully that the issue be deferred.[457]

It was shortly after this that Heitland made the sudden transition from undergraduate to fledgling don. Although by no means a shrinking violet, he hardly dared to open his mouth for fear of saying the wrong thing to the wrong person, so charged was the atmosphere, and it grew worse as months went by, then a year, and then another, without the Seniors showing any signs of acting on the matter. Eventually, in April 1873, the issue was taken up by twenty-six former Fellows (including Robert and Joseph Mayor), who sent a memorial to the Seniors, not directly but via James Atlay, now bishop of Hereford. It was a strongly worded protest deploring the fact that, 'at the very time the Chapel has just been re-erected with unusual magnificence, the voice of the preacher should cease to be heard within the Chapel walls', and it ended with an implied threat to discourage relatives, friends, and pupils from applying to St John's unless sermons were resumed.[458] In his covering note Atlay added the following gloss.

> Moving as the Memorialists do, in various grades of Society, it may perhaps be that we hear more frequently than the residents what the outside world says and thinks about College life; and I doubt whether there is any reproach more constantly levelled against the Universities (...) than their apparent want of care for the souls of the men who they are training for active life. Words of Counsel the Undergraduates frequently hear from their Tutors, (...) but they do not receive that public exhortation and instruction to which they have been accustomed at school and at home, and they feel the loss.

He ended by saying that the anger was widespread, and that the memorial-

---

[456] Pearson to Bateson, 13 Sept. 1869: SJCA, D104.134; Russell, 'Diary of events', 25 Oct. 1870.

[457] Russell, 'Diary of events', 5 and 20 Dec. 1870.

[458] Memorial from former Fellows to Master and Seniors: SJCA, D103.75.

ists could easily have obtained more signatories.[459] Two Tutors, Bonney and Sandys, backed up his plea, protesting that their pupils were likely to suffer far more from the loss of spiritual exhortation 'than from any divergence of opinion [among] the preachers', but when a motion to resume sermons was put to the Seniority on 31 May, it secured only four votes and so went down.[460]

This casual dismissal of the pleas for sermons to resume was accompanied by two other contentious decisions: to abolish a vacant Lectureship in Moral Sciences and to appoint only one instead of two Lecturers in Theology. The latter was especially bad news for Henry Melvill Gwatkin, a young Fellow who by 1873 had become desperate to marry his fiancée, but who was equally desperate not to lose his Fellowship before landing a theology lectureship, and determined also to hang in long enough to play a part in the 'fearful row' that he could see was coming. His letters to 'Darling Lucy' convey just how poisonous the atmosphere was at this time, though they make no pretence of impartiality, not least because he was sure that the forces of darkness were out to deprive him of a lectureship. With regard to the Seniors' meeting of 31 May, he judged that his 'enemies' (whom he also called 'the owls') had had 'cunning enough just to do all the mischief possible without a general revolt'. Nevertheless,

> All we can see yet is a general outburst all over the college. Even the moderate men are tired of their meddling jobbery: and the churchmen are ready to join us against men who prefer abolishing sermons to the chance of any but ritualists having a turn in the pulpit.[461] [...] Of course Reyner & Co are delighted with themselves. I never saw them in such uproarious glee as yesterday in hall. The college may go to the dogs, if only *they* can take it there. You must know that their first two steps [on lectureships] are in the teeth of the advice of all the lecturers, asked by themselves; and the third [on sermons] is so utterly against the statutes that the Master has openly declared that the Visitor can only reverse it ... If the storm does burst – and I never before saw anything nearly so threatening – it will be in a context of such bitterness as I do not like to think of.[462]

At this point the serious plotting began.

[459] Atlay to Bateson, 12 Apr. 1873: SJCA, D103.74. As a Fellow (1842–59) and prominent Tutor (1847–59), Atlay had opposed the reform party *toto cælo* on the 'tenure of fellowships, the marriage question, the Tuition, and the advisability of retaining as many Clergymen in our body as we can'. Once, when Joe Mayor had conceded the point that 'no married Fellow shall reside in College', Atlay had added the rider, 'or any where else': James Atlay to Joseph Mayor, 20 Nov. 1858: Mayor Papers, B16/122.

[460] Bonney and Sandys to the Master and Seniors, 2 Jun. 1873, and the same to the memorialists, 16 Jun. 1873: SJCA, D103.76.

[461] Gwatkin's use of the word 'ritualists' is problematic since, although 'Reyner & Co' were high churchmen, there is no evidence that they belonged to the growing movement within the Anglican church calling for the introduction of Catholic liturgical practices. Maybe Gwatkin was deliberately exaggerating for effect (in the manner that a conservative might refer to socialists as communists), or maybe he wished to imply that anyone who opposed sermons must *ipso facto* be possessed of ritualistic instincts.

[462] Henry Gwatkin to Lucy de Lisle Brock, 1 June 1873, Emmanuel College, Cambridge: Papers of Henry Melvill Gwatkin, ECA Col.9. 39c. 319.

Bonney and Sandys mean to make all the disturbance they can: and almost the entire college will support them. It is to begin by a protest before the owls on Wednesday, and to be followed up by a general explosion at the meeting in October, publication of all the nasty charges they have made themselves liable to, and in the last resort, a row in Parliament. Well darling, I must retain my fellowship for the present. I have little hope for myself, but the owls are arrant cowards, and may throw the church over any day to save their precious hides; and I *must* speak at the meeting in October.[463]

In September 1873 William Hudson, Philip Main, Alfred Marshall, J. E. Sandys, and Bonney put forward three issues for discussion at the forthcoming general College meeting, held under Statute LV: tenure of Fellowships, University contributions, and – portentously – 'the more efficient government of the College'. They also demanded that the meeting 'have power to adjourn as often as may be found necessary', another way of saying that the Seniors should not be allowed to talk resolutions out as in previous years.[464] It all made for what Russell described as a 'very stormy meeting' of twenty-six Fellows, including five non-residents, in the following month. The meeting began with Reyner, Frederic Wace, Ernest Levett, and Frank Watson seeking to abort proceedings on the grounds that the demand by Hudson and his colleagues for a discussion under Statute LV contravened Statue LVI. Russell, of course, was in full agreement with them, as his account of proceedings on 28 October makes clear.

> The Master was beginning to read Counsel's opinion given to Trinity College to shew that it was within our Statutes to call under Statute 55 for a meeting of Master and Fellows of Statute 59, when he was asked again to carry out Statute 56 so that the Master and Seniors could say whether the propositions could be put to the meeting: it was suggested that the propositions should be put and the question be taken afterwards, but it was answered that the very thing protested against was the putting the propositions at all: the Master tried to begin discussion again and was evidently trying to force on the propositions: there was strong and repeated remonstrances from Wace, Levett, Watson, Reyner, and Hill and charges of discourtesy to the Master by Bonney, Pearson, Marshall, Hudson. Wood said the cause of all this was the Master beginning to read that Counsel's opinion. The Master speaking, Reyner spoke also but was met by cries of 'order' till he sat down: and, I protesting against discussion till the objections made had been decided, the propositions were supported by Sandys, Marshall, Bonney, Hudson and spoken against by Reyner, (after Sandys), Frank Watson, Levett: I protesting against any discussion – saying it need cause no surprise if those who objected refused to consider the propositions put at all, that it was clear that an attempt was making to force them on to gain a year that they might be voted on next year (some had wanted

---

[463] Gwatkin to Lucy Brock, 2 June 1873, Gwatkin Papers, ECA Col.9. 39c. 320. Gwatkin went on to become Dixie Professor of Ecclesiastical History (1891–1916) and a Fellow of Emmanuel.

[464] W. H. H. Hudson to Bateson, 18 Sept. 1873: SJCA, D103.63.

a meeting called directly): but bringing the question of legality, as the Master had done, before this meeting instead of before the Master and Seniors which was the only body to decide it was naturally and practically to prejudice the question on its merits, &c &c.

Russell's concern for due process was undoubtedly sincere, but to his antagonists it entirely missed the point. What follows is Gwatkin's more colourful account of the meeting.

Before Sandys had spoken a word, up jumps Wace with a protest that the meeting had no power to discuss the matter with half a dozen legal doubts. He is supported by several more on his side. We said nothing at all. Then the Master rose. But when he came to the words – 'I will now tell the meeting the reasons why I think the propositions *can* be discussed' – he was interrupted by Reyner Russell Watson Wace and Levett all at once. The scene was fearful, and at last the Master sat down – 'I appeal to the courtesy of the meeting, whether the chairman is to be allowed to finish his sentence' – and it was nearly an hour before he spoke again. These five spent their time in a quick series of furious declamations, usually two together. We only interposed occasionally to demand that the chairman be heard. Reyner was utterly wild – 'the Master has no right to speak' – 'a gang of conspirators, of whom the Master is one'. At last the meeting calmed. Moderate men demanded a hearing for the Master. Pearson and Mayor administered a tremendous rebuke to Levett and Watson. The offenders one by one made ungracious apologies, except Reyner. At last the Master rose again, and was at once interrupted by Reyner. But *now*, Wace & Co helped to hiss him down, & he had to be quiet while the Master gave his decision, & called on Sandys to open the proceedings. Even then the whole pack protested throughout against the Master's ruling, & nothing but the marked disfavour of the meeting prevented Reyner from clamouring us down. So now we were free to speak. Sandys began with an extremely conciliatory speech. Nothing was to be said of the past. Then Russell with technical objections: the other side except Reyner absolutely refused to touch the merits of the case, & confined themselves to protesting against the Master's decision. Then came Bonney – conciliatory again. Then a long rambling speech from Reyner, declaring the whole thing a job, to fill our own pockets, & and containing more personal abuse than I ever heard before in 15 minutes time. It is well for him that we were on the conciliatory tack, for I never saw a finer opening for a crushing answer. Then came a very long series of short speeches from everyone, in which the chief points were the enemy's determined policy of fighting with legal quibbles – it was useless to clear up any doubts, for the arguments were repeated over and over again as if we had not heard them. And the way the moderate men came steadily over to our side. In fact, the strongest things said were by some of them, such as Griffith and Hill at the end. [...] Now there is no *direct* gain in all this, for the owls have yet to decide whether the proposals can be voted on next year; and as Hill said in almost so many words, their decision is a foregone conclusion.

They will never allow them to come to vote. But we have played moderates ourselves, and got a most discreditable scene out of them, which has shaken their moral weight in a way nothing else has done for years. The persistent abuse of Reyner and the persistent quibbling of the others have helped us wonderfully.[465]

Gwatkin's overall impression was that the row had a 'soothing effect', except with respect to Reyner, and indeed it seems surprising that the Senior Bursar should have continued in post for another three years, given the complete breakdown of his relations with the Master.

Although the two sides lined up according to how they had divided over sermons in Chapel, the point at issue was now a more fundamental one concerning governance. Could propositions put in writing to all Fellows by the Master under Statute LVI be discussed by all Fellows at an annual general meeting called under Statute LV? Wood, Reyner, Pieters, and Russell said they could not, Bateson, Mayor, Bonney, and Bushby voted in favour. (General consternation greeted Bushby's vote, as it tends to do when someone acts contrary to expectation. The poor chap was forced to admit that he would have voted on the other side had he understood what was going on, but had mistakenly supposed that they were voting to elect a McMahon Student.)[466] Bateson then suggested that the Masters and Fellows might deliberate on issues under Statute LIX instead, but Wood objected that such meetings were only called for fixing the seal. When recording all this in his diary, Russell got even more worked up over the heretical suggestion that such meetings might adjourn and reconvene *themselves*:

> This Meeting of course to judge itself when adjournment no longer 'necessary', i.e. when the *clique of residents* (no one else but the resident clique would attend long) had carried all its points under name of General College Meeting. The Master and Seniors are virtually asked to play into the hands of a clique, (…) the world to be told (…) that certain Fellows are obstructives. Master and Seniors are asked to assent to I and II in absolute ignorance, i.e. to put things with their eyes blindfolded into the hands of a clique to do as they like like a Long Parliament, and call their conclusions those of General College Meetings.[467]

The Seniors met on 2 December and, urged on by Reyner and Russell, pronounced that the recent general meeting had acted *ultra vires* in discussing two illegal propositions. This determination prompted a further memorial from Sandys and thirteen other Junior Fellows demanding that the question of

---

[465] Gwatkin to Lucy Brock, 28 Oct. 1873: Gwatkin Papers, ECA Col. 9. 39c. 324.

[466] Edward Bushby was one of Bonney's ultra-conservative bugbears. 'He was now much advanced in years and seemed to be quite incapable of realizing how greatly the University and the outside world had changed since he had taken any part in educational work. Besides this he had in other ways altered for the worse. Always parsimonious, he had gradually become miserly, to such an extent at last as to be an unpleasant neighbour from his habits at table and his dirty clothing.' Bonney, *Memories*, 39–40. McMahon studentships are awards for lawyers in training.

[467] Russell, 'Diary of events', 28 Oct. 1873: SJCL, U22.

28 The Pensionary (about 1870) on the site later occupied by the Divinity School, in the sixteenth century occupied by paying students (pensioners): SJCL, Arch. V.13

legality be referred to legal counsel: 'We venture to call [the Seniors'] attention to the dilemma in which they have placed those Fellows of the College who question whether that decision is in accordance with law; and who are thereby compelled either to submit to what they regard as a wrong, or to introduce an element of vexation and discord into the College by appealing to the interposition of the Visitor.'[468] This was no mere bluff, since in February 1874 six of the 'rebels' went ahead and appealed to the bishop of Ely. In their submission they hovered between the narrower legal-ecclesiastical question of the 'the non-appointment of College Preachers' according to Statute XIV, and the wider constitutional difficulty caused by 'the persistent opposition of an accidental majority of the governing body to a large majority of the Society assembled in a general College meeting'.[469] The Seniors wrote two responses to this appeal and submitted only the second. The first response, not sent, was a highly technical historical and legal vindication of their actions in respect of Statute XIV, and

[468] CB, 2 Dec. 1873; Russell, 'Diary of events', 23 Dec. 1873: SJCL, U22; Reyner and Russell to Bateson, 2 Nov. 1873: SJCL, U22. Russell noted gnomically in his diary, 'This Memorial was not alluded to at any Seniority Meeting again, perhaps because Mr Gladstone's Ministry resigned in January /74.'

[469] Mayor, Bonney, Pearson, Hill, Sandys, and Griffith to the Visitor, n.d.: SJCA, D103.73.

designed to show that they were not in breach, though it ended more rhetorically by claiming that, in the current state of religious conflict, the preaching of sermons, 'so far from providing "definite religious teaching" for the younger members of our Society, (...) tends rather to convert the College Chapel into a battle-field for conflicting opinions'. The sent response, much shorter, ditched all the technicalities and stated bluntly:

> The Master and Seniors take exception to this appeal, *in limine*, on the ground that under the Statutes of the College the appellants are not entitled to make, or the Visitor to entertain, such Appeal (...) The Visitor is empowered to intervene only when requested to do so by the Master and five of the Senior Fellows concurrently, or by seven of the Senior Fellows if the Master should not concur.

In other words, the juniors could neither debate their grievances within the College, nor appeal to authority without.[470] The rebels naturally protested but, having deliberated, the bishop pronounced in November that he would have to postpone judgment pending a decision of the Seniority 'on the constructions of such of the Statutes as may be pertinent'.[471]

At which point both the wider and the narrower issues disappear from the archives. With regard to the latter, Reyner's departure in 1876 must have lowered the temperature, and in October of the following year Chapel sermons were at last resumed. The wider dispute had certainly not been resolved, but Junior Fellows may well have decided that there was no point in continuing to attend general College meetings if they were not to be allowed to discuss sensitive matters, let alone vote on them. The meeting of 1875 considered the possibility of shortened services, as mentioned above, but none of the juniors bothered to turn up in 1876, and the meeting was prorogued without discussion. Given recent excitements, it looks suspiciously like a boycott. No one turned up in the following two years either, but by this time there was a more straightforward reason, for in 1877 an Act of Parliament established another University Commission. It prompted a series of meetings of all Fellows, starting in October 1877, to consider the shape of yet another set of statutes, and it offered Juniors the prospect that satisfaction could be obtained from without.[472]

Consideration of the new statutes belongs mainly to the next section, but one point is pertinent here. The detailed work was carried out by Bateson and Bonney in conjunction with G. W. Hemming QC, a member of the College and one of the commissioners appointed under the Universities Act of 1877. It was common ground that governance should be vested in an elected Council rather than a Seniority, but Bonney – ever the country backbencher – supported a proposed Statute XVI, the purpose of which was to give the Fellowship at large, acting in general College meetings, a right to challenge the governing body's decisions. Bateson was adamantly opposed to this as being inconsistent with

---

[470] Master and Seniors to the Visitor, n.d.: SJCA, D103.77–8. Their claim was that the Visitor's powers in respect of appeals were the same as under the pre-1860 Statutes.

[471] Bishop Woodford to Bateson, 26 Feb., 13 May, 10 and 27 Jul., 21 Nov. 1874: SJCA, D103.64, 67–70.

[472] Russell, 'Diary of events', 31 Oct. 1876, 30 Oct. 1877, 29 Oct. 1878: SJCL, U22.

the statute on the government of the College, already agreed. The latter statute had been framed on the principle of representation, every Fellow of the College having a vote as to who should be on the Council 'and the whole of the elective members being liable to be displaced at the end of their term of service'. In modern terms he might as well have substituted the words, 'on the principle of elective dictatorship', for in his view the Council once elected should have total power over the government of the College, including 'the administration of all the property and income thereof, also power to fix the stipends and salaries of the College officers as they should think fit; and generally'. Yet contrariwise, the proposed Statute XVI would allow a general College meeting of Fellows to 'nullify any act of the Governing Board and practically supersede it'.

> In short what by the first made Statute is dignified by the name of the Governing Board [i.e. Council] by the second becomes a Committee only of the whole number of Fellows, and the benefits which are ordinarily experienced from representative institutions, such as the conduct of affairs by men chosen for their fitness, a sense of responsibility on the part both of the electors and the elected, and some moderate interval of time for the exercise of authority by those who are appointed to govern, all these seem likely to disappear through the power of interference given by the later Statute to the constituency by a decisive vote at a term's notice.

In explicating this point, Bateson chose diplomatically to highlight probable clashes between resident and non-resident Fellows.

> A Master and a body of Fellows of a College are jointly interested in the conduct of a great educational institution, in which the questions that arise from time to time are often semi-political or semi-theological and liable to be discussed with heat and passion. On such occasions it is important that time should be given to cool the disputants. It would, I think, be inexpedient to allow a sudden appeal from the regularly appointed representative Body to a General Meeting of the whole Society, in which there may be many persons brought together from various parts of the country who may not have heard the arguments for the decision which is objected to and who may be ready to give a hasty vote on the *ex parte* solicitation of friends.

It was diplomatic of Bateson to pretend that the problem over Statute XVI was the difference in perspective between the current twenty-six resident and thirty non-resident Fellows, but in reality that was never a serious problem, since the latter had never counted for very much, despite their superior numbers, and they would count for less in the future as the notion of an academic career took hold. What really bothered Bateson about the proposed Statute XVI was that it might encourage the historic struggle between Junior Fellows and Seniors to transmute into one between elected Councillors and the rest. So much is clear from another passage in the same letter:

> Under it we shall have a double system of government one by representatives the other by interferences of the whole body. Hitherto the government has been in the hands of the eight senior residents (…) The operation

of the proposed Statute will encourage a dissatisfied minority of the Governing Body to call in those who are outside of the Governing Body (...) in order to set aside the acts of the majority of their colleagues.[473]

As Bateson knew only too well by now, democracy might have its dangers, but these paled in comparison with the 'double system of government' that had plagued the College for over a decade.

Yet to all intents and purposes Bateson lost his last constitutional battle. Although the proposed Statute XVI was jettisoned, it was replaced by Statute LIX, which gave any eight Fellows the right to requisition a general College meeting, and stated that if a proposition consistent with the statutes was supported by a minimum of sixteen Fellows, and also by at least two-thirds of those present at two such consecutive meetings, then the Council could not hold up its implementation for longer than three months (excluding vacations). Despite the qualifying clauses, this created exactly what Bateson did not want: double government.

On 27 March 1881 Bateson, who had suffered from bronchitis all that term, had a sudden seizure and died aged sixty-eight from an aneurism of the aorta. He had been a somewhat divisive figure politically, but had striven manfully and tactfully over the previous decade to prevent the College from falling apart. Bonney commented that regard for him 'seemed to increase year by year, so that he was probably never more beloved than during the last few months of his life'.[474] The funeral was more than usually splendid, with a great procession stretching all round Second Court. Everyone was very quiet, very emotional, partly because they were not just burying a Master, they were burying the hatchet. It was a moment of catharsis.

10.   POVERTY AND CONTRACTION, 1881–1900

I was at dear old St John's yesterday, and was not merely horrified, I was positively disgusted and made almost sick when I looked through our beautiful covered bridge into the River beneath. The pupil I was showing round, will I trust be some day an honoured member of the College and University, he was delighted with his visit. But when we stayed on our bridge and looked down onto the water, he made an exclamation, which was only natural, and which I could neither answer nor pass off, but which told me very plainly that he had seen the one point in which our Johnian drainage is a disgrace to the College.

W. L. Wilson to Charles Taylor, 31 Mar. 1885, D104.27.

Our College at present is no place to form the manners of a gentleman: nothing but vulgarity, bad taste, sharp practice and petty wrangling.

H. S. Foxwell to Joseph Larmor, 4 Oct. 1893,
SJCL Miscellaneous Letters: FO2, 2.

---

[473] W. H. Bateson to ?, ?7 Jan. 1878: SJCA, D103.98.
[474] [T. G. Bonney], 'The Master of St John's: obituary', *CR* ii (1880–1), 258–9.

The fraught election to succeed Bateson can be understood in part as the final act in the chapel wars. It began on the morning of 12 April 1881 as a six-way contest, but two candidates were eliminated at the first round, leaving Bonney with 14 votes, Parkinson with 6, and two other candidates not yet mentioned in this chapter: Charles Taylor, who came top with 22, and Benjamin Cowie with 15. When the remaining candidates were pitted against each other, Bonney lost narrowly to Cowie and Taylor and won narrowly over Parkinson; Cowie easily beat Parkinson and lost easily to Taylor, who in turn slaughtered Parkinson. The latter was discarded, after which another straight vote gave Taylor 14, Cowie and Bonney 11 each. The meeting recommenced after lunch, afforced by two additional non-resident Fellows. This gave Taylor 16 as against Cowie's 12 and Bonney's 10. At 2.30 p.m. the Fellows moved into chapel for the election, but the first scrutiny was inconclusive (Taylor 16, Cowie 14, Bonney 12). A second scrutiny was held which this time gave Taylor a majority, with 22 votes against Cowie's 13 and Bonney's 7, after which Taylor was summoned and the ritual of inauguration began. It had been a tight squeeze and a tense one, and one can almost detect a sigh of relief in Russell's written comment on the final stages, 'Everything very quiet but orderly.'[475]

This was the last election fought under rules which stipulated that the winner must be a clergyman. The sense in which it was also the last act in the chapel wars is that it was fundamentally a contest between Bateson and Cowie, with the latter standing proxy for Reyner. At least, they were the only candidates for whom there was genuine enthusiasm. Of the final three, the brash and charismatic Bonney had a strong following among the Junior Fellows, but after the strife of recent years even they for the most part wanted a quiet life, and many of them opted for the more anodyne Taylor.[476] Benjamin Morgan Cowie, who finished as runner-up, had been a Senior Wrangler and a Fellow (1839–43), and was currently making a reputation for himself as an active dean of Manchester. He was very interested in liturgy, and was ritualistic in his tastes, though not immoderately so,[477] and he appealed to those who had formerly followed Reyner's lead thanks to his uncompromisingly orthodox theology, which was fixed on 'the truth that the death of Christ is a vicarious sacrifice' that redeems the debt incurred by sinful men.[478] His support was solid in the sense that the fourteen or so who voted for him were very reluctant to vote for either of the others; on the other hand, Cowie was unlikely to attract any waverers, and once it had become clear that Bonney was not going to make it, about half of his votes went to Taylor. It would be misleading to say that the latter *emerged* as the

---

[475] Russell's 'Diary of events', 12 Apr. 1881: SJCL, U22. Russell, whose diaries provide these inside details, voted for anyone but Bonney at each opportunity.

[476] Heitand wrote, 'I can say with confidence that Bonney would have been Master but for the fear he inspired in many of the more active juniors': *Eagle* xliii (1923–4), 263.

[477] He had urged St John's to respond to the admission of non-Anglicans by instituting theological instruction and by increasing the frequency of Holy Communion: B. M. Cowie, *A Commemoration Sermon Preached on the Feast of S. John, Port Lat. 1871* (1871), 13–15.

[478] B. M. Cowie, *On Sacrifice, the Atonement, Vicarious Oblation, and Example of Christ, and the Punishment of Sin: Five Sermons Preached before the University of Cambridge* (Cambridge, 1856), 35, 47.

compromise candidate, given that his biggest lead was won in the first round, yet that is how he should be regarded in relation to the ecclesiastical disputes of the previous decade. Neither a liberal theologian like Bonney nor a severely orthodox churchman like Reyner, he rather conformed to that middle-of-the-road religiosity that had long been a St John's hallmark. 'He had an intense Church feeling, without the slightest appearance of ecclesiasticism, (…) and his moderation, which was no part of a policy, but was natural to the man, was an invaluable quality in the head of a large college containing many varieties of religious opinion.'[479]

Another sign perhaps of the ill feeling of the times was that, having lost, Taylor's two closest internal rivals at once departed the scene. Stephen Parkinson resigned his Fellowship for the second time in 1882,[480] while Bonney retained his status but went off to live in London, where he found his life 'more free and happy than it had been for some years in Cambridge'. He had in fact been the Professor of Geology at University College since 1877, and had willingly commuted for five years. However,

> the choice of [Bateson's] successor showed me that, for reasons on which I had better not enter, it would be the wiser course not to continue even an intermittent residence in Cambridge. I foresaw what would be the consequence of the election, and that I should soon be forced into becoming 'leader of the opposition'. Of that sort of thing I had already had more than enough.[481]

He would return to live in St John's eventually, but not until the next century.

Forty-one years old at the time of his election, Taylor had started out as a mathematician, and had conformed to College tradition by producing works on geometry that were either textbooks or else had a strong historical as distinct from analytical bent.[482] After switching subjects he had been appointed Lecturer in Theology in 1873, and had won considerable acclaim with his edition of the *Sayings of the Jewish Fathers, in Hebrew and English, with Critical and Illustrative Notes* (1877).[483] He came to prominence within the College in 1877–8 by taking an active part in the discussions on statute revision, and in the following year he was chosen, alongside Bonney and Bateson, as a College representative in conferring with the University commissioners.[484] As Master he was to prove

---

[479] Anon., 'The Revd. Charles Taylor, D. D.', *Eagle* xxx (1908–9), 64–85, 197–204 at p. 78..

[480] A former sizar, Senior Wrangler, and President (1864–70), Parkinson had also been a notably successful Tutor, and after he resigned his Fellowship by marriage in 1871 the Seniors allowed him to continue in that role (and also to remain in residence) by making him a Praelector. CB, 30 Sept. 1871.

[481] Bonney, *Memories*, 42–3.

[482] Even his first and most ambitious book, *Geometrical Conics, including Anharmonic Ratio and Projection* (1863), was mainly derived from earlier work by George Salmon of Trinity College, Dublin.

[483] The establishment of new triposes in Moral and Natural Sciences in 1851 was followed by others in Law (1858), Theology (1874), and History (1875).

[484] 'The best news I have heard from Cambridge since I left', wrote Marshall from Bristol. 'I don't think any other set of three would be nearly as good as this set': Marshall to Foxwell, 14 Feb. 1879: *Correspondence of Alfred Marshall*, I. 106.

generous with his money, both to College and University – had it not been for a donation in 1894, for example, it would have been necessary to sell consols in order to clear an overdraft on the Education Fund.[485] He was, moreover, well liked for his good-humoured, equable, and even-handed management of affairs, but he was also somewhat semi-detached. Elegant and even stately, the contrast between him and Bateson was not unlike that between Tatham and his predecessor, Wood. Like Bateson, the latter had had little physical presence but his activity and involvement brought him veneration, whereas Taylor and Tatham were men who shone on public occasions but took only a superficial interest in management. To add to the symmetry, both Tatham and Taylor surrendered much of the initiative to their Bursars, who duly succeeded them as Master.

Taylor's immediate task was to preside over the transition to new statutes, a process which Heitland called 'the years of conflict', and which was more commonly referred to for a long time afterwards as simply 'the revolution'. The 1872 commissioners (who included Bateson) had been much more aggressive towards the colleges than their predecessors two decades earlier. Their report led directly to the Oxford and Cambridge Act of 1877 and to the appointment of statutory commissioners (again including Bateson) to ensure its implementation. Every college was invited to draw up revised statutes that they hoped would prove acceptable, and to appoint three representatives to negotiate with the University commissioners.[486] The bitterest pill was that colleges must in future 'pay annually to the University the sum authorized by the Statutes of the University'. This was unwelcome in principle, since the money would inevitably eat into dividends, and it also seemed frighteningly open-ended in practice. The total sum to be handed over was phased so as to increase gradually over twelve years, and each college was to contribute a proportion according to its income, which in the first instance (1883) meant that St John's had to contribute £644, or just over 16 per cent of the total.[487] This would rise to £1,151 in 1885, and reach about £4,800 by 1897, when it was expected to level off. (In the event it remained static through most of the 1890s, and stood at only £1,613 in 1900. This was not good news, however, since the smaller than anticipated contribution reflected the collapse – wholly unanticipated in 1882 – of the College's income.) Somewhat desperately, a decision was taken in December 1881 to petition the Privy Council for a stay of execution on account of the agricultural depression and decline in college revenue. Thirty-four Fellows supported this move, but it was strongly criticized by a minority, which included Heitland, Mayor, and Liveing, and in a somewhat humiliating climbdown it was resolved not to proceed with the petition.[488]

The commissioners' aim in establishing a University contribution was to

---

[485] CM, 391/9 (17 Nov. 1893).

[486] But only two in the case of those colleges like St John's that had a representative on the University Commission.

[487] It would have been £1,000 more than this except that a deduction was allowed on the grounds that the College was supporting five professors. For an explanation of how the size of contributions was calculated, see Howard, *Finances*, 224–5.

[488] 'Papers regarding the passing of the new Statutes with annotations by Heitland, 1877–82': SJCA, D44.3.3.

enable Cambridge to compete with the civic universities and London colleges. They conceived the main necessities as being to build scientific laboratories, to establish three grades of University teaching officer 'on a scale sufficiently substantial to open a real career',[489] and more generally to encourage 'Germanic-style' research. Their stipulations in respect of colleges were mainly designed to improve their function as teaching institutions, and in particular to bring them up to the level of certain Oxford colleges, where the Tutors were both more numerous and more involved, academically as well as pastorally. Possession of a Fellowship was no longer to be confined to men who were celibate and in Holy Orders. Anyone who did not hold a University or College office, either academic or administrative, was to relinquish his Fellowship after six years, thereby ensuring the gradual elimination of the non-resident (and by definition non-teaching) Fellows.[490] And governing bodies were to have control over all matters connected with appointments to tutorships and lectureships. In St John's, as elsewhere, these forced adjustments were painful to many. The presumption that all Fellows should be involved in undergraduate education in some way cut across the tradition that Fellowships were unconditional prizes, and could properly be used to maintain gifted young men while they trained for the Bar or for some other career or profession. From the College's point of view, such men brought contact with the world, hopefully perhaps even access to the corridors of power, and there were also fears that gifted young men would cease to compete in future if the only career open to them was that of a don. In the protracted battles that now occurred over the statutes, according to Heitland 'some non-resident Fellows, young barristers, fought hard for the interests of their class, and their training gave them a great advantage in dealing with men of purely Academic experience'.[491]

The other main feature of 'the revolution' was the decision, alluded to in the previous section, to vest executive governance in an elected Council of twelve Fellows and the Master. This was not a direct consequence of the commissioners' recommendations, but was rather a belated attempt to resolve the tensions of almost three decades. The transition was effected more seamlessly than many had feared, partly because the eight Fellows who had sat on the previous governing body were permitted to serve on the new Council in the first instance. The three most senior of these Seniors were appointed for four years, three others for three years, and two for two years. This left one Fellow to be elected for two years and three for one year, and the successful candidates – respectively Hill, Smith, Sandys, Heitland – were, as Russell commented approvingly, the 'residents next in order to the acting Seniors, Cox having been but short term in residence, and Pendlebury deaf and otherwise not caring to be elected'.[492] Because it was a larger body, and because there were many transitional arrangements that had to be agreed to, the new governing body was probably more loquacious than the old. Also Taylor as chairman seems to have been willing

---

[489] George Hemming to Bateson, 19 Nov. 1878: SJCA, D90.579.
[490] The tenure of Fellowships was reduced from six to three years in 1912.
[491] Heitland, *After Many Years*, 157.
[492] Russell's 'Diary of events', 24 May 1882: SJCL, U22.

to let members express themselves freely. This irritated Heitland, whose telegraphic diary entries provide one of two first-hand accounts of proceedings. 'Much drivel and waste of time'; 'futile'; 'talky-talky'; 'long and muddled discussion, confused result'; 'much jaw'. But then the dyspeptic Heitland's irritation seemed to increase by the month, and signified less and less.[493]

One feature of the Council's constitution which did cause dissatisfaction, and which was still unresolved in 1900, was the system of election by cumulative voting. This meant that each Fellow had as many votes as there were vacancies (usually three, once the system was up and running), and might if he pleased give them all to the same candidate. Until 1885, when single-member constituencies and a system of 'one man one vote' was instituted, plural voting also applied in British general elections (though without the cumulative element), and was heavily criticized as giving rise to 'caucus politics', a reference to the situation in America where elected representatives were often merely delegates of those who voted for them, and it was on similar grounds that it came into disrepute in St John's. In 1888 MacAlister resigned his Council seat in order to force the issue. He complained that 'a chance combination of cumulative votes has come to have an altogether inordinate weight, with the result of producing very undesirable surprises', a tactless remark at which Larmor took umbrage – not surprisingly given that he had benefited from such votes in the previous year's election. MacAlister in fact had a lot of time for Larmor, and his point was a more principled one. 'When a member of the Council knows that he is elected by a small group of Fellows he must find it difficult not to regard himself as the delegate of his constituents rather than a representative of the whole body (...) [It] is unfair to the member of Council so elected, and bad for the College.' To emphasize the point he wrote to Larmor, 'I was told last night that some of the junior [fellows] were expressing dissatisfaction that you did not consult them enough.' This was, in essence, a replay of the 1870s wars. Back then there had been complaints against a gerontocracy; now the complaint was against an elective dictatorship. On the one side there was Main requesting the release of 'information with regard to actions which the Council is taking from time to time and which are of interest and importance to the Fellows generally', and on the other there was MacAlister railing against 'a notion that keeps cropping up that no step should be taken without first consulting certain of the Fellows not on the Council'.[494]

As with the admission of female students almost a century later, the creation of Fellows' wives did not turn St John's upside down. The old bachelor John Mayor commented that 'the society here is becoming very pleasant' as a result. But then the old romantic had never been a crusty old bachelor, and he had as usual an idiosyncratic reason for welcoming the presence of 'young married folk, among whom "high thinking" may be presumed and plain living is a [financial] necessity'. There seems to have been little hesitation in granting J. E. Sandys'

[493] Heitland's private diary, 9 Dec. 1895, 28 May, 5 Nov. 1897: SJCL, Heitland's Papers B (Box 2). See also P. T. Main, 'Notes of College Council business, 1884–1894': SJCL, W2.

[494] Main to Taylor, 23 Feb. 1892: SJCA, D92.20.15; MacAlister to Larmor, 30 Apr., 1, 2 May 1888, Larmor to MacAlister, 1 May 1888: SJCL, Larmor Collection, MA1, 1–6.

request to be allowed to continue as Tutor after his marriage in 1880, and before very long it seems likely that possession of a wife would come to be regarded as a tutorial asset.[495] Meanwhile, only Heitland seems to have taken seriously the commissioners' recommendation that the tutorial system should be brought into line with the Oxford practice (which was also the ancient practice at St John's) of associating Tutors more closely with teaching while reducing their pastoral functions. If anything there was movement in the opposite direction. Whereas in the past most Tutors had been chosen from among those who already held Fellowships, there was now a strong feeling that, if St John's was once again to make a mark in the world, it would need to reach out to the top schools, and that the way to do that might be to bring in one or two Tutors from outside. In 1882 Torry had his eye on two likely candidates for such a role: Frederick Watson, a former Fellow and now rector of Sharston, and Robert Scott, a non-resident Fellow who had till recently been Assistant Master at Christ's Hospital.[496]

It *was* agreed that the Junior Bursar might take over responsibility for allocating rooms, but suggestions that responsibility for undergraduates' financial affairs might be transferred to a Bursarial Tutor were strongly resisted as likely to undermine 'a valuable relationship between the Tutor and his pupil or his pupil's parent'.[497] (The switch eventually occurred in 1900, by which time the dire state of tutorial finances had made Tutors more willing to surrender to bureaucratic centralization.) Another suggestion was to abandon recruitment by individual Tutors in favour of a centralized admissions process, and to allocate students among the Tutors in equal numbers. This was rebuffed by Torry and others with the rallying cry, 'Free Trade in Tutors'. Although the present competitive system might seem illogical, in so far as it led to some Tutors having bigger sides than others, yet 'so long as they represent the effect of his labour or influence in attracting men to the College, and do not become an absolutely unwieldy amount, there seems no valid reason for transferring them to someone else's care'.[498]

In 1883, following 'the revolution', there remained nine Fellows who operated under the pre-1860 Statutes, and who were entitled to certain small payments for boars' meat, livery, and corn. They, like those Fellows elected under the 1860 Statutes, were also still entitled (under new Statute XLI) to either a life Fellowship or a College living if they were in Holy Orders, and if laymen to a tenure of seven years (instead of six) from taking their MA degrees. They retained the extra half dividend if Seniors, and the maximum limit on their ordinary dividend remained £300, whereas Fellows under the new statutes could not draw more than £250, with the addition of just one-fifth to those who served on the Council.[499] (Though no one knew it at the time, these stipulations as to maxima

---

[495] CB, 14 Jun. 1880. Not that, in Sandys' case, matrimony did anything to soften a stiffness of manner characteristic of a tutor of a previous generation.

[496] Torry to Taylor, 24 Oct. 1882: SJCA, D103.147.

[497] Torry to Taylor, 21 Oct. 1882: SJCA, D103.146.

[498] A. F. Torry, 'Free trade in tutorships: to the members of the College Council', 21 Jun. 1882: SJCA, D103.145.

[499] The differential in dividend continued from 1882 until 1896 and varied between £20 and £30.

would soon become irrelevant.) All 'New Fellows', meaning those elected after 13 March 1878, had no choice but to come under the new statutes, whereas 'Old Fellows' had to decide whether to transfer to them if they wished, thereby taking a pay cut in return for being allowed to marry.[500] To some the answer was obvious. MacAlister was the youngest of the Old Fellows, 'the last "vested iniquity," as I was described by an outspoken junior colleague. So I transferred to the new statutes, and was free to take an active part in the "youth" movement, which soon brought about great reforms in the College.'[501] As a rising star in his profession, MacAlister could afford to be principled, but others had to make some awkward calculations. Torry had a particularly horny dilemma. He was a Lecturer under the old statutes and very keen to accept a proffered Tutorship, but he was even keener to get married. This meant transferring to the new statutes, under which his Tutorship would no longer constitute a qualifying office for permanent Fellowship. He departed in 1886. Later, in 1895, Edwin Clark was told by the University that the only way in which he could claim full fees for his lectures was by transferring to its new statutes, but as this would involve 'a certain loss of leisure and liberty' as well as considerable 'diminution of income', St John's dividends being so low, he came close to resigning his Fellowship.[502]

The presence in the same common room of Fellows with such different entitlements was bound to lead to tension. For example, when Marshall had to resign his Fellowship on getting married in 1877, he had no cause for complaint, but when another economist, Foxwell, had to do the same in 1898, he was ruefully aware ('my usual luck') that his many colleagues holding under the 1882 Statutes were marrying with impunity.[503] Torry meanwhile fussed endlessly about the interpretation of the new statutes in so far as they affected 'Old Fellows' like himself. He understood that, if he were to become a Senior according to the old rules, he would no longer automatically be a member of the executive body (which was now the Council), but would be entitled to his additional 50 per cent on the dividend, and, if he were to be elected a Councillor, would he be entitled to the additional 20 per cent as well?

> Statute 53 provides: That no member of the Council who is or may become a Senior Fellow under or in virtue of the former Statutes shall be entitled to receive *both* the additional *half dividend* (...) and the additional *one-fifth* (...) This would seem to imply his *right* to receive the one-fifth if he has not the half. It does *not* seem to imply that the right to succeed hereafter to the half dividend should invalidate the right to receive the one-fifth in the meantime. I interpret the proviso as against receiving *both* simultaneously, and not against the exercise *of both rights*, one at one time and the other subsequently.[504]

---

[500] In 1886 there were seventeen 'Old Fellows' and thirty-six 'New Fellows', while three Fellowships were vacant.

[501] MacAlister, *Sir Donald MacAlister*, 311.

[502] Edwin C. Clark to Taylor, 22 May 1895: SJCA, D92.25.22.

[503] Foxwell to Larmor, 7 Aug. 1897: SJCL, Miscellaneous Letters, FO2, 5.

[504] A. F. Torry, 'To the Council: preservation of the "interests" of Fellows elected before March 1878': SJCA, D103.114.

Then there was the question as to which Fellows were to finance the additional one-fifth by a deduction from their dividends.

> Are the payments of the 'additional one-fifth dividend to each member of the Council' to be charged upon the Fellows under the New Statutes only, as being charges not contemplated under former Statutes? They must be so charged, unless they can be reckoned under the head of a) ordinary expenses b) stipends or salaries contemplated in Statute 48 (previous Statutes 1860).[505]

The fine print of Torry's inquiries is not all that significant, but the fact that Fellows were forced to jockey for financial advantage in such a way inevitably damaged morale, especially as a favourable interpretation of the statutes for one member had negative implications for many others. Nor were Torry's concerns merely academic, since he was next in line to inherit when Mason's position on the old Seniority became vacant shortly afterwards. 'Does the extra half dividend paid to a Senior become payable to me from 2 May, the day on which Mr Mason placed himself under the New Statutes? (...) Mr Mason's right to an extra half dividend having "*determined*" I believe I am no longer debarred from it.'[506] In such situations, everyone was eyeing everyone else suspiciously.

Another dispute, similar in principle but of much greater moment because the sums involved were larger, concerned new Statute XLII on the liability of Fellows to pay a share of the College's contribution to the University. The pre-1860 Fellows were clearly exempt, and the 1882 Fellows were just as clearly liable, but what of those like Torry who operated under the 1860 Statutes? A point in their favour was that the contribution was 'essentially a part of the New Statutes, being one of the main purposes' of the 1877 Act. Yet on the other hand, as Torry conceded, the new Statute XLII 'only repeats a provision of Statute XLVIII (1860 Statutes) viz:– "And subject (...) to such payment (if any) as may become due to the University Chest to be applied to purposes for the benefit of the University at large."'[507] It was clearly a grey area, and on 15 February 1884 the Council pronounced that 1860 Fellows ought to pay: 'Agreed that the University Contribution be charged upon the divisible revenue of the College *before* the calculation of the dividends payable to the Fellows under the Statutes of 1860 and 1882' (italics added). This determination must have been challenged, very possibly by Torry or Foxwell, for advice was taken and on 30 May the Council climbed down:

> [Agreed] that in consequence of the opinion of Prof Cayley[508] the order dated Feb. 15, 1884 be rescinded (...) [Agreed] that the Bursar be instructed to pay each of the Fellows holding under the Statutes of 1860 such sum as will raise his dividend for the year ending St Thomas 1883 to £230 free of income tax. [Agreed] that, in consequence of Prof Cayley's opinion, the

[505] SJCA, D103.114. On this matter the Council found in Torry's favour: CB, 24 Apr. 1883.

[506] Torry, 'To the Council', 7 May 1883: SJCA, D103.116.

[507] SJCA, D103.114.

[508] Probably Arthur Cayley DCL, Trinity, Sadlerian Professor of Mathematics 1863–95.

contribution to the University be charged only upon the dividends of such of the Master and Fellows as have their interests regulated by the Statutes of 1882. [Agreed] that the dividends of [the pre-1882] Master and Fellows shall in each year be calculated before deducting the amount of the contribution due to the University in that year.[509]

Although Fellows had reserved rights under Section 34 of the 1877 Oxford and Cambridge Act, it was decided on the advice of counsel that 'Old Lecturers' held office 'under the pleasure of the Master and Seniors' (Statute XVIII of 1860), and therefore that they must come under the provisions of new Statute XV.8. This was cruel, since under the 1860 Statutes a Lecturer had held his post until deprived of it by a majority of the Seniors, whereas under the new Statute XV.8 he had to cease after twenty years unless 'expressly appointed to continue' by the votes of at least nine members of Council: a tall hurdle.[510] The first person to be affected by this rule was Frederic Charles Wace, who had been elected a Fellow in 1860 and appointed a Lecturer in Mathematics in 1864. He had forfeited his Fellowship by marriage in 1875 but was allowed to continue in his lectureship, until being informed in 1884 that his twenty years were up, and that the nine votes requisite to reappoint him had not been forthcoming. He was shattered by the news, and even more so when told that his pension was to be a meagre £150 for just five years.

> I have hitherto at no time raised objection to any action of the College with respect to Lectureships (…) I have preferred to rely on the good feeling of the Governing Body of the College, being persuaded, that in carrying out the changes rendered necessary by the New Statutes they would feel it a duty incumbent upon them to minimize as far as possible any case of hardship that might arise, that they would be inclined to err if at all on the side of liberality, especially in dealing with those whose status has been so materially altered (not by any action of their own but by that of a body before whom they had no opportunity of stating their case), knowing moreover that such a course could not establish a precedent for the future, as similar conditions are not likely again to arise.

Although Wace might not have been aware of it, he had in fact been living on borrowed time for almost a decade, since the decision to keep him on board in 1875 had been heavily criticised at the time, leading the Seniors to resolve then and there that in future any lecturer who vacated a fellowship would be deemed to have vacated his lectureship as well.[511] In view of this Wace should probably have seen his enforced demission coming, though his bitter response to the ungracious manner in which it was carried out seems entirely understandable.

> But I am even more disappointed with the manner in which the offer [of pension] is made to me. The resolution in which it is embodied, does not contain any expression of thanks for past services, or of regret at their

---

[509] CM, 73/6 (13 May 1884).
[510] CMM, 83/9, 87/8, 88/5 (17 Oct., 7 and 14 Nov. 1884).
[511] CB, 5 Nov. 1875.

unusual compulsory termination. Is it intended to supplement it by any further resolution of a complimentary character, conferring it may be some nominal or titular position in virtue of which I might be allowed to retain all or some of the few privileges I have hitherto enjoyed as Lecturer, or am I to infer that my connection with the College is to be brought to a close without a word of even the scantiest civility? I must at any rate apply for some formal certificate of service. It will be necessary for me to take the earliest opportunity which may present itself of applying for some other employment, either in Cambridge, or more probably elsewhere, and I should require some such certificate as a testimonial.[512]

All he got from the Council in response to his letter was a grudging expression of gratitude and a warning that the matter was closed. His place on the teaching staff was taken by Joseph Larmor, an immeasurably more distinguished mathematician, a fact which no doubt helps to explain his brutal treatment as well as his pained response.

At least Wace was able to receive a pension as a result of being forcibly transplanted onto the 1882 Statutes. Because 'New Fellows' were no longer required to be in Holy Orders, and there was no longer any need for a fund to purchase advowsons, it had been decided that the property and income of the old Livings Fund should be transferred to a Pensions Fund, which should also receive the dividends of any vacant Fellowships. The Council was empowered to grant (for as long as they wished) a pension (of not greater value than the current dividend) to any Tutors, Lecturers, or other officers, whether or not they were Fellows, provided that the officer had like Wace been in post for at least fifteen years. In November 1886, following the rapid downturn in College income, a general meeting of the Governing Body agreed ('by all present and voting save one') on a new Statute LIV. It noted that the Elizabethan Statutes, like those of 1848, had allowed for 'a diminution in the number of Fellowships in case of decrease of revenue or other great misfortune', whereas the 1882 Statutes seemed to prevent any such adjustment, first by fixing the number of Fellowships, and then by directing that the income of unfilled Fellowships could not be used for current needs, but had to be paid into the Pension Fund. These Statutes therefore failed to address a situation such as had now occurred, when it was 'no longer possible to provide for each Fellow a sufficient dividend'. In such straitened circumstances it was proving difficult to 'encourage those to remain members of our Body who are best fitted to promote the interests of our College as a place of Education Religion Learning and Research'. Hence the need for the proposed Statute LIV:

> If it shall at any time appear to the Council that the revenues of the College do not produce the amount required to afford to every Fellow an income of £200 a year (exclusive of rooms and commons but inclusive of other allowances) they may by a resolution in which not less than nine votes shall have concurred declare that a Fellowship then vacant is suspended. And the dividend of any vacant Fellowship so suspended shall

[512] Wace to Taylor, 11 Oct. and 26 Dec. 1884, 7 Apr. 1885: SJCA, D103.112, D92.55.2–3; D92.55.4–7.

not be paid to the capital of the Pension Fund but shall in each year be wholly assigned to the payment or part payment to the University of the sum authorised and directed by the Statutes of the University to be charged upon the College.

Very likely Foxwell was the single dissentient referred to above. He had been elected a Fellow in 1874, and had served as a Tutor and Lecturer before taking up a position as Professor of Political Economy in London University in 1881. Still in residence, he was frustrated by the policy of suspending Fellowships, since as an 'Old Fellow' he was anxious to become a Senior,[513] but Statute LIV struck him as worse than frustrating, being in his view contrary to the spirit (and possibly the terms) of the Oxford and Cambridge Act of 1877. Accordingly in 1886 he petitioned the Universities Committee of the Privy Council, his legal grievance being that, whereas all Fellows would suffer from the depletion of the Pension Fund, only the 'New Fellows' would benefit from the decision to use the income of suspended Fellowships for the purposes of University Contribution ('Old Fellows' having been exempted from payment for the latter). In their reply to the Privy Council Committee, the Master and Fellows submitted that the proposed Statute LIV was 'necessary and expedient' for maintaining the core functions of the College. Furthermore,

> It is just and equitable that the dividends of a suspended Fellowship should be applied … for the benefit of the New Fellows only. The Pension Fund was first created under the Statutes of 1882 for the purpose of making provision for the New Fellows in lieu of the rights possessed by Old Fellows under the previous Statutes. The benefit of the Pension Fund does not enure to the Old Fellows, or if it does so enure, their prospective interest therein is subject to any alteration which may be duly made in the Statutes relating thereto even if such alteration is in fact for the benefit of the New Fellows or otherwise.

In the view of the Master and Fellows, Foxwell was seeking to avoid the 'onerous provisions' of the 1882 Statutes, while at the same time benefiting from its advantages.[514] From the very beginning of the saga Bateson had been determined 'to prevent Fellows under the existing Statutes on their repeal having the advantages of both codes'.[515] Reading between the lines, it seems likely that Foxwell was being punished for having insisted on exempting 'Old Fellows' from University Contribution. The College eventually won the case in the Privy Council, but as the proceedings had held up the implementation of the 'necessary and expedient' Statute LIV for three years, Foxwell's presence in the College cannot but have created a good deal of awkwardness.

The root of the problem was summed up in two Council determinations.

---

[513] His ill luck was such that a Senior Fellowship did not become available until 1898, the year in which he had to give up his Fellowship altogether because of his marriage.

[514] *The Universities Committee of the Privy Council in the Matter of the Universities of Oxford and Cambridge Act, 1877, and of the Petition of Robert Rumsey Webb MA, and of Herbert Somerton Foxwell, MA, Fellows &c.*: SJCA, D44.9. The irresolute Webb had embarked on the case with Foxwell, but had dropped out at an early stage.

[515] Bateson to Taylor, 29 Dec. 1880: SJCA, D103.176.

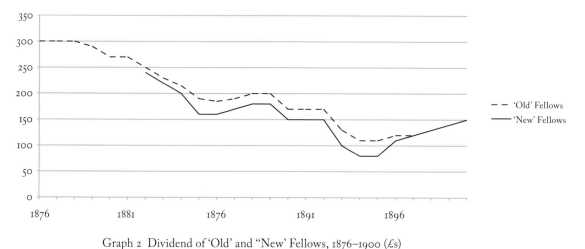

Graph 2 Dividend of 'Old' and "New' Fellows, 1876–1900 (£s)

According to the first, all 'Old Fellows' not holding an office that 'under the present Statutes entitles the holder to retain his Fellowship notwithstanding lapse of time', nor having held any such office 'so long that they would under these Statutes be entitled to retain their Fellowships for life, should be deemed (…) to be holding on limited tenure', in other words six years. The second stipulated that the Council was not debarred from extending the tenure of an 'Old Fellow'.[516] In other words, it gave the Council an arbitrary power to play favourites. In 1884 Wace was told to go, whereas three years later J. E. Sandys, in a similar position, had his lectureship in classics extended after twenty years. With reform had come flexibility, and with flexibility had come partiality. This was what the College had warned the Graham Commission would happen back in the 1850s.[517]

Clearly the adjustment to new statutes would have proved problematic in any circumstances, but it was made very much more so by a wholly unanticipated crisis in the College's finances, one measure of which was the size of the dividend which, having stood at £300 from 1872 to 1878, then sank steadily to £150 in 1890, and collapsed to £80 (its nadir) in 1894, one year after wheat prices had also touched their lowest point.[518] (See Graph 2.)

Because several Fellowships were suspended,[519] the total cost of the dividend to the College fell even more drastically, from £18,000 to £5,000. Heitland was not correct to say that 'the dividends of the Fellows bore the whole brunt of the great Depression' (since the proportion of internal revenue and tuition fees to total income rose from about 27 per cent to one-third during 1883–93), but it must certainly have felt like that.[520]

There is no mystery about the fall in the dividend, for the simple fact is that

[516] CB, 2 Mar. 1883.
[517] See above, p. 287.
[518] These figures are for Fellows operating under the new statutes. Fellows under the old statutes received slightly more, as Graph 2 demonstrates.
[519] See below, p. 394.
[520] Heitland, *After Many Years*, 168.

spending continued while revenue declined. On the debit side of the ledger, the interest on the Chapel debt continued to drain £1,735 p.a. (equivalent to a £30 loss of dividend for each Fellow) until 1896, when it was liquidated, slightly earlier than expected, by a transfer from the Composition Fund. However, this did not deter the Fellows from embarking on other building schemes, such was their optimism about the future until it was rudely jolted by a collapse of rents from 1886 onwards. The most important of these schemes was the Penrose Building, erected between 1885 and 1888 at a cost of £10,346. It was designed in what has been described as 'an inoffensive neo-Tudor', its main elevation opposite the west end of the Chapel consisting of red brick with stone dressings. A great deal of offence was exchanged during the course of planning, however, as was only to be expected in such a quarrelsome common room. All seemed to proceed smoothly at first. A committee consisting of Hill, Scott, MacAlister, and Liveing won general support for the idea that the College should build three large lecture rooms, topped by eighteen residential sets on the first and second floors. The need for lecture rooms had long been pressing, while the upstairs rooms would nearly restore the supply of accommodation to where it had been before the building of the new Chapel had displaced twenty-two students into lodgings. Fellows were also reassured that the £9,000 needed to complete the building could be squeezed from the Coal Fund, and from Dr Wood's Fund and the Ely Lease Fund. A second committee (Liveing, Heitland, Webb) recommended as architect F. C. Penrose, surveyor of St Paul's Cathedral and an astronomer in his spare time. His design was warmly welcomed, the only dissent coming from Foxwell, who wanted something more 'modern', and from Bonney, who always hated spending money on bricks and mortar. A much later, more serious, and mysterious intervention came from the Master, who made it known in Council quite late on that he would contribute £5,000 on condition that the building was reduced to a single-storey block of lecture rooms. When news of this offer leaked out, the word went round that the Council had rejected the Master's offer precipitately 'and suppressed all mention of it'. Heitland responded with a furious paper, in which he pointed out that the Master's offer had not been made until the designs had been posted for three weeks and were on the point of being approved.

> From first to last the Master, being present at all the meetings of the Council, has never moved the rejection of a single proposal relating to this subject, and I have been used to think a member of any responsible body who takes no divisions and records no protest is considered to have at least acquiesced in their decisions. Can business be conducted on any other principle? Yet I understand the Master now to favour the discussion of alternatives in general by a perpetually changing body of at present fifty-seven members. Alternatives were considered by the proper body, the First Committee.[521]

Heitland continued, 'What is it that an objector wants? A new design, a new architect, or simply delay?' Presumably – though it seems not to have been

---

[521] Heitland, 'Printed paper to the Master and Fellows', 30 Jun. 1885: SJCA, D33.11.39; Crook, *Penrose to Cripps* (Cambridge, 1978), 4–10.

stated – what Taylor really wanted was that undergraduates should not be able to look out onto his garden. However, he was unable to prevent the building from going ahead, and despite some further hold-ups during the course of construction – it looked at one point as though Penrose might have to be replaced as a result of tensions between College, architect, and contractor – the building opened, not much over budget, in 1888. There were further ironies in that, while the lecture rooms were far from being white elephants like the Chapel,[522] the rapid development of University premises reduced the crying need for them that had previously existed, while the fall in student numbers over the following decade was to render the new sets, for a while at least, redundant.

The next single biggest item of expenditure was to rebuild and re-equip the kitchens with mod-cons such as gas-powered roasting ovens, and to erect new offices and stores for them in Back Lane, at a total cost of about £6,000 in 1893–4. Approximately £4,000 was spent four years later on general sewering and redraining, perhaps putting an end to the sights that had so disgusted W. L. Wilson and his young charge in 1885. A realization that the fabric required sundry other repairs led to an annual maintenance grant of £1,000 being paid to the Junior Bursar, not to mention other *ad hoc* disbursements. The Junior Bursar in question was Heitland, who was always more relaxed with inanimate objects than he was with colleagues (it was joked that he 'loved a ladder'), and turned out to be both energetic and effective. Indeed, he served longer in that office (1886–1901) than any of his predecessors, and was later authoritatively described 'as in some sense the creator of the "department" [his own coinage], in its modern function and efficiency'.[523] The same source comments on his 'almost hectic activity', as recorded in the pages of his working notebook.

> When something needed doing quickly, Heitland was not the man to stand on his dignity. If there was no one else on hand, he did the job himself. Thus: 'Aug. 17 1886. Heavy rain – at 8. p.m. Merry[524] told me wet coming through into Buttery – Saw it all up E 1st Court. Aug. 19. Went out on gutter, found cisternhead choked with paper and dirt. Cleared it myself.

He wrote a long report on every aspect of the fabric, a great deal of which he pronounced 'terrible, terrible', and he had a (possibly justified) phobia about fire. However, energy in a Junior Bursar always turns out to be expensive. In 1891 he tried unsuccessfully to persuade the Council to provide him with a clerical assistant; in 1892 electric light was installed in Hall, Chapel, and the First Court lamps; in 1897 the porters were supplied with hats; and in the following year an undergraduate set at the foot of K First Court was turned into a bicycle store. This was a smart move in a decade of bicycling mania, when the machines that cluttered rooms and corridors were regarded as a great anti-social nuisance. Heitland made one of his heavy jokes about the conversion, commenting that he had been unable to persuade anyone to live in a room so 'small and very

---

[522] Tottenham to Taylor, 2 Oct. 1890: SJCA, D92.18.34.

[523] Anon., 'Heitland as J. B.', *Eagle* li (1938–9), 132–43, at p. 136.

[524] College butler, 1876–1911.

inconvenient besides being damp and unwholesome' as K1. 'To put a freshman in them without seeing them (or rather his parents seeing them) *might* chance to bring one unpleasantly near to manslaughter'.[525] That last comment was more macabre than funny, given that a brilliant Evangelical undergraduate, Kirke White, had apparently died in those rooms eighty-four years earlier.[526] Finally, and very creditably in view of the financial situation, Heitland persuaded the Council to establish a Reserve Fund for repairs and improvements to the College buildings and grounds.[527]

Turning now to the revenue side of the account, two factors stand out: the decline in student numbers and the collapse of rental income. Despite quite sharp year-on-year fluctuations, the undergraduate intake fell from about 120 in the early 1880s to about seventy in 1893, where it remained in 1903 after a very slight recovery in the later nineties. To make the picture worse, these were years during which numbers in the University as a whole continued to rise – from 2,653 in 1879–80 to 2,985 in 1900–1. The figures were known and commented on, and helped to breed a sense of anxiety with regard to the College's academic standing. In 1904 when MacAlister, the College's most glamorous and famous Fellow, quit his Tutorship in order to become President of the General Medical Council, the committee appointed to find a replacement was clear that someone must be brought in from outside.

> In the judgment of the Committee the present condition of the College must give rise to grave anxiety (...) Besides [the] numerical decline a serious feature of our present state appears in the fact that, of the men who enter at the College, not many come from good schools and very few from the larger Public Schools. It seems to the Committee useless to expect any sensible rise in the entry while the proportion from the good schools is so small. Parents, and the boys themselves are well aware that a College so composed fails to provide some of the most important elements of a University career. As these advantages are now to be had at several other Colleges on terms scarcely higher than those at St John's, the difference in expense, if any, is no longer sufficient to enable us to hold our own. The Committee regard it as essential that the new Tutor should be directly connected with one of the great Public Schools, and that he should be a man likely to attract boys of the same class.[528]

Loss of fee income was serious, but the dominant factor in St John's troubles was the so-called great agricultural depression. Until the mid-1870s rents had continued to rise at the expiry of each lease, and farmers had tumbled over themselves to get tenancies, allowing Reyner to be choosy (as over their

---

[525] Heitland to Taylor, 5 Mar. 1890: SJCA, D92.18.7.

[526] Chantrey's medallion portrait of White was transferred from All Saints' Church on its demolition in 1870 to the ante-Chapel of St John's.

[527] CM, 170/4 (18 Feb. 1887).

[528] Report of the Committee on Tutorships, 17 Mar. 1905: SJCA, SBF54. The committee had a likely man in mind to replace MacAlister, but he was demanding £800 p.a. and the College could afford only £500.

religious affiliation, for example). A series of wet seasons then checked progress, it was assumed temporarily, but by the time of the next good harvest the situation had changed forever owing to imports of cheap, American, prairie-grown wheat. The response throughout most of the Continent was a return to agricultural protection, but Britain's policy-making elite was in thrall to free trade – no one more so than the College's own Alfred Marshall – while its dominant interests (the City of London, Lancashire cottons) were mainly dependent on open-market competition. Wheat prices fell from an average of 57s per imperial quarter in 1871–4 to 27s 7d in 1893–6, after which they bounced along just above the bottom until the First World War. The result was severe depression, followed by arrears and then bankruptcies, in the cereal growing districts, and especially on the heavy clay soils. Two of the worst affected areas in the 1880s were Cambridgeshire and Huntingdonshire, while one of the worst affected in the 1890s was Kent, these three being the counties in which (apart from Yorkshire) St John's held the most property. So, along with King's and Queens', it was one of those colleges that were very badly hit while others remained immune, perhaps because their farming land was devoted to livestock farming, which remained relatively prosperous. (Trinity, for example, was relatively unscathed, partly because it still had an unusually high proportion of beneficial leases, and so was able to reap the same benefit from the switch to rack rents that St John's and many other colleges had reaped earlier.)[529]

Rental receipts fell from a high water mark of £26,000 in 1876 to £17,000 in 1894, while the cost of collection did not fall at all. Meanwhile income from tithes declined from £4,300 to £3,200, the damage being exacerbated by the fact that from 1891 all tithes were payable by the landlord. Overall external revenue fell by one-third over twenty years. The Bursar who first had to deal with this sudden downturn in fortunes was the saintly cleric, John Pieters, who was commonly known as 'Plucky Pieters'. This moniker may have been a sarcastic allusion to his notorious timidity. It may, more respectfully, have referred to his willingness to take on hopeless mathematicians as private pupils. Or it may refer to the fact that so many of his hopeless private pupils were plucked in their examinations. As Bursar he was given a far sterner test than any of the men whom he coached. Having taken over at what his successor in that office would call the 'high water' point financially, he saw the College's income from rents fall from £26,000 to £21,000, while the charge for estate repairs rose from £3,000 to £4,600 a year (with frequent changes of tenancy requiring fresh expenditure on repairs and extensions). In these circumstances no Bursar could have acted with more kindness and consideration towards the tenants, as most of them tacitly acknowledged by revering him, and extensions of payment were

[529] Neild, *Riches and Responsibility*, 90. Abstracting Trinity, Caius, and King's from the equation, rural income from land of Cambridge colleges declined by 40 per cent between 1871 and 1893: Dunbabin, 'Oxford and Cambridge college finances'. Heitland, *After Many Years*, 168–9, reported that Henry Sidgwick had 'tried to get a system whereby richer colleges paid a greater share of the University contribution, but (...) it was not possible to procure a general consent to accept charitable aid, and the generous design came to nothing'. Was he saying that St John's spurned alms from Trinity?

freely granted.[530] No doubt Pieters was too kind for the College's good, but the crash came so fast he had hardly time to think, and his departure from office in 1883, a nervous wreck, seems to have been entirely his own decision. 'Mr Pieters, kind-hearted a man as ever lived (...) told me that he could not face the tenants come up with tears in their eyes begging that they might throw up their leases.'[531] Dogged by a sense of constant failure, he married in 1883 and retired to Bournemouth, where it is to be hoped that he slept soundly.

It is unclear who decided to bring in a Bursar from outside the resident Fellowship (though it is known that the post was first offered to Webb, who refused it). Robert Forsyth Scott was the first lay Bursar and went on to become the first lay Master. He had come up in 1871, had led a 'vigorous undergraduate life' in which he managed to combine rowing and wrangling. (He only made the third boat but came fourth in the tripos.) Between then and before returning to St John's he had been a schoolmaster and then a barrister. Torry had marked him out as a likely Tutor in the previous year. Photographs suggest a strikingly handsome (or at any rate handsomely striking) man, though one who clearly preferred his right profile to his left, and despite the fact that he was a son of the manse there was something slightly proletarian about his appearance – a miner perhaps, or a Lawrentian gamekeeper (see fig. 34). Glover was particularly struck by his twinkle-eyed kindness.

> When the agricultural depression began in earnest (...) Scott was equal to it. Everything that kindness and geniality and devotion to the College could do, he did. And he enjoyed any gleam of absurdity or nonsense that came [as when one tenant wrote to him as 'the Senior Boozer'] (...) One feature of his work was his tolerance of interruption. Few men had more work or more difficult; but, if you invaded the Bursary, you would see him look up over his glasses, and lay down his pen, with an air of relief, as if he were sick of solitude and wanted nothing more than a half-hour's crack' (...) He was so human (...) As one looks back upon the many years, one sees a figure always genial, always ready with some amusing story, always sympathetic with normal youth (less so with premature apostles or prigs of any age), always open-eyed for service to the College, devotion to which was the very core of his life and character.[532]

The latter quality was apparent from the passionate interest he took in the

---

[530] 'It would be far better for all parties that the rent should be paid before the Audit. To assist you in this the College is prepared to make you a return of £30 being about 20 per cent on the half year's rent to Mich. last, provided it be paid on or before Sunday March 5 so as to be in time for the Audit': Pieters to Ephraim Batterson, 7 Feb. 1881: SJCA, SB21/Girton.

[531] Liveing in *Eagle* xxxv (1913–14), 86; R. F. Scott, 'John William Pieters', *Eagle* xxiii (1901–2), 81–2.

[532] Glover, *Cambridge Retrospect*, pp. 90–5. The amusing stories that Glover refers to were frequently smutty, but they would not have been so in Glover's company. There was a chameleon quality to Scott, who would probably have regarded Glover, not without genuine affection, as the type of prig that Glover thought him unsympathetic to.

history of St John's,[533] but he also served the University as a proctor and member of the Council of the Senate, he was a town councillor, and he was a major in the Volunteers. He had the inner confidence to appear self-deprecating, as in the following insincere apology to one of his pricklier colleagues: 'My dear Larmor, Many thanks for your letters. I quite understand that what you wished to slate were my views and not myself personally. And I hope that you will continue to trounce me as long as you think I deserve it. Perhaps I am thick skinned and so require an extra dose!'[534] He could occasionally be slapdash. Apparently he was mortified for ever after by an early moment of carelessness in leasing land for a house in Grange Road, his fatal folly being to rely on the goodwill and decency of a Fellow of Trinity. The result is a kink in the middle of Grange Road that remains an eyesore and threat to cyclists to this day.[535] But above all he was cheerful in the face of corporate adversity, and this had a tonic effect on morale. Whatever might be the judgment on his later period as Master, there can be no doubt that he was a magnificent Bursar.

As well as being a prodigiously hard worker,[536] Scott subjected himself for many years to what anyone else would have regarded as a punishing regime of farm visiting, but he evidently relished the regimen.[537] To take a period at random, during July 1892 he visited Holbeach (Lincs) on the 1st, Ramerick (Herts) on the 5th, Little Stonham (Suffolk) on the 7th, Paxton (Hunts) on the 8th, Thorington (Essex) on the 11th, Wootton Rivers (Wilts) on the 12–13th, Steeple and Southminster (Essex) on the 14th, Ridgewell (Essex) on the 18th, Great Shelford (Cambs) on the 19th, Raveley, Broughton, and Great Stukeley (Hunts) on the 22nd, Ospringe and Luddenham (Kent) on the 25th, Higham (Kent) on the 28th, all of these inspections being written up in sixty-six pages of detailed notes. The latter reveal a number of things about Scott himself, his paternalist instincts, his antiquarian bent – he took a close interest in the tenants' families and back stories, and got to know them personally as no previous Bursar had done – and also the fact that he was a bit of a farmer *manqué*. This is clear from his accounts of the farms that had to be taken in hand. The first such farm was at Tuxford in Nottinghamshire, where the College had to supply capital in stock and implements. No sooner was Tuxford let again than a neighbouring farm at West Markham had to be put in the hands of local agents, leading to a loss of £1,123 over four years. A farm in Little Raveley cost the College more than £425 in 1885–8. ('This was the first farm in hand in which I took an active interest, visiting it repeatedly and going into all questions.') Then in Michaelmas 1890 the 240-acre Girton farm had to be taken in hand for two years at a loss of more

---

[533] Between 1891 and 1915 he contributed any number of 'Notes from the College records' to *The Eagle*.

[534] Scott to Larmor, 2 Feb. 1892: SJCL, Miscellaneous Letters, R. F. Scott, 2.

[535] Philomena Guillebaud, 'West Cambridge, 1870–1914: building the bicycle suburb', *Proceedings of the Cambridge Antiquarian Society* xcvi (2007), 193–210 at pp. 207–8.

[536] During Heitland's great illness he took on the additional work of Junior Bursar without any fuss.

[537] On visiting Holt in Norfolk, the Revd Edward Brumell, a former Fellow, 'told me that no Bursar had been to see the place since he came to Holt. This includes Bateson, Reyner and Pieters.' R. F. Scott, 'Senior Bursar's diary, 1891–3', 10. Aug. 1891: SJCA, SB1.21.63.

than £1,673, 'the heaviest loss on any farm I had to deal with, being between £3 and £4 an acre p.a.'

> We got the farm in a very bad state and left it much improved (...) Wilson, the outgoing tenant, was a cross-grained ill-natured man. He was always grumbling and pressing for concessions. I suspect that he had made up his mind to go some time before he actually gave notice (...) He is said to have bragged to his friends of the trouble he was causing the College, and to have stated that if he had foreseen that I should have to farm the land he would have left it in even worse condition. It was as a matter of fact left in a very foul state. One troublesome feature was this. Much of the heavy land on the farm was infested by wild onions (...) The corn crops were infested with it (...) Thus the wheat especially was unsaleable as when it was ground the flour stunk of onions. We had to get it ground to feed to pigs and cattle. Then the millers declined to grind the corn as it made their stones stink of onions (...) Being near the College I was in the habit of going over the whole farm about once a week.[538]

Although Scott was exhilarated by the practical side of having farms in hand, he was only too aware of the negative consequences: 'a steady loss to the College which has never been less than £1 per acre per annum'. Admittedly, most of the farms taken in hand had been steadily run down over a number of years, and so 'part of the loss was accounted for by the capital sunk in improving them', but more fundamentally Scott, who was a strong Conservative in politics, believed that farms managed by agents would never prosper. 'You cannot get a man to work so hard for another as he would for himself, and the feeling that it is a Corporation which will suffer and not a visible individual does not stimulate them to greater effort.'[539] Such thoughts must have lain behind his determination to grant building leases on some of the College's less fertile estates for residential development.

The Kentish Town estate was almost completed by the time Scott took over, so he looked instead to the West Road, Grange Road, and Madingley Road areas of west Cambridge. As the historian Philomena Guillebaud has pointed out, hitherto all the colleges owning land west of the river had been very reluctant to build on fields that they cherished as their parkland or 'green belt', and now it was only 'economic necessity' that 'forced the invasion of this treasured area'. Gonville and Caius College and Corpus Christi led the way in the 1860s and 1870s, and there is a single piece of evidence to suggest that St John's thought of emulating them: Anne Clough's letter to Bursar Reyner in 1873 in which she stated that she had heard rumours to the effect that the College was considering a change of land-use policy in Madingley Road.[540] Whether or not that was the case, nothing was done about it until Scott's time, though Miss Clough's inquiry was not wasted since it prompted the College to

---

[538] R. F. Scott, 'Memorandum on the finances of unlet or vacant farms, 1895', Senior Bursar's Diary, 1899–1908: SJCA, SB1.23.338–50.

[539] R. F. Scott, 'Statement made by the Senior Bursar at the Final Audit of 1893 on March 13, 1894': SJCA, D100.70.i–xxi at p. xvi.

[540] Anne Clough to Reyner, 7 Aug. 1873: SJCA, SB21/Cb/N.11.1.

grant a lease of two-and-a-half acres east of Grange Road to the future Newnham College in 1875.[541] This was done at Bateson's prompting, and he was no
doubt prompted in turn by his wife, a leading member of the committee to
promote higher education for women. Despite his general conservatism, Reyner
was helpful to the project, and suggested the site that was eventually chosen on
Malting Lane. St John's first intensive (and very 'superior') housing development occurred shortly afterwards on Grange Road, which was greatly extended,
and on a number of new roads to the west. A further development of slightly
less 'superior' houses took place along Madingley Road on the site of the 290-
acre Grange Farm, which had been in a failing state for fifty years (in a 'wretch-
edly foul state all over', according to Carter Jonas) and had long been a source
of bursarial despair.[542] The College's decision (copied by other colleges) that all
the houses should be built of red brick and tiled, and designed according to the
Arts & Crafts or Queen Anne styles, gave the suburb a pleasantly uniform character that remained until the later part of the twentieth century. Guillebaud has
argued forcefully against the myth that the motivation behind the development
was the need to build houses for dons who were at last allowed to marry.[543]
Being desperate to ensure a superior class of resident in their 'treasured area',
it was stipulated that the houses were to be large and of high quality,[544] even
though this meant that they would be beyond the pockets of most married dons,
the vast majority of whom went off to live in new middle-class areas east and
south of the town. The Grange Road area would morph into 'donsville' in the
following century, but for the most part only as academics managed to trade up
from more humble properties.[545]

The success of West Cambridge must have inspired Scott to undertake what
Glover called 'the biggest venture of his bursarial life' – the development of land
at Sunningdale in Berkshire into a golf course and expensive housing. A twenty-
one-year lease was granted to a small syndicate in 1889, but the impact of this
decision was not felt until the twentieth century. Meanwhile, following a fall
in consols he sought to boost income by more daring investments, for example
in the Manchester Ship Canal and Forth Bridge Railway Companies.[546] The
policy was to bear fruit from about the turn of the century. There was also an
occasional act of munificence to ease the strain. The most significant by far were

[541] The freehold was sold to Newnham College in 1900.

[542] SJCA, SB21/Cb/W22.80 [5 Apr. 1884].

[543] Only one St John's don truly fits the bill, C. E. Haskins, who married in 1886 and
in the same year moved into Lady Margaret Road. Alfred Marshall moved into
Madingley Road in 1885, but he had married eight years earlier.

[544] A minimum of one-acre plots and a minimum price tag of £1,500 for the Grange
Road estate, and half-acre plots and £1,000 on the Madingley Road estate.

[545] Guillebaud, 'West Cambridge, 1870–1914', on which this paragraph relies extensively.

[546] Scott, 'Senior Bursar's diary', 4 Apr. 1892: SB1.21.153–4. See Foxwell to Scott, 7 Mar.
1894: SJCA, D92.1.153: 'I imagine we only accumulated such masses of Consols in
the palmy days, when our income overflowed the £300 limit, and the Bursars saw no
necessity to trouble themselves to think about a more profitable investment. What
we really pay for in buying Consols is the extraordinary facility for instantaneous
realisation with small loss. This is all important to bankers, and to some other financial businesses, but of no consequence to us.'

two unrestricted gifts of £2,000 and £10,000 in 1888 and 1894 from a wealthy Canadian businessman and philanthropist, Sir Donald Alexander Smith (later Baron Strathcona).[547] There was a whiff of simony about the transaction, since he evidently gave the cash in return (rather than in gratitude) for having been granted College membership, and this may explain why he insisted on secrecy in contrast to the very public manner in which he donated money to McGill and Aberdeen Universities. The donation was a coup for MacAlister, who had already secured an honorary doctorate for his close friend, besides investing 'all his spare money' in one of Smith's great ventures, the Canadian Pacific Railway. (The latter punt would seem to have been profitable, for MacAlister went on to speculate in property, leasing and building four houses in Madingley Road between 1897 and 1903, in addition to the one that he and his wife already inhabited.) Smith's money helped to redeem the Chapel debt, but it was greeted sourly by Heitland, as was his wont. '£10,000 is good of course, but does it carry with it any likelihood of strengthening the FK interest? If so, the sum is £190,000 short.'[548]

Ultimately, of course, the only way out of the difficulty was to save money, for which reason the most important and pondered over document of the decade was Scott's printed 'State of the College' report of 1894. His verdict on the past management of the College was stinging, though gently and even hesitantly delivered.

> I am inclined to think, but as the other side cannot now be heard, you must receive this statement with caution, that the high dividends paid between 1872 and 1878 were hardly justified. And that some portion of them came out of capital or accumulation (…) Again you must receive my statement with caution (…) but one cannot help feeling that if a more generous policy [towards tenants] had ruled in the good times and the dividends been £10 lower then they might have been higher now.[549]

Looking forward, Scott saw no prospect of increased rents ('Indeed to be candid one hardly sees how a tenant can pay rent at all'), and no prospect of diminished expenditure, since even the impending liquidation of the Chapel debt (equivalent to £30 off the dividend) would merely double the amount of the College's University contribution (equivalent on £20 dividend).[550] The Grange Farm, Madingley, and Sunningdale all offered hope for the future but it would take a long time for serious profits to materialize. Nor could Scott see any prospect of significant economies in the running of the College. Yet – and this was the point he did not spell out but left to be inferred – if St John's was to regain its old eminence, then it was essential to improve the quality of those Lecturers and Tutors who did the academic work. This would require an increase of stipend,

---

[547] CM, 220/3 (25 Jul. 1888); Donna McDonald, *Lord Strathcona: A Biography of Donald Alexander Smith* (Toronto and Oxford, 1996), 427.

[548] Heitland to Scott, 8 Aug. 1894: SJCA, D92.1.183. It is unclear what the intriguing term 'FK interest' refers to.

[549] Scott, 'Statement at the Final Audit of 1893', 13 Mar. 1894: SJCA, D100.70.viii–x.

[550] By March 1896, four years ahead of schedule, Scott had succeeded in paying off the Chapel debt.

but that could only be obtained at the expense of the dividend (effectively the pension) of older Fellows who had borne the burden and heat of an earlier day.

> I myself think that the real remedy lies in decreasing the number of Fellowships (at any rate for a time) and so increasing the value of those which remain. If a steady policy of this kind were adopted a Fellowship would be more difficult to get but it would be of greater value and a greater honour. I know that several Fellows of the College object to this course and it is one which should not be embarked on without careful considera-tion and a strong feeling in its favour.[551]

Had Scott been willing to spell out his reasoning more candidly it might have gone something like the following. 1. Reduce the number of Fellows. 2. Increase the stipends of those that remain, so as to attract a higher quality of Fellow than at present. 3. More distinguished Fellows will make St John's famous again. 4. It will then be possible to attract more paying undergradu-ates. 5. Eventually the College might get back on an even keel. A 'long dis-cussion' followed Scott's presentation, 'the facts touched upon being the advis-ability of suspending fellowships, and the accounts and state of the Steward's department', thereby revealing the Fellowship's characteristic fascination with detail rather than the larger picture and its commitment to tactics rather than to strategy.[552]

It followed from Scott's gloomy report that efficiency and retrenchment had to be the orders of the day. The first step was to revise the methods by which the College's accounts were audited. This was partly just a matter of adapt-ing to changed circumstances. These were, firstly, the proliferation of separate accounts[553] in place of the old general corporate revenue account – this was in obedience to the instructions of the 1871 University commissioners – and sec-ondly, the move from beneficial leases (under which tenants had to pay for expenses and outgoings) to a system of rack rents where the various payments and allowances became a matter of annual routine. It meant that vouchers were being scrutinized several times over, including by the Deans, which left no time, in Scott's words, 'to obtain a general view of College finance'. Scott was not one to shirk responsibility, but he can be forgiven for having wanted a few others to share some of it. It was therefore decided to bypass the Deans and to require a report each year from a committee comprising an auditor and two other Fel-lows, only one of whom could also be a member of the Council.[554] Larmor's scheme for merging the offices of Junior Bursar and Steward came to nothing[555] – at least until 1987 – but it had been agreed for some time that 'the accounts of

---

[551] Scott, 'Statement at the Final Audit of 1893', xxi–xxii.

[552] And also a perennial tendency of colleges to blame their Stewards: CM, 405/3 (13 Mar. 1894).

[553] Such as, for example, the accounts of separate trusts and estates; distinct accounts for land, houses, and ground rents; the education and service accounts which had formerly been kept by the Tutors and the Junior Bursar, and the kitchen's commercial accounts.

[554] Scott to Taylor, 18 Apr. 1891: SJCA, D92.19.24.

[555] 'Report of the Committee on the Unification of College Finance', 24 Nov. 1893: SJCA, D100.64; CMM, 378/13, 412/6 (2 Jun. 1893, 25 May 1894).

the various College departments should be brought under the control of a single financial authority', and this led eventually to the establishment of a central College office for the various internal accounts.

In the circumstances it is hardly surprising that St John's should have departed the nineteenth century in an atmosphere of backbiting and resentment (or in 'ructions again', as Heitland wrote in his diary).[556] There is no evidence to suggest that Taylor or Scott came in for criticism,[557] but the lesser officers were fair game. Taylor commented privately that there were 'agitators' on the Council who were impatient 'to get rid of' Heitland as Junior Bursar,[558] and it was symptomatic, perhaps, that the committee to consider the unification of finance did not contain any officers, prompting one Fellow to complain that it 'will arrive at no useful or acceptable result'.[559] (Incidentally, it cannot have helped the officers that there was something of a power vacuum at the top. With a semi-detached Master and a remote farm house of a President, the College in the 1890s would appear to have been run mainly by Larmor, MacAlister, and Scott.) It was only in such a febrile atmosphere that something so mundane as a pillar box could have caused so much agitation. The details are murky but it would appear that Heitland colluded with the Post Office in the erection of such a receptacle in the street just outside the Great Gate. It provoked widespread dismay, and prompted fifteen Fellows to write (twice) urging the Council to have it repositioned, which was eventually done. (According to one of many rumours about the affair, the box was torn from the ground forcibly and pitched into the river, but this cannot be substantiated.) The anti-pillar box party claimed to act on aesthetic grounds, arguing that the clash between pink brickwork and scarlet-painted iron 'must take away the charm and the stateliness of the gateway',[560] but Heitland insisted that he was the victim of a personal vendetta. Some Fellows might well have feared that the Junior Bursar would cite the proximity of the box as a reason why they should post their own mail, thus allowing him to save on porters' wages. Whatever the problem was exactly, Heitland almost certainly exaggerated it, and yet the Master felt that he had 'a right to an apology in the matter of the Pillar-box, and any unprejudiced person, not carried away by the excitement of the moment, would admit it'.[561]

In fact, if anyone had cause to feel paranoid it was the Deans, William Cox and Alfred Caldecott, who met with a good deal of animus, much of it stoked by Heitland. It may be that they were not well suited to the job. Much later Glover, drawing on his undergraduate memories, described Cox as a 'gloomy

---

[556] Heitland's diary, 11 Jun. 1897.

[557] In 1886 Scott read the Council some letters from tenants to illustrate the difficulty of collecting rents. This led Heitland to propose a motion of full confidence in Scott's handling of affairs which was carried *nem. con.*: CM, 136/6 (12 Feb. 1886).

[558] Taylor to Scott, 21 Mar. 1891: SJCA, D92.19.21.

[559] Bateson to Taylor, 12 Feb. 1892: SJCA, D92.20.9.

[560] Fifteen Fellows to Taylor, 27 Feb. 1891, in Beatrice Bateson, *William Bateson, FRS, Naturalist: His Essays and Addresses together with a Short Account of his Life* (Cambridge, 1928), 50–1.

[561] Charles Taylor to R. F. Scott, 21 Mar. 1891: SJCA, D92.19.21.

and unsympathetic would-be authority'. 'Cox should never have been Dean; he didn't do as Dean, and his colleague was beyond words worse.'[562] Very possibly they were mainly to blame for the prolonged period of warfare between themselves and the undergraduates, but even if so they had reason to resent the gleeful way in which so many of their colleagues sided with the latter. Likewise, the Council may have been justified in engineering Cox's dismissal (after twelve years in post) in 1894, but the careful (i.e underhand) way in which it planned the coup cannot but have been hurtful. Step one was to line up a successor. On 27 April Mayor's motion that H. T. E. Barlow should be appointed Junior Dean was carried narrowly, and on 11 May the Council (but no one else) was informed that Barlow had accepted, whereupon it unanimously agreed to accept MacAlister's motion that, whenever a President, Bursar, Steward, or Dean completed five years, the Council should 'take into consideration the question, "Whether it is desirable that *XXX* should be re-elected".'[563] On 25 May it was decided to send copies of the Mayor and MacAlister motions to the Deans with a covering letter, and on 18 June Cox's resignation letter was received. This sequence of events prompted Main to comment sourly that 'the game most popular with the Council in their leisure-moments seems to be false accusations against the Deans'. And certainly, for all that the individual officers might have given cause for criticism, anti-clericalism was almost certainly a factor, especially on the part of MacAlister and Heitland, whose motion twelve years previously that one of the deans should be a layman had been only very narrowly defeated, by 13 votes to 12.[564]

Cox continued to teach divinity until 1905 when, following complaints that his lessons 'were as a rule above the men's heads', he declared himself 'quite prepared to be automatically and silently extinguished as a College Lecturer'.[565] Caldecott's demise was altogether less graceful. He had been promoted to Senior Dean following Cox's defenestration in 1894, but he must have realized that the knives would soon come looking for him as well, and just six days into the job he asked to be presented to the living of Staplehurst, recently vacated by the death of Reyner. 'I should have wished some day to return to parochial work, as Theology in the department which I study is not needed for lecturing and I have never felt that the deanship taken alone was of a permanent character.'[566] However, the Council turned down both this and later requests for a living that was both close to London and sufficiently rich to support a curate. 'I might have been unreasonable', he wrote reproachfully to Larmor, 'but I did think some ten

---

[562] Glover, *Cambridge Retrospect*, 39–40.

[563] Tellingly, MacAlister was persuaded to withdraw an earlier motion to similar effect but directed against the deans alone.

[564] Laicization on these lines occurred in 1902, see below, p. 408. Main to Scott, 26 Jan. 1894: SJCA, D92.1.145; Cox to Taylor, 9 June 1894: SJCA, D92.24.32; CM, 408/8, 410/4, 412/4, 415/20, 27 Apr., 11 and 25 May, 18 June 1894.

[565] Cox to Larmor, 30 May [?1905]: SJCL, Miscellaneous letters, W1.Cl–Cu, Cox, 3.

[566] Caldecott to Larmor, 24 June 1894: SJCL, Miscellaneous letters, W1.Ca–Ch, Caldecott, 1.

years of Fellowship and nearly four of office would have been worth *something* (i.e. not less than zero!).'[567]

Caldecott's personal disappointments are not all that significant, but his case is interesting for what it says about the current state of religion in the University, as well as about relations between Church and College. With regard to the first, he unburdened himself to Larmor over his reasons for wishing to leave.

> An average man cannot just now do justice to a clerical position in Cambridge except on the basis of 'Scholarship', so called, whereby only a remote and incidental position is possible for Rational and Moral Theology. For myself I have felt obliged to acquiesce in this, and have laid down the lines of a book which would stand in lieu of lectures as my contribution to research and teaching. But when I considered the weakness of the College equipment for taking its part in the Theological teaching [of the University] I could not resist the feeling that I was in the way, a feeling confirmed when my mind reverted to that other direction indicated by yourself, the insufficient endowment of rising young scientific men in the College, and the possibility of laicizing my present position.[568]

As Caldecott could see, the secularizing process meant that religion's main claim to attention was now as an academic discipline, and that left few senior positions available in universities for people like himself who simply had strong spiritual convictions.[569] On the question of worship as distinct from teaching, it was evidently Larmor's view that the College should renounce its alliance with the established Church and 'organize religion for itself'. Caldecott's response to that suggestion was brusque: 'The kind of religion that could be organized by our present "Fifty-Six" is to me beyond conceivability, and I therefore think there is nothing feasible between continuing the alliance and pure secularization.' Yet the latter step was surely ruled out by the existence in college of about fifty undergraduates who intended to take Anglican Orders. 'The Bishops and their advisers will continue to lay down the conditions of admission to ordination, and if St John's no longer approves itself to them, the exodus to Pembroke and Selwyn and even to Trinity will continue and increase.'

If the 1890s was a bad decade in which to be a Dean, it was also a bad time to be Steward, whose hapless role is always to be damned, either by the penny-pinchers, or by the gourmands, or more often by both. The Steward from 1892 onwards was William Bateson. It will be remembered that he had come into the office having staged a coup against his predecessor W. F. Smith, whom he had accused of laxity.[570] Up to a point Bateson proved to be conscientious in detailed matters but he failed to get a grip, and within one year of his appointment the following resolution of the Audit Committee was carried *nem. con.*

[567] Caldecott to Larmor, 23 Jan 1895: SJCL, Miscellaneous letters, W1.Ca–Ch, Caldecott, 3.

[568] Caldecott to Larmor, 8 Jan. 1895: SJCL, Miscellaneous letters, W1.Ca–Ch, Caldecott, 2.

[569] A point brought home to him by his failure to be appointed to a recent College lectureship in theology.

[570] See above, p. 273.

That as soon as possible after the affairs of the Farm and Dairy are wound up a statement of the then state of the department under the control of the Steward should be laid before the Fellows, together with a concise statement of the financial position at the time the present Steward entered on his duties. Professor Liveing asked that the Steward be asked to report on the state of his department.[571]

During the four following years the Steward's department (which comprised the wine cellar and kitchen garden as well as the kitchens themselves) fell seriously into the red, not helped of course by the collapse in student enrolments. Mortified, Bateson moved for a reduction in his own stipend from £200 to £150, and though he could not find a seconder, the fact that he felt compelled to make the gesture says much about the poisonous atmosphere that prevailed.[572]

Meanwhile the Tutors, equally unhappy, were moved to protest in 1898 that for the first time in its history the College was unable to let all its rooms. In the past, when unlet rooms were rare, and could reasonably be supposed to have resulted from an oversight on the Tutor's part, it was the latter who had borne the loss, but the current spate of vacancies was such as to 'swallow up the whole profits of the Tutorship for the year', meaning that 'a sufficient supply of Tutors will not easily be found.'[573] The main reason was the fall in undergraduate numbers from about 400 to 270, but there was also the dilapidated state of College rooms, which were for the most part either 'dear, inconvenient, or unhealthy'. Staircases and passages were in a neglected state, largely owing to economies on works staff, while many of the rooms themselves were lined with dark and gloomy panelling, which was expensive to paint. Many of the sets were bitterly cold, especially those in high-ceilinged New Court, where condensation dripped down the walls in winter. There was therefore an increasing tendency for local students to live with their parents, and for others to live out of College, where they might take baths and read by electric light. It was therefore agreed in 1900 that, in respect of unlet rooms, the College should bear the loss of rental income as well as paying into the Service Fund a sum sufficient to guarantee the bedmakers' wages.[574]

The Committee on Tutorships reported in 1905 that, 'as a consequence of this fall in entry, the Education Fund has also declined, and the stipends of the educational staff have reached a limit which is dangerous to efficiency.'[575] Since 1884 Lecturers had been paid, not directly out of general revenue, but from an Education Fund into which the undergraduates paid their tuition fees and the College contributed £520 annually. In 1893 the Education Committee reported that the Fund was in deficit by £140, and would have been even more indebted without the generous personal donations of Mason (£25) and Main (£75). It then

---

[571] CM, 406/1 (14 Mar. 1894).

[572] Heitland's diary, 4 Mar. 1897. The fact that Bateson remained Steward until 1908 suggests that no one was clamouring to take his place. See below, p. 484.

[573] Sandys, MacAlister, and Graves to the Council, 25 May 1898: SJCA, C12.10.5(i).

[574] Sandys, MacAlister, and Graves, 'Memorandum to the Council', 25 May 1898: SJCA, C12.10.5; Scott, 'Vacant rooms in College', 25 May 1898: SJCA, C12.10.6(i); 'Report by the Tutors and Senior Bursar on vacant rooms in College', 1898: SJCA, C12.10.5.

[575] 'Report of the Committee on Tutorships', 17 Mar. 1905, p. 3: SJCA, SBF54.

posed two questions: 'In this state of things, what is (a) the chance of being able to exercise some choice in the matter of admissions (as distinct from taking anyone who applied), (b) the existing Lecturers' security for their stipends?' That was the year in which Scott, saying the unsayable, called for a systematic policy to reduce the number of Fellows. Almost immediately afterwards the classic Haskins died, suddenly and early, which helped to create a £160 surplus in the Education Fund for 1894, but such divine interventions could not be relied on. In 1893 it was adjudged (almost unanimously and after much barrack room 'jaw') that the Council was empowered by statute to suspend Fellowships for a limited period. That legal point settled, a lengthy discussion took place as to the wisdom of suspending whenever a vacancy occurred. MacAlister and Liveing seem to have been especially hawkish, but slashing motions were usually carried by 10 votes to just 1 or 2, so that eight Fellowships out of the fifty-five were suspended between 1893 and 1899.

Suspensions might have relieved the financial problems but they naturally put a strain on teaching provision, and this at a time when costs were rising anyway owing to the fact that, as Miller puts it, 'the old coaches like Love and Webb were giving place to the new [stipendiary] supervisor, whom MacAlister and Baker were making the characteristic college teacher'.[576] The resulting financial squeeze forced the Education Committee into any number of balancing acts, not to say fudges. Between 1880 and 1896 financial support to students fell from £6,700 to £3,900. In 1892 a decision not to replace two vacated Lecturerships, in classics and physics, was accompanied by a vague suggestion that 'the Committee be empowered to propose some arrangement by which lectures in Physics may be provided in College during the ensuing academical year'.[577] When, later that same year, Haskins' sudden death created another vacancy in classics, it was decided ('as a temporary expedient') to elect into a Fellowship the only Classical Lecturer who did not at that time have one, Charles Graves.[578] However, this would not bring him any immediate financial benefit, since the *quid pro quo* was that his Lecturer's stipend was to be docked by £150, thus enabling the Education Fund to remain in balance. Two years later still, the Fellows in that subject were moved to remonstrate on the fact that candidates for the classical special examination 'have had to prepare the work by themselves, to provide a private coach, or have, in some cases, been taken, practically as private pupils, by one of the Classical Lecturers without remuneration'.[579]

These difficulties were reflected in tripos results, hitherto the one enduring source of college pride throughout a difficult century. Only thirty-one Johnians achieved Firsts in classics (as against eighty-two from Trinity), and of those

[576] Miller, *Portrait of a College*, 112.

[577] 'Report and minutes of the Education Committee', 12 Mar. 1892: SJCA, CC1.3, 18.

[578] SJCA, SB1.17; 'Report of the Education Committee', 1892–3: SJCA, CC1.19. Graves had first been elected a Fellow in 1863 but had surrendered by marriage in 1865. He later served as Tutor (1895–1905).

[579] Classical Lecturers (Graves, Sandys, Tottenham, Sikes) to Council, 29 May 1895: SJCA, CC1.3. In the previous year (12 Feb. 1894) the Education Committee had concluded that the only way to provide lectures for the special examination was by discontinuing little-go lectures in Lent and Easter: SJCA, CC1.3.

thirty-one only two were in the top division (as against twenty-five from Trinity); worse still, the thirty-one Firsts were outweighed by thirty-six Thirds. Mathematics held up much better, but even here there was a falling off from the glory days. Between 1890 and 1899 sixty-one Johnians achieved Firsts in the mathematics tripos as against eighty-two from Trinity and 280 overall, the real story being the improved performance of a number of other colleges. Crushingly, only one Johnian in that period was Senior Wrangler.

When, in 1909, a committee reported on the educational state of the College, it was in no doubt that financial constraints were playing a malign part in the College's declension, not least by giving the undergraduates a comparatively poor deal. Each student paid £5 in tuition fees to the Education Fund, yet received back no more than £3 in the form of a grant, meaning that there was an 'intercepted £2'. In classics, mathematics and theology, the College was, 'in a manner self-sufficing', but it was not so in economics, history, law, modern languages, moral sciences, or oriental studies, the teaching being in large part 'done outside' with the students themselves paying the fees, subject to a miniscule grant from the Education Fund.

> It will appear that although Trinity, King's, Caius and Pembroke charge a larger Tuition fee than St John's they make a larger return to the student since, in addition to the cash grant, supervision is provided free or under cost price to a much greater extent than with us; while at Emmanuel the student pays the same Tuition fee, receives a larger grant in cash and is subsidised from the grant in respect of what is practically private tuition.[580]

'Long desultory jaw about decline of St John's College, with many futilities of suggestion and explanation. No result.'[581] Having entered the nineteenth century in what was arguably pole position, St John's entered the twentieth in something approaching turmoil. There were diversions, however. It is interesting to compare the 1875 and 1893 menus for the *Ante Portam Latinam* Feast. The first, devised at a time when the dividend was £300 and the College on the crest of an economic wave, indicates a substantial but reasonably manly repast.

Potage printanier
Potage de fausse tortue (lié)

———

Saumon bouilli sauce persil
Soles frites sauce anchois
Salade de concombres

———

Agneau rôti
Aloyeau de bœuf rôti
Hanche de mouton

———

[580] Scott, Blackman, Leathem, Glover, Hart, 'Report on the Education Fund', 1909: SJCA, SBF77.
[581] Heitland's diary, 5 Nov. 1897.

Pouding Victoria
Paté de groseilles
Gelée au noyeau
Crême à la vanille
Pâté de rhubarb

The 1893 menu, concocted at a time when the dividend was £100 and still going downwards, suggests an altogether more lavish and fittingly *fin de siècle* banquet. From a much later perspective it looks like nothing so much as a camp culinary distraction from the howling of the wolves at the gates.

Royans à la gourmet

———

Consommé de volaille à l'impériale
Purée de haricot verts à la française

———

Saumon, sauce génoise
Concombres
Blanchailles

———

Boudins de homard à la Cardinale
Côtelettes de caille à l'Egyptienne

———

Selle d'agneau
Salade de tomates, Salade à la française
Poulets printaniers rôti
Jambon d'York sauté
Pommes de terre nouvelle, Choux fleurs au gratin
Epinards

———

Langue de bœuf fumée
Asperges au beurre
Aspic de thon aux crevettes

———

Poudin à l'Impératrice
Gelée de fraises au vin de champagne
Petits soufflés glace marasquin

———

Beignets de gruyère à la Pluton

———

Dessert

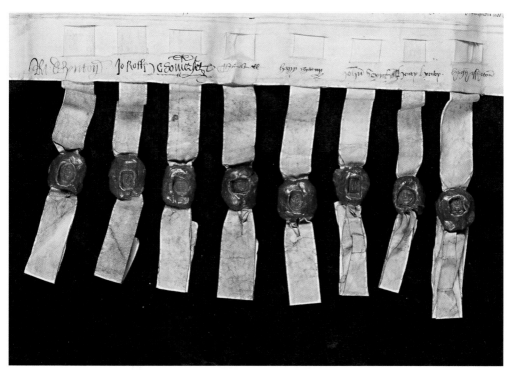

I The personal seals of Lady Margaret's executors, attached to the College's foundation Charter 9 April 1511: SJCA, D4.17. Amongst the seals, from left to right, are those of (1) Richard Fox, bishop of Winchester; (2) John Fisher, bishop of Rochester; (6) Sir John St John, Lady Margaret's chamberlain; (7) Henry Hornby (her Chancellor; Master of Peterhouse); (8) Hugh Ashton (her Comptroller or Chief Accountant)

II The signature of Roger Ascham incised in the fireplace of the Old Treasury, First Court
Photograph: Paul Everest

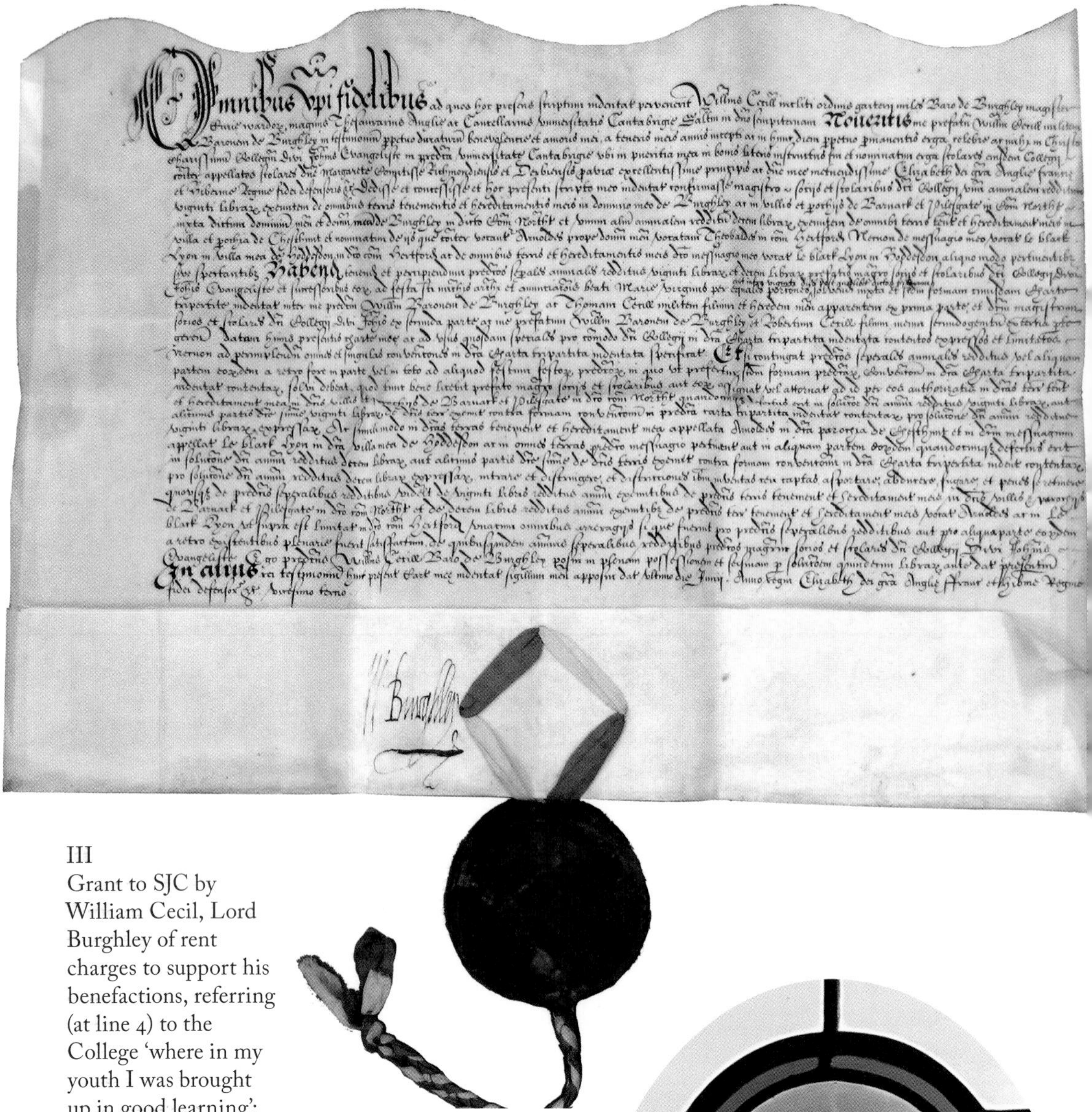

III
Grant to SJC by William Cecil, Lord Burghley of rent charges to support his benefactions, referring (at line 4) to the College 'where in my youth I was brought up in good learning': SJCA, D42.26

IV
Combination Room window roundel of Henrietta Maria commemorating her betrothal to the future Charles I in that room, 1624

V SJCL, MS C9, fo.35v: the 'Southampton Psalter'
(Irish; 10th century). The Library's oldest complete manuscript
(part of the Crashaw-Southampton bequest).

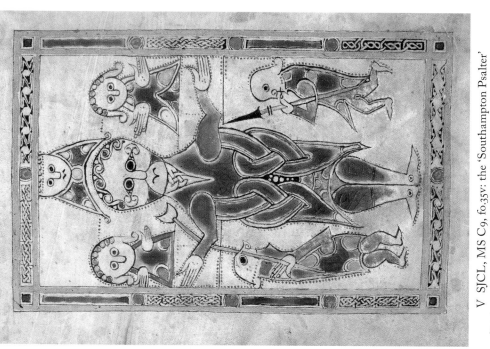

VI '... the tombstone where he lies': Baker's sadly neglected slab
tomb on the lawn of First Court where once the Chapel stood.
Photograph: Paul Everest

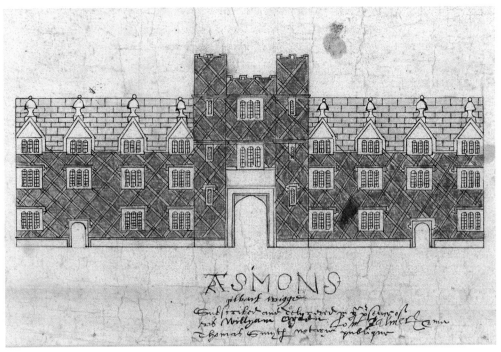

VII Elevation of the west range of Second Court drawn by Ralph Simons, 1598.
Simons was one of the architects-cum-builders of Second Court,
working with Gilbert Wigge whose name also appears here: SJCL, Bb.7.6

VIII Is it a hyena? Or could it be a bear? Early 17th-century wall painting in K4 Second Court
(See Mark Nicholls, *Eagle* [2003], 38–40.)

IX Matthew Prior, poet and diplomat, BA 1687
Portrait by Alexis Simon Belle

X The Upper Library looking west
From Rudolph Ackermann, *History of the University of Cambridge* (London, 1815)

XI
William Bateson
(Master, 1857–81)
Sketch by E. H. Palmer

XII
A study in dejection. J. E. B.
Mayor reflects on the presumed
theft of the manuscript of his
Latin dictionary, by then sixty
years in the making. (After
advertising all over Europe for
its return, he would discover
that it had been used by his
bedder to prop up an ailing
piece of furniture in his own
keeping room.)
Crayon sketch by Victoria
Monkhouse: SJCL, Port.
XIV.9

XIII The College Bread and Broth Charity, *c.* 1920. Picture by Agatha Shore.
An obligation inherited from the old Hospital, the distribution was always done on
thirteen successive Thursdays in the bleak mid-winter. See p. 640.

XIV Ever anxious to oblige: Norman Buck, Assistant Librarian,
retired in 1982 after fifty-three years service in the College.

XV
'Far brighter than these gaudy melon-flowers': Boys Smith at the Conference of European Vice-Chancellors and Rectors, Göttingen, September 1964. Photograph: G. S. Boys Smith

XVI *(below)*
Full Circle. June 1985. After Cardinal Basil Hume's commemoration of John Fisher's 450th anniversary Harry Hinsley makes a further telling point.

XVII The College from the Backs, showing New Court to the left and Third Court to the right, with St John's Chapel Tower rising in the background. Photograph: Alice Hardy.

XVIII View of First Court from the Chapel Tower. Photograph: Alice Hardy.

XIX The School of Pythagoras

XX Chapel Gargoyles. Photograph: Paul Everest

XXI Hall Turret and Bell Tower. Photograph: Paul Everest

XXII The College from the top of the Chapel Tower

XXIII The Great Gate

V

THE TWENTIETH CENTURY

Peter Linehan

INTRODUCTION

Peter Hennessy

THE College had a remarkable twentieth century. It touched the world and the world touched it in many ways that were unforeseeable and almost inconceivable in 1900. Two of its Nobel Laureates changed for ever our understanding of the physical world and its possibilities. Paul Dirac was one of the pioneers of quantum mechanics who, in Max Born's words, in the late 1920s and early 1930s 'brought order and meaning into the chaos of atomic phenomena',[1] and John Cockcroft, who 'split' the atom at the Cavendish Laboratory in 1932, went on to shape atomic weapons research in the wartime Manhattan Project and was a founding father of the British nuclear weapons programme after 1945.[2] In national terms, St John's rose mightily within the general 'rise of professional society'[3] and 'meritocracy',[4] and, generation on generation, peopled the higher ranks of the great professions with a distinction and an impact out of all proportion to its size. As Renford Bambrough (Dean of Johnians' bodies though not their souls) could claim without excessive exaggeration, at 'every institution where the Number One is a figurehead, like a great department of state in Whitehall, the Number Two was educated at St John's College, Cambridge.'[5]

Johnians lubricated pivotal working parts of the British Empire from the Colonial Office to the Sudan Political Service and when the time came also helped ease the enterprise into relatively dignified dissolution; some were instrumental in tilting the UK towards Europe and keeping it there; others in the Treasury grappled with Britain's relative economic decline or laboured mightily to prevent the cold war from morphing into a hot one; still more oversaw the transformation of the City of London and the world's financial institutions. The twentieth-century College produced an archbishop of Canterbury (Donald

---

[1] Max Born, *My Life and Views* (New York, 1968), 105; see also Peter Goddard, 'Paul Dirac', *Eagle* lxxi, no. 294 (1986), 69–77; Graham Farmelo, *The Strangest Man: The Hidden life of Paul Dirac, Quantum Genius* (London, 2009).

[2] Margaret Gowing, *Britain and Atomic Energy 1939–1945* (London, 1964). For his postwar work see Gowing, *Independence and Deterrence, Britain and Atomic Energy 1945–1952*, I. *Policy Making*; II. *Policy Execution* (London, 1974).

[3] The phrase is Harold Perkin's, *The Rise of Professional Society England since 1880* (London, 1989).

[4] The concept was popularized and satirized by Michael Young in *The Rise of the Meritocracy* (Harmondsworth, 1961).

[5] In conversation with the author in the early 1970s.

Coggan), a Governor of the Bank of England (Mervyn King), *the* pioneering 'tele-don' (Glyn Daniel) and the most cerebral England Cricket Captain ever (Mike Brearley). Johnians, too, in great numbers, quickened the life of the mind in universities and research labs across the globe.

Something like this could be said of several other Cambridge colleges. Yet there is a special spirit of place about St John's, both in the glorious setting of brick and stone, architecture and water in which it housed its members and in the Johnian *mentalité* – a certain idea of life and learning lightly worn, easy for fellow initiates to recognize but extraordinarily difficult to capture in words without gush or cliché. This has been true in different ways of St John's through-out its centuries. But in the twentieth, the quiddity of the College acquired a special vividness tinged with poignancy because of the two world wars which emptied its staircases in a way that had not happened since the plague cleared out the University in the seventeenth century. The pair of total wars affected everybody in College from the bedmakers, the kitchen staff, the gardeners, the undergraduates and postgraduates to the Master and Fellows.

The College in the twentieth century is a story too of substantial changes and reforms in Cambridge, the British university system generally and society as a whole – all of which were felt throughout St John's. But it is also a tale of those special micro-relationships that perhaps linger longest in the memories of individual Johnians, only fragments of which can be captured in a general history of the College. And, given the great surge in numbers, especially after the Second World War, more members of the College passed through the Great Gate beneath the arms of Lady Margaret and the statue of St John the Evange-list in the twentieth century than in the four preceding it.

Apart from those (hopefully few) who had a bad time between St John's Street and the Backs, the College (as George Orwell wrote of England during the war) has something about it which 'is continuous, it stretches into the future and the past, there is something in it that persists, as in a living creature'.[6] Or as R. H. Tawney put it during another of Britain's twentieth-century wars, 'Only those institutions are loved which touch the imagination.'[7] All of these ingre-dients – tangible and intangible alike – we attempt to capture in the pages that follow. In our different ways, the College has touched our imaginations consist-ently and powerfully since we first came up (Linehan in 1961; Hennessy in 1966).

Yet how much of the coming century could have been imagined in the John's of 1900? Minds gathered together in the Governing Body were naturally greatly absorbed by the present and still had much to absorb from the great reforms of the nineteenth century, led so effectively by W. H. Bateson during his long Mastership. Its forty-four-strong Fellowship in 1900 contained several who were among the first generation to make the transition 'from clergyman to don'.[8] Once the religious tests had gone, an entirely different intellectual

---

[6] George Orwell, 'The Lion and the Unicorn' (first published in 1941), in Peter Davison (ed.), *Orwell's England* (London, 2001), 252.

[7] R. H. Tawney, 'A national College of All Souls', *Times Educational Supplement*, 22 February 1917.

[8] Christopher Brooke, *A History of the University of Cambridge*, IV. *1870–1900* (Cambridge, 1992), 1–19.

trajectory was possible. The college nonetheless remained a great and regular replenisher of the Anglican tank. The 1900 *Eagle* records sixteen ordinations the previous December (eight priests; eight deacons) and a dozen ecclesiastical appointments.[9]

The surge of intellectual energy recruited and released in the late nineteenth century paid off, too, in the early twentieth in the shape of new triposes. Johnian influence was probably most pronounced in the creation of the economics tripos in 1903 in the person of Alfred Marshall (a protégé of Bateson's from the time, as a Merchant Taylor's schoolboy, he was awarded a College mathematics Exhibition in 1861) whose *Principles of Economics* when published in 1890 had set a new standard for his discipline.[10] (He had succeeded to the University's Chair of Political Economy in 1885 after holding a College Lectureship since 1868.)[11]

In describing him in a famous 1924 biographical essay, John Maynard Keynes established a kind of gold standard not just for economists, but with modifications, for the donnish trade as a whole. The 'master-economist', wrote Keynes,

> must reach a high standard on several different directions and must combine talents not often formed together. He must be mathematician, historian, statesman, philosopher – in some degree. He must understand symbols and speak in words. He must contemplate the particular in terms of the general, and touch abstract and concrete in the same flight of thought. He must study the present in the light of the past for the purposes of the future. No part of man's nature or his institutions must lie entirely outside his regard. He must be purposeful and disinterested in a simultaneous mood; as aloof and incorruptible as an artist, yet sometimes as near the earth as a politician.

Did Marshall, in Keynes' view, match up to this specification?

> Much, but not all, of this ideal many-sidedness Marshall possessed. But chiefly … he was conspicuously historian and mathematician, a dealer in the particular and the general, the temporal and the eternal, at the same time.[12]

High praise for a great Johnian tripos-builder.

The College, however, had not shown itself to be a master of sound, practical economics. In a very nineteenth-century way, it had built to last, but it had overextended itself on its capital works especially where 'the temporal and the eternal' met in the new Chapel. The great agricultural depression of the 1880s was beyond the reach of anyone to remedy. Given its reliance on land as *the* source of its wealth, St John's was hit especially hard, even though, as Senior Bursar, R. F. Scott struggled mightily to restore the College's position. Yet as the century turned, John's was feeling the effect of fewer Fellowships, Scholarships and

---

[9] 'Our Chronicle', *Eagle* xxi (1899–1900), 244.

[10] Alfred Marshall, *Principles of Economics* (London, 1890). For Bateson's interest see John Maynard Keynes, *Essays in Biography* [1933] (London, 1972), 164, n. 2.

[11] Keynes, *Essays in Biography*, 212–15.

[12] Ibid., 173–4.

Exhibitions,[13] and, in that delicate Cam-side membrane which calibrates who's up and who's down, Trinity increasingly gave the impression of being the dominant member of the big three (King's being one-third).[14]

What, then, of the 237-strong undergraduate body in 1900? The numbers show it was far from a boom-time for recruitment. On the eve of the First World War there were only about 274 junior members in residence.[15] What kind of young men were they? Was, for example, the College still holding true to its foundress's intentions of putting down ladders of opportunity north of the River Trent for clever, but far from wealthy, boys? To what extent did the patchwork of financial provision compensate for the pronounced inequalities of late Victorian, Edwardian and early Georgian Britain between the turn of the century and the Great War?

What were the preoccupations of this surprisingly rich mix of junior members apart from the normal combinations of high-mindedness and hedonism, self-assurance and anxiety that, generation on generation, fashions clever young men clustered close in the special intimacy of a College? War, certainly. Not the still unimaginable prospect of trenches stretching from the English Channel to the Swiss Alps that awaited so many of them. But the Boer War in South Africa was vivid enough and deeply worrying for those, almost certainly then a majority, who cared deeply about the fortunes of the British Empire.

[13] Miller, *Portrait of a College*, 96–7.
[14] Brooke, *History of the University of Cambridge*, IV. 67–9.
[15] Ibid., 98.

A New Century

It is not by the direct method of a scrupulous narration that the explorer of the past can hope to depict that singular epoch. If he is wise, he will adopt a subtler strategy. He will attack his subject in unexpected places; he will fall upon the flank, or the rear; he will shoot a sudden, revealing searchlight into obscure recesses, hitherto undivined. He will row out over that great ocean of material, and lower down into it, here and there, a little bucket, which will bring up to the light of day some characteristic specimen, from those far depths, to be examined with a careful curiosity.

Lytton Strachey, *Eminent Victorians* (1918), Preface

O N 19 June 1902 twenty or so Fellows and sixty-odd 'members of the College on the Boards' assembled in Hall for the first-ever Old Johnians' Dinner.[1] As to the seating arrangements, T. R. Glover (one of the Fellows present) recorded in his diary that he thought himself fortunate.[2] Amongst others present, to Scott and Glover (frequently) and to Jumbo and Sandys (much less often) we shall return. As they settled down to exchange gossip over their port and cigars, the news will have spread of the death on the previous day of Samuel Butler.

In their different ways, R. F. Scott and T. R. Glover both typified a new phenomenon on the Cambridge scene, or at any rate one no older than the new (1882) Statutes. This was the don whose profession no longer required him to go off to a parish in his early thirties or at least as soon as he felt the need for female companionship. Now he might stay on into and beyond middle age, marry, and make his whole career in Cambridge.[3] Although not every under-graduate would judge this dispensation a distinct advantage, there were plenty who did. The steady collective gaze of the teams of muddied oafs and flannelled fools assembled for the team photographs of various club in the early 1900s gave no intimation of the College's financial and academic insecurity as described above.[4] Which was, of course, natural: as also was the presence in almost all of them, as either performer or coach, of the athletically omnicompetent Anglo-Irishman and teacher of law, Loftus Bushe-Fox, described on his death as 'the moral force which directed and controlled the undergraduate life of the College', the chief work of whose life had been 'to unite the senior and junior members

---

For reading drafts of this and some or all of the following chapters I am indebted to Stephen Anderson, Owen Chadwick, Peter Clarke, Simon Conway-Morris, Graham Harding, Jonathan Harrison, Ronald Hyam, Edmund King, Elliot Ross, Malcolm Schofield, my oldest Cambridge friend John Sheldon, David Thistlethwaite, and Malcolm Underwood.

[1] *Eagle* xxiv (1902–3), 105–6.

[2] 'Evening dinner a pleasant time – especially [C. S. H.] Brereton across table and [T.] Darlington', but less so with the speeches ('Jumbo absurd. Gorst and Sandys fair. Scott's speech easily best').

[3] Cf. A. J. Engel, *From Clergyman to Don: The Rise of the Academic Profession in Nineteenth-Century Oxford* (Oxford, 1983), 273–85, 294 (Appendix II).

[4] Pp. 367ff.

of St John's in a far closer understanding than hitherto'.[5] The encomiast was J. H. Beith (the novelist and playwright Ian Hay) with whom 'Bushie' had been engaged in 1900 in running a joint poll coaching firm for the academically confused.[6] Appointed College Law lecturer in 1902 (at the age of 39) and Fellow and Junior Dean 1903, in 1905 'Bushie' was made a Tutor and in 1906 became a husband. Albeit other Cambridge colleges exhibited more extreme forms of the type, not everyone at St John's was equally delighted. 'I hated the idea of promoting a boating coach to one of the principal offices in College', E. W. MacBride (Fellow, 1893–7; embryologist and extreme eugenicist) complained from McGill University. 'It seemed to me to be a lowering of academic ideals.'[7] And it was not as if the towpath provided compensation, with the history of LMBC in the Mays down to 1914 providing an uninterrupted saga of exceptional promise regularly unfulfilled, and the reasons adduced for this indicating the contagious consequences of Professor MacBride's intrusive academic ideals.[8]

The tension between the MacBride and the Bushe-Fox views of things was to have its effects down to 1914 and beyond. Sometimes it was creative.

The College's long twentieth century had begun with the establishment of an Audit Committee in 1891 and, in response to a deficit in the Steward's department, proposals in 1892–3 for the amalgamation of the offices of Steward and Praelector and Junior Bursar as a single College office 'in which all the business management of the College can be carried on'.[9] Since for the Tutors in particular the implications of these measures were far-reaching, the composition of the two-man committee to which the matter was referred in 1898 was no doubt intended to reflect the balance of opinion within the Fellowship between the traditional way of doing things and a degree of rationalization of College procedures.

Running to thirty-two pages, and containing rather more material than the Governing Body had previously been expected to ingest at a single gulp, the Committee's report proffered the agreed solution of its two members, J. R. Tanner and Joseph Larmor (to both of whom we shall also shortly return) as to the best way forward for the College. Since it is impossible to separate out the strands of the arguments in which they may have engaged, it must suffice to state the problem, summarize their report and record their recommendations:

[5] *Eagle* xxxvii (1915–16), 380, 383.

[6] 'As far as I remember, the joint *repertoire* of our firm included Classics, Mathematics, and all those multifarious and snippety mysteries which comprise the General Examination for the Ordinary B.A. Degree. The division of labour was that I took all the Classics, and Bushey the Mathematics. (After an acrimonious discussion, we agreed to regard Paley and History as Classics, and Logic and English Literature as Mathematics.)': *Eagle* xxxvii. 381.

[7] Letter to Glover, 2 Nov. 1906. Cf. J. A. Mangan, '"Oars and the man": pleasure and purpose in Victorian and Edwardian Cambridge', *British Journal of Sports History* i (1984), 253–66 (for Jesus College examples).

[8] 'The First Boat suffered much through disease and examinations', it was complained in 1909, while three years earlier 'the fact that five members of the crew were taking Triposes was not conducive to the best results. Moreover, last but by no means least, "Bushie" was taken ill and was unable to coach': R. H. Foster, W. Harris *et al.*, *The History of the Lady Margaret Boat Club, 1825–1926* (Cambridge, 1936), 220, 207.

[9] Motion at General College Meeting, 1 Feb. 1892; CM, 378/13 (2 Jun. 1893).

29 Booted and spurred. Mr Bushe-Fox in his element, May 1907: SJCL, Port. XXIV.10

recommendations which, the Governing Body was assured, were 'on the whole shared by the Committee' – that is, by both its members.[10]

The problem was the accretion of almost four centuries of College history. For example, 'at present the President appoints bedmakers and the Senior Bursar pays them; the Junior Bursar appoints gate-porters, clerks, and gardeners; the Senior Bursar appoints coal-porters; and the Steward appoints kitchen staff.'[11] This was unsatisfactory. 'Probably the best system in principle would be one under which the whole College staff was directly controlled by one official' – or, if not one, two, with the Junior Bursar assigned the conjoint responsibilities envisaged in 1892–3. The Committee realized 'that a Junior Bursar appointed under the system described would, as a rule, have to be on the spot; that he must be a man of business-like habits, with a capacity, if not a genius, for government.' And there was, and there remained, the rub. For 'it [was] easier to find half a dozen men who are willing to spend part of their time in managing small offices than one who will devote the whole of his to controlling a large office.' Having confirmed that they were looking for a paragon, the Committee called off the search. Having envisioned the ideal (and with W. E. Heitland currently in office), it now proposed lesser measures – or 'half measures', as it generously suggested, namely a 'Tutor-Bursar, who should have no other business than the financial part of tutorial work'.

[10] 'College Office, and Liability of Tutors' (Aug. 1898) [SJCA, SBF51/Internal Reports], 2.

[11] Thus (one example amongst many), in March 1896 the Bursar's Clerk's salary increase was charged to the Coal Account: CM, 470/10.

That, the 'Tutor-Bursar' (Tutorial Bursar, as he came to be known), and the location in a single College office of both Bursars, either on the south side of First Court or above the Buttery and Kitchens, were the report's principal recommendations. But kitchens mean smells, and since nothing could have been better calculated to alienate Scott from the entire scheme, it was adept (of Tanner perhaps) to have manœuvred Larmor into endorsing the proposal to move the Senior Bursar from the sylvan delights of I New Court to a garret suffused with the odour of boiling cabbage. Quite apart from the interests of College officers who would have to spend their every day there, would it be acceptable for important College tenants to be received in the equivalent of a room above a chop-house? Nor, surprisingly, was it to prove easier to establish a College office than to finesse with the susceptibilities of College officers. So a rabbit-warren of an office was established in First Court with the Kitchen remaining unreformed and its ledgers in disarray. Not until the 1980s were the functions of Junior Bursar and Steward combined in a single officer, while to this day the Praelector remains his own man. Likewise the Bursary, which after 1898 stayed put where it had been ever since the building of New Court. The Tutorial system, though, was another matter.

Hitherto a Tutor's income had depended directly on the number of pupils he had in residence. If therefore, as the Report stated, 'a case should arise in which a Tutor was a poor man, entirely dependent on the profits of his side, it is easy to see that the interests of the College might be neglected under the influence of motives of human action which are at any rate quite normal.'[12] In other words, the Tutor's pecuniary interest in the size of his side might be expected to induce him to keep a worthless pupil in residence merely in order to pay his own tradesmen. Thus was 'the bone lazy' Donald MacAlister remembered by a future Fellow of the College[13] – though not of course by Mrs MacAlister.[14] The truth probably lay roughly equidistant from both extremes – albeit he was sufficiently well informed about his pupils to prevent one from taking his own life by removing both revolver and razors from his room, and another from contracting an injudicious alliance with a tobacconist's assistant.[15] Tobacconists' assistants were a notorious snare and hazard. The author of a contemporary *vademecum* was emphatic:

Don't take a girl from the Tobacconist's or Confectioner's home.

More than that,

---

[12] 'College Office, and Liability of Tutors', 11–13.

[13] 'Tutors were paid a fee for each pupil and he gathered an immense crowd to whom he gave little attention': W. G. Constable to Guillebaud, 2 Apr. 1969 (SJCL, Constable Papers, 1/8). Constable: matric. 1906 (the year after MacAlister's resignation of his tutorship); Slade Professor of Fine Art and Fellow, 1935–8; Honorary Fellow, 1955.

[14] 'His pupils and their parents liked him and respected him, and his "side" was always crowded.' With a side of two hundred or more, 'he seemed to know all about every man': E. F. B. MacAlister, *Sir Donald MacAlister of Tarbert, by his wife* (London, 1935), 129–30.

[15] Ibid., 137–8.

Don't by any chance speak to girls without introduction. However innocent may be the motive, such practices are the worst distraction a student
can foster. We know that it is only natural that a man should require
ladies' society, and that if he cannot meet ladies of his own station in life,
he is driven into less desirable circles. We are also of opinion that the
Dons, by arranging attractive 'At Homes' and 'Social Gatherings,' could
do a good deal to lessen a great evil; but notwithstanding we strongly
advise you – Don't make chance acquaintances.[16]

But eighty years before co-residence the virtuous alternative, 'social gatherings'
with the Tutor, could set snares and hazards too. According to his own wife,
the dry Sunday lunches and suppers to which they were summoned six at a
time were regarded by MacAlister's pupils as 'a boring duty, a necessary evil
to be endured as patiently as might be, and to be got through as quickly as
possible.'[17]

Purgatorial repasts such as these would hardly have satisfied the youthful Gorst and the other young bloods whose excesses had filled the pages of
the Deans' Books in the 1870s. But (to return to the Larmor-Tanner report),
although they remained responsible for their pupils' bills and debts, 'the days of
wealthy Tutors with large sides and ample working capital' were past. Moreover,
Tutors were not competent to keep accounts and make out bills. That was clerks'
work, and what was now required was for such operations to be centralized
in a College office, for the Tutor's financial liability to be transferred to 'the
College in general', and for the size of sides to be equalized and fixed stipends
established, with Tutors paid 'by stipend instead of profits'. If this new dispensation could be adopted unilaterally, the choice would be between three Tutors
each with about eighty pupils or two with about 125, with in either case more
responsibility for advising men on their work falling on Directors and Lecturers within the various subjects. Such was the ideal. But, of course, no such new
beginning *ex abrupto* was possible. As usual, existing interests had to be allowed
for. Willing to wound and yet afraid to strike, the Committee was therefore 'not
prepared to make any recommendations which would have the effect if adopted
of at once establishing a new system.'[18]

Of J. E. Sandys, who had been appointed Tutor in 1870 at the age of twenty-
five, his obituarist reported that 'to the ordinary man he was cold, impassive,
ineffective and unintelligible, not quite human. As a matter of fact he was by
nature intensely generous, affectionate and warm-hearted.'[19] Unfortunately
though, most undergraduates *were* ordinary men. On Sandys's resignation of
his Tutorship in 1900, Larmor, assisted by the geneticist William Bateson (son

---

[16] *The Fresher's Don't, by A Sympathiser (B.A.)* [Arthur John Story, BA 1896], 7th edn,
Redin & Co., Trinity Street, Cambridge, 10 (copy amongst Constable's papers).

[17] 'We never offered our students wine: Donald did not want it to be possible for any
young man to say that he had tasted wine first at our house.' Instead, at the table of
the future President of the General Medical Council, 'cigarettes (not so universal
then as now) were always passed round after luncheon': MacAlister, *Sir Donald
MacAlister*, 133.

[18] 'College Office, and Liability of Tutors', 23, 25–6.

[19] N. G. L. Hammond, *Sir John Edwin Sandys* (Cambridge, 1933), 23.

of W. H. Bateson, Master), attempted to reduce the number of tutorial sides from six to two, and failed. Instead, on Sandys's motion, Tanner was appointed as Tutorial Bursar, and E. E. ('Billy') Sikes succeeded to the Tutorship after Tanner had declined it.[20] However, when MacAlister resigned his Tutorship at Michaelmas 1905, Bateson and Larmor were more successful in securing the succession of Bushe-Fox while MacAlister continued in the Directorship of Medical Studies to which he had been appointed in 1901 on demitting his college lectureship. This he had done on the grounds that it was beyond any individual to provide all medical students of the College with instruction in that subject: an important concession which acknowledged changes in the teaching aspirations of Cambridge colleges in these years.[21] Recognition of the need for development in the direction of a more coherent system of College-based teaching across all subjects was high on the agenda of Larmor, the modernizing advocate who remained its active and vocal promoter. A great galvanizer, on the Council Larmor was for ever watchful, advancing as much of his scheme as was possible. But as always it was not so much the recommendations of committees and the decrees of the Council that counted as the Fellows' response to them and the effectiveness of the Master at the helm. In the cause of effectiveness in 1908 the 'Larmor gang' would attempt to get Larmor into the Lodge.

I.   SIGNS OF THE TIMES

Was ever known
The witless shepherd who persists to drive
A flock that thirsts not to a pool disliked?[22]

As the old century ended, its contradictions rested on new foundations. In March 1896 the new Chapel, which had been built in order to accommodate greater numbers, was finally paid for.[23] Three years later the Senior and Junior Deans ceased to maintain their register of chapel attendance. As that record reveals, within the hallowed space, and especially within Iniquity Corner (the corner invisible to the authorities) there had long been mutiny, murmurings, the cracking of nuts audible, not to mention the reading of Milton and worse, and men having to be carried out dead drunk. Such memories became the anecdotes

---

[20] Ibid., 75; CMM, 528/2, 533/4 (Jan.–Mar. 1898), 542/7, 593/6, 600/14. After a tangled series of negotiations Tanner was also appointed as Assistant Tutor and coadjutor to C. E. Graves: CM, 594/3. In 1882–3 there had been six tutors (with Hill, Sandys, Heitland and Ward functioning in 1885–6, and Mason and Smith not). For Larmor (1857–1942), see *ODNB* (I. Falconer).

[21] CMM, 706/10, 718/7; Miller, *Portrait of a College*, 103–5.

[22] Wordsworth, *The Prelude*, III. 411–13.

[23] Howard, *Finances*, 211.

of later generations.[24] Moreover, the record kept by the Deans' chapel-markers was widely regarded as unreliable, not least by the Deans themselves. Nor was a casual disregard for the duty of attendance or for standards of seemly behaviour thought to constitute an impediment to the prospect of ecclesiastical preferment. On being admonished for talking, the son of the Venerable Isaac Wood, archdeacon of Chester, protested that 'there is no harm in it as he cannot regard it as a Church, the attendance in the one case being compulsory & in the other voluntary.'[25] Such attitudes were widespread. A sermon preached in 1868 to the serried ranks of future archdeacons put it bluntly: 'Do you think that you can entirely transform yourselves, and change your characters, at one special period of your life, the time of ordination', J. B. Pearson, Fellow, enquired of an audience in whom 'self-indulgence – sometimes in its lowest form – is the one object kept in view, who care nothing for their neighbours save as instruments for their own gratification?' 'Depend upon it', he reminded them, 'that you will be then very much what you are making yourselves now.'[26]

In these circumstances, the passage of the University Tests Act in 1871, just two years after the completion of the new edifice, proved fatal, with Nonconformists of every colour flourishing, and Swedenborgians, Huntingdonians, Irvingites, RCs and Jews lumped together with those whose credal affiliations could be described as 'Hindoo', 'Oriental', 'Japanese' and non-denominational.[27] Ructions amongst the Senior set the tone. It was hardly to be wondered at that J. S. Allen (later New Zealand's High Commissioner in London) should have celebrated liberation by 'romping in the court & throwing his surplice on a lamp-post' when, in protest against the 1871 legislation, the President himself (J. S. Wood) was boycotting the place, 'as if he considered it profaned by this action of Parliament'.[28] On his first Sunday in residence

---

[24] 'In Combination Room Dean of Worcester (W. Moore Ede) genial old man. His tale of old chapel and voice from Iniquity Corner in pause of service "What's trumps?"': GD, 5 Feb. 1927. Cf. the report of the behaviour of audiences at the lectures of celebrated divines in the 1870s: 'not edifying (...) the frivolous read novels, the utterly profane played surreptitious games of cards, the rest slept' (F. J. Foakes Jackson in 1931, cit. Mangan, 'Oars and the man', 248. (Not that Foakes Jackson himself was not above reading 'his letters and the litany simultaneously': ODNB [P. Gardner-Smith and H. Chadwick]).

[25] T. C. Wood in 1854–5: SJCA, DS 3.4. By CM, 527/8 (Jan. 1898) the Junior Bursar was authorized to dismiss J. W. Metcalfe, marker ('so many Markers being no longer wanted', a gloss to the minute in Scott's hand).

[26] 'The Church's Need of Excellence. A Sermon preached in the Chapel of St John's College, Cambridge, on Sunday evening, Mar. 22, 1868' (Cambridge, 1868), 12–13. Cf. W. E. Heitland, *After Many Years: A Tale of Experiences and Impressions Gathered in the Course of an Obscure Life* (Cambridge, 1926), 177–8.

[27] E.g. W. J. Sollas ('Christian but could not call himself of any denomination'): SJCA, DS 3.6. (1871): later Fellow, FRS, Professor of Geology and Palaeontology at Oxford (Venn, *Alumni Cantabrigienses*, II.v. 589).

[28] SJCA, DS 3.6 (1875); Venn, *Alumni Cantabrigienses*, II.i. 36; above, pp. 335–6; T. G. Bonney, *Memories of a Long Life* (Cambridge, 1921), 41. Wood rehearsed his objections to the 1871 Statutes in his published Letter to the Visitor. J. E. B. Mayor's obituary of him (*Eagle* xvii [1892–3]) discusses the matter at his customary length, adding, irrelevantly, that Wood had discharged the office of proctor 'with conscientious care, being able to restore several penitent daughters to their homes' (p. 654).

the undergraduate T. R. Glover, a devout Baptist, attended his own service in the morning and recorded his surpliced attendance at College evensong as a 'masquerade'.[29]

In 1902 measures were taken to amend the statute requiring both Deans to be in Holy Orders, in order 'to allow the College greater liberty in the choice of Deans'.[30] In 1912 J. H. Clapham of King's wrote to Tanner as follows:

> Dear Tanner,
>
> Can you give me a bit of tutorial information? We are having a little mild trouble here in the enforcement of the rule about getting up in the morning. Years ago – forty years – we allowed men to sign a book instead of going to six o'clock chapel. This is now regarded as a hardship in some quarters. I want to find out what other Colleges do. I imagine that you have chapel rules. What do you require of men in the morning?
>
> From what I can gather our rule which in its day was a liberal one is now more paternal than the rules of most places

(which of course in King's would never do).

So secular, liberal King's was reduced to turning for advice to stick-in-the-mud St John's on the age-old question of how to get men up in the morning, and the St John's answer was neither fear of God nor dread of the Dean but rather the difficulties involved in slipping in late beneath the lecturer's notice. 'Chapels but not nec[essary] in morning. And cases get found out by lecturing attendances', Tanner's summary of his reply reads.[31] (Not that they did.) 'Things have altered a great deal since our undergraduate days', the Master informed a potential benefactor anxious to establish a prize for which attendance at chapel would be an alternative qualification to prowess on the river or the cricket field. 'The matter is now more of moral persuasion than disciplinary rule. Men are told that it is hoped and expected that they will attend but the matter is almost voluntary.'[32] 'Would you mind reconsidering this point and putting Football at the end of the list?', Scott asked. This was in 1916. Things may have altered but even so, the Old Guard were against having a dissenter, Benians, as Dean, even as a makeshift war-time measure.[33] In the following year, thirty years after coming up, Glover seconded the motion abolishing compulsion: 'Council (...), without discussion, abolished compulsory chapel – 115 years after Wordsworth

---

[29] GD, 30 Sept. 1888. For Glover (1869–1943), see H. G. Wood, *Terrot Reaveley Glover* (Cambridge, 1953); *ODNB* (I. Falconer).

[30] CM, 653/3(i).

[31] SJCA, TU12.14.16 (23 Jan. 1912). Cf. the letter of a pupil to his old tutor twenty years on from the University of Edinburgh and comparing it to Cambridge, almost entirely to the latter's disadvantage. 'They are up on Cambridge in one respect however; instead of the "signing on" method for lectures, whereby any number of names can be written down by one person, the lecturer after the lecture collects cards from each member of the class!': D. W. P. Bythell to Wordie, 19 Nov. 1932 (SJCA, tut. file/ Bythell, D. W. P.).

[32] Letter to Rev. R. I. Woodhouse, 22 Feb. 1916: SJCA, M.2.1, pp. 198–9. Mark the '*almost* voluntary'.

[33] GD, 12 Jun. 1918: 'Tanner and now Sikes against Ben as Dean, on chapel issue; can't have dissenter, who doesn't go but responsible for services.'

advocated it. So we speed on.'[34] For some years a register of Sunday attendance continued to be kept, though if Cecil Beaton (possibly not the most reliable of witnesses on such matters) is to be believed, the task can hardly have been arduous.[35]

Although the Fellowship in the first decade of the century may seem to us a more divided body than in more recent times, we must allow for the possibility that the historian's access to the diaries that some of its members kept and to the letters many of them exchanged may have the effect of magnifying such divisions. We are unusually well informed about these years and the tittle-tattle exchanged because, as well as maintaining one of the most detailed of such diaries (uninterrupted between his Bristol schooldays in 1883 and his death sixty years later), T. R. Glover was kept up to date with college news while teaching in Canada between 1896 and 1901 and evidently preserved every communication he received. Even so, of those years no less than the present, we must beware of accepting at face value the evaluation of the friends and contemporaries of academic colleagues (as to 'negative acidulated criticism' as their collective characteristic, for example)[36] – or for that matter the accounts of them in the diaries that their pupils kept too.

That said, the captious Senior Fellow who wanted to know what was going now to happen to the Chapel was very much a figure of the age in which for some at least the coincident conclusion of the century and of a seemingly endless reign served to concentrate the mind. The College about which the literary J. R. Tanner wrote to Glover in the year of the Old Queen's diamond jubilee sounded like a society *in extremis*. 'Things are getting worse, and the college staff is being swamped by incompetence & decrepitude. The courts are populous with squalid hags who squeak and gibber in corners, only scattering to carry away their spoil under cloaks of darkness.'[37] A similar story was related by Heitland, Glover's old Tutor and the College's ancient historian and Junior Bursar, who at the start of the academic year 1898–9 prophesied that it would be a 'trying & anxious' one. 'Many things loom on the sky', he reported. 'What

---

[34] GD, 7 Mar. 1919; CM, 1048/8: 'On the motion of Dr Shore [Junior Bursar], Mr Glover seconding, it was agreed by 10 votes, 3 not voting, that the attendance at College chapel of members of the College *in statu pupillari* be no longer compulsory.' In 1951 Benians recalled the voting on the issue differently and in more dramatic terms, describing one dissenting Senior Fellow asking what the other Fellows now intended to do with the chapel: 'Cambridge in the last half century', *Eagle* lv (1952–3), 13. (This sounds like Heitland.)

[35] Boys Smith, *Memories*, 29–30; 'extraordinarily few people there': CBD, 21 Jan. 1923 (on the previous October 29 he had noted the preacher's 'terrible face and voice'). For Beaton, see below, pp. 476–9. According to Ken North, a chorister at the time, later Kitchen clerk, and an accurate man: 'In my days in the Choir attendance at Chapel was compulsory on a set number of nights each term': SJCA, Arch.2.8.1.

[36] Thus the zoologist E. W. MacBride (Fellow, 1893–9; FRS, 1905) to Glover, 2 Jan. 1906: 'I take your view about our dons. I fear I should not like to be back as a Johnian Don. (...) The contrast between them and the broad-minded go-ahead dons of Trinity is painful to a Johnian.' On grounds of assiduity (though not of acidulousness), MacBride was inclined to make an exception of William Bateson.

[37] Tanner to Glover, 19 Feb. 1897; cit. (adapted) T. R. Glover, *Cambridge Retrospect* (Cambridge, 1943), 116.

with quack remedies for College failure, jobs in prospect, general weakness and apathy &c &c, life in SJC is certain not to be a happy one.' As always, the unforgiving Heitland, to whom the Council had recently agreed to allow a male bedmaker, drew on his 'freakish and often mordant humour' to blame his colleagues. 'As a member of the Church of England I am not required to believe the creeds myself', he was later heard to observe. 'But I am entitled to have clergy who do.'[38] Above all, he did not care 'to live among that gang of nondescripts who form the Johnian undergraduates of this latter day.'[39] For a man so firmly persuaded that 'to enter into details on paper is not necessary and not wise', he was none the less unusually ready to particularize, celebrating as 'our corner stone', H. T. E. Barlow (whose own obituarist would describe as 'reserved and difficult to know', cynical, morbid and despondent,[40] making him sound suspiciously like Heitland himself), and declaring his classical colleague C. E. Graves 'one of the weakest failures about the place'. 'By this time next year', he concluded delphically, 'great changes will have happened, and I may have queer things to report before then.'[41]

Some idea of both Heitland's astringency and the frailty to which Tanner was referring of College government under Charles Taylor is provided by a report in the Council's minutes of October 1896 on the subject of the Lecture Room grates:

> Mr Heitland drew attention to the grates in Lecture Rooms I and IV. It was suggested that the matter be left in the hands of the Junior Bursar.
>
> Mr Heitland moved that the matter be put in the hands of a Committee. This was carried.
>
> After considering the question as to who should form the Committee the resolution was rescinded and it was agreed to leave the matter in the hands of the Junior Bursar.[42]

As stated, the Junior Bursar in question *was* Heitland, a circumstance on more

---

[38] GD, 26 Jun. 1918.

[39] CM, 501/2 (12 Mar. 1897). Cf. W. F. Reddaway's recollection of the remark of an Emmanuel friend with whom he was passing through St John's, to the effect that 'in no other [College] should we see an undergraduate sitting on a railing picking his teeth with a penknife': *Cambridge in 1891* (Cambridge, 1943), 4.

[40] BA 1885. College Lecturer in Ecclesiastical History 1896–1900, Junior Dean 1894, Proctor 1896–7, rector of Marwood, Devon 1900–2, of Lawford, Essex, 1902–6, died 1906: *Eagle* xxviii (1906–7), 86. Glover retained happier memories of him but could not regard him as distinguished: ibid., 87.

[41] Heitland to Glover, 21 Sept. 1898. Cf. Heitland's obituary of Graves in *Eagle* xlii (1921–2), 58–60: a very different story ('It was in the personal contact with pupils that his qualities shewed themselves at their very best'). For Heitland (1847–1935), see his memoir, *After Many Years* (which disappointed by its uncharacteristic discretion: Boys-Smith, *Memories*, 56–7); *ODNB* (P. Searby). As to the 'gang of nondescripts', Heitland was perhaps influenced by the class lists of the recent Classical tripos, in which St John's had indeed fared notably badly in comparison with Trinity: *CUR* (1897–8), 1028–9.

[42] CM, 484/9 (23 Oct. 1896). 'Taylor a very bad chairman': GD, 24 Oct. 1902; 'perhaps unique among inefficient chairmen', GD, 6 Dec. 1907.

30 P. H. Mason, President 1882–1902. 'Peter ought to resign,' Scott sighed. 'In a well managed college he would be made to do so...': SJCL, Album 10/44b

than one occasion regretted by his senior colleague.[43] An inveterate fusspot who when not trying could be mischievous and who 'pursued "scamped work" like an Inquisitor', Heitland may also have been in possession of an ability to impart to the Council minutes something of the collective weariness and despair that his remorseless raising of trivial issues induced among Council members.[44]

The denizens of the Combination Room over which the acerbic classic cast his jaundiced eye comprised the old guard and the not so old, the men with whom Glover had began to have dealings on his election to the Fellowship in 1892 and those he met on his return to it nine years later. At the head of the first division stood the notably eccentric Peter Mason, lecturer in Hebrew, who in the capacity of Senior Dean had had to deal with the insolent Langley.[45] Singular in appearance for his sharp features, black skull-cap and silvery hair, inventor of a design of roller-skate whose principal defect was a tendency to break the

[43] 'He would do much better at that sort of work than defacing the College building and grounds', Scott to Glover, 29 Dec. 1898, apropos Heitland's decision not be a candidate for the new chair of Ancient History.

[44] E.g. CM, 542/8: 'Mr Heitland mentioned several difficulties which had arisen with regard to the windows [inserted in Scott's hand: *one of the* windows] in the Chapel Tower. It was agreed to leave the matter in the Junior Bursar's hands to do the best he could' (3 Jun. 1898). See 'Heitland as J. B.', *Eagle* li (1939), 136; Crook, *Penrose to Cripps*, 17–19.

[45] Above, p. 305.

ankles of its user, and President of the College since 1882, the allegedly courteous Mason was the officer in charge of the 'squalid hags'.[46] But because he was a professional invalid, in 1900 he did not come into College for months on end. Instead, the College went to him: in March the Council met at his house in town.[47] When he did preside at table his 'trick of spitting his food into an envelope which he keeps on the table beside him' was not to everyone's taste.[48] 'Peter ought to resign', Scott sighed. 'In a well managed college he would be made to do so, *sed aliter* in St John's.'[49] But how, the long-serving Bursar perhaps reflected, could a college be managed at all which bore the additional burden of a Master such as Charles ('Jumbo') Taylor, a man combining inability to conduct a meeting or deliver a speech to old members with virtual invisibility to those in residence?[50] In Scott's view, the muddle Taylor made over Glover's re-election to the Fellowship 'would disgrace a parish council'. Five years later the same thing was repeated. To A. C. Benson he appeared 'a glorious spectacle (...) immensely fat, very pink in the face, with a large sensual mouth full of jagged teeth.'[51] As to Mason, although successively stripped of his responsibility for the hags, the College laundresses, the college Register and the choosing of College guests for the Port Latin feast, in May 1902 he was nevertheless again re-elected President. And when five months later he did resign, at the age of seventy-five and reportedly with bad grace,[52] he was replaced by a man two years his *senior*.

Mason's successor in the office was the Esperanto *aficionado*, Old Catholic sympathizer and high-ranking (but unwittingly beefed up) vegetarian, J. E. B. ('Johnny') Mayor, Kennedy Professor of Latin since 1872 (and continued in the chair because the University could not afford a successor likely to be more

[46] *Eagle* xxxiv (1912–13), 230, 248; Glover, *Cambridge Retrospect*, 81–3. Reddaway recalled that 'the effect of his old-world courtesy upon undergraduates was to prompt them to cap him from both sides at once, so as to enjoy his neck-breaking efforts to return both salutes at once': *Cambridge in 1891*, 3. In 1882 he had been a candidate for the Chair of Hebrew. A summary of that process ('copied [into R. F. Scott's letter book] from a sheet of paper in the handwriting of Dr Charles Taylor (...) found by me among some scattered papers in the [Master's] Lodge') shows that after three ballots Mason and Kirkpatrick lay equal, resulting in no election: SJCA, SB1.23.325.

[47] CM, 595. 'Such a strange object', A. C. Benson of Magdalene found him on dining at St John's: 'propped up in a chair with a skull cap': Benson Diary, 134, fo. 30 (2 Dec. 1912).

[48] GD, 8 Apr. 1902.

[49] Adding gloomily, 'still he may live a long time yet': Scott to Glover, 20 Mar. 1900. Tanner had previously written that 'Mason has been seriously ill, but is now much better and has resumed control of the bed-makers, so reform in that department is likely to be delayed': Tanner to Glover, 19 Feb. 1897.

[50] For Taylor's hermit's existence, see Wilson Harris, *Life So Far* (London, 1954), 49: 'Once a year he gave a perpendicular (so-called because there was nowhere to sit down)'; R. Paranjpye, 'Sixty Years Ago', *Eagle* lviii (1958), 4. The Sandys also held 'perpendiculars': Glover, *Cambridge Retrospect*, 47. In Glover's undergraduate diaries of 1888 to 1892 Taylor is all but invisible.

[51] GD, 12 Oct. 1901; 15 & 24 Nov. 1906: Benson Diary, 69, fo. 61 (May 1905); 75, fos. 67–8: 'fascinated by sight of this strange, dark, vain, pompous ogreish man' (Nov. 1905).

[52] CMM, 570/9, 572/3, 594/11, 650/1; GD, 22 Oct. 1902 ('Peter Mason has sent a reluctant and rather unpleasant resignation to the College Council'). 'I should still have liked to have a finger in the pie', he remarked: *Eagle* xxxiv (1912–13), 247–8.

expensive), celebrated for the special sort of marmalade he made but failed to market, a man whose thought-processes were sufficiently ramified to make Mason's meanderings appear almost systematic.[53] In 1951 E. A. Benians would remember the meeting of Fellows summoned in 1907 to decide on a wedding present for Taylor. 'Mayor presided and an hour passed, pleasantly for me, but somewhat restively for busier people, while he sketched the history of household furnishing from Roman times.' Nor was that the end of it.[54] As the Master of Trinity described him after his death, Mayor was a 'good old man', 'loved and revered' and 'the ideal Scholar and Student of an earlier age'.[55] So it may have seemed from over the wall. To too many colleagues in his own College, however, Mayor, although a man of many parts, seemed neither to belong to his own age nor even to be securely anchored in the sublunary world. Despite his heroic achievements as annalist of the College and his work as University Librarian in the face of a restrictive syndicate, his 'want of a sense of proportion (and humour) could hardly be exaggerated'.[56] 'The list of his work', Glover wrote on his death, [was] 'endless, and yet Rumour [spoke] vaguely of books left in the press, dropped for the moment for some fresher interest, and not taken up again.'[57] According to Heitland, Mayor was off the Council in 1898 'because no man wanted him on and many wanted him off' – though 'of course', as he was willing to concede, 'the evil is not in Mayor'. While 'of no use', he was to be regarded rather as a symptom of the deeper malaise than its cause. 'The actively mischievous people sit on', Heitland noted.

The 'actively mischievous' that Heitland had in mind must have been the surviving Seniors for whom the new (1882) statutes had prescribed a process of withering away though without insisting upon it. By Statute VII (Government of the College), the control exercised by the eight of them over a Council comprising the Master and twelve Fellows might have disappeared within four years. But out of a body of forty-four in 1900 there were still seven of them extant, and although over the previous eighteen years the Council's average

[53] For the marmalade and Keiller's threat of legal action for selling it in their jars: J. Henderson, *Juvenal's Mayor: The Professor who Lived on 2d. a Day*, Proceedings of the Cambridge Philological Society, Suppl. vol. no. 20 (Cambridge, 1998), 65 n. 13; above, pp. 319–20.

[54] Benians, 'Cambridge in the last half century', 13–14. For more on this occasion see C. W. Guillebaud, 'Some personal reminiscences of Alfred Marshall', *Eagle* lxiv (1971), 97–8; also J. Henderson, *Mayor's Juvenal* (Bristol, 2007), vii–xxiii.

[55] *Eagle* xxxii (1910–11), 73–4.

[56] D. McKitterick, *Cambridge University Library: A History: The Eighteenth and Nineteenth Centuries* (Cambridge, 1986), 537–40, 650–6; M. R. James, *Eton and King's* (London, 1926), 182.

[57] Unsigned article in *The Athenæum*, 10 Dec. 1910. The Dean, H. F. Stewart, evidently suffused with the Christmas spirit, remarked that 'Glover confesses to the article (...) and is pleased to be congratulated on it', continuing: 'I really think it is very good and gets closer to the dear old man than I thought G. could ever be', Stewart to Tanner, 24 Dec. 1910: SJCA, TU12.12.225. Cf. Glover on Mayor in *Cambridge Retrospect*, 85–7. To Glover, who found him insupportable ('a little man, and like a schoolmaster'), it came as a 'great relief' when in 1918 Stewart returned to Trinity, whence Tanner had spirited him in 1907: Stewart to Tanner, SJCA, TU12.9.52; GD, 12 Feb. 1917; 7 Jun. 1918.

age had dropped, the less antique members of that body continued to plump for very senior figures as President. Statute IX stated that the President should be elected annually from among its members, but did not state who the electors were. The Council's view was that it was themselves, and accordingly, on Mason's resignation, 'they appointed John Mayor President'.[58] Mayor, the man whom four years earlier no one had wanted on the Council, was in his seventy-eighth year. Together with G. D. Liveing and, to Glover's exasperation, Mason, he had been re-elected to the Council earlier that year.[59] And when Mayor died in 1910 the Council which Glover and the young men had voted in opted for Liveing.[60] 'This means change', Glover had predicted on hearing of Mayor's death.[61] But the replacement of an eighty-four-year-old by a colleague approaching eighty-three was rather a case of institutionalized gerontocracy – a tendency encouraged by the practice of cumulative voting (the divisive procedure whereby a Fellow might cast all his votes for a single candidate) and the polarization to which it might lead.[62] 'We may not assume, of course, that such men were obstructive of all change', Edward Miller has assured us. Nor in Liveing's case was there any diminution of power – as the legibility, lucidity and content of a letter written just after his eighty-sixth birthday amply testify.[63] Still, despite the *quid pro quo* provided in 1911 by the addition of A. C. Seward to the Council it must have afforded Heitland rueful satisfaction that the College's Presidents elected in the first quarter of the century were all successively older than their predecessors.[64]

Heitland was an inveterate schemer and connoisseur of faction. His September 1898 jeremiad to Glover was not his first pronouncement on the subject. Thirty years later he would 'claim credit to have been the proposer of the first move towards engaging Tanner in the service of the College' and

[58] GD., 24 Oct. 1902. Earlier that year Taylor had wondered whether Mayor should replace Mason if both were elected to the Council and had asked Tanner to take soundings. 'I do not think the change on the whole desirable unless the wish for it is general', Taylor to Tanner, 20 May 1902: SJCA, TU12.4.49. In Sikes's judgement he was the only possible alternative: letter to Tanner, 5 Jun. 1902: SJCA, TU12.5.145.

[59] 'We lost. (...) Liveing 18, Mayor 15, Mason and Dyson 14. So the silly old man got in on his seniority and the plumping of the three next stupidest men in College': GD, 31 May 1902. It was in different terms that Glover wrote to Mayor's younger brother, Joseph, after the old man's death: 'No one else held in his unique way the regard and affection of everybody': Trinity College Cambridge, B16/220 (27 Apr. 1911).

[60] For Liveing (1827–1924): *ODNB* (W. C. D. Dampier and F. A. J. L. James).

[61] GD, 1 Dec. 1910. 'But we still have three octogenarian fellows', Glover added. That was not the problem though. The problem was the octogenarian mind-set of the younger men.

[62] On cumulative voting, a practice permitted by Statute VIII but abandoned in the course of discussions leading to the adoption of distributive voting in the 1926 statutes (IX.4): 'a bad mistake' according to Glover (GD, 13 May 1924); above, p. 372.

[63] Miller, *Portrait of a College*, 111; SJCA, TU12.16.101: 'having fallen and hit my head a tremendous thwack on the edge of the foot walk. I got up without help and walked home. (...) It does not prevent my following all my usual occupations' (letter to Tanner, 23 Dec. 1913).

[64] GD, 24 Jan. 1911, 10 Feb. 1911 (Liveing elected by Council on motion of Larmor). For Seward (1863–1941), Professor of Botany, 1905, Master of Downing, 1915: *ODNB* (H. H. Thomas and A. McConnell).

praise him for his role in reforming the tutorial body.[65] Nearer the time he saw things differently. 'As to College, yes, we have made great progress in *power*, but the real bother is to find men to carry on the work of the place – younger men, that is. For Tanner is not [a] big enough man to be our only hope, and there are no means of giving new men permanent positions at present. It will need patient staunchness to get through the next 4 or 5 years.' Heitland was hoping to draw Graves into his camp and 'to act with [him] in some matters' (evidently Graves had not yet been found to be beyond redemption) since 'he seems by no means anxious to be led by the Larmor gang.'[66] Snipings such as these impart something of the flavour of *fin de siècle* St John's.

As the new century began, Barlow, Heitland's 'corner stone', left Cambridge in order to prop up the faithful of Devonshire, Graves soldiered on,[67] Heitland himself resigned the Junior Bursarship, married and moved out of college, and Glover returned from Canada to a College lectureship.[68] Thereafter the attitude of Glover's reporting changes, from that of the outsider looking in to that of the insider looking under stones.

'Jumbo's is a good life actuarially considered', Tanner confided to Glover in the summer of 1906, referring to their sixty-seven-year-old bachelor Master.[69] The Old Order might continue for ever. At that juncture, no actuary would have allowed for Taylor's marriage in the following year to a lady less than half his age.[70] To the future Master of Magdalene the news served only to confirm his opinion of the melancholy decline of St John's. 'They seem to have no guiding spirit', he observed. 'The old, corpulent, apoplectic Master is going to be married! Rather horrible.'[71] Since Taylor, an alpine climber until late in life, was so notably stout that his colleagues, it was reported, declined to be roped to him 'for fear he should drag them down a crevasse', amongst others greater interest attached to the motives of the lady in the case. 'Mrs Taylor is reported to have explained she married Master as she wished for a larger sphere', Glover was informed by A. A. Bevan of Trinity: 'ambitions, he said, rarely so literally fulfilled.'[72] In the following spring there was gossip of a baby expected at the Lodge, by which when her husband mentioned it to her Alice Glover was

[65] 'The new Tutorial system was largely the result of his wise and genial direction – and what an improvement it is on the old!': *Eagle* xlvi (1930–31), 185.

[66] Heitland to Glover, 9 Aug. 1895.

[67] Above, p. 410. C. E. Graves, BA (2nd Classic) 1862; Fellow, 1863; Tutor, 1895–1905; married (1865) daughter of Richard Gwatkin (1810); Fellow SJC. For an altogether more favourable estimate (authoritative because his own) of one 'whom students reckoned at St John's / Among the decent sort of Dons', see Glover, *Cambridge Retrospect*, 51–4.

[68] CMM, 614/10, 619/4.

[69] Letter dated 12 Jun. 1906 (GC).

[70] News of 'a Mrs Taylor at the Lodge' had come as 'rather a bolt from the blue': Sikes to Tanner, 21 Sept. 1907: SJCA, TU12.9.198.

[71] Benson Diary, 97, fo. 21r. (11 Oct. 1907). Benson had previously remarked on the sad eclipse of 'this great palace of learning, with its magnificence, its great church, inhabited by a dwindling & grubby throng': ibid., 78, fo. 57r. (9 Feb. 1906).

[72] F. J. Lias to Glover, 20 Dec. 1934; GD, 1 Nov. 1907.

31 Off to the palace. The Master and the Hon. Mrs Taylor in court dress, 1908: SJCA, M10.1.2

profoundly shocked,[73] and a month later a playful May Week exchange in the course of which the Master's long-protected alias was revealed.[74] Meanwhile, Scott reflected on his bursarial predecessors. 'They wore themselves out quickly in those days [he had been Bursar for twenty-four years]; but (...) I don't want my grey hairs put down to old age, but debauchery. You never know when they'll chuck you in these days of Workmen's Compensation Acts.'[75]

Three months later Taylor expired in Nuremberg, albeit of apoplexy rather than debauchery, and the latent tensions within the Fellowship surfaced. While the obituarists paid proper tribute to Taylor's scholarship, generosity and 'College patriotism',[76] the College clans and alliances within the Fellowship pre-

[73] GD, 20 May 1908.

[74] GD, 20 Jun. 1908: 'Leathem tells me tale of College ball. A man dancing with a girl spoke warmly of Mrs Taylor – "and Jumbo's not a bad old sort." Who was *he*? This learnt, the girl, who was her sister, told Mrs Taylor. The two to Master: "Oh! Charles! We've found out what your nickname is." Great amusement. Mrs Taylor asked Tanner if he had heard it. "Yes (cautiously) he had." How long? 18 years.'

[75] GD, 14 May 1908.

[76] *Eagle* xxx (1910–11), 77–81. For his scholarly role, see S. C. Reif, *A Jewish Archive from Old Cairo: The History of Cambridge University's Genizah Collection* (Richmond, 2000), 59–63; R. Loewe, 'Taylor's teachers and pupils', in S. Reif (ed.), *Charles Taylor: A Centenary Seminar and Exhibition, St John's College, Cambridge, 2 November 2008* (Cambridge, 2009), 22–9.

32 Hunger mounts. Having the First Boat to breakfast, June 1908: SJCL, Album 38/16

pared for the election of his successor. With an electorate of forty-six the contest between the Scotsman and the Ulsterman – Scott, the Senior Bursar who had increasingly taken charge of College affairs of late, and Larmor, the Lucasian Professor – was one in which every vote would count. In College legend, as related by Claude Guillebaud, it was decided by one unidentified Fellow changing sides, and provided C. P. Snow with that dramatic element of his novel, *The Masters*.[77] In some ways it foreshadowed later contests, real or imaginary, between the establishment, particularly the tutorial establishment, and the rest, between the Old Guard and the Young Turks, which would be played out again in one form or another in 1952, 1959 and 1969. In the previous year Larmor had expressed himself 'not very well pleased with the present government by tutors'.[78] Now, with an election imminent, T. H. Havelock stated the corollary: 'I don't think a Master in a large College can play the part of a Tutor.'[79]

[77] Speech at eightieth birthday dinner, 27 Dec. 1970.

[78] GD, 12 Feb. 1907.

[79] Letter to Benians, dated 26 Aug. 1906, stressing Larmor's administrative skills and knowledge of university affairs beyond Cambridge, 'not to mention his friendship with our Chancellor' (EABP). For Havelock (1877–1968), Research Fellow, 1903–9; Professor of Applied Mathematics, Durham College of Physical Science in Newcastle upon Tyne, 1915: *ODNB* (P. H. Roberts).

The circumstantial account in Glover's diary is the only one we have of the course of events between 13 August, when news of the Master's death at Nuremberg on the previous day reached Cambridge,[80] and the 31st when, in the depths of the Long Vacation, the Fellows elected his successor. Scott emerged immediately as a front-runner, with some favouring William Bateson, the former Master's son ('too masterful already' according to Glover). There may have been something of a 'Two Cultures' feel to the contest too. There was certainly quite a lot of acid lying around in puddles and no small risk of onlookers getting splashed.[81] The choice soon came down to Scott or Larmor. Glover himself agonized and eventually plumped for Larmor. By Saturday 29 August the Larmor 'gang' was confident, and after successive ballots in the Combination Room that evening, remained so, with twenty-nine Fellows present and the votes cast: first, Scott 13; Larmor 12; Bateson 4; then, Larmor 14; Scott 13; blanks 2. But on the Sunday Larmor was 'wrought into feeling'. 'C^d he work with hostile tutors etc., c^d he keep Professorship? C^d he retire & let us make it unanimous for Scott, who he saw was feeling it?'[82] And on the Monday, with thirty-seven Fellows present, in a final straw vote in the Combination Room there were 19 for Scott and 18 for Larmor.

> Then to Chapel. On way I told Larmor [of the latest vote] and his face lit up with relief, and he came to Chapel and voted for Scott. Result: Scott 21, Larmor 17. Scott was admitted and knelt in prayer. John Mayor outdid himself in muddling senility. Larmor has come through nobly, and I respect him more than before.[83]

Glover's respect for Larmor and his judgement never waned; he would consult him at every critical stage of his career and when he died describe him as 'my best friend in SJC for many years'.[84]

The outcome was hardly the eirenic one that Larmor's relieved countenance had seemed to presage. To the Tutors during the contest, to Tanner for example, even Bateson would have been preferable to Larmor. 'Scott was made Master by Larmor as Taylor was by [T. G.] Bonney', Heitland would later pronounce.[85] Larmor they saw, with some reason, as the enemy, or at any rate as someone intent on shaking them up. It was a Tutor, the quite recently appointed R. P. Gregory, whose change of vote was thought to have tipped the scales of his-

---

[80] GD, 13 Aug. 1908 ('this very startling').

[81] Regarding Heitland's tale (related GD, 23 Aug. 1908) of Bateson's young son turning over his kitten 'and saying "Oh! Female!" – paternal style', for example, Glover's account of the occasion needs to be scrupulously adhered to in the matter of punctuation.

[82] GD, 30 Aug. 1908. 'I was moved by him', Glover admitted.

[83] GD, 31 Aug. 1908.

[84] GD, 20 May 1942; 'His friendship helps me to keep sane' (30 Nov. 1918); (on being invited to serve on a government committee on Classical teaching), 'Larmor said accept, and I accepted.' (15 Nov. 1919). 'You have done more than anybody to keep me reasonably contented and happy in St John's this long time': Glover to Larmor, 21 Jun. 1932. For Larmor's bequest to him, received five days before his own death: GD, 21 May 1943.

[85] GD, 16 Aug. 1908; 27 Aug. 1926.

tory.[86] Without knowing the particulars, that was how Guillebaud told the story.[87] Tanner's pronouncement that the 'contest has done good, as we all came together and showed one another how reasonable we can be' said less about the protagonists and their relationship than about Tanner's ability to adjust reality to his own satisfaction.[88]

Three years later J. H. A. Hart confessed what he claimed to have come to regard as his error on that occasion,[89] while for the rest of his time in Cambridge Larmor, the Adullamite Ulsterman, remained spiky and resentful.

2. SCOTT IN THE LODGE

If I may offer suggestion, I would suggest that like Scott in 1908 you should wait in your rooms, and be fetched. This will let the undergraduates in, and make it a memorable moment for them to look back to, beside being a gesture toward the unity of the whole society.[90]

Scott was the College's first lay Master and the first married man elected to the office since John Newcome in 1735.[91] A lawyer by training, as Bursar he had steadied the finances and initiated a move from agricultural rents into securities.[92] Between 1896 and 1904 he had managed to increase the Fellowship dividend from £80 to £200. But in the same period, one in which in the University as a whole numbers of undergraduates were increasing, the annual entry to St John's had fallen from 104 in 1880 to 73 in 1900. To a degree, however, quantity was offset by quality as a larger proportion of the College's scholarship fund came to be used to attract able boys of limited means from schools with no historic connexion with the College to apply for open entrance awards. Between 1882 and 1912 the number of such awards increased from eleven to twenty-seven, with subjects other than classics and mathematics – natural sciences, history and modern languages, for example – increasingly represented.[93] For examination

[86] GD, 1 Sept. 1908: 'It seems that Gregory changed his vote between Saturday and Monday – momentumque fuit mutatus Gregory rerum' (adapting Lucan on the role of Curio in the Roman civil wars of the first century BC).

[87] '... it was never known with any certainty who it was who had defected from the Larmor camp. For Sir Joseph Larmor himself it was a tremendous blow, and I felt that he was an embittered man till the end of his days, with a deep personal resentment against Scott as Master, which was very evident at meetings of the Council': Guillebaud, 'Reminiscences of Alfred Marshall'.

[88] GD, 1 Sept. 1908. Cf. 15 Jun. 1910: 'Two dicta by Tanner: "The minute might be altered; it does not represent what actually happened"; "Other considerations come in, but generally the order of merit holds."'

[89] '... and don't want to make another mistake': letter to Larmor, 6 May 1911: SJCL, Larmor, Miscellaneous papers.

[90] Glover to Benians, 6 Dec. 1933 (EABP).

[91] Baker-Mayor, II. 1027.

[92] Howard, *Finances*, 237–8.

[93] Ibid., 226–40; Miller, *Portrait of a College*, 96–9.

purposes, in March 1898 St John's joined the Six (the group headed by Pembroke; the group *not* led by Trinity). These were not times for shrinking violets: in 1907 an application for an allowance for a St John's candidate who had undergone surgery on the first day of the examination was refused.[94] But as Tanner, who played a prominent part in the process, remarked during the dark days of the late 1890s, 'these things are only for a season, and we shall live down the College past if we are allowed another twenty years'.[95]

'As an administrator he took a broad view of things and was content to leave the details to others', one obituarist reported of Charles Taylor. Another observed that 'there is (...) something to be said for the old-fashioned view of the duties of a Cambridge Head when the occupant of the office is a man of learning.' From members of the College Council the verdict had been less indulgent. 'The wear and tear of these weekly meetings is beyond belief, & I shall die of them – like President Faure of the Dreyfus case', Tanner had complained to Glover in 1897.[96] Scott's manner was in total contrast. A man of business rather than scholarship, he found other people's business his bread and butter. Scott did his homework. Just as while still Bursar he had played the Master (for it was he, not the Council's chairman, who controlled the Council minutes), so as Master he played the Vice-Chancellor. When the Lord Archbishop of Melbourne wrote requesting him to intercede with the Council of the Senate in favour of an honorary MA for W. F. Tucker, archdeacon of Ballarat ('a gentleman by birth and in mind and manner' and 'most prominent as an Imperialist and a devoted lover of English life and ideals, one who years ago left the College before taking his degree and came to Australia'), and the Master of Peterhouse was minded to rubber-stamp the request, Scott it was whose enquiries established that the reason why the venerable gentleman had not taken his degree was that, after spending two years over Little Go, failing the Special Examination in Theology and managing only a fourth in the General, he had not been qualified to do so – and who therefore suggested a Lambeth degree instead.[97]

Scott's wonderful 'Notes from the College Records' were the authentic product of a facts man, a man who had thought himself a slow worker 'when Maitland used to sit on my sofa in I New Court and read the Cartulary of the old Hospital as if it was the Saturday Review', the Gradgrindian accumulator rather than creative artist: an organized John Mayor, in short, with the difference that there was a thoroughness, even a measure of ruthlessness, about him. It was only semi-jovially that the incumbent of the local parish of St Sepulchre's, the fence to the glebe of which Scott had destroyed, wrote regretting that St John's should be linked 'even for a moment, with the predatory methods

---

[94] CM, 533/3; Peter Linehan, 'Piam in memoriam: Group III 1894–1986', *Cambridge* 35 (1994–5), 70–2.

[95] Tanner to Glover, 19 Feb. 1897.

[96] *Eagle* xxx (1908–9), 78–9; Tanner to Glover, 19 Feb. 1897.

[97] Archbishop of Melbourne to Scott, 7 Dec. 1917; Scott to E. W. Lockhart, 31 Jan. 1918; A. W. Ward to Vice Chancellor [A. E. Shipley], 2 Feb. 1918: SJCA, D90.1280–84; Scott to Archbishop [H. L. Clarke, 7th Wrangler, BA 1874], 12 Feb. 1918 (SLB); *Eagle* xliv (1926), 323–5.

of border warfare to which, no doubt by hereditary instincts, their Bursar is attached.'[98] The character and variety of his correspondence is reflected in his letter book and elsewhere where letters about livings,[99] parents breaking the rules by entering their sons for Oxford as well as Cambridge awards, and potential benefactions jostle with those concerning Lord Walsingham's offer of bulbs of *Lilium giganteum* for planting on the Backs (where they would never have grown),[100] and the payment to bedmakers of amounts of deferred pay, which because they were women Scott considered they ought not to be entrusted with.[101]

That last expression of opinion points to a feature of Scott's administration of the College of which there are many other evidences, namely his desire to intervene in the affairs of its every department. 'Bedmakers have to be comic and dishonest. It is expected of them. In a picture of university life it is their only function', a contemporary novelist observed.[102] Scott would have agreed. Just a month after his election, the business of the bedders arose while the contentious issue of his successor as Bursar was still undecided, with four names under more or less desultory consideration.[103] Not until 20 November did Leathem emerge as victor, and even then Scott hung on to the Bursary records, ostensibly in order to enable the new man to break the news as a festive gesture into the following month. Even into the new year Leathem was having to ask Tanner for sight of his copy of the Council minutes: 'We have been rather held up through not being able to see them', he admitted.[104] When the Council had been established in 1883, only by the Master's casting vote had it been agreed that its *acta* should be circulated to Fellows,[105] and only very recently that they should receive a copy of the abstract of its proceedings.[106] Even so, it remains remarkable that in

[98] Scott to Tanner, 3 Jan. 1917: SJCA, TU12.19.2; S. G. Ponsonby to Scott, 26 Apr. 1894: SJCA, SB21/Cb/N/11.387 [letter book no. 2650]. In his Ford Lectures of 1897, published as *Township and Borough* (Cambridge, 1898), F. W. Maitland had made much use of the Cartulary of the Hospital.

[99] 'If it were not for decorum an article in the Eagle on the troubles of patrons would be readable. The number of decent folk who have delicate wives and only desire a move on their account is marvellous. But when all that bishops, archdeacons and the like can say on their behalf is that they have delicate wives one feels inclined to bring out some notes on "Effective Advocacy"', Scott to Tanner, 3 Jan. 1917: SJCA, TU12.19.2.

[100] For advice whereupon I am indebted to Prof. David McMullen.

[101] 'I have never thought and do not think now that it is wise to hand over, what for these women are, very large sums': Scott to W. Bateson, 3 Oct. 1908 (SLB). For the Report of the Service Committee, see above, p. 269.

[102] E. M. Forster, *The Longest Journey* (London, 1907), chap. 1.

[103] J. G. Leathem and Bushe-Fox (both Fellows); L. Horton-Smith (Fellow, 1900–4), currently at the Bar; J. Lupton (Fellow, 1896–1901), currently assistant master at St Paul's ('ideally unsuitable', according to Glover). Scott's initial preference was for Horton-Smith, whom Bateson and Co. (Larmor, Liveing, Glover) favoured to the end (because Bateson 'doesn't want a man from the North of Ireland'; i.e. Leathem): GD, 16 Oct.–20 Nov. 1908.

[104] Scott to Tanner, 2 Jan. 1909 ('I thought that the fact of the endless Christmas cheques going out in his name was a convenient way of marking the change'): SJCA, TU12.11.X; Leathem to Tanner, 13 Jan. 1909: TU12.11.21.

[105] Howard, *Finances*, 218.

[106] On a motion of T. J. Bromwich carried by 23 votes to none: GD, 20 Nov. 1908.

33 Long Vac. Cricket 1898: Dons v. Undergraduates. Standing fifth from left, T. J. Bromwich; fourth from right, H. H. Brindley; seated fourth from right, J. H. Beith; fifth from right, H. T. E. Barlow; fifth from left, J. R. Tanner; third from left, L. H. K. Bushe-Fox. 'Undergraduates won very easily': SJCL, Album 25/321

1908 the College's principal financial officer should have been expected to manage without access to his own agenda.

In addition to these self-imposed burdens was that of the Vice-Chancellorship, which Scott bore between 1910 and 1912. 'I never seem to be at the end of V.C.'s job', he complained towards the end of his first year of office. 'I believe the ideal V.C. is a canon of some distant cathedral': a strange remark but one indicating at least a degree of weariness.[107] In the previous December Glover had discovered him in rare holiday mood, 'free for the moment of cares of V.-C. with bowler instead of top hat, and this on the back of his head in the privacy of Chapel Court.'[108] 'I like Scott', Benson mused towards the end of 1912: 'he is so handsome and modest and full of humour.'[109]

But that, it is to be supposed, was not the impression he gave on any of the

[107] Letter to Tanner, 28 Aug. 1911: SJCA, TU12.13.353.
[108] GD, 15 Dec. 1910.
[109] Diary, 134, fos. 29–30.

days on which the College Council was meeting[110] – or on which the Hon. Mrs Margaret Taylor was visiting. Although the young widow of the old Master was naturally anxious to ensure that her late husband was properly commemorated in his College chapel, her successive initiatives in the matter were calculated to drive an already over-taxed Master and Vice-Chancellor to distraction. Spiky writing and an emphatic way of expressing herself enhanced the effect. Her first thought had been a pulpit, from which she was forced to withdraw as Scott sought to interest her in a window. Regarding the design of this and the selection of Johnian worthies for inclusion, it also fell to the Master to mediate between the lady on the one hand and on the other a Council on which, as he wearily explained, 'it was inevitable that by a critical body of men some remarks should be made.'[111] Her promotion of 'a group of the most distinguished of those who were members at the time of the building and opening of the Chapel' was not materially assisted by her observation that 'some members have hardly felt themselves able to carry out [the Evangelist's] precepts to the letter.' Her desire for the inclusion in stained glass of her husband's immediate predecessor raised further problems.[112] And no sooner had that exchange been brought to a more or less harmonious conclusion than, in a private and confidential letter in which the stylistic cadences of the late Queen were made to harmonize with the sentiments of Mrs Proudie, the certain lady opened up a new front concerning a 'calamitous' appointment at the College's mission church at Walworth.[113]

3.   THE EDWARDIAN COLLEGE

'The team was fairly successful, but lost nearly all matches.' The report on the 1906 Long Vac. cricket season may be thought to epitomize the College's rather limited aspirations as well as its achievements at a time when the strength of the temptation to take a desultory breakfast or other than a light lunch was summarized by the availability of such delicacies as ptarmigan, capercailzie and lark pie on the Kitchen's seventeen-page 'tariff of approximate prices for private supply'. Other than for the First VIII, the sharpened appetite for fitness in response to the recent disasters in South Africa seems to have had a somewhat limited appeal in St John's.[114] To judge by Benson's account of the future Sir

[110] 'Of all the bodies I frequent I think our Council indulges most in the irrelevant': letter to Bushe-Fox, 2 Aug. 1912: SJCA, TU13/Scott R. F./14.

[111] 'I conclude that the Pulpit idea has practically fallen through and that really a certain lady had better forget that she has any likes and dislikes', Margaret Taylor to Charlotte Tanner, 28 Jun. 1909: SJCA, TU12.11.202; Scott to Mrs Taylor, 4 Dec. 1909 (SLB).

[112] Mrs Taylor to Tanner, 12 Nov. 1909: SJCA, TU12.11.295; Scott to Tanner, 4 Jan. 1910: 'The more I think of Dr Bateson the more difficulties I see': TU12.12.5.

[113] 'A rumour has reached me (…). I trust this is *quite* without foundation': Mrs Taylor to Tanner, 3 Dec. 1912: SJCA, TU12.14.245. For the window, see W. A. C[ox], 'The new window in Chapel: Legends of St. John (II.)', *Eagle* xxxi (1909–10), 374–6.

[114] Cf. P. R. Deslandes, *Oxbridge Men: British Masculinity and the Undergraduate Experience, 1850–1920* (Bloomington, IN, 2005), 60.

John Squire, who called on him early that same year, a culture of unavailing heartiness was rather the mark of the place.[115] The lacklustre consequences of this life of grace as they extended to the examination halls as well as the playing field were indicated by Tanner when, on failing to receive any indication of the College's intention to continue his lectureship, Glover resolved to apply for a Glasgow chair. 'We should be more sorry to lose you than I can very well describe to you', he wrote. 'Live teaching is not any too common and it would be most difficult to fill your place. There are plenty of dead dogs about, but this element is already sufficiently represented on the Foundation.'[116] In the event, Glover stayed. But, as he himself reported, tripos results remained in the doldrums, with the Classics class list 'depressing' both in 1908 and 1909, those in other subjects 'disheartening', and in 1910 with a man contemplating changing to Classics from Modern Languages suggesting that 'he might go to another college where the teaching would be better'.[117] Evidently, leadership was needed. Also evidently, Sikes was not thought of as the man to provide it, being at the bottom of the poll in the Council election in 1909 and again in the following year coming in last with the added indignity this time of even trailing behind Mayor.[118] Would Tanner provide it then?

If the 1908 election contributed to the plot of *The Masters*, Joseph Robson Tanner was the prototype of solid Arthur Brown, the Senior Tutor of Snow's college. To the surprise of outsiders there was no collective desire to promote him to the highest office in St John's.[119] The man looked back to as 'the most helpful of the tutors' (by contrast with that 'cold fish' E. E. Sikes),[120] Tanner enjoyed the reputation of being for ever obliging, the man in touch with all the right sort of schools, the man to get to support your application for a headmastership, and, once you had secured it, to turn to for assistant staff. Once only was his recommendation rejected, when the High Master of Manchester Grammar School (himself Sheffield-born and Shrewsbury-educated) objected that the Londoner proposed by Tanner was lacking in smoothness, with 'just the faults to which my boys are most subject'.[121] Tanner was the 'profes-

---

[115] He 'arranges his hair so oddly, so aesthetically', Benson noted. 'He seemed to dislike the social tone of John's': Diary, 79, fo. 16. J. C. Squire ('a good minor poet and central figure in Georgianism, a brilliant parodist, and an entertaining critic') had obtained a second in History in the previous year: *ODNB* (E. Blunden and C. L. Taylor).

[116] *Eagle* xxviii (1906–7), 119; Tanner to Glover, 12 Jun. 1906; Glover to Tanner, 14 Jun. 1906: SJCA, TU12.8.216.

[117] GD, 18–19, 22 Jun. 1909; 8 Dec. 1910.

[118] GD, 5 Jun. 1909; 4 Jun. 1910.

[119] 'I have never got over the fact that at the last vacancy Tanner hadn't a chance': B. Goulding-Brown to Benians, 25 Dec. 1933 (EABP).

[120] Constable to Guillebaud, 2 Apr. 1969: SJCL, Constable papers, 1/8.

[121] 'I lay a good deal of stress on purity of accent and smoothness, if not exactly refinement, of manner. Folk here are so angular and self-made': J. L. A. Paton to Tanner, 24 Sept. 1907: SJCA, TU12.9.201. Paton (Fellow, 1887–95), 'among the great headmasters of his time', 'a blend of Dr Arnold and King Arthur' and author of *On Discipline* etc., was considered for an Honorary Fellowship in 1927 but found no support: Venn, *Alumni Cantabrigienses*, II.v. 45; J. Bentley, *Dare to be Wise: A History of the Manchester Grammar School* (London, 1990), 89–105; SJCA, SB1.23, p. 335. By 1911 the man whom Paton had rejected was a headmaster himself.

sor from Cambridge', the constitutional historian who had been engaged in 1894 to instruct the future George V on the subject of the Monarchy, an exercise which he based on Bagehot's *English Constitution*.[122] His division of the subject of the Crown's value into its 'dignified' and its 'business' (rather than Bagehot's 'efficient') aspects faithfully reflected Tanner's view of his own tutorial role.

As Lecturer in History since 1883 and Fellow since 1886, Tanner the man of business accumulated a huge mass of correspondence, almost 5,000 items of it on all manner of tutorial and para-tutorial business. With characteristic generosity, Heitland had described Tanner in 1898 as 'good μέχρι του ['up to a point'] but lack[ing] strength and rather by way of seeing great truths just too late.'[123] Heitland was not alone in that opinion. But it was not the view of the wider world. 'I cannot thank you too warmly for your kindness to both the lads', wrote one satisfied parent. 'I can only feel that you are an ideal Tutor: giving no sanguine hopes, but fostering those who have little hope in themselves.'[124] There were scores of such testimonials, and not only from the clergy and grandees. Just a week later a protective mother wrote to thank him for helping her son return to 'the manly straightforward course' after becoming ensnared in a sentimental liaison.[125] 'For the kindly interest you have given my boy', another parent, describing himself as 'a working carpenter' delayed in writing because 'breaking up at the school where I am employed presses pretty heavily upon me', had been similarly grateful. This boy (whose scholarship 'did not go far enough') had not even been Tanner's pupil.[126] With those who were, he was assiduous about keeping in touch and they with him, in splendidly unbuttoned letters. 'How is Bushey getting on as J[unior] D[ean]?', one of them, by now a master at Durham School, enquired. 'It was a great thing appointing him. Was it your idea?'[127] Would he care to take an unappetizing-sounding boy from Worksop College whose lack of star quality his Johnian headmaster could be entirely frank about with Tanner?[128] In an epistle of twelve sprawling sides,

---

[122] Harold Nicolson, *King George the Fifth: His Life and Reign* (London, 1952), 61–3.

[123] Heitland to Glover, 21 Sept. 1898. The same judgement might equally be applied to Heitland's own obituary note of the man (above, pp. 414–15).

[124] Rev. J. Bentley to Tanner, 25 Jan. 1910: SJCA, TU12.12.44.

[125] Letter of 1 Feb. 1910: 'We felt that now he was 21 years of age we were obliged to use some stern measures to bring him to reason, so as to safeguard his future career', she explained. The young man was to die at Taranto in the last month of the coming War (SJCA, TU12.12.56).

[126] E. C. Booker to Tanner, 25 Jul. 1903: SJCA, TU12.5.205.

[127] J. H. Beith to Tanner, 25 Oct. 1903: SJCA, TU12.5.273. Beith (as said, the novelist and playwright Ian Hay) continued: '*Re* Hawks: – It is not an extravagant, and not particularly expensive, club. Thirty shillings a term, some of which can be got back in the way of stamped letters, free teas etc. (...) They are pretty strict now about the athletic qualification, and the mere fact that a man possesses a dog and wears hunting breeches no longer ranks as a qualification for membership.'

[128] 'He is the son of a tradesman, a thoroughly good fellow but one who does not make up for his lack of social qualities by athletic abilities. Nor indeed by literary, though he will manage the examinations well enough, and might with advantage read History though he may only get a 3rd. I am afraid that at a small College he would be 'ragged' – and at a big College there is the fear that he would escape the social

full of local colour and sententiousness ('manhood is worthless unless a price be paid'), G. W. Williams, who had not been his pupil either and who had preferred taking up the White Man's burden to Part II of the Natural Sciences tripos, reported from South Africa how he had recently been riding back across the veld at one in the morning.

> It was inky dark so by way of encouraging(?) my horse and myself I commenced singing. I was gaily shouting the old L.M.B.C. boating song ['Vivat laeta Margareta', words by T. R. Glover] at the top of my lungs when, in the pause as my horse breasted the rise I heard the sound of another horse. I continued singing and presently out of the darkness came the challenge: 'Halt! Brother Johnian.' I reined in and found that I was held up by one of the police. 'Haven't heard that for 10 years,' he said.[129]

Tanner would not have been much surprised by this chance meeting of two Johnians in the middle of the East Rand in the middle of the night, as though in Petty Cury at two in the afternoon. To him nothing could have seemed more natural, as no doubt would the paean to the changelessness of things contained in the letter's coda:

> I suppose Cambridge will be as ever – but then the Varsities never change. (…) The Spirit of Things remains unaltered. The red Tudor courts still glow redly at sunset as the last sun lights the upper windows. The Backs are ever green, the same type of man still walks the court at midnight, relegating the world to its true position in the cosmos and advising the Almighty on things mundane and spiritual. (…) How are the rest of you (…) dear Mr Graves, best of sportsmen and kindliest of tutors? Gad! I'd give a lot, Sir, to put in a week again there. (…) To see the river again and hear the rhythmic pulse of racing oars or watch the yellow light quiver on the water beneath the Bridge of Sighs.[130]

The conjecture that the same type of man was still walking the court and advising the Almighty at midnight would probably have met with Heitland's rueful acquiescence. It was precisely the sort of thing that he had recently been bewailing. But Tanner, whose in-tray provided a clearing house for such sentiments, was more indulgent.[131] Could he recommend someone to act as tutor to a twenty-two-year old who was 'neither a lunatic nor a black man, but an ordinary mortal who rather thinks cricket is the only thing worth living for' as well as the son of a wealthy father, enquired another, specifying 'a high principled

---

advantages which are precisely what he requires': letter from F. A. Hibbert (BA 1889), 30 Jan. 1903: SJCA, TU12.5.34.

[129] 'He was up in the early 90's but as he didn't tell me his name I didn't ask it' (an altogether Johnian attitude): Williams to Tanner, 23 Sept. 1904.

[130] Ibid. Tanner replied on New Year's Day 1905.

[131] After a First in Part I (1900), Williams had kept a few days of the following Lent term and then gone to South Africa where he distinguished himself both militarily and as a mining engineer for his research on cyanide solutions: 'On active service', *Eagle* xxiii (1901–2), 343–6, xxvi (1904–5), 258.

religious man, who is a gentleman and sportsman, with a fair knowledge of history'? Of course he could.[132]

Amongst Tanner's pupils, former pupils and Johnians in general at the time there seems to have been no shortage of high principled religious men able to boast that particular array of qualifications who, like their fathers before them, felt able to approach 'Rob' Tanner with confidence and in the assurance of a prompt reply. So did others, with no particular association with the College. As a rule they received the sort of flexible response for which Mr Booker, the Dulwich carpenter, was grateful, a response at the opposite end of the spectrum of such things from the eyrie occupied by a contemporary Tutor of Christ's, whose declaration, 'I cannot reconcile myself to take a youth who has not a clean record from a public school', as well as uncannily anticipating the prissiness of Snow's Despard-Smith, suggests that Lady Margaret's two Cambridge foundations may have been moving in different directions in these years.[133] Yet with Scott continuing to guard the approaches to the College by scrutinizing applicants for indications of Oxford proclivities, it was more than ever necessary to have an emollient figure in reserve. It was in this connexion, that of the old problem of a boy playing the system by seeking to resign a Cambridge award in order to accept a better Oxford offer, that, just for once, Tanner thought it necessary to preserve a draft of his reply to the headmaster of Hampton Grammar.[134] History does not relate when relations with that school were restored.

The protest from Hampton Grammar resonated with contemporary anxiety in government circles regarding a number of questions which the Royal Commission on the Civil Service in 1912 had conceived as to 'the facilities which exist (...) to enable persons of slender means to obtain University education'. The view of the unsympathetic Sikes was that in his experience 'slender means' were 'too often accompanied by slender intellectual merit'.[135] It was fortunate therefore that it was Tanner rather than his acerbic colleague who was charged with formulating the University's collective response, and that the reflections jotted by him on the copy of the Vice-Chancellor's response that served as *aide-mémoire* for the latter's meeting with the commissioners summarized the experience of colleagues in other colleges as well as his own.[136]

[132] P. H. Bown (BA 1898) to Tanner, 10 Jul. 1905: SJCA, TU12.7.112; annotated by Tanner 'Suggested Norbury': F. C. Norbury (BA 1904), at the time a Classics master at Oundle, and another casualty of the War.

[133] J. W. Cartmell to Tanner, 14 Nov. 1906: SJCA, TU12.8.347. 'A rather grubby little man who comes from Bolton Grammar School' was how A. E. Shipley, soon to be Master of Christ's, described one of his pupils, letter to Tanner, 3 Nov. 1909: SJCA, TU12.11.283.

[134] W. A. Roberts to Tanner, 3 Apr. 1909: 'I find it almost impossible to believe that a Cambridge tutor could so far forget himself as to indulge in spite and petty feeling at the expense of a boy of 17', though he had to concede that 'strict etiquette demanded that he should have informed you [of his intention to apply to Oxford]'. In his much corrected draft reply, Tanner contented himself with repeating that a Cambridge award abandoned was an award wasted: SJCA, TU12.11.126.

[135] Undated, 'unofficial' note to Tanner: SJCA, TU12.15.16.

[136] Annotated text of Vice-Chancellor's letter to the Secretary of the Commission, 19 Nov. 1912: SJCA, TU12.15.30.

'Are poor men assimilated?', Tanner asked, and answered that 'on the whole poverty as such' was 'no bar'; that while 'many men of good antecedents and education' were 'poor in a sense', 'poor antecedents' themselves were 'no drawback'. (On the draft he had already extended the category of 'working men' to comprise not only 'small farmers, village shopkeepers and schoolmasters' but also 'policemen, commercial travellers and office clerks, and working men belonging to various trades, *e.g.* shoemaker, carpenter, blacksmith, general labourer, agricultural labourer, engine-driver, coal-miner, warehouseman, carman').[137] There was a 'freemasonry' between men of the same type of school and 'nothing that character cannot easily break through'. There was 'no class feeling': men were 'taken on their merits'. While 'athletic success' was 'a passport at once, the same [was] true of all other kinds of success.' Moreover, the 'stimulus of slight handicap' was 'not bad for character'. On the whole therefore Tanner's outlook was optimistic, though even he was prepared to admit the existence of 'a class of exhausted hermits who do not get assimilated'.

'Exhausted hermits' were not in Sikes's calculations when, for the purposes of the Asquith Commission after the War, he put together a rough list of the twenty-four 'most important schools' with total of fifty-one members in residence. Hampton Grammar School was not one of them. What might be called the 'Aldenham to Westminster list' consisted entirely of public schools. 'Among these schools', Sikes informed Tanner while the earliest post-War list was being filled, 'there are several men (average of 3 or 4 from each) from each of the following – Malvern, Rugby, Marlborough, Haileybury, Oundle, Bedford, Dulwich, Fettes, Clifton.'[138]

Indeed, of a hugely inflated 1919 intake of 227 from 163 different institutions at home and abroad,[139] those eleven schools accounted for thirty-two of that year's freshmen. A further nineteen came from the ten schools with closed awards to the College (not that the College was significantly represented on the governing bodies of those schools at this time: indeed Sikes at Aldenham was the *only* such Fellow-governor).[140] By comparison, the College's long-established relationship with the northern grammar schools where there was not that representation provided just four men from three establishments.[141]

'In spite of their being the public school boys – some of them – whom Sikes and others yearn to have about the College', Glover did not find the first-year Classics a particularly attractive group.[142] Even so, Sikes's categories do not presuppose a junior membership exclusively of the economically comfortable

---

[137] Amongst others on Tanner's euphonious list who did not make it through to the final selection were 'mould-fillers' and 'plasterers'.

[138] Letter dated 13 Feb. 1919: SJCA, TU12.21.90.

[139] Appendix 5.

[140] C3.7 ('Register of Fellows and Scholars, 1860–1965'), pp. 677–90.

[141] Two from Wheelwright Grammar, Dewsbury, and one each from Nelson School, Wigton, and RGS Lancaster.

[142] GD, 25 Jan. 1905. Sikes was 'not a bad sort *per se* – but rather a snob and apt to dictate': GD, 8 Feb. 1905. In his 1919 letter to Tanner, Sikes had not counted in most of the smaller public schools, he explained, 'although the men from these, as you know, are nearly always of a high type.'

34 Eagles Club 1899. R. F. Scott with eyes half-left; pair at end of middle row unidentified.

classes. A rather more nuanced picture emerges from the particulars prepared by Scott and sent to the commissioners. According to these the seventy-five freshmen admitted in 1912 came from sixty-two schools, and the sixty-five in 1913 from forty-eight, with thirty-six and twenty-one respectively coming from institutions other than public schools.[143] Chapter and verse are provided by both *The Fresher's Don't* and the College's tutorial files. While the one advised the newcomer, 'Don't, should you have left a Public School, air this fact before the less fortunate Freshers', in the other tale after tale is found of attempts to scrape funds together, battles to accumulate the wherewithal, well-off maiden aunts coming to the rescue, parental self-sacrifice, and failure.[144] 'It is with great regret that I am forced to sever my connection with the college; but as you know engineering firms in this country have not yet realised the advantage of encouraging university men.'[145] Altogether happier in its outcome was the case of the 'brilliant boy – quite the best I have ever had to deal with', the son of the Bournemouth journeyman carpenter whose non-Johnian headmaster feared had not done justice to himself in the 1908 scholarship examination. 'I say this (...) in justice to a boy to whom a University Education will mean so much in his career. A fairly long list of pupils of mine have gone to St John's; but I shall be

---

[143] D.44.14. These figures ignore foreign undergraduates and those admitted for second first degrees.

[144] 'They will not appreciate it, nor like you the better', above, p. 405; cf. Boys Smith, *Memories*, 23.

[145] H. B. Jenkins to MacAlister, 19 Sept. 1905: SJCA, TU11.10/Jenkins, H. B.

much surprised if Grigg does not do better than any of his predecessors.'[146] As Sir James Grigg's subsequent career as a Whitehall permanent secretary and Churchill's war-time Secretary of State for War testifies, he did.

It was 'with of course no wish to influence the election in any way' that Grigg's headmaster had written. (Dear me, no!) None the less, if the mutually beneficial machinery was to remain in working order there was always a case for a spot of the old oil. Or, at least, one for keeping grit out of the works. When Sikes reported on the spartan conditions of the Charterhouse changing rooms therefore ('I should think Charterhouse is good enough for a strong boy, and may be, now, for a delicate boy'), he stipulated that his opinion must go no further, conscious no doubt of the influence associated with the Charterhouse-led 'Clarendon group'.[147] Not that Charterhouse was one of Sikes's favoured twenty-four. Likewise, in the case of Felsted, which not only was, but which also 'sends us boys', and where one of the masters was the elder son of the father who had failed to clear his younger son's college account, would it, Sikes wondered, be altogether 'in the interest of the College to press matters too far'?[148]

Tanner's resignation as Tutor in 1912, at the early age of fifty-two on account of chronic insomnia, was widely deplored, with Bonney declaring it a 'calamity, especially at the present juncture' (for Bonney – 'old cantank' to the staff – *all* 'present junctures' brought calamities in their wake),[149] Hart, a 'thunderbolt', and Leathem, 'rather a shock'.[150] Notwithstanding the differences that divided them (since 'as perhaps has sometimes been clear, I have not always gone all the way with you in tutorial policy'), Glover cordially acknowledged the Tanners' kindness 'around the years 1888–1892 and other years, when you headed me off the path that leads to breakdown'. Tributes such as that from a colleague on whom his autocratic habits (or tendency to unprincipled flexibility) had sometimes jarred, provide an indication of Tanner's value to the place, which in this particular case took the form of persuading his high-striving fourth-term pupil

[146] E. Fenwick to Tutor, 9 Dec. 1908: Sir (James) Grigg (1890–1964): SJCA, TU 13/ Grigg, P. J.

[147] Sikes to Tanner, 6 Jan. 1903: SJCA, TU12.5.5. 'Will you kindly be careful not to mention my name (if you use this information) for the sake of the College, as I am trying to get up a connexion with the School.' In 1861 the 'Clarendon group' (comprising Charterhouse, Eton, Harrow, Merchant Taylors', Rugby, St Paul's, Shrewsbury, Westminster and Winchester) had provided Oxford with one-third of all its undergraduates: J. R. de S. Honey and M. C. Curthoys, 'Oxford and schooling', *History of the University of Oxford*, VII, ed. M. G. Brock and M. C. Curthoys (Oxford, 2000), 566; above, pp. 299–300.

[148] Sikes to Tanner, 27 Oct. 1908: SJCA, TU12.10.272 ('he might do us mischief there').

[149] Letters of 8 & 9 Mar. 1912: 'You were doing more than any other man among the Fellows to raise [the College] from the depression into which it had fallen – a depression, the causes of which, and the remedies for which, the majority of [members of the Council] apparently do not realize. (…) I am now less than ever sanguine that I shall live to see the College restored to something like its former position in the University', letter of 8 Mar. 1912: SJCA, TU12.14.65. On the following day he returned to the charge ('the more I think of it the more I feel that your enforced retirement from the Tutorship is the greatest misfortune, save one, which could happen to the *personnel* of the College'): TU12.14.66 (note the 'save one'); SJCA, Arch.2.6: W. T. Thurbon, 'Memoir', 4.

[150] SJCA, TU12.14.53–4 (1 Mar. 1912).

to cut down his daily stint of work from eight hours to nearer six by taking him for lengthy walks as far afield as Linton and Abington and entertaining him to tennis in the garden of his home, the Stone House on the Madingley Road.[151] 'Walking was safe and reasonable in those days before motors.'[152] 'Strenuous walks with a fellow undergraduate of like persuasion' – or, as in this case, with a Tutor – were an activity that marked off the reading man from those described by Heitland 'with no ideas to exchange and prone to intellectual rest' as well as needful of what another has described as more powerful 'analgesics against the pain of occasional contemplation'.[153]

In a graceful tribute a group headed by the mathematician R. P. Paranjpye (bracketed Senior Wrangler, 1899; Fellow, 1901; the first Indian – according to Glover, the first 'native' – elected to the Fellowship of any Oxford or Cambridge college) presented Mrs Tanner with a gift of Indian silver.[154] Having since 1885 been the Indian Civil Service teacher of Indian history, Tanner had been long active in promoting interest in the Subcontinent and long remained in correspondence with many of his old pupils both there and beyond. In his will he would dispose of a silver box presented to him by the Crown Prince of Japan (on the occasion of the Crown Prince Hirohito's recent visit to Cambridge, presumably in return for the nuggets of constitutional procedure contained in Tanner's admonitory lecture on the Relations of Crown and People of England).[155]

For another nine years Tanner continued as Tutorial Bursar (or 'Bursarial Tutor'),[156] at the beginning of his tenure of which office his aptitude for figures had succeeded in the unusual achievement of causing an Audit Committee to break into verse:

> What is this very novel manner
> Adopted by our Mr Tanner?
>
> A full analysis displayed,
> The sums to washerwomen paid,
> With some most careful estimates
> Of profits drawn from fines and gates.

---

[151] SJCA, TU12.14.55 (9 Mar. 1912). Tanner's advice 'not to over-work or under-eat and to avoid nervous break-down': GD, 30 Nov. 1889; the Linton grind, just before his tripos (GD, 13 May 1891); in same term, tennis (in which he is 'invariably on the losing side': GD, 8, 14 May, 5 Jun. 1891). In the course of another restorative ramble, on 26 November 1891, he fell in with a 'go-ahead little boy' called Maynard Keynes.

[152] Glover, *Cambridge Retrospect*, 82.

[153] Heitland, *After Many Years*, 115; Mangan, 'Oars and the man', 248–9.

[154] Paranjpye and others to Mrs Tanner, 14 Mar. 1913: SJCA, TU12.16.31. For the earlier presentation by Tanner's pupils in residence, see *Eagle* xxxiv [1912–13], 365); GD, 4 Nov. 1901.

[155] D22.60; GD, 18 May 1921. This was the occasion of the celebrated encounter in First Court described by J. T. Combridge (BA 1921): 'There was only one path down the centre of the court. The Crown Prince would naturally expect anyone else on it to keep out of his way; with equal certainty Dr Bonney would give way to no one on his ground': 'Dr Bonney and the Crown Prince', *Eagle* lxviii, no. 288 (1980), 32.

[156] GD, 22 Nov. 1907.

> The strictest arithmetic law
> Revealed in *his* accounts no flaw –
> Addition right and right subtraction
> Gave auditors full satisfaction.
> But what astounded them the most:
> Of all his ledgers *none* was lost.
>
> And that is the astounding manner
> Used in his books by Mr Tanner.[157]

We know more about Tanner than we do about most of his contemporaries because unlike them (and in particular unlike the longer-lived and rather less emollient E. E. Sikes) he left all that paper behind him. From it there continues to exude an impression of Elgarian warmth which, together with the old dog licences preserved there, makes Tanner ('Papa', as he was known to the undergraduates) a very Edwardian figure, easily imaginable imparting his benediction to those lethargic afternoons when the only question was whether the cricket or the tennis team would be the more successful in mopping up surplus talent from amongst unoccupied oarsmen: the afternoons faithfully recorded in the *Eagle* of these years, with their accounts of cricket matches against the dons and the servants interspersed with reports of the College Mission and LMBC, and LMBC as usual occupying the lion's share of both the sporting budget and the magazine's pages.[158] In D. ('Ivor') Day, Honorary Secretary of CUBC, 'the glory of the Blue reached its perfection.'[159] When Day's father (G. D. Day) had visited Cambridge for the May races in 1911 and watched his elder son, G. L. ('Loo') Day rejoicing in his First Boat colours (though not perhaps in his going down a couple of places), he remarked how very much pleased he was with

> all the Men I have met in the week & feel it is bound to tell on the College in the future that you have such a number of simple minded (*sic*) manly young Fellows who seem to bear the brand of clean living so clearly. I think they are as nice a type of young English Gentlemen as anyone could wish to meet or to be the Friends of ones Boy.[160]

The following year brought more effusive OJs, Edgar T. Woodhead for example, whose 'pleasure in visiting the scenes of my undergrad days culminated when the races began':

---

[157] SJCA, TU12.2.74 (undated).

[158] GD, 19 Aug. 1911; *Eagle* xxx (1908–9), 119.

[159] *Eagle* xxxv (1913–14), 359.

[160] Letter to Tanner, 11 Jun. 1911: SJCA, TU12.13.270. The same letter refers to the father's launching of Ivor into St John's society, evidently during that same May week. ('I hope you did not think that we had "abused the process of the Court" as we say. I gathered from your previous report that Ivor had only a slightest off chance but I thought that the experience would be good for him & that he would lose nothing by coming up.') He certainly lost nothing. In fact, to the extent that both the Day brothers were Tanner's pupils and would become the brothers-in-law of L. E. Tanner, another of Tanner's pupils as well as his nephew, there is a powerful odour of nepotism about the entire procedure. In September 1924 Tanner would appoint G. L. Day one of the executors of his will (D22.60). See also *Eagle* xxxii (1910–11), 323–3.

35 Long Vac Cricket no date (*c.* 1900). Seated, first from left, E. E. Sikes; standing fourth from left, J. R. Tanner; seated third from right, L. H. K. Bushe-Fox: SJCL, Album 36/9

Seeing the boats swish round Ditton and chase each other up the Long Reach, the sound of the familiar roar from the bank when a 'bump' became likely, made me almost forget the 25 years and to wish once more to be rowing '3'! I even attempted to run with the 1st boat, but alas my course was short and Oh! how stiff my ankles for days![161]

a passage irresistibly reminiscent of Leslie Stephen's description of 'the rowing man', the clerical old member of the previous generation, back amongst his own for the bumps:

To-morrow he will be again a domestic parson, teaching a Sunday school. To-day he has got back into his old life. He resided at the University for, say, 800 days, excluding Sundays and vacations. Of those, he passed 790 on the river, and during nine of the remainder he was laid up with a strain caused by his exertions. The remaining day, which he wasted in lionizing his mother and sisters, he will regret as long as he lives. Years afterwards he will date events by the University races of the time. The Crimean War, he will say, broke out in the year of the 'the eighteen-inch race', *i.e.* the race when Oxford beat Cambridge at Henley by that distance.[162]

[161] Letter to Tanner, 17 Jun. 1912: SJCA, TU12.14.146.
[162] *Sketches from Cambridge, by a Don* (London, 1865), 19.

36 The Life of Grace. A New Court dinner party just before the First War. Note both the floral wallpaper and the controlled resignation of those present as they contemplate the prospect of yet another evening of unalloyed pleasure: SJCL, Album, 18/25

Needless to say, even in this not overly academic company some of the young gentlemen failed to remain afloat. However, diplomatic understatement was equal to masking the reasons for the disappearance from the Cam of, for example, one who 'unfortunately' had to be 'about his business' and of the 'unexpected and much lamented departure' of another – though the latter who had left in order to train for the Roman Catholic priesthood nevertheless managed to return for Henley.[163] Secretaries of clubs either departed with the club's funds, or ('owing to circumstances') failed to collect them in the first place.[164] One of these, the Portcullis, a society for sharing the loving cup and reading and discussing plays and other literary exertions started with five undergraduates in 1907, soon settled with twelve including a couple of the more biddable Fellows (Benians and Glover), and in 1910 demonstrated both its seriousness of purpose by instituting an annual five- or six-course dinner in a member's room and its essentially undergraduate character by failing to record the first of them.[165] The practices of another, the rather less cerebral Punchbowl, included

[163] *Eagle* xxx (1908–9), 114; xxxi (1909–10), 126 (C. J. W. Henslow); 32 (1910–11), 126.
[164] *Eagle* xxix (1907–8), 105, 260.
[165] The Club's Minute Book: SJCA, SOC.24.1.

a good deal of drinking the king's health and emptying the vessel after which it was named, staying up all night, singing, and room cricket played with coal shovels and apples.[166] In the Debating Society by contrast the cautious side of the house generally had the better of it.[167] The programme of the May Week concert – the LMBC concert as it still proclaimed itself, with the Boat Club anthem sung by the First May colours 'with that sense of duty which is their property', 'the fitting crown to an evening's music in the College Hall' – was complained of for being too *musical*, the Club drawing the line at 'set choral works' and 'concerted instrumental pieces'. 'May Term audiences are supposed to be not too fond of long or serious works', it was noted in 1907, while two years later it was observed: 'The L.M.B.C. concert (...) is intended to be a social function; but this year it suffered from being treated too much as one of the College's musical events, which it obviously is not.'[168]

Appropriately enough, in June 1913 the protest at intellectualism experienced its apogee and fused with the sense of endless Edwardian afternoons in the visit of the seventeen-year-old Kabaka of Uganda in his 'oriental dress', described in the sort of terms adopted by headmasters attempting to persuade Tanner to take their not terribly bright head of house.[169] As the strains of Herr Moritz Wurm's Blue Viennese Band faded away over the survivors of the pre-War May Balls, to the septuagenarian Bonney it seemed that modern undergraduates were 'a trifle more luxurious than in my days – rather more inclined to recline on soft cushions, basking on bank or in boat, to look on at games instead of playing them, to drive about in cabs, which, except to go to the station, were rarely used by us.'[170] Already there were complaints about noise from the Backs, in particular from waterborne gramophones.[171] Rowdiness, not all of it seasonal, was never far beneath the surface. The letters home of Gilbert Waterhouse report drunken scenes around a boat club bonfire fed by college furniture and lavatory seats, the systematic wrecking, involving fireworks and flooding, of a meeting of mathematical undergraduates organized by Louis Mordell ('the Yankee sent over here by a syndicate to capture the last senior wranglership'), celebration of 'the feast of St. John Porter Latin, whatever that is', and coal dropped on passing punts. In addition to consuming the head porter's hat as well as 'all wooden College property which was not very firmly secured', the bonfire in Third Court

---

[166] In Feb. 1914 its last pre-War meeting 'broke up after a rowdy and most enjoyable evening': Minute Book (SJCA, SOC.16.1).

[167] E.g. *Eagle* xxxi (1909–10), 137.

[168] *Eagle* xxviii (1906–7), 122; xxix (1907–8), 400; xxx (1908–9), 234; GD, 14 Jun. 1909 ('College Concert with Boat Song as one bright item, I heard'). The Musical Society's claim on the General Athletics Club in 1930 'to defray the expenses of the May Concert' was refused *inter alia* because 'the seating accommodation at the concert was so poor as to make it physically impossible for more than half of the subscribers to attend': GAC, min. of 8 May 1930.

[169] *Eagle* xxxv (1913–14), 112–13: 'The young King is some six foot two in height, and is a keen golf and football player.'

[170] *Eagle* xxxi (1910–11), 330; xxxiii (1912–13), 436; 'A septuagenarian's recollections of St John's', *Eagle* xxx (1908–9), 309.

[171] H. F. Stewart to Tanner, 11 Apr. 1909: SJCA, TU12.11.131.

37 Visit of the Kabaka of Buganda, June 1913. Although not a candidate for admission, His vigorous Majesty was thought to evince certain Johnian characteristics.

after the 1901 Lents almost accounted for the Library.[172] Criminal acts reported to the College by the constabulary and conscientiously filed away by Tanner consisted of wilfully extinguishing a public gas lamp (the offence that provided that generation with the sort of relief later to be enjoyed by discharging fire extinguishers, and compounded on one occasion by the malefactor offering the officer half a sovereign 'on the nail' to let him go) and the theft of railway lamps by a hockey team returning from Oxford.[173] Consorting with loose women remained the business of the proctors.

By now, academically things were on the mend somewhat. If the number of Research Fellows elected annually was limited that was largely because so was

[172] 'We had a nine course dinner in Hall, followed by a reception in the Fellows' Combination Hall. It was a squash and no mistake: about 250 people, all smoking cigars': 'Nothing new under the sun …': *Eagle* (1993), 24–8. Cf. *Eagle* (1995), 48–50 (S. Priston); xxx (1908–9), 233. Waterhouse was subsequently Professor of German at Queen's University, Belfast. For Mordell (1888–1972; Third Wrangler in Part I of the Mathematical tripos, 1909, Sadleirian Professor of Pure Mathematics, Cambridge, 1945–53): *ODNB* (J. W. S. Cassels).

[173] SJCA, TU12.7.177; TU12.9.35. A. J. Mason (Vice-Chancellor) to Tanner, 2 Mar. 1909, forwarding an estimate from the Great Western Railway ('Compartment in coach 2121 reserved for St John's F.C. Doorlight broken and frame damaged. Cost of repairs 5/11d.'): TU12.11.104. Complaints about Cambridge teams returning from Oxford were not unprecedented: CM, 623/4(ii) (3 May 1901).

38 'Triumph. Triumph!' The last Wooden Spoon (the prize awarded to the man at the bottom of the Mathematical Class-List) is borne away by its winner, C. L. Holthouse, June 1909: SJCL, Album 38/28. Bequeathed to the College by Mr Holthouse, the trophy now hangs in the Small Combination Room.

the number of candidates.[174] As regards distinction, in 1911 Bonney's verdict was for once wholly favourable. Measuring it in terms of numbers of Fellows of the Royal Society and the recently founded British Academy (not always the safest index, of course), with sixteen of forty-six the contrast with 1853 was striking. Then a Fellowship of fifty-four had contained just one FRS and about one-fifth of the whole number were dismissible as 'men of no account'.[175] Donald MacAlister's appointment as Principal of Glasgow University in 1907 provided an early example of the influence of the Johnian diaspora in academic institutions at home and abroad of which the rest of the century would furnish so many more examples. Meanwhile amongst those elected to the Fellowship in the years before and after the Quatercentenary were men who had first come to the place as entrance scholars,[176] men such as Ernest Alfred Benians and Harold Jeffreys. Both were the sons of schoolmasters. Jeffreys was almost a caricature

[174] Statute XVII. In the years 1908–11, four, seven, eight and seven: SJCA, Fellowship papers/D96.

[175] 'The Quatercentenary Sermon', *Eagle* xxxiii (1911–12), 15. With a Fellowship three times as large, in 2010 the numbers were nine and eleven respectively, with two Fellows of the College Fellows of both. The comparison may be thought to be of interest.

[176] Miller, *Portrait of a College*, 99ff.

of the scholarship boy, worrying about being overcharged on his first term's college account after spending only 4½d on a quarter of butter.[177] Benians was different.

4. EAB

At Bethany House – the school at Goudhurst, Kent where he was a pupil and his father, W. A. Benians, its first headmaster – 'the gentle Ben' had begun teaching at the age of fourteen and thereafter never stopped. Behind the kindly, quizzical exterior, the insistently intellectual high moral seriousness was ever present. As the embodiment of Heitland's hoped-for 'man to carry on the work of the place', Benians, the protégé of Alfred Marshall and H. S. Fox-well, was to remember the period 1906–14 as one of 'quiescence'. 'We talked of reforms, but they seemed remote and not very important. (...) Finance was then a hard master and any suggested change was treated as impracticable.'[178] The content and flavour of the surviving correspondence of these years suggest otherwise.[179]

Although Benians's correspondence richly deserves a study of its own, there are aspects of it that have an immediate bearing on the present work. For a boy from a Nonconformist non-establishment school hardly a generation old to have prevailed in the Cambridge History Scholarship competition was a remarkable enough triumph both for himself and for his school. What made that success significant for the College was the missionary dedication to educational improvement that Benians had inherited from his father together with a native understanding of young people that was unparalleled amongst his St John's contemporaries.

Although an entrance scholar, Benians was a poor boy. At the start of his first term he wrote to his father about possible economies: no ptarmigan or lark pie for him![180] Two days later he reported on his success in persuading the bedder not to bring him such a large daily loaf (for her own benefit) and on meeting his agonizingly shy Tutor and his wife: 'They simply did not know what to talk about. Dr Sandys has an exceedingly bad name among the students for his iciness.' His stratagems for saving pennies on the books needed for his Part I indicate real poverty.[181] He was also the son of a very possessive mother whose

---

[177] CM, 534/2; *Eagle* xxxi (1909–10), 260; Jeffreys to Tanner, 6 Jan. 1911: SJCA, TU12.13.6. For Jeffreys (1891–1989; Minor Scholar in Mathematics, 1909; Fellow, 1914; Plumian Professor of Astronomy and Experimental Philosophy, Cambridge, 1946): *ODNB* (A. Cook).

[178] Benians, 'Cambridge in the last half century', 17; Linehan, 'Piam in memoriam', 74–5.

[179] Unless otherwise indicated, all material in the following pages is derived from the uncatalogued Benians papers (EABP).

[180] 'I do not know whether you will find it cheaper to send me things for breakfast and dinners even [if] I sign off. There are a *few* cheap reasonable things in the Kitchen tariff: Hot, Boiled salt beef 10d lb (...) Among the furniture is Table 8/– (very dear)' (6 Oct. 1899): SJCL, Misc. Letters/Benians, 1.

[181] SJCL, Misc. Letters/Benians, 2, 3 (8, 10 Oct. 1899).

expectation of long weekly letters was matched by her insistence on regular lengthy home visits.[182] As a first-year graduate student suffering from eye-strain, her son was urged to bring his work back for her to do,[183] and as a rising academic star to 'try *less* of the "pernicious weed"', not to adopt an academic stoop, and 'to take Easton's Syrup of Hypophosphites'.[184] Filial son though he was, he evidently needed props other than his parents. These he found in the friendship of his contemporaries and pupils, chief amongst whom was Hugh Russell-Smith, his junior by seven years. In the summer of 1909, shortly after Russell-Smith's graduation, the two were planning a camping holiday together in Scotland. Despite the references in their correspondence to a number of historical questions that the younger man was supposed to wrestle with over the vac., it was already clear that a relationship of equality had already outgrown that of teacher and pupil.

Amongst the Benians's papers there is a copy of the papers read at the dinner of the Portcullis Club in Benians's rooms on 12 March 1910,[185] including those of the Chairman, Russell-Smith (his 'Apology for Bluntness') and the host's own whimsical 'Milk Carts'. Then, J. B. Sterndale Bennett (the composer's grandson) rose to describe his vision of a meeting of the club in a Piccadilly restaurant forty years on, attended by, amongst others,

> a grave, rather bent old gentleman, with a face furrowed with learning, and eyes gentle, but penetrating. This is Dr. Benians, the well-known and well-loved Master of the Associated Colleges Ltd., Cambridge. He is famous in Cambridge for the lenity with which he regards the peccadilloes of his young subjects, and is said to scandalise his Fellows by holding assemblies of undergraduates in the small hours of the morning. At the moment he is engaged in a minute examination of a piece of tracing paper on which is sketched a map of the Campaigns of Louis XI. This is, no doubt, connected with the historical atlas which he has been so carefully compiling for the last forty years.

Here was a third-year undergraduate guying a don something like ten years his senior but confident that he was willing to be guyed and aware that he was already on his way to achieving legendary status.

The same camaraderie is evident in the letters Benians received from Russell-Smith in 1911–12 while the former was embarked upon an Albert Kahn-funded world tour and the other was substituting for him as college lecturer[186] and angling for a College Research Fellowship. At such times it is not unusual for academic aspirants to look for and to think they have discovered encouragement

---

[182] E. g. 'Steph and Doro have been so very good all the time, in a way which only those on the spot have the chance to be' (25 Nov. 1926).

[183] 'If you brought your work home, could I write or revise under your direction?' (19 Oct. 1903; also 20 and 22 Oct. 1903).

[184] 'that is supposed to be the thing for brain fag' (12 May 1906).

[185] Printed for Private Circulation (Cambridge: W. P. Spalding, 43 Sidney Street).

[186] CM, 857/3 (27 Jan. 1911).

in the *obiter dicta* of their seniors.[187] But in the spring of 1911, in thanking Benians for his 'splendid long letter from Trieste', this junior signs off 'Enough, Good Bye. Love, HFRS', which is not so usual, while the tone of the letter of the following December in which he informed his mentor of his disappointment in the competition conveys the ease of a relationship at a stage of the two men's careers that ordinarily might not have made for ease.[188] Though his fellow Portcullis member, Glover, thought well of him too, describing him as a 'future Fellow, a real sound man' and 'one of our best types and individuals', Russell-Smith would surely not have addressed Glover in such terms.[189] The same letter also provides a privileged view of the College's social mores at the time:

> People are awfully nice up here in encouraging me to go hard for a fellowship next year. Bushie and Sikes are extremely hopeful of my claims. Tanner – well he's Tanner. I have heard from Hart all about the election discussions etc. He's really an ass to tell me, but it may interest you, and I know that you won't let it go any further. It appears, as I expected, that Tanner was my enemy throughout. In appointing referees he refused to have more than one given me (although others objected to this) on the grounds that I was too young & inexperienced to be taken as a serious candidate. When I went up to see him, he informed me of this voluntarily (which is to his credit) and added that he was going to press the Council to appoint three for me next year. Hart tells me my referee was Gwatkin,[190] and both he, Sikes & Bushie say that his report was extremely favourable; and both Bushie and Hart inform me that for a time my claims were seriously discussed. Then Tanner stepped in again & of course I got the boot.[191] In fact I gather (chiefly from Hart) that without Tanner it would have been a very close touch. I don't know why he objects to me, unless it is because I once laughed at Button [A. E. Button, matric. 1908] in his presence before I knew he was his nephew.

Equally informative were his reports of the boat-burning earlier that year:

> There was a fire in the courts. All the boys were pleased and some drunk. The Dean [H. F. Stewart] was vexed. I got hauled for bagging a forth-seat. The Dean et-tu-Bruted me for ten minutes & said he was surprised & pained for one who is employed by the college to help to destroy college property, but thought it would be not dignified to gate me. (He called the

---

187 Thus, 'The VC and Glover both told me to send in for a fellowship this year. Glover in comparing me with Previté-Orton remarked, "I wish I could show some of your work to Larmor." (...) Tanner looked really and genuinely pleased, when I told him about the Allen [Scholarship]. The first time.' (Russell-Smith to Benians, 6 Mar. 1911).

188 Letters of 14 Mar. and 3 Dec. 1911.

189 Glover to Larmor, 5 Dec. 1911.

190 The omniscient H. M. Gwatkin who reported that he thought the dissertation submitted to 'shew very sound and careful work' (SJCA, D93 file 25).

191 Elected were C. W. Previté-Orton (1877–1947; Professor of Medieval History, Cambridge, 1937: Peter Linehan, 'The Making of the *Cambridge Medieval History*', *Speculum* 57 [1982], 463–94; *ODNB* (R. B. Dobson) and R. Whiddington (1885–1970; Fellow, 1911–19; Cavendish Professor of Physics, University of Leeds, 1919; *ODNB* [N. Feather and I. Falconer]): CM, 877 (6 Nov. 1911).

burning of 4th seats 'indelicate'!) He is a little shit to rub it down that I am no longer an ordinary undergraduate. The whole affair on Saturday night was rather a disgusting orgy, but things are quieting down now. (...) Love to Rupert. (...) Don't drink too much beer at Munich & don't let Rupert do so either.[192]

and, while Benians was progressing from Trieste to St Petersburg, of a 'Cambridge evening' off Jesus Lane with some prelates in the making:[193]

I need some time to recover from this evening. It's been a good evening – a Cambridge evening – a scrap at 1 Malcolm Place – those present (besides myself) being Burton,[194] Marchand,[195] Ragg,[196] Algy[197] & P. J. Lewis.[198] We had some ordinary fighting (in fancy dress) in the course of which we broke the glass front of a bookcase & I threw Ragg down a flight of stairs into the landlady's kitchen. Then the real fun came, when we went up into Marchand's bedroom to change. Lewis, Ragg & I were locked in. Marchand won't sleep tonight. We did our work, then let Ragg out of the window, who rushed up & let us out, so that we just got back to college by 12 o'clock.

Likewise, the morning after the night before's College quatercentenary:

The College achieved its 400th year on Saturday, which was celebrated by a dinner – speakers the Master, the Visitor, Burton (who was excellent). The wine I think was bad, as I felt very ill after it, woke at 4 next morning with indigestion, rose at 6 & walked it off among the cuckoos and cowslips, bathed at Grantchester with Rupert (who is now back) & Dudley, had breakfast & lay in their garden with them etc. etc. Rupert is in fine form, told us about Munich etc. & generally played the child;[199]

not to mention an energetic May Week:

I had a simply splendid May Week, roof clomb (*sic*) all Saturday night, thoroughly enjoyed the Ball (contrary to expectations) & did not go to bed at all that night – proceeding to the river & finally breakfasting at the Orchard instead, had river picnics in one of which I was pushed in by Burton but repaid him twofold – and generally unstuffed myself.[200]

---

[192] Letter of 22 Feb. 1911 (top and bottom of last sheet of letter torn off).

[193] Letter of 29 April 1911.

[194] H. P. W. Burton, Hereford Cathedral School, later prebendary of Louth, Lincoln Cathedral.

[195] G. I. C. Marchand, Aldenham, later brother-in-law of Burton.

[196] H. R. Ragg, Hereford Cathedral School, later bishop of Calgary.

[197] Perhaps the sixteen-year-old W. S. A. Robertson (Queens'), 'one of the pioneers of the Franciscan movement in the Anglican Church (...) A darting, mercurial figure, always the centre of a humming circle of friends, young and old, he found willing accomplices in his plots and parties': http://www.franciscan.org.nz/algy.html.

[198] P. J. Lewis, Hereford Cathedral School, at the time master at Malvern College.

[199] Letter of 8 May 1911. Later that month Benians was briefly back in Cambridge: GD, 29 May 1911.

[200] Letter of 18 Jun. 1911.

All of which sheds light not only on College politics but also on the social circles through which the College's young meteor was moving. As to the first, when Russell-Smith was courted by Emmanuel in the summer of 1912 Tanner would redeem himself by resigning his own College lectureship in order to make room for him and later by not standing in the way of his election to the Fellowship.[201] 'Russell Smith is to be lecturer here on same terms as Benians – this possible because Tanner resigns his stipend as lecturer. I saw him and tried to express sense of service done to College by his act.' The 'keep Russell-Smith campaign' was one with whose progress Benians had been kept in touch over the previous year as he progressed from the Munich *Karneval* in March 1911 (where he coincided with Rupert Brooke, Russell-Smith's friend and contemporary at Rugby, the 'Rupert' referred to in the correspondence) via North America and the Far East to Egypt, leaving his young friend in charge of the production of his atlas volume for the *Cambridge Modern History*: those tracing-paper maps which had occasioned such mirth at the meeting of the Portcullis.[202]

In Munich, Brooke reported, Benians had been 'too shy to wear clothes of a riotous kind'.[203] But far removed though he may have been from the neo-pagan spirit in which Brooke claimed to have seduced Hugh's younger brother in the autumn of 1909, in terms of physical proximity he was not.[204] According to Brooke, after spending the night with him Denham Russell-Smith 'had to bicycle into breakfast with Mr Benians'.[205] For all his lack of exuberance and absence of interest in dressing up, Benians stood for the casting off of provincial shackles. He was the personification of liberation, but of a discreet sort, and above all of liberation by travel. 'I thank you for having originally suggested it: another thing you have done for me', Russell-Smith wrote from Harvard in the spring of 1912.[206]

---

[201] GD, 14 Jun. 1912; Russell-Smith to Benians (9 Jun. 1912); CMM, 896/5 (12 Jun. 1912), 901/3 (4 Nov. 1912). On 22 Jul. 1912 Tanner wrote to Benians: 'The Council did nothing about Russell Smith. A delicate operation was being carried through & it did not seem wise to complicate the situation. (…) If Russell-Smith's backers claim too much, they may end by losing what they want [in the Fellowship election].' On this occasion the referees were C. H. Firth ('The conception is better than the execution, that is to say there are a considerable number of errors and omissions. The authorities used are rather uncritically employed. (…) If it had been submitted to me here [Oxford] as a dissertation for the degree of Bachelor of Letters, I should consider that it reached a sufficiently high standard of merit to obtain the degree') and W. R. Sorley ('I have gone on the assumption that all human works are imperfect – even fellowship dissertations. But I regard the essay on Harrington as constituting a very strong claim for election to a fellowship, and the Essay on Religious Liberty as adding to the strength of that claim').

[202] Letter of 18 Jun. 1911, reporting on dinner of *History* contributors: 'Wine good & well circulated. No dons drunk. I was the only person under 30 in the room.'

[203] Geoffrey Keynes (ed.), *The Letters of Rupert Brooke* (London, 1968), 282.

[204] Paul Delany, *The Neo-Pagans: Friendship and Love in the Rupert Brooke Circle* (London, 1987), 77–82.

[205] Ibid.

[206] 'It' being his visit to the United States to search for Harrington material on the proceeds of the Allen Prize: Russell-Smith to Benians, 18 Mar. 1912. Cf. his *Harrington and his* Oceana: *A Study of a Seventeenth-Century Utopia and its Influence in America* (Cambridge, 1914), p. vii.

39 The Master (R. F. Scott) with Eagles, 1909; H. Russell-Smith on Scott's right: SJCL, Album 23/31c

There was a bracing, uninhibited freshness about the friendship of 'Dear Benians' and 'Dear Hugh', which was how the two addressed each another. Benians's idyll was set in his native weald. From Kobe in the autumn of 1911 he wrote: 'What I want is brown leaves, autumn winds, a country walk with you',[207] which sounds more like G. M. Trevelyan than R. C. Brooke. At the edge of an age at which notions of friendship acquired new connotations, inevitably there was a different brand of openness about Benians's relationship with his mother. 'How do you like this verse?', he inquired, writing to her from Corfu and adding that he wished he had Russell-Smith with him: 'Then I should enjoy it.'[208] By mid-April they were together at Naples, and evidently he did.[209]

[207] 'So don't forget me. Yours affectionately EAB' (offering best wishes for the Fellowship election: 'I tried three times myself'): letter of 23 Sept. 1911.

[208] 'Over land and over sea / The primrose calls me back to thee. / The violet whispers on the breeze, / Hasten over land and seas. // You don't like it. Very well then. I won't say more.' (letter of 22 Mar. 1912).

[209] Letter to mother (Elizabeth Benians), 17 Apr. 1912.

40 Father of the College, June 1905: T. R. Glover as Praelector, with four supplicants for the BA degree identifiable from back of photograph as (left to right): J. Wilson Harris (son of house decorator; Classics; journalist and author, editor of *Spectator*); R. E. T. Bell (son of merchant; Classics; rural dean of Henley); W. Coop (son of cattle dealer; Classics; died of wounds received in France 1915); J. Lusk (son of master baker; Mechanical Sciences; Chevalier de la Légion d'Honneur; died of wounds received in France 1915): SJCL, loose item in Glover's diary for 1905

5.   WAR

In 1897 Tanner had reckoned that twenty years were needed for the College past to be 'live[d] down'.[210] But the College was not to be allowed them. Perhaps Peter Mason hadn't been so off-beam after all in the opinion reported by his obituarist of 'a certain friendly Power [that] had carefully studied the geography of this country with a view to its invasion'.[211] The mood had changed from Kenneth Grahame to Erskine Childers. Browsing on quail stuffed with olives and plovers' eggs in aspic, Fellows and guests at the eight-course Port Latin feast of May 1914 had aroused their jaded appetites.[212] In the following December, at the time of Harold Jeffreys's election to the Fellowship, the Kaiser's War was already three months old. Four months after that Rupert Brooke died off Gallipoli. 'It seems too unutterably sad and wrong', Russell-Smith wrote to

[210] Above, p. 420.
[211] *Eagle* xxxiv (1912–13), 249. The threat had been discussed by the College History Society in Feb. 1911: Previté Orton to Tanner, SJCA, TU12.13.85.
[212] SJCA, CC5.3.

Benians.[213] In early July 1916 Russell-Smith himself died, of wounds received at the front.[214] Even Heitland was moved:

> He went, and comes not back again:
> Yet sure he has not died in vain
> For Peace and Right, whose cruel price
> Is glorious manhood's sacrifice.[215]

The start of hostilities changed everything, transforming the College and diminishing the relative importance of academic activity.[216] Clubs and societies which had proliferated over the previous decade disappeared for ever, with the Portcullis just one of the casualties. In order to discover who would be coming up for the Michaelmas term in mid-September 1914 Scott sent a circular to men about to begin their second and third years 'and to such Freshman as have entered and not withdrawn. I definitely know only of one – Howell.'[217] But M. I. B. Howells (matric. 1914) would be killed in action in the following year and have his name added to the lists of war dead published regularly by the *Cambridge Review* and the *Eagle*. Glover's account of the early weeks of the War reported the characteristic attitudes of the College's leading lights: 'Sikes *ipsissimus* – athletes and public school men gone to war, not board school men, they would be up next term, after main chance – also fussing about our doing extra work to make up for men being away' (24 September); Scott, 'full of anxiety for future of College – 100 men short = £1500 short on Education Fund, room rents also – and prospects to be bad for some years to come' (9 October); 'Tanner has been trying, it would appear from what he says, to push Gregory's pupils into OTC, and resented two declining without giving what he thought reason enough. He grows stupider year by year' (12 October). On the 13th he saw Larmor, 'who is a relief when one has had too much tutor. Saw Sikes later and was glad to think of Larmor.'

The childless Scott shared all the patriotic assumptions of the elderly. 'The parents who are sending their sons up in many cases were quite apologetic', the Tutor of Trinity informed him.[218] A single index may serve for many: in the five years after 1914 numbers of candidates for the history tripos across all the colleges dropped from 194 to 52, 22, 7, 13 and 17. The 'Our War List' of those

---

[213] Letter of 27 Apr. 1915.

[214] On 6 Jul. 1916: Nellie Russell-Smith (Hugh's mother) to Benians, 7 Jul. 1916. Benians's undated draft reply to her (the most heavily emended item in the correspondence) concludes: 'I do not know and cannot know how much you have lost and suffer. I know only my own feelings about him and how constant and returning they are, how grief and disappointment and loneliness struggle with happier and braver feelings. I know how much better a friend he was than I deserved, how much I admired and loved him, how much I expected of him, how beautiful his memory is to me, how certain I am that we must meet again.' See also his calmer appreciation in *Eagle* xxxviii (1916–17), 94–9.

[215] Ibid., 33.

[216] Thus the unsigned note 'The College and the War', which sought to 'give posterity a fair idea of the conditions under which we are living today': *Eagle* xxxvi (1914–15), 329–32.

[217] Scott to Tanner, 17 Sept. 1914: SJCA, TU12.17.42.

[218] Ibid.

on active service occupied five pages of the Michaelmas term 1914 issue of the *Eagle* including, amongst the names of those killed, that of H. V. Roseveare, for whom that ought to have been his first term of residence.[219] In the following term a committee charged with the preservation of its treasures, 'appointed to consider what action to take in view of possible injury to the College by hostile aircraft', reported, *inter alia*, that a third night porter had been appointed, while in the *Eagle* the obituaries began to appear, amongst them those of D. I. Day, the flower of LMBC, as well as his younger brother Miles, poet and fighter pilot.[220] By the summer of 1915 the 'Johniana' section was reduced to war honours and little else other than a tennis report including a notice that one of the courts had been assigned to 'our Belgian visitors'.[221]

By then other visitors had arrived, officers of the 2nd Welsh Brigade RFA who dined with the Fellows, and men of the Fourth Cheshires and the Third Monmouths who slept in the boathouse and the pavilion respectively – 'and that has brought the [GAC] a small but welcome revenue', the *Eagle*'s calculating chronicler reported, as well as recording that the May Term had ended 'without the colour and animation of May week, without races, concerts, and balls, aunts and cousins and sisters, but in the gloom of examinations whose importance it is hard to feel, we realise still more keenly the distance that divides us from the past'. 'This year has seen no "crocks" or "Lents" or May races, no league matches, no giving of "colours" or election of club officers.' 'The river has been deserted and the boat-houses occupied by soldiers.'[222] 'College, of course, is empty and Hall has died of inanition', Bonney reported to Glover, who was with the YMCA in India, informing him of Gregory's breakdown with acute indigestion and the 'more serious' case of another young colleague, Bushe-Fox.[223] Over the three terms of 1914–15 numbers descended from 161 to 121 to 116. Emptiness and desolation were everywhere.

The College continued on reduced power since, of course, members of the staff had joined up too. In a pencil-written letter dated 'somewhere in France Friday' one of them, G. E. ('Sonny') Frost, junior clerk in the College Office, provided an up-beat account of the 'jolly fine weather' he was enjoying and the 'fairly decent time' he was having, concluding by thanking Tanner 'and Mr Lockhart [Chief Clerk] for the way you are treating Mother'.[224] 'Elsie the cook's young man killed', Glover reported in May 1917. 'They were to marry in September.'[225]

From the beginning, particularly amongst the elderly, there was the expectation that all Johnians, and especially all British Johnians, would do their bit. 'Met the general's wife [Gen. Wellesley Paget] in morning, very full of

---

[219] *Eagle* xxxvi (1914–15), 107–11.

[220] Poems of his first published in the *Spectator* are in *Eagle* xxxix (1918–19), 222–4.

[221] Ibid., xxxvi (1914–15), 206–10, 366.

[222] Ibid., 236, 329–31.

[223] Letter of 2 Jan. 1915.

[224] SJCA, TU12.17.34: '... on the whole we are looked after better than some people imagine, and for myself I feel as well as I have ever felt and I am sure this life suits me if it wasn't so uncertain.' See *Eagle* xxxvi (1914–15), 252.

[225] GD, 11 May 1917.

recruiting', Glover recorded at the outset. 'Gave me an advertisement she had had printed: "Wanted petticoats for young men who have not joined the army or navy".'[226] When in the course of a scintillating speech at the Union Prof. A. C. Pigou of King's denied the fact of the Belgian atrocities, A. E. Shipley, the Master of Christ's and noted authority on diseases of the grouse, deplored the bad effect of such talk 'on the Indian students and the pimply anaemics left here' and urged Tanner to join him in denouncing the pacifist professor in the *Morning Post*. 'If the idea that Pigou represents Cambridge gets abroad, well there will be a land-slip to Oxford', Shipley predicted, while Scott contrasted, to his disadvantage, Pigou's 'war work' with that of the Tanners, who for two years had 'given up a large part of their house and great deal of their time to looking after the welfare of Belgian refugees'.[227] In 1915 there was of course little prospect of a land-slip to anywhere other than France, and in April 1916 when F. P. White, a research student of the College, appealed to the borough tribunal for absolute exemption from military service on grounds of conscience and heart disease, he encountered hostility and the suspicion that St John's was a nest of subversives:

> Mr Vinter: You are a member of the little society in St John's of conscientious objectors? – There is no society.
>
> I thought there had been meetings and resolutions passed? – Not at St John's.
>
> Mr Stephenson: How is it that they all come from St John's?
>
> The Chairman: Have you made any sacrifice for your conscience at all? – I certainly drink tea,[228] but there were jobs going as assistant naval instructors starting at £400 a year, and I most certainly would have got one of those had I applied.
>
> Mr Stace: And that is the sacrifice!
>
> Appellant: I don't think that I shall call it a sacrifice, but evidence of my objection.
>
> The Chairman: You have not denied yourself any things upon which taxes are paid? – No. I do not see how one is to live.
>
> There is water, nature's drink. – No answer.[229]

[226] GD, 28 Aug. 1914.

[227] Shipley to Tanner, 11 Mar. 1915: SJCA, TU12.18.16; *CR*, xxxvi (1914–15), 252; Scott to Vice-Chancellor (T. C. Fitzpatrick), 10 Sept. 1916 (SLB): 'What "War work" for example has Professor Pigou done? Apart from the "Joy rides" in his motor car of which we hear so much I should have thought that he used every artifice to avoid war work.' Cf. J. Saltmarsh and P. Wilkinson, *Arthur Cecil Pigou, 1877–1959 … A Memoir* (Cambridge, 1960), 8–9.

[228] Anticipating the standard question, the answer to which led to the charge that since tea was taxed the non-combatant tea drinker was willing to pay for others to fight.

[229] *Cambridge Daily News*, 21 Apr. 1916. The appeal was refused. Cf. Russell-Smith to Benians, 15 May 1916: 'I've just had your letter announcing your exemption from military service. I'm glad, as you wouldn't like it. I was immensely amused with the reports of the tribunals given in the Magazine you sent me. They should be cut out and kept for their historical as well as general interest.'

The case of Ebenezer Cunningham, Fellow since 1904 and lecturer since 1914, differed to the extent that having initially been allowed to do teaching work, on the appeal of the military member of the tribunal he was sent to dig trenches at Chivers' farm at Impington, and on the intervention of Glover, who 'shared the opinion of other members of St John's that it was not consistent with the dignity of the College that one of its Fellows should be thus engaged', was then transferred to a YMCA office job in London. Although by his own account at the end of the War he was cordially received back at St John's, there were those there, Glover was later to tell him, 'who would "rather have seen [his] head on a spike at the gate".'[230] As Glover, another pacifist, discovered, the animus endured. In 1916 Leathem would not agree to allow his lecturing in the United States to count as war work; in 1917 he confessed to being 'rather alarmed' by the rumour that he 'laughed in his sleeve at the army'; and when three years later he stood for election as University Orator he was initially refused the support of William Ridgeway, the Disney Professor of Archaeology, on the grounds that 'as an incorrigible Radical by nature and utterly unmoved by the great war, like almost all others of your kind, you would not be in sympathy with many of the best recipients of Honorary degrees, such as the great soldiers and sailors who have kept the roofs over our heads.'[231] As to undergraduate COs, did this mean 'Conscientious Objectors' or 'Complete Outcasts'?, Scott enquired, thereby identifying himself with the collective view of the borough tribunal, and required any such wishing to come into residence to give a solemn undertaking not to engage in propaganda of any sort or connect the name of the College with their cause in any way.[232]

As the conflict dragged on, Glover identified Tanner and his 'fierce commonplaceness' as the mouthpiece of intolerance. 'As trustees for the College we [the Fellows] could not afford luxurious consciences', he was heard to pronounce: this in the case of a man imprisoned for his views whom he wanted 'excluded forever in the College interest'. 'If the College is going to expel honest opinion, and keep Stewart and the like, why should one wish to belong to it?', Glover wondered,[233] though he did not wonder audibly. On the question of who should be appealed for at the Tribunal the Master of St John's was 'shuffling' and 'cowardlier all the time', he noted in the following year.[234] But Scott was in the majority, and his sentiments survived the armistice. That autumn Glover recorded 'hearing how ex-officer undergraduates shaved head of Brown (who would not stand for God Save the King in Chapel) and painted it red',[235] while

[230] E. Cunningham, 'Memoir', SJCA, Arch.2.12a, pp. 53–7.

[231] Scott to Glover, 29 Mar. 1916 (in his view 'you ought to finance yourself independently of the College'); GD, 13 Oct. 1917; Ridgeway to Glover, 1 Jan. 1920; Glover, *Cambridge Retrospect*, 77; Wood, *Glover*, 128.

[232] Scott to Glover, 11 Jul. 1916, 31 Aug. 1917 (SLB). Cf. Wood, *Glover*, 116–17, Brooke, *History of the University of Cambridge*, IV. 335–40.

[233] GD, 28 Sept. & 24 Nov. 1916; 8 Jan. 1917. Tanner's fire was principally levelled at a former Fellow, J. A. Crowther (1908–14; in 1917 University Demonstrator in Physics) who was found to be medically unfit to fight: GD, 8 Mar., 21 Apr. 1917.

[234] GD, 24 May 1918.

[235] '(This last, Sikes says, is wrong, though believed)': GD, 23 Nov. 1918, apparently referring to A. J. C Brown (matric. 1917), later a translator of Pasternak.

in March 1919 a lynch-mob of fifty or more Caius and other undergraduates and naval men raided the College intent on 'maltreating' the classics under-graduate H. D. F. Kitto.[236] On an enquiry whether the reconstruction work an applicant had been engaged on with the Relief Committee volunteers in France could be counted as war service for purposes of exemption from Little Go, two months later the University Registrary sought confirmation from his Tutor that 'the man about whom you are writing was not a Conscientious Objector'.[237]

Repugnance at the idea of feasts at such a time drew on the same store of sentiments. In 1900 the Lent Term feast had been cancelled and a sum equivalent to its exceedings over an ordinary dinner donated to relief of the war-wounded from South Africa.[238] No less was expected in the first year of the Great War, so when in May 1915, in the week after the sinking of the *Lusitania*, the Secretary of the University Press, misinformed that Glover had supported the idea of a Port Latin feast, sent him an epistolary white feather:

> Hitherto (…) if I may be permitted to say so (…) I have looked on you as a friend. I must appear to you to be a most awful prig, but, in view of the fact that, when the best blood of England and Canada is being shed, you should think it right to support a College feast, I am sorry we must in future be simply members of the same university.[239]

Having been put right on the matter, on the following day he wrote again, apologizing and withdrawing 'everything I have said or thought on the matter' but nevertheless stressing his strength of feeling at the indecency of continuing with '"business as usual" at the present time'.[240] Consistent with such feelings was the Press's cancellation in 1916 of a volume of the *Cambridge Medieval History* written largely by 'enemy aliens' and two years later the College's rejection of the suggestion by W. A. Cox, one of the surviving Seniors, that local MAs be invited to dinner on 6 May.[241]

---

[236] They were seen off by C. B. Rootham ('a brave act'): GD, 7 Mar. 1919. On 24 Jan. 1918 Glover had recorded that Kitto's 'c. o. troubles have given him little chance to come on.' (Kitto: Professor of Greek, Bristol Univ., 1944.)

[237] J. N. Keynes to Benians, 15 May 1919: SJCA, TU Brown/ Sidney Kemp.

[238] CM, 589/8.

[239] A. R. Waller to Glover, 9 May 1915. In fact, Glover assured him, the occasion had been a 'quiet' one, with only College members, including undergraduates, in the Combination Room: GD, 6 May 1915. The Feast Book (SJCL, MS U40) records a five-course 'Exceeding Dinner' ('Undergraduates the same dinner without dessert. No anthem') by contrast with the nine-course affair of twelve months before. May 1915 was hardly the time for 'œufs de pluviers en aspic aux crevettes'.

[240] GD, 10 May 1915 ('a letter of moderate remonstrance' to Waller); Waller to Glover, 10 May 1915 ('… and I feel I could only unburden my soul to one whom I knew intimately'). In 1926 the Port Latin feast would be cancelled as 'unfitting' (draft letter, Sikes, 4 May 1926: SJCA, TU12.30.3). The General Strike also interfered with cricket fixtures and the programme of the Musical Society: *Eagle* xliv (1924–6), 308, 313.

[241] Linehan, 'Making of the *Cambridge Medieval History*', 463–4; Cox to Scott, 11 Mar. 1918, stressing that he did not propose 'to "revive the old Sixth of May dinner" in any sense' but presuming that there would be some sort of dinner in Hall on that day, 'probably a little better one with flowers, a speech or two possibly, & sound wine &

In order to save heating the Chapel, in the winter of 1916–17 morning prayer had been read in the Library and evensong conducted in the Combination Room. In the following year normal services were further reduced in consequence of the departure of both Dean and Chaplain to Fellowships elsewhere, Stewart to Trinity and B. D. T. Smith to Sidney Sussex, necessitating the suspension of Statute XXXVIII's requirement of morning prayer altogether on the understanding that Bonney, though now in his eighties and non-resident, would cope with evening services as he had 'nobly' volunteered to do.[242] Even worse threatened when at the age of forty-seven the College's lynchpin, E. W. (Ned) Lockhart, was placed in medical grade I and passed fit for military service.[243] The College which had kept its supreme servant busy and therefore sufficiently fit to be so graded was, for that very reason, in danger of losing his services. Having joined it at the age of fifteen, by 1918 Lockhart had been in the College for thirty-two years, as Library Clerk and Tutors' Clerk (1886), College Butler and General Superintendent of the Kitchen Department in succession to J. E. Merry (1911) and *de facto* Chief Clerk, serving as a model of that tradition of devoted, life-long service of which the coming century would provide further examples. When, in the first of these capacities, he had in 1900 requested a rise in his annual salary from £65 to £100, the Library Committee had gone so far as to describe as 'a misfortune' the possibility of losing the services of 'one who has, for so many years, done his work with great ability and fidelity, and who has had under his hands every volume in the Library and catalogued a large proportion', and the Council had accepted the offer of J. B. Mullinger (Librarian, 1883–1905) to provide from his own pocket £20 of the increase requested.[244] On his death in 1917 Mullinger would leave Lockhart £600 and all the contents of his house other than his silver plate.[245] Such was his reliability as amanuensis that scholars of the calibre of C. H. Firth entrusted him with the copying of seventeenth-century ballads;[246] such his indispensability that on the very day on which he wrote to the Visitor about chapel services the Master informed the military authorities that without Lockhart it would be impossible to continue to provide the cadets inhabiting New Court with their more mundane requirements.[247] Lockhart stayed. We shall meet him again.

For some Fellows, by early 1918 the pleasure of the company of military men at dinner was beginning to pall. Glover remarked that he now understood why an officer's mess had a band. 'It is like a restaurant now at

---

cigars – *We* shall I suppose have that': SJCA, D90.1288, p. 3. To his mind, the only question was, should the MAs bring coupons?

[242] *Eagle* xxxix (1917–18), 38; Scott to Visitor (F. H. Chase, bishop of Ely), 20 Jul. 1918 (SLB). A further difficulty arose regarding the release from military service of Smith's successor, R. P. Dodd MC, an army chaplain: Scott to Archbishop of Canterbury (Randall Davidson), 28 Jan. 1919 (ibid.).

[243] 'And what will the College be like without him?', Glover wondered: GD, 19 Jul. 1918.

[244] CM, 597/10.

[245] Will proved 12 Feb. 1918 (D11.33–4).

[246] Firth to Tanner, postcard of 14 Aug. 1910: SJCA, TU12.12.144.

[247] Scott to Col. H. J. Edwards, 20 Jul. 1918 (SLB). The reasons adduced were suggested by Edwards himself.

SJC.'[248] The continuing presence in College of naval officers after the Armistice created problems of a different sort, causing Scott to write to the authorities insisting that 'they shall be made to understand that as regards College life they are under our control and that if occasion arises the College has the power of removing them at once without question and without appeal.'[249] Glover as proctor had frequent dealings with them. In the spring of 1919 the College was seeking to put the War behind it, with Hall crowded again 'as one has not seen it since May term 1914', tipsy soldiers in the streets and the local prostitutes back in business, and on the feast of St John Bonney welcoming the warriors back. In October, at a service for the fallen in the Chapel 153 members of the College (including twenty of Glover's classical pupils) and of the Choir School and College Servants were remembered, amongst them G. E. Frost.[250]

1918 found Scott in his seventieth year, plagued by neuritis, and running down. Small matters were allowed to loom large: the gift of the Brucciani bust of Lady Margaret to the Chapel for one. When the Council came to discuss the wording and positioning of the inscription Larmor raised a number of objections and, in Scott's words, 'a good deal of heat developed'.[251] Scott's capitulation to the benefactor's preferences was taken by the growing number of his critics as further evidence of the feebleness they increasingly regarded as sapping his authority. Business was not brisk. In the December of that year the Council met three times in eight days. In the previous spring 'useless' and 'as futile as ever' were just two of Glover's descriptions of the Master. Meanwhile Heitland discoursed on Mrs Scott's failure to provide him with the moral stiffening he needed and on Leathem's 'thirst for power', while Glover noted Leathem's 'fretful arbitrariness' and Leathem told Glover that he was 'so sick of the Council he would leave SJC if he could.' In short, the College was settling down to the familiar divisions of peace-time.[252]

One such *casus belli* arose early in the year from the discovery of inequities in the payment of stipends, with the Master, Senior Bursar, Dean and 'one or two other officers' having their income tax paid for them and other Fellows not.[253] Another related to matters word of which had reached the ears of the Commemoration preacher in 1917. 'For ourselves', W. A. Cox had concluded his

---

[248] '… and Harker does not help to make it gay': GD, 18 Jan. 1918. For Alfred Harker FRS, 'one of the most taciturn of men', see G. G. Coulton, *Fourscore Years: An Autobiography* (Cambridge, 1943), 315.

[249] CM, 1041/12 (16 Dec. 1918); Scott to J. W. S. Anderson, The Admiralty, 6 Jun. 1919 (SLB). Sixteen sets of rooms were allotted to them on two New Court staircases: letters of 26 Dec. 1918 and 6 Jan. 1919 (ibid.).

[250] GD, 25 Apr., 3 May ('A captain of Gordon Highlanders, gownless, a bit tipsy, shouting he was not a conscientious objector, Ivy Cook at her old ways; a jolly rackety crew dancing jazz in Trinity St.'), 6 May, 26 Oct. 1919; *Eagle* xli (1919–20), 12–21, 52–3.

[251] CMM, 1021/2, 1022/5; M7.3.

[252] GD, 8 Feb., 26 & 30 Apr. 1918, 1 Mar. and 6 Jun. 1919.

[253] 'No visible reason other than usage [viz. payment from different funds]. The Master was definite in wishing that passed over – rarely definite': GD, 8 Mar. 1918. The matter ebbed to and fro, with Glover and Larmor leading the charge until in May 1918 it was agreed to appoint no more men with tax-free stipends: CM, 1024/4 (3 May 1918); GD, 24 May 1918. Details of the emoluments of the Master and Fellows had been circulated in November 1915, marked 'Very Confidential': SJCA, D90.921–2.

sermon on that occasion, 'we hope that our Courts and Halls will soon be filled again with students of the arts of peace, and that the broken thread of our old life will be gathered up. We hope, too, for various improvements in our studies and methods; and some of the best heads are already planning, rightly and wisely planning them.'[254]

6. RECONSTRUCTION

While hostilities continued, Tanner and Sikes (those 'best heads') hesitated to promote such improvements. At the outbreak of war, despite Larmor's attempt to reduce their number further, there had been three Tutors – Sikes, Bushe-Fox and Gregory – and, in Gregory's absence on military service, in October 1914 Tanner was temporarily recalled to the tutorial colours.[255] But the premature death of Loftus Bushe-Fox in March 1916 left just Sikes. Ten years after the College's oarsmen had flocked to Bushey's wedding, their successors could not be at his funeral. With undergraduate numbers low and falling, however, despite his disposition to be 'anxious and worried' 'just Sikes' was considered sufficient.[256] Then came the armistice and later that same month the death of Gregory.

To an institution bracing itself for the warriors' return the loss of its two younger Tutors was a grievous blow. 'His place will be hard to fill', it was written of Gregory, dead at thirty-nine after being gassed in France, 'particularly in these days when there is an exceptional need for virile teachers and men of wide and strong human sympathies.'[257] In addition, in association with Sikes in a tutorial duumvirate Gregory was to have played a central role in post-bellum St John's. Such was the preference expressed by Sikes – for 'not more than two Tutors (eventually, perhaps, one)', evidently including himself – in the course of a root-and-branch consideration of the tutorial structure associated with a discussion of teaching in Natural Sciences. This had been prompted in a memorandum presented to the Council in January 1918 by 'the increasing public interest in [the subject] and the great part which the College has already played in the advancement of scientific knowledge'.[258] During the year-long debate that followed, Sikes spoke in favour of 'the creation of a new type of College Officers, for whom I can find no other name than that of Assistant Tutors (broadly speaking, existing Directors of Studies in the larger subjects, four or five of them)', Tanner pronounced against an Oxford-style supreme Senior Tutor (who would 'possess the virtues and will probably develop the defects of the Managing Director of a Public Company or the General Manager of a Railway', a

---

[254] *Eagle* xxxviii (1916–17), 272–3.

[255] Undated notice with corrections in Sikes's hand (Sikes and Bushe-Fox to have eight freshmen each; Tanner to see other years until Gregory's return): SJCA, TU12.17.54 (?Oct. 1914).

[256] Leathem to Glover, 26 Apr. 1916; *Eagle* xxvii (1905–6), 409; Scott to Glover, 29 Mar. 1916; Anon., 'The College in war time: 1915–1917', *Eagle* xxxix (1917–18), 36–8.

[257] *Eagle* xxxvii (1915–16), 379–87; xl (1919), 117–20 (119; A. C. Seward).

[258] 'The Tutorial System' (SJCA, D90.938); CM, 1015/6 (25 Jan. 1918).

man 'officialised', 'entirely sacrificed to the system', 'a mere bureaucrat'), and the Council committed itself to the proposition that 'there should be closer personal touch than heretofore between junior members of the College working in any particular subject and Fellows interested in the same subject', namely a system of mentoring *avant la lettre*. At the end of it, in December 1918 approval was given to the establishment of a Praelectorship in Natural Science (to be occupied by a man 'whose position and influence are primarily due to his interest in research work'), W. H. R. Rivers was appointed to the new office, and the tutorial system was restructured round it, with up to five Tutors to be appointed over time 'as opportunity offers and suitable men become available'. This team was expected *inter alia* 'to play an important part in "keeping the place together"', with (*pace* Tanner) a Senior Tutor at their head, and with more of their routine tasks hived off to the Tutorial Bursar and the College office.[259]

As in 1900, there were those who hoped that the Praelectorship scheme would lead to further and significant changes. The mathematical Bursar, the Ulsterman Leathem, who had been one of the signatories to the January memorandum, and who earned Glover's easily earned disfavour during the passage of the measure,[260] was jubilant about the outcome and chided Tanner for not giving it greater prominence.[261] 'Meanwhile Rivers is hard at work, and there is already a new spirit in the College', he declared, while acknowledging the 'division of opinion that undoubtedly exists' regarding the first of a series of General College Meetings entitled 'College problems of reconstruction'.[262] These divisions ran at least three ways, with the traditionalist Tutors warily eyeing the modernizing scientists, and figures such as Glover (who found Rivers 'a bit doctrinaire and dogmatic')[263] hovering uneasily between the camps. Moreover, despite being Larmor's close ally Glover was haunted by a lingering suspicion that Larmor's associates, though doubtless first-class, were not first-rate.[264] Such sentiments were not uncommon. In the election of a Chancellor of the University in the year of Scott's victory over Larmor a vain attempt had been made to

---

[259] Tanner, 'Memorandum on the Tutorial System': SJCA, SBF54/Nat. Sci., CMM, 1023/3, 1025/7, 1039/6, 1041/4; 'Natural Sciences Teaching and the Tutorial System' (Committee report to GB, 2 Dec. 1918).

[260] 'Discussion [at College Council] of Leathem's Praelector in Sciences – Leathem as uncompromising as any Carson or John Dillon – won't abate jot or tittle of his will': GD, 26 Apr. 1918.

[261] Letter of 13 Jan. 1919: 'I wish we had announced the Rivers appointment first alone. As an isolated item it would have caught the eye and made more impression': SJCA, TU12.21.5; *Eagle* xliii (1923–4), 140.

[262] Leathem to Tanner, 17 Jan. 1919: SJCA, TU12.21.7; General College Meeting *Acta* of 16 Jan. 1919.

[263] GD, 17 Nov. 1919.

[264] GD, 31 Oct. 1919: 'How untrained the N. Sci. men are in mind and style'; 1 Nov. 1919: 'The essays written by the N. Sci. candidates generally show poor quality in literacy and thought'; 3 Nov. 1919: (of the four newly elected Fellows), 'Appleton (Physics) and Engledow (Mendelism) (…) wrote very trivial essays and evidently have not done any real thinking'; 19 Nov. 1919: 'New fellows are unsolved problems and I fancy there is a heavy philistine element among them.'

run a 'literary man' against the successful candidate, Rayleigh.[265] 'Strange, in an age of progress, when Cambridge is monotonously devoting her fellowships to young men trained in the Cavendish or bred to Mendelize, that people should still believe in the value of culture!', it had been observed in March 1915 of the establishment of the College's Patchett scholarships for proficiency in Greek and Latin.[266] In the event it all proved to be something of a false dawn owing to the cessation of Rivers's inspirational teaching on his death in June 1922 and the dimming of the lustre of the title through its association with Bromwich (of whom more below) as Praelector in Mathematics.[267] Paradoxically, it was the adaptation of the tutorial role necessitated by the establishment of the Praelectorship in this specific sense that was to have greater significance for the College in the coming decades.

Tanner signed the December 1918 report and continued as Tutorial Bursar until November 1920 when he resigned both from that office and as Honorary Lecturer in History.[268] It was typical of the man's hospitality that early in 1919 he and his wife should have had as house guests a near-contemporary, who quite expected his host to have forgotten all about him, and the son whom that father was anxious to have follow in his footsteps. As to the visiting boy, parent and teacher were both cautious in their estimates, the first describing him as unlikely to secure more than a good second ('for his mind is not built to specialise over much, and with plenty of intelligence it is character which will be his stronger side'), while the other (the headmaster of Sherborne), while referring to him as 'one of the best and nicest (…) I have ever had in my house', was careful not to over-egg the pudding – though he was inclined to think that 'his influence, whatever it is, will always be for good'.[269]

Whatever that influence may have been, and an unsystematic estimate suggests that it may have been not inconsiderable, Tanner may be said to have been fortunate in not being elected Master. Certainly it appears that Scott's reputation was not enhanced by the experience. Nor arguably would the reputations of any of those elected after him, at least in our period, in which only Benians and Boys Smith would fully realize the promise descried in them by others. An enthusiastic golfer throughout his career, Tanner spent most of the last ten years of his life improving his swing at Aldeburgh (in his years of maximum

[265] J. H. Gray to Tanner, 30 Mar. 1908, seeking his support for Lord Alverstone ('a keen billiards player': *ODNB*) and asking 'whether you don't see a fearful danger to the literary side of the University in the election of a scientist entirely in the hands of scientists?': SJCA, TU112.10.11. In the event there was no contest. Cf. Wood, *Glover*, 145–6.

[266] *CR*, xxxvi (1914–15), 230.

[267] 'Perhaps if everybody supervised in his [Rivers's] way there might be more to be said for the system': F. C. Bartlett's obituary of 'the best possible kind of friend to a few': *Eagle* xliii (1923–4), 12–14; also lxii, no. 269 (1968), 156–60. For his delight in and commitment to the Praelectorship: Shore, *Eagle* xliii. 11.

[268] SJCA, TU12.23.11–12.

[269] Boys Smith, *Memories*, 24; E. P. Boys Smith to Tanner, 7 Jan. and 1 Feb. 1919 (SJCA, TU12.21.2, TU12.21.89); Nowell Smith to Scott, 8 Feb. 1919: '… without being clever or quick – but rather slow – is nevertheless intelligent and refined. He may be too retiring to make any mark on the college, but I hope he will find congenial friends who will draw him out': SJCA, TU14.2/Boys Smith, J. S.

activity, his friend James Adam had known how to whet his appetite).[270] Yet
while reducing his handicap he contrived to remain a substantial figure on the
Cambridge scene. Having already been recruited by the University Press to sal-
vage the *Cambridge Medieval History*,[271] in 1926 and 1927 he was pleased to be
recalled to act as deputy for the ailing Regius Professor of Modern History, J. B.
Bury. 'Now he is not trying to run College, one finds him very mellow and
companionable; his gifts of sloth don't block you, and his charm *is* available',
Glover observed, generously for him.[272] Though later he would take the lead
in arranging a plaque for him in the chapel, the terms in which he remembered him at the time of his death (January 1931) were dispassionate rather than
affectionate.[273]

'It looks as if my boy will be very fortunate in the moment for going up to
Cambridge', Boys Smith *père* reflected early in 1919. With the War over, the
place would be 'just entering in full on a period of singular interest, with men
returning from service, and new vistas of thought and work opening out as perhaps never before.'[274] The record provides some support for this optimistic view.
In the University the two years after 1919 saw numbers of candidates for the history tripos increase from 17 to 168 and then 284. With 210 freshmen in residence
– to be compared with 75 in 1909 and 146 in 1929 – the first Michaelmas term
of peace was heralded by the innovation of a series of fortnightly lectures in
Hall intended for the whole College, alternating with concerts by the Musical
Society. From the ashes of the literary Portcullis Club there arose the debating
Gadflies, and as smoking concerts flourished, the Hall rang regularly with all
the airs from that infernal nonsense *Pinafore*.[275] Though Cunningham's recollection was that 'some things were lost',[276] with most of his contemporaries the
spirit of Boys Smith *père* prevailed. But not with Scott. Despite his inauguration
of the Lectures series with an account of the College's history, for him the lustre
of the age had departed.

[270] 'If I should become Professor James Adam, we will play GOLF twice a week': Adam
to Tanner, 28 Dec. 1905: SJCA, TU12.7.221. Adam was a candidate for the Regius
Chair of Greek, unsuccessful in the event: D. Robinson in C. Stray (ed.), *The Owl of
Minerva: The Cambridge Praelections of 1906* (Cambridge, 2005), 47–68.

[271] Linehan, 'Making of the *Cambridge Medieval History*', 472–7.

[272] GD, 9 Nov. 1921. Later he would remark on Tanner's admonition of him for
addressing Sikes at Hall as 'Sikes' rather than 'Mr President' as the action of the
'elder statesman as old buffer': GD, 30 Nov. 1925.

[273] 'His kindness to my father got my name entered for SJC schols in 1887; he was a good
friend in my younger days, though we differed after my return on SJC affairs, and
some others. Not a great man at all, he did a lot for SJC, in pulling it up from decline.
SJC has also suffered from his timidity, with Scott and Sikes always timid. But he
was kindly': GD, 16 Jan. 1931; 20 Oct. 1934.

[274] E. P. Boys Smith to Tanner: SJCA, TU12.21.89 (1 Feb. 1919).

[275] *Eagle* xli (1919–20), 38–43; xlii (1921–2), 198–203, 313–15; xliii (1923–4), 134–7.

[276] 'Manners changed, and even language lost some of its grace. The Lady Margaret
Boat Club was greeted for the first time as "Lady Maggie", and suchlike horrors':
'Memoir', SJCA, Arch.2.12a, p. 58.

I. MR GLOVER AND HIS DIARIES

SINCE there is rather a lot of T. R. Glover in what follows, it may be as well at this point to provide a word of explanation. The reason why there is rather a lot of him is that his diary, which he customarily wrote up every morning before breakfast, is the fullest continuous account of the College and its affairs between 1900 and 1943.

Glover was a man whose self-esteem was in constant need of injections of encouragement. As an undergraduate he had been an obsessive keeper of his own intellectual pulse, maintaining a weekly record of his hours spent studying, and clocking up 1,150 hours for Part II Classics. Perennially fretful about the sufficiency of his income, in his thirties he was regularly recording the mean temperature, lateness of trains, cost of taxis and attendance at his lectures. Haunted by the dread of penury, he jotted down the increased balance in his current account, 'for which one may be thankful', he noted at the outset of his career, adding: 'I hope I may not be fond of money, but death and fatherless children are ideas I do not forget.'[1] Here was a scholar whose moral health and peace of mind depended on his royalties returns. With Cavendish College bankrupted off the Cambridge map by 1900 and Magdalene tottering, the need for financial circumspection was acute. Fashion was seditious and needed close watching. Had not his own Uncle Hunter's petticoat business been 'killed by women wearing divided skirts instead'? *Facilis descensus Averno.* The following years brought reports of an unidentified former Fellow in the workhouse,[2] and of another (or perhaps the same man, Glover's classical predecessor, 'the once brilliant and popular H. R. Tottenham') dependent for sustenance on handouts from communal kitchens.[3] Along the way fears of revolution may further have increased the anxiety.[4]

Having him to dinner in the Magdalene lodge during the War, Benson found Glover 'a curious mixture of artist & puritan & philanthropist & egotist –

---

[1] GD, 1 Jun. 1892, 5 May 1901 (just a month before his failure to secure a University lectureship in Ancient History). Cf. his remarks in *Cambridge Retrospect*, 2–3, 106–7.

[2] GD, 7 Feb. 1902. 'There is an ex-Fellow, a high Classic, in the Workhouse now, poor beast he cannot get an old age pension. The Chaplain to the Workhouse suggested that he might come back as a classical lecturer but I said that at this time we were not wanting any. He is not on Boards and so (...) will not get asked to Old Boys dinner': Scott to Tanner, 5 Jul. 1908: SJCA, TU12.10.145.

[3] Cox to Scott, 11 Mar. 1918: SJCA, D90.1288. For Tottenham, see GD, 2 Feb. 1937 ('a Trinity man, pushed on to Mayor and SJC [...], lazy, clever, funny, likeable; married [...]; she died; he back to SJC, drank, was sacked 1901, and I came back'); more circumspectly, his obituary in *Eagle* 1 (1937), 70–1; more cordially, his remarks in *Cambridge Retrospect*, 58–62.

[4] 'The end is even nearer than we thought', R. V. Laurence of Trinity (later director of the future King George VI's studies) informed Tanner on 20 Aug. 1911, at the time of the threatened Railway Strike. 'Few echoes of the revolution have yet reached here [rural Hinton] but it is well to be prepared': SJCA, TU12.13.341.

with a dash of the bounder'.[5] Seven years later he had come to 'detest' him '& all
his works'.[6] By 1922, in his mid-fifties and with a wife and six children to support, Glover was despondent, increasingly curmudgeonly and frequently 'wondering whether, with income just now enough, and if I lose University lectureship, which is likely, some in time to come by inheritance, I can risk Cambridge
without a chair. It is all on plane of finance, and no clear light where most use, if
any use for me really left at all.'[7] In 1911 A. E. Housman had beaten him to the
Kennedy Chair of Latin,[8] and in 1919 he had withdrawn his application for the
Dixie (Ecclesiastical History), only to see J. P. Whitney ('prolix circumambient
irrelevant old dear') clamber aboard.[9] So the professorship of Ancient History
was the 'big issue' for 1925, though this time he was already preparing his hide
for the flaying and anticipating disappointment. 'I am making up my mind not
to chafe at doing without it, as it seems very likely I must. Years that bring the
philosophic mind.' 'Do they?' though, he wondered.[10] Then, sure enough, the
blow fell: F. E. Adcock was elected and the shutters closed. 'So', he reflected,
contemplating the illimitable acreage of 9 a.m. Greek and Latin Composition
classes reaching before him as far as the horizon, 'it is Comps for life.'[11] 'Perhaps [the electors] thought a neutral tint would be safer – a characteristic Cambridge view', he would later observe of another non-election, that of William
Ridgeway to the Regius chair of Greek.[12] What for the moment made that disappointment the sharper was the sense that this was one Cambridge chair contemplated by him that would not have necessitated exile from St John's. These
were Oxford sensibilities in a Cambridge setting.[13]

Later that year, indeed, he reported the opinion of a friend that he would
have done better at Oxford. 'But w^d be a square peg in round hole anywhere',

---

[5] 'I found his table [talk] fairly interesting, but his manners are poor – he is utterly
inattentive – he pursues his own thought & admires his own fancy. Still he is an able
man with a sort of stiff culture – & he gives me the idea of a moth trying to break
out of a chrysalis of narrow religious traditions. He has considerable intelligence but
curiously little charm of any kind': Diary 163, fo. 38 (24 Jan. 1917). Glover himself
enjoyed the evening: GD, 24 Jan. 1917.

[6] Benson Diary, 177, fo. 25 (31 Oct. 1924).

[7] GD, 13 May 1922.

[8] 'Fateful day', he noted on the day of the election, on receiving a 'dark nod only' from
the Registrary (E. Harrison) cycling past: GD, 18 Jan, 1911.

[9] GD, 9 Nov. 1927. Nearer to the time he was less indulgent: 'A dishonour to the Chair
and the first two professors': GD, 12 Apr. 1919. 'I used to dream of that Chair', he
wrote to Tanner (9 Apr. 1919: SJCA, TU12.21.125). His reasons for not persevering
with his application are hinted at (letters written but not posted etc.) in repeated
diary entries between January and April 1919; Wood, *Glover*, 141–2.

[10] GD, 1 Jan. & 10 Feb. 1925.

[11] GD, 26 Feb. & 3 Mar. 1925: 'I feel greatly at loose end for object in life now, if I am
to reach my father's age and fill in 25 more years somehow' (this at the very time of
Armitage's inglorious departure: below, p. 471).

[12] Glover, *Cambridge Retrospect*, 78: '"Safety first" is a Cambridge watchword, not quite
a heroic note.'

[13] 'I incline to stand for Chair [Regius of Greek], if it does not mean quitting St. Johns':
GD, 26 Sept. 1921.

he reflected.[14] Lacking the complacency needed for membership, he was never elected to the Book Club, the impotent successors of the old Seniors whose members' energies were now focused on vintages, for him a *closed* book. Glover was always vulnerable and, whenever he felt misprized, took comfort by casting himself as the outsider for whom the attractions of Canada and the United States were all but irresistible.[15] But interest in the psychology of the man is not the reason for this excursus into his career. It is instead, at least in part, what that psychology represents about the anxieties experienced by a whole generation of Cambridge scholars, at St John's as elsewhere, and about the strains that the New University Statutes of 1926 introduced into the University–College relationship.

'I have overestimated myself or wasted my gifts', Glover reflected at that time.[16] Albeit over the previous twenty-five years his family and the Baptist Union had compensated for academic disappointment, with the University's new arrangements sweeping away the blowsy security of the old it was the precariousness that came with them that lent a special edge and significance to Glover's musings, and distinguishes his diaries as a source from the *Reminiscences* of Henry Gunning, the confident placeholder of the previous century. The fact that at the age of sixty-three a scholar of Glover's seniority and achievement should have been kept in uncertainty as to his prospects for reappointment by the University for a further five years was not without significance for the health of the College. Forever on the *qui vive* for a sharp exchange,[17] Glover was nevertheless prepared to give Scott, and (at a stretch) even the College kitchens, credit.[18] By the same token, his diaries deserve credibility, even if (or, rather, precisely because) by contrast with his treatment of Baptist Union affairs and his fond descriptions of the artless antics of his young children, in the case of the College their usual mode and manner were critical. He was no respecter of Fellows. As Larmor warned him, he irritated the College bureaucrats.[19] In College terms there was something of the village atheist about the eminent Baptist. With his teetotal judgements dulcified on feast nights by potations from 'a syphon of soda and a jug of neat lemon juice', his jottings are littered with irreverent references to 'little White' ('appearance dreadfully against him'), to 'thinker Jeffreys' ('a man who has information behind a bad delivery'), to Winfield (a 'dull and commonplace person'), to the 'seedy' Ernest Foxwell ('a professional crank'), to the 'silent' Briggs '(the botanist)', and to Palmer, who 'chattered inanely'.[20] Recording

---

[14] GD, 27 May 1925. Cf. C. Stray, 'Curriculum and style in the collegiate university: Classics in nineteenth-century Oxbridge', *History of Universities* xvi/2 (2000), 200: 'There are certainly Cambridge classical scholars who might have been happier at Oxford: the most obvious example is perhaps ... T. R. Glover.'

[15] 'I have found Cambridge disappointing in various ways – Tory and uninspired, & also we are so conspicuously outsiders there': to his Mother, 20/21 Jul. 1903 (GC).

[16] GD, 8 Jun. 1926.

[17] E.g. regarding Larmor's objection that a certain previous decision of the Council had been provisional: Rivers: 'The one definite action of Council.' Larmor: 'If I had known, I should have raised this then.' Blackman: 'You did': GD, 9 Dec. 1921.

[18] 'Master spoke amusingly; dinner good': GD, 7 Nov. 1922. Cf. Wood, *Glover*, 222–3.

[19] GD, 8 Nov. 1926.

[20] GD, 12 Dec. 1922, 25 Jun. 1926, 23 Nov. 1924 ('At tea Thinker Jeffreys & [H. H.] Scullard (SJC) & [H. T.] Deas (Caius) 3 mutes on one sofa'); report of Ken North,

Paul Dirac on the occasion of his election to a Research Fellowship in 1927 as 'some sort of foreign N. Sci. man',[21] Glover noted the young physicist's enquiry after he had read the post-prandial grace, 'whether I had ever read Latin before', jotting down Dirac's opinion that 'he could do it better'.[22] He kept a wary eye on the clergy, particularly clerical deans, and *very* particularly Dean Stewart. Nor when he looked beyond the walls was he any more indulgent, on taking the 'bed-makers' own' tram home allowing himself the Gilbertian observation 'Few bedmakers are lovely or impressive.'[23] Miss Murray of Girton was 'dim'; Mrs Portway rather so.[24] But his old pupils treasured his eccentricities. Prompted by a wireless broadcast in the mid-thirties, one of them wrote commenting that his and Bernard Shaw's were the only talks worth listening to right to the end, recalling Glover's very first words to him ('Hullo! I suppose you are Oakley? Have you started your winter underclothing yet?') and remembering his lectures of a quarter of a century before.[25] As well as a curmudgeon, he was a conscientious purveyor of local and university gossip: regarding the vicar of Fulbourn offering twopenny dancing classes with a reduction for those taking Holy Communion; Scott's report of the Professor of Chemistry's domestic arrangements; the theft of Lapsley's clothes whilst 'bathing at sheds' and their later discovery at the door of his rooms in Trinity; the Master of Emmanuel's antecedents;[26] sundry tales of proctoring by the 'damn sound proctor' (namely himself);[27] and

Kitchen Clerk: 'Memoir' (SJCA, Arch.2.8.1); GD, 5 & 14 Nov. 1921, 16 Oct. 1922, 1 Jun. 1925, 16 Jan. & 27 Mar. 1933 ('Dined in Combination Room next Rapson, too near Palmer'). On dining in College after an absence of seventeen days, Palmer asks him, 'Do you notice much change in the College?': GD, 28 May 1936.

[21] GD, 7 Nov. 1927. Cf. Cunningham's recollection of Dirac's first evening as a Fellow: 'T. R. Glover said to him, "I hear you are the most eminent Bristolian in the College" (Glover was himself one). But Paul replied, "I did not know there were any others." Glover, taken aback, went on, "Well, there is Dr. Rootham" (Rootham was then the leading figure in Cambridge music). "Who is Dr. Rootham?" asked Paul': 'Memoir', SJCA, Arch.2.12a, p. 66.

[22] 'Modest man, too! Possibly right': GD, 22 Mar. 1933. He was perhaps alluding to the adoption of the 'new pronunciation' in the Senate House; at this date Glover had been Public Orator for fourteen years. On an earlier occasion, on being asked by Cockcroft at the beginning of dinner whether he considered himself an educated man, at the end of it Dirac answered in the negative 'because I don't know Latin': B. Jeffreys, *Eagle* lxii, no. 294 (1986), 69.

[23] GD, 31 May 1904. Cf. Glover, *Cambridge Retrospect*, 116–17.

[24] GD, 29 Oct. 1921, 5 Jun. 1925.

[25] During which 'we were irreverent enough to count the number of references to Canada and to Wordsworth. Tonight Canada scored 3, but what has happened to Wordsworth? He almost always beat Canada in the old days': F. C. Oakley (BA 1911) to Glover, 19 Dec. 1934. Cf. GD, 17 Jul. 1926 ('So early to bed in woollen pyjamas').

[26] GD, 24 Apr. 1902, 7 Nov. 1921 ('Master says that Prof. Sir William Pope [Prof. of Chemistry] keeps mistress and that was the cause of G. M. Bennett's quarrel [Fellow SJC, 1917–23]'), 9 Jun. 1927, 17 Sept. 1935, death of Peter Giles 'bastard of Aberdeenshire peasant and a good scholar' (Glover had heard this from J. R. P. Sclater while *en route* to Canada: GD, 2 Sept. 1925. Cf. *PBA* xxi [1935], 406 [equivocal notice]).

[27] 'Man outside theatre in Clare gown, which he thought was Emmanuel, and so he said he was Emmanuel – being Pembroke'; musical comedy at theatre 'plotless, pretty, trivial, the choruses all girls and legs'; 'Carnival scene, dancing, girls in shirts, green

his daughters turning Anglican, drinking sherry at weddings and powdering their faces,[28] all mixed up with everything else.

2. THE POST-BELLUM COLLEGE: THREE FELLOWS

For the post-war Scott the keynote was caution. 'Prefers caution to action, as always', Glover concluded after hearing his ruling as chairman of the University Lodging House Syndicate as to the location of a refuge for illegitimate children amongst University lodgings.[29] In fairness to Scott it must be said that, as well as by rheumatism and neuritis,[30] his life was made miserable by College problems, above all by those associated with two Fellows periodically in and out of lunatic asylums, and a third whose activities were largely extra-institutional.

As to the first of these – J. H. A. Hart, lecturer in Theology – the teetotal Glover had entertained doubts ever since discovering the man's wife at her supper with 'liqueur repairing [the] exhaustion of philanthropy'. From that day on – indeed until Hart's death as rector of the College living of Brandesburton almost fifty years later, when the local paper remembered him as a 'picturesque and revered figure' whose 'partiality to conversing in Greek or Hebrew [was] said to have embarrassed not only the rural clergy, but at least one archbishop' – either occasionally or serially Hart was to cause the College severe embarrassment.[31] According to Wilson Harris, the problem was religion.[32] In fact, Hart's difficulties were as much social as religious in nature and nonconformist with a small 'n'.[33] Indeed, for the son of the minister of the Independent Church at Oundle, the two aspects of the matter were formally inseparable. It is for that reason, as well as as an example of problems that may not have been peculiar to Hart in early twentieth-century St John's, that his case is entered into here.

with red beneath etc, prettier effect than diamond-patterned jazz lights. Saw crowd out. Bromwich is reported sane again': GD, 30 May, 11 and 17 Nov., 5 Dec. 1919.

[28] GD, 12 Jan. 1931, 28 Jun. 1941.

[29] GD, 9 Oct. 1919.

[30] GD, 25 Jan. 1918.

[31] 'Curious world. Sorry to see it': GD, 22 Apr. 1904 (Mrs [Katharine] Hart was a niece of the formidable H. M. Gwatkin); *Hull Daily Mail*, 17 Oct. 1952: 'a well known figure in black cassock and shaggy beard (...) [and] well known for his generosity, he was more than once the recipient of charity from passers by.' The *Eagle* carried no obituary. Brandesburton was not the most fortunate of college livings. Between 1848 and 1852 it had provided the discredited Charles Blick with a refuge: above, p. 233.

[32] 'Glover, in fact, taken for what he was, fitted in perfectly well at John's High Table, apart from one or two slight personal tensions. There was J. H. A. Hart, for example, long, lean, melancholy of aspect and a good Hebrew scholar. There was no reason why anyone should not like Hart. Most people, in fact, did like him. But for Glover the mark of the beast was on him. He had been born into a sound Nonconformist family and brought up on sound Nonconformist lines. In spite of that he had not only joined the Church of England but taken Orders in it. A renegade in Glover's eyes; it was more than Glover could quite forgive. There was no open warfare, but an alert armed neutrality on either side': Wilson Harris, *Life So Far*, 54–5 (mistakenly on the date of Hart's apostasy).

[33] Whence his complaint that 'the Theology faculty (...) put pressure on him to be ordained and cannot do anything for him if he isn't': GD, 8 Jul. 1904.

41 J. H. A. Hart, 'long, lean, melancholy of aspect and a good Hebrew scholar. There was no reason why anyone should not like Hart': SJCL, Port. IX.6

A Fellow of the College since 1902 and Librarian from 1905 (but at an annual stipend of only £50, half what Mullinger had received),[34] on the religious question Hart remained as the Faculty found him. 'Dark, obscure, askew', as Glover described him,[35] he launched himself on his low-level trajectory across the Johnian firmament. While boasting of having been 'more than ordinarily indiscreet at the Council', he would complain to Tanner of being overworked, underpaid and undervalued as a scholar.[36] By the summer of 1909 things were beginning to go wrong. To Russell-Smith, to whom he had leaked particulars of the Council's discussion of his prospects of election as a Research Fellow, he seemed 'an ass' for doing so. Then, one of his dinner guests 'carried off a silver matchbox' from the Combination Room and questions were raised about 'a curious series of malicious damage' done to books in the College Library. Although this was eventually otherwise accounted for, by May 1914, just three months after the birth of his youngest son, there was 'a good deal of talk in College' about his state of health and the 'general feeling' that his 'excitement, extravagance, and needless drinks [pointed] one way',[37] and that that way madness lay. By

---

[34] GD, 16 Oct. 1905.

[35] GD, 22 Oct. 1908.

[36] 'People in America and Germany know of my work but the College Council seems contemptuous of my teaching': SJCA, TUII.194 (14 Jun. 1909).

[37] Above, p. 440; GD, 13 Oct. 1911, 10 Oct. 1912, 19 May 1914.

mid-June 1914 his erratic behaviour had reached crisis point.[38] Six weeks later he was dispatched to Bedlam, and from there under escort to St Andrew's, Northampton, with only the clothes he stood up in and not so much as a toothbrush to his name.[39] 'Sad end', Glover remarked. In fact it was a sad beginning.

In the following summer Hart was doing vegetable gardening at his Norfolk home and enquiring after the possibility of similar work in the College garden, and a year later, having consulted Rivers's colleague the neurologist Henry Head, declared himself fit to resume his duties that Michaelmas. Head, however, was rather less sanguine regarding his prospects.[40] And as 1917 advanced, with Hart hoarding secret caches of drink and borrowing from the staff to purchase it, caution seemed justified.[41] A limit was reached and, at the end of January 1918, crossed when, on receipt of a complaint from the commanding officer of the military cadets stationed in St John's regarding Hart's 'mistaken hospitality' in plying the young men with excessive amounts of drink in his College rooms, Scott summoned Hart to the presence.[42] Hart's letter to Scott after the ensuing interview indicates how the conversation had gone:

> If we had no children I would resign my fellowship but I must hold it until I can find some other source of maintenance. With regard to the matter of my taking too much wine I can only plead that my wife has not yet discarded me though she knows or might know whatever I have done since I was admitted Fellow by Doctor C. Taylor in 1902 *decessore* John Lupton *pro domina fundatrice*. Perhaps I might suggest that if my character is worth defending I might appeal to the Visitor and cross-examine your witnesses by counsel or a next friend. As it is we go home when I can get journey money so that I may break down (as you say) somewhere else or find a means to pay my debts. I am, Your's faithfully, J. H. A. Hart.[43]

[38] Letter to Scott (17 Jun. 1914) complaining of 'the sore caused by the way in which my wife was approached (...). Resignation seemed my only course', recording the help received from Rivers, and reporting learning of his brother's death in Toronto: 'So I went off to some friends at Lowestoft on the Tuesday following and thence to Danzig on a cargo-steamer at their suggestion': M7.2.1.7.

[39] 'Learnt from Blackman and Leathem in turn that Hart is definitely insane – illusions and violence at St Pancras Hotel, and taken to Bedlam. Sad end. Sent Mrs Hart £10 to cover big things he had given me in past': GD, 31 Jul. 1914; Hart to Leathem, 19 Nov. 1914, penning some lines of verse on the recently deceased Lord Roberts of Kandahar, and concluding: 'Acheronta pertransivi'.

[40] Hart to Scott, 30 May 1915 (M7.2.1.14), 5 Jun. 1916; Head to Scott, 5 Jun. 1916 ('There is no doubt he is eccentric and erratic, but, as you say he was never like other people. [...] I think he will probably be able to take up work again next term. I am presuming that the classes will be small'): M7.2.2.12–13.

[41] GD, 5 Nov. 1917: Hart 'doing a lot of queer things'; Scott 'disturbed'; 16 Nov.: 'Shore tells me Hart's bedmaker wants to leave him – secret in his cupboards, i.e. cases of liquor from London. Poor fellow'; 23 Nov.: 'So he goes on, drinking and getting madder, unhelped'; 21 Dec.: 'Lockhart on Hart's doings – Hart has repaid him all but £70.' To his brother, T. B. Hart, Scott later reported that as well as borrowing from a college servant he had tried to do so 'from the merest acquaintances': SJCA, D90.1035 (16 Sept. 1919).

[42] Col. B. T. Ready to Scott, 31 Jan. 1918; Maj. A. L. Peebles to Scott, 1 Feb. 1918: M7.2.3.1–2.

[43] M7.2.3.3b (1 Feb. 1918); GD, 6 Feb. 1918.

Influenced by Leathem's judicious opinion,[44] if not cowed by Hart's half-veiled threat of involving the Visitor, the Council havered for months before agreeing at the end of July to require the resignation of his lectureship in return for a yearly pension of £100 for life and a three-year 'Taylor Research Fellowship in Divinity of £150 *per annum*.'[45] Glover, who considered Scott 'quite a nonentity in the chair' and his handling of the matter 'useless', reported on meeting after meeting at which the 'whole thing weltered, and then all [was] shelved for [a] fortnight,[46] while the saturnine Hart continued to haunt him, 'sour and contemptuous and "sick unto death"'.[47] Not until October did the Council learn that, having accepted its July offer, Hart was now off its hands and, as Leatham had acidly remarked to him, was 'free to devote all [his] energies to the really useful work of producing food for the nation.'[48]

By now, however, another problem was demanding Scott's attention, that of T. J. I'A. Bromwich, sometime Senior Wrangler, reported for various acts of insanity as well as for spreading the rumour that the Junior Bursar was 'marking down all the Fellows gradually for the asylum', for inciting undergraduates to throw one of his colleagues (J. R. Marrack) into the Cam for contemplating divorce, and for instructing the Head Porter to arrange a military funeral for yet another (Ernest Foxwell, the author of *English Express Trains*).[49] The letter from the Lowndean Professor, H. F. Baker, at the start of the Michaelmas Term 1919, enquiring why 'the College' had not done more for his mathematical colleague (Bromwich) over the recent vacation, touched Scott to the quick and occasioned a rather good question. What precisely, the Master wanted to know, did Baker suppose 'the College' amounted to in vacations? 'After the reception my efforts to avoid a scandal in Hart's case had met with I had determined to have nothing to do with Bromwich's case and to [t]his I adhered for some time.' But when Dr Bromwich called at the Lodge two and three times a day and often sat and babbled for something like an hour, and when Fellows of St John's and other colleges as well as College servants and police officers came complaining about him, he it was, he the Master, who had had to bear the brunt. Signed 'Yours faithfully', Scott's reply to Baker reveals the extent of the former's irritation and weariness as 'the College' returned to its old ways and Bromwich did to his.[50]

---

[44] 'The incident of the cadet is of so doubtful interpretation that we are bound in fairness to banish it from our minds in considering what course may now be rendered necessary by other circumstances. We know in what state the cadet left Mr H—'s rooms, we do not know in what state he entered them': M7.2.3.8 (27 Feb. 1918).

[45] In April the proposal had been £250 for three years and no pension.

[46] GD, 8 Feb; 1 Mar. ('Council 1¾ hours talking about Hart. H. F. Baker for letting him stay lecturer permanently but not lecture; Rootham not convinced he is mad yet; Larmor, mad only ⅓ of his time'); 19 Apr.; 14 Jun. 1918.

[47] GD, 10 Jun. 1918: 'Call from Hart to offer me 2 books, one by G. Friedlander, "he knows a damned sight more than you" … ejaculating "Christ Almighty!".'

[48] Letter of 20 Apr. 1918.

[49] Who 'instead of dying [was] presiding at examinations': GD, 18 & 26 Jun. 1919; 6 Oct. 1919 ('Bromwich after great extravagance and no savings, in asylum; Hart too').

[50] Letter of 6 Oct. 1919. Bromwich's sad decline continued, as reported by Glover on successive days in late May 1923: 'has felt it his duty to warn Charlesworth against Sikes and me'; 'is denouncing Shore as Autocrat of SJC, and me as his Viceroy';

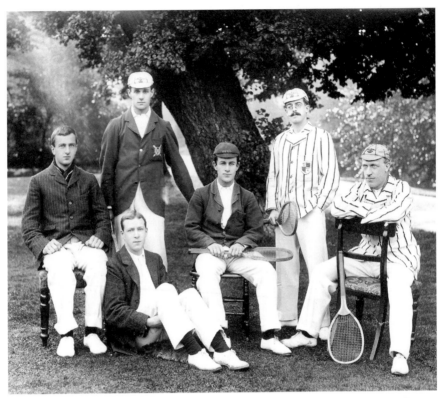

42 Tennis VI no date (*c.* 1900), including T. J. Bromwich and L. H. K. Bushe-Fox:
SJCL, Album 36/7

Although rowing and field sports and the reports of them in the *Eagle* were soon revived in the post-bellum College ('a hard worker, but apt to wash out at the finish'), such was the hiatus in the collective memory of the place, 'so many things [had] lapsed into oblivion', that as the Tanners were entertaining the Boys Smiths there was no one in College able to remember the rules of the Eagles Club, of which only two pre-War members had returned to College in 1919.[51] As the College obituaries of them emphasized, two of those who would have been able to do so, Bushe-Fox and the botanist Gregory, had both been vigorous as well as (though not everyone thought so) credible academics, but, above all, youngish, at least in spirit. 'There is always a disposition in certain quarters to regard a senior member of a College who takes the chair at Bump-suppers and constantly accepts invitations to undergraduate dinner-parties as a person not quite alive to the dignity of his position', the obituarist of the first of

'trying to rouse tutors and fetching in Dr Canney at 2am for a sick man, who proved well and asleep', culminating in a night in the police station before being committed to St Andrew's, Northampton.

[51] *Eagle* xl (1918–19), 141–5, 187; xliii (1923–4), 2; Eagles Club Minute Book (SJCA, SOC.21.1). The Eagles Club had been founded in the Lent term 1876 for lawn tennis players and with a limit of forty players: *Eagle* x (1876–8), 127–8. By 1883 its range had increased.

these wrote.[52] But, he insisted, the criticism could not be applied in the case of one whose 'very presence (...) was a guarantee that, though everyone was going to enjoy himself hugely, the academic proprieties would not be outraged.'[53] Gregory's obituarist described him in similar terms, as 'manly, direct and unconventional'.[54]

With the 'exceptional need for virile teachers and men of wide and strong human sympathies' in mind, the two men chosen to replace them were E. A. Benians and B. F. ('Basil') Armitage. Regarding the first of these College memory is clear. From all who knew him, the recently married Benians, elected in December 1918 to take office from that Christmas, drew tributes.[55]

Armitage was unconventional too, though not in the way that Gregory had been. Indeed, if unconventionality had been the only requirement Armitage would have survived his critics. It was in other respects that he failed to measure up to what the College had had in mind. As a Natural Sciences undergraduate and Tanner's tutorial pupil, by Hart's reckoning he was one of the elect.[56] Yet already his career was distinguished by havering and wavering, missed appointments, unanswered letters, unpaid bills, interventions in his favour by Dean Stewart, conviction for wilfully causing an obstruction in Jesus Lane 'by means of a certain bicycle', crises of confidence, thoughts of change of subject, and imagined calls to the religious life. The trouble had started before he had come up. Even to a medically unqualified Tutor it ought to have been clear that the 'unsettled state' into which he had slumped, the sense that he was 'groping about in a sort of fog', and the preoccupation with his own lines of thought which, when combined with dedication to the (running) track, and a bit of swimming and debating, had led to his missing laboratory sessions and in 1913 graduating without honours, were less than ideal auguries for an academic-cum-pastoral career.[57] Yet it was none other than Rivers, the distinguished experimental psychologist and anthropologist, Praelector in Natural Sciences and Gregory's successor on the Council, who caused it to be believed that Jesus College and University College London were bidding for Armitage's services and in May 1919 secured unanimous support for his election to a Tutorship and Fellowship for

---

[52] Though 'such persons do undoubtedly exist, and sometimes they are not desirable persons', he conceded: *Eagle* xxxvii (1915–16), 380–1.

[53] 'Not, be it observed, from any pedantic reverence for the letter of the law or its administrators, but out of respect and affection for the guest of the evening': ibid.

[54] *Eagle* xl (1918–19), 117.

[55] Above, p. 438ff.; CM, 1041/9.

[56] 'Nat. Sci. is the theology which is making real progress', Hart to Tanner, 14 Jun. 1909: SJCA, TU12.11.194.

[57] Many letters to Tanner of the years 1908–11, in SJCA, TU12.10–13. *passim*, e.g. 28 Feb. 1911: 'I missed the Chemistry lecture at the beginning of last week because a man, who was staying for a few days in Camb. ~~arrived~~ (and whom I had to see ⁿᵒᵗ ᶠᵒʳ ᵖˡᵉᵃˢᵘʳᵉ) arrived 35 mins. late for breakfast, and as his ~~was~~ time was full up for his remaining days I found it difficult to ask him to go': TU12.13.97. His success as a three-miler is recorded in the entry in *Eagle* (xxxi [1909–10], 267–8) which also chronicles N. B. Jopson's victory in the Freshman's 200 Yards; *Eagle* xxxii (1910–11), 244–5, 250, 329. After the inglorious conclusion of his undergraduate career he remained in Cambridge, engaging in conversation: 'Tea with B. F. Armitage talking of life and Christianity here', Glover noted on 12 Nov. 1913.

the statutory five years from that midsummer.[58] According to Donald Portway, the future Master of St Catharine's, who thought he had been offered the post, it was Armitage's bachelorhood that tipped the balance.[59]

There followed a series of approaches by Scott to the RAMC authorities requesting Lieut. Armitage's early demobilization in order to enable him to 'take charge of our medical and natural science' needs, and a flurry of letters from Armitage denouncing the corps as unbusinesslike and stating that his CO simply couldn't do without him.[60] Reaching Cambridge in the first week of October, he was just in time for term.[61] Apart from recording its further appointment of him to a supervisorship in Anatomy that October, again at Rivers's behest, for almost five years the Council minutes are silent on the subject of the nonchalant Mr Armitage: a telling indication of the inadequacy of college records for the purposes of college historians.

Off the record, it was a different story. Already, within two years, his credibility was reported to be chipped if not frayed.[62] Egregiously misquoting the College prayer, Armitage had promised at the time of his appointment to do his best 'for the furtherance of "good living and sound learning" in our old and famous foundation'. In the summer of 1924 he remained intent on at least part of his mission, conspiratorially assuring the Master that a particular pupil ought to have got a (low) First, informing him that he was off to Shrewsbury for the bumps and the ball, and protesting (perhaps a shade too ingratiatingly) the need for rest from his tutorial labours.[63] In correspondence with colleagues he regularly stressed the 'very serious view' he took of the need for scrupulous attention to his pupils' financial affairs. This no doubt was one of the reasons why parents continued to ask the Master 'to have their sons under him', as the Chaplain, E. E. Raven, assured Glover in early February 1924, shortly before the Council renewed his Tutorship for a further five years.[64] Splendidly installed in spacious quarters at E8 New Court, Armitage was full of optimism, declaring it his intention to 'continue to do my best for my college' and adding mysteriously: 'it is certainly pleasanter working with support than in the curious atmosphere of the past – the reasons for which, however, I fully understand.'[65] If this sounds ominous, it was, as had been revealed by the 'very melancholy story' he had told to the Master of Magdalene a few days earlier. With an annual income

[58] CM, 1056/2; GD, 26 & 30 May 1919.

[59] D. Portway, *Militant Don* (London), 1964, 93–4. Forty years on it continued to rankle with Portway that the College had failed to reimburse the expenses incurred in travelling from Devon for interview.

[60] Armitage to Scott, 7 Aug. 1919: SJCA, D90.1014.

[61] Armitage to Scott, May–Oct. 1919: SJCA, D90.1001–27; letter of 8 Jul. 1919 (SLB).

[62] 'Bromwich again in excited state, talking at large of undergraduates' disbelief in Armitage (which is pretty well established)': GD, 22 Jul. 1921.

[63] Armitage to Scott, 7 Jun. 1919 and 17 Jul. 1924: SJCA, D90.1003, 1511. ('I usually get some good men for the College on these occasions! I must have a break from some very heavy Tutorial work too.')

[64] E. g. letter to Tanner, 21 Jan. 1921: SJCA, TU 12.25.23; GD, 6 Feb. 1924.

[65] CM, 1175/3 (15 Feb. 1924); Armitage to Scott, 17 Feb. 1924: SJCA, D90.1446. 'I also have not cared for all the curious fads through which we have to plough our way', he added.

of about £600 he had 'spent recklessly, furnishing, entertaining' and was now £700 in debt and overdrawn by another £600 (almost £40,000 in today's money). 'He broke down and cried – said he lived in horror', Benson recorded, whom he then proceeded to touch for a loan of £100.[66] As to Armitage's credentials Benson was right – and not only regarding the loan, half of which, he later discovered, was spent on a subscription to the Athenaeum.[67] Then, in early November, just four months into his second lease, Armitage was brought to face the inevitable, submitting a letter of resignation, effective from June 1925.[68]

So what had happened in those four months? What, in particular, had caused Glover to describe him in August as a 'sickening fool'?[69] Because Glover was not on the College Council he had to depend on others for information, and others were not telling all. Thus on 25 October, 'Sikes says Council getting Armitage to go by December but conceals rest.' Part of the rest was that Scott had been desired by the Council to inform Armitage that 'they were unanimously of opinion that it would be well for [him] to submit [his] resignation.'[70] But a week later, 'Armitage, asked to resign, has not done so.' The Master was blamed for his 'foolish timidity'; he had had to be directed to press Armitage.[71] By now the Council had the measure of their man. Even so, he held out for another two weeks and two meetings. Only on 20 November was Glover able to record that his resignation was 'announced'.

In his reply to a letter from R. W. Seton-Watson of University College London a fortnight later, Scott summarized the whole sorry story and revealed that, having promoted Armitage's cause, almost immediately Rivers had revised his opinion, before the end of that first term telling 'some of us' that 'the appointment was a mistake and Armitage a failure'. Armitage himself was still 'under [the] delusion that matters as he puts it will "blow over"', Scott added.[72] Though as supervisor in a subject in which he himself had failed to satisfy the examiners he ought to have been at least well enough qualified to advise the weaker brethren, he had not even done this. He was negligent, frequently

---

[66] 'But even so bragged and boasted of having re-made the College. Said everyone was against him, and that they were all fools or rogues. Yet he spoke confidently of his being elected Master at the next vacancy. The man is I think more than slightly crazy, with a sort of megalomania. He seems to have been cadging round for money; but one can't really trust a word he says. There is a writ out against him. I ended by "lending" him £100 which I shall never see again. But he has no resources and no friends. I don't see how he is to be extricated. (...) The whole of his talk vain, inaccurate, disingenuous and egotistical': Benson Diary, 173, fos. 19–20 (25 Jan. 1924).

[67] Benson Diary, 174, fo. 41 (12 May 1924): 'I said plainly I hadn't given him money for that.'

[68] CM, 1192/3 (3 Nov. 1924).

[69] GD, 10 Aug. 1924 (recording a conversation with Arnold Lunn in Switzerland).

[70] GD, 25 Oct. 1924; Scott to Armitage, 25 Oct. 1924 (SLB).

[71] GD, 1 Nov. 1924; Scott to Armitage, 1 Nov. 1924 (SLB): 'I was directed to forward to you the following resolution: "That Mr Armitage be asked to reply definitely to the letter sent to him by the Council before the Council meeting to be held on Friday November 7th."'

[72] Scott to Seton-Watson, 3 Dec. 1924 (SLB). The reason for Seton-Watson's entitlement to an explanation is unexplained.

43 Eagles Club 1924. Scott with his usual hat. Also in evidence: middle row: E. E. Sikes, R. B. T. Craggs, E. E. Raven, L. H. Macklin, B. F. Armitage, unidentified; front row: second and third from left: G. A. Tait, O. R. Fulljames; second from right F. M. Eagles: SJCL, Album 17/15

absent,[73] unbusinesslike (the charge he had himself levied against the Medical Corps five years earlier) and irresponsible. Examination entries to the University had remained unentered and letters from schools unacknowledged until the climax had been reached earlier that term

> when there was an unfortunate disciplinary incident, with the details of which I need not trouble you. But the result was that our Council were confronted with the alternative of asking Armitage to resign or having at least one other officer tendering his resignation. They chose the former.

They did so regardless of the claims of illness that Armitage's father[74] and Armitage himself occasionally alleged, and despite his 'many good qualities' and being 'on excellent terms with the undergraduates and (...) well-meaning'. The whole business was 'most unfortunate and perhaps the most deplorable feature is the total inability of Armitage to recognise his short-coming' and the plain fact that he was 'frankly unsuited for the post of College Tutor in these days'.[75] But as to the nature of the final, fatal, clinching incident, Scott remained silent.

[73] 'As for his plea that he has had no proper holiday, that is simply ridiculous', Scott wrote, itemizing Armitage's absences in 'Western America', Switzerland etc.: ibid.

[74] E.g. William Armitage to Tanner, 15 Apr. 1922: SJCA, TU12.26.17.

[75] Scott to Seton-Watson, 3 Dec. 1924 (SLB).

A degree of compensation for his reticence is provided by two undergraduates who had different sorts of dealings with the man, and whose diaries contain something of the sort of information that Armitage's tutorial colleagues will have been beginning to assemble. One was Cecil Beaton. Beaton was Armitage's pupil, so on his first day of residence dutifully waited on him, reflecting before doing so:

> I'm really terribly lucky to be up here without having passed the exam & I'm awfully lucky in getting these nice rooms & they are so central. I *am* glad Daddy has such good whisky, because I think that's the reason that Arm: allows me here.[76]

He found 'Arm:' 'delightfully vague' and 'quite charming'. And the impression lasted, for all of a week.

Then though, after asking Beaton to call on him after Hall, Armitage kept him waiting for three hours. Beaton's unvarnished report of it demonstrates both the impossibility of (some) dons and the heroic patience of (some) undergraduates:

> I went to Armitage's rooms but such a crowd waiting that I rushed back again after Hall. Armitage was quite charming (...). He was amusing about Papa and Mama – & I liked him immensely. He asked me if I'd like to motor over to Harrow with him to see Juggins! Delightful! He asked me to come round again that night about a quarter to nine (...) Back in Armitage's room (...) I waited and waited & it was so cold. A telephone message to say Armitage would be in in another ¼ hr; ½ an hour & he wasn't there. Then at last he arrived & in his room spoke to another man, presumably his secretary until ¼ to 12! I was livid. So cold waiting, & wandering round the room looking over & over again at all the wretched things – 3 hours waiting. I was annoyed – & so cold & sleepy. When at last he did see me he nearly went to sleep – & yawned all the time! I thought he was very rude, but poor man I s'pose he was very busy, and it was nice of him to see me like this. (...) He looked at me and said 'You are a queer fish!' but I felt he was a damnably rude queer fish! Anyhow I liked him and I know he likes me, & particularly wants me to meet nice people who will do me *good*.[77]

And so things continued. Another week on and Beaton was coming round to the view that his Tutor had 'a terrible knack of keeping people waiting'.[78] When he came for his *exeat* at the end of his first term, he was regaled with an opprobrious account of someone about to become Armitage's colleague in

[76] CBD, 4 Oct. 1922. Here and elsewhere there is a problem with Beaton's assurance that the content of the published version of his diaries 'remains unaltered, though from time to time I have fused a number of entries to form a single recollection of a person or place': *The Wandering Years: Diaries: 1922–1939* (London, 1961), Introduction. E.g. ibid., 4: 'I'm fortunate to be up here at all, without having passed the exam, but I really feel that I'm up here on the strength of my father's charm.'

[77] CBD, 11 Oct. 1922. The entire incident is omitted from *The Wandering Years*.

[78] CBD, 18 Oct. 1922.

the Fellowship, described as 'very common, the son of a cheap village parson'.[79] Thereafter, Beaton seems rather to have lost interest in his Tutor, perhaps sensing in that preternatural way of his a certain lack of social grace in the man,[80] until calling on him late one afternoon during his first May Week he found him 'still in his pyjamas' – though 'he hopes to be able to come to the dance.'[81]

Whatever dance Armitage was hoping to come to, it wasn't the St John's Ball, which had finished earlier that day under the baton of Clifford Essex and his Band and Armitage's Presidency.[82] And the fact that the *Eagle*'s account of the occasion credits him with nothing beyond that office probably signifies how much of a cipher he had now become, undergraduates being generally rather good at identifying dead wood. The second diarist, L. H. Macklin, Beaton's senior by a year and as remote from him in sense and sentiment as any two undergraduates could be, was one of the stewards on that occasion. Although not one of Armitage's pupils, he was nevertheless in the habit of dropping in on him after a spot of night-climbing for a cup of tea, a cigar, a ceremonial wine, some amiable conversation[83] ... or for the loan of the keys of the powerful motor car that, according to Claude Guillebaud, Armitage had persuaded the dealers to let him have the use of in return for the business he said he could bring their way,[84] and which, so Macklin relates, he lent him and his friends when, after pronging a doubtless despondent Bump Supper and smoking a 'critical or scornful pipe over the descent of the First Boat every night',[85] 'having pranced round the Pemmer bonner' they returned to College, 'just in time to keep a 12'. Accordingly 'at 1.30 I left the Front Gate on a hare-brained expedition: Frank Law,[86] Fergus

[79] CBD, 7 Dec. 1922: 'Armitage said he didn't care for Arundell ...'. Beaton had thought D. D. Arundell (Fellow and Deputy Organist; 1923–9, whose father was nothing of the sort) 'quite good looking' though 'a trifle affected with the biggest trousers I've ever seen' and 'no manners': CBD, 3 & 30 Nov. 1922.

[80] To judge by A. Clara Armitage's painfully inscribed pencil-written letter to Tanner of February 1911, Armitage's native heath was that of Mr Salteena rather than of Old Salopian Balls and powerful motor cars. '[Hearing] of you that you are of a "kind and understanding heart", I will introduce myself to you as "Bernard Armitage's mother", which most boys think is the suitable attitude for a mother to assume!', she wrote, before, coming to the point (her son's unpaid account), regretting not having met Tanner in person on her recent visit to Cambridge ('but B. was never able to "point you out" to me'), and, sounding now like a parody of someone out of middle-period Dickens, concluding: 'I hope Bernard is being a credit to his parentage!': SJCA, TU12.13.62.

[81] CBD, 14 Jun. 1923: 'What a lot of fuss he makes about nothing.'

[82] *Eagle* xliii (1921–2), 137. In 1920, at the first May Ball since before the War, 'Mr Armitage appeared to think that his life depended on everyone having partners: if it did he saved it.': *Eagle* xli (1919–20), 233–4. The absence of reference to him in later years may suggest that he was less active and visible thereafter; cf. *Eagle* xlii (1920–1), 316; 43 (1921–2), no report.

[83] LHMD, 18 Nov. 1922, 16 Feb. 1923.

[84] Personal communication *c.* 1970.

[85] 'The First Boat was one of the worst the club has ever had': Foster *et al.*, *History of the Lady Margaret Boat Club*, I. 267; *Eagle* xliii (1923–4), 122–4.

[86] Matric. 1919, Captain of Boats in 1922–3 (whose 'enthusiasm and optimism [...] amazed those who realised the difficulties of his task': *Eagle* xliii (1923–4), 122–4), later ophthalmologist of distinction, d. 1987.

Dunlop,[87] Mick (D. H.) Sanderson[88] and I were let out by Armitage the Tutor to go for a run in his racing car, a 40 h.p. Hispano-Suiza.' Of 'our wild dash to Hunstanton', Macklin relates,

> at an average of 40 mph, with the speed needle occasionally touching 65, through the pitch darkness, of seeing the dawn break in the park at San-dringham, of trying to sleep on the beach at 4 am and of climbing into the Links Hotel to sleep in the lounge at 5, of our breakfast at 7, and of the run back to Cambridge, a distance of 65 miles which we covered in one hour 35 mins, I need hardly write; they are well imprinted on my memory.[89]

Quite possibly they came to be imprinted on the memory of Armitage's colleagues too, and, assuming that he was aware of them, figured amongst the reasons why a week later Glover gave him 'the long-delayed explanation' for concluding that he should not remain a Tutor.[90]

By then Armitage had already been regaling the Master of Magdalene with a colourful account of his 'wholly obscure and quarrelsome' College colleagues: 'Larmor secluded, shy, obstructive, complacent', Benson recorded him complaining:

> Liveing and Bonney over ninety. The rest mostly inefficient. Bromwich insane. Armitage talks as though he were himself invested with irresisti-ble influence and secret power. The dons conspire against him in vain. He unmasks and repudiates them. When he makes up his mind that a man is useless, that man has to go. He spoke of Cunningham as going about, talking and laughing and affecting to arrange matters, but A. adds 'He little knows he is doomed.' Rootham, whatever office is vacant, announces at large that he is too busy to accept it. (…) A. says with a smile that at all events since his accession the dons wash.[91]

When more than a year later the blow eventually fell, the ostensible grievance was extreme incompetence both in the discharge of his office and the conduct of his own affairs. But Beaton, who lamented the loss, had heard that there was more to it than that. 'Butler told me a lot about Armitage's debts but that isnt the only reason why he's gone. Poor old Armitage.'[92] What he thought the other reasons were, Beaton did not reveal.

Armitage's 'chief defect', Seton-Watson was informed, was 'want of method and concentration on the work in hand'. 'We have', said Scott, 'a special short-hand clerk and typewriter at the service of the Tutors, but if a man will not avail himself of this what can be done?' What

---

[87] Matric. 1919, not Lord Morton of Henryton of that name but the future President of the Slough Philharmonic Orchestra, d. 1980.

[88] Matric. 1920, farmer, d. 1969.

[89] LHMD, 9 Jun. 1923.

[90] GD, 15 Jun. 1923. On 23 May Glover, Armitage and Charlesworth had combined in urging Scott to have something done about Bromwich.

[91] Benson Diary, 170, fo. 46r (27 May 1923). (Bonney at this date was eighty-nine.)

[92] CBD, 2 Mar. 1925 (presumably R. D. W. Butler, matric. 1919).

44 G. D. Liveing (right).
Portrait by Sir George Reid

indeed?[93] Correspondence had accumulated and overwhelmed him; he had failed to master routines: defects of character which had been all too evident in his undergraduate years. The handing over of the side to his successor was strictly in keeping with all that had gone before. 'The one thing you have to be sure of is to keep your pupils' papers in order', he declared to Martin Charlesworth, flinging open a drawer of his desk and revealing quantities of ... socks.[94]

But it wasn't only socks that remained to be revealed. 'More (privately) on Armitage, who appears to have been partly mad, frightfully extravagant (bill of £150 at Roe's I learnt yesterday & no funds) and to have lied and done worse. Insanity has been a curse to SJC', Glover reported. It was one thing after another.[95] Benson, on whom Armitage called at this time, concurred: he was 'wholly unfit for any responsibility'.[96] In April there was talk of his being

---

[93] Scott to Seton-Watson, 3 Dec. 1924 (SLB). Armitage's only typed letter in the files is one of 1 Dec. 1920 to Lockhart reporting his discovery that part of his duty of interviewing entrance candidates had been taken over by Appleton (the future Nobel laureate), and enquiring why this had happened: SJCA, TU12.24.91.

[94] Recollection of W. O. Chadwick (conversation with the Author, 17 Sept. 2007).

[95] GD, 4 Mar. 1925. Roe's was Gilbert Roe, the furniture dealer.

[96] £1,500 in debt 'and he has I fancy taken to drink. I could not get him to the point. He was for ever pulling out papers, talking about all that he had done for St John's, the intrigues against him, his inadequate income (£700 a year), his necessary expenses

'£2000 in debt, writs coming in, a quiet settlement with creditors at 3/6 in £, sale next week of all his effects; and this a year after Sikes and the rest carried his re-appointment with 5 disagreeing.'[97] The fact that Sikes had not been one of those five (or three) may be attributable to either tutorial solidarity or anxiety not to be mistaken sartorially for Mr Toad, something of Armitage's raffishness having rubbed off on the older man, persuading him to overhaul his wardrobe.[98] Be that as it may, his initial stance can hardly have enhanced his reputation, furiously though he strove to distance himself from the wreckage thereafter.[99] Having found refuge with Stewart, the former Dean ('Oh dear! Let us have dignified Deans!'), Armitage continued to haunt the scene from the wings, engaging the assistance of the faithful Lockhart in outwitting the bailiffs ('It was very good of you to have given all that time to it, & to have watched my interests so carefully') as he moved from pillar to post ('next address Poste Restante Bexhill-on-Sea'), proffering advice to Cunningham on financial matters ('I think you ought to be very careful that *all* his bills are always paid up to date'), contemplating resuming his medical career and instructing Lockhart to procure old Third MB exam papers from Deighton Bell ('Please do not tell D. Bell & Co. who they are for'), and advising the proprietors of the *Daily Telegraph* on the design of their newspaper ('Under Lord Burnham's regime it was very bad in this respect'). 'Guts! Guts! Guts! dash, and drive – that is what is needed', he communicated from the Cavendish Club, W1, in June 1927. He was writing about the LMBC, though it might equally have been about himself.[100]

That was not quite the end of Armitage. On Benians's election as Master in 1933 he reappeared, anxious to explain 'the frightful state of confusion [he had been in] like a nightmare of the past', and intent on describing how much better he was now. Four months later there followed a painful seventeen-page apologia appealing to their shared 'happy Portcullis days' and begging Benians to support the application he had been 'advised' to make for appointment as

(...) He said that all he wanted was a guarantee. He said he had a good appointment promised him, that there are writs out against him, and if the College doesn't help he will be done for. One can't trust a word he says, unfortunately. He says his furniture is worth £1500, but he has taken no steps to sell it. (...) He owes me £80, which he promised to repay 8 months ago. He has no conscience, he is helplessly extravagant, and is wholly unfit for any responsibility': Benson Diary, 179, fo. 18r. (15 Mar. 1925).

[97] Benson Diary, 11 Apr. 1925. Despite repeating Glover's testimony of 15 Feb. 1924 ('Council reappointed the ass Armitage though 5 against [Shore, Blackman, Bartlett, Engledow, Creed]'), '5 disagreeing' cannot be right. CM, 1175/3 records a vote of 9 to 3, by Statute XX the minimum required for reappointment. At the same February meeting the Council refused to reconsider Bromwich's case, despite Bromwich's threat of causing a public scandal: CM, 1175/2 and attachment.

[98] 'Sikes looked in about 7pm in golf coat; he says youth of his acquaintance disapprove of our costumes, don't approve brown boots with gray trousers, and other ways of ours': GD, 23 Sept. 1922.

[99] 'We have had a rather hectic fortnight, tutorially; but all is now over, including the worst of BWFA's leavings to us': Sikes to Glover, 21 Mar. 1925 (SJCL, unclass., Sikes papers; no such letter survives amongst Glover's).

[100] SJCA, TU12.29.10–11; 31.6; 31.22; 32.31.

medical tutor at Magdalen College Oxford.[101] In 1945 he was told he was not to dine at the Fellows' table in future.[102] Later on, contemporaries and ex-pupils would report rumours even darker than administrative incompetence, hint at a somewhat louche reputation, talk of intimacy with the Prince of Wales, and of borrowing from pupils, even of homosexual tendencies – though had such really been the case it is hardly likely that Hilary Macklin would have been in the habit of dropping in on him at three in the morning for a chat about 'the College in general'.[103] Quite the contrary: on Macklin's evidence the rootless Armitage was seen as a pathetic and largely harmless figure of fun.[104] Rather like Widmerpool, Anthony Powell's equally socially buoyant but rather more upwardly mobile creation, Armitage had a way of cropping up. In 1955 the newly appointed headmaster of Gresham's School Holt received a 'prodigious letter from an Old Johnian, whom I feel sure I ought to know by repute if not to speak to'.[105]

The Armitage affair has been gone into at some length for one reason above all, namely what his appointment to the Tutorship in 1919, being 'personally unknown to the majority of the Council' as Seton-Watson was informed, tells us about the government of the College less than half-way through Scott's Mastership.[106] It was this, rather than Armitage's inability to recognize his own shortcomings, that was its 'most unfortunate and perhaps most deplorable feature'. Moreover, the fact that at the Council meeting in question Tanner, Armitage's former Tutor, evidently said nothing about the man's habit of living his life in arrears says something about Tanner.[107] A further insight is provided by the coincidence in the autumn of 1924 of Armitage's dismissal and flight with the last weeks of Liveing after he was run over by a woman cyclist while on his way to work. By now approaching ninety-seven – 'he had known Tatham elected Orator in 1815', Glover noted – the stricken President offered the Master his resignation, only to be told by Scott, not entirely jokingly perhaps, that if he accepted the President's the College would ask for his.[108] The tension between Scott and Larmor had not abated. In 1917 Liveing himself had

[101] Armitage to Benians, 7 Dec. 1933; 27 Mar. 1934 (EABP). With all its crossings-out, Benians's draft reply, perhaps never brought to a fair copy, might be thought a masterpiece of tutorial dissembling.

[102] Charlesworth to Armitage, 31 May 1945, attached to CM, 1801/11.

[103] LHMD, 23 Jun. 1923. For the strength of Macklin's feelings on that subject, see below, n. 128.

[104] 'Armitage came in last night to [G. A. D.] Tait's rooms, where he and I were working – at about 11pm and stayed talking the most extraordinary nonsense, and being very laughable till 2 am': LMHD, 26 Nov. 1922. Later that morning they breakfasted with him, Sir Arthur Stanley (Governor of Victoria) and others.

[105] '... Armitage by name. If I do manage to come up in the near future, I should be glad if you could spare a moment to tell me something about him': L. Bruce Lockhart to Wordie, 15 Jul. 1955: SJCA, tut. file/Bruce Lockhart.

[106] Scott to Seton-Watson, 3 Dec. 1924 (SLB).

[107] CM, 1056/2. It was Tanner's penultimate meeting.

[108] GD, 11 & 27 Oct., 26 Dec. 1924. He had been in mid-season form at the previous 6 May, according to Benson: 'A wonderful sight, like a Blake picture of Job. After dinner he *ran* back to the University Arms': Diary, 174, fo. 37 (6 May 1924).

45 Men of confidence. Sir Joseph Larmor (right) and Arthur Balfour, former Prime Minister, at the Royal Society Jubilee, 1913. But Larmor would not walk with his Master.

written to Larmor on behalf of 'a very large number of the resident fellows of our College' urging the knighted Unionist MP for the University to agree to offer himself for membership of the Council at the forthcoming election. The result of that contest was greeted by an unnamed junior Fellow as 'a sweeping Progressive victory'.[109] At Liveing's funeral Larmor declined to walk with Scott, despite Cunningham's efforts to repair the breach, and thereafter – reportedly from 'distaste for being 2nd to Scott' – spurned the invitation to follow Liveing as President. 'They jar each other', Benians observed.[110] After much to-ing and fro-ing over a period of two months, with Larmor pressing for Glover, Sikes was elected President on the day on which Armitage's resignation was recorded. Charlesworth, Armitage's successor as well as his polar opposite, was a convivial rather than an outlandish figure. Outlandish Tutors would be out of fashion for some time at St John's.[111]

---

[109] In the name of twenty-two fellows (half the Fellowship), the President's observation – that 'I do this very willingly because I feel with the other fellows that we specially need the help of your experience and judgment at the present time and the near future' – might have been construed as implying less than total confidence in the Master: letter of 9 May 1917 (SJCL, Misc. Letters/Liveing, 9). Result: Larmor 23; Glover 14; Rootham 14; Baker 13; Marr 12: GD, 2 Jun. 1917.

[110] GD, 23, 24, 26 Jan. 1925.

[111] GD, 27 Feb. 1925; CM, 1201/2–4.

3. TWO UNDERGRADUATES

Alike only in their unawareness of these developments, the undergraduate dia-
rists Macklin and Beaton were polar opposites too. While contemplating how
to deal with an absolute blister or give a temporary girl-friend the old heave-ho,
the former's pronouncements provide a rather B. Woosterish account of himself.[112] The other reeks of Firbank. Shipwrecked for three years (and in Beaton's
case emerging from the experience without so much as a degree) in 'a university town of which we know very little' (Macklin's words,[113] much as remains
the case today), neither socially or emotionally did the pair have anything in
common. Their interests diverged as widely as their upbringing. Whereas (as
he remarked on his third day at St John's) Beaton 'used to worry and wonder if
people had soft lips etc. [but now wondered] about their temperament', what
preoccupied Macklin as he returned into residence for his second year was the
thought of seeing his friends again that evening and re-rowing the Henley
course together.[114] While Beaton was wondering how cottagey to make his
lodgings and what pastel shades to experiment with next, Macklin's practical
mother was there advising her son on the subject of cushions and curtains.[115] As
Macklin and two friends biked to Ely on the Sunday two weekends later, and
after an 'epic' ride with one front lamp between them returned to St John's just
in time for Macklin (a choral scholar) to make evensong, Beaton was in Oxford
in the arms of his 'perfect' boy-friend.[116] While the one derived pleasure from
rowing for the first time on a sliding seat, the other experienced fulfilment on
dry land.[117]

Macklin, who as a boy had lost his father and in the last month of the War
his elder brother,[118] and the medical condition of whose younger sibling made
him especially protective of his mother, was particularly at home in his College
room on the November Sunday on which

> I had some people to breakfast with [B. E. A.] Vigers: then a good chapel
> with Harwood in E minor for the service; and then a thoroughly cosy and
> comfortable afternoon in an armchair by a warm fire after a simple lunch
> and some candles, a pleasant companion – John [R. M.] Simmons – a
> copy of the 'Observer', a pipe and a good book: what more could a man
> want? (26 Nov. 1922)

or on an October Friday, savouring

---

[112] 'Berridge is a bounder (...), he must be cut'; 'A fellow can't go to a girl and tell her
flatly that he doesn't care for her in the way she seems to care for him': LHMD, 10 &
12 Oct. 1922, 9 Mar. 1923.

[113] LHMD, 14 Jan. 1922. (Macklin was up from 1921 to 1924; his diary runs from
September 1920 to February 1924.)

[114] CBD, 6 Oct. 1922 (omitted from *The Wandering Years*); LHMD, 7 Oct. 1922.

[115] Beaton, *The Wandering Years*, 6; LHMD, 7 Oct. 1922.

[116] Ibid.

[117] LHMD, 16 & 21 Feb. 1922; CBD, 22 Oct. 1922.

[118] *Eagle* xxxix (1918–19), 228–34.

the joy of Cambridge when a new term and a new year begins ... A cosy fireside with its environment of treasured possessions – my own and no one else's – and the smoke of half a dozen pipes (12 Oct. 1923).

The domestic tendency amongst undergraduates was materially encouraged by the practice of retaining particular rooms for two years or even longer, thereby keeping the same gyp and coming to regard him as your retainer.[119] What more *could* a man want? Well, not much – unless one were a Beaton, whose family was intact and prosperous and for whom pipes in any numbers, if not candles, were anathema.[120]

Another thing Beaton could not abide, no doubt because his father favoured it, was Scotch,[121] which was the occasional tipple of the Stormy Petrels too, just as the pouch of shag was their regular solace. Members of the Stormy Petrels Club divided their time between Drones-like nocturnal japes involving boulders of coal cascading down the well of the Wedding Cake, decoration of the pinnacles of New Court with eighteen of Trinity's wooden lavatory-seats (a feat of such 'skill and daring' that even Johnian loyalists attributed at least part of the credit to Trinity),[122] and the removal of the oak of a hapless officer of the Christian Union and in accordance with college tradition its affixing to Dean Creed's door at the top of E Second,[123] not to mention play-reading evenings.[124] Dean Creed, who, coming from Caius and being elected on the very day on which compulsory chapel was abolished and his natural quarry liberated, may not have been prepared for such rough-and-tumble, was certainly not the 'stupid little man' that Beaton thought him.[125] His walking of Macklin round the Backs, for example, was a well-judged exercise in decanal destabilization.[126] But 'Jimmy' Creed was no match for the Stormy Petrels, who after their evening's exploits

---

[119] Thus Macklin kept at K7 Second from Michaelmas 1922 until Easter 1924, while his successor in the set, A. N. Newell, enjoyed it for twice as long. On the importance of such 'undergraduate sanctuaries', see Deslandes, *Oxbridge Men*, 63, 71–2.

[120] 'People smoked pipes (at the Harrow dinner) which I thought was disgusting': CBD, 3 Nov. 1922.

[121] 'God forbid that he [his boyfriend] should take to whiskey', he declared: 'I must talk to him lest he kills his soul with heartiness': CBD, 13 Oct. 1922.

[122] LHMD, 3–4 May 1922, reporting an overheard conversation between Sikes and Palmer, the Head Porter, to the effect that 'there must have been at least 8 or 9 men in it [in fact, 3 or 4], and that they must have been some Johnians and some Trinity, as the raid could not have been carried out without collaboration in both Colleges. We consider this a very high compliment to our skill and daring.' Cf. GD, 3 May 1922: 'Heard how Trinity men put 27 seats from Trinity closets on pinnacles of our New Court last night': revealing that Macklin had the edge in respect of the counting of lavatory seats and Glover in that of chronology.

[123] LHMD, 16 Feb., 2 Dec. 1922. The practice was not exclusive to St John's (above, p. 303): in 1880 an incident at University College Oxford led to the sending down of the whole college and national interest in the matter: L. Mitchell, 'The Screwing-up of the Dean', *University College Record* xi (1995–6), no. 4, pp. 69–81.

[124] 'We decided to adopt a more serious tone, and have some literary readings – and not only social rags and binges': LHMD, 16 Oct. 1922.

[125] CM, 1048/9; CBD, 25 Oct. 1922.

[126] 'I cannot quite understand his motive in asking me', Macklin remarked, a shade disingenuously perhaps: LHMD, 20 Feb. 1923.

were wont to return to the security of their snug College room as though to the refuge of a Greyfriars study.[127]

As the Petrels concluded their latest dawn-raid or session of sitting up putting the College to rights there would have been nothing to be seen of the languid Beaton, whose idea of a strenuous morning was to snuggle down under the covers with the next chapter of *Sinister Street* before betaking himself to the ADC where most of his waking hours were spent, a place apostrophized by Macklin as a haunt of 'homosexualists', in the company of Steven ('Queenie') Runciman and other exotics.[128] To that extent Beaton was fortunate to escape the fate of the 'rather offensive aesthete' whose 'extraordinarily long hair' provoked the Petrels into cutting a lock of it 'by way of a gentle hint'.[129] Beaton was committed to aesthetics, whatever they were,[130] and was reading for the Ordinary Degree. While Beaton scoured the city for goldfish to keep him company, Macklin preferred budgerigars from Gamages, presumably for their more wholesome reputation rather than on account of the loneliness that had haunted Thomas Whytehead a century before. (Neither species had it yet occurred to the College to prohibit.)[131] Only in the most strained sense might they be said to have shared an interest in music, in which both as a choral scholar and otherwise Macklin was a significant contributor to the place and, in the spirit in which pre-War oarsmen had complained about the excessive musicality of the May Concert, also the occasional severe critic of the Organist Cyril Rootham, 'that conceited faddist' whose aversion to familiar hymn-tunes he blamed for the thinness of chapel attendance. 'As it is without doubt desirable to make the Chapel a centre of College life, and a type of esprit-de-corps', Macklin affirmed, 'the wishes of the majority should be more closely consulted.'[132]

Macklin's vision of a chapel-centred college was perhaps overly nostalgic. Since the removal of that compulsion, Hall provided the one remaining collegiate forum, or focus of discontent. Thus, in the Michaelmas Term 1920 an increase of the charge for dinner to 3s 2d occasioned a protest by the undergraduate Kitchen Committee. Pressing for a three-course 3s meal with better food, it was signed by M. P. Roseveare and just four undergraduates, perhaps because it was suppressed by the authorities before the mutiny spread, perhaps because

---

[127] Creed 'was not really at his best in dealing with unruly undergraduates, though' – according to J. F. Bethune-Baker – 'they recognised and respected his principles and sense of justice', *PBA* xxvi (1940), 520.

[128] CBD, 14 Oct. 1922 ('Sinister Street'), 1 Nov. 1922: '... did rather a dreadful thing. I lay on the bed under the eiderdown & slept till after ¼ past 4!'; 'The place smells of that most nauseating of vices – homosexualism': LHMD, 18 Nov. 1923; CBD, 30 Nov., 3 Dec. 1922.

[129] LHMD, 21 Oct. 1922: 'I then retired to bed, being, I regret to say somewhat jagged and having had considerable difficulty in mounting my staircase even with the aid of a broomstick which I had somehow acquired.'

[130] 'It's a very muddling subject aesthetics': CBD, 21 Jan. 1922.

[131] CBD, 17 Jan. 1922; LHMD, 4 Apr. 1922. Cf. above, p. 294, and Tanner's Tutors' Instructions: 'Dogs are not allowed in College; but a man may keep a cat with the permission of his Tutor. Permission to keep more unusual animals (e.g. monkeys) must be obtained from (and will be refused by) the Junior Bursar': SJCA, TU1.9.18 (Apr. 1912).

[132] Above, p. 433; LHMD, 23 Nov. 1922.

Benians was successful in removing the cause of it.[133] But Hall meant one thing for the secure young boat-club blood and quite another for the distracted aesthete who in the course of his first fortnight of residence found the place full of people who 'looked and spoke so common' and, apart from the Grassy Corner Pudding, food that was 'perfectly filthy'. In any case, he didn't go there for sustenance but to gaze at nice-looking boys[134] and the 'really sweet' old men on the daïs serene.[135] Hall was not for the arty. 'Hall was fairly amusing this evening', Beaton conceded. 'I s'pose it was because I was feeling rather hearty.'[136] But for Beaton sensations such as that were unfamiliar. And between him at one extreme and the Stormy Petrels at the other lay the great mass of undergraduates whose names are writ on the pages of the JCR Suggestions Book of the period.

4. THE DOMESTIC SCENE

After all, it was 'only thirty years from the Middle Ages', Rivers observed to Glover early in 1904 in the course of a 'private homily' on the subject of 'progress in the University'. He was evidently referring to the end of 'medieval celibacy'.[137] With many of the dons now married, Hall as an institution was going the way of Chapel. Even before the War the diet, the company and the home fires had been taking their toll. Alison 'would not go to hall as he disliked the stodge & found dons oppressive. I can understand it,' wrote Glover. 'Marriage has thinned and dulled the table.' Leisurely commensality had surrendered to matrimony. On acquiring a wife the geologist J. E. Marr had even resigned from that sanctuary of tradition, the Book Club.[138] Married Fellows were labelled 'day boys'. 'I cannot afford this Term to give two hours every evening to come to Hall', H. F. Baker decided in 1906, and ten years earlier, when L. E. Shore had attempted to liven things up by instituting 'Invitation nights' (to include an extra course, simple dessert, wine and whist), it came to nothing. Although a majority of Fellows declared themselves in favour of the measure in principle, in practice discussion came to centre on the impossibility of finding an evening of

---

[133] SJCA, TU12.24.90; below, n. 172. Previously there had been four courses for 2/9d: TU12.24.20.

[134] CBD, 6, 8, 9 & 15 Oct. 1922: 'v. good looking youth sat opposite but he was so coldblooded I was nearly ill'. Cf. the explanation provided by the headmaster of Eastbourne College (Stephen Foot) for Hugh Casson's having left school early: 'Small and rather good looking he was in fact rather too attractive for Public School life. (…) The difficulties of an attractive boy at the Public School age are much greater than at any other time in his life': letter to M. P. Charlesworth, 13 Jul. 1928 (SJCA, tut. file/H. Casson).

[135] 'One (don) in particular might have been painted by Tintoretto: he had a straight nose and deep, hollow eyes with huge pouches under them': CBD, 1 Dec. 1922. This sounds like Liveing.

[136] CBD, 17 Oct. 1922. Ten days earlier he had agreed with a friend 'how it would have been much nicer [at Harrow] if we'd been more hearty.'

[137] GD, 22 Mar. 1904.

[138] GD, 26, 28 Apr. 1902. Marr: *ODNB* (D. Oldroyd). By 1902 'the Book' was powerless other than in the eyes of Fellows not members of it. And so it remains.

the week likely to prove generally acceptable, and no one voted for Sundays.[139]
By then numbers in the Long Vac were already down to single figures.[140] Earlier still, when Hall on Sundays was at 6 p.m. and Chapel at 7.15, a proposal
headed by Alfred Marshall to move the hour of eating to a later hour had been
thwarted by the opposition of the servants. Likewise for the undergraduates,
the hour of whose dinner had been under consideration since February 1889.
Following a petition of the Dinner Committee and about 130 'other students', in
1881 undergraduates were enabled to sign themselves out from Hall on up to two
days a week, but not on Sundays. In 1889, on the motion of Heitland and Bateson, the hour of the Sunday second Hall was moved from 4 to 6 with evensong
following, and ten years later to 7.15 (changed in 1908 to 7.30), with evensong
preceding.[141]

One further disincentive to dining was provided by the availability of lunch,
a communal concession to the later hour of dinner (albeit at the individual's
own expense, not taken as part of Fellow's commons);[142] another by the danger
of encountering there one or other relict of a past age. Of these probably the
most notable was A. J. Stevens, memorably recalled by John Boys Smith, his
neighbour in Third Court, with a mixture of indulgence and despair:

> When he died [in 1931] and the rooms [occupied by him since 1883] were
> being cleared, a robin's nest was found behind one of the pictures (I saw
> it myself), and on a leather-covered settee, the leather grown colourless,
> there was a sharply defined patch still bright red, where papers had lain
> through the years as colour faded from the areas around them.[143]

For Boys Smith, Stevens personified the worst features of the old system of Life
Fellowships. So did he for Stevens's companions at table, where during Mason's
presidency he regularly read the post-prandial grace, very badly, the personification of Macaulay's 'pitiable being, an old fellow of a college'. 'Dear old Stevens
was up all this Vac.', Scott informed Glover in 1897. 'He has now added two
sniffs to his other variations on the ordinary form of Grace after Meat so that
the performance is more unique than ever.'[144] 'The marriage of so many of the
livelier members of the society has left Hall rather dull', Glover observed on
his return from Canada – though 'the old unpunctuality due to desire to avoid

[139] GD, 10 Jan. 1907; 26 Apr. 1902; Baker to Tanner, 7 Jan. 1906: SJCA, TU 12.8.25;
SJCA, D100.69.b ('Invitation nights'; 1896); CM, 463/12.

[140] Fellows Menu Book, 1919–21 (SJCA, SD17.1).

[141] CMM, 412/5 (25 May 1894); 429/9; D100.60, 'Report of the Committee appointed to
consider the hours of Hall on Sunday' (Dec. 1894); Tutors' Instructions 1883, SJCA,
TU1.9.13, pp. 28–9; CMM, 237/5, 241/5, 790/5, 796/4.

[142] CM, 1272/3(b) (20 Jan. 1928). As to junior members, 'lunch in hall draws some 100
men a day, a change in social habits since our undergraduate days': GD, 25 Oct. 1929.
Eight years earlier, Glover had taken 'lunch in hall, for the first time', he said (incor-
rectly): ibid., 28 Jan. 1921 (cf. 17 Jan. 1908: 'Lunched in Hall – new experiment').

[143] *Memories*, 55–6. See also Glover, *Cambridge Retrospect*, 83–4.

[144] *The Letters of Thomas Babington Macaulay*, ed. T. Pinney, I (Cambridge, 1974), 107
('without domestic ties or liberal views or capacities of literary enjoyment, or sense
of benevolent pleasures', 11 Nov. 1818); Glover, *Cambridge Retrospect*, 83–4; Scott to
Glover, 13 Jan. 1897 (GC).

46 One undergraduate (F. M. Eagles) and three Fellows (Udny Yule, E. E. Raven, F. P. White). A party in Penzance in the early 1920s: SJCL, Album 12/42c

sitting next to Mason and Stevens still survives – perhaps accentuated even.'[145] What with Mullinger's moodiness, which was liable to turn murderous at the slightest provocation,[146] morale doubtless plummeted even lower as knowledge spread that Stevens had waived his right of option to presentation to vacant college livings. 'Does nought know it is not an integer?', Sikes had recently been moved to wonder out loud regarding the failed mathematics master dubbed by his pupils 'The Bloke', as the awful prospect of another Long Vac. of dinners in his company loomed: 'a dreary experience only relieved by the sparkle of Stevens' wit', Heitland, not significantly sweetened by the connubial contentment provided by the suffragist wife he had married in 1901, would remark. 'I wonder how I lived all those years in College and survived it.'[147]

---

[145] GD, 2 Dec, 1901.

[146] Mullinger's outburst in C[ombination].R[oom] last night – liable to flare up denouncing the persecution he undergoes, latest being [W. A.] Cox rubbing his beard beside him in Hall' (GD, 4 Feb. 1903); 'Mullinger of SJC has a devilish temper – threw a knife at his sister-in-law & I believe killed her – he went to prison but was not deprived at SJC. If undergrads sneeze, smile, laugh or cough before him he's likely, frail & lame as he now is, to threaten them with the thrashing of their lives': Benson Diary, 69 fo. 34r–v, 14 May 1905); *Eagle* xl (1918–19), 51–6 (obit. J. E. Sandys), on the subject of Mullinger's *History of the University of Cambridge* but omitting mention of his extra-mural activities and, extraordinarily, with hardly a word on his *History* of the College; Venn, *Alumni Cantabrigienses*, II.iv. 495.

[147] Scott to Stevens, 18 Feb. 1919 (SLB); GD, 5 Jun. 1918; Heitland to Glover, 1 September 1928. In 1901 at the age of fifty-four Heitland had married Margaret Bateson, the former Master's daughter.

5. A NEW DISPENSATION?

Heitland's astonishment at his own forbearance begs more questions than one. Stevens was not the only disincentive to dinner in Hall. Since 1882 the evenings had offered alternatives: as well as a rush to the altar there had been a tendency towards the family dining room.[148] On being visited at home by Glover some years earlier, Heitland 'blazed out' that 'he had left College to get away from people', which in his case was to a house in Wordsworth Close on St John's land off Grange Road.[149] His choice of location for domestic bliss, much admired by Benson when he visited him there in December 1916,[150] was significant. In 1919 it was shared by the overwhelming majority of those of his colleagues who lived out of college as well as by Glover's parents-in-law, the Fews, though not by Glover himself whose settlement elsewhere would later be identified by Larmor as a reason for his failing to prosper as others had.[151] Twenty years earlier Glover had been 'making enquiries about [the] desirability of building a house in Huntingdon Road',[152] which at that time was beginning to develop as something of a haven for Fellows of St John's with, according to the *Resident Members' List*, by then four of them there or thereabouts. In the event, Glover continued to rent his (different) Glisson Road house from the church to which he was so closely attached. But his failure to pursue the Huntingdon Road possibility may have been as much attributable to economic imperatives as to religious allegiance. In the 1930s it was still possible for Z. N. Brooke, a Fellow of Caius with a university lectureship, to purchase for 'something over £3,000' 'a house in the most desirable region of west Cambridge, with what amounts to eight bedrooms, allowing for two maids, the family, a guest room and a dressing room.'[153] But to Glover – and more particularly to Mrs Glover – immediate post-War Cambridge had less to offer. With servants demanding exorbitant wages, Alice Glover was doing servants' work, she complained. 'Why did we vote Labour?', she wanted to know.[154] With 'girl carriage-sweepers in trousers' to be seen at Cambridge station, life was full of surprises, fuller than the Glovers would have wished.[155]

[148] Glover, *Cambridge Retrospect*, 105.

[149] Ibid., 42.

[150] '... very quiet & with free air all round – I indeed rather wish that I had taken a house like this on first coming to Cambridge, & had remained a leisurely Don! I liked the arrangements, all so elderly, the books & papers, the cat asleep, firewood stacked in the verandah ...': Diary, 162, fo. 47 (1 Dec. 1916).

[151] 'I saw Larmor in p.m. I said Mary [Glover] thought I ought to have gone to Oxford. JL: "It's a good thing you didn't, you'd have been a second rate politician now." JL thinks we might have done better *not* in Glisson Road': GD, 5 May 1921. H. G. Few and family resided spaciously at 'Berrycroft', Grange Road.

[152] GD, 12 Aug. 1901.

[153] Brooke, *History of the University of Cambridge*, IV. 285.

[154] GD, 7 Feb. 1919, recording receipt of letter from Alice: '"I begin and end each day with grates and spend a large part of my time in the scullery"; no servants in view; they want £30, and the spirit they are all in doesn't make A. wish to live with them. "Why did we vote for labour?"' Glover's net income from the College in 1909 was £268.

[155] GD, 28 Jan. 1918. 'I grow rusty, and am old for these dear lads from officer's messes. Especially when I am told that etiquette of introduction between girls and men is

The extension northwards of Grange Road in the years before 1914 by means of the widening of the bridle road and footpath between West Road and Madingley Road was a development fuelled by the new demand for donnish *Lebensraum* and abetted by the invention of the pneumatic bicycle tyre.[156] At the College Council in 1897 'a long conversation took place as to the accommodation in College for bicycles belonging to the Fellows'.[157] (Not that the short distances into College, whether from Grange Road or Glisson Road, actually required a bicycle.[158] Glover, for example, usually walked in and out, often twice a day.) And then there were punctures. When in his first year back in Cambridge, rather than going for long walks, he took to the saddle and ventured out as far afield as Willingham and St Ives in the afternoon (though of course never on Sunday afternoon), all too often he found himself deflated and having to push his intractable machine all the way back home.[159]

While doubting whether anyone cared to hear him, Heitland was of opinion that the position of Fellows, and especially resident Fellows, had been brought down to 'a lower level than that existing even after the Statutes of 1882': a development he thought 'probably due to indifference rather than intent'.[160] The offer made by Edwin Cash, the Head Cook in 1892, to take on the role of caterer at a valuation to be agreed with the College, 'provided that no limit is placed upon the use of the kitchen for outside trade', indicated the extent of the commercial possibilities that had made (as they have continued to make) some of Cambridge's kitchen managers into millionaires, with fortunes accumulated in some cases by describing as 'goods supplied' in undergraduates' kitchen accounts money lent to them at exorbitant rates of interest.[161] Here, as in the Oxford colleges of the day, 'college service was almost a model of an informal black

beginning to lapse, and girl or man strikes up talk without introduction': GD, 15 May 1919.

[156] P. Guillebaud, 'West Cambridge 1870–1914: building the bicycle suburb', *Proceedings of the Cambridge Antiquarian Society* xcvi (2007).

[157] CM, 507/12 (28 May 1897): 'Decision on the matter was postponed' – and continued to preoccupy the Council for the following two years (cf. CM, 574/11).

[158] 'I do not care for much additional exercise, when I walk from house to St John's, thence to Newnham and so home, and to College and back in pm or evening': GD, 12 Nov. 1901. On 22 May he had done the Grantchester grind ('only seems rather further nowadays than of old'). The younger, fitter Macklin managed to cycle the 18 miles from Sandy (Beds.) in 70 minutes: LHMD, 4 Aug. 1922.

[159] E.g. 6 Jun. 1901: puncture at Willingham, 'so did not enjoy the ride home'; 'Another puncture' (26 Aug.); 'Puncture' (27 Aug.); 'To crown all, bicycle punctured and must be pumped every trip' (1 Oct.), despite having had his 'valves Anglicized' as recently as 27 September. In the case of West Cambridge the state of the road surfaces was constantly complained of by residents: Guillebaud, 'West Cambridge', 202–3.

[160] Letter to Benians, 4 Jun. 1920 (EABP). 'If I am plainly told that my interest in College matters is viewed as needless interference, I shall certainly save myself trouble', he stated. But (hardly surprisingly) 'as yet I have had no such assurance.'

[161] Cash to Steward, 30 Jan. 1892 (a letter written on paper headed 'St John's College Kitchen Cambridge, Telegraphic address CASH, CAMBRIDGE'): SJCA, SD.8.1. The offer was declined: E. Cunningham, 'Memoir', SJCA, Arch.2.12a, p. 71. As a young Fellow in the 1850s H. J. Roby (above, pp. 276–7) had striven valiantly against the prevailing system: *Eagle* xxxvi (1914–15), 203.

economy.'[162] And even within a College-controlled system there was profit to be made, by embezzlement. Everything depended on control, of which there was none. As emerged in 1902, when on H. F. Baker's inspection of the balance sheets and the 'extraordinary number of errors in the figures submitted' a £15,000 deficit was 'reduced to 17/4d', the Steward did not inspect the Kitchen accounts.[163]

The Steward in 1902 was Bateson; in 1908 F. F. Blackman succeeded Bateson; in 1914 Brindley succeeded Blackman, and in November 1915 a Kitchen Committee was appointed with instructions 'to enquire into the possibility of effecting considerable economies in the organization of the College kitchens'. But since the kitchens continued entirely without organization, the likelihood of achieving anything whatsoever, least of all of persuading the commander of the cadets that his charges were receiving value for money, remained meagre. Although the institution of monthly accounts was ordered, because the figures produced could not be trusted the accounts were not adopted. The Committee's minutes, recorded in Brindley's inauspicious hand in a school exercise book with pages missing, chronicle a continuing saga of discrepancies disregarded and decisions deferred, with at the end of almost every item of business the undertaking given that 'the Steward would obtain further information'. By Glover's account of its meetings, the combination of Brindley as Steward and G. W. Parsley, Cash's successor as Head Cook, was unsatisfactory for everyone other than Brindley and Parsley: 'Brindley only echoes head cook'; 'Apple dumpling following apple pie on Sunday – and Parsley telling Brindley "of course, Sir, I can cook what you tell me".'[164] An investigation of staff payments undertaken in February 1919 concluded that 'the form of return was so varied that the result is admittedly of no value to speak of.'

That spring there was talk in the Combination Room of Bushe-Fox when an undergraduate 'slipping grass-snake into salad at hall and having Merry sent for to explain why such things were sent into dinner'.[165] But by the time of Parsley's retirement the provender lacked even that degree of variety. And now there was urgent need to compensate for the departure of the cadets whose provisioning had shown that the problem about the kitchens was not that they were not profitable but that they were not profitable *to the College*. Hence the experiment, adopted in 1919, of a 'kitchen superintendent', the redoubtable Mrs Masters, under whose direction a possibility

[162] J. M. Crook, *Brasenose: The Biography of an Oxford College* (Oxford, 2008), 251; L. W. B. Brockliss, *Magdalen College Oxford: A History* (Oxford, 2008), 687–9.

[163] SJCA, CC3.24 (1903, added note); GD, 21 & 28 Nov. 1902; CMM, 660/2, 661/4 (including a resolution that 'the information given to the Audit Committee hitherto drawn out on loose sheets be made up and entered in a book kept for the purpose').

[164] GD, 4 Jan. & 20 Feb. 1917. At Hall on 24 February 'Parsley flung flour limits to the winds – stupid creature.' When in the following December Brindley asked for Parsley's salary to be raised the Committee recommended that his work be lightened and that he be given a holiday: SJCA, CC8.1.

[165] GD, 18 Apr. 1919. J. E. Merry was in the College service from 1853 and butler from 1876 until his death aged seventy-three in 1911: *Eagle* xxxiii (1911–12), 65–7.

of improvement was initially noted. 'Different foods taste differently now', Glover was surprised to discover – though for Beaton's tastes not differently enough.[166]

But the improvement didn't last; in college kitchens servicing Fellows only too ready to be disappointed it never does.[167] The request of the BAs before the War for their own table in Hall, unencumbered by Scholars, had been a territorial claim, not a gastronomical statement.[168] Moreover, Tanner's annotation on the letter that conveyed it – 'Excl[n] of Sch[rs] from table at wh. they have prescriptive rights. But see Steward' – drew attention to a further problem: 'seeing the Steward' led nowhere. In 1919 the only argument for retaining Brindley, who for the previous five years had been 'regaling Fellows with tales of College offal uncleared, maggots breeding, and his own personal labours in digging it out', was that there was no one willing to take over from him.[169] Brindley's obituarist would tell of his driving a railway engine from London to Liverpool during the General Strike and breaking the speed record on account of not knowing where the brakes were; others would hint at earlier derring-do in hostile waters.[170] But this sounds as little like Brindley the Steward as it does of Brindley of the 'inevitable' voice, the man whose 'literal mind, cramped ideas of patriotism, and loose tongue' had been so dangerously conspicuous when Larmor had brought some Japanese guests to Hall early in the War.[171]

'Anomalies' and 'discrepancies' in kitchen receipts and the storeman's records remained rife. When the £662 deficit for the first four months of 1919–20 was found to have *doubled* twelve months later, despite an increase in the provision of meals to undergraduate rooms (supposedly the kitchens' most profitable business), it was agreed to seek the services of a professional accountant and to 'have the Kitchen bank pass book laid on the [Committee's] table from time to time.' While in the Committee's suspicions incompetence was replaced by knavery, there was desultory discussion of the 'beer bottle deficit' (suspicion coming to rest on the bedders making off with the empties), of the relative merits of pickling and jam-making as a means of keeping staff occupied out of season, of the prohibition of the Hall waiters' practice of sending round a tumbler for tips, of the advantages of the use of carbon paper by the Order Clerk, and of the affordability of the annual outing to Yarmouth. The Steward's announcement at one meeting that the staff were pressing for deferred payments was withdrawn at the next after consultation with the Vice-Chairman of the Joint Committee of College Officers and Kitchen Servants (the Larder Cook and future Kitchen Manager, Albert Sadler). When the cost of Hall was raised,

---

[166] CM, 1061/6 (25 Jul. 1919); GD, 6 Oct. 1919; Audit Committee report, Nov. 1919 (SJCA, CC3.57): 'she is energetic, efficient, resourceful, thoroughly interested (...) a number of improvements (...) staff well in hand and working in a most amicable manner.'

[167] GD, 13 Mar. 1923 ('Dined in hall and found menu poorer than Jesus or Queens').

[168] R. Whiddington to Tanner, 1 Mar. 1911: SJCA, TU12.13.99.

[169] GD, 15 Feb. 1918, 11, 13 Jun. 1919, castigating Brindley's 'foolish muddling'; 28 Jan. 1921 ('no hope of getting clear of Brindley').

[170] *Eagle* lii (1941–7), 278; W. T. Thurbon, 'Brindley & the Riddle of the Sands', *Eagle* lxvii (1975).

[171] GD, 9 Nov. 1914, 3 Mar. 1919.

Benians objected that the increased revenue was being used to pay the pensions of servants long departed, whereupon it was lowered again and a vegetarian option secured, doubtless for Benians's Indian pupils.[172] Perhaps J. Lyons & Co. might be interested in taking the whole thing over, it was suggested (presumably with nippies to provide for the undergraduates in Hall).[173] It was not. Nor was the recently graduated A. S. (Jock) Le Maitre, to whom the Stewardship and Tutorial Bursarship combined were offered.[174] In between the two October 1921 meetings Mrs Brindley hanged herself.[175] So matters remained, with the College food-chain disrupted and tedium relieved only by Bonney's periodic letters of complaint about everything from the Scotch broth to the coffee.[176] However, by the time of Bonney's death at the end of 1923, within a matter of months of celebrating his eighty-ninth birthday with a seven-course dinner in bed, matters seemed to be improving. With Ebenezer Cunningham in charge, the Audit Committee's only substantial complaint was about cockroaches peeping out of the mashed potatoes or embedded in the bread. By then though Mrs Masters was beginning to lose her grip and, like the cockroaches themselves, peculation was again colonizing warm corners in which to flourish out of sight of both the Steward and the auditors.[177]

On hearing in 1898 of Scott's engagement to be married Heitland had confined himself to the bleak observation that 'another man going out of College', made 'the question of pernoctation more pressing than ever'.[178] By interpreting the statute that required *any* College Officer to sleep aboard for five nights a week as applying to only eight persons (President, Deans, Tutors principally), the Council in 1897 had made the duty correspondingly irksome for those to whom it applied. By August 1905 it had devolved on four officers: the Dean (Dyson), for five nights a week, and three Tutors (Tanner, Bushe-Fox and Sikes) for three each.[179] So the Junior Bursar pressed for the Steward to shoulder part of his share of the duty, in the hope that doing so might encourage him to

---

172 Not that some sort of system was not long overdue. 'Both of these ought to be considered for pensions', it was conceded in the case of servants each with more than forty years' service: Kitchen Committee minutes (SJCA, CC8.1), min. of 19 Oct. 1920.

173 'Hall, then up at Blackman's with Robespierre [=Brindley] Bartlett and Benians. Bartlett had sounded Lyons as to whether they would take Kitchen over, and they definitely don't want to. Scott and Heitland have suggested this sort of thing': GD, 4 May 1921.

174 GD, 22 Apr. (committee appointed), 14 Oct. & 17 Nov. 1921; CMM, 1116/9; 1123/7. Instead, Le Maitre (BA 1920) made his career in the civil service, rising to be Under-Secretary to the Board of Trade in 1947–8.

175 Kitchen Committee minutes, 18 Jan. 1917 – 1 Feb. 1923 *passim*; GD, 26 Oct. 1921.

176 For which see Glyn Daniel, *Some Small Harvest* (London, 1986), 283–6. 'His complaints to the Steward about dinner at St John's, made publicly, were endless': Benson Diary, 173, fo. 14 (16 Jan. 1924).

177 SJCA, CC3.75; GD, 5 Mar. 1924 (Cunningham 'doing things in Kitchen beyond Brindley's dreams – even clearing cockroaches'); Cunningham, 'The College in 1911', *Eagle* lix (1960–63), 165; below, p. 506.

178 Scott to Glover, 11 Jul. 1898 (GC).

179 Statute XX (1882); CM, 494/3; SJCA, Tanner's Scrap-book.

dine in and even keep an eye on the servants (whose work 'wants looking after closely').[180]

Yet the relationship between the domestic and the collegiate was not a simple one. In the quatercentennial year Bonney looked back on the changes the College had experienced over the previous three decades and declared its corporate life to have been 'to some extent weakened'. Undergraduates might be thought to have suffered, at least indirectly, from the reduction in the number of resident Fellows, he said. On the other hand they stood to profit from having contact with Fellows in a family setting and from the narrowing of the gap there had been between them and the dons since the time when social intercourse had been 'less frequent and more formal' (a development which some of Mac-Alister's and Armitage's pupils would have been ready either to deny or ruefully to confirm).[181] And meanwhile even that domestic scene was made subtly to conform to collegiate models. In the same volume of the *Eagle* that contained Bonney's musings the announcement was recorded that the set of silver stoups presented to Tanner and his wife on the occasion of his retirement were 'as exact replicas as possible' of those used at the Fellows' table.[182]

In this company, Martin Charlesworth, who had migrated from Jesus in 1923 after two years as *ad hoc* Lecturer in Classics, struck a new note. On first meeting him at a tea-party at the Glovers (an occasion described by Glover himself, whose role in the appointment had been decisive, as 'a jocund and happy time'), and on receiving an invitation to breakfast and staying on for a sing-song round the piano immediately following, Macklin unhesitatingly declared him 'awfully jolly' and 'a kindred spirit in every way'.[183] For the next thirty-two years such was the abiding impression: jollity, jocundity, music and breakfasts. Like Macklin, Douglas Wass, who came up in 1941 to read mathematics, was immediately struck by Charlesworth's exuberant humanity:

> Martin was easily the most amusing and delightful of all the senior members of the College. He was a classical scholar of some distinction and could easily have neglected the scientists and mathematicians, but he didn't. He was immensely interested in all the undergraduates and delighted in getting to know them – and getting to know what made them tick. I do not think that his office as President laid on him any duty *vis-à-vis* the junior members of the College. If anything that office made him more the shop steward of those senior members who did not have any particular College office. But he had a youthful interest in young people and went out of his way to engage them. He would drop in on one's rooms at breakfast and immediately embark on some anecdote or classical story which was relevant to what was happening in the wider world.[184]

---

[180] Shore to Tanner, 23 Jul. 1908 (when Blackman was on the point of taking over from Bateson as Steward): SJCA, TU 12.10.164.

[181] 'The Quatercentenary Sermon', *Eagle* xxxiii (1911–12), 16.

[182] *Eagle* xxxiv (1912–13), 365.

[183] GD, 13 Aug. 1922; LHMD, 15 Aug. & 9 Oct. 1922; Glover to Charlesworth, 9 Dec. 1921, and Charlesworth to Glover, 29 Dec. 1921 (GC both).

[184] Letter to Peter Hennessy, 30 Dec. 2007.

47 SJC Classical Society dinner, June 1927. Seated left T. R. Glover;
centre right E. E. Sikes; far right M. P. Charlesworth: SJCL, insert in Glover diary

In November 1924 Charlesworth stood for election to the Council of the
Senate on the Conservative ticket and, just as St John's was divesting itself of
Armitage, failed in the attempt. A month later, he was offered a professorship
at Princeton at $4,000 p.a. ('Some have luck', murmured Glover), and declined
it.[185] By the end of that year Armitage's replacement as Tutor had decided where
his future lay.

With Benians alongside him, Charlesworth had as his chief E. E. Sikes,
who on the Council's election of him as President in succession to Liveing
initially made it clear that it was not his intention to resign his Tutorship.[186]
Describing himself (with rather heavy jocularity) as a 'comparatively young
man' and stating his determination to soldier on until the settlement of 'the
present tutorial difficulties',[187] perhaps he had hopes of further advancement. In November 1924 Glover had described Scott's performance at a
General Meeting of the Fellows as 'hardly in control', and shortly thereafter
recorded Sikes's less than loyal description of the Master whose number two
he was on the point of becoming.[188] However, if Sikes did indeed imagine
such prospects they cannot have been improved either by his symbolic isola-
tion on the periphery of things in his eyrie at I 8 New Court or by the return
to the Fellowship of Sir Humphry Rolleston, the Regius Professor of Physic,

[185] *CUR* (1924–5), 235; GD, 24 Oct. & 3 Dec. 1924.
[186] GD, 5 Jun. 1925. In the following summer he did so.
[187] Sikes to Scott, 5 Mar. 1925: SJCA, D90.1582.
[188] GD, 10 Nov. 1924; below, n. 303.

in the spring of 1925. Rolleston 'will very likely be the next Master', Glover prophesied.[189]

In 1925 Rolleston was sixty-three, at that time an age at which any man with no further terrestrial ambitions might have thought of his old College as a future twilight home.[190] But things were about to change.

6. THE NEW STATUTES
(with Peter Hennessy)

Quite apart from the Johnian blood spilt in the Great War, the Kaiser was to have a considerable, if delayed, impact on Cambridge and the College. Because out of World War I there came a Royal Commission on Oxford and Cambridge Universities, chaired by the former prime minister, H. H. Asquith, which would shape the finances and the governance of universities, faculties and colleges alike into a new regime that survived in its essentials remarkably unchanged for the next seventy years.

The deal was simple. Oxford and Cambridge, reeling from the impact of war and rising costs, had asked for state assistance. They would get it provided they let the Royal Commissioners in 'to enquire into the financial resources of the Universities and of the College and Halls therein, into the administration and application of these resources, into the government of the Universities, and into the relations of the Colleges and Halls to the Universities and to each other.'[191] King George V commissioned Asquith on 14 November 1919, just over a year after the Armistice was signed, and he laboured for three years. But the genesis of the inquiry lay two years back in early 1917, long before victory was assured.

Unusually for a British education minister, a University man held the job in Lloyd George's war and post-war coalition government. H. A. L. Fisher, the Liberal MP for Sheffield, Hallam, who would go on to be Warden of New College, Oxford, and to write *A History of Europe* that would become a staple of countless sixth forms until well after the Second World War, was convinced that the days of British universities as 'self-governing independent republics' was over and that even Oxford and Cambridge could no longer live off their private endowments or 'cope with the developing requirements of applied science without help from the State'.[192]

With a speed breathtaking to those familiar with early twenty-first-century Whitehall procedures, the President of the Board of Education persuaded the Treasury to act. 'Their needs were crying', Fisher later wrote of the ancient universities.

> Without immediate financial aid it would have been impossible for them to carry on their current scientific work. Austen Chamberlain was

[189] GD, 24 Mar. 1925; *ODNB* (M. W. Weatherall).

[190] True, the 1882 Statutes set no retiring age for the Master, but Statute V did include 'provision in case of [his] Incapacity'.

[191] *Royal Commission on Oxford and Cambridge Universities: Report*, Cmd. 1588 (London: HMSO, 1922), 3.

[192] H. A. L. Fisher, *An Unfinished Autobiography* (Oxford, 1940), 114–15.

fortunately Chancellor of the Exchequer. He was himself an alumnus of Cambridge and the son of the founder of Birmingham University [Joe Chamberlain]. Few words were necessary to convince such a man of the needs of the two universities. After twenty minutes I left the Treasury Chambers with an assurance of a certain grant of £30,000 a year for each university pending the report of the Royal Commission, which we agreed between us must necessarily be set up.[193]

Out of the same settlement came the University Grants Committee in 1919 as an arms-length body between the state and higher education 'to reconcile the need for the Exchequer to subsidize universities as a national system with the need to maintain the autonomy of the universities as indispensable for the function they performed'.[194]

For the self-governing independent republic of St John's College, Cambridge, autonomous is not exactly what its Master and Fellows felt over Christmas 1919 when a letter arrived from the Asquith Commission outlining a 'Preliminary List of Questions' to heads of colleges and halls. Every particle of income, every item of financial practice including the selection, ordering, sourcing and purchase of food for the kitchens, was to be disclosed. Similar levels of detail were demanded on undergraduate recruitment, teaching, the rhythm of a Fellow's life and emolument, the treatment of 'poor students' and their support, ditto for those coming from '(a) the Dominions, (b) Colonies and Protectorates, (c) India, and (d) Foreign Countries'. This was Intrusion with a capital 'I', far outstripping the inquisitiveness of the nineteenth-century Royal Commissions. And the College did not care for it.

Scott allocated various Fellows to draft answers to particular questions.[195] On one question – the position of women in Cambridge – there developed a profound rift between Scott and Heitland which came to a head in the autumn of 1921 when both took their arguments directly to the Royal Commissioners. Twice within a year (December 1920 and October 1921) the Cambridge Senate (unlike Oxford) had rejected proposals to admit women to full membership of the University, an outcome which 'greatly embarrassed' the Royal Commission then nearing the end of its work.[196] Heitland's passionate letter was sent a week after the 1921 vote which had led to a mob of male undergraduates gathered outside the Senate House, inspired by the improbably named Corpus MA, the Reverend Mr Pussy Hart, Vicar of Ixworth, who told them 'Now go and tell Girton and Newnham', to cross the Backs to storm Newnham and pull down its gates.[197]

That Cambridge women would receive only titles of degrees, plus, no doubt, the activities of the Revd Mr Pussy, inspired Heitland to tell the Royal

[193] Ibid., 115–16.

[194] John Carswell, *Government and the Universities in Britain* (Cambridge, 1985), 10.

[195] SJCA, D44.14. 'Royal Commission on Oxford and Cambridge Universities … Paper No. 2. Preliminary List of Questions addressed to Heads of Colleges and Halls. 23 December 1919.' Scott has scribbled the initials of respondent Fellows alongside each question.

[196] Brooke, *History of the University of Cambridge*, IV. 326.

[197] Ibid.

Commissioners that '[r]ecent events here are generally allowed to have disgraced the name of Cambridge. Instead of idle lamentations, I have tried to look below the surface and set out some of the causes of evil that have long been at work.'[198] Heitland believed reactionary elements mobilizing the non-resident MAs were behind the failure to do justice to women – that and the long-term effects of 'the fostering of College-patriotism … a fine thing in itself' which, however, can lead anyone to the view 'that things were about their best in his time' and that the 'slightest suspicion that College interests, as he understands them, are thought by his College Dons to be threatened by a proposed change in the University, alarms him and rouses him to vote against it'.

Heitland noted that the non-resident MA possessed a vote on University, but not College, matters. Such opposition to change deserved some respect, he went on, and 'has its uses as a check upon hasty legislation and the adoption of interested fads. But it is heedless of present facts, and is led by vague cries and deaf to argument. For instance, it ignores the fact that the Women's Question is fifty years old, while it swallows readily the false and malignant assertion that the women want to force their way into men's Colleges.'[199]

Scott, by contrast, was co-signatory with seven other senior university figures, of a letter of 22 November 1921 to the Royal Commissioners which pointed out that since the 1882 reforms it had been Cambridge men who had been 'the leaders of the movement for the higher education of women in this country' and that '[i]n view of what Cambridge has done, and is still doing, for the higher education of women, it is perverse to assert that the present attitude of the Senate is due to prejudice or any other cause than a deliberate judgement as to what is best in all the circumstances of the case.'[200]

For Scott and his colleagues, the possession henceforth by Cambridge women of the 'title of the degree' rather than 'the complete degree' would not confer upon them a lesser distinction. The ladies of Girton and Newnham, 'although in a different position from members of the University, are not put in an inferior position as compared with women students at other universities. They will be under the discipline of their own Colleges; but they will have the same opportunities for study and research as students of the University, and they will receive the hall-mark.' Scott and Co. concluded, with, one suspects, more than a dash of wishful thinking, by recognizing that '[a]s long as women students can get degrees from Oxford and cannot get them from Cambridge, they will be at a disadvantage in the latter University: but there is no good ground for supposing that any disadvantage will continue to be felt after the new statute has come into operation.'[201]

For Heitland, the handling of the Women's Question had exposed the 'grave defects of our constitution. (…) Self-government, our boasted privilege, has made a public show of its failure. (…) Will not the Commission lend a hand

---

[198] W. E. Heitland to the Members of the Universities Commission: D44.15.1 (27 Oct. 1921).

[199] Ibid.

[200] Ibid.

[201] Ibid.

to rescue us from the bog of blunders perpetrated by ourselves? Will they not examine the working of our constitution (…) The question at issue is far more than the mere question of admitting women to full membership. We need a reasonable and workable form of government.'[202] Did the Commission ride to the rescue?

On the Women Question, their report was feeble and ambivalent. Mindful that Cambridge was not the only UK university not to offer women equality with men, they believed that women should be entitled to be admitted on the same conditions as men to membership of the University, but with conditions. For example, the Cambridge characteristic of being 'mainly and predominantly a "men's University"' should be preserved and a cap of 500 women undergraduates imposed[203] (with the influx of returning servicemen, the undergraduate population of Cambridge had reached 5,733 by Michaelmas Term 1920).[204] This finding, among others, was probably in the mind of Asquith's biographer, Roy Jenkins (himself a future Chancellor of Oxford), when he wrote that though the former premier 'discharged his duties with some enthusiasm', he was 'in fact, a bad appointment. As Gladstone had been before him, and Lord Attlee was to be after him, Asquith was a natural conservative on most subjects outside politics. This was particularly so on anything touching both scholarship and his early life, and he led the Commission into producing an unadventurous report.'[205]

The Cambridge sections of the Royal Commission's report were largely written by a combination of Sir Hugh Anderson, neurophysiologist and Master of Caius, and the great social historian G. M. Trevelyan, who would return to Cambridge as Regius Professor of Modern History in 1927, becoming Master of Trinity in 1940.[206] (The historical portion with which the report opens is especially well crafted and reveals the spoors of Trevelyan.) The document recognized the impact upon both universities of what was already being seen as *the* lost generation 'sent down by the Kaiser', as Harold Macmillan would later characterize it:[207] 'the Schools both at Oxford and Cambridge are now seriously impeded in their efficiency and progress by the loss of many of those who were their most promising students and most brilliant young teachers.'[208] As we have seen, this was a judgement cruelly apt in the case of St Johns. The Royal Commissioners also stressed the pre-eminence of the ancient universities within the still relatively tiny UK system of higher education (certainly when compared to the United States or Germany) and what they called the 'special value to the nation'[209] of the 'two senior Universities of the Empire'.[210]

---

[202] Ibid.

[203] Cmd. 1588, p. 173.

[204] Ibid., 26.

[205] Roy Jenkins, *Asquith* (London, 1967), 546.

[206] Brooke, *History of the University of Cambridge*, IV. 364–9.

[207] *Teste* Sir Anthony Kenny.

[208] Cmd. 1588, p.46.

[209] Ibid., 43.

[210] Ibid., 45.

For all Jenkins's criticism of the Asquith Report as 'unadventurous', it did lead to a rebalancing of power between colleges and university which was very much in the University's favour. The new public money went to the University; the colleges remained autonomous but were required to find Fellowships for University lecturers appointed by the new subject faculties. Real voting power was withdrawn from non-resident MAs and confined to those resident and working within the University and the colleges (no doubt to Heitland's relief). Greater efforts were enjoined in the recruitment of poorer students. The colleges' and the universities' statutes were to be refreshed (a process completed by 1926) overseen by Statutory Commissioners as laid down by the Universities of Oxford and Cambridge Act.[211]

In February 1923 Scott established a committee of three (himself, Benians and Engledow) to examine the Asquith Report's recommendations and to advise the Council on its impact within the College. Their final assessment in May 1923 was especially concerned with the cost and the absorption of new Fellows whose tenure, terms and conditions were 'associated with official posts in the College, or with University lectureships or University Demonstratorships'. New salary structures and the extension of the 'Federated Superannuation System' to college and university appointments drove a coach and horses through the old dividend system.[212] The new, university types billeted on the College reflected the strong recommendation of the Asquith Commission that Cambridge boost its research contribution to the nation to avoid the danger of too much of everybody's time being absorbed by teaching.

St John's, however, genuinely feared a draining of the collegiate spirit through the creation of a two-tier Fellowship and Scott made this plain to the new Cambridge Statutory Commissioners after two meetings of the Governing Body on 23 November and 1 December 1923:

> The Governing Body view with misgiving the proposal to create a class of Fellows, namely Professors and Readers whose income (apart from a nominal allowance) will be entirely independent of the College, and who will have the same powers, but not the same interests and responsibilities, as other Fellows, in College policy.
>
> The solidarity of the interests of the Fellows has hitherto been a characteristic feature of College life. The new proposal would divide the community into two sections, one of which would depend for their income on the stability of College finance and the other of which would be independent of this consideration.
>
> 'The latter class might not feel entitled or inclined to take the same part in College affairs as such Fellows have done in the past.[213]

The question of primary or overlapping loyalties – to College, department

---

[211] For parliamentary debate on the Bill see House of Commons, *Official Report*, 22 Jun. 1923, cols. 1825–1909.

[212] *Report of the Committee on the Recommendations of the Universities Commission*, 8 May 1923: D44.15.2.

[213] Ibid.: 'Universities of Oxford and Cambridge Act 1923. Memorandum by the Governing Body of St. John's College, Cambridge.' 1 Dec. 1923.

or lab – has run like a thread through Cambridge history since the 1920s often expressed as a fear that College life might, for some, be but a hotel matter of room and food.

Some, like Glover, felt that Cambridge ceased to be Cambridge when the 1920s reforms entered the University and collegiate bloodstreams. In the memoir that he published shortly before his death in the middle of World War II, the venerable classicist unsheathed his pen, declaring that 'after the first German war, a new Universities Commission made drastic endeavours to re-model Cambridge, top, bottom and middle. For centuries the centre of academic life had been the College (and a very good centre, too, with its diversities of types); now it was to be the "faculty" (a group of people of one interest).' 'We have a lot of Mathematicians and Natural Science men who have been nowhere and seen nothing and read nothing', Glover complained, 'and older Mathematicians (except Larmor) not much better.' 'Hall gets rather dull', he grumbled. 'Uninformed young scientists pall.' 'The "lab" was really more to the new type of man than the College, and very often he came from outside and knew little of our traditions.' 'Theorists' and 'reformers' whose 'ideal seemed to be the transformation of Cambridge into a copy of the huge American "State University"' proclaimed 'the triumph of practical efficiency over humanism, and the substitution of science for culture'.[214] Dirac, for example, an enigma to all his colleagues, needed to be told 'who Erasmus was and when'.[215]

Glover deplored the pollution of the old sanctuaries by the new jargon spouted by 'scientific semi-nobodies'.[216] Yet his closest College friend was a distinguished scientist, and it was with Larmor, Benians and (sometimes) Charlesworth that he regularly dined at the lower of the Fellows' tables, as part of a conspiratorial quartet.[217] When Rivers died he mourned the College's loss of 'a foremost man of science, who has been a great help to us', and when William Bateson, Heitland's brother-in-law, followed him he was quick to acknowledge 'a great man, the outstanding figure in SJC in my early years at High Table – candid, rough and kindly, a little of a bully but a great man.'[218]

Glover's is a picture that does not quite fit either the Cambridge experience of most Johnians over the ninety years since the Asquith Commission sat or the mind of Trevelyan or Anderson. But undergraduates, then as now, tend to take little interest in inquiries and statutes unless they touch directly on student funding matters or transforming questions such as the admission of women. Cambridge's version of the 'roaring twenties', one suspects, played more powerfully for the young members of the College (and not just for the 'Stormy Petrels') than the impact of 'lab' men on the Governing Body. For as the Royal Commission Report put it, somewhat coyly, '[m]ost of the Oxford and Cambridge

---

214 GD, 2 Mar. 1921; 10 Nov. 1924; 12 Feb. 1927; Glover, *Cambridge Retrospect*, 110.

215 GD, 11 Jun. 1930.

216 GD, 11 Feb. 1927.

217 GD, 22 May 1930; 19 Jan. 1931; 25 May 1931 ('Hall, at foot with Larmor's group – "you're all there" he [Larmor] said; Ben and MPC; and a good deal of fun'); 16 May 1932 ('Hall, 2nd table, Ben, MPC, and the impenetrable voiceless stranger who does engineering, Gough').

218 GD, 5 Jun. 1922, 8 Feb. 1926.

graduates are serious and hard-working students, if not entirely divested on all occasions of the exuberance natural to congregated youth.'[219] And in the 1920s that exuberance, as Macklin and Co. demonstrated, could take some richly imaginative forms.

At the undergraduate level, the most visible and enduring change the 1926 statutes brought was the centrality of the supervision system to their College and Cambridge experience. Miller was right to judge Glover's sustained complaint about the new post-twenties' dispensation as 'excessively pessimistic':

> The arrangements that came into force in 1926 were more efficient, but that does not by itself discredit them. They were indispensable to exploit the new dimensions of scientific study, as the college had already recognised by closing its laboratories. They did not involve losing the intimacy of college teaching: from some points of view this was better secured by the supervision system than by the old regime of college lectures. Finally, a community of undergraduates engaged in many different studies, living together and adding to each other's experience, is much more than a boarding house. Acceptance of the new character of college teaching, combined as it was with the retention of the old character of colleges as places in which undergraduates educate each other, was a better thing than clinging in new and changing times to a world which had passed.[220]

As Gandhi liked to remark, structures do not create character. But, as the 1926 statutes demonstrated, they can easily add to the cost of the intimate living which does.

For St John's the task of coping with the financial implications fell upon Sir Henry Howard who became Senior Bursar in 1923 and remained in office for twenty years. Howard had 'a long experience of financial administration in India behind him'[221] and left a detailed record of the impact of the 1926 changes upon the fortunes of a College about to experience the fiscal consequences of yet another slump in agricultural prices and land values (though the bursarial efforts of Scott and Leathem left it better placed to absorb the blow than had been the case in the 1880s and after).[222]

NEW FELLOWSHIP STRUCTURE, OCTOBER 1926

TITLE A: Three year appointment for recent graduates (extendable in special cases) to concentrate on 'the advancement of learning and research'.

TITLE B: For holders of College Offices (5 years renewable). Also for 'men of exceptional distinction' recruited for research or teaching purposes.

TITLE C: For University professors and 'other persons holding University offices' who are 'ineligible for Fellowships with Dividend'.

---

[219] Cmd. 1588, p. 26.
[220] Miller, *Portrait of a College*, 120–1.
[221] Boys Smith, *Memories*, 45.
[222] Howard, *Finances*, 250–51, 258.

TITLE D: Fellowships with life tenure. Masters and Fellow, who have held qualifying College offices for 20 years, automatically qualify on retirement.

TITLE E: For Title B Fellows 'who have ceased to be Fellows under Title B before the age of retirement is reached, and generally of other persons whom it shall appear to be in the interests of the College so to elect'.

The old dividend system of Fellows' remuneration ran on for most Fellows, except for the new Title Cs made up of professors and others holding University offices, seven of whom the College was now obliged to take in. But new and higher levels of pay came with the 1926 statutes as well as membership of the national university superannuation scheme.[223]

Howard found the new rates for St John's contribution to Cambridge University funds especially vexing, noting in 1935 that the 1926 statutes had 'thrown a heavy additional burden on the College, the amount payable in respect of the first year of the new Statutes being £6191 compared with £3369 for the last year of the old. The payment dropped to £5326 for 1929–30, as a result of some falling off in net income, and of allowances granted on account of heavy repairs to the College fabric [in First Court and redecoration of the Hall], but it has since risen, being £6613 for 1932–33.'[224]

The 1926 changes also affected the powers of the College Council which was now required to 'prescribe the extent and conditions under which expenditure may be incurred by the Bursars or other administrative officers, and the extent to which control over expenditure generally shall be exercised by the Senior Bursar.'[225] Scholarship and Exhibition provision was also changed in line with Royal Commission recommendations, with extra money substituted for the practice of rent-free rooms, the money for them coming from a special scholarship and exhibition fund account.[226]

By the time the new statutes came into force on 1 October 1926, state aid to Cambridge University as a whole had risen to £85,000 a year, the largest proportion of which (£28,000) was allocated for stipends, £20,000 for the faculties, £10,000 for the pension scheme, £10,000 for the proposed new University Library, £4,000 for the Board of Extra-mural Studies and £4,000 for the women's colleges.[227] The cluster of 'republics' by the Cam was never quite so 'independent' again. Yet the new state-sanctioned financial regime would never succeed in easing the anxieties of the ever frugally retentive Glover.

---

[223] Ibid., 248–54.

[224] Ibid., 254.

[225] Quoted ibid., 24.

[226] Ibid., 253–4.

[227] *The Victoria History of the Counties of England: A History of the County of Cambridge and the Isle of Ely*, III. *The City and University of Cambridge*, ed. J. P. C. Roach (London, 1959), 293.

7. A CHANGE OF KEY

The wider University world, within which the inner emotional geography of St John's played itself out, experienced a considerable shift in the years following the Armistice. As Scott's powers faded, the state began to demand reform and a raising of the game all round.

On the introduction of electric light into College rooms in 1911 an anonymous writer in *The Eagle* had been at pains to explain that it was 'no loss to St John's to be one of the last Colleges to [do so], since, owing to the delay, we have been able to put it in on a greatly improved system':[228] an artless expression of that perennial Johnian genius, of which the rest of the century was to furnish further examples, for making a virtue of procrastination by letting others venture first into the unknown. With many sets left empty during the War, the opportunity was also taken of letting some College rooms furnished, which, together with the establishment of separate charges for shoe-cleaning, window-cleaning, carpet beating, water, staircase lighting and a College matron (not with a view to healing the sick but 'to improving the standard of cleanliness in the College rooms and to affecting economies in the expenditure of the undergraduates on household utensils and cleaning materials'), had been one of the measures proposed by the Committee on Charges to Undergraduates which had reported in October 1916.[229] In October 1920 it was decided to convert three large sets of rooms into double sets: a development necessitated by pressure of numbers created by returned warriors all doing two-year courses, and one requiring a relatively heavy investment by the College in furniture.[230] Multiple occupation was one novelty, distinguishable from the occupation of E 8 New by the three Blackman brothers between 1892 and 1895, making the set almost a family peculiar.[231] Another was the beginning of the end of the age-old system whereby at each change of occupancy the incoming resident purchased his predecessor's furniture at a valuation provided by Messrs. Eaden Lilley, while adding to the movables as he wished. Although the practice of private furnishing continued, with Macklin and Charlesworth finding the choice of curtaining material a suitable subject for conversation, it was an indication of the transition from the expansive, careless extravagance of the elegiac era to a regime of closer calculation that, as Cunningham reported on leaving the Tutorial Bursarship, whereas in 1918 only eight sets were subject to the new College-funded arrangements, owing largely to his own activity in that office by 1927 the number had risen to 121.[232]

---

[228] *Eagle* xxxiii (1911–12), 25. For particulars of the process see Crook, *Penrose to Cripps*, 22–4. As a young Fellow, Glover first saw the Hall lit electrically on 16 Jan. 1893.

[229] SJCA, CC4.10; CM, 985/12.

[230] Tanner to Scott, 6 Oct. 1920: SJCA, TU12.24.64. In the event it seems that only two sets were converted: I4 First and B1 New.

[231] Heitland, *After Many Years*, 119. Born six years apart, all achieved Firsts in the Natural Sciences tripos, and two were distinguished plant physiologists and Fellows (the oldest, F. F., 1895–1947; the youngest, V. H., 1898–1904). Later, Armitage was there.

[232] LHMD, 15 Aug. 1922: 'We entered into the subject of cretonne patterns with mutual sympathy'; Senior Bursar's Note on the Accounts for the year ended 31 July 1935.

In evidence given to the Royal Commission on the Civil Service in February 1914 Tanner had stated that

> he had known poor students get through the University course on about £140 or £150 a year, but the student would be a great deal happier with something like £200 a year. Even that would admit of no extravagance.[233]

After the War concern increased for the welfare of the lowest form of pond life, Tanner's 'exhausted hermits'. In May 1920 the Council established a committee 'to consider in consultation with the undergraduates, means by which, through self-help, pooling of work, etc., the costs of College life can be substantially reduced'.[234] Undergraduates were beginning to experience an existence different from that of their Edwardian predecessors. Guillebaud, who came up in 1909 and was a Tutor from 1926 and Senior Tutor 1952–6, commented on the 'immense increase in the proportion of the men entering Cambridge [at this time] who come up from the elementary and smaller secondary schools, as a result of the extension of scholarships given by County Councils and the State.' Yet the gulf to be crossed remained considerable. On arriving at St John's from Barry County School for Boys one such award-holder, Glyn Daniel, was invited to dine *chez* Wordie, his Tutor, and was instructed to come in black tie. Years later he remembered the occasion, 'the first time I had worn a dinner jacket, boiled shirt, and stiff collar'.[235]

For Jasper Rootham, the Organist's son who came up from Tonbridge School in 1929, three years before Daniel, Cambridge, and St John's in particular, was the place where 'the tide of grammar school and public school, of north and south and indeed of east and west too, began to flow together'.

> The mixture varied between the inarticulate, bespectacled and poverty-stricken scientist from a school that nobody had ever heard of in Dumfriesshire who had won the top scholarship in physics, to the well-dressed, well-fed, well-heeled vulgarian from a public school who had satisfied the examiners with his hand-off or his leg-break, and little else. Brilliantly articulate Indians, a high proportion of whom became Presidents of the Union, cricket Blues, or hockey Blues, found themselves on the same staircase as knobbly-kneed hookers from Giggleswick, with a knack for anatomy, vast hunks of Afrikaner manhood, allegedly studying law if they could take off from the line-out and the loose-scrum, and a portly Jew from St. Paul's, who when he was not contributing savagely

---

[233] 'Witness considered it better that men from poorer schools should enter fully into the general life of the place than that they should form a class apart living under special conditions. Questioned as to the advisability of reducing the cost of living all round at the University the witness said the effect would be to depreciate the whole standard of living of men who were not required from pecuniary considerations to live at a reduced standard': SJCA, TU12.15.43.

[234] CM, 1083/16 (14 May 1920).

[235] C. W. Guillebaud, 'Then and now', *Eagle* lviii (1958–9), 160; Daniel, *Some Small Harvest*, 59. The gross annual income stated by Daniel's father in July 1934, £394 (SJCA, TU16/Daniel) is to be compared with that of Edward Miller's (below, p. 533).

amusing articles to the University periodicals or drinking beer by the quart from a glass Wellington boot, was studying with devotion the holy writings of his faith.[236]

For the members of this diverse constituency (or at least for some of them), by 1927 the Steward was proposing a 'Junior Common Room', extra student sets and the provision of a Library reading room for study needs.[237] Again, the process of social modulation is almost audible. The College Reading Room established in 1902 in what is now the Old Music Room, was a sanctum administered by a committee comprising a Senior Treasurer appointed by the Council (initially, and inevitably, Tanner) and representatives of the General Athletic Club and the Debating Society, serviced by a bedder and the Library Boy appointed at 3s 6d each per week to lay and light the fire and keep it in, clean the room, arrange the newspapers, wind the clock, replenish the match stands, keep an eye on the cigarette machine, and tidy the place up at intervals throughout the day. A list of papers taken in October 1907 records eleven dailies (including two copies of *The Sportsman*), fifteen weeklies (amongst them the *Oxford Magazine* but not the *Cambridge Review*) and various monthlies, not least *C. B. Fry's*.[238] But because it proved increasingly squalid and unsatisfactory the room was unable to compete with the Union Society just across the road, to which since at least the middle of the previous century unathletic members had migrated of an afternoon for the purpose of writing letters and scouring the weeklies, and in 1932 a move was made into the former bicycle store on the ground floor of I and K First, with the Committee under different auspices (two senior members, appointees of the editors of the *Eagle*, the General Athletic Club and what was to become the Associated Societies, with power to co-opt).[239] It was the refurbished Committee's first senior treasurer, J. S. Boys Smith, who was responsible for the adoption of the name 'Junior Combination Room' for the old Reading Room in which little or nothing was now perused, let alone read.[240] Describing that survival from an earlier age as 'the worst room of its type in the University', and denouncing the niggardliness and 'persistent inactivity of Authority', the author of the call to action published in the *Eagle* stressed the need for provision for those living in distant lodgings and described 'the lazy charm of deep chairs by a drowsy fireside, of quiet reading and talking in the evening after Hall' as something 'well-nigh unknown to the modern generation'.[241] Whereas less than a decade before Macklin's College room had provided such a haven, now College rooms were no longer represented

---

[236] J. Rootham, *Demi-Paradise* (London, 1960), 63.

[237] CM, 1252/6 (18 Feb. 1927).

[238] SJCA, CC 17.6. Changes to this list in subsequent years and the particulars of other publications acquired would provide the social historian with ample food for thought.

[239] CM, 1367/9; *Eagle* xlvii (1932–3), 55–7 (J. S. Boys Smith); Crook, *Penrose to Cripps*, 12–13, 66.

[240] 'My principal motive was to preclude the use of the Oxford term "Junior Common Room" which seemed likely to creep into use': Henry and Crook, *Use and Occupancy of Rooms*, I. 14.

[241] *Eagle* xlv (1927–9), 303–7 (K. A[dam], President of the Union Society and future head of BBC Television).

as places of solace but rather as chilly refuges left unimproved for history's sake.[242]

Not chilly for everyone though. Not for the Punchbowl Club, for example, revived in 1924, the minutes of whose meetings, charged with the exuberance of youth, are redolent rather of warm evenings and the braying of young gentlemen whose antics disproved Belloc's dictum on the sound of broken glass as an upper-class monopoly. If not claret breakfasts, it was 'punch, beer and obscenity evenings, a lot of staying up all night' and the simulation of sexual congress that dominated the agenda of Punchbowl meetings.[243] R. L. Howland, elected a full member in October 1925, considered it prudent to resign two years later in advance of joining the Fellowship two years after that. In November 1928 the Punchbowl's minutes fall silent. The following month saw the establishment of the Nashe Society. As the revival of the former Wordsworth Society (of which no trace remains), the Nashe was dedicated to the 'reading of plays and dissertations, and the discussions of matters of literary, scientific and artistic interest'.[244] If the one be regarded as at the opposite end of the spectrum of boisterousness from the other, the case of 'The Crickets', another well-established society which by 11 March 1928 had reached its 129th meeting, was less easily located. The Crickets were ostensibly dedicated to the innocent pursuit of Sunday-evening play-reading to the accompaniment of coffee, cigarettes and chocolate biscuits. Yet the Secretary of the Club and its host on that occasion, E. N. Avery, nevertheless thought it his duty to report that 'the furniture [of A 12 New] stood up to its task nobly.' 'Proceedings opened quietly.' Whereafter,

> members turned their attention to a collection of *pornographical* literature fresh from Paris and Mr Harbinson, who is reading French, evinced a deep knowledge of the colloquial language contained therein. It was some time before we could get on with the play, Pinero's *Playgoers*, which deals with a domestic episode. Mr Harbinson in the part of 'Pussy' the mistress, shewed that he knew what the character implied ...

Other activities included practising the steps of the Charleston and strumming the banjulele.[245]

Not everyone's evenings were devoted to such exertions. For some undergraduates were mathematicians, and for these the Adams Society had been founded in February 1923, under the aegis of Ebenezer Cunningham. On reaching its seventy-first meeting ten years later, paradoxically it allowed itself its first annual dinner, a festive occasion at which Cunningham regaled the company with some verses *à la* Lewis Carroll:

---

[242] Ibid., 304: 'We suffer in our rooms old-fashioned extravagant grates, and ancient, draughty windows because their artistic effect may compensate for their practical inefficiency. But the Reading Room is not even old.'

[243] Minute of 25 April 1925 recording dinner in the room of Mr R. E. M. Pilcher (E 10 New): SJCA, SOC.16.1.

[244] Minutes of the Nashe Society (SJCA, SOC.22.1). In February 1929 the Nashe was treated to a paper by Mr Anthony Blunt on 'Austrian Baroque'.

[245] Minutes of the Crickets Club (SJCA, SOC.6.7). Sometime in 1928/9 these peter out, the later pages of the book being used as a scrapbook for Club menus of 1943–5.

You may know, said Dirac, I was born in Geneva,
　At Bristol first solved an equation.
I then came to Cambridge and caught quantum-fever;
　The after effects were Lucasian.

Nineteen months later the Society had occasion to congratulate the Lucasian Professor on the award of his Nobel Prize.[246]

To the same period belongs a rare testimony to those to whom fell the task of servicing and clearing up after the young gentlemen. 'This is a most remarkable year', it was recorded on a scrap of paper bearing the date 11 March 1929. 'Today as above the Undergraduates are out on the river in white Flannels boating yet it is only three weeks ago that they were busy skating on the same water. We poor Devils are busy floor bumping.' Of the authors of this, who signed themselves J. Blackburn and R. Piggott, nothing more is known than their names.[247] Not so of the two post-War figures who stand as representative of an older way of doing things and of the engineers of change respectively. The first of these, the inimitable Lockhart, sometime Library Clerk, now Chief Clerk-cum-College Butler and omnicompetent factotum, demonstrated the same easy social skills in gracefully acknowledging receipt of seasonal gifts from his superior as he had in assisting Armitage to wrong-foot the bailiffs, in both capacities revealing himself as the equal of the resourceful butler of English country house fiction of the period, the counsellor of the reprobate younger son and keeper of his confidences.[248] As acutely conscious of the niceties of the College hierarchy as he was of the foibles of its Fellows, Lockhart found time to engage in correspondence with old members sweltering in the heat of Barbados in terms calculated to stir memories of the Cam and the courts forty years before.[249] 'Please ... let me have a good long letter when you have time', the sometime Fellow J. H. A. Hart wrote from distant Blakeney and Bakewell, along with a request for pipes and tobacco from Colin Lunn, and newspapers and magazines from the Cambridge Union. To Macklin he was 'the Steward'.[250] 'Careful as always about small matters, when from his sick-bed he dutifully sent his deputy a note reminding him to attend to the distribution of the Poor's Soup and the various needs of

[246] Adams Society Minute Book: SJCA, SOC23.1.1.

[247] SJCA, Arch 2.15.

[248] Letters thanking Tanner for a present of pheasants, 28 Dec. 1908: SJCA, TU12.10.369 ('We hope to make their better acquaintance tomorrow'); TU12.24.3 (17 Jan. 1920); above, p. 473.

[249] 'Thank you very much for your long and interesting letter. (...) I think that in 1888 we managed to get a pretty good bonfire going in 2nd Court, and it was allowed to go on quite a decent time before a porter noticed something and reported to the Senior Dean, then Cox, who with wonderful deliberation came along when the show was nearly over, so that he was quite sure of not catching dear old Bushe-Fox dancing round the fire linked with me': R. Radclyffe Hall (BA 1888) to Lockhart, 6 Sept. 1926: SJCA, TU12.30.15.

[250] SJCA, TU12.25.43, 51 (Jul.–Aug. 1921). Before his downfall Hart had borrowed substantial sums from Lockhart, and in the course of it had used him as an emissary in his dealings with Scott: GD, 21 Dec. 1917; M.7.2.3.26 (Hart to Gregory, 20 Sept. 1918); LMHD, 14 Jun. 1922.

Fellows and staff, Lockhart was at pains to explain that he was 'enclosing this with Harry's in order to save a stamp'.[251]

The second was the Fellow in charge of many of the processes of improvement in these years: the physiologist L. E. ('Daddy') Shore, a long-running Junior Bursar (1901–33) and a man of many proposals. Most of these were long-running too, none more so than that for the construction of a bath house, first mooted in 1901 at a time when rumour had it that Johnians did not wash.[252] In March 1914 progress had been made to the extent of an agreement 'that any scheme for Baths should not include a Swimming Bath'. (With the swimming bath party led by Liveing and Bonney, inevitably it failed.)[253] Then came the War. In 1922 the bath house was opened, whereafter the steamy edifice behind New Court was said to ring every morning with the strains of Wagner, Gilbert and Sullivan, and 'I want to be happy' while Larmor (initially the sturdiest opponent of the innovation) made his way there in cap and macintosh for his ritual ablutions.[254] For a brief period Shore's bath-house provided a shared collegiate focus for Fellows and undergraduates, rather in the way that shared lavatories once had.[255]

When the Council refused his request to spend £20,000 on the project the Bursar's plea of every age was heard: 'At any rate let us build something.'[256] Even when he was allowed to spend less, 'the old dear' (Glover's name for him) did not stint.[257] But Shore's schemes had a tendency to go wrong.[258] Those for the repair and redecoration of the Hall and for a summer house in the Fellows' Garden drew much hostile fire: 'the little dean [Creed] preparing another stroke against dear old Shore, about trees in grounds and Howard saying Shore overspends his allowance in College'; 'Howard rising in wrath against Shore, because hall floor to be repaired without tenders.'[259] His tendency to race ahead

---

[251] Beneath which is written 'CHARACTERISTIC!!!': Letter to G. W. Rawlinson, 4 Mar. 1925: SJCA, TU12.29.5. For the distribution to the local needy of The Poor's Soup, a charitable duty inherited by the College from the preceding hospital, see W. T. Thurbon, 'The College Bread and Broth Charity', *Eagle* lxix, no. 292 (1984), 16–23.

[252] Reddaway, *Cambridge in 1891*, 4. Cf. GD, 21 Oct. 1908: 'Registrary [at Senate House] complimented me [as Praelector] on the appearance of the men – had not yet come to "the soapless Colleges"; when he did he would send a cake of soap to the Master of each concerned.' The canard survived: see above, n. 91.

[253] General College Meeting, 13 Mar. 1914. Bonney: was 'a great controversialist with the misfortune always to be on the losing side': BSP, C. T. Nicholas to J. S. Boys Smith, 27 Feb. 1984.

[254] Crook, *Penrose to Cripps*, 27–9; *Eagle* xliv (1924–6), 183; lii (1941–7), 187.

[255] Under Scott's direction, in Sept. 1897 the Fellows' rears had been moved from Third Court to New Court: D33.13(3): Sewage Diary (an under-rated source). There is urgent need for a thorough investigation of the social consequences of shared lavatory and bathing facilities in the College.

[256] GD, 24 Oct. 1919. In the following month the Governing Body threw out his proposal to build a new wing: GD, 21 Nov. 1919.

[257] 'Saw SJC new baths building – Shore has not stinted money': GD, 16 Jun., 6 Oct. 1922.

[258] Thus, 'Shore's bath boiler out of order at once': GD, 9 Oct. 1922.

[259] GD, 11 Feb. & 24 Apr. 1925; also 29 May & 11 Nov. 1925. Cf. Crook, *Penrose to Cripps*, 51.

recklessly (or not to restrain others from doing so) was well, and almost fatally, demonstrated in the matter of the death-watch-beetle-infested timbers of the Old Library, saved from being consigned to the flames only by the Cunningham-like vigilance of the medievalist G. G. Coulton.[260] During Shore's tenure of office the need for constant vigilance must have seemed paramount, not least vigilance lest hares started by him got lost sight of. In 1915, while describing him 'drawing on his inexhaustible stores of procrastination', on the same page of his letter book Scott, recorded some verses of Glover, penned perhaps with 'Iolanthe' and Captain Shore in mind, commemorating the opposite side of him:

> 'There's a Zeppelin overhead' –
> 'You leave it to me', Shore said.
> 'And the bombs rain fast from the skies' –
> 'Trust the J. B.', Shore cries.
> 'And the Chapel tower's ablaze' –
> 'I'm the man with the hose' – Shore says.
> And the flames.
> But all the rest
> By the Censorship is suppressed.[261]

So the War had not killed humour in the College altogether. After it though there was sometimes the implication that a corollary of Shore's energetic interventions fore and aft was his opposition to any scheme or initiative not his own – apropos a ladies' lavatory for the May Ball for example.[262] Not that that prevented Glover – who relieved the tedium of one Council meeting by composing a sonnet about the man 'who ten thousand things at once would do':

> Who yearns to face the junior Fellows' rage,
> Coalporters mocking warmth with slack in sacks,
> Bedmakers voluble in garrulous rage,
> Cadets, Deans, Tutors – frontal and flank attacks?
> 'Leave it to me!' in quiet tones saith he;
> The Junior Bursar cries: 'Leave it to ME!') –

from coming to regard the mettlesome Shore, the College's Tigger to Scott's Eeyore, as 'one of the kindest of men'.[263]

---

[260] Crook, *Penrose to Cripps*, 67–70; GD, 28 Feb. & 2 Mar. 1925; C. W. Previté-Orton, 'The College Library and its renovation', *Eagle* xlv (1927–9), 296–302. As late as 16 Mar. 1928 Glover reported that 'a terrible restoration, with girders, [was] necessary for the true roof' (GD). For Previté's failure as Librarian to rein in the Junior Bursar, see Linehan, 'Making of the *Cambridge Medieval History*', 491.

[261] SJCA, SB1.23, p. 326.

[262] Leathem to Glover, 12 Feb. 1923: 'Arrangements in the cloak room at the ball are hideous.'

[263] Printed anonymously in *Eagle* xl (1918–19), 116; GD, 5 Dec. 1919; 20 Apr. 1925. Cf. Wood, *Glover*, 147–8; Boys Smith, *Memories*, 63; Benians (obit.) in *Eagle* lii (1941–7), 387–8.

8.　A MASTER 'SEEN IN THE DISTANCE'

'Council amusing for once', Glover grudgingly reported in October 1919.[264] With tedium casting its pall over all too many meetings, this was unusual as Scott aged and drift and indecision placed light relief at a premium. The norm was the reversal of decisions arrived at only a fortnight before[265] and the *longueurs* of petty estate matters interspersed with the affairs of Fellows: '½ hour over question of trying to buy Jolley's place in Bridge St. and another to get corner which sticks into our domain; more re little White and his brains or pains.'[266] The post-bellum Scott did not cut the dominant figure he once had. At Leathem's funeral his reading of 1 Corinthians 15 was 'bad, acid, soul-less'. Illness prevented him from attending events such as the LMBC centenary dinner and made him increasingly impatient. In his anxiety not to be overwhelmed by the detritus of ages he threw away papers that were still current.[267] Albeit his diplomatic hand had not lost its cunning, with advancing years he became ever more autocratic, ruling increasingly by intimation – and, as Thomas Baker wrote of the reign of Henry VIII, 'intimations then were to be complied with'.[268] When during Joynson-Hicks's reign as Home Secretary, an undergraduate was reported to him for having ordered 'a number of grossly indecent books' from 'a well-known (Parisian) dealer in obscenities', he was able to persuade the authorities that, as a student of human physiology and captain of his school cricket XI, the offender was obviously 'not of the decadent type', so that no further action was necessary. In intervening thus with the authorities Scott was following the example of his predecessor Francis Turner who had been similarly of opinion that in the case of former pupils of good schools allowance must needs be made for roguery. But he made a point of not mentioning the matter to the man's Tutor, J. M. Wordie, treating him as Beaton had regarded him, as 'a rather insignificant man'.[269]

Although by then Scott was seventy-seven, to the boy's father (a former Fellow) he wrote that 'you and I have been young and can allow for youth I hope.'[270] If so, the Master was more indulgent than the proctors were (as the son of the Lord Bishop of Bangor was soon to discover a couple of years later on first being caught strolling on Christ's Piece with a girl called Doris and then detected in

---

[264] 'Passionate outcry by tutors against sale of bootlaces in kitchen "beneath the dignity of a great college"': GD, 24 Oct. 1919; 13 Oct. 1922: 'Scott in chair, for once taking a view.'

[265] Regarding the election of Winfield, 'Bartlett and Baker changing': GD, 11 & 25 Nov. 1921.

[266] GD, 9 Jun. 1922. (This in the pre-Manserghian age, when meetings lasting for as much as two or three hours were thought excessive: ibid., 30 Apr. & 11 Jun. 1926.)

[267] GD, 22 Mar. 1923; *Eagle* xliv (1924–6), 202; 'Perhaps I am precipitate but the spectacle of the mass of old examination papers left first by Mayor and then by Mason made me think how awkward it might be if these things fell into the hands of a comic journalist or any other unscrupulous person': Scott to Tanner, 22 Dec. 1923: SJCA, TU12.16.99. (A Fellowship dissertation had gone missing.)

[268] Baker-Mayor, I. 105.

[269] Director of Public Prosecutions to Scott, 21 and 29 Mar. 1927; Scott to DPP, 26 Mar. 1927: SJCA, D90.1603–16; CBD, 18 Oct. 1922. Cf. above, p. 131.

[270] SJCA, D90.1610.

conversation with a barmaid at 'The Eagle')[271] or than he himself was when it came to dealing with colleagues. Neither for his colleagues or for himself was there any easing up. Thus, on receiving further complaints that November regarding two books dealing with what the man from the DPP said was 'the disgusting subject of female flagellation', he would no doubt have recalled yet another case twelve months earlier and noticed that in both cases the culprits were Old Rugbeians – and also made a note for himself, because as Master he was still dealing with all routine admissions correspondence.[272]

To a modern observer, Scott may appear to have been interested to an unusual degree in matters of race. 'The number of "Blacks" is now so large that we are thinking of having a black Tutor', he had written (perhaps playfully) in his bursarial days.[273] As Master he continued to indulge such foibles, concerning interracial marriage, for example,[274] and the hue of the offspring of native Jamaicans in particular.[275] In the latter regard it was presumably at his instigation that Tanner was directed to make enquiries regarding one of them in particular,[276] and hardly likely that Tanner would have done so of his own volition, any more than he would have favoured restrictions regarding Indian candidates, a group in whom he had always expressed special interest.[277] To censure Scott for failing to aspire to the exacting standards of twenty-first-century *Guardian* readers would be to do so for failure to transcend widely shared attitudes of his age, displayed for example at the June 1907 Congregation when on presenting his

---

[271] J. A. Venn to Wordie, 2 Nov. 1929; J. W. C. Turner to Wordie, 18 Nov. 1929 ('I report the matter to you as in the opinion of the Proctors it is undesirable that undergraduates should frequent places of this kind'): SJCA, tut. file/N. G. Davies. It was for academic reasons that Davies went down at the end of his first year.

[272] On this occasion Wordie *was* consulted: SJCA, D90.1658–60.

[273] Letter to Glover, 18 Dec. 1897: 'There is to be a white Reservation in the New Court & we are drafting a new set of College rules for persons in statu pup. Waist cloths must be worn at Lectures & in Hall etc. etc. Ju ju in the College Chapel on Tuesdays.'

[274] A recent College preacher's 'remedy for the "colour bar" [was] that black and white should intermarry freely and criss cross', he informed Bushe-Fox on 2 August 1912. 'Fortunately you and I are not in a position to humour him': SJCA, TU13/Scott R. F./14.

[275] 'Have you followed the correspondence in the *Daily Mail* in which Gregory is mixed up? Where the question whether mullatos obey Mendelian law has been discussed. I have been quite interested in the question whether Jamaica blacks have white children': letter to Tanner, 11 Sept. 1909: SJCA, TU12.11.235.

[276] 'I have ascertained that Sharp [T. H. Sharp, BA 1913] is quite white, with no trace of negro blood. He appears to belong to an eccentric but extremely clever family': J. N. Keynes [Local Examinations and Lectures Syndicate] to Tanner, 2 Mar. 1910: SJCA, TU12.12.17.

[277] Cf. Scott to Tanner, 1 Jun. 1910: 'With regard to Mr Rice and his Indians I have told him that we only take a certain number of Indians, giving preference in the first place to those recommended to us by members of our own Society': SJCA, TU12.12.126. By CM, 859/7, 'on the motion of Mr. Bushe-Fox it was agreed that in each year there be admitted to the College not less than one or more than two Indian students' (24 Feb. 1911). Cf. Bushe-Fox to Tanner, 4 Sept. 1907, apropos the 'new idea that there is a special prejudice against Indians at St John's. I thought it was because we treated blacks as brothers and "Fellows" that the white man looked elsewhere for a College': SJCA, TU12.9.188; 'St. John's has always had a special attraction for Indian students': R. P. Paranjpye, *Eighty-four, Not Out* (Delhi, 1961), 34.

first-class men Glover was 'chaffed' for the fact that five of them were 'natives of Asia', one 'a Chinaman' and four Indians.[278]

The zeal with which over Christmas and the New Year 1929–30 he pursued the Tutorial Bursar was another matter, however. With Ebenezer Cunningham, whose integrity was protected by a steely determination, Scott had long been at odds. No sooner was Cunningham appointed Tutor and Tutorial Bursar in 1921 than he was pressed into resigning the former office on the grounds that as a pacifist he was bad for trade.[279] By Cunningham's own account:

> It was one of the functions of the Tutors to make touch with schools, and in those days the 'public schools' ranked very high in the estimation of the Tutors, who found kudos in bringing students from schools of high social esteem. I was surprised one day to receive a suggestion that I should resign the office. I could not understand it at the time, but I gradually came to feel that there were those in authority who felt that it was not in the interest of the reputation of the College in the public eye that one of the Tutors should be an ex-conscientious objector.[280]

Despite his initial reluctance to exchange the Tutorship for the Steward-ship in succession to Brindley, Cunningham, who had not come from a school of 'high social esteem',[281] 'swallowed his pride' and set about sluicing out the Augean stables inhabited by Cash, Parsley and Merry, the successors of Peach and Miss Mutton, and by Hulks and Death, the head gardeners. In that role his attention to detail focused on profiteering both internal and external,[282] profiteering which applied even to the special Asiatic variety of St John's cock-roach hitherto harvested by the College store-man and sold on to his brother, an assistant at the University's Elementary Zoology laboratory. Cunningham set about eliminating these, as he thought successfully.[283] Instead of seeking a successor for the Kitchen Superintendent, who had come to be regarded as

---

[278] GD, 18 Jun. 1907; figures not confirmed by the record (*CUR* [1906–7], 1226ff). Cf. Tanner's report at the start of the following year: 'We matriculated 62 – only one native of India and one Chinese': GD, 21 Oct. 1907.

[279] (According to Benians) 'Master will not work with Cunningham as tutor, refuses to continue with tutors': GD, 4 Mar. 1921 (only a fortnight after Cunningham's appointment to the office): CM, 1102/3 (18 Feb. 1921). Cf. GD, 25 May 1923: 'after long wrangle [Council] made error of appointing little White lecturer by 6–4 (2 not voting) (...) Cunningham forced White on us by threat to resign Stewardship.'

[280] SJCA, 'Memoir', Arch.2.12a, p. 70.

[281] He and F. P. White both haled from Owen's School, Islington.

[282] '... first I looked at the meat bill, which seemed to me very large. I instituted a book for the recording of all supplies, with their quality, kind, weight and price. I did not have to look at the book again, but the meat bill the next year was down by £300': SJCA, 'Memoir', Arch.2.12a, pp. 74–5; above, p. 268.

[283] Ibid., 75–7. The creatures were Brindley's 'chief subject for lectures' and he 'would be very sorry if they was done away with', the store-man, 'Tip' Drury, advised Cunningham. Cf. Glover, *Cambridge Retrospect*, 55; *ex inf.* Dr G. C. Evans; SJCA, Arch.2.12a; Daniel, *Some Small Harvest*, 288. After reports that Drury had been writing off stores without authority, the Kitchen Committee had previously over-ruled Brindley's recommendation of a wage-rise (minutes of 23 Nov. 1922 and 1 Feb. 1923: SJCA, CC8.1). As a breeder of earwigs (GD, 20 Jan. 1921), Brindley's qualifica-tions for the office of Steward were unrivalled.

48 The College Gardeners, with Ralph ('Alteration is awful') Thoday and Bob Fuller third and fourth from right: SJCL, GPH5.9. The Gordon Lennox Cup for 1954, around which the group stands, was awarded to the College by the Royal Horticultural Society for the best display of fruit (Grapes, Apples and Pears) by an amateur exhibitioner.

'virtually a fifth wheel in the coach', in November 1931 the Steward promoted the Larder Cook, Alfred Sadler, to Head Cook and put him in charge of operations. When Death's successor failed to provide adequate produce from the College's vegetable garden on Storey's Way, he was replaced as Head Gardener by Ralph Thoday, whose Cox's Orange apples and vegetables would carry off first prizes from Royal Horticultural Society shows for year after year. Where Thoday sowed Sadler reaped, and for nearly thirty years the College was to remain deeply in debt to both of them.[284]

[284] CM, 1359/3. Thoday died in May 1981. See J. S. Boys Smith, *Eagle* lxix, no. 290 (1982), 18–20 (Memorial Service Address). Cf. GEDD, 2 May 1981 (on exclusions of mourners from funeral): 'A mistake: he ought to have said that he wanted me to be there but he felt if he said that it would be a reflection on Briggs, Boys Smith and all the rest of them'; J. S. Boys Smith, 'Portrait of a Head Gardener', *Eagle* liv (1950–51), 144–7; *Some Small Harvest*, 271–2, 281–2.

Despite feeling himself prevented by his principles from providing particulars of the wine served at feasts, Cunningham was highly regarded as Steward and enjoyed an enviable reputation for competence. The effectiveness of his taking a lively interest was quickly demonstrated.[285] It therefore came as a severe blow to him while on vacation in Switzerland in August 1927 to receive a wire from Scott informing him of the discovery of defalcations by his clerk.[286] Despite the deficiencies of the auditor (on which he remarked), he felt it a 'serious reflection' upon his Stewardship that the fraud, which was found to have been 'going on for some years', should have remained undetected – though the guilty party had been under suspicion since at least 1920, as Scott was no doubt aware.[287] The principal consequence of the incident was to expose Cunningham to Scott's censure, and in 1929 this came to a head when the unpaid account of a state scholar was raised on the University's Board of Education, of which Scott was chairman. The language in which Scott contemplated addressing a colleague whose record in such matters was exemplary would have been excessive in addressing an obtuse freshman. 'I almost despair of making clear to you the views of the Board', he wrote in a letter he thought better of sending (as an example of therapy by letter-book this is itself revealing). But no such second thoughts had intervened in the case of an earlier six-page screed in which he had demanded explanations, impugned the Tutor's good faith ('the omission to inform me was no doubt unintentional') and imputed to dishonesty the undergraduate's failure to pay his bill: 'These State Scholars come from a class whose parents have never paid for the education of their children and do not see why they should be called upon to commence to do so.'[288]

Even allowing for the time of year, these symptoms of Scott's distemper make him sound querulous as well as weary. Glover's account confirms that by the late 1920s the sometime purveyor of racy anecdotes whose election as Master had spurred the whisky distillers to seek his patronage was slowing down.[289] Memory of the days when he 'was a bachelor, shaved in cold water before his bed-maker came, made his lunch of bread and marmalade, and dined at 4.30 Hall', was now fading.[290] Perhaps the optimism he had expressed in the midst

---

[285] Cunningham to Boys Smith, 28 Oct. 1930; GD, 15–16 Mar. 1923, 21 Nov. 1924 ('a very good report on his kitchen work – real enterprise'); 20 Nov. 1925: 'Cunningham applauded genially for his capital management of Kitchens'.

[286] To the tune of £120-odd in the current year, a figure later revised to £368: Scott to Cunningham, 23 Aug. 1927, adding that he and the Senior Bursar had agreed that it would be 'inadvisable for several reasons to take legal proceedings': a judgement implying continuing misgivings about the state of kitchen finances: SJCA, SB1.23, pp. 34–5.

[287] Cunningham to Scott, 31 Aug. & 5 Sept. 1927; Kitchen Committee minutes (SJCA, CC8.1), 16 Dec. 1920, 17 Feb. 1921.

[288] Scott to Cunningham, 22 Jan. 1930 (SLB); Cunningham to Scott, 23 Dec. 1929–30 Jan. 1930: SJCA, D90.D1775–7.

[289] GD, 21 Mar. 1904: 'Hall. Scott full of tales, one of 2 girls and "an unmitigated aunt". Great tales of John Mayor's (…) dictionary lost-and-found as deputy for leg of chest of drawers': Scott to Tanner, 16 Sept. 1908 ('two enterprising firms have offered to supply the Lodge with whiskey'); GD, 11 Jun. 1939; Glover, *Cambridge Retrospect*, 92 (for the letter received at the Bursary addressed to 'The Senior Boozer').

[290] H. F. Baker to Benians, 14 Dec. 1946: SJCL, Misc. Letters/Baker, 5.

of thanking well-wishers on his election had not been translated into deeds.[291] In wanting the Port Latin Feast to go ahead during the General Strike (a portentous event for some) he was almost alone and was 'very disagreeable' about being in an 18 to 2 minority.[292]

But even so, even at the age of eighty-two he was still capable of making 'one of his happiest little speeches'[293] – and remained determined not to let go, continuing routinely to scrutinize undergraduate application forms and in red ink to indicate solecisms or inconsistencies therein. Increasingly suspicious of all other officers, he came more and more to depend upon his Bursar, Howard, and Howard's *alter ego* (and deputy in the Lent Term of 1931 whilst Howard was in South Asia advising the Burmese authorities on their future financial relations with India), Ifor Evans.[294] In accordance with its custom of retaining a Welshman as whipping boy, the College's inner cabinet responded by charging Evans with insubordination and overreaching himself in his behaviour towards Larmor.[295] The Scott–Larmor imbroglio of 1908 lasted as long as Scott did.

Even in the last months of his life, when he informed Benians from hospital that on medical advice he wished to give up 'the direct superintendence of State Scholars' forthwith, Scott could still not quite bring himself to hand it over to Cunningham completely.[296] And no sooner was he back in the Lodge than he decided to soldier on until October.[297] In modern parlance he would be politely described as a micro-manager. But if by 1930 he was tiring of the Fellows so were they, or at least some of them, of him, chafing at the knowledge that under the new statutes the College would never again be ruled by a Master in his eighties. Even so, the institution over which he had presided for perhaps too long continued to draw on intellectual streams as wide as they were deep and to harbour those encouraged in the expectation of dynastic advantage to treat the place as a refuge for three years of inertia or over-indulgence while in the same court men were engaged in work that would change the world. The report from the Head Master of Westminster on one applicant, the son of an Old Johnian, who, after a succession of tripos failures and near misses in these years, would

---

[291] 'One cannot help being touched by the outburst of good feeling and it does look as if we had [*sic*] a chance if it can only be laid hold of': letter to Tanner, 16 Sept. 1908, SJCA, TU 12.10.220.

[292] GD, 3 & 5 May 1926: 'Whole position more critical than when James II left London.'

[293] GD, 14 Oct. 1931, on the occasion of the admission of new Fellows; CM, 1354/1.

[294] GD, 4 Dec. 1931: 'Talk with Larmor: says Master's character changing, noted chivvies officials to keep them to their work. (Yes, says Ben, he has his knife into the tutors nowadays); says Howard and Ifor Evans run everything.'; 5 May 1932: 'Larmor feels on SJC Council high hand of Charlesworth, Evans and Howard behind them. (Howard always seems to me an able civil inhuman sort of creature)'; Thurbon, 'Memoir', 5. In 1934 Evans became Principal of University College of Wales, Aberystwyth: Boys Smith, *Eagle* lv (1952–3), 161–3; Boys Smith, *Memories*, 65–7.

[295] GD, 6 Jun. 1932: 'MPC[harlesworth] spoke of attitude and words of Evans to Larmor on Council as unsuitable, and rebuked by Howard and Ben'; 8 Jun. 1932: 'Raven doesn't and never did trust Evans, he said.'

[296] Scott to Benians, 19 Jul. 1933: 'To me the Tutorial Bursar is naturally indicated as the person to replace me. I can coach him at first and in any case will always be available for advice' (EABP).

[297] Scott to Benians, 28 Jul. 1933.

after 1945 proceed to a University post, the Fellowship of the College and membership of the Book Club, speaks volumes: 'He is a nice, good fellow; a gentleman in every sense; not prominent in any way, but a worthy and pleasing person of the kind that one likes to have to make up the backbone of the community.'[298]

It was, 'of course, only too easy just to go on doing the minimum of work and secure a comfortable Third Class', Charlesworth remarked to one of his pupils in 1931,[299] while in the following year a landlord in Portugal Place had occasion to complain of a group of his lodgers, and of one of them in particular, for 'coming home drunk practically every night and doing much damage to his rooms and causing great disturbance to the house'.[300] But all this belongs to just one section of the College triptych. Elsewhere in 1930 we have Hugh Sykes Davies as a second-year undergraduate securing both the first of his firsts and the first of his wives,[301] and three years later that 'foreign N. Sci. man' Paul Dirac winning the Nobel Prize for Physics at the age of thirty-one, the earliest of five such Johnian laureates between then and 1979.

Of these, Dirac, Cockcroft and Mott had all come into residence as either undergraduates or advanced students between 1922 and 1924 (by which time the fourth of them, E. V. Appleton, was already working with Rutherford in the Cavendish). Dirac, the son of a Bristol schoolteacher, and Appleton, the son of a warehouse clerk, in particular had been dependent on the system of academic awards in which the Asquith Commission of those years had been so interested. But in Dirac's case the part played by his academic protector was also crucial. That protector had been Cunningham. Cunningham it was who in June 1929 had suggested that to save him having to 'divert his energy to the discussion of Tripos problems with the ordinary student', a Praelectorship in Mathematical Physics should be created for him. Cunningham's steering of that proposal through the perilous Scottian rapids had coincided with the issue of the unpaid State Scholar's bill and will have constrained him to do all that was humanly possible not to alienate further the irascible Master.[302] For the benefit of his subject the Steward chose to bear the brunt. Of such concatenations does college life consist, and of such coincidences involving the likes of Dirac, Cockcroft and Mott with 'the ordinary student' coasting towards a comfortable Third the College has always had its share.

[298] H. Costley-White to [Wordie], 1 May 1930.

[299] Letter to T. M Arnison, 18 Mar., 1931, continuing: 'but I hope you will not do that, considering that you hold a special scholarship from Sedbergh to the College, and have therefore been given rather preferential treatment.'

[300] 'I am afraid that they are getting so bad that perhaps you would help me': landlord of Royston House, Portugal Place to Tutor, 2 May 1932. One of these, C. M. Glover, was a cousin of the abstemious Fellow of that name, another of whose relations, R. L. (Roy) Glover ('a lazy idler'; 'a thorough little fool': GD, 6 May, 30 Jun., 8. Dec. 1926) had got into scrapes earlier.

[301] 'I had felt that my papers [in Part I Classics] were the essence of mediocrity, fit to earn a good second – the sort of papers Pitt the Younger might have done.' The marriage ceremony was to be performed by his Methodist father, 'who thereby does great violence to my Oedipus complex': undated letters to Charlesworth (summer 1930).

[302] Cunningham to Scott, 18 Jun. 1929: SJCA, D90.D1726. The title was granted in 1931–2.

Although not Senior Tutor *de iure*, Sikes had been the longest in office when the returns for the Asquith Commission had had to be prepared. Yet the Master would not let go. He insisted on attending to the task himself. Six years later Sikes was heard to remark on the need for 'a man who knows old Johnians (...) to pull College together in view of Scott's decay'.[303] Possibly not for the first time, he was perhaps thinking of himself. As to Scott (though not to Sikes), Glover agreed: the Master was ever 'more helpless and the Council discursive'.[304]

When on 18 November 1933, in his eighty-fifth year and after twenty-five as Senior Bursar and as many again as Master duly celebrated by the Governing Body,[305] the end came, Glover readily acknowledged that Scott had 'always served St John's, his one great loyalty'. But for all that it was a case of 'at last'. Writing from Egypt, the youthful Colin Bertram, who had come up in 1929, testified to Scott's remoteness from the everyday life of the place. In the same sense, of the final twenty-five council meetings of his Mastership he had been absent from fourteen.[306]

'Armitage speaks of the Fellows of St John's as wholly obscure and quarrelsome', the Master of Magdalene had reported ten years earlier.

> It is sad that so great a place should be so disunited & undistinguished & feeble – unknown dons, poor quality of undergraduates, general weakness & unproductiveness. The Master is lost in indolence, a good-natured babbler. *Never* leaves Cambridge, but goes to University Arms for a fortnight while house is cleaned.'[307]

Perhaps not surprisingly in view of the identity of Benson's informant, as to Scott's holiday arrangements this was a calumny: in 1908 he had been to Margate.[308] Benson's description of Scott in the following year – 'a very amusing and lazy man' – was equally wide of the mark. R. F. Scott was famously industrious, uncritically so even – and (as Benson himself reported apropos his raillery at the expense of the Master of Trinity, Montagu Butler) no sluggard in the practical repartee department either.[309] Those who encountered him only in his final years as a stocky figure plagued by kidney and prostate problems[310] with a bowler hat seemingly welded to his head and a list of weaknesses which did not include sensitivity to others, saw less than half the man whose time extended back to an age when full academical dress was worn in the Cambridge streets and smoking while wearing it was an indictable offence. At that time,

---

[303] GD, 3 Feb. 1925. To the extent that it was Scott who had begun the tradition of Old Johnian dinners this was unfair.

[304] GD, 4 Dec. 1925.

[305] CM, 1409/1; H. F. Howard, *Eagle* xlviii (1934–5), 9.

[306] GD, 20 Nov. 1933; Bertram to Wordie, 7 Dec. 1933: 'I was sorry to hear that the Master had died, though I must confess that I had only once seen him in the distance in his garden' (tut. file/G. C. L. Bertram); CMM, 1388–1412.

[307] Benson Diary, 170, fo. 46r (27 May 1923).

[308] Scott to Tanner, 16 Sept. 1908: SJCA, TU12.10.220.

[309] Benson Diary, 174, fo. 37: 'one of the idlest men in Cambridge, I think, but excellent company' (6 May 1924); David Newsome, *On the Edge of Paradise: A. C. Benson: The Diarist* (London, 1980), 187.

[310] GD, 22 Jan. 1926.

after entertaining the University (or possibly the Lady Margaret) Boat, Scott had regaled his guests with cigars as they left and advised them as they did so that on their way out of College they would find his colleague the Senior Proctor lurking at the gate.[311]

In preparations for the election that followed Sikes's hand was guided by Charlesworth as Secretary of the Council.[312] Howard had no interest in the matter and was thought to favour Benians. Sikes's preference was for Engledow.[313] But as Glover described it the outcome was otherwise:

> ... Chapel for Election of Master. Sikes floundering, [Charlesworth], Raven, etc. fussing; 45 for Benians, 1 not voting.[314] Benians installed, briefly said Thank you; graceless huddled ceremony. (...) Evening, Fellows gathered in Combination Room; so to Hall. Sikes started grace before we were in & rather brief in proposing Master's health at dessert. Ben spoke rightly. (...) Colette Benians [young daughter] concerned as to moving. What of the swings and the rabbits?[315]

---

[311] Howard, *Eagle* xlviii, 5. One version of the story, one which although consistent with Lockhart's pheasants is otherwise incompatible with the liberal training regime even of earlier centuries, has this scene enacted after *breakfast*; Glover, *Cambridge Retrospect*, 93.

[312] Letters of Charlesworth to Sikes, 4 & 6 Dec. 1933: SJCA, SBF76.

[313] GD, 25 Feb., 22 & 27 Nov. 1933.

[314] Amongst Benians's papers is a list of Fellows with the names of the forty-five ticked. Seven were not ticked: R. R. Webb, Sir Duncan MacAlister, Larmor, J. T. Ward, H. S. Foxwell, Benians himself, L. Rosenhead.

[315] GD, 7 Dec. 1933. 'If a vote or two went elsewhere', he had written on the previous day, 'it may save you from King Herod's fate' (EABP).

I. BENIANS

SWINGS and rabbits were the order of the day and altogether suitable symbols of the new regime. 'Some years ago', one of the new Master's oldest collaborators on the reform of the history tripos confided to him on Christmas Day 1933, 'ONE WHO THINKS HE KNOWS said to me', "unless Benians makes a bad mistake he cannot help being Master of St John's" – though, 'knowing something of the last two elections and of the last two Masters', he admitted, 'I was only able to hope.'[1] In 1906, Benians's election to the Fellowship had been to Glover's satisfaction 'and most other people's'.[2] Likewise in 1933.

To judge by the scores of letters that came flooding in, all Cambridge and beyond had been looking forward to the outcome. G. M. Trevelyan wrote to say that it was because he was sure that Benians would be elected Master that he had sought to dissuade him from standing for the vacant Vere Harmsworth Chair (of Imperial and Naval History), also that of course he must stay on the History Board 'till we have got the Reforms through'.[3] From the headmaster of the College Choir School came a picture drawn by the boys and a 'little tea-pot stand' made by them (harbingers of many such diplomatic offerings and hardly the sort of thing it would have been sensible to have troubled Scott with);[4] from Henry Roseveare (BA, 1904), Benians's near-contemporary, a letter measuring him against his two predecessors (to Benians's distinct advantage);[5] and, on the day of the election itself, another from the faithful Lockhart, on behalf of himself and his fellow servants: 'It is all the more pleasing to me personally as I have known you from your earliest undergraduate days and seen you climb up gradually step by step in the College to the very highest position it is possible to attain.'[6] 'Now that I am asking for payment of Income Tax', even the man responsible for collecting it from the Fellows weighed in.[7] The succession of the blithe Benians to the black-letter Scott was universally acclaimed. It can only

---

[1] Letter from B. [G]oulding-[B]rown (1881–1964), for whom see D. Newsome, 'Two Emmanuel historians', *Emmanuel College Magazine*, Quatercentenary Issue (1984), 104–6 (25 Dec. 1933). (Unless otherwise indicated, all material cited in this chapter is derived from the uncatalogued Benians papers.)

[2] GD, 5 Nov. 1906. A year earlier there had been 'great disappointment' on that score: GD, 6 Nov. 1905.

[3] 'They are more yours than any one else's, and I have great hopes that that work of yours will be crowned': letter of 2 Jan. 1934. See *CUR* (1908–9), 968–9; J. O. McLachlan, 'The origin and early development of the Cambridge Historical Tripos', *Cambridge Historical Journal* ix (1947–9), 97.

[4] Letter of 22 Dec. 1933.

[5] 'I cannot imagine your being at all like either, unless the cares of a Tutor have made you lose that geniality of temper, which I remember, not to speak of the smile which comes back to my mind's eye': letter of 5 Jun. 1934.

[6] 'We all have the utmost respect, love, and regard for you, and hope you will live to enjoy for many many years your well earned promotion': letter of 7 Dec. 1933.

[7] Letter of J. W. Turner, 11 Jan. 1934.

have been by a slip of the pen that H. S. Foxwell, the new Master's old mentor, while describing the election as 'in many ways ideal', went on to observe that 'None of us is too old or too young to feel in intimate relations with you.'[8] Evidently most did.

Larmor, like Foxwell an absentee from the election, wrote anxiously from Co. Down enquiring whether Scott had left an autobiography, asking after 'the illustrious Dirac' (to whom, he said, sometime earlier he had offered his rooms, 'but he spurns the suggestion') and concluding with some general and largely illegible remarks about the hopelessness of everything.[9] Such was not the tenor of the new Master's first evening in office. In the Combination Room 'Ben spoke rightly', Glover noted, though he omitted to record the gist of his remarks – which inasmuch as they so deeply moved at least one of his hearers is the more to be regretted.[10] However, the association with Benians of things heard but not reported, things that made a profound impression yet never got written down, was altogether characteristic of a man to whom as well as a reputation for cordiality a degree of remoteness forever attached. Since going round the world on the Kahn Fellowship in 1911–12 had involved resigning his college lectureship, by accepting it he had taken a risk. But the risk had been a calculated one, and before he was half-way back he had been reappointed.[11] The Kahn was to prove a good investment. As well as providing him with a wider perspective, it put him in touch with influential people especially in America and Asia, and endowed him with a powerful allure. The career of the circumnavigator with connexions everywhere, royally received at every port of call, the scholar with matching interests reaching far beyond the European limits of Cambridge history was that of a man of sharply distinguishable profile from that of his magisterial predecessor shackled to his College desk for half a century, poring over the College records for leisure. Benians possessed a deeper hinterland and scanned wider horizons. Through his 'Notes from the College records', which had monopolized the pages of the *Eagle* for decades, Scott had looked backwards. Benians was steeped in the College past too. But his vision was also lateral and it comprehended areas which Cambridge History had yet to colonize and into which it was he who would lead the explorers.[12]

Another aspect of the man, frequently commented upon, was a

[8] Letter of 11 Dec. 1933.

[9] Letter of 9 Dec. 1933: 'The earth will thus not perish by general refrigeration but by a scientific catastrophe, when a new evolution will gradually arise. All which I pray may be outside your time. Yours truly, J. Larmor.' 'Dirac has just gone off to get his Nobel Prize', Benians replied on 16 December. 'He is at a loss to know what to do with the money!'

[10] 'After the election of this afternoon I hastened to my rooms and, quite frankly, I wept. When I heard your speech this evening, I very nearly broke down again, but for the presence of Frank Engledow, who told me that yours was a point of view he had long felt, but never had expressed': Ifor Evans to Benians, 7 Dec. 1933.

[11] CMM, 857/3, 885/8; Scott to Benians, 3 Feb. 1912; Benians to Tanner, 28 Feb. 1912: SJCA, TU12.14.50.

[12] See Ronald Hyam, 'The study of imperial and commonwealth history at Cambridge, 1881–1981: Founding fathers and pioneer research students', *Journal of Imperial and Commonwealth History* xxix (2001), 76–9.

quasi-numinous quality which found expression in the exclusive attention received by the individual before him.[13] Such was the lightness of touch when writing, the tremulousness almost, that often the pen seems only to have flickered over the paper, scarcely touching it – which for the historian presents difficulties of course. But the illegibility of his much corrected drafts, as well as a system of shorthand all his own, were marks of the man whose desire it was to give delight and hurt not, just as the retention of those drafts signified dissatisfaction with anything other than the *mot juste*. Here was a man with a hinterland, a man with a genius for friendship and a writer of prose shot through with velleities and veins of poetry revealing an alertness to language and its cadences and a historical sensibility which, as Vice-Chancellor in 1940, a year with, as he said, 'no close parallel in our history', he was to deploy to such effect.[14]

Here was the gilded youth whom the workmanlike Tanner had described as 'sound and steady rather than brilliant',[15] the man who already before the War had been asked to overhaul the teaching of history in the University of Bombay and considered for chairs at Belfast and Birmingham, and after it measured for the Secretaryship of the Cambridge General Board in 1926, and in 1929 for the Vice-Chancellorship of Reading,[16] the warmth of whose smile his undergraduate contemporary Roseveare remembered decades later, the 'gentle Master' whose greeting Owen Chadwick would describe as a benediction,[17] whom every committee wanted as a member and every applicant for advancement as referee since a single phrase from Benians was worth an essay from the next man. 'Cicero was the Benians of the Roman Republic', Charlesworth explained to some mathematical neighbours at Hall in 1930: 'all the sweet reasonableness and the equity, but Ben lacks the colossal vanity.'[18] During the years of both peace and war he was the gracious host, to visiting potentates and sultans, to the Congress of Universities of the British Empire (in 1936), to Danish delegations and, in particular, to members of the Dominion and American armed forces. As well as taking the lead in promoting the study of American history in the University, Benians came to be regarded as unofficial consul for American affairs in the city and beyond. 'I am told that you are more likely than anyone in Cambridge to know what the USA plans with regard to the Bull are and who controls them in this country', the Bursar of St Catharine's wrote to him in 1945 regarding the

---

[13] As by Boys Smith, *Memories*, 24–5.

[14] *CUR* (1940–41), 131–2. Thus his reply to the fraternal greetings of the National Alumni Association of Princeton University, 'to you who stand on the firing line in defence of our common heritage of liberty and freedom' and to the founder of the periodical *La France Libre* ('It is impossible to think of a world in which France is not free to continue her beneficent services to mankind; least of all can we contemplate it in the old Universities of England which owe to the University of Paris the beginnings of their life'): cable of 10 Jun. 1940; letter to A. Labarthe, 11 Sept. 1940.

[15] Reference to A. W. Ward regarding candidature for Allen Scholarship, 3 Feb. 1905: SJCA, TU12.7.20.

[16] GD, 2 Jun. 1913 (17 Jun. 1926). Revealingly, Glover considered the post less arduous than a tutorship: 'he might get some History done' (16 Mar. 1929).

[17] 'The Commemoration Sermon' [1952], *Eagle* lv (1952–3), 25.

[18] GD, 3 Jun. 1930.

Bull Hotel, a St Catharine's property.[19] In the same year St John's received the first Pitt Professor of American History into its Fellowship and in the following year established a Dominion Fellowship, representing its Master's parallel commitment to those two aspects of extra-European study and scholarship.[20]

On his return home in December 1912 the India Office had appointed Benians Local Adviser to Indian Students, on account of which and of his academic obligations in May 1916 the Cambridge Borough Tribunal granted him exemption from military service.[21] The University's Indian students were certainly in need of an adviser, not to say a protector, and this was a role that Benians, like Tanner before him, had been fulfilling. To a statement in the *Athenaeum* two years earlier, that 'despite certain individual successes, there [had] been a large proportion of Indians who gained nothing from the intellectual studies' of Oxford and Cambridge, he had responded with a characteristically generous-minded rebuttal of the consequential proposition that the Government of India 'abandon their policy of encouraging students to come to England'.[22] And that remained his role, notwithstanding the implication of the privacy of his Tribunal hearing that at the core of his duties was something even more pressing and confidential than the survival of the economics tripos,[23] and despite his mother's curiosity on the matter, just as she had previously been about his never-ending work on the *Cambridge Modern History* atlas volume.[24] 'How is it that you still have the Indian work?', she wanted to know. 'I thought you had given that up now. Will nobody take it on?', she asked when urging him and his new wife to come to her for the birth of their first child: an invitation that the couple declined, just as her son had initially refrained from revealing the identity of his fiancée. 'Am I right in guessing *her* to be Miss Glover?', Mrs Benians enquired. No, she wasn't. She was Miss Sylvia Dodds, 'one of the rippingest girls in College', Glover's Girton pupils assured him, Benians's junior by about seventeen years and 1918's only First in Part II History. In the period of his walking out with her (with Eileen Power, another former Kahn Fellow, acting as chaperone),

[19] J. H. Hutton to Benians, 21 Aug. 1945.

[20] CMM, 1776/11 (4 Aug. 1944); 1873/4. See F. Thistlethwaite, *Cambridge Years* (Cambridge, 1999), 34–5.

[21] *Cambridge Daily News*, 10 May 1916. The case was heard in private.

[22] *CR* xxxv (1913–14), 195, 222. This was the 'capital paragraph' prompted by Glover's report that his five proctorial colleagues were 'all curiously touched with idea of excluding Indians if possible from University': GD, 26, 27 Jan. 1914. Cf. the words of R.Paranjpye ('Looking back at my life in Cambridge I cannot say that I took a very prominent part in college or university life except among my Indian fellow-students, but I found many good friends there'): *Eighty-four, Not Out*, 35; and the more cautious approach adopted by Balliol: J. Jones, *Balliol College: A History*, 2nd edn (Oxford, 2005), 253–4. In the sharpest of contrasts to the case of Paranjpye is that of the New Zealander W. T. Ritchie (matric. 1901), a first-generation emigrant from Scotland, rugby blue in 1904 playing at wing three-quarter, and Scottish international in the same position in 1905. Photographs of his undergraduate years are in SJCL, Album 35.

[23] 'The tribunal called him up; he asked VC not to request exemption this time; went to Burg and because of his knee was cleared C3, so stays for his proper work with Indians here': GD, 26 Jun. 1917. But Glover may not have known all.

[24] 'Are you very tired of the map work? You must be' (letter of 4 Feb. 1908).

Benians had shared his views on marriage with Glover. 'Men generally marry for companionship', Glover reported him remarking, 'and, in his observation, generally don't get it in marriage.'[25]

With his still young wife and growing family, his background in education, his experience as Senior Tutor (an office instituted for him in 1926, and for the time being no more than a *primus inter pares*, though doubtless to the consternation of those who shared Tanner's fear of creating 'a mere bureaucrat')[26] and his cosmopolitan range, Benians brought to the Master's Lodge a breath of fresh air which, to judge by the departing chatelaine's discouraging description of the place, was much needed.[27] After the gloomy days of Scott's later years the radiant uplands beckoned. Johnians were in the ascendant. Dirac had recently shared the Nobel Prize; in May 1934 J. G. W. Davies bowled Bradman for a duck at Fenners (the achievement registered even with Glover) and the new Master instituted the custom of Council tea. In 1935 Benians was being sounded out by his neighbour A. B. Ramsay, the Master of Magdalene and Chairman of the University Conservative Association: never mind what his politics were, was he willing to be drafted as the University's next MP?[28] It has been said of Ramsay that he 'had no pretensions to be a serious academic; he was therefore considered a suitable college master.'[29] The same could not be said of Benians.

2. NEW BUILDING AND OLD HABITS

In February 1929 T. R. Glover had acquired a copy of the early edition of Wordsworth's *Prelude* in which (III.48) the poet's 'three Gothic courts' appeared as 'three gloomy courts':[30] a description of the easterly part of the College at that date altogether more accurate. In particular, there were virtually no traces of colour visible above the Great Gate, which was 'not what Bishop Fisher saw, or intended that future generations should see'.[31] After Scott's long decline it was time not only to freshen the place up but even to keep it standing. On the day after his election the new Master presided over a meeting of the Council at

---

[25] Letters of 18 Jan. 1918 and 7 May 1919; GD, 27 Feb. 1918. Perhaps Glover shared her maternal suspicions, whence his reaction when Benians told him of the engagement: 'I was stirred, for I feel it like losing him and marriage rots life so, when it is not right': GD, 23 Feb. 1918; 14 Nov. 1917.

[26] CM, 1237/6 (23 Jul. 1926); above, p. 453. The hyper-sensitive Glover did not even notice the development.

[27] Lady Scott to Benians, 7 Dec. 1933 (day of election): 'Do come in as soon you can manage to look over the Lodge though it is in an awful mess at present.'; to Mrs Benians, 1 Jul. 1934: '*We* had hordes of black beetles that took a long time to eradicate. It is *not* pleasant to come home from a party and find the front stair black with cockroaches, and then leaping into bed to find them there too': SJCA, M10.1.9.

[28] GD, 9 May 1934; 22 Nov. 1934 ('such is March of progress'); 26 Jan. 1935 ('Ramsay asked Ben what are his politics'). In 1911 R. F. Scott had been spoken of in that connexion: GD, 16 Jan. 1911.

[29] R. Hyam in *ODNB*.

[30] GD, 27 Feb. 1929.

[31] *Eagle* xlix (1935–7), 5.

which, at the end of the term which had begun with the appointment of John Cockcroft as Junior Bursar in succession to Shore, the Old Buildings Committee reported on the ruinous condition of the College's bricks and mortar. The account of subsidence and of stonework, brickwork, floor beams and roof timbers all in a 'dangerous' or 'crumbling' state was alarming and required immediate action. Accordingly, a consultant architect in the person of Sir Charles Peers was appointed for a period of five years.[32]

Although there is no need to repeat A. C. Crook's technical account of that period of activity, two complicating considerations do deserve mention. One, nourished by memories of the still recent Library ceiling episode, was a widespread suspicion of root-and-branch measures, whether essential or not, combined with a ready susceptibility to rumour.[33] The other was the inevitability of delays caused by the academic exercise of aesthetic judgement over such matters as restoration and, already, the issue that was to divide the Fellowship until after the War, the lightness or darkness of the mortar to be used in pointing and repointing the brickwork.[34] The sequence of motions and amendments on the subject of the First Court lawns debated at the Governing Body meeting of 8 August 1935, culminating in the motion 'That nothing be done', adequately demonstrated the strength of the equipollent forces engaged in such controversies.[35]

Even so, over the next five years more was achieved than in any similar period since the 1860s. The Council minutes of the period regularly recorded the progress: of the turrets surrounding the Great Gate taken down and rebuilt with sixteenth-century bricks salvaged from near and far; of the stonework above the Gate repaired and repainted (a procedure described as 'in one sense conservative, in another revolutionary') after delays caused by damage done by the composition of the lime pickle used in the preparatory cleaning process; of the rafters and hammer beam trusses of the beetle-infested Hall cleansed; and structural problems affecting both the ceiling and the floor of the Combination Room addressed.[36]

While these works were in progress activity opened up on another front

---

[32] CMM, 1402/5, 1415/3; *Eagle* xlix (1935–7), 78; M. Oliphant and Lord Penney, 'John Cockcroft', in *Biographical Memoirs of Fellows of the Royal Society* xiv (1968), 153–4.

[33] E.g. on death of Rutherford: 'Will Cockcroft now go higher and SJC find a new JB to rebuild us again?': GD, 20 Oct. 1937; 'Briggs (...) says Cockcroft wanted to take down Combination Room ceiling in squares, clean it and put it back! They stopped this': GD, 27 May 1936. Cf. Crook, *Penrose to Cripps*, 51–4, 82–92.

[34] Wordie to Benians, 23 Aug. 1938.

[35] In this case it was then decided 'not to proceed further until plans had been prepared for the rebuilding of the block at the north end of First Court': CM, 1471/10. Cf. Crook, *Penrose to Cripps*, 91–2. In March 1938 the Council agreed, on the recommendation of the Old Buildings Committee, '(1) to pave the foundations of the old Chapel, using the paving stones to be taken up from the New Court Cloisters; (2) to re-lay a number of the tombstones; (3) to remove two badly decayed stones without names, and to mark the sites; (4) to re-cut some of the lettering on the tombstone of Thomas Baker': CM, 1559/6. But no action followed.

[36] CMM, 1421/9, 1428/11, 1434/4, 1463/7; 'A Letter from Cambridge', *Spectator*, 7 Jun. 1935; GD, 26 Jan. 1938: 'Architect finds beams of Combination Room floor no longer rest in wall on court side! And long haven't.' For the state of the turrets see Crook, *Penrose to Cripps*, plate 1 opp. p. 166.

ST JOHN'S COLLEGE

MEETING OF THE GOVERNING BODY

On Tuesday, 30 July 1935, at 2.30 p.m.

A meeting of the Governing Body of the College was held in the Combination Room on Tuesday, 30 July 1935. The following were present:

The Master, The President, Mr Harker, Prof. Baker, Dr Shore, Prof. Rapson, Mr Cunningham, Dr Coulton, Mr White, Mr Wordie, Prof. Winfield, Mr Yule, Mr Charlesworth, Sir H. F. Howard, Mr Raven, Dr Previté-Orton, Mr Guillebaud, Mr Boys Smith, Dr Cockcroft, Mr Brindley, Dr Redman, Mr Gatty, Mr Bailey, Mr Wormell, Dr Goldstein, Mr Jackson, Dr Oliphant and Prof. Constable, twenty-eight in all.

1. The Report of the Council to the Governing Body on New College Buildings was discussed. The further consideration of this Report was adjourned to the meeting of the Governing Body on October 15.

2. The Report of the Garden Committee on Grass Plots in First Court was discussed.

Dr Shore proposed and Mr Charlesworth seconded:
"That only the two grass-plots on each side of the main pathway in First Court be joined together."

To this an amendment was proposed by Dr Coulton, and Mr Gatty seconded:
"That the whole scheme, as prepared by Sir Charles Peers, be carried out this summer."

Upon the amendment being put to the vote, 14 voted in favour and 11 against; the amendment was therefore carried.

The amendment was then put as a substantive motion:
"That the whole scheme, as prepared by Sir Charles Peers, be carried out this summer."

To this an amendment was proposed by Mr White, and Mr Yule seconded:
"That nothing be done."

Upon the amendment being put to the vote, 10 voted in favour and 14 against; the amendment was therefore lost.

An amendment was proposed by Dr Shore, and Mr Bailey seconded:
"That only the two plots on each side of the main footpath be joined together during this Long Vacation."

Upon the amendment being put to the vote, 7 voted in favour and 15 against; the amendment was therefore lost.

The motion was now put to the vote and carried by 15 votes to 9.

E. A. BENIANS
Master

30 *July* 1935

49 'That nothing be done': the St John's Circumlocution Office in control
(Governing Body minutes, July 1935)

in connexion with plans for the first new buildings for more than a century. 'Owing to our preoccupation with the problems of our new buildings we have not I am afraid made much progress with the old buildings in the last two years', Benians wrote to Peers at the end of 1938, thanking him for his advice and asking if he would be willing to be consulted 'in future' when the College turned to 'our other courts'.[37]

A Council committee 'to consider the steps to be taken towards the utilization of the College Precincts for further buildings and other purposes' had been appointed in May 1930 with Benians one of its members.[38] However, it was not until February 1932 that its recommendations were referred to the Governing Body, by which time the College had acquired the last of the Bridge Street tenements occupying the frontage between St John's Street and Magdalene Bridge. Again, a description of what then ensued, or the essence of it, is already available.[39] But, again too, it is necessary to emphasize the interconnectedness of other matters either raised at the Governing Body or emerging later, the rival attraction of building to the west of the river behind New Court and the recently opened bath-house, the issue of the College's right of way across Magdalene territory, and the question whether or not to relocate and diminish the Master's Lodge. ('I can't help feeling it a little absurd of these bourgeois people in possession of these great houses', Benson had remarked of the Scotts in 1911.)[40] Principal amongst these other matters was the problem of numbers for on this the case for expansion largely depended. After the failure of the attempt by the acrimonious Larmor (Glover supporting) to scupper development in a northward direction,[41] the Fellowship were left to contemplate the proposition that there was need for 'additional accommodation of about 12 Fellows sets and 100 other sets': a calculation based on the assumption that 'a man should have at least two years in College and Scholars their whole time'; that 'all Fellows are entitled to room in College if in residence', and that there were 400 men and forty-five Fellows to provide for.[42] Additional luxury items such as a ladies' cloakroom were postponed, while a 'sick room' or 'sick-bay'[43] (what today would be called a 'health centre') was added later.

In April 1938 the Senior Tutor, J. M. Wordie, reported that the College was expecting about 150 freshmen at Michaelmas, a number well in excess of the 'about 135' approved by a Council minute of 1927.[44] Even at Michaelmas 1927,

---

[37] CM, 1583/10 (9 Dec. 1938); letter of 14 Dec. 1938.

[38] CM, 1323/6.

[39] Crook, *Penrose to Cripps*, 99–110.

[40] Diary, 119, fo. 19–20.

[41] Governing Body *Acta*, 19 Feb. 1932 ('usual College meeting atmosphere of sniggering inattention': GD, *ad diem*).

[42] 'New College Buildings. First Report of the Committee …', 1–2; *Eagle* l (1937–8), 254.

[43] Thus Miller, *Portrait of a College*, 118.

[44] Which had been followed by another concerning the bulging of the wall at the north-east corner of Second Court due to settlement of portion of the roof: timely reminder of the connexion between numbers and space and of the pressure of one on the other: CMM, 1253/9, 10; 1562/12.

the number admitted was 147.[45] But would that pressure of numbers continue? Prompted by Larmor's February 1932 prophecy of 'a considerable falling off in the number of entries', a month later the statistician G. U. Yule produced a survey the conclusion of which was 'that the proportion of freshmen age coming forward circa 1975 [would] be only half that with which we have been provided during recent years.'[46] In the same sense, F. L. Engledow felt obliged to alert the Senior Bursar to 'one of the most profound changes in the history of civilisation [which was] slowly taking place in the form of a sharp decline in birth rate' and accordingly to advise him against acquiring more land for house-building.[47]

Here was evidence of the College's ability if not to think outside the box then at least to speculate within a long-term development. Of the various alternative and modified schemes provided by the architect, Sir Edward Maufe, the scaled-down one eventually decided upon was for completion of Chapel Court on the site of the razed Bridge Street tenements and retention of the Master's Lodge where it was.[48] The decision, taken in October 1937, stipulated completion by July 1939. In May 1940 the names 'Chapel Court', 'Forecourt' and 'North Court' were adopted for the new buildings. Their total cost (something over £110,000) was met from reserves accumulated by prudent husbandry over the previous decade.[49]

Significant assistance was provided by the benefaction of Baron Courtney of Penwith, former Fellow, who had died in 1918. But the Senior Bursar, Sir Henry Howard, had no such expectations of the modern generation, and to judge by the example of two recently deceased long-lived Fellows of the College his scepticism was justified. Neither Liveing nor Heitland, whose rendering of 'Jerusalem, my happy home' had enlivened the corridors of the Evelyn Nursing Home during his last days, bequeathed anything to the place. Glover attributed the latter omission to his old Tutor's general disaffection with a college of nonentities.[50]

Another sign of the times was the installation by some resident Fellows of private bathrooms and lavatories, largely at their own expense, in despair of improvement of the noisome state of the College's communal facilities in Second Court which the Fellows' Amenities Committee in its earliest report

[45] *Resident Members [List] of the University*, 1927, xxiii–xxiv.

[46] 'Note on a Possible Fall in the Number of Undergraduates owing to the Fall of the Birth-rate' [Mar. 1932] (SJCL, W3 [Yule]), 1, 7. Cf. his *The Fall of the Birth-Rate: A Paper Read before the Cambridge Eugenics Society, 20 May 1920* (Cambridge, 1920); *ODNB* (F. Yates and A. Yoshiaka).

[47] 'I imagine that in fifty years' time our population will commence a short period of constancy and will thereafter show an extremely rapid decline': Engledow to Howard, 23 Feb. 1932 (SJCL, Yule papers); *ODNB*: Engledow (G. D. H. Bell).

[48] Crook, *Penrose to Cripps*, 107–8, whose account is not entirely helpful. The scheme illustrated in *Eagle* 1 (1937–8), opp. p. 253, is likely to have given readers a wrong impression of what was intended.

[49] CM, 1636/2. Between June 1925 and July 1937 the value of the College's securities had increased by some 76 per cent, from £566,270 to £999,650: CM, 1516/7.

[50] '£26,000, but not 1d. to SJC; his house hereafter to Newnham Coll. He had his temper, & SJC for 40 years does little to endear – ruled by timid people, and timid people are not generally gracious; & WEH was easily, and early, chafed ...' GD, 18 Oct. 1934, 21 Sept. 1935.

St John's College, showing the New Buildings

JOHNIAN SOCIETY

LUNCHEON IN HONOUR OF

THE RIGHT HONOURABLE SIR JAMES GRIGG, K.C.B., K.C.S.I., M.P.

HONORARY FELLOW OF ST JOHN'S COLLEGE, CAMBRIDGE

Secretary of State for War

at the Connaught Rooms, Great Queen Street, London

President: MAJOR-GENERAL IAN HAY BEITH, C.B.E., M.C.

MENU

Hors d'Oeuvres

⁂

Roast Turkey

Roast Potatoes   Brussels Sprouts

⁂

Empire Fruit Flan

⁂

Coffee

7 JANUARY 1944

50 The Johnian Society at War: Empire fruit flan and an artist's impression of
the New Buildings that never were, repeating that published in *Eagle* 1938,
and reprinted doubtless in order to confuse the Hun

had described as 'deplorable and entirely unworthy of a great institution'.[51] Of this cellular development Ifor Evans, Charlesworth and Boys Smith were the pioneers and collegiality the inevitable casualty.[52] The rooms of non-residents were less sacrosanct. During Sikes's term's leave of absence in 1934 his were used for the accommodation of guests and even as the setting for one of Brindley's dinner parties; and Sikes was President.[53] Larmor was another matter. On resigning his chair in October 1932 he had retired to Northern Ireland, leaving uninhabited the enormous set at K6 Second Court which he had occupied since 1885. Yet when the installation of a bathroom there was mooted, his response was swift: 'In view of Sir Joseph Larmor's letter, it was agreed to make no structural alterations in his rooms at present.'[54] Despite pressure on space, there was no arguing with the vested interests of the irascible Ulsterman. Until his death in 1943 Larmor's name remained over the door of the set of rooms whose emptiness had meanwhile come to be seen as a threat to College, and even national, security.[55] Wordie, as Senior Tutor, was 'against worrying Larmor, Webb and Ward about their rooms in College',[56] with the consequence that, when Larmor, Webb and Ward had passed beyond reach of being worried, the extent of redecoration and plumbing required was such as to make it seem inequitable for the new occupants to bear the full cost.[57] In Webb's case this meant making good more than forty years' neglect.[58] But thus the process was hastened towards the

[51] Work there had been abandoned in 1914. 'No other society in Cambridge and no reasonably decent private family would tolerate such a state of affairs', the undated report (SJCA, CC88.1) concluded. The Committee's observation in January 1928 that 'conditions of life in College in many ways approximate[d] to those prevalent in a small French provincial town' was not intended as a recommendation. In July 1930 the insanitary Third Court facilities attracted the same criticism, such cleaning as they received being 'mainly confined to a hasty polishing of the door handles'. See Crook, *Penrose to Cripps*, 62.

[52] 'There was no bathroom in the College' during his period of residence (1906–10), Lord Morton of Henryton believed. The closest convenience for a resident of First Court was in the Hawks Club (then in All Saints' Passage): 'St John's fifty years ago', *Eagle* lviii (1958–9), 9–10.

[53] CMM, 1441/18, 20 (11 Oct. 1934), 1443/7 (25 Oct. 1934).

[54] CMM, 1471/13 (8 Aug. 1935), 1472/9 (10 Oct. 1935).

[55] Below, p. 549.

[56] GD, 15 May 1935. For the last two, see *Eagle* lix (1935–6), 122–3, 272–3; Boys Smith, *Memories*, 16, 38. R. R. Webb, 'the last of the great mathematical coaches' (a sixty hours a week man in his prime), Fellow since 1872 and Senior Fellow at the time of his death in 1936, had kept at I 7 New since 1883; and J. T. Ward (Fellow since 1876; d. 1935) at M 5 Second since 1903. Webb's bequest to the College of a collection of items already held in the Library was declined: CM, 1511/10. In a letter to Benians of 3 Aug. 1936 A. A. Robb alleged that there was money hidden in a secret compartment of Webb's desk.

[57] CM, 1508/12 (30 Oct. 1936) concerning Boys Smith, the new occupant in this case, who as well as being in the vanguard of the bathroom movement had already redecorated his old set twice at his own expense (see his *Memories*, 35, 39). In February 1937 the system was regularized by CM, 1520/9. In 1930 Ifor Evans had borne £350 of the £500 cost of restoring Mayor's old set: GD, 7 Jun. 1930.

[58] And 'what rooms they were. A single picture on the walls, the only books the Records of the Mathematical Society, no touch of domesticity': L. R. Phelps (former Provost of Oriel College, Oxford) to Benians, 30 Jul. 1936: a letter which, 'with its

51 Whipsnade Zoo Outing, 1931. From left C. W. Guillebaud; M. H. A. Newman; further to right (without coat) E. Cunningham; on extreme right (with cap & rucksack) J. S. Boys Smith & talking to him & wearing stiff felt hat C. B. Rootham. Back to camera (perhaps) F. L. Engledow: SJCL, Misc IVb

College rather than the individual being held responsible for the furnishing and decoration of Fellows' rooms, in accordance with what was already happening in the case of undergraduate accommodation.

The departure from the scene of the last of the Fellows elected under the old Statutes, many of them men with apparently little appreciation of life outside their College rooms, was compensated for by the arrival of the likes of Hugh Sykes Davies in 1933, talented, lazy, self-indulgent youngsters with the sort of modern conscience the mid-1930s were eagerly awaiting.

> What is Hugh Sykes's little game,
> Why does he thus deny his name?

an anonymous versifier in the *Eagle* inquired.[59] The same number contained an account of the Nashe Society in which it was recorded that, having received Dr Leavis and Mr Sykes Davies, the Society was hoping to be 'privileged to entertain Mr Eric Gill the sculptor'[60] – as it did, putting paid to further club activities.[61] In the estimate of some 'the greatest artist–craftsman of the twentieth

typical Oxonian superiority' and its 'tissue of lies' in describing Webb's arrangements, Larmor 'rather resented' (letter to Benians, 1 Aug. [1936]).

[59] *Eagle* xlvii (1932–3), 13, presumably alluding to HSD's demotic suppression of the double-barrel.

[60] Ibid., 28–9.

[61] 'It is regretted that none of the many invitations for visitors during the rest of the term were accepted': ibid., 100–1.

century', Gill was engaged in carving the Fisher arms in Chapel Court. He was not Glover's idea of engaging company.[62] But that was the way the College was going, against the pull of Glover's tide.

An index of the change of both key and direction was provided by the transition from Sikes's Presidency to that of Martin Charlesworth. By 1935 when Sikes came up for re-election for a final two years, there were those who 'resented' the holding of Council meetings in the Master's Lodge, as the President's infirmity dictated. A President incapable of managing the stairs to the Combination Room was a wounded hart.[63] But despite being 'the old man by now', and 'fumbling', Sikes soldiered on.[64] The extension was favoured by Glover whose diary was by now full of complaints about Charlesworth, the man he had been responsible for bringing to St John's, and whose 'recapture' by Jesus he had resisted. The initial *casus belli* appears to have been Charlesworth's failure to reply to the other's invitations and objections raised to the installation of a lavatory in Glover's gyp room (at his own expense of course), which the older man interpreted as a conspiracy to unseat him.[65] But these were merely symptoms, not the cause of his resentment at the 'most distasteful' prospect of the other's election as President, in 1937 to the extent of his running the once-despised Winfield against him. The relative closeness of that contest indicates that the bonhomie for which Charlesworth was celebrated was not to everyone's taste.[66]

Glover's alienation from his junior colleague ('I don't enjoy his patronage and correction', he complained) stemmed from a lack of self-esteem, a 'sense of belonging to an unneeded past', fuelled by the suspicion that as Director of Studies Charlesworth was either keeping the best men for himself or sending them elsewhere for lectures and supervision.[67] Charlesworth's priestly ordination in the College chapel in a 'very long and involved service, very Jacobean and musical' which left Glover 'more stout for Geneva', hastened the process.[68] The causes of such a parting of the ways might be thought trivial. In fact, divisions such as this, and their causes, are the very stuff of an institution's experience

---

[62] GD, 7 Jul. 1939: 'a pity that Eric Gill should be commissioned to make some of his unpleasant statues for [New Buildings]'; 'Hall – like Noah's Ark – Eric Gill as Tolstoy etc.' (8 Aug 1939); 'Eric Gill dead who did the squalid sculpture in SJC; I wish it had been 2 years earlier' (19 Nov. 1940).

[63] On 19 Nov. 1934 he had asked for meetings to be held in the Lodge 'as the late Master used to do'. But that had been on account of the Master's condition, not the President's. By the 28th he was withdrawing the request ('I quite understand the difficulty of having the Council in the Lodge').

[64] GD, 19 Apr. 1935; 7 May 1935; 12 Nov. 1935.

[65] GD, 30 Nov. 1929; 18 Jun. 1936 ('I grow very tired of MPC and Co.'); 6 and 7 Oct. 1936.

[66] GD, 8 Mar. 1929; 3 Mar. 1937 ('I have ceased to value his Lloyd Georgian friendship; this more than ever makes me want to clear out for good'); 1 Jun. 1937 (Charlesworth victorious by 25 votes to 17). In the following year Glover was relishing the possibility of Charlesworth's election as Master of Jesus: GD, 3 Nov. 1938; cf. 17 Apr. 1940.

[67] GD, 25 Nov. 1940; 12 Jan. & 11 Jun. 1935; 19 Feb. 1937 (his class shrunken but loyal): 'How small the crumbs of praise with which I must nourish my self-esteem'; 19 Oct. 1937: 'I found my 2nd year hastening at 12 to Charlesworth's crowded room in Mill Lane ... wishful, it seemed, not to have to sit on floor.'

[68] GD, 10 Mar. 1940.

and its history. Though not capable of being chronicled in detail, the existence, absence, or breakdown of human relationships, and the foibles and feuds that last decades, long after their origins have been forgotten, provide the framework within which places like colleges operate. Glover supplied one prism.[69] Others have long since been put away in drawers.

For most of the younger Fellows and undergraduates a gregarious, socializing President, the first in residence since Mayor had surrendered his rooms to his books, was a blessing. By Glyn Daniel in particular the very unWelshness of Charlesworth's hospitality was especially appreciated.[70] With their Baptist backgrounds, both Daniel and Clifford Evans evidently found the contact liberating – to the dismay of Glover who expressed astonishment at the one's lack of a copy of the Bible and the other's treatment of a party of research students to 'cocktails' ahead of the Commemoration Dinner.[71] Also unnerving to him was his younger colleagues' knowledge of the men 'and their circumstances, family, football, Oxford group etc.'[72] To Owen Chadwick, at the time a candidate for Part I of the Classical tripos and obliged by a misunderstanding with the Proctors to spend a term away from the University, Charlesworth's supervisions on Epicureanism at the Arrington village pub provided a lifeline. On transferring from Classics to History, the instruction on the Middle Ages provided by Hugh ('Hugo') Gatty proved educational in a rather looser sense, focusing more on eighteenth-century porcelain than on medieval popes and emperors, and, in the recipient's view was none the worse for that.[73] The precept of the 1930s, which continued to have its devotees for sometime after, that you taught the man not the subject, could serve as code for not teaching him anything.[74] Gatty's career shows that, alongside Charlesworth, Cockcroft and Dirac, room could still be found in the St John's Fellowship for dilettantes of the old school. A Harrovian like Beaton (though made of sterner stuff), he was an advertisement for what could be achieved by a graduate with a brace of II.2s

[69] Apart from Scott and Larmor: Sikes and H. S. Foxwell; Heitland and H. S. Foxwell (the unnamed 'sneak' mentioned by the former to R. Tate, 'Recollections', *Eagle* liii [1948–9], 11); GD, 10 Feb. 1927 (Heitland talking of being 'turned off Council by trick of "the noisome" (meaning H. S. Foxwell)'; 7 Jun. 1929 ('Shore told me that the 40 year feud between Heitland and Foxwell is ended – WEH sought peace'); Sikes and Tanner vs MacAlister: GD, 2 Dec. 1904 ('Tanner owned Litt.D. was to compete with Donald [Macalister] as tutor'); 21 Oct. 1929 (Sikes 'always acrid; like Tanner, against DM – little creatures against big'); Glover and H. A. Harris (noted Daniel, *Some Small Harvest*, 191–2): 'odious', 'obscene and mismanager', 'lewd': GD, 8 Mar. & 8 Aug. 1939; 'In Combination Room, MPC, well aware I didn't wish it, forced the man Harris on me; he was not obscene': GD, 24 May 1940.

[70] Daniel, *Some Small Harvest*, 88–9 *et passim*.

[71] Ibid., 193; GD, 8 May 1939 ('… who behaved accordingly. Foolish, pretty lad, son of Geo. Evans …').

[72] GD, 6 Dec. 1937.

[73] *Ex. inf.* Owen Chadwick.

[74] The attitudes of the generalist may have endured longer in St John's than elsewhere. In October 1962 the Director of Studies in History (F. H. Hinsley) patiently informed his second-year undergraduates that if they chose to 'do modern' that term they would go to Mr Miller because he was a medievalist, and if they decided to 'do medieval' then they would come to him because he was a modernist: a proposition so manifestly reasonable that all readily assented.

and a II.1 to his credit, provided at least one of his Fellowship referees (in this case Guillebaud) was able to descry 'signs of real promise for the future' somewhere in the writings he submitted.[75]

Another of Yule's statistical exercises demonstrated that, according to two methods of calculation, in June 1936 the College was top of Cambridge's academic league and second according to a third. Success bred success, Wordie observed, with the schools 'getting the idea that in Classics and Maths SJC takes the trouble to *teach* the men', and therefore entering their ablest boys there. But Benians was sceptical, and in an undated letter of that year urged Wordie to pursue a more active policy with regard to public school headmasters ('I am not sure that we have been pulling our weight in this respect'). Nevertheless, the following December saw six classics scholarships awarded and in June 1937 two starred Firsts in that subject, which since neither had come up as a Scholar, represented value added, Glover noted.[76] In 1935 St John's had collected seven of the forty-five Firsts awarded in Part I Classics. But tripos is not the last judgment, not even Part II. B. M. W. Knox, 'a clever lad of working-class origin, keen on Communism or something', who was classed II.1 on that occasion (the consequence perhaps of regularly preferring a lie-in to Glover's composition class)[77] would proceed via the French battalion of the XIth International Brigade and a much-decorated World War to a distinguished academic career at Yale and Harvard. If the fact that Trinity outscored St John's by forty-eight seats to one in the 1935 General Election reflected a lack of political contacts it provided no indication of an absence of political interest.[78] Nor for some was tripos the highest of priorities. Although in 1927 it surprised Glover to learn that the LMBC VIII that had gone head of the river in the previous year for the first time since 1872 was wholly made up of honours men, David Haig-Thomas – who came up in 1928 and would row for Cambridge and for Great Britain in the Los Angeles Olympics of 1932 – would, like both his father and grandfather before him, go down without a degree.[79] F. R. (Freddie) Brown, Haig-Thomas's junior by a year and a future captain of the England Cricket XI, suffered the same misfortune after a series of exploits with, again, more than a touch of the Drones Club about them.[80] N. W. D. Yardley (matric. 1934), however, who was to enjoy the same distinction in later life, did significantly better. While wrestling with the complexities of the Previous and Ordinary examinations, he accumulated Blues

---

[75] D93 file 46.

[76] 'The Standing of the College on the Tripos Results of 1936 and 1937' (SJCL, Yule papers); GD, 19 Dec. 1936; 18 Jun. 1937.

[77] Thereby providing a stick for Glover to beat Charlesworth with ('Knox the scholar doesn't like getting up; MPC has his own ideas of guiding youth – to choose as it pleases': GD, 25 Jan. 1935); also 21 and 28 Feb., 7 Mar. 1935.

[78] *CR* lvii (1935–6), 127.

[79] GD, 7 Jun. 1927; D. Haig-Thomas, *I Leap Before I Look* (London, 1936), 82: a volume of reminiscences notable for its tourist's knowledge of College matters, e.g. the old *canard* that swan was served at the May Ball, 'provided by the King's swan master' (p. 190). 'Rubbish!' reads the marginal remark in the College Library copy in the hand of the normally ultra-restrained N. C. Buck (Sub-Librarian).

[80] F. Brown, *Cricket Musketeer*, London 1954, 115; F. Hoyle, *Home is Where the Wind Blows: Chapters from a Cosmologist's Life* (Mill Valley, CA, 1994), 111.

for squash, hockey and Rugby fives as well as cricket, and in the 1937 season, in the term of his final examinations, found time to play fourteen matches at Fenners (where, of course, in those halcyon days cricket did not stop for tripos), scoring almost 650 runs. In December 1933 the Admissions Committee ('that formidable body which really only consists of the four Tutors')[81] had agreed to postpone part of Yardley's Previous examination so that he might be free to play squash with the Prince of Wales on the latter's visit to his school (were such to prove His Royal Highness's desire), and in the Easter term of 1938 allowed him to return after graduation and a winter tour of India with Lord Tennyson's XI for the sole purpose of enjoying a further season with the Varsity side, caressing the ball effortlessly wide of extra cover's left hand.[82] Writing on behalf of the son of a friend in the following spring, an Old Johnian was moved to describe the boy, also a pupil at Yardley's school, as 'just the kind of lad likely to do the College credit, being moderately good at work and above the average in sports.' The boy got in,[83] and doubtless caressed the ball effortlessly too. The tutorial fixer in both cases was Wordie. As a rule though it was the congenial R. L. (Bede; familiarly 'Bonzo' or 'The Howler') Howland, himself an Olympian shot-putter in 1928, who maintained olympian standards at the margins of academe, being known throughout his tutorial career (1931–65) to be sympathetic to sporting prowess and likelier than some to prove benevolent to the Norman Yardleys and David Haig-Thomases of succeeding generations.

At a time when Firsts were as elusive as Thirds are today, there were rewards for those who managed to get one. On the initiative of Charlesworth and Boys Smith, in 1934 the Foundation Dinner at which Master, Fellows and Scholars dine together at the end of the Michaelmas Term, was instituted. Significantly, Boys Smith remembered the idea occurring to them whilst motoring in France in the company of a couple of their pupils, one of them H. St. J. Hart, son of the former Fellow J. H. A. Hart.[84] Eleven years earlier, when Winfield had proposed something similar, Scott had shuddered at the thought, recalling how 'the experiment of inviting the Scholars to a College Feast was tried a good many years ago':

> The result was disastrous. As it was impossible to 'ration' the amount of wine to the Scholars a good many got drunk. Some mobbed the College

[81] Charlesworth to J. H. A. Hart, 27 May 1931 (tut.file/H. St J. Hart).

[82] Headmaster of St Peter's School, York, to Wordie, 5 Dec. 1933 (SJCA, tut. file/ Yardley).

[83] A supporting letter from the boy's own father listed his many sporting achievements, adding: 'This all looks as if I want him to be considered on his athletic prowess only but, really, I think he has also a very good brain. His academic studying would have been much higher if he had paid more attention to accuracy and detail but perhaps he has been rather too occupied with his duties as Captain of Athletics, for two year as Head of his House, and, latterly, as Head of the School. Probably his studies have suffered in consequence but I am certain this will be remedied in future.' (It was not. But National Service compensated for academic failure, earned him an Ordinary degree and, eventually, a deputy Lord-Lieutenancy.)

[84] Boys Smith, *Memories*, 65, perhaps conflates two things here. Although the personnel named confirm that the French trip must indeed have been in 1936, the dinner dated from 1934: CM, 1442/12 (19 Oct. 1934); GD, 4 Dec. 1934; 5 Dec. 1935.

guests as they were leaving and I remember that Dr Taylor was most indignant at what happened to Dr Butler [the Master] of Trinity and had to apologise to him. But what was perhaps worst was that some of the men in returning to their lodgings fell into the hands of the police. One of the Tutors was sent for post haste to bail them out and when the matter came before the magistrates and the cause of the disturbance came out one of the magistrates pointedly remarked that the people who ought to be before the Court were the Fellows of St John's who had led the men astray.[85]

In the other direction, when arrangements for the Quatercentenary Feast were being discussed, Heitland had expressed alarm at the prospect of finding himself 'sandwiched between two teetotal undergraduates' – which perhaps explains why in 1927 it was customary for senior and junior members to be seated at separate tables at the annual Commemoration Dinner, and why it remained so until well after the War.[86] In terms of commensality the Foundation Dinner (the Scholars' Dinner as it came to be known) reflected a change in the relationship of Fellows and undergraduates – not, to be sure, a change that went so far as chumminess but one that paralleled the contrast between Armitage's loan of his powerful motor-car to a quartet of postprandial undergraduates and the ferrying of a group of tripos candidates on the weekend before their Part II examinations to the Bell at Clare and the hospitality afforded them there by Boys Smith, Charlesworth and Gatty.[87]

The particulars of Boys Smith's dealings with Henry St. J. Hart (matriculated 1931) provide a further testimonial, and a remarkable one, to the trouble to which this Tutor at least was prepared to go on behalf of the welfare of a pupil. Two years after his departure from the St John's Fellowship, Hart senior had sought to relaunch his academic career by appointment as a theological lecturer at Durham: an attempt fatally blasted by Scott's report to the Professor of Divinity there of the events of 1914–18 in terms which went well beyond the evidence presented to the Council at the time.[88] After several years of scraping a living at Leeds by dint of 'odd jobs' at the grammar school with which to supplement his income as a 'pensioner' of the College (the description provided on

---

85 Scott to Winfield, 3 Mar. 1925 (SLB). Winfield had suggested that inviting Scholars 'to a separate table at one of the College feasts' would be appreciated 'as a mark of the distinction of their position', which they 'would probably recollect in after life': Winfield to Scott, 2 Mar. 1925: SJCA, D90.1577.

86 GD, 11 Nov. 1910; 7 May 1902, 7 May 1927.

87 BSP, H. J. Habakkuk to G. Boys Smith, 6 Nov. 1991: 'All six of us went into the examinations in high spirits, and I have always remembered with gratitude this characteristic piece of thoughtful generosity.'

88 '... brilliant, learned, but always a little different from other people (...) His mental state gave him unpleasant trains of thought from which alcoholic stimulant gave him relief. Thus he was always tippling. The College was then full of cadets and the officers in charge complained to me that he was always having the cadets round to his room and tempting them with liquor (...). His mental instability is hereditary for his father was for years in confinement, he may be still unless he has died (...) I am afraid another breakdown is impending': Scott to Dawson Walker, 8 May 1920: SJCA, D90.1036.

Henry's application form), in 1929 he overcame his Nonconformist scruples and applied for Anglican Orders, managing, Scott's demurral notwithstanding, to persuade the archbishop of York of his complete restoration 'to health and stability', and in 1931, the year in which Henry came up, was appointed vicar of the College living of Holme-on-Spalding-Moor.[89]

But Scott had been right to demur. Early in December 1932, a further breakdown followed, with the father confined to a nursing-home in York ('called a Retreat which is fortunate and should be the only name given it', the son stipulated. 'He *may* recover'), and the son, Henry, then towards the end of his fourth term, a victim of his violence. 'There are things that happened on Sunday night which I can never forget and I am not fit company for myself', he wrote to Boys Smith, with whom he must have communicated earlier since the letter also contained details of the Christmas services in Yorkshire which the other (Chaplain and Assistant Tutor at the time) had already volunteered to provide.[90] The son's optimism proved unjustified. As well as accepting Boys Smith's invitation for a fortnight in Wales over Easter (neither the first break the Tutor had provided nor the last),[91] his letter of the following March reported the abuse heaped upon his mother before his father's internment.

By 18 June, when Henry wrote to thank Boys Smith for all the support that had secured him his recent First in Part 1A Theology,[92] 'the abuse which my father sends me so liberally' showed no sign of abating, he had 'started playing ducks and drakes with money he cannot spare', and his certification was imminent. However, a fortnight later (2 July) father had escaped that fate by discharging himself and disappearing with more than £200. Thereafter letters for Boys Smith arrived from Henry thick and fast. 'This waiting is an absolute nightmare of the worst possible order not even dispelled by the contemplation of Holy Hebrew words', he complained on 8 July – though all those letters were generously larded with Hebrew glosses, Syriac fragments, scholarly niceties, the denunciation of slovenly scholarship, and chunks of the poet Horace. If JHAH turned up in Cambridge, Lockhart was to take him in charge and confine him at his Shelford home (5 July). On the 14th Mrs Hart reported to Boys Smith his intention of bequeathing his entire estate to a certain lady in Northampton and then doing away with himself.

By now Hart Senior was known to be somewhere in Ireland, and on the following day Boys Smith was on the case in Yorkshire, crossing to Dublin

[89] J. H. A. Hart to Benians, 15 Jan. 1929, 'and gather that I am regarded as competent': SJCA, TU14/Hart, R. W. K.; SLB, 18–19 Dec. 1929: Scott to William Temple and reply. Cf. his protestation to Tanner on 22 Jan. 1906: 'I think sometimes I would look better in the shop window dyed black and marked Reverend – but I can't bring my conscience to let me take Orders by way of Adv[ertisemen]t and the official cure of souls would be the last straw': SJCA, TU12.8.55.

[90] Letters dated 5 & 7 Dec. 1932: tut. file/Hart, H. St. J. (the source for the account in the following paragraphs).

[91] Letter dated 19 Mar. 1933: 'This is the first time I have written to you since we went to Keswick in Cumberland and cackled on the top of Scawfell (I believe you only grinned): *gratias tibi ago maximas.*'

[92] 'to you, *blandissime doctorum* especially, for information, supervision and exercise on the mountains of Merionethshire'.

with Henry on the following day and spending the next two searching with him there.[93] Soon after, further disaster intervened. On 4 August Henry's older brother, Richard, died of gunshot wounds, apparently self-administered, on board a yacht at Burnham on Crouch skippered by R. M. Jackson (BA 1924; supervisor in Law at St John's; Fellow 1946–86). The tragedy both provided further testimony of Boys Smith's tutorial commitment (in driving Henry and his mother to North Norfolk for the funeral), and served to smoke out Arthur (as he now took to signing himself) from his Irish redoubt. Via his Howdon solicitor, before the end of the month he was reported (in Boys Smith's words) to be 'attributing RWKH's death to Hutchinson and RMJ by some plot'.[94]

In a subsequent letter to Jackson himself, dated 9 September from far-distant Achill Island Co. Mayo and forwarded by the recipient to Boys Smith, Hart indicated that he had 'no wish to visit England again',[95] *item* to Lockhart: a prospect not uncongenial to young Henry, especially after the discovery of the truth regarding his father's financial affairs.[96] With Archbishop Temple Boys Smith explored the question of Hart's resigning his parish and found the archbishop in favour. But then, the errant vicar returned, as though nothing had happened. Was it the news of R. F. Scott's death that had brought him back? No: 'I came back Thursday 30th Novr as Mrs Hart had arranged till end of November for the work to be done as the Bishop of Hull approved', he wrote to Boys Smith ('My dear Supplanter, Faber, or what?')[97] Forever anxious to dodge services, with his antennae if anything sharpened by his recent excursion, less than a week later he was engaged in luring Boys Smith northwards to cover for him at Christmas and in proposing thereafter to motor across the North Yorkshire Moors with Henry and himself and Yadça (the family cat) in the back for further company.[98]

[93] Envelope of notes, scraps in Hart file.

[94] BSP, Henry Hart to Mrs G. Boys Smith, 6 Nov. 1991; MS note by Boys Smith, 30 Aug. 1933. M. Hutchinson was Hart's GP (letter to Boys Smith, 5 Dec. 1932, regarding Hart's recent breakdown).

[95] He had been informed of the death on August, he said, 'and it is only this morning that it occurred to me that I should write to you to say this' (viz. that he had previously received a post-card from Richard dated 22 July).

[96] 'What a liar he has been in these matters': 15 Sept. 1933. In an undated letter from Dublin (acknowledged 28 Nov. 1933), addressed 'Dear Chaplin' (*sic*), one 'Kenneth' (presumably a member of the College but unidentifiable) reported having lunched with Hart and to having found him perfectly normal, though 'he mentioned that he had been deceived into accepting a living in Yorkshire supposed to be worth £700 a year when it was really only £100, which I thought rather strange.' (In fact, in August 1931 the annual net value of the living had been estimated at £913-odd: Smith-Woolley & Co. to Scott [SJCA, SBFL/5B(1) Holme-on-Spalding-Moor I (1857–1954).]

[97] Letter dated 8 Dec. 1933 (marked by Boys Smith 'Ackd 12 Dec.' One would give much for sight of that reply): 'Hy seems by his own and others' reports to grow by your parental care in knowledge and competency.' He was giving his copy of Raleigh's *History of the World* which 'thanks to you I secured for Richard at Lincoln' to a professor of psychology and philosophy at University College Galway who had been 'very kind'. 'They practise their religion there. Well, do come if you can. Everyone seems delighted at having me back ...'

[98] 'I don't think I should be *tertium quid* if you let me bring Yadça to sit with me behind Hy and you. Besides if your talk soars beyond my scope I can always think up verses

If Boys Smith was at risk of being seduced by blandishments such as these, Henry's Christmas letter will have steadied him.[99] Such was the young man's attachment to his mentor that when in the following year he triumphed again in Theology IB his father, describing himself as 'the discard', wrote of him to Boys Smith as 'largely your fabrication' and as '[owing] his First largely to you'.[100] A year later, after another First in Oriental Studies, Hart, signing himself 'your affectionate pupil', invited him for a walking holiday with him in the hills round Münster and confided that he had bought a suit ('according to your advice, a good one').[101] By the beginning of 1936 Boys Smith is 'Dear IHN', and in June, on Hart's appointment as Fellow and Chaplain of Queens', 'My dear John (I have written it at last)'. The last letter in his tutorial file, addressed to his Tutor, ends: 'and my love to yourself'.[102] Regrettably, Boys Smith's letters to his pupil were not copied into that file. But the essence of them was remarked on in particular by Henry's non-academic younger brother:

> I am interested in the way you write particularly, Sir, as a business man; for in such a capacity it is essential to employ as much amateur psychology in letter writing as one can command. Now your letter, as it stands, would not appear to be surprisingly elevating: yet I found it extremely comforting for some reason, & can only presume that you possess the elusive faculty, which I set out to obtain and cannot, of suiting your letter writing to the individual *primarily*.[103]

The quality of 'wise helpfulness' to which Colin Bertram would pay tribute at the end of Boys Smith's long life[104] was never better deployed than in these painful circumstances.

Not every pupil was as interesting as H. St. J. Hart, of course, nor for that matter was every parent as demanding as that 'picturesque and revered figure', as the local paper would describe his father.[105] Another (who *was* interesting)

---

or sing songs': ibid. Thoughtfully, he had excluded the possibility of an expedition at that time of year to the living of Aberdaron in West Wales: 'a coveted rectory (?sinecure)'. (Alas, the College's living there had been sold to the Church Commission in 1911.)

[99] 'This is the first opportunity I have had of writing unsupervised. (...) He has no manners but fortunately feels it necessary to behave in front of me. He (...) eats like a pig and talks like a gramophone. I hope you will not judge these statements harshly: I realize that they are hardly respectful – if you had been through the last twelve months in my place I think you would feel much the same. See Isaiah VI.11 down to the question mark.' ['Then said I, Lord, how long?']

[100] Letter to Boys Smith, addressed 'Dear Bezaleel' (Moses' clerk of works for the construction of the Tabernacle), 21 Jun. 1934.

[101] Letters dated 20 & 26 Jun., 9 Jul. 1935.

[102] Letters dated 17 Mar., 24 Jun., 24 Sept. 1936.

[103] A. N. Hart to Boys Smith, 31 Dec. 1935.

[104] BSP, letter to G. Boys Smith, 5 Nov. 1991.

[105] Of whom the College had not heard the last: 'I am very anxious about the parish of Brandesburton, in the gift of St John's College', the archbishop of York, Cyril Garbett, wrote to Benians on 14 Aug. 1945, reporting that Hart was 'mentally failing and is in various ways eccentric and difficult'. ('I have had several serious complaints about him. I tried to see him last Sunday, but though I have reason to believe he was

was the applicant from Morpeth Grammar School, the son of a 'farm steward and shepherd', as the son's application form described him, with a net annual income of £115 and three siblings to provide for, the future Fellow of the College and Master of Fitzwilliam, Edward Miller. Even for a boy of Miller's intellectual distinction, therefore, a £40 entrance exhibition was not enough.[106] It would have to be stretched, and in his case (as in many others) it was Boys Smith who supervised the stretching.[107] It was in his tutorial dealings with the College and the University that Boys Smith won the spurs that would serve him so well in later years. In this case, with the assistance of the school, the local educational committee and the College, eventually £200 was raised, which, with rooms at 10 guineas a term, enabled Miller to come up. 'It will not be easy to cover all your expenses with this sum', his future Tutor conjectured. 'But I believe it is sufficient to make it worth while your coming into residence, which I hope you will be able to do.'[108]

Although Ted Miller will have needed to count the pennies, at least until his string of Firsts and starred Firsts brought their monetary rewards – and it is cheering as well as instructive to observe the tone of his communications with his Tutor warming and lightening over the years – for the composite undergraduate of the 1930s life was a simpler affair. A normal day might begin with a party breakfasting off victuals brought in by kitchen porters – though even this simple ceremony could have its hazards: coffee adulterated by mulligatawny soup, for example.[109] To judge by the head count provided in the 'Register of Services 1934–1955',[110] he is hardly likely to have attended 8 a.m. Holy Communion beforehand. With the development of faculties most lectures were delivered on University premises rather than in colleges, thereby rendering them even more resistible to the likes of Bernard Knox. In similar vein, to Knox and so many of

in the rectory I had no answer to repeated knocking and ringing. The present position is now causing widespread scandal.') In the following June Hart was reported to be begging 'in cafés and banks with a collecting box, in Hull and Beverley', the compensation provided by the War Ministry in respect of its occupation of his rectory not having been spent other than on repairs to the fabric. In 1948 the archbishop exercised his powers of removal, making him Hart's 'present enemy': T. W. F. Sparrow (Hart's adjutor) to Boys Smith; 16 Jun. 1947; E. E. Raven to Benians, 15 Oct. 1948; Archbishop of York to Benians, 12 Jun. 1948; Boys Smith to Benians, 17 Aug. 1948 (all SJCA, SBFL2/Brandesburton). Such was the revered figure celebrated by the *Hull Daily Mail* in October 1952: above, p. 460. He had been rector of Brandesburton since 1941.

[106] Miller to Tutor for Admissions, 25 Dec. 1933, informing him of the need to apply for an Oxford scholarship 'for my parents may find it impossible to raise sufficient money to send me with only the aid of the Exhibition'. In the event he did not apply to Oxford: tut. file/E. Miller.

[107] At the instigation of Miller's headmaster (G. F. Howell), who strove heroically on his behalf, informing Boys Smith of the father's 'great agitation' on receiving the College's (customary) request for caution money to the tune of £22-odd. For a man with a weekly income of £2.10.0 this was an impossible demand: 'We are hard put to it to collect the money necessary to make Miller's University course possible' (letter of 15 Mar. 1934).

[108] Boys Smith to Miller, 11 Aug. 1934.

[109] Daniel, *Some Small Harvest*, 88–9.

[110] SJCA, DS5.1.

his generation, in the summer of Habakkuk and Co.'s pre-tripos excursion into Suffolk, Miller, at the time a devout Marxist, was at work accommodating the perversely ambiguous activity of the nobility during the Wars of the Roses to the demands of the dialectic as prescribed by J. H. Plumb's proposed Communist history of England.[111]

As always, there were those for whom the field or the river provided distraction in the afternoons. Successive numbers of the *Eagle* of these years record the draining of the lower field (an operation completed during the 1920s by means of contributions from College members) and the recovery from Peterhouse of the area to the south of the driftway (developments owing much to the exertions of F. C. Bartlett and F. L. Engledow). In May 1930 the old pavilion was found to be 'in a dangerous state and [showing] signs of collapse' and in the following November the decision was reached to rebuild it at a cost of about £3,000.[112] With its completion in 1934 facilities here were ideal – for batsmen.[113] Only bowlers had cause to quarrel with the 'otherwise perfect Len Baker', groundsman *par excellence*.[114] New hard courts and, on the College side of Queen's Road, squash courts, prompted by a gift from Sir Jeremiah Colman, which produced a 'wave of squash consciousness', and improvements to the baths,[115] inadequate though they remained for some,[116] completed the arrangements available to those with sufficient energy to derive benefit therefrom.

One of these was Louis Leakey, who claimed to have been threatened as recently as 1926 with being sent down for wearing tennis shorts in the College courts. He now found things greatly, and suddenly, changed,[117] the end of the draconian application of the rules coinciding with J. M. Creed's resignation from the office of Dean, an office in which he had not been happy, and the succession of the Chaplain E. E. Raven, a quickish left-arm bowler as an undergraduate, but one whose 'cheerless rooms' even the austere Glover thought

[111] Although by then his views had changed, Miller's earlier pro-Soviet sympathies were remembered in the post-War nickname 'Ludmilla': R. R. Branford to F. Thistlethwaite, 22 Jun. [1947]: SJCA, tut. file/Branford; Barbara Harvey and Peter Linehan, 'Edward Miller 1915–2000', *PBA* cxxxviii (2006), 234, 239.

[112] General Athletics Club Minute Book (SJCA, SOC.3.3c), mins of 8 May and 17 Nov. 1930.

[113] CMM, 1199/11, 1412/17, 1425/7, 1426/7; J. S. Boys Smith, 'The College grounds and playing fields', *Eagle* liv (1950–51), 311. So perfect was the surface of the square that it was 'sometimes almost an impertinence to ask the bowler to perform': *Eagle* xlviii. 43.

[114] *Eagle* xlviii. 174. There was further cause for complaint when the team boards from the old pavilion were found to have been destroyed by fire in the contractors' yard: CM, 1465/9 (23 May 1935).

[115] CMM, 1449/12, 1451/5, 1455/2, 1459/2; *Eagle* l (1937–8), 55.

[116] '8 baths, 6 for undergraduates, is entirely insufficient for a College with a membership of 500 residents', J. A. F. Ennals complained in the JCR Suggestions Book, 15 Jan. 1939. Morning opening times of 2½ hours allowed individuals just two minutes each, he calculated.

[117] 'By 1932, more than half the tennis players had adopted shorts, and a few even appeared on the courts bare to the waist without any protest from the authorities': L. S. B. Leakey, *By the Evidence: Memoirs, 1932–1951* (New York & London, 1974), 17. Shortly before, 'the foolish Head Porter, Captain Palmer', had challenged Glover's teenage son for entering the college in a blazer before 1 p.m.: GD, 27 May 1931.

to remark upon.[118] Reports from the 1937–8 season included accounts of the Hockey and Rugby Clubs, both of which could run to three teams, a club tour during which some hockey was played, and a stirring account of the defeat suffered in the Rugby cuppers final.[119]

'Only those who have had the pleasure of being at Henley with him can know how the presence of Sir Henry as coach and mentor, one might almost say, assures success', reported the chronicler of LMBC of Sir Henry Howard.[120] Whether mounted upon quadruped or bicycle, a Senior Bursar of another age, ever since his arrival in the College, Howard had played a key role in the boat club's improving fortunes. His resignation as coach in 1937 over a theological disagreement regarding slide-length and his eventual replacement by Roy Meldrum and E. A. Walker (Vere Harmsworth Professor of Imperial and Naval History) are matters for LMBC's own chronicler since, as Lady Margaret's canon lawyers would have advised her, it is not licit to set one's sickle to another man's field.[121]

After the river, tea, followed for some by beer,[122] or for rather fewer perhaps by Chapel,[123] where until his sudden decline Cyril Rootham remained dominant.[124] Thereafter Hall, with G. E. Briggs succeeding Cunningham as Steward in 1935: a move welcomed by Glover who haled Briggs's first feast, a seven-course affair, as 'very well done' – until the oysters struck.[125] Of the lower tables reports are lacking, which is generally a good sign, though club dinners were well spoken of, for example the inaugural dinner of the History Society in December 1933, an occasion attended by Benians days just before his election.[126] Then as now, the ordinary meetings of societies proved less of a draw, regardless of the speaker's distinction, with 'good papers and poor audiences' every Secretary's lament (the History Society's on this occasion).[127] Meanwhile, the

---

[118] GD, 16 Nov. 1911; *Eagle* lv (1952–3), 84.

[119] *Eagle* l (1937–8), 291, 295–6.

[120] *Eagle* xlviii (1934–5), 41.

[121] 'Thus over a question of two inches of slide came the end of an era in Lady Margaret rowing': J. F. Hall-Craggs *et al.*, *The History of the Lady Margaret Boat Club*, II. *1926–1956* (Cambridge, 1957), 71–2, 290–2.

[122] In June 1936 the Scholars' Buttery was re-opened 'for the service of beer': CM, 1500/9. A call for a College bar in June 1939 (JCR Suggestions Book) received the answer that there were no rooms available. Glover would blame the Boat Club (as well as 'a drifting habit of mind') for having enticed his nephew by marriage Ll. V. Bevan away from teetotalism: GD, 15 Jul. 1940.

[123] The College clergy regarded the wearing of surplices as a deterrent to attendance and wished to discontinue the practice, whereat the Council provided a cupboard with space for sixty garments: E. E. Raven to Benians, 4 Mar. 1935; CM, 1464/8. To judge by numbers recorded in the 'Register of Services', this was ample provision.

[124] Glover on Rootham: *Eagle* l. 304–6.

[125] GD, 26 Oct. 1935. Cf. 28–31 Oct., 14 Nov. 1935: a register of those who had been laid low after opting for the molluscs rather than the grapefruit before the Consommé Chancelière and the rest of it. 'Briggs expressed no regret', Glover informed Larmor on 5 November. Thereafter Glover rarely reported on a college feast without recalling 'the fatal feast with the oysters' (GD, 27 Nov.).

[126] 2 Dec. 1933: *Eagle* xlviii. 52.

[127] *Eagle* xlix (1935–7), 26; l. 43.

MENU

Geierslayer Sonnseite, 1933	Huîtres au naturel Pamplemousse au Marasquin

*

Consommé Chancelière
Potage Bonvalet

*

Paupiettes de Sole Richelieu

Richebourg, 1923	*
Niersteiner Rehbach, 1929	Suprêmes de Perdreau au cerise
Pommery and Greno, 1926	*

Selle de Mouton rôti
Pommes à la crème   Choux de Bruxelles

*

Soufflé glacé à la Carmen

*

Canapés Féodora

o◯o

Dessert

Dow, 1912	*
Sherry, 1891	
Chât.Rauzan-Ségla, 1929	Café

52 'The fatal feast with the oysters': G. E. Briggs's début as Steward, 26 October 1935

Classical Society revived the custom of reading plays, after which Charlesworth treated it to refreshment and sweet music while the Theological Society set-tled down to a sermon by Peter Laslett (a third-year undergraduate) on the text that 'the woman's place is in the home'.[128] Alternative attractions might include a gathering of the Nashe Society,[129] an assembly of the more exclusive and short-lived (Johnian) Apostles (a twelve-member club which though ostensibly 'for the purpose of debating on any subject', chose to ignore the international

---

[128] *Eagle* xlviii. 110; xlix. 30; l. 287 ('Mr Laslett pointed out that the way to check the decline in the birth rate lay not in the discouraging of the use of contraceptives, but in a practical return to the theory that the woman's place is in the home and not in the factory').

[129] Whose fiftieth meeting in March 1936 drew a crowd of eighty-nine, and which was later addressed by such luminaries as William Empson, Dylan Thomas and Christo-pher Isherwood: Minute Book (SJCA, SOC.22.1).

scene),[130] a smoking concert with pianistic pyrotechnics by Charlesworth and Max Newman amongst the Fellows and support from any of a galaxy of undergraduate performers,[131] or, for a change, the Union or a cinema. Later in the evening literary types might cheer themselves by complaining about the perennial tendency of the Boat Club and the Musical Society to monopolize the pages of the *Eagle* and discuss the ever-interesting question why the magazine of so vital a society was so dull.[132] For the more strenuous, or for the soothing of troubled nerves, there was of course always the option of a spot of night-climbing.[133]

In some of these activities, those conducted at ground level at least, Benians played a prominent part. As President of the Eagles Club (the 'chief function' of which, according to Howland, was, simply 'to exist'), he established the custom of inviting its junior members to dessert in the Combination Room.[134] He was especially adept at providing the graceful improvised speech or the extempore address, a skill acquired at undergraduate club dinners before 1914. His speeches as President of LMBC brought the historian's recommendation of taking the long view to the task of encouraging jaded Bump Suppers when the club was dispirited and needed cheering up, as during the great slide controversy was quite often the case.[135] Not so with regard to the tripos, however, in which, to judge by the results of the last occasion before the War, success had not been entirely undermined by exertion in other activities. (See Table 1.) In 1932 the College had secured six of the nine Firsts awarded in Part I Classics, and three of the four in Part II. In 1938–9 fifteen of the College's fifty-seven Fellows were Fellows of the Royal Society or of the British Academy.[136]

Meanwhile, those such as Haig-Thomas who had succeeded in sublimating their academic ambitions by fishing for dace from their New Court windows could concentrate on giving the College porters a good run for their

[130] Established in November 1934 and surviving for just over two years, it debated such urgent issues as whether it preferred moonlight to sunlight and the proposition 'that pessimism is justifiable in the present age', otherwise concentrating on sex, religion and the royal family. It folded (or at least its records ended) after thirteen meetings: SJCA, SOC.9. Amongst its leading lights was Harry Rée (matric. 1933).

[131] Notably Guy Lee, R. B. Marchant and Frank Thistlethwaite.

[132] *Eagle* 1 (1937–8), 40: a letter from R. G. Benians (nephew of the Master) asking for 'a snappy editorial', the reduction 'to an absolute minimum' of 'contributions by elderly Dons', and an altogether more 'scurrilous' magazine. The June 1933 number contained a parody on LMBC's Henley Fund Appeal announcing the contribution of 'the Committee of the Old Johnian Hawaii Fund (...) towards sending our Fellows' Ukelele Team to Hawaii this summer as usual': *Eagle* xlvii. 223 ('They have excellent rhythm, are potentially very fast, and during the last few weeks have been getting well together').

[133] Of which Whipplesnaith's guide, *The Night Climbers of Cambridge* (Cambridge, 1937), may be said to have been symptom rather than cause (by contrast with its effect when reissued in 2007).

[134] J. G. W. Davies (Club Secretary) to Benians, 26 Apr. 1934; CM, 1545/9; *Eagle* lxxi, no. 295 (1987), 56.

[135] Hall-Craggs, *History of the Lady Margaret Boat Club*, II. 122, 174. Various jottings for these speeches, largely illegible, survive amongst his papers.

[136] Cf. above, p. 437.

Table 1 Some St John's tripos results, 1939

	I	II.1	II.2	III	Total classed
Classics Part I	3/34	3/29	3/16	1/11	10/90
Classics Part II	1/21	4/23	0/7	5/53	10/104
History Part I	5/17	0/41	2/57	3/59	10/174
History Part II	2/15	0/51	4/73	3/29	9/168
Mathematics I	2/23	0/23		3/20	5/66
Mathematics II	3/22	3/19		4/16	10/57

Key: St John's/all Colleges

money[137] – though, if reports of Captain Palmer were anything to go by, in this they were likely to be disappointed. Palmer was 'a perfect man for his job', Haig-Thomas himself reported. 'He was the height of discretion himself, provided nothing really bad was going on. He never saw anything that it would be better for the Head Porter not to see, and for this he was greatly respected by all the undergraduates'[138] – not least doubtless by Macklin and the Petrels. It was to the imperturbable Palmer that it fell in late 1927 to exclude the deranged Bromwich from the precincts.[139] His Assistant J. R. ('Jesse') Collins (d. 1928), a man as much celebrated for his encyclopedic memory for old members as for his prodigious stoutness, was remembered 'wandering through a crowd of undergraduates, exhilarated by success on the river and the fumes of a bump supper, a very Falstaff sent to judgment', all the while representing, according to his obituarist, 'that type of faithful service which we are frequently assured is defunct'.[140] Like both Collins and Bob Fuller fifty years later, Palmer was not a porter built for speed. When in the early twenties a 'Brighter Hall Movement' was started, its high point was the detonation of a thunderflash in the gallery followed by the appearance of a large effigy of the Head Porter.[141] In the course of 1935 Palmer received grants for medical expenses and six months' leave to go with his wife on a three-month cruise to South Africa. But the change did not mend him, and in the following June he resigned, to be replaced by Regimental Sergeant-Major G. C. Bowles.[142]

Such concern for the welfare of its members and employees was not new in the College. When Leathem, the Senior Bursar, had needed surgery in 1921 the Fellows had clubbed together and sent his wife £150, and after his death the Council contributed £1,000 to a fund to educate his children.[143] The solicitude

---

[137] Haig-Thomas, *I Leap Before I Look*, 24–5.

[138] Ibid., 27. Sergeant-Major J. H. Palmer of the Royal 10th Hussars, at the time serving with King Edward's Horse, had been appointed in 1911: CM, 870/2. He had fought in the Boer War and again in the Great War, during which he was commissioned.

[139] CM, 1270/15; GD, 20 Dec. 1927.

[140] *Eagle* xlv (1927–9), 217–19.

[141] GD, 5 Nov. 1922; SJCA, Arch.2.6 (Recollection of W. T. Thurbon, *c.* 1974).

[142] CMM, 1465/2, 1475/5, 1476/2, 1499/11; 'Eyes not right yet', Glover reported on 22 Apr. 1936 (GD). On 23 Dec. 1940 'Howland and I met [Palmer] who proudly said he had lost 5 stone out of 16, and showed us how his paunch was gone' (ibid.); CM, 1504/8.

[143] GD, 23 Mar. 1921 ('to cover this bout'); 27 Apr. 1923.

53 Long service. College Staff Sports Club, 1932–3. Seated, 2nd from right the omnicompetent E. W. (Ned) Lockhart (1886–1936); standing, back row first from left Norman Buck (Library boy since 1929)

shown to Captain Palmer, therefore, was an example of the extension of that concern to members of the staff. During the Junior Bursarship of Cockcroft, whose own advancement in the domestic hierarchy the Council acknowledged by new stipend levels agreed in August 1935, such relief was increasingly systematized.[144] Lockhart's departure in September 1936 after more than fifty years of Figaro-like service as Library Clerk, Tutors' Clerk, Chief Clerk and College Butler was significant, not least for the manner of his going: a commemorative minute of the Council augmented by an invitation to the Port Latin Feast.[145] But not even Cockcroft was able to shovel every relic of the College's eleemosynary past onto a single annihilating bonfire. The assistance given to Scott in his dotage by W. E. Wolfe, Assistant Bursar's Clerk and Bursar's Clerk (1914–55), was rewarded by a £30 bonus but more significantly by the 'very substantial help' towards the education of his son at St John's.[146] The son of G. W. Rawlinson, clerk in the College office, was similarly assisted at Nottingham University

[144] CM, 1471/3: Steward £200; Tutorial Bursar £200; Junior Bursar £300 increasing to £350.
[145] Lockhart to Cockcroft, 14 Sept. 1935 (EABP); CM, 1473/10 (18 Oct. 1935); Benians to Lockhart, n.d.
[146] CM, 1413/7 (23 Nov. 1933); W. E. Wolfe to Benians, 22 Jun. 1938 (EABP). See Boys Smith, *Memories*, 81–2.

54 F. W. Robinson,
College Butler,
'whose waistcoat was
reputed to be boiled up
to make the Poor's Soup':
The Eagle 1955

AN IMPRESSION OF THE COLLEGE BUTLER

College.[147] Every term the Council wrote off debts incurred by the sons of casualties of the economic depression.

When R. R. Webb became incapable of looking after himself his gyp W. S. Matthews took him into his own house. In the case of H. H. Brindley it was the reverse, with F. W. Robinson, the heavily stained College Butler whose waistcoat was reputed 'to be boiled up to make the Poor's Soup', moving into New Court to care for him.[148] Even so, in Cockcroft's new business-like regime it was no longer a case of the Librarian paying part of his staff's salary out of his own pocket.[149] At the end of 1934 when the 'zealous and intelligent' current Library Boy reached the age of nineteen, measures were taken to create a proper salary scale for him. Thus the College retained the services of Norman Buck, throughout the next half-century the College Library personified.[150] In the following year similar provision was made for A. J. Sadler, A. E. Martin, H. Pettitt and E. W. Austin, the anchor men of the Kitchens, the College Office and the Maintenance Department for the next generation; R. Toller, the craftsman who gilded the College arms on the Great Gate; and C. C. Scott, Senior

[147] CM, 1573/25 (1 Oct. 1938).

[148] Boys Smith, *Memories*, 16, 60; R. Papworth, 'Pig Club memories', *Eagle* (1996), 20.

[149] Cf. above, p. 449.

[150] The 'Library Committee's Report on the MacAlister Bequest', 19 Dec. 1934; recommended raising his 26s weekly salary by increments of 4s (the University Library rate) rather than 1s as hitherto: CM, 1451/6.

Assistant Librarian.[151] A general pension scheme for servants was introduced in May 1934,[152] partly to compensate for the recent abolition of tipping, a practice reckoned to be worth between £20 and £30 a year to porters and £10 to shoe-blacks (whose paid duties also included carpet-beating, furniture-moving and waiting in hall). Henceforth only gyps and bedmakers were to be allowed to accept gratuities, though the Head Porter was allowed to retain cigars presented to him by departing alumni.[153] The changes were designed to leave those affected significantly better off.[154] Glover's gyps, Poole and Smoothey, were of course always ready to grumble about Cockcroft's innovations, particularly when they felt confident of a sympathetic audience, which was usually. And no doubt, as before, there were those who found ways of combining the advantages of the old dispensation with the benefits of the new.[155]

In the same spirit, an entertainment allowance was established for the Master and the College assumed the cost of maintaining his house and garden.[156] Unlike his two predecessors, Benians had a young family to provide for and no substantial private income,[157] and, as all inhabitants of Master's Lodge have since found, the combination of official residence and family home involves numerous compromises of an expensive sort. In 1937 Cockcroft was well supported in his proposal to knock the place down and build elsewhere.[158] 'Please do not think I am interfering but servants do try one so!', Lady Scott wrote to Mrs Benians at the time of their moving in.[159] But the Benianses will have been unaccustomed to anything more than the one or two servants customary to married Fellows at the time and the requirement to maintain an establishment sufficient to run a minor baronial residence without a minor baronial income to match could not be done other than with assistance.

As was evident from the response to the quatercentenary of John Fisher's death and his canonization in May 1935, in some quarters old attitudes died hard. Although the College's decision not to make an offer for the Torrigiano bust of Fisher was as much influenced by doubts about its authenticity (now themselves doubted) as by the natural disinclination of Fellows to exert themselves in the

---

[151] CMM, 1463/3, 1448/6, 1550/10. See also *Eagle* lviii (1958–9), 223.

[152] CM, 1430/4.

[153] 'Report on the Tipping and Emoluments of College Servants' and schedule listing the perquisites declared by the College's six porters, five shoe-blacks and eleven others, attached to CM, 1412/3 (17 Nov. 1933).

[154] For example, the Butler brothers (W. G. and C. H.), previously paid £2 3s 2d as porters plus perquisites of 18s or 18s 6d, had their weekly wage raised to £3 plus about 10s for waitering. Two who declined to quantify the value of tips received had their wages left unchanged.

[155] GD, 20 Nov. 1937; 19 Sept. 1939; above, pp. 266–9.

[156] CMM, 1568/13, 1577/15 (10 Jun., 28 Oct. 1938); GD, 25 Nov. 1938 ('meeting to vote relief to Master. I raised question if form of words used was watertight against Inland Revenue').

[157] Scott's annual emoluments had been 'governed by a special statute of 1859 read with the statutes of 1882.' In 1910 they amounted to £1,504, in 1915 £1,588 and in 1933 provided a net sum in excess of £2,650: SJCA, D90.921; CM, 1415/5 (23 Nov. 1933).

[158] Crook, *Penrose to Cripps*, 42–5, 107.

[159] M10.1.6 (24 Apr. 1934).

55 Torrigiano's 'Fisher': the bust not acquired by the College in 1935

month of August,[160] for Protestant hard-liners within the Fellowship the occasion was one for the reflection that the Lady Margaret's confidant had been a papist and therefore a traitor to her grandson Henry VIII. Larmor and Glover gave public expression to their wounded sensitivities, bridling at the suggestion that the University had been represented at the Roman ceremonial and entering the lists of the *Times* correspondence columns in the good old cause.[161] Benians it was who 'expurgated' Glover's letter to the *Tablet* on the subject of papistical lies,[162] and in a lecture of 'austere felicity' delivered at the memorial celebrations in the College Hall on 24 July supplied the eirenic touch. This he did not for religious reasons of his own – for, as he would inform a seeker after alms,

[160] CM, 1474/11; Benians to F. F. Blackman, 19 Oct. 1935; P. Linehan, 'An opportunity missed? The Torrigiano "Fisher" and St John's', *Eagle* lxxi, no. 294 (1986), 13–18; P. Galvin and P. Lindley, 'Pietro Torrigiano's portrait bust of King Henry VII', *The Burlington Magazine*, cxxx (1988), 901. Cf. A. Goronwy-Roberts, *Mask: Torrigiano's bust of Fisher reconsidered* (London, 1992).

[161] GD, 20–29 May 1935; *Tablet*, 8 Jun. 1935. Might Benians signify 'our acceptance of St John of Rochester' by announcing at his forthcoming lecture the formal change from St John's to St Johns'?, Blackman asked mischievously. 'How would [Glover] rise to that bait, do you think?': Linehan, 'Opportunity missed?', 14.

[162] GD, 24 May 1935. This letter was not published.

he was not a member of the Church of England[163] – but on behalf of the Cambridge college which could reasonably 'claim to be most in [Fisher's] debt and in the strictest sense his child';[164] also simply because that was Benians's way.

Both then and over the next five years there were other signs of the College's coming to terms with its medieval ancestry. A photograph of the Hall portrait of Fisher was requested by the Vatican and in return copies of the papers relating to the canonization were secured via the British Legation to the Holy See.[165] Because it was not College practice to name courts or buildings after persons, in May 1940 the Governing Body resolved by 13 votes to 7 to call the recent extension not 'Fisher Court', as it was coming to be referred to since that was how it had been described two and three years earlier, but 'North Court'.[166] John Fisher would have to wait another forty or more years for a building of his own in St John's, which he may well have thought a happier location than the alternative.

3. FOUR FAT YEARS

In pursuit of his interest in North American affairs, in the autumn of 1936 Benians and his wife set off for the States, leaving Sikes in charge of the College and Lockhart in charge of the post.[167] At the end of October Sylvia Benians was seriously injured in a motor accident. Although she made a recovery and they were both back by the end of term, or perhaps because they were, it took even sympathetic colleagues some time to understand how much the experience had aged him.[168]

With the establishment of annual elections to the JCR Committee in February 1938, democracy – and, in the circumstances of the time, politicization – invaded that body.[169] Ten years earlier the Council had 'decided not to accede to the request' of the Secretary of the University's Marshall Society 'to entertain a party of London dockers to luncheon or dinner in the Hall on a Sunday in the Lent Term'.[170] At that time, according to Guillebaud, 'the Russian experiment has aroused very great interest inside the University.'[171] Now, although not

[163] Letter to Rev. P. H. Potter, 26 Feb. 1938.

[164] 'The Quatercentenary celebration of St John of Rochester', *Eagle* xlix (1935–7), 73–5 (describing the occasion). Benians's address was published as *John Fisher* (Cambridge, 1935).

[165] CMM, 1455/8, 1471/16 ('Canonization of Cardinal John Fisher'). (Neither for the first time nor the last the nomenclature adopted by the Secretary of the College Council differed from that preferred by the Editor of the *Eagle*.)

[166] GD, 30 May 1940. Cf. CM, 1541/3 (15 Oct. 1937) and Maufe's drawings dated March 1938 (MPSC12.9).

[167] Benians to Sikes, 7 Sept. 1936; Benians to Lockhart, n.d.: honoraria to the two, £150 and £50 respectively: CMM, 1516/15, 1517/4 (Jan. 1937).

[168] CMM, 1508/3, 1514/16; GD, 22 Dec. 1936 (after admission of Fellow): 'Ben not impressive'; 17 Mar. 1937: 'He looks worn and old, with experiences in USA last autumn.'

[169] CM, 1555/14.

[170] CM, 1290/14 (16 Nov. 1928).

[171] 'Then and now', *Eagle* lviii (1958–9), 160.

everyone shared either Dirac's enthusiasm for the achievements of Soviet communism or the liberal Glover's evaluation of Mussolini and Hitler as 'in different ways doing the same thing, restoring order and confidence to a nation, whatever critics at home or abroad say',[172] certain senior members were devoting their energies to the needs of German refugee scholars and Basque children, while amongst undergraduates much of the zeal which once had fuelled the College Mission at Walworth was being directed instead to more secular concerns. The opinion of the College 'on whether a Boys' Club, or some other form of activity, provides the best expression of the social interests of the College', which was the question put to a General Meeting of the College Mission in April 1938, had already received the uncompromisingly stern reply: 'We are dealing with men, not boys.'[173] By spreading its efforts in 1920 from the parish of Walworth to the Maurice Hostel for boys at Hoxton the Mission had overextended itself. In June 1939 the Council made it an annual grant of £50 for three years but with the express warning that 'it should not base its plans for the future' on further assistance thereafter.[174]

'The stress and anxiety which have overwhelmed us all during these last days of vacation', referred to by the Vice-Chancellor (H. R. Dean, Master of Trinity Hall) in his address to the Senate on 1 October 1938, found echo in St John's where 'owing to the uncertainties of the international situation' Benians brought forward the first Council meeting of the year to that day, in particular in order to discuss air raid precautions, the provision of black-out curtains, and the accommodation ('at a day's notice') of 150 London school boys, as well as to hear of the Senior Bursar's sale of securities reserved for the payment of the new buildings.[175] At the suggestion of the Lowndean Professor of Astronomy and Geometry, H. F. Baker,

> It was unanimously agreed that the Master should write a letter to the Prime Minister in the following terms: 'The Council of the College, meeting this afternoon, wished me to express to you their admiration and gratitude for the services you have rendered to humanity by the courage and wisdom with which you have guided us through the critical days just passed.'[176]

That sentiment may have reflected the consensus.[177] But the consensus was not

---

[172] GD, 9 Oct. 1934. Larmor had earlier speculated that Dirac was 'promoting the Bolshevic [*sic*] erudition which already holds the record for the highest atmosphere': letter to Benians, 9 Dec. 1933; 18 Jun. 1935.

[173] Max Newman to Benians, 15 Dec. 1934; 1532/5 (3 Jun. 1937); letter of Benians and others, declaring 'common cause, that of maintaining Democracy' with 'the struggle of the Spanish people': *CR* lx. 107–8 (18 Nov. 1938); 'A Camp for Unemployed Men', *Eagle* xlix (1935–7), 89; 230–3; li (1938–9), 27–30; J. M. Preston, 'Lending a hand', *Eagle* lxix, no. 292 (1984), 11–13; T. E. B. Howarth, *Cambridge between Two Wars* (London, 1978), 178–9.

[174] CM, 1602/8. The Hoxton Mission was closed by bombing in 1940 and its activities in Walworth terminated in 1955: CM, 2052/7.

[175] *CUR* (1938–9), 155; CM, 1573/4, 7.

[176] CM, 1573/5, paraphrasing Baker's letter to Benians of same day (EABP).

[177] Wood, *Glover*, 216.

```
          1 Quickstep.....................Jeepers Creepers    ..............................
          2 Fox Trot ... I've Got a Pocketful of Dreams       ..............................
          3 Waltz ....................... Waltz of My Heart    ..............................
          4 Quick Step ...................... It's in the Air  ..............................
          5 Fox Trot ...... You're as Pretty as a Picture      ..............................
  1st   ⌠  6 Tango .......................... La Cumparsita     ..............................
 Supper ⎨  7 Fox Trot .................. Lovely Debutante       ..............................
 11.30  ⎪  8 Quick Step ......................... Woe is Me     ..............................
        ⌡  9 Fox Trot.................... Delta Serenade        ..............................
         10 Fox Trot ................. Ninepins in the Sky      ..............................
  2nd   ⌠ 11 Quick Step........... Gotta get some Shuteye       ..............................
 Supper ⎨ 12 Waltz ........................... Little Sir Echo  ..............................
 12 45  ⎪ 13 Quick Step ........I Miss You in the Morning       ..............................
        ⌡ 14 Fox Trot ...................... Deep Purple        ..............................
         15 Quick Step .....................How'm I Doing       ..............................
  3rd   ⌠ 16 Fox Trot .. ......................Black and Tan    ..............................
 Supper ⎨ 17 Waltz.........One Day when we were Young           ..............................
 2.15   ⎪ 18 Quick Step....................That's a Plenty      ..............................
        ⌡ 19 Waltz ............................... Blue Danube  ..............................
         20 Quick Step .......... Hold Tight, Hold Tight        ..............................
         21 Fox Trot...................... Deep in a Dream      ..............................
         22 Waltz...........I can give You the Starlight        ..............................
         23 Rhumba.................... Mulatto Rhumbero         ..............................
         24 Quick Step ....................... ...John's Idea   ..............................
         25 Waltz .............................Umbrelle Man     ..............................
         26 Fox Trot........... ......... ...........Could Be   ..............................
         27 Quick Step...............................Medley     ..............................
         28 Gallop ................................. John Peel  ..............................
```

AULD LANG SYNE

Special numbers will be played by request

SYDNEY LIPTON AND THE GROSVENOR HOUSE BAND

THE FOOTLIGHTS' BAND   [P.T.O.

56 Before the Lights Went Out. The Last Waltz.
May Ball 13 June 1939: SJCA, Arch. 2.8.2

universal. One of those upon whom F. L. Lucas of King's called for signatures to his protest against Chamberlain and Munich was G. G. Coulton, who signed and, in a letter to Benians asking that with Europe 'under war conditions' there should be no 'unusual outlay' at the forthcoming celebration of his eightieth birthday, protested at the Council's initiative, which 'others even in the College' had 'criticized very freely', denouncing it himself as 'not only a dangerous precedent, but one which riper thought can hardly approve'.[178]

Coulton was very much a symbol of the College's inter-war years and, as was remarked at the time of his election to the Fellowship in 1919 at the instigation of Tanner and Glover, a prime example of its 'second to none' commitment to 'disinterested scholarship'.[179] A graduate of St Catharine's and a controversialist

---

[178] Coulton to Benians, 26 Nov. 1938. While hawking a letter of protest around Cambridge earlier that term, Lucas had observed the contrast between 'dear old Dr. Y [evidently Coulton] sitting like an aged monk in dressing gown and slippers, a plate with the remains of lunch under his chair, and his table covered with a chaos of the most improbable débris', who signed, and Dr. X, 'the Wellsian atom-splitter' (?Cockcroft), who refused to: *Journal under the Terror, 1938* (London, 1939), 281–2.

[179] Coulton, *Fourscore Years,* 314.

on many fronts, this wandering scholar was the native counterpart to the academic refugees from persecution abroad. Ordinarily, the point of entry for
scholars of distinction was the annual Research Fellowship competition, for
which in the 1930s the number of candidates, rarely exceeding a dozen, was
as small as their quality was distinguished. The three-year tenure, extendible
to six, was of particular value to those whose research was unconventional or
involved long periods of work in distant regions or areas of research in which, as
in the case of the anthropologist Gregory Bateson, 'the collection of (…) data
is necessarily a slow and laborious business.'[180] Another beneficiary of a similar
sort was the archaeologist and palaeo-anthropologist L. S. B. Leakey, whose
access to his college rooms enabled him to work through the night without disturbing his family, and from whom the Council received monthly field-reports
on the progress of his East African researches.[181]

4. THE SECOND WORLD WAR: MEN AND BOYS

In June 1939, a second-year undergraduate with the initials F. H. H., a Research
Fellow of the next generation, penned some 'Lines on the Establishment of
Special Crisis Services of Prayers for Peace' (of which, given his attitude to
Eliot, Lucas would have violently disapproved) and as to the Great Pointing
Controversy the decision was taken in favour of the light-coloured option.[182] 'In
sharp contrast to the confusion and uncertainty which [had] marked the crisis
of September 1938', as the new-model Hun reached the gate the departing Vice-
Chancellor insisted that 'members of the University [were] prepared and ready
to undertake unaccustomed duties.'[183] With its reports of F. H. Hinsley's paper
for the History Society on 'The Constitutional Problem in the Reign of Stephen'
(for Hinsley *all* historical issues were 'problems') and his willingness 'to defend
his own original viewpoint against all-comers',[184] and of Binks (W. O.) Chadwick's sterling contribution to victory in Rugger cuppers, the pages of the
most recent *Eagle* had shown few signs of anything out of the ordinary.[185] For
Benians, however, Dean's successor as Vice-Chancellor for the usual two-year
stint, those duties promised to be particularly onerous.

In St John's the Council constituted the College's senior officers as an
'Emergency Committee' which, meeting daily throughout September 1939,

---

[180] F. C. Bartlett to Benians, 28 Feb. 1934. Bateson, the son of an also much-travelled
data-collecting Fellow and grandson of a Master of the College, had expressed the
hope that his report on research undertaken would not 'hurt the religious feelings of
any member of the Council' (letter to Benians, 23 Feb. 1934).

[181] Leakey, *By the Evidence*, 16; Leakey to Benians, n.d. but late 1934.

[182] *Eagle* li (1938–9), 111–12 (and on this evidence alone adjudged by none other than
J. A. W. Bennett 'an astringent poet of promise': 'One hundred and twenty years of
The Eagle', *Eagle* lxviii, no. 288 (1980), 7); CM, 1603/8(i) (9 Jun. 1939).

[183] *CUR* (1939–40), 158.

[184] *Eagle* li. 171.

[185] *Eagle* li. 158 ('He earned the distinction of being the first known paper reader in our
Society whose opponents felt it necessary to bring with them documentary evidence
to sustain their objections').

made arrangements for the getting-in of palliasses and the lining of black-out curtains by bedders and Fellows' wives, and decreed that members of staff needing to be in College by night for ARP purposes might bring their spouses with them – while strictly adhering to the principle of single occupancy for undergraduates.[186] Eight days later the unthinkable was being contemplated: 'the position was such that it appeared possible that colleges would have to put two men in a set in college.'[187] Although its remit extended to such extraneous business as the scattering of the ashes of the petrologist Alfred Harker,[188] the Committee's main agenda concerned the problem of balancing the accommodation and teaching requirements of returning undergraduates (whose numbers remained uncertain, despite the current exemption from call-up of those under twenty) against the needs of the 125 RAF cadets billeted in New Court, where their use of wireless sets and appropriation of property from undergraduate gyp rooms were giving cause for concern. An enquiry from the borough authorities regarding shelter for local people in the cellars (to which, as Howard responded, although the space available was insufficient for its own people 'in common humanity it would not be the intention of the college to prevent') raised fears lest any application for materials with which to complete the new buildings at North Court might provide the Government with the opportunity to make a claim on them.[189] Regarding the order that dinner bells be silenced, the Committee declined to comply, on the grounds that 'our bell which was sounded at grace was actually a chapel bell.'[190]

On this matter (as on all others) the Committee was advised by Boys Smith in advance of the resignation of his Tutorship and his succession to Cockcroft as Junior Bursar on 1 October.[191] On 6 October the Council had from him a full account of all arrangements made over the previous five weeks. A remark by Glover suggests that, if only occasionally, the College's next Master but one was already shaping up to the task.[192] Inasmuch as the present Master (and Vice-Chancellor) was currently under heavy pressure from the new Master of Christ's and Regius Professor of Divinity, the pacifist C. E. Raven, this was just as well. So concerned was Raven (elder brother of the Dean of St John's) about the moral perils of the 'anarchic conditions' created by the black-out that

---

[186] CM, 1607/4 (3 Aug. 1939); 'Minutes of Emergency Committee' (SJCA, CC15.1), Min. 2 of 15 Sept. 1939.

[187] The information that there might be 400 undergraduates in residence, all in double sets, contributed to Glover's sense of despair. 'Which Greek island gave hemlock to men of 70?', he asked, and answered: 'It was Ceos (Zia) at 60': GD, 21 Sept. 1939.

[188] Fellow, 1885–1939 (*ODNB:* D. Oldroyd).

[189] Howard to Borough Surveyor, 22 Sept. 1939.

[190] Min. 4 of 9 Sept.; min. 2 of 16 Sept.: 'Agreed, despite a communication from the Air Raid Wardens of the borough concerning the ringing of Hall bells, to continue to ring the Grace bell.'

[191] CMM, 1600/2, 1602/2; Boys Smith to Benians, 29 May and 6 Jun. 1939; CM, 1608/15, 16.

[192] 'Chat also with Boys Smith, genial today and like himself (instead of Harrison)': GD, 13 Sept. 1939. Cf. Glover on E. Harrison (the University Registrary): 'not a genial nature, born to be an official'; 'very type of inhuman and unmannerly official': 11 Aug. 1926, 26 Oct. 1926.

57 E.A. Benians, Master (left), during the War: as usual, listening

within a fortnight of entering office he was writing to inform the Senior Proctor
that the vicar of Holy Trinity had been solicited by loose women no fewer than
three times between his vestry and the Christ's Lodge and that he himself had
been accosted within ten yards of his College gate.[193] The Master's gimlet gaze
then spotted a chink of light – of blue light – in the College billets of the RAF
cadets. As his confederate Glover wanted to know, why was 'central authority
insisting on blue lights and on making "camp conditions" in college rooms, with
all this risk to moral life' (blue lighting of course being regarded as bad for the
eyes and, as Vyvyan Adams MP protested in the House to the Secretary of
State for Air, therefore liable to lead to a breakdown of social order).[194] Cambridge, it seemed, was in danger of becoming a garrison town, with all that that
implied.

   The Senior Proctor was unable to find evidence of the 'particular evil' to
which the Master of Christ's had referred. What concerned him was the 'rep-
rehensible' practice of wearing cloth caps and felt hats with academical dress.[195]
As the year of Battle of Britain opened, and Benians, as returning officer, was

---

[193] 'Freshmen are being molested and seized by the arm in Petty Cury': Raven to E. E.
    Rich, 12 Oct. 1939.
[194] Raven to E. E. Rich, 13 Oct. 1939. Was the Secretary of State 'aware that members
    of the Royal Air Force stationed in colleges at Cambridge University are allowed no
    other illumination than blue lighting in their rooms; that this restriction prevents
    reading; that in consequence these men have no recreation after dark other than that
    offered by the cinemas and the streets and that the social consequences are serious?':
    House of Commons, Official Report, 25 October 1939, cols. 1374–5. A promise of
    white lights was promptly secured: GD, 25 Oct. 1939.
[195] Rich to Raven, 13 Oct. 1939; Rich to Benians, 24 Jan. 1940.

studiously distancing himself from supporting a proposal that Sir John Reith
be slipped in as MP for the University,[196] rumour was rife. In May Glover was
informed of a Willingham report of his own arrest as a German spy.[197] On
the day before and the day after, H. F. Baker, by now less convinced of Chamberlain's far-sightedness, wrote to Benians with a series of questions which
with invasion imminent became actual. 'Should the hoarding be allowed to
remain round the New Building? Should the door between B New Court and
Magdalene be kept locked?' Had the antecedents of all kitchen employees been
considered? 'In case of a major attack from the air' (disregarding the fact that
by then it would be rather late for anyone to do so), 'would Professor Cockcroft
agree to advise?' 'The windows on the south side of the Second and First courts
are open to easy approach from the Trinity Bowling Green. Should they not
be protected (especially in empty rooms such as Larmor's)?'[198] Although the
Junior Bursar (on Boys Smith's election as Ely Professor of Divinity that April,
A. T. Welford) was not persuaded by the suggestion that the *Wehrmacht* might
be halted at B New Court or even contained within the Trinity Bowling Green,
in June it was nevertheless agreed to close the College to the public and control
access of College people to points west of the Bridge of Sighs by a system of
passes administered by RAF sentries.[199]

Whether or not it was Baker's strategic vision that was responsible for the
agreement to explore the problematic question of establishing a common gate
with Trinity in the boundary wall in Kitchen Lane,[200] meanwhile the issue of
conscientious objection had arisen again, on this occasion concerning M. A.
Cunningham (son of Ebenezer) whose attitude the local tribunal under J. H.
Clapham's chairmanship had found 'patronising'. When consulted on the question of the College's legal liability for undergraduates injured in an air raid,
Winfield unnecessarily raised the case of those living in lodgings and thereby
prevented by University regulations from being on the streets at night, 'even
for the purpose of seeking a public shelter'.[201] Moreover, the available shelter
accommodation in College was wholly inadequate for the 185 members expected
to be living there – or such was the unequivocal view of the Senior Tutor and
others at the start of the Michaelmas Term 1940.[202] Soon after, the bombing of

[196] Lord Birdwood to Benians, 11 Jan. 1940 ('I cannot help thinking he would be a most
excellent and distinguished representative for our University'); Benians to Birdwood,
16 Jan. 1940.

[197] '(and apparatus found installed in cellar)': GD, 29 May 1940.

[198] Letters of 28 and 30 May 1940. Although Larmor had previously offered to vacate his
rooms at K6 (Emergency Committee, 14 Sept. 1939, min. 3), they remained empty
until Easter 1943 when four undergraduates moved in.

[199] Boys Smith to Benians, 25 May 1940 (two days later the office passed to Welford:
CM, 1634/3); notice dated 17 Jun. 1940: CM, 1639/3.

[200] CMM, 1643/4 (10 Oct. 1940); 1654/6; 1661/4. The iron footbridge on the Backs, later
described by Boys Smith as 'a convenience and pleasure to many, and a happy mark
of co-operation between the two Colleges' (*Eagle* liv [1950–51], 310), having presumably been closed against the enemy, as it is today against tourists.

[201] S. J. Bailey (Tutor) to Benians, 26 Apr. 1940; Winfield to Benians, 27 & 30 Sept. 1940;
Benians to Winfield, 27 Sept. 1940.

[202] Wordie and others to Benians, 1 Oct. 1940.

Coventry persuaded Glover that there was 'nothing to stop them sacking Cambridge any night they wish, or any town north of London'.[203]

On the cessation of hostilities Benians would reflect 'how regularly college life [had] functioned' while hostilities had lasted. 'The undergraduate took life as he found it and made it worth while. To his ordinary academic work were added military duties in the STC and fire-watching at night.'[204] As Wordie's annotated copies of *The Resident Members' List* reveal, numbers were not nearly so sharply reduced as they had been in 1914.[205] College sport continued to be played, which to some locals beyond military age seemed scandalous, leading to demands that the University disperse and undergraduates be sent to fight rather than indulging in 'such trivialities as tennis and the tripos'. In the summer of 1940, indeed, it was quite widely believed that closure was imminent, and in the following year Benians was warned of growing resentment amongst RAF personnel and Dominion forces at the spectacle of pampered students lounging on the lawns.[206] At times the impression of modified ordinariness must have been tested, as when the Regional Commissioner reviewed procedures to be followed in the event of *Sturm und Drang*.[207]

Because any reduction of numbers affected income, in the autumn of 1940 a Council committee demanded economies on all fronts – to little effect. The Dean's reaction confirmed that domestic in-fighting continued undisturbed regardless of hostilities elsewhere. The proposals regarding the porters required 'a great deal more thought – and knowledge of detail – than the Committee's report seems to possess', the normally placid Raven ventured to suggest, while those concerning the Chapel and the Choir School were said to have been made in ignorance of arcane financial arrangements only discoverable by enquiry.[208] In the event, the only saving achieved by this initiative was in the secretarial department.[209] Expectations of cost-cutting in the porters' lodges following the recent appointment of a Lady Superintendent, Miss Price, to take charge of the bedmakers in the place of the Head Porter, were soon disappointed by the extra demands created by the expansion of the College's precincts.[210]

---

[203] GD, 16 Nov. 1940.

[204] 'The College during the War', *Eagle* lii (1941–7), 306–9. In October 1941 Dr Frank Hollick had been put in charge of the College fire squad: CM, 1680/12.

[205] In the Michaelmas Term of 1938 the numbers of BAs/graduate students and undergraduates in residence were 58 and 389; in 1939, 40 and 343, with the combined first and second years at the earlier date (269) shrinking to 244. Corresponding figures for 1940 were 20 and 190, and for 1941, 9 and 180. See Boys Smith, *Memories*, 85–6.

[206] J. A. Ryle to Benians, 23 May 1940; Benians to Ryle, 25 May 1940 (draft reply, reply not sent); GD, 4 Jun. 1940; A. B. Ramsay to Benians, 14 Jul. 1940; letter of R. W. Stanners (25 Apr. 1941): 'The contrast between service conditions and the languors of the Backs and the long lazy leisure of cricket on carefully tended grounds which remain intact amidst hoardings blazing with prayers that we shall dig for victory, is a very evil thing which will work mischief.'

[207] 'Minutes of a Conference on the Position of Colleges in Cambridge during Blitz and Invasion', 12 May 1942: attached to CM, 1705/2.

[208] CMM, 1645/2, 1648/2, 1651/3; Raven to Benians, 14 Nov. 1940; below, p. 577.

[209] CM, 1652/3.

[210] CM, 1646/5 (1 Nov. 1940). The advertisement had been for a 'Matron': CM, 1641/11(a).

Elsewhere the belt-tightening process was more pronounced. 'Some of us', John Crook, who was up between October 1939 and June 1941, later recalled, 'were convinced that there was a causal relationship between the mowing of the lawns on Mondays and the serving of "creamed spinach" on Tuesdays.' 'This War is beginning to bite', Winfield is reported to have observed on being informed by the Hall waiter of the withdrawal of the choice of hot or cold apple pie. At successive meetings of the Council in the autumn of 1942 it was decreed that on Sunday nights no more wine was 'to be furnished' in the Combination Room 'than [was] sufficient for circulation twice'. Worse, it was reported as probable that the College would have to share a carpenter with Trinity.[211]

With the recently named Chapel Court turned into a vegetable patch, nowhere perhaps was the extent of such privations and restrictions more painfully, or graphically, exhibited than in that infallible index of undergraduate opinion, the JCR Suggestions Book. 'None at all', H. M. Pelling insisted in March 1940 in response to a request for suggestions of pictures to be purchased to adorn the walls of the JCR. 'This is not the time to spend money.' Although Pelling's economical instinct may have coincided with Benians's,[212] the fact that the iconophobe had to repeat his words twice may suggest that his was not the universal view. J. A. Crook wanted 'landscape' and J. R. Goody hot baths after games in the afternoon (5 November 1939). With widely supported demands for a Students' Representative Council to replace the JCRC (18 November 1939), it seemed possible that War might be followed by Revolution.[213]

'This is a residential College: Tutors, College Officers and other senior members are easily accessible to discuss matters', the JCR apparatchik intoned. 'So WHAT!!', came the response. With the Movement's leader, Pelling again, dubbed 'Uncle Joe' (2 Feb. 1941), and demands being made for him to be 'c-st-ated' (9 Mar. 1941), perhaps the danger had passed. In the interval (24 Feb. 1941), Pelling adduced 'some sinister reason' for the appearance in the JCR of the *Spectator* instead of the *New Statesman*. The emollient explanation (that the 'sinister reason was a mistake in delivery. What a nose for the smelling of rats') was provided by the Secretary, R. E. Robinson, another future Fellow. A year later, at the lowest point in the history of the world for some time, however, the demand for shoes to be cleaned in time for 9 o'clock lectures and the news that five more baths were available in the new buildings signalled that that danger had been averted (26 October, 6 November 1940) – as indeed may the fact that a defence of the RAF cadets had been initialled by, amongst others, ...

---

[211] Crook, 'Memories of St John's. The Second World War and immediately after', 1–2; CMM, 1710/19 ('except on the instructions of the Master, President or Senior Fellow presiding'); 1711/6.

[212] Letter to Boys Smith (marked 'Not sent. Told him this'), 7 Dec. 1939 regarding a new drawing room carpet for the Lodge: 'I think the Fellows might feel, as in fact I feel myself, that in the present uncertainty we had better not spend money on that. It may cost us more if we wait, but on the whole I think I favour spending no more on the Lodge furnishing just now than we feel obliged to.'

[213] SJCA, CC8.5.

H. M. Pelling.[214] Later complaints that undergraduates were being inconvenienced by the cadets' unlicensed use of the New Court baths elicited the response that, anyway, the baths were reserved for the dons (1 December 1943, 7 February 1944). Other favourite topics included rationing, especially coal rationing, the assumption that the Steward was up to no good with the ration books, privation in general, and the contrasting merits of the *Daily Mail* and the *Daily Worker*.[215]

By this local constituency the College was accused for passing the buck, for holding 'that universal scapegoat', the War, responsible for everything from the texture of the soup in Hall[216] to the state of the Third Court lavatories (2 February 1941). But by early 1941 the College really was at War. Almost every Council meeting recorded the departure of Fellows on war service, seventeen of them in October 1942, for example. Of those mentioned in preceding pages, Rée had gone to France, where he would organize sabotage for the resistance, Hinsley and Marchant to crack codes at Bletchley; Miller (by now a Research Fellow), Goody, Pelling and Crook to the army (and in the cases of Goody and Crook to prisoner of war camps), and Robinson to train as a bomber pilot.

Many did not return: in December 1946 a memorial service was held 'for the members of St John's College and Choir School and for College servants who had died on active service'.[217] Others, who had the choice, decided not to. One of the 1939 intake who had joined the Navy in 1940 had been persuaded by his success as an Entertainment Office to make theatre his career, so went off to RADA instead and later found fame as the asinine Colonel Reynolds in the 1970s sitcom *It Ain't Half Hot Mum*.[218] After one year of Cambridge, another, whose Johnian father had written in June 1939 to inform Wordie of his decision to do his military training 'after his Varsity entry rather than before', departed for the same service.[219] In April 1946 his father indicated that, despite all it meant for dynastic sentiment, he would not be coming back but would be going to the job he had waiting for him.[220] 'I had expected you to reply as you have done', Wordie wrote, 'as war service for many has been in the nature of a University.'

[214] Against 'priggish and intolerant suggestions [which] will (...) be allowed to remain in this book to the lasting shame of the College' (for example, that they had spread jam on the tables in Hall, taken ladies up the Chapel tower, and played gramophones on the Backs [22 January, 15 & 19 May 1941]).

[215] In February 1940 the Fellows voted by 15 to 7 in favour of the *Daily Worker*: SJCA, CC38.2 (Fellows' Amenities Committee Minutes).

[216] SJCA, CC8.4 (19 Feb. 1940).

[217] Eight years later 110 names were added to the War Memorial in the chapel on the panels designed by Sir Edward Maufe: CMM, 2032/6, 2035/2(ii). More were added in later years, and in response to information supplied by families and friends have continued to be subsequently.

[218] D. M. Hewlett to Wordie, 26 August 1948.

[219] 'As I feel he will then be fitter to cope with the very mixed company with which he will have to deal. (This is not intended to be a slur on John's!)'

[220] 'In a way his years in the Navy have had a certain value he would have enjoyed at Cambridge, at any rate its more social aspect, though of course he will have missed many of its other advantages. Perhaps the next generation – if any – will carry on the family connection with John's.'

For those who did return to complete their triposes there were all the tensions associated with readjustment. Squadron Leader R. E. (Robbie) Robinson, back to read for Part II of the Historical tripos, called on his Director of Studies, Frank Thistlethwaite, most of whose War had been spent behind a desk. Thistlethwaite remembered the other's smart salute as he departed. Robinson's recollection was of being told to wear a gown the next time he called.[221] As well as indicating that a historian's memory is no better than another man's, the encounter epitomized some of those tensions, not all of them creative, in the post-War College, as remembered by Logie Bruce Lockhart in his memoir of the 'chaotic year' spent sharing a room with Robbie:

> Our routine was morning work and afternoon exercise, followed by a couple of beers at the Hawk's Club between six and half past seven, often meeting with Sandy Smith. We would sing a strange variety of music. Sometimes it would be a Bacchic rendering of the Seventh Symphony with a vocal version of all orchestral instruments. Sometimes Robbie would attempt to change our 'privileged background viewpoint' by a melancholy rendering of 'Please don't burn our shit house down.' (...) By his own account, he must have had a tough upbringing in Battersea, paying for extra books and tuition at the Grammar School by milk or newspaper rounds. He had strong feelings about social injustice, and he flirted at different times with the Plymouth Brothers and Communism. It might seem unusual that his closest friends were ex-Public School boys; but in the immediate aftermath of the war, the main division at Cambridge was not Public Schoolboys v the State Schools, but ex-Service men v 'the children'. The war had changed us profoundly. Sandy Smith did not get his MC at Pegasus Bridge for a picnic, nor did Robbie get his DFC for joyrides. Those of us who had returned from the war were drawn together by our experiences and our age. We more or less kept to College or University rules with wry amusement; we kept strange hours. Most of us looked down on the nineteen year olds straight from school, and even on the dons who had not been to war, with what in retrospect seems to have been surprising arrogance. What right, we felt, had they got to talk about death, disease and poverty, life, suffering, hatred and love, sex and sadism? We felt that they were darkening counsel by knowledge without understanding, and that they were using words without the density of meaning which experience gives to them.
>
> After dinner we nearly always worked together from eight to midnight in a silence interrupted only by brief requests for an opinion or factual information, or a ten minute session of room cricket.[222]

---

[221] F. Thistlethwaite, *Our War, 1938–1945* (Cambridge, 1997), 169; personal information. Cf. George Shepperson's recollection of 'some of the Fellows of Cambridge colleges' attempting to subject ex-servicemen 'to petty measures of discipline such as the wearing of gowns on every possible occasion', in Shepperson *et al.*, 'J. W. Davidson at Cambridge University: some student evaluations', *History in Africa* xxvii (2000), 217.

[222] 'Robbie as an undergraduate', *Eagle* (2000), 15–17; see also obit., *Eagle* (1999), 110–15; *Independent*, 25 Jun. 1999 (Peter Linehan). L. Bruce Lockhart (BA 1946) had served with the 9th Sherwood Foresters and 2nd Household Cavalry (Lifeguards);

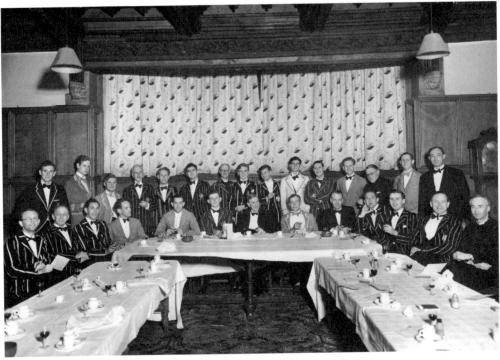

58 The Eagles Dinner 1946, the Old Music Room

Standing: A. W. Scott, R. G. Watkinson, Rev. J. N. Duckworth, Prof. P. H. Winfield, R. A. Roseveare, P. G. Allan, Rev. E. E. Raven, N. Thomas, J. K. Moss, J. J. H. Rymer, A. G. Aitchison, L. Bruce Lockhart, Rev. M. P. Charlesworth, H. Symons, R. L. Howland. *Seated:* A. L. R. Perry, E. Cunningham, R. G. Salmon, R. M. Argyle, E. Bole (Magdalene Coll.), B. M. W. Trapnell, E. A. Benians (in the Chair), J. S. Paton Philip, Colonel J. H. V. Ivory, R. E. Robinson, D. H. Clarke, S. J. Bailey, Rev. J. S. Boys Smith

(As has been written of contemporary Oxford: 'Ex-majors with MCs, wives and moustaches had little in common with 17-year-old boys who carried green ration-books entitling them to extra bananas.')[223] But, to continue with Bruce Lockhart:

> We hardly attended any lectures, except to get a booklist at the beginning of the year, so we were able to read an unusually large number of books. (...) Our view on lectures was that little was to be gained from attending them. Most lecturers, although they might have written good books, were poor public speakers. (...)
>
> If you went to a lecture at 9am and another at 11, you wasted the time from 10 to 11 and from 12 to 1 by going to the Whim or to the Baron of Beef, because there wasn't enough time to bike back to college and to set about a serious job of work in between lectures. (...) Supervisors' tutorials

headmaster of Gresham's School, Holt, 1955–82. R. A. A. (Sandy) Smith, Oxford and Buckinghamshire Light Infantry, worked in India and Pakistan, 1946–68.

223 Keith Thomas, 'College life, 1945–1970', in B. Harrison (ed.), *The History of the University of Oxford*, VIII (Oxford, 1994), 208. 'But would you fly with him?' was forever after Robinson's ultimate question about a man.

were potentially far more valuable, but the standard varied from the sublime to the ridiculous.

By a junior membership comprising such veterans (for whom 'climbing into college would otherwise have been an adventure, whereas after several years in the Marines it was an unnecessary bore') alongside recent sixth-formers ('the children'),[224] there were freezing conditions to be endured[225] and the continuing shortage of pretty well everything. In respect of its junior membership, the Council had informed the University at the beginning of 1944 that, while the College was willing to admit increased numbers of students immediately after the War, thereafter it was determined to return to the limits imposed by its buildings and endowments, limits which 'cannot be increased if the traditional character and standard of a Cambridge education are to be maintained', namely 450[226] – of whom, be it noted, in accordance with the policy enunciated in 1927 more than 400 would be undergraduates. In October 1947, while acknowledging the need eventually to respond to continued growth of properly qualified applicants, this intention was reaffirmed.[227] But numbers continued to rise, placing intolerable pressures on premises and facilities. By the summer of 1946 'the more studious undergraduates' (the 'grey men') were asking for an increase in reading room accommodation, and in October 1949, with numbers in the 650s, there were calls (unavailing) for four Halls of an evening rather than three.[228]

Also heard, both before and after Briggs's replacement by Glyn Daniel as Steward in 1946, were complaints about what was on the plates during these compulsory repasts when there was room for plates on the table. As Daniel himself observed later, many of the undergraduate complainants had been majors and colonels with experience of running army messes.[229] At the time, the thought may not have consoled him. Would the Steward indicate whether the College was a 'catering establishment'? Where did he 'buy (or rent) his sausages'? In the Kitchen Suggestions Book of the period complaints about the state of the waiters' finger-nails and generally filthy conditions jostle with grumbles about the frequent appearance of 'Vienna steaks', grapefruit and custard, ants and cockroaches, and mouse faeces in the porridge (not that vermin were any respecters of the College hierarchy).[230] The origin of the 'widespread

---

[224] Trevor Bailey (matric. 1946), *Wickets, Catches and the Odd Run* (London, 1986), 39. Of 298 in October 1945 (26 BAs and Research Students, 272 undergraduates); 522 twelve months later (85 and 437).

[225] See 'Winter, 1946–7, in College': *Eagle* liii (1948–9), 13–16.

[226] The Council 'think these limits were reached with the expansion that followed the last war': Benians to Registry, emphasizing that 'we have no building programme on view at the present time': undated attachment to CM, 1756/2 (21 Jan. 1944).

[227] CM, 1863/2 (31 Oct. 1947); Benians to Registry, 1 Nov. 1947.

[228] Gatty (Librarian) to Benians, 31 Jul. 1946; Kitchen Suggestions Book 1938–49 (SJCA, CC8.4), 18 Oct. 1949.

[229] Daniel, *Some Small Harvest*, 287.

[230] 'That the JB be asked to remove the rats and mice from the top of the screen in the Hall, as they tend, at present, to fall on to the Fellows when the latter are lunching or dining in Hall' (J. W. Davidson, recommendation to Fellows' Amenities Committee agenda, 24 Mar. 1949).

suffering' caused by the Steward's game pie and of the antecedents of the pigeon that had given rise to 'severe gastric disarrangements' seemed to have been found in a box labelled 'Frozen Rooks' spotted in Kitchen Lane by an eagle-eyed undergraduate. Daniel's later insistence that suspicions were allayed by his explanation of the matter[231] is not confirmed by the primary sources. Not every one of those majors and colonels may have been satisfied by his response to the suggestion of T. E. Bailey on 4 March 1947 that the game pie recently served had contained 'crow, sparrow and birds of similar description', that 'crows have only been served once this academic year in Hall: that was to Fellows when it was described by the name of "Rook Pie". I well remember how extremely good it was.' On the other hand, nor were compliments to the chef, Sadler, rare, as on the 'superlative excellence' of Hall on 9 February 1946. Meanwhile general relief could occasionally be provided in the shape of roast pork from the College Pig Club's pigs reared on the College orchard by Ralph Thoday and protected by him by one or another stratagem from the attention of the man from the Ministry of Food.

For years the College had relied for the recruitment of intellectual talent on the annual Research Fellowship (Title A) competition in which selection was based primarily on dissertations or other writings submitted. In view of the falling number of such candidates (from eleven in 1940 to five in 1943), and in order to allow also for those doing National Service who intended to return to academic study after the War to be considered, in 1943 the rules were changed, enabling such Section II candidates (as they were classified) to submit instead a *curriculum vitae* and the names of two or three referees.[232] The credentials of Section II candidates were therefore for other persons to establish, and although a number of those chosen were to have distinguished careers in the College and elsewhere, not all were in that category – any more than all those elected under the old dispensation had been. In practice, as emerges from an anxious letter of one of the electors, the process had become one of comparing one candidate's research achievement and potential with another's apparent teaching (Title B) qualifications. 'I am worried, as I think most of us are, about this Fellowship election', E. A. Walker wrote to Benians on the day of the 1943 election. On purely academic grounds the New Zealander J. W. Davidson seemed to him clearly the best. But on teaching grounds he was outshone by one of the Section II candidates. Walker wanted both of them of course, though if pressed he would plump for Davidson.[233] In the event, the Council preferred two Section II men.

Davidson, one of the College's earliest graduate students from New Zealand, was shattered by his failure. In a long letter to his mother he unburdened himself:[234]

[231] Daniel, *Some Small Harvest*, 287–8.

[232] CM, 1728/2 (26 Feb. 1943). The shrinkage of candidates of the traditional sort continued: five in 1944; six in 1945; four in 1946.

[233] Letter of 1 May 1943. For Davidson and his strengths and weaknesses, see Hyam, 'The study of imperial and commonwealth history at Cambridge', 81–3.

[234] Letter to E. M. Davidson, 16 May 1943: Davidson Papers, National Library of

It had always been a subject of comment with us how the College Council chose a certain proportion of mediocrities as Fellows. These things – alas! – are not managed by the good scholars of the College – e.g. by men like Prof. Winfield. Such men have too much to do in their own subjects to sit much on Committees and to be College Tutors. (The Tutors, 4 in number, are the backbone of College government.) The St John's Tutors are, in general, very pleasant men but of little standing as scholars – my former Tutor, Mr Bailey, is the most remarkable in these respects (very amiable but most mediocre); Mr Wordie (my present Admiralty overlord)[235] is the one for whom I have most respect. In addition to these four the others most concerned were Mr Charlesworth (shrewd but unbalanced) and the Master (again a man whom I like much but one keen above all for compromise, or avoiding disagreements). (…) All that I am trying to show is that there are likely to be a good many unsatisfactory decisions – unspectacular men choosing others like themselves to carry on the College in a hum-drum way. They choose a good many first-rate scholars at one time or another, but often they think more (it seems) of a candidate's supposed ability to 'fit in', to sit on committees, do routine teaching. This has all been common subject of discussion for a long time – St John's seems to have something of a reputation in Cambridge for this sort of thing.

As to the two people elected on that occasion,

[they] have neither done any original work at all nor been in a position to show whether they are really good or not. One I knew well – a man who gave up history for law because, as he said, the intellectual standard was lower there. After he took his B.A. (a first class) he didn't begin research but spent another year on 'examination' work for an LL.B. and got only a 2nd. Then he was called up and has been in an anti-aircraft unit ever since. He has always said very frankly that he wanted to be a don – just to live the life of Cambridge, rather than to engage in any particular study. He had no real enthusiasms it seemed always; he was always very 'correct' in all that he did, very respectful towards those in authority. We were always a little amused – he is so efficient and yet so totally uninspired.[236]

When a disappointed Fellowship candidate writes to his mother in New Zealand he is not on oath. But his reflections are none the less of interest. In a competition such as this Dirac would probably not have prospered. In the following year, 1944, Davidson did. The experiment with Section II candidates was not persevered with after the War. The prevailing view was the one enunciated by H. A. Harris, that 'We are not so badly off as we might be.'[237]

Australia, MS 5105, Box 65. See D. Munro, 'Becoming an expatriate: J. W. Davidson and the Brain Drain', *Journal of New Zealand Studies* ii–iii (2003–4), 30.

[235] Under Wordie's direction, Davidson had been engaged in the preparation of Naval Intelligence Handbooks at the Scott Polar Institute.

[236] Evidently a reference to Capt K. Scott, later Lecturer in Law, whose letters to his Tutor (S. J. Bailey) from Deolali in 1945 rather confirm Davidson's opinion. The other election was of J. C. (later Sir John) Gunn.

[237] Letter to Benians, 20 Apr. 1945: 'Miller, Deer, Evans, Glyn Daniel and Hoyle maintain my confidence in the future'. All these were Section I Fellows.

59 Best hats and Back to Normal. The Annual Staff Outing sets off, 1945

Such was the crush of numbers in the post-War years that Cambridge-domiciled academics who wanted their sons to have rooms in college had to be prevailed upon to take other undergraduates into their own homes in lieu, while those living out had to learn to make the best of whatever was available. In offering to one such 'rather humble lodgings' in Aylestone Road, his Tutor sought to cheer him by mentioning the compensating advantage 'that it is near the river if you want to go swimming before breakfast'.[238] By the same token, landladies could afford to be choosier than they had been twenty years before. Mrs Cherry, for example, wrote as follows of one fourth-generation Johnian with a speech impediment and his fellow lodger.

> Will you please tell them they are not to use the paraffin stove. Mr Cherry and myself have both told them about it and after which they took it to the bedroom every where smells strong of paraffin and all the years I have let, I have never never had rooms left in the condition they leave these in what with bacon amongst dirty linen in the cupboard. The funny talker finishes in June so I prefer the other to go too.[239]

Even so, during 1945–6 the return to peacetime conditions proceeded, with staff salaries raised to match the increase of the number of students to be serviced, the annual staff outing to the seaside (suspended for the course of

238 G. C. L. Bertram to A. J. G. Cellan-Jones, 16 Jul. 1951.
239 Letter to G. C. L. Bertram, 24 Mar. 1952.

hostilities) reinstated, and undergraduates having their shoes as well as their windows cleaned.[240] College societies began to flourish, in some cases falteringly. In May 1946 the Nashe Society briefly resurfaced for the first time since Isherwood's visit nine years earlier, and with J. R. Goody at the helm as Secretary, debated whether to continue as a dining club or to allow a literary element its head, whereafter the minute book falls permanently silent.[241] It was in the course of this transformation that, according to legend, the Committee, prosperous ever since, had its origins in a protest against the preciousness of the also recently founded Swans.[242] With its mixture of senior and junior members dining together, the Committee afforded an opportunity for social mingling rare in those hierarchical days, paralleling what the Pig Club provided for College officers and senior members of the College staff.[243] Meanwhile, on the other side of Queen's Road, substantial reparations received from the Air Ministry and the Home Guard in respect of use of the pavilion and the old Peterhouse ground put the Field Clubs on a sounder financial basis than they had previously enjoyed.[244] Though not on the St John's pitches, Trevor Bailey – as an exserviceman a two-year BA man, and a soccer player in the winter – embarked upon a six-days-a-week, six-hours-a-day Easter-term cricketing routine.[245] For whatever reason, it seems that Bailey did not meet that earlier exponent of medium-fast bowling when 'Round-the-Corner Smith', now Sir Aubrey Smith, the gilded survivor of the College's Victorian past, returned that summer to the scenes of the triumphs of his youth, visited the Master and revisited his old rooms, where *The Prisoner of Zenda* was photographed peering in disbelief at the College's still medieval installations, before crossing the road and purchasing from Messrs Buttress's twelve College ties for his Hollywood Cricket Club and a pair of college socks for himself.[246]

Further evidence of a return to pre-War practices was provided by two associated notices, one (featuring a member of an earlier Johnian generation) from the Boat Club log, the other from the JCR Suggestions Book. The first recorded how:

[240] CMM, 1797/4, 1802/5–8, 1829/7.

[241] Under the same auspices, in January 1947 the Nashe evaporated – or mutated into the Lady Margaret Players (SJCA, SOC.22.1). Cf. *Eagle* lii (1941–7), 333; liv (1950–51), 326, 386.

[242] According to a version of events which, in the absence of the records, lost when the Club Secretary was sent to prison in the early 1960s, has to be allowed a measure of credence.

[243] For the origins of the Pig Club and its survival 'as a society for convivial purposes' after the removal of its *raison d'être* in 1954 ('there being abundant precedent in the University for bodies – such as Colleges – which continue in existence although the original purpose of their foundation has been lost sight of'), see G. E. D[aniel], 'The Pig Club', *Eagle* lvi (1954–5), 146–8; Peter Linehan, 'The Pig's Golden', *Eagle* (1996), 9–13.

[244] CM, 1846/9.

[245] Bailey, *Wickets, Catches*, 40. But it was Bailey himself who, despite the Tutors' willingness to let him do so, chose not to tour the West Indies with the MCC in January–April 1948: Bailey to F. Thistlethwaite, 28 Aug. 1947; Thistlethwaite to Bailey, 16 Sept. 1947 (tut. file/T. E. Bailey).

[246] *Cambridge Daily News*, 21 Jun. 1947; Allen, *Sir Aubrey*, 162–3.

During [the May Term 1949] a practice was instituted of the First Boat entertaining the coaches to a lavish dinner before going into training. It was on this night that L. H. Macklin, having broken two windows of his old rooms, rushed into the Porter's Lodge and threw down 10/–. The Porter, Mr Butler, said: 'Windows are only half-a-crown, Sir'; hereupon Macklin went out and broke another. He attempted to break a fourth, but missed.[247]

The second was written by J. C. Bray, an Australian ex-POW, who had noticed that since Robinson's commencement of his duties as College Butler the porters had ceased being employed as waiters in Hall and wanted it to be known that

> there [was] no college in the University with a more helpful and consider-
> ate body of porters than St John's, and it would be a heavy loss indeed if
> any of them expressed dissatisfaction over their wages and left for more
> lucrative employment.

In order to pay them more, and thereby to keep them, the College should adjust their wages, 'even to the extent, if necessary, of making a moderate increase in the service or establishment charge'.[248]

For all his prim insistence that porters' wages were no business of undergrad-uates, the JCR Duty Officer's endorsement of Bray's proposal signified the jun-ior membership of the College's transition, cautious though it was, from feudal conditions to welfare arrangements appropriate to the age of Beveridge. 'And very good of you, Sir', the porter on duty on the evening of Macklin's visit would no doubt have volunteered. Curiously, history as viewed from the Head Porter's office ran counter to the dialectic. 'It has not been our custom to recruit Head Porters from our existing porters' staff and any move in that direction would carry consequences far beyond any temporary gain', Dean Raven had stated in 1940:[249] despite which, when Bowles resigned in 1952, he was succeeded by W. G. Butler, who having been the Head Porter's assistant since 1946 was a man with just the antecedents of which Bray would thoroughly have approved.[250]

Benians's sense of the College was a catholic one. On receiving a long, mean-dering screed concerning the doings of her 'young gentlemen' from a former landlady down on her luck and requesting assistance for her sick daughter who had 'got a coal bin lid on her thumb nail and a cold', remedial action followed within a couple of days.[251] A severely pragmatic romantic, on another occasion he remarked: 'My experience with cooks is that one must either put up with

---

[247] Hall-Craggs, *History of the Lady Margaret Boat Club*, II. 138–9.

[248] JCR Suggestion Book (SJCA, CC8.6).

[249] Letter to Benians, 14 Nov. 1940.

[250] CMM, 1826/9, 1994/10; JB 16.4. Gate porter since 1920, he was the nephew of Herbert Butler, gyp; hall waiter (1920–43) and Head Porter 1952–61. His younger brother, Cecil (Head Porter, 1967–9 [CMM, 2408/6, 2477/13], had started as a kitchen porter: above, n. 154.

[251] Forwarded to Junior Bursar, 9 Jan. 1935, with illegible hieroglyph. On January 11, 'Yours Respectfully Mrs Crabb' thanked him for his 'kind answer', and went on to deplore the failure of one of her lodgers to pay her for doing his washing and to sing the praises of another ('a pleasure in the house'). (The pair went on to become a writer of White Papers and a Chief Constable respectively.)

the cook or with the cooking.'[252] Such was his attitude to the College and its quiddities. But such was his commitment to it and to college teaching – 'the duty and the liberty of teaching', no less – that, on Previté-Orton's elevation to the chair of Medieval History in 1937, alongside all his other duties, Benians agreed to undertake the directorship of historical studies.[253] A month earlier, a suggestion made by the Professor of Botany that undergraduate teaching be transferred from College to University really stirred him.

> The question (...) is a fundamental one. What [the professor] proposes in Botany might be proposed in every subject and the Colleges might be asked to surrender all their teaching. But education is placed first in the objects for which the College exists. We cannot give up the duty and the liberty of teaching. (...) Our business in all subjects is to educate our men as well as we can in collaboration with but not under the direction of the University, to provide entirely, or partly, or not at all for their teaching as we think fit. Otherwise the Colleges become only boarding houses.[254]

Late in life he remembered his own undergraduate experience:

> Supervision was weekly for the first term, and occasional for the remainder of that year, and, after that, it came to an end. (...) The scientists disappeared to their laboratories during the day and complained that they got nothing from the College. A duality was already apparent.[255]

The duality already apparent was the social phenomenon regularly testified to by the prickly Glover. Glover feared a take-over of the place by the scientists.[256] It was a fear soon to find further expression.

Despite growing numbers, which required him to warn some old members that although the College would like to welcome 'their boy' times had changed ('I am very much interested to hear of the boy's musical interests, but in present circumstances doubt whether they can help him very much', he wrote to one in June 1946),[257] he continued to remain accessible to all. He was seen on the touchline. Returning the compliment, undergraduates invited him and his wife to tea. The fact that 'even in wartime' he and the senior members found time to maintain the custom of entertaining junior members of the Eagles Club to dessert in the Combination Room was particularly appreciated. Harry Rée asked

---

[252] Undated letter (Jan. 1938) regarding a cook who had not justified her testimonial.

[253] CM, 1537/15.

[254] Draft letter to Wordie (10) Jun. 1937.

[255] Benians, 'Cambridge in the last half century', 12–13.

[256] '... this progressive place seems to be on the verge of deciding that Celtic language and literature are not needed, as against the many branches of anatomy, chemistry and worse things': Wood, *Glover*, 210. Thus, 'Two men with comps (or for "supervision" as they now call it, in imitation of N. Sci. crowd, alas!'): GD, 8 May 1925; 3 Nov. 1938: 'Arts need fortifying in this welter of N. Sci.'; 23 Jul. 1929 (at Hall): 'Young science ... grows tiresome. Palmer especially shallow.'

[257] One on whose behalf he did intervene, albeit tepidly, was the nephew of his old friend Hugh Russell-Smith: letter to Wordie, 14 Jun. 1946. His support was unavailing. The confident tone of the letter sent on behalf of the supplicant's cousin in 1939 ('My son will be coming up to John's next October, and I have just written to Wordie about it') indicates the difference the War had made.

if he might call to discuss a scheme for stimulating interest in the College club at Hoxton 'and generally of fostering the College spirit'.[258] If the first of these looked unpropitious there would be no lack of enthusiasm to the second. The Master's address to the freshmen was 'really grand', Dean Raven enthused: 'really superlative and has given [them] something they will never, I think, entirely forget.'[259] Despite giving up Scott's practice of maintaining the Admissions Register,[260] Benians continued to inspect the relevant paperwork and to keep a close eye on the social composition of the junior membership. Amongst his papers is a hand-written list of the various professions (fifty-two in all) of the fathers of the 1951 freshmen, bakers, millers and miners as well as barristers and stockbrokers. Thus informed, he was able to demonstrate to the father of Kenneth Craik, the Research Fellow in Applied Psychology tragically killed in 1945, that it was in fact not at all surprising that his son should have been admitted to the College 'without the traditions of an English public school behind him'.[261] As to those who had done so by means of the award of State Scholarships, he was clear that their selection was vindicated by academic success. Asked by the Chairman of a Panel of Investigators whether State Scholars showed 'signs of excessive fatigue' or tended to be 'worked out', whether there was 'any unusual degree of failure' amongst them 'indicating a faulty method of selection', and whether too many were reaching Cambridge 'with public assistance who are not really worth it, and would be better advised to attempt something else', Benians could reply with a No to each question, bolster his conclusions with College figures, and (shades of Tanner's 'exhausted hermits') conclude that 'taken as a whole, the results strike me as the results of an able and well-selected body of men.'[262] In the middle of the War he took the lead in promoting the case for a General Examination as an option in the Entrance Scholarship Examination, having in mind 'that some boys probably ought to delay specialization longer than they do, until they have acquired a broader foundation of knowledge and their minds are more mature', boys like Benians himself, in short, whose education was of the liberal, unspecialized, unprivileged sort that he had received at his own father's little school at Goudhurst; boys, that is, likelier to have been found perusing his Horace in a tavern, *à la* Matthew Prior, than cracking nuts in the chapel.[263]

When conflict ended the danger of over-specialization as well as the eirenic side of him were again on display. In the College Hall in which while hostilities had continued members of the Allied forces had regularly dined,[264] he addressed a gathering of German prisoners of war at the conclusion of a

[258] Card of B. W. T. Ritchie, 12 Feb. 1938; letters of R. I. Stokes, describing the invitation as 'perhaps slightly "unconstitutional"' (Feb. 1945), B. M. W. Trapnell, 9 Oct. 1944; Rée, 6 Nov. 1934.

[259] 'It just came out grand. Thank you, Master': Raven to Benians, 9.Oct. 1945: SJCL, Misc. Letters/Raven.

[260] Letter to Wordie, 24 Mar. 1939.

[261] J. B. Craik to Benians, 14 May 1945.

[262] Cyril Norwood to Benians, 14 Mar. 1938; Benians to Norwood, 22 Mar. 1938.

[263] Attachment to CM, 1721/3 (19 Dec. 1942); above, pp. 136, 406.

[264] Benians, 'The College during the War', 307.

Summer School organized by the University's Board of Extra-Mural Studies. After welcoming the enforced visitors to Cambridge and celebrating the glories of the universities of Germany, Benians directed their attention to what it was that mattered most to him.

> Each of us here is a member not only of the University but of a College, and I think it is very fitting that you should come to hold your last meeting this evening – this social evening – in the heart of one of the Colleges. In our Colleges we have the management of our own affairs, we mingle men who are students of all subjects, arts and sciences, in a common life.[265]

For Benians, an evening such as this was no perfunctory exercise.[266] It was part of the process of restoring things, colleges included, to where they ideally belonged. In his Commemoration Sermon two months earlier he had described the essence of the matter:

> A College is not a factory, or a mint, or a sub-department of Government; but, as Newman said, 'an alma mater, knowing her children one by one.'[267]

Benians's commitment to the College ideal deserves reiteration in every generation.

On 23 October 1950 Benians entered his seventieth year, in the course of which the Statutes required him to retire, unless renewed for a period, as the Governing Body was enabled to do. By an overwhelming majority, on 28 October his tenure was prolonged for three years from 1 October 1951. In an (as usual) conscientiously corrected draft of a letter to Claude Guillebaud, he expressed his satisfaction at being asked to stay on.[268] Three days later Martin Charlesworth died, aged fifty-five. On 2 December 1951 Edward Raven followed him: President and Dean both gone. On the day after that the Benianses attended the annual dinner of the Lady Margaret Players. It was the last function in College that they attended together.[269] On 20 December, by now mortally stricken with stomach cancer, the haggard Master presided over what was to be his final College Council.

On odd scraps of paper that came to hand during his final days his wife jotted down his spiritual testament, the reiteration of the principles which had guided his entire career:

> Feb. 2 'It was the College who made him Master so he gave his time to

---

[265] 'Prisoners of War', typescript, 30 Jul. 1947. Benians had substituted 'in a common life' for 'which may save us perhaps from the modern danger of over-specialisation'. His text, as usual, was much revised.

[266] 'I think it was especially kind of you to remain with us throughout the whole evening and I am sure that this was appreciated by everyone': F. E. Bell (Board of Extra-Mural Studies) to Benians, 1 Aug. 1947.

[267] *Eagle* liii (1948–9), 1–6, at p. 3.

[268] 'For me the years here have been very happy, ~~for I have felt always the good will and affection of the Fellows,~~ and though I should have been well content to go at the appointed time, I can't but be pleased that ~~they~~ Fellows should ask me to stay a little longer' (30 Oct. 1950).

[269] Note by Sylvia Benians on letter of invitation from R. Busvine, 22 Nov. 1951.

the College and never attempted to do much outside. The College job appealed to him, and he didn't see why as they paid him.'

'College a great institution which could do so much if it tried. If everybody neglected College work to do outside things, College would suffer. If you can get ~~any~~ everybody to believe College is a wonderful institution, it can do things no other body can.'[270]

'Does so much for Fellows if they only get 3 years, it makes them different men. This was one of the things he tried hard for – that College should take a lot of junior Fellows, then they could go out to the academic world of England.'

'His speeches, where these would be found. These ought to be kept for 50 years as an interesting social document showing how a Master spoke to Fellows, undergraduates and College societies.'

'The evening of the night he died he became conscious for a few moments and I told him you had liked the Valentine.[271] His face brightened and he smiled – so pleased. It was the one day I said 'it comforts me to be in the College – it seems in a way immortal. And you are one in the ~~great~~ long series of Masters.' He said 'Yes. Nothing can ever take that away from me and it is the only memorial I want.'

Amongst his own jottings, preserved by his widow together with hers of his remarks, is an undated one, deciphered in part by her as follows:

What is a College? Is it that group of buildings charged with memories in every angle? Or is it that group of people with whom we lived through three swift years? The buildings are there still: but the people are gone.

When he had met him at a Trinity dinner party in the spring of 1914 the then Master of Magdalene had found Benians 'wholly silent', speaking too softly and too infrequently. He had 'looked nice but I'm told he is dull – such an odd theory of hospitality to go to dine, eat and drink, and say nothing!'[272] By contrast, Benson's successor had wanted him as the University's MP.[273] Both had misjudged the man and his potential. As remarked some pages earlier, when the relationship of the College – *his* College – to the University was the issue, Benians was tinder dry and liable to take fire. As to the essence of him, the words of the chapel memorial come closest: 'The words of wise men are heard in quiet', the text of Ecclesiastes 9:17, implying as it does his invariable courteousness, and his deference to and consideration for others.

He died on 13 February 1952. Near the end he asked for his ashes to be scattered privately in a corner of the cricket field, 'unless', he specified – and this was characteristic – 'Fellows would not like this.' The Fellows did not object, and twenty-seven years later those of his widow joined them there.[274]

---

[270] It was sentiments such as these perhaps that had so affected Ifor Evans in 1933.

[271] Referring to a squib dedicated to G. M. Trevelyan (publ. *CR* lxxxiii [1951–2], 280).

[272] Benson Diary, 145, fo. 36 (13 May 1914); likewise, ibid., 161, fo. 53: 'A nice fellow but rather speechless'.

[273] Above, p. 517.

[274] CM, 2731/33 (4 Oct. 1979).

I. THE MASTERSHIP OF WORDIE

THOUGH many of them may have feared as much, those present at the Council meeting of 20 December 1951 were not to know that it was Benians's last. But College life continued. That same afternoon note was taken of the imminent retirement of Bowles, the Head Porter.[1] Early in the following term a new Dean, J. S. Bezzant, was appointed, and the Junior and Tutorial Bursar, K. Scott, resigned in circumstances concerning which the Council record refrained from particularizing.[2] With Wordie, already Senior Tutor, having succeeded Charlesworth as President a year before, and Boys Smith alone remaining in place, all this represented a pretty thorough sea-change – though, not for the first time in St John's, to some of its Fellows it may all have seemed less that than a rearrangement of the deck-chairs along the esplanade. Earlier, Charlesworth may have looked the coming man. But to Glyn Daniel and others (Charlesworth included) discussing the matter in 1948 it had not seemed so. To them Wordie appeared the favourite.[3] And, in the election itself, an occasion reminiscent of 1908 rather than 1933, so he proved.

A meeting of Fellows on 19 February, the day after the old Master's funeral, saw the emergence of three candidates, namely Wordie, Cockcroft, and Boys Smith, all of whom were 'seriously considered' according to Frank Smithies, though with Boys Smith very much the also-ran. The contest between the first two of these was to some extent paradoxical in so far as the qualifications of Mr Wordie, the good College man, were those of an unbureaucratic administrator rather than an academic, whereas Sir John Cockcroft, who as Junior Bursar had once had charge of the College's roofs and drains, had shared the Nobel Prize for Physics in 1951 and enjoyed celebrity status as one of the founding fathers of nuclear physics. However, whatever advantage all this may have afforded was offset by Cockcroft's absence from the College after 1938 as well as by a measure of uncertainty, useful to his opponents, regarding Churchill's willingness to release him from the Directorship of the Atomic Energy Research Establishment at Harwell.[4]

'Bought a sponge at Boots', the complete diarist Frank Smithies began his account of 10 March, a day which for the generality of Fellows was to end rather more eventfully, with straw votes in the Combination Room, although inconclusive, proving favourable to Cockcroft.[5] At the election itself, on the

---

[1] CM, 1978/13.

[2] CMM, 1981/5 (25 Jan. 1952), 1982/ 9 (8 Feb. 1952).

[3] GEDD, 1 Mar. 1948.

[4] On 24 February Smithies was assured by R. A. Lyttleton, Cockcroft's agent, that Cockcroft could accept the Mastership if elected. Yet on 4 March there was 'still no definite news' on the matter (same source). Cf. Oliphant and Penney, 'John Cockcroft', 183–5.

[5] SJCL/Smithies/J21; (i) Cockcroft 24; Wordie 22; Boys Smith 15; (ii) Cockcroft 33; Wordie 23; Boys Smith 5, according to Daniel, the Secretary of the Council, whose figures differ slightly from Smithies': *Some Small Harvest*, 188.

13th, with 64 of the College's 69 Fellows present, the first ballot produced a dead heat with 30 votes for each of the front-runners, and four for Boys Smith. At the second, held after a brief adjournment which some of the worsted party would later complain had cheated them of victory, Wordie prevailed by 33 votes to 31, and, as President, duly declared himself elected Master.[6]

Wordie's reputation had been made at the world's chilliest extremes, as geologist and chief of scientific staff on Shackleton's *Endurance* expedition in 1914 and thereafter. He would have climbed Everest too, but for medical advice in 1921–2 not to venture into high altitudes.[7] Accordingly, in 1923 he had settled at the more richly oxygenated level of a St John's Tutorship and, despite approaches to consider the Principalship of McGill University of Montreal, there he stayed.[8] At the time of his election, the Master who came in from the cold had been a Tutor for twenty-nine years, Benians's successor as Senior Tutor for nineteen,[9] and Charlesworth's as President for two. If James Wordie left a spiritual testament, which seems unlikely, his widow burnt it along with the rest of his College papers. Partly for that reason, this account of his years in office will be brief.

'As a member of the College Council and as Master he sometimes had difficulty in finding arguments in support of a line of action which he felt the College ought to follow', his anonymous obituarist wrote, whereas 'his filing system seemed (...) to depend on memory, for his large table was littered with papers from which he never failed to extract the document required.'[10] However, a chaotically disorganized desk does not necessarily betoken a richly furnished mind. As another Fellow, one of the Tutors and a sometime protégé with whom later he had a mighty falling-out, put it, rather less indulgently: 'He relied, in Council meetings, very largely upon the President, his number 2, in a way not in accordance with St John's customs.'[11] Shrewd, devious and endowed with a gift for intrigue, he was 'a dyed in the wool traditionalist', according to Bertram, who was in a position to know.[12] Glover had agreed, at least sometimes.[13] The

[6] Ibid., 189. Again Daniel's count is awry. The account in M. Smith, *Sir James Wordie Polar Crusader: Exploring the Arctic and Antarctic* (Edinburgh, 2004), 253, allegedly provided by John Crook, is wrong in every particular – as also is the assertion that Wordie had 'turned down an earlier invitation' to be Master.

[7] Smith, *Sir James Wordie*, 144.

[8] In this connexion Glover was consulted by his Canadian friends regarding Wordie's 'religious position': GD, 4 Apr. 1935. Cf. Smith, *Sir James Wordie*, 194, who refers to the office as the Chancellorship.

[9] Extended in both capacities for a further five years from Michaelmas 1948: CM, 1872/4(ii), 12 Feb. 1948.

[10] *Eagle* lix (1960–63), 319 (probably B. H. Farmer; cf. *ODNB*).

[11] Colin Bertram, cit. Smith, *Sir James Wordie*, 256. For the progress of their row, resulting in Wordie's removal as Chairman of the management committee of the Scott Polar Research Institute of which Bertram was Director: ibid., 225ff. The latter refers to this as 'an unhappy time': C. Bertram, *Antarctica, Cambridge, Conservation and Population: A Biologist's Story* (Cambridge, 1987), 64–5. The need for him to petition the St John's Council, chaired by Wordie, for an allowance to compensate for his losses in resigning the Directorship in 1956 made it the more so: CM, 2105/5.

[12] Smith, *Sir James Wordie*, 242.

[13] 'a call from Wordie, who is now Senior Tutor (...) gained more from his silence than his speech', GD, 17 Feb. 1934.

60 Eagles Club 1956. J. M. Wordie in the chair.
Left to right: E. Miller, N. B. Jopson. Behind Wordie: E. Cunningham, E. A. Walker, J. S. Boys Smith. At left S. J. Bailey, R. E. Robinson; at right: R. L. Howland, K. Scott: SJCL, Album, 17/27

contrast with his predecessor could hardly have been sharper. Maurice Wilkes, his tutorial pupil in the 1930s, found him 'alert and shrewd, though lacking in social graces'.[14] It is difficult to imagine Benians 'barking' at an undergraduate who had complained about having to cross the court for his ablutions, or answering him as Wordie did, or dividing his pupils into as few as two or three categories.[15] For Benians, humanity was far more richly variegated than that modified Manichaean arrangement implied. A Glasgow graduate, Wordie had come to St John's in 1910 as an advanced student, and was therefore the first modern Master of St John's without experience of life as a St John's undergraduate. Aged sixty-three at the time of his election, Wordie had no academic position to resign. By now he was a fixture and thereafter a virtual inevitability. Ten years older than Benians had been when he replaced Scott, it was probably ten years too late when he arrived at the Lodge. Significantly wealthy,[16] he left the College nothing.

[14] *Memoirs of a Computer Engineer* (Cambridge, MA, & London, 1985), 10.

[15] Smith, *Sir James Wordie*, 221: 'When I was with Shackleton we did not wash or clean our teeth for two years – the natural greases kept us clean.' Ibid., 256, for his categorization of his pupils as either 'a good man' or 'a strange man'. There was a further possibility: 'May make a schoolmaster.'

[16] 'Well off', according to Tanner's note on Wordie's tutorial form: SJCA, TU20/ Wordie. J. M.

Wordie's Mastership was characterized by seven years of largely uneventful Council meetings, the principal agenda of which were implicit in the replacement of the Tutorial Bursar by a Bursar for Buildings, a change made even before his election.[17] 'We see no present possibility of completing the building plans we formed 15 years ago', Benians had written to the Central Bodies (the University authorities) in 1949, restating the College's determination to return to pre-War numbers of junior members as soon as the current bulge had passed through the system. Yet even in those circumstances, over the previous two years that desirable objective had increased by fifty to 500.[18] Likewise, when during the Wordie years the prospect returned of resuming those plans it remained collegiate orthodoxy that the purpose of increasing the Johnian curtilage was not to accommodate the ever greater numbers for which the University unceasingly pressed. It was to bring the College's men in from unacceptably distant lodgings.

Yet for all its protestations, in common with other such institutions at Cambridge and beyond throughout the 1950s the College continued to adapt to such demands. The process of attrition continued. In April 1955 it was 'agreed to approve the recommendation of the Tutors that it is desirable to maintain the total number [of junior members] at about 600'; a new plateau: 'it being recognized (1) that the number will fluctuate slightly about that figure in consequence particularly of the choice given to most of those admitted to the College to take their National Service either before or after residence and (2) that the increase in the population of undergraduate age which will take place in a few years time may then justify some increase above 600': another plateau reached, all within a single sentence.[19] And when that summer the University returned to the charge with an enquiry whether the College would be willing to expand numbers 'in order to meet the expected increase of applicants after 1960 owing to the larger number of births during the later years of the War', the reply was to reiterate its policy of maintaining an average of 600 'over a period of years' while conceding that it might be possible to go to 620 or 630 'during the anticipated period of pressure'.[20]

Unfortunately, periods of pressure were *always* anticipated – unless of course they were actual, and therefore inevitable. In December 1958, after two years in which because of the virtual abolition of National Service numbers had reached 679 and 720, it was again asserted that, even when new accommodation did become available, they should 'ultimately revert to ... about 600'.[21] 'Having regard to the College as a society' (Benians's constant preoccupation), it was only in respect of its desirable number of Fellows that the College held the line. In Benians's time that number was thought to be not more than seventy-five, 'alike in the interests of the College and in the interests of the academic world generally', of which number one-fifth should be Research

[17] CMM, 1985/2, 1986/3 (7, 14 Mar. 1952).
[18] Letter to H. Kidd, First Assistant Registrary, 29 Oct. 1949, attached to CM, 1920/7.
[19] CM, 2060/11 (22 Apr. 1955).
[20] CM, 2070/24 (6 Oct. 1955).
[21] CM, 2157/4 (8 Jan. 1959).

Fellows.[22] At the time of Wordie's election in 1952 there were sixty-nine Fellows. Six years later, when he resigned, the figure was seventy-one.

As a bridle on the likes of Wordie, who during the War had managed a side of hundreds without evident exertion, two years earlier the maximum period of tutorial service had been set at twenty years.[23] Increasing numbers of junior members called for extra Tutors to service them,[24] and extra Tutors cost money. In this context, the economic imperative operated in both directions. As the National Service years ended declining numbers necessitated higher charges, as indicated and quantified in a supplement to the December 1958 report on numbers, the last of Wordie's Mastership. As the decade advanced charges were raised with increasing frequency and the JCR Committee became correspondingly vocal on the subject.

It did so against a background of the also costly process of putting the College to rights, a process interrupted in 1939 and resumed in 1951 in respect of the resurfacing of Second Court and the repair of its cobbles, which had been repeatedly excavated since 1945 for the installation of gas, electric, water and telephone services. The Governing Body's divisions on the issue, concerning the laying of paving stones along the axes of the court – a process achieved 'successfully because', in the words of its historian G. C. Evans, 'slowly' – are perpetuated in the interruption of the pavement a yard or so short of M staircase where F. S. L. Hollick, tribune of the anti-paving party, kept both then and for long thereafter.[25] European dictators might come and go, but the colour of the pointing of Second Court remained controversial.[26] It says something about changing perceptions as well as about changing times that in 2008 the College should have had First Court repaved in conformity with disability legislation with only a summary reference to its own Governing Body, so-called.

Not that the paving issue drove the pointing parties wholly into the shade. Indeed one of the recommendations of the 1956 'Report on the Structural Condition of the Buildings in Second Court' was that, as in First Court, its 'sombre appearance' should be relieved by the use of light pointing.[27] But here it was not cosmetic matters that were the issue. What weighed here was the ruinous state of the buildings themselves, graphically illustrated by photographs of rafters apparently resting on thin air and seemingly only kept aloft by their inhabitants' simple faith in the College. In consequence, the range between First and Second Court, and much of Second Court itself, and following from that Third Court, were taken apart and put together again. Photographs of the Kitchen

---

[22] CM, 1963/7 (3 May 1951), regarding report of Committee on Fellowships under Titles B and E.

[23] CM, 2068/3 (22 Jul. 1955).

[24] In 1957 an increase of four to ten in all was recommended to the Council, which agreed to three, noting that the proposal was based on projected figure of 700 undergraduates: CMM, 2117/18, 2127/8.

[25] GB, 8 Jun. 1951; G. C. E[vans], 'The Cobbling of Second Court', *Eagle* lv (1952–3), 171–7. Crucial in the process was the search for an element of *pinkness* in the paving stones.

[26] Until the summer of 1964: CM, 2331/3.

[27] [Noël Dean], 'Report ...', March 1956, 37.

61 Second Court under restoration in the late 1950s

range demonstrate the thoroughness of the operation. For this part of his serv-ices to it, the College has every reason to remember with gratitude Alec Crook, whose account of these operations and of the problems encountered in the course of them is unlikely to be bettered.[28] Between 1956 and 1968 upwards of £325,000 were spent on the work. Throughout this decade or more old mem-bers with an appetite for such things were kept informed of the progress of its process, as well as of incidental discoveries made *en route*, by Clifford Evans's regular and regularly ruminative articles in the *Eagle*.[29] Like everything else in St John's, they were not beyond parody.[30]

Brandishing a £5 annual contribution as bait, one Old Member (and future arbiter of Good Taste), wrote in January 1958 in response to the appeal for funds for the repair of the old buildings and the provision of new, recently published in *The Times*:

The buildings that have been run up by the College in the course of

---

[28] Crook, *Penrose to Cripps*, 160–76; above, p. 518.

[29] For one example, on K6 Second Court, see 'A Set of Rooms. Some discoveries and puzzles', *Eagle* lvi (1954–5), 60–68, 150–60.

[30] Of which B. G. C[artledge], 'A set of tiled rooms', *Eagle* lvii (1957), 15–17 – a descrip-tion of the Third Court lavatories – provides a nice example.

the last 75 years are (with, I think, only one exception) so disgraceful that I hesitate to subscribe to what might turn out to be a similar act of desecration. On the other hand, if it is thought the College's intention to abandon all thought of Flemish bricks, hand made tiles & Sir Edward Maufe, and instead to build in a wholeheartedly C.20 way (employing an architect likely to be approved by, say, Dr Pevsner), then I would gladly give as much as I can afford, or possibly more than I can afford.[31]

In a scrawl on the letter, for the Master's benefit, the man's former Tutor (F. Thistlethwaite) remarked that he was 'both rich & difficult & would repay a good deal of humouring'. Apart from its content, choice example as it provides of the perils of dealing with a clientele as well educated as it was occasionally well informed about such things as the presence of Dr Pevsner on the premises,[32] the reader will wish to know that the answering of it was handled not by the Master but by the Senior Bursar, whose reply, penned within three days, constituted a masterpiece of diplomatic discretion, ranging over such subjects as contemporary silver design as exemplified by recent pieces of Sir Joseph Larmor's Plate, and the use of 'smithy dust' in black pointing with particular and judicious reference to the College Rental of 1793.

Revealing as it does the regular recurrence of a limited number of parochial issues, the JCR Committee Minute Book of the period is recommendable as further reading to complement *The Glittering Prizes*. Despite an occasional shaft of frankness of the sort mealy-mouthed College records normally contrive to conceal,[33] the agenda were routine, the state of the croquet equipment vying for attention with the collapse of the picture loan scheme; the Steward's resistance to requests for a bar in the JCR, the Dean's to approaches on gate hours,[34] and membership of the National Union of Students. As often as not, almost as many senior members as junior were present at its meetings, the attendance of the former not yet resented by the undergraduates. Indeed, in February 1956 there was pressure for the Fellows (but not from them) to dine weekly with the undergraduates, an initiative reported to be favoured by the Master.[35] The suggestion of the Senior Tutor (Guillebaud) two years before that at the undergraduate Commemoration of Benefactors 'the Fellows and undergraduates, in dining together, should not dine at separate tables', had met with 'general agreement'.[36] Now the junior members wanted more of it. However, a proposal

---

[31] Adding for good measure: 'I also believe that it was at one time the Master's wish that 2nd Court should be re-pointed with black mortar. I should not wish to have any part in this sad project': letter of 21 Jan. 1958 (D33.17.18).

[32] Nikolaus Pevsner, Slade Professor and Title E Fellow, 1950–55; Honorary Fellow, 1967.

[33] E.g. 'Nothing could possibly be done [about the Library] until Mr Wight (*sic*) retired' (March 1960).

[34] Extended from 10 to 11 p.m. in April 1956: CM, 2085/9. In February 1959 the JCR Committee's request for the Bridge Street door to be left open until that hour was refused.

[35] SJCA, CC17.2, covering the years 1955–60: minutes of 21 Feb. and 1 May 1956.

[36] CM, 2034/3 (30 Apr. 1954).

that the two constituencies should share 'an ordinary undergraduate dinner' at
a form of domus evening in the following October elicited from the Governing
Body the response that 'there was need for some action to assist closer contact
between senior and junior members of the College, though not perhaps along
the lines proposed.' Although refraining from instructing Fellows with entertainment allowances how to encourage 'private contacts' with undergraduates,
the committee charged with 'Promoting Closer Contact between Senior and
Junior Members' did venture to suggest that it would be 'of no small value' if
when entertaining their pupils they were to introduce other Fellows into the
company 'as liberally as possible'. Shades of Martin Charlesworth! Beyond that,
while observing that 'one part of the desire of the junior members of the College to meet the Dons is basically a wish for social recognition, a feeling that the
College is two societies instead of one, and the only practicable line of solution
for this problem lies in communal entertainment', it recommended the holding
of dessert parties for fourth-year undergraduates, BAs and research students.[37]

Although this was not what had been asked for – and quite possibly prompted
the suggestion that 'to increase confidence' in the College Council amongst junior members extracts of its minutes should be made available to them[38] – it did
at least represent some acknowledgement of the role of postgraduate students
in the College community, the cohort which in 1947 and again in 1949 the College had stipulated should constitute no more than about one sixth of the junior
membership.[39] While the 'Closer Contact' committee may have recognized that,
'as was emphasized by several members of the Governing Body', socially 'the
Research Students from elsewhere are the least catered for', in correspondence
with the University about junior member numbers in the following year all reference was to *under*graduates, with no mention at all of other categories:[40] an
expression of deeply ingrained and persistent attitudes, the College's graduate
student community might have been forgiven for concluding. While graduate students were not accommodated within the courts of the College (as has
remained the case almost to this day), not even the first hostel reserved for their
use was regarded as their exclusive preserve, the committee charged with the
conversion of the house at 69 Grange Road being directed to provide accommodation 'for Research Students *or other junior members*'.[41] Although I 1 First
Court, declared a junior common room in 1957 and by popular acclaim dedicated to Samuel Butler – in preference to Peter Mason (the singular President),
the Earl of Southampton, Vivian Fuchs, or Richard Bentley (the beleaguered
Master of Trinity) – was colonized by graduate students from the beginning,

---

[37] GB, 8 Jun. 1956; Report dated 31 Aug. 1956; CMM, 2097/20, 2102/16, 2123/10. The
Committee had specified *third*-year undergraduates (as indeed was the reality in the
late 1960s).

[38] Minute of 15 Oct. 1957: the proposal of J. H. Cockcroft, one of the two nephews of
Sir John currently junior members of the Committee, President of the Cambridge
Union (1958) and Conservative MP for Nantwich (1974–9), did not recommend itself
to J. R. Bambrough, one of the Committee's Seniors.

[39] CM, 1863/2; 1920/7.

[40] CM, 2127/8.

[41] CM, 2183/7 (23 Oct. 1959).

in 1960 the request for official approval of their *de facto* occupation of the space separating it from the JCR led to border warfare between the two constituencies and resistance to the graduates' wish to use their territory for dinner parties and the entertainment of ladies: a sequence of events which, since graduate students did not yet have their own committee, can only be reconstructed from the JCRC minute book.[42] Despite the assertion made almost a half-century earlier, that 'anything that encourages post-graduate research is looked upon [at St John's] with more favour than undergraduate and early B.A.',[43] the impression remains that regardless of the Governing Body's fine professions on their behalf, in the bipolar world inhabited by the College Council graduate students remained an anomaly, neither one thing nor the other. Some progress would be made under the next Master. Then they would instead be regarded merely as a problem.

Undergraduates were mostly British and therefore predictable, and because predictable manageable. They went home in vacations, or if they had no home to go to on this side of the equator, they went somewhere else. When in April 1958 the JCR Committee asked about the occupation of rooms by overseas undergraduates during vacations, it was informed that 'the Master was against it on the grounds that it was good for people to get away from Cambridge during the vacations.' But the senior member whom undergraduates, whether from home or abroad, were destined to have dealings with during Wordie's mastership was not the Master. It was the Dean.

J. S. Bezzant (Stanley to intimates; 'Bezz' to the collegiate rest) was as familiar a part of the St John's landscape of the period as the First VIII peering into the Cam from the Old Bridge after Hall. As a naval chaplain during the War he had gone down with the *Repulse* and lost a lung. To undergraduates of St John's during his regime he was arbitrariness with a (more often than not) human face, effortlessly combining, to their discomfiture, his reputation as one of the century's great liberal theologians with the capriciousness of an oriental despot. As the College officer responsible for both worship and discipline, the last of the its omni-competent Deans indeed, Dean Bezzant could treat with disdain its Senior Tutor and Junior Bursar. 'Bezzantries' abounded; stories about him were legion, many of them as exaggerated as the man himself, the Dean who was capable of sending down thirty-odd men about to sit down to a bumps supper ('and I mean it') and then spending the rest of the night penning them letters on his special thick writing paper, in the reading of which each recipient could discern the prelude to the inevitable climbing-down process.[44] One of those letters, sent to the Captain of Boats, K. W. Blythe, after an unusually lively bumps supper in June 1957 summarizes the man as neatly as such a man might ever be summarized:

[42] JCRC, min. of 16 Feb. 1960. Since October 1957 the postgraduates had been demanding exclusive use of a room for drinking coffee. The ensuing debate over the sort of coffee it should be reveals exclusively postgraduate preoccupations. See Henry and Crook, *Use and Occupancy of Rooms*, I. 21–2.

[43] H. F. Stewart to J. B. Mayor, 29 Dec. 1911, apropos the establishment of a prize in memory of J. E. B. Mayor: Trinity College Cambridge, B16/221.

[44] For which see Linehan in D. Morphet (ed.), *St John's College* (London, 2007), 182.

I feel very strongly about what happened on Saturday-Sunday night. The Master was unwell and was kept awake by the long-continuing series of explosions, as were many others who were not in a drink-induced sleep. As for the oar on the chapel tower, the Master, being a good Scottish Presbyterian, takes a more serious view of it than I do: he used the word 'sacrilege' about it, which I regard as excessive. I think it would be wise of you to call at the Lodge and repeat the apology which I understand you made to Prof. Ratcliff.

As well as enclosing his usual cheque for the Henley Fund – 'and, as I have already said to you, I shall be gladly willing to repeat (or even increase) it', his letter, addressed 'Dear Ken', breathed fire, brimstone and threats: 'Henceforward, anyone caught in any climbing activity, or arranging any explosions, will find his membership of the College terminated at once, and therefore, also, his membership of the University': all of which of course can only have acted as stimulus and added savour to the prospect of future breaches of the rules. A month later Bezzant presented the College's bill for removing the oar, followed by an offer to reimburse Blyth an equal sum.[45] As those close to him will have understood, Bezzant's erratic behaviour stemmed from a ravaged family life, of which his delight in the antics of young children gave some indication.[46] Not surprisingly, callow undergraduates were less adept at interpreting the conflicting signals. After his retirement in 1964 the decanal office was separated into its disciplinary and its sacerdotal components and a secular Dean of the night established alongside a religious (even spiritual) Dean of the light.[47] In view of the choppy period ahead this was probably not before time.

Bezzant's reign coincided with the last years of the old dispensation before the impact of changes in British society, which would transform the College both within the walls and beyond, began to be felt. A notice circulated to members of the Council in November 1958 provides one glimpse of a world that was about to be lost. Headed 'Plans for the Future of the Master's Lodge', it described arrangements for a forthcoming visit to that building, concluding: 'The President [G. E. Briggs] suggests that members of the Council may care to take with them someone who has the responsibility of running a house.'[48] Further afield, such persons, the connoisseurs of domestic expertise, were regularly described as wives.

Another is afforded by a letter sent *c.* 1950 by R. L. Howland, Guillebaud's successor as Senior Tutor, to the headmaster of a Leading Public School where he had recently spent a week-end in the course of which half-time on the rugby field was spent in casting an eye over an athletically well-endowed candidate, a procedure resembling a Tattersalls yearling sale, from which the young man

---

[45] Letters of 17 Jun., 19 and 22 Jul. 1957 ('If there is any real difficulty about this £2.14.6, *you* send a cheque to Mr Evans and *I* will reimburse *you*'). Cf. CM, 2031/7(b): 'Dean to inform College clubs and societies that it would be the intention of the Council to considers subsequent applications only if conduct on such occasions was satisfactory' (19 Feb. 1954).

[46] See K. Sutton's sensitive obituary: *Eagle* lxii (1967–8), 124–6.

[47] CM, 2308/7.

[48] Building Committee Minutes, SJCA, CC16.2.

had emerged with the offer of a place. But alas, on returning to College, Howland had discovered that the five seat in the First VIII had 'already been promised by another Tutor'. The postscript is eloquent: 'As I sign this it occurs to me that we did not consider the question of a subject for the boy to read.'[49] 'Slow to act unless there was something important to be done', as Guy Lee was to write of him, with victory in both Soccer and Rugby cuppers and the First Boat going head in the Mays, 1959 was a Golden Year for College sport and therefore for Howland.[50] The (successful) recommendation in that year for the granting of a Larmor Award to an oarsman with a Third who had 'shown high quality in accepting calmly and without bitterness the disappointment of twice so nearly missing Putney' may serve as a memorial to a world whose values were coming under increasing scrutiny.

In June 1963, on Briggs's retirement from the Presidency, Howland added that office to his tally after a late spurt which dashed Glyn Daniel's hopes of securing a stepping-stone to the Mastership at the next vacancy.[51] Here the friendly evaluation of Sir Richard Cherrington, FRS, FBA, DSc [sic], MA, Daniel's fictional counterpart, may not be out of place.[52] But be that as it may, despite the campaign of strenuous lunching already planned and the furnishing of the Third Court room adjacent to his which he proposed to annex more or less settled, it was not to be. Daniel consoled himself with a remark made to him by F. H. Hinsley on the night before the election: 'My dear boy, this is why you will not succeed tomorrow: because this is a mediocre society and they will vote for a mediocrity.'[53] Two years later Howland resigned the Senior Tutorship on appointment as Warden of Madingley Hall, the University's 'House of Residence' for graduate students and venue for courses run by the Board of Extramural Studies.

2. THE CHOIR SCHOOL AND NEW BUILDING

It was during Bezzant's time as Dean that the imminent retirement of its headmaster brought the future of the little two-room College Choir School in Bridge Street, and therefore that of the Choir itself, into question.

By 1954 Mr Sam Senior had been in charge of the Choir School for a period of forty-two years, and for most of that time he had been intent on its

---

[49] Letter no longer extant at either St John's or the Leading Public School.

[50] *Eagle* lxxi (1987), 59; lviii (1958–9), 179, 192, 201.

[51] 'The real fear answer (sic) in my mind is that I will get this job and that I will do it bloody well so help me Ruth [Daniel's wife] and God and that as a result, unless memories fail incredibly I should be thought a possibility to succeed Boys Smith': GEDD, 27 Nov. 1962.

[52] 'A most brilliant scholar. A most accomplished man. He has travelled everywhere and knows all sorts of people. He keeps a good table, a good cellar and is still the hardest worker in College. (...) The Presidency of Fisher College will go to him at Dr Quibell's death or retirement. You might think he has everything. And yet ...': G. E. Daniel [under pseudonym Dilwyn Rees], *The Cambridge Murders* (London, 1945), chaps. 4.i, 18.i.

[53] GEDD, 2 Jun. 1963.

aggrandizement. When in 1921–2 the tempestuous C. B. Rootham had produced a scheme for a school for 200 boys in the Hermitage (now Darwin College), 'with choir as nucleus', opponents had identified the schoolmaster as the prime mover. 'Senior's vaulting ambition is revealed as the motive force behind Rootham – who seems to be megaphone for other people', Glover opined.[54] On that occasion a tutorial veto on the loss of undergraduate accommodation proved decisive with the Council, and Senior had to be satisfied with permission to engage a French teacher in order to enable his charges to qualify for admission to the Perse School when their voices broke and they left his tutelage at the age of fourteen or fifteen ('even though it appears *no* boy there now wants special teaching to go on with education').[55] Four years later, an *ad hoc* committee reported that, although the school was 'on the whole satisfactory' and 'Mr Senior [had] earned the reputation of being successful with backward boys', it was 'not in the interest of the school that he should admit especially backward boys as fee-paying pupils.'[56] According to George Guest, Senior 'was permitted to augment his salary by admitting as many non-singing boys as he liked'.[57] This was Senior's understanding of the situation too. But it was not what the College understood, nor was it the College's wish that in consequence the inmates should be so tightly packed in that each of them had to walk across the desks in order to reach his own place. However, with thirty-four boys on the roll at this stage, twenty-two of them choristers or probationers, it was the fees paid in respect of the other twelve that kept the enterprise going – or, as some considered, Mr Senior, who retained those fees, in clover.[58]

In 1927 the number of fee-payers was fixed at the level it had then reached, twenty out of a total of forty-two.[59] From the report for the year 1931–2 it emerged that all instruction was provided by Senior and his wife with the occasional assistance of passing choral students who, when the schoolmaster had to take to his bed for a fortnight, assumed entire responsibility for an enterprise the financial side of which continued to leave something to be desired, notably in respect of financial particulars.[60] When in 1940 these were received, and it appeared that the Schoolmaster's emoluments had risen to £675 (a sum

---

[54] GD, 3 Feb. 1922.

[55] GD, 28 Jan. 1922; CMM, 1116/3, 1125/7.

[56] Report of 20 Jan. 1926; CM, 1223/7 (5 Feb. 1926).

[57] G. H. Guest, *A Guest at Cambridge* (Orleans, MA, 1994), 23.

[58] GD, 5 Feb. 1926: 'choir schoolmaster who rolls up £480'. (This was more than three times Glover's receipts for the year in dividend and chamber allowance, and almost half that of a busy teaching Fellow, such as Z. N. Brooke of Caius: Brooke, *History of the University of Cambridge*, IV. 284.) Cf. Boys Smith, *Memories*, 219: 'Mr Senior was permitted to take a limited number of additional boys and to charge them fees at his discretion, which he retained. The College had no official cognizance of the amount of these fees and they did not appear in the books of the College or the statements of school expenditure.'

[59] With Senior's emoluments and allowances amounting to £625: Report dated November 1927; CM, 1280/14 (8 Jun. 1928).

[60] £330 of the £605 the school had cost the College 1931–2 was accounted for by Senior's salary and rent-free house. The accounts for the year contain mention neither of income from the fee-payers nor of its destination (Report, 8 Mar. 1933).

considerably in excess of the Senior Bursar's dividend), that at £24 the cost to the College of educating a chorister was a 'very high figure in view of the scope of the education provided', and that total College expenditure had risen to upwards of £1,700, the conclusion of the Committee on Economy was clear: the school should be closed. The proposal, declared 'disastrous' for Chapel music by Robin Orr, Rootham's successor as Organist, was deflected by Dean Raven's well-founded insistence that the committee was not fully informed of the financial complexities of the matter – as well it may not have been.[61]

Additionally the choral tradition that the choir represented excited hostility within the College, particularly within its Low Church party. Glover, for one, 'hated' Rootham's music and was deeply suspicious of every Dean's every move, noting Creed 'getting £30 for Senior to sing in Chapel which he might do himself'.[62] According to Macklin, a member of that choir, it was on account of Rootham's musical tastes that the Chapel remained largely empty.[63] On the other hand, by Guest's account, so pronounced were the Nonconformist sympathies of the Chapel establishment that on his arrival in 1938 Orr had to fight off a demand for congregational singing ('even of the canticles') and on his return in 1945 found 'Master, President, Dean and Chaplains, together with a number of Fellows' all of that mind.[64] By then the 1944 Education Act had established the transition to secondary education at the age of eleven, thereby compounding the problems of a school whose songsters were at that age approaching their best.[65] By 1953 the place had reached bursting point, with eighty boys on the roll, sixty of them paying fees to the Schoolmaster, and all at an annual cost to the College approaching £2,000: a hypertrophic growth on the College's flank to which Senior's approaching retirement at last made it possible to contemplate the necessary surgery.

It was plain that neither in its existing form nor on its existing premises could the school continue.[66] A scheme for educating the choristers at the Perse schools was found to be unworkable. The question then put to the musicians, whether the College's choral tradition could be maintained without a choir school, was of course one expecting, and receiving, the answer No. Asked by a 'distinguished botanist' (Briggs, the President), to prove it, Guest did, by securing testimonials from various great musical names of the day, culminating in Rootham's old friend, Ralph Vaughan Williams. The acquisition meanwhile of

---

[61] Raven to Benians, 14 Nov. 1940.

[62] GD, 29 Jan. 1922; 29 May 1921 ('Bullied by the Dean [Creed] I went to College Chapel, an appallingly tiresome service, all Rootham and choir, dull *Te Deum*; I wonder at the patience of Master and Sikes etc.'); 13 Nov. 1925. His obituary of Rootham, *Eagle* l (1937–8), 305–6, is in a different key and stresses their shared Bristolian origins.

[63] Above, p. 478.

[64] Guest to F. H. Hinsley, 25 Jan. 1982: SJCA, SBFP/Orr; Robin Orr, *Musical Chairs: An Autobiography* (London, 1998), 35–6 ('What even I, as a lapsed Scots Presbyterian, could only describe as very low church indeed'), 53. Cf. Pilkington's denunciation of 'swete Organes for the eare' as popish idolatry (above, p. 61), the 'Welsh Baptist or northern mill town' option contemplated in the early 1870s (above, p. 358).

[65] Choir School Committee, Report of 24 May 1949. A related problem with regard to the Act was the condition of the premises.

[66] 'The accommodation was limited and old-fashioned, and so, I think it must be said, was the education': Boys Smith, *Memories*, 219.

the unexpired term of the lease of St John's House, the Sandys' former residence in Grange Road, provided a solution with which in July 1954 the College felt able to accept.[67] In a letter to Boys Smith penned on the evening of the decision Bezzant paid tribute to the other's contribution to the outcome of the 'long and worrying business'.[68]

While moving the school from its old cramped premises to spacious new quarters in the verdant west, Guest emerged from Orr's shadow and modulated to a new key, moulding the choir in his own image and likeness: more a case of 'reculer pour mieux reculer' than 'a minimis incipe', therefore. After that the School was rarely out of the Council minutes. Guest's application for the BBC to broadcast choral evensong on two evenings in the coming term (his earliest venture into the medium, following Rootham's lead) had been received at Benians's last Council meeting.[69] One of Boys Smith's first acts as Master would be to take charge of the choir's contractual arrangements.[70] Despite its roll breaking the one hundred barrier in each of the terms of the year 1955–6, it now transpired that 'the School, under existing arrangements, did not promise to provide the required number of singing boys to maintain the Chapel choir at a good standard.' Thus the inevitable corollary of Hadley's views on Cambridge accent, the creation of a boarding house, was mooted. By Michaelmas 1957 provision had been made for up to twenty-six boarders and capital expenditure on the School was mounting.[71] All this must be accounted the achievement of the Wordie years.

By 1957, however, Wordie was losing what little flexibility he had brought to the Mastership. The man who in younger days had scrambled up the outside of the chapel tower[72] was now increasingly censorious of such activities and scarcely capable of managing the stairs to the Combination Room. Meanwhile, albeit cautiously, the old order was yielding place to the new. While all the Johnian conventions remained in place – as exemplified by Lord Morton of Henryton's direction in 1956–7 that the scholarship funded

[67] Choir School Committee minutes, 1953–4; Guest, *A Guest in Cambridge*, 27; letters from composers etc. (SJCA, DS2.13, including the maxim of the precentor of Caius, P. A. S. Hadley, that without a choir-school it would be better to have no boys in the choir, 'especially inferior boys [particularly those with Cambridge accents]'; Hadley's expressions of opinion had a way of carrying the argument, not least on account of his unnerving practice of driving sharp instruments into his leg for emphasis, to the discomfiture of choristers and others unaware that the limb was made of wood); GD, 30 May 1935 (after hearing 'Rootham's choir on tower [sing] very squeaky anthem, with instrument sounding like concertina', Glover recorded Vaughan Williams at Hall with Rootham), also 28 May 1936 ('big burly ill-shaved man, like a farmer'); CM, 2041/10 (9 Jul. 1954); report of Choir School Committee, 16 Jul. 1954; CM, 2042/3 (23 Jul. 1954).

[68] 'It is only fair to Guest (...) to add that last night [he] also expressed his admiration of your attitude about the whole outcome. (...) I think he spoke *sincerely*' (BSP). Cf. Boys Smith, *Memories*, 219–23.

[69] CM, 1978/5; 1486/12 (13 Feb. 1936).

[70] Boys Smith to Guest: BSLB 1.276, 388 (9 Mar. 1960).

[71] CMM, 2102/6, 2101/4; School Commitee, min. of 2 Mar. 1956. By 1967 capital expenditure had reached £48,000.

[72] Smith, *Sir James Wordie*, 20.

by him be awarded to an undergraduate of 'reasonable efficiency in work, ability in some form or forms of University sport, character, and qualities of leadership',[73] and the mention in the Council minutes of Chris Brasher's gold medal in the Melbourne Olympics[74] – Wordie's world was becoming more complicated. The Council was happy to accept the Morton bequest – but not that of Mrs M. P. Meres, which would have excluded Jews and coloureds from its beneficiaries.[75] Then, sign of the times, as an emergency measure an evening entertainment for Fellows' Ladies was established as from October 1956.[76]

At roughly this juncture an old member whose son had apparently just been rejected by the College without interview wrote to Wordie as follows:

> He is an average boy and has no obvious attainments in his career so far ... I quite understand that the pressure of entrants is likely to be high ... I do suggest however that unless the college is prepared to take a proportion of the average and normal in its intake, even if it means rejecting a proportion of the apparently brilliant, life at Cambridge will lose much of its value and it will become a very distorted place. I myself was a very undistinguished member of the college and I am fairly certain you will not remember being my tutor in the early '30s but I derived considerable benefit from my 3 years ... These things are always awkward and no doubt you get many letters from other Johnian fathers similarly disappointed but I do think Hinsley's letter to the boy's housemaster and his rather casual suggestion that some other college might do – to a family whose every male member for the last 80 years has gone to John's – might have been better done.

Wordie replied that Hinsley's letter was a standard one and that no decision had yet been made. The boy was admitted and (as he recalled years later) found

> Cambridge, or, more correctly, St Johns College, (...) a fun place to spend three years and, as was the fashion in those far-off days, not taken terribly seriously as a place of study. Sufficient hard work to pass one's degree yearly exams of course but not a lot more.

But times had changed, and not so subtly, since the days when Wordie had felt able to assure an applicant's headmaster *tout court* that 'the fact that his father was here will of course be in his favour.'[77]

At the earlier date, 'Would you like me to bring up my son, for you to have a look at him?', one OJ might enquire of the Master, while another asserted that 'the boy's great grandfather and great-great grandfather were also Johnians'

[73] CMM, 2094/10, 2109/14. Morton's provision 'even though the boy thus selected is intellectually inferior to other candidates' (letter to Boys Smith, 27 Mar. 1956) was not taken into the regulations. 'No pupil's achievement has astonished me more', Glover had remarked of the benefactor's: GD, 4 Mar. 1939.

[74] CM, 2100/4 (30 Nov. 1956).

[75] CMM, 2065/4, 2069/5, 2218/8 (conditions declared 'void for uncertainty', Nov. 1960).

[76] CM, 2095/4 (20 Jul. 1956).

[77] Wordie to Headmaster of Uppingham, 12 May 1928: tut. file/D. W. P Bythell.

(though Wordie was not so sure about this)[78] and asked for financial assistance for 'the boy'. 'It is suggested that Johns may do things for Salopians that other Colleges might not', the headmaster of Shrewsbury had written. 'Is this a libel, or an optimistic hope?'[79] Ten years later the description by Master or Senior Tutor of an OJ father's son as 'your boy' is heard less and less. 'We shall of course have the college connection in mind and this may make the difference', Wordie as Senior Tutor assured a public school headmaster regarding one of the 1949 contingent. But he was the last of that family for whom it did. 'Surely family ties mean something to the Admissions Committee?', wrote one Old Sedberghian on behalf of another, an OJ who had been told that the College had no place for his son. 'Furthermore the boy is no fool and is a keen and able entomologist', he added clinchingly;[80] which settled the matter, securing him a place. But, although there were always allowances to be made,[81] and although diplomats might have a diplomatic way of promoting a cause,[82] nevertheless the clouds were gathering. Certain schools with close awards might continue to play the system for all it was worth (Sedbergh itself, for example, securing ten places in 1949, or ten years later Marlborough eleven),[83] yet by and large it was only those few whose governing bodies also included a Fellow that were enabled to realize the advantages of the connexion, and even that only rarely.[84] Everything was becoming more complicated. On the one hand, the heir to 10,000

---

[78] F. M. Cheshire to Wordie, 4 Jan. 1937; Wordie to H. Paulley, 21 Oct. 1938: 'I am very glad to have a letter from one with such a long continued association with the College and I presume your great-grandfather must have joined early in the nineteenth-century. The latest volume of admissions which has been printed stops at 1802 and he is not there unless under another name': tut. files/Cheshire, A. W.; Paulley, C. J. A. Paulley, who came up in 1939, was killed in action in Italy in 1944. All quotations in this paragraph are from tutorial files of 1939 and 1949 freshmen.

[79] 'We shall certainly consider sympathetically any application from a Salopian but I am afraid we cannot promise him any financial assistance on that score', Howland to C. W. Mitford; letter of 23 Jun., 1938.

[80] G. Ghey to Wordie, 17 Jun. 1947: 'I wonder if you will remember me, but we met to play fives vigorously together in 1924 and 1925': tut. files/Alexander, A. V; Charters, J. D.

[81] 'His poor performance in the Scholarship Examination', it was explained of a future Deputy High Court Judge, 'may, to a limited extent, be explained by his duties as school captain of rugby football, in a particularly difficult term, when an inexperienced side and the vagaries of the weather combined to present problems which few captains have had to face': Headmaster of Oundle to Wordie, 21 Mar. 1948: tut. file/Read, L. F.

[82] 'Of course, you will agree that as an Old Johnian, I have a special claim on the college for the admission of my son' (and also a nephew, as it happened): M. A. H. Ispahani (Pakistani ambassador to United Nations and USA) to Wordie, 6 Dec. 1947: tut. file/Ispahani, M. M.

[83] E.g. Rev. P. Newell (Sedbergh) to Charlesworth, 23 Nov. 1946, recommending one of his charges as a 'very sound fellow in his way, and musical, but not really a scholar. I feel that the Lupton Hebblethwaite [closed award] is about his limit.'

[84] Of the ten schools to which the College appointed governors, in six cases it was represented by non-Fellows between 1900 and 1946. The principal exceptions were Aldenham (Sikes, 1907–40), Sedbergh (Charlesworth, 1933–52), Shrewsbury (The Master *ex officio*), Stamford (Howland, 1946–64): C3.7 (Register of Fellows and Scholars 1860–1965), 677–90.

acres who failed the First Examination in Agriculture twice, 'his main failing being that he does not realize the need to *learn* things';[85] on the other the hardship cases in which the College helped out: the boy whose father was unable to provide the necessary caution money (who finished as a headmaster) or the son of a butcher who had left home with another woman and a canteen-worker who got a First and qualified as a veterinary surgeon.[86]

The establishment in April 1955 of an Investments Committee, for the moment comprising only Fellows, acknowledged another aspect of the same process of diversification and the College's response to it.[87] But although Boys Smith as Senior Bursar may have been well advised, it took judgement of his own to appreciate the value of the advice of others. With foresight, he had in 1948 prevented the laying by the Bedfordshire, Cambridgeshire and Huntingdonshire Electricity Company of a high-tension cable across College territory.[88] Now, ten years later, with rumours of a new foundation in honour of Sir Winston Churchill beginning to circulate, and in response to the College's public appeal for funds for both the restoration of Second and Third Courts and new buildings, an approach was made to Wordie by Humphrey Cripps (BA 1937) offering to provide from the Cripps Charitable Foundation the £350,000 needed for the latter if the cost of the former (£150,000) could be met by the appeal. In the same letter Cripps urged the College Council to 'give serious consideration' to an approach to Merton College, Oxford for the purchase of their land beyond New Court.[89] Earlier efforts to acquire this property had invariably encountered the objection that it had been in Merton's ownership since that college's very foundation. But for St John's never before had the stakes been so high, which makes it the more remarkable that, despite the need for extreme circumspection, as much as four months were allowed to elapse before the Master discharged a ranging shot into Oxford territory.[90]

At this stage, Boys Smith – and he alone – was taken into Wordie's confidence, 'in order that', as the latter said, 'two people here should be aware of the proposals'.[91] In a pencil-written note (undated but from its content evidently belonging to this stage of the story) Boys Smith provided, perhaps for his own benefit, an *aide-mémoire* and summary of the various imponderables:

1. We must show immediate appreciation: this may be the largest benefaction the College has ever received.

2. We must get him morally committed, and must do so *before Churchill College becomes public*.

---

[85] Tut. file, Lord Stafford (supervision report, Easter Term 1951).

[86] Of the butcher's son (whom the Ministry of Education were initially unwilling to allow to transfer his State Scholarship to Cambridge) Bertram noted: 'I get very tired of trying to help the working man's child which has been my earnest desire.'

[87] CM, 2061/3.

[88] 'from the Madingley Road to Thompson's Lane, through the Pickerel Garden, under the river and through the garden of the Master's Lodge': CM, 1870/9 (23 Jan. 1948).

[89] Cripps to Wordie, 11 Apr. 1958: D33.18.41.

[90] Letter dated 18 Aug. 1958: Crook, *Penrose to Cripps*, 137.

[91] Wordie to Cripps, 14 Apr. 1958 (note: proposals, in the plural): D33.18.41.

3. It is difficult for us to make any concrete plans before his gift is *certain* [and] we can make it known, at least within the College. Because sites can only be decided upon by general College discussion, and with professional advice, the sooner the Council, at least, can be told the better.

4. *Merton.* The timing of the approach is difficult. Do we make it now, or when Holland-Hibbert retires?[92] Do we make it on the basis of Rothschild's suggestion, or expressly on the ground of the need for new buildings? To introduce the argument of new buildings would be much more effective if we could be sure it was the best site and could say that we should be able to build in the near future. We cannot do this until Cripps's benefaction is certain.

5. *Trusts.* We must tell him of the Trusts that are helping us and of the Pilgrim Trust.

6. *Companies.* Cripps is quite right here. The question is what more we can do. Churchill College is a complication here.

I believe a further talk with Cripps would be helpful, both in itself and to confirm his interest. (…)

Facilitated by the sale to the trustees of Churchill College of the College's site on Storey's Way, the purchase of the Merton property in April 1959 left St John's poised for the expansion of the following decade.[93] Yet only on the day

---

[92] The Hon. Wilfred Holland-Hibbert, Estates Bursar of Merton (1932–60).

[93] Crook, *Penrose to Cripps*, 133–59; CM, 2164/1 (vii) (i) (27 Feb. 1959); Boys Smith, *Memories*, 236–45, esp. pp. 244–5: 'It is true that the price paid to Merton (£80,000) was closely similar to the price (£82,500) received from the Churchill Trustees; but this was entirely fortuitous.' The decision had already been taken to close down the Kitchen Garden there on Thoday's retirement in September 1960: CM, 2154/4. Cripps's own account of the matter, written after Boys Smith's death, deserves quotation *verbatim*: '… I had indicated to Wordie (my old Tutor) that I would try and find the money (£350,000) which was the estimate for new buildings required by the College. They told me, in strict secrecy, that a new college was being planned and would carry an illustrious name (Churchill) by (…) Cockcroft and that they both felt it proper to advise me about what was likely to be made public later, and to free me from my promise to help St John's, so that I could contribute to Churchill. I felt that their offer to me showed great consideration and generosity on their part. I questioned them on the need to help St John's, and on be [*sic*] assured that the College Appeal was necessary. On being satisfied I remember saying "Charity begins at home" and I refused to be released. (…) The next question was the site for the New Buildings – which could be built on 4 different situations. The preferred choice was on the 5 acres we did not own – and then began the effort to acquire it – being land held by Merton, Oxford for well over 700 years. Wordie told me that the College had been negotiating to acquire the land for well over 100 years without success. I outlined to him that it would only be acquired if, instead of using agents, the College found its most able Fellow, that it ascertained the present rent roll from the properties on the land, and then sent this man – who turned out to be John – to offer Merton a capital sum, the interest from which if invested would double Merton's income. I recall the figures. Our valuers put a figure of £50000 for the 5 acres. Merton asked £100,000. I said I would find the extra money to top up what the College would contribute. The outcome was John bought it for £80,000 – and the Fellows were so pleased that they paid for it in full. At the same time St John's sold 40 acres (along the Madingley Road) to John Cockcroft for Churchill College and almost gave it to him at £2000

following Wordie's resignation in October 1959, six months after the conclusion of those delicate negotiations, was the extent of the Cripps Foundation's munificence made known to the Council, and although the fading Master had been prevented by illness from attending meetings of the Council since May 1958, not until the following spring did Cripps allow him to inform even the President, G. E. Briggs (who by then had been running the College for a matter of months) and the Fellowship of the gift.[94] Glyn Daniel's good story of Wordie's unemotional response to Cripps's offer of a million pounds ('Have a glass of sherry, Mr Cripps, medium or dry?') seems to be principally that, a good story altogether compatible with Wordie's 'thin Toryism' as Glover had described it, but hardly with the chronology of these events as Boys Smith records them.[95]

Wordie's lack of interest in continuing beyond September 1959 enabled the Council to propose a change of the statute governing the retirement of the Master whereby the Governing Body's discretionary power to extend his tenure to the age of seventy-five would be replaced by an automatic extension of seven years if he had been elected between the ages of sixty-three and sixty-eight. But the Governing Body was unwilling to have this, and instead in December 1958 set seventy as the absolute limit of tenure.[96] In the following May it had before it a proposal to pre-elect a successor in mid-June. With the vote producing a tie, the motion was not carried.[97] Something of what lay behind this is revealed by the musings in Glyn Daniel's journal, recording the events 'for my memoirs and posterity'. While favouring Cockcroft, Daniel reflected on his own prospects.[98] What he did not want was Boys Smith – though it is not at all clear at this stage whether his lucubrations refer to Boys Smith or to the prospect of himself as Master shouldering the task of reining in Boys Smith as Senior Bursar. 'If the fortunately improbable occurred, what would we do with Boys Smith?', he asked himself. 'Fight him, insist on policy issues, fixed council meetings etc. and many committees. But fortunately this won't occur. Let us hope for Cockcroft.'[99]

---

per acre – making £80,000 which was used to buy the Merton land ...': BSP, letter to G. Boys Smith, 16 Dec. 1991. (Lord Rothschild was then the tenant of Merton Hall.)

[94] Cripps to Wordie, 6 Apr. 1959. He had asked to be allowed to do so in the previous autumn but had been asked not to do so 'for a few weeks' (letters of 8 and 17 Oct. 1958): D33.18.41.

[95] GD, 23 May 1928; CM, 2180/6 (2 Oct. 1959); Daniel, *Some Small Harvest*, 190; Boys Smith, *Memories*, 237. As Daniel observes, Boys Smith does not tell that story.

[96] GB, *Acta* of 4 Dec. 1958, 30 Jan. & 6 Mar. 1959.

[97] GB, *Acta* of 20 May 1959.

[98] GEDD, Nov. 1958 ('I suppose I have to face a grouping which would ask me at 44 to be Master'), 21 May 1959.

[99] Ibid. Daniel's animus perhaps dates from the palpable and public put-down on the occasion of Benians's funeral when, as Secretary of the College Council and in the absence of a Junior Bursar, he took it upon himself to select pall-bearers from members of the Council, only to be overruled by Boys Smith's appointment for the honour of a team of senior Fellows: SJCA, SBF76/Benians. Cf. Daniel's strikingly different account of the matter: 'John Boys Smith rang me and said. "You have to cope with all this – the funeral and the election of a new Master. (...) Please, you must do it all. Indeed as acting J. B. you have to do it all"': Daniel, *Some Small Harvest*, 187.

But that was a vain hope. Churchill had reserved Cockcroft for himself. On 30 October the Fellows elected Boys Smith at the first round.[100]

3. JSBS: THE MASTERS' MASTER

It has often been asserted that it was with alacrity that in November 1943 John Boys Smith accepted the invitation to move from the Ely Chair of Divinity to the Senior Bursarship of St John's. In reality, only after a good deal of agonizing did he abandon God for Mammon.[101] True, it had been with that possibility in mind that in the previous June he had asked not to be considered for the office of University Registrary in succession to E. Harrison. But that had been in the expectation that the sixty-nine-year old Henry Howard would continue as Senior Bursar for sometime yet. The plan had been 'to keep Henry on under the Emergency Statute [the Universities and Colleges Emergency Provisions Act] and meanwhile to look round for a young man who could take it on after the war.'[102] Howard's death on 19 October 1943 created an unexpected vacancy therefore, one which had to be filled at once, and (for such was the view of the Council's committee) filled by Boys Smith. Now in his forty-third year, Boys Smith was the obvious choice and the Committee would be recommending him, Benians informed his former pupil on 25 October: 'You are the man in war or peace we should wish to offer the office.'

Initially, the Ely Professor concurred, inclining towards acceptance. Prior to calling on Benians 'to talk the matter over' on the following day, he wrote that he believed he would be 'happy in the work'.[103]

> I think too I should find enough opportunity to keep my theological and philosophical interests alive, at least as a personal sphere of interest; to sacrifice them completely would be like starvation to me, and I could hardly face it, but, as far as my own happiness is concerned it is the main-tenance of the personal interest, rather than anything more public, which counts with me. For good or ill (and no doubt it is both), I have not been, and shall never be, a one-line specialist; and, though I think I can be use-ful as a teacher, my personal interest is in asking questions and trying to satisfy my own mind, rather than in teaching as such.

[100] Smithies Diary records the voting: Boys Smith 40; Mansergh 18; Hinsley 1. Mansergh had joined the College Council in the previous June. On 30 October Daniel was in Czechoslovakia.

[101] Boys Smith, *Memories*, 45.

[102] Benians to D. W. Ward (corrected draft dated '?Oct. 43') in reply to Ward's letter of 21 Oct. 1943 offering himself for the post and stating that 'many years ago' (after Leathem's death, in fact: GD, 20 Apr. 1923) Scott had asked him whether he was prepared to take it on; also that more recently Ifor Evans had made similar enquiries ('in which I do not know whether he was speaking solely for himself or whether he was directly or indirectly inspired'). Ward (Fellow, 1909–15, and the son of a railway clerk) was currently working for the Ministry of Economic Warfare. Unless other-wise indicated, all material in this section is derived from EABP or BSP.

[103] Letter of 27 Oct. 1943.

But there were three considerations that suggested otherwise:[104] the need for people with theological interests akin to his, of which 'the supply [was] small'; his own hesitation over making such an 'unusual' change after only three years in the Chair; and the likely displeasure, or worse, of the Divinity Faculty.

Whatever may have passed between Master and ex-pupil that Thursday morning, later the same day the Council minuted its approval of an unspecified 'recommendation' from its committee which can only have been for the appointment of the Ely Professor.[105] But that was not the end of the matter. The Bursar-elect was correct in his conjecture that the Faculty would not be pleased to lose him, not least because he was 'one of very few who would survive [the approaching period of retirements] and so have the task of maintaining continuity', as C. E. Raven, Master of Christ's and Regius Professor of Divinity, confirmed when he called on Benians on the following Monday. Although Benians's scrawled memorandum of their exchange is even less legible than usual, it is at least clear that Raven 'spoke very strongly' on the matter. For the Faculty, continuity was essential. 'The Colleges must make sacrifices for the University.' To poach Boys Smith would be 'an unfriendly act'. 'I said we too had a conscience', Benians had responded. But the pressure told. On 3 November Boys Smith wrote again to Benians, declining appointment – not, he insisted, on account of 'what has been said from the side of the Faculty – that, now at least, carries little weight with me – but the feeling that my heart is really in my present work and interests.'

On the same day Benians acknowledged this in a letter the draft of which reads as follows:

I am so glad that you have been able to reach a decision that you feel the right one. I wish it had not been so difficult for you. But in such a choice, so far as I can judge, what is going to satisfy ~~you~~ yourself in the long run should be your guide. Faculty situations change, the opinions of one's colleagues change, but one's own nature changes less, at least at your age. I did not say what I am sure you know, how rejoiced I ~~(and not I only)~~ should have been if we had been working together for the College for the remainder of my time, for I should not forgive myself later if I had used words which ~~might~~ had influenced you towards a decision you had begun to regret. I wished only that you should see the thing in its certain and lasting aspects and not be overweighed by temporary and contingent considerations. But I know we shall always have a share in your affections and your help and ~~I am entirely happy in the thought that you have reached your own conclusion.~~ You know that our affection and respect for you will remain the same. Yours ever

---

[104] Three but not four: 'I am not influenced by any possibilities of ecclesiastical preferment. They have no attraction for me. If they ever came, I should probably decline them; I should certainly *want* to decline them. I fear my own self and a bishop (or even a dean) are so far of a different order that they would never coalesce to make one person, and a dual life would be neither good nor endurable.'

[105] CM, 1748/2.

In every line and phrase this was exactly the letter to write. Its every hesitation shows how well Benians knew his man and that side of him so clearly revealed in, for example, the lyrical account he himself would later give of the strength of his 'intimate feeling for the country, its sights, its sounds, its smells'.[106] The claims of loyalty and conscience and the understated allusion to the disagreement between the two men were calculated to reopen the question and require further consideration. 'Some of us believe the best way we can serve the College is by our personal devotion here', Glyn Daniel would later be told by him on declining an offer of the Junior Bursarship, remembering it not as 'a reproof' but as 'a statement of faith', but also recalling being almost in tears as he left the presence.[107] In November 1943 there were no tears. Instead the message found its mark and, as it percolated into its recipient over the next two days, worked its magic. On the 4th Boys Smith's refusal was reported to the Council and Briggs was appointed as caretaker.[108] On the morning of the 5th Boys Smith called on the Master to say that he had changed his mind and was reassured that the offer was still open. A week later Boys Smith was appointed Senior Bursar from 1 January 1944.[109]

As well as providing further evidence of Benians's genius for dealing with colleagues, this sequence of events is recounted here both in order to indicate a degree of conscientious wrestling with himself which most observers of Boys Smith as Master would have thought uncharacteristic, and also on account of the principles enunciated by Benians in the course of his confrontation with Raven. For these were principles central to his understanding of the relationship of College and University. And so they were for Boys Smith, to whom offers of advancement elsewhere over the next sixteen years – to the Secretary Generalship and the Treasurership of the University in late 1952, when he might have been thought susceptible on account of Wordie's recent election, and to the Mastership of Selwyn in September 1955 – caused altogether less anguish. By then it had long been clear, to him as it was to others,[110] that his final destination was the St John's Master's Lodge. On his arrival there hundreds of letters of congratulation awaited him, one addressed 'My dear Master and Holy Man'. In Oxford the appointment had restored confidence 'in the rationality of the cosmos'. Nearer home the Master of Trinity expressed concern lest his new neighbour should bring 'discredit on your more indolent colleagues by working double overtime'.[111] Two messages in particular deserve special mention: one was from Harold Pettitt (formerly Deputy Chief Clerk of St John's, now Chief Clerk of nascent Churchill College), rejoicing that the College was 'again in the very best hands'; and the other from

[106] Boys Smith, *Memories*, 102–4.

[107] Daniel, *Some Small Harvest*, 186.

[108] CM, 1749/6.

[109] CM, 1750/3 (with Briggs as *locum tenens* until then).

[110] Bezzant, who before appointment had jibbed at the prospect of retirement at sixty-five, indicated that if the election had turned out differently he would probably have gone early: SJCL, Misc. Letters/Raven, letters to Benians, 5 Dec. 1951; BSP, letter to Mrs G. Boys Smith, 30 Oct. 1959.

[111] BSP, D. N. Crotori, 3 Nov.; Henry Chadwick, 2 Nov.; Lord Adrian, 31 Oct. 1959.

Sylvia Benians. 'May I now tell you what Ernest said shortly before he died?', she asked.

> He talked often of the College in those days, and one morning said he wondered who his successor would be – then added: 'I know whom they will choose if they are wise.' 'Who?', I asked. He answered: 'Boys Smith.'[112]

With Wordie's retirement, interest in new building and *the* New Building quickened. Within two months the Tutors were reporting to the Council on the future residential requirements of a total of 600 junior members (500 under-graduates and a hundred graduate students) by 1964 or 1965. Although that document was entitled 'New Accommodation for Undergraduates', one of its emphases was the importance of enabling 'affiliated students and research students from other universities, particularly from universities abroad, [to] have at least their first year in College.'[113] Another was the need for 'extra bathrooms and lavatories' within the new buildings, with the implication that existing communal facilities were to be replicated.[114] In the event, neither of these objectives was realized. Whereas previously freshmen had been delicately informed of the College's supply to them of furniture 'including bed-room crockery', after 1967 every floor of every staircase of the Cripps Building was to be provided with its own installations for ablutions, and, although within the new dispensation room would indeed be found for affiliated students, research students were to remain without the walls, as most of them still do. 'In the problem of the relationship between an enormously increased graduate population, at all levels, and the traditional organization of the University, lies the most serious issue of the future', it was observed by a surveyor of the wider scene writing in the first year of Boys Smith's Mastership.[115] As Boys Smith would himself remark, by 1967 graduate students had come to constitute about a quarter of the junior membership of the College.[116] Meanwhile the College's response remained minimal: recognition of the Samuel Butler Room (but that alone) as the exclusive preserve of the graduate constituency,[117] and the elimination of 'other junior members' from the list of those for whom the hostel at 69 Grange Road (Whitfield House) was intended. Now it was 'for use as a hostel primarily for Research Students in scientific subjects who have to spend the greater part of the year in Cambridge'.[118] The 'whole problem of Research Students is very much in mind in connexion with schemes we are beginning to consider for new College

---

[112] 'I have long wanted you to know this', she continued, 'but perhaps even now you would think it shouldn't go beyond yourself and Gwenda.' Both letters (BSP) are dated 30 Oct. 1959.

[113] As late as July 1966 it was envisaged that graduate students would live in Cripps: CM, 2395/8.

[114] Memorandum dated 13. Nov. 1959, §§3, 6.

[115] *Victoria History of Cambridge*, III. 312.

[116] 'The Constitution and Government of the College', *Eagle* lxii (1967–8), 94.

[117] BSLB: Boys Smith to J. C. Hall, 20 Feb. 1960, promising confirmation in a Council minute (which never eventuated) and specifically excluding from the terms of the grant what had been the bedroom and gyp room of the former set.

[118] BSLB: Boys Smith to F. Hollick, 16 Feb. 1960.

buildings', Boys Smith wrote to K. W. Blythe, one of those problematic juniors.[119] But it was not until almost twenty years later, by which time there were about 200 of them in residence, that the post of Tutor for Graduate Admissions was established, to handle issues specific to their recruitment, admission and welfare.[120]

In 1958 of course the Tutors were still in the dark about the scope and extent of the new development. There was uncertainty even as to the site until at meetings of the Governing Body on 12 October and 9 November 1960 large majorities voted for the area centred on the land purchased from Merton College.[121] This stimulated Colin Bertram to submit a paper on the subject of 'Functional Flexibility', in which, since 'we ourselves are diverse' the need for diversity was stressed and Fellows were urged to imagine 'a building whose lifetime will be far greater than the life of other buildings erected today, with the possible exception of churches and cathedrals'.[122]

In not every particular have such expectations been realized. However, since A. C. Crook's description of the construction of the Cripps Building (in his estimation, 'perhaps the finest building the College possesses') is already on record there is no need here to retell that story down to its formal opening by Cyril Cripps in May 1967.[123] Instead, and in particular because the period of its construction was almost exactly co-extensive with Boys Smith's Mastership, it may be useful to consider the role that the Cripps Building came to play in the quickening social developments of the period.

By bringing its entire undergraduate membership within the walls the College may be said to have colluded with the subversive tendencies of the age. Now that the chilly cycle-ride out to Cherry Hinton straight after Hall and the landlady's 10 p.m. curfew were things of the past, undergraduate visionaries could settle down with coffee and other stimulants all through the night and concentrate high-mindedly on refashioning the world, and thereby the College. The severe Lent Term of 1963 had prepared the ground, the frozen ground. Twelve months earlier, *experto crede*, the undergraduate inhabitants of E Third had been just about content with one cold tap between them. The conditions of 1963 showed that the College had not learnt any lessons from the winter of 1947 when for most of the Lent term Richard Goody had been able to preserve a snowball in mint condition in his First Court room, or even from the freezing 1890s for that matter.[124] Now, while in New Court sets the toothpaste froze and the perilous condition of the staircase confined Dean Bezzant permanently to his rooms, the Cam was converted into a pedestrian thoroughfare and men

---

[119] Letter of 3 Mar. 1960.

[120] CM, 2707/8 (29 Jul. 1978).

[121] At the earlier meeting, at which the voting was 47 to 3, only F. H. Hinsley had spoken in favour of the site to the east of the river bounded by Bridge Street: an option far more heavily favoured in the 1930s. 'Thinks removal of Lodge not a disadvantage', Boys Smith noted. Dirac wanted there to be a swimming pool.

[122] 'New College Buildings', 15 Nov. 1960.

[123] Crook, *Penrose to Cripps*, 180–204.

[124] *Ex inf.* J. R. Goody. Cf. 'Winter, 1946–7, in College', *Eagle* liii (1948–9), 13–16, when 'ice on the river surprisingly never became solid'.

walked on water – *and so did women*, both into and out of College. In that 'Annus mirabilis', as Philip Larkin would later describe it, for some of both sexes (as they still were then; 'gender' being in the process of discovery) this proved a liberating experience. Not long after the river had returned to its normal state, around the time 'between the end of the Chatterley ban and the Beatles first LP', requests, and then demands, for the removal of irksome guest and gate rules began to be heard. Rarely has history's susceptibility to the vagaries of climate been so clearly demonstrated. The then influential history journal, *Annales*, might have taken Cambridge's correspondence course. There had been nothing like this since the recent hostilities when the iron railings had been removed from the Backs.[125]

4. SHIFTING FOUNDATIONS

To all outward appearances the mid-1960s College remained the same community of British Warm, Harris tweed, cavalry-twilled, pipe-smoking opinion. The Willows (the Sunday cricket side of dons, dons' sons and junior members which pitted itself against Cambridgeshire village teams and, because it selected itself by signing up on the list at the bottom of A First Court) might well comprise J. M. Brearley alongside a culturally curious Alaskan), continued to prosper. So too, of an evening, did sundry College societies, notable amongst them the History Society, whose Kiplingesque evening of 'Songs of Empire' may be said to have changed history itself.[126]

And other changes were afoot. In January 1965 the Council offered no objection to the University's proposal to dispense with the requirement that junior members wear academical dress in the streets after dark. In October 1961 it had opposed the change.[127] Soon after, in the earliest edition of the College's *Student's Handbook* (1968) the long-standing prohibition on the wearing of athletic dress in the courts was quietly dropped – though while members were allowed to have guests of either sex on the hard (field) courts at any time (rather than on weekdays only, the rule since 1949),[128] on the courts on the Backs only in May Week would they be admitted, and then only in whites. Even so, standards were slipping. Whereas white tie was prescribed for the new Fellows' Ladies' Night in 1961, in the following March the requirement was relaxed for the Port Latin.[129]

1961, of course, was the College's 450th birthday, an occasion commemorated by Edward Miller's splendid *Portrait of a College*, and on 20 May an evening entertainment on the Backs with a running buffet supper including both

[125] *Eagle* lii (1941–7), 308.

[126] Recording held at SJC Library, and, as is the case with all the most intriguing historical records, undated, for good measure unreported in the *Eagle*, and not to be confused with 'Songs of Slaughter' (performed in Michaelmas Term 1967: *Eagle* lxii, no. 269 [1968], 200).

[127] CMM, 2250/7, 2346/9.

[128] CM, 1907/6.

[129] Entertainments Committee, min. of 5 Aug. 1961; CM, 2354/3.

62 The Annual Cricket Match: 1st VIII vs College staff, 1961

lemonade and orangeade, red *and* white wine, claret cup and, at 10.15, punch. Madrigals, an operetta and fireworks (including a 'Humorous Mechanical Device' and a representation of 'The Lady Margaret') completed the occasion, to which junior members had been invited each to bring *'one* lady guest'. Musical works for the 450th were commissioned from three notable composers for a total sum less than that paid to the Organist and performers for a recording by the choir of twentieth-century British church music in the following year and only slightly in excess of the Dean's £150 entertainment allowance for 1961 itself.[130]

Although, as the fees received reveal, the choir continued to go from strength to strength, by the early sixties the chapel had long since ceased to provide a social focus. The main conclusions of the questionnaire concerning Chapel services issued in 1964 were that there was a larger number of early-risers on Sunday then than now, an impressive range of churchmanship, and deep theological division on the question of chapel breakfast.[131] Eating and teaching were limited as substitute exercises, with the former remaining hierarchical and, other than for members of clubs and societies such as the Committee, commensality a rarity, at least until the introduction of dessert parties

[130] CMM, 2251/9 (Robin Orr 50 guineas, Michael Tippett 100 guineas, Herbert Howells *gratis*), 2273/13 (total: 224 guineas; Organist 75 guineas), 2253/4.

[131] SJCA, DS1.5 (ninety respondents). While one denounced 'the idea of turning the Holy Eucharist into a social breakfast club' as 'repugnant', another thought it 'an extremely good idea, contributing to chapel community'. Another, quoting 1 Corinthians 11:23–6, was conscious of 'a tremendous lack of Christian fellowship – not only at breakfast but in the service itself'.

in the Combination Room for third-year undergraduates.[132] Not every Tutor was equal to the exertions of the rumbustious R. E. Robinson and those of his pupils for whom, to the despair of successive Senior Tutors and Junior Bursars, no festive evening was complete without a spot of room cricket. Indeed, few at all were. Except for the 'God squad', communal breakfast was a thing of the past. When in the spring of 1967 the prestigious Bilderberg Conference came to stay in the brand-new Cripps Building, the Kitchen Manager had to knock up the residents of Bridge Street for the loan of an egg-cup to contain the duke of Edinburgh's breakfast.[133] At lunchtime, by contrast, the College was extending itself just a little, at least on special occasions. In 1962 the glass of wine in the Combination Room offered to parents on the day of General Admissions was replaced by lunch, but with only College officers and their wives invited.[134]

But some things never change. Note, for example, the excitement of an Australian affiliated student on the occasion of his first bump (on Pembroke III):

> Then the final effort when life itself seemed to stop, the pain of exhaustion and, just past the Railings, that jerk in the boat, like nothing else on God's earth, that signifies that our bows had scraped the rudder ahead. We made a glorious bump, smashing our bow right off with the impact. That moment was one of the greatest I have ever experienced. I was literally gulping down tears of joy. Nick Walkinshaw's only heartfelt comment was 'an EPIC row'.[135]

This sounds suspiciously like timeless Cambridge, indistinguishable from the Cam eighty years before – as does the Steward, Norman Henry's bet of a case of champagne that Hugh Sykes Davies would not 'capture and kill a rat in the area of the kitchen premises within one month'.[136] But in fact some change *was* beginning to be observable.

5.   THE SAME, CONTINUED

As Lord Devlin was to pronounce in 1973, the Family Law Reform Act 1969, which, following the Latey Report on the Age of Majority, lowered the age of majority to eighteen, 'profoundly affected the theoretical basis of university discipline'.[137] For the College its consequences were likewise far-reaching – far more so, it was John Crook's unvarying contention, than the admission of women a decade later. Moreover, by the beginning of the seventies the new buildings had shifted the College's centre of gravity westward, with (by Clifford Evans's count) 420 undergraduate rooms in nine courts compared with 180

---

[132] CM, 2271/12 (June 1962).

[133] *Ex. inf.* Sid Dring, Kitchen Manager.

[134] CM, 2260/5.

[135] J. S. Sheldon (BA 1963), diary entry, 3 Mar. 1962. See Jane Milburn and J. F. Hall-Craggs, *History of the Lady Margaret Boat Club*, III (Cambridge, 2008), 69; N. J. C. Walkinshaw (BA 1962). Cf. above, p. 432.

[136] Fellows' Betting Book, 17 Jan. 1967.

[137] Lord Devlin, *Report of the Sit-in in February 1972 and its Consequences*, §143.

in four thirty years earlier.[138] Other changes too were in train. Of these the *Eagle* provided a barometric reading. Whereas in 1960–61 it had been possible for the Rugby club to run as many as four XVs, by 1968 its secretary was blaming another lack-lustre performance in cuppers on a 'general apathy' probably traceable to 'the present college tendency towards "frightening" sportsmen the moment they arrive so that studies are performed from fear rather than love and any time spent practising for a team game is regarded as time away from books rather than as useful recreation.'[139] This may not have been all though. The publication in the College Chronicle section of the magazine of entries by the National Union of Students in 1966 and the Labour Club in January 1967 reveals other influences at work. Undergraduates were becoming more interested in aspects of the place previously regarded as none of their business. 'There is always scope for any Labour Club member in the College to talk on any subject he wishes', stated a claim regularly substantiated at meetings of the JCR Committee in the early seventies.[140] The following number confirmed the trend, with its cover adorned by a picture of a pretty young woman in place of the proprietary bird of prey that had graced it for over a century, and its contents dominated by the results of a visionary survey showing almost two-thirds of the respondents to be in favour of co-education. Although the questions asked were about sharing bathrooms and the JCR with women (75 and 90 per cent in favour respectively) and not about sharing beds, it was even so all a far cry from the prelapsarian world represented by the headmaster of Colyton Grammar School's letter to the Master on the eve of the last War enquiring whether his Newnham daughter, Daphne, might be allowed to join the Girtonians whom Mrs Benians invited to tea 'in order to help to civilize (...) the young men at John's'.[141] Not even the Master's 1966 Commemoration Sermon had been able to steady the ship, rally the troops or spare the place more surveys.[142] The next issue contained those of yet another, promoted by the JCR and concerned with the College as it was. In January 1969 even the magazine's format changed.

As recently as 1955 the *Eagle*'s pages had contained an account by Claude Guillebaud of admissions procedures during his time as Senior Tutor which belonged to a timeless past, to a world in which the means-test treated middle-class and professional parents 'with real harshness' and (albeit 'the absolute number of men from public schools [had] not declined at all') 'many parents of public schoolboys constituted the new poor.' Even so, the world of 1955 was one in which not only could you trust your suppliers –

> We hardly ever interview. We go on the results of the General Certificate of Education and on the Headmaster's recommendation – principally the latter, and it is remarkable how rarely we consider we have been let down.

---

[138] G. C. Evans, 'Master', *Eagle* lxiii (1969–70), 14.

[139] *Eagle* lix (1961–2), 252; lxii (1967–8), 269.

[140] *Eagle* lxii (1967–8), 70.

[141] Ibid., 84–6; D. McKay-Ohm to Benians, 9 Oct. 1939 (EABP).

[142] *Eagle* lxii (1967–8), 41–6.

– you did.

> All sorts of considerations can influence the decision in the case of any given application – the factor of heredity, past and possible future, relations with the Head or Housemaster concerned; College connections where they exist; the question of a future career; and so on.

The self-satisfied tone reads very much like that of an after-dinner speech to the Old Boys, which was what it had started as.[143] Likewise the contribution six years later of Colin Bertram, Guillebaud's successor but one, and a second-to-none Johnian patriot, in a piece replete with what were to become the familiar Bertramesque themes of 'wise ponderings', 'stimulated assertions', 'the rather humble [i.e. modest] matriculation requirements of the University'; freedom; 'polishing', 'integration', genetical speculation, and vigour ('this last factor often exemplified by skill in games').[144]

Now the idiom was different, now there were fewer easy answers. The questionnaire distributed to undergraduates by the JCR Committee in February 1967, a matter of months before the opening of the Cripps Building, contained questions whose only purpose was to supply the College authorities 'with some statistical information on the attitudes and trends within the College'. But despite the entire operation being directed by a third-year undergraduate of impeccable academical credentials, M. J. Field, and although the agenda – on the Tutorial System and Senior–Junior Member relations; Rules and Regulations; Facilities; Hall and Buttery; Education; the College Community – had been drafted by a group including the Dean of Chapel (S. W. Sykes) and the Master's son, S. W. Boys Smith, it was to prove an agenda for activists, one of whom (another of the draughtsmen) was reported to have contended that 'many people' were ashamed of being 'Johnsmen'. Even before the responses had been analysed (with financial assistance from the tutorial body) a militant group was insisting that the JCR must act on the results, and the University Labour Club chairman G. J. Whitty was reported to be counselling against compromise with the College Council or any other form of backsliding.[145]

When the largely unsurprising answers provided were both analysed and published, the *Eagle*'s editors (Senior and Junior) declared the picture that emerged 'a very reassuring one'.[146] To others it will have seemed less so. For it was neither the revelation that over half of the 450-odd respondents (about 80 per cent of the undergraduate population) were 'on speaking terms with less [*sic*] than 3 dons',[147] nor even that most of them broke most of the College's rules most of the time (in particular those concerning ladies at night), that was most deeply shocking. What was was that junior members should be calling the shots and setting the agenda at all, the realization that the consequences of the

---

[143] 'Thirty Years of Tutorial Policy', *Eagle* lvi (1954–5), 123–31.

[144] 'College Recruitment', *Eagle* lix (1960–63), 187–97.

[145] *Varsity*, 25 Feb. 1967.

[146] 'The JCR Survey', *Eagle* lxii (1967–8), 139–48.

[147] There were many who considered the absence of a question about the value of night-time conversations with W. R. (Reuben) Peck, the Cripps Lodge porter, a fatal omission. See Peter Linehan, 'Reuben Peck, 1913–91', *Eagle* (1991), 41–2.

63 Keeping an eye on Cripps:
Reuben of Quy: W. R. Peck,
Cripps porter, 1963–78.
Photograph courtesy of
Mrs J. W. Rolph

social changes permeating British society were now lapping at the perimeter of
the College and seeping into its foundations. Forms of address reflected social
norms with which a significant proportion of freshmen had long been unfamiliar. It had always taken time for those unaccustomed to the usage at school to
understand that 'Dear Smith' was a more familiar form of address than 'Dear
Mr Smith'. To increasing numbers of members of an all-embracing age the
time-honoured convention was coming to seem chilly and condescending.

In a situation which some of the Council's members regarded as unprecedented in the College's history, precedent required either a rapid response or
sublime indifference braced by the firm conviction that it would all go away.
Instead, just in advance of the publication of the survey's results, in May 1967
the Council constituted a committee to advise it on 'the question of the relation of Senior and Junior members within the Society',[148] and, while the mili-
tantly apathetic amongst its undergraduates defended the College's morale and
its Dean J. R. Bambrough in the pages of *Varsity*, at the committee's request a
meeting of Fellows was summoned for 'an informal exchange of views'. At this
post-tripos gathering (according to Hugh Sykes Davies the first such discussion
in thirty-four years, that is, since the death of R. F. Scott, not the greatest of
consultants)[149] a number of those present conjectured that current problems had

---

[148] CM, 2418/11 (12 May 1967: Master, Senior Tutor [Bertram], Sykes Davies, Robinson,
Hinde, Sykes, Linehan).
[149] Memorandum of meeting by G. C. L. Bertram.

their origin in the recruitment of men who had not attended boarding school. More optimistic spirits pinned their hopes on the sense of camaraderie associated with the recently opened JCR bar, the provision of cafeteria facilities, and indoor games. The Senior Tutor speculated further:

> In general the pressures of life upon both Senior and Junior members of our community are greater than in the past and that is unfortunate at a time when the Junior Members are perhaps more articulate and certainly have enhanced expectations, both as to the amount of informal contact they should have with their Seniors and as to their standards of living. For a variety of reasons concerned with the difficulties and frustrations of the world (of which able young men are properly very conscious) perhaps a greater proportion discover loneliness than in the past. In simplest terms, too, the wider the recruitment of the University, the less the probability of school friends being in Cambridge to help conquer initial loneliness.

Then, in July 1968, well over a year later, the Council invited Claude Guillebaud to report on just one aspect of the present discontents, namely the 'working of the tutorial system'. Guillebaud's report was delivered in January 1969. With the lowered age of majority about to destroy the *in loco parentis* case for the tutorial system, the author was at pains to demonstrate to junior members that the system had in reality 'a quite different basis and justification'.[150] Guillebaud's objective was not ignoble. But in the circumstances of the time that was no longer enough. Guillebaud's satisfaction with the system with which he was so well, perhaps too well, acquainted was total. His recommendations for improvement – as to the size of typeface used in the recently issued 'General Information for Freshmen', for example, or for discontinuing the wearing of gowns on tutorial visits – were largely cosmetic. Others called them whitewash. The author's complaisance with his handiwork emerges clearly from his correspondence with an old friend and contemporary. 'Although we have not had any serious student unrest here in Cambridge, we are certainly not exempt from the tendency of youth to question the merits of established institutions', he informed W. G. Constable (Honorary Fellow). 'Amongst these is the Tutorial System as it operates in most Cambridge colleges, including St John's; though in this particular case I think it would be true to say that the initiative came from some of the Fellows rather than from the Junior Members themselves.' As to Guillebaud's recommendations, none of them were 'at all revolutionary, as might be expected when coming from one who had himself been a Tutor for many years'.[151] Others further distant from Guillebaud's world or outside it altogether reached the same conclusion and wondered whether, for all his experience of chairing tribunals and the like, it had been entirely wise to ask an ex-Senior Tutor in his eightieth year to take a fresh look at the 'institution'.

With Guillebaud still at work, at the beginning of the Michaelmas Term 1968 Boys Smith announced his decision to retire in the following October,

---

[150] C. W. Guillebaud, 'Report to the Council on the Working of the Tutorial System in St John's College', 8.

[151] Letter of 10 Mar. 1969: SJCL, Constable Papers, 1/7.

two years ahead of time.[152] Amongst his papers is preserved the handwritten, corrected text of the personal statement he read out at the subsequent meeting of the Governing Body. It was as always an elegant piece, and, especially in its emendations, as carefully considered as anything he had ever set his hand to.[153] He sought to make what he had to say 'as matter-of-fact' as he could. A recent spell of illness had made him aware that his physical capacities were not what they once had been. There were two 'more special considerations'. One was that for him the duties of the Mastership had been 'paramount' and to be discharged actively.

> There are many ways of being the Head of a House and it would be pre-sumptuous of me to suggest that one way is always better than another. But I think I know what is the best way for me, and I should not wish to hold office in semi-retirement.

The other was to provide the Fellows with the opportunity of pre-electing his successor (as in his own case they had chosen not to do). He referred also to the support and co-operation that the Fellows had always given him, for that too (he stated) was a matter of fact. As to that, Glyn Daniel wrote, thanking him for 'the admirable clarity and unemotionalism' of his 'difficult speech' and expressing appreciation of 'the courage and wisdom of [his] decision'.[154] But Boys Smith made no allusion to other members of the College community. It was others who referred to the larger picture: Hugh Sykes Davies, for example, whose nose for the whiff of trouble brewing was keen if not infallible. To the departing Master ('For me, of course, you will be in a sense the last real Master'), he confided that he regarded as a possibility 'that your successor may, at some time in his tenure, be besieged in the Lodge or otherwise molested by demon-strators, because they believe him to be "the administration", the remote source of real power – though it makes me feel uncomfortably like Enoch Powell to say this.'[155] That flourish apart, Sykes Davies was not so far from the mark. The departing Master had sensed an unseasonal change of temperature in the air.

6.   HOW STRANGE THE CHANGE

The JCR questionnaire and its aftermath was only one of the ingredients of the turbid brew into which Sykes Davies was more or less gingerly peering. For those Fellows who had only recently adjusted to the 1926 Statutes, developments of the year 1968–9 constituted an abomination, one that certainly justified Boys Smith's decision to make it his last in the Lodge. Since the informal arrange-ments with which the JCR at K First Court had managed to stumble along

---

[152] CM, 2455/4 (4 Oct. 1968).

[153] Thus, in relation to consulting the Council, the words 'and to seek their concurrence with the procedure I had in view' are replaced by 'about the procedure' *tout court*.

[154] BSP, letter of 5 Oct. 1968, addressed 'My dear John (because this is a personal letter from a very old friend)'; GEDD, 5 Oct. 1968 'a moving speech full of emotion from his point of view'; 'voice broke'.

[155] Letter of 2 Dec. 1968.

since 1932[156] were thought to be inadequate to the post-Crippsian dispensation, in 1966 the Council proposed that the social management of both places be vested in a JCR Committee with an 'up-to-date' constitution but with the management of the Cripps bar, initially a bar no bigger than a man's hand, in the form of a cupboard containing one bottle of sherry and one of port, under the control of the Steward and with service provided by a College porter.[157] Further consideration of the matter had resulted in October 1968 in a compromise whereby the Committee secured both its constitution (as yet a deceptively slight single-sheet-of-paper affair, lucid precursor of its clause-clogged successors) and variation of the previous arrangements to the extent of permission to the JCR both to run and staff the bar and to retain its net profits. *De facto*, the Steward's ultimate control of the bar was lost sight of. Inevitably it was on this territory that over the coming years battle would be joined.[158] And by then, the constitution – which already made provision for affiliation to the Student Representative Council (the earliest University-wide students' organization, established in 1964 with an ambitious agenda of its own) – had been amended to enable it to send observers to meetings of the National Union of Students[159] while a year later the SRC transformed itself into an assembly (SRA) supposedly attended by three or four delegates from each college. The next step towards the discovery of the general will was taken in October 1970 with the emergence of the Cambridge Students' Union (CSU) and government not by an assembly of representatives but by general meetings attended by members of non-University bodies (the local Arts and Technology College and Homerton College, then still a teacher training college).

Parallel with these developments were others which persuaded some that the seeping process was beginning to do damage at the foundations. The same Council meeting that ruled on the profits of the Cripps bar acceded to the request of graduate students to dine together with the Fellows periodically[160] and – a departure ahead of its time and testimony to Boys Smith's fineness of judgement – established a standing committee of senior and junior members ('the Consultative Committee'), at whose initial meeting in November 1968 the first item on the agenda was financial (charges to undergraduates) and the others, defined for discussion by the junior members, were representation, College teaching, and discipline. Concerning the last of these it was the Senior Bursar, T. C. Thomas, who suggested the establishment of a disciplinary committee to be interposed between the Dean and the Council. Discussion of this occupied successive meetings of the committee until the end of the following April.[161]

[156] In December 1938 an annual election of Junior Members of the Committee had been instituted: CM, 1555/14.

[157] CM, 2404/5 (2 Dec. 1966); Boys Smith to S. W. Sykes (Chairman, JCRC), 12 Dec. 1966: SJCA, CC17.5.

[158] CM, 2456/4 (10 Oct. 1968).

[159] CM, 2450/7 (7 Jun. 1968).

[160] CM, 2456/5: four times a term, a proposal approved at the Governing Body of 18 October by 39 votes to 3.

[161] CM, 2456/6; SJMC (SJCA, CC18.1).

When the junior members suggested, astonishingly, that their representatives on the Disciplinary Committee be appointed by the Tutors, again it was Thomas who observed that such a proposal was liable to be interpreted as a denial of junior members' 'authority in the matter'.[162] But, as his Mastership neared its end and the nattily suited members of that committee continued to tramp in and out of the Master's Lodge, in step with the trade union leaders in and out of Harold Wilson's 10 Downing Street, Boys Smith cannot but have sensed that the age of deference was approaching closure. By then, the Old Schools Sit-in of January 1969, ostensibly in protest at the closure of the London School of Economics by its Director, had demonstrated the ability of local malcontents to exploit entirely alien issues for their own purposes within the University. And although on that occasion the protestors had delicately spared the Senate House (reportedly out of consideration for a concert of the Purcell Society), if within the University (Boys Smith may well have asked himself), and with suits now being exchanged for denim moreover, or less even, then why not also within its colleges?

Within St John's the Governing Body discussed both the Guillebaud Report and the responses to yet another questionnaire, this one conducted by yet another committee (on Educational Needs) on the subject of College teaching. And so through the long spring the process rolled on, the progress of the season marked chiefly by the beginnings of discussions of the Kitchen Lane development (eventually to provide an alternative venue to Hall),[163] the establishment of the Disciplinary Committee to provide a course of appeal from decisions of the Dean,[164] and in mid-May the appointment as Head Porter of R. F. (Bob) Fuller to provide well over six foot of substantial reassurance.[165]

No sooner had all this been achieved than after being delated by their bedmaker two third-year undergraduates, A. and C., appealed to the Council against a penalty imposed on them by the Dean. Since the newly elaborated disciplinary procedure was not yet in place, the Council found it necessary as an act of clemency to rescind part of this:[166] an outcome which had the effect of entrenching the practice of appealing against decanal penalties, especially minor monetary penalties, on a more or less routine basis in order to make nonsense of the entire process.[167] One of those present at the appeal recalls the whiteness of the Master's knuckles as he grasped the edge of the table. The 'Swinging Sixties' were taking their toll. Things had changed since 1951 when Boys Smith had informed the then Master that, in the view of the University's principal officers, 'a Dean (disciplinary) [did] not as such hold a substantial administrative office'. As recently as 1963, on at least two occasions Dean Bezzant had had undergraduates sent down for acts of frailty of nature such as those committed by A. and C.[168]

---

[162] Letter to Boys Smith, 5 Mar. 1969 (papers of Disciplinary Committee).

[163] CM, 2472/17 (7 Mar. 1969).

[164] CM, 2476/18 (9 May 1969).

[165] CM, 2477/13.

[166] SJMC, 5 Jun. 1969, min. 4(b); CM, 2479/3.

[167] I am obliged to Dr G. A. Reid for sight of his 'The Disciplinary Committee', his thirty-nine-page summary of the matter presented to the Council on 13 January 1994.

[168] Letter to Benians, 29 Sept. 1951 (Raven-Bezzant file); CMM, 2292/2, 2296/2.

64 Hall laid up, judging by its benchlessness, for an other than ordinary dinner, October 1964. Photograph courtesy of Messrs Campbell, Smith & Co.

They had been unusual, and were unlucky.[169] But be that as it may, within the year his successor, J. R. Bambrough – a man whose 'lack of mannerism', according to his obituarist, 'sometimes seemed itself a mannerism' – would be being asked 'to tabulate penalties as they related to breaches of discipline': to provide a tariff, in short. His response reveals how far and how fast matters had changed:

[169] In fact, not at all unusual and, to judge by the account of life in St John's provided in Frederic Raphael's *The Glittering Prizes* (1976), *very* unlucky. The fact that in 1952–3 F. M. Raphael shared a landing in E New Court with the newly arrived Dean Bezzant provides additional *frisson*, as no doubt did the author's choice of Charlesworth as the name of the bigoted headmaster in chapter 1 of his novel. (Raphael came up in October 1950, the month of Martin Charlesworth's death.)

The Dean found it difficult without prior notice to answer these questions, and it was agreed that the Junior Members would tabulate specific instances of breaches of regulations to enable the Dean, at a subsequent meeting of the Committee, to give specific answers in so far as it was possible and generally desirable to do so.[170]

In short, the Dean was on the back foot and ducking.

Inexorably, Boys Smith's last year wore on. Early in July it was agreed to bring junior members onto a number of College committees. Amongst those thought by the Senior Bursar suitable for such enrichment were the Archives and Records Committee ('a good research student capable of reading medieval documents might be useful occasionally!') and the Silver Audit ('this could be educational for someone who was really interested – and who could count spoons!').[171] Later that month, for the last time in Boys Smith's Mastership the issue of ladies at board and women in bed was addressed.

Long-term developments were already having their effects upon dining arrangements. For the Seniors, the shift was well underway from a dining College (with Friday the favoured evening) to a lunching College.[172] The service of wine on Mondays rather than Fridays had been experimented with in October 1961 as a means of attracting Fellows to the earlier evening.[173] In the same year, in order to accommodate all the junior members at two sittings instead of three, the width of the three existing tables was narrowed and a fourth one added: 'a mistake', as the Steward of the day would later admit. 'Some called it vandalism.'[174] Since, as others observed, even with undergraduates occupying the high tables at the earlier sessions the need for three halls remained, it was also pointless. Meanwhile, grace and gowns were dispensed with at the earlier sittings,[175] and waitresses were employed to minister to the young gentlemen.[176]

A war-time suggestion 'that ladies be allowed to dine in Hall' had been dismissed by the then Secretary of the JCR as 'fatuous'.[177] A generation later, undergraduate opinion had changed. But although, despite the crush, the male guests of undergraduates were welcome on three nights a week, ladies were allowed only twice a term – and initially were placed in a form of purdah on

---

[170] *Times*, 5 Feb. 1999 (M. C. Scholar); SJMC, 21 Jan. 1970, min. 3.

[171] CM, 2481/4 (11 Jul. 1969); Thomas to Boys Smith, 18 Mar. 1969 (SJMC file).

[172] In May 1958 and August 1963 Fellows were limited to taking no more than four of their commons meals per week as lunch: GB, 30 May 1958; CM, 2307/19.

[173] CM, 2242/6.

[174] CMM, 2232/13, 2242/6; Thistlethwaite, *Cambridge Years*, 124.

[175] 'Surely', crowed D. E. H. T[histlethwaite] – no relation of the Steward of that name – on behalf of the Philistines' Society, 'even Third Hall will conform soon!': *Eagle* lxiv (1970–71), 79.

[176] CM, 2312/3, next to a minute on the colleges' response to the Robbins Committee on Higher Education (Nov. 1963). The unsettling effect of the first occasion on which women waited at a club dinner (that of the Room Cricket Society in 1969: its only dinner ever) resulted in damage to the recently redecorated Wordsworth Room and the banning of the Society in perpetuity.

[177] SJCA, CC8.5 (JCR Suggestions Book, 1938–44); 21 Nov. 1941: suggestion of N. K. Harris (matric. 1940), later headmaster of St Christopher's School, Letchworth.

the guest table.[178] As to the High Table, in the year after women achieved full membership of the University the Governing Body had braced itself to include them in the guest lists for luncheons on special occasions and to invite Fellows' wives and other ladies to dinner once a year. But in early 1949 it had rejected the proposal of the Entertainments Committee to invite the heads of Girton and Newnham to the Port Latin Feast on 6 May.[179] It was not long since one of Glover's circle had described Dorothy Garrod's election as Cambridge or Oxford's first woman professor as the 'beginning of the end'. While contributing generously to the establishment of the future New Hall, the College was altogether slower to offer women places at its own table.[180] It was as if the young gentlemen were unaccustomed to exposure to the conversation of ladies, even *d'un certain âge*. When in November 1958 the College Historical Society was addressed by the illustrious Professor Cam of Girton and Harvard, then safely in her seventies, she was trumpeted as 'the first woman ever' to do so.[181] What with Stipends, the Cripps Building, the Kitchen Lane development, the end of Fellows' dividend and changes in the Admissions procedures on its agenda, the mid-1960s Governing Body somehow lost sight of the ladies. In October 1962 the question of their presence at the Fellows' table was deferred for 'further consideration' in the following month, when by 34 votes to 7 the Governing Body went so far as to intimate that discussion of the matter would be welcome. And so it continued for another six months, by which time Fellows had been invited to state their 'personal attitude' on the matter and discussions had commenced on the proposal that Seniors and Juniors both invite ladies on the same night, six times a year.[182] Five *years* later, there was a majority of Fellows in favour of adding another such evening in the Long Vacation.[183] Meanwhile, however, the Council had inadvertently invited Dame Honor Fell to deliver the 1968 Linacre Lecture, failing to observe that Professor Fell was a lady as well as a Dame.[184]

---

[178] CMM, 2261/9 (Mar. 1962), 2310/9 (Oct. 1963); *Freshmen's Handbook*, Oct. 1968.

[179] CMM, 1903/4, 1904/5.

[180] GD, 6 May 1939; CM, 2014/6 (May 1953); *Eagle* lviii (1958–9), 182.

[181] By the undergraduate treasurer, Ronald Hyam. A fearless feminist, on being denied entry to an academic meeting at Harvard on the grounds that she was a woman, Helen Cam had splendidly riposted to the usher: 'I am not a woman; I am a professor.' Likewise, when Miss Alison Duke (another sturdy Girtonian) attended the Classical Society Annual dinner in 1959, she was said to be 'the first member of the opposite sex to do so *ex hominum memoria*': *Eagle* lviii (1958–9), 182.

[182] CMM, 2276/13, 2279/4; GB, 25 Jan. 1963 (the same meeting gave unanimous approval to the less controversial motion for the foundation of a new College, Darwin), 10 May 1963, 7 Jun. 1963; CMM, 2286/2, 2304/2, 2305/25–6. On the question whether Fellows should be permitted to invite ladies to dine as their guests on specified evenings during term, 19 were 'strongly in favour', 26 'in favour', 3 'indifferent', 8 'against' and 20 'strongly against'. At the Governing Body of June 1963 (according to Glyn Daniel!) it was Boys Smith's 'rage' at the proposal of one Fellow that those desiring female company should be enabled 'to dine free with women in a private room', on the grounds that 'women in Hall was an affront to his wife', that occasioned the decisive straw vote (GEDD, 15 Jun. 1963). Daniel regarded the outcome as consolation for his disappointment over the Presidency since, despite Aubrey Silberston's initiative in the matter, 'of course [it all] started with my letter of two years ago.'

[183] CM, 2428/2 (October 1967).

[184] CM, 2429/7.

Asked by some junior Fellows whether she ought to receive an invitation, after much deliberation one of the denizens of the last ditch, F. P. White, conceded that she should, adding: 'But she should not accept it.' Dame Honor, however, was made of sterner stuff.

When in 1939 the College had decreed that ladies leave by 10 p.m., a future Chairman of the Anti-Apartheid Movement commented that it seemed to be 'a step in the wrong direction'.[185] But it was not as if there had not been fair warning. As long ago as 1898 there had been warnings of the alarming prospect of ladies attending the Congress on Zoology and Physiology needing to be fed in Hall.[186] By the autumn of 1967 the issues of gate hours and guest hours were both very much on the agenda and demonstrating an increasingly symbiotic relationship. After a series of grudging extensions over the previous decade the hours of closure were set at midnight to 6 a.m.[187] But in the view of increasing numbers of junior members the Council's most recently published hours of curfew were little other than an opening bid. Thus, in early June 1969 undergraduate representatives asked for the removal of gate hours and the extension of guest hours to 2 a.m. and their complete abolition at the weekend.[188] And just two days later the case of A. and C. gave the cause its martyrs. Bertram's submission to the Council with its recurrent mantra requiring all activities within the College to advance its statutory purposes of 'education, religion, learning and research' revealed a man struggling with unfamiliar concepts and outmatched by quick-witted youth. His compromise ('integration', as he called it) opposed all change whatsoever, thereby leaving the impression that sexual licence, not security, was the only issue that mattered. The letter sent to him two days later by four of his colleagues showed that the tutorial body was split down the middle. As the dissidents observed, the recent case of A. and C. had ensured that because it would appear that 'the rule is only enforced on the whim of the individual bed-maker' there would be constant appeals against decanal rulings on the matter.[189] The inevitable consequence was that co-residence replaced co-education on the College's agenda.

[185] SJCA, CC8.5, 15 Jan. 1939: observation of J. A. F. Ennals (matric. 1936).

[186] CM, 530/4.

[187] CM, 2424/4 (21 Jul. 1967).

[188] SJMC, 5 Jun. 1969, min. 4.

[189] Bertram, 'Gate hours and Guest hours', 21 Jul. 1969; 'Further comment from certain Tutors': SJCA, CC18.2, 23 Jul. 1969; CM, 2482/4 (25 Jul. 1969) and attached papers.

The Modern College

I. THE AGE OF BROTHER CHAIR

> An historian dealing with characters long dead may legitimately assign motives, speculate on rumours and even indulge in a little scandal-mongering. It is neither courteous nor helpful nor wise for him to do so when he is dealing with the fringe of the present.
>
> Steven Runciman, *The White Rajahs*, 1960, Preface

DURING Boys Smith's last year of office allegations of irregularity regarding the conduct of recent Mastership elections were regularly made by R. A. Lyttleton and Hugh Sykes Davies, according to whom the holding of informal meetings in advance of proceedings in the Chapel and, in the case of an inconclusive voting or indeed of any voting after the first scrutiny, the reading out of the number of votes cast, were both in breach of statute. In January 1969 the Council rejected both contentions.[1] In the previous November an informal discussion of the traditional sort had ensued, in the course of which Sykes Davies urged the need for a good-looking Master in order to improve the appearance of the portraits on the stairway up to the Combination Room, Ronald Robinson likened the whole process to the election of an African chief, and Nicholas Mansergh conjectured that diminishing pressures might make it unnecessary for the next Master to be a full-time officer. The outcome was the pre-election of Mansergh himself on 6 June 1969 and his prompt resignation of his chair. The first Oxford graduate since 1670 to find favour with the electors, he had been a Fellow of the College and Smuts Professor of the History of the British Commonwealth since 1953.[2]

As the Anglo-Irish chronicler of Indian independence, Mansergh (who would in due course make a striking enough portrait) was no stranger to sectarian politics. Aided by a disarmingly patrician manner (family motto 'Tout Jour Pret': 'Ever Ready'), and with his historical expertise distilled in his recently published *The Commonwealth Experience*, he had been prepared by knowledge and experience of that disparate community for the role of a Head of House in the 1970s. In 1959, to the consternation of some of the Fellows' wives, he had run against Boys Smith, and now his victory was trumpeted by those hitherto disappointed of the prospect of rerunning the last two elections as heralding a triumph over the monstrous regiment of Bursars and Tutors tantamount to a new creation. 'College Master breaks tradition', the *Guardian*'s Science correspondent announced. 'Since 1541 the masters of St John's have risen, apparently exclusively, from the ranks of college bursars or tutors.' Here at last was a 'decidedly non-establishment figure' whose pre-election (many Fellows would be hoping) meant 'not simply a new broom but a real break with the retarding

---

[1] CM, 2468/3, 4 (30 Jan. 1969).

[2] With ninety of the ninety-seven Fellows present, Farmer 35; Mansergh 49; Thomas 6.

stranglehold of college tradition'.[3] The monstrous regiment itself was not so sure. 'I would expect him to serve the College well as Master, but I doubt whether he will turn out to be of the same calibre as either Benians or Boys Smith', Guillebaud confided to W. G. Constable.[4]

In fact, although previously rather little known in the College at large,[5] Nicholas Mansergh – 'Old Nick' as he came to be familiarly known – was to prove an ideal Master during a more than usually turbulent decade. Admittedly there was a price to be paid. Council meetings under the chairmanship of one able to make four syllables out of 'ping-pong' tended to resemble those of Charles Taylor at the beginning of the century. Fellows accustomed to Boys Smith's crisp and decisive chairmanship had to adjust to meetings which began after lunch and ended sometime after dinner.[6] 'Is not a Master, is a jollyfish [*sic*]', Jean-Bertrand Barrère, the Professor of French Literature, was heard to opine in a moment of extreme anguish at one meeting of the Governing Body. But Boys Smith could never have simulated Mansergh's impassiveness on being addressed by one of the undergraduate comrades on the Consultative Committee as 'Brother Chair'. Letting everyone have his say takes time, and it was the intention of Mansergh, the remorseless constitutionalist, that everyone should. Olympian detachment such as his had kept the Commonwealth going. While remaining maddeningly inscrutable as to his own opinions, meanwhile he was tirelessly wearing down committee-mongering junior apparatchiks and trouncing them at their own bureaucratic game. Above all, he recognized the significance for the College of Lord Devlin's criticism of the University's handling of its junior members, namely 'that (...) having made arrangements to obtain student opinion, [it] has not formed any clear idea of what, if anything, to do with it when it gets it.'[7] Nor was it only junior members whom the system seemed not so much intent on keeping at arm's length but rather content to do so. It was as recently as Benians's time that the Council had raised 'no objection' to Fellows receiving relevant material in advance of the Audit meeting of the Governing Body.[8]

---

[3] *Guardian*, 9 Jun. 1969. Both the date 1541 and the statement that this was the 'first pre-election made possible by changes in the statute in 1944' are erroneous.

[4] Letter of 16 Jun. 1969 (Constable Papers, 1/9).

[5] Even amongst the undergraduate historians, as was demonstrated when at one of their annual dinners in the early 1960s at which the guest speaker entertained the company with his brilliant mimicry of the seniors present (prompting F. H. Hinsley, for example, to insist that 'it's only a caricature, my boy') his impersonation of Mansergh (whose voice was once likened to the sound of sheep on a distant mountain) alone fell flat – until, on rising to make an unexceptionable comment on the speaker's reference to Pandit Nehru, Mansergh was greeted with delighted applause, providing thereby an example, rare in St John's, of Life imitating Art. Having come onto the College Council in June 1959 he had resigned from it in Oct. 1961: CM, 2242/4.

[6] Despite the resolution of February 1970 establishing closure at 4.45 p.m.: CM, 2499/10.

[7] Devlin, §§122, 200.

[8] CM, 1857/8 (July 1947).

Accordingly, the man whose preferred recreation (after lawn tennis) was consultation, was unwilling to take lessons in procedure from elderly law Fellows, as one of them who presumed to proffer advice had it sonorously indicated to him towards the end of the new Master's first term.[9] Further comeuppance was forthcoming when the same person called for Junior Fellows to be reminded of the lessons of appeasement and insisted that the 'militants' constituted only a small minority of the junior membership:[10] the invitable corollary of his definition of militancy as the displacement activity of men uninterested in work and unwilling to get up in time for a 9 o'clock lecture. In reality, it was not only militants, however defined, who at both the JCR and Consultative Committee level engaged in a College debate which throughout the following decade had as one of its perennial features the interconnectedness of everything from solidarity with 'the oppressed car workers of North East Bolivia' (February 1975) to the state of the New Court lavatories. Despite the introduction of agenda in February 1971, a typical JCR or Consultative Committee menu might include the vote of a recent Open Meeting on South Africa, demand for a contraceptive-vending machine,[11] guest hours, emergency heating regulations, bedders' wages and College lawns.[12] Such was the confusion of issues that any attempt to present them serially or strand by strand would misrepresent their frenzied collective impact. As the Consultative Committee wrestled one issue to the ground, hydra-like another arose. Thus, with the Disciplinary Committee more or less established, guest and gate hours had returned to the agenda,[13] to be followed by Admissions policy (February 1970); room allocation (April 1970); Kitchen charges; junior member attendance at meetings of the Governing Body and the College Council (or Governing Body and College Council) as well as return matches with senior members at 'JCR discussion sessions'. As the undergraduates themselves observed, it was with themselves that most items for discussion originated. Wherever they convened, though – and *where* was symbolically significant – just about the only thing the two parties were ever able to agree on was the Undesirability of Noise.[14] On matters of procedure however –

[9] R. M. Jackson to Mansergh, 5 Dec. 1969: M6.3/1 (Governing Body papers).

[10] 'the point (...) is one, on the evidence that was laid before me and my predecessor by the elected representatives of the Junior Members, to which, with whatever regrets, I find it hard to subscribe': Mansergh to Jackson, 9 Dec. 1969. (Incidentally an early example of the use of initial capital letters for 'Junior Members': a theological issue akin to that of omission of the definite article before 'Council' (below, n. 131), regarding which confusion reigned in these years.)

[11] 'Not an – er – contra –er – ceptive – er – machine', as Mansergh periodically insisted, to little avail.

[12] JCR President (N. A. Burton) to Mansergh, 20 Nov. 1973, in language like that of some functionary of a Minister of State addressing a provincial governor ('I have been instructed by the JCR Committee to convey to you the following ...'): SJCA, CC 18.1.

[13] Minutes of 29 Apr. and 5 Jun. 1969.

[14] Min. 5 of 9 Mar. 1970. At the beginning of Mansergh's mastership meetings shifted from the Lodge to the Senior Tutor's office or J. C. Hall's set. This was a mistake. In April 1970 they returned to the Lodge. In November 1971 (presumably at a time of extreme republican fervour) the Committee assembled in an undergraduate set (K6 Second).

on the request for circulation of an account of his impressions of meetings of the Governing Body, for example, or for public hearings or publication of proceedings of the Disciplinary Committee – Mansergh proved adamantine.[15]

The extent of the ramifications of student concern was adumbrated by the Senior Tutor, G. C. L. Bertram, in a paper on the subject of Gate and Guest Hours, one of two papers commissioned by the Council for presentation at Mansergh's first Council meeting in October 1969.

Gate hours were easy enough to change. It was the associated issue of *guest* hours that seemed to present problems and raise the metaphysical question with which the bewildered Bertram wrestled manfully as to the precise moment at which 'seeming' visitors were transformed into guests. The transformation process appeared to have something to do with the act of lifting one leg off the floor, although 'problems arise when a Visitor attempts to turn into a Guest, usually at short notice'[16] – particularly when in such numbers as to exceed the supply of additional guest rooms. The accommodation of *male* guests in an undergraduate room would therefore be allowable, it was conceded, 'on occasion or in emergency' – always provided the emergency had been notified 'as long in advance as is conveniently possible'.[17] But in the face of the growing conviction that, whether they called them guests or visitors, the dons had no moral authority to impose different rules on men and women, and the Tutors no business in monitoring late-comers on the grounds that they might need 'help or advice', both these measures proved insufficient.[18] In a paper presented to the Consultative Committee in February 1970, entitled 'Should Guest Hours be Abolished?', it was stated that many women were already spending nights in College, and that their presence promoted stable relationships and discouraged the use of prostitutes. A guest rule containing the word 'male' was no more than a 'charter for homosexuals'. As stated by a petition of a group of undergraduates opposed to change, 'the main question' was 'widely, though tacitly agreed to concern the matter of women staying overnight in the rooms of junior members.'[19] Since that question was seen by both sides as one of principle, compromises involving tinkering with the witching-hour were equally unacceptable to both, as was the proposal, seriously made, to confine the 2 a.m. closure to members (that is to say *male* members) of the University.[20]

Indeed (and this was understood by all parties), unsoundness on the issue

---

[15] SJMC, mins. of 22 Oct. 1970; 11 Feb. 1971; 9 Nov. 1971 (SJCA, CC18.1); CM, 2542/7. 'I will hope to convey later on and more formally the reactions of the Council to your letter and to the particular points in it', he wrote to N. A. Burton on 18 Jan. 1974. 'In the meantime, following the precept of the "old diplomacy", I am placing the whole question on ice.'

[16] 'Gate Hours and Guest Hours: recommendations from the Tutors and Dean', 26 Sept. 1969: SJCA, CC18.2 (G. C. L. Bertram).

[17] With sleeping bags provided at a charge of half a crown to cover 'wear and tear': 'Arrangements for Guests in College', draft, 17 Oct. 1969: CC18.1.

[18] 'Gate Hours and Guest Hours', 26 Sept. 1969, §4(d): CC18.2.

[19] Dated 27 Nov. 1969, forwarded to Mansergh by the Acting Senior Tutor, J. C. Hall.

[20] Hall to Mansergh, 30 Oct. 1969 adducing as the 'principal argument in its favour, that our men ought to be enabled to continue discussions in their rooms with members of other Colleges until after midnight': 'I think such a rule could be made to work.'

of guest hours threw everything else into confusion: that way lay anarchy and sexual licence. In Mansergh's first term, J. C. Hall consulted Alan Welford (sometime Tutor, Professor of Psychology at the University of Adelaide) on the subject. The response was bleak. 'Many women guests will undoubtedly be predators earnestly seeking a husband', the antipodean answer came. 'They are likely to look upon an extra two hours, especially in the small hours of the morning, as a good opportunity for breaking down resistance.'[21] 'If students are to work well they need adequate and regular sleep', Welford insisted. 'It would not be an unreasonable thing to suggest; it would really not be very different from the boat club going into training.' This was not the analogy which would have recommended itself to undergraduates of the sort that the Senior Tutor had in mind.

Hall shared the tidings from Adelaide with Bertram, and in return was asked whether the age of majority in Australia was 'now 18 too, or still 21, and adding that he was sending a 'draft paper to help, I hope, us to clear our minds further'.[22] The content of this draft recorded the impact of Welford's warning. In it 'almost predatory', 'time-wasting' women sapped the 'academic potentialities' of young men (who although legally 'adult' were 'certainly no more full of personal wisdom than their predecessors') by depriving them of sleep after that hour at which 'Visitors merge into Guests'. If all other colleges thought otherwise should not the schools be informed that St John's was 'a more monastic community (...) with all the believed ultimate academic advantages and ephemeral seeming disadvantages of such a system'?[23] 'In these days of Latey changes,[24] social evolution, and the manner of behaviour of young men and women', Balliol had already been written to, as a college whose arrangements 'are sometimes referred to here as being indicative of something or other, or "advanced" in a sensible way, etc. etc.' With its tidings of a college bar out of control and the admission that, because undergraduate rooms were 'regarded as sacrosanct, and scouts can no longer reasonably be expected to report to the Dean', the ban on ladies staying overnight was 'very much of a face-saver', Balliol's reply was not encouraging.[25] Likewise the news from another Oxford college, Wadham, where there was no distinction of women guests from men, and members were allowed to 'come and go as they wished' at any hour. The Senior Tutor of Wadham's scepticism 'whether anybody's habits of working, drinking, wenching,

---

[21] 'If you say this at the governing body you will undoubtedly be laughed to scorn, but few men, especially those who have not worked as Parish clergy and College chaplains, realise the extent of the truth of what I have said': letter dated 24 Nov. 1969.

[22] 'The structure of this draft paper – swinging from side to side – is quite deliberate but not necessarily effective': Note dated 12 Dec. 1969: SJCA, STF2007/16.

[23] It was some consolation that meanwhile, 'quite certainly no College can properly move beyond this position without discussions among the Tutorial Representatives': 'Gates and Guests: an appraisal of the future', 12 Dec. 1269: SJCA, STF2007/16.

[24] For Sir John Latey's *Report of the Committee on the Age of Majority* (Cmnd. 3342, 1967); see B. Harrison, *Seeking a Role: The United Kingdom, 1951–1970* (Oxford, 2009), 263.

[25] Bertram to Senior Tutor of Balliol, 10 Dec. 1969; R. M. Ogilvie to Bertram, 12 Jan. 1970: STF2007/16.

card-playing have been changed at all' was not altogether welcome to the Senior Tutor of St John's.[26]

In the minds of the same constituency when activated, the question was that presented in May 1973 as an amendment to a motion before the Governing Body for repeal of the 'male only' rule, namely whether the statutory objectives of the College included promiscuity. Accordingly, instead of admitting women, somewhat later the possibility of a 'limited agreement' with the Ladies of New Hall was floated, whereby an invitation would be extended to 'a limited number of Fellows of [that college] (perhaps 4) to dine on our High Table on Fridays during term, the expense being borne by New Hall' and a number of 'undergraduate volunteers, preferably between 30 and 50, would be accommodated during their second year in the other College and would take all meals in that College exclusively.' In the context of the more thoroughgoing changes in some people's minds such arrangements might be thought to have advantages. Above all, 'sports teams would not suffer and no irrevocable step would have been taken.' Even so, any such course of action was risk-laden. With regard to mixed classes for members of the two colleges, for example, Directors of Studies would need to be asked

> what they believe the long term effects of such collaboration might be, and in particular whether a symbiosis might occur that would prove difficult to terminate at a later date, but which might (or might not) be advantageous.[27]

With symbiosis a danger never to be underestimated in a community such as a college, guest hours inevitably remained on the agenda throughout the 1970s, became hopelessly confused with the debate on co-residence, and disappeared only when that issue was finally decided.[28]

Co-residence was the subject of Bertram's other paper presented to the Council in October 1969, which the Council caused to be circulated to the Governing Body in amended form 'as a personal statement';[29] it is not difficult to see why. Unrealistically, its author hoped to conceal his own views. In fact he did more. 'Co-Residence in relation to St John's' was a statement for a passing age and a generation about to be deprived of its responsibilities as surrogate parents, vaguely conscious that they and their predecessors had been collectively negligent in discharging those responsibilities, and, as Claude Guillebaud had revealed earlier that year, anxious to atone for that lapse by continuing to exercise them.[30] However, everything was changing: for example, the customary

---

[26] Ibid: Senior Tutor of Wadham to Bertram, 17 Dec. 1969.

[27] 'Committee on the Education of Women in the University, Note of Partial Dissent', 6 May 1976: CCF/Education of Women (proposal of J. C. Hall); 'Ways in which St John's might be able to collaborate with New Hall' (undated, initialled JCH).

[28] It was raised again by Hall in the autumn of 1975 in connexion with his proposal to postpone a decision until the following term: a proposal rejected by the Governing Body on 27 November.

[29] CM, 2484/6 (6 Oct. 1969). The paper had its origins in a working paper prepared for a discussion between the Tutors and the JCR Committee on 15 June 1969, nine days after Mansergh's pre-election: SJCA, STF 2007/5.

[30] Above, p. 595.

practice of addressing a pupil as 'Dear Smith' was now considered chilly (particularly if Smith came from what might be termed a 'humble' school). 'The *in loco parentis* principle is now gone – entirely in theory and almost entirely in practice', Lord Devlin was soon to pronounce in respect of the University at large.

> It would be helpful if the vestiges were formally abandoned. A great deal of concern in the minds of those students who discuss questions of discipline is, I believe, due to the suspicion that those in authority in the University secretly cling to what students regard (…) as an outworn idea. The abandonment of *in loco parentis* would leave membership of a society as the only justification for disciplinary rules. On this students ask two questions. First, why and how is a university a society? Second, if it is a society, why are the rules not made by all the members? (§143)

Bertram's presentation of his ideas stands as an early artless, albeit honest, attempt to comprehend such questions and provide some tentative answers.

His survey went as follows. At present only Kings and Churchill had plans to admit women undergraduates (he thought it an open question whether they were to have women Fellows too), but 'doubtless other Colleges [were] pondering this same problem.' Any statutory change must be 'demonstrably helpful' to *all* its statutory purposes – education, religion, learning and research – not just education, and not just for the convenience of the concupiscent few. Young women were not to be admitted just for 'the social convenience of young men'. If they were, they would displace the same number of men, which would be wasteful since, 'observing the fact that so high a proportion of young women, through marriage, quickly drop out of the national availability of professional expertise, (anyhow for a number of years) some may feel that it would be unfortunate if Cambridge Colleges ceased to give opportunity for so many men Undergraduates.' Anyway, what business of undergraduates was it to make such proposals? Undergraduates should recognize their limitations. They were here for only about 500 days over three years (and deprived of female company for only nine hours in every twenty-four for that matter). Contrast the forty years of some senior members, 'as specialists in education, religion, learning and research': 'undergraduates are ephemeral indeed.' If the worst came to the worst and change did happen, might it perhaps be reversed later? Could men and women use the same system of scholarship examination? ('The attempt would be interesting.') If not, analogically with the world that was familiar to him, at first the College would need to rely on the recommendation of certain Headmistresses. 'There is no doubt of the availability of able young women who would like to come to Cambridge – however great the difficulty of selection of some of them instead of their not quite so able brothers whom, it may be argued, at present we admit.' 'For nearly all the scientists to be men and nearly all the Arts people to be women (…) may or may not be regarded as helpful to a really liberal education.' Would the men treat the women as skivvies, counting on their 'ready compliance (…) in many aspects of life, for example washing, mending and meals?' There were already 'socially available' women at Homerton, Addenbrooke's and the language schools. Old Johnian headmasters might be upset. 'Healthy vigour (if not overdone)' must not be discouraged (though 'the degree of participation in or the quality of sport may or may not be correlated with co-residence'). A co-residential college would house academic couples (North Court seemed suitable). Otherwise, Bertram assumed, it would be a segregated college with strict rules about visiting at particular hours. 'There is a relevance here to our present considerations about Guest Hours', he noted, correctly.

In another lengthy memorandum entitled 'Focus on Administration', Bertram expatiated further on the whole range of deplorable developments within the modern College: an account which, despite its inadequacies, he believed would 'have a usefulness, if only in describing and recording something of how things are managed in 1971'. Wherever he looked Bertram observed increasing complexity and rapidity of change. A handful of College officers were 'running an enormous and very diverse business on a shoestring'.

> There are few bigger hotels in the country but only some barracks, hospitals and prisons. We feed our 'inmates' and many others too; we run conferences on our premises; we welcome many in guest rooms; we act as house agents for dozens of flats and married quarters. Yet, after selecting who shall be admitted to the College (in itself a substantial task) we go so far as to try to give them a choice of rooms as well as to educate them.

Hamstrung by 'the modern fashion for participation by Junior Members', administrators were robbed of any chance of doing their own research. In this context one alarming development was the Consultative Committee, 'the arena' into which the Senior Bursar 'has had to come' to discuss with junior members 'detailed aspects of their monetary and other affairs'. This was disproportionate. After all, 'a Prime Minister does not discuss with her the inflation in Mrs Jones' grocery bills.'

So what remedies were there? Well, 'men might be told where they will keep in College instead of being offered some freedom of choice.' This would be one consequence of adopting 'a fully hierarchical administration; a bureaucracy, comparable perhaps with a hospital, organized so that 'the Fellows would be provided with premises, in which to exercise their skills upon young men selected by the Tutors, and in which to pursue their researches and teaching freed from all non-scholarly duties.' Personally, Bertram favoured persisting with the 'non-hierarchical mode'. But 'if size and complexity continue to mount' that option would disappear, and the prison – rather than the hotel – model would become inevitable.[31]

Two principles were discernible in these elegiac ponderings. One was

---

[31] SJCL, Bertram box: a paper brought to the Council in the Michaelmas term 1971 after consideration by the Master and some others and deletion of some remarks 'concerning the Steward and his department (...) made because of the (in my view) irrational emotions aroused in many by any consideration of food and its provision.' By CM, 2551/9 (20 Jan. 1972) the paper was referred to a Council Committee on Administration within the College which in due course recommended shifting various of the chores complained of from the Senior Tutor's department to the Junior Bursar's: CM, 2566/13 (5 Oct. 1972).

concern for the existing women's colleges; this would continue to be voiced over the coming decade.[32] The other was the paramount importance of ensuring that any change satisfied the College's statutory objectives, which 'all Fellows (...) have sworn an oath on admission to promote.' A third combined both.[33] But, as even the undergraduate supporters of the *status quo* observed, that argument would not only prevent *all* change, it would reduce to rubble many of the social amenities achieved over the previous century or more. And 'the situation of the College as a place of learning at such times as May Week would be comic.'[34]

However, in these years 'no change' seemed to be the authorities' default position. On being informed that some colleges with grounds on the Backs were likely to permit the passage of perambulators through their grounds, the Council promptly 'agreed to make no such change in respect of the courts and grounds of St. John's'.[35] To the young men here for only 500 days and deprived of female company for 500 nights, the outlook was depressing, and especially so in view of the wait-and-see philosophy espoused by Bertram. The attitude of R. G. Harding, Junior Treasurer of the JCR, as he remembers it now, was doubtless that of many:

> My own motives were rather base. Having been at a boys grammar school and living out in the Essex countryside I lacked the social skills necessary to successful dating and thought that were there girls in college (which was clearly going to happen – if not at St Johns then somewhere else) meeting them would be easier and more 'natural'. To the College Council I argued that it would improve academic standards.[36]

However, together with the interests of the women's colleges, it was the Asquithian strategy that found favour when on 14 November 1969 the Governing Body discussed co-residence ('coexistence' according to Glyn Daniel's journal) for the first time. 'Would there be important loss, or gain, in a particular College observing change in others in practice before itself taking a grave decision?', Bertram wondered, unwittingly echoing the argument from electricity adduced in 1911 that it was no loss to the College to be one of the last to adopt that convenience, 'since, owing to the delay, we have been able to put it in on a greatly improved system.' But in 1911 the question had not been asked, as it was now of the latest novelty, whether the use of electricity was compatible with the College's statutory objectives.[37]

---

[32] E.g. Bertram to Mansergh, 28 Oct. 1977: 'I still believe that, as a College, we can more advance women's education by financial help to Women's Colleges than by admitting women to our own Society': M6.5.

[33] 'And even if we do the latter (...) I would hope that we can continue to help impoverished Women's Colleges, for they will still have a special part to play within the University and the realms of Women's Education, Religion, Learning and Research': M6.5.

[34] 'Should Guest Hours be Abolished?' (a paper prepared by members of the Consultative Committee, Feb. 1970), referring to min. 4 of the meeting of the Consultative Committee, 12 Feb. 1970: SJCA, CC18.1.

[35] CM, 2535/13 (13 May 1971).

[36] Letter to Author, 12 Dec 2007.

[37] Above, p. 497.

Small wonder therefore that the November 1969 meeting of the Governing Body (at which there was no motion) proved inconclusive[38] and that at its successor on Guest Hours in the following month those Fellows who were interested at all favoured either the retentionist or the total abolitionist position, and that the Council's agreement to 'certain changes' (subsequently decoded as adoption of the 2 a.m. curfew) was regarded by a number of them as unprincipled compromise.[39] Early in the following term the result of a junior member referendum mandated the JCR Committee to campaign for guests to be allowed to stay overnight 'regardless of their sex'.[40] Regardless of that mandate (a sophisticated device unheard-of four years earlier), throughout the 1970s the rules remained unchanged, the social arrangements of junior members (or at least of those of them fortunate in their bedders), continued undisturbed,[41] while amongst those interested attention shifted to the spectacle of co-residence becalmed somewhere between Governing Body, Council and one or other of its committees.[42] In March 1974 one freshman's observation that 'some colleges should remain "for men only" and why not ours?' ('I wonder how St John Fisher would have felt about the suggestion') was greeted by the Senior Tutor as a significant contribution to the search for a solution of 'the co-residence problem (*sic*)': 'this is just the sort of viewpoint which our Committee are glad to hear of.' In the course of that and the following year a succession of Governing Body meetings debated a series of motions and amendments on and around the subject (including one proposed by Dr G. A. Reid in November 1975, later described as 'of immense and at this distance of time impenetrable complexity'),[43] in which the issue was frequently decided by the narrowest of margins. Meanwhile Mansergh proved adamant in resisting the suggestion that in the fast-moving mid-seventies St John's should agree to join a queue of colleges prepared to hold fire until after 1980. It was perhaps as well for the College to have an Oxford man at the helm at such a time.[44] For all this, in November 1977 a motion for the crucial change of statute, although approved by 50 votes to 30, failed to secure the necessary two-thirds majority.

---

[38] Bertram's notes on the occasion begin: 'S.T.'s introduction. Long pause. Hollick …', and record Daniel (who believed himself to be a keen advocate of change) as being 'not for or against': SJCA, STF 2007/5.

[39] CM, 2492/4; G. A. Reid to Mansergh, 10 Dec. 1969; R. N. Perham, P. A. Linehan and A. G. C. Renwick to Mansergh, 12 Dec. 1969.

[40] By 289 votes to 123, with three spoilt papers: SJMC, 21 Jan. 1970. In November 1972 the exercise was repeated (by 233 votes to 106).

[41] In May 1978 the Governing Body agreed by 39 votes to 17 to remove the word 'male' from the 2 a.m. rule.

[42] At the Consultative Committee in Feb. 1972, with Bertram's 1969 paper as its discussion document, the Junior Members asked for a Joint Committee on the matter, and were refused. In May 1973 the Tutors were appointed to serve as such a committee and asked to report within twelve months: SJCA, CC 18.1; CMM, 2554/23, 2582/5.

[43] Thus F. H. Hinsley in a manuscript *aide-mémoire* apparently compiled for use by him at the Governing Body of October 1980.

[44] His objection was, he insisted, 'fundamental': letter to Chairman of Colleges' Committee, D. W. Bowett (President of Queens'), 14 Apr. 1975: SJCA, STF 2007/5.

As always on such matters, the *Eagle* preserved its reputation as a sometimes tongue-in-cheek journal of record.[45] The picture of nappies drying in the breeze was an inevitable consequence of Colin Bertram's vision of married couples residing in a gated-off North Court, the benefits of which the Senior Tutor of all people was well placed to appreciate.[46] But let it not be thought that the College was preoccupied with these matters to the exclusion of all others. During 1970, after it had been shown that St John's was one of the colleges most restrictive in respect of lady guests, no more than two meetings of the Governing Body were needed to secure agreement that they might dine at High Table on Tuesdays and Thursdays throughout the year.[47] Meanwhile junior members were permitted to bring their ladies in on any evening. But the pleasure of that was unfortunately compromised by relations with the Steward. In March 1970, three months after the retirement of his short-lived predecessor (J. A. Charles), W. D. Armstrong migrated from Churchill. Armstrong was a conscientious man of high standards and great probity, massively knowledgeable on the subject of VAT, and to that extent ideally qualified to supervise the transition from the old catering regime to the new cafeteria dispensation housed in the Buttery Dining Room. His conclusion that 'in the New Court Cellars Discothèque a punch made of foreign wines might be sold to members of the University and their guests', for example, exemplified the level of that conscientiousness. It was a level with which the College was not altogether familiar. Unfortunately, moreover, although efficient, Armstrong was not notably clubbable, but rather peevish and prickly, easily goaded and wholly lacking in diplomatic skills. In short, he was not the ideal person to deal with volatile, sharp-witted undergraduates – or even Fellows, for that matter, 'some old and some young' whose 'ignorant criticism (sometimes written) from a truly blinkered purview' drew Bertram's fire in his 'Focus on Administration'. After all, 'those who suffered imprisonment in wartime, (…) have special thankfulness for the good and ample food which is set before them.'[48]

However, evocation of POW privations – or even of the Franco-Prussian

---

[45] As in the case of David Thistlethwaite's cover for vol. lxiv, no. 276 (Jun. 1971) showing the College façade advertising discos, bars, 'ALL-NITE FUN 'N' GAMES' etc., which caused at least one senior Fellow to protest to the President, indicating *inter alia* that irony may sometime be wasted even on astronomers.

[46] In October 1961 there had been thirty-eight married students, ten of them undergraduates and two affiliated. Eleven years later there were fifty-five (four and seven respectively). In the early 2000s one of the Fellows was both surprised and affronted to learn that she would not be able to live in College with her husband and infant.

[47] A. Silberston to Mansergh, 9 Jan. 1970: M6.3/1; CM, 2507/20. In January 1970, after a flurry of amendments, a proposal that they might do so on any weekday, 'provided that (a) they are ladies who on that day have given or are about to give a seminar, lecture, supervision or the like in the University or the College, and (b) it being understood that they will not take wine in the Combination Room', was approved by 22 votes to 21, a majority considered by the Council 'inconclusive': CM, 2499/6. This decision prompted the gnomic observation of G. E. Briggs and S. J. Bailey 'that a voting of the Governing Body that fails to achieve the necessary majority as laid down in Statute VIII(9) is no more inconclusive than a voting that achieves such a majority' (letter to Mansergh, 11 Feb. 1970).

[48] Above, p. 610.

War[49] – was not calculated to cut much ice with a generation for which Paris had quite different connotations, not least because although in the summer of 1972 a Kitchen Consultative Committee had been established 'to provide a regular channel of communication between the Steward and the members of the College',[50] friction soon led to the early retirement of the Kitchen Manager, Sid Dring, 'after', in the Steward's own words, '45 years devoted service to the College', and problems proliferated with the contract catering firm brought in by him in July 1973 to do the job that Jo. Lyons had shrunk from in 1921.[51] By early 1974 Armstrong was embroiled with the junior members over a ½p delivery charge for a pint of milk, leading *Scan*, the JCR newsletter, to complain that he regarded them as 'his natural enemies'.[52] With rising prices at a time of rapid inflation, closures of Hall, and continuing complaints about portion control, dirty cutlery and birds in the Buttery, allegations flew to and fro, and at the end of that year Armstrong resigned.[53]

Yet not all was gloom and woe. Though now club and society reports in the *Eagle* rarely acknowledged the fact, senior members continued to exert themselves in helping to keep such activities going. Traditions held, and the old guard grumbled on, as the new Steward soon discovered. 'As Palmer is no longer with us and Briggs not often, the post of principal critic of Hall may fall on me', Harold Jeffreys informed R. T. B. Langhorne soon after the latter's arrival as Steward and Junior Bursar (the two offices having been 'united' on the recommendation of the Committee on Administration within the College).[54] Fellows and junior members continued to play cricket together in the Long Vac. XI and (until undergraduate ineptitude let things slip) the Willows, and to drink together thereafter in the local pub. Rather less often, they did so in the Combination Room to which, in the hope of creating bonds while time still remained for them to develop, it had recently been decided to invite second-year rather than third-year men for wine and nuts with the Fellows.[55]

It was a convivial party of this sort that assembled on the evening of 13 February 1970, a month after the referendum on guest hours and a month before

---

[49] 'I cannot restrain myself from a childhood memory, of fifty-five years ago. I stood in a queue for margarine at a Grocer's in Petty Cury. Supplies ran out and there were murmurings among the waiting people. I was with an elderly French woman who thereupon stepped into the middle of the street and harangued us: we should not grumble about margarine; in her youth she was thankful, in the siege of Paris, to queue for rats': ibid.

[50] CM, 2562/4; Kitchen Consultative Committee Minutes (SJCA, CC 21.1).

[51] KCC, Note dated 23 Oct. 1972 (W. D. Armstrong); G. E. Daniel, 'Mr. Sid Dring', *Eagle* lxv (1972–3), 88–9; CM, 2583/8 (14 Jun. 1973); above, p. 486.

[52] *Scan*, 7 May 1974: 'We want to be treated as equals whose opinions and criticisms are welcome and not to be fobbed off with meaningless discussions on consultative committees. (…) Time is running out.' Cf. Bon Viveur, 'SJC – or Mysteries of the Organisms', *Eagle* lxv (1972–3), 50.

[53] KCC, 25 Nov. 1974, mins. 4, 6, 8. Though technically misinformed, the Eagles Club's vote of thanks to the Council for not renewing the Steward's tenure was unmistakable as to the sentiment it expressed.

[54] Letter of 24 Feb. 1975, complaining of the bluntness of the knives, the fizziness of bottled beer and the absence of mutton from Hall: SJCA, SDF 1987/11.

[55] CM, 2463/6 (5 Dec. 1968).

W. D. Armstrong's installation. The author of these pages (who had presumably deserved the privilege by having offended the then acting Steward) found himself sitting at a table occupied by members of the College 'hard left' and remembers some generally good-natured chaffing and watching them enjoying the College's port, cigars and walnuts while denouncing its feudal shortcomings. Unbeknown to at least one of those present, meanwhile there were developments at the local Garden House Hotel in protest at an event organized by the Greek Tourist Office at a time when Greece was governed by colonels. With 'the exuberance natural to congregated youth' remarked by the Royal Commissioners earlier in the century gaining the upper hand,[56] the proctors soon found it impossible to contain the situation, and before long the Riot Act was read.

By the next morning the 'Garden House Affair' was national headlines,[57] with consequences including a number of undergraduates arrested at the scene receiving custodial sentences, one of them, a member of the College, having to take his Part II in Wormwood Scrubs (temporarily deemed part of the University for the purposes of tripos regulations), and a limited embitterment of relations within select sectors of the student body. For the malcontents it was therefore a godsend. Within the College, it provided the Left Lunch Club, the canteen of the elect, with an occasion for instructing the generality of undergraduates not to fraternize with Fellows and calling for the resignation of any Fellows associated with the proctorial body.[58] Sadly, some of the former were influenced. Six days later, as many as seventy-two junior members turned up for the AGM of the General Athletics Club, not normally a college crowd-puller, to hear 'some "basic" questions about sports' raised by one non-sportsman, including a plea to eliminate the competitive element therefrom as bourgeois, and the proposal of another, for which also rather little support was forthcoming, that 'the general public should be able to use the field in the Long. Vac.'[59]

Devlin estimated the proportion of the University student body intent on destroying the 'power structure' of university government as 'a tiny fraction'.[60] By that reckoning, the Johnian contingent would have amounted to six or seven. There may have been twice that number, many of them the sons of bank managers. But that must remain an impression. Certainly the moulders of opinion worked hard to activate a largely inert junior membership, instructing it when it might and might not have dealings with the dons, namely supervisions and fraternization respectively. The remainder of the Winter of Discontent proved reasonably mild. The First XV won half its matches, the VIII did creditably in

[56] Above, p. 495.

[57] For an inadequate account of the incident based largely on newspaper reports, see D. Crook, 'The Cambridge Garden House Hotel Riot of 1970 and its place in the history of British student protests', *Journal of Educational Administration and History* xxxviii (2006), 19–28. Cf. 'Riot! What riot? The Garden House in perspective', a broadsheet published a week after the event by the University Socialist Society and others (copy in SJCA, CC17.5.1).

[58] D. J. Griffiths to Mansergh, 28 Feb. 1972, conveying the text of a motion to this effect passed at a recent meeting of the JCR.

[59] GAC, min. 7 of 16 Feb. 1970: SOC.3.3c.

[60] 'if it were as large as 100, it would only be 1 per cent' (§76).

both the Lents and the Mays, in order to retain the lowest (thirteenth) place on the river a scratch crew of Fellows (helped along by some class-unconscious undergraduates) offered themselves as propitiatory sacrifice in the Mays and for their pains finished up as sixth boat (it might have been 1870), and against the Buccaneers G. R. G. Keeble and D. H. Quinney put on 256 for the second wicket.

Later that year, on the night of 21–2 November, the Sit-in infection entered the College at its weakest spot, the Cripps JCR, 'for abolishment of guest hours' in the words of the report on the incident supplied by the Head Porter, Bob Fuller. About forty 'sitters' and five ladies were present and stated that they would be staying all night, Fuller recorded. 'WITH R. PECK ONE OF THE NIGHT PORTERS', he continued,

> I STAYED OUTSIDE OF THE JCR TO SEE THINGS REMAINED ORDERLY BY THIS TIME ABOUT 100 STUDENTS MOSTLY FROM THE RUGBY CLUB AND BOAT CLUB SOME WITH STINK BOMBS OFFERED ME THEIR SERVICES TO REMOVE THE SITTERS (THIS WAS DECLINED) AT 0200 HRS I ENTERED THE JCR ASKING ALL LADIES TO LEAVE, LADIES OUT OF COLLEGE BY 2AM, I LEFT ALSO 13 STUDENTS MR DINGWALL THEN TOLD ME HE WANTED TO KNOW WHERE THE DEAN MR BAMBROUGH WAS ALSO THE TUTORS AFTER BEING TOLD IN BED AT THAT TIME OF THE MORNING (...) THE SIT IN ENDED AT 0225 WHEN THE 5 LADIES LEFT BY CRIPPS LODGE.[61]

For those twenty-five illicit minutes the Dean found five undergraduates principally responsible and fined them 50p apiece. The five of course appealed to the Disciplinary Committee, thereby providing it with its first piece of business, whereupon the punishment was confirmed. On being reminded that on accepting a place at the College they had contractually bound themselves also to accept its rules, the appellants responded in their newsletter by inviting readers to

> Cast your mind back. You were offered a place in a letter which made no mention of any petty or arbitrary rules. It merely offered you the chance of pursuing your education in this College. It did not tell you that they were going to go on treating you like a schoolboy who mustn't say boo to teacher. It didn't tell you that an 'academic community' is a pretty exclusive club which counts you out, where you're only a junior member who has to obey any capricious rule somebody else makes for you. That's a funny sort of contract.[62]

As Devlin would paraphrase the question: 'If the University is a society, why are the rules not made by all the members?'

No JCR Committee, least of all one capable of spawning something called the 'Direct Action Sub-committee' (a concept worthy of Peter Simple's column

---

[61] SJCA, Arch.2.4.
[62] *St John's Left Newsletter*, 18 Feb. 1971.

in a daily paper which few of them would have admitted to having read)[63] could hope to contain the impatience of those of its constituents with questions such as these. One of them, indeed, the Secretary of the JCR Committee no less, had already been rebuked for claiming the Committee's sanction for a referendum on Guest hours without reference to the sub-committee and failing to provide the necessary paperwork.[64] Meanwhile two things happened. One was the JCR Committee's creation of sub-committees at a rate that not even the College Council could aspire to.[65] The other was the arrival of a tribe of devout observers who, having demanded entrance to JCR meetings and been denied it, entered anyway[66] and stayed in single figures as the representatives of a very English sort of insurrection, in a parody of a parish meeting sitting sadly at the back while in the arena the senatorial aristocracy gravely debated such issues as the 1970 South African Cricket tour, abolition of the 'incomprehensible grace' at first and second Halls, the 'greater democratisation and accountability of the May Ball Committee' (March 1972), the provision of soft lavatory paper and the insufficiency of the laundry room's supply of left-handed irons. Hence, as Colin Bertram would remark twenty years later: 'We never had a riot in the College.'[67]

The JCR Committee was in choppy water, and, as its judicious response to the Garden House fracas indicated, knew it.[68] As the foaming radicals ridiculed its procedures as social democratic posturings, the undergraduates on the Consultative Committee were asking why they were being kept waiting for copies of the Notes on the Accounts prepared 'for Fellows of the College only'.[69] (Of the Master's promise to investigate the complaint nothing further was heard.) Three months later the Governing Body rejected the Consultative Committee's proposal to remove the word 'male' from the Guest Hour rules. In the following year a committee was appointed under the chairmanship of the President (J. A. Crook) to consider the issue of junior member representation, which had been first raised in early 1969. But the doctrine ultimately devised by the JCRC's 'Constitutional Commission', of rule by Open or General meeting,[70] ensured that it would come to little or nothing. For just as the

[63] SJCA, CC17.4. JCRC, min. 12 of 23 Nov. 1970, rebuking someone (unnamed) for having claimed this sub-committee's approval of the recent sit-in, juxtaposed to min. 13 concerning the price of JCR Christmas cards.

[64] JCRC, min. 9 of 4 Dec. 1969.

[65] E.g. mins. 4, 5, 7 of 24 Feb. 1970.

[66] 'This decision [not to admit them] was then conveyed to a small group waiting outside in the rain. Undeterred by the decision they invited themselves in to seek an explanation for the decision. Official business was halted at this point, until they condescended to leave the meeting': min. 5 of 2 Feb. 1970. From 16 February 1970 their presence was recorded without further explanation.

[67] Speech at eightieth birthday dinner, 27 Dec. 1991.

[68] 'While sympathizing with the motives behind last Friday's demonstration, [the Committee] deplores its violent nature': min. 25 of 16 Feb. 1970.

[69] *John's Left Newsletter*, 21 Feb. 1970; SJMC, min. 2 of 21 Jan. 1970; GB, 8 May 1970.

[70] 'The JCRC will no longer make policy decisions, but will execute mandates given to it by the general meetings': JCRC, min. 6(e) of 19 Nov. 1973; 'The New Constitution – What's It All About?', Oct. 1974.

practice of 'mandation' had paralysed the process towards the abolition of guest hours, so too did its spectre, defined by that committee as the 'very observable' danger that the JCRC 'might at any moment so change as to become a body wholly subject to mandate by majority votes of an "open meeting".'[71] Of this danger more than one example had already been provided.[72] And the evidence continued to accumulate. In March 1972 thirty people attended a gathering that committed the College to financial support for a university-wide 'Open Union' (later Cambridge Student Union: CSU) and to denunciation of the proctorial body. Two years later, a motion to picket the University of Essex displaying the 'John's Open Meeting Banner' was approved by 9 votes to 5 with 16 abstentions, only for it then to be discovered that no such banner existed.[73] Four years after that, a further attempt, based on the contention that the right of junior members to 'effective participation in the decision-making process of the College Community, in so far as those decisions directly concern them', was 'embodied in the constitution of the College' (to wit, Statute I), failed to get airborne.[74]

In consequence, representation was achieved only in its most dilute form, namely by the presence of junior members at the Council's discussion of recommendations of the joint committee, and the bemused JCR President resumed his search for the precise whereabouts of Johnian power and influence. With the assistance of his opposite numbers in other colleges, by November 1974 he had concluded that what was required was either binding decisions by the Consultative Committee (which would prevent a repetition of the May 1970 reverse), or, alternatively, one or two voting junior members of the College Council and the Governing Body. Meanwhile, in order to ease the way there should be 'Open Halls', with 'Fellows and students sitting together' and Fellows' wives should be invited to JCR events.[75]

As an alternative to bodies, rules and representation, the reversion to human remedies is notable. For life went on, with the evidence of the *Eagle* for what it is worth, providing a rather different impression from that of the JCRC minutes – though even there signs of finer instincts were occasionally evident.[76] Throughout these years, not least when the JCR itself was out of funds, the regularity of contributions to the Porters' Fund revealed a nicely calculated blend of

[71] Report of the Committee Appointed under CM, 2542/7, received 9 Dec. 1971 (CM, 2548/5), §5(c)(iii).

[72] E.g. Open Meeting pressure for '50% voting Junior Member representation on the College Council': JCRC, 23 Nov. 1971, min. 13 (considered inappropriate by the JCRC since the matter of representation was currently under consideration by the Council).

[73] JCRC, 6 Mar. 1972, min. 11; Open Meeting, 22 Apr. 1974, item 6.

[74] SJMC, 7 Mar. 1978, min. 8; 25 Apr. 1978, min. 4 (The 'question of representation of junior members at meetings of College Council was discussed and Mr Morely [*recte* (D.) Morley, President of JCR] promised that the JCRC would bring forward proposals for consideration'). The rest is silence.

[75] JCRC, 19 Nov. 1974, min. 7. Concern at the 'lamentable lack of communication and contact between Senior and Junior Members' had been expressed in min. 14 of 15 Feb. 1971.

[76] E.g. introduction of black swans to the Cam; the donation of the fee from University Challenge to the family of a recently incapacitated College bricklayer: JCRC, 24 Feb. 1970, min. 14; 31 May 1972, min. 7 (cf. CM, 2543/27).

prudence and generosity. Thanks largely to the JCR Committee, 'St John's can rarely have been such a pleasant place to live in as it is now', the junior editor enthused in 1970. 'With the liberality of the rules now so much part and parcel of our lives here it is sometimes difficult to credit that it could ever have been different.'[77] The juxtaposition in the next number of Julian Browning's yielding Firbank- or Beaton-like contribution ('There was little correspondence worth reading in Soraya Pacini's escritoire, but Lysander, with unusual consistency, was leaving no envelope unopened') to that of the remorseless R. W. J. Dingwall, impresario-in-chief of the recent Sit-in ('This period has seen the statement of fundamental conflicts of ideology') catches the contrast admirably.[78] 'You get a definite sense of satisfaction with the *status quo*', the next junior editor remarked in January 1972, instancing the 'handful of people' at the Great Sit-in and popular revolt against a proposal to affiliate or contribute to CSU. 'Or perhaps the college is just becoming bored with politics.'[79] Even so, as the then senior editor (the present writer) observed in his turn, the spirit of grim sanctimony was still abroad: 'The chilling evocation of "College spirit" receives the welcome it deserves.'[80] One manifestation of this in the first half of 1974 was the relegation of the JCRC's senior members to the end of the list of those attending its meetings: the rather pitiful protest of a Secretary whose *Eagle* editorial remains as an impotent expression of exasperation at the constricting effect of the College's 'revered "academic and sporting traditions", its hallowed "statutes".'[81] The Committee's high-minded action in depriving its Senior Treasurer of authority to sign their cheques had the unfortunate consequence of an unsettled account with the telephone company, and in consequence no public phones for junior members throughout the following year.[82]

It was the relief that it afforded from all this that made the Cripps bar saga such a welcome diversion. By 1972–3 the bar that had started as a cupboard in the corner of the JCR offering a choice of sherry or port (by contrast with the buttery opposite Hall in which sherry, beer, boot polish and even corn flakes were available) had in a single year converted a £300 profit into a £450 loss (8 October 1973) – and was fast developing into a hostelry with the unusual distinction of losing more money the longer it stayed open. It was also established as a symbol of junior member independence and testimony to the truth of the proposition that not even good undiscounted A level scores provide any

[77] *Eagle* lxiv (1970–71), 48 (K. C. B. Hutcheson).

[78] 'Fans folded in the shade' *or* 'The unlikely prospect – a tale for graduates', *Eagle* lxiv, 127–9; 'Retrospective', 129–31.

[79] *Eagle* lxv (1972–3), 2 (S. Magee); JCRC, 19 Oct. 1970, min. 11; 26 Oct. 1970, min. 4(i); 23 Nov. 1970, min. 16.

[80] 'What is now axiomatic is that no College may be permitted to lag behind King's College in its implementation of an advanced educational programme. *Pietas*, like leg-pulling, is proscribed': *Eagle* lxvi (1974), 2.

[81] '"Statutes" and "standards" are merely a disposable mystique which hinders us from resuscitating our living tradition': *Eagle* lxvii, no. 283 (1975), 2 (F. Hodcroft). For the JCRC's 'strong feeling' that the statutes preventing subsidization of food costs 'ought to be abolished until the level of student grants is revised', min. 5 of 15 Mar. 1974.

[82] Junior Treasurer, JCRC (V. K. Cross) to Mansergh, 2 Feb. 1972 (attachment to CM, 2552/20). Cf. JCRC, 7 Oct. 1974, min. 3.

indication of ability to run a pub. To problems of forged chits and finding the rent to pay the Steward, during the next two years was added the discovery that an agreement had been signed by the committee's predecessors committing them to purchase almost 173,000 pints of beer over a six-year period, as well as problems associated with the damage and loss of certain 'pleasure machines' (hired exclusively for the playing of pin-ball and electric ping-pong). Even so, and even despite the still outstanding debt to the brewers,[83] by February 1975 the bar was said to be making a profit and, despite the unwelcome discovery of an unpaid newspaper bill of almost £1,000, in 1976–7 was heaving with customers. Unfortunately, however, many of these had nothing to do with the College and with some of them wielding bicycle chains the Cripps bar now represented a risk to domestic safety as well as to the Steward's licence. Further deficits in 1978 and 1979 led to the threat in the Steward's Audit Note of disestablishment in the event of any recurrence.[84]

In May 1973 the Governing Body had discussed co-residence again, with this time the benefit of a focused and cogent paper on the subject by the JCR President, N. A. Burton, 'Co-residence in Relation to St John's College', signifying an interest in junior member opinion unimaginable four years earlier. By further contrast, on this occasion there was no input at all by the Senior Tutor, J. C. Hall (who had succeeded Bertram in October 1972) informing the Master that the Tutors preferred not to submit a paper.[85] In fact, although again there was no motion to vote on, it was by then evident that a majority of both the Tutors and the Fellowship at large were in favour of change and that the earlier sense of heady anticipation was giving way to one of boredom.

There was more than a hint of that about the title of an article on the subject in the 1976 *Eagle*.[86] Whereas, as an additional pro-proctor, five years earlier the present writer had spent time in the vicinity of the barricades, disarming the grimly axe-wielding, Hampstead-dwelling daughters of bishops and merchant bankers, returning now as Senior Proctor he found all the intensity of that time strangely vaporized, the sulphurous atmosphere dispersed, and the President of the Student Union willing to agree to an annual cricket match (mixed of course) against the ancient enemy. He might even have supposed that the danger had passed. With only three of the old men's colleges having 'gone mixed', others may have thought as much. If so, they deluded themselves. In fact, amongst other men-only colleges the race was on and it was one for the swift, unhampered now by strident radicals and their demands. As Jeffery asked, with at least three-fifths of its entry coming from mixed state schools and in 1975 one-third of those mixed comprehensives, could St John's afford to stand aloof? These were questions of concern not just to the Tutors.

In Boys Smith's last year the Educational Needs Committee had promoted discussion of teaching methods amongst Fellows. By the following year junior

---

[83] JCRC, min. of 9 Oct. 1975.

[84] C19.52, 53.

[85] Letter of 14 May 1973. In the previous month Mansergh had rejected his proposal simply to recirculate Bertram's 1969 material: SJCA, STF 2007/5.

[86] Keith Jeffery, '... not co-residence again', *Eagle* lxvii, no. 284 (1976), 39–41.

members were seeking to go further and investigate Admissions Policy, hitherto a sacrosanct tutorial preserve. At its February 1970 meeting the Consultative Committee discussed three aspects of this: the range of schools from which the College was recruiting; and the related issues of third-year sixth forms and the Colleges' Joint Examination (CJE: originally the Scholarship examination, by now a hybrid affair also used for entrance purposes). This interest coincided with an enquiry by a committee chaired by Prof. J. H. Horlock, Fellow of St John's, and its recommendation that henceforth the primary purpose of the CJE be 'to select candidates for admission, with selection for awards as a secondary purpose', thereby reversing the established St John's position as enunciated by Bertram, namely, to rely on A levels 'in maximum degree' for pensioner entry and to maintain the Open Scholarship examination 'for the encouragement of the highest standards'. While recording the College's 'gratefulness' to Horlock and his committee, therefore, and assisted by some truly challenging logic, St John's wanted it to be known that the proposal to abandon those standards was anathema.[87]

But in this as in the matter of co-residence, again Bertram and his like-minded successor found themselves left behind by the tide of things which swept single-sex colleges and open scholarships away together. By the end of the 1970s the CJE had become a scholarship examination for entrance purposes and was well on its way to total extinction in favour of the then gold-standard A level. The colleges readiest to divest themselves of their obligations to their scholarship groups were equally prepared to disregard more recent agreements to form an orderly queue to admit women. In all, while faithful St John's, doggedly clinging to its ancient covenants, brought up the rear, self-interest proved supreme.[88] All in all, Mansergh proved himself a great Fabian tactician. A distinguished lawn-tennis player in his youth and middle years, with his heavily spun backhand chopped high and deep into the undergraduates' half of the court, he proved devastating at exploiting the inveterate tendency of headlong youth to rush the net while facing the sun. Despite the interminable reference hither and thither of proposals for change, by the end of his Mastership the only one of any substance to have been proceeded with was for the removal of the requirement to wear gowns in Chapel.[89] As his obituarist observed, 'the seventies were not easy years and the qualities of liberal humanity and fair-minded tolerance that were Mansergh's served his college peculiarly well: interests *were* reconciled; the college *was* held together while solutions were found.'[90] And during his decade, although events abroad may have made colleges shiver as

---

[87] 'Some able dons reach the House of Lords, but many dons never do. That is no reason why none should or that the House of Lords should be abolished! The argument over Entrance Scholarships seems to us somewhat comparable': G. C. L. Bertram, 'St. John's Comments on Horlock II, paragraph by paragraph', §7 (SJCA, STF 2008/1); CM, 2549/5 (18 Dec. 1971).

[88] Linehan, 'Piam in memoriam', 77–8; Brooke, *History of the University of Cambridge*, IV. 531.

[89] CM, 2510/5 (on the recommendation of the Dean), 27 Jun. 1970.

[90] D. Harkness, *PBA* lxxxii (1993), 426–7. See also *ODNB* (R. Hyam) and K. Jeffery, *Dictionary of Irish Biography* (Cambridge, 2009).

they peered into the abyss, at St John's at least no fiercer display of fervour and commitment was experienced than the scalding Commemoration Sermon of 1977 in which Guy Lee poured coals of fire upon Dean Basil Hall's proposal to tamper with the recitation in Chapel of the roll of benefactors on the Sunday nearest the Feast of St John ante Portam Latinam.[91]

2. CO-RESIDENCE AND CAREFULNESS: THE HINSLEY YEARS

'But, er, there is, er, no hurry', Mansergh would reassure guests towards the end of a College feast when reminding them of the availablity of further refreshment in the Combination Room. As a matter of fact, however, increasingly there was, and by 1979, when the bloodhound was replaced in the Lodge by a terrier, a sense even of urgency was beginning to permeate the College. The retirement of the scion of the Anglo-Irish gentry and his replacement by the son of a wagoner 'at the coal department of the Walsall Cooperative Society' (as the Admissions Register had listed him in 1937), a boy whose headmaster at Queen Mary's Grammar School had described as coming from a 'rather starved home' with 'no cultural background save what we have been able to give him', signalled a sudden change at least of gear. 'Fasten your seat belts', F. H. Hinsley advised members of the Council as he took the chair for his first meeting as Master.[92]

Not that Harry Hinsley was a hurrier by nature. Inexorable rather, he had won an entrance Exhibition in December 1936. With a First in Part I History to his credit and just a fortnight after moving into his first College room, in October 1939 the wagoner's son was recruited on Charlesworth's recommendation to the GCCS (Government Code and Cipher School), predecessor of GCHQ, at Bletchley Park's naval section. Here the third-year undergraduate[93] soon established himself as 'the leading expert on the decryption and analysis of German wireless traffic, and, particularly after the capture of German Enigma

[91] 'This noble roll of names, however, has lately been found a stone of stumbling and a rock of offence in our neo-Gothic Zion. Some have even suggested that it should no longer be read. The young, we are told, find it dull; and the young, as a certain Provost has revealed to us, are wiser than their elders': *Eagle* lxviii, no. 286 (1978), 4–5. Described by Dr Seedy (an eighteenth-century visitor to the twentieth) as 'the finest I have heard in Chapel (…). The Other Dean and his whole Committee for Publick Prayer anathematized and comminated by the Librarian': 'The Seedy Chronicles', ibid., 22.

[92] A. E. Clark to Boys Smith, 3 Dec. 1936: Tut. file/Hinsley, F. H. In a recorded interview with Jonathan Steinberg near the end of his life (Nov. 1991), from which other unattributed material in what follows is derived, Hinsley described himself as born into 'pretty low, poor circumstances', his father as a 'labourer', his mother as engaged in domestic work (school-cleaning) and his first home as 'pretty well a slum'. According to family legend, he regularly cycled from Walsall to Cambridge at the start and end of every term. Personal recollection.

[93] Not second-year, as stated by R. T. B. Langhorne, *PBA* cxx (2003) [obit.], 264, *q.v.*, and *ODNB*. See also H. Sebag-Montefiore, *Enigma: The Battle for the Code* (London, 2000).

code machines and materials, which allowed their settings to be broken, played a vital role in supplying the Admiralty with crucial intelligence analysis derived from Admiral Doenitz's signals.' Known at Bletchley as 'the Cardinal', by the end of 1939 he was, in his own words, 'the leading expert outside Germany on the wireless organization of the German Navy'.[94] His was a good war. Wearing his first suit, purchased from Burberry ('a *be*spoke suit, very smart it was'), and with Peter Laslett, his Johnian senior by two years, carrying his bag – and how cruelly deep those two years of juniority must have cut – in late 1943 the traffic analyst was sent to liaise with the U. S. Navy in Washington. In complementary ways this was a seminal experience, for both Hinsley and his bagman. Dispensed by war-time regulations from the requirement to complete his tripos, in May 1944 he was elected to a Research Fellowship. Before the end of the year he was enquiring whether that promotion might be combinable with election as a Member of Parliament.[95]

In the thirty-five years since his return from Bletchley, Hinsley had come to enjoy the reputation of a Fellow whose interventions at meetings of the Governing Body were frequently memorable and often lengthy. After one virtuoso performance he sought to placate Dean Bezzant with the explanation that the discursiveness of his comments had had to do with his stopped watch. 'It's not a watch you need, Harry', Bezzant responded. 'It's a calendar.' He always had a view to express. Thus 'the discussion' of R. W. Southern's paper on the 'Letters of Heloïse and Abelard' at the College History Society was 'enlivened by Mr Hinsley's unorthodox thesis that the affair never became as Platonic as history would have us believe.'[96] Another tale, to the truth of which the present writer can testify, belongs to the day in November 1967 when Hinsley declared at lunch that Prime Minister Wilson would never devalue the pound: 'He simply wouldn't dare, my boy.' The effect was electric. Clutching their wallets, the Fellows as one made for their branches of Barclays and Lloyds to save what they could from the wreckage. Later that day the pound was devalued. While Hinsley remained confident in his predictions, and was indeed at his best before an undergraduate or graduate audience, the common opinion of his colleagues was that he was perhaps cannier at anticipating the past than the future.

No doubt, thoughts such as these were in the minds of at least some of those as they entered the Chapel on 16 November 1978 to elect a successor to Mansergh. Three days before, the final straw-vote in the Combination Room had placed Hinsley third amongst four contestants with less than a quarter of the vote. Now, with 103 Fellows present, there ensued a classic play-off. Starting this time second of four (but only just), by the narrowest of margins Hinsley emerged the victor at the third ballot before, as President, memorably declaring

---

[94] 'This may sound an arrogant claim, but it does not amount to much': F. H. Hinsley, 'BP, Admiralty, and naval Enigma', in F. H. Hinsley and A. Stripp (eds.), *Codebreakers: The Inside Story of Bletchley Park* (Oxford, 1993), 77.

[95] Letter to S. J. Bailey, 6 Dec. 1944: SJCA, TU22/Hinsley, F. H. As an undergraduate he had intervened occasionally in Union Society debates: *CR* lix (1937–8), 37–8, 58 (stressing 'the importance of youth in the preservation of England's glory'), lx (1938–9), 255, 276.

[96] *Eagle* lvi (1954–5), 221.

the election of 'me' and, for clarification, 'myself' as Master. This time there was no report in the *Guardian* from its Science correspondent.

At his first Council meeting in July 1979 the new Master gave notice that the ruminative browsings of his predecessor's reign were a thing of the past. Meetings would now begin at four because since time immemorial that had been the hour before which smoking was not allowed, and Hinsley was an impenitent pipe-smoker. As Thatcher's contemporary and her equal in determination to prune away the lushness of the previous decade, he was also rather famously economical, parsimonious even. 'Another £20 down the drain', he lamented as a third opinion on a Research Fellowship dissertation was consigned to the waste paper basket. 'Would Dr Linehan please put *half* a scuttle of coal on the fire', he enquired at a Council meeting one freezing and candle-less December afternoon early in his pontificate. Hinsley's 'powers as an interpreter of decrypts were unrivalled and were based on an ability to sense that something unusual was afoot from the tiniest clues', it has been said of him.[97] Likewise with respect to the spending of money. In the spring of 1981, as K. G. Budden was preparing the Commemoration Sermon in which he would predict that in 2981 the reading out of the list of benefactors would take 'at least two hours' to complete,[98] the Council established an Economies Committee because, with draft budgets for 1981/2 showing anticipated deficits of £20,000 on the Tuition account and £58,000 on Internal Revenue, 'it had become clear that, beginning in July 1981, government economies were going to prevent both the College Fee and the Student maintenance grant from keeping pace with inflation'.[99] This was a situation that Hinsley rather relished. After all, here was a man who had traversed Europe in the 1939 Long Vac. on just £5. What appealed to him rather less, but had to come first, was the unfinished business of co-residence.

That question was the Governing Body's first item of business for the year 1980–81. On 9 October it assembled to debate yet again and to vote on 'the draft Amending Statute permitting the admission of women to membership of the College'. As, for the last time perhaps, Johnian freshmen trudged off to the field with only drop goals in mind, the Secretary of the Council (an astronomer and normally, therefore, one of the more accurate members of the Fellowship) and his co-teller attempted to count the in some cases palsied hands of the eighty-seven standing (or almost standing) Fellows present, and delivered the result to the (non-voting) Master. Carried, the Master declared, by 57 to 28: carried therefore by the necessary two-thirds majority, but *only just*, so that after eleven years, and at the third attempt, the lengthy debate was concluded.

Or was it? The worsted minority thought not. In the gloaming of Second Court they stood in a fairy ring, counting one another, and proving what they had already suspected: that there were twenty-*nine* of them.[100] As was stated

---

[97] Langhorne, *PBA*, 264.

[98] *Eagle* lxix, no. 290 (1982), 4. Cf. GEDD, 5 May 1981: 'He told us the list of benefactors in a thousand years time would take *3* hours to read.'

[99] CM, 2767/7(a), 5 Mar. 1981.

[100] As was stated in a subsequent enquiry by the Master (which also revealed an 'understandable' 'confusion' between one Fellow who was marked absent though present and another marked present although absent) 'there might be substance in [that]

thereafter, conducting a count in an unlit room on an autumn afternoon was not as easy as it sounded. Indeed, as the second teller observed, it is 'extremely difficult to count a random scatter of Fellows in assorted shapes and sizes, some partly hidden behind others, some grimacing, some smirking, some mouthing figures themselves.' As Hinsley himself insisted, often: 'You see my difficulty.' In short, and as a matter of fact, the motion had failed.

Or had it? Amongst its supporters there were those who insisted that, since disagreement had not been voiced at the meeting, the published result must stand. There was, after all, still another statutory hurdle to be cleared, namely another vote and approval by the same majority at a second meeting to be held within thirty days.

Or was there? Was there even the need for two meetings? As the Senior Bursar (C. M. P. Johnson) noted in a draft document ('Procedure for amending College statutes'), precedent was inconclusive. But be that as it may, as the second teller observed, there was danger here of the College making itself a laughing-stock. 'Whether an error was made may be an interesting open question for future College historians', one of the fifty-seven (if it really *was* fifty-seven) wrote: 'But I do not see how the matter can be reopened now.'[101]

In advance of the November meeting statistics circulated showing unmixed St John's lying seventeenth out of twenty-four amongst the colleges in terms of attractiveness to the nation's sixth-formers.[102] Of this information, as also of what was to follow, captious interpretation was widespread. On the one hand it was again stressed that there was no need for hurry ('the matter is not urgent. [...] If not carried now it can, and no doubt will be raised again'), and that 'it would be difficult to point to an institution of comparable size where education has contributed more to the public well-being' and 'the maintenance and advancement of our civilisation'; to say nothing of the benefits to persons of undergraduate age of 'leaving experimentation with sexuality and all that goes with it to a later stage.'[103] To which the majority riposted that about three-quarters of the College's teaching Fellows, representing 'a very substantial majority of those Fellows most closely concerned with College teaching', had indicated otherwise.[104] In the event, again there was confusion, although not

claim': memo. dated 19 Jan. 1981: M4. *Stop Press* (the undergraduate newspaper) of 18 October reported the voting as 56–28 without mention of any 'confusion'.

[101] P. Goddard to Master, 9 Oct. 1980: M4. And to their credit, the Adullamites – '*everyone* who was in distress (...) and *everyone* who was *discontented*' (1 Samuel 22:2) – agreed, choosing not to go to the Visitor but to remain in their cave instead. Even so, there were those intent on making roaring noises – or at least who said that they were.

[102] With 2.19 applicants per place, with the most popular (Churchill) enjoying 4.63 and the average at 2.7. The fact that mixed Trinity lay in eighteenth position was the only feature of the figures to provide universal satisfaction in St John's.

[103] G. C. Evans, J. C. Hall, A. A. Macintosh, 'Admission of Women to the College', 3 Nov. 1980: M4. According to the student newspaper, which had much fun with this manifesto, 'those in favour have changed the voting procedure so that everyone will have to stand up to register his vote', which would 'prove difficult for one Emeritus Professor who will be attending on a stretcher': *Stop Press with Varsity*, 8 Nov. 1980, 9.

[104] E. D. James and 28 others, 'Admission of Women to the College', 10 Nov. 1980: M4.

such as to vitiate the result.[105] On the previous day the undergraduates, who were having rather greater success with their voting procedures, had voted 165 to 122 in favour of change, with 9 abstentions.[106] As the editor of *Scan*, B. Andradi, remarked, as well as recording that several Fellows had been 'very upset' at the decision and one of them 'almost in tears': 'It is interesting to note that a greater percentage of fellows seems to be in favour of co-residence than junior members of the College.'[107] The Great Cause was showing signs of having entered its post-apostolic period. Sensing that history had passed the place by, the active sort of junior members consoled themselves by resuming responsibility for the wider world and agreeing (by 5 votes to 3) to delate one of their number to the Dean for forging chits in the Cripps bar. As well as pressing for the transfer of the College's account from Barclays in view of the bank's unsoundness on South Africa, in the course of 1978 the JCRC agreed, *nem. con.*, to send Mr Brezhnev (the leader of the Soviet Union) a telegram scolding him for contravening human rights but to spare President Carter like censure in respect of the United States administration's support for the Nicaraguan and Paraguayan regimes (motion defeated by 11 to 12 with 2 abstentions).[108] By now even Glyn Daniel was off the boil. On learning from Norman Henry of the 9 October outcome, he had written:

> The real thing is that I am no longer a passionate advocate of women's admission but can see no reason why it should not happen. So my vote must be cast for the admission of women.[109] I particularly want women fellows and I want especially to [*sic*] old toads who decline to have women in on Saturdays and Sundays![110]

There was always a sense of balance about Daniel's reports of matters of high import.[111] 'What goings on but at least at long last it has happened', he remarked of the narrowness of the outcome; then, four days later, having dined in in order to view Michael Noakes's portrait of Hinsley: 'very good but how sad that he

---

[105] Voting was done by card, but the Secretary of the Council, an opponent of the motion, first placed his own card on the wrong pile and then failed to transfer it to the other before the result of the vote was declared as 59 to 28. But even with an outcome of 58–29 the motion would have had a sufficient majority. At the Governing Body of 21 May 1981 one motion confirming the November voting to have been as declared (59–28) was passed by 25 votes to 24, and another amending the record of the voting at the October meeting as 57–29 was by agreement withdrawn.

[106] President of JCR (R. Scarlett-Smith) to Master, 12 Nov. 1980.

[107] *Scan*, Nov. 1980 (U3), giving the JCR referendum figures as 190–120.

[108] JCRC, mins. 780504, 780207, 780708.

[109] In fact he was absent from both votes.

[110] GEDD, 9 Oct. 1980: 'Obviously NH thought I was on his side because he referred to "us".' Not so: 'Glyn Daniel rang me up from Exeter to know the result; if he had been here that would have settled it against us': Henry to G. A. Reid, 10 Oct. 1980.

[111] Regarding the murder of Lord Mountbatten, for example ('the most hideous day in the Irish terrorist war … the hideous horror of it and the senselessness'): 'We were all shocked by the news but recovered to take Olaf Pedersen out to dinner in Strudels …: very good smoked mackerel and his veal dish in orange sauce; ½ carafe of white wine and bottle of Bull's Blood': GEDD, 28 Aug. 1979.

is our Master!'[112] Meanwhile, Hinsley himself characteristically informed the *Times* that he was 'neither pleased nor displeased' at the outcome. 'Suffused as usual with enthusiasm for the future', commented one wry Oxford observer of the Cambridge scene.[113] So finally St John's made the break, just ahead of Magdalene and Peterhouse.

On 1 October 1981 Hinsley was elected Vice-Chancellor and on the same day the first woman member of the College, Dr K. M. Wheeler, was admitted to the Fellowship together with nine female graduate students. Twelve months later these were followed by the first contingent of women undergraduates, forty-four in all, six the daughters of Johnian fathers. 'Had Daphne been a boy she would naturally have come to John's', Daphne's OJ father had written in 1939.[114] Naturally – though it would have come as something to a surprise to the undergraduate *enragés* as they celebrated their victory over the forces of darkness that amongst the earliest generations of ladies admitted after 1982 were the grand-daughters of Fellows who had been most conspicuous in their opposition to change.[115] In the interim the Fellowship prepared itself for the change of life for which it had opted, immersing itself in discussion of the number of full-length mirrors that the ladies would require (a vaguely unhealthy obsession amongst academic males almost everywhere in these years).[116] On arrival, however, the ladies themselves got down to essentials, such as arranging netball practice and humouring the Head Porter, Bob Fuller, whose public expressions of dismay at their admission to the place were not to everyone's taste.[117] The diary and correspondence of one of them who, 'as a young woman who had grown up in rural Devon [had] never been on a train and never even heard of profiteroles',[118] came up to read Anglo-Saxon, Norse and Celtic in 1985, reveals both how large a step into the unknown that was for some of them and how soon they settled in, being impressed by the fineness of the male Johnian mind, to the extent indeed of marrying one: a development adding further layers of complexity to the task of the College's dynastic historian.[119] As else-

---

[112] GEDD, 13 and 17 Nov. 1980.

[113] Angus Macintyre to the author, undated postcard. For a comparable botched vote on the issue at Macintyre's own college nine years earlier, see Brockliss, *Magdalen College Oxford*, 785–6.

[114] Above, p. 592.

[115] See Appendix 4.

[116] E.g. Jones, *Balliol College*, 313; R. Darwall-Smith, *A History of University College Oxford* (Oxford, 2008), 515.

[117] In November 1983 the Entertainments Committee agreed 'that the present Head Porter's address to the junior members was now out of all proportion, and that he should be invited to speak for ten minutes before (Matriculation) dinner while sherry was served', and in the following year that his successor 'should not be invited to address the Freshmen in future years'. Fuller's retirement in June 1985 was followed ten months later by his death and a funeral attended by hundreds of College and Cambridge folk: '"Big Bob" remembers' (memoirs), *Eagle* lxx, no. 293 (1985), 18–22; obits., *Eagle* lxxi, no. 294 (1986), 78–81.

[118] Rachel Beckett (*née* Lewis) to the Author, 5 Dec. 2002.

[119] 'I have been in some very enjoyable intellectual conversations', she wrote home after her first week. 'It is lovely to be with such clever people and, although many are cleverer than I am as far as I can judge from their very advanced ways of thinking

where, co-residence boosted numbers at St John's – and not only numbers of women:[120]

Table 2 Numbers of men and women at St John's, 1981–5

	Fellows			Junior Members		
	Men	Women	Total	Men	Women	Total
1981	114	1	115	714	9	723
1982	116	1	117	679	56	735
1983	118	2	120	609	114	723
1984	119	2	121	548	173	721
1985	115	2	117	557	197	754

In the absence of a woman Tutor there was agitation in March 1984, supported by sixty-three of the eighty-two female undergraduates in residence, for a 'female adviser' or 'counsellor', whose counsel, once she had been appointed, was almost never sought.[121] With the appointment of a woman as Tutor from October 1988 and the realization that efficiency was not gender-related, the clamour subsided. By 1987 not only had they got the netball as well as other vigorous activities going, they had made themselves sufficiently indispensable to the place to walk off with all five of the Larmor awards for that year, bestowed, as Larmor had prescribed, upon those junior members 'adjudged most worthy either for intellectual qualifications to be estimated on a wide basis or alternatively in moral conduct and practical activities'.[122] What Larmor himself would have thought of this particular outcome must be left to the imagination. Likewise, the class lists' account of women's academic contribution to the place, about which so much had been heard in recent years, lies beyond the limits of this volume.

But that was as far as change was going to go. Partly on the grounds of the 'definite educational value' to them of 'greater responsibility for the administration of the College community', in 1972 the JCR Committee's grandiloquent, social-democrat-flavoured blueprint had stated as its 'long-term aim' the transfer of 'day to day responsibility' for that community 'onto the shoulders of the Junior Members',[123] and at a General Meeting in 1978 its membership had

(they have mostly been to public schools and have very WELL TRAINED minds), they are not awesome and do not make one seem inferior'. 'They are still normal human beings', she conjectured. I am particularly grateful to Rachel Beckett for access to extracts from her diary and letters of this period.

[120] 'Co-residence and application for admission': Senior Tutor's paper for Council, 8 Nov. 1984. J. C. Hall witnessed only the beginning of this process, having retired in the previous September. That year's list contained the College's first 'Ms'.

[121] SJMC, 15 Nov. 1983, min. 4 (Senior Tutor insisting that 'any specifically [*sic!*] female counsellor would have to act largely as a broker for advice'). The counsellor proposal, first made in November 1982, was acceded to in March 1984: SJMC, 16 Nov. 1982, min. 7; CM, 2835/3(b) (15 Mar. 1984).

[122] CMM, 2904/4(d) (14 May 1987), 2925/5. Cf. *Eagle* lxx (1985), 40: 'Team sport in the year 1984/5 has been attended with general success, and the ladies' achievement more than matches that of the gentlemen.'

[123] 'To this extent we *do* question the complete sovereignty of the Senior Members in the government of the College': 'Junior Member representation at the College Council' (SJCA, CC18.1).

committed it to 'campaign for full observer status on the College Council and the Governing Body'. But in view of the extent of post-Devlin lassitude (the motion succeeding by 16 votes to 3), that was the end of the matter.[124] Indeed, as reflected in the title of its manifesto, 'Junior Member Representation *at* the College Council', by 1972 the pass had been sold. The JCR paper of the previous year, which lay behind it, had been headed 'Representation *on* the College Council'. In the copy of this that entered the record, 'on' had been replaced in Mansergh's hand by the eirenic 'at'.[125] Amongst those interested in the matter the theological significance of the correction was well understood. Although by 1978 the JCR's call had reverted to a claim to 'full observer status *on* both the College Council and Governing Body', by then the Johnian dialectic had passed on.

In 1983 the thrilling possibilities of 1978 were briefly revived. There was talk of such exemplars as colleges with 'compulsory observation rights', of claims to 'a right to effective participation in the decision-making process of the College Community', of authority allegedly enshrined in Statute I ('The Foundation of the College shall consist of the Master, the Fellows, and the Scholars') for junior membership of both Council and Governing Body, and, as an interim measure while the statutory implications of all this were being investigated, the concession of entitlement to 'receipt of their full agenda and minutes (including a record of the discussion of unreserved business)'.[126] But none of this cut much ice. By contrast with his predecessor, Hinsley as Master deputed the chairmanship of the Senior and Junior Committee to a distinguished Law Fellow, Prof. S. F. C. Milson.[127] This hands-off policy further defused the issue. In comparison with some earlier proposals, the formula first adumbrated in October 1982 and eventually adopted was as anodyne[128] as the contention that the Senior and Junior Committee 'had an important role to play in the processes of decision making' was optimistic.[129]

[124] SJMC, 21 Oct. 1978, min. 5; CM, 2712/16.

[125] JCRC, min. 780705 (16 Nov. 1978); SJCA, CC18.1 (29 Apr. 1971).

[126] 'Junior Member representation on College decision making bodies', Feb. 1983: attachment to CM 2811/9(a), 17 Feb. 1983.

[127] CM, 2732/13 (30 Jul. 1979). At the Senior and Junior Committee the view was soon expressed that: 'junior members would welcome the presence of the Master at meetings in order to hear the arguments of members': 20 Nov. 1979, min. 4.

[128] CM, 2802/8(d) (SJMC, 12 Oct. 1982, min. 6). The Presidents of the JCR and SBR Committees together with a member of the JCR Committee, ordinarily the Secretary, were to be invited to attend the Council 'whenever the Minutes of the Committee of Senior and Junior Members are to be received, and for the discussion of other items of business which are of direct concern to Junior Members, in particular discussion concerning the amendment of Standing Orders relating to Junior Members. The Master shall, in consultation with the Council, determine whether particular items of business are of direct concern to Junior Members, it being understood that the President of the JCR Committee and the President of the SBR Committee may at any time bring items to the Master's attention': CM, 2815/9 (28 Apr. 1983) [whence Standing Order A.2.4].

[129] Senior Tutor P. Goddard at SJMC, 15 Nov. 1983, min. 3. On 19 May of that year the Governing Body had voted by 30 to 21 in favour of considering a draft standing order to enable the Master to invite Junior Member representatives to the Governing Body 'as observers when he judged that Junior Members had an interest in items on the

A subsequent attempt to gain entry to the Governing Body was repulsed without serious loss.[130]

Indeed, in all important respects bar one (that surest of signifiers, the omission of the definite article before the word 'Council'),[131] by now the torch of radicalism was passing from the Senior and Junior Committee to, of all people, the Tutors. While the female junior members themselves were busy about a female counsellor and vegetarian options in the Buttery Dining Room,[132] even before the first contingent of women had graduated, their Tutors all but unanimously proposed the abolition of the single-sex sharing rule, and the Council, taken by surprise no doubt, concurred.[133] However, the Governing Body was made of sterner stuff and voted the proposal down.[134] In the following year the issue again spluttered briefly into life, before finally going nowhere while undergraduate attention allowed itself to be diverted to the issue of tourists.[135] In 1970 the inconceivability of anything other than same-sex sharing had been regarded as axiomatic and therefore as constituting a diriment impediment to the abolition of guest hours and to interference with 'the traditional life of the College'. Any change designed to permit the accommodation of guests would surely lead all right-minded men to abandon their luxurious room-mates and go to live in lodgings.[136] The Tutors had now turned the domestic syllogism on its head. How far we had come in the last fourteen years. Or had we?[137]

The 1979 Audit Note had threatened closure of the Cripps bar in the event of another deficit there. In 1980, however, the Audit Committee decided otherwise, partly because the JCR Bar Account was *almost* in profit, partly in view

agenda or could be useful by contributing their views.' The Junior Members' representatives were to be asked to prepare a statement of their case, which the Master undertook to incorporate into a paper for the Governing Body. Like other similar proposals of the sort, nothing further was heard of the matter.

[130] SJMC, 28 Feb. 1984, min. 5, noting that its 'more moderate tone' than one previously produced on the subject, gave it 'a greater chance of a favourable reception'.

[131] A seditious and infectious usage fostered by these discussions, which over the next twenty-five years would invade every department of the College. For an early instance (though surely not the first), 'In Council': SJMC, 12 Oct. 1982, min. 2. The whole question urgently requires further study.

[132] SJMC, 15 Nov. 1983, min. 5.

[133] With women in the minority in the second year (when it was, as it remains, customary for undergraduates to share), many, it was contended, 'consequently are and will be in the position of knowing rather few women in their year but a comparatively large number of men', so that 'the prohibition of mixed sharing presents a special difficulty for our women undergraduates': CM, 2835/8 (15 Mar. 1984).

[134] CM, 2836/3(b); GB, 17 May 1984 (proposal defeated 34 to 23); SJCA, SBFG/1980–2000/Rooms/Mixed Sharing.

[135] SJMC, 26 Feb. 1985. Cf. CM, 2856/11b (14 Mar. 1985).

[136] SJCA, STF 2007/16: J. C. H[all], 'Should Guest Hours be Abolished?' 30 Jan. 1970, §§1, 2.

[137] In fact, as the committee appointed to investigate the matter discovered (CM, 2838/4(b), 13(e), the proposal was both impracticable and unwanted: of the 51 per cent of undergraduates who responded to the question asked, only 19 per cent 'thought the present arrangements for sharing in the second year unsatisfactory to any extent': CM, 2848/13(b).

of the 'uncertain state' of the 'parent catering establishment'.[138] Meanwhile, the Senior and Junior Members Committee was being assured that the bar's financial problems 'had now been solved – it was believed forever.'[139] For the moment therefore the sanction was not applied. But the outlook was ominous.

Reporting in May 1981, in the term before women arrived, the Economies Committee looked for savings on the cost of teaching and direction of studies. Introducing the concept of 'half-lecturers' (ideally suited to an age of half-scuttles of coal), the committee recommended a fixed establishment of teaching Fellows; subject to annual review. The Cambridge Colleges Examination (CCE), currently costing the College almost £1,000 per annum, was to be 'self-supporting' and means to be found of transferring the cost of teaching and library items to the Endowment account and of pruning the staff bill, in particular by reducing bedmaker service (here cutting into live tissue as well as confirming something that undergraduates had long suspected: that 'the Committee recognizes that the bed-makers provide an important service for Tutors'). The provision of accommodation for language schools was recommended, as well as bed and breakfast for tourists. In the same spirit the Note to Fellows after the 1981 Audit agreed to 'continue to accept profitable conference bookings even at the price of some inconvenience' and to 'bear in mind' the 'feasibility and cost of using University rooms, particularly in the Divinity School, as an alternative to the building of a new room in College.'[140]

Concern about economies in general combined with anxiety regarding suitable arrangements for the ladies – foreshadowed at the very meeting at which the Cripps bar's 'rather seedy atmosphere' was declared in need of attention.[141] Thus, the days of the old bar were numbered and its closure anticipated in favour of the creation of that 'new room in College' on the site on which it stood. After a series of occasions involving local youths carrying offensive weapons and intervention by the constabulary, interspersed with Rugby Club Black Velvets prior to the Advent Carol Service and riotous Soccer Club evenings resulting in hospitalization, the end came mercifully quickly with the Council concluding that the site was unsuitable for further use as a bar.[142] There were no flowers. The further decision, reached by the Governing Body in May 1982, to raze the old building to the ground and sow the ground with salt before erecting a new one, allowed for a bar to continue to function there for the next two terms, but only under the strict control of the Steward.[143] It also incidentally confirmed the futility of the view expressed some ten years before that, with the restoration of the Second Court and the erection of the Cripps Building, 'the College had seen the last of major building works for some decades to come.'

---

[138] C19.54.

[139] Min. 3 of 18 Nov. 1980 (CM, 2760/7[c]).

[140] CM, 2772/11(b), 28 May 1981; Audit Note, 11 Jan. 1982, §§8, 10.

[141] 'In the long term radical redevelopment was desirable, particularly at a time when the social composition of the College was about to change': SJMC, min. 3 of 18 Nov. 1980.

[142] SJMC, 4 Mar. 1980, min. 1; CM, 2770/6(d) (30 April 1981). The JCR bar closed with a debit balance of almost £6,000: Steward's Note 1980–81 (C19.55).

[143] CM, 2795/13(d) (27 May 1982).

As the Report on the separation of the offices of Junior Bursar and Steward had wearily observed: 'This view was perhaps an over-optimistic one.'[144]

The demise of the Cripps bar, that symbol of student independence, produced a call in *Scan* for 'a smear campaign against the College in the local and national press' as 'the only threat that we can not only execute but that will also frighten the fellows'.[145] Providing a dry run for arguments based on exegesis of Statute I (regarding the entitlement of the College's junior members to a role in its government), another contributor, espousing 'basic democratic principle', alleged 'alienation (and) indirect intimidation' and revived the claim that 'junior member observers should sit on the College Council and Governing Body as of right, subject only to exclusion from reserved business.'[146] Meanwhile, the (Acting) Steward appeared to be in no hurry about finding a barman to run the bar in the brief period before the bulldozers moved in.[147]

There were two aspects to all this. One was the security of the College in general and along its entire perimeter, as evidenced by the need to provide new protection at the front between Chapel Court and its adjacent car park against hooligans associated with the temporary success of Cambridge United football club.[148] The other was the fast-dilapidating state of the Cripps Building. With women about to arrive and the Economies Committee poised to begin work, in February 1981 the Buildings Committee asked for a detailed report to be sent to Humphrey Cripps, copy to the architects requesting their comments, together with an estimate of the cost of repairs that had accrued since 1967.[149] The expense of correcting the 'Cripps outrage' and its catalogue of 'shoddy work' (leaking roofs, faults involving up to 90 per cent of baths and showers, plumbing, electricity, damp), as listed in the Audit Report for 1979–80, was calculated in the following year at about 10 per cent of the cost of a building only fifteen years old.[150] Within weeks of its opening, for example, it had been discovered that, when delivered to the building site, the channel-devices designed to prevent the wiring of the under-floor heating from fusing had been appropriated by the joiners and tacked around the window frames, in consequence of which all the windows had been rendered unopenable and all the wood-block floors needed to be excavated. And now the demolition of the Cripps JCR revealed 'possibly serious faults' in the building's concrete slabs, evidenced by water damage and

---

[144] Report of Committee appointed by CM 2721/6 (15 Mar. 1979).

[145] 'The effects may still be around years after we've left. Saying "Please" to the fellows will not work. We must attack them by threatening the standards of the College – it is our only option.' (12 Feb. 1982; P. Mayne).

[146] 'Torn between the lure of "democratic principle" and the benefits of "efficiency", how far should we go, using what methods?', R. P. McDowell had asked (8 Nov. 1982) and sought an answer by means of a questionnaire entitled 'Student Representation in St John's: the History and the Facts'.

[147] KCC, min. 84.28 (30 Nov. 1984). In the previous summer the Council had concurred with Hinsley regarding the need to resist junior member pressure on the matter: C. M. P. Johnson to Secretary of Council (P. T. Johnstone), 29 Jun. 1984 (Council and GB File 1980–91).

[148] CM, 2877/11 (26 May 1983).

[149] BC, 16 Feb. 1981, min. 4.

[150] Audit Report, 1979–80, §3 (SJCA, CC3.170); 1980–81, §§19–29 (£571,000).

rust stains.[151] 'Because of the detailed design faults which [had] emerged' there, it was accordingly decided to entrust the revision of the building not to Powell and Moya but to Peter Boston of Saunders Boston & Co.[152] Comprising an auditorium which doubles as a venue for bops and basketball, seminar, drawing and music rooms – and of course a bar (but this time under the Steward's management), though no JCR[153] – the new complex was opened by the Visitor on 16 August 1988, three years and four months after the Governing Body's almost unanimous decision to proceed with the work. At a cost of £1.7 million, the Fisher Building was designed as 'a prestige building, and' – as the new Domestic Bursar, Col. Richard Robinson, gave fair warning – 'it should be maintained that way'.[154] Student architectural opinion held it to be 'not a great building but a sensible one. Retiring, perhaps a little modest, apologetic even, its architectural aspirations are not high' – therefore altogether Johnian perhaps: β??α possibly – but of course, hardly worthy to keep company with the Cripps Building itself (that 'extremely distinguished piece of architecture, almost without contemporary peer', never mind its numerous structural peccadilloes).[155]

In 1939 Fisher's name had been thought too Romish to be imposed on what came to be North Court. But even before having a building named after him the College's second and arguably foremost benefactor had been adjudged worthy of celebration. On 8 June 1985 the 450th anniversary of his martyrdom had been commemorated with a service of thanksgiving in the Chapel and an address by Cardinal Basil Hume followed by a party on the Backs for senior and junior as well as old members.[156] In the following month the first all-Johnian wedding was celebrated in the College Chapel.[157]

[151] BC, 24 Oct. 1985, min. 5; 19 Mar. 1986, min. 2 (CM, 1879/9(a), 17 Apr. 1986).

[152] Report of the Committee to Recommend an Architect for the Cripps JCR: CM, 2809/7(c) (19 Jan. 1983). Cf. the altogether up-beat account of the 'magnificent' building in K. Powell, *Powell and Moya: Twentieth Century Architects* (London, 2009), 72–8, with its description of the Fisher Building as 'ungainly'.

[153] Particularly in view of the haven of quiet, calm, TV-less deliberation that it was supposed to provide, at the December 1981 Governing Body the present writer likened the establishment of the JCR alongside the Second Court to the juxtaposition of a nunnery to a barracks. This proved prophetic. No notes regarding the 'considerable misgivings' expressed at this meeting were preserved by Hinsley (see R. T. B. Langhorne, 'The inception of the building', *Eagle* lxxi, no. 295 [1987], 4–5). At the next, in May 1982, the motion was approved by 39 to 15.

[154] SJMC, 28 Apr. 1987, min. 4.

[155] J. Lambert, 'Comment', *Eagle* lxxi, no. 295 (1987), 18–22. Cf. 'Stranger in the College', David Thistlethwaite's brilliantly subversive, perhaps Martin Heidegger-influenced, account (*Eagle* lxviii, no. 288 [1980], 9–16): 'some explanation is due from somewhere to those for whom a year in Cripps is an inexplicably disturbing experience' (9); 'the fact that Cripps has no wall' (9); 'like an essay in which the writer has left out all the punctuation' (13); 'an embassy of the modern movement, a stranger unintroduced' (13); 'a building composed entirely of windows' (14); 'You have one friend, but he doesn't stay long (the armchair has virtually no back to it). You stick to your subject, so the shelves provided will hold all your books' (16); 'gradual replacement of the concept "member" with the concept "student"... so lovingly and conscientiously embodied in the new building' (16).

[156] 'John Fisher, 1469–1535', *Eagle* lxxi, no. 294 (1986), 3–18.

[157] CM, 2855/10(a), 28 Feb. 1985.

By 1979, when Hinsley moved into the Lodge, the College kitchens were in crisis and the six-year-old arrangement with the company contracted as the College's caterers was under huge strain. On top of the revelation in the Audit Committee's Report for 1980–81 of the outgoing Catering Manager's purchase of 'an incredible miscellany of spirits and liqueurs' and the probable 'total loss' (to the tune of almost £20,000) that this represented, the discovery of systematic peculation after the same manager's dismissal in July 1980 resulted in the College's termination of its agreement with the catering company, followed by the initiation of legal proceedings by the company against the College, counteraction by the College, and the discovery of 'massive' losses on the storeman's departure without giving notice, 'having got behind with his record-keeping'. These were practices worthy of the 1880s, with consequences certainly equalling, possibly even exceeding, those associated with 'Tip' Drury and the great cockroach-farming scandal of the 1920s. 'Management has been weak and inadequate', the Audit Committee soberly concluded. A 'degree of formality' was needed in the Steward's dealings with the Manager. Accumulated deficits of £294,000 since 1971–2 were reported on the Kitchen Maintenance Account, and of £327,000 on the Kitchen Reserve Account.[158] At every level control was lacking. The report of the Acting Steward (C. M. P. Johnson) at a meeting of the Kitchen Consultative Committee, that of the twelve gross (1,728) pint glasses bought at the start of term only some three dozen remained, must have fallen on deaf ears.[159] Anyway, this loss was relatively venial. There was a long way back to come. For a College, even a great College, marches on its stomach.

Of all of which one of the consequences, the separation of the Junior Bursarship from the Stewardship, had occurred at the Junior Bursar's request at the very beginning of Hinsley's Mastership.[160] Towards its end, the two offices were recombined, bolted together indeed, and from March 1987 entrusted to Colonel Richard Robinson, the College's first non-academic Domestic Bursar.[161] Never again would its Bursars, Senior or Domestic, bestride the towpath between luncheon and tea *à la* Sir Henry Howard – or even the touchline for that matter. Another change on that front, another rejection of the concept of substantial college office as an amateur occupation, occurred six months into Hinsley's reign when, in a paper on Entrance Awards (the thrust of which, since the two strategies were presented as alternatives, was to sacrifice Entrance Awards rather than admit women), it was noted that all the academically best-performing colleges had both specialist Admissions Tutors and specialist Senior Tutors. In fact, St John's ended up with women members from 1981, an Admissions Tutor from 1985,[162] and, in common with all the other colleges, no entrance examination

---

[158] Audit Report, 1980–81 (C19.55), §16; Steward's Note 1981–2 (K. J. Pascoe); Audit Report, 1981–2, §§50–55.

[159] Min. 80.15 of 6 Jun. 1980.

[160] Langhorne's letter to Mansergh stating the conviction that 'the best interests of the College' were no longer served by his continuing to hold both offices, was dated 7 March 1979: SDF1987/11.

[161] CMM, 2726/6 (7 Jun. 1979), 2887/4(a)(ii) (24 Jul. 1986), 2894/4.

[162] CMM, 2848/6, 2850/3(c), with Dr Malcolm Schofield the first holder of the office.

after 1986.[163] While some things (the loyalty of cockroaches to the kitchens, for example)[164] never changed, the merits of rationalization vied with the need for economies. Calvinist tendencies in unexpected places harmonized happily with the Master's inclinations. The 'unfortunate impression created' (at least amongst junior members) 'by the apparent extravagance of College feasts amid a general climate of austerity' was effective (just) in preventing the addition of another such bacchanal (courtesy of the Cripp's [*sic*] Foundation and planned to include junior members) to the College calendar.[165] Stringency struggled with tradition. The Natural Sciences Fellows were unanimous in rejecting the concept of notional establishments. In July 1983 five junior members were sent down for academic failure.[166] Infirmity of purpose as to where the principal porters' lodge should be located indicated what one Senior Fellow described as degeneration of the College's central nervous system, with the closure of the Forecourt Porters' Lodge and the reduction of the portering staff by two recommended by the Economies Committee in May 1981. The 'many complexities' attaching to the question as acknowledged by the Dean and the Junior Bursar two years later led two years after that to the reversal of the policy on the recommendation of the then Head Porter and the transfer to the Forecourt of operations previously located in the Front Lodge. The failure in 1986 of the Old Guard to persuade the Governing Body to admit its earlier error, devise some 'salutary casuistry by which a wealthy College can be enabled to keep faith with the benefactors who made it wealthy' and prevent the demotion of the Great Gate 'to the status of a postern' calculated to turn the front of Lady Margaret's college 'into a side-alley', was followed in 1987 by the refurbishment of the Front Lodge, its restoration as the distribution point for junior member mail, and the return of the portering establishment to its 1981 figure.[167]

As attendance in Hall improved porters began to be seen there, wine replaced beer as the usual beverage, in some cases in glasses unusually large for the purpose, and together with the quantities consumed bad behaviour increased.[168] Although the business of the Senior-Junior Committee subsided

---

[163] CM, 2812/5(c); GB 19 May 1983 (voted out by 45 to 15). For the end of the CCE – originally an examination for awards which after 1979 ceased to be awarded – see Linehan, 'Piam in memoriam', 70–78.

[164] SJMC, 28 Jan. 1986, min. 2.

[165] SJMC, 17 Nov. 1981, min. 7 (M. Whitton); GB 24 Feb. 1983 (26 to 25 against a new feast; 28 to 7 in favour of attendance by 'other Junior Members besides the President of the JCR Committee and the President of the SBR Committee'; EC, 19 Nov. 1982, min. 7 ('Cripp's Feast'), 25 Nov. 1983.

[166] Director of Studies in Natural Sciences (J. A. Charles) to Master, 28 Jul. 1982; CM, 2821/1.

[167] Above, p. 631; CM, 2817/11 (J. Staunton and R. T. B. Langhorne, 'Security in the College', 11 May 1983 (CM, 2817/11); 'An analysis of the security, function and the utilization of portering staff at St John's College' (B. G. Dove), 30 Nov. 1985 (CM, 2876/10(b); GB, 15 May 1986 (4 votes against); J. A. Crook and P. A. Linehan to Master, 17 May 1986: SJCA, SBFG 1980–2000/Council & Governing Body Papers 1980–86; R. H. Robinson, 'College Porter Organisation and Lodges', 22 Jun. 1987 (CM, 2907/10).

[168] KCC 28 Nov. 1983, min. 83.20(a): size of wine glasses at BA and Guest tables increased to 6 oz 'as for the Fellows' Table'; 83.23(iii). A second glass of wine at the

with the demise of the Cripps bar, the Kitchen Consultative Committee was always active. It needed to be. In the Lent Term 1986, rowdiness in Hall – food-throwing and the use of water pistols, together with other expressions of higher intelligence at the recent Christmas festivities – occasioned a fierce notice by the Dean and others, as well (regrettably) as the need to have a porter on duty there during the course of hostilities.[169] Doubtless such exuberance was the undergraduates' way of acknowledging the Kitchen's response to a question-naire of that term, with the combination of improved quality and no signing-in resulting in the doubling of Hall attendance in the first five months of 1987 over that of the previous year. With the novelty of the Buttery Dining Room alter-native fading, by the following Michaelmas term Hall was oversubscribed.[170] Although there would be no going back to the culinary delights of 1906, when ptarmigan, capercailzie and lark pie had graced the bill of fare, by April 1980 the choice available in the BDR – 'Welliburgers' at 33p, Road [*sic*] in the Hole at 23p, or (for those on a more limited budget) Jelly at 8p – was already having the effect of enhancing the attractiveness of Hall.

In these circumstances, and encouraged perhaps by indications of complai-sance, not to say complacency, in high places, the rugby club in particular but the hockey players too '[sank] to new depths of debauchery in the bar', the Dean and Tutors assembled a catalogue of incidents involving sexual harassment and drunken brutality (extending even as far as the Netball Club dinner) and the Council responded by approving a draconian programme of measures designed to control 'sessions' in the buttery and other tribal practices recently and help-fully placed in their anthropological context in a fundamental Part II disserta-tion by a College member of the University front row.[171] Meanwhile, however, the mercurial career of C. R. Andrew had been demonstrating real talent as well as the possibilities available behind the scrum and beyond the buttery, not-withstanding his observations on 'the importance placed [by the University] on scholarship over sportsmanship', the liberality (even in the 1980s) of the *exeat* system, and in so far as his own future career was concerned the wisdom of Uni-versity regulations that prevented him from participating in a disastrous British Lions tour at the time of his final examinations.[172] Thirty-five years earlier, the Tutors had been prepared to let Trevor Bailey spend a long Lent term before his

---

Fellows' table was subsequently authorized by CM, 2828/8 (16 Dec. 1983), 2829/7. When graduate students began to dine with them in 1968 Fellows had been asked not to ask for more than one glass: CM, 2456/5. Only in 1949, during Daniel's Steward-ship, had wine been introduced for them on two nights a week as substitute for beer or cider; extended to every evening in 1965: CMM, 1922/13, 2359/3 (wine to the value of 2s 3d, the price of the pint of beer currently served).

[169] CM, 2875/7.

[170] KCC, 20 May 1987, min. 87.3 and Annexe A (CM, 2905/7[c]); 27 Oct. 1988, min. 88.15.

[171] *Eagle* lxxi, no. 295 (1987), 31; 'Drink and anti-social behaviour', 25 Apr. 1988; CM, 2928/8; SJMC, 7 Jun. 1988, min. 9 (protesting at stringency), 15 Nov. 1988, min. 3; CM, 2939/11(a) (i), 24 Nov. 1988 (modification); J. P. Freeman, 'The Eagle and the Red Boy' (1987), being a study of the ritual significance of 'sessions', developed in accordance with the sociological precept of rendering 'intelligible lives unintelligible to those who lived them' (pp. 4, 7–13).

[172] Rob Andrew, *A Game and a Half: An Autobiography* (London, 1994), 91–8.

final examinations on an MCC tour of the West Indies. On that occasion it was Bailey himself, aware of the need for a degree as a passport to school-mastering, who decided otherwise.[173] By contrast, in the summer of 1981 the successor of the Councils which had congratulated Neville Chamberlain and Chris Brasher on their respective triumphs at Munich and Melbourne[174] was not moved to accord like recognition to J. M. Brearley on his triumph in regaining the Ashes.

At a different, earlier in the day, level of existence, the combination of graduate appetites and the enticingly entitled Tutor for Graduate Affairs (an innovation of 1978)[175] resulted in the establishment of the July buffet lunch for graduate students and their families, though not without a struggle. Initially a sit-down affair in Hall, and timed to exclude the possibility of children attending, in 1987 the 'summer function' took the form of a tea party in the Fellows' Garden. But the hour of liberation approached. 'It was noted that the arrangements would be similar to those for the buffet lunch for new graduands [*sic*] on the occasion of General Admission':[176] a triumph over the Master's tendency to economy which acknowledged, albeit a shade grudgingly, the role of graduate students within the College's junior membership of which by now they comprised not less than a third, with the proportion of women graduate students growing too: since 1982 from 11 per cent to almost half the graduate body in 2009–10.[177] More significantly, this development has been recognized by the implementation of a policy of admitting only those graduates for whom, whether married or single, comfortable accommodation was available either along the Madingley Road, up Mount Pleasant, or elsewhere within walking distance of the College. It was the 1984 Audit Committee's recommendation 'that the College acquire another hostel for graduates' that led to the discovery that 'in proportional terms' only five colleges had a worse record than St John's in the accommodation of single graduates.[178] A year later St John's was half-way up the ladder,[179] and by 1988 was one of the most sought-after of colleges by graduate applicants,[180] with the beginning of each Michaelmas term thereafter revealing a lengthening queue on the Tutor for Graduate Admissions' staircase of travel-stained supplicants whose chosen havens' promises of accommodation had proved as evanescent as the early autumn mist enveloping them. The next twenty years have seen a

---

[173] Above, pp. 559 n. 245.

[174] Above, pp. 544, 579.

[175] And responsible for the admission but not the pastoral care of all graduate students which remained dispersed amongst the body of tutors in accordance with the express 'desire' of the tutors in 1972 'not to follow the example of virtually all other Colleges and appoint a "Tutor for Graduate Students"': 'Report of the Committee on Administration within the College' (Oct. 1972).

[176] Though the provision of bouncy castles and conjurors lay still further in the future: EC, 18 May 1984, 28 Nov. 1986 (CM, 2895/6[b]).

[177] Appendix II.

[178] 'Graduate Accommodation' = CM, 2856/8 (14 Mar. 1985).

[179] 'Graduate Accommodation' = CM, 2885/13 (10 Jul. 1986).

[180] CM, 2906/11 (policy of providing accommodation for 85 per cent of single graduates adopted (11 Jun. 1987); need for increase of this provision: CM, 2923/8 (4 Feb. 1988).

surge of graduate student numbers and thereby the College both transformed and enhanced.[181]

Another novel domestic preoccupation of the 1980s was fire precautions. Remarkable though it is that by the time that adequate fire-fighting arrangements were provided all of Oxford and Cambridge's ancient colleges had not already been reduced to ashes, when in the case of modern St John's the need for the removal of bars from ground-floor windows, for the installation of fire alarms and for night-time fire practice had all been signified in 1976 it was not the College authorities that had raised the alarm; it was the JCR Committee.[182] And the undergraduates' warnings deserve to be emphasized, since in the aftermath of the near-fatal conflagration at B1 New Court in the early morning of 21 January 1984 they were not. Instead, in a flurry of activity, both a committee and a sub-committee were established (Safety and Fire Precautions, the latter meeting for the first time in the following December), extinguisher-mindedness took hold with extreme disciplinary measures threatened against club dinners for tampering, fire drills instituted and the Fisher Building designed, as the Cripps Building had not been, in order to allow for the entrance of the brigade's engines. By the winter of 1988–9 the Head Porter was in an agony of indecision whether to admonish a student for letting his toaster catch fire or praise him for dealing with the consequences, and was planning one 'simulated disaster' involving the brigade on an evening in February ('it was agreed that Rag Week should be avoided') and another, complete with smoke machines, in Third Court during the examination term. By now undergraduate interest in such exercises was reported to be fading as fast as the Council's concern was on the increase.[183]

Just as with fire, so with Library facilities the call for more reading room space rose from below, in this case from undergraduates on the Library Committee in January 1986. Earlier than that, the original demand for a computerized catalogue had come from Directors of Studies, many of whom, it emerged at the meeting of the Library Committee in question, were unaware that the Third Court entrance had ceased to be used seventeen years before.

Adjacent Council minutes of April 1986 referred to both this and the latest Cripps horrors.[184] A year later, on the windy night of 13 April 1987, a substantial

---

[181] See Appendix II.

[182] JCRC, min. 760505. In Feb. 1901 Heitland had reported the sixth fire in College in his fifteen years as Junior Bursar: CM, 615/7. At that time, bonfires in the courts had provided an additional hazard. On 22 Feb. 1896 Heitland described a great conflagration in New Court on the previous evening, for which the Boat Club were evidently responsible and in the course of which five cupboard doors, two cupboards, two Fellows' coal bins, five closet seats, eight earth-box lids and other items were consigned to the flames: letter to Master (SJCA, SB2.29, no. 3963).

[183] Report to Council (Strictly Confidential), 31 Jan. 1984, SJMC, 31 Jan. 1984, min. 3; CM, 2848/16, 2918/11(e), Audit Note to Fellows 1985, §4; Fire-Precautions Sub-Committee, 6 Dec. 1988, min. 4, 1 Feb. 1989, min. 3 (CM, 2946/10(f): 'It was agreed that the Committee's proposals for such exercises should be brought to the attention of the Council before they take place.'

[184] CM, 2879/9a, 9b.

chunk of masonry fell from the north elevation of the chapel tower.[185] In earlier centuries this last would have occasioned consideration of the community's collective wickedness, perhaps even of the need for a general penance. In July 1987 it necessitated the summoning of a meeting of the Governing Body, produced from the Domestic Bursar a substantial repair and cleaning bill, and in some minds raised the possibility of an appeal to old members.[186] After all, between 1970 and 1987 had not the College assisted the University, other Cambridge colleges and other good causes to the tune of almost £1.4 million?[187] – no inconsiderable sum with the cost just of replacing the chapel's friable gargoyles (only to look on which was liable to bring one of them crashing down) set at £4,795 per gargoyle and that of making the entire Chapel safe even for sinners, few of whom ever entered it, estimated at £459,000 (not at all bad in comparison with the £575,000 needed for the Cripps roof, by now considered at risk, not only of flood, but also, for good measure, of fire).[188]

That left the issue of Library improvements, which ever since the earliest murmurings had become the cynosure of enlightened opinion within the College. For some, for Guy Lee for example, the issue was simple, and in College terms economical: the bookstore should be housed in the Chapel tower. Alternatively, it was seriously proposed that the everyday library should be situated above the Cripps car-park, partly in the belief that such would be the effect of the first sight upon freshmen and freshwomen as they first approached the College that their eyes would be drawn thither, rendering them insensible to such other snares and pleasures that the place might seek to tempt them with. And such indeed, by 31 votes to 25, was the consequence of the vote of the Governing Body on 2 March 1989. Between then and 18 May there must therefore have been further conversations, since at the next meeting it was decided, by 35 to 27, to keep the Library where it had been since 1624 – though how any sort of new Library was to be afforded was just one of the issues awaiting the new Master, R. A. Hinde, on his assumption of office on 31 July 1989. He had been pre-elected on 17 November 1988.

---

[185] CM, 2903/10 (30 Apr. 1987).

[186] CM, 2909/10 (23 Jul. 1987).

[187] Use of Endowment Income Committee, July 1983.

[188] BC, 26 Nov. 1987 (CMM, 2918/11[c]), 29 Jan. 1988; 2928/9(b), 28 Apr. 1988; Fire-Precautions Sub-Committee, 9 Jun. 1987.

EPILOGUE

Peter Linehan

You see, my boy, sometimes no evidence is more significant than any evidence.

F. H. Hinsley, *obiter*

HARRY Hinsley's retirement in July 1989 and (just months short of his eightieth birthday and of the feast of St John in December at which octogenarian Fellows have their health drunk and are invited to respond with some reflections on their years in the College) his death in February 1998 left various questions unanswered because unasked. However this may have been viewed by the College, it is surely how Hinsley himself would have wanted it, not least because it left history rather puzzled and, if only very cautiously, looking forward. The year 1990 saw two changes which together drew a line across the College's understanding of itself: one, after almost 800 years, the commutation to a money payment of the old Bread and Broth charity;[1] the other the appropriation of the *Eagle* by Hinsley's successor and its transformation into the 'official annual record of the College',[2] thereby depriving the College's historian of one of his most fruitful sources, as may be seen in the foregoing pages of this account, notwithstanding the terms of T. R. Glover's recommendation of the magazine seventy years earlier, namely 'its tradition of dullness'.[3]

Since Glover's undergraduate years when he had thought the sight of a Clare man 'conspicuously' kissing a girl at an open window something worth recording, both the College and society at large had undergone transformation.[4] On the eve of Benians's election in 1933, Glover, by then past his middle years, had in mind a demonstration of college unity on the morrow.[5] With these sentiments, consistent though they were with the passing round of the loving cup

---

[1] CM, 2976/5 (i) (19 Jul. 1990); Thurbon, 'The College Bread and Broth Charity', 16–23. 'The Poor's Soup', *Eagle* (2000), 35–7.

[2] *Eagle* lxxii, no. 298 (1990), 2; stating that the acquisition of the magazine had been decided upon by 'the College', revealing an evident confusion with the College Council. What had survived since 1858 as 'A magazine supported by members of St. John's College' now changed its self-description to 'A magazine for members of St John's College, Cambridge' and became the responsibility of the Johnian (later the Development) Office. 'Would that we had in Trinity the tradition of a college magazine like the *Eagle*', T. C. Nicholas had written to Guy Lee on 13 Feb. 1984 (BSP), foreshadowing Professor Hilton's perceptive remarks (above, pp. 295–6).

[3] *Eagle* Minute Book 1890–1923 (SJCA, CC6.1): '... which he claimed was permanent in any magazine of value' (26 Nov. 1922).

[4] GD, 7 Apr. 1893; GD, 6 May 1890 (on visiting Girton): 'Forgot gloves so could not dance.'

[5] Above, p. 419.

after Hall in the College's earliest days as prescribed in John Fisher's statutes,[6] Benians had not concurred. By then changes inimical to the old College had already been absorbed. After 1927 colleges gradually lost control of their households. With rare exceptions, academic appointments were made by University committees exclusively concerned, at least ostensibly, with intellectual merit. Increasingly, the 'good College man' was squeezed out. Eventually, after 1986 the Research Assessment Exercise would even cause collegial tendencies to be treated as a negative indicator. No matter that talented applicants were encouraged to apply for University lectureships by the prospect of picking up a College Fellowship. Once appointed, those of them contemplating accepting a Tutorship or other College office were liable to be informed by the RAE officer of their faculty that their card had been marked. Consequently, after rising from the lunch table (from which since sometime in the 1980s the same Low Church spirit succeeded in banishing beer) Fellows no longer stroll off for a spot of croquet in the Wilderness of a summer afternoon.

In the 1920s the soda-water-tippling Glover (for whom of course the banishment of beer would have provided cause for celebration) lived in a rented house with servants and walked or cycled to College and back, sometimes as many as four times a day. Half a century later the establishment of Trinity's Science Park and of St John's Innovation Centre was driving young academics further and further out, way beyond the range of the bicycle and far too remote from the city centre to make the entertainment of pupils, tutorial or other, a possibility. The operation of the academic diaspora is evident from the addresses provided by successive *Resident Members' Lists* across the decades.[7]

	North and West of SJC	South	East	City Centre	in College	in villages
1919	14	4	2	–	24	–
1929	10	10	2	–	25	1
1939	22	11	5	–	13	5
1949	23	13	5	7	10	5
1959	29	15	5	4	8	5
1969	29	11	10	4	14	18
1979	27	11	15	7	23	18
1989	33	16	5	3	26	24

For neither academic nor non-academic staff could the introduction of the College's House Loan Scheme in the 1980s reverse the inflationary effects of such developments. The servantless contrast with the 1930s was acute, even for those in leafy West Cambridge. According to A. J. P. Taylor, academic complaints about the decline of civilization meant only that 'university professors used to have domestic servants and now do their own washing-up.'[8] For those in College, some issues have remained perennial, of course: the swimming-pool

[6] *Early Statutes*, 164.

[7] These figures provide only an indication of distribution with the 'College' figures inflated since, for whatever reason, a number of Fellows gave the College rather than their own residence as their address.

[8] *Observer*, 21 Jun. 1959; cit. A. Sisman, *A. J. P. Taylor: A Biography* (London, 1994), 332. Cf. above, pp. 479–80.

issue for example,[9] or the commitment of some bachelor Fellows to maintenance of the stringent standards set by T. G. Bonney. 'The woast meat in this College is a *public* scandal', E. C. Ratcliff was heard to declare at the lunch table sometime in the mid-1960s.[10]

W‍HAT then *is* a college at the beginning of the twenty-first century? What does the concept which caused Scott in his time to seek a definition and which, in his, Benians toyed with, amount to now?[11] Is it simply where its members live? Where they eat? Or drink? Or what they use as a *poste restante* at which to collect their mail? Or perchance to park their car? For some, especially for those driven by local property prices to live miles out, a parking space may be the essence of it. For others, Fellows particularly, and above all Fellows absorbed in university business, it is a place to have lunch and to which to bring guests and not to introduce them to their neighbour. Leaving aside medieval discussions of the matter, we are on safe ground in insisting on the importance not of lunch but of dinner, of Hall: 'one of the most fundamental activities in the life of a corporate society', as the *Eagle* editorial bravely stated as the revolutionary brickbats were already raining down.[12] In that same editorial was an approving reference to John Crook's recent Commemoration Sermon in which the demise of the College 'as a corporate entity' had been contemplated together with its disappearance 'into the pages of history along with the Greek city-state and the steam locomotive'. 'And the onus, the grave onus, is on us', the preacher, in characteristically optimistic mood, had continued. And sure enough, in January 1973 the Buttery Dining Room was opened and in 1982 the concept of compulsory Hall was abandoned. *Compulsory* Hall: how very odd and foreign the idea seems now.

Reviewing the recent past, in which he found little consolation, Crook had stated as 'most fundamental of all (...) the unexpressed presupposition (...) now for the first time exposed to challenge – the premise that was the major premise for all our benefactors, that a College is *ex hypothesi* a good thing.'[13] Here he was on firm ground, for there was no one more firmly committed to the College's invisible reality than John Crook, or more regular in his attendance at Old Johnian dinners throughout the decades during which the presence of other Fellows has declined from thirty-nine out of seventy-one in 1950 to twelve out of 142 in 2009, and of those twelve hardly one under the age of sixty. Likewise the last two decades have witnessed a steep decline in attendance on ordinary nights, and in 2007 new measures were proposed as a means of reversing a trend which in fact went back decades. For it was not so much the pressures of the

---

[9] E.g. CM, 3140/3(c): 'Agreed gratefully to accept the gift and to credit it to the Goody (Lavatory Improvements and Swimming Pool) (Accumulation) Fund. Agreed further, following a request from Professor Goody, to rename the fund the "Goody Swimming Pool [formerly (Lavatory and Swimming Pool) (Accumulation)] Fund].'" (18 Mar. 1999).

[10] Cf. Bonney on the subject of scotch broth: above, p. 486.

[11] Above, pp. 412, 564.

[12] *Eagle* lxiii, no. 272 (1969), 58.

[13] Ibid., 78.

Research Assessment Exercise that was responsible for the decline, as the then President suggested, as those of modern matrimony, probably an irreversible tendency. A century has passed since Glover remarked on the consequences of marriage for Hall.[14]

For the unmarried, gas-rings have meanwhile done the trick and for such as prefer high tea anyway the availability of the Buttery Dining Room from 6 o'clock onwards has proved a godsend. More than this, though, the principle of commensality has been fatally undermined. Times have changed. With the demise of chapel as a collective ceremony, only Hall remained. But now, regardless of Fisher's injunction (fig. 3), the College's high priests themselves spurn it. Deans don't dine much; Tutors neither, the Stewards less (and serves the Poor's Soup on *Tuesdays*). Even special events for junior members are eschewed by college officers. On ordinary evenings the principle of commensality is compromised by the departure of the Fellows while the rest of the company is still in mid-meal. The practice of Hall is no more than an etiolated admission of collegiality. Only for junior members does it correspond to anything substantial.

Parallel with the decline of their attendance at dinner has been a steady reduction in the proportion of Fellows attending meetings of the Governing Body[15] along with the abandonment of the old notice boards by the Great Gate, now bereft of team notices and subject to appropriation by the most questionable of interlopers. In 1901 telephonic communication was established between the Front Lodge and New Court, and a decade later Glover recorded the installation of an 'instrument called telephone'. Howard though would not allow the Bursary phone to be connected to the public exchange: 'He used to say that it would encourage tenants to ring up the Bursary. It was better that they should call or write.' The adventure of phoning had to await the arrival of Boys Smith in 1944.[16] And twenty years later, except in the case of birth or death, undergraduates did not ring home; they wrote – or failed to, just as they had done, or failed to, a hundred years before when the penny post had become available.[17] But since the 1980s e-mail has established itself and is now used even for invitations to collegiate entertainment, even for meetings of the Book Club, even in requests to the Dean to permit or not to prohibit something. So team and fixture lists are no longer posted on notice-boards, with the inevitable consequences – for all that, support on 'touchline and towpath', what in another age described itself as 'College patriotism',[18] remains vocal. Sooner or later, no doubt, e-mail

---

[14] 'College Functions and the Fellows' Table', 26 Apr. 2007; above, p. 479.

[15] From 67.5 per cent in 1949–50 to 35 per cent in 2009–10: a trend only briefly interrupted by votes on the admission of women and on the installation of a peal of bells in the chapel tower in 1979–80.

[16] CM, 629/3 (26 Jul. 1901); GD, 12 Nov. 1912; Boys Smith, *Memories*, 80–81.

[17] Above, p. 294.

[18] Above, pp. 416–17. For the same quality discernible in J. J. Lister, see *Eagle* xlv (1927–9), 44, and in the versatile J. W. Dale, who in 1869 'most patriotically gave his services to our boat, although he was playing in the University cricket eleven': Hall-Craggs, *History of the Lady Margaret Boat Club*, II. xx. Cf. the case of the Jesus man who in 1876 abandoned a cricket match and, although quite untrained, subbed for a sick colleague in his winning college eight, dying a dozen years later: Mangan, 'Oars and the man', 252. Likewise, Hart to Tanner, 15 Sept. 1911: 'We all depend on you, as

will supplant supervision as part of the process towards an entirely atomized College. In some respects this would be regrettable.

The most pronounced expression of that process is on the domestic front, a development already identified forty years ago: 'as castles were, so our rooms should be', R. G. Harding declared during the rumblings of discontent.[19] The 'ensuitement' of sets was the natural conclusion of the process of cellular development of which Boys Smith's bathroom had been the harbinger. Although by October 2009 there were as many as twenty-seven Fellows in residence, many of these, as well as referring to their rooms as 'flats' or 'apartments', never dined, lunched or attended Fellows' meetings or, on an otherwise uneventful afternoon, even the election of a Master. St John's had turned its back on Larmor and baths with the boys. Notwithstanding the collective dyspepsia of the bachelor Fellows, inasmuch as the Council's chief criterion in filling the ranks has become a declared unwillingness to perform teaching duties, the neglect by some of the social responsibilities of Fellowship is now inevitable. 'Twas ever thus, though once it had been their wives in Chesterton who had emptied the High Table.[20]

Not that it hadn't been seen coming. Amongst the reasons for objecting to the changes in guest hours in 1970 had been 'the tendency towards regarding a junior member's set as a flat with a private key but without service': a concept barely imaginable, and, from a landlord and tenant point-of-view, certainly 'untenable both for the College and for Junior Members'.[21] Nothing daunted, the domesticators advanced, with the early-evening exhalations associated with self-catering rendering some staircases redolent of Soho chop-houses on summer afternoons. With ovens in demand, by 1985 there were proposals for mixed sharing in the undergraduates' third year.[22] In 2009 double beds were the issue. How different, how very different, from Samuel Butler's bliss in a room of his own, or Macklin's snug apartment, or Glyn Daniel's description of the don's lair at the opening of *The Cambridge Murders* with its roaring fire and sherry, no doubt from a private solera.[23]

Daniel's story told of a dinner-centred College in which a beaker of amontillado by the fire was the invariable preliminary. Though excellent of course, it was a *solitary* lunch that Sir Richard Cherrington, the great detective-archaeologist, took in Fisher College's Combination Room, followed by the uncustomary indulgence of a glass of port.[24] But that was a 1938 lunch viewed from a 1945 perspective. In 2010 there is precious little port after lunch, at least

you know to your cost, for precepts and for example of unselfish patriotism': SJCA, TU12.13.366.

[19] 'It is always said that an Englishman's home is his castle. This is now doubtful but it is an ideal that could be realised in Cambridge – as castles were, so our rooms should be. Just so long as we all remember that many castles here have thin walls': *Eagle* no. 275 (Jan. 1971), 86.

[20] Above, p. 480.

[21] 'Should Guest Hours be Abolished?': SJMC (16 Feb. 1970).

[22] Above, p. 630.

[23] 'How can a boy fail to feel an ecstasy of pleasure on first finding himself in rooms which he knows for the next few years are to be his castle?': Butler, *The Way of All Flesh*, chap. 45; above, pp. 476–7; Daniel, *The Cambridge Murders*, chap. i. ii.

[24] Daniel, *The Cambridge Murders*, chap. 4.

in the Combination Room, and scant prospect of solitariness either. Sometimes, indeed, the room can rather resemble a commuter train compartment, a time-capsule devoid of introductions. When the option of taking lunch as commons was introduced in 1958, an attempt was made to protect dinner as an institution by limiting to four per week the number of lunches allowed.[25] Over time that strategy was deemed to have failed. For most Fellows the College is a 9-to-5, five-days-a-week, lunchtime place. Time was when Fellows would sit around in the Combination Room after dinner and review the world. More recently, the young Title A Research Fellows were the life and soul of the party. But it was not always so,[26] and over the last twenty-five years the Fellows' postprandial wine circle, now reduced to Sundays, has been scantily attended.[27]

Meanwhile, and in accordance with the foregoing, the College's ten Tutors, the people looked to in 1918 as principally responsible for 'keeping the place together' have moved their Saturday morning meetings to a weekday after-noon.[28] Although no longer *in loco parentis*, in other respects however, in matters of admission for example, the Johnian Tutor's role has little changed – whereas in Trinity it is the Director of Studies who reigns supreme. Significantly, none of the present team of Tutors was an undergraduate of the College, and of the current forty-six Directors of Studies just five were: a development matched by the decline in what might be termed 'cradle membership' of the Fellowship, with twenty-nine such Fellows out of 143 in 2009, compared with fifty-three out of seventy-four fifty years earlier:[29] a symptom rather than a cause of change, akin to the twenty-nine foreign nationals from seventeen countries as against the seven from five at the earlier date.[30]

Another development of this increasingly cosmopolitan college has been the transformed role, especially since the arrival of women, of the nurse and the chaplain. In many respects the Nurse, in the late 1950s a chilly spinster who regarded the taking of an aspirin as an act of moral turpitude, and the Chaplain have come to supplement the Tutors or, other than for formal purposes, even to supplant them. Both deserve their capital letters. Early in 1989 the then Chaplain, Nurse and President of the JCR had declared their role to be 'very ambiguous'. 'In disciplinary cases in the past, some Tutors have supported their students, others have reprimanded them, while still others have offered no advice or support whatever', they stated.[31]

---

[25] Above, p. 600.

[26] GD, 27 Dec. 1935: those dining 'mostly the married lot; not the transient juniors who are so dreadful.'

[27] Audit Note to Fellows 1985, para. 9: 'That efforts should be made to increase the appeal of the Wine Circle.'

[28] Above, p. 452.

[29] Not to mention 349 out of 353 between 1801 and 1870: above, p. 284, n. 223.

[30] A notable variant to this tendency is provided by the College's Title A (Junior Research) Fellowships, eligibility for which was extended in 1991 to include gradu-ates of all UK universities in addition to Oxford and Cambridge. Of the ninety-five elected since then, just five have come from this wider world by contrast with twenty-nine cradle Johnians and sixty-one from other Oxbridge colleges.

[31] 'Counselling and Welfare Support for Students in St John's', 2 Mar. 1989; CM, 2947/13 (16 Mar. 1989).

65 The essence of the place: John Crook, Fellow, 1951–2007. Photograph by Mr Justice Morris Fish

'The very survival of a College still depends – perhaps more than ever depends – on there being some who will make it, I do not say the sole, but at any rate for a period the primary object of their care', J. A. Crook observed in 1969. 'Men have two kinds of time: their tired time and their creative time; and the College needs some who will devote to it, I do not say all, but at any rate for a period part at least of their creative time – or at the very least it needs one such person.'[32] As a provider of 'creative time' – what would now be termed quality time – John Crook himself was second to none. Preaching today, he would not speak of 'men'. Since 1990 indeed it has been a female, the College Nurse, who has come to supply a large part of that need.

By 1990 of course other changes were under way, hastened as well as necessitated by the management revolution which gave the College its first non-academic domestic officer, the Domestic Bursar, the renaming of the Kitchen Office as 'the 'Catering and Conference Office', and weekly Heads of Department meetings for non-academic staff both in and out of term. 'My early impressions of moving from a military environment to an academic one', Col. Richard Robinson recalls,

> were of warmth, friendship and understanding. However, with regard to the management of the day to day administration of the College, whilst the assistant staff were extremely hardworking it was clear that there was a disturbing lack of co-ordination of, and liaison between the many departments. There existed an element, if I may use the military term (!) of a 'private army' mind-set, and an acceptance of 'crisis management'. Improvement in this area I saw as my priority task, and this was achieved, principally, by three specific measures i.e. the introduction of a weekly

[32] 'Commemoration of Benefactors 1969', *Eagle* lxiii, no. 272 (1969), 80.

meeting of *all* departmental heads, at which problems were aired and future activities discussed; by a limited enhancement of the Domestic Bursar's personal staff in order that they were in a position to exercise the overall co-ordination role; and by myself providing a higher profile in the day to day administrative activities of the College (getting out and about!).[33]

Amongst the Domestic Bursar's many responsibilities were those connected with conferences and tourists. In 1985 it had been agreed 'that conferences should be encouraged as an important source of income (…) and that reduced charges should be made to academic conferences.'[34] But not all parts of the College were suitable: such customers would not tolerate the 'medieval' provision of one cold tap per staircase. However, Cripps changed that – and even before Cripps it had become necessary to establish a *cordon sanitaire* protecting term-time from the incursion of conference delegates.[35] Of this process undergraduates were the term-time beneficiaries and the College the victim: the former as inhabitants of the progressively 'en-suited' accommodation, the latter in consequence of the pressures applied to send junior members packing as soon as term ended, and of moving alternative seating in and out during vacation periods on account of the sedentary needs of geriatric conference delegates and the alleged inconvenience of their enjoying the privilege of sitting on benches while dining in the late-medieval Hall.[36] In the great debates of these years conference-related arguments might be deployed on either side of any issue: in favour of guest hours, for example, on the grounds that if they were abolished and guests took up residence outraged bedders would leave, sets would become flats, their decoration would deteriorate; and the conference trade would suffer.[37] In fact, of course, none of this happened. Bedders didn't leave. They remained as 'cleaners' and turned a blind eye to everything other (it was hoped) than squatting, just as they proved capable of adapting to funny smells on staircases and to not taking in the young gentlemen's laundry now that the young ladies had College washing machines in which to do what once upon a time Glover's mother received in the weekly post.[38] By now indeed, washing machines were just about the only object of domestic furniture not trundled into College during term-time. Whereas fifty years before, most of what most undergraduates brought with them was contained in a trunk sent by train (for which purposes the Porter's Lodge maintained a weighing machine), the hypertrophic growth of material possessions now required parents (comprehensive parents rather

---

[33] R. H. Robinson to the Author, 16 Feb. 2010. See also 'Colonel Richard Robinson', *Eagle* (2000), 25–9.

[34] Audit Note to Fellows 1985, para. 5. Non-academic conferences had been accommodated since at least 1956: CM, 2097/24 (Engineering Designers; 5 Oct. 1956); CM, 2099/12 (British Wood-Preserving Association; 2 Nov. 1956).

[35] CM, 2373/7 (Nov. 1965).

[36] Cf. Philistines' Society report (D. E. H. T[histlethwaite]: *Eagle* lxiv, no. 274 [1970], 79): 'Our other demand of this year will probably be implemented next term – the covering of the unhygienic wooden tables in hall with formica.'

[37] SJMC, 16 Feb. 1970.

[38] 'Wrote Mother & sent her a lot of socks – 2 lbs or so': GD, 1 Nov. 1893.

than the impecunious independents as a rule) to provide a large Volvo, or even a brace thereof, for the conveyance of all the electronic equipment, aspidistras and other aids to survival for as much as eight weeks away at a time.

Parallel with the growth of conferences was the practice of charging tourists for entrance and, inexorably, the extension of the tourist season throughout the Easter term, which initially the junior members had strongly resisted.[39] In the early sixties two of the Fellows having complained of an 'increase in the number of persons visiting the College', a man had been appointed to patrol the grounds during spring and summer afternoons.[40] Thereafter, the opening first of the M11 motorway and then of the Channel Tunnel necessitated further defensive initiatives. Yet after the 1987 Audit Committee's urging of a 'more positive policy towards tourism', the College was eventually thrown open to tourists, though in view of the JCR's opposition, only 'on the basis that [the arrangement] may be terminated at short notice in the event of nuisance being caused by tourists visiting the College'.[41] Although the combination of huge increases in the number of tourists year on year and, in comparison with its neighbours', the College's exceptional open-gates policy have amply demonstrated the need for some such closure, the proviso has remained a dead letter ever since. As they are punted along the Backs, visitors may have their attention drawn to New Court, the building chosen by Hitler to be his headquarters, they are solemnly assured: an urban myth dating from about 1997. Regarding the authentic use of the Combination Room for the planning of D-Day they tend to be less well informed.[42]

Most colleges are institutionally conservative places. Ralph Thoday's pronouncement at the Pig Club, also in 1997, that 'Alteration is awful', affirmed a profound Johnian truth.[43] Because of the requirement of Statute VIII(9) that to be binding on the College, any motion has to be 'carried by a majority of the whole Governing Body or by a majority of at least two-thirds of the persons present and voting', any change of established practice is difficult to achieve. The issue of Ladies Dining provides an example from Mansergh's Mastership.[44] Similarly when, as President, John Crook attempted to change the wording of the post-prandial grace, from the injunction to pray for all Christians to one to pray for all men, the Fellowship was divided from top to bottom.

Yet despite all this there has been change. Whereas it was in continuation of 'Father's old society up here' that Hilary Macklin had founded the semi-secret Stormy Petrels in the 1920s,[45] after the 1950s the old dynastic assumptions as to 'my boy' and his inherited expectations, then and later so casually deployed, withered on the vine. In more recent times some Senior Tutors have continued to acquire, or perhaps have been born with, special skills in sniffing out such relationships. Perhaps to cheer himself in those troubled times, in his annual

[39] CM, 2856/11(c)(i), 24 Mar. 1985.

[40] CMM, 2240/18 (28 Jul. 1961), 2262/16 (13 Apr. 1962).

[41] CM, 3047/14[c]), 10 Mar. 1994.

[42] See J. S. Boys Smith, 'The Combination Room and 'D' Day', *Eagle* lxii (1967–8), 218–22.

[43] Linehan, 'The Pig's Golden', 12.

[44] Above, p. 613.

[45] LHMD, 17 Feb. 1922.

report on Admissions between 1970 and 1973 Colin Bertram took to noting the number of sons of old members on the list. Thereafter, however, the practice lapsed, although even into the eighties certain admissions papers would reach the tutor responsible inscribed 'Johnian father', '?Johnian father', even 'Johnian uncle'. After all, it had done the College no harm that John Boys Smith's father was a member, albeit in the eyes of some his coming from a southern school would have ruled him out. Well into the twentieth century Lady Margaret's north–south distinction and Fisher's partiality for those 'northern tuffe laddes' retained their adherents. 'I don't find any originality or vigour in these south country boys', the Head Master of Dean Close Cheltenham, himself an exiled northerner, had confided in Donald MacAlister in 1900.[46]

Time was when the linkage was via best friends' sisters: 'By Gad, [G. A. D.] Tait is lucky in his sisters; both are perfectly topping', Hilary Macklin declared in the summer of 1922.[47] But the first batch of Johniennes themselves carried Johnian genes. And in 2009 an undergraduate, probably the first with both mother and father members of the College, matriculated.

In fostering matrimony (or its informal substitute) between natives of Yorkshire and Devon (for example) first-generation mixed colleges have provided the same service as England's reformation parliaments once did.[48] Meanwhile, whereas for years until the 1990s the sons of Fellows and the grand-daughters of Masters continued to grace the courts, such sightings have proved far fewer. Since the College has no means of keeping track of such relationships, nephews and nieces are harder to spot, of course, and complications such as divorce hamper discovery. Only years after the event did the College come to know that Alex Blackburn, whom it had admitted in 1995, was Lady Margaret's sixteenth great-granddaughter. All told, dynasty appears to be in rather sharp decline.[49]

That consideration apart, from analysis of the admittedly patchy and inevitably subjective information supplied by the Fellows themselves, of the 496 elected between 1900 and 1989, ninety-six appear to have belonged to the lowliest categories of the Registrar-General's classification, with the balance supplied by categories I and II (professional occupations and managerial and lower professional occupations respectively).[50]

---

[46] SJCA, TU 11.2/Bennett, G. A. (Jun. 15, 1900). Cf. Martin Charlesworth's letter of recommendation for T. M. Arnison (13 Mar. 1931): 'I do not think he would hinder his prospects by taking a tutorship this vacation, and I am certain he would get on quite well with most families, though it is fair to add that he is more a north-country than a south-country type'; above, pp. 20, 132.

[47] LMHD, 19 Jun. 1922; D. Winterbottom, *Bertram Hallward* (Nottingham, 1995), 50. Likewise, Hugh Russell-Smith wrote to Benians from Torquay in December 1912 that 'I have been making myself the happiest person in the world by winning the most glorious girl that was ever born.' This was Dorothy Tait. Meanwhile Russell-Smith's sister Elsie had become engaged to G. I. C. Marchand (BA 1910): EABP.

[48] A. F. Pollard, 'The Reformation Parliament as a matrimonial agency and its national effects', *History* xxi (1936–7), 219–29.

[49] A survey of Parents' Graduate Status conducted in June 2009 and responded to by 270 out of the 569 undergraduates then in residence (47 per cent) revealed that sixteen were the children of Johnian fathers and nineteen those of members of other Cambridge colleges. 80 per cent had at least one graduate parent.

[50] Cf. above, p. 207 for eighteenth-century equivalents.

| | Occupations of some Fellows' parents | | | | |
	Non-manual skilled	Manual skilled	Semi-skilled	Unskilled	Total of Fellows elected
1900–4	2	1	1	–	14
1905–10	1	–	2	–	9
1911–20	1	4	–	1	24
1921–30	2	4	1	–	26
1931–40	5	3	–	1	25
1941–50	2	2	2	1	54
1951–60	5	4	5	1	65
1961–70	7	6	4	–	87
1971–80	5	11	1	–	105
1981–9	4	6	–	1	87

Of these latter groups, forty-eight were the sons of school-teachers, twenty-nine those of ministers of religion and twenty-six the sons and one the daughter of academics (the first of these being elected in 1944).[51] Distributed across the whole spectrum were the sons of an ex-shoe riveter, a bristle merchant, a grey cloth maker-up (in his time, a Head of House and Vice-Chancellor of the University), two writers to the signet (one of them also a Head of House), an orchestral pianist, one gentleman (namely Sir Henry Howard, Senior Bursar), and one baronet (a South African).

Modest though such figures may appear in 2011, only those unaware of the eventual impact of the 1944 Education Act, party politicians in particular, will go so far as to brand them scandalous. A century ago, T. R. Glover (the son of a Baptist minister) recorded with astonishment the marriage of an undergraduate of Trinity Hall to a "'floor-girl' from Peter Robinson's [the department store], daughter of a lodging-house keeper'.[52] Today, most Cambridge colleges would be falling over themselves to include such a trophy in their statistics. Contrast this with the recollection of Glover (C. W. M.), a graduate of 1962: 'Cambridge, or, more correctly, St Johns College, (…) was a fun place to spend three years and, as was the fashion in those far-off days, not taken terribly seriously as a place of study. Sufficient hard work to pass one's degree yearly exams of course but not a lot more.' The reaction to this of Glover (T. R.), his first cousin once removed, who in a single undergraduate term had recorded himself as spending 371¼ hours at his books, may be easily enough imagined.[53]

And all this time the staff looked stoically on, observing the modern equivalent of Wordsworth's

> Half-and-half idlers, hardy recusants,
> And honest dunces   (*Prelude*, III.68–9).

[51] The failure of these figures to amount to the total stated is due to the vagueness of some description supplied, especially in the case of Fellows from abroad.

[52] GD, 11 Aug. 1908.

[53] http://www.pa59ers.com/potpourri/folders/go6-Glove/go6.html (Phillips Academy of Andover Class of 1959 website). Cf. GD, 19 Mar. & 23 Apr. 1892.

The College staff are the College's bedrock. They are not to be treated like Art and Culture in the old Oxford Histories, bobbing along after the main narrative like dinghies in the wake of a destroyer. They are here, it is here almost at the end that they belong, because this is a place of honour. For they it is – the legions of clerks, porters, secretaries, gardeners, cooks and the rest – to whom over the years it has regularly fallen to tidy up after the Senior and Junior Members have made a mess of things. While dons and undergraduates have come and gone, they have remained, and have done so for decades: Cecil Butler, Head Porter, after more than fifty years' service;[54] Sheila Smith, ultimately the earthly representative of successive Senior Tutors, for forty-seven;[55] Wally Reynolds, the College cabinet maker and craftsman without peer, creator of the Combination Room table and much else besides;[56] Norman Buck with his fifty-three years of service in the Library acknowledged by scholars from all over the world, the Governing Body's acclamation and the University's award of the degree of MA *honoris causa*;[57] and, amongst many others, the two bedders of the present writer's youth, Pleasance (as she always insisted on being addressed: 'not Mrs Pleasance, Sir, *if* you please'), the bucket-carrying lady of many layers of overcoat from the pockets of which new-laid eggs or fresh weasel for the breakfast table might be produced, and Maud Chandler who, on retiring after twenty-six years of service and it being suggested that she deserved 'a suitable form of appreciation for long service', was in due course rewarded with a letter of thanks from the Master of the day,[58] for which she was no doubt duly grateful – though many, many more there are whose name is writ in water.

When at Easter 1920 Bill Thurbon joined the College Office staff as a 15/- a week seventeen-year-old he did so under the wing of Ned Lockhart, Chief Clerk and since 1911 College Butler. Lockhart would serve the College in numerous capacities for fifty years; likewise Thurbon as Bursary assistant from 1931 and Bursar's Clerk from 1955. Thurbon had heard about the vacancy 'from the wife of a policeman to whom G. W. Rawlinson (who kept the Day Book and Bill Book) had mentioned it'.[59] This was recruitment the old-fashioned, tried and trusted way, which today would probably be illegal. Likewise Ken North, for years the anchor-man of the Kitchen Office who after a period in the College choir until his voice broke at fourteen (1923–6) and a spell at Eaden Lilley's

---

[54] CM, 2477/13.

[55] And like Lockhart before her, the College's guest at the Port Latin Feast in the year of her retirement (2008), an invitation, unlike Lockhart's, not recorded in the Council minutes: above, p. 539.

[56] To whom in February 1981, at the request of the Council, a 'letter of appreciation' of his construction of the new doors at the east end of the room was sent by the Master: CM, 2765/4(b). A man of astonishing versatility, he created the rounded protuberances on rectangular wooden boxes to hold rolled archive documents with large seals, and built a large wooden map cabinet as well as the table, for which see G. C. Evans, 'The Combination Room table', *Eagle* (1996), 49–51.

[57] GB, 24 Feb. 1983; *CUR* (1982–3), 225–7; 'Library Memories', *Eagle* lxix, no. 291 (1983), 14–20; obit. (A. G. Lee and others), *Eagle* lxxi, no. 297 (1989), 36–8.

[58] CM, 2381/1(b), 2 (4 Feb. 1966), 2403/17 (25 Nov. 1966).

[59] *Ex inf.* M. Underwood (conversation of 24 Mar. 1992); Thurbon 'Memoir'; CM, 2453/16 (27 Jul. 1968).

66 *Homo bursarius*:
a youthful W. T. Thurbon

grocery department, became Kitchen Clerk in October 1935, 'really thanks to the grocery manager at Lilley's, a cousin of Alfred Sadler, the Kitchen Manager'.[60] Ditto Roy Papworth, Chief Clerk at the time of his retirement in 1993 after forty-two years in the College office: 'It was through somebody knowing somebody who knew Mr Wolfe [Thurbon's predecessor as Bursar's Clerk] that I first heard of the vacancy in the College Office.'[61] Time was when the recruitment of porters was similarly kept within the extended College family. To Bob Fuller's chagrin, by 1975 that system was changing.[62]

During the time of these great stalwarts, office life – like College life in general – had regard to the legitimate claims of the afternoon. In 1951 when Papworth joined the office, the Chief Clerk Arthur Martin and Harold Pettitt, his deputy, 'didn't return after lunch until about 5 o'clock having spent the afternoon in their gardens.' So long was Martin's Gilbert Road garden 'that he would ride up and down it on his bicycle when feeding the hens.' During his hours in College, he didn't miss much from his E First Court eyrie: 'when he spotted his prey he would utter a loud cry and bound out of the door and down the stairs, usually catching his quarry before he reached the screens' (his occasional prey was K. Scott who as Junior Bursar looked in about once a week).[63] Even bookish Bill Thurbon had to adjust to the Arcadian regime.[64]

But even Arcady has its drawbacks. Because Wolfe had been agnostic in respect of adding machines his retirement unleashed a revolution in bursary practice. Ken North shared Wolfe's reservations, in his case as to decimalization, so at its introduction he resigned. E. A. Wood, Lockhart's successor as Chief Clerk (1936–45), 'did not believe in volunteering for anything', the generally charitable Thurbon, the high-ranking Scout, recorded reprovingly.[65] As Edward Miller observed of these men and women, their 'contribution to the corporate life of the college has been inestimable':[66] inestimable and fondly appreciated by senior and junior members alike. The death of Jim Williams, groundsman from 1963 to 1999, resulted in a clutch of obituaries in the *Eagle* from members of all ages, all of singular perceptiveness.[67]

WE began this part of the History with the first Old Johnians' Dinner on the day after Samuel Butler's death. There have been many dinners along the way, memorably the allegedly centennial gathering of the

[60] K. North, 'Memoirs', SJCA, Arch.2.8.1.

[61] 'Pig Club memories', *Eagle* (1996), 17; also Boys Smith, *Memories*, 80–82.

[62] 'While he dislikes specifically advertising for porters, he has recently been forced to do so': D. Souter, 'Bob's your uncle', *Eagle* lxvii, no. 283 (1975), 22.

[63] Papworth, 'Pig Club memories', *Eagle* (1995), 23–5. For Martin, forty-two years in the College; Chief Clerk from 1946 to 1968, see *Eagle* lxix, no. 291 (1983), 59 (obit. W. T. Thurbon); CM, 2460/18 (15 Nov. 1968).

[64] With original hours of 9–1 and 5–7.30, he only began working in the afternoon 'because Lockhart, whose home was at Shelford used to lunch in College, and then like[d] to go out in the afternoons, particularly in the rugger season': Thurbon, 'Memoir', 4.

[65] Ibid., 13, 17. Cf. *Eagle* liii (1948), 69.

[66] Miller, *Portrait of a College*, 123–4.

[67] *Eagle* (2006), 92–8.

General Athletic Club in 1998, to which many old members said they would
only come if a spot of room cricket was included in the entertainment, whereupon the Master, aware as he was of the game's pariah status, felt obliged to
coax it out of the closet, thereby providing yet another example, to parallel
the introduction of electric light and the admission of women, of the recurrent truth that, given time, in the College's long history the once unthinkable eventually becomes ineluctable.[68] In Johnian terms the embourgeoise-
ment of an activity once proscribed was the equivalent of the conversion of
Emperor Constantine for the Western Church. (No such request was received
in respect of court golf, be it noted. Likewise stories of the night have been
largely absent from this History, making it at best only about two-thirds of an
account of its subject. It is this that makes the Macklin diaries a source of such
importance.)[69]

Of other recent changes of the last half-century more than enough has
already been said in these pages. The damp, faintly gassy, Proustian smell of
the gyp room, little changed since Benians's undergraduate days,[70] now gone,
all gone, dispersed by central heating. The December scholarship exams held
in College, which introduced sundry seventeen-year-old hopefuls, some of
them for the first time away from home for as much as three days, to that chilly
atmosphere, to breakfast in Hall and exposure to other people's insistent confidence; and the old buttery, dispensing corn-flakes, boot polish, sherry and bitter, but all *so very slowly*: both gone. The last Hall during the evenings of the
May races, then postponed until 7.45 on the assumption that no true-blooded
Johnian would have much appetite for half-warmed provisions before knowing
that the First VIII was home and dry and the Hall waiters were assured of their
winnings on the outcome: likewise, together with indistinct memories of John
Betjeman's

> Kitchen din,
> Cups and plates
> And the getting of bump suppers for the long-dead generations
> Coming in,
> From Eights.[71]

(Except of course that it wasn't Eights.)

In the transformation of the relationship between senior and junior members
brought about by the changed age of majority, unsurprisingly the College has
changed as society has changed. These days junior members, especially graduate
students, may be on first-name terms with their Seniors. That was only one of

---

[68] Cf. above, p. 600.

[69] Providing, incidentally, some of the earliest evidence for the pre-history of Room
Cricket: 'The Opera went as usual: [O. R.] Fulljames and I had a great rag during
Act I, playing "French cricket" in the wings in a corner with several of the girls, using
as a ball one of the peaches from the dish of sham fruit in Act III': LHMD, 16 Feb.
1922.

[70] 'Most men affected the cold sponge in the morning': Benians, 'Cambridge in the last
half century', 13.

[71] 'I. M. Walter Ramsden ob. March 26, 1947 Pembroke College, Oxford'.

the things that John Crook was right about, just as his counter-suggestibility so strongly resembled that of his antecessor William Heitland whose colleagues 'learned how to exploit his contrarian tendencies by urging him to do the opposite of what they really wished him to'. On occasion, the authentic Crookian cadences are clearly audible in Glover's reports of his tutor's reactions.[72] For that matter, contrast the blend of cautious familiarity, deference and strictly hierarchical matiness exemplified by the young Glover during that tutor's convalescence at Hastings in 1893.[73] Drinking patterns have also changed. For Macklin a quart of beer (two pints) was a lot of beer.[74] Since his time wine has supplanted beer in Hall and until 2008, when (not for the first time)[75] the practice was stopped and a Hall strike threatened, Hall having replaced Chapel as the College's place of protest, a bottle of cheap plonk per person became established as the ration. Most of May Week in the twenty-first century is self-catering too, with Eagles in flip-flops and long shorts and Flamingoes (their female opposite numbers) in sari-like garments (at most) bearing bags full of vodka and lemonade back from Sainsbury's. In the 1960s the Kitchens set up Eagles' parties, the young gentlemen wore proper shoes, blazers and flannels, their ladies floated diaphanously across the lawns, and the Flamingoes hadn't yet been thought of.

It may be reassuring, therefore, to reflect that some things never change. The question asked by the Senior Treasurer of the Magdalene Field Clubs in the 1970s on the occasion of that college's entering into the agreement to share the St John's facilities, whether St John's had any spare stabling, indicates the existence of a chasm between the two institutions even wider than Magdalene Street. In a southwards direction, meanwhile, although borrowed from Balliol's homage to its neighbour of the same name, the end-of-the evening singing of Gordouli:

> If I were a bloody Trinity Man, I would, I would,
> I'd go into a public rear, I would, I would,
> I'd pull the chain and disappear, I would, I would,
> One – Two – Three:
> Bloody Trinity … (and so on),

commemorates a rivalry centuries old, as old as the blood on the cobbles in the early seventeenth century and the competition over class-lists for so much of the nineteenth.[76]

Not altogether new is the world-wide fame of the College Choir and its mundane manifestation, the Gentlemen of St John's. The pupils of Guest and

---

[72] Above, p. 321. Cf. GD, 12 Mar. 1891, on winning the Browne Medal for Greek epigram: 'Called (…) on Heitland who did not think much of my epigram.'

[73] 'In morning found WEH on beach and with him & Berry built a ditch, a pond and a "barrage"': GD, 10 Apr. 1893. On their return to London Heitland travels first class, Glover third, whereafter Glover spends an evening 'playing tiddlywinks with Scott and Sikes': GD, 17 Apr. and 2 Jun. 1893. *Autres pays, autres mœurs.*

[74] Yet while rowing in the Third VIII he would drink port of an evening: LHMB, 22 May & 8 Feb. 1922.

[75] See above, p. 312.

[76] Above, pp. 130, 394–5. For the origins of the Oxford vendetta, see Hopkins, *Trinity*, 307–9.

its subsequent directors, not least those members of the choir whose musical prowess was not matched by academic achievement, have transcended the tradition that dominated chapel services from the construction of the new building until the late 1940s and have colonized England's great cathedrals.[77] When, with the retirement of George Guest imminent, in 1989 the new Master, as head of a now co-residential College, felt obliged to question the continuation of a men-and-boys-only choir the bombardment launched by George Guest made Vaughan Williams etc. in 1954 appear pre-bow and arrows. 'The choir is without equal in the world', wrote one supporter in the USA. To tamper with its constitution would be 'an astonishing act of vandalism' marking the College as 'a most Philistine society', averred Robin Orr. 'There must be many thousands of people around the world who are aware of the existence of St John's solely by virtue of its Choir.' As to the fate of some choral students at the hands of tripos examiners, the skills of the former 'are different in kind, but *not inferior* to those of other serious artists and scholars/academics'. 'It might be interesting to know the academic results obtained by members of the LMBC 1st boat, or by those who achieve distinction in other forms of sport in St John's', the former college organist helpfully suggested.[78] Twenty years on, such comparisons may be seen to be otiose. Although chapel services remain hardly better attended by members of the College than they were a century and more ago, in 2011 the College choir is securely established as one of the glories of the wider world.

With a travel grant of course, undergraduates these days will readily travel to London or, in the Long Vac., to Mongolia or Ecuador. It will not occur to them to visit villages five or ten miles from Cambridge; and after three years they won't even know in which direction such places are. In 2011 undergraduates who a century ago would have walked there and back in an afternoon have yet to discover the delights of the 'Queen's Head' at Newton. But that is *Daily Mail* talk. Better to hearken to that old curmudgeon, Heitland. For Heitland undergraduates (graduate students had yet to be invented) were 'habitually loyal and responsive to trust'.[79] In the same vein, a century ago precisely Russell-Smith wrote thus to Benians: 'But for the fact that the freshers seem a better lot, John's would be now with the dogs. It may recover.'[80] Similar sentiment suffused Benians's own life work. 'If everybody neglected College work to do outside things, College would suffer', he was heard to say on his deathbed. 'If you can get everybody to believe College is a wonderful institution, it can do things no other body can.' Convictions such as that may seem embarrassingly dated now, may be thought to smack of *Greyfriars* even, as may its reformulation by successive commemoration preachers over the years to the effect that for one reason or another the College's undergraduates are its surest benefactors.[81]

There are forces at work in the University corroding the colleges that protect it. There are faculties and departments which pressurize their lecturers not to

[77] Above, pp. 575–7.
[78] SJCA, DS2.14.
[79] Heitland, *After Many Years*, 230.
[80] Letter of 15 Oct. 1911 (EABP).
[81] *Eagle* xlix (1935), 10 [Yule], lv (1953), 178 [Guillebaud]; (1997), 18 [Linehan].

give college supervisions or accept college appointments. But undergraduates won't live at their faculties, or eat there, or sleep there, or play for them. It is colleges that draw their strength from their junior roots, and their junior members, the crooked timber of Johnian humanity, that supply it. Though the College may die at the top and shed its upper branches, it sends up strong growth from beneath. The College's soundest ethos is its very lack of one. It is the freedom that it provides every one of its members to find his or her own level and direction. As Nicholas Mansergh, its thirty-ninth Master, declared of the Commonwealth, the College is 'an end sufficient in itself'.[82]

Without lapsing further into sententious mode, it may surely be claimed that any College takes time, that there need to be those willing to devote to it that quality time of which John Crook spoke, and that those so prepared need to outnumber those who are only aboard for the benefits it bestows, and who, when anything collegiate or demanding of time is mooted, prove conspicuous by their absence. Doubtless within the next 500 years the balance of things will be revealed. If the first 500 have a lesson to convey, perhaps it is that in its dealings with funding councils and governments the college which was effectively founded by a man who, exceptionally in his time, refused to comply with the demands of tyranny, will in the years ahead do well to remember his example. In discussions of the future prospects of the country's great universities the fate of the great monasteries in the 1530s is often enough prayed in aid. But let it also be remembered that it was by intimation that government in the 1530s proceeded – 'and intimations were then to be complied with'.[83] No doubt, now as then, supping with the Secretary of State is necessary. That certainly was Nicholas Metcalfe's strategy, making it hard at first glance to believe that the Master spent any time in Cambridge at all.[84] His fate, and that of Fisher too, serves only to demonstrate the uncertain outcome of too comfortable an association with the powers that be.

---

[82] P. N. S. Mansergh, *The Commonwealth Experience* (London, 1969), 413.
[83] Above, p. 504.
[84] Above, p. 28.

APPENDICES

The Social, Intellectual and Professional Arithmetic of the College, 1900–89

Peter Hennessy

THE College possesses an essence, a specialness which can be felt and described in words not quantified. Yet, like all institutions, it has a social arithmetic that can be measured – the social and geographical origins of the undergraduates; their funding; subjects studied and subsequent careers pursued. Thanks to pioneering work by Lucy Rhymer, Dawn Dodds and Fiona Colbert, it has been possible to create a statistical picture of the Johnian intakes of 1900 and at decennial intervals between 1909 and 1989.

The coverage is not perfect. There are gaps. And the foundress, Lady Margaret Beaufort, added a quirk with her definition of the six northern counties of England whence she particularly hoped scholars would be drawn. The northerly and middle terrain was straightforward enough: Durham; Northumberland; Cumberland; Westmorland; Yorkshire and Richmond (then a separate entity). Yet south of the Mersey and the Humber she has included Derbyshire and Nottinghamshire but not Cheshire or Lincolnshire. But, faithful as ever to the foundress, it is her definition of the north that we had adopted for the purposes of geographical identification. The state/private school split is difficult to define from the data available, but the attempt to do so is made.

Fig. 1 depicting undergraduate and postgraduate admissions 1900–89 illustrates a strong upward march of numbers with two surges influenced by returning servicemen in 1919 and 1949 and two step changes (even allowing for the post-War bulges) after the First and Second World Wars. As we shall see, these shifts were influenced by increased availability of state or local authority funding, especially so after the passage of the Education Act in 1944.

Table 1 on the geographical spread of the eight intakes shows a consistent domination by the South of England and the North usually surpassing the Midlands but only getting close to the South in 1939 (which is a freakish year as war was declared on 3 September between admission and matriculation in October).

Table 2 shows, in terms of social origins, the overwhelming predominance of young men from professional middle class homes which is hardly dented by the wider opportunities available from the mid-1940s though the lower clerical/professional proportion demonstrates a steady rise as the proportion of grammar-school-educated entrants rises and the effects of the 1944 Act work through the UK's educational system. The proportion of recruits from the manual working class is minute throughout but the skilled working class fares rather better though rarely nudging the 10 per cent mark. Each year, however, has a special story to tell and it is to these that we now turn.

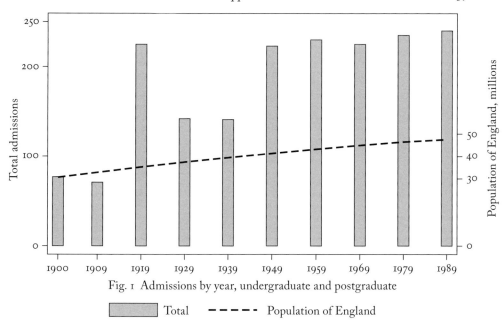

Fig. 1 Admissions by year, undergraduate and postgraduate

▓ Total　　— — — Population of England

Table 1 Geographical origins of students
as a percentage of those with available information

Year	South	Midlands	North	Scotland Ireland & Wales	Common-wealth	Overseas
1900	49.4%	19.5%	15.6%	9.1%	6.5%	0.0%
1909	57.7%	18.3%	14.1%	8.5%	1.4%	0.0%
1919	58.2%	9.3%	17.3%	9.8%	3.6%	1.8%
1929	50.0%	11.3%	19.0%	9.9%	5.6%	4.2%
1939	34.0%	12.8%	29.1%	9.2%	12.1%	2.8%
1949	42.9%	10.5%	21.9%	11.0%	8.2%	5.5%
1959	49.6%	16.2%	12.7%	6.1%	10.5%	4.8%
1969	53.8%	11.6%	19.1%	5.8%	4.0%	5.8%
1979	46.0%	6.8%	22.1%	8.9%	8.1%	8.1%
1989	48.9%	10.4%	14.9%	5.9%	6.8%	13.1%

Table 2 Parental social class as a percentage of those with available information.

Year	Private means	Professional middle class	Self-employed	Lower clerical & professional	Skilled working class	Manual working class
1900	6.2%	51.9%	16.0%	4.9%	17.3%	3.7%
1909	3.9%	63.2%	15.8%	7.9%	7.9%	1.3%
1919	3.8%	45.1%	17.7%	24.9%	8.0%	0.4%
1929	4.2%	63.9%	17.4%	9.7%	3.5%	1.4%
1939	1.4%	65.2%	17.4%	7.2%	8.0%	0.7%
1949	0.9%	59.2%	14.8%	13.5%	9.4%	2.2%
1959	0.4%	63.4%	8.8%	18.5%	7.5%	1.3%
1969	0.0%	58.8%	9.3%	23.9%	7.5%	0.4%
1979	0.0%	72.8%	5.7%	9.6%	10.5%	1.3%
1989	0.0%	78.6%	2.7%	10.5%	7.3%	0.9%

1900

The turn-of-the-century College naturally reflected late-nineteenth-century patterns. For example, it still had the air of a clergy factory, with the Church still by far the most prominent professional destination even though only two of the 1900 intake read Theology (Natural Sciences being the dominant tripos as it was to remain throughout the ninety years surveyed). The tables for 'Subject Read' and 'Professional Destinations' reflect those for whom data are available rather than the complete cohort – and this is true for the tables to come. The 'Subject Read' tables do not distinguish between undergraduate and postgraduate recruits.

SUBJECT READ, 1900	
Natural Sciences	16
Classics	11
History	5
Law	5
Mathematics	4
Mechanical Sciences	3
Theology	2
Moral Sciences	2

In 1900, drawing on the best figures manageable from those for whom data are available, 35 of the intake were from private schools plus three receiving private tuition; 20 were from grammar schools (most of which pre-1944 included fee-paying pupils).

PROFESSIONAL DESTINATIONS, 1900	
Clergy	21
Medicine	9
School teaching	9
Law	7
Civil Service	5
University teaching	3
Industry/Commerce/Finance	2
Armed Forces	2
Tea Planting	1

There is no trace of state or local authority funding in the pattern of scholarships, exhibitions and sizarships awarded in 1900, though this has begun to change by 1909 as we shall see.

1909

By 1909 there was a new tripos available, Economics, very much the intellectual child of the world-renowned Alfred Marshall, perhaps the most famous member of the College's Fellowship.

SUBJECT READ, 1909	
Natural Sciences	16
Mathematics	10
Classics	10
History	7
Economics	5
Languages	3
Theology	2
Engineering	1
Moral Sciences	1
Agriculture	1

In terms of schooling, the best available figures indicate 43 from private schools plus two receiving private tuition; 15 from grammar schools.

PROFESSIONAL DESTINATIONS, 1909	
Clergy	12
Industry/Commerce/Finance	8
School teaching	7
Armed Forces	7
Civil Service	5
Colonial Service	5
Medicine	4
University teaching	4
Law	3
Journalism	1

In 1909 the traces of state/local authority funding are discernible though the numbers are small: two Board of Education-supported students; one on a Kent County Council Scholarship.

1919

In addition to its considerable number, the 1919 intake had a still wider range of triposes from which to choose including English, Geography and Anthropology. The War, too, had altered permanently the balance between God and Mammon in terms of career destination. The dominance of the clergy was over, though they still managed to cling to third place. The schools balance was 135 from private schools, 11 from private tuition, and 31 from grammar schools.

SUBJECT READ, 1919

Natural Sciences	38
Mathematics	24
History	17
Classics	14
Languages	8
Law	7
Economics	7
Mechanical Sciences/Engineering	3
English	2
Medicine	1
Theology	1
Anthropology	1
Moral Sciences	1
Geography	1

PROFESSIONAL DESTINATIONS, 1919

Industry/Commerce/Finance	31
School teaching	28
Clergy	18
Medicine	15
University teaching	14
Colonial Service	10
Civil Service	7
Law	4
Journalism/Writing	3
Farming	2
Police	2

State funding was suddenly a strong presence in 1919. Some 82 of the new undergraduate and postgraduate members benefited from grants, chiefly paid by the Board of Education with a few from the Board of Agriculture.

1929

1929 can be treated as a normal inter-war year neither boosted by Great War veterans as in 1919 nor depleted by early volunteers for World War II as in 1939. The schools balance was 91 from private schools, 7 from private tuition, and 21 from grammar schools.

SUBJECT READ, 1929	
Natural Sciences	17
Law	13
Languages	12
History	11
Classics	9
Mathematics	9
Mechanical Sciences/Engineering	7
English	5
Economics	4
Geography	1
Architecture	1
Agriculture	1

PROFESSIONAL DESTINATIONS, 1929	
School teaching	15
Industry/Commerce/Finance	14
University teaching	11
Law	8
Medicine	7
Armed Forces	6
Clergy	4
Civil Service	3
Colonial Service	3
Local Government	3
BBC	2
Acting	1
Veterinary	1
Librarian	1
Museum Keeper	1
Architect	1
Politics	1

Only nine of those students for whom we have data received State, Colonial Office or local authority funding in 1929.

1939

1939 was the year the flow of students from Lady Margaret's six northern counties peaked with 41 (to 48 from the South of England; 29 per cent to the South's 34 per cent). The gap between grammar schools and private schools had narrowed, too, with 82 coming from private schools, and 29 from grammar.

SUBJECT READ, 1939

Natural Sciences	19
Mathematics	12
Economics	11
Mechanical Services/Engineering	10
Law	9
Classics	8
Geography	6
Languages	5
History	4
English	2
Moral Sciences	1
Agriculture	1
Architecture	1

PROFESSIONAL DESTINATIONS, 1939

University teaching	20
Medicine	16
Industry/Commerce/Finance	16
Armed Forces	11
Civil Service	10
Schoolteaching	8
Law	5
Colonial Service	2
Farming	2
Music	2
Local Government	1
Clergy	1
Acting	1

In terms of funding, 29 of the 1939 intake received state or local authority support of some kind; a noticeable increase since 1929.

1949

The 1949 intake saw the tail-end of the returning servicemen and the first effects of the extra state/local authority funding available as a result of the 1944 Education Act (known as the 'Butler Act' after its progenitor, R. A. Butler) which provided free secondary schooling for all (including all but the 'direct grant' grammar schools) and a substantial and sustained increase in the availability of public funding for students moving on to higher education. The private/state school split for the 1949 cohort was 130 from private and 51 from grammar schools.

SUBJECT READ, 1949

Natural Sciences	40
Mathematics	23
Mechanical Services/Engineering	20
Languages	18
History	15
English	14
Classics	10
Economics	9
Law	7
Geography	6
Agriculture	2
Archaeology & Anthropology	1
Theology	1
Architecture	1
Estate Management	1

PROFESSIONAL DESTINATIONS, 1949

Industry/Commerce/Finance	58
University teaching/Administration	34
Schoolteaching	21
Medicine	14
Civil Service	9
Law	8
Clergy	6
Colonial Service	4
Armed Forces	4
Media/Writing/Publishing	3
Farming	2
Veterinary	1
Musician	1

The real impact of the 1944 Act is visible in the funding figures for 1949. Of the 168 students for whom we have financial details, 100 were state/local authority supported in one form or another, thirteen of them by the Further Education and Training Scheme for Ex-Servicemen (the UK equivalent of the US GI Bill).

1959

The 1959 intake gives a picture of the College as it had developed fifteen years after the 1944 Education Act with the resulting relative meritocracy visible, though grammar schoolboys had still some way to go to catch up with the privately educated (this took another decade, as we shall see shortly). Of those for whom we have data, the 1959 split was 119 from private schools, 49 from grammar schools.

SUBJECT READ, 1959

Natural Sciences	54
Mechanical Sciences	28
Mathematics	19
Languages	18
History	17
Classics	16
Economics	14
Geography	9
Agriculture	8
Geography	6
Law	7
Colonial Service Course	7
English	6
Architecture	4
Music	4
Oriental Studies	3
Theology	2
Estate Management	2
Moral Sciences	2
Anthropology	1

PROFESSIONAL DESTINATIONS, 1959

Industry/Commerce/Finance	56
University teaching	54
Schoolteaching	15
Medicine	9
Civil Service	7
Law	6
Colonial Service	4
Clergy	4
Armed Forces	4
Charity	2
Veterinary	2
Farmer	1
Singer	1
Actor	1
Television	1

Of the 164 new undergraduate and postgraduate members for whom we have financial information, 128 were in receipt of state funding of one kind or another.

1969

This was the intake when the grammar schools almost pipped the private schools. Rab Butler's boys fell a mere three short, with 84 from private schools, 81 from grammar schools.

SUBJECT READ, 1969	
Natural Science	34
Engineering	27
Mathematics	21
Medicine	20
History	17
Economics	15
Law	13
English	11
Certificate of Education	10
Languages	10
Classics	8
Geography	8
Theology	5
Archaeology & Anthropology	5
Philosophy	4
Architecture	3
Music	3
Criminology	1

PROFESSIONAL DESTINATIONS, 1969	
Industry/Commerce/Finance	56
University teaching	25
Medicine	15
Law	14
Civil and Diplomatic Services	9
Schoolteaching	7
Clergy	5
Television	3
Veterinary	2
Architect	2
Musician	2
Health Service	1
Local Government	1
Publishing	1
Politician	1
Poet	1

1979

Of the 199 undergraduates and postgraduates for whom we have data 142 were in receipt of state funding of one kind or another.

SUBJECT READ, 1979

Natural Science	46
Engineering	38
Mathematics	22
Medicine	15
History	10
Economics	16
Law	23
English	7
Certificate of Education	3
Languages	6
Classics	7
Geography	7
Theology	4
Archaeology & Anthropology	8
Philosophy	6
Architecture	1
Music	4
Veterinary Medicine	1
Land Economy	1

PROFESSIONAL DESTINATIONS, 1979

Industry/Commerce/Finance	66
University teaching	20
Medicine	12
Law	18
Civil and Diplomatic Services	5
Schoolteaching	13
Clergy	2
Television	2
Veterinary medicine	3
Architecture	2
Musician	2
Local Government	1
Record Producer	1
Farmer	1
Cartoonist	1
Racing Driver	1
Journalism	1
Armed Forces	2
Museum Curator	1

1989

By 1989 the 'subjects read' reflect a proliferation of courses within the tripos framework such as international relations at postgraduate level, often studied by members of the Armed Forces on secondment.

SUBJECT READ, 1989	
Natural Science	61
Engineering	26
Mathematics	22
Medicine	14
History	11
Economics	14
Law	18
English	8
Certificate of Education	2
Languages	19
Classics	5
Geography	7
Theology	2
Archaeology & Anthropology	4
Philosophy	5
Architecture	1
Music	5
Social & Political Science	4
International Relations	4
Veterinary Medicine	3
History of Art	2
Management	2

PROFESSIONAL DESTINATIONS, 1989	
Industry/Commerce/Finance	85
University teaching	29
Medicine	14
Law	18
Civil and Diplomatic Services	5
Schoolteaching	8
Clergy	1
Veterinary	1
Musician	2
Health Service	1
Publishing	1
Farmer	1
Politician	1
Armed Services	2
Police	1
Journalism	4
Actor	1
Museum/Art Curator	2

APPENDIX 2

Recruitment, 1904–2009

Peter Linehan

	Undergraduates			BAs + Research			Total
	men	*women*		*men*	*women*		
1904–5			*208*			*44*	*252*
1909–10			*228*			*35*	*263*
1914–15			*153*			*15*	*168*
1915–16			*78*			*14*	*92*
1916–17			*33*			*6*	*39*
1917–18			*34*			*6*	*40*
1918–19			*50*			*4*	*54*
1919–20			*357*			*19*	*376*
1924–5			*342*			*45*	*387*
1929–30			*417*			*38*	*455*
1934–5			373			37+21	431
1939–40							370
1944–5							282
1949–50			*532*			*177*	709
1954–5			499			76	575
1959–60			602			110	712
1964–5			550			152	702
1969–70			525			156	681
1974–5			521			176	697
1979–80			527			171	698
1982–3	470	43	513	187	23	210	723
1983–4	419	84	503	165	30	195	698
1984–5	376	135	511	161	36	197	708
1985–6	386	151	537	157	49	206	743
1986–7	378	163	541	173	53	226	767
1987–8	365	161	526	195	41	236	762
1988–9	366	162	528	153	75	228	756
1989–90	373	156	529	159	73	232	761
1994–5	355	184	539	199	85	284	823
1999–2000	346	210	556	211	102	313	869
2004–5	319	219	538	171	126	297	837
2009–10	346	229	575	181	156	337	912

Figures in italics are derived from Resident Members List, which are at variance with College figures where these are available: e.g. for 1934–5: 416+60. In the case of figures for the early 1980s (cf. p.»628) such variation must derive from differing methods of counting.

APPENDIX 3

Cambridge University and St John's College Tripos Performance by Decade, 1899–2009

Stephanie Rucker-Andrews

The following tables represent tripos examination results achieved by Cambridge University and St John's College students, thus allowing for comparison by class. The results include all parts of the honours tripos exam for each subject (not only the final year). All subjects offered at Cambridge University have been included. Results were gathered from *The Cambridge University Reporter* Class Lists for each corresponding year, with the exception of 2009, when electronic results were available directly from the Office of Student Records and Administration.

FIRST CLASS

Year	All Subjects				Arts/Humanities				Maths/Sciences			
	CU		SJC		CU		SJC		CU		SJC	
	#	%	#	%	#	%	#	%	#	%	#	%
1899	213	22.0%	29	30.2%	113	17.0%	14	23.7%	100	32.7%	15	40.5%
1909	277	20.0%	23	25.0%	110	12.8%	3	8.1%	167	31.5%	20	36.4%
1919	118	29.8%	15	60.0%	21	12.1%	1	16.7%	97	43.5%	14	73.7%
1929	408	17.7%	42	21.6%	250	15.5%	22	17.1%	158	22.9%	20	30.8%
1939	412	15.7%	33	17.2%	246	13.0%	22	17.6%	166	22.6%	11	16.4%
1949	441	12.8%	45	16.5%	263	10.7%	22	13.4%	178	18.3%	23	21.1%
1959	433	10.5%	35	11.9%	213	7.8%	15	8.3%	220	15.9%	20	17.7%
1969	722	12.1%	57	15.0%	222	7.7%	9	5.8%	500	16.2%	48	21.3%
1979	915	12.6%	58	13.3%	285	8.2%	14	8.2%	630	16.6%	44	16.7%
1989	1,256	15.7%	93	20.5%	332	8.1%	18	9.5%	924	23.6%	75	28.5%
1999	1,823	19.5%	116	23.9%	610	14.0%	39	17.0%	1,213	24.4%	77	30.1%
2009	2,085	21.0%	105	20.6%	847	17.5%	43	17.3%	1,238	24.4%	62	23.8%
Total	9,103	16.3%	651	19.0%	3,512	11.7%	222	13.1%	5,591	21.8%	429	24.8%

SECOND CLASS

Year	All Subjects				Arts/Humanities				Maths/Sciences			
	CU		SJC		CU		SJC		CU		SJC	
	#	%	#	%	#	%	#	%	#	%	#	%
1899	283	29.2%	24	25.0%	183	27.6%	12	20.3%	100	32.7%	12	32.4%
1909	474	34.1%	33	35.9%	300	35.0%	20	54.1%	174	32.8%	13	23.6%
1919	102	25.8%	3	12.0%	40	23.1%	1	16.7%	62	27.8%	2	10.5%
1929	388	16.9%	37	19.1%	142	8.8%	10	7.8%	246	35.6%	27	41.5%
1939	287	10.9%	27	14.1%	59	3.1%	4	3.2%	228	31.0%	23	34.3%
1949	352	10.2%	41	15.0%	9	0.4%	0	0.0%	343	35.3%	41	37.6%
1959	96	2.3%	5	1.7%	0	0.0%	0	0.0%	96	6.9%	5	4.4%
1969	640	10.7%	46	12.1%	0	0.0%	0	0.0%	640	20.8%	46	20.4%
1979	672	9.2%	81	18.6%	0	0.0%	0	0.0%	672	17.7%	81	30.7%
1989	596	7.4%	39	8.6%	0	0.0%	0	0.0%	596	15.2%	39	14.8%
1999	410	4.4%	23	4.7%	0	0.0%	0	0.0%	410	8.3%	23	9.0%
2009	787	7.9%	39	7.7%	65	1.3%	2	0.8%	722	14.2%	37	14.2%
Total	5,087	9.1%	398	11.6%	798	2.7%	49	2.9%	4,289	16.7%	349	20.1%

CLASSED II.1

| Year | All Subjects | | | | Arts/Humanities | | | | Maths/Sciences | | | |
| | CU | | SJC | | CU | | SJC | | CU | | SJC | |
	#	%	#	%	#	%	#	%	#	%	#	%
1909	11	0.8%	0	0.0%	11	1.3%	0	0.0%	0	0.0%	0	0.0%
1919	11	2.8%	1	4.0%	11	6.4%	1	16.7%	0	0.0%	0	0.0%
1929	242	10.5%	17	8.8%	242	15.0%	17	13.2%	0	0.0%	0	0.0%
1939	466	17.7%	25	13.0%	433	22.9%	22	17.6%	33	4.5%	3	4.5%
1949	776	22.6%	58	21.2%	727	29.5%	50	30.5%	49	5.0%	8	7.3%
1959	1065	25.8%	75	25.5%	832	30.3%	55	30.4%	233	16.8%	20	17.7%
1969	1453	24.3%	100	26.4%	979	33.8%	63	40.9%	474	15.4%	37	16.4%
1979	2286	31.4%	125	28.7%	1,489	42.8%	78	45.6%	797	20.9%	47	17.8%
1989	3225	40.2%	192	42.4%	2,232	54.5%	131	68.9%	993	25.3%	61	23.2%
1999	4,514	48.4%	229	47.1%	2,851	65.3%	140	60.9%	1,663	33.5%	89	34.8%
2009	4,885	49.3%	255	50.1%	3,223	66.6%	168	67.5%	1,662	32.8%	87	33.5%
Total	18,934	33.9%	1077	31.4%	13,030	43.3%	725	42.8%	5,904	23.0%	352	20.3%

CLASSED II.2

| Year | All Subjects | | | | Arts/Humanities | | | | Maths/Sciences | | | |
| | CU | | SJC | | CU | | SJC | | CU | | SJC | |
	#	%	#	%	#	%	#	%	#	%	#	%
1909	11	0.8%	0	0.0%	11	1.3%	0	0.0%	0	0.0%	0	0.0%
1919	32	8.1%	0	0.0%	32	18.5%	0	0.0%	0	0.0%	0	0.0%
1929	354	15.4%	30	15.5%	354	22.0%	30	23.3%	0	0.0%	0	0.0%
1939	625	23.8%	45	23.4%	590	31.2%	43	34.4%	35	4.8%	2	3.0%
1949	1,060	30.9%	74	27.1%	977	39.7%	67	40.9%	83	8.5%	7	6.4%
1959	1,494	36.2%	113	38.4%	1,108	40.4%	75	41.4%	386	27.8%	38	33.6%
1969	2,082	34.8%	110	29.0%	1,284	44.3%	64	41.6%	798	25.9%	46	20.4%
1979	2,432	33.4%	120	27.6%	1,412	40.6%	64	37.4%	1,020	26.8%	56	21.2%
1989	2,300	28.7%	102	22.5%	1,372	33.5%	39	20.5%	928	23.7%	63	24.0%
1999	1,878	20.1%	89	18.3%	833	19.1%	47	20.4%	1,045	21.0%	42	16.4%
2009	1,549	15.6%	76	14.9%	639	13.2%	32	12.9%	910	17.9%	44	16.9%
Total	13,817	24.8%	759	22.1%	8,612	28.6%	461	27.2%	5,205	20.3%	298	17.2%

A Note on Second Class results

In 1899 Second Class exams in 1899 were not split between II.1 and II.2 in any subject. Several subjects continued to issue Second Class results for all or part of their tripos examinations even after II.1 and II.2 classifications were introduced. These subjects were: 1909–89: Maths; 1909–39 and 2009: Classics; 1909–49: Mechanical Sciences; 1909–49 & 1969–2009: Natural Sciences; Theological: 1909–39; 1909, 1919: Modern and Medieval Languages; 1909: General Examination and History; 1919: English and Law; 1929: Geography; 1909, 1929: Moral Sciences; 1929, 1939: Oriental Studies; 2009: Medical and Veterinary Sciences.

In some subjects, Second Class results were reserved for specific parts of the tripos examinations and 'split second' classifications were given for other parts (Moral Sciences, Classics, Medical and Veterinary Sciences and Natural Sciences). Therefore, these subjects are also included in the II.1 and II.2 tables. A review of the original data set reflects exactly which classes were used for each subject and their individual tripos parts.

THIRD CLASS

Year	All Subjects				Arts/Humanities				Maths/Sciences			
	CU		SJC		CU		SJC		CU		SJC	
	#	%	#	%	#	%	#	%	#	%	#	%
1899	323	33.3%	30	31.3%	241	36.3%	20	33.9%	82	26.8%	10	27.0%
1909	442	31.8%	29	31.5%	289	33.7%	8	21.6%	153	28.9%	21	38.2%
1919	114	28.8%	4	16.0%	60	34.7%	1	16.7%	54	24.2%	3	15.8%
1929	722	31.4%	52	26.8%	498	30.9%	40	31.0%	224	32.4%	12	18.5%
1939	774	29.4%	55	28.6%	539	28.5%	33	26.4%	235	32.0%	22	32.8%
1949	758	22.1%	49	17.9%	480	19.5%	24	14.6%	278	28.6%	25	22.9%
1959	973	23.6%	62	21.1%	588	21.4%	36	19.9%	385	27.7%	26	23.0%
1969	926	15.5%	50	13.2%	399	13.8%	16	10.4%	527	17.1%	34	15.1%
1979	863	11.8%	44	10.1%	269	7.7%	14	8.2%	594	15.6%	30	11.4%
1989	532	6.6%	16	3.5%	149	3.6%	2	1.1%	383	9.8%	14	5.3%
1999	372	4.0%	13	2.7%	70	1.6%	4	1.7%	302	6.1%	9	3.5%
2009	271	2.7%	19	3.7%	60	1.2%	4	1.6%	211	4.2%	15	5.8%
Total	7,070	12.7%	423	12.3%	3,642	12.1%	202	12.0%	3,428	13.3%	221	12.8%

A Note on Honours results

The Honours and Honours with Distinction classifications have been reserved for final-year exams in the following subjects. (In 2009 'Honours with Merit' was also distinguished from Honours and Honours with Distinction in the data received from the Office of Student Records and Administration. Honours with Merit classifications were added to the Honours in this table, thus maintaining the two categories.)

   1939–2009 Maths, Part III
      1969 Mechanical Sciences, Part II
 1989, 1999 & 2009 Manufacturing/Manufacturing Engineering, Part II
      1999 Electrical & Information Sciences, Part II
   1999 & 2009 Engineering, Part IIB

	HONOURS WITH DISTINCTION				HONOURS			
Year	Maths/Sciences				Maths/Sciences			
	CU		SJC		CU		SJC	
	#	%	#	%	#	%	#	%
1939	14	1.9%	4	6.0%	13	1.8%	2	3.0%
1949	21	2.2%	2	1.8%	11	1.1%	2	1.8%
1959	16	1.2%	3	2.7%	51	3.7%	1	0.9%
1969	28	0.9%	3	1.3%	88	2.9%	8	3.6%
1979	16	0.4%	2	0.8%	37	1.0%	3	1.1%
1989	21	0.5%	5	1.9%	51	1.3%	2	0.8%
1999	86	1.7%	4	1.6%	223	4.5%	11	4.3%
2009	90	1.8%	2	0.8%	220	4.3%	13	5.0%
Total	292	1.1%	25	1.4%	694	2.7%	42	2.4%

APPENDIX 4

Johnian Dynasties, 1900–99

Peter Linehan

Year	Member was child of OJ	Member was grandchild of OJ	Member had sons at SJC	Member had grandchildren at SJC	Member was wife/widow/ partner/ fiancé(e) of
1900	5	4	6	I	
1904	6	I	10	3	
1909	5	–	–	I	
1914	2	–	8	I	
1919	24	2	67	8	
1924	11	–	18	3	
1929	13	I	19	4	
1934	7	–	14	I	
1939	11	2	16	3	
1944	9	I	15	–	
1949	26	3	11	4	
1954	23	5	17	I	
1959	34	2	7	–	
1964	20	5	9	–	
1969[a]	13	I	5	–	
1974	10	2	5	–	
1979	20	3	–	–	
1984	14 = 6s+8d	4	I	–	28
1989	17 = 11s+6d	7	–	–	30
1994	7 = 4s+3d	I	–	–	20
1999	11 = 6s+5d	–	–	–	15
2004	8 = 5s+3d				
2009	6 = 4s[b]+2d				

a According to Admissions Statistics presented annually by the Senior Tutor, numbers in 1970 to 1973 were 21; 16; 10; 18 (SJCA, STF2007/1). On the retirement of Dr Bertram, after 1973 the calculation discontinued.

b Including one with both parents Johnian.

Many of the figures above are derived from information provided by members themselves. They are therefore only as reliable, and as unforgetful, as their authors.

Schools Feeding the College: Individuals and Institutions

Peter Linehan

	Grammar	6th-form College	Independent	State	University	Other	Total
1900	18 (16)		29 (24)	–	8 (8)	18	73
1909	16 (11)		42 (29)	–	4 (4)	13	75
1919	31 (25)		125 (68)	4 (4)	26 (25)	41	227
1929	15 (16)		93 (52)	–	12 (10)	26	146
1939	27 (22)		81 (57)	2 (2)	18 (18)	11	139
1949	42 (38)		130[a] (66)	3 (3)	25 (22)	16	216
1959	38 (32)		125[b] (78)	5 (2)	27 (22)	15	210
1969	66 (52)		84 (57)	11 (3)	41 (35)	12	213
1979	33 (21)	5 (4)	104 (73)	27 (26)	48 (40)	20	237
1989	36 (31)	11 (11)	89 (72)	37 (32)	38 (22)	27	238
1999	14 (14)	10 (7)	76 (54)	35 (33)	82 (71)	15	232
2009	20 (18)	14 (11)	61 (51)	33 (32)	89 (69)	19	236

Numbers in parentheses indicate institutions; other numbers indicate individuals

a Including 10 from Sedbergh
b Including 11 from Marlborough

Individuals from schools with closed awards and/or SJC governors:
1900: 8; 1909: 7; 1919: 28; 1929: 26; 1939: 34; 1949: 38; 1959: 36; 1969: 16

The Finances of St John's College
during the Twentieth Century

Edmund Rogers

ENDLESS money, as Cicero famously suggested, forms 'the sinews of war'. One might also say that it constitutes the sinews of learning. A wealthy academic institution is, of course, better placed to attract the brightest minds, offer the highest quality teaching, and adequately fund the learning and research that push back the boundaries of human knowledge. The twentieth century marks a particularly interesting period in the financial history of universities and colleges: rapid economic and social change, the growth of the state's role in funding higher education, and the democratization of higher education. Several former Bursars of St John's have already charted parts of the College's financial history in that hundred-year span. H. F. Howard's *Account of the Finances of the College of St John the Evangelist*, published in 1935, told the story up to 1926, when the New Statutes altered the presentation of accounts. Given the difficulties in comparing accounts before and after this year, it marked a neat cut-off. J. S. Boys Smith, Bursar from 1944 to 1959, produced a detailed account of his tenure in 1983, but this, of course, tells only a small part of the College's twentieth-century story.[1]

The period witnessed the increasing sophistication of College accounting, with major University-wide reforms in the 1920s altering the form and presentation of each college's financial position. Systematic and sophisticated accounting practices do not, however, necessarily bring clarity, especially to the non-expert. Expenditures and revenues are often arbitrarily classified, and leap from one account to another, creating a confusing financial maze. As one of the College's Audit Committees commented in its report for 1929–30, the 'various Internal Accounts of the College form a motley and somewhat disconnected conglomerate'.[2] This is not, therefore, the place for a thorough and detailed (and thus rather dry) description of every item of expenditure and every source of revenue in every financial year. The aim here is to provide a broad-brush depiction of the changing nature of St John's wealth and income over the twentieth century; to ascertain the level of pecuniary commitment to its historic obligations to 'education, religion, learning, and research'; and to situate its financial story within the contexts of University, nation, and the wider world. For the sake of the general reader (and the mental and physical health of the historian), the focus falls on the College's financial position at ten-year intervals from 1899–1900 to 1999–2000. Although such an approach can, of course, only provide a partial illustration of St John's wealth, income, and educational expenditure in this period, these decennial 'snapshots' offer sufficient insight into evolving

---

[1] J. S. Boys Smith, *Memories of St John's College Cambridge, 1919–1969* (Cambridge, 1983).

[2] Report of the Audit Committee on Internal College Accounts for year ending July 1930 (SJCA, CC 3, 97), 1.

bursarial strategy and performance in an era of sometimes staggering economic and social change.

———

In the closing years of the nineteenth century the College finances, so dependent on revenue from its landed estates, had just begun to benefit from the end of Britain's protracted agricultural 'depression'. From the 1870s to the mid-1890s, British farming endured a fundamental shift in global trade and production, as cheap food imports from the New World flooded into the Mother Country's ports. Britain became dependent on imported food, and agricultural rents, the main source of income for the oldest and biggest Oxbridge colleges, fell into a lingering depressed state alleviated only by the high prices and turn towards domestic production of the World Wars.[3]

As a result of the problems in British agriculture, bursars at Oxford and Cambridge colleges pressed for the Board of Agriculture to loosen the statutory restrictions on college investments. Consequently, the Universities and Colleges Estates Act 1898 granted new powers to colleges to invest part of their foundation assets in securities, although such investments could only be made with the consent, and in the name of, the Board of Agriculture. Like trustees, Bursars were also legally obliged to confine themselves to fixed-interest stocks, and to eschew the potentially lucrative but volatile returns from equities.[4] This ability to diversify away from land rents would become crucial during the tumultuous years between the wars.

From what sources did St John's derive its income at the turn of the century? Rents from real property, both land and houses, were the College's largest source of external, or endowment, income (that is, not trust fund income; see Fig. 2). Of this revenue from property, that from land or buildings leased at 'rack rent' – at the full market rental value, as opposed to a value fixed over a long leasing period – accounted for the majority (Fig. 3). Switching to rack rents had proved a winning formula for many Oxbridge colleges as they sought to sustain their agricultural incomes.[5] In the early twentieth century St John's found itself in a comfortable financial position, enjoying for the most part a steadily, although not rapidly, rising real income. However, this resulted from the expanding contribution of rents from houses on long lease, whilst there was a notable *decline* in real income from lands let at rack rent and, for much of the early twentieth century, interest from securities (Fig. 4). The investment reforms of 1898 were not yet proving to be of great financial use.

War in 1914 brought tremendous economic disruption. Even as revenues from securities and rack-rented land rose from 1916 (Fig. 5), rapid inflation meant that the real value of this income plunged (Figs. 1 and 6). The uncertainties of the war prompted a greater degree of prudential foresight, and to provide for the

[3] Report of the Audit Committee on the Senior Bursar's Accounts for the year 1898–9 (SJCA); S. B. Saul, *The Myth of the Great Depression, 1873–1896* (Basingstoke, 1985); R. R. Neild, *Riches and Responsibility: The Financial History of Trinity College, Cambridge* (Cambridge, 2008), 83.

[4] Ibid., 87–8.

[5] Ibid., 90.

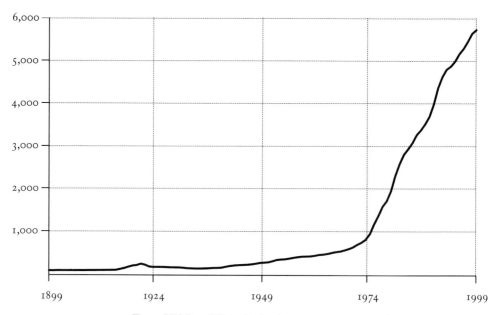

Fig. 1 UK Retail Price Index (average 1982–4 = 100%)
Source: Measuring Worth, http://www.measuringworth.org

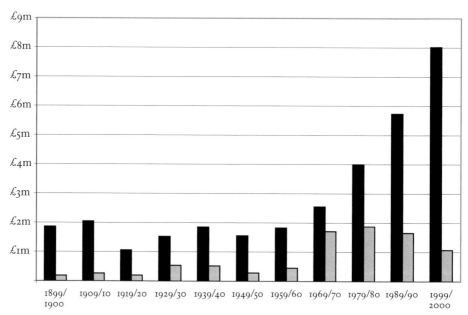

Fig. 2 External income, 1899/1900 to 1999/2000 (2007 £s)

■ Total estates income   ▨ Dividends, interest, etc.

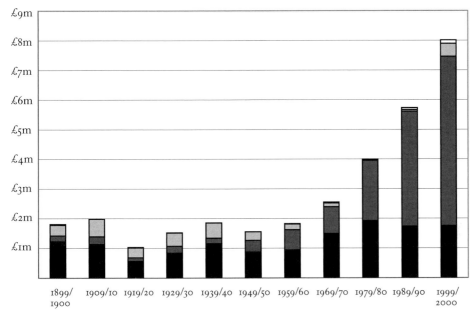

Fig. 3 Sources of external estate income, 1899/2000 to 1999/2000 (2007 £s)

■ Rack-rented land ■ Rack-rented property

▨ Property on long lease ☐ Other

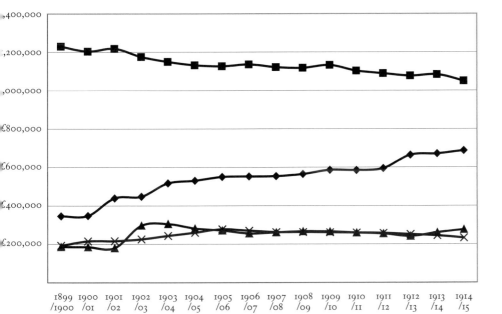

Fig. 4 Sources of real income, 1899/1900 to 1914/15 (2007 £s)

■— Lands at rack rent ✳— Houses on rack rent

◆— Houses on long leases ▲— Interest

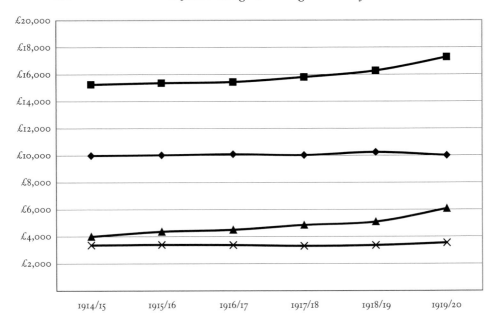

Fig. 5 Sources of wartime income (current £s)

━■━ Lands at rack rent   ━✕━ Houses on rack rent

━◆━ Houses on long leases   ━▲━ Interest

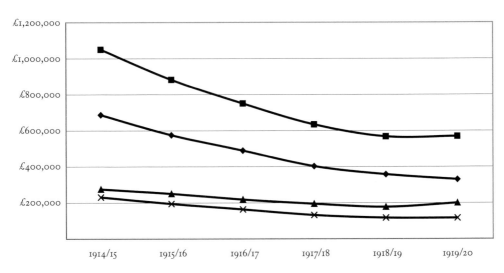

Fig. 6 Sources of wartime income (2007 £s)

━■━ Lands at rack rent   ━✕━ Houses on rack rent

━◆━ Houses on long leases   ━▲━ Interest

future repairs and improvement of estates a General Reserve Fund (GRF) was established in 1917, to which large sums were transferred over the following few years. With an expensive College bath scheme, maintenance of estates, and provision for new studentships on the horizon (in the case of the first of these an ever receding one), the Audit Committee noted that 'the importance of this large general reserve cannot be overestimated.'[6] Careless and wasteful spending was, more than ever, unacceptable. One abnormally large increase in expenditure in 1919–20 was deliciously Oxbridge: the leap in entertainments expenditure since the previous year from £292 to £462, which the Audit Committee attributed 'almost wholly to the fact that the College has purchased considerable quantities of champagne and sherry'.[7]

The end of the war did ease some of the financial pressures on the College, however. Income from room rents more than doubled between 1918 and 1919, and there were welcome increases in property rents and dividends.[8] A post-war influx of undergraduates also prompted a rise in the tuition fee from £7 to £8, giving a healthy boost to the Education Fund. 'It appears that a great deal is now being done for the men in the way of provision both of lectures and supervision, and I think that the very moderate increase in the tuition fee is more than justified', the College auditor reported to Master and Fellows.[9]

The tuition fee rise was also justifiable in light of the inflationary boom that characterized Britain's immediate post-war years (Fig. 1), as pent-up wartime demand combined with speculative investment to create a rapidly bubbling economic brew. This exuberance was, however, quickly followed by the savage unemployment and deflation of the 1920s. The decade was a brutal one in Britain, more so than in many other developed economies, since the government chose to pursue tight monetary and fiscal policies in order to restore sterling's prized pre-war value in gold. Harsh deflation meant that the real value of both the College's external income and its spending on statutory responsibilities surged during the 1920s (Figs. 1, 7 and 8). High interest rates were a boon to investors in government bonds like St John's, but they also squeezed producers as prices fell. The financial position of the universities in the wake of the war and its economic aftermath was a matter of great concern amongst dons, Fellows, and statesmen. The Royal Commission of 1919–22 chaired by the Liberal prime minister deposed during the war, H. H. Asquith, recommended that the universities of Oxford and Cambridge receive government financial support in light of insufficient relief from other sources. This 'bail out', as it were, was but an early step towards the universities' ultimate dependence on the public purse.[10]

---

[6] H. F. Howard, *An Account of the Finances of the College of St John the Evangelist in the University of Cambridge, 1511–1926* (Cambridge, 1935), 241–2; Report of the Audit Committee on the Senior Bursar's Accounts, 1920 (SJCA, CC3 39–58), §3. To the GRF was transferred £1,750 in 1917, £3,550 in 1918, and £5,300 in 1919.

[7] Report of the Audit Committee on the Senior Bursar's Accounts, 1920 (SJCA, CC3.39–58), §1.

[8] Report of the Auditor to the Master and Fellows of St John's College, for the year 1919 (SJCA), 1.

[9] Report of the Auditor to the Master and Fellows of St John's College, presented November 1920 (SJCA), 1.

[10] Neild, *Riches and Responsibility*, 86.

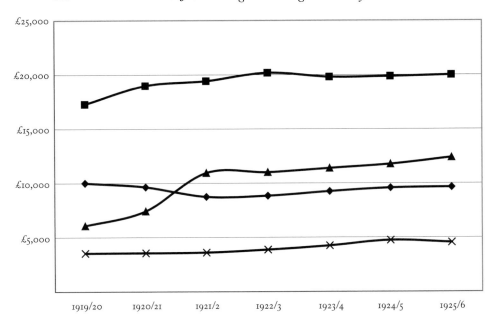

Fig. 7 Sources of income, 1919/20 to 1924/5 (current £s)

■ Lands at rack rent　✕ Houses on rack rent
◆ Houses on long leases　▲ Interest

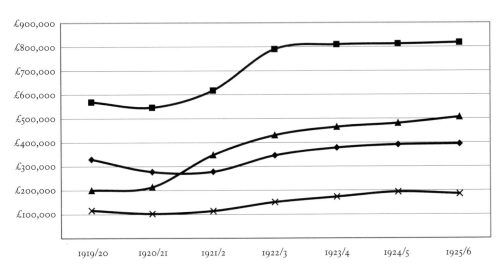

Fig. 8 Sources of income, 1919/20 to 1924/5 (2007 £s)

■ Lands at rack rent　✕ Houses on rack rent
◆ Houses on long leases　▲ Interest

Plunging world commodity prices during the 1920s added to the deflation-ary pressure and hit farmers hard. Whilst the state had sought to prop up crop prices during the war through the Corn Production Act 1917, and again with the Agriculture Act 1920, these legislative supports were withdrawn in 1921. Such conditions were, of course, problematic for a large agricultural landowner like St John's. Land rents were stagnant for most of the decade, and the extreme downward direction of the global economy from 1929 only added to the reasons for a Bursar to worry. The seriousness and uncertainty of the times is reflected in Howard's notes for 1929–30. Many of the College's tenants had requested permanent reductions in their rent, but it was 'obviously preferable', thought Howard, to offer a temporary abatement which, unlike a 'permanent' reduction, could 'probably be discontinued without serious difficulty if and when better times return'. The Bursar recognized that the College would not benefit from having tenantless farms on its hands in such unpropitious economic times, and that it would be 'clearly advantageous to do what we can to keep our existing tenants where they are solvent'. Whilst he saw 'no sure ground for confidence that the worst is past', he did not believe that a situation whereby 'a large por-tion of the agricultural community over a great part of the world is providing food for the rest of the population at a loss' could possibly go on forever.[11]

However, as Howard explained, the distribution of College income had 'radically changed' since the late nineteenth century. Whilst over 60 per cent of revenue in 1894 had been derived from farm property, 'the position is now reversed and more than 60 per cent is practically immune from the vicissitudes of the seasons and of the world's markets.'[12] Roughly 35 per cent of gross income now came from dividends and interest, compared to under 10 per cent at the turn of the century. But this income, as we know all too well, was hardly invin-cible. The health of the College's finances was inevitably affected by the volatile market conditions of 1929. Although the epochal Wall Street crash of October 1929 dominates popular ideas about the beginning of the Great Depression, it was preceded in Britain by the 'Hatry Crash' of 20 September, when Clarence Hatry's business empire collapsed in a fraudulent heap. For the Bursar of St John's, the resultant fall in price of long-term 'gilt-edged' securities offered a good opportunity to sell off the College's War Loan holdings, which the gov-ernment would have the option of paying off after 1929, and to buy up local authority bonds cheaply in order to give the College investments a permanent gilt-edged 'footing'.[13]

As well as backing state support for the universities, the Royal Commis-sion of 1919–22 also expressed dismay at the use of college endowment incomes to subsidize kitchens, tuition fees, charges, and room rents, thus benefiting all students, rich and poor alike, rather than targeting help at the most needy. The Commissioners recommended that in future the colleges should open a win-dow onto this practice by presenting separate accounts for internal revenue,

[11] Note on the Senior Bursar's Accounts, for the year ending 31 July 1930 (SJCA), 2.
[12] Ibid., 3.
[13] Ibid., 1.

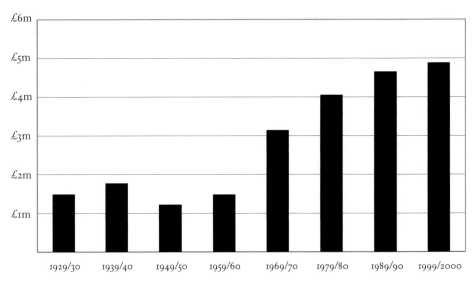

Fig. 9 Net endowment income, 1929/30 to 1999/2000 (2007 £s)

tuition, and kitchen.[14] Consequently, from 1926, the form in which the St John's accounts were presented changed markedly. Endowment income – that is, from the College's holdings of property and securities – was now recorded in the External Revenue Account, whilst the income of the many and varied College trust funds fell under a separate heading. As the Royal Commission had suggested, an Internal Revenue Account listed income from room rents and other charges; a Tuition Account recorded fees and teaching expenditures; and the Kitchen Account divulged the financial self-sufficiency, or otherwise, of the College kitchen.

As the Annual Financial Review for 1989–90 explained, the 'most realistic measure' of the College's 'overall investment yield' is 'the surplus on Account 1A', the External Revenue Account. This surplus represents 'the net general endowment income (as opposed to Trust Fund income) of the College', unaffected by new money from gifts or bequests which is 'by custom treated as Trust Fund money'. Because the endowment income is subject to measures to protect its real value, such as sinking funds and property improvements, St John's financial officers have regarded it as a useful gauge of the College's pecuniary well-being.[15] Fig. 9 shows the changes in net endowment income, adjusted to 2007 prices, from 1929–30 to 1999–2000.

As is clear, the period of the Second World War marked a substantial drop in real endowment income. Austerity was the defining word of the 1940s, and war saw good housekeeping become synonymous with duty to king and country. The Senior Bursar expressed concern early on in the conflict that 'war conditions' had 'operated to accentuate difficulties' in the already unbalanced Internal Revenue and Tuition Accounts. Suggesting that the Internal Revenue deficit should be covered as far as possible by making economies in the Endowment Account,

---

[14] Neild, *Riches and Responsibility*, 86.
[15] St John's College Annual financial review 1989–90 (SJCA), 7.

he emphasized that it was 'as much in our interest as it is a National obligation to exercise the most rigorous economy over the whole field of our expenditure'.[16] Likewise, on the Audit Committee, R. J. Getty and E. A. Walker agreed with the Bursar that drawing on the College's capital to cover deficits could create more problems in future, and St John's must therefore exercise the same patriotic restraint as ordinary Britons. 'Individual citizens are urged daily to limit personal expenditure and to save for victory; and, if victory comes in answer to the nation's response, the College by having faced this national obligation will at the same time be in a better position to meet further difficult years for the world at large.'[17]

For Getty and Walker, the war represented a possible window of opportunity for both the country and the College finances. They pondered how the conflict might mark a new dawn for British agriculture, and how the College might capitalize on this. The 'cloud of the counter-blockade' would 'have its silver lining in increased agricultural activity at home', and possibly lead to a more permanent agricultural revolution in Britain as 'temporary "digging for victory"' developed into a fully fledged 'back to the land' movement. Although the onset of war had created uncertainty, they believed that now was the time for St John's to invest in land.[18] Whilst this long-held dream of many a British social reformer for a popular 'back to the land' movement once again failed to come to fruition, agricultural land continued to account for a significant portion of College revenue. Boys Smith, presenting his own bursarial record for prosperity, later explained in his memoirs that 'improved agricultural conditions' ensured annual increases in the College's net income on its External Revenue Account during the war years.[19] However, once wartime inflation is taken into consideration, it can be seen that the real value of that income was actually falling:

Net income on External Revenue Account, current £s and 2007 £s

	Current £s	2007 £s
1938–9	39,114	1,789,964
1939–40	39,663	1,762,477
1940–1	41,389	1,619,783
1941–2	42,192	1,497,432
1942–3	43,749	1,461,486
1943–4	43,809	1,411,987
1944–5	44,069	1,391,121
1945–6	44,147	1,365,467

Sources: Boys Smith, *Memories*, 86;
2007 values calculated using Measuring
Worth (http://www.measuringworth.org)

By the end of the 1940s the Audit Committee was more worried by a trend of rising expenditure that if left unchecked would soon see it outrunning

[16] Note on the Senior Bursar's Accounts, for the year ending 31 July 1940 (SJCA), 8.
[17] Report of the Audit Committee on the Senior Bursar's Accounts for the year ending 31 July 1940 (SJCA, CC3–123), 1–2.
[18] Ibid., 4.
[19] Boys Smith, *Memories*, 85.

income. The Committee felt 'little confidence that dramatic saving is possible', but advised the College 'to make quite small economies where possible'. Commitments to support the 'less well endowed Colleges' through the University Contribution, and to sustain the outflows from the Scholarships and Exhibitions Fund, meant only a few options for economizing were left. One idea was to do away with the Choir School, which was beginning to seem a burdensome anachronism in the era of the 'eleven plus'. In the end, the risk was taken to establish a new St John's College School in 1954, which soon proved to be more financially self-sufficient.[20] As in the aftermath of the previous war, one further area of College expenditure appeared irresponsibly high; the Entertainments Committee was advised to 'exercise some restraint in the future in its provision'.[21]

At the close of the 1950s in real terms the College's endowment income still lay below even the level enjoyed when depression had struck in 1929–30. However, during the 1960s endowment income leapt magnificently and continued to soar, albeit more gradually, over the ensuing decades (Fig. 9). What were the reasons for this? The College's property holdings certainly performed well (Fig. 2). In the post-war era, property on long lease faded into relative insignificance, as rack-rented residential and commercial real estate played an increasingly important role in swelling the College's external income, and in the 1980s overtaking rack-rented land as the majority source of revenue from property (Fig. 3). But the real success story of the 1960s was the College's income from securities.

In his financial history of Trinity College, Robert Neild cites the importance of the liberalization of trust law in the 1960s. From 1961, trustees were permitted to invest up to half their funds in securities, and in 1966 this was raised to three-quarters. Furthermore, the Universities and Colleges Estates Act 1964 freed college investment practices from Ministry of Agriculture oversight.[22] However, these broad national reforms followed, rather than instigated, a financial revolution that had already taken place at the college level; a revolution in which St John's and Boys Smith enthusiastically participated. In 1964, the Ministry happily relinquished legal responsibility for more daring investment practices to which it had for some time consented and which it admitted to not really comprehending.[23]

In the wake of a favourable legal opinion in 1949, Corpus Christi College had led the way in formulating an Investment Statute, made under the legal framework of the Universities of Oxford and Cambridge Act 1923, which extended bursarial investment powers beyond those permitted under ordinary trust law, and loosened the Ministry of Agriculture's control over investment decisions. Several more colleges followed suit, and in 1953–4 Boys Smith drafted and promoted an Investment Statute for St John's. Approved in January 1955, the Statute gave the Bursar what he had wanted: greater freedom to invest the

---

[20] Above, pp. 577–8.

[21] St John's College, Report of the Audit Committee, 1949/50 (SJCA, CC3, 139), 1–2.

[22] Neild, *Riches and Responsibility*, 88.

[23] Boys Smith, *Memories*, 199.

College's funds in a wider and more profitable range of assets. On top of this, he also masterminded the establishment of the Consolidated Trust Fund, which allowed the College to administer its myriad trust funds as one, allotting to each its share of the proceeds of investment.[24] With these reforms in place, Boys Smith instigated a bold shift in strategy, boosting the College's holdings in securities, especially (and predictably) equities.[25] Following his election as Master in 1959, the Audit Committee praised 'the skill and sound judgment with which he managed the College finances during his term of office as Senior Bursar'.[26] Although under his tenure St John's began to employ professionals to advise on investment decisions, it was unquestionably to Boys Smith's confidence, initiative, and bursarial acumen that the College's financial successes in these years is to be credited.

The prerogatives of share ownership brought new issues into debate amongst the Fellows. How should the College make use of the rights and powers associated with equities? The Audit Committee suggested how St John's ought to take up the mantle of activist shareholder:

> There are probably one or two public companies whose policy, though financially successful, finds general disfavour amongst a majority of Fellows; and it would seem to follow that, if the College becomes a member of such a company, it must be prepared to use its voting power at general meetings to oppose the Board. The alternative is not to invest in the company. The issue is raised, we suggest, by our membership of Daily Mirror Newspapers Ltd.[27]

One can only assume that the *Mirror*'s leftish hue and unequivocal support for the Labour Party perhaps jarred with the views of certain Fellows.

During the 1960s, the College felt the benefits of Boys Smith's reforms. Income from dividends and interest surged (Figs. 2 and 9), thanks to investment of the proceeds from property sales during a period of high interest rates.[28] The real value of trust fund income also leapt to unprecedented heights, beginning an enduringly upward trend (Fig. 10) and validating the creation of the Consolidated Trust Fund. Expenditure on education steadily declined, in real terms, over the course of the 1940s and 1950s, but as the College's real income galloped ahead in the 1960s there was a dramatic recovery in the growth of real expenditure on the College's statutory responsibilities (Fig. 11). Even as Britain endured double-digit inflation in the 1970s (Fig. 1), spending on 'education, religion, learning, and research' kept pace with, and even outran, rising prices. These trends in income and expenditure continued into the 1970s and 1980s, with educational expenditure rising to meet widening participation in higher education. Although the Thatcher years are often regarded as an era of relative impoverishment for British universities as the Conservative government pledged to bring

---

[24] Ibid., chap. 11.

[25] Ibid., 282.

[26] St John's College Audit Committee Report 1959–60 (SJCA, CC3 150), 1.

[27] Ibid., 3–4.

[28] Notes on the Senior Bursar's Accounts for the year ended 31 July 1970 (SJCA, C18.6), 8.

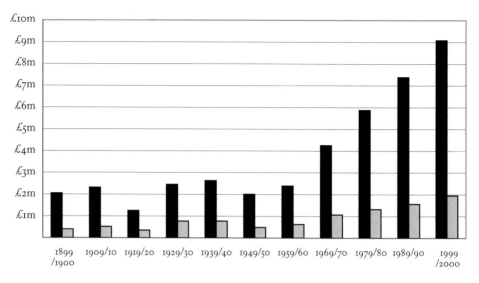

Fig. 10 External revenue and trust fund income, 1899/1900 to 1999/2000 (2007 £s)

■ External revenue ▢ Trust funds

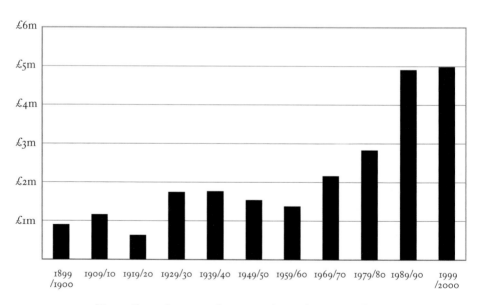

Fig. 11 Expenditure on education, religion, learning and research,
1899/1900 to 1999/2000 (2007 £s)

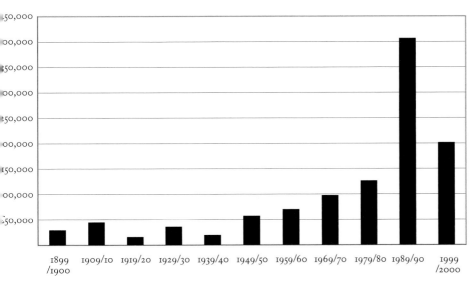

Fig. 12 Expenditure on entertainments, 1899/1900 to 1999/2000 (2007 £s)

public expenditure to heel, shrewd Oxbridge bursars with large endowment funds to play with were able to make a killing in booming stock markets. The 1980s were the years when British champagne consumption skyrocketed, and at the end of the decade the real value of the College's entertainment expenditure mirrored the nation's ebullient mood; a mood that was, of course, soon to end in the painful hangover of recession (see Fig. 12).

The 1990s witnessed a dramatic reversal of the trend towards securities income, as revenue from rack-rented property surged ahead of dividends and interest. The College wisely invested in booming commercial property, and the 1980s and 1990s also saw the appearance of 'Innovation and business' developments in the Johnian portfolio. In 1989–90 gross income from 'Innovation and Business Parks' amounted to £527,986: 10 per cent of gross external income, or 8 per cent net. A decade later, revenue under the heading 'Innovation Centre' totalled £2,058,445: 21 per cent of gross income, and 17 per cent net.[29] St John's had come full circle, passing through a transition from land to securities as its main source of income, and now back into property.

As the twentieth century ended and the twenty-first began, the College was beginning to experience the financial implications of the 1997 Dearing Report on higher education. The New Labour government acted on the Report's recommendations that variations in public funding for university tuition should occur only when there was an 'approved difference in the provision' and 'society, through the Secretary of State' deemed such variations a 'good use of resources'. Oxbridge colleges consequently had to demonstrate that all revenue raised from the publicly funded undergraduate College fees was applied to educational purposes. This meant a shake-up of the St John's accounts. Whilst

[29] St John's College Annual Financial Review (1990), 4 (SJCA); Annual Financial Review (2000) (SJCA), 7.

College fee income had previously been split between several accounts – Internal Revenue, Kitchen, and Tuition – now the Tuition Account would be the sole beneficiary. Consequently, many items of expenditure, including porters' wages and payments to teaching staff, were now also transferred to the Tuition Account. However, the changes left the College with a number of internal accounting imbalances which needed to be addressed as the century drew to a close.[30]

Dearing also prompted a fresh look at the University Contribution. The Contribution was introduced under the 1882 Statutes; as defined in the College's own Annual Financial Review, it is 'a tax charged on College income derived from property used for a collegiate purpose'.[31] The New Statutes which took effect in October 1926 resulted in a markedly higher contribution, although the extra outlay for the College was somewhat offset by the transfer of lecturers to the University payroll.[32] The New Statutes fixed the net assessable income bands for determining each college's contribution at the first £5,000, the next £5,000, and the excess over £10,000. As we shall see, although the rates at which College income was assessed were altered throughout the century, it was only in 1999–2000 that these thresholds were raised to more realistic levels. If the University Contribution is thought of as a tax, wealthier colleges like St John's were therefore beneficiaries of what economists call 'fiscal drag', whereby the thresholds for progressive rates of income taxation do not adjust in line with inflation, thus automatically decreasing the burden of tax.

Following a Council of the Senate report in 1966, the financial relationship between the University and the colleges underwent a major reform. The extent to which the colleges' aggregate contributions were applied to University purposes was to diminish over a twenty-year period, and the balance paid into a newly established Colleges Fund to make grants to colleges for both recurrent and non-recurrent expenditure. By 1986–7, payment for University purposes was supposed to cease, and the rates on which college income was 'taxed' were to be 2 per cent on the first £5,000, 5 per cent on the next £5,000, and 10 per cent on the rest, falling from rates of 4, 11, and 21 per cent, albeit with repayments back to the colleges. However, this scheme was amended in 1976. Repayments to the colleges were phased out by 1979–80, and a more gradual reduction in the rates took place from 1986–7:

---

[30] Annual Financial Review (2000), 1–2, 28; 'Oxbridge fears college fee crisis', *Times Higher Education Supplement*, 3 Oct. 1997; 'Blair backs down over Oxbridge fees', *Independent*, 28 Feb. 1998; 'Oxbridge college fee changeover', *Times Higher Education Supplement*, 20 Mar. 1998. The report by the National Committee of Inquiry into Higher Education, chaired by Sir Ron Dearing, can be found at http://www.leeds.ac.uk/educol/ncihe/.

[31] Annual Financial Review (2000), 4.

[32] Audit Committee Report, 1929–30 (SJCA, CC3, 95), 1–2; Howard, *Account*, 253.

	First £5,000	Next £5,000	Excess over £10,000
1986–7	4%	11%	21%
1987–8	4%	10%	19%
1988–9	3%	9%	17%
1989–90	3%	8%	15%
1990–91	2%	7%	13%
1991–2	2%	6%	11%
1992–3	2%	5%	10%

In 1995, the lower rate was reduced to 0 per cent, as by then the revenue from that source was trifling.

In real terms, the University Contribution gradually dwindled as a share of the College's assessable income between the 1970s and the end of the century, although its real value was still greater in 1999–2000 than it had been from the 1920s to the 1950s (see Fig. 13). However, the Contribution was set to take on much greater significance. Following the Dearing Report, negotiations with the government over public funding for the Oxbridge College fee reached a settlement in 1998. State support for the fee would be transferred from Local Education Authorities to the Higher Education Funding Council for England (HEFCE), and gradually reduced by one-third over a period of ten years from 1999–2000. The Universities of Oxford and Cambridge themselves, *not* the constituent colleges, would now receive grants from HEFCE just like any other university. The Bursar of St John's, George Reid, was also chair of the Colleges Committee's Fees Sub-Committee, and responded to the Department of Education's announcement of the changes on 8 December 1998 with brutal honesty yet determined optimism:

> We realise that these are difficult times for the sector but this settlement is a substantial cut in our public funding; we can't absorb that cut without it having an impact. We shall work hard to manage the change and are pleased to have a clear planning perspective of ten years for that purpose. All colleges are conscious of the difficulties of the settlement and will work together to resolve them. We are determined to ensure that each student has the same quality of education, whichever their Cambridge college, and will use the ten years ahead to cope with these cuts.[33]

In order to preserve that famous 'quality of education' across all the colleges, rich and poor, the ambitious goal for the University was to double the income of the Colleges Fund over a ten-year period. But how was this to be achieved? In readiness for the new funding regime, the Fees Sub-Committee had set about planning an overhaul of the University Contribution in May 1998. The formula approved by the colleges in February 1999 was to increase the bands of net

---

[33] 'Advice on Oxford and Cambridge college fees accepted', HEFCE press release, 8 December 1998, http://www.hefce.ac.uk/news/hefce/1998/oxbridge.htm; 'Cambridge responds to future funding formula', University of Cambridge News Centre, 8 December 1998, http://www.admin.cam.ac.uk/news/press/dpp/1998120801.

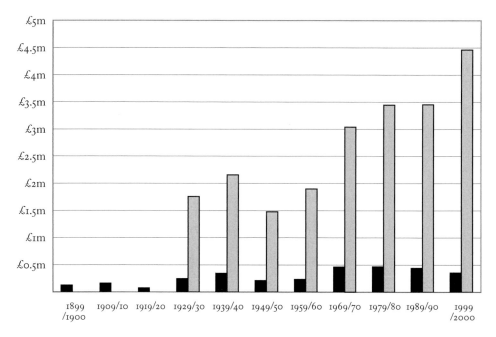

Fig. 13 St John's University Contribution and Net Assessable Income,
1899/1900 to 1999/2000 (2007 £s)

■ University contribution   ▨ Net assessable income

assessable income from £5,000 to £250,000, and to temporarily raise the rates of contribution as follows:

	First £5,000	Next £5,000	Excess over £10,000
1999–2000	4%	10%	19%
2000–1	3%	9%	18%
2001–2	3%	9%	17%
2002–3	3%	8%	16%
2003–4	2%	8%	15%
2004–5	2%	7%	14%
2005–6	2%	7%	13%
2006–7	2%	6%	12%
2007–8	2%	6%	11%
2008–9	2%	5%	10%

In this way, the wealthier colleges like St John's committed themselves to offering greater financial sustenance to their poorer counterparts in order to preserve the 'vitality of the collegiate University'.[34]

The shadow of 'Blair's Britain' also hung over Fellows' discussions of the College's various property development schemes. The impending arrival of the new millennium in Britain had come to represent not a bright new future, but

---

[34] *CUR*, 17 March 1999, 'Second Report of the Council on Amendments of Statute G, II', Appendix; 'Blair backs down over Oxbridge fees', *Independent*, 28 Feb. 1998.

rather wasteful and ill-advised public projects, epitomized, of course, by the infamous Millennium Dome. The question of what to do with the 'Triangle Site' opposite the College's main entrance would eventually be solved in 2004, when work began on converting the site's listed properties into a medical centre, commercial space, and student accommodation. Before that, £142,000 was spent on drawing up plans only to be abandoned. However, in its 2000 report the Audit Committee spotted 'a crumb of Bursarial comfort' in the fact that this outlay had revealed the 'impropriety' of committing 'vastly larger sums to what we now believe – as some suspected all along – would have resulted in a "Cambridge Dome"'.[35]

Similarly, New Labour's reputation for managing public opinion resulted in 'spin' creeping into the lexicon of College financial management. The Audit Committee was concerned by adverse public reactions to College property development plans, particularly at Waterbeach, and that the 'image' of St John's therefore needed to be protected. 'Although we deplore the need to undertake window-dressing exercises in an effort to keep the public happy,' the Committee emphasised, 'we think that the need is a real one.' Perhaps employing a public relations professional or firm to engage in 'what Downing Street detractors would call spin' would help 'to put a pleasing gloss' on the College's activities? The College Council did not agree with the Audit Committee on the necessity of this, suggesting that the role of the Development Office was already growing to encompass public relations.[36]

An ancient institution such as St John's represents a direct and palpable link to a distant past, embodying a world of different values even as it adapts itself to changing realities. Inevitably, there will be tensions between its roots in a simpler pre-capitalist age, and the hyper-commercial modernity in which it now finds itself. Indeed, some Fellows found it difficult at times to reconcile the College's centuries-old charitable status with its role as landowner and landlord. In the Audit Committee's view, the development of the Triangle Site would need to be '"sold" to the public as an enhancement of the locality rather than appearing as an imposition if we as a College are not to be seen as ready to stoop to whatever desecration may be a corollary of our pursuit of lucre.' What Fellows most feared, however, was the reaction to a possible sale of Sunningdale Golf Course, which had been in the College's portfolio since the Berkshire club's establishment in 1900. Although the Audit Committee deemed this transaction to be 'possibly justifiable in the narrow financial interests of the College Estates', it had the 'potential to generate adverse publicity on a scale similar to that of the question of female membership of the M.C.C.!'[37]

Property development was, however, still a means to the same old statutory ends. As income from investments surged in the 1980s and 1990s, so too did spending on education, religion, learning, and research (see Fig. 11). For all the concern about the 'pursuit of lucre', St John's rounded off the twentieth century and began the twenty-first with the same dedication to its duty to educate.

[35] Audit Committee Report 2000 (SJCA, C19.74), 1.

[36] Ibid., 2–3; G. A. Reid, 'Audit 2000 Note to Fellows' (SJCA, C19.74), 1.

[37] Ibid., 2–4.

As concerns about student debt mounted in Britain, the Fellows approved the launch of a new appeal to endow the Access Exhibition Fund. It was felt that 'ensuring that the undergraduate students from poorer family backgrounds leave Cambridge with no greater burden of debt than their better-off contemporaries is one likely to prove attractive to many Old Johnians'. Indeed, as the Bursar informed the Fellows in his 2000 report, gifts for that purpose had already been received.[38] That same year, a gift of $253,215 from the American Friends of Cambridge University, made possible by the generosity of an anonymous donor, provided for the EAGLE Project to help Lambeth school children aspire to university.[39] At the beginning of the twenty-first century, just as one hundred years before, St John's, supported by the generosity of its alumni, was using its substantial resources to help the least-advantaged youth acquire the education they deserved.

Over the century the College travelled a long way from being a passive collector of agricultural rents and interest on low-yield bonds, becoming by the late 1980s a sophisticated investor in commercial properties and securities. How far the global financial crisis that broke in 2008 has affected St John's wealth and income, particularly from the property sector, will be left for a future historian of the College to write about. For now, perhaps the words of the optimistic Audit Committee in 1940 will suffice: 'Depressions fortunately do not last for ever.'[40]

---

[38] Ibid., 3.

[39] Annual Financial Review (2000), 23.

[40] Report of the Audit Committee on the Senior Bursar's Accounts for the year ending 31 July, 1940 (SJCA, CC3–23), 4.

BIBLIOGRAPHY

GENERAL

Baker, Thomas, *History of the College of St John the Evangelist, Cambridge*, ed. J. E. B. Mayor, 2 vols. (Cambridge, 1869)

Baker-Mayor: *see preceding item*

Brooke, Christopher, *A History of the University of Cambridge*, IV. *1870–1900* (Cambridge, 1992)

Collegium Divi Johannis Evangelistae, 1511–1911 (Cambridge, 1911)

Cooper, C. H., *Annals of Cambridge*, 5 vols. (Cambridge, 1842–1908)

Crook, A. C., *From the Foundation to Gilbert Scott: A History of the Buildings of St John's College, Cambridge 1511 to 1885* (Cambridge, 1980)

—— *From Penrose to Cripps* (Cambridge, 1978)

Early Statutes of the College of St. John the Evangelist in the University of Cambridge, ed. J. E. B. Mayor (Cambridge, 1859)

Henry, N. F. M., and A. C. Crook (eds.), *Use and Occupancy of Rooms in St John's College*, Part I: *Use from Early Times to 1983*; Part II: *List of Occupants, 1936–1976* (Cambridge, 1985)

Howard, H. F., *An Account of the Finances of the College of St John the Evangelist in the University of Cambridge, 1511–1926* (Cambridge, 1935)

Mayor, J. E. B., *Admissions to the College of St John the Evangelist in the University of Cambridge*, ed. R. F. Scott, 4 parts in 3 vols. (Cambridge, 1882–1931)

Miller, Edward, *Portrait of a College: A History of the College of Saint John the Evangelist Cambridge* (Cambridge, 1961)

Morgan, V. H., *A History of the University of Cambridge*, II. *1546–1750* (Cambridge, 2004)

Mullinger, J. B., *St John's College* (London, 1901)

Raven, E. E. (comp.), *List of Rooms in St John's College, 1895–1936* (Supplement to *The Eagle*: Cambridge, 1936)

Scott, R. F., 'Notes from the College records', *Eagle* xx–xxxvi (1891–1915)

Scott-Mayor: *see* Mayor, J. E. B.

Searby, Peter, *A History of the University of Cambridge*, III. *1750–1870* (Cambridge, 1997)

Venn, J., and J. A. (comp.), *Alumni Cantabrigienses: A Biographical List of all Known Students, Graduates, and Holders of Office at the University of Cambridge … to 1900*, Part I in 4 vols., Part II in 6 vols. (Cambridge, 1922–54)

Willis, R., and J. W. Clark, *The Architectural History of the University of Cambridge*, II (Cambridge, 1886)

THE SIXTEENTH CENTURY

Primary Sources

SJCA

C1	Statutes
C3.1	Register of Admissions of College Officers, Fellows, and Scholars
C7.11	Thin Red Book
C7.12	Thick Black Book
C12	Prizing Books
C17.2	Statement of Revenues and Charges, 1556
C17.23	Accounts of Oliver Scales, Clerk of Works, 1512–14
C17.24	Valuation of College Estates, 1517–18
D3	Miscellaneous Early Deeds
D4.17	Foundation charter, 1511
D6 and D14	Early Deeds and Memoranda
D56 and D57	Miscellaneous deeds, accounts, and other correspondence
D58, D59, and D64	Deeds and Papers relating to Benefactions
D94	Letters to the Master, and others
D102.1	Accounts of Lady Margaret's Household, 1509
D105	Letters to the Master, and others
D106 and D107	College Accounts
M3	Masters' Account Rolls
SB3	Bursars' Account Rolls
SB4	Annual Accounts of the College, the 'rentals'

SJCL

MS 263	Spanish Antiphoner

CAMBRIDGE UNIVERSITY ARCHIVES

College I.7	Roster of Members of St John's College, 1559
CUR 93	Guard-book of Papers relating to St John's College
VCCt IV.22	Records of the Vice-Chancellor's Court
VCCt Wills I-II	Registers of Wills Proved in the Vice-Chancellor's Court

CAMBRIDGE UNIVERSITY LIBRARY MANUSCRIPTS

Mm.2.23	Thomas Baker's Manuscripts

BRITISH LIBRARY

Additional MS 6059	Calendar from William Cecil's prayer book
Harleian MS 7039	Thomas Baker's manuscripts
Lansdowne MSS 6–79	Papers of William Cecil

THE NATIONAL ARCHIVES

SP1	State Papers of the Reign of Henry VIII
SP7	Wriothesley Papers, 1536–40
SP10	State Papers Domestic, Edward VI
SP12	State Papers Domestic, Elizabeth I

Published Sources

Alford, S., *Burghley: William Cecil at the Court of Elizabeth I* (New Haven & London, 2008)

—— *Kingship and Politics in the Reign of Edward VI* (Cambridge, 2002)

Ascham, R., *Apologia pro coena dominica* (London, 1577)

—— *The Whole Works of Roger Ascham*, ed. J. A. Giles (London, 1856)

Bale, J., *Scriptorum illustrium Majoris Brytanniae ... catalogus* (Basel, 1557–9)

Brigden, S., *London and the Reformation* (Oxford, 1989)

Bullock, G., *Oeconomia Methodica Concordantiarum Scripturae Sacrae* (Antwerp, 1572)

Caius, J., *Historiae Cantabrigiensis Academiae* (London, 1574)

Calendar of Entries in the Papal Registers Relating to Great Britain and Ireland: Papal Letters (London, 1893–)

Calendar of State Papers Domestic Series of the Reign of Edward VI, ed. C. S. Knighton (London, 1992)

Calendar of State Papers Domestic Series of the Reigns of Edward VI, Mary, Elizabeth, ed. R. Lemon (London, 1856)

Cheke, J. (trans.), *D. Ioannis Chrysostomi homiliae duae* (London, 1543)

Christopherson, J., *Jephthah*, ed. F. H. Fobes (Newark, DE, 1928)

Collinson, P., *The Elizabethan Puritan Movement* (Oxford, 1967)

Collinson, P., D. McKitterick, and E. Leedham-Green, *Andrew Perne: Quatercentenary Studies* (Cambridge, 1991)

Cranmer, T., *Miscellaneous Writings and Letters*, ed. J. E. Cox (Cambridge, 1846)

De obitu doctissimi ... Martini Buceri (London, 1551)

Digby, E., *De arte natandi* (London, 1587)

—— *Dissuasive from Taking away the Lyvings and Goods of the Church* (London, 1589)

—— *Theoria Analytica* (London, 1579)

Dobson, B., 'The foundation', in D. Reynolds (ed.), *Christ's: A Cambridge College over Five Centuries* (London, 2004), 3–34

Duffy, E., *Fires of Faith* (New Haven & London, 2009)

—— *The Stripping of the Altars* (New Haven & London, 1992)

Elton, G. R., *The Parliament of England, 1559–1581* (Cambridge, 1986)

Fincham, K., and P. Tyacke, *Altars Restored: The Changing Face of English Religious Worship, 1547–c. 1700* (Oxford, 2007)

Firpo, M., *Pietro Bizzarri: esule italiano del cinquecento* (Turin, 1971)

Fisher, J., *Assertionis Lutheranae Confutatio* (Antwerp, 1523)

—— *Concio quam anglice habuit* (Cambridge, 1521 [i.e. 1522])

Foxe, J., *The Acts and Monuments*, 4th edn, ed. J. Pratt (London, [1877])

Frere, W. H. (ed.), *Visitation Articles and Injunctions of the Reformation Period* (London, 1910)

Gardiner, S., *The Letters of Stephen Gardiner*, ed. J. A. Muller (Cambridge, 1933)

Garrett, C. H., *The Marian Exiles: A Study in the Origins of Elizabethan Puritanism* (Cambridge, 1938)

Godfrey, G., *Garrett Godfrey's Accounts, c. 1527–1533*, ed. E. Leedham-Green, D. E. Rhodes, F. H. Stubbings (Cambridge, 1992)

Grace Book B, ed. M. Bateson, 2 vols. (Cambridge, 1903–5)

Grace Book Δ, ed. J. Venn (Cambridge, 1910)

Grindal, E., *The Remains of Edmund Grindal*, ed. W. Nicholson (Cambridge, 1843)

Howell, W. S., *Logic and Rhetoric in England, 1500–1700* (Princeton, 1956)

Hoyle, R. W., *The Pilgrimage of Grace and the Politics of the 1530s* (Oxford, 2001)

Hudson, W. S., *The Cambridge Connection and the Elizabethan Settlement of 1559* (Durham, NC, 1980)

Jones, M. K., and M. G. Underwood, *The King's Mother: Lady Margaret Beaufort, Countess of Richmond and Derby* (Cambridge, 1992)

Jones, N., *The English Reformation* (Oxford, 2002)

King, J. N., *English Reformation Literature* (Princeton, 1982)

Kitching, C. J. (ed.), *The Royal Visitation of 1559: Act Book for the Northern Province* (Gateshead, 1975)

Lake, P., *Moderate Puritans and the Elizabethan Church* (Cambridge, 1982)

Lamb, J. (ed.), *A Collection of Letters, Statutes, and Other Documents … Illustrative of the History of the University of Cambridge* (London, 1838)

Latimer, H., *Sermons and Remains of Hugh Latimer*, ed. G. E. Corrie (Cambridge, 1845)

Leedham-Green, E. S. (ed.), *Books in Cambridge Inventories* (Cambridge, 1986)

—— (ed.), *Verses Presented to Queen Elizabeth I (CUL MS Add. 8915)* (Cambridge, 1993)

Letters and Papers, Foreign and Domestic, of the Reign of Henry VIII, ed. J. S. Brewer *et al.*, 21 vols. (London, 1862–1910)

Lever, R., *The Most Ancient and Learned Playe, Called the Philosophers Game* (London, 1563)

Lever, T., *A Sermon Preached the Thyrd Sondaye in Lente before the Kynges Maiestie* (London, 1550)

Lewis, J., *The Life of Dr. John Fisher*, ed. T. H. Turner, 2 vols. (London, 1855)

Logan, F. D., 'The first royal visitation of the English universities, 1535', *English Historical Review* cvi (1991), 861–88

MacCulloch, D. A., *Thomas Cranmer: A Life* (New Haven & London, 1996)

—— *Tudor Church Militant: Edward VI and the Protestant Reformation* (London, 1999)

Matricule de l'Université de Louvain, ed. E. H. J. Reusens *et al.*, 10 vols. (1903–80)

Nelson, A. H. (ed.), *Records of Early English Drama: Cambridge*, 2 vols. (Toronto, 1989)

Nicholl, C., *A Cup of News: The Life of Thomas Nashe* (London, 1984)

Peck, F. (ed), *Desiderata Curiosa*, 2nd edn (London, 1779)

Pilkington, J., *Aggeus the Prophete declared* (London, 1560)

Porter, H. C., *Reformation and Reaction in Tudor Cambridge* (Cambridge, 1958)

Rex, R., *The Theology of John Fisher* (Cambridge, 1991)

—— 'The crisis of obedience: God's word and Henry's reformation', *Historical Journal* xxxix (1996), 863–94

Select Committee on Education, *Fifth Report from the Select Committee on Education* (London, 1818)

Seton, J., *Dialectica* (London, 1545)

Starkey, D., *The Reign of Henry VIII: Personalities and Politics* (London, 1991)

Thistlethwaite, N., 'St John's College Organs, 1528–1994', *Eagle* (1995), 54–60

Underwood, M. G., 'Behind the Early Statutes', *Eagle* lxix, no. 291 (1983), 3–9

——'The Old Treasury and its graffiti', *Eagle* lxviii, no. 288 (1980), 23–6

Valor Ecclesiasticus (London, 1810–34)

Vie du bienheureux martyr Jean Fisher, ed. F. van Ortroy (Brussels, 1893)

Vita et obitus duorum fratrum Suffolciensium (London, 1551)

Wabuda, S., *Preaching during the English Reformation* (Cambridge, 2002)

Watson, T., *A Humanist's Trew Imitation: Thomas Watson's Absalom*, ed. J. H. Smith (Urbana, 1964)

Whatmore, L. E., 'A sermon of Henry Gold, vicar of Ospringe, 1525–27, preached before Archbishop Warham', *Archaeologia Cantiana* lvii (1944), 34–43

Whitaker, W., *Praelectiones*, ed. J. Allenson (Cambridge, 1599)

White, R., 'The carols of Richard White', in J. H. Pollen (ed.), *Unpublished Documents Relating to the English Martyrs*, I. *1584–1603* (London, 1908), 90–99

——'A True Report of the Life and Martyrdom of Mr. Richard White, Schoolmaster', *The Rambler* iii, part vii (May 1860), 233–48 and 366–88

ODNB articles on: R. Alvey (C. S. Knighton); R. Baynes (J. Wright); W. Bill (C. S. Knighton); G. Bullock (R. Rex); J. Cheke (A. Bryson); J. Christopherson (J. Wright); H. Constable (C. Sullivan); Henry Courtenay, earl of Devon (J. P. D. Cooper); R. Croke (J. Woolfson); E. Digby (N. Orme); B. Dodington (E. Leedham-Green and N. G. Wilson), T. Linacre (V. Nutton); A. Fraunce (W. Barker); Roger Hutchinson (J. F. Jackson); R. Jermyn (J. Craig); Roger Kelke; (B. Lowe); A. Langdale (J. Wright); Thomas Lever (B. Lowe); E. Lewkenor (J. W. Brigden); R. Lupton (S. Wright); Andrew Perne (P. Collinson); L. Pilkington (R. L. Graves); J. Pilkington (D. Marcombe); E. Sandys (P. Collinson); J. Stanley (D. G. Newcombe); J. Taylor (M. Bowker)

THE SEVENTEENTH CENTURY

Primary Sources

SJCA

BB2 and 3	Records of the Brewhouse and Bakehouse Bursar
C3.1 and 2	Registers of Admissions of College Officers, Fellows, and Scholars
C5.1	Orders made by the government of the College from 1628
C8.1	Register copies of leases and other deeds of property
C12.1 to 3	Registers and inventories of chambers
C13.6.1	Extract copy of College Balance Book
C17.7	College Balance Book
D30	Rentals, terriers and surveys mainly of land in Cambridgeshire
D57	Miscellaneous deeds, accounts and correspondence
D94 and D105	Letters to the Master, and others
SB4.3 to 4.10	Annual accounts of the College, the 'rentals'

SJCL

Bb.7.6	Accounts, letters and drawings relating to the building of Second Court
U.20.68	*A confession of faith, put forth by the elders and brethren of many congregations of Christians, (baptized upon profession of their faith) in London and the country: with an appendix concerning baptism,* London, 1688, a volume formerly owned by Titus Oates and Thomas Baker
MS H.31	Charles Yate's notes on eminent members of the College
MS K.18	The College Library 'Liber Memorialis'
MS O.65	Matthew Robinson, 'Strena Poetica', 1646
MS S.26.2	Autobiography of Matthew Robinson

CAMBRIDGE UNIVERSITY ARCHIVES

CUR 44.1	From the series of Cambridge University Registry Guardbooks
Lett. 11a.A.8.a	Files of letters
VCCt.I.9	Records of the Vice-Chancellor's Court

CAMBRIDGE UNIVERSITY LIBRARY, WESTERN MANUSCRIPTS

Add. MS 2677	Commonplace fragments relating to royal visits by James I and Charles I

THE NATIONAL ARCHIVES

SP (State Papers) 14/176; SP 38/8

Printed Sources

Batho, G. R., 'Gilbert Talbot, seventh earl of Shrewsbury (1553–1616): the "great and glorious earl"?', *Derbyshire Archaeological Journal* xciii (1973), 23–32

Beeching, H. C., 'Was Ben Jonson a Johnian?', *Eagle* xxvi (1904–5), 357–8

Bennett, G. V., 'The Seven Bishops: a reconsideration', in D. Baker (ed.), *Religious Motivation: Biographical and Sociological Problems for the Church Historian* (Oxford, 1978), 267–87

Bowle, J. (ed.), *The Diary of John Evelyn* (Oxford, 1985)

Clark, S., 'Inversion, misrule and the meaning of witchcraft', *Past and Present* 87 (1980), 98–127

Cooper, T., *The Journal of William Dowsing* (Woodbridge, 2001)

Cowan, B. W., *The Social Life of Coffee: The Emergence of the British Coffeehouse* (London, 2005)

Cressy, D., 'Levels of illiteracy in England, 1530–1730', *Historical Journal* xx (1977), 1–23

Cunich, P., *et al.*, *A History of Magdalene College Cambridge, 1428–1988* (Cambridge, 1994)

Curtis, M. H., *Oxford and Cambridge in Transition, 1558–1642* (Oxford, 1959)

Douglas, D. C., *English Scholars, 1660–1730* (London, 1951)

Fincham, K., *Prelate as Pastor: The Episcopate of James I* (Oxford, 1990)

Foster, A., 'Church policies of the 1630s', in R. P. Cust and A. Hughes (eds.), *Conflict in Early Stuart England: Studies in Religion and Politics, 1603–1642* (Harlow, 1989), 193–223

Fox, A., *Oral and Literate Culture in England, 1500–1700* (Oxford, 2001)

Glasgow, E., 'Ben Jonson and St John's', *Eagle* lxxi, no. 295 (1987), 66–70

Hatcher, J., *The History of the British Coal Industry*, I. *Before 1700* (Oxford, 1993)

Heywood, O., *Life of John Angier of Denton* (Manchester, 1937)

Hoyle, D., *Reformation and Religious Identity in Cambridge, 1590–1644* (Woodbridge, 2007)

Jackson, C. (ed.), *The Diary of Abraham de la Pryme, the Yorkshire Antiquary* (Durham, 1870)

Jukes, H. A. L., 'Peter Gunning, 1613–1684: churchman, scholar, controversialist', *Proceedings of the Cambridge Antiquarian Society* lv (1962), 36–52

Kishlansky, M., 'Charles I: a case of mistaken identity', *Past and Present* 189 (2005), 41–80

Korsten, F., *A Catalogue of the Library of Thomas Baker* (Cambridge, 1990)

Lake, P., *Anglicans and Puritans? Presbyterianism and English Conformist Thought from Whitgift to Hooker* (London, 1988)

—— 'Calvinism and the English Church, 1570–1635', in M. Todd (ed.), *Reformation to Revolution: Politics and Religion in Early Modern England* (London, 1995), 179–207

Leedham-Green, E., *A Concise History of the University of Cambridge* (Cambridge, 1996)

McClure, N. E. (ed.), *The Letters of John Chamberlain*, 2 vols. (Philadelphia, 1939)

[Marsden, J. H.], *College Life in the Time of James the First, as Illustrated by an Unpublished Diary of Sir Symonds D'Ewes* (London, 1851)

Mears, N., '*Regnum Cecilianum*? A Cecilian perspective of the court', in J. Guy (ed.), *The Reign of Elizabeth I: Court and Culture in the Last Decade* (Cambridge, 1995), 46–64

Miller, Edward, 'Fish Ponds Close and its pondyards', *Eagle* lix (1960–63), 353–62

Moore Smith, G. C. (ed.), *Club Law: A Comedy* (Cambridge, 1907)

Mullinger, J. B., 'Was Ben Jonson ever a member of our College?', *Eagle* xxv (1903–4), 302–5

Nelson, A. H. (ed.), *Records of Early English Drama, Cambridge*, 2 vols. (Toronto, 1989)

O'Day, R., *Education and Society, 1500–1800: The Social Foundations of Education in Early Modern Britain* (London, 1982)

Parkinson, R. (ed.), *The Autobiography of Henry Newcome* (Manchester, 1852)

Robinson, Matthew, *Autobiography of Matthew Robinson*, ed. J. E. B. Mayor (Cambridge, 1856)

Sayle, C., 'Bibliotheca loquitur', *Eagle* xvii (1891–3), 376–7

Scott, R. F., 'Some aspects of College life in past times', *Eagle* xliii (1923–4), 160–75

Seaward, P., *The Cavalier Parliament and the Reconstruction of the Old Regime, 1661–1667* (Cambridge, 1989)

Sharpe, J., *Remember Remember the Fifth of November: Guy Fawkes and the Gunpowder Plot* (London, 2005)

Shepard, A., *Meanings of Manhood in Early Modern England* (Oxford, 2003)

——'Contesting communities? "Town" and "Gown" in Cambridge, c. 1560–1640', in Shepard and P. Withington (eds.), *Communities in Early Modern England: Networks, Place, Rhetoric* (Manchester, 2000), 216–34

Smith, G. C. M. (ed.), 'John Gibson's manuscript', *Eagle* xvii (1891–3), 246–68

Stone, L. (ed.), *The University in Society* (Princeton, 1975)

Stray, C., 'From oral to written examinations: Cambridge, Oxford and Dublin, 1700–1914', *History of Universities* xx (2005), 76–130

Sugg, W., *A Tradition Unshared: A History of Cambridge Town and County Cricket, 1700–1890* (Cambridge, 2002–4)

Thomas, R., 'The Seven Bishops and their petition, 18 May 1688', *Journal of Ecclesiastical History* xii (1961), 56–70

Torry, A. F., *Founders and Benefactors of St John's College, Cambridge* (Cambridge, 1888)

Twigg, J., *The University of Cambridge and the English Revolution, 1625–1688* (Woodbridge, 1990)

Tyacke, N., *Anti-Calvinists: The Rise of English Arminianism, c. 1590–1640* (Oxford, 1987)

Vallance, E., '"An holy and sacramentall faction": federal thought and the Solemn League and Covenant in England', *English Historical Review* cxvi (2001), 50–75

Venn, J. A., *A Statistical Chart to Illustrate the Entries at the Various Colleges in the University of Cambridge, 1544–1907* (Cambridge, 1908)

Wallis, P. J. *William Crashawe: The Sheffield Puritan* (Sheffield, 1963)

——'The library of William Crashawe', *Transactions of the Cambridge Bibliographical Society* ii (1954–8), 213–28

Watson, G., 'Charles and Henrietta', *Eagle* (1998), 40–8

Willis, R., and J. W. Clark, *The Architectural History of the University of Cambridge* (Cambridge, 1886)

Worthington, J. (ed.), *The Works of the Pious and Profoundly Learned Joseph Mede* (London, 1677)

ODNB articles on: P. Gunning (K. W. Stevenson); R. Senhouse (P. E. McCullough); H. Welby (D. Souden)

THE EIGHTEENTH CENTURY

Primary Sources

SJCA

Admonition Book (to 1780)

Conclusions Books 1736–86; 1786 onwards

Drawer 83: Shrewsbury school dispute

Examination Books C 15 5

Oaths Book

SJCL

Commonplace Book of William Selwin (O.60)

Letters of Rowland Hill (Misc. Letters Hill)

Notes by William Powell and other material on Todington case (D.89. 194–200; D.108. 119–21)

BRITISH LIBRARY

Add. MSS 32457: Conyers Middleton etc. (incl. 2nd Earl of Oxford)

Add. MSS 4318: Samuel Squire

Add. MSS 35639, 35640: Hardwicke MSS: Charles Yorke

MS sketch of Squire's life inserted in LR.271.e.5

ROYAL HORTICULTURAL SOCIETY LIBRARY

Accounts of Capability Brown

CAMBRIDGE UNIVERSITY LIBRARY

Grace Book I

Printed Sources

Academiae Cantabrigiensis Luctus in obitum Frederici celsissimi Walliae Principis (Cambridge, 1751)

Best, G. F. A., *Temporal Pillars* (Cambridge, 1964)

Besterman, T. (ed.), *Voltaire's Correspondence*, 136 vols. to date (Geneva, 1953–)

Bewley, C., and D. Bewley, *Gentleman Radical: A Life of John Horne Tooke, 1736–1812* (London, 1998)

Boys-Smith, J. S., 'The alterations made in the Fellows' Garden and the College grounds in 1822–3', *Eagle* liii (1950), 147–61

—— 'The College grounds and playing fields', *Eagle* liv (1950–51), 300–5

Brewer, S. (ed.), *The Early Letters of Bishop Richard Hurd, 1739–1762* (London, 1995)

Brown, John, *An Estimate of the Manners and Principles of the Times*, 2 vols. (London, 1757)

Clark, J. C. D., *English Society, 1688–1832* (Cambridge, 1985)

Clifford, J., *Capability Brown* (Princes Risborough, 2001)

Darwin, C., *The Life of Erasmus Darwin*, 2nd edn (London, 1887)

Findon, J. C., 'The Nonjurors and the Church of England, 1689–1716' (D.Phil. thesis, Oxford University, 1978)

Fowler, L., and H. Fowler, *Cambridge Commemorated* (Cambridge, 1984)

Gascoigne, J., *Cambridge in the Age of the Enlightenment* (Cambridge, 1989)

——'Mathematics and meritocracy: the emergence of the Cambridge mathematical Tripos', *Social Studies of Science* xiv (1984), 547–84

Gunning, H., *Reminiscences of the University, Town and County of Cambridge from the Year 1780*, 2 vols. (London, 1854)

Hague, W., *William Wilberforce* (London, 2008)

Hoadly, B., *A Preservative against the Principles and Practices of the* NONJURORS *both in Church and State* (London, 1716)

Hochstrasser, T., '"A College in the Air": myth and reality in the foundation story of Downing College, Cambridge', *History of Universities* xvii (2001–2), 81–120

Humphreys, R., *Sidney Sussex College: A History* (Cambridge, 2009)

Jenkin, R., *The Reasonableness and Certainty of the Christian Religion*, 5th edn, 2 vols. (London, 1721)

Johnston, K. R., *The Hidden Wordsworth* (Bloomington, IN, 1998)

Jones, H. D., *John Balguy: An English Moralist of the 18th Century*, Abhandlungen zur Philosophie und ihrer Geschichte, Heft 2 (Leipzig, 1907)

Legg, L. G. Wickham, *Matthew Prior: A Study of his Public Career and Correspondence* (Cambridge, 1921)

Linehan, Peter, 'Unfinished business', *Eagle* (2001), 32–9

Luckett, R., *Handel's Messiah: A Celebration* (London, 1992)

Maitland, F. W., *Township and Borough* (Cambridge, 1898)

Mayor, J. E. B., *Cambridge under Queen Anne* (Cambridge, 1911)

Monk, J. H., *The Life of Richard Bentley*, 2 vols. (London, 1833)

Needham, P., *A Sermon Preached before the University of Cambridge* (Cambridge, 1716)

Newcome, J., *The Sure Word of Prophecy*, 2nd edn (Cambridge, 1724)

[Newcome, Susanna(h)], *An Enquiry into the Evidence of the Christian Religion* (Cambridge, 1729)

——*The Plain Account of the Nature and End of the Sacrament &c. not Drawn or Founded, upon Scripture*, Parts I and II (Cambridge, 1734, 1738)

Newman, Richard, *St John's Triangle, Cambridge: An Archaeological Excavation and Watching Brief*, 2 vols. (Cambridge, 2008)

Page, A., *John Jebb and the Enlightened Origins of British Radicalism* (London, 2003)

Pollbooks for the Cambridge University Elections of 1780, 1784, 1790

Porter, R., *The Greatest Benefit to Mankind* (London, 1997)

Powell, W. S. (ed. T. Balguy), *Discourses on Various Subjects* (London, 1776)

——*An Observation on the Design of Establishing Annual Examinations at Cambridge* (Cambridge, 1774)

Rook, A. (ed.), *Cambridge and its Contribution to Medicine* (London, 1971)

Scott, R. F., 'Some aspects of College life in past times', *Eagle* xliii (1923–4), 160–75

Sedgwick, R. (ed.), *The History of Parliament: The House of Commons, 1715–1754*, 2 vols. (London, 1970)

Selincourt, E. de, and C. L. Shaver, *The Letters of William and Dorothy Wordsworth*, vol. I (Oxford, 1967)

Souden, J., *Wimpole Hall* (London, 1991)

Squire, S., *Works*, 4 vols. bound together in British Library

Stray, C., 'From oral to written examinations', *History of Universities* xx/2 (2005), 76–130

Taylor, S. J. C., 'University reform and the Cambridge regulations of 1750' (unpublished article)

Thomas, P. D. G., *The House of Commons in the Eighteenth Century* (Oxford, 1971)

Tovey, D. C. (ed.), *Gray's Letters*, 3 vols. (London, 1900–12)

Uglow, J., *The Lunar Men: The Friends who Made the Future* (London, 2002)

Venn, J. A., 'Matriculations at Oxford and Cambridge, 1544–1906', *Oxford and Cambridge Review* (1908), 48–66

Virgin, P., *The Church in an Age of Negligence* (Cambridge, 1989)

Walsh, J., C. Haydon, and S. Taylor (eds.), *The Church of England, c. 1689–c. 1833* (Cambridge, 1993)

White, R. J., *Dr Bentley: A Study in Academic Scarlet* (London, 1965)

Winstanley, D. A., *The University of Cambridge in the Eighteenth Century* (Cambridge, 1922)

Wordsworth, C., *Scholae academicae* (Cambridge, 1887)

—— *Social Life at the English Universities in the Eighteenth Century*, 2 vols. (London, 1874)

Wordsworth, J., M. H. Abrams and S. Gill (eds.), *The Prelude, 1799, 1805, 1850* (London, 1979.)

Wordsworth at Cambridge [= *Eagle* liv (1950–51), 73–143]

Wraxall, N. W., *Historical Memoirs of My Own Time*, ed. R. Askham, 2 vols. (London, 1904)

[Yorke, C., *et al.*], *Athenian Letters: Residing at Athens during the Peloponnesian War*, 4 vols. (London, 1741–3)

ODNB articles on: F. Norton (P. Laundy); S. Squire (R. Browning)

THE NINETEENTH CENTURY

Primary Sources

SJCA

CB	Conclusion Book, 1800–1900
CM	Minutes of College Council and reports to same, 1882–1900
C12.10	Report and documents relating to vacant rooms in College, 1898
CC1.1.21	Reports and minutes of Education Committee, 1860–1900
CC4/4.1	Reports of committees and other papers concerning the reform of management and the wages and duties of servants, 1854–1916
CC5	Records of the May Ball Committee, 1886–1914
D33.1–14	Papers relating to major building projects within the college precincts
D44.1–47, 44.2–10	Papers relating to University Commissions, 1855–1900, including
D44.3.3	Volume of papers relating to the passing of new Statutes, annotated by W. E. Heitland, 1877–82
D69	Papers relating to the government of Shrewsbury School, 1800–50
D76.62–5, 83–387	Correspondence concerning Pocklington Grammar School, 1800–62
D78.61–146	Correspondence concerning Sedbergh School, 1800–84
D79.1–89	Correspondence with University Commissioners on revision of statutes regarding scholarships from grammar schools, 1856–1861
D88.1–39, 44–79	Papers concerning Shrewsbury School (1–39) and Public Schools Bill, 1866–7
D89.13, 35–8, 59–67, 81–147	Papers relating to the appeal of Revd Dr Wood (Bursar), 1795–1840
D90.51–904	Correspondence of Masters and Bursars, 1800–1900
D92.1.1–429,	Correspondence of Bursars (including internal administration estates, schools, University matters, appointments, etc.)
D92.17.1–30.87	The same continued
D100	Reports of Service Committee, 1888 (155) and Unification of Finance, 1893 (64); Audit statement 1893 (70)
D101	Miscellaneous papers on college, university, and estate business, including pamphlets relating to Revd Dr Wood's case (4) and resolutions on a new chapel, 1861 (5)
D103.1–225	Papers and correspondence on aspects of University/College relations, including reform of statutes, fellowships, chapel
D104	Papers relating to the reform of statutes; tutorial, teaching, and examination arrangements; Junior Bursar's business; etc.
D105.255–63	Correspondence of James Wood with the Home Department regarding the limitation of fellowships to particular counties, 1819–20
DS1	Order book and memoranda of the College deans, 1806–7
DS3.2–6	Junior Dean's registers, 1826–1900: chapel attendance and conduct
DS4.2–5	Senior Dean's papers, 1828–96

JB2	Junior Bursar's order book etc., 1823–99
JB3.1.	Junior bursar's accounts, 1807–29
M1.3	Abstract letter book of James Wood, 1808–36
M1.7	W. H. Bateson's Letter Books, 1856–66
M1.10.3–10	Memoranda: breakdown of charges for commons (fellows, pensioners, sizars, etc.) and costs, 1822–5
SB1.4–11	Senior Bursar's memoranda and estate inspection notes, 1800–1900, including SB1.6 Reyner's estate diary (1857–76), SB1.21–3 Scott's estate diary (1891–1908)
SB2.1–22	Letters from the Senior Bursar, 1846–1900
SB11	Annual summaries of the accounts of the Senior Bursar, 1800–87
SB21	Estate papers, correspondence regarding farm buildings, tenancies, local schools, 1830–1900
SB21/Sun	Senior Bursar's papers relating to the Sunningdale estate
SB21/Cb/W/22	Grange Farm estate papers
SBF54	Reports of Committee on Tutorships
SBF77	Report on the Education Fund, 1909
SD7.2–12	Miscellaneous accounts relating to the Steward and his office, including book of tradesmen's receipts, 1800–1900
SOC3.1–3	Records of the General Athletic Club, etc., 1878–1900
SOC7	Records of the O. D. S., Trinity & St John's Debating Society, 1849–51
SOC8	Records of the St John's Debating Society, 1870–1922
TU.1.1.2	Letter Book of James Wood, 1792–1807
TU1.3.2	Payments to bedmakers and laundresses, 1839–53
TU4	Tutors' admission papers: James Atlay, Edward Brummell, 1847–56
TU5A	Tutors' admission papers: James Atlay, T. M. S. Field, 1853–9
TU5B	Tutors' admission papers: Francis France, 1853–62
TU5C	Tutors' admission papers: Joseph Mayor, 1861–4
TU6 (1–12)	Admission and tutorial papers: Stephen Parkinson, 1864–83
TU7 (1–18)	Tutorial files: J. E. Sandys, 1871–1900
TU8	Tutorial files: Edwin Hill, 1877–88
TU9	Tutorial files: W. E. Heitland, 1875–92
TU10 (2–6)	Tutorial files: Joseph T. Ward, 1883–95
TU10 (7–10)	General correspondence and bills: Joseph T. Ward
TU11	Tutorial files: Donald MacAlister

SJCL

Post-medieval Manuscripts

K. 36	James Wood, Papers on subjects in divinity, church government, and education
K. 43–4	William Craven, Notes and drafts of sermons (–1815)
O. 78	Correspondence of George Shaw (undergraduate), 1840
S. 66	John Kaye and James Wood, Sermons and other papers, 1785–1819

U. 22	Henry Russell, Diary of events connected with St John's College, 1865–84 (an exceptionally detailed and valuable insider's account of meetings of the Seniority, the Council, the Fellows, and of Chapel services, Hall meals, College functions, etc.)
U. 40–1	Feast books of St John's College, 1873–1920
W. 2	Diary of Joseph Timmis Ward (undergraduate and graduate), 1874–6
W. 2	P. T. Main: Notes on College Council business, 1884–1894
W. 14–15	Edward H. Palmer, Notebooks, 1868, and scrap-book, 1862–80 (relating almost exclusively to his travels abroad, but containing sketches and water colours of members of St John's)
W. 28	Journal of John Rogers (undergraduate), 1820–4
W. 33	Journal of Francis P. B. N. Hutton (undergraduate), mainly 1846–9

Personal and Family Papers

Papers of Edwin Abbott Abbott, *c.* 1875–1928 (GBR/0275/Abbott)

Papers of John Couch Adams, 1701–1996 (GBR/0275/Adams)

Papers of Arthur Carrighan, 1802–1953 (GBR/0275/Carrighan)

Papers of Terrot Reavely Glover, 1850–1955 (GBR/0275/Glover) (including detailed diaries of the 1890s)

Papers of William Emerton Heitland, 1864–97 (GBR/0275/Heitland) (including diary of a holiday on the Isle of White with Tom Hughes, and a diary of notes on Council meetings, 1895–7: C, Box 2)

Papers of Sir John Frederick William Herschel, 1812–71 (GBR/0275/Herschel)

Papers of Sir Joseph Larmor, 1908–42 (GBR/0275/Larmor)

Notebooks of John Eyton Bickersteth Mayor, *c.* 1660–1910 (GBR/0275/Mayor)

Papers of James Bass Mullinger, 1873–1915 (GBR/0275/Mullinger)

Letters of Stephen Abbott Notcutt (undergraduate), 1883–1977 (GBR/0275/Notcutt)

Papers of Henry John Temple, 3rd Viscount Palmerston, 1812–65 (GBR/0275/Palmerston)

Papers of Stephen Parkinson, *c.* 1845–89 (GBR/0275/Parkinson)

Papers of Richard Pendlebury, 1872–1902 (GBR/0275/Pendlebury)

Papers of Sir John Edwin Sandys, *c.* 1870–1934 (GBR/0275/Sandys)

Papers of William Selwyn, 1875–6 (GBR/0275/Selwyn)

Papers of Joseph Robson Tanner, *c.* 1881–1926 (GBR/0275/Selwyn)

Papers of Sir Charles Taylor, 1861–1909 (GBR/0275/Taylor)

Papers of John William Whittaker, 1798–1838 (GBR/0275/Whittaker)

Papers of James Wood, 1754–1817, n.d. (GBR/0275/Wood)

Sir Joseph Larmor Collection

W1.K-LU.Liveing.1–9/Larmor–Liveing, 1881, 1884–1917, 1919

W1/D-F.Foxwell H. S.1–16/Larmor–H. S. Foxwell, 1893–1923

M1.Ma-Mi.MacAlister.1–15/ Larmor–MacAlister, 1888–1927

W1.Sa-Se.Scott/Larmor–Scott, 1892–1922

TO4/A. F. Torry to Larmor, 1882–8

SO1/1–2/Letters to Lamor

W1.Ma-Mi.Main.1–2/MA7/10b/12/ P. T. Main to Larmor, 1896–9

W1.Ma-Mi.Mason.1/MA13/Larmor/P. Mason to Lamor, 1889

W1.Na-Be.Bateson, 1–12/W. Bateson to Larmor, 1889–1918

W1.Cl-Cu.Cox.1–3/CO9/W. A. Cox to Larmor, 1899

W1.Ca-Ch.Caldecottt.1–5/CA1/Caldecott to Larmor, 1894–1897

BA8/1/7–8, W. H. Bateson to P. T. Main, 1869

W1.Ta-Tu.Taylor.1–34, C. Taylor to Larmor, 1884–1905

GR2/25, BE/8/3/Larmor to C. Taylor, 1888, 1890

EMMANUEL COLLEGE, CAMBRIDGE

Papers of Henry Melvill Gwatkin, ECA Col.9. 39c

TRINITY COLLEGE, CAMBRIDGE, LIBRARY

Mayor Papers, 1838–*c.* 1900 (B7–16) (extensive correspondence of Robert Bickersteth Mayor, John Eyton Bickertseth Mayor, and Joseph Bickersteth Mayor)

Published Sources

Allen, David Rayvern, *Sir Aubrey: Biography of Charles Aubrey Smith, England Cricketer, West End Actor, Hollywood Film Star* (London, 1982)

Allen, Peter, *The Cambridge Apostles: The Early Years* (Cambridge, 1978)

Anderson, Olive, 'The growth of Christian militarism in mid-Victorian Britain', *English Historical Review* lxxxvi (1971), 46–72

——'The Administrative Reform Association, 1855–1857', in Patricia Hollis (ed.), *Pressure from Without in Early Victorian England* (London, 1974), 262–88

Anon., 'Our chronicle', *Eagle* vi (1869), 254–6

——'The Revd. Charles Taylor, D. D.', *Eagle* xxx (1909–10), 64–85, 197–204

——'Presentation of the Master's portrait', *Eagle* xxxv (1914), 78–88

——'Heitland as J. B.', *Eagle* li (1938–9), 132–43

Babington, A. M. (ed.), with preface by J. E. B. Mayor, *Memorial Journal and Botanical Correspondence of Charles Cardale Babington* (Cambridge, 1897)

Barber, Lynn, *The Heyday of Natural History, 1820–1870* (London, 1970)

Barker, Juliet, *The Brontës* (London, 1994)

Barrow-Green, June, '"The advantage of proceeding from an author of some scientific reputation": Isaac Todhunter and his mathematics textbooks', in Jonathan Smith and Christopher Stray (eds.), *Teaching and Learning in Nineteenth-Century Cambridge* (Woodbridge, 2001), 177–203

Bateson, Beatrice, *William Bateson, FRS, Naturalist* (London, 1928)

Bateson, William H., *Six Sermons* (Cambridge, 1881)

Blackman, Helen, 'A spiritual leader? Cambridge zoology, mountaineering and the death of F. M. Balfour', *Studies in History and Philosophy of Science*, Part C*: Studies in the History and Philosophy of Biological and Biomedical Sciences* 35 (2004), 93–117

Bonney, Thomas George, *A Letter to the Master and Fellows of St John's College* (Cambridge, 1867)

——*The Influence of Science on Theology* (Cambridge, 1885)

——*Memories of a Long Life* (Cambridge, 1921)

——'The Master of St John's: obituary', *CR* ii (1880–1), 258–9

——'A septuagenarian's recollections of St John's', *Eagle* xxx (1909), 294–310

Boys Smith, J. S., 'The College seeks help from Lord Palmerston', *Eagle* lvi (1954–5), 185–93

Brock, M. G., and M. C. Curthoys (eds.), *The History of the University of Oxford*, VI–VII. *Nineteenth-Century Oxford* (Oxford, 1997–2000)

Brockliss, L. W. B., 'The European university in the age of revolution, 1789–1850', in Brock and Curthoys, VI. 84–9

Browne, Janet, *Charles Darwin: Voyaging: Part I of a Biography* (London, 1995)

Burkhardt, Frederick, James A. Secord *et al.* (eds.), *The Correspondence of Charles Darwin* (Cambridge, 1985–)

Bury, J. P. T., M. E. Bury and J. D. Pickles (eds.), *Selected Passages from the Diary of the Rev. Joseph Romilly*, 2 vols. (Cambridge, 1967–2000)

Butler, Samuel, *The Way of All Flesh* (London, 1903)

Chandos, John, *Boys Together: English Public Schools, 1800–1864* (London, 1984)

Coleridge, S. T., *On the Constitution of Church and State According to the Idea of Each* (1830), ed. John Colmer, vol. 10 of *The Collected Works of Samuel Taylor Coleridge*, ed. Kathleen Coburn and Bart Winer (London, 1969–)

Correspondence Respecting the Proposed Measures of Improvement in the Universities and Colleges of Oxford and Cambridge, 12 Jan. 1854, Parliamentary Papers 1854, l

Cowie, B. M., *On Sacrifice, the Atonement, Vicarious Oblation, and Example of Christ, and the Punishment of Sin* (Cambridge, 1856)

——*A Commemoration Sermon Preached on the Feast of S. John, Port Lat. 1871* (Cambridge, 1871)

Cox, D. R., 'Biometrika; the first 100 years', *Biometrika* 88 (2001), 3–11

Cox, George W., *The Life of John William Colenso*, 2 vols. (London, 1888)

Craik, Alex D. D., *Mr Hopkins' Men: Cambridge Reform and British Mathematics in the 19th Century* (London, 2007)

Croome, A. C. M. (ed.), *Fifty Years of Sport: Oxford and Cambridge*, 2 vols. (London, 1913)

Crowe, Michael J., *Calendar of the Correspondence of Sir John Herschel* (Cambridge, 1998)

Curthoys, M. C., 'The careers of Oxford men', in Brock and Curthoys, VI. 477–510

Dunbabin, J. P. D., 'Oxford and Cambridge college finances, 1871–1913', *Economic History Review* 2nd ser., xxviii (1975), 631–47

——'College estates and wealth, 1600–1815', in Sutherland and Mitchell, 269–301

'E.B.C.', *Victoria and Albert at Cambridge: The Royal Visits of 1843 and 1847 as they were Recorded by Joseph Romilly, Registrary of the University of Cambridge* (Cambridge, 1977)

Engel, A. J., *From Clergyman to Don: The Rise of the Academic Profession in Nineteenth-Century Oxford* (Oxford, 1983)

Garland, M. M., *Cambridge before Darwin: The Ideal of a Liberal Education* (Cambridge, 1980)

Gillham, Nicholas W., 'Evolution by jumps: Francis Galton and William Bateson and the mechanism of evolutionary change', *Genetics* 159 (2001), 1383–92

Glover, T. R., *Cambridge Retrospect* (Cambridge, 1943)

Grattan-Guiness, I., 'Mathematics and mathematical physics from Cambridge, 1815–40': a survey of the achievements and of the French influences', in Harman, *Wranglers and Physicists*, 84–111

Grave, W. W., *Fitzwilliam College Cambridge, 1869–1969* (Cambridge, 1983)

Groenewegen, P. D., *A Soaring Eagle: Alfred Marshall, 1842–1924* (Aldershot, 1995)

Guillebaud, Philomena, 'West Cambridge, 1870–1914: building the bicycle suburb', *Proceedings of the Cambridge Antiquarian Society* xcvi (2007), 193–210

Gunning, Henry, *Reminiscences of the University, Town and County of Cambridge from the Year 1780*, 2 vols. (London & Cambridge, 1854)

Hammond, N. G. L., *Sir John Edwin Sandys* (Cambridge, 1933)

Harman, P. M. (ed.), *Wranglers and Physicists: Studies on Cambridge Physics in the Nineteenth Century* (Manchester, 1985)

Heitland, W. E., *After Many Years: A Tale of Experiences and Impressions Gathered in the Course of an Obscure Life* (Cambridge, 1926)

—— 'Josiah Brown Pearson', *Eagle* xix (1897), 89–91

—— review of Bonney's *Memories*, *Eagle* xlii (1921–2), 283–7

—— 'Thomas George Bonney', *Eagle* xliii (1923–4), 262–4

—— 'George Downing Liveing', *Eagle* xliv (1924–6), 96–9

Henderson, John, *Juvenal's Mayor: The Professor who Lived on 2d. a Day* (Bristol, 1998)

Herschel, John F. W., review of Humboldt's *Kosmos*, *Edinburgh Review* 87 (1848), 170–229

Hill, Edwin, 'Revd Henry Russell', *Eagle* xxv (1904), 198–200

Honey, J. R. de S., *Tom Brown's Universe: The Development of the Victorian Public School* (London, 1977)

—— and M. C. Curthoys, 'Oxford and schooling', in Brock and Curthoys, VII. 545–69

Jackson, J. R., 'The first athletic sports in Cambridge', *Eagle* xvi (1891), 358–61

Joyce, Thomas, 'College life at Cambridge', *Westminster Review* 35 (1841), 456–81

Kirke-White, Henry, *Remains*, rev. edn (Cambridge, 1839)

Latham, H., 'University expenses', in *The Student's Guide* (1862), 50–66

Lubenow, W. C., *The Cambridge Apostles, 1820–1914: Liberalism, Imagination, and Friendship in British Intellectual and Professional Life* (Cambridge, 1998)

MacAlister, E. F. B., *Sir Donald MacAlister of Tarbert, by His Wife* (London, 1935)

McDonald, Donna, *Lord Strathcona: A Biography of Donald Alexander Smith* (Toronto & Oxford, 1996)

Macleod, Roy and Russell Moseley, 'Breaking the circle of the sciences: the natural sciences tripos and the "examination revolution"', in Roy Macleod (ed.), *Days of Judgement: Science Examinations and the Organization of Knowledge in Late Victorian England* (Driffield, 1982), 189–212

Marshall, Alfred, *Principles of Economics* (London, 1890)

Martin, Ged, *The Cambridge Union and Ireland, 1815–1914* (Edinburgh, 2000)

Mayor, J. E. B., *Social Changes in Sixty Years* (Manchester, 1897)

—— Obituary of The Rev. John Spicer Wood D. D., *Eagle* xvii (1893), 654–64

Mayor, Joseph B., 'College reform in the fifties', *Eagle* xxxi (1910), 189–94

Merivale, Judith Anne (ed.), *Autobiography of Dean Merivale, with Selections from his Correspondence* (London, 1899)

Moore, Christopher Oldstone, 'The beard movement in Victorian Britain', *Victorian Studies* 48 (2005), 7–34

Murphy, Michael J., *Cambridge Newspapers and Opinion, 1780–1850* (Cambridge, 1977)

Neild, Robert, *Riches and Responsibility: The Financial History of Trinity College, Cambridge* (Cambridge, 2008)

Oldham, J. Basil, *A History of Shrewsbury School, 1552–1952* (Oxford, 1952)

Parker, Rowland, *Town and Gown: The 700 Years' War in Cambridge* (Cambridge, 1983)

Pearson, Karl, *The Life, Letters, and Labours of Francis Galton*, 4 vols. (Cambridge, 1914–30)

Pevsner, Nikolaus, *The Buildings of England: Cambridgeshire*, 2nd edn (Harmondsworth, 1970)

Pigou, A. C., and J. M. Keynes (eds.), *Memorials of Alfred Marshall* (London, 1925)

Porter, Roy, 'The Natural Sciences tripos and the "Cambridge school of geology", 1815–1914', *History of Universities* ii (1982), 193–216

Poynter, F. N. L. (ed.), *The Evolution of Medical Education in Britain* (London, 1966)

Ray, G. N. (ed.), *The Letters and Private Papers of William Makepeace Thackeray*, 4 vols., I. *1817–1840* (London, 1945–6)

Reisman, D., *Alfred Marshall's Mission* (London, 1890)

Report of Her Majesty's Commissioners Appointed to Inquire into the State, Discipline, Studies, and Revenues of the University and Colleges of Cambridge: together with the evidence and an appendix, Parliamentary Papers 1852–3, xliv [Graham Commission]

Report of the Cambridge University Commissioners, Parliamentary Papers 1861, xx

Report of the Commissioners Appointed to Inquire into the Property and Incomes of the Universities of Oxford and Cambridge and of the Colleges and Halls Therein, Vol. III: Returns from the University of Cambridge, and from the Colleges therein, Parliamentary Papers 1873, xxxvii [Cleveland Commission]

Robson, Robert, 'Trinity College in the age of Peel', in Robert Robson (ed.), *Ideas and Institutions of Victorian Britain: Essays* (London, 1967), 313–35

Roby, H. J., *To the Master and Fellows of St John's College, Cambridge: of the Government and Tuition* (Cambridge, 1857)

—— *Remarks on College Reform* (Cambridge, 1858)

—— *Reminiscences of My Life and Work: For my own Family Only* (privately printed, Cambridge, 1913)

—— 'College reform under the Cambridge University Act of 1856', *Eagle* xxxi (1910), 195–209

Rolleston, Humphry, obituary notice for Sir Donald MacAlister, *British Medical Journal* (1936), 1154

Rothblatt, Sheldon, *The Revolution of the Dons: Cambridge and Society in Victorian England*, 2nd edn (Cambridge, 1981)

Russell, H., *The New Chapel of St. John's College, Cambridge* (Cambridge, 1869)

Russell-Gebbett, Jean, *Henslow of Hitcham: Botanist, Educationalist and Clergyman* (Lavenham, 1977)

Sandys, J. E., *In Memoriam William Henry Bateson* (Cambridge, 1881)

Scott, R. F., 'The Rev George Fearns Reyner D. D.', *Eagle* xvii (1893), 403–8

—— 'John William Pieters', *Eagle* xxiii (1902), 81–3

Selwyn, William, *The New Chapel of St John's College Cambridge: A Word Spoken at the Annual Commemoration of Benefactors, 1861* (Cambridge, 1869)

Sherrington, W. S., 'Edward Palmer', *Eagle* xii (1883), 238–40

Smith, Jonathan and Christopher Stray (eds.), *Cambridge in the 1830s: The Letters of Alexander Chisholm Gooden, 1831–1841*, History of the University of Cambridge, Texts and Studies v (Woodbridge, 2003)

—— *Teaching and Learning in Nineteenth-Century Cambridge*, History of the University of Cambridge iv (Woodbridge, 2001)

Special Report from Select Committee on Oxford and Cambridge Universities Education Bill, together with Proceedings of the Committee, Minutes of Evidence, Parliamentary Papers 1867, xiii

Stanley, A. P., *The Life and Correspondence of Thomas Arnold*, 2 vols. (London, 1845)

Stephen, Leslie, *Life of Henry Fawcett*, 3rd edn (London, 1886)

Stray, Christopher, 'Curriculum and style in the collegiate university: classics in nineteenth-century Oxbridge', *History of Universities* xvi (2000), 183–218

——'The first century of the classical tripos (1822–1922): high culture and the politics of the Curriculum', in Christopher Stray (ed.), *Classics in 19th and 20th Century Cambridge: Curriculum, Culture and Community* (Cambridge, 1999), 1–14

——'From oral to written examinations: Cambridge, Oxford and Durham, 1700–1914', *History of Universities* xx (2005), 76–130

——'Non-identical twins: classics at nineteenth-century Oxford and Cambridge', in Christopher Stray (ed.), *Oxford Classics: Teaching and Learning, 1800–1200* (London, 2007), 1–13

——'The shift from oral to written examination: Cambridge and Oxford, 1700–1900', *Assessment in Education* 8 (2001), 33–50

Sutherland, L. S., and L. G. Mitchell (eds.), *The History of the University of Oxford*, V. *The Eighteenth Century* (Oxford, 1986)

Thompson, David Michael, *Cambridge Theology in the Nineteenth Century: Enquiry, Controversy and Truth* (Aldershot, 2008)

Torry, A. F., *College Economy and University Extension: A Letter to the Master of St John's College, Cambridge* (Cambridge & London, 1868)

Trevelyan, G. M., *Trinity College: An Historical Sketch* (Cambridge, 1946)

Underwood, Malcolm, 'Restructuring a household: service and its nineteenth century critics in St John's', *Eagle* lxxii, no. 298 (1990), 9–19

——'The revolution in college teaching: St John's College, 1850–1926', in Jonathan Smith and Christopher Stray (eds.), *Teaching and Learning in Nineteenth-Century Cambridge* (Woodbridge, 2001), 107–21

——'A Tutor's lot', *Eagle* lxix, no. 292 (1983–4), 3–8

Vance, Norman, *The Sinews of the Spirit: The Ideal of Christian Manliness in Victorian Literature and Religious Thought* (Cambridge, 1985)

Walters, S. M., *The Shaping of Cambridge Botany* (Cambridge, 1981)

Weldon, F. W. R., 'Some Remarks on Variations in Plants and Animals', *Proceedings of the Royal Society of London* lvii (1894–5), 379–82

Whitaker, John K. (ed.), *The Correspondence of Alfred Marshall, Economist* (Cambridge, 1996)

Wilson, James Maurice, *James M. Wilson: An Autobiography, 1836–1931* (London, 1932)

——*A Letter to the Master and Seniors of St John's College on the Subject of the Natural and Physical Sciences in Relation to School and College* (London, 1867)

——'H. J. Roby', *Eagle* xxxvi (1914–15), 202–6

Winch, Donald, *Wealth and Life: Essays on the Intellectual History of Political Economy in Britain, 1848–1914* (Cambridge, 2009)

Winstanley, D. A., *Early Victorian Cambridge* (Cambridge, 1940)

——*Later Victorian Cambridge* (Cambridge, 1947)

Wood, J. S., *The Position of Members of the Church of England in a College of the University of Cambridge* (Cambridge & London, 1882)

——'William Selwyn', *Eagle* ix (1873–5), 298–322

Woodruff, A. E., in *Dictionary of Scientific Biography*, ed. C. C. Gillispie, 16 vols. (New York, 1970–80), VIII. 39–41

Wroth, Rachel, 'Servants at St John's College, Cambridge, 1850–1900' (dissertation for the Advanced Diploma in English Local History, University of Cambridge Board of Continuing Education, 1998)

ODNB articles on: J. C. Adams (R. Hutchins); Charles Cardale Babington (D. E. Allen); William Bateson (Robert Olby), Samuel Butler (J. H. C. Leach), Edwin Clark (Wilfrid E. Rumble), Herbert Somerton Foxwell (A. L. Bowley and Richard D. Freeman), W. Garnett (D. Knight); J. W. F. Herschel (Michael J. Crowe), B. H. Kennedy (T. E. Page; J. H. C. Leach); J. Larmor (I. Falconer); Alfred Marshall (Rita McWilliams Tullberg); T. E. Page (N. Rudd), H. J. Roby (C. Stray); T. Whytehead (R. Scott)

INTRODUCTION, TWENTIETH CENTURY, & EPILOGUE

Primary Sources

SJCL

Cecil Beaton Diaries

G. E. Daniel, 'Commonplace Book *mit* Journal'

T. R. Glover correspondence (letters in) unclassified

T. R. Glover Diaries, 1888–1943

Hilary Macklin Diaries

F. Smithies, Diary

Miscellaneous papers: H. R. Baker; E. A. Benians; W. G. Constable; J. Larmor, G. D. Liveing; E. E. Raven; U. Yule

MS U40: Feast Book

SJCA

Arch.2.4	Memoirs of Bob Fuller, Head Porter
Arch.2.6	W. T. Thurbon, 'Memoir'
Arch.2.8.1	Ken North; 'Memoirs'
Arch.2.12a	E. Cunningham, 'Memoir'
C3.7	'Register of Fellows and Scholars, 1860–1965'
C19.52, 53, 55.	Annual Accounts and Papers, 1976–7, 1977–8, 1978–9, 1980–81
CC3.24	Report of the Audit Committee, 1903
CC3.75	Report of the Audit Committee on the Kitchen Accounts, 1922–3
CC3.170	Audit Report, 1979–80
CC4.10	Committee on Charges to Undergraduates (1916)
CC5.3	Menu for Port Latin Feast, 1914
CC6.1	*Eagle* Minute Book, 1890–1923
CC8.1	Kitchen Committee minutes, 1915–23
CC8.4	Kitchen Suggestions Book, 1938–49
CC8.5	JCR Suggestions Book, 1938–44
CC8.6	JCR Suggestions Books, 1944–7
CC15.1	Minutes of Emergency Committee', 1939
CC16.2	Building Committee Minutes
CC17.2	JCRC Minute Book, 1955–1960
CC17.4	JCRC Minute Book, 1969–80
CC17.5.1	JCRC papers, 1967–73
CC 17.6	JCRC Account Book
CC18.1	SJMC minutes, 1968–76, 'Junior Member representation at the College Council'
CC18.2	Gate and Guest hours papers
CC 21.1	Kitchen Consultative Committee Minutes
CC38.1, 2	Fellows' Amenities Committee Minutes, 1928–95
SBFG1980–2000	Council and Governing Body file, 1980–91
D11.33–4	Will of J. B. Mullinger

D22.60	Copy will of J. R. Tanner, 1924
D33.13(3)	Sewage Diary, 1897
D33.17.18	Letters from donors to College Appeal, 1958–66
D33.18.41	Cripps Building papers, 1958–61
D.44.13–15	Royal Commission on Oxford and Cambridge Universities, 1919
D90.765–1167	R. F. Scott papers, 1880–1932
D93	Research Fellowship reports, 1884–1978
D96	Fellowship papers, 1887–1970
D100.69.b	Invitation Nights, 1896
DS1.5	Chapel questionnaire, 1964
DS2.13	Choir matters, 1954
DS 3.4; 3.6; 4.5	Books of the Junior and Senior Deans
DS5.1	Register of Services, 1934–55
M.2.1–2	R. F. Scott letter books, 1908–24, 1925–33
M4	Co-residence material, 1980
M6.3/1; M6.5	Governing Body papers, 1967–70, 1977–82
M7.2.1	Correspondence re conduct of J. H. A. Hart, 1913–15
M7.3	Correspondence re Chapel bust of Lady Margaret, 1916–19
M10.1	Correspondence Dame Jessy Scott and Mrs Benians, 1934
MPSC12.9	E. B. Maufe drawings (March 1938)
SB1.23	Senior Bursar's Estates Diary, vol. 4, 1899–1908, with notes of College affairs kept up by Scott to 1932
SB21/Cb/N/11.387	Letter, S. G. Ponsonby, Trinity College, to Scott, 26 April 1894
SBF51	'College Office, and Liability of Tutors' (1898)
SBF54	Nat. Sci.; Tanner, 'Memorandum on the Tutorial System'; 'Natural Sciences Teaching and the Tutorial System', 1918
SBFG/1980–2000	Rooms/Mixed Sharing
SBFG 1980–2000	Council & Governing Body Papers, 1980–86
SBFL2	Living of Brandesburton (1852–1952)
SBFL/5B(1)	Living of Holme-on-Spalding-Moor I (1857–1954)
SBFP	Fellows' papers
SD.8.1	Steward's Order Book, 1873–91
SD17.1	Fellows Menu Book, 1919–21
SDF 1987/11	Kitchen papers, 1974–9
SOC.3.3c	GAC Minute Book, 1929–59
SOC.6.7	Minutes of the Crickets Club, 1924–8
SOC.9	Apostles Minute Book, 1934–7
SOC.16.1	Punchbowl Club: Minute Book, 1910–28
SOC.21.1	Eagles Club Minute Book, 1919–75
SOC.22.1	Minutes of the Nashe Society, 1928–47
SOC.23.1.1	Adams Society Minute Book, 1923–47
SOC.24.1	Portcullis Club Minute Book, 1906–14
STF2007/16; STF2007/5; STF2008/1	Senior Tutor's files
TU1.9.18	Tutors' instructions etc., 1912
TU1.9.20	Tanner's scrap-book, 1905–12

TUɪɪ   Tutorial papers of Donald MacAlister, 1893–1905
TUɪ2   Tutorial and other papers of J. R. Tanner, 1895–1931
TUɪ3   Tutorial papers of L. Bushe-Fox
TUɪ4   R. F. Scott, General letters

Fellows' Betting Book (Green Room)

Committee minutes: Buildings Committee; Choir School Committee; Disciplinary Committee; Entertainments Committee; Fire-Precautions Sub-Committee; JCR Committee; Senior and Junior Members Committee/Consultative Committee; Use of Endowment Income Committee

OTHER CAMBRIDGE COLLECTIONS

Magdalene College Cambridge: A. C. Benson Diaries, 180 vols.
Trinity College Cambridge, B16: J. B. Mayor Papers

PRIVATE COLLECTIONS

E. A. Benians papers
J. S. Boys Smith papers
Rachel Lewis (BA 1989), Diary
J. S. Sheldon (BA 1963), Diary

Unpublished Sources

J. A. Crook, 'Memories of St John's. The Second World War and immediately after' (n.d.)

J. P. Freeman, 'The Eagle and the Red Boy': Pt II Archaeology and Anthropology dissertation (1987)

G. A. Reid, 'The Disciplinary Committee' (1994)

Published Sources

Andrew, Rob, *A Game and a Half: An Autobiography* (London, 1994)

Anon., 'A Camp for Unemployed Men', *Eagle* xlix (1935–7), 88–90; 230–3; li (1938), 27–30

—— 'The College and the War', *Eagle* xxxvi (1914–15), 329–32

—— 'Heitland as J. B', *Eagle* li (1939), 132–43

Bailey, Trevor, *Wickets, Catches and the Odd Run* (London, 1986)

Beaton, Cecil, *The Wandering Years: Diaries, 1922–1939* (London, 1961)

Benians, E. A., *John Fisher* (Cambridge, 1935)

—— 'Cambridge in the last half century', *Eagle* lv (1952–3), 11–22

—— 'The College during the War', *Eagle* lii (1941–6), 306–9

—— 'Commemoration Sermon 1947', *Eagle* liii (1948–9), 1–6

Bennett, J. A. W., 'One hundred and twenty years of *The Eagle*', *Eagle* lxviii no. 288 (1980), 3–8

Bentley, J., *Dare to be Wise: A History of the Manchester Grammar School* (London, 1990)

Bertram, Colin (G. C. L.), *Antarctica, Cambridge, Conservation and Population: A Biologist's Story* (Cambridge, 1987)

—— 'Antarctica sixty years ago. We the obligate Pinnipedophagi', *Polar Record* xxxii, no. 181 (April 1996), 101–83

—— 'College Recruitment', *Eagle* lix (1960–63), 187–97

Bonney, T. G., *Memories of a Long Life* (Cambridge, 1921)

—— The Quatercentenary Sermon', *Eagle* xxxiii (1911–12), 11–20

Born, Max, *My Life and Views* (New York, 1968)

Boys Smith, J. S., *Memories of St John's College Cambridge, 1919–1969* (Cambridge, 1983)

—— 'College grounds and playing fields', *Eagle* liv (1950–51), 300–12

—— 'The Combination Room and 'D' Day', *Eagle* lxii (1967–8), 218–22

—— 'The Constitution and Government of the College', *Eagle* lxii (1967–8), 87–94

Brockliss, L. W. B., *Magdalen College Oxford: A History* (Oxford, 2008)

Brooke, C. N. L., 'The churches of medieval Cambridge': *History, Society and the Churches: Essays in Honour of Owen Chadwick*, ed. D. Beales and G. Best (Cambridge, 1985), 49–76

Brown, Freddie, *Cricket Musketeer* (London, 1954)

Browning, Julian, 'Fans folded in the shade' *or* 'The unlikely prospect – a tale for graduates', *Eagle* lxiv (1970–71), 127–9

Bruce Lockhart, L., 'Robbie as an undergraduate', *Eagle* (2000), 15–17

Carswell, John, *Government and the Universities in Britain* (Cambridge, 1985)

Cartledge, B. G., 'A Set of Tiled Rooms', *Eagle* lvii (1956–7), 15–17

Chadwick, W. O., 'The Commemoration Sermon' [1952], *Eagle* lv (1952–3), 23–6

Combridge, J. T., 'Dr Bonney and the Crown Prince', *Eagle* lxviii, no. 288 (1980), 32–3

Colbert, Fiona (ed.), *Register of Twentieth-Century Johnians, I. 1900–1949* (Cambridge, 2004)

Coulton, G. G., *Fourscore Years: An Autobiography* (Cambridge, 1943)

Cox, 'W. A., The new window in Chapel: Legends of St. John (II.)', *Eagle* xxxi (1909–10), 364–76

Crook, D., 'The Cambridge Garden House Hotel Riot of 1970 and its place in the history of British student protests', *Journal of Educational Administration and History* xxxviii (2006), 19–28

Crook, J. A., 'Commemoration of Benefactors 1969', *Eagle* lxiii, no. 272 (1969), 77–80

Crook, J. Mordaunt, *Brasenose: The Biography of an Oxford College* (Oxford, 2008)

Cunningham, E., 'The College in 1911', *Eagle* lix (1960–63), 155–65

Daniel, Glyn, *Some Small Harvest* (London, 1986)

—— 'Mr. Sid Dring', *Eagle* lxv (1972–3), 88–9

—— 'The Pig Club', *Eagle* lvi (1954–5), 146–8

—— 'Portrait of a Head Gardener', *Eagle* liv (1950–51), 144–7

Darwall-Smith, R., *A History of University College Oxford* (Oxford, 2008)

Delany, Paul, *The Neo-Pagans: Friendship and Love in the Rupert Brooke Circle* (London, 1987)

Deslandes, P. R., *Oxbridge Men: British Masculinity and the Undergraduate Experience, 1850–1920* (Bloomington, IN, 2005)

Devlin (Lord), *Report of the Sit-in in February 1972 and its Consequences: CUR* ciii (Special no. 12; 14 Feb. 1973)

Dingwall, R. W. J., 'Retrospective', *Eagle* lxiv (1970–71), 129–31

Dobson, R. B., 'The Jews of medieval Cambridge', *Transactions of the Jewish Historical Society of England* xxxii (1990–92), 1–24

Engel, A. J., *From Clergyman to Don: The Rise of the Academic Profession in Nineteenth-Century Oxford* (Oxford, 1983)

Evans, G. C., 'The Cobbling of Second Court', *Eagle* lv (1952–3), 171–7

——'The Combination Room table', *Eagle* (1996), 43–51

——'Master', *Eagle* lxiii (1969–70), 9–16

——'A Set of Rooms: some discoveries and puzzles', *Eagle* lvi (1954–5), 60–68, 150–60

Evans, G. R., *The University of Cambridge: A New History* (London, 2009)

Farmelo, Graham, *The Strangest Man: The Hidden Life of Paul Dirac, Quantum Genius* (London, 2009)

Fisher, H. A. L., *An Unfinished Autobiography* (Oxford, 1940)

Forster, E. M., *The Longest Journey* (London, 1907)

Foster, R. H., and W. Harris *et al.*, *The History of the Lady Margaret Boat Club, 1825–1926* (Cambridge, 1926)

Galvin, P., and P. Lindley, 'Pietro Torrigiano's portrait bust of King Henry VII', *The Burlington Magazine* cxxx (1988), 892–902

Glover, T. R., *Cambridge Retrospect* (Cambridge, 1943)

Goddard, Peter, 'Paul Dirac', *Eagle* lxxi, no. 294 (1986), 69–77

Goronwy-Roberts, A., *Mask: Torrigiano's Bust of Fisher Reconsidered* (London, 1992)

Gowing, Margaret, *Britain and Atomic Energy, 1939–1945* (London, 1964)

——*Independence and Deterrence: Britain and Atomic Energy, 1945–1952*, I. *Policy Making*; II. *Policy Execution* (London, 1974)

Guest, G. H., *A Guest at Cambridge* (Orleans, MA, 1994)

Guillebaud, C. W., 'Then and now', *Eagle* lviii (1958–9), 159–60

——'Some personal reminiscences of Alfred Marshall', *Eagle* lxiv (1970–71), 97–9

——'Report to the Council on the Working of the Tutorial System in St John's College' (1969)

——'Thirty Years of Tutorial Policy', *Eagle* lvi (1954–5), 123–31

Guillebaud, Philomena, 'West Cambridge, 1870–1914: building the bicycle suburb', *Proceedings of the Cambridge Antiquarian Society* xcvi (2007), 193–210

Haig-Thomas, David, *I Leap Before I Look* (London, 1936)

Hammond, N. G. L., *Sir John Edwin Sandys* (Cambridge, 1933)

Harkness, David, 'Philip Nicholas Seton Mansergh, 1919–1991', *PBA* lxxxii (1993), 415–30

Harrison, B., *Seeking a Role: The United Kingdom, 1951–1970* (Oxford, 2009)

——(ed.), *The History of the University of Oxford*, VIII (Oxford, 1994)

Harvey, Barbara, and Peter Linehan, 'Edward Miller, 1915–2000', *PBA* cxxxviii (2006), 231–56

Heitland, W. E., *After Many Years: A Tale of Experiences and Impressions Gathered in the Course of an Obscure Life* (Cambridge, 1926)

Henderson, J., *Juvenal's Mayor: The Professor who Lived on 2d. a Day*, Proceedings of the Cambridge Philological Society, Suppl. vol. no. 20 (Cambridge, 1998)

——*Mayor's Juvenal* (Bristol, 2007)

Hinsley, F. H., 'BP, Admiralty, and naval Enigma', in F. H. Hinsley and A. Stripp (eds.), *Codebreakers: The Inside Story of Bletchley Park* (Oxford, 1993)

Hall-Craggs, J. F. *et al.*, *The History of the Lady Margaret Boat Club*, II. *1926–1956* (Cambridge, 1957); III. *1957–1982* (Cambridge, 2008)

Honey, J. R. de S., and M. C. Curthoys, 'Oxford and schooling', in M. G. Brock and M. C. Curthoys (eds.), *History of the University of Oxford*, VII (Oxford, 2000), 545–69

Hopkins, C., *Trinity: 450 Years of an Oxford College Community* (Oxford, 2005)

Howarth, T. E. B., *Cambridge between Two Wars* (London, 1978)

Hoyle, F., *Home is Where the Wind Blows: Chapters from a Cosmologist's Life* (Mill Valley, CA, 1994)

Hume, G. B, Cardinal, 'John Fisher, 1469–1535', *Eagle* lxxi, no. 294 (1986), 3–18

Hyam, Ronald, 'The Study of Imperial and Commonwealth History at Cambridge, 1881–1981: Founding Fathers and Pioneer Research Students', *Journal of Imperial and Commonwealth History* xxix (2001), 75–103

James, M. R., *Eton and King's* (London, 1926)

Jeffery, Keith, '… not co-residence again', *Eagle* lxvii, no. 284 [1976], 39–41

Jenkins, Roy, *Asquith* (London, 1967)

Jones, J., *Balliol College: A History*, 2nd edn (Oxford, 2005)

Keynes, Geoffrey (ed.), *The Letters of Rupert Brooke* (London, 1968)

Keynes, John Maynard, *Essays in Biography* [1933] (London, 1972)

Lambert, 'J., Comment', *Eagle* lxxi, no. 295 (1987), 18–22

Langhorne, R. T. B., 'Francis Harry Hinsley, 1918–1998', *PBA* cxx (2003), 263–74

—— 'The inception of the building', *Eagle* lxxi, no. 295 (1987), 4–10

Leakey, L. S. B., *By the Evidence: Memoirs, 1932–1951* (New York & London, 1974)

Lee, A. G., 'Commemoration Sermon, 1977', *Eagle* lxviii, no. 286 (1978), 3–7

Linehan, Peter, 'Commemoration of Benefactors, 4 May 1997', *Eagle* lxxii (1997), 10–19

—— 'The Making of the *Cambridge Medieval History*', *Speculum* 57 (1982), 463–94

—— 'An opportunity missed? The Torrigiano "Fisher" and St John's', *Eagle* lxxi (1986), 13–18

—— 'Piam in memoriam: Group III, 1894–1986', *Cambridge* no. 35 (1994–5), 70–78

—— 'The Pig's Golden', *Eagle* (1996), 9–13

—— 'Reuben Peck, 1913–91', *Eagle* (1991), 41–2

—— 'Professor Ronald Robinson', *Independent*, 25 June 1999

Loewe, R., 'Taylor's teachers and pupils', in S. Reif (ed.), *Charles Taylor: A Centenary Seminar and Exhibition, St John's College, Cambridge, 2 November 2008* (Cambridge, 2009), 22–9

Lovatt, R., 'Hugh of Balsham, bishop of Ely, 1256/7–1286', in R. Horrox and S. Rees Jones (eds.), *Pragmatic Utopias: Ideals and Communities, 1200–1630* (Cambridge, 2001), 60–83

Lucas, F. L., *Journal under the Terror, 1938* (London, 1939)

MacAlister, E. F. B., *Sir Donald MacAlister of Tarbert, by His Wife* (London, 1935)

Macaulay, Thomas Babington, *The Letters of Thomas Babington Macaulay*, ed. T. Pinney, I (Cambridge, 1974)

McKitterick, D., *Cambridge University Library: A History: The Eighteenth and Nineteenth Centuries* (Cambridge, 1986)

McLachlan, J. O., 'The origin and early development of the Cambridge Historical Tripos', *Cambridge Historical Journal* ix (1947–9), 78–105

Maitland, F. W., *Township and Borough* (Cambridge, 1898)

Mangan, J. A., '"Oars and the man": pleasure and purpose in Victorian and Edwardian Cambridge', *British Journal of Sports History* i (1984), 246–71

Mansergh, P. N. S., *The Commonwealth Experience* (London, 1969)

Marshall, Alfred, *Principles of Economics* (London, 1890)

Mitchell, L., 'The Screwing-up of the Dean', *University College* [Oxford] *Record* xi no. 4 (1995–6), 69–81

Morphet, D. (ed.), *St John's College Cambridge: Excellence and Diversity* (London, 2007)

Morton of Henryton, 'St John's fifty years ago', *Eagle* lviii (1958–9), 9–12

Munro, D., 'Becoming an expatriate: J. W. Davidson and the Brain Drain', *Journal of New Zealand Studies* ii–iii (2003–4), 19–43

Neild, R. R., *Riches and Responsibility: The Financial History of Trinity College, Cambridge* (Cambridge, 2008)

Newsome, David, *On the Edge of Paradise: A. C. Benson: The Diarist* (London, 1980)

—— 'Two Emmanuel historians', *Emmanuel College Magazine*, Quatercentenary Issue (1984), 104–14

Nicolson, Harold, *King George the Fifth: His Life and Reign* (London, 1952)

Oliphant, M., and Lord Penney, 'John Cockcroft', in *Biographical Memoirs FRS* xiv (1968), 139–88

Orr, Robin, *Musical Chairs: An Autobiography* (London, 1998)

Papworth, R., 'Pig Club memories: some reminiscences by a former President of the Club', *Eagle* (1995), 22–9; (1996), 14–21

Paranjpye, R., *Eighty-four, Not Out* (Delhi, 1961)

—— 'Sixty Years Ago', *Eagle* lviii (1958–9), 4–8

Pearson, J. B., 'The Church's Need of Excellence. A Sermon preached in the Chapel of St John's College, Cambridge, on Sunday evening, Mar. 22, 1868' (Cambridge, 1868)

Perkin, Harold, *The Rise of Professional Society England since 1880* (London, 1989)

Portway, D., *Militant Don* (London, 1964)

Powell, K., *Powell and Moya: Twentieth Century Architects* (London, 2009)

Preston, J. M., 'Lending a hand', *Eagle* lxix, no. 292 (1984), 11–13

Previté-Orton, C. W., 'The College Library and its renovation', *Eagle* xlv (1927–9), 296–302

Reddaway, W. F., *Cambridge in 1891* (Cambridge, 1943)

Reif, S. C., *A Jewish Archive from Old Cairo: The History of Cambridge University's Genizah Collection* (Richmond, 2000)

Robinson, D., 'James Adam "in the arena of the South": an Aberdeen Platonist in Cambridge', in Stray (ed.), *The Owl of Minerva*, 47–68

Rootham, J., *Demi-Paradise* (London, 1960)

Royal Commission on Oxford and Cambridge Universities: Report, Cmd. 1588 (HMSO London, 1922)

Rubin, M., *Charity and Community in Medieval Cambridge* (Cambridge, 1987)

Russell-Smith, H., *Harrington and his* Oceana: *A Study of a Seventeenth-Century Utopia and its Influence in America* (Cambridge, 1914)

Saltmarsh, J., and P. Wilkinson, *Arthur Cecil Pigou, 1877–1959, Fellow and Professor of Political Economy: A Memoir* (Cambridge, 1960)

Scott, K., 'The foundation of the Hospital of St John the Evangelist', *Eagle* lxvii, no. 283 (1975), 3–4

Scott, R. F., *St John's College, Cambridge* (London, 1907)

Sebag-Montefiore, H., *Enigma: The Battle for the Code* (London, 2000)

Shepperson, G., *et al.*, 'J. W. Davidson at Cambridge University: some student evaluations', *History in Africa* xxvii (2000), 215–27

Sisman, Adam, *A. J. P. Taylor: A Biography* (London, 1994)

Smith, M., *Sir James Wordie, Polar Crusader: Exploring the Arctic and Antarctic* (Edinburgh, 2004)

Souter, D., 'Bob's your uncle', *Eagle* lxvii, no. 283 (1975), 21–2

[Stephen, Leslie], *Sketches from Cambridge, by a Don* (London, 1865)

Strachey, Lytton, *Eminent Victorians* (London, 1918)

Stray, C., *The Owl of Minerva: The Cambridge Praelections of 1906* [*Proc. Cambridge Philological Soc.* supplementary vol. 28] (2005)

—— 'Curriculum and style in the collegiate university: Classics in nineteenth-century Oxbridge', *History of Universities* xvi/2 (2000), 183–218

A Sympathiser (BA) [Arthur John Story], *The Fresher's Don't*, 7th edn (Cambridge, 1896)

Tate, R., 'Recollections', *Eagle* liii (1948–9), 7–11

Tawney, R. H., 'A National College of All Souls', *Times Educational Supplement*, 22 February 1917

Thistlethwaite, D., 'Stranger in the College', *Eagle* lxviii, no. 288 (1980), 9–16

Thistlethwaite, F., *Cambridge Years* (Cambridge, 1999)

—— *Our War, 1938–1945* (Cambridge, 1997)

Thomas, Keith, 'College life, 1945–1970', in B. Harrison (ed.), *History of the University of Oxford*, VIII, 189–215

Thurbon, W. T., 'Brindley and the Riddle of the Sands', *Eagle* lxvii, no. 283 (1975), 5–6

—— 'The College Bread and Broth Charity', *Eagle* lxix, no. 292 (1984), 16–23

—— 'The Poor's Soup', *Eagle* (2000), 35–7

Twigg, J., 'Evolution, obstacles and aims: the writing of Oxford and Cambridge college histories', *History of Universities* viii (1989), 179–99

Underwood, M. (ed.), *Cartulary of the Hospital of St John the Evangelist, Cambridge* (Cambridge, 2008)

The Victoria History of the Counties of England: A History of the County of Cambridge and the Isle of Ely, III. *The City and University of Cambridge*, ed. J. P. C. Roach (London, 1959)

Whipplesnaith, *The Night Climbers of Cambridge* (Cambridge, 1937)

Wilks, M. V., *Memoirs of a Computer Engineer* (Cambridge, MA, & London, 1985)

Wilson Harris, H., *Life So Far* (London, 1954)

Winterbottom, D., *Bertram Hallward: First Vice-Chancellor of the University of Nottingham, 1948–1965: A Biography* (Nottingham, 1995)

Wood, H. G., *Terrot Reaveley Glover* (Cambridge, 1953)

Young, Michael, *The Rise of the Meritocracy* (Harmondsworth, 1961)

Yule, U., *The Fall of the Birth-rate: A Paper Read Before the Cambridge Eugenics Society, 20 May 1920* (Cambridge, 1920)

ODNB articles on: F. Engledow (G. D. H. Bell); F. J. Foakes-Jackson (P. Gardner-Smith and H. Chadwick); T. R. Glover (I. Falconer); A. Harker (D. Oldroyd); T. H. Havelock (P. H. Roberts); W. E. Heitland (P. Searby); F. H. Hinsley (R. T. B. Langhorne); H. Jeffreys (A. Cook); J. Larmor (I. Falconer); G. D. Liveing (W. C. D. Dampier and F. A. J. L. James); P. N. S. Mansergh (R. Hyam); L. Mordell (J. W. S. Cassels); C. W. Previté-Orton (R. B. Dobson); A. B. Ramsay (R. Hyam); A. C. Seward (H. H. Thomas and A. McConnell); J. C. Squire (E. Blunden and C. L. Taylor); R. Whiddington (N. Feather and I. Falconer); J. M. Wordie (B. H. Farmer); U. Yule (F. Yates and A. Yoshiaka)

INDEXES

I. ST JOHN'S COLLEGE

II. MEMBERS

B(ursar); **C**(ommoner); **F**(ellow); **H**(onorary); **J**(unior); **M**(aster); **P**(resident); **T**(utor); **S**(enior); **Sch**(olar); **St**(eward)

Except where otherwise indicated, date given is that of matriculation or incorporation [or admission to status], i.e. first sighting by College

Abbott, Edwin Abbott (1857), **F**, 352; **HF**

Aberdeen, 4th earl of [George Hamilton-Gordon; 1800], Prime Minister (1841–6), 165, 216

Adam, K. (1926), 499

Adams, John Couch (1839), **F**, Lowndean Prof. of Astronomy and Geometry, 1859–92), 275, 277, 317, 329–30; **HF**

Aitchison, A. G. (1945), fig. 58

Alison, H. C. (1874), 479

Allan, P. G. (1944), fig. 58

Allen, C. (1738) **F**, xvii

Allen, J. S. (1874), 407

Allen, James (1751), Methodist, 199

Allen, W. (1877), 302

Alvey, Henry (1564), **F** (1571), **P**, ambitious Puritan agitator, 84–5, 88, 89; Fellows' preferred candidate for Mastership (1596), 85, 89–90, 113–14; adapts to new regime, 92

Alvey, Richard, **F** (adm. 1537–8), Protestant refugee, 39

Ambrose, John (1624), **F**, 118–19, 148

Andradi, P. B. M. (1979), 626

Andrew, C. R. (1982), 636

Appleton, E. V. (1911), **F**, 453; Nobel laureate, 472, 510; **HF**

Argyle, R. M. (1937), fig. 58

Armitage, B. W. F. (1909), **F**; fig. 43; rise and fall of, 465–74; parents, 468, 470; and C. Beaton, 469–70; and L. H. Macklin, 470–1

Armstrong, W. D. (1945; Christ's), **F**, **St**, 613–14

Arnison, T. M. (1929), 510, 649

Arrowsmith, John (1616), **M** (1644–53), 111, 139–42, 145

Arthur, Thomas, **F** (adm. 1518–19), College preacher, 25; abjured heresy, 25–6; playwright, 26

Arundell, D. D. (1919), **F**, 470

Ascham, Roger, **F** (adm. 1534), 22, 33, 35, 40, 42, 46; pl. II; encomium of College, 41; treatise against the Catholic mass, 47; author and royal tutor, 132

Ashton, James (1744), undergraduate, perhaps murdered, 183

Atkins, H. J. (1870), 301–2

Atlay, James (1836), **F**, **T**, 268, 359–60

Avery, E. N. (1926), 500

Babington, C. C. (1826), **F**, Prof. of Botany, 325–6, 332, 341

Babington, Churchill (1839), **F**, Disney Prof. of Archaeology, **JB**, 267, 277, 325, 338; **HF**

Bagnall, H. H. (1863), 301

Bailey, S. J. (1919), **F**, **T**, 549, 557, 623; figs. 58, 60

Bailey, T. E. (1946), 555, 556, 559, 636–7

Bainbridge, G. (1835), **F**, 268

Baker, H. F. (1884), **F**, Lowndean Prof. of Astronomy and Geometry, 317, 326, 394, 463, 479, 504; and Kitchen accounts, 484; on College's defences (1940), 549; *see also* Munich crisis

Baker, L. P. (1803), **F**, 235

Baker, Thomas, (1674), **F**; historian of the College, xv, xviii, 3–4, 14, 83, 172, 184, 185, 504; fig. 12; pl. VI; 'socius ejectus', 157; books bequeathed to the Library, 104; transcribes diary of William Dowsing, 138; comments on College income, 95; on Fellows, 112; hostility to Owen Gwyn, 114–15; opinion of Second Court, 99, 101; records gifts and loans to Charles I, 136–7; sympathy for Anthony Tuckney, 149; and for Titus Oates, 158; and William Beale, 139–40

Balguy, Thomas F. (1734), 199, 206

Bambrough, J. R. (1945), **F**, 397, 572; **D**, 594, 598–600, 616

Barlow, H. T. E. (1882), **F**, **JD** (1894), 391; 410, 415; fig. 33

Barrère, J. B. (1957), **F**, Prof. of French Literature, 604

Bartlett, F. C. [Sir Frederic; 1912], **F**, 454, 473, 486, 504, 534; Prof. of Experimental Psychology, 546

Barwick, John (1631), **F**, 140, 145

III. GENERAL

Persons' Colleges shown given are those of their matriculation.

Abbot, George, archbishop of Canterbury (d. 1633), 116

Abjuration Act (1701), 169

Academic and teaching professions, 246–7, 249, 308, 317–19, 366

academical dress, 589

Acta eruditorum (1734), 185

Adam, James (Gonville & Caius), candidate for Regius Chair of Greek, 1906, 455

Adams, Vyvyan, MP, 548

Adamson, John, showman, 133

Adcock, F. E., Prof. of Ancient History, 457

Addison, Joseph, poet, ode in *Spectator* (1712), 190

Adington, Henry, Viscount Sidmouth, 230

Adkin, Tom (Corpus Christi), 184

Administrative Reform Association, 267–8

Adrian, Baron, Master of Trinity, 586

Aeschylus, 175

Agriculture Act (1920), 683

Aikin, Annie, Mrs W. H. Bateson, 258, 387

Airy, George, 330

Albert, Prince, Chancellor of Cambridge University (1847–61), 239 274, 282

Aldenham School, 428, 580; 'Aldenham to Westminster list', 428

Alverstone, Viscount (R. E. Webster; Trinity), 454

American colonies, 187

American Friends of Cambridge University, 694

American Independence, War of, 204, 210

Anderson, Sir Hugh, Master of Caius, 492

Anne, Queen of England, Scotland (from 1707 of the Union of England and Scotland), and Ireland, reign of, 169–70, 186

Arlington, 1st earl of [Henry Bennet], 131

Armagh, archbishopric of, 210

Arnold, Thomas, 295, 300, 302

Ashton, Hugh, controller of Lady Margaret Beaufort's household, 7, 15, 24; pl. I

Asquith, H. H., 489; Royal Commission on Oxford and Cambridge Universities, 510, 511, 681, 683–4

Audley End, Essex, 104

Babbage, Charles, 317, 329

Bacon, Francis, 121

Balfour, Arthur, Prime Minister, fig. 45

Balfour, Frank, 317, 331

Ball, W. W. Rouse, responsible for kink in Grange Road, 385

'Bangorian Controversy', 172–3

Baring-Gould, S., 297

Bateson, Margaret (Mrs Heitland), 481

Beaufort, Lady Margaret, mother of King Henry VII; impressed by John Fisher, 5; influenced by him, 6; her Oxford advisers, 7; her vision for the College, 8; her last will and testament, 10, 11; portrait hung in Hall, 92; frontispiece

bee-keeping, 113

Beerbohm, Max, 309

Bell, F. E. (Board of Extra-Mural Studies), 563

Benians, Sylvia Mrs (*née* Dodds), 516, 541, 587, 592; injury of, 543

Benson, A. C., Master of Magdalene, diarist, on Armitage, 472–3; on Benians, 564; on Bonney, 486; on Glover, 456, 466–7, 471; on Heitland's domestic arrangements, 482; on Liveing, 474; on P. Mason, 412; on SJC, 415; on Scott and SJC, 422, 511; on SJC Master's Lodge, 520; on J. C. Squire, 424; on C. Taylor, 412, 415

Bernis, Cardinal François-Joachim de Pierre de, 203

Bevan, A. A. (Trinity), 415

Beverley (Yorks.), Fisher's connections in, 15

Bible societies, 212

bicycles, 483

Bird, John (adversary of Waidson), 142

Birdwood, Baron, Master of Peterhouse (1930–8), 549

Bishop's Stortford, 217

Boleyn, Anne, Queen, supports students at College, 35

Bonaparte, Napoleon, 222

Booker, E. C. (father of E. Booker [BA 1903]), 425

Boulton, Matthew, 179

Bowett, D. W., President of Queens', 612

Brancker, T., 250